DATE DUE

NO 28 05		

DEMCO 38-296

The Right Guide

A Guide to Conservative and Right-of-Center Organizations

Edited by Derk Arend Wilcox

Economics America, Inc.
Ann Arbor, Michigan

While every attempt has been made to ensure the accuracy of the information in this publication, Economics America, Inc. does not guarantee that all information herein is correct. The publisher accepts no payment for listing; and inclusion in this publication does not imply endorsement of the organization.

This publication is designed to provide authoritative information. It is sold with the understanding that the publisher is not engaged in rendering legal, accounting, or other professional service. If legal advice or other expert assistance is required, the services of a competent professional should be sought.

Corrections brought to the attention of the publisher, once verified, will be included in future editions.

This publication is a creative work fully protected by all applicable copyright laws, as well as missappropriation, trade secret, unfair competition, and other state, federal, and international laws. The authors and editors have added economic and intellectual value to the underlying factual material. That added value includes but is not limited to: classification, selection, coordination, expression, and organization. In addition, no information from this work may be entered into any database for any purpose.

The copyright holder will rigorously defend, protect and litigate all of its rights in this publication.

The paper used in this publication is acid free and meets the minimum requirements of American Standard for Information Sciences--Permanence of Paper for Printed Materials, ANSI Z39.48-1984.

Printed in the United States by Braun-Brumfield, Inc.

TABLE OF CONTENTS

Who These Organizations Are and Why They Matter

The distinction between the Left and the Right began as a reference to seating arrangements of the French Assembly in the 1790's. The monarchists sat on the right, the republicans on the left. Modern usage usually breaks down into conservatives and liberals, Republicans and Democrats, reactionaries and radicals, capitalists and socialists. The organizations in The Right Guide represent differing approaches and philosophies.

The traditional core of conservatism is that human nature is fixed. Society is a gradually evolving system, and resists planned attempts to substantially alter economic, familial, class and other social structures. According to this view, humans act economically in their own self-interest, individuals and families make up the basic building block of society, and history, religion and tradition provide the best guide to improvement. This differs significantly from the 'progressive' world view that holds that human nature is malleable, and that society can be engineered based on a plan developed by experts - then instituted and maintained with political will.

In the 1950's, due in large part to William F. Buckley, Jr.'s, efforts at National Review, 'classical liberals' - or libertarians, became a part of the movement due to the common enemy of communism abroad and increasingly socialistic programs at home. The alliance has not always been cozy, but many of these groups work together or independently toward similar goals and objectives. Others feud bitterly and resent any insinuation that they are associated with the other. The enormous diversity within the political Right is one important reason why we publish The Right Guide. As the movement grows, and individual organizations increase in size and influence, the unifying themes become more difficult to classify. These facts are known by some leaders in the policy community, but not at the activist level.

How were organizations selected? The Right Guide was produced with the help and cooperation of most of the listed organizations. Information was solicited from each organization that is included (although this solicited information is not the sole source). All groups contacted were aware of the focus and scope of the Guide. Knowing this, organizations chose to respond and wanted to be listed. Others were reluctant. We examined these organizations' officers and directors, as well as financial supporters and positions, for connections and links to other conservative organizations. Most organizations in The Right Guide take positions on current issues and it is relatively easy to match positions with their place on the political spectrum. When in doubt, we referred to published material from the American Conservative Union and Americans for Democratic Action. Both organizations monitor votes in Congress, and scales the votes on what most people would call the Left and Right. (Of course neither of these two organizations necessarily agrees with our classifications.)

Virtually every piece of conservative or free-market-based legislation that passes or is considered by the federal and state governments is first created by the organizations listed in The Right Guide. Most of the elements in the Republican's "Contract With America" were first advocated by these organizations, as was NAFTA, and many elements of the 1996 welfare reform legislation, school choice, medical savings accounts, privatization, the Strategic Defense Initiative (Star Wars), or any number of other policy initiatives that have become a part of our cultural, legal and political system.

These organizations have been critical in defeating legislation as well. The campaign conducted by these organizations to defeat the Clinton Health Care Plan will serve as a model of opposition for years to come. They have also defeated Presidential appointments.

Listed organizations are increasing their litigation activities as well. Long a staple of the Left, litigation is being used by the Right to challenge legislation's constitutionality, and to create a body of precedent-setting law that works in much the same way as legislation does to influence the public. This litigation has resulted in expanded property rights, reforming the Endangered Species Act, and holding in check the excesses of 'political correctness' on college campuses.

Organizations in The Right Guide serve as the training ground for elected officials' staffs, and in many cases, congressmen and senators worked for these groups prior to their election to office. Many of the organizations provide testimony, hold press briefings, and in general, provide intellectual ammunition for Right-oriented policy.

The workings of these organizations vary. Much of what goes on fits in with the traditional view of the way a 'think tank' operates. A public-policy question is examined, alternate views are considered, and recommendations or conclusions are made. But, unlike this traditional view, and unlike their brethren in academia, the process does not stop there. These organizations promote their research. First, they typically publish their work in their own periodical or publication. Then they produce an op-ed for general consumption that appears in newspapers. Next, the ideas will be promoted in friendly media sources - often this means talk radio, especially with the Right. Certain groups on the Right, such as the 'Religious Right' and 'Gun Lobby,' will take the ideas to their grassroots supporters, who will write letters to the editor, their congressmen, etc.   The whole procedure does an end-run around traditional policy-making participants, such as academia and the mass media.   After the idea has been promoted, they then return to those participants, producing academic-format research for the professors, and catching the attention of the television networks and other mass media.   The Right has been promoting and honing these skills, and continues to expand, particularly at the state and local level.

Averaging fiscal years 1994-95, the lobbying and research/educational organizations profiled in The Right Guide, as a group, had average annual revenues of $824 million.   They spent $266 million on lobbying.   The philanthropies that funded them had assets of $5.1 billion.   As detailed in the **Profiles**, the vast majority of these organizations' revenues are increasing at a greater rate than the economy or inflation.   While all these financial figures are still considerably less for the Right than their counterparts on the Left (as detailed in the companion volume - The Left Guide), they represent a considerable sum and indicate that these organizations will be a critical force in the political system for the foreseeable future.

The Editor

HOW TO USE THE RIGHT GUIDE

Most users will probably turn to the **Profiles** section and find the information they need. Only if they cannot find the organization or information they need will they read this section.

PROFILE SUBJECT INDEX

The **Profile Subject Index** is designed to help researchers locate organizations by an area of interest rather than by a specific organization's name. It is especially useful when researchers are dealing with a new subject matter.

PROFILES

This section contains information on most of the active right-of-center organizations. Information in the **Profiles** is organized as follows:

SAMPLE PROFILE

Acton Institute for the Study of Religion and Liberty

161 Ottawa Ave., N.W., Suite 301
Grand Rapids, MI 49503   **Phone:** (616) 454-3080   **E-Mail:** info@acton.org
USA   **Fax:**   (616) 454-9454   **Internet:** http://www.acton.org/

Contact Person: Kris Alan Mauren, Executive Director.
Officers or Principals: Kris Alan Mauren, Executive Director ($47,500); Rev. Robert A. Sirico, CSP, President/Chairman ($0); Jeff D. Sandefer, Vice Chairman ($0); Dr. Alejandro Chafuen, Secretary; Gerald P. O'Driscoll, Jr., Treasurer; Brett A. Elder, Operations Manager.
Mission or Interest: "To educate the religious and broader communities about the moral basis for personal and economic liberty."
Accomplishments: The keynote speaker at the Institute's 1996 annual dinner was Nobel Laureate in economics, Dr. Gary Becker. The 1994 dinner featured Justice Clarence Thomas. In 1996 the Institute started the Center for Economic Personalism, an "academic Center that promotes rigorous scholarly activity with the aim of generating new economic models synthesizing free-market economic theory and the central tenets of Christian social thought." The Institute has been prominent in the welfare reform debate. In 1995 it created the National Welfare Reform Initiative, which was launched with the "Welfare that Works" conference in Washington, DC. Conference attendees included: House Speaker Newt Gingrich, Gov. John Engler (R-MI), Mayor Stephen Goldsmith (R-Indianapolis), Dr. Marvin Olasky, Dr. Gertrude Himmelfarb, and Robert Woodson. More than 12,000 people worldwide receive the Institute's newsletter. In 1994 the Institute spent $497,530 on its programs.
Total Revenue: 1994 $788,863 22%(2) **Total Expenses:** $640,107 78%/12%/10% **Net Assets:** $514,412
Products or Services: Annual Samaritan Awards given to successful private charities that "practice effective compassion." In 1995 the Institute awarded $40,000 in prizes to ten winners. Quarterly three-day conference, "Toward a Free and Virtuous Society," for theology students and seminarians. Three times a year "Spirituality in a Capitalist Economy" retreats for business leaders. Conferences, Lord Acton Lecture Series, annual dinner, and several publications.
Tax Status: 501(c)(3) **Annual Report:** Yes. **Employees:** 13 **Citations:** 26:138
Board of Directors or Trustees: Dr. Edwin Feulner (Heritage Found.), Dr. Leonard Liggio (Atlas Economic Research Found.), Dr. Gerald O'Driscoll, George Strake, Jr., Betsy DeVos, David Padden, James Johnston. Advisors include: Dr. William Allen, Doug Bandow, Dr. Rocco Buttiglione, Sr. Connie Driscoll, Rabbi Daniel Lapin, Dr. Jennifer Roback Morse, Dr. Ronald Nash, Michael Novak, Rev. Dr. Edmund Opitz (Foundation for Economic Education), Rev. James Schall, Dr. Julian Simon, Hon. William E. Simon.
Periodicals: *Religion & Liberty* (bimonthly journal), and *Acton Notes* (monthly newsletter).
Internships: Yes, unpaid year-round.
Other Information: Established in 1990. Named for Baron John Emerich Edward Dalberg-Acton (1834-1902). Lord Acton was a prominent historian and social philosopher. According to Lord Acton, "Religious liberty is the generating principle of civil liberty; and civil liberty is the necessary condition of religious liberty." Lord Acton is perhaps best known for his quotation, "Power tends to corrupt; absolute power corrupts absolutely." The Institute received $714,020, or 91% of revenue, from contributions and grants awarded by foundations, businesses, and individuals. (These grants included $20,000 from the M.J. Murdock Charitable Trust, $10,000 from the Earhart Foundation, $5,000 from the Richard & Helen DeVos Foundation, $5,000 from the Aequus Institute, and $800 from the Charles G. Koch Charitable Foundation. In 1995, $100,000 from the Scaife Family Foundation, $80,000 from the Lynde and Harry Bradley Foundation, $40,000 from the Claude R. Lambe Charitable Foundation, $15,500 from the John M. Olin Foundation, $10,000 from the Sunmark Foundation, $10,000 from the Philip M. McKenna Foundation, $5,000 from the Roe Foundation, and $1,000 from the John William Pope Foundation.) $22,664, or 3%, from speaking engagements. $17,651, or 2%, from interest on savings and temporary cash investments. $12,148, or 2%, from the Lord Acton Lecture Series. $8,210, or 1%, from student conferences. The remaining revenue came from the sale of publications and other inventory.

This profile was selected because it not only has an entry in every category, but it also has additional information that will be explained in the following pages. Some of the organizations do not have an entry for one or more of the categories. This is due to the inability of the staff and editors to ascertain that particular information. All pertinent information obtained was included.

Name: The organization's official name is given, along with an acronym or initials if they are commonly used. "The" is excluded if it is the first word in the name. Some names have been modified slightly to make them easier to find. For example: the Michigan affiliate of the National Right to Life is called the "Michigan Right to Life Educational Foundation," but is listed as the "Right to Life, Michigan Educational Foundation" in order to place it alphabetically with its other affiliates. In situations where there are numerous affiliates, such as Right to Life, the national headquarters are listed first, followed by the affiliates in alphabetical order. If researchers cannot find the organization they are looking for, it is best to check the **Keyword Index** under various words in the organization's name.

Address: The official address is always used. Sometimes small groups use the home or office address of a key official. A personal address is used if it is the only one provided.

Phone: The voice phone is listed with its area code.

Fax: The facsimile number is provided when available. If the number is listed as "same," it is the same as the voice number. It is always best to call first and get permission before sending something via fax.

E-Mail: The number to reach the organization via computer is provided when available.

Internet: This is the internet web-page address that many organizations have. Unlike an e-mail address, the web-page is not used for two-way communications, although that option is sometimes available. The web-page contains various pre-set information and graphics about the group, and often includes access to its studies, reports, and activities. Organizations find this a very cost-effective and immediate way to inform members and interested parties, so these web sites are becoming more common. Even if there is no address listed here, it is recommended that you call the voice number and ask if they have an internet site.

Contact Person: The person listed is usually best suited to answer researchers' questions quickly. Most questions can be referred to specialists or the chief official if needed.

Officers or Principals: Lists some of the key officials associated with the organization. These are usually people who are directly involved in the day-to-day operation of the organization. Included under this listing are the salaries and compensation for the three highest-paid employees of the *nonprofit* organizations. If one or more of the three highest-paid employees is not paid anything then it is listed as ($0). It is not uncommon for only one, two, or even none, of the officers or staff to be paid. If there is no amount listed in parentheses for the first three officers or principals, then we were unable to locate their compensation; it does not necessarily mean they were unpaid. If there are more than three who earn over $100,000, that information is included. Disclosure laws differ for organizations with various IRS tax statuses. Notably, organizations with 501(c)(4) status are only required to disclose the compensation of its officers, while 501(c)(3) nonprofits must disclose officers' compensation *and* the five highest-paid employees who receive more than $50,000. (See **Tax Status** below for more information.) Unless otherwise noted, the amounts given are for the year listed under **Total Revenue**.

Mission or Interest: A brief statement of objectives. Some organizations have many detailed goals and others express their aspirations in more abstract or ethereal terms. Whenever the organization's own words seem to capture their essence best, we put these in quotes.

Accomplishments: Lists what the organization or The Right Guide's editors believe to be the organization's most significant or interesting results. Space usually limits the information that can be presented. How the organization spent its revenues is typically listed here. This is where the recipients of philanthropic foundations' grants are listed.

Total Revenue: Includes "Contributions, Gifts, Grants, and Similar Amounts Received" for 501(c) organizations. This does not include the value of services donated by volunteers. The amount listed here is for a single fiscal year. Some organizations do not end their fiscal year December 31. For these organizations we have listed them as FY (for Fiscal Year), and then whatever month their fiscal year ended. So an organization whose total revenue was $788,863, and whose fiscal year ended December 31, 1994, is listed simply as "1994 $788,863," as in our example. However, if that same organization ended their fiscal year in September, it will be listed as "FY ending 9/94 $788,863." Some organizations receive government grants. These grants usually come from the federal government, but many receive grants from state and local governments as well. Government grants are listed by total amount and percentage of total revenue that this constitutes. If the Acton Institute had received $20,000 in grants, following the **Total Revenue** it would have read "$20,000, or 3%, from government grants." More detailed information on these government grants, when available, is listed under **Other Information**. Listed information reflects the latest data on file with the Internal Revenue Service. For more information on what constitutes revenue, consult "Instructions for Form 990" from the IRS. Following the **Total Revenue** (and government grants where applicable), The Right Guide lists growth rates for most organizations. In our example, "22%(2)." What this means is that over the period covering the last three years, 1992 →₁→ 1993 →₂→ 1994, there were two measurable changes, and the average of these increases was 22%. If the organization's revenues had decreased over the corresponding period of time, it would have read "(-22%)(2)." For 501(c)(3) organizations, if there is no growth rate listed after **Total Revenue**, consult **Other Information**. There may be a listing under this heading for the growth rate for contributions and grants received by the organization in question. Since these contributions and grants usually make up the largest source of revenues, this measurement makes an excellent substitute. Changes in revenue for grant-making philanthropies are not included, but their changes in assets are listed under **Net Assets**.

Total Expenses: "Program Services, Management and General, and Fundraising Expenses" for 501(c) organizations. This is how much the organization spent to operate in the given fiscal year. The fiscal year for **Total Expenses** is the same as for the period listed in **Total Revenues**. The three percentages following the expenses constitutes the breakdown of expenses by Program Services/Management and General/Fundraising Expenses - in our example, "78% /12% / 10%." These percentages should add up to 100%; however, in some cases rounding-off may cause discrepancies. In some instances, payments to affiliates is a substantial expense, and is not reflected by these three percentages, causing a large difference between the sum and 100%. It should be noted that there is often crossover between these categories. (For example, the publication of a newsletter will fall under the heading of "Program Services," but this newsletter will also usually contribute to fundraising efforts.) For more information on what constitutes expenses, consult "Instructions for Form 990" from the IRS.

Net Assets: "Net Assets or Fund Balances, end of year." The net assets include the current year's excess (or deficit) of revenue over expenses plus the net assets (or deficit) carried over from the previous fiscal year. Grant-making private foundations' net assets are listed at their market value, as opposed to their book value. In our example, the Acton Institute had net assets of $514,412. Rather than accumulating assets, some organizations are net debtors at the end of the fiscal year. The Right Guide lists net debt in parentheses, with a negative sign, like this: (-$514,412). This is unlike standard accounting procedures, where either a negative sign or parentheses denotes negative value, and both together would signify a positive value. We hope this does not cause confusion among users of the Guide familiar with accounting procedures. However, most users of the Guide will probably not be familiar with standard accounting procedures, and for that reason both a negative sign and parentheses are used to make it easier to determine at a glance that the organization is a net debtor at the end of that fiscal year. For grant-making philanthropies, we measured the change in assets, similar to the change in **Total Revenues** for other organizations. This is because these philanthropies rely on a base of accumulated assets, rather than annual revenues, for their programs, and a better measure of the organization's well-being is the change in assets.

Products and Services: Includes tangible activities and objects produced or offered by the organization. **Periodicals** are listed separate from this heading. Lobbying expenditures are listed here for 501(c)(3) organizations, who are allowed to spend a portion of their expenses on lobbying without paying a tax penalty (see **Tax Status** for more information on 501(c)(3) lobbying). There are two types of lobbying, grassroots lobbying and direct lobbying. Grassroots lobbying refers to the organization's efforts to generate interest on the part of the general public regarding a specific piece of legislation. This might include postcard and letter-writing campaigns, rallies, demonstrations, billboards, or newspaper and magazine ads that urge you to call or write your representative. Direct lobbying is either face-to-face contact between the organization's lobbyist and the legislator, or direct contact by the organization with the legislator or his office through phone calls or letters.

Tax Status: Many organizations are for-profit businesses that maintain operations based on the sale of their goods or services. They are listed as simply "For profit." The most frequently listed nonprofit tax status is 501(c)(3). Briefly, this means that contributions to the organization are considered charitable donations and thus deductible for taxpayers who itemize. A 501(c)(3) organization may engage in educational activities, but may not directly try to influence a particular piece of legislation. That is, they may publish a nonpartisan analysis of particular legislation, but they may not directly say this legislation should not be enacted. To do so would be considered lobbying. There are exceptions to this rule. 501(c)(3) organizations may spend approximately 15% to 20% of their expenses, up to a maximum of $1 million, on lobbying without paying a penalty, depending on the amount of their expenses. The second most frequently listed tax status is 501(c)(4). These are also nonprofit; however, individuals may not (in general) deduct payments to these groups, but in some cases businesses can deduct payments to them as ordinary and necessary expenses. A 501(c)(4) organization may lobby on behalf of, or against, specific legislation if it is to promote the general social welfare, and not the benefit of a single industry. Another common tax status is 501(c)(6) which is granted to business leagues. These organizations represent a common business interest and may lobby on behalf of that interest. In general, donations to 501(c)(6) organizations are not deductible, although a portion of membership fees may be. We have made no attempt to verify all the organizations' tax status with the IRS, and users of The Right Guide should verify this information and obtain qualified tax counsel in all cases. There are many other forms of tax-exempt status. Researchers are referred to IRS Publication 557, "Tax-Exempt Status for your Organization," for more information.

Report: Indicates the availability of an annual report from the organization.

Employees: Usually includes full-time staff. However, some probably list part-time and volunteers too. Researchers should recognize that many organizations have a tiny or nonexistent full-time staff but have extensive programs. Some accomplish their goals through unpaid volunteers and others use consultants, leased, temporary and contract personnel.

Citations: The Right Guide, using a database and search procedures provided by DataTimes®, searched the full text and abstracts of over 150 daily newspapers nationwide for citations of the 250 largest organizations, as determined by yearly revenues. The citations were taken from a one year period, from April 17, 1996 to April 17, 1997. Grant-making foundations were omitted. The figure listed, "26:138," represents the total number of citations "26", and the rank out of 250, " 138." So, the Acton Institute was cited 26 times, and this ranked 138th out of 250. When affiliated organizations have the same name except for one word, as in the case of Citizens for a Sound Economy and Citizens for a Sound Economy *Foundation*, a search for the first name would find citations for the second, and so the same figure is given for both of the affiliates. Some organizations that would have been included in the 250 were excluded because their names are also common figures of speech, and the search could not distinguish between the two. Examples of this include National Affairs, Family Foundation, Human Life, and others. Not all organizations seek the public's attention, so the number of citations may not reflect those groups' influence or ability. Also, organizations' publications or specific programs may have been cited rather than the organization itself. Despite these qualifications the editors and publisher find these measures informative, and a useful guide to the relative influence of the various organizations.

Board of Directors or Trustees: Lists members of the board. Many organizations have a long list of distinguished board members, but only a partial list is included here due to space limitations. In private enterprise, board members are usually paid for service. Nonprofit board members are usually significant donors, high-level employees of major corporations, or leaders of other advocacy organizations. Many organizations now have a separate board of academic advisors for intellectual guidance. Sometimes these academic advisors are listed under this heading or else under **Other Information.**

Periodicals: Lists regularly produced publications. Books, pamphlets, papers and studies are listed under **Products and Services.**

Internships: Indicates if the organization has an active interest in obtaining summer or temporary interns. Sometimes the interns receive a modest stipend. Students who are knowledgeable about the organization's interests, the subject areas that interest the organization, and who have skills such as word processing, spread sheets and office procedures have the best chance at these openings. Others should inquire about unpaid internships. Most organizations would consider an application for an unpaid summer internship from a college student.

Other Information: This section contains information that does not fit under other headings. The year the organization was established is often included here as well as background information on the organization, key employees, and founders. More detailed information regarding sources of funding is covered including contributing foundations and details regarding assets.

STATUS UNKNOWN

This section contains an alphabetical list of groups identified as right-of-center, a fact the editors of The Right Guide have been unable to confirm. Despite written requests for information, no response was received. Some of these groups are in operation, but uninterested in appearing in the Guide, or the organization is defunct and our inquiries were not returned. The last known address, phone number and contact person is recorded. Be aware that these groups may be less responsive to your interest. We, of course, welcome any information on these organizations that would be of value to researchers.

NO FORWARDING ADDRESS

This section lists organizations believed to be right-of-center, but mail sent to the address listed was returned as "no forwarding address." Whether these organizations are still functioning at other addresses or are suitable for listing is unknown. The last known addresses for these groups are listed. The editors earnestly solicit information about these organizations for future editions.

DEFUNCT

These organizations, unlike those in **Status Unknown** and **No Forwarding Address**, have been confirmed to no longer operate. We provide the last known address for purposes of identification and to assist researchers who may study the life cycle of these groups. The organizations listed here have become defunct in the last few years. The editors welcome information on other groups that have ceased operations or that are successors to the ones listed in this section.

PERIODICALS

This section contains an alphabetical list of the serial publications produced by the organizations listed in the **Profiles** section, whether they are members-only newsletters, or magazines and newspapers available at your local newsstand.

OTHER INFORMATION SOURCES

The Right Guide is the most comprehensive guide to right-of-center organizations. However, there are other publications of a specialized nature that cover other aspects of the progressive movement, or that would interest users of The Right Guide. We include these sources so that researchers have, in a single source, the most complete guide to the Right.

GEOGRAPHIC LIST

Organizations from the **Profiles** section are listed geographically by the 50 states and the District of Columbia. Page numbers are not inlcuded. Researchers can use this section to find local organizations, or to study the distribution of advocacy organizations.

KEYWORD INDEX

Keyword indices may be unfamiliar to those who do not regularly use library reference materials. This index lists groups not only alphabetically by the first word in the name, but also by all other key words in the organization's name (words such as the, of, for, etc., are not indexed). For more complete information on how to use this section, see the **Keyword Index** title page immediately preceding the keyword index.

PROFILE SUBJECT INDEX

The organizations in the **Profiles** section are listed in alphabetical order by name. The **Profile Subject Index** lists organizations by subject so that researchers who are not looking for a particular group, but rather are looking for information on a particular topic, can find a variety of organizations dedicated to that area of interest. For example, researchers looking for information on school vouchers will find groups who advocate this policy in the **Education** section, under the subsection **School Choice**, in the **Profile Subject Index**.

MULTI-CATEGORY
Organizations under this heading have a very wide range of interests. Researchers can contact these groups about any of the areas listed in the Profile Subject Index, although none have programs in all areas. Organizations listed here are good first contacts in researching either established or new subject areas.

ABORTION
Following are the organizations that are considered conservative or libertarian, and cover both sides of the abortion issue. While many organizations in The Right Guide take positions on the issue, these organizations make it their primary focus.

ABORTION-RIGHTS ADVOCATES

ANTI-ABORTION ADVOCATES

ANTI-COMMUNISM

These organizations are dedicated to fighting communism abroad and ferreting out communist influences at home. With the crumbling of communist governments throughout the world, the missions of these organizations have become ambiguous. Many are taking advantage of the new openings in the former communist countries to bolster their historic documentation of the tragedies that constituted communist rule - they are also adding to the documentation of the complicities of certain individuals and governments during the Cold War. Some focus on human rights in communist and formerly-communist countries. Others focus on the influence of Marxism and other forms of collectivism in academia and culture.

ART, ENTERTAINMENT, LITERATURE, AND CULTURE

The listed organizations critique current culture - the arts, entertainment, popular culture, literature - and its effects on society. Many of them see underlying cultural influences as much more important to the shaping of our society than any current partisan fight. They are proponents of preserving cultural heritage and developing contemporary art and literature based on traditional criteria, not on shock value or political relevance.

CRIME AND LAW ENFORCEMENT

The following organizations focus on the day-to-day workings of law enforcement, criminal law, and the prison system. They pursue solutions based on a belief in the limits of government, constitutional rights, and the criminal - not society or weapons - as the center of law enforcement efforts.

ECONOMICS

ECONOMIC THEORY

This group of organizations focuses on underlying universal laws of economics. Unlike the groups listed in **Public Policy Economics**, these organizations do not focus on the debate of the day and are usually not good sources for facts and statistics on current situations. Organizations listed here represent differing opinions and schools of thought, such as Austrian economics, supply-siders, the public choice school, and others. Many of these organizations advocate a gold-based currency standard, as opposed to the United State's current system of fiat currency, but for a complete listing of such organizations, see the subheading **Gold-Backed Money**. For more information on some of the basic concepts held by these various approaches, researchers are encouraged to examine the New Palgrave Dictionary of Economics.

GOLD-BACKED MONEY (anti-Federal Reserve)

Organizations under this heading generally advocate a monetary standard based on the value of gold or some other commodity. They reject the current monetary authorities of the United States, who issue paper money based on the credit and good faith of the United States government, and is not redeemable through the Treasury (as it once was) for a fixed quantity of gold. They are anti-inflation, and blame the current Federal Reserve system for inflation, business cycle fluctuations, and recessions. They also oppose the Federal Reserve for other reasons. The fact that the Federal Reserve is directed by a board of governors who are not elected by the general public, that it is a private not public agency, and as an institution it is not a part of the constitution, are all reasons for opposition. The advocacy of gold- or silver-backed money is frequently associated with populists, although not all of the organizations listed here can be described as such. However, most of the organizations listed under the **Populists** heading can reliably be expected to support a metallic currency.

LABOR AND EMPLOYMENT POLICY

These organizations focus on economic policy and legal developments regarding labor and employment. Many focus on the activities of labor unions, and represent the businesses and industries that employ an organized labor force. Others focus on employment regulations, such as the minimum wage and occupational safety laws.

PRIVATIZATION

The following organizations are involved in advocacy and the practical aspects of assigning various functions now handled by the government to the private sector. They develop ways to make government more efficient and more responsive to public needs. By breaking the government monopoly on services, costs can often be reduced. Privatization is also used to reduce the number of politically-powerful public-sector unionized employees; the only employment sector that has experienced recent growth in unionization. Most of these organizations have a nation-wide focus. For information on specific state and local areas, organizations listed under the **State and Local** heading can reliably be expected to support privatization and have programs and information in this area.

PUBLIC POLICY ECONOMICS

Organizations under this heading focus on current public policy and economic problems in the United States. Taxes, deficits, regulations, capital accumulation, and trade are among the many issues these groups study. In addition, most of them develop solutions based on competitive, free-market fundamentals. These organizations typically focus on the national economy. For those working in specific states or regions, see the **State and Local** heading.

REGULATIONS

Organizations here are opposed to excessive government regulation, whether for environmental, safety, or consumer protection. Most view regulations as an unnecessary infringement upon the workings of a market economy. They maintain that these regulations increase the cost to the consumer, impede economic growth, and may not have the desired effect of making citizens safer. Even worse - they maintain - these regulations impede innovation and new developments, in industries such as pharmaceuticals and manufacturing, that would improve health and well being.

TAXATION

These organizations specialize in public policy related to taxation. They produce studies, lobby government officials, and organize against taxes at the grassroots level. While virtually all organizations in The Right Guide advocate reduced taxation - for these organizations it is their primary focus, or they feature specific programs with this goal.

EDUCATION

COLLEGE AND UNIVERSITY PROGRAMS AND AFFAIRS

Many organizations here have college-level degree programs with conservative or free-market leanings at various colleges and universities. Others are research institutes affiliated with a college or university. (The affiliated university is included in parentheses.) There are also groups which specialize in aiding college students in various ways, such as combating 'politically correct' administrators and instructors, protecting the rights of students to free speech and free inquiry, and promoting higher standards of scholarship. Others promote a particular conservative or libertarian cause or causes that are of interest to college students.

GENERAL EDUCATION

The organizations listed here promote a variety of approaches to improving education at the kindergarten through high-school levels. Some advocate tougher standards, concentration on the fundamentals, and the teaching of the free-enterprise system. Others want schools to eliminate such programs as sex education and value-neutral instruction. All operate from a conservative perspective.

HOME SCHOOLING

These groups advocate, defend, or facilitate the instruction of children at home, by their parents. They produce teaching materials and books, legal and academic defenses for their practices, and set up networks between home schooling parents.

SCHOOL CHOICE

Organizations listed here advocate and defend the idea of parents choosing the schools their children attend, and competition among schools to attract students. Many provide funding for low-income students to attend private schools. Frequently these programs are set up to prefigure or duplicate proposed school-choice legislation, so as to demonstrate the viability of such legislation.

ENVIRONMENT

GENERAL ENVIRONMENT

The organizations listed here take a variety of approaches to preserving the environment and facilitating economic growth. The common core among these organizations is their desire to use the market price mechanism to allocate scarce resources, and private property as the primary institution to protect and conserve resources. Most organizations here oppose the left-leaning environmental, or 'green,' movement and its reliance on government control and regulations. Many are concerned with the perceived politicization of science associated with the environmental movement, and advocate public policy set on a stricter criteria of scientific certainty. For more information, see the organizations listed under **Property Rights** and the subheading **Regulations**, under **Economics**.

WISE-USE GROUPS

The Wise-Use or Multiple-Use movement focuses on the rights of people to use natural resources, as well as conserve them for future generations. These groups are often made up of those who work in extraction industries (mining, forestry, cattle, trappers, etc.) and the companies they work for, as well as sportsmen (hunters and fishers). They also represent those who live on or near federally protected lands, and those who use these lands for recreation. Though pro-business, they have been criticized by some free-market advocates for supporting special government privileges and subsidies for their industries and lifestyles.

FIREARM OWNERS' RIGHTS

These groups are dedicated to the preservation of the right to own and lawfully use firearms. They promote the individuals' right of self-defense and the defense of their family and property. They view the Second Amendment right to keep and bear arms as a fundamental right which insures all of the other rights.

FOREIGN POLICY / NATIONAL SECURITY

CIVIL DEFENSE

These groups promote the knowledge, preparation, and products the civilian population would need in case of a nuclear, biological, or standard war on American soil. They believe that preparation decreases the chances of war. They also plan for the eventuality of natural disasters.

GENERAL FOREIGN POLICY AND NATIONAL DEFENSE

The concern of these groups is the foreign policy and national security of the United States, its allies and other friendly nations.

FOUNDATIONS AND PHILANTHROPIES

The following organizations use their assets to fund numerous activities in various fields. They support organizations in this directory, as well as others. Most do not make grants to individuals per se, but some do award scholarships and fellowships. Although all the foundations listed here award grants to support conservative or free-market activities, often it is only a very small proportion of their total grant-making budget. Other organizations under this listing monitor the grant-making activities of these and other foundations, as well as corporate philanthropy.

GENDER BASED

These groups advocate a certain position or philosophy based on, or directed to, a particular gender. Some advocate policies based on perceived gender inequities, others on the necessity of preserving certain historical and social-based gender roles. Some simply put forth a conservative or free-market agenda and direct it to one of the sexes in particular.

HEALTH CARE

The organizations listed here are involved with the health-care sector in some way. Many are concerned with health care from a consumer safety point of view, some from an ethical point of view, others pursue market-based reforms. All operate on the principle, to some degree, that health care is provided in a market which is controlled by supply and demand. This view is in stark contrast to the progressive, or 'school of public health' view, where health care is a public good distributed according to need.

HOMOSEXUALITY AND SOCIETY

These groups are conservatives or libertarians concerned with the status and rights of homosexuals in society. Some oppose open homosexuality and assist homosexuals to become heterosexuals, if possible. Others advocate homosexuality as natural and fully deserving of the same status as heterosexuals. The listed groups who oppose homosexuality do not deny constitutional rights to homosexuals, and those who support homosexuals' rights to not advocate special privileges or protected status.

IMMIGRATION

The aims of these organizations vary greatly, but the majority advocate the restriction of immigration for cultural or economic reasons. Some support immigration on behalf of a certain constituency, but none represent a (libertarian) open-border policy. Researchers looking for arguments on behalf of open-border immigration are referred to the writings of Dr. Julian Simon, author of The Economic Consequences of Immigration and The Ultimate Resource. Another source on open-border immigration might be one of the libertarian organizations listed in this directory who, although they do not specialize in it, may have studied the issue.

INTERNATIONAL

All of these groups operate outside the United States, or are located in the U.S. and focus on the affairs of other countries. They pursue as many different aims as there are organizations. Researchers should recognize that they vary in their adherence to what we call conservatism or free-market economics in the United States. In previous editions, The Right Guide had a much larger International section. Due to the explosion of free-market organizations worldwide, the Guide has had to reduce the scope of this section. The organizations listed here were chosen because of their contributions to, and connections with, conservative and free-market organizations and research in the United States. For this reason, most of the organizations here are English-speaking, or regularly produce translations. The organizations listed here that are located in the United States are excellent sources for contacting foreign organizations involved in conservative and free-market policy. In particular, the Atlas Economic Research Foundation, Foundation Francisco Marroquin, and the Institute for Contemporary Studies are recommended sources for more organizations and contacts.

LEGAL

These organizations focus on the United States' legal system. They work in a variety of areas, from criminal justice to property rights and constitutional law. Some perform research and others litigate cases that they feel are in the public interest, choosing cases that will have maximum impact on the legal system.

LIBERTARIAN

Libertarians generally believe that the only legitimate function of the government is the protection of the rights of the citizen. Specifically, they often focus on the right to own and dispose of property, right of free association, free speech, limited government, low taxes, deregulation, privatization, democracy and religious freedom. There are many different approaches to libertarianism, and not all hold the same beliefs or take the same approach. However, we think most points of view are represented in the organizations listed here.

MEDIA

These organizations are involved in researching and documenting leftist bias in the mainstream news and entertainment industry. (For conservatives and libertarians who are forming their own media outlets, please see PUBLICATIONS and TELEVISION AND RADIO PROGRAMMING).

OBJECTIVISTS

Objectivists adhere to the philosophy that existence is a given and that reality is knowable through the faculties of logic. Objectivism has become synonymous with the philosophy of Ayn Rand, and most groups listed here are followers of her teaching. During her lifetime she was best known for her novels <u>Atlas Shrugged</u> and <u>The Fountainhead</u>. Now some might say her nonfiction philosophic work, developing justification for individual liberty, is the source of her fame.

PARTISAN POLITICS

Most of the groups in this guide are political in nature, but the groups listed here are directly involved in electoral politics. They are either themselves direct advocates of, or associated with, a political party, or are in some way connected to the process of electing candidates or passing legislation, or are constant observers of these processes.

POPULISTS

Many of these organizations, although opposed to large and intrusive government, are unlike most of the other organizations listed in The Right Guide in that they are more likely to attribute the growth of government to a centrally controlled source that is pushing for a single, socialist, world government. They attribute various sources as being behind this conspiracy, and distrust the perceived elites in politics, academia and industry. Others have become so distrustful of the federal government (and to a lesser extent, state and local governments), and see no hope for electoral reform, that they no longer acknowledge governmental authority over their lives. These individuals no longer pay taxes or seek the licencing, registration, and oversight that the government requires. Although many are thought of as militant 'survivalists,' this is rarely the case. The populist movement has grown tremendously over the past few years. By the very nature of these organizations, they tend not to incorporate or create a formal operational status. Despite this, we believe that The Right Guide includes a representative group of populist organizations and publications; and in particular, that these are the groups that frequently operate with the larger conservative and free-market movement, and should serve as a starting place for researchers.

PROPERTY RIGHTS

The groups listed here are dedicated to preserving private property rights, with an emphasis on the Fifth Amendment to the Constitution. Most of these organizations believe that currently the greatest threat to private property is the environmental, or 'green,' movement.

PUBLISHERS

The following organizations are primarily involved in the publication of either books, magazines, or newspapers. While most of the groups in this directory publish something, it is not their primary function. However, those listed under this heading specialize in publishing per se. (For a complete listing of all periodicals, including newsletters, see the **Periodicals** section.) Many of these publishers will furnish sample copies of periodicals for potential subscribers. Also included under this heading are writings and articles produced for computer-only services.

RACE AND ETHNICITY BASED

These conservative organizations appeal to and are concerned with issues of specific interest to segments of the population based on race or ethnic background. Generally, these groups see government as a problem rather than a solution to economic and social advancement, and oppose government programs to remedy group racial inequalities.

RELIGION AND PUBLIC LIFE

These organizations advocate religious values, approaches, and religion itself as an important component of both private and public life. They are aware of constitutional questions and legality. That is, although they may advocate adoption of laws that conform to their religious beliefs (usually Christian), none advocate a political relationship between government and a specific sectarian organization. (See also **Traditional Values** for organizations with similar interests, but who are less expressly religious.)

SENIOR CITIZENS' POLICY

These organizations focus on public policies that affect older Americans; specifically, on Social Security and Medicare. They typically advocate policies based on free markets.

STATE AND LOCAL

The following are public policy groups that concentrate on state and local issues. Many have a specific geographic interest, or specialize in public policy issues in a single state. The state or region they concentrate on is in parentheses. Researchers in any state should feel free to contact any of these groups about their home state's problems and possible solutions. Organizations that are state- or region-based and pursue a single issue, such as **Anti-Abortion** or **Property Rights**, will be listed under that corresponding heading, rather than under **State and Local**. The organizations here are subdivided into **Economic and Fiscal Policy**, and **Social Policy and Traditional Values** - although there is often overlapping interests between the two divisions.

ECONOMIC AND FISCAL POLICY

SOCIAL POLICY AND TRADITIONAL VALUES

TELEVISION AND RADIO PROGRAMMING

These organizations produce programming for radio and television. Although more and more groups are producing programming on video tape or can be heard on a single radio station, these groups are on cable or satellite television, are syndicated, or can otherwise be seen and heard nationwide.

TRADITIONAL VALUES

The groups listed here support traditional values in public and private life. Traditional values are difficult to define in a concrete way, there is no catechism of traditional values. When these groups refer to traditional values they are usually referring to the values, primarily related to the family, which evolved from the experience of many generations, usually under religious influence. (See also **Religion and Public Life** for similar organizations that are more expressly religious.)

PROFILES

This section contains information obtained from various reliable sources, including the organizations themselves. Where a quotation appears, unless otherwise attributed, it indicates that the statement comes directly from the organization. The **Profiles** section presents the basic information most researchers need; the organization's mission, accomplishments, key personnel, address, phone and fax numbers. We also included more in-depth and difficult to obtain information in the **Profiles**; financial information, salaries, and sources of funding. While we have listed the major areas of interest, most organizations have more interests then could be listed in the profile. Almost all of the organizations will respond to telephone or written inquiries. Most organizations are pleased to help, especially if you mention The Right Guide as your contact.

60 Plus Association

1655 N. Fort Meyers Dr., Suite 355
Arlington, VA 22209   **Phone:** (703) 807-2070
USA   **Fax:**   (703) 807-2073   **Internet:** http://www.60.org

Contact Person: James L. Martin, President.
Officers or Principals: Hon. Roger H. Zion, Honorary Chairman.
Mission or Interest: Supports public policy on behalf of senior citizens based on "free enterprise, less government, less taxes." Opposition to inheritance taxes. Supports Social Security privatization.
Accomplishments: Claims over 475,000 members
Products or Services: "Guardian of Seniors' Rights" award given to elected representatives. Voters' guides.
Tax Status: 501(c)(4)
Periodicals: *Senior Voice* (monthly newsletter).
Other Information: Chairman Roger Zion was a Republican Congressman from Indiana from 1967-75.

A. B. Laffer, V. A. Canto & Associates

5405 Moorehouse Dr., Suite 340
San Diego, CA 92121   **Phone:** (619) 458-0811
USA   **Fax:**   (619) 458-9856

Contact Person: Victor A. Canto, President.
Officers or Principals: Arthur B. Laffer, Chairman.
Mission or Interest: Economic and investment consulting services for businesses, individuals, and governments. Active in the United States, Canada, Europe, and the Pacific Rim
Products or Services: Seminars and workshops, economic analysis.
Tax Status: For profit.
Other Information: Arthur Laffer is a well-known supply-side economist and creator of the "Laffer Curve". Supply-side economists focus on marginal income tax rates, and hold that high rates serve as a disincentive to work, reducing labor supply and output. The Laffer Curve diagramed a curve showing that as marginal tax-rates rose, tax revenues would actually fall, after a point, because of lowered production. Laffer served on President Reagan's team of Economic Policy Advisors from 1981-89.

Abraham Lincoln Foundation for Public Policy Research

10315 Georgetown Pike
Great Falls, VA 22066   **Phone:** (703) 759-4599
USA

Contact Person: Jay A. Parker, President .
Officers or Principals: Jay A. Parker, President ($163,652, this represents compensation for 1993 plus the previous two years); James B. Taylor, Secretary/Treasurer ($10,225); Ashley D. Strand, Director ($1,335); Alice M. Mackey, Vice President.
Mission or Interest: "America's Black Conservative Voice of Action."
Accomplishments: J.A. Parker is "the longest active, black conservative." Rallied opposition and collected more than 500,000 citizen petitions opposing District of Columbia statehood. Filed a 'friend of the court' legal brief to stop the House from giving voting power to representatives from U.S. territories and the District of Columbia. Collected cards in support for Rep. Gary Franks (R-CT), a black conservative. (Franks was voted out of office in 1996.)
Total Revenue: 1993 $1,182,039 (-6%)(1) **Total Expenses:** $1,172,264 64%/6%/30% **Net Assets:** $40,988
Tax Status: 501(c)(4)   **Citations:** 281:33
Periodicals: *Judicial Watch* (newsletter).
Other Information: Jay Parker is also president of the 501(c)(3) Lincoln Institute for Research and Education. The Foundation received $1,002,493, or 85% of revenue, from contributors. $179,123, or 15%, from royalties. The remaining revenue came from interest on savings and temporary cash investments.

Abundant Wildlife Society of North America

12665 Highway 59 N
Gillette, WY 82716   **Phone:** (307) 682-2826
USA   **Fax:**   (307) 682-3016

Contact Person: Troy R. Mader, Director of Research.
Officers or Principals: R. A. "Dick" Mader, Founder/President.
Mission or Interest: Promotion of conservation, management, and the 'wise use' of wildlife. Preserve uses of wildlife - hunting, fishing, trapping - as part of America's heritage. "We take our name from the fact that its been through man's management that we have the abundant wildlife we have today."
Accomplishments: Led demonstrations against wolf transplants in Yellowstone National Park. Financed a booth in Yellowstone to inform visitors of the impact of wolves and show how the Endangered Species Act is used by our government to acquire control of land. Featured in a *Wall Street Journal* article. Delivered nearly 40,000 petition signatures opposing wolf recovery to the U.S. Fish and Wildlife Department

Products or Services: Brochures, special reports, media events, more.
Tax Status: For profit. **Annual Report:** No. **Employees:** 6
Internships: No.
Other Information: Established in 1989.

Academics for the Second Amendment

P.O. Box 131254
St. Paul, MN 55113   **Phone:**   (612) 641-2142
USA

Contact Person: Prof. Joseph E. Olson, President.
Officers or Principals: Prof. Joseph E. Olson, President ($0); Prof. Robert Cottrol, Director ($0); Prof. James Viator, Director ($0).
Mission or Interest: Academic research and education regarding the Second Amendment. "The view that the Second Amendment. . . guarantees only the states' right to maintain formal militias has attained a surprising respectability. That may be more explicable as an expression of the hostility many academicians feel toward guns and their owners than as unbiased constitutional interpretation. The Second Amendment does not guarantee merely a 'right of the states,' but rather a 'right of the people'."
Accomplishments: In the fiscal year ending August 1995, the organization spent $30,414 on its programs. These programs included an academic conference on the "Second Amendment and the Bill of Rights" featuring 20 participants, and a conference on "Firearms and Society" featuring 14 participants.
Total Revenue: FY ending 8/95 $33,015 **Total Expenses:** $31,311 **Net Assets:** $14,004
Products or Services: Conferences and research.
Tax Status: 501(c)(3)
Other Information: Established in 1992. Prof. Olson teaches law at Hamline University in Minnesota. He also serves on the Board of Directors of the National Rifle Association. Academics for the Second Amendment received $32,708, or 99% of revenue, from contributions and grants awarded by foundations, businesses, and individuals. (These grants included $10,000 from the Firearms Civil Rights Legal Defense Fund, and $5,000 from the Second Amendment Foundation.) The remaining revenue came from interest on savings and temporary cash investments.

Access Research Network (ARN)

P.O. Box 38069
Colorado Springs, CO 80937   **Phone:**   (719) 633-1772   **E-Mail:** arn@arn.org
USA   **Internet:** http://www.arn.org/arn

Contact Person: Dennis Wagner, Publisher.
Officers or Principals: Paul A. Nelson, Editor; William A. Dembski, Stephen C. Meyer, Jonathan Wells, Associate Editors.
Mission or Interest: Organization that focus on the origins of life and of human beings. Challenges the views of evolutionists, such as Darwinians, who hold that human life and origins are the result of chance and error with no intelligent design guiding it. Publishes *Origins & Design*, "an interdisciplinary, peer-reviewed quarterly with two related goals; (1) to examine theories of origins, their philosophical foundations, and their bearing on culture, and (2) to examine all aspects of the idea of design, Both 'origins' and 'design' are intellectual grounds on which theology, philosophy, and the natural sciences find themselves with an equal interest."
Accomplishments: Editorial advisors Michael Denton and Michael Behe presented their research at a conference hosted by the Ethics and Public Policy Center
Tax Status: 501(c)(3)
Board of Directors or Trustees: Editorial Advisory Board includes: Michael Behe (Biochemistry, Lehigh Univ.), Tom Bethell (*American Spectator*), John Angus Campbell (Speech and Rhetoric, Univ. of Memphis), Kenneth de Jong (Linguistics, Indiana Univ.), Michael Denton (Biochemistry, Univ. of Otago), Brock Eide (Committee on Social Thought, Univ. of Chicago), Doug Geivett (Philosophy, Talbot School of Theology), Loren Haarsma (Neuroscience, Tufts Univ.), Brian Harper (Applied Mechanics, Ohio State Univ.), Mark Hartwig (Social Sciences, Foundation for Thought and Ethics), Phillip Johnson (School of Law, Univ. of California, Berkeley), Robert Kaita (Plasma Physics Laboratory, Princeton Univ.), Dean Kenyon (Biology, S. F. State Univ.), Ernst Lutz (Senior Environmental Economist, The World Bank), J. P. Moreland (Philosophy, Talbot School of Theology), Bijan Nemati (Physics, Univ. of Oklahoma), John Mark Reynolds (Philosophy, Biola Univ.), Siegfried Scherer (Taxonomy/Molecular Evolution, Technical Univ. of Munich), Charles Thaxton (Chemistry, Prague), Hubert Yockey (Information Theory/Molecular Biology, Bel Air, MD), Stan Zygmunt (Physics and Astronomy, Valpraiso Univ.).
Periodicals: *Origins & Design* (quarterly academic journal).
Other Information: Correspondence should be addressed to editor Paul Nelson at: 600 Davis St., 3rd Floor West, Evanston, IL 60201, (847) 733-9417, e-mail "pnelson2@ix.netcom.com". Associate editor William Dembski is affiliated with the Center for Philosophy of Religion at the University of Notre Dame, Stephen Meyer with the Department of Philosophy at Whitworth College, and Jonathan Wells with the Department of Molecular and Cell Biology at the University of California.

Access to Energy

P.O. Box 1250
Cave Junction, OR 97523   **Phone:**   (503) 592-4142
USA   **Fax:**   same

Contact Person: Dr. Arthur B. Robinson.
Mission or Interest: Newsletter promoting technology and science. Dr. Robinson believes that environmentalism is corrupting science for political benefit and is one of the most dangerous threats to freedom. Disseminates facts and scientific inquiry into issues regarding nuclear and other forms of energy, and on the environment
Tax Status: For profit.
Periodicals: *Access to Energy* (monthly newsletter).
Other Information: *Access to Energy* was founded and published for 20 years by Petr Beckmann, until his death on August 3, 1993. Since then it has been taken over by Dr. Arthur Robinson, the founder of the Oregon Institute of Science and Medicine. Dr. Robinson was once Scientific Director of the Linus Pauling Institute, until he disproved Pauling's claim that high doses of vitamin C can prevent or cure cancer.

Accrediting Association of Bible Colleges
130-F North College St.
P.O. Box 1523
Fayettville, AR 72702   **Phone:** (501) 521-8164
USA

Contact Person: Randall Bell, Executive Director.
Officers or Principals: Randall Bell, Executive Director ($46,800).
Mission or Interest: A source of information on evangelical colleges. They set standards, accredit and evaluate member and candidate schools.
Accomplishments: In the fiscal year ending August 1995, the Association spent $280,974 on its programs.
Total Revenue: FY ending 8/95 $328,712 5%(2) **Total Expenses:** $322,434 87%/13%/0% **Net Assets:** $205,575
Tax Status: 501(c)(3)   **Citations:** 7:182
Other Information: Formerly called the American Association of Bible Colleges. Not all bible colleges are conservative or free-market oriented. Many are as liberal or 'politically correct' as secular schools. The Association received $298,100, or 91% of revenue, from membership dues. $21,297, or 6%, from the sale of publications. $7,445, or 2%, from interest on savings and temporary cash investments. The remaining revenue came from contributions and grants.

Accuracy in Academia (AIA)
4455 Connecticut Ave., N.W., Suite 330
Washington, DC 20008   **Phone:** (202) 364-4401
USA   **Fax:**   (202) 364-4098

Contact Person: Deborah Lambert, Secretary.
Officers or Principals: John LeBoutillier, President ($0); Charlotte McCormick, Vice President ($0); Donald Irvine, Treasurer ($0); Wilson C. Lucom, Vice President; Reed Irvine, Chairman.
Mission or Interest: "To expose the politicization of academia, and restore scholarship to universities. . . AIA investigates reports from students of seriously slanted or inaccurate information being imparted by classroom instructors. . . When we receive a complaint, we request and review the course catalog description of the class, the syllabus and reading list, students' class notes, and any hand-outs; we also contact other students in the class. . . We attempt to discuss the class with the professor. . . publicizes cases of biased teaching."
Accomplishments: Exposed specific cases of academic politicization and helped restore academic ethics through public pressure. Dr. Thomas Sowell (Hoover Institution) says of AIA's newspaper, "If sanity ever returns to the academic world, part of the credit will go to a small newspaper called *Campus Report*." In the fiscal year ending June 1995 AIA spent $440,260 on its programs.
Total Revenue: FY ending 6/95 $401,215 23%(2) **Total Expenses:** $454,134 97%/3%/0% **Net Assets:** $118,318
Products or Services: Investigation of students or faculty who have been penalized for "politically incorrect" views. Investigation of 'slanted or inaccurate' information imparted by classroom instructors.
Tax Status: 501(c)(3) **Annual Report:** Yes. **Employees:** 3   **Citations:** 4:196
Board of Directors or Trustees: Addie Letwin, Dr. Judith Reisman, Fred Decker, James Guirard, Kenneth Campbell.
Periodicals: *Campus Report* (monthly newspaper).
Internships: Yes, interns accepted for one semester terms.
Other Information: Affiliated with the 501(c)(3) Accuracy in Media and Center for the Defense of Freedom at the same address. AIA received $405,733, or 99% of gross revenue, from contributions and grants awarded by foundations, businesses, and individuals. (These grants included $1,000 from the John William Pope Foundation.) The remaining revenue came from dividends and interest from securities, interest on savings, and other miscellaneous sources. AIA lost $9,351 on the sale of inventory.

Accuracy in Media (AIM)
4455 Connecticut Ave., N.W., Suite 330
Washington, DC 20008   **Phone:** (202) 364-4401   **E-Mail:** 76307.3462@compuserve.com
USA   **Fax:**   (202) 364-4098

Contact Person: Donald Irvine, Executive Secretary.

Officers or Principals: Joseph Goulden, Public Affairs Director ($55,498); Donald Irvine, Executive Secretary ($48,712); Reed Irvine, Chairman ($29,111); Murray Baron, President; Wilson C. Lucom, Vice President; Samuel Shepard Jones, Jr., General Counsel.

Mission or Interest: Media watchdog. Exposes and documents bias in the news media.

Accomplishments: AIM has been actively calling for increased media attention into the case of the apparent suicide of White House Deputy Counsel Vincent Foster. AIM causes thousands of letter to be sent to sponsors of badly flawed programming. Representatives from AIM regularly appear on radio and TV talk shows. In the fiscal year ending April 1995 AIM spent $1,254,676 on its programs.

Total Revenue: FY ending 4/95 $1,524,605 (-3%)(5) **Total Expenses:** $1,686,212 **Net Assets:** $1,940,934

Products or Services: Books and tapes. Speakers, conferences, "AIM NET" computer bulletin board, Media Monitor radio show, weekly column. Representatives attend the shareholder meetings of several large media corporations to critique their performance and to introduce resolutions urging improvements. AIM produces "The Other Side of the Story," a television program for National Empowerment Television.

Tax Status: 501(c)(3) **Annual Report:** Comprehensive yearly audit available. **Employees:** 17 **Citations:** 146:48

Board of Directors or Trustees: Dr. Paul Busiek, Beverly Danielson, Frank Fusco, John Hueter, John Uhlmann, Dr. Charles Moser.

Periodicals: *AIM Report.*

Internships: Yes, for writing and research.

Other Information: Established in 1969. Affiliated with the 501(c)(3) Council for the Defense of Freedom and Accuracy in Academia at the same address. AIM received $1,315,334, or 86% of revenue, from contributions and grants awarded by foundations, businesses, and individuals. (These grants included $355,000 from the Carthage Foundation, $20,000 from the F.M. Kirby Foundation, $15,000 from the Scaife Family Foundation, $10,000 from the Milliken Foundation, $5,000 from the Aequus Institute, $3,000 from the Vernon K. Krieble Foundation, and $2,000 from the Ruth and Vernon Taylor Foundation, and $500 from the United Educators Foundation.) $72,324 net, or 5%, from the sale of inventory. $65,312, or 4%, from capital gains on the sale of securities. $53,680, or 4%, from dividends and interest from securities. The remaining revenue came from royalties, conference fees, and other miscellaneous sources.

Acton Institute for the Study of Religion and Liberty

161 Ottawa Ave., N.W., Suite 301
Grand Rapids, MI 49503   **Phone:** (616) 454-3080   **E-Mail:** info@acton.org
USA   **Fax:** (616) 454-9454   **Internet:** http://www.acton.org/

Contact Person: Kris Alan Mauren, Executive Director.

Officers or Principals: Kris Alan Mauren, Executive Director ($47,500); Rev. Robert A. Sirico, CSP, President/Chairman ($0); Jeff D. Sandefer, Vice Chairman ($0); Dr. Alejandro Chafuen, Secretary; Gerald P. O'Driscoll, Jr., Treasurer; Brett A. Elder, Operations Manager.

Mission or Interest: "To educate the religious and broader communities about the moral basis for personal and economic liberty."

Accomplishments: The keynote speaker at the Institute's 1996 annual dinner was Nobel Laureate in economics, Dr. Gary Becker. The 1994 dinner featured Justice Clarence Thomas. In 1996 the Institute started the Center for Economic Personalism, an "academic Center that promotes rigorous scholarly activity with the aim of generating new economic models synthesizing free-market economic theory and the central tenets of Christian social thought." The Institute has been prominent in the welfare reform debate. In 1995 it created the National Welfare Reform Initiative, which was launched with the "Welfare that Works" conference in Washington, DC. Conference attendees included: House Speaker Newt Gingrich, Gov. John Engler (R-MI), Mayor Stephen Goldsmith (R-Indianapolis), Dr. Marvin Olasky, Dr. Gertrude Himmelfarb, and Robert Woodson. More than 12,000 people worldwide receive the Institute's newsletter. In 1994 the Institute spent $497,530 on its programs.

Total Revenue: 1994 $788,863 22%(2) **Total Expenses:** $640,107 78%/12%/10% **Net Assets:** $514,412

Products or Services: Annual Samaritan Awards given to successful private charities that "practice effective compassion." In 1995 the Institute awarded $40,000 in prizes to ten winners. Quarterly three-day conference, "Toward a Free and Virtuous Society," for theology students and seminarians. Three times a year "Spirituality in a Capitalist Economy" retreats for business leaders. Conferences, Lord Acton Lecture Series, annual dinner, and several publications.

Tax Status: 501(c)(3) **Annual Report:** Yes. **Employees:** 13 **Citations:** 26:138

Board of Directors or Trustees: Dr. Edwin Feulner (Heritage Found.), Dr. Leonard Liggio (Atlas Economic Research Found.), Dr. Gerald O'Driscoll, George Strake, Jr., Betsy DeVos, David Padden, James Johnston. Advisors include: Dr. William Allen, Doug Bandow, Dr. Rocco Buttiglione, Sr. Connie Driscoll, Rabbi Daniel Lapin, Dr. Jennifer Roback Morse, Dr. Ronald Nash, Michael Novak, Rev. Dr. Edmund Opitz (Foundation for Economic Education), Rev. James Schall, Dr. Julian Simon, Hon. William E. Simon.

Periodicals: *Religion & Liberty* (bimonthly journal), and *Acton Notes* (monthly newsletter).

Internships: Yes, unpaid year-round.

Other Information: Established in 1990. Named for Baron John Emerich Edward Dalberg-Acton (1834-1902). Lord Acton was a prominent historian and social philosopher. According to Lord Acton, "Religious liberty is the generating principle of civil liberty; and civil liberty is the necessary condition of religious liberty." Lord Acton is perhaps best known for his quotation, "Power tends to corrupt; absolute power corrupts absolutely." The Institute received $714,020, or 91% of revenue, from contributions and grants awarded by foundations, businesses, and individuals. (These grants included $20,000 from the M.J. Murdock Charitable Trust, $10,000 from the Earhart Foundation, $5,000 from the Richard & Helen DeVos Foundation, $5,000 from the Aequus Institute, and $800 from the Charles G. Koch Charitable Foundation. In 1995, $100,000 from the Scaife Family Foundation, $80,000 from the Lynde and Harry Bradley Foundation, $40,000 from the Claude R. Lambe Charitable Foundation, $15,500 from the John M. Olin Foundation, $10,000 from the Sunmark Foundation, $10,000 from the Philip M. McKenna Foundation, $5,000 from the Roe Foundation, and $1,000 from the John William Pope Foundation.) $22,664, or 3%, from speaking engagements. $17,651, or 2%, from interest on savings and temporary cash investments. $12,148, or 2%, from the Lord Acton Lecture Series. $8,210, or 1%, from student conferences. The remaining revenue came from the sale of publications and other inventory.

Ad Hoc Committee in Defense of Life

150 E. 35th St.
New York, NY 10016   **Phone:**   (212) 679-7330
USA

Contact Person: James P. McFadden, President.
Officers or Principals: James P. McFadden, President ($0); Edward A. Capano, Vice President/Treasurer ($0); Edward W. McFadden, Secretary ($0); J.P. McFadden, Chairman; Thomas Bolan, Counsel.
Mission or Interest: "To educate people of all races and creeds concerning the importance and inviolability of human life and to foster a reverence for the inherent dignity of all human life however threatened or impaired."
Accomplishments: Its publication, *Lifeletter*, was described by *The Washington Post* as, "The nation's leading anti-abortion newsletter." In 1995 the Committee spent $95,854 on its programs. This included a grant of $4,000 for the Life Advocacy Alliance.
Total Revenue: 1995 $215,418 **Total Expenses:** $204,916 47%/32%/21% **Net Assets:** $38,921
Tax Status: 501(c)(3)   **Citations:** 0:233
Board of Directors or Trustees: Faith Abbott, George Boelger, Priscilla Buckley, William Drake, M.D., Don Farrell, John Finn, John Hackett, M.D., Anne Higgins, James Holman, Alice Maier, M.D., Thomas Nix, Jr., M.D., Joseph Stanton, M.D., Robert Walsh, M.D., Grace Wolfe, M.D.
Periodicals: *Lifeletter* (newsletter).
Other Information: Affiliated with the 501(c)(3) Human Life Foundation and National Committee of Catholic Laymen. They have a second office in Washington, DC: 1187 National Press Building, Washington, DC 20045, (202) 347-8686. The Committee received $214,399, or 99% of revenue, from contributions. The remaining revenue came from interest on savings and temporary cash investments.

Adam Smith Institute

23 Great Smith St.
London SW1P 3BL, England   **Phone:**   (44) 071-222-4995
UNITED KINGDOM   **Fax:**   (44) 071-222-7544

Contact Person: Scott Fowler.
Officers or Principals: Dr. Madsen Pirie, President; Sir Austin Bide, Chairman; Dr. Eamonn Butler, Director.
Mission or Interest: Research institute working on policy innovation based on free-market principles.
Accomplishments: Has played a major role in the privatization program both in the United Kingdom and internationally. Over one hundred of the policies they supported were adopted by the U.K. government in the 1980's. Prime Minister John Major said, "I think it can be fairly said that Britain has led the way on privatization, supported by the work of the Adam Smith Institute."
Products or Services: Produces regular policy reports and holds conferences on public policy issues.
Tax Status: Nonprofit. **Employees:** 6
Board of Directors or Trustees: Sir Ralph Bateman, KBE, Sir John Greenborough, KBE, Robert Bee.
Other Information: Nobel Laureate F. A. Hayek was the Chairman of the Academic Board until his death.

Adolph Coors Foundation

(see Castle Rock Foundation)

Advocates for a Competitive Economy

2300 N St., N.W., Suite 600
Washington, DC 20037   **Phone:**   (202) 663-9011   **E-Mail:**   moodyjim@aol.com
USA   **Fax:**   (202) 223-1512

Contact Person: Jim Moody, Chairman/CEO.
Mission or Interest: "Through direct advocacy and litigation - less government regulation, taxation, spending; more economic and political rights." Currently working to end restrictions on "commercial and compelled" speech.
Accomplishments: "Ended government cartels in citrus, hops, cherries, eggs and tree fruit. Other projects: deregulation of airlines, communications, peanuts, and sugar. Lots of litigation under the False Claims Act and Freedom of Information Act."
Tax Status: For profit. **Annual Report:** No. **Employees:** 2
Internships: Yes, for law students and graduate students in public-choice economics.

Advocates for Self-Government

1202 N. Tennessee St., Suite 202
Cartersville, GA 30120   **Phone:**   (404) 417-1304   **E-Mail:**   pschmidt@world.std.com
USA   **Internet:** http://www.his.com/~atlas/

Contact Person: Carole Ann Rand, President.
Officers or Principals: Carole Ann Rand, President ($44,949); David Dawson, Secretary ($0); Britt Miller, Treasurer ($0), George Schwappach, Director.

Mission or Interest: "To present the freedom philosophy honestly and persuasively to opinion leaders so that they can encounter, evaluate, and if appropriate, embrace the ideals of self-government." To accomplish that end they teach communication, outreach, and leadership skills to libertarians.

Accomplishments: In 1993 they gave extensive leadership training to 24 libertarians who will charter local Advocate service clubs. Carole Ann Rand spoke to over 500 libertarians on how to improve their communication skills. In 1994 the Advocates spent $20,547 on its programs.

Total Revenue: 1994 $125,896 (-15%)(1) **Total Expenses:** $131,233 16%/78%/6% **Net Assets:** $9,524

Products or Services: Speaker training, audio tapes and workbooks. "Operation Politically Homeless" outreach event kit. Seminar study group where newcomers evaluate libertarian ideas.

Tax Status: 501(c)(3) **Employees:** 3

Periodicals: *Liberator* (quarterly).

Internships: Yes.

Other Information: The Advocates received $105,760, or 84% of revenue, from contributions and grants awarded by foundations, businesses, and individuals. $12,773 net, or 10%, from the sale of inventory. $5,550, or 4%, from leadership training summit fees. The remaining revenue came from speakers fees, interest on savings, and temporary cash investments.

Aequus Institute

250 W. First St., Suite 330
Claremont, CA 91711   **Phone:** (909) 625-6825
USA

Contact Person: Larry Arnn, Executive Director.

Officers or Principals: Dr. Larry Arnn, Executive Director ($8,000); Dr. Edwin Feulner, Secretary ($8,000); Patrick Parker, President ($8,000); David Keyston, Vice President.

Mission or Interest: Grant-making foundation that funds the "study of Christian Science religion, the free market system and related areas."

Accomplishments: In 1994 the Institute awarded $509,700 in grants. Recipients included; $100,000 each for the Claremont Institute's Golden State Center for Policy Studies (executive director Dr. Larry Arnn is the president of the Claremont Institute) and the Heritage Foundation (secretary Dr. Edwin Feulner is the president of the Heritage Foundation), $65,500 for the Intercollegiate Studies Institute, two grants totaling $35,000 for the Atlas Economic Research Foundation, $15,000 for the Center for Security Policy, $11,500 for the Mont Pelerin Society, $10,000 each for the Competitive Enterprise Institute and Henry Salvatori Center, $8,000 for the Council for National Policy, $7,500 for the Capital Research Center, $5,000 each for Accuracy in Media, the Acton Institute, Institute for Humane Studies, National Defense Council Foundation, Pacific Research Institute, the Philadelphia Society, Reason Foundation, and Hillsdale College, $2,500 for the Education and Research Institute, $2,000 for the Center for Individual Rights, $1,000 each for the Center for Economic and Policy Education and Crispus Attucks Institute, and $500 for the Foundation Francisco Marroquin.

Total Revenue: 1994 $462,103 **Total Expenses:** $783,973 **Net Assets:** $4,871,276 (-5%)(2)

Tax Status: 501(c)(3)

Other Information: Established in 1990. The Institute received $435,029, or 71% of gross revenue, from capital gains on the sale of assets. $167,242, or 27%, from dividends and interest from securities. $5,567, or 1%, from interest on savings and temporary cash investments. The Institute lost net $146,775 on the sale of books and pamphlets.

Aid & Abet Foundation

P.O. Box 8787
Phoenix, AZ 85066   **Phone:** (602) 237-2533   **E-Mail:** patriotz@aol.com
USA   **Fax:**   (602) 237-2444

Contact Person: Officer Jack McLamb (Ret.), Executive Director/Editor.

Officers or Principals: Theresa Huebner, Executive Secretary.

Mission or Interest: Publish *Aid & Abet Police Newsletter*, a populist newsletter to assist officers of the law in keeping informed with important local, national and world issues that affect life in the United States. Although directed at law enforcement officials, anyone can subscribe.

Accomplishments: They say untold numbers of American lawmen, as well as private citizens are learning about true law and proper law enforcement as it was intended for America in its founding

Products or Services: Periodic newsletter, tapes, live lectures, radio talk show interviews and newspaper interviews.

Tax Status: Unincorporated. **Annual Report:** Yes. **Employees:** All volunteer.

Periodicals: *Aid and Abet Police Newsletter*.

Internships: No.

Other Information: Officer Jack McLamb (Ret.) is the most highly decorated police officer in Phoenix's history. The *Aid and Abet Police Newsletter* covers a variety of topics pertaining to law enforcement. Prominent among these topics is resisting what Officer McLamb sees as a slide toward "Socialistic World Government." To resist this he urges law enforcement officials to be practicing Christians, and to uphold their sworn oaths to defend the constitution - even if infringing on constitutional rights appears to make their police work easier.

Alabama Family Alliance

P.O. Box 59468
Birmingham, AL 35259   **Phone:**   (205) 870-9900
USA   **Fax:**   (205) 870-4407

Contact Person: Gary J. Palmer, President.
Mission or Interest: Traditional-values and free-market organization focusing on Alabama
Tax Status: 501(c)(3)
Periodicals: *Alabama Citizen* (monthly newsletter, inserted in Focus on the Family's *Citizen*).
Other Information: Member of the State Policy Network. Also affiliated with Focus on the Family, although they receive no direct financial support. In 1995 the Alliance received $2,500 from the Roe Foundation.

Alex C. Walker Educational and Charitable Foundation

c/o PNC Bank, One Oliver Plaza, 28th Floor
210 6th Ave.
Pittsburgh, PA 15222   **Phone:**   (412) 762-3866
USA   **Fax:**   (412) 762-6160

Contact Person: H.C. Flood, Jr., Vice President.
Officers or Principals: T. Urling Walker, Trustee ($1,582); Dr. Barrett C. Walker, Trustee ($1,582).
Mission or Interest: "Solution of social and economic problems through free market methods." Grant-making foundation that includes conservative and free-market organizations in its awards.
Accomplishments: In 1994 the Foundation awarded $209,200 in grants. Recipients included: $85,000 for the Heritage Foundation, $10,000 each for the Brookings Institution, Rockford Institute, National Center for Policy Analysis, and George Mason University's Law and Economic Center, $7,500 for the Cato Institute, $5,000 each for Americans for the Competitive Enterprise System, Competitive Enterprise Institute, and the Reason Foundation, $2,000 for the Capital Research Center, and $700 for America's Future. The Foundation also awarded $16,000 to the Nature Conservancy.
Total Revenue: 1994 $451,883 **Total Expenses:** $242,255 **Net Assets:** $5,073,293 (less than -1%)(2)
Tax Status: 501(c)(3)
Other Information: The PNC Bank manages the Foundation and received a fee of $16,575 in 1994. The Foundation received $231,454, or 51% of revenue, from capital gains on the sale of securities. $208,559, or 46%, from dividends and interest on securities. $11,870, or 3%, from interest on savings and temporary cash investments. The Foundation held $2,749,679, or 54% of assets, in corporate stocks. $1,672,068, or 33%, in government obligations. $628,510, or 12%, in corporate bonds.

Alexis de Tocqueville Institution (AdTI)

1611 N. Kent St., Suite 901
Arlington, VA 22209   **Phone:**   (703) 351-4969   **E-Mail:** jberthoud@aol.com
USA   **Fax:**   (703) 351-0090

Contact Person: John Berthoud, Vice President.
Officers or Principals: Cesar Conda, Executive Director ($82,300); Merrick Carey, President ($78,500); Bruce Bartlett, Senior Fellow ($60,333); Clifford Sobel, Chairman; Gregory Fossedal, Executive Chairman.
Mission or Interest: "Study, promote and extend the principles of classical liberalism: political equality, civil liberty and economic freedom. Conducts research on five key areas of concern to policy makers: 1) education, 2) immigration, 3) national defense, 4) taxes and economic growth, and 5) deregulation." Promotes policies in accordance with the views of French philosopher/journalist Alexis de Toqueville, who said, "The species of oppression by which democratic nations are menaced is unlike anything which ever before existed in the world. It does not tyrannize, but it compresses, enervates, extinguishes and stupefies a people, till each nation is reduced to be nothing better than a flock of timid...animals, of which the government is shepherd."
Accomplishments: Was at the forefront of an amendment introduced by Sen. J. Bennett Johnston (D-LA) and Rep. John Mica (R-FL) to compel the EPA to produce cost-benefit and risk analysis before issuing regulations. Analyzed the fiscal impact of enacting the legislative agenda of the National Education Association and AFL-CIO. Studied privatizing the Defense Department. Numerous op-eds and articles. In the fiscal year ending November 1994 the Institute spent $400,060 on its programs, up 82% from the previous year.
Total Revenue: FY ending 11/94 $565,841 88%(1) **Total Expenses:** $536,312 75%/16%/9% **Net Assets:** $218,925
Tax Status: 501(c)(3) **Employees:** 6   **Citations:** 85:73
Internships: Yes, during the school year and during summer.
Other Information: The Institute hired Frank Miele of Sunnyvale, CA, as a consultant and paid him $32,500. The Institute received $579,589, or 99% of gross revenue, from contributions and grants awarded by foundations, businesses, and individuals. (These grants included $30,000 from the Joyce Mertz-Gilmore Foundation -- which gives almost exclusively to left-of-center organizations. In 1995, $20,000 from the Lynde and Harry Bradley Foundation, $10,000 from the John M. Olin Foundation, and $10,000 from the John William Pope Foundation.) $6,533, or 1%, from dividends and interest from securities. The remaining revenue came from interest on savings and temporary cash investments. The Institute lost $20,584 on the sale of securities.

Allegheny Foundation

Three Mellon Bank Center
525 William Penn Place, Suite 3900
Pittsburgh, PA 15219   **Phone:**   (412) 392-2900
USA

Contact Person: Joanne B. Beyer, President.
Officers or Principals: Richard M. Scaife, Chairman; Donald C. Sipp, Treasurer.
Mission or Interest: Grant-making foundation that includes conservative organizations in its awards.
Accomplishments: In 1995 the Foundation awarded $2,080,500 in grants. Recipients included: $400,000 for the Intercollegiate Studies Institute, $100,000 for the Allegheny Institute for Public Policy, $85,000 for the Lincoln Institute of Public Opinion Research, $75,000 for the American Legislative Exchange Council, $40,000 for the Landmark Legal Foundation, and $10,000 for the Philanthropy Roundtable.
Total Revenue: 1995 $1,161,199 **Total Expenses:** $2,382,537 **Net Assets:** $30,284,745
Tax Status: 501(c)(3)
Other Information: The Foundation received $1,158,608, or 99.7% of revenue, from dividends and interest from securities. The Foundation held $26,900,615, or 89% of assets, in corporate stock.

Allegheny Institute for Public Policy

7 Parkway Center, Suite 612
Pittsburgh, PA 15220   **Phone:**   (412) 937-4526
USA   **Fax:**   (412) 928-1501   **Internet:** http://www.@nauticom.net/aipp/users

Contact Person: Jerry Bowyer, President.
Officers or Principals: Robert Chamberlain, Chairman; William J. Donahue, Vice Chairman; Jerry Fulmer, Treasurer;   Ron Stiller, Secretary.
Mission or Interest: "Formed to fill the gap, namely the lack of academically credible conservative polemic in Western Pennsylvania. Because regional policy issues were discussed within a very narrow ideological range, nothing remotely like a 'movement-conservative' philosophy held a significant role in elite planning or academic circles. . . The Allegheny Institute makes possible the addition of a conservative voice on local issues in an academically credible setting." Focus on county, city and local government in Pennsylvania.
Accomplishments: Released over 16 reports, and hosted a privatization workshop for county officials
Products or Services: "Institute Fax" weekly updates, numerous publications and news releases, workshops and seminars. Weekly syndicated television talk show, "Focus on the Issues."
Tax Status: 501(c)(3) **Annual Report:** Not yet. **Employees:** 2
Board of Directors or Trustees: Ruth Ann Baker, George Cahill, Richard Potter.
Periodicals: *Update on the Institute* (monthly newsletter).
Internships: Yes, for graduate students of public policy during the school year and summer.
Other Information: Established in 1995. In 1995 it received $107,500 from the Carthage Foundation, $100,000 from the Scaife Family Foundation, $100,000 from the Allegheny Foundation.

Alliance Defense Fund

7819 E. Greenway Rd.
Scottsdale, AZ 85260   **Phone:**   (602) 953-1200
USA   **Fax:**   (602) 953-6530

Contact Person: Alan Sears, President.
Officers or Principals: Alan E. Sears, President ($137,785 "includes one-time payment of bonus and carryover 1994 payroll"); Tom Minnery, Chairman ($0); E. Brandt Gustavson, Vice Chairman ($0); Tim Wildmon, Secretary; Mark Maddoux, Treasurer.
Mission or Interest: "Building the permanent national alliance of ministries and other supporters funding the legal protection of religious freedom, human life and family values." Assists litigation supporting religious freedom and traditional values, and opposing abortion and pornography. Also supports legal training for other organizations.
Accomplishments: In 1995 the Fund spent $859,486 on its programs. The largest program, with expenditures of $522,402, was the awarding of grants to other organizations. Recipients of these grants included; ten grants totaling $142,856 for the American Center for Law and Justice, seven grants totaling $69,739 for the Minnesota Family Council, $32,195 for the Christian Legal Society, three grants for $29,617 for the Western Center for Law and Religious Freedom, $25,000 for the National Institute of Family and Life Advocates, $25,000 for the Liberty Council, two grants totaling $24,675 for Americans United for Life, two grants totaling $18,915 for the Center for Individual Rights, four grants totaling $14,996 for the Anchorage Grace Brethren Church, two grants totaling $10,250 for the National Family Legal Foundation, $9,597 for the Center for Law and Religious Freedom, $8,000 for the National Law Center for Children and Families and $4,975 for the Coalition for Children. Other programs included public education efforts, public relations, and the development of a National Legal Advisory Group.
Total Revenue: 1995 $2,534,732 **Total Expenses:** $1,444,518 59%/11%/29% **Net Assets:** $1,823,178
Tax Status: 501(c)(3) **Annual Report:** Yes. **Employees:** 5   **Citations:** 16:160

Board of Directors or Trustees: James Bramlett (Campus Crusade for Christ), Allen Burkett (Christian Financial Concepts), Samuel Ericsson (Advocates Intl.), Clark Hollingsworth (Coral Ridge Ministries), Ray Miller (Fellowship of Companies for Christ), Charles Ohman (Jack Van Impe Ministries), William Pew.
Internships: No.
Other Information: Established in 1993. The Fund received $2,477,861, or 98% of revenue, from contributions and grants awarded by foundations, businesses, and individuals. (In 1994 these grants included $25,000 from the Richard & Helen DeVos Foundation. These grants have grown from $249,211 in 1993 and $1,380,353 in 1994; a two-year average growth rate of 115%.) $53,886, or 2%, from interest on savings and temporary cash investments. The remaining revenue came from rental income.

Alliance for America Foundation

P.O. Box 449
Caroga Lake, NY 12078   **Phone:** (518) 835-6702
USA   **Fax:** (518) 835-2527

Contact Person: Harry McIntosh, Executive Director.
Officers or Principals: Norman Murray, President ($0); David Guernsey, Vice President ($0); Don Powell, Vice President ($0); Bruce Vincent, Secretary; Tom Hirons, Treasurer.
Mission or Interest: "Putting people back into the environmental equation." They work to protect the rights of property owners and advocate the wise use of natural resources.
Accomplishments: Nationwide umbrella organization with chapters in all 50 states, representing over 500 organizations nationwide. They have hosted an annual "Fly-In for Freedom" since 1991. This Fly-In brings people adversely affected by environmental regulations to Washington, DC to talk to members of the U.S. Congress.
Total Revenue: 1995 $66,001 **Total Expenses:** $67,891 **Net Assets:** $10,852
Products or Services: Nationwide "Fax Alert System," briefing papers. In 1995 the Foundation spent $1,728 on the direct lobbying of legislators.
Tax Status: 501(c)(3) **Annual Report:** Yes. **Employees:** All volunteer.
Periodicals: *Alliance for America Newsletter.*
Other Information: Established in 1992. The Foundation received $62,008, or 94% of revenue, from contributions and grants awarded by foundations, businesses, and individuals. (These contributions and grants have increased by an average of 2% a year since its founding.) $3,902, or 6%, from the sale of inventory. The remaining revenue came from investment income.

Alliance for Medical Savings Accounts

23712 Clarkson
Southfield, MI 48034   **Phone:** (810) 357-7852
USA   **Fax:** (810) 357-7833

Contact Person: Michael J. O'Dea.
Mission or Interest: Dedicated to promoting Medical Savings Accounts as the free-market solution to reform health care.
Accomplishments: Several of O'Dea's articles have been published in national Catholic newspapers, including *The Wanderer* and *The National Catholic Register*. O'Dea has also been active in exposing how the major insurance companies require policy holders to pay for abortion coverage
Tax Status: For profit.
Other Information: Medical Savings Accounts, or "Medical IRA's," have received support from William F. Buckley, Rush Limbaugh, Sen. Phil Gramm (R-TX), and other conservative luminaries. Several states have already passed laws that would clear the way for Medical Savings Accounts to be put in place if the federal government changes the tax code to allow for it. Some states have passed resolutions calling on the federal government to enact such a law. The Kassebaum-Kennedy Health Care Act of 1996 included provisions for a limited number of Medical Savings Accounts to be allowed by the federal government, on a trial basis.

Alliance of California Taxpayers & Involved Voters (ACTIV)

P.O. Box 330
Aptos, CA 95001-0330   **Phone:** (408) 688-8986
USA   **Fax:** (408) 622-9138

Contact Person: Jane Armstrong, Chairman.
Officers or Principals: Lee A. Phelps, Founder.
Mission or Interest: Government watch-dog dedicated to saving taxpayers' money and restoring accountability to government. Focus on California.
Accomplishments: Helped qualify the "Three Strikes and You're Out" proposition on the 1994 California ballot. Led the campaigns for term-limits Propositions 140 and 164. Active in reducing California's income and inheritance taxes
Tax Status: California PAC. **Annual Report:** No. **Employees:** All volunteer.
Board of Directors or Trustees: Advisors include: David Keating (Exec. Vice Pres., National Taxpayers Union), Lewis Uhler, Jr. (Pres., National Tax Limitation Committee), Joel Fox (Pres., Howard Jarvis Taxpayers Assn.), Richard Gann (Pres., Paul Gann Citizens Committee), J. G. Ford, Jr.

Periodicals: *ACTIV News* (bimonthly newsletter).
Other Information: ACTIV cooperates routinely with American Legislative Exchange Council, Americans for Tax Reform, California Taxpayers' Assn., Center for California Taxpayer, Citizens Against Government Waste, Heritage Found., National Taxpayers Union Found., Pacific Legal Found., Pacific Research Inst., Tax Foundation, and U.S. Term Limits.

Alliance of Libertarian Student Organizations

25 Red Lion Square
London WC1R 4RL, England
UNITED KINGDOM

Mission or Interest: To organize student libertarian meetings and to make the case for a free society to students
Products or Services: Various student publications. Regular meetings and large libertarian student conferences. Pamphlets and leaflets.
Tax Status: Not exempt.
Periodicals: *The Libertarian Student, The No Statesman Magazine.*
Internships: No.
Other Information: Affiliated with the Libertarian Alliance. They welcome contact with foreign students. The title of their magazine, *The No Statesman Magazine*, is a parody of the British Leftist-socialist magazine, *The New Statesman.*

American Academy for Liberal Education (AALE)

1015 18th St., N.W., Suite 204
Washington, DC 20036
USA

Contact Person: Jeffrey Wallin, President.
Officers or Principals: Jeffrey Wallin, President ($110,000); Deal Hudson, Secretary ($29,708); Herman Belz, Chairman ($0); Jacques Barzun, Honorary Chairman; Chester Finn, Jr., Treasurer.
Mission or Interest: A new academic institution supporting higher education by offering its accreditation to member institutions "to raise the standards of undergraduate education." Accreditation is given based on academic merit and not 'politically correct' considerations.
Accomplishments: In the fiscal year ending August 1995 the Academy spent $322,347 on its programs. The AALE has been recognized as an accreditation agency by the U.S. Department of Education. Has admitted four institutions as candidates for accreditation. Numerous other institutions have expressed interest in AALE's programs.
Total Revenue: FY ending 8/95 $360,154 744%(2) **Total Expenses:** $395,405 82%/14%/5% **Net Assets:** $277,292
Tax Status: 501(c)(3)   **Citations:** 6:189
Board of Directors or Trustees: Dr. Elizabeth Fox-Genovese (Emory Univ.), Dr. Paul Gross (Dir., Center for Advanced Studies, Univ. of VA), Dr. John Harris (Asst. Provost, Samford Univ.), Hon. Richard Lamm (Dir., Center for Public Policy Contemporary Issues, Univ. of Denver), Martin Peretz, Dr. Shelby Steele, Charles Sullivan (Georgetown Univ.), Edward Wilson (Harvard Univ.).
Other Information: Established in 1992. The National Association of Scholars assisted in founding the AALE. The Academy received $342,250, or 95% of revenue, from contributions and grants awarded by foundations, businesses, and individuals. (These grants included $75,000 from the Sarah Scaife Foundation, $50,000 from the Lynde and Harry Bradley Foundation, and $5,000 from the John William Pope Foundation.) $17,904, or 5%, from interest on savings and temporary cash investments.

American Association for Small Property Ownership (AASPO)

4200 Cathedral Ave., N.W., Box 515
Washington, DC 20016   **Phone:** (202) 244-6277
USA   **Fax:**   (202) 363-3669   **Internet:** http://www.smallpropertyowner.com/~aaspo

Contact Person: F. Patricia Callahan, President.
Mission or Interest: Preserving the rights of small property owners as a prerequisite to entrepreneurship and strong economies in local communities. Challenges rent control and excessive regulation and taxation of property ownership.
Accomplishments: Awarded the "Best Independent Real Estate Newsletter" by the National Association of Real Estate Editors. Produced "Case Studies of Rent Control in Boston" that appeared in October 1994. This study is credited with being influential in the passage of a statewide referendum to repeal rent control in Massachusetts. AASPO efforts in Massachusetts attracted much attention and representatives were featured on numerous media outlets in the New England region. AASPO has attracted some national media attention and has been featured in *The Washington Times* and *Insight*. Plans to create a legal division, the Private Property Legal Foundation
Products or Services: Many studies on property rights issues. AASPO is working to establish a national network of community-based property rights organizations nationwide. Through an on-line computer system they hope to provide resources, information and training for activists.
Tax Status: 501(c)(3)
Periodicals: *Small Property Owner* (newsletter).
Other Information: AASPO has a Boston office, phone (617) 266-5444, fax (617) 266-8298.

American Association of Christian Schools (AACS)

P.O. Box 2189
Independence, MO 64055   **Phone:**   (816) 795-7709
USA   **Fax:**   (816) 795-7462

Contact Person: Gary A. Deedrick, Administrative Assistant.
Officers or Principals: Dr. Carl Herbster, President; Dr. Arno Q. Weniger, Vice President; Dr. Charles Walker, Educational Director; Rev. Duane Motley, Legislative Director.
Mission or Interest: Numerous services to protect and improve Christian schools. Schools that are affiliated with the National or World Council of Churches, the ecumenical movement, or the modern charismatic movement are not considered for membership.
Accomplishments: Serves over 120,000 students enrolled in member schools throughout the United States
Products or Services: Several books, an annual directory of member schools. Teacher placement service. Conferences. Representation in state and federal governments.
Tax Status: 501(c)(3)   **Annual Report:** No.   **Employees:** 10
Board of Directors or Trustees: Rev. Duane Motley, Dr. Leon Moody, Rev. Al Monson, Dr. Walter Brock, Dr. Dick Mercado, Sr., Dr. Malcolm Cummings, Dr. John Vaughn, Dr. Charles Walker, Dr. Earle Goode, Dr. Collins Glenn, Dr. Wayne VanGelderen, Sr., Dr. Ed Johnson, Rev. Lynn Sparkman, Dr. Marion Fast, Dr. Arno Weniger, Jr., Dr. Richard Grammer, Rev. Ken Stephens, Dr. Charles Herbster.
Periodicals: *Capitol Comments* (monthly), *Parent Update* (monthly).
Internships: Yes, during the summer at their Washington, D.C. legislative office.
Other Information: Established in 1972. Operates a legislative office in Washington, D.C., P.O. Box 15304, Washington, D.C. 20003. Phone (202) 547-2991, fax (202) 547-2992. AACS is made up of state associations, with 38 state offices.

American Center for Law and Justice (ACLJ)

1000 Regent University Dr.
P.O. Box 64429
Virginia Beach, VA 23467   **Phone:**   (757) 579-2489
USA   **Fax:**   (757) 579-2836

Contact Person: James E. Murphy, Vice President of Administration.
Officers or Principals: Colby May, Trial Attorney ($165,000); Jay Sekulow, Chief Counsel ($158,209); Keith A. Fournier, Executive Director ($158,209); Patrick Monaghan, Trial Attorney ($150,000); Benjamin Bull, Trial Attorney ($142,800); Gary Sekulow, Vice President ($135,000); Stewart Roth, Trial Attorney ($115,000); Pat Robertson, President; John Stepanovich, Norman Berman, James Murphy, Vice Presidents.
Mission or Interest: A public interest law firm and educational organization devoted to preserving religious liberties and promoting pro-family and anti-abortion causes.
Accomplishments: Have represented several cases before the U.S. Supreme Court. Won the right for individuals to distribute religious literature at game sites of the 1996 Olympics. Dispute resolution allowing a student-led prayer at a school graduation ceremony. Many significant victories from the U.S. Supreme Court, other federal courts, state courts, and administrative hearings. In the fiscal year ending March 1995 the ACLJ spent $8,892,499 on its programs.
Total Revenue: FY ending 3/95 $10,311,161 13%(2) **Total Expenses:** $10,961,372 81%/6%/13% **Net Assets:** $13,8786
Products or Services: Engages in litigation and provides legal support and advice. Maintains a listing of Christian Affiliate Attorneys for referrals. Various pamphlets.
Tax Status: 501(c)(3)   **Annual Report:** Yes.   **Employees:** 50+   **Citations:** 329:29
Internships: Yes, for law students.
Other Information: ACLJ describes the current state of legal attitude toward religion as "Religious Cleansing" - an effort to remove all traces of religious observance from public life. The ACLJ contracted Gene Knapp for public relations and paid him $51,400. The Center has offices in Georgia, Alabama, Kentucky, Arizona, and the District of Columbia. The ACLJ received $10,282,854, or 99.7% of revenue, from contributions and grants awarded by foundations, businesses, and individuals. (These grants included $142,856 from the Alliance Defense Fund.) The remaining revenue came from interest on savings and temporary cash investments.

American Christian Cause

208 North Patrick St.
Alexandria, VA 22314   **Phone:**   (703) 548-1421
USA

Contact Person: Rev. Robert G. Grant, Ph.D., President.
Officers or Principals: Rev. Robert G. Grant, Ph.D., President ($0); Rev. Don Sills, Vice President/Treasurer ($0); Sandra M. Ostby, Secretary ($0).
Mission or Interest: Pursuing moral accountability based on a biblical viewpoint. "Issues include education of our children, sex and AIDS education, drugs and violence, television and crime."
Accomplishments: In the fiscal year ending September 1995, the organization spent $158,097 on its programs.
Total Revenue: FY ending 9/95 $251,583 1%(2) **Total Expenses:** $251,643 63%/12%/25% **Net Assets:** $3,506

Products or Services: Educational materials and programs.
Tax Status: 501(c)(3)   **Citations:** 0:233
Other Information: Affiliated with the Christian Voice. The Cause received $251,583, or 100% of revenue, from contributions and grants awarded by foundations, businesses, and individuals. (These grants included $22,045 from Americans for Moral Government.)

American Christian History Institute

P.O. Box 648
Palo Cedro, CA 96073   **Phone:** (916) 547-3535
USA

Contact Person: James B. Rose, President.
Officers or Principals: James B. Rose, President ($21,500); Mary-Elaine Swanson, Vice President ($0); Barbara Rose, Secretary ($0); Marcene Bolton, Treasurer.
Mission or Interest: Research and educational foundation for the purpose of documenting and teaching America's Christian history, government, and education.
Accomplishments: In the fiscal year ending September 1995 the Institute spent $62,711 on its programs.
Total Revenue: FY ending 9/95 $107,004 (-6%)(2) **Total Expenses:** $62,711 67%/33%/0% **Net Assets:** $190,828
Products or Services: Published A Guide to American Christian Education for the Home and School - The Principle Approach, hardbound, in addition to several paperback books on geography and America's history. Conferences, more.
Tax Status: 501(c)(3) **Annual Report:** No. **Employees:** 1
Internships: Yes, seminars and day school.
Other Information: The institute received $55,750, or 52% or revenue, from contributions and grants awarded by foundations, businesses, and individuals. $15,136, or 14%, from conference and seminar fees. $13,311, or 12%, from speaker's fees and honorarium. $11,732, or 11%, from dividends and interest from securities. $10,862 net, or 10%, from the sale of inventory. The remaining revenue came from interest.

American Civil Defense Association, The (TACDA)

118 Court St.
Starke, FL 32091   **Phone:** (904) 964-5397   **E-Mail:** TACDA2000@DACCESS.NET
USA   **Fax:**   (904) 964-9641   **Internet:** http://www.daccess.net/TACDAtacda.htm

Contact Person: Walter Murphey, Executive Director.
Officers or Principals: Walter Murphey, Executive Director ($23,243); Kathy Eiland, Secretary/Treasurer ($10,588); Kevin Briggs, President ($0); Kenneth P. Brown, Vice President.
Mission or Interest: Promotes national defense and security through "known means of protection that will effectively protect the United States and make aggression against it a clearly unacceptable risk." Also concerned with preparedness in the face of terrorism, and natural and man-made disasters. Promotion the Strategic Defense Initiative space-based missile defense system.
Accomplishments: "Over thirty years of active campaigning for measures against disaster." In 1995 TACDA spent $76,541 on its programs; up from $36,687 in 1993. Featured speakers at their 1996 conference were; Dr. Edward Teller (developer of the hydrogen bomb), Dr. Reed Blake (Brigham Young Univ.), Sam Cohen (developer of the neutron bomb), Dr. Gerald Looney (Doctors for Disaster Preparedness), Charles Wiley (Accuracy in Media), Brian Bex, and Ambassador Henry F. Cooper (Chairman, High Frontier). The conference was co-sponsored with Accuracy in Media, American Strategic Defense Association, America's Future, High Frontier, and Live Free. Conference topics include the threats from chemical and nuclear terrorism, civil defense in other countries, shelters, and information "need(ed) to survive in a new world of mass casualty weaponry."
Total Revenue: 1995 $118,888 34%(2) **Total Expenses:** $103,018 74%/26%/0% **Net Assets:** $33,574
Products or Services: METTAG emergency medical tags and related products. Seminars, speakers, publications, etc.
Tax Status: 501(c)(3) **Annual Report:** No. **Employees:** 5
Board of Directors or Trustees: Nancy Greene (widow of actor Lorne Greene), William McCampbell (former employee of the Federal Emergency Management Agency), Hon. Donald Mitchell (former congressman), James Newman, Dr. Giuseppe Satriano, Thomas Strider, Edwin York.
Periodicals: *Journal of Civil Defense* (quarterly journal), *TACDA Alert* (monthly newsletter).
Internships: No.
Other Information: Founded in 1962 as the Association for Community-Wide Protection from Nuclear Attack. The *Journal of Civil Defense* began publication in 1968. TACDA received net $95,859, or 81% of revenue, from the sale of products. $11,926, or 10%, from member dues. $6,033, or 5%, from contributions and grants awarded by foundations, businesses, and individuals. $4,604, or 4%, from sales and subscriptions of the *Journal*. The remaining revenue came from interest on savings and temporary cash investments, and other miscellaneous sources.

American Civil Rights Institute

P.O. Box 188350
Sacramento, CA 95818   **Phone:** (916) 444-2278
USA   **Fax:**   (916) 444-2279   **Internet:** http://www.acri.org

Contact Person: Jennifer Nelson, Executive Director.
Officers or Principals: Ward Connerly, Chairman; Thomas Rhoades, Co-Chair.
Mission or Interest: "Work toward eliminating racial and gender preferences at the state and federal level."
Tax Status: 501(c)(3) (tax status pending) **Annual Report:** Not yet. **Employees:** 2
Internships: Yes.
Other Information: Established in 1997 by the people who successfully passed California's Proposition 209, a measure that made discrimination based on race or gender (affirmative action quotas) illegal in California state schools and government. Information and legal documents pertaining to Prop. 209 and its legal defense can be accessed on the internet at "http://www.wdn.com/cir/ccri.htm", a web-page set up by Center for Individual Rights. Affiliated with the 501(c)(4) American Civil Rights Coalition at the same address.

American Conservative Union (ACU)

1007 Cameron St.
Alexandria, VA 22314   **Phone:** (703) 836-8602   **E-Mail:** acu@conservative.org
USA   **Fax:**   (703) 836-8606   **Internet:** http://www.conservative.org

Contact Person: Jeff Hollingsworth, Executive Director.
Officers or Principals: David A. Keene, Chairman ($0); Thomas S. Winter, First Vice Chairman ($0); Leroy Corey, Second Vice Chairman ($0); Jameson Campaign, Jr., Secretary; Donald Devine, Treasurer.
Mission or Interest: Lobbying to further conservative causes.
Accomplishments: "Oldest conservative lobbying organization." The ACU is well-known for its *Ratings of Congress* which, since 1971, have ranked congressional members as liberal or conservative based on votes on key issues. They have over 100,000 members in over 40 state groups. Helped defeat President Clinton's health-care plan through the ACU organized "Citizens Against Rationing Health Care" coalition, nationwide 'town hall meetings' and the "Health Care Truth Tour." Supported "The Contract With America." Actively opposed the SALT treaties, the giving away of the Panama Canal, and supported U.S.-backed rebels in communist-controlled countries.
Total Revenue: 1993 $9,484,686 **Total Expenses:** $10,340,082 **Net Assets:** (-$1,306,729)
Products or Services: Long distance network. Lobbying, publications, video and audio tapes, coalition building. Annual "ACU Ratings of Congress." Hosts the annual Conservative Political Action Conference (CPAC).
Tax Status: 501(c)(4) **Employees:** 5
Board of Directors or Trustees: Jeffrey Bell, Charles Black, Morton Blackwell (Leadership Inst.), Ed Capano (*National Review*), Muriel Coleman, Becky Norton Dunlap (National Wilderness Institute), M. Stanton Evans (Consumers' Research), Alan Gottlieb (Second Amendment Foundation), Louis Guerra, Sen. Jesse Helms (R-NC), Rep. Duncan Hunter (R-CA), Tom Huston, Hon. Louis Jenkins (former Rep., R-LA), James Lacy, Michael Long, State Sen. Serphin Maltese (R-NY), Joseph Morris (Pres., Lincoln Legal Found.), Ralph Reed, Jr. (Exec. Dir., Christian Coalition), Craig Shirley, Hon. Steve Symms (Chair., American Policy Center), Lewis Uhler (Pres., National Tax Limitation Committee), Hon. Malcom Wallop (former Sen., R-WY).
Periodicals: *Battleline* (newsletter).
Other Information: Established in 1964 just a week after the decisive defeat of Sen. Barry Goldwater for President. Founding members included John Ashbrook, L. Brent Bozell, John Chamberlain, and William F. Buckley, Jr. Affiliated with the 501(c)(3) ACU Foundation at the same address. Also affiliated with the ACU Political Action Committee. The ACU received $9,395,432, or 99% of revenue, from contributions. The remaining revenue came from mailing list rentals.

American Council for Capital Formation (ACCF)

1750 K St., N.W., Suite 400
Washington, DC 20006   **Phone:** (202) 293-5811   **E-Mail:** info@accf.org
USA   **Fax:**   (202) 785-8165   **Internet:** http://www.accf.org

Contact Person: Mark A. Bloomfield, President.
Officers or Principals: Mark A. Bloomfield, President ($329,007); Mari Lee Dunn, Vice President ($127,513); Dr. Margo Thorning, Chief Economist ($116,364); Dr. Charls E. Walker, Chairman; Ernestine Johnson, Assistant Secretary/Treasurer.
Mission or Interest: To refocus the U.S. tax and environmental policy debate in a pro-capital-formation direction. Advocates lowering the capital-gains tax and reducing the deficit.
Accomplishments: Played a leading role in the 1990 debate on the appropriate taxation of capital gains through studies and congressional testimony. ACCF officers have been widely quoted in leading daily newspapers, business magazines, and respected tax-policy journals. In 1995 the Council spent $510,032 on its programs. The largest program, with expenses of $343,603, was the production of a newsletter and other publications.
Total Revenue: 1995 $861,940 32%(2) **Total Expenses:** $761,212 67%/18%/15% **Net Assets:** $448,014
Products or Services: Publications, symposiums. Capital Formation Breakfast Series discussion program. Economic Policy Evenings for members of Congress, the media, and business leaders. Lobbying. In 1995 the Council spent $165,099 on lobbying, this was up 249% from 1994, and much more than in 1993, when the Council spent less than $2,000.
Tax Status: 501(c)(6) **Annual Report:** Yes. **Employees:** 10   **Citations:** 32:125

Board of Directors or Trustees: Hon. Beryl Athony, Jr., Hon. Lloyd Bentsen (Secretary of the Treasury, 1993-94), Hon. William Brock, III (Secretary of Labor, 1985-87), John Byrne, Hon. Carroll Campbell (Pres. American Council of Life Insurance), Philip Carroll (Pres./CEO, Shell Oil), Charles DiBona (Pres., American Petroleum Inst.), David Drury (Principal Financial Group), Hon. Kenneth Duberstein (White House Chief of Staff, 1988-89), James Ericson (Pres./CEO, Northwestern Mutual Life), Matthew Fink, Keith Fox, Robert Galvin (Chair, Motorola), Hon. William Gray, III (United Negro College Fund), George Hatsopoulos, Jeffrey Henley (CFO, Oracle), Allen Krowe (Vice Chair, Texaco), Marc Lackritz, Dr. Kenneth Lay, Donald Lucas, Frederic Malek, Edward Mitchell, Hon. W. Henson Moore (American Forest & Paper Assoc.), James Morgan, John Murphy, John Nolan, Dr. Richard Rahn, Ronald Readmond (Vice Chair, Charles Schwab), Jack Rehm, James Rogers, Dr. Barry Rogstad (American Business Conference), Hon. William Ruckelshaus (Administrator, EPA, 1983-85), Dr. H. Onno Ruding (Vice Chair, Citicorp/Citibank), Hon. William Seidman, Hon. George Shultz (Secretary of State, 1982-89), Hon. Robert Strauss, Hon. Paul Volcker (former Chairman of the Federal Reserve Board), Hon. John Whitehead (Deputy Secretary of State, 1985-89), Herbert Winokur, Jr.

Periodicals: *Capital Formation* (bimonthly newsletter).

Other Information: Affiliated with the 501(c)(3) American Council for Capital Formation Center for Policy Research at the same address. In 1995 the two affiliates had combined net revenues, expenses, and assets of $1,590,404, $1,474,726, and $952,596. The Council received $789,525, or 92% of revenue, from contributions and grants awarded by foundations, businesses, and individuals. $40,000, or 5%, from management fees. $17,564, or 2%, from interest on savings and temporary cash investments. The remaining revenue came from Breakfast Series fees and other miscellaneous sources.

American Council for Capital Formation Center for Policy Research

1750 K St., N.W., Suite 400
Washington, DC 20006   **Phone:** (202) 293-5811   **E-Mail:** info@accf.org
USA   **Fax:**   (202) 785-8165   **Internet:** http://www.accf.org

Contact Person: Mark A. Bloomfield, President.

Officers or Principals: Mark A. Bloomfield, President ($0); Mari Lee Dunn, Vice President ($0); Ernestine R. Johnson, Assistant Treasurer($0); Dr. Margo Thorning, Director of Research; Dr. Charls E. Walker, Chairman.

Mission or Interest: "To help redefine and restructure U.S. tax, regulatory, and environmental policies so that this country can increase the pace of economic growth, provide high-quality jobs and compete effectively in world markets." Research and education affiliate of the American Council for Capital Formation.

Accomplishments: In 1995 the Center spent $489,089 on its programs. The largest program, with expenditures of $429,986, was a series of seminars attended by congressional committees, administrative staff, and academics that discussed capital formation and economic growth as it relates to tax and environmental policies. Each seminar was transcribed and published as a monograph. Attendees included Senate Majority Leader Trent Lott (R-MS), House Majority Leader Dick Armey (R-TX), Sen. William Roth (R-DE), Sen. Carol Moseley-Braun (D-IL), Vice President Al Gore, and Senate Minority Leader Tom Daschle (D-SD). The Center awarded a $2,500 research grant to the National Bureau of Economic Research.

Total Revenue: 1995 $728,464 10%(5) **Total Expenses:** $713,514 69%/16%/16% **Net Assets:** $504,582

Products or Services: <u>An Economic Perspective on Climate Change Policies</u> and many other books and publications.

Tax Status: 501(c)(3)   **Citations:** 32:125

Board of Directors or Trustees: Dr. B. Douglas Bernheim (Stanford Univ.), Hon. Michael Boskin (Hoover Inst.), Dr. David Bradford (Woodrow Wilson School, Princeton), Dr. George Carlson, Maxine Champion (Vice Pres., Government & Intl. Relations, Nestle USA), Ernest Christian, Jr., Dr. Kathleen Cooper (Chief Economist, Exxon), Dr. Theodore Eck (Chief Economist, Amoco), Dr. Lawrence Goulder (Stanford Univ.), Dr. John Graham (Harvard School of Public Health), Dr. Robert Hall (Hoover Inst.), Prof. Arnold Harberger (UCLA), Paul Huard (Senior Vice Pres., Policy and Communications, National Association of Manufacturers), Hon. Manuel Johnson, Dr. Dale Jorgenson (Harvard Univ.), Dr. Alan Manne (Stanford Univ.), Dr. Charles McLure (Hoover Inst.), Dr. Rudolph Penner (KPMG Peat Marwick), Larry Pollock (Vice Pres., Weyerhaeuser Co.), Dr. Roger Porter (John F. Kennedy School of Government, Harvard Univ.), Dr. James Poterba (MIT), John Renshaw, Dr. Richard Schmalensee (MIT), Dean John Shoven (Stanford Univ.), Dr. Norman Ture (Inst. for Research on the Economics of Taxation), Hon. Murray Weidenbaum (Center for the Study of American Business).

Other Information: Established in 1977. Affiliated with the 501(c)(6) American Council for Capital Formation at the same address. In 1995 the two affiliates had combined net revenues, expenses, and assets of $1,590,404, $1,474,726, and $952,596. The Center received $680,500, or 93% of revenue, from contributions and grants awarded by foundations, businesses, and individuals. (These grants included $2,000 from the Ruth and Vernon Taylor Foundation. In 1993 these grants included $45,000 from the Starr Foundation.) $22,938, or 3%, from interest on savings or temporary cash investments. $19,130, or 3%, from the sale of seminar monographs. The remaining revenue came from registration fees, and other miscellaneous sources.

American Council for Health Care Reform

5155 North 37th St.
Arlington, VA 22207   **Phone:** (703) 534-6028
USA   **Fax:**   (703) 534-0242

Contact Person: Sylvia Magers.

Officers or Principals: Joanna L. Shaker, Secretary/CEO ($21,250); William H. Shaker, Executive Director ($0); Arthur Obester, Director ($0).

Mission or Interest: Dedicated to a free-market solution for health care problems. Against any government action which would restrict consumers' choice of doctors and hospitals.

Accomplishments: Were a party to the law suit which forced Hillary Rodham Clinton's task force to make public their documents. Distributed information about "Medical Savings Accounts," or "Medical IRA's," to thousands of people. Has received praise from Ronald Reagan and Senator Orin Hatch (R-UT). In 1994 the Council spent $2,797,991 on its programs; an increase of 2,174% over $123,180 the previous year.

Total Revenue: 1994 $3,177,011 951% **Total Expenses:** $3,474,142 81%/8%/12% **Net Assets:** (-$134,216)

Products or Services: Health Care Reform, 1994: The Options, guidebook.

Tax Status: 501(c)(4) **Employees:** 12 **Citations:** 1:225

Internships: Yes.

Other Information: Established in 1983. Affiliated with the 501(c)(3) American Foundation for Health Care Reform. The Council received $3,158,344, or 99% of revenue, from contributions and grants awarded by foundations, businesses, and individuals. $16,412, or 1%, from the sale of books. The remaining revenue came from miscellaneous sources.

American Council on Economics and Society

34152 Doreka Dr.
Fraser, MI 48026
USA

Contact Person: Harry C. Verser, Jr., Executive Director.

Mission or Interest: Studies social institutions, such as the legal system, and how they affect the economic system. Awards grants for that purpose.

Accomplishments: Were preparing a book called The Future of Justice, with the late Russell Kirk as principal researcher. Funding for this project was provided by the Earhart Foundation. In 1994 the Council spent $82,841 on its programs, mostly for grants and scholarships.

Total Revenue: 1994 $83,170 **Total Expenses:** $87,214 **Net Assets:** $44,601

Products or Services: They operate the Library of Conservative Thought, which is supported by the John M. Olin Foundation.

Tax Status: 501(c)(3)

Board of Directors or Trustees: Horace Mann, Jeff Nelson, Don Byrn, Craig Fuller.

Other Information: In 1994 the Council received $5,000 from the Earhart Foundation.

American Council on Science and Health (ACSH)

1995 Broadway, 16th Floor
New York, NY 10023-5860   **Phone:** (212) 362-7044
USA   **Fax:** (212) 362-4919

Contact Person: Elizabeth M. Whelan, President.

Officers or Principals: Elizabeth M. Whelan, President ($155,503); Edward G. Remmers, Vice President ($116,043); Ann Perry ($54,049).

Mission or Interest: "To provide consumers with up-to-date, scientifically sound information on the relationship between chemicals, foods, nutrition, lifestyle factors, the environment and human health."

Accomplishments: ACSH has been singled out by *The Wall Street Journal* as the group "that knows the difference between a health threat and a health scare." *The Washington Post* said, "ACSH has become perhaps the most prominent National group to defend controversial chemicals." The Council's position papers are peer reviewed by 20-100 scientists and experts. In the fiscal year ending June 1994 the Council spent $887,406 on its programs.

Total Revenue: FY ending 6/94 $1,407,215 7%(5) **Total Expenses:** $1,338,394 66%/17%/16% **Net Assets:** $986,029

Products or Services: Publications, special reports.

Tax Status: 501(c)(3) **Annual Report:** Yes. **Employees:** 10 **Citations:** 148:47

Board of Directors or Trustees: Dr. Robert Upchurch, Dr. Joseph Boezelleca, Dr. Roger Maickel, Dr. Stephen Sternberg, Lorraine Thelian, Dr. Raymond Gambino, Dr. Robert White, Albert Nickle, Dr. F.J. Francis, Jerald Hill, Dr. Alan Moghissi, Dr. R.T. Ravenhold, Dr. Frederick Stare, Dr. Norman Borlaug, James Cunningham, Taiwo Danmola.

Periodicals: *Priorities* (quarterly magazine).

Internships: Yes, candidates are welcome and should submit applications.

Other Information: Established in 1978. The Council employed the Alexandria, VA firm of Hugh C. Newton and Associates for public relations, and Louis J. Cordia (Reagan Alumni Association) for consulting. Each were paid $35,000. The Council received $1,351,877, or 96% of revenue, from contributions and grants from foundations, businesses, and individuals. (These grants included $30,000 from the Starr Foundation, and $15,000 from the F.M. Kirby Foundation. In 1995, $50,000 from the John M. Olin Foundation, and $37,500 from the William H. Donner Foundation. Grants have historically been awarded by food and chemical companies such as the NutraSweet Company, Dow Chemicals, General Mills, Professional Lawn Care Association of America, American Cyanamid, Archer Daniels Midland, Ethyl Corp., and others. The Council is careful to reveal these funding sources, and has demonstrated independence from them, releasing reports that have at times been critical of their products.) $55,338, or 4%, from interest on savings and temporary cash investments.

American Defense Institute (ADI)

1055 N. Fairfax St., 2nd Floor
Alexandria, VA 22314   **Phone:**   (703) 519-7000
USA   **Fax:**   (703) 519-8627

Contact Person: Michael McDaniel, Executive Director.
Officers or Principals: Michael McDaniel, Executive Director ($31,530); Capt. Eugene "Red" McDaniel, USN (Ret.), President ($0).
Mission or Interest: "Works to increase public awareness of national security issues and educate young people about their responsibilities for protecting America's freedom." Opposes the "use of the military for social experimental programs" and for "putting our troops under U.N. command."
Accomplishments: ADI has been influential in the SDI missile defense program and in the movement to account for POW's in Vietnam. In 1994 ADI spent $420,394 on its programs. The largest program, with expenditures of $195,317, was the Pride in America program "to develop from among America's young men and women tomorrow's leaders."
Total Revenue: 1994 $551,751 (-37%)(2) **Total Expenses:** $609,506 69%/11%/20% **Net Assets:** (-$47,425)
Products or Services: Military Voter Registration project. Fellowships for graduate students in the areas of national defense and foreign policy. Annual Outstanding Leadership Award.
Tax Status: 501(c)(3)   **Citations:** 32:125
Board of Directors or Trustees: Stuart Johnson, H.J. Koehler, III, Glen Urquhart.
Periodicals: *ADI News* (quarterly newsletter).
Internships: Yes.
Other Information: Established in 1983. Previously affiliated with the 501(c)(4) American Defense Foundation, which disbanded in 1995, giving its $43,344 in assets to the Institute. Capt. McDaniels was an A-6 Intruder pilot who was shot down over Vietnam. He was held as a prisoner of the North Vietnamese for over six years, where he faced brutal torture. His story is told in his book, Scars and Stripes. ADI received $532,902, or 97% of revenue, from contributions and grants awarded by foundations, businesses, and individuals. (These grant have been steadily declining since the dissolution of the Soviet Union. Since 1990 they have decreased by an average of 23% each year. In 1995 they included $50,000 from the Carthage Foundation.) $12,210, or 2%, from mailing list rentals. The remaining revenue came from interest on savings and other temporary cash investments, and other miscellaneous sources.

American Education Association

P.O. Box 463
Center Moriches, NY 11934
USA

Contact Person: Rudolph P. Blaum, President.
Mission or Interest: Expose and oppose the effects of Progressive Education and Secular Humanism on American society. Promote biblically based moral values. Uphold the U.S. Constitution. "Oppose 'The New World Order'."
Accomplishments: "Provided basic research on which the Lamb's Chapel v. Center Moriches School District case was based. Supreme Court ruled unanimously in favor of Lamb's Chapel, establishing the right of religiously oriented organizations to use school facilities." Participated successfully in legislative campaigns, notably "Stop E.R.A."
Products or Services: Distribution of information "ignored by the major media." Periodic newsletters and literature to members.
Tax Status: For profit. **Annual Report:** No. **Employees:** All volunteer.
Board of Directors or Trustees: Dr. Timothy Mitchell, Chairman, Mrs. Evelyn Haglund (Principal, Christian School), Dr. Genevieve Klein (Regent Emerita, New York State), Robert Peters.
Periodicals: *American Education Association Newsletter* (monthly).
Internships: No.
Other Information: "Founded 53 years ago by employees of the New York City public school system because of their concern for the destructive impact that Progressive Education (Now Secular Humanism) would have on the future of America." Mr. Blaum is a former New York City Police Captain.

American Enterprise Institute for Public Policy Research (AEI)

1150 17th St., N.W.
Washington, DC 20036   **Phone:** (202) 862-5800   **E-Mail:** aei@aei.org
USA   **Fax:**   (202) 862-7177   **Internet:** http://www.aei.org

Contact Person: Leah Seppanen, Executive Assistant.
Officers or Principals: Christopher C. DeMuth, President ($329,560); David Gerson, Executive Vice President ($179,642); Douglas Besharov, Scholar ($119,560); Michael Novak, Scholar ($118,137); Robert Bork, Scholar ($110,773); Charles Murray, Scholar ($110,297); Wilson H. Taylor, Chairman; Tully M. Friedman, Treasurer. (Compensation from 1993.)
Mission or Interest: "Sponsors original research on government policy, the American economy, and American politics. AEI research aims to preserve and to strengthen the foundations of a free society - limited government, competitive private enterprise, vital culture and political institutions, and vigilant defense - through rigorous inquiry, debate, and writing."

Accomplishments: Senator Phil Gramm (R-TX) has said, "(AEI) has a special place because they were the first in Washington political debate to defend American capitalism and to recognize that if America is going to be saved, it is going to be saved at a profit." AEI has published many influential books through its own press or through the Free Press. Titles include <u>The End of Racism</u> by Dinesh D'Souza, <u>Values Matter Most</u> by Ben Wattenberg, <u>Neo-Conservatism</u> by Irving Kristol, <u>The Bell Curve</u> by Charles Murray and Richard Hernstein, <u>Good Intentions: The Failure of the Clinton Approach to Foreign Policy</u> by Jeane Kirkpatrick, and others. In 1995 AEI spent $2.9 million, or 23% of expenditures, on economic policy studies; $2.3 million, or 18%, on social and political studies; and $1.9 million, or 15%, on foreign policy and defense policy studies. In 1995 AEI published more than 600 studies and articles in professional journals, general circulation magazines, and the daily press. AEI internships were highly ranked in <u>America's Top 100 Internships</u> (Random House, 1993).

Total Revenue: 1995 $15,117,010 10%(2) **Total Expenses:** $12,633,796 **Net Assets:** $9,000,000 (est.)

Products or Services: Directory of scholars, seminars, conferences, reports, catalog of books and publications.

Tax Status: 501(c)(3) **Annual Report:** Yes.

Employees: 125; in 1993 AEI had 62 employees paid over $50,000.   **Citations:** 1,589:5

Board of Directors or Trustees: Edwin Artzt (CEO, Proctor & Gamble), Joseph Cannon (Chair/CEO, Geneva Steel Co.), Hon. Dick Cheney (former Secretary of Defense, 1989-93), Albert Costello (Pres./CEO, W.R. Grace & Co.), Harlan Crow, Steve Forbes (Pres./CEO, Forbes, Inc.), Christopher Galvin (Pres./COO, Motorola, Inc.), Harvey Golub (Chair/CEO, American Express Co.), Robert Greenhill, M. Douglas Ivester (Pres./COO, Coca Cola Co.), Martin Koffel, Bruce Kovner, Kenneth Lay, Marilyn Ware Lewis (Chair, American Water Works Co.), Alex Mandl (Pres./COO, AT&T), Craig McCaw, Paul O.Neill (Chair/CEO, ALCOA), George Roberts, John Rowe, Edward Rust, Jr. (Pres./CEO, State Farm Insurance Co.), James Shadt (Chair/CEO, Reader's Digest Assoc.), John Snow (Chair/CEO, CSX Corp.), William Stavropoulos (Pres./CEO, Dow Chemical Co.), Prof. James Q. Wilson (UCLA).

Periodicals: *The American Enterprise* (bimonthly magazine), and *AEI* (monthly newsletter).

Internships: Yes. 40-50 interns are accepted out of a pool of approximately 200.

Other Information: AEI was established in 1943. AEI was recently embroiled in controversy following the publication of <u>The Bell Curve</u> and <u>The End of Racism</u>. Black conservative and professor of economics at Boston University, Glenn Loury resigned from AEI's Council of Academic Advisors, citing those two books. Loury called <u>The End of Racism</u> "a racist book, whose mean-spiritedness obfuscates the need for thoughtful and constructive debate. . . " and that "It is now fashionable on the Right to attribute the catastrophe unfolding in the urban ghettos to some combination of mistaken liberal policies and the deficiencies of inner-city residents themselves. . . Some conservatives now write about 'the problem of black crime,' about 'the crisis of black illegitimacy,' about 'the threat of black social pathology.' But what has race *per se* to do with these problems? These are problems of sin, not of skin. . ." AEI's Council of Academic Advisors includes: James Q. Wilson (UCLA), Gertrude Himmelfarb (CUNY), Samuel Huntington (Harvard), D. Gale Johnson (Univ. of Chicago), William Landes (Univ. of Chicago Law School), Sam Peltzman (Univ. of Chicago Graduate School of Business), Nelson Polsby (UC, Berkeley), George Priest (Yale Law School), Murray Weidenbaum (Washington Univ.). In 1995 AEI received $13,605,309, or 90% of revenue, from contributions and grants awarded by businesses, 43%, foundations, 36%, and individuals, 11%. (These grants included $740,000 from the Lynde and Harry Bradley Foundation, $649,185 from the John M. Olin Foundation, $210,050 from the Smith Richardson Foundation, $125,000 from the Scaife Family Foundation, $10,000 from the Forbes Foundation, $10,000 from the Castle Rock Foundation, $5,000 from the Gates Foundation, $2,000 from the Sunmark Foundation. In 1994, $415,000 from the Sarah Scaife Foundation, $112,500 from the Lilly Endowment, $77,453 from the Henry J. Kaiser Family Foundation, $55,000 from the Earhart Foundation, $15,000 from the Philip M. McKenna Foundation, $6,500 from the F.M. Kirby Foundation, $5,000 from the Anschutz Foundation, and $3,000 from the Vernon K. Krieble Foundation. In 1993, $300,000 from the Starr Foundation.) The remaining revenue came from conferences, the sale of publications, dividends and interest on securities, and other miscellaneous sources.

American Enterprise Publications

177 N. Spring Rd.
Mercer, PA 16137   **Phone:** (412) 748-3726
USA   **Fax:**   (412) 748-5373

Contact Person: Tom Rose, President.

Officers or Principals: Ruth Rose, Vice President.

Mission or Interest: Publishes books to foster a better understanding of the free-market system, from a biblical basis.

Accomplishments: Publishing for over 20 years. Books "used in colleges, high schools and by home-schoolers."

Products or Services: Books by Tom Rose on economics and business, including; <u>Economics: Principles and Policy from a Christian Perspective</u>, <u>The American Economy from a Christian Perspective</u>, <u>How to Succeed in Business</u>, and others.

Tax Status: For profit. **Annual Report:** No. **Employees:** 2

American Family Association (AFA)

P.O. Drawer 2440
Tupelo, MS 38803   **Phone:** (601) 844-5036
USA

Contact Person: Rev. Donald Wildmon, President.

Mission or Interest: A media and entertainment industry watch-dog group. "To promote the Biblical ethic of decency in American society with primary emphasis on TV and other media."

Accomplishments: Claims more than 500,000 members. Hosts a daily radio show carried by over 150 radio stations. AFA is credited with starting the campaign against the National Endowment for the Arts. Instigated numerous boycotts against businesses and entertainment companies for promoting sex and violence. Boycotted K-Mart because of their refusal to get its subsidiary, Waldenbooks, to stop carrying "*Playboy, Penthouse,* and other pornographic magazines." *U.S. News and World Report* reported that "In certain regions of the country, the (K-Mart) boycott affected the amount of traffic, without a doubt." Less successful has been their boycott of television shows such as NYPD Blue; in fact the boycott may have called more attention to the show, raising ratings. Still, the AFA maintains that it has caused advertisers to leave, causing a $40 million loss in potential revenue. Rev. Wildmon was a co-chair of Pat Buchanan's 1996 Presidential campaign.

Periodicals: *American Family Association Journal.*

Other Information: Established in 1977. The AFA and Rev. Wildmon were criticized for their association with the Pat Buchanan Presidential campaign by the Center for Public Integrity. The Center (which misidentified Rev. Wildmon as "Douglas" Wildmon, not Donald, and stated that the AFA was founded in 1988, not 1977) accused Rev. Wildmon of having said that the film "The Last Temptation of Christ" was funded by "Jewish money," a charge Wildmon denies and has challenged the Center to document, which it has not.

American Focus
P.O. Box 711599
Santee, CA 92072   **Phone:** (619) 448-0544
USA   **Fax:**   (619) 448-5196   **Internet:** http://www.Americanfocus.com

Contact Person: James G. Knox.

Mission or Interest: James Knox's commentaries about America and "the certain loss of our Republic" from a populist point of view. Previously in newsletter form, *American Focus* is now available exclusively in the *National Educator* and on his own web-page.

Other Information: Knox does not consider America a lost cause, but he does see it in grave danger. He sees this country's best hope in a coalition of "knowledgeable and skilled patriots," among whom he includes Howard Phillips' Conservative Caucus, Bo Gritz and the Populist Party, the Libertarian Party, the American Conservative Party, Pat Buchanan and other Republicans willing to "buck" their party.

American Freedom Coalition
7777 Leesburg Pike, Suite 314N
Falls Church, VA 22043   **Phone:** (703) 790-8700
USA   **Fax:**   (703) 790-8711

Contact Person: Michael Leone, Executive Director.

Officers or Principals: Michael Leone. Executive Director ($70,647); Dr. Robert G. Grant, President/Treasurer ($0); Philip Sanchez, Vice President ($0); Robert Wilson, Chair.

Mission or Interest: "Restoration of traditional American values through lobbying and voter education."

Accomplishments: During Operation Desert Storm the Coalition aided in over 54 rallies nationwide. In the fiscal year ending March 1995, the Coalition spent $206,133 on its programs.

Total Revenue: FY ending 3/95 $451,487 **Total Expenses:** $459,851 45%/55%/0% **Net Assets:** $83,921

Tax Status: 501(c)(4)   **Citations:** 4:196

Other Information: The Coalition made several interest-free loans to its officers; $19,900 to Michael Leone in 1992 and two loans of $4,500 each to Dr. Robert Grant in 1992. The Coalition received $401,578, or 89% of revenue, from contributions and grants. $49,098, or 11%, from list rentals. The remaining revenue came from interest on savings and temporary cash investments.

American Health Legal Foundation
1601 N. Tucson Blvd., Suite 9
Tucson, AZ 85716   **Phone:** (800) 635-1196
USA

Contact Person: Jane Orient, M.D., Secretary/Treasurer.

Officers or Principals: John Boyles Jr., M.D., President ($0); Victor Duvall, M.D., Vice President ($0); Jane Orient, M.D., Secretary/Treasurer.

Mission or Interest: Legal foundation dedicated to defending the rights of doctors and patients from intrusive government controls.

Total Revenue: 1994 $306,942 61%(2) **Total Expenses:** $268,758 65%/4%/31% **Net Assets:** $90,001

Products or Services: Financial assistance to patients and physicians engaged in litigation to defend their rights.

Tax Status: 501(c)(3)   **Citations:** 0:233

Board of Directors or Trustees: W. Daniel Jordan, M.D., Donald Quinlan, M.D.

Other Information: Established in 1989. Affiliated with the 501(c)(6) Association of American Physicians and Surgeons located at the same address. The Foundation received $305,899, or 99.6% of revenue, from contributions and grants awarded by foundations, businesses, and individuals. The remaining revenue came from interest on savings and temporary cash investments.

American Immigration Control Foundation (AICF)

P.O. Box 525
Monterey, VA 24465   **Phone:**   (540) 468-2022   **E-Mail:**   aicf@cfw.com
USA   **Fax:**   (540) 468-2024   **Internet:** http://www.cfw.com/~aicf

Contact Person: John Vinson, President.
Officers or Principals: John Vinson, President ($30,000); John Roddy, Secretary/Treasurer ($0); Samuel Francis, Chairman ($0); Brent Nelson, Director.
Mission or Interest: "To raise public awareness of the damage that excessive immigration poses to American culture and heritage."
Accomplishments: AICF's newsletter has a claimed circulation of 150,000. Its work has been cited in the national press. Former New Hampshire Governor Meldrim Thomson, Jr., said "frankly, I can't think of (a cause) more important to the health and future of our nation than AICF's effort to control illegal immigration." In 1995 AICF spent $945,804 on its programs. This included grants of $25,000 for the Representative Government Education Foundation and $15,000 for the American Policy Institute.
Total Revenue: 1995 $1,275,729 (-24%)(2) **Total Expenses:** $1,427,911 66%/4%/30% **Net Assets:** $319,301
Products or Services: Numerous essays and books, including: America Balkanized - Immigration's Challenge to Government by Robert Nelson, The Path to National Suicide: An Essay on Immigration and Multiculturalism by Lawrence Auster, and Immigration Out of Control by John Vinson.
Tax Status: 501(c)(3) **Annual Report:** No. **Employees:** 2   **Citations:** 3:204
Board of Directors or Trustees: Brig. Gen John Smith, USA (Ret.), Maj. Gen. Carl Sutherland, USA (Ret.), Brig. Gen. Benjamin Talley, USA (Ret.), Brig. Gen. Maurice Tawes, USA (Ret.), Hon. Meldrim Thomson, Jr. (former Gov., NH), Lt. Gen. William Train, USA (Ret.), Prof. James Whisker (W. Virginia Univ.), Chilton Williamson, Jr. (senior editor, *Chronicles*), Prof. Clyde Wilson (Univ. of South Carolina), Brig. Gen. Laurence Wright, USA (Ret.).
Periodicals: *Border Watch* (monthly newsletter).
Other Information: AICF hired the Fairfax, VA firm Advanced Response Marketing Associates to handle direct-mail advertising and fundraising, and the Raleigh, NC firm Publication Support Services to handle management and technical support. The two firms were paid $193,908 and $62,447 respectively. AICF received $1,192,231, or 93% of revenue, from contributions and grants awarded by foundations businesses, and individuals. $49,359, or 4%, from mailing-list rentals. $21,884, or 2%, from the sale of publications. $12,255, or 1%, from interest on savings and temporary cash investments.

American Institute for Economic Research

P.O. Box 1000
Great Barrington, MA 01230   **Phone:**   (413) 528-1216   **E-Mail:**   mdavis@aier.org
USA   **Fax:**   (413) 528-0103   **Internet:** http://www.aier.org

Contact Person: Lawrence Pratt, Director of Research.
Officers or Principals: Robert A. Gilmour, President; Edward P. Welker, Vice President; Frederick C. Harwood, Secretary.
Mission or Interest: "To disseminate useful knowledge, based on scientific research, about current issues relating to public policy, personal finance, and fundamental economic and monetary trends."
Accomplishments: Cited in numerous publications
Tax Status: 501(c)(3) **Annual Report:** No. **Employees:** 30
Periodicals: *Research Reports* (bimonthly newsletter), and *Economic Education Bulletin* (monthly newsletter).
Internships: Yes, Summer Fellowship Program for graduate students in economics.
Other Information: Owns a for-profit investment advisory company, American Investment Services. In 1994 the Institute received $500 from the United Educators Foundation.

American Jewish Committee / *Commentary*

165 E. 56th St.
New York, NY 10022   **Phone:**   (212) 751-4000
USA   **Fax:**   (212) 751-1174

Contact Person: David A. Harris, Executive Director.
Officers or Principals: David A. Harris, Executive Director ($230,645); Jaime Kelstein, Director, Resource Development ($204,338); Norman Podhoretz, Editor in Chief, *Commentary* ($197,435); Shulamith Bahat, Associate Executive Director ($169,132); Clifford B. Surloff, Director of Finance; Eugene DuBow, Director, Community Services; Robert S. Rifkind, President; Harold Tanner, Chair; E. Miriam Alperin, Treasurer; Harris L. Kempner, Secretary.
Mission or Interest: "Protects the rights and freedoms of Jews the world over; combats bigotry and anti-Semitism and promotes human rights for all; works for the security of Israel and deepened understanding between Americans and Israelis; defends democratic values in American public policy; and enhances the creative vitality of the Jewish people." Publishes *Commentary*, a magazine of conservative opinion, typically from a Jewish perspective.
Accomplishments: *Commentary* was seminal in publishing 'neo-conservatives' - conservatives who were formerly on the Left. Contributors to *Commentary* have included Paul Johnson, Edward Luttwak, Midge Decter, Jeane Kirkpatrick, Carol Iannone, Mona Charen, Elliot Abrams, Alan Bloom, and others. The leftist Jewish magazine *Tikkun* was started in reaction to the influence of *Commentary*. In the fiscal year ending June 1995, the Committee spent $15,854,073 on its programs.

Total Revenue: FY ending 6/95 $22,150,062 **Total Expenses:** $19,856,725 80%/7%/13% **Net Assets:** $24,049,903
Products or Services: Publications, seminars, grants, and lobbying. The Committee spent $124,658 on lobbying, $34,996 on grassroots lobbying and $89,662 on the direct lobbying of legislators. This was 30% increase over the previous year, and 193% over two years prior.
Tax Status: 501(c)(3)   **Citations:** 920:10
Board of Directors or Trustees: Bruce Ramer, Jack Lapin, S. Stephen Selig, III, E. Robert Goodkind, Jane Silverman.
Periodicals: *Commentary* (monthly magazine).
Other Information: *Commentary* is one of the best-known magazines of conservative opinion. Central to its success, and movement from leftward to right, was its long-time editor Norman Podhoretz. During the sixties Podhoretz turned *Commentary* away from being a journal of strictly Jewish cultural concerns to a greater involvement in politics of the day. At the time Podhoretz opposed the Vietnam War and wrote about race relations and civil rights. This move was seen as a shift to the Left. But Podhoretz expressed concern with the excesses of the 'counter-culture,' and the shift from civil rights and non-discriminatory public policy to government mandated quotas and outcomes. This, along with the view that the United States military could play an important role in shaping the world for the better, marked the shift to the Right which attracted many conservative writers to *Commentary*. The American Jewish Committee, however, is not necessarily a conservative organization despite the views of its flagship publication. Among the grants it awarded was $10,000 for the Fund for Peace - a left-leaning organization which created, among other things, the Center for Defense Information. The Committee received $18,531,817, or 82% of revenue, from contributions and grants awarded by foundations, businesses, and individuals. (These grants included $75,000 from the Lynde and Harry Bradley Foundation, $60,000 from the John M. Olin Foundation, $50,000 from the Smith Richardson Foundation, $25,000 from the Gilder Foundation, $15,000 from the Carthage Foundation, $1,500 from the Milliken Foundation, and $1,000 from the Forbes Foundation.) $1,221,842, or 5%, from magazine subscriptions. $1,198,028, or 5%, from membership dues. $713,402, or 3%, from dividends and interest from securities. $352,411, or 2%, from capital gains on the sale of securities. The remaining revenue came from rental income, seminars, and other miscellaneous sources. The Committee held $14,711,228, or 61% of assets, in securities. (These securities were 52% corporate stock, 42% domestic government bonds, 5% Israel bonds, and 1% corporate bonds and loans.)

American Justice Federation

3850 S. Emerson Ave., Suite E
Indianapolis, IN 46203   **Phone:** (317) 780-5204
USA   **Fax:**   (317) 780-5209

Contact Person: Linda Thompson.
Officers or Principals: Al Thompson.
Mission or Interest: Populist organization promoting Constitutional rights and public knowledge of those rights.
Accomplishments: Produced two videos on the government's handling of the Branch Davidians' standoff in Waco which ended in their deaths, "Waco, The Big Lie," and "Waco II, The Big Lie Continues." These videos allege a deliberate attempt on the part of government agents to kill the Branch Davidians and cover up the agents' actions
Products or Services: Computer network called the "Associated Electronic News," publications, videos. Matches persons needing legal aid securing their constitutional rights with lawyers willing to accept the case *pro bono*, for a reduced fee, or strictly as a contingency-fee case.
Tax Status: For profit. **Annual Report:** No.
Periodicals: *American Justice News* (newsletter).
Internships: No.
Other Information: Linda Thompson is a key figure in the conspiracy and populist movement that believes a "New World Order" is currently posing a threat to Americans and their freedoms. She was arrested in 1993 for impeding the progress of Hillary Rodham Clinton's health-care bus tour.

American Land Rights Association (ALRA)

30218 N.E., 82nd Ave.
Battle Ground, WA 98604   **Phone:** (360) 687-3087   **E-Mail:** alra@pacifier.com
USA   **Fax:**   (360) 687-2973

Contact Person: Chuck Cushman, Executive Director.
Officers or Principals: Elizabeth West, Assistant Director; Bruce Grefrath, Washington Representative.
Mission or Interest: "ALRA helps protect private property owners from government regulation or acquisition. . . helps all private property owners in dealings with the Federal government with a special emphasis on those impacted by the Endangered Species Act, the Clean Water Act and the Environmental Protection Agency."
Accomplishments: Fax network with over 18,000 members. "Has been involved in helping land owners in most Federal land acquisition areas for the past 25 years. These include old and new areas managed by the National Park Service, U.S. Forest Service, Bureau of Land Management, Fish and Wildlife Service, and Corps of Engineers. ALRA has saved thousands of property owners from land acquisition. It has helped curtail the use of Wilderness areas, national parks and wildlife refuges as tools for needless land use control." Testified before Congress on several occasions
Tax Status: Nonprofit. **Annual Report:** No. **Employees:** 8
Board of Directors or Trustees: Don Fife, Wayne Hage, Bray Kreig, Rollo Pool.

Periodicals: *Land Rights Advocate* (monthly newsletter).
Internships: Yes, in Battle Ground, WA and the District of Columbia.
Other Information: Formerly called the National Inholders Association, and was originally formed to assist 'inholders' - people "who own land or some economic interest within or adjacent to a Federally managed area". ALRA has a Washington, DC, office: 233 Pennsylvania Ave., S.E., Suite 301, Washington, DC 20003, (202) 544-6156, fax (202) 544-6774. Cushman was a successful insurance salesman before becoming a property-rights activist. Cushman's father owned a cabin in Yosemite, which was claimed by the Park Service, burned to ground and bulldozed. Cushman himself bought a cabin within the park, and when the Park Service tried to eliminate the entire town in which it was located, Cushman led the battle against it. Cushman is a leading speaker on the property-rights circuit, and environmentalists charge that, although he explicitly urges non-violent action, violence often takes place in the communities were he has visited. Jill Hamburg of the Center for Investigative Reporting says, "to environmentalists, he may be the most dangerous man in America." In 1994 the Association received $6,000 from the Coalitions for America.

American Legal Foundation

2009 Massachusetts Ave., N.W.
Washington, DC 20036   **Phone:**   (202) 588-0302
USA   **Fax:**   (202) 588-0386

Contact Person: Daniel J. Popeo, Director.
Officers or Principals: Constance C. Larcher, Director ($0); John A. Popeo, Director ($0).
Mission or Interest: To provide financial support for the Washington Legal Foundation.
Accomplishments: In 1995 the Foundation awarded a grant of $100,000 to the Fund for American Living Government.
Total Revenue: 1995 $281,564 **Total Expenses:** $152,707 98%/2%/0% **Net Assets:** $1,231,588
Tax Status: 501(c)(3)
Other Information: Affiliated with the 501(c)(3) Washington Legal Foundation. The American Legal Foundation received $252,000, or 86% of gross revenue, from contributions and grants awarded by foundations, businesses, and individuals. (These grants included $100,000 from the Carthage Foundation.) $29,247, or 10%, from interest on savings and temporary cash investments. $11,696, or 4%, from dividends and interest from securities. The Foundation lost $11,379 on the sale of assets.

American Legislative Exchange Council (ALEC)

910 17th St., N.W., 5th Floor
Washington, DC 20006   **Phone:**   (202) 466-3800
USA   **Fax:**   (202) 466-3801

Contact Person: Noel Card, Director of Public Affairs.
Officers or Principals: Sam Brunelli, Executive Director ($184,259); Matthew Bordonaro, Development Director ($80,363); Robert Bennett, Chief of Staff ($76,596); State Sen. Ray Powers, National Chairman; State Rep. Dale VanVyven, First Vice Chairman; State Sen. Joseph Manchin, II, Second Vice Chairman; State Rep. Bonnie Sue Cooper, Treasurer.
Mission or Interest: "To advance the Jeffersonian principles of free markets, limited government, federalism, and individual liberty, through a non-partisan, public-private partnership between America's state legislators and concerned members of the private sector, the federal government and the general public." Organization of state legislators from all parties who adhere to these principles.
Accomplishments: Members include approximately 2,400 state legislators from all 50 states and both major parties. In 1994 ALEC spent $4,374,903 on its programs. The largest expenditure, $2,342,530, was on conferences and seminars that "provide opportunities for legislators to communicate across state lines, share experiences and work in unison with corporate leaders to create effective public policies." $969,217 was spent on task forces that focus on tax and fiscal policy, financial services, energy, education, health care, transportation and the environment. Other programs focused on publication and public affairs, and membership services and development.
Total Revenue: 1994 $4,335,658 ($96,083, or 2%, from government grants) 4%(2) **Total Expenses:** $4,612,074 95%/5%/0%
Net Assets: $133,666
Products or Services: Conferences, publications, model legislation, legislative expertise. Awards the annual Thomas Jefferson Freedom Award for the individual who best exemplifies the ideals of Jeffersonian democracy. Also presents the Adam Smith Free Enterprise Award for the individual who best exemplifies a commitment to free markets.
Tax Status: 501(c)(3)   **Annual Report:** No.   **Employees:** 27   **Citations:** 111:57
Board of Directors or Trustees: State Rep. David Halbrook (MS), State Rep. Halvorson (IA), State Rep. Bobby Hogue (AR), State Rep. Perry Hooper, Jr. (AL), State Sen. Owen Johnson (NY), State Sen. Dean Rhoads (NV), State Assemblyman Robert Straniere (NY). ALEC is advised by a Private Enterprise Board whose members include: Ronald Scheberle, Chairman (GTE Telephone Operations), Allan Auger, Vice Chairman (Coors Brewing Co.), Fred Ferguson (Price Waterhouse), John Brust (ALCOA), Jane Cahill (Coastal Corp.), Marie Chelli (Joseph E. Seagram & Sons), Louie Curto (Shell Oil Co.), Thomas Hardeman (United Parcel Service), Rebecca Linn (Steel Can Recycling Inst.), Gerald Mossinghoff (Pharmaceutical Manufacturing Assoc.), Margot Parker (General Motors), F. John Potts (Household Intl.), Ed Powers (K-mart), Ray Snokus (Houston Lighting & Power), John Venardos (Pfizer Specialty Chemicals Group), Tina Walls (Philip Morris).
Periodicals: *FYI* (monthly magazine), *The State Factor* (monthly research report).
Internships: Yes, year-round.

Other Information: Established in 1973. Affiliated with the ALEC Foundation at the same address. ALEC contracted researcher Wendell Cox, of Wendell Cox Consultancy of Belleville, IL, and paid him $153,259. ALEC received $2,088,307, or 48% of revenue, from conference and seminar fees. $1,520,372, or 35%, from contributions and grants awarded by foundations, businesses, and individuals. (These grants included $75,000 from the Allegheny Foundation, and $5,000 from the Grover Hermann Foundation. In 1995, $50,000 from the Castle Rock Foundation, $5,000 from the Sunmark Foundation, and $1,500 from the Roe Foundation.) $562,026, or 13%, from task-force revenues. $96,083, or 2%, from government grants. $42,125, or 1%, from membership dues. The remaining revenue came from interest on savings and temporary cash investments, the sale of publications, and the sale of inventory.

American Life League (ALL)

1179 Courthouse Rd.
Stafford, VA 22554   **Phone:**   (540) 659-4171
USA   **Fax:**   (540) 659-2586

Contact Person: Judith A. Brown, President.
Officers or Principals: Francis Norris, Manager of Operations ($85,567); Robert L. Sassone, Director ($78,000); Richard C. Rue, Executive Vice President ($75,000); Scarlett Clark, Secretary; Judith A. Brown, President.
Mission or Interest: "Holds the position that human life is a gift from God, and that the sanctity of innocent human life should be defended from the moment of fertilization until the author of Life calls us home, without regard to age, health, or condition of dependency." Opposed to abortion and euthanasia. Produces educational materials and participates in legal action.
Accomplishments: Claims 300,000 members. ALL filed charges asserting that the Freedom of Access to Clinics Act violates the First Amendment and that it exceeded Congress' authority under the Commerce Clause. American Life League v. Reno was joined on the other side by the Center for Reproductive Law and Policy and the NOW Legal Defense and Education Fund. ALL lost in the Fourth Circuit Court of Appeals and the Supreme Court refused to hear the case. Two days after his inauguration, President Clinton issued an executive order calling for government funding of fetal tissue and human embryo research; ALL "helped to generate more than 100,000 letters of opposition" during the public comment period. In 1995 ALL spent $5,398,492 on its programs. The largest expenditure, $4,077,076, went toward the production of educational programs "relating to family issues." $1,019,266 was spent on publications, and $302,150 was spent producing video tapes, and television and radio programming.
Total Revenue: 1995 $7,930,105 9%(2) **Total Expenses:** $7,754,918 70%/9%/21% **Net Assets:** $1,115,784
Products or Services: "Celebrate Life" and other videos, publications, litigation, and lobbying. ALL spent $113,720 on lobbying, $76,659 on grassroots lobbying and $41,675 on the direct lobbying of legislators. This was down 4% from the 1994 and down 18% from 1993.
Tax Status: 501(c)(3)   **Citations:** 213:37
Board of Directors or Trustees: Fr. Dennis O'Brien, William Colliton, M.D.
Periodicals: *ALL About Issues* (quarterly magazine).
Internships: Yes, during the summer.
Other Information: Established in 1979. Affiliated with the 501(c)(2) ALL Endowment that holds the title to property on behalf of ALL. In 1995 the Endowment held $390,580 in assets. ALL contracted Marion Edwyn Harrison of Falls Church, VA, for legal services and paid her $96,351. ALL rented office space from the husband of the president, Judith Brown, for $65,000. ALL also incurred fees totaling $2,531,633 from the firm of Anthony Kane & Associates, a firm in which Mr. Brown has controlling interest. The League's assets included three cars, including a 1994 Lincoln Mark VIII purchased new in 1994. ALL received $7,788,984, or 98% of gross revenue, from contributions and grants awarded by foundations, businesses, and individuals. $124,959, or 2%, from the sale of pamphlets. The remaining revenue came from the sale of videos, subscriptions, interest on savings, dividends and interest from securities. ALL lost $2,495 on the sale of securities.

American Policy Center

13873 Park Center Rd., Suite 316
Herndon, VA 20171   **Phone:** (703) 925-0881   **E-Mail:** APC@Nicom.com
USA   **Fax:**   (703) 925-0991   **Internet:** http://www.AmericanPolicy.com

Contact Person: Thomas A. DeWeese, President.
Officers or Principals: Thomas A. DeWeese, President ($0); Gregory Ellis, Vice President ($0); Virginia DeWeese, Secretary ($0).
Mission or Interest: The promotion of free enterprise, limited government and limited regulation over commerce and individuals. Opposed to U.S. involvement in the United Nations and "Outcome-based Education."
Accomplishments: Claims over 65,000 supporters. In 1996 the Center hosted a conference in Turin, New York, on Outcome-based Education. The conference was initiated by local parents. Due to the Center's participation, syndicated radio host Gary Nolan broadcast live from the conference. Many parents at the conference took the pledge, "that from this day forward we're going to run the psychologists and social planners out of the classrooms and start teaching children to read and write again." The Conference received widespread print media coverage in New York. Distributed a nationwide survey on immigration reform. Collected over 10,000 signatures to block statehood for Washington D.C. Held many conferences, including one which brought together the National League of Cities, the National School Boards Association, and several experts on the environment to discuss the effects of heavy-handed environmental regulations. In 1994 the Center spent $102,701 on its programs. The largest program, with expenditures of $75,250, was a petition drive that delivered over 200,000 petitions to House Speaker Thomas Foley calling for the replacement of Rep. Ron Dellums (D-CA) of the House Armed Services Committee. $14,951 was spent on a nation-wide survey regarding the public's attitude toward the policies of then-Surgeon General Joycelyn Elders. $9,000 was spent on *EPA Watch*, and $3,500 to co-sponsor the Conservative Political Action Conference (CPAC).

Total Revenue: 1994 $344,024 (-39%)(1) **Total Expenses:** $310,621 33%/19%/48% **Net Assets:** (-$27,200)
Tax Status: 501(c)(4) **Annual Report:** Yes. **Employees:** 5   **Citations:** 10:173
Board of Directors or Trustees: Board of Advisors includes: Maj. General Robert Blount, MC USA (Ret.), Dr. Arnold Beichman (Hoover Inst.), Capt. G. Russell Evans, USCG (Ret.), General Andrew Gatsis, USA (Ret.), Phillip Abbott Luce, Lt. General Willard Pearson, USA (Ret.), General Crawford Sams, USA (Ret.), Maj. General William Temple, USAF (Ret.).
Periodicals: *EPA Watch* (bimonthly journal that surveys the environmental regulatory activities of the EPA, the Department of the Interior, OSHA, the White House, Congress, and other federal, state and local agencies), *The DeWeese Report* (monthly newsletter) and *Insider's Report* (monthly newsletter).
Internships: No.
Other Information: Established in 1988. Affiliated with the 501(c)(3) American Policy Foundation, the 501(c)(3) Putting Liberty First, and the for-profit DeWeese Company. The Center received $325,690, or 95% of revenue, from contributions. $18,334, or 5%, from mailing list royalties.

American Policy Foundation
13873 Park Center Rd., Suite 316
Herndon, VA 20171   **Phone:** (703) 925-0881   **E-Mail:** APC@Nicom.com
USA   **Fax:** (703) 925-0991   **Internet:** http://www.AmericanPolicy.com

Contact Person: Bonner H. Cohen, Vice President .
Officers or Principals: Bonner H. Cohen, Vice President ($23,333); Carl Craig, Director ($23,000); Thomas A. DeWeese, President/Treasurer ($0); Carolyn Craig, Secretary.
Mission or Interest: Provides research and educational services for the American Policy Center.
Accomplishments: In 1995 the Foundation spent $174,351 on its programs. The largest program, with expenses of $65,000, was editorial research for *EPA Watch*, a publication of the affiliated American Policy Center. $53,654 was spent producing a newsletter sent to 18,000 supporters, members of congress and the news media. $47,197 was spent on a survey of 150,000 Americans and their views on education. $8,500 was spent on a conference co-sponsored with the National School Boards Association. Speakers included Elizabeth Whelan (American Council of Science and Health), Patrick Michaels (*World Climate Review*), Robert Gordon (National Wilderness Inst.), Kent Jeffries (National Center for Policy Analysis), and others. The Foundation also awarded two grants for environmental research; $25,000 for vice president Bonner Cohen (making his total receipts from the Foundation $48,333), and $2,470 for Stewards of the Range.
Total Revenue: 1995 $317,914 119%(2) **Total Expenses:** $337,516 52%/13%/36% **Net Assets:** $30,399
Tax Status: 501(c)(3)   **Citations:** 10:173
Other Information: Established in 1993. Affiliated with the 501(c)(4) American Policy Center, 501(c)(3) Putting Liberty First, and the for-profit DeWeese Company. The Foundation received $317,027, or 99.7% of revenue, from contributions and grants awarded by foundations, businesses, and individuals. The remaining revenue came from interest on savings and conference fees.

American Portrait Films
503 E. 200th St.
Cleveland, OH 44119   **Phone:** (216) 531-8600
USA   **Fax:** (216) 531-8355

Contact Person: Roy Tidwell, General Manager.
Officers or Principals: Mark Tichar, Director of Sales; Susi Tedrick, Marketing.
Mission or Interest: Produces anti-abortion and traditional values videos.
Accomplishments: Produced the well-known anti-abortion movie, "Silent Scream."
Products or Services: Movies and videos for churches, home schoolers, families and schools. In addition to "Silent Scream" they produced "Your Crisis Pregnancy" and "Hard Truth," which was used by candidates nationwide during the 1992 elections.
Employees: 10

American Renewal
801 G St., N.W.
Washington, DC 20001   **Phone:** (202) 393-2100
USA   **Fax:** (202) 393-2134

Contact Person: Gary L. Bauer, President.
Officers or Principals: Gary L. Bauer, President ($24,000); Betty L. Barrett, Secretary ($5,000); Kristi Hamrick.
Mission or Interest: Lobbying affiliate of the Family Research Council. "Educate the public on traditional family values through advertisements in major U.S. newspapers."
Accomplishments: In 1996 Kristi Hamrick appeared on CNN's Inside Politics to debate Patricia Ireland of NOW on the subject of Paula Corbin Jones lawsuit alleging that President Clinton sexually harassed her. In 1994 the organization spent $169,527 on its programs. The previous year the organization conducted no programs. It appears, however, to be accumulating assets, from $25,009 in 1992, to $366,277 in 1993, to $437,012 in 1994.
Total Revenue: 1994 $265,575 (-23%)(1) **Total Expenses:** $194,840 87%/13%/0% **Net Assets:** $437,012
Tax Status: 501(c)(4)   **Citations:** 98:66
Board of Directors or Trustees: Alan Dye, Charles Watkins.
Other Information: Affiliated with the 501(c)(3) Family Research Council at the same address. American Renewal received $257,890, or 97% of revenue, from contributions. $7,685, or 3%, from interest on savings and temporary cash investments.

American Security Council (ASC)

5545 Security Circle
P.O. Box 8
Boston, VA 22713   **Phone:**   (703) 547-1750
USA

Contact Person: John M. Fisher.
Officers or Principals: John M. Fisher, CEO ($0); Hon. Duncan Hunter, President ($0); Steven R. Fisher, Vice President/Secretary ($0); Dr. Henry A. Fischer, Treasurer.
Mission or Interest: To maintain a strong defense and a secure America.
Accomplishments: "Widely recognized by every U.S. President since Lyndon Johnson, and by hundreds of members of Congress for its expertise in national defense and military matters, ASC has taken the lead in critical issues of national security ranging from opposition to the nuclear freeze, to support for the Strategic Defense Initiative." Former President Ronald Reagan said to the ASC. "Your work on Capitol Hill and with the public at large has been a principal factor in returning America to the days when she was militarily strong and morally principled."
Total Revenue: FY ending 8/93 $1,274,984 **Total Expenses:** $1,654,886 **Net Assets:** (-$671,826)
Products or Services: Various studies, testimony before Congress. Projects such as the "National Campaign to Keep the Ban on Homosexuals in the Military," and the "Coalition for Peace Through Strength." Rates members of congress based on their votes affecting national security.
Tax Status: 501(c)(6)   **Citations:** 5:192
Other Information: Affiliated with the 501(c)(3) American Security Council Foundation, and the for-profit American Security Press at the same address. Admiral Thomas H. Moorer, USN, (Ret.), who chairs their National Campaign to Keep the Ban on Homosexuals in the Military, is a former Chairman of the Joint Chiefs of Staff (1970-74). The Council received $963,375, or 76% of revenue, from the sale of mailing lists. $308,089, or 24%, from contributions and grants from foundations, businesses, and inidividuals. The remaining revenue came from interest on savings and the sale of assets.

American Security Council Foundation

5545 Security Circle
P.O. Box 8
Boston, VA 22713   **Phone:**   (703) 547-1750
USA

Contact Person: Gregg Hilton, Executive Director.
Officers or Principals: George T. Webb, Director of Development ($47,110); Gregg Hilton, Executive Director ($41,320); Daniel Kalinger, Executive Vice President ($29,445); John M. Fisher, Chairman; Hon. Duncan Hunter, President; Steven R. Fischer, Treasurer.
Mission or Interest: Research and education affiliate of the American Security Council.
Accomplishments: In the fiscal year ending August 1994 the Foundation spent $770,895 on its programs.
Total Revenue: FY ending 8/94 $227,541 **Total Expenses:** $970,268 79%/15%/5% **Net Assets:** $5,231,983
Tax Status: 501(c)(3)   **Citations:** 5:192
Board of Directors or Trustees: Adm. Thomas Moorer, USN (Ret.), Phyllis Roberts.
Other Information: Affiliated with the 501(c)(6) American Security Council at the same address. The Foundation received $95,044, or 40% of gross revenue, from interest on savings and temporary cash investments. $72,725, or 30%, from contributions and grants awarded by foundations, businesses, and individuals. $22,096, or 9%, from a litigation settlement. $19,100, or 8%, from rental income. $10,437, or 4%, from mailing list rentals. The remaining revenue came from other miscellaneous sources.

American Sentinel

Radio Center, Suite 2E
3229 South Boulevard
Charlotte, NC 28209   **Phone:**   (704) 525-8807   **E-Mail:** sentinel@igc.apc.org
USA   **Fax:**   (704) 525-6779

Contact Person: Lee Bellinger, Publisher.
Officers or Principals: Kenneth F. Fairleigh, Publisher; Andrew C. White, Business Correspondent.
Mission or Interest: Newsletter with a populist-conservative viewpoint that focuses on "the activities of big government and its proponents."
Accomplishments: Publishing since 1971. Approximately 10,000 subscribers
Tax Status: For profit. **Annual Report:** No. **Employees:** 4
Periodicals: *The American Sentinel* (monthly newsletter).
Other Information: Established in 1971. Previously called the *Pink Sheet on the Left*. Editor Lee Bellinger served as a legislative assistant to Rep. Toby Roth (R-WI) on military and intelligence issues, and as an aide to Rep. Dan Coats, now a Senator (R-IN).

American Society for the Defense of Tradition, Family and Property (TFP) / Foundation for a Christian Civilization

P.O. Box 1868
York, PA 17405   **Phone:**   (717) 225-7147
USA   **Fax:**   (717) 225-7382

Contact Person: C. Preston Noell, III, Director, Office of Public Liaison.
Officers or Principals: Raymond F. Drake, President/Treasurer; Steven Schmieder, Vice President; Matthew Carlson, Secretary.
Mission or Interest: "A civic, cultural and educational organization (that) draws its inspiration from the traditional teaching of the Roman Catholic Church." The Foundation for a Christian Civilization is the incorporated name for the U.S. affiliate of the international group, Tradition, Family, Property.
Accomplishments: Former Congressman Robert K. Dornan (R-CA), called TFP, "A great organization that defends tradition, family and property with zeal and fervor." Long-time support of independence for the Baltic countries; TFP collected over 5.2 million signatures worldwide supporting Lithuanian independence in 1990, a feat recognized by the Guinness Book of World Records as the largest petition drive in history. Highly visible public protests of the movies "Hail Mary" and "The Last Temptation of Christ." TFP activists are often recognizable at anti-abortion rallies and other events by their red capes and their yellow-lion-on-a-red-banner standard. Has taken out full-page ads in the *Wall Street Journal* analyzing the collapse of communism in 1989-90. Today there are 25 TFP organizations internationally. Prof. Corrêa de Oliveira, the founder of the Society for the Defense of Tradition, Family and Property world-wide, has written many books including The Church in the Communist State: The Impossible Coexistence, and his most recent, Nobility and Analogous Traditional Elites in the Allocutions of Pius XII. Nobility makes the case for a "natural social hierarchy" and has received praise from numerous Catholic theologians and American conservatives Morton C. Blackwell of the Leadership Institute and Paul Weyrich of the Free Congress Foundation.
Tax Status: 501(c)(3) **Annual Report:** Yes. **Employees:** 50
Periodicals: *TFP Newsletter, TFP Campus Update, TFP Prolife Update.*
Other Information: The international TFP was established in 1960 in Brazil by Prof. Plinio Corrêa de Oliveira. The United States branch was established in 1973.

American Sovereignty Task Force

P.O. Box 65631
Washington, DC 20035   **Phone:**   (703) 241-3700
USA   **Fax:**   (818) 223-8080

Contact Person: Carl Olson, Chairman.
Officers or Principals: Carl Olson, Chairman ($0); Mark Seidenberg, Vice Chairman ($0); Charles Cliff, Secretary ($0).
Mission or Interest: "To assure that the U.S. government maintains sovereignty over all American territory and cedes it only by treaty."
Accomplishments: Worked to prevent the giveaway of the Navassa Island to Haiti, Hawaiian islands to the Solomon Islands and other countries, numerous islands and seabeds to Cuba, and eight Alaskan islands in the Arctic and Bering Sea to the Russians. Focused attention on inaccuracies in high school geology textbooks. Called for an investigation into Russian gulags found on Wrangell Island in the Arctic. In 1994 the Task Force spent $3,448 on its programs.
Total Revenue: 1994 $251,173 216%(3) **Total Expenses:** $8,657 40%/49%/11% **Net Assets:** $247,518
Tax Status: 501(c)(3) **Annual Report:** No. **Employees:** 2   **Citations:** 0:233
Internships: No.
Other Information: Affiliated with State Department Watch. The Task Force received $250,390, or 99.6% of revenue, from contributions and grants awarded by foundations, businesses, and individuals.

American Spectator Educational Foundation / *American Spectator* (TAS)

2020 N. 14th St., Suite 750
Arlington, VA 22216   **Phone:**   (703) 243-3733   **E-Mail:**   amspec@ix.netcom.com
USA   **Fax:**   (703) 243-6814

Contact Person: Wladys Pleszczynski, Managing Editor.
Officers or Principals: R. Emmett Tyrrell, Jr., President/Chairman ($223,584); Ronald E. Burr, Secretary/Treasurer ($202,789); David Brock, Writer ($195,000).
Mission or Interest: Produces *The American Spectator*, or TAS, a magazine of news, humor, investigative reporting, and conservative opinion.
Accomplishments: TAS has been the fastest growing magazine of opinion, growing from a paid circulation of 32,598 in 1992 to 270,622 in 1995; an average of 79,341 new subscribers per year over three years. The success has been largely due to an emphasis on investigative reporting, including David Brock's article on the Clarence Thomas - Anita Hill dispute that grew into the best-selling book, The Real Anita Hill. Other stories included the 'Troopergate' story - an article on President Clinton's activities as Arkansas' governor, also by David Brock, and James Ring Adams' articles on Whitewater and related affairs. Features regular appearances by writer/humorist P. J. O'Rourke, actor/financial writer Ben Stein, and Grover Norquist of Americans' for Tax Reform. The average TAS reader is male, has a college degree, is married, 48 years old, and has a household income of $51,540. In the fiscal year ending June 1995, the Foundation spent $7,790,217 on the production of *The American Spectator*. $108,662 was spent on other projects. The magazine brought in $8,217,183 in subscriptions, advertising, mailing lists, and related items; a net gain of $426,966.

Total Revenue: FY ending 6/95 $9,961,139 **Total Expenses:** $8,431,688 94%/4%/2% **Net Assets:** $368,810
Tax Status: 501(c)(3)   **Citations:** 683:14
Board of Directors or Trustees: Theodore Forstmann, Jerry Gerde, Robert Groseth (Northwestern Univ.), Peter Hanaford, Dave Henderson, Jeane Kirkpatrick (American Enterprise Inst.), John Lehman, Jr., Shane O'Neil, Hon. Frank Shakespeare (former Ambassador to the Holy See), William E. Simon (former Treasury Secretary, 1974-76), Dr. Alan Somers, Thomas Tarzian, Gen. William Westmoreland, USA (Ret.).
Periodicals: *The American Spectator* (monthly magazine).
Other Information: Established in 1967 at Indiana University as *The American Alternative*. TAS contracted Stephen S. Boynton of the District of Columbia for legal services, and compensated him with $537,500. TAS received $6,674,822, or 67% of revenue, from subscriptions. $1,574,187, or 16%, from contributions and grants awarded by foundations, businesses, and individuals. (These grants included $350,000 from the Carthage Foundation, $185,000 from the Sarah Scaife Foundation, $165,000 from the Lynde and Harry Bradley Foundation, $75,000 from the John M. Olin Foundation, $10,000 from the Grover Hermann Foundation, $5,000 from the Milliken Foundation, $5,000 from the Philip M. McKenna Foundation, and $2,000 from the Sunmark Foundation.) $963,901, or 10%, from advertising sales. $554,361, or 6%, from mailing list rentals. The remaining revenue came from dividends and interest from securities, the sale of books, articles and reports, and other miscellaneous sources.

American Studies Center / Radio America

1030 15th St., N.W., Suite 700
Washington DC 20005   **Phone:** (202) 408-0944
USA   **Fax:**   (202) 408-1087

Contact Person: James C. Roberts, President.
Officers or Principals: James C. Roberts, President ($137,475); Marc Lipsitz, Vice President ($0); Frank Donatelli, Secretary ($0); Patricia Roberts, Treasurer ($0); Gene Pell, Blanquita Cullum, Radio Hosts; Dave Teevwen, Program Director.
Mission or Interest: Promotion of conservative ideas, traditional values, and American history through radio programming.
Accomplishments: Over 350 radio stations across the country broadcast a weekly or daily Radio America production. Recently launched 24-hour programming. Produced award-winning radio documentaries including "Reagan Reconsidered: The Life and Legacy of Ronald Reagan", "D-Day: They Were There", and "World War II Chronicles". Radio host Blanquita Cullum is also president of the National Association of radio Talk Show Hosts. The Center's National Heritage Library contains over 1,200 volumes on American history and culture which are donated by members.
Total Revenue: 1995 $2,049,192 **Total Expenses:** $2,186,227 25%/26%/49% **Net Assets:** $137,006
Products or Services: Radio America programing that includes: "Dateline:Washington" with Gene Pell, "B.Q. View with Blanquita Cullum", "What's the Story" with Fred Barnes of the *Weekly Standard*, "This Week from Washington" with Stephan Halper, "Reflections" sponsored by the United Seniors Association, and "Small Business Focus" sponsored by the National Federation for Independent Business.
Tax Status: 501(c)(3) **Annual Report:** Yes. **Employees:** 15   **Citations:** 74:84
Board of Directors or Trustees: John Roberts.
Internships: Yes, priority given to broadcast majors.
Other Information: Also houses The Founders Society "dedicated to preserving and protecting the legacy of our Founding Fathers," and The World War II Veterans Committee. The Center contracted the McLean, VA, firm of Bruce W. Eberle & Associates for fund raising and the McLean firm of Omega List Company for mailing list maintenance; the two firms were paid $138,357 and $48,048 respectively. The Center received $1,621,951, or 79% of revenue from contributions and grants awarded by foundations, businesses, and individuals. (These grants included $115,000 from the John M. Olin Foundation, $50,000 from the Carthage Foundation, and $20,000 from the William H. Donner Foundation. In 1994, $6,000 from the Grover Hermann Foundation, and $5,000 from the J.M. Foundation. These contributions and grants have been increasing by an average of 10% over the last five years.) $314,606, or 15%, from mailing list rentals. $106,102, or 5%, from "production income". The remaining revenue came from advertising, interest on savings, and the sale of publications and videos.

American Survival Guide

774 S. Placentia Ave.
Placentia, CA 92870   **Phone:** (714) 572-6887   **E-Mail:** Jim4ASG@aol.com
USA   **Fax:**   (714) 572-4265

Contact Person: Jim Benson, Editor.
Officers or Principals: Scott Stoddard, Managing Editor
Mission or Interest: "A monthly magazine distributed nationally and internationally devoted to urban and wilderness survival matters such as natural and human-caused disasters and socio-economic upheaval (riots, economic collapse, etc.). Preservation of the U.S. as a constitutional republic, promoting maximum individual freedom and the capitalist/free-market economic system." Originally a gun magazine called *Shooters' Journal*, its emphasis has shifted more to the political arena, with regular articles on both political philosophy and practical electoral matters with a libertarian/conservative emphasis.
Accomplishments: Paid circulation of over 55,000. Regularly features articles by Ph.D.s and other credentialed experts
Tax Status: For profit.
Periodicals: *American Survival Guide* (monthly magazine).

Internships: No.
Other Information: Established in 1979 as *Shooters' Journal*, then changed its name to *American Survival Guide* in 1985. Published by McMullen Argus Publishing, best known for its car and truck publications such as *Popular Hot Rodding* and *Street Rodder*.

American Textbook Committee

2957 Old Rocky Ridge Rd.
Birmingham, AL 35243   **Phone:** (205) 879-9222
USA

Contact Person: R. Nelson Nash, President.
Officers or Principals: W. Jack Sexton, Secretary/Treasurer.
Mission or Interest: "To foster the writing of textbooks, especially in the political, social, and economic areas, that will be suitable for use in private, Christian, and all other schools and homes where patriotic American and traditional values hold sway, and for study by interested adults." Publishes the books of Dr. Clarence Carson, a former professor of history.
Accomplishments: Many of Dr. Carson's books have been distributed by the Conservative Book Club
Products or Services: Textbooks of conservative viewpoint by Dr. Clarence Carson, including the five-volume series - A Basic History of the United States, Basic Economics, The War on the Poor, and Basic Communism: Its Rise, Spread and Debacle in the 20th Century.
Tax Status: 501(c)(3) **Annual Report:** Yes. **Employees:** 1
Internships: No.

American Vision

10 Perimeter Way, Suite B-175
Atlanta, GA 30339   **Phone:** (404) 988-0555
USA   **Fax:**   (404) 952-2587

Contact Person: Ralph C. Barker, Vice President.
Officers or Principals: Gary DeMar, President ($35.500); Ralph C. Barker, Vice President ($35,000); Ira Moore, Chairman ($0).
Mission or Interest: Their calling is to help Christians of all denominations develop a biblical world-view and rebuild our nation in every area according to the blueprint of scripture. "We are one of the very few ministries in America providing the type of approach to Christian living that we espouse. Our approach is that God is not neutral about any area of life and that He has given us clear instruction on how to handle everything from inflation to war to government. We believe our culture is falling apart because Christians do not understand this basic truth. Our job is to help educate and train them."
Accomplishments: Twelve books published, monthly newsletters, and annual 'boot camps' for young students to prepare them for survival in the hostile college environment. They have become a national resource for many other ministries and pastors.
Total Revenue: 1994 $256,921 (-8%)(1) **Total Expenses:** $203,176 **Net Assets:** $256,916
Products or Services: Books, tapes, seminars, newsletters. Source of information for almost any topic from a biblical perspective, i.e. government, economics, law, art, family, business, occult, etc.
Tax Status: 501(c)(3) **Annual Report:** No. **Employees:** 5
Board of Directors or Trustees: James McMullen, Robert Brame, Mark Schweizer.
Periodicals: *The AV Report* (monthly newsletter).
Internships: No.
Other Information: Established in 1979. The organization received $206,750, or 80% of revenue, from contributions and grants awarded by foundations, businesses, and individuals. $39,700, or 15%, from royalties. $8,401, or 3%, from interest on savings and temporary cash investments.

Americanism Foundation

48 N. Linwood St.
Norwalk, OH 44857   **Phone:** (419) 668-8282
USA   **Fax:**   (419) 663-3723

Contact Person: N. M. Camardese M.D., President and Founder.
Officers or Principals: Mayely Waite, Vice President ($0); Wilbur Edwards, Treasurer ($0); Mark O'Brenovich, Secretary ($0).
Mission or Interest: "Preserving, protecting, and passing on the great heritage of freedom and traditional American and family values, particularly to the youth of America."
Accomplishments: The Foundation has won the George Washington Honor Medal from the Freedoms Foundation at Valley Forge. Since its creation, the Foundation's speakers have addressed more than 50,000 high school students In the fiscal year ending June 1993 the Foundation spent $25,614 on its programs.
Total Revenue: FY ending 6/93 $32,402 **Total Expenses:** $25,614 **Net Assets:** $9,258
Products or Services: Annual Leadership Award for high school students.
Tax Status: 501(c)(3) **Annual Report:** Yes. **Employees:** 2 part-time.
Internships: No.

Other Information: Established in 1979. Dr. Camardese fled to America from Mussolini's Italy. He served in the military and worked his way through school to obtain his M.D. Since then he has devoted himself to civic duty, and has won numerous honors, including "Man of the Year" in Norwalk. Currently, he also serves as president of the Association of American Physicians and Surgeons. The Foundation received $17,873, or 55% of revenue, from contributions and grants awarded by foundations, businesses, and individuals. (These contributions and grants have been erratic and have averaged $14,791 over the previous four years.) $14,442, or 44%, from program service revenues. The remaining revenue came from investments.

Americans for a Balanced Budget (ABB)

101 D St., S.E.
Washington, DC 20003   **Phone:**   (202) 544-2601
USA

Contact Person: Tony Zagotta, President.
Officers or Principals: Tony Zagotta, President ($54,000); David Miner, Chairman ($47,000); Emily McGee, Program Director ($24,000); Colin Chapman, Executive Director; Charles Harvey, Director.
Mission or Interest: Supports balancing the federal budget by cutting taxes and reducing spending further.
Accomplishments: Claims over 200,000 members. During the 1996 campaign ABB conducted media campaigns and focus groups to counter television ads financed by the AFL-CIO regarding reductions in Medicare spending. ABB claims to have spent a million dollars on an ad campaign during the election season to support a balanced budget and tax cuts. In 1995 ABB's promotional materials included a letter by then Senate Majority Leader Bob Dole. In 1995 ABB spent $296,549 on its programs.
Total Revenue: 1995 $449,777 39%(3) **Total Expenses:** $398,948 74%/19%/7% **Net Assets:** $67,105
Tax Status: 501(c)(4)   **Citations:** 110:59
Other Information: Established in 1990. President Tony Zagotta is a former chairman of the College Republicans. ABB received $448,777, or 100% of revenue, from contributors.

Americans for Constitutional Democracy

19325 S.W. Edy Road
Sherwood, OR 97140   **Phone:**   (503) 625-2181
USA

Contact Person: James Greenfield, President.
Mission or Interest: Restore limited government as set up by the Constitution. Repeal the 16th amendment, abolish the IRS, eliminate all unconstitutional functions performed by the Federal government, restore and reinvigorate the Bill of Rights.
Accomplishments: Numerous media appearances, public speaking engagements and publication of several articles. Working on an independently produced, feature-length film version of "The Taxman Cometh."
Total Revenue: FY ending 6/95 $10,000 **Total Expenses:** $10,010 **Net Assets:** $190
Products or Services: Audio tape, "The Taxman Cometh - Notes from the Underground Economy."
Tax Status: 501(c)(3) **Annual Report:** No.
Other Information: Established in 1991. The organization received $10,000, or 100% of revenue, from contributions and grants.

Americans for Free Choice in Medicine (AFCM)

1525 Superior Ave., Suite 100
Newport Beach, CA 92665   **Phone:**   (714) 645-2622   **E-Mail:**   afcm@netcom.com
USA   **Fax:**   (714) 645-4624   **Internet:** http://www.afcm.org

Contact Person: Scott Holleran, Executive Director.
Officers or Principals: Scott Holleran, Executive Director ($16,256); Joan Wise, Director of Operations ($8,712); Arthur Astorine, Jr., M.D., Founder/Chairman Emeritus ($0); Peter C. LePort, M.D., Co-founder/Chairman; Cristina Rizza, M.D., Co-founder/Treasurer.
Mission or Interest: "To educate the public about health care industry issues. AFCM offers a 100 percent pure free-market plan for health care which encourages tax-free medical savings accounts as a blueprint for weaning America's health-care system off the federal government."
Accomplishments: Nobel Prize-winning economist Milton Friedman said, "I thoroughly agree with the principles of free choice underlying AFCM's mission statement." A 1994 Costa Mesa 'Town Hall' meeting co-hosted by AFCM, featuring Dr. Leonard Peikoff (author, Objectivism: The Philosophy of Ayn Rand) drew over 600 citizens.
Total Revenue: FY ending 8/96 $40,604 **Total Expenses:** $41,225 **Net Assets:** $6,596
Products or Services: Forums, lectures, and debates. Many booklets.
Tax Status: 501(c)(3) **Annual Report:** No.
Periodicals: *AFCM Pulse* (quarterly newsletter).
Internships: Yes, unpaid.
Other Information: Established in 1993. The organization received $40,382, or 99% of revenue, from contributions and grants awarded by foundations, businesses, and individuals. (These contributions and grants have been decreasing since its founding in 1993 by an average of 7% per year.) The remaining revenue came from investment income.

Americans for Hope, Growth and Opportunity (AHGO)

1400 Route 206 North
P.O. Box 38
Bedminster, NJ 07921   **Phone:**   (908) 781-5111   **E-Mail:**   Forbes@AHGO.org
USA   **Fax:**   (908) 781-6001   **Internet:** http://www.AHGO.org

Officers or Principals: Steve Forbes, Honorary Chairman.
Mission or Interest: "A conservative, grassroots organization created to champion a positive, forward-looking agenda to take America into the 21st century." Supports: A lower, flat-rate income tax, a monetary standard that "tie(s) the value of the dollar to a fixed measure," medical savings accounts, school choice, privatized Social Security, term limits, a reduced role for the United Nations in U.S. foreign policy, and a ballistic missile defense system
Tax Status: 501(c)(4)
Periodicals: Quarterly newsletter.
Other Information: Established in August 1996 by former Presidential hopeful, Steve Forbes. Steve Forbes is CEO/president of Forbes, Inc., and editor-in-chief of *Forbes* magazine. Until founding AHGO, Forbes served as co-chairman of Empower America.

Americans for Moral Government

2055 Kedge Dr.
Vienna, VA 22181   **Phone:**   (703) 281-7378
USA

Contact Person: Gary L. Jarmin, Director.
Officers or Principals: Gina A. Jarmin, Director ($0); Gary L. Jarmin, Director ($0); Matthew D. Smyth, Director ($0).
Mission or Interest: "Educating and activating Americans toward constructive action on key issues, especially as regards the threat to a free democratic and God centered value system." Awards grants to other organizations.
Accomplishments: In 1995 the organization awarded $125,066 in grants. Recipients were organizations associated with Dr. Robert Grant; $66,036 for Christian Voice, $36,985 for the American Business Council, and $22,045 for the American Christian Cause.
Total Revenue: 1995 $120,203 **Total Expenses:** $125,066 99%/1%/0% **Net Assets:** (-$2,377)
Tax Status: 501(c)(4)
Other Information: Affiliated with the for-profit JAR-MON Consultants, Inc. Americans for Moral Government received $120,000, or 99.8% of revenue, from contributions. The remaining revenue came from interest on savings and temporary cash investments.

Americans for a Sound AIDS / HIV Policy

P.O. Box 17433
Washington, DC 20041   **Phone:**   (703) 471-7350
USA

Contact Person: Anita Smith, Assistant Director.
Officers or Principals: Patricia Ware, Executive Director ($52,500); Anita Smith, Assistant Director ($29,708); W. Shepard Smith, Jr., Director ($17,000).
Mission or Interest: To influence national policies and opinions on AIDS, and do so using scientific fact, not special-interest politics.
Accomplishments: In 1994 the organization spent $495,337 on its programs. The largest program, with expenditures of $384,405, was the production of educational materials. This included a grant of $129,800 to the AIDS National Interfaith Network. $104,197 was spent on the "Children's Fund" providing contributions and support for children infected with HIV.
Total Revenue: 1994 $517,306 ($248,865, or 48%, from government grants) (-1%)(2) **Total Expenses:** $548,448 90%/9%/1%
Net Assets: (-$98,684)
Products or Services: Books, publications, seminars and conferences.
Tax Status: 501(c)(3)   **Citations:** 15:163
Periodicals: Newsletter.
Other Information: The organization received $262,363, or 51%, from contributions and grants awarded by foundations, businesses, and individuals. $248,865, or 48%, from government grants. The remaining revenue came from conference and seminar fees, and the sale of publications.

Americans for Tax Reform (ATR)

1320 18th St., N.W., Suite 200
Washington, DC 20036   **Phone:**   (202) 785-0266   **E-Mail:**   AmTxReform@aol.com
USA   **Fax:**   (202) 785-0261   **Internet:** http://www.Emerald.Net/ATR/

Contact Person: Grover Norquist, President.
Officers or Principals: Peter Ruff, Executive Director ($30,000); Grover Norquist, President ($0).

Mission or Interest: Lobbying affiliate of the Americans for Tax Reform Foundation. Lobbies on behalf of lower taxes and less government regulation.

Accomplishments: In 1994 ATR spent $734,092 on its programs. The two main programs were the "Taxpayer Protection Pledge" that the organization persuades political candidates to sign. Signees pledge to oppose tax increases. Almost every Republican member of the House and Senate has taken the pledge, along with about five House Democrats. Also campaigns against a Value Added Tax, or VAT, which ATR sees as a way to raise taxes and hide the true cost from taxpayers.

Total Revenue: 1994 $844,610 184%(2) **Total Expenses:** $898,031 82%/18%/0% **Net Assets:** $102,535

Tax Status: 501(c)(4)   **Citations:** 429:22

Other Information: Established in 1985 at the suggestion of the Reagan administration to build coalition support for the 1986 tax reform bill. Affiliated with the 501(c)(3) Americans for Tax Reform Foundation at the same address. President Grover Norquist is a featured columnist for *The American Spectator*. Norquist practices a 'take no prisoners' form of activism; "How do you ever expect to gain allies [if what you say is] 'I'm standing in the train tracks and the train is going to run me over, but the right and virtuous thing for you to do is stand with me while we lose?'. . . I think you run up 100 yards and blow [up] the train tracks and then see what the train thinks about that." ATR received $843,238, or 99.8% of revenue, from contributions and grants. The remaining revenue came from interest on savings and temporary cash investments.

Americans for Tax Reform Foundation

1320 18th St., N.W., Suite 200
Washington, DC 20036   **Phone:**   (202) 785-0266
USA   **Fax:**   (202) 785-0261   **Internet:** http://www.Emerald.Net/ATR/

Contact Person: Grover Norquist, President.

Officers or Principals: Grover G. Norquist, President; Audrey Mullen, Executive Director; Jim Lucier, Research Director.

Mission or Interest: Research and education affiliate of Americans for Tax Reform.

Accomplishments: Promoter of "Tax Freedom Day," and the "Cost of Government Day." Tax Freedom Day is the day on which the average American's "tax obligations are fully paid to the government" (currently in the first week of May), and Cost of Government Day is that plus the cost of "government-imposed financial obligations," or regulations (currently in the second week of July). President Grover Norquist was referred to in a *Washington Post* feature story as "a combination architect, gatekeeper, drill sergeant and mother hen of the right." In 1995 the Foundation spent $85,770 on its programs.

Total Revenue: 1995 $301,949 **Total Expenses:** $120,440 71%/29%/0% **Net Assets:** $182,374

Tax Status: 501(c)(3)   **Citations:** 429:22

Periodicals: *American Tax Reformer* (bimonthly tabloid), *Anti-VAT Report* (newsletter).

Other Information: Affiliated with the 501(c)(4) Americans for Tax Reform at the same address. Norquist is the author of Rock the House, an analysis of the 1994 elections. The Foundation received $301,949, or 100% of revenue, from contributions and grants awarded by foundations, businesses, and individuals. (These grants included $100,000 from the John M. Olin Foundation, $40,000 from the Lynde and Harry Bradley Foundation, $5,000 $5,000 from the John William Pope Foundation, and $5,000 from the Roe Foundation. In 1994 the Foundation received $15,000 from the J.M. Foundation. These contributions and grants have been increasing by an average of 35% per year over the last five years.)

Americans for Voluntary School Prayer

1105 E. Commonwealth
Fullerton, CA 92631   **Phone:**   (714) 284-5990
USA   **Fax:**   (714) 871-4221

Contact Person: Susan Hirzel.

Officers or Principals: Bill Dannemeyer, David Barton, Co-Founders.

Mission or Interest: "To develop Congressional and state legislative support for reclaiming religious liberty, voluntary school prayer in America."

Accomplishments: "Helped to procure 122 co-sponsors for HJ Res. 127 authored by Rep. Istook (R-OK), in the 104th Congress."

Products or Services: A Guide to the School Prayer & Religious Liberty Debate booklet and other publications.

Tax Status: 501(c)(4) **Employees:** 1

Internships: No.

Other Information: Bill Dannemeyer was a former member of the House of Representatives (R-CA), from 1979-1992. As a legislator, he had an ACU rating of 95%.

Americans United for Life (AUL)

343 S. Dearborn St., Suite 1804
Chicago, IL 60604   **Phone:**   (312) 786-9494
USA   **Fax:**   (312) 341-2656

Contact Person: Clarke D. Forsythe, President.
Officers or Principals: Clarke D. Forsythe, President ($65,000); Paige Comstock Cunningham, former President ($64,000); J. Damron, Director, Development ($50,770); Tom G. Murray, Secretary/Treasurer; P. Linton, Associate General Counsel; D. Mackura-Tromski, Senior Legislative Counsel.
Mission or Interest: "The legal arm of the pro-life movement. . . from a human rights, civil rights, medical and sociological viewpoint."
Accomplishments: America's oldest anti-abortion organization. In 1991 AUL sponsored a Gallup Poll that found that 78% of Americans thought that abortion was wrong, but that a majority viewed it as a 'necessary evil.' AUL filed a citizen petition against the Food and Drug Administration regarding the approval of the abortifacient RU-486. The petition held that there are numerous health risks associated with this drug and that "the FDA has short-circuited the review process." In 1993 AUL spent $737,993 on its programs. The largest expenditure, $495,307, was on legal research and litigation. $223,590 was spent on public affairs and education. $19,096 was spent on researching public attitudes on abortion.
Total Revenue: 1993 $1,109,042 (-50%)(1) **Total Expenses:** $1,178,795 63%/6%/32% **Net Assets:** $286,125
Products or Services: Litigation, research, and lobbying. In 1993 AUL spent $119,220 on the direct lobbying of legislators. This was an increase of 159% over the previous year.
Tax Status: 501(c)(3)   **Citations:** 32:125
Board of Directors or Trustees: Prof. Robert Destro (Columbus School of Law, Catholic Univ.), Eugene Diamond, M.D., Thomas Donnelly, Karol Emmerich, Mildred Jefferson, M.D., Dr. Kenneth Mitzner, Rev. John Neuhaus (Inst. on Religion and Public Life), Herbert Ratner, M.D., Rep. Chris Smith (R-NJ), Prof. Lynn Wardle (Brigham Young Univ.), Dr. Richard Wirthlin, Msgr. John Woolsey (Archdiocese of New York).
Other Information: Established in 1971. AUL received $1,097,564, or 99% of revenue, from contributions and grants awarded by foundations, businesses, and individuals. (In 1995 these grants included $24,675 from the Alliance Defense Fund.) The remaining revenue came from dividends and interest on securities, and the sale of inventory. The large drop in revenue from 1992 was due to a decrease in contributions and grants. During the previous three years AUL averaged in $2,383,128 in contributions, 117% more than in 1993.

America's Future

7800 Bonhomme Ave.
St. Louis, MO 63105   **Phone:** (314) 725-6003   **E-Mail:** eamiller@basenet.net
USA   **Fax:**   (314) 721-3373   **Internet:** http://www.basenet.net/~eamiller/af/af.html

Contact Person: Robert Morriss, Chairman.
Officers or Principals: Phyllis Schlafly, Treasurer ($0).
Mission or Interest: "Emphasizing benefits of our constitutional form of government and our free enterprise system. . . We perceive as the most serious threat to our freedom and way of life the ideologies of collectivism and state socialism."
Accomplishments: Recently changed headquarters and updated the format and graphics of its newsletter and publications. "Providing political commentaries to more than 125 radio stations across America, and more than 300 daily and weekly newspapers." Celebrated its 50th anniversary in 1996. On the occasion of America's 40th anniversary in 1986, Sen. Jesse Helms (R-NC) said, "I know of no other organization that has more uniquely and effectively promoted and defended the fundamental principles of the Miracle of America than America's Future." Produced textbook evaluations and bibliographies compiled by the late Dr. Russell Kirk.
Total Revenue: 1995 $154,043 (-36%)(1) **Total Expenses:** $192,088 79%/21%/0% **Net Assets:** $22,663
Products or Services: "Behind the Headlines" radio commentaries and syndicated columns distributed free of charge to newspapers and radio stations nationwide. Numerous pamphlets on education, national defense, and other topics.
Tax Status: 501(c)(3) **Annual Report:** Yes.
Board of Directors or Trustees: D. Clifford Allison, Dr. Anthony Bouscaren, William Gill, Sen. Jesse Helms (R-NC), Wesley Hillendahl, Dr. Anthony Kubek, John Metzler, Mrs. Herbert Philbrick, Elizabeth Racer, Brig. Gen. Robert Richardson III, Henri Salvatori, Maj. Gen. John Singlaub, Raymond Telles, James Tyson, W. Raymond Wannall, John Wetzel, Philip Clarke.
Periodicals: *America's Future* (bimonthly newsletter).
Internships: No.
Other Information: Founded in 1946. 1995 was its first year in Missouri; previous locations were New York and Pennsylvania. America's Future received $149,039, or 97% from contributions and grants awarded by foundations, businesses, and individuals. (These grants included $5,000 from the John M. Olin Foundation. In 1994, $50,000 from the George Edward Durell Foundation, $2,500 from the Milliken Foundation, and $700 from the Alex C. Walker Foundation. These contributions and grants have been falling by an average of 18% a year for the last five years.) $3,638, or 2%, from newsletter subscriptions. The remaining revenue came from interest on savings.

America's Future Foundation

1508 21st St., N.W.
Washington, DC 20036   **Phone:** (202) 530-9860   **E-Mail:** amfuture@earthlink.net
USA   **Fax:**   same

Contact Person: Mary C. Riner, Executive Director..

Officers or Principals: Christopher S. Siddall, President; Samuel Casey Carter, Treasurer; Mary Caroline Riner, Executive Director/Secretary.

Mission or Interest: "Supports limited government, free markets, personal responsibility, moral virtue, world leadership, and technological progress by educating and mobilizing today's young Americans." Appeals to and organized by 'generation X' members.

Accomplishments: "America's Future Foundation fills a gap in the conservative movement between college activists and the leaders already on the front lines. . . Through the generosity of The Fund for American Studies, America's Future Foundation has brought together a core group of young policy analysts and other experts who meet monthly to discuss new policy initiatives. Featured speakers have included former U.S. Attorney General Edwin Meese, III; Grover Norquist, President of Americans for Tax Reform; Karlyn Bowman, Resident Fellow for Political Studies at the American Enterprise Institute; Ramesh Ponnuru, *National Review's* national reporter."

Products or Services: E-mail and fax updates. Roundtable meetings, conferences, and seminars.

Tax Status: 501(c)(3)

Board of Directors or Trustees: John Barry, Suzanne-Kirby Carter, Brian Jones, Lisa Kardell, Adam Kaufman, Scott Lansell, Patrick Mancuso, Christian Tellalian, Geoffrey Underwood.

Periodicals: *Doublethink* (quarterly newsletter) and *Brainwash* (monthly 'zine).

Other Information: Established in 1995.

Amy Foundation

P.O. Box 16091
Lansing, MI 48901-6091   **Phone:**   (517) 323-6233
USA

Contact Person: Walter J. Russell, President.

Officers or Principals: Walter J. Russell, President ($0); Phyllis M. Russell, Vice President ($0); Dale G. Walter, Secretary/Treasurer ($0).

Mission or Interest: Foundation which presents the Amy Writing Awards for scriptural quotes and Biblical morality in writings which appear in a secular forum. Also supports small writing groups which meet and write letters to the editor in their local communities.

Accomplishments: Awarded over $34,000 in prizes during 1995. Past winners of the Amy Writing Awards included; Richard John Neuhaus (Institute on Religion and Public Life), Charles Colson (Prison Fellowship), William R. Mattox, Jr. (Family Research Council), and Cal Thomas (syndicated columnist). During the fiscal year ending August 1995 the Foundation awarded $65,530 in grants. Recipients were mostly religious groups in the Lansing, Michigan area. Recipients included: $1,300 for the Rutherford Institute, $1,200 for Prison Fellowship, $500 for the Foundation for Traditional Values, and $50 for Citizens for Traditional Values.

Total Revenue: FY ending 8/95 $226,871 **Total Expenses:** $230,385 **Net Assets:** $6,929 112%(2)

Products or Services: Amy Writing Awards: $10,000 for first place, $5,000 for second place, $4,000 for third, $3,000 for fourth, $2,000 for fifth, and ten other prizes of $1,000 each.

Tax Status: 501(c)(3)

Board of Directors or Trustees: Distinguished Judges included: Dr. Carl F. H. Henry (editor, *World*), Prof. Clifford Kelly (Regent Univ.), Sam Moore (Thomas Nelson Publishers), Dean Will Norton, Jr. (College of Journalism, Univ. of Nebraska), Wesley Pippert (Director, Univ. of Missouri School of Journalism), Millie Samuelson (Central College, KS).

Periodicals: *Church Writing Group Newsletter* (quarterly).

Other Information: The Amy Foundation and Writing Awards were established by Michigan businessman W. J. Russell and his wife Phyllis in 1976, and named after their daughter. The Foundation received $226,871, or 100% of revenue, from contributions and grants from individuals and companies, the largest percentage from W. J. Russell.

Anschutz Foundation

555 17th St., Suite 2400
Denver, CO 80202   **Phone:**   (303) 293-2338
USA

Contact Person: Sue Anschutz-Rodgers, President.

Officers or Principals: Philip F. Anschutz, Chairman ($0); Sue Anschutz-Rodgers, President ($0); Nancy P. Anschutz, Vice President ($0); Hugh C. Braly, Secretary/Treasurer; Sarah Anschutz, Director.

Mission or Interest: Grant-making foundation that includes conservative organizations in its awards.

Accomplishments: In the fiscal year ending November 1994, the Foundation awarded $177,500 in grants. Recipients included: $7,500 for the Free Congress Foundation, $5,000 each for the American Enterprise Institute, Defense Forum Foundation, Empowerment Network Foundation, Mountain States Legal Foundation, Pacific Legal Foundation, Washington Legal Foundation, and the Claremont Institute, and $2,500 for the Capital Research Center.

Total Revenue: FY ending 11/94 $244,568 **Total Expenses:** $365,184 **Net Assets:** $1,164,326 (-3%)(2)

Tax Status: 501(c)(3)
Other Information: Established in 1984. The Foundation received $189,747, or 76% of revenue, from the sale of oil and gas royalties. $53,563, or 22%, from dividends and interest from securities. The remaining revenue came from interest on savings and temporary cash investments. The Foundation held $649,000, or 56% of assets, in oil and gas royalties. $513,750, or 44%, in government securities.

AntiShyster

P.O. Box 540786
Dallas, TX 75354   **Phone:** (214) 418-8993   **Internet:** http://www.antishyster.com
USA

Contact Person: Alfred Adask, Editor/Publisher.
Officers or Principals: Debra Bertke, Administrative Assistant.
Mission or Interest: Populist/libertarian magazine whose "principle theme is that the American legal system is essentially an extortion racket whose purpose is not to dispense justice, but rather, to generate fat fees for lawyers," according to *The National Law Journal*. AntiShyster describes itself as "one of the two or three best legal reform publications in the U.S.A. (some say *the* best). Unlike most of our competitors, we don't 'sell' conspiracy theories and fear - instead, we endeavor to provide understanding, *workable strategies*, and hope."
Accomplishments: *The Los Angeles Times* calls it "The Constitutionalist. . . movement's academic nerve center." AntiShyster claims a paid circulation of approximately 12,000. "We were the first magazine to publicize information concerning Common Law Liens, Commercial liens, the 'Missing 13th Amendment', Barratry, and challenges to Legislative Jurisdiction - and every one of these strategies has helped keep government at bay while increasing the Patriot community's confidence and ability to act."
Tax Status: For profit.
Periodicals: *AntiShyster: A Critical Examination of the American Legal System* (bimonthly journal).

Applied Foresight, Inc.

5511 Malibu Dr.
Edina, MN 55436   **E-Mail:** 71510.1042@compuserve.com
USA

Mission or Interest: Applied Foresight has two computer services for sale of interest to conservatives and libertarians. "ShareDebate International" carries fiction and non-fiction original and reprinted writings. Writers include Stuart Butler, George Gilder, Milton Friedman, the Republican Liberty Caucus, Murray Rothbard, Joe Sobran and many more. ShareDebate also carries numerous debates on topics of interest to conservatives and libertarians. They also offer Hillsdale College's newsletter, *Imprimis*, electronically on "Imprimis Online." Both ShareDebate International and Imprimis Online are available on diskette as well as online computer network. Back issues are available for both
Products or Services: Computer services.
Tax Status: For profit.

Aristos Foundation

P.O. Box 1105
New York, NY 10101   **Phone:** (212) 678-8550   **Internet:** http://www.aristos.org
USA

Contact Person: Michelle Marder Kamhi, Vice Chairman.
Officers or Principals: Louis Torres, Chairman; Richard W. Disbrow, Treasurer.
Mission or Interest: Dedicated to the preservation and enhancement of traditional values (as opposed to modernism and post-modernism) in the arts, and to objective standards in scholarship and criticism. "We aim to further objective standards in arts scholarship and criticism; to champion humanistic values in the arts of the twentieth century; and to expose fraudulence and intellectual bankruptcy of the contemporary arts establishment now entrenched in the nation's cultural, educational, governmental, and corporate institutions."
Accomplishments: *Aristos* is indexed in the ARTbibliographies Modern, and the American Humanities Index. Cultural historian Jacques Barzun has said, "Reading some of your issues has given me pleasure and instruction." The Foundation has produced a series on Ayn Rand's philosophy of art. Louis Torres and Michele Marder Kamhi have collaborated on a book entitled, What Art Is: Ayn Rand's Philosophy of Art in Critical Perspective, due to be published by Open Court in 1998
Products or Services: Art journal, speakers' bureau.
Tax Status: 501(c)(3) **Annual Report:** No. **Employees:** 2
Periodicals: *Aristos: The Journal of Esthetics* (bimonthly journal)
Internships: On a volunteer basis.
Other Information: Established in 1987, but the journal *Aristos* was established in 1982 by Louis Torres.

Arizona School Choice Trust

8711 E. Pinnacle Peak Rd., Suite 203
Scottsdale, AZ 85255   **Phone:** (602) 340-9302
USA   **Fax:**   (602) 501-2949

Contact Person: Jack McVaughn, President.
Officers or Principals: Jack McVaughn, President ($0); Sydney Hoof Hay, Executive Director ($0); Rick Tompkins, Vice President ($0); Thomas Rouse, Treasurer; John Karow, Secretary.
Mission or Interest: Provides scholarships for low-income families (mostly of Latino descent) to attend the private school of their choice.
Accomplishments: In 1996 the Trust provided scholarships for 100 children; the Trust had provided a *total* of 100 scholarships in the previous three years. The Trust awards half the child's tuition, or a maximum of $800. It has over 200 children on waiting lists.
Total Revenue: 1995 $67,349 **Total Expenses:** $37,749 **Net Assets:** $70,414
Products or Services: Scholarships.
Tax Status: 501(c)(3) **Annual Report:** No. **Employees:** 1
Internships: No.
Other Information: Established in 1992. Affiliated with CEO America. The Trust received $66,668, or 99% of revenue, from contributions and grants awarded by foundations, businesses, and individuals. This was 90% more than the previous three year's average. The remaining revenue came from investment income.

Arkansas Policy Foundation (APF)

8201 Cantrell Rd.
Pavilion in the Park, Suite 325
Little Rock, AR 72227   **Phone:** (501) 227-4815   **E-Mail:** aggiemw2@aol.com
USA   **Fax:**   (501) 227-8970   **Internet:** www.tristero.com/praxis/apf

Contact Person: Michael W. Watson, President.
Officers or Principals: Michael W. Watson, President ($39,585); Wythe Walker, Jr., Chairman ($0); J. French Hill, Treasurer ($0); Karen Henry, Secretary.
Mission or Interest: State-based policy Foundation. "Conservative, free-market oriented, committed to reducing government and dedicated to preserving individual freedom and responsibility."
Accomplishments: In 1995 the Foundation spent $61,902 on its programs. $35,130 was spent producing and distributing over 30,000 copies of research papers, executive summaries, and surveys. $17,494 was spent on speakers and issues forums attended by 430 individuals. Appeared in over 50 print and broadcast media engagements. William Bennett of Empower America said of APF, "The Arkansas Policy Foundation can do a lot of good for Arkansas, as well as the entire conservative movement."
Total Revenue: FY running from 2/95 to 12/95 $144,526 **Total Expenses:** $109,547 57%/34%/10% **Net Assets:** $34,979
Products or Services: Survey of business' attitudes toward taxes, fiscal issues, public school performance, and other topics.
Tax Status: 501(c)(3) **Annual Report:** No. **Employees:** 3
Board of Directors or Trustees: David Howell, Blant Hurt, Fritz Steiger, Steve Stephens.
Internships: No.
Other Information: Established in 1995. A member of the State Policy Network. The Foundation received $144,526, or 99% of revenue, from contributions and grants awarded by foundations, businesses, and individuals. (These grants included $10,000 from the Roe Foundation, and $1,000 from the Charles G. Koch Charitable Foundation.) $801, or 1%, from interest on savings and temporary cash investments.

Associated Conservatives of Texas (ACT)

2029 Levee St.
Dallas, TX 75207   **Phone:** (214) 278-2511   **E-Mail:** act@why.net
USA   **Fax:**   same

Contact Person: Sandra Crosnoe, Director.
Officers or Principals: David Rucker, David Hall, Directors.
Mission or Interest: "An independent grassroots network which blends fiscally and socially conservative individuals into a unified force working together to achieve limited government with: high ethical standards, personal responsibility, strong national defense, and fiscal integrity." Active in the 'Fully Informed Jury Movement.'
Accomplishments: Hosts the only touring replica of the Liberty Bell. This bell was one of 70 commissioned for the bicentennial, and the only one that now tours. "During the Civil War the Bell traveled from city to city 'proclaiming liberty' for the country's black inhabitants. It achieved iconic status relative to the abolitionist cause. Today, the replica of the Liberty Bell travels from city to city 'proclaiming liberty' for the unborn as well as those already born." Influential criticism of former President George Bush and other moderate Republicans in Texas
Products or Services: E-mail network, several brochures, The Rat in the Hat children's book, "Project Truth" graphic anti-abortion video, more.
Tax Status: Unincorporated. **Annual Report:** No. **Employees:** All volunteer.

Board of Directors or Trustees: Advisors include: Joseph Foreman (Missionaries to the Preborn), Don McAlvaney, R. E. McMaster (*The Reaper*), Rep. Ron Paul, M.D. (R-TX), Howard Phillips (Conservative Caucus), Larry Pratt (Gun Owners of America), Llewellyn Rockwell (Mises Inst.), Otto Scott (*Compass*).

Other Information: Conducts multiple projects through "Issues Coordinators." These include: Alfred Adask (legal reform), Lance Bedford (computer bulletin board systems), Wayne Burnham (right-to-bear-arms issues), Dorita Head (family and education issues), Bill Keffer (tax reform), Deborah McClelland (pro-life issues), Tom Glass (Fully Informed Jury Association), Tom Staley (national sovereignty issues).

Association of American Physicians and Surgeons (AAPS)

1601 N. Tucson Blvd., Suite 9
Tucson, AZ 85716   **Phone:**   (800) 635-1196
USA   **Fax:**   (520) 326-3529   **Internet:** http://www.primenet.com/~snavely

Contact Person: Jane Orient, M.D., Executive Director.

Officers or Principals: Don Printz, M.D., President ($0); W. Daniel Jordan, M.D., Secretary ($0); R. Lowell Campbell, M.D., Treasurer ($0).

Mission or Interest: A professional organization for medical doctors. "To protect the practice of private medicine, preserve freedom of choice for patients and doctors, and educate physicians and the general public."

Accomplishments: Forced the Clinton administration to release the documents pertaining to Hillary Rodham Clinton's Health Care Task Force. Using the documents, the AAPS revealed and charged that Task Force Leader, Ira Magaziner, falsely claimed in a sworn affidavit that the Task Force was comprised of Federal employees and therefore allowed to operate in secret; a claim he must have known to be false since some of his colleagues from a private sector consulting firm were included. The AAPS brought suit against the Clinton Administration in AAPS v. Clinton, and the suit was dismissed when the administration finally turned over most of the records. The judge referred the question of criminal perjury on the part of Magaziner to Attorney General Janet Reno.

Total Revenue: FY ending 10/95 $725,613 39%(2) **Total Expenses:** $691,933 **Net Assets:** $277,168

Products or Services: Membership services and Lobbying: in the fiscal year ending October 1995 the AAPS spent $56,323 on lobbying and political expenditures.

Tax Status: 501(c)(6)   **Citations:** 21:146

Board of Directors or Trustees: V. L. Goltry, M.D., Bruce Schlafly, M.D., James Weaver, M.D., Claud Boyd, Jr., M.D., Curtis Caine Sr., M.D., Donald Quinlan, M.D., Nino Camardese, M.D., John Boyles Jr., M.D., Joseph Scherzer, M.D., James Cot, M.D., John Dwyer, M.D., Michale Schlitt, M.D.

Periodicals: *AAPS News* (monthly newsletter), *Medical Sentinel* (quarterly journal).

Internships: No.

Other Information: Established in 1943. In addition to its lobbying, the AAPS maintains a political action committee, the AAPS-PAC. In the 1993-94 election cycle the AAPS-PAC gave $25,500 to candidates for political office, all of them Republican, 84% of whom were challenging incumbent Democrats. The AAPS received $609,175, or 84% of revenue, from membership dues. $68,778, or 9%, from program services, including an annual meeting, regional meetings, and the sale of literature. $25,907, or 4%, from contributions and grants awarded by foundations, businesses, and individuals. $16,255, or 2%, from interest on savings and temporary cash investments. The remaining revenue came from other miscellaneous sources.

Association of Libertarian Feminists (ALF)

P.O. Box 20252, London Terrace
New York, NY 10011
USA

Contact Person: Joan Kennedy Taylor, National Coordinator.

Mission or Interest: "To encourage women to become economically self-sufficient and psychologically independent; to publicize and promote realistic attitudes toward female competence, achievement, and potential. To oppose abridgement of individual rights by any government on account of sex. To work toward changing sexist attitudes and behavior exhibited by individuals. To provide a libertarian alternative to those aspects of the women's movement that tend to discourage independence and individuality." Supports abortion rights

Products or Services: Discussion papers.

Tax Status: Not exempt. **Annual Report:** No.

Board of Directors or Trustees: Coordinating Committee; Sieglinde Kress, Lee Nason, Sharon Presley, Andrea Rich (Laissez Faire Books), Rebecca Shipman.

Periodicals: *ALF News* (quarterly newsletter).

Internships: No.

Other Information: Established in 1975 by Tonie Nathan, the first woman in American history to receive an electoral vote when she ran for Vice President on the Libertarian ticket, and a "maverick" Republican (Roger MacBride, now with the Republican Liberty Caucus) cast his electoral vote for Nathan and Presidential candidate John Hospers.

Association of Objectivist Businessmen (AOB)

P.O. Box 370
Beverly, MA 01915   **Phone:**   (508) 922-4381
USA   **Fax:**   (508) 922-4810

Contact Person: Ken West, President.
Mission or Interest: Promoting Ayn Rand's philosophy of Objectivism and free-market economics to the business community. "There is a worthy battle to be fought in our culture, a battle to provide a moral sanction for the heroic producers of our age. Ayn Rand's philosophy of Objectivism, and the intellectuals who stand on her shoulders, give us the ammunition we need."
Accomplishments: Membership directory.
Periodicals: *AOB News* (bimonthly newsletter).
Other Information: Established in 1988.

Athens Institute

1800 Diagonal Rd., Suite 600
Alexandria, VA 22314   **Phone:**   (703) 684-3130
USA   **Fax:**   (703) 548-9446

Contact Person: John F. Groom, President.
Mission or Interest: Study the efforts and output of conservative public policy organizations, their methods and their use of changing technologies.
Accomplishments: William E. Simon, president of the John M. Olin Foundation, said of their study *Publishing, Communications, and Public Policy*, "The Athens Communications Study is a highly informative survey of the programs and practices of free market institutions. This study is well worth reading by all those who are devoted to the cause of free markets and limited government."
Total Revenue: 1993 less than $25,000
Products or Services: Studies and publications including, *Communications and Public Policy and the Media, Volume 1: Public Policy and the Media.*
Tax Status: 501(c)(3)
Other Information: Groom Books also operates at the same address as the Athens Institute. John Groom serves on the Board of Directors of U.S. Term Limits.

Atlantic Legal Foundation (ALF)

205 E. 42nd St., 9th Floor
New York, NY 10017   **Phone:**   (212) 573-1960
USA

Contact Person: Douglas Foster, President.
Mission or Interest: "To advocate the principles of limited government, the free market system, and the rights of individuals."
Accomplishments: Challenging various affirmative action programs in New York state. Helped preserve the right of 'cottage industries' to contract home-based workers to perform work such as sewing. ALF represented 18 scientists, including six Nobel Laureates in Daubert v. Merrell Dow Pharmaceuticals, a case that helped define scientific standards for court admissibility
Tax Status: 501(c)(3)
Other Information: In 1994 the Foundation received $40,000 from the Lilly Endowment, $25,000 from the Sarah Scaife Foundation, $20,000 from the F.M. Kirby Foundation. In 1995, $15,000 from the John M. Olin Foundation, $5,000 from the Forbes Foundation, and $4,000 from the Philip M. McKenna Foundation.

Atlantis Project, The

4132 S. Rainbow Blvd., Suite 387
Las Vegas, NV 89103   **Phone:**   (702) 897-8320   **E-Mail:** oceania@world.std.com
USA   **Fax:**   (702) 897-4172

Contact Person: Dawn Lambert.
Officers or Principals: Eric Klien.
Mission or Interest: The Atlantis Project intends to build a floating city in the Caribbean, called Oceania, which will be founded on the principles of "free thought and free markets." They have already written Oceania's Constitution and laws, carefully worded to insure future inhabitants enjoy the same freedoms as the founders do. The ambitious project is to be built by the Swedish firm that built what is now the Saigon Floating Hotel, as well as many floating structures such as military barracks and oil platforms.
Accomplishments: They have received much publicity and raised $100,000. Their architect is nearly finished with the model
Tax Status: Nonprofit. **Annual Report:** No. **Employees:** 5
Periodicals: *Chain Breaker* (bi-monthly newsletter).
Internships: No.
Other Information: Eric Klien founded this project because he discovered "massive election fraud" in the U.S. system, and realized that the government could not be changed peacefully. This is his solution. It was originally called Gult's Gulch Development Corporation, after the fictional community in Ayn Rand's novel, Atlas Shrugged.

Atlas Economic Research Foundation

4084 University Dr., Suite 103
Fairfax, VA 22030   **Phone:** (703) 934-6969   **E-Mail:** atlas@his.com
USA   **Fax:**   (703) 352-7530   **Internet:** www.his.com/~atlas

Contact Person: Dr. Alejandro A. Chafuen, President.
Officers or Principals: Dr. Alejandro A. Chafuen, President/CEO ($74,999); Carl Helstrom, Secretary/Treasurer ($40,171); Leonard Liggio, Executive Vice President ($13,615).
Mission or Interest: Promotion of free markets and the rule of law throughout the United States and the world. Atlas assists in the formation of free-market think tanks. Special emphasis is made on state-based think tanks in the U.S., and Latin American countries abroad.
Accomplishments: Atlas helped to establish over 100 organizations worldwide. In 1994, eighty institutes received development awards and grants. Five institutes received monetary prizes as part of the "Sir Antony Fisher International Memorial Awards" for high-quality research publications. Six new institutes in Bangladesh, Canada, Turkey, and the United States, received grants to cover start-up costs. The total amount awarded in contributions and grants was $1,798,228. Atlas spent $95,149 on workshops discussing new management techniques, privatization, and the link between economics and morality. One workshop introduced a new video tape on the life and ideas of Nobel Prize winning economist Friedrich Hayek. $93,549 was spent advising "more than 100 institutes internationally to develop projects and solve management problems.
Total Revenue: 1994 $2,050,642 8%(1) **Total Expenses:** $2,231,088 91%/4%/5% **Net Assets:** $1,989,383
Products or Services: Sir Antony Fisher Memorial Awards for "outstanding institute publications." 1996 recipients included Simple Rules for a Complex World by Richard Epstein (Cato), Revolution at the Roots (Reason Foundation), The Academy in Crisis edited by John Sommer (Independent Institute), and Trade Protection in the United States by Charles K. Rowley, et al, (The Locke Institute).
Tax Status: 501(c)(3)   **Citations:** 8:178
Board of Directors or Trustees: Dorian Adams, Timothy Browne, Francis O'Connell, Jr., Walter Grinder (Inst. for Humane Studies), Alejandro Garza Laguera, George Pearson (National Foundation for Teaching Entrepreneurship), James Pope, Rene Scull, William Sumner.
Periodicals: *Highlights* (quarterly newsletter).
Internships: Yes.
Other Information: Established in 1981. The Atlas Economic Research Foundation was founded by the late Sir Antony Fisher. Sir Fisher founded the Institute of Economic Affairs in London in 1955, and was instrumental in the development of most state-based public policy institutions in the United States. His financial support was crucial to their early development and survival. Atlas received $1,982,639, or 95% of revenue, from contributions and grants awarded by foundations, businesses, and individuals. (These grants included $375,000 from the Lilly Endowment, $61,750 from the Earhart Foundation, $48,000 from the Lynde and Harry Bradley Foundation, $35,000 from the Aequus Institute, and $10,000 from the Charles G. Koch Charitable Foundation. In 1995, $225,000 from the Carthage Foundation, $20,000 from the Sunmark Foundation, $20,000 from the John William Pope Foundation, $5,000 from the Heritage Foundation, and $5,000 from the Roe Foundation.) $52,600, or 3%, from dividends and interest from securities. $28,818, or 1%, from interest on savings and temporary cash investments. $14,662, or 1%, from program services, including publication sales and conference fees. The remaining revenue came from various other miscellaneous sources. The Foundation lost $28,747 on the sale of securities.

Awake America

P.O. Box 22431
St. Louis, MO 63126   **Phone:** (314) 843-8369
USA

Contact Person: Winston Smith.
Mission or Interest: Populist organization opposing non-gold-backed money, big government, and the "New World Order." "Exposing deception; financial, political and spiritual."
Accomplishments: "Brought information to readers that is available from no other source."
Products or Services: Books and tapes on "monetary realism and spiritual realism."
Tax Status: Not incorporated.   **Annual Report:** No.
Periodicals: *These Orwellian Times.*
Internships: No.

Ayn Rand Institute: The Center for the Advancement of Objectivism

4640 Admiralty Way, Suite 715
Marina Del Rey, CA 90292   **Phone:** (310) 306-9232
USA   **Fax:**   (310) 306-4925   **Internet:** http://www.aynrand.org

Contact Person: Dr. Michael S. Berliner, Executive Director.
Officers or Principals: Dr. Michael S. Berliner, Executive Director ($65,000); Donna Montrezza, Treasurer ($36,550); Richard E. Ralston, Secretary ($34,500); Peter Schwartz, Chairman.

Mission or Interest: Dedicated to promoting the works of novelist/philosopher Ayn Rand (1905-1982) and her philosophy of Objectivism.

Accomplishments: In 1994 the Institute spent $449,814 on its projects. The largest project, with expenditures of $203,921, was the Objectivists Graduate Center that "provides advanced seminars and tutorials in a program of intense training for future Objectivist scholars in philosophy and cognate fields." $151,137 was spent on high-school essay contests. "Nearly 10,000 high-school students are introduced each year to The Fountainhead and Anthem through annual essay contests." Winners receive prize money. $25,607 was awarded to Objectivist clubs on college campuses. $14,763 was awarded in academic grants for Objectivist papers. Other projects included publications, conferences, scholarships, and other promotions.

Total Revenue: 1994 $911,633 18% **Total Expenses:** $945,516 48%/48%/4% **Net Assets:** $514,947

Tax Status: 501(c)(3)   **Citations:** 17:156

Board of Directors or Trustees: Harry Binswanger, Ph.D. (author, The Biological Basis of Teleological Concepts), David Hirschler, Peter LePort, M.D. (Americans for Free Choice in Medicine), Aline Mann (Vice Pres./Assoc. General Counsel, Goldman, Sachs & Co.), John Ridpath, Ph.D. (York Univ., Toronto), Leonard Peikoff, Ph.D. (Chairman Emeritus and Executor of the Estate of Ayn Rand).

Periodicals: IMPACT (monthly newsletter).

Other Information: Rand is perhaps best known for her novels, The Fountainhead and Atlas Shrugged. She also wrote nonfiction outlining her philosophy, including Introduction to Objectivist Epistemology, The Virtue of Selfishness, Capitalism: The Unknown Ideal, and others. Objectivism's essential tenets are, "Reality is objective; facts exist independent of anyone's beliefs, fears, or wishes... Reason is man's only source of knowledge and his basic tool of survival... Man is an end in himself - which means that each individual must live by his own mind for his own sake, neither sacrificing himself to others nor others to himself." The logical result of this is laissez-faire capitalism; but "Objectivism is opposed to both Conservatism and Libertarianism. Objectivism stands for reason, not religion and tradition - for freedom, not the welfare status quo - and for a philosophical defense of capitalism, not anarchism or nihilism." The Institute received $896,403, or 98% of gross revenue, from contributions and grants awarded by foundations, businesses, and individuals. $12,133, or 1%, from interest on savings and temporary cash investments. The remaining revenue came from the sale of books. The Institute lost $1,126 on the sale of securities.

Banfield Analytical Services

300 West 60th Street, Suite 202A
Westmont, IL 60559   **Phone:**   (630) 960-1552   **E-Mail:** ECBanfield@aol.com
USA   **Fax:**   same

Contact Person: Eric C. Banfield.

Mission or Interest: A for-profit sole proprietorship which specializes in public-policy issues. Mr. Banfield writes freelance articles, gives speeches and lectures, and provides testimony for regulatory and legislative bodies. Specializes in risk-management, financial and economic education, and public policy analysis. Analysis influenced by Austrian economics.

Accomplishments: Mr. Banfield has delivered addresses to the Federal Reserve Bank of St. Louis, the University of Chicago and various other state and local conventions. He has appeared on C-Span and other television and radio stations, mostly in the Midwest. He has been published by The Wall Street Journal, American Banker, Liberty, Intellectual Ammunition, International Financing Review, The Freeman, Liberty, Treasury and Risk Management, and has written policy studies for the Cato Institute and the Heartland Institute

Tax Status: For profit.

Basic Freedoms

3405 Rochester Ave.
Iowa City, IA 52240   **Phone:**   (319) 351-8118
USA

Contact Person: Joe Zajicek, President.

Officers or Principals: Roberta Whitson, Director; Berle Schmidt, Director.

Mission or Interest: Property rights advocacy. "Originally specialized in combating zoning injustices. Now, are concerned with government acquisition and/or control of private property."

Accomplishments: Helped keep zoning out several Iowa counties

Tax Status: Nonprofit. **Annual Report:** No. **Employees:** All volunteer.

Board of Directors or Trustees: George Webber, Holland Cornick.

Other Information: They oppose zoning restrictions, which "reduce the housing stock and contribute to homelessness." Their motto; "Our liberties we prize and our rights we will maintain."

Beacon Hill Institute for Public Policy Research

Suffolk University
8 Ashburton Place
Boston, MA 02108   **Phone:**   (617) 573-8750   **E-Mail:** bhi@acad.suffolk.edu
USA   **Fax:**   (617) 720-4272   **Internet:** http://bhi.sclas.suffolk.edu

Contact Person: Ellen F. Foley, Director of Communications.
Officers or Principals: David G. Tuerck, Ph.D., Executive Director; Frank Conte, Editor.
Mission or Interest: "Focuses on federal, state and local economic policies as they affect citizens and businesses, particularly in Massachusetts. The Institute uses state-of-the-art statistical, mathematical and econometric methods to provide timely and readable analyses that help voters, policy makers and opinion leaders understand today's leading public policy issues."
Accomplishments: Produced three studies on "charitable-giving tax credits" - tax incentives awarded to taxpayers who give to qualified private charities, which have been cited in *U.S. News & World Report, the Chronicle of Philanthropy, Los Angeles Times Magazine, Alternatives in Philanthropy, Boston Herald*, and others. Executive Director Tuerck has testified on behalf of these tax credits before the U.S. Senate Labor & Human Resources Committee, Subcommittee on Children and Families. Held a conference on "Compassionate Welfare Reform" featuring Arianna Huffington (Center for Effective Compassion), Rep. Joe Knollenberg (R-MI), Lou Nanni (Center for the Homeless), Robert L. Woodson (National Center for Neighborhood Enterprise), John Fund (*Wall Street Journal*), Peter J. Ferrara (Americans for Tax Reform), John Goodman (National Center for Policy Analysis), Robert Rector (Heritage Found.), and others
Products or Services: Econometric models of state tax and revenue proposals.
Tax Status: 501(c)(3) **Annual Report:** No. **Employees:** 4
Periodicals: *NewsLink* (quarterly newsletter).
Internships: Yes, for students pursuing a master's in economics at Suffolk University.
Other Information: Affiliated with, and incorporated under, Suffolk University. In 1995 the Institute received $3,000 from the Roe Foundation.

Becket Fund for Religious Liberty

2000 Pennsylvania Ave., Suite 3200
Washington, DC 20006   **Phone:** (202) 955-0095   **E-Mail:** mail@becketfund.org
USA   **Fax:** (202) 955-0090   **Internet:** http://www.becketfund.org

Contact Person: Kristiana Arriaga.
Officers or Principals: Kevin Hasson, President
Mission or Interest: Legal action group defending religious freedom. "The Becket Fund strives to defend religious liberty from the radical secularization that American society has experienced in the recent past. We defend those who are discriminated against because of their religious convictions as well as those whom civic government would deny their exercise of religion."
Accomplishments: The Fund was involved in the case of Karl Metz, an employee at the Department of Agriculture who was demoted for stating that, due to his religious beliefs, he was opposed to the Department's promotion of homosexuality. After Becket took his case, and threatened to sue the Department, Metz was reinstated. In Rigdon v. Perry the Fund filed suit on behalf of military chaplains against military. The case was a result of Pentagon's issuing a directive barring military chaplains from discussing legislation during sermons or counseling. The directive was in response to the Catholic Church's "Project Life Postcard Campaign" in opposition to the 'partial-birth abortion' procedure. "Pope John Paul II has expressed 'a particular word of appreciation to The Becket Fund for its many efforts in defense of religious freedom in the United States and around the world."
Products or Services: Annual Canterbury Medal awarded "in recognition of political courage in the defense of religious liberty." The first recipient of the award, in 1997, was Mayor Bret Schundler (R-Jersey City, NJ). Mayor Schundler received the award for his display of a crèche and a menorah on city property, as part of a larger holiday display, despite opposition from the ACLU. The Award dinner featured His Eminence John Cardinal O'Connor (Archbishop of New York) and Dr. Ronald B. Sobel (Senior Rabbi, Congregation Emanu-El) as Honorary Chairmen. The Hon. Jack Kemp was featured as a keynote speaker.
Tax Status: 501(c)(3)
Other Information: Named after the Archbishop of Canterbury, Thomas a Becket (1118-70), who was executed after resisting King Henry II's interference in the Church's affairs. In 1995 the Fund received $50,000 from the John M. Olin Foundation, and $42,000 from the Lynde and Harry Bradley Foundation.

Beeson Report

42640 W. 10th St.
Lancaster, CA 93534   **Phone:** (800) 462-4700
USA

Contact Person: Ty Beeson, Publisher.
Officers or Principals: Jeannette Beeson, Editor.
Mission or Interest: Bimonthly newsletter "raising the standard to educate people on issues that affect their lives." Advocates traditional, biblical morality.
Periodicals: *Beeson Report* (bimonthly newsletter).

Berean Call, The

P.O. Box 7019
Bend, OR 97708
USA

Contact Person: Dave Hunt.

Mission or Interest: A newsletter of conservative Protestant theology, opinion and news.

Accomplishments: Dave Hunt is the author of numerous books including How Close Are We?: Compelling Evidence for the Soon Return of Christ, Whatever Happened to Heaven?, Sanctuary of the Chosen, and The Seduction of Christianity (also available in Spanish)

Products or Services: In addition to various books, *The Berean Call* sells monthly selections of video and audio tapes on various subjects.

Tax Status: Nonprofit.

Periodicals: *The Berean Call* (monthly newsletter).

Other Information: The name "Berean" comes from the New Testament Bereans of Acts 17:10,11. The Bereans searched the scriptures daily, to determine the validity of what they were being taught. Part of *The Berean Call*'s mission is to save Catholics, whom Dave Hunt describes as having been, "the major purveyor of a false gospel."

Bionomics Institute

2173 E. Francisco Blvd., Suite C
San Rafael, CA 94901
USA

Phone: (415) 454-1000   **E-Mail:** info@bionomics.org
Fax: (415) 454-7460   **Internet:** http://www.bionomics.org

Contact Person: Michael Rothschild, President.

Officers or Principals: Michael L. Rothschild, President ($60,000); Stephen Gibson, Executive Director ($57,250); Mark Edwards, Treasurer ($0); Leigh S. Marriner, Secretary.

Mission or Interest: "Bionomics suggests a new economic paradigm. Where mainstream economics is based on concepts borrowed from classical Newtonian physics, bionomics is derived from the teachings of modern evolutionary biology. Where orthodox thinking describes the economy as a static, predictable engine, bionomics sees the economy as self-organizing, complex information ecosystem. Where the traditional view sees organizations as production machines, bionomics sees organizations as intelligent social organisms."

Accomplishments: Rothschild has addressed the Mont Pelerin Society. In the two years from September 1993 to September 1995, the Institute has grown at an average rate of 133% per year. Rothschild's book, Bionomics: Economy as Ecosystem, has been praised in *The Wall Street Journal, Liberty, Human Events, Reason, Library Journal, The Boston Globe, Houston Chronicle, The Washington Times,* and others. In the fiscal year ending September 1995, the Institute spent $334,160 on its programs. The largest expenditure, $165,000, went for an annual conference in Redwood City, CA, and a conference in Washington, DC. $103,526 was spent on research and publications, development of a web site, and other programs. $45,000 was spent translating Bionomics into Chinese, Spanish, and Russian. $20,000 for the production of a film for television.

Total Revenue: FY ending 9/95 $512,355 133%(2) **Total Expenses:** $445,546 75%/15%/10% **Net Assets:** $179,434

Tax Status: 501(c)(3) **Annual Report:** No. **Citations:** 3:204

Board of Directors or Trustees: Mike Ford, Jr., Peter Gruber, Terry Huffington, Allan King, Leo Linbeck, Jr., Daniel Lynch, Bill Melton, David Padden, John Porter, Mark Tebbe.

Periodicals: *Bionomic Perspectives* (quarterly newsletter).

Other Information: Established in 1991. Bionomics was originally subtitled "The Inevitability of Capitalism," but Rothschild found that this turned away many readers who would have otherwise given the book fair consideration. The Institute received $479,144, or 94% of revenue, from contributions and grants awarded by foundations, businesses, and individuals. (These grants included $100,000 from the Gordon and Mary Cain Foundation.) $30,385, or 6%, from conference admission fees. The remaining revenue came from interest on savings and temporary cash investments.

Black Economic Times

2303 W. Ledbetter, Suite 432
Dallas, TX 75224
USA

Phone: (214) 467-3607
Fax: (214) 331-0782

Contact Person: Chevis King, Jr., Publisher.

Mission or Interest: Publish *The Black Economic Times*, a biweekly newspaper of free-market entrepreneurship produced for a black audience. King also promotes his "Beacon Economic Plan" that encourages blacks to patronize black-owned businesses and to save and invest. King calculates that adherence to his plan would produce 5,700 new jobs in the Dallas/Fort Worth area and greatly increase black-owned and run businesses, especially in the manufacturing sector.

Accomplishments: *The Black Economic Times* was featured in *The Wall Street Journal*

Products or Services: Chevis King can be heard daily, along with co-host Joe Howard, on radio KSKY, 660 AM, in the Dallas/Fort Worth area.

Tax Status: For profit.

Periodicals: *Black Economic Times* (biweekly newspaper).

Other Information: Their motto is "It's not just business, it's a way of life."

Blackstone Audio Books

P.O. Box 969
Ashland, OR 97520   **Phone:**   (800) 729-2665   **E-Mail:**   baudiob@mind.net
USA   **Fax:**   (541) 482-9294

Contact Person: Penny Curtis.
Officers or Principals: Craig W. Black, President/Owner
Mission or Interest: Increase public exposure to books of conservative ideas through the media of audio cassettes. Many books on politics, philosophy, history, and economics with a conservative focus.
Accomplishments: "Produced over 1,000 unabridged recordings of great books."
Products or Services: Catalog of full-length book recordings on cassettes.
Tax Status: For profit. **Annual Report:** No. **Employees:** 12
Board of Directors or Trustees: John Jacobson, Thomas Allen.
Internships: No.
Other Information: Established in 1988. Formerly "Classics on Tape."

Bluestocking Press

P.O. Box 2030
Shingle Springs, CA 95682   **Phone:**   (916) 621-1123
USA   **Fax:**   (916) 642-9222

Contact Person: Jane A. Williams.
Mission or Interest: Books and educational materials for all ages. Materials cover free-market economics, American history, law, reasoning, and other subjects for kindergarten through adult.
Accomplishments: Publisher of the "Uncle Eric" books by Richard J. Maybury, which have been praised by former Treasury Secretary, William E. Simon, *School Library Journal*, Ron Paul, and many others. Products and reports which help home schoolers. Also offers the complete works of Laura Ingalls Wilder, including her "Little House" series, as well as works by her daughter, Rose Wilder Lane
Products or Services: "The Authentic Jane Williams' Home School Market Guide," an annual directory of stores, catalogs, web sites, curriculum reviewers, exhibit opportunities and more. Catalog of books, tapes, games, more.
Tax Status: For profit. **Annual Report:** No.
Internships: No.
Other Information: Bluestocking Press is named after Mrs. Elizabeth Montague's Bluestocking Society of the 18th century. The society was devoted to discussion of intellectual and literary matters, and was identified by their blue stockings.

Blum Center for Parental Freedom in Education

Marquette University
Brooks Hall, Suite 209
Milwaukee, WI 53201-1881   **Phone:**   (414) 288-7040   **E-Mail:**   blumcenter@vms.csd.mu.edu
USA   **Fax:**   (414) 288-3170

Contact Person: Quentin L. Quade, Director.
Mission or Interest: Research and promotion of School Choice programs
Products or Services: Numerous studies, books, model and proposed legislation, reports and more.
Tax Status: 501(c)(3)
Other Information: The Blum Center is named after Virgil C. Blum, S.J. Affiliated with, and incorporated under, Marquette University.

Books for All Times

P.O. Box 2
Alexandria, VA 22313   **Phone:**   (703) 548-0457
USA

Contact Person: Joe David.
Mission or Interest: Books and materials on education. Focus on different learning styles and supportive of school choice programs. Opposes 'whole language' and 'creative spelling' methods.
Accomplishments: "We produce a newsletter, *Education in Focus*, and have published several books which have received good public exposure, all on education."
Products or Services: The Fire Within ("exposes public 'education' for the fraud it really is - a coercive institution of indoctrination" - Libertarian Digest), and other books.
Annual Report: No.
Periodicals: *Education in Focus* (quarterly newsletter).
Internships: No.

Boston Review

E53-407, MIT
Cambridge, MA 02139
USA

Phone: (617) 253-3642   **E-Mail:** review@mit.edu
Fax: (617) 252-1549

Contact Person: Betsy Reed.
Officers or Principals: Joshua Cohen, Editor-in-Chief; Betsy Reed, Managing Editor.
Mission or Interest: "Magazine of ideas committed to the democratic ideal of an open public forum."
Periodicals: *Boston Review*.

Brotherhood Organization of a New Destiny (BOND)

1312 S. Ogden Dr.
Los Angeles, CA 90019
USA

Phone: (213) 939-2160   **E-Mail:** bond411@aol.com
Fax: (213) 939-4199

Contact Person: Pat Roney.
Officers or Principals: Jesse Lee Paterson, President; Malcolm Jones, Vice President; Kerr Johnson, Secretary.
Mission or Interest: "Rebuilding the family by rebuilding the man." Conservative organization focusing on the problems of the black community and specifically, black males. Founder Jesse Patterson said "When I first began to overcome, I wasn't aware of black conservative thinkers because the media had not shown us any. Conservatism was something I came to without knowing it. I just knew I had to change my life."
Accomplishments: Peterson and BOND have been featured in *Issues & Views* and *Insight*.
Tax Status: 501(c)(3)   **Annual Report:** No.
Periodicals: Newsletter.
Internships: No.
Other Information: Affiliated with *Minority Mainstream* and Project 21.

Brownson Institute / *Crisis*

1511 K St., N.W., Suite 525
Washington, DC 20005
USA

Phone: (202) 347-7411
Fax: (202) 347-1128

Contact Person: Deal W. Hudson, Editor.
Officers or Principals: Alice Osberger, Treasurer ($28,800); Michael Novak, Ralph McInery, Founders/Publishers ($0); Samuel Casey Carter, Associate Editor; Gwen Vereen Purtill, Managing Editor.
Mission or Interest: Publish *Crisis*, a monthly magazine of conservative lay-Catholic opinion.
Accomplishments: *Crisis* contributors include Paul Johnson, William Bennett, Hadley Arkes, George Weigel, Linda Chavez, Herb London, Piers Paul Read and, Russ Hittnger. Over 12,000 subscribers. In 1994 the Institute spent $284,681 on its programs. This included a conference on the Pope's Encyclicals.
Total Revenue: 1994 $452,295 (-18%)   **Total Expenses:** $465,186 100%/0%/0%   **Net Assets:** $82,274
Products or Services: E. L. Wiegand distinguished lecture series. Crisis Books, which publishes translations of works by Michael Novak into Chinese, Hungarian, and Polish; also sole U.S. distributor of Claridge Press Books, U.K.
Tax Status: 501(c)(3)   **Citations:** 0:233
Periodicals: *Crisis* (monthly magazine).
Other Information: The Brownson Institute is located at P.O. Box 495, Notre Dame, IN 46556, but correspondence should be sent to the Washington, DC, address. The Institute received $219,615, or 49% of revenue, from contributions and grants awarded by foundations, businesses, and individuals. (In 1995, these grants included $90,000 from the Lynde and Harry Bradley Foundation, and $30,000 from the John M. Olin Foundation.) $180,505, or 40%, from magazine subscriptions. $30,192, or 7%, from mailing list rentals. $15,135, or 3%, from advertising. $12,355, or 3%, from the sale of Crisis Books. The remaining revenue came from interest on savings and temporary cash investments. The total cost of publishing *Crisis* was $180,505, and the revenues (including advertising, mailing lists, etc.) were $221,902; a net gain of $22,172.

Buckeye Institute for Public Policy Solutions

131 N. Ludlow St., Suite 317
Dayton, OH 45402
USA

Phone: (513) 224-8352   **E-Mail:** BuckeyIns@aol.com
Fax: (513) 224-8457

Contact Person: Brad Beckett, Communications Director.
Officers or Principals: Andrew L. Little, President/Treasurer ($35,795); Samuel R. Staley, Vice President, Treasurer ($14,596); Julie Kochendorfer, Administrative Director ($13,070); William Killgallon, Chairman.
Mission or Interest: "To provide Ohio's leaders and citizens with new ways of thinking about problems facing our state and local communities. . . To provide market-driven solutions and alternatives for state and local problems."

Accomplishments: "Buckeye's reports and studies have helped shape policy in Ohio in areas such as School Vouchers, Charter Schools, Medical Savings Accounts, and tax issues." The Institute has been cited in numerous newspapers state-wide, including the *Akron Beacon Journal, Cincinnati Enquirer, Cincinnati Post, Cleveland Plains Dealer, Columbus Daily Reporter, Columbus Dispatch, Dayton Daily News, Toledo Blade*, and others. Institute representatives have appeared on radio and television stations state-wide.

Total Revenue: 1994 $112,141 **Total Expenses:** $98,825 63%/18%/18% **Net Assets:** $11,591

Tax Status: 501(c)(3) **Annual Report:** No. **Employees:** 5

Board of Directors or Trustees: Robert Breen, Alex Chafuen (Atlas Economic Research Foundation), Daniel Peters (Proctor & Gamble Co.), John Blundell (Inst. for Economic Affairs). Academic Advisors include professors; William Binning (Youngstown State Univ.), Gina Dow (Denisen Univ.), Ralph Frasca (Univ. of Dayton), Janice Gabbert (Wright State Univ.), William Irvine (Wright State Univ.), John Kelley (Shawnee State Univ.), Robert Kohl (Defiance College), Abraha Miller (Univ. of Cincinnati), Dennis Miller (Baldwin-Wallace College), Henry Moon (Univ. of Toledo), William Peirce (Case Western Reserve Univ.), Robert Premus (Wright State Univ.), John Rapp (Univ. of Dayton), Robert Scherer (Wright State Univ.), Larry Schweikart (Univ. of Dayton), John Soper (John Carroll Univ.), Richard Vedder (Ohio Univ.).

Periodicals: *Perspective on Current Issues* (monthly newsletter), *Policy Note* (monthly), *The Ohio Education Report* (quarterly).

Internships: Yes.

Other Information: Established in 1984 as the Buckeye Center, then changed its name in 1995 to the Buckeye Institute. The Institute assumed the corporate identity of the Urban Policy Research Institute, a dormant organization. Member of the State Policy Network. The Institute received $111,874, or 99.7% of revenue, from contributions and grants awarded by foundations, businesses, and individuals. (These grants included $10,000 from the J.M. Foundation. In 1995, $14,600 from the Castle Rock Foundation, $7,500 from the Roe Foundation.) The remaining revenue came from interest on savings and temporary cash investments, and other miscellaneous sources.

Buffalo Creek Press

P.O. Box 2424
Cleburne, TX 76033 **Phone:** (817) 641-4908
USA **Fax:** (817) 641-0901

Mission or Interest: Publisher and distributor of books with a conservative or populist point-of-view. Focus on the government's use of emergency war powers during peacetime.

Accomplishments: <u>Constitution: Fact or Fiction</u> by Dr. Eugene Schroder, <u>War and Emergency Powers Book of Supporting Documents</u>, "War and Emergency Powers" video and audio cassettes, and other books and publications

Tax Status: For profit.

Business Coalition for Affordable Health Care

122 C St., N.W., Suite 815
Washington, DC 20001 **Phone:** (202) 628-3690
USA **Fax:** (202) 628-3698

Contact Person: Kevin L. Kearns, Chairman.

Officers or Principals: Dan Perrin, Executive Director; Dolores Daly, Congressional Liaison.

Mission or Interest: A coalition representing over 1.6 million businesses. They advocate the adoption of Medical Savings Accounts (MSAs) and equal treatment for medical expenses under the tax code.

Accomplishments: The Coalition's Steering Committee includes: the American Legislative Exchange Council, American Medical Association, American Small Business Association, Association of Concerned Taxpayers, Citizens for Affordable Health Care, Council for Affordable Health Care, Council for Affordable Health Insurance, Council for Citizens Against Government Waste, National Association of the Self-Employed, Small Business Survival Committee, U.S. Federation of Small Business, U.S. Business & Industrial Council, and many other groups representing business and consumer interests

Products or Services: Lobbies. Distributes packages of articles from numerous sources showing the successes and potential of implementing Medical Savings Accounts.

Tax Status: 501(c)(6)

C. S. Lewis Institute

4208 Evergreen Lane, Suite 222
Annandale, VA 22003 **Phone:** (703) 247-3866
USA **Fax:** (703) 247-3847

Contact Person: Tim Couch, Chairman.

Officers or Principals: Art Lindsley, Ph.D., Scholar-in-Residence.

Mission or Interest: "Founded to challenge and educate those who seek a living faith in the modern world. Named after C.S. Lewis, scholar of English literature, apologist and ardent follower of Jesus Christ, the Institute has enabled men and women to develop, like Lewis, an articulate, persuasive response to the questions and concerns of our modern world." Offers "graduate education, public seminars, retreats and individual discipleship."

Accomplishments: The Institute's first chancellor, the late Dr. Richard Halverson, was formerly the Senate Chaplain.
Total Revenue: 1996 $180,000 (est.)
Products or Services: Various classes, including a Master's Degree through the Trinity Evangelical Divinity School in Deerfield, IL, or Reformed Theological Seminary in Maitland, FL.
Tax Status: 501(c)(3)
Board of Directors or Trustees: Otis Bowden, Dr. Nigel Cameron, Stephen Hase, Jim Johnson, Rev. Dennis Hollinger, Dr. Sherrie MacKenzie, Rev. John Yates, Dr. Frank Young.
Periodicals: *C.S. Lewis Institute Report* (quarterly newsletter).
Other Information: Established in 1976 under the incorporation of the International Foundation. As of January 1997, the Institute became a separate incorporated entity. Clive Staples Lewis (1898-1963) was the author of numerous books including his popular Chronicles of Narnia which includes the well-known The Lion, the Witch, and the Wardrobe, works of science fiction, and Christian apologetics such as The Screwtape Letters.

California Desert Coalition (CDC)

6192 Magnolia Ave., Suite D
Riverside, CA 92506   **Phone:**   (909) 684-6509
USA

Contact Person: Marie Brashear, Secretary.
Officers or Principals: David Hess, Chairman ($0); James Williams, Vice Chairman ($0); Ron Fite, Second Vice Chairman ($0).
Mission or Interest: Formed to lobby against the "California Desert Protection Act." Part of the Wise Use movement, they stress land-use issues.
Accomplishments: In 1995 the Coalition spent $29,247 on its programs.
Total Revenue: 1995 $39,575 (-19%)(2) **Total Expenses:** $34,145 86%/14%/0% **Net Assets:** (-$4,158)
Tax Status: 501(c)(4)
Periodicals: *Desert News Letter*.
Other Information: Established in 1986. The Coalition received $39,575, or 100% of revenue, from contributions.

California Public Policy Foundation

P.O. Box 931
Camarillo, CA 93011   **Phone:**   (805) 445-9138
USA

Contact Person: John Kurzweil, President.
Officers or Principals: John Kurzweil, President ($31,793); William Saracino, Secretary ($0); Eugene Foley, Treasurer ($0).
Mission or Interest: California public policy with a free-market emphasis.
Total Revenue: 1995 $61,122 **Total Expenses:** $55,674 **Net Assets:** $19,393
Tax Status: 501(c)(3)
Board of Directors or Trustees: Prof. William Allen (UCLA), Robert Naylor.
Periodicals: *California Political Review* (bimonthly).
Other Information: The Foundation received $36,521, or 60% of revenue, from contributions and grants awarded by foundations, businesses, and individuals. $24,553, or 40%, from program services including the sale of publications. The remaining revenue came from interest on savings.

California Rifle and Pistol Association

271 E. Imperial Highway, Suite 620
Fullerton, CA 92635   **Phone:**   (714) 992-2772
USA   **Fax:**   (714) 992-2996

Contact Person: James H. Erdman, Executive Director.
Officers or Principals: James H. Erdman, Executive Director ($63,871); Bill Chapman, President ($0); Martin Miller, Vice President ($0); Robert Frushon, Secretary; George V. Barr, Treasurer.
Mission or Interest: Engages in lobbying and educational activities that promote the ownership and safe use of firearms.
Accomplishments: In the fiscal year ending September 1995 the Association spent $232,588 on its programs.
Total Revenue: FY ending 9/95 $844,878 3%(2) **Total Expenses:** $946,261 25%/44%/31% **Net Assets:** $1,353,753
Products or Services: Statewide shooting competitions. Educational materials.
Tax Status: 501(c)(4)   **Citations:** 31:130
Periodicals: *The Firing Line* (monthly newsletter).
Other Information: The Association received $333,847, or 40% of revenue, from membership dues. $231,795, or 27%, from contributors. $176,850 net, or 21%, from special fund-raising events. $39,503, or 5%, from shooting competition fees. The remaining revenue came from dividends and interest from securities, advertising and other miscellaneous sources.

California Taxpayers Association

921 11th St., Suite 800
Sacramento, CA 95814   **Phone:**   (916) 441-0490
USA

Contact Person: Larry McCarthy, President.
Officers or Principals: Larry McCarthy, President ($126,209); Rebecca Taylor, Senior Vice President ($83,985); Carol Ross Evans, Vice President ($83,970); Betty Rickard, Secretary.
Mission or Interest: California tax reduction lobbying organization.
Accomplishments: In 1994 the Association spent $1,009,092 on its programs.
Total Revenue: 1994 $1,277,187 5%(2) **Total Expenses:** $1,284,283 79%/13%/9% **Net Assets:** $97,655
Tax Status: 501(c)(4)   **Citations:** 55:95
Board of Directors or Trustees: J. David Aylmer (Rockwell International), Kate Bartolo (Gov. Relations, Walt Disney Co.), Kenneth Brown (Ernst & Young), Darrell Burruss (Chevron), Stephen Chaudet (Lockheed Corp.), Michael Curtis (Exxon), Bruce Daigh (Price Waterhouse), Joseph Dooling (Hughes), Kevin Farr (Mattel), Daniel Flynn (Dow Chemical), Steven Friedlander (Xerox Corp.), Alan Gordon (Wells Fargo & Co.), Richard Groudan (Texaco), Richard Hall (Intel), Jerry Ham (IBM), Bruce Smith (Shell Oil Co.), many other prominent members of the California business community.
Periodicals: *Cal-Tax News*, and *Cal-Tax Letter*.
Other Information: Affiliated with the 501(c)(3) California Tax Foundation. The Association received $1,106,878, or 87% of revenue, from membership dues. $134,702, or 11%, from publication sales. The remaining revenue came from dividends and interest from securities, conference fees, interest on savings, seminars, and other miscellaneous sources.

Calvert Institute for Policy Research

2806 N. Calvert St.
Baltimore, MD 21218   **Phone:**   (410) 662-7110   **E-Mail:** calvert@attach.net
USA   **Fax:**   (410) 662-7112   **Internet:** http://www.calvertinstitute.org

Contact Person: Douglas P. Munro, Ph.D., Executive Officer.
Officers or Principals: Ronald W. Dworkin, M.D., Ph.D., Financial Officer ($0); Douglas W. Hamilton, Jr., Chairman ($0); Douglas P. Munro, Ph.D., Executive Officer ($0).
Mission or Interest: "The promotion of free-market approaches to policy making in Maryland, with an emphasis on urban policy in relation to taxation and education. . . Seeks to make Maryland worthy of its fond nickname - 'The Free State'."
Accomplishments: Called attention to the fact that "Baltimore has the third highest bureaucrat-to-resident ratio in the U.S." Helped disseminate information on the economic consequences of a city income tax proposed by Mayor Shmoke (the proposal was defeated). Advocacy for school choice programs including providing the Mayor's Task Force on School Choice with relevant information. State Senator Christopher J. McCabe called its newsletter "a unique and valuable academic resource for Maryland legislation...extensively researched and exceptionally written."
Total Revenue: 1995 $11,080 **Total Expenses:** $3,677 **Net Assets:** $7,403
Tax Status: 501(c)(3) **Annual Report:** No. **Employees:** 2
Board of Directors or Trustees: Jeffrey Bergner, Ph.D., Joseph Brown, Jr., Peter Centenari, Jairo Garcia, M.D., Barclay Greene, III, Robert Greene, William Hall, Jr., Carol Hirschburg, Jeffrey Kramer, M.S., Kenneth Nohe, William Zitzmann, M.D.
Periodicals: *Calvert Comment* (periodic op-ed articles), and *Calvert News* (quarterly journal).
Internships: No.
Other Information: Established in 1995. Named after George Calvert (1580-1632), founder of the Maryland Colony "and author of its experiment in freedom of conscience."

Capital & Liberty

P.O. Box 694
Wayne, MI 48184   **Phone:**   (313) 326-7227
USA

Contact Person: Craig L. Seymour.
Mission or Interest: "Opposition to statism, especially gun control and violations of private property rights. Promotion of laissez-faire capitalism as the only system which does not require the violation of individual rights."
Accomplishments: *Claustrophobia*'s magazine reviewer describes *Capital & Liberty* as "a healthy balance of capitalism and libertarianism. . . *Capital & Liberty* is off to a great start."
Tax Status: For profit. **Annual Report:** No.
Periodicals: *Capital & Liberty* (ten issues a year).
Internships: No.
Other Information: Published by Seymour Enterprises. Craig L. Seymour was the 1994 Libertarian candidate from Michigan's 13th district for the U.S. House of Representatives.

Capital Research Center (CRC)

727 15th St., N.W., Suite 800
Washington, DC 20005
USA

Phone: (202) 393-2600
Fax: (202) 393-2626

E-Mail: 74157.1070@compuserve.com
Internet: http://www.capitalresearch.org

Contact Person: Natasha Clerihue, Director of Communications.
Officers or Principals: Terrence M. Scanlon, President ($88,829 for less than a full year); Robert Huberty, Researcher ($52,000); Lorraine Overbeck, Chief Financial Officer ($25,000); Daniel J. Popeo, Vice President/Treasurer; Constance C. Larcher, Secretary.
Mission or Interest: "Watchdog" organization created to study the influence of nonprofit advocacy organizations. "The goal of CRC is to educate taxpayers, corporate shareholders, foundation grant makers, donors and government officials on the activities of advocacy groups." Special focus on corporate donations to anti-business organizations on the Left.
Accomplishments: CRC polls the 250 largest American corporations for philanthropic activity. The results showed that in 1993 corporate donations to advocacy organizations went 77.56% to left-of-center organizations, with only 19% going to right-of-center organizations. CRC has presented the results of its polling to directors and shareholders in an effort to change these patterns by showing that the left-of-center programs funded by the philanthropic actions of the corporations are not in the best interest of the corporation and its shareholders. Work by CRC on the activities of government-funded advocacy groups was used extensively during the 104th Congress by Representatives David McIntosh (R-IN), Ernest Istook (R-OK), and Senator Alan Simpson (R-WY). The *Chronicle of Philanthropy* called CRC "an intelligence agency for lawmakers."
Total Revenue: 1994 $1,119,390 25% **Total Expenses:** $943,509 82%/9%/9% **Net Assets:** $886,526
Products or Services: Patterns in Corporate Philanthropy by Austin Fulk and Stuart Nolan. Other studies.
Tax Status: 501(c)(3) **Annual Report:** Yes. **Employees:** 11 **Citations:** 52:96
Board of Directors or Trustees: Hon. Edwin Meese, III (former Attorney General, 1985-88), Barbara Van Andel-Gaby (Vice Pres., Corporate Affairs, Amway Corp.), Marion G. Wells (Lillian Wells Found.), Hon. William Simon (former Secretary of the Treasury, 1974-77).
Periodicals: *Organization Trends* (monthly report), *Foundation Watch* (monthly report), *Culture Watch* (monthly), *Alternatives in Philanthropy* (monthly report), and *Philanthropy, Culture, and Society* (monthly essay).
Internships: Yes, year-round unpaid internships and paid summer internships.
Other Information: Established in 1984. CRC received $1,106,587, or 99% of revenue, from contributions and grants awarded by foundations, businesses, and individuals. (These grants included $275,000 from the Sarah Scaife Foundation, $50,000 from the Lilly Endowment, $25,000 from the John M. Olin Foundation, $10,000 from the Samuel Roberts Noble Foundation, $7,500 Aequus Institute, $3,500 from the F.M. Kirby Foundation, $2,500 from the Milliken Foundation, $2,500 from the Grover Hermann Foundation, $2,500 from the Anschutz Foundation, and $2,000 from the Alex C. Walker Foundation. In 1995, $50,000 from the Scaife Family Foundation, $47,420 from the E. L. Wiegand Foundation, $35,000 from the Philip M. McKenna Foundation, $25,000 from the Lynde and Harry Bradley Foundation, $12,000 from the Sunmark Foundation, $10,000 from the William H. Donner Foundation, $10,000 from the Claude R. Lambe Charitable Foundation, $10,000 from the John William Pope Foundation, and $9,000 from the Roe Foundation.) The remaining revenue came from the sale of publications.

Capitol Resource Institute

1314 H St., Suite 203
Sacramento, CA 95814
USA

Phone: (916) 498-1940
Fax: (916) 448-2888

E-Mail: capitolres@aol.com

Contact Person: Lori Ann Pardau, Executive Secretary.
Officers or Principals: Michael D. Bowman, Executive Director; Peter L. Henderson, former Executive Director ($69,693); Randy Thomasson, Assistant Director.
Mission or Interest: "To strengthen the families of California through education, training, and helping citizens who desire to see Judeo-Christian values conveyed into spheres of American Society."
Accomplishments: Dr. James Dobson, of Focus on the Family, said the Institute, "provides crucial leadership for the development of pro-family coalition work in California. . . they have been an example for other pro-family groups in other states." Yearly "City on the Hill" conference. Coalitions, legislation, press releases, columns in local papers. In 1994 the Institute spent $412,905 on its programs.
Total Revenue: 1994 $412,905 12%(2) **Total Expenses:** $404,170 62%/30%/7% **Net Assets:** $67,607
Products or Services: Legislative update, Educator's Tool Kit, and various conferences and seminars. Weekly media releases, primarily radio. Lobbying: in 1994 the Institute spent $15,680 on lobbying.
Tax Status: 501(c)(3) **Annual Report:** No. **Employees:** 8 **Citations:** 14:165
Periodicals: *California Citizen* (monthly newsletter).
Internships: Yes, internships available for college credit, also, seasonal intern employment, and volunteer positions.
Other Information: The Institute received $353,465, or 86% of revenue, from contributions and grants awarded by foundations, businesses, and individuals. $29,578, or 7%, from conference fees. $20,750, or 5%, from product sales. The remaining revenue came from interest on savings, and other miscellaneous sources.

CapitolWatch

601 Pennsylvania Ave., N.W.
South Bldg., Suite 900
Washington, DC 20004   **Phone:** (202) 544-2600   **E-Mail:** SDH5555@aol.com
USA   **Fax:**   (202) 544-9647

Contact Person: Jason Henderson.
Officers or Principals: S. Dennis Hoffman, Chairman ($35,000); Michael W. Thompson, Director ($1,703); Hon. Beau Boulter, Chairman ($0); Allen Brandstater, President.
Mission or Interest: "Common sense economic policies of lower taxes and limited government."
Accomplishments: Claims over 70,000 members. Chairs the Coalition Against Corporate Welfare, a coalition that includes Citizens Against Government Waste, Citizens for a Sound Economy, American Conservative Union, and eight others. "Former Representative Beau Boulter is a constant figure in Congress lobbying for lower taxes and against government hand outs." His recent testimony before the House Budget Committee was featured in *Time*. In 1995 CapitolWatch spent $1,018,012 on its programs. $760,746 was spent on lobbying and citizen involvement, and $257,266 was spent on research and education.
Total Revenue: 1995 $1,401,522 23%(2) **Total Expenses:** $1,401,687 73%/13%/15% **Net Assets:** (-$666,377)
Tax Status: 501(c)(4) **Annual Report:** No. **Employees:** 3   **Citations:** 3:204
Board of Directors or Trustees: J. Curtis Herge, Howard Moye, Robert Watters.
Periodicals: *CapitolWatch* (newsletter).
Internships: Yes, stipends based on need.
Other Information: Formerly called the American Defense Lobby. President Allen Brandstater's radio show is heard throughout southern California. CapitolWatch received $1,340,825, or 96% of revenue, from contributions and grants. The remaining revenue came from rents, interest on savings and temporary cash investments, and other miscellaneous sources.

Cardinal Mindszenty Foundation (CMF)

P.O. Box 11321
St. Louis, MO 63105   **Phone:** (314) 727-6279
USA   **Fax:**   (314) 727-5897

Contact Person: Eleanor Schlafly, President.
Officers or Principals: John D. Boland, Editor ($9,892); Rev. John A. Houle, S.J., Vice President ($0); Claire L. Shields, Secretary ($0); John O. Shields, Treasurer; Elaine Middendorf, Producer of Radio Programming.
Mission or Interest: "To educate people concerning threats to our faiths, families and freedom." Especially concerned with the re-emergence of the Communists in the governments of former Soviet-bloc nations.
Accomplishments: In 1996 CMF's conferences featured syndicated columnist Walter E. Williams as keynote speaker. In 1995 CMF spent $137,357 on its programs.
Total Revenue: 1995 $193,422 **Total Expenses:** $177,936 77%/12%/11% **Net Assets:** $140,505
Products or Services: One-day seminars in cities nationwide. A weekly radio interview program, "The Dangers of Apathy," and audio cassettes of past programs. Cassettes include columnist Cal Thomas, Michael Medved, David Horowitz, Phyllis Schlafly, George Gilder, Rev. Robert Sirico, and others.
Tax Status: 501(c)(3) **Annual Report:** No. **Citations:** 14:165
Board of Directors or Trustees: Martin Duggan, Rev. Alexander Ratiu, Rev. Abbot L. K. Parker.
Periodicals: *Mindszenty Report* (monthly newsletter).
Internships: No.
Other Information: Established in 1958 as a Catholic anti-communist organization. Named after a Catholic prelate who clashed with the Communist government in Hungary. With the collapse of the Soviet bloc its focus has expanded. The Foundation received $117,350, or 58% of gross revenue, from contributions and grants awarded by foundations, businesses, and individuals. (These grants included $500 from the Sunmark Foundation.) $45,162, or 22%, from seminars and other programs. $35,801, or 18%, from membership dues. $4,837, or 2%, from interest on savings and temporary cash investments. The Foundation lost $9,728 on the sale of inventory.

Carthage Foundation

Three Mellon Bank Center
525 William Penn Place, Suite 3900
Pittsburgh, PA 15219   **Phone:** (412) 392-2900
USA

Contact Person: Richard M. Larry, Treasurer.
Officers or Principals: R. Daniel McMichael, Program Consulting/Secretary ($58,400); Donald Sipp, Vice President ($36,225); Richard M. Scaife, Chairman ($0); George R. McCullough, Vice Chairman; Richard M. Larry, Treasurer. (Salaries are from 1993.)
Mission or Interest: Grant-making foundation that awards money to conservative organizations.

Accomplishments: In 1995 the Foundation awarded $6,954,300 in grants. Recipients included: $720,000 for the Free Congress Foundation, $635,000 for the Heritage Foundation, $450,000 for the Washington Legal Foundation, $355,000 for Accuracy in Media, $350,000 for the American Spectator Educational Foundation, $250,000 for the Center for the Study of Popular Culture, $230,000 for the Western Journalism Center, $225,000 for the Atlas Economic Research Foundation, $215,000 for the Hudson Institute, $150,000 for the Center for Individual Rights, $125,000 each for the Federation for American Immigration Reform, Social Philosophy and Policy Forum, and the Landmark Legal Foundation, $120,000 for the Institute for Humane Studies, $107,500 for the Allegheny Institute, $100,000 each for the American Legal Foundation, Defenders of Property Rights, Foundation for Research on Economics and the Environment, Independent Women's Forum, Institute for Foreign Policy Analysis, National Center for Public Policy Research, and Center for Security Policy, $80,000 for the American Foreign Policy Council, $75,000 each for Americans Back in Charge, and National Defense Forum Foundation, $62,000 for the National Legal and Policy Center, $60,000 each for the Pacific Academy for Advanced Studies, and Pacific Forum CSIS, $59,500 for Women for Freedom, and $50,000 each for the American Defense Institute, American Statesman Institute, Center for Immigration Studies, Committee for a Constructive Tomorrow, Fully Informed Jury Association, Institute for Policy Innovation, Legislative Studies Institute, and American Studies Center.
Total Revenue: 1995 $7,482,179 **Total Expenses:** $6,410,184 **Net Assets:** $16,491,405 28%(2)
Tax Status: 501(c)(3) **Annual Report:** Yes.
Other Information: Established in 1964. The Foundation received $6,479,211, or 87% of revenue, from contributions and grants, primarily from Richard M. Scaife. $553,474, or 7%, from dividends and interest from securities. $449,494, or 6%, from capital gains on the sale of securities. The Foundation held $14,901,777, or 90% of assets, in corporate stock.

Cascade Policy Institute

813 S.W. Adler, Suite 707
Portland, OR 97205   **Phone:** (503) 242-0900   **E-Mail:** 71401.2764@compuserve.com
USA   **Fax:** (503) 242-3822   **Internet:** http://www.CascadePolicy.org

Contact Person: Tracie Sharp, Executive Director.
Officers or Principals: Steve Buckstein, President ($41,200); Tracie Sharp, Executive Director ($34,750); Bill Udy, Secretary/Treasurer ($0); David Gore, Director.
Mission or Interest: Provide market-oriented answers to Oregon's public policy questions regarding education, the environment, health care, taxation, and fiscal issues.
Accomplishments: National recognition and distribution for "Marketplace Schools" (a new education design). Enhanced accountability in state government division of audits. Hosted a conference on Medical Savings Accounts. Numerous media citations and op-eds in Oregon's newspapers. In 1995 the Institute spent $201,562 on its programs.
Total Revenue: 1995 $233,479 10%(3) **Total Expenses:** $236,787 85%/6%/9% **Net Assets:** $26,087
Products or Services: Studies, press releases, seminars and conferences. Cascade sponsors a "Better Government Competition" for Oregon, much like the one initiated by Massachusetts' Pioneer Institute. "Independence Scholarship Essay" competition for high school students. Three students are awarded $1,000 each in scholarships, and their school library is awarded a $100 gift certificate for Laissez Faire Books. Cascade's radio commentaries can be heard on KBNP (1410 AM) in Portland.
Tax Status: 501(c)(3) **Annual Report:** No. **Employees:** 4   **Citations:** 43:106
Board of Directors or Trustees: Academic Advisors include: Michael Bliziotes, M.D. (Oregon Health Sciences Univ.), Fred Decker, Ph.D. (Oregon State Univ.), James Huffman, J.D. (Northwestern School of Law, Lewis and Clark College), Richard Mildner, Ph.D. (Portland State Univ.), William Mitchell, Ph.D. (Univ. of Oregon), Lon Peters, Ph.D. (Reed College), Anthony Rufolo, Ph.D. (Portland State Univ.), Jim Seagraves, Ph.D. (North Carolina State Univ.), Fred Thompson, Ph.D. (Williamette Univ.).
Periodicals: *Education Insight*, and *Cascade Update* (three times-a-year).
Internships: Yes, one intern 12-15 hours weekly.
Other Information: Established in 1991. Member of the State Policy Network. The Institute received $214,111, or 92% of revenue, from contributions and grants awarded by foundations, businesses, and individuals. (In 1995 these grants included $20,000 from the Castle Rock Foundation, and $10,000 from the Roe Foundation. In 1994, $30,000 from the M.J. Murdock Charitable Trust.) $13,300, or 6%, from program services including publication sales and event admissions. $6,068, or 2%, from interest on savings and temporary cash investments.

Castle Rock Foundation

3773 Cherry Creek N. Dr., Suite 955
Denver, CO 80209   **Phone:** (303) 388-1636
USA   **Fax:** (303) 388-1684

Contact Person: Linda Tafoya, Executive Director.
Officers or Principals: William K. Coors, President ($0); Peter H. Coors, Vice President ($0); Jeffrey H. Coors, Treasurer ($0).
Mission or Interest: Grant making foundation affiliated with the Coors family. Awards grants to conservative and free-market organizations.
Accomplishments: In the fiscal year ending November 1995, the Foundation awarded $2,218,100 in grants (all other financial information is from the fiscal year ending November 1996.) Recipients included: $152,000 for Hillsdale College, $150,000 for the Free Congress Foundation, $100,000 for the Heritage Foundation, $50,000 each for the American Legislative Exchange Council, Center for the Study of Popular Culture, Intercollegiate Studies Institute, and the Nevada Policy Research Institute, $40,000 for the Education and Research Institute, $35,000 each for the Mountain States Legal Foundation and the Madison Center for Educational Affairs, $30,000 each for the Foundation for Teaching Economics and Independence Institute, and $25,000 each for the Center for Individual Rights, Defenders of Property Rights, Leadership Institute, National Association of Scholars, National Center for Public Policy Research, Pacific Legal Foundation, and Southeastern Legal Foundation. The Foundation also made a loan of $900,000 to the Free Congress Foundation at 6%.

Total Revenue: FY ending 11/96 $4,883,179 **Total Expenses:** $1,574,457 **Net Assets:** $58,379,551 17%
Tax Status: 501(c)(3) **Annual Report:** Yes. **Employees:** 4
Board of Directors or Trustees: Holland Coors, Robert Windsor.
Internships: No.
Other Information: Established in 1993. The Castle Rock Foundation was created with an endowment of $36,596,253 from the Adolph Coors Foundation. With the creation of the new Foundation, the Coors Foundation ceased to award grants to public policy organizations, and concentrates on conservation, cultural institutions, medical research, and education. Although the executive director/secretary, Linda Tafoya, does not receive compensation from the Castle Rock Foundation, she has historically been paid by the Adolph Coors Foundation, where she continues to serve as secretary. In the fiscal year ending November 1996, the Foundation received $4,089,565, or 84% of revenue, from capital gains on the sale of assets. $793,614, or 16%, from dividends and interest from securities. The Foundation held $55,774,414, or 96% of assets, in corporate stock.

Catalyst Institute

33 North LaSalle St., Suite 1920
Chicago, IL 60602   **Phone:** (312) 541-5400   **E-Mail:** 102173.2646@compuserve.com
USA   **Fax:**   (312) 541-5401

Contact Person: Paul R. Knapp, President.
Officers or Principals: Paul R, Knapp, President/CEO ($232,764); Suzanne Hammond, Managing Director ($86,916); Gus R. LeDonne, Treasurer/CFO ($44,853); Mary Jones Miller, Managing Director.
Mission or Interest: "Offering research, advisory and consulting services to financial markets and institutions worldwide. The organization conducts issue-oriented research and strategic planning studies."
Accomplishments: "Has established itself as the world's leading financial services think tank." In 1994 Catalyst spent $847,069 on its programs. The largest program, with expenditures of $454,834, was consulting work for the U.S. federal government dealing with Savings and Loan organization sales by the FHLBB. "This work reduced government oversight and bureaucracy and saved taxpayers in excess of $100 million." $262,894 was spent on researching the private and social costs of teenage childbearing. Other studies focused on capital markets and economic growth, alternatives to government-financed low-income home ownership, and various facets of financial markets.
Total Revenue: 1994 $1,353,679 -6%(2) ($391,957, or 29%, from government contracts)
Total Expenses: $1,343,297 63%/23%/14% **Net Assets:** $133,823
Products or Services: Various reports and books.
Tax Status: 501(c)(3) **Annual Report:** No. **Employees:** 6   **Citations:** 11:170
Board of Directors or Trustees: J. Carter Beese, Jr. (Former Commissioner, U.S. Securities and Exchange Commission), Peter Borish, Joseph Carr, James Cochrane (Senior Vice Pres., Research and Planning, New York Stock Exchange), Ann Wood Farmer, Michael Hoffman, Case Hoogendoorn, Manuel Johnson (Center for Global Market Studies, George Mason Univ.), Leo Melamed (Chairman Emeritus, Chicago Mercantile Exchange), Adlai Stevenson (former U.S. Senator, D-IL), Didier Varlet.
Internships: No.
Other Information: Formerly the Mid-America Institute for Public Policy Research. Catalyst contracted Cyrus Gardner of Herndon, VA, and University of Michigan Professor of Business Economics (and former Catalyst director) Roger Kormendi for consulting work done for the Resolution Trust Corp. study concerning Savings and Loan sales by the FHLBB. The consultants were paid $103,256 and $92,925 respectively. Catalyst received $570,602, or 42% of revenue, from contributions and grants awarded by foundations, businesses, and individuals. (These grants included $100,000 from the Sarah Scaife Foundation.) $391,957, or 29%, from government contracts. $356,331, or 26%, from the sale of research and analysis. The remaining revenue came from interest on savings and temporary cash investments, and other miscellaneous sources.

Catholic Campaign for America (CCA)

1620 I St., N.W., Suite 916
Washington, DC 20006   **Phone:** (202) 833-4999
USA   **Fax:**   (202) 833-5569

Contact Person: Michael A. Ferguson, Executive Director.
Officers or Principals: Frank J. Lynch, Chairman; Amb. Thomas P. Melady, National Committee Chairman; Richard V. Allen, Treasurer; Michelle B. Prunty, Communications Director; Joseph Cosby, Field Director; Ed Ceol, Development Director; Monica Check, Controller.
Mission or Interest: "Educating the public regarding the Catholic perspective on social issues affecting the country and the world and organizing and mobilizing the public to bring about social change." Opposes abortion and euthanasia, and supports school choice.
Accomplishments: Opposed the "anti-Catholic, anti-family policies" of U.S. Surgeon General Jocelyn Elders and opposed the nomination of Dr. Henry Foster to replace her. Supports a ban on 'partial birth' abortions. Holds "Catholic town meetings" and "Celebrate Your Catholic Faith Nights." Monitored the U.N. Conference on Population and Development in Cairo and the Fourth U.N. Conference on Women in Beijing and reported these events to Catholics in the U.S. and before congressional committees. In 1995 the Campaign spent $775,961 on its programs; an increase of 186% over the previous year.
Total Revenue: 1995 $1,159,143 67%(3) **Total Expenses:** $1,031,531 75%/19%/6% **Net Assets:** $312,562

Products or Services: Bestows the annual "Catholic American of the Year Award." The first winner in 1993 was former Governor Bob Casey (D-PA). In 1994 it was given to Rep. Henry Hyde (R-IL). Also presents an annual "Catholic Contribution Award" to non-public figures who make significant contributions. Published a book, <u>Catholics in the Public Square</u>. The CCA did not engage in lobbying in 1994, but in 1996 lobbied on behalf of the ban on 'partial birth abortions.'

Tax Status: 501(c)(3) **Annual Report:** Yes. **Employees:** 8   **Citations:** 21:146

Board of Directors or Trustees: Anthony Abraham, Mary Cunningham Agee (Nurturing Network), Richard Allen (Asst. to the President for Natl. Security, 1981-82), Hon. William Bennett (Empower America), Mary Ellen Bork (John Carroll Society), John Brennan (Trustee, The Papal Foundation), Elmer Hansen, Jr. (Trustee, The Papal Foundation), William McCann, Thomas Monaghan (Pres./CEO, Domino's Pizza), Robert Mylod, George Newman, William Sasso, Hon. Frank Shakespeare (former Ambassador to the Holy See),

Periodicals: *Campaign Update* (bimonthly newsletter).

Internships: Yes.

Other Information: Founded in 1992. In 1994 the CCA received $738,248, or 99.9% of revenue, from contributions and grants awarded by foundations, businesses, and individuals. (In 1995 these grants included $3,000 from the Lynde and Harry Bradley Foundation.) The remaining revenue came from other miscellaneous sources.

Catholic Family News (CFN)

P.O. Box 743
Niagara Falls, NY 14302   **Phone:**   (905) 871-6292
USA

Contact Person: John Vennari, Associate Editor.

Mission or Interest: Monthly newspaper that is a "hard-hitting, orthodox alternative to the wishy-washy liberalism of the so-called 'Catholic' press."

Accomplishments: "Has assembled the largest group of Catholic writers in history. Writers such as Heiland, Rini, Demers, Faust, Engle, Goldsboroug, Wickens, Trinchard, Cotter, Ferrara, Leonard, O'Connor, and many more yet to come."

Periodicals: *Catholic Family News* (monthly newspaper).

Other Information: Published by Catholic Family Ministries.

Catholics United for Life (CUL)

6375 New Hope Rd.
New Hope, KY 40052   **Phone:**   (502) 549-7020
USA

Contact Person: Theo Stearns, President.

Officers or Principals: Patrick Monaghan, General Counsel; Prof. Charles E. Rice, Chairman, Legal Committee.

Mission or Interest: Catholic anti-abortion organization that litigates and produces educational materials.

Accomplishments: Works with the American Center for Law and Justice through its ACLJ-New Hope Project. This project was formerly called Free Speech Advocates, and was created by Prof. Charles E. Rice (Univ. of Notre Dame Law School) in 1984.

Products or Services: Catalog of books and pamphlets.

Tax Status: 501(c)(3)

Other Information: Established in 1973. CUL also participates in the distribution of *Culture Wars*. In 1995 the organization received $3,000 from the Lynde and Harry Bradley Foundation.

Cato Institute

1000 Massachusetts Ave., N.W.
Washington, DC 20001   **Phone:**   (202) 842-0200   **E-Mail:** cato@cato.org
USA   **Fax:**   (202) 842-3490   **Internet:** http://www.cato.org

Officers or Principals: Edward H. Crane, President ($140,000); William Niskanen, Chairman ($100,000); David Boaz, Executive Vice President ($82,472); Roger Pilon, Director, Constitutional Studies; Brian Smith, Vice President, Administration; Ted Carpenter, Director, Public Policy; Stephen Moore, Director, Fiscal Policy.

Mission or Interest: "Dedicated to the traditional American principles of limited government, individual liberty, and peace. . . The Institute's name comes from Cato's Letter's, libertarian writings circulated in the American colonies in the 18th century. The pamphlets helped lay the philosophical foundation for the American Revolution and greatly influenced the author of the Declaration of Independence, Thomas Jefferson."

Accomplishments: Considered by most to be the leading libertarian think tank. In 1994 the Cato Institute released the "Cato Handbook for Congress" for the 104th Congress. The Handbook detailed $1.1 trillion in budget cuts. The Handbook received extensive media coverage, including two articles in the *Washington Post*. Cato has been advocating the privatization of Social Security. *The National Journal* said "in the center of the action is the not-for-profit Cato Institute, which launched a project to push. . . the idea of privatizing the system." Cato has been called "Washington's hottest think tank" by the *Boston Globe*, and *New York* magazine said "since the (1994) election, Cato has been at the white-hot center of the revolution." Cato's Web site won the Four-Star Magellan award for excellence. In 1994 Cato spent $3,251,745 on its programs. The largest expense, $2,447,796, was the production and distribution of publications. The rest was spent on ten conferences and seventy-five forums.

Total Revenue: 1994 $6,436,365 14%(4) **Total Expenses:** $5,992,843 54%/35%/11% **Net Assets:** $7,694,221
Products or Services: Conferences, seminars, research and publications. Science Without Sense by Steven Milloy, Educational Freedom in Eastern Europe by Charles Glenn, and other books.
Tax Status: 501(c)(3) **Annual Report:** Yes. **Citations:** 1,429:6
Board of Directors or Trustees: Peter Ackerman (Rockport Financial), K. Tucker Andersen, James Blanchard, III (Jefferson Financial), John Blokker, Frank Bond, Gordon Cain (Chari, Sterling Group), Richard Dennis, Theodore Forstmann (Forstmann & Little Co.), Ethelmae Humphreys, David Koch (Pres., Koch Industries), John Malone, David Padden, Howard Rich (Pres., U.S. Term Limits), Frederick Smith (Chair, Federal Express Corp.).
Periodicals: *The Cato Journal* (biannual academic journal), *Regulation* (quarterly academic magazine).
Internships: Yes.
Other Information: Established in 1977. Cato received $5,951,988, or 92% of revenue, from contributions and grants awarded by foundations, businesses, and individuals. (These grants included $140,000 from the Gordon and Mary Cain Foundation, $135,000 from the Sarah Scaife Foundation, $10,000 from the Grover Hermann Foundation, $7,500 from the Alex C. Walker Foundation, $5,000 from the Vernon K. Krieble Foundation, $3,000 from the Ruth and Vernon Taylor Foundation, and $3,000 from the Earhart Foundation. In 1995, $500,000 from the Claude R. Lambe Charitable Foundation, $500,000 from the David H. Koch Charitable Foundation, $50,000 from the John M. Olin Foundation, $35,000 from the John William Pope Foundation, $18,000 from the William H. Donner Foundation, $15,000 from the Sunmark Foundation, and $5,000 from the Roe Foundation.) $312,832, or 5%, from the sale of publications. $118,122, or 2%, from conference registration fees. The remaining revenue came from mailing list rentals, royalties, interest on savings, and rental income.

CAUSE Foundation

1112 ½ Montreat Rd., Suite 1
Black Mountain, NC 28711   **Phone:** (704) 669-5189
USA   **Fax:**   (704) 669-5191

Contact Person: Kirk David Lyons, Executive Director.
Officers or Principals: Kirk David Lyons, Executive Director; Dr. Neill Payne, Director; David Hollaway, Director.
Mission or Interest: Legal foundation established to defend Constitutional rights, even for unpopular causes.
Accomplishments: Have attracted attention for defending the rights of members of the Ku Klux Klan. They were key in securing defense lawyer Dick DeGuerin for Branch Davidian leader David Koresh and his lieutenant, Steve Schneider, during the standoff in Waco, Texas. Kirk David Lyons of the CAUSE Foundation is currently representing the plaintiffs in *Gyarfas v. U.S.*, Case No. W93-CA-334, United States District Court, Western District of Texas, Waco Division. The plaintiffs are survivors of the fire at the Branch Davidian compound in Waco, Texas, that burned to the ground after the FBI launched a chemical assault on the compound. The suit is a civil action against various government agencies and employees
Tax Status: 501(c)(3) status pending
Other Information: Kirk Lyons describes why he is willing to take on cases the liberal organizations, such as the ACLU (of which he is a member), usually shun, "The greatest threat to liberty in the world today is the American government. . . So that means we're going to be defending people who are not in the mainstream, that are not popular, that are not even likeable. . . But if they do not have rights. . . to a fair trial, then nobody does. . . As long as they are persecuted for their beliefs, somebody needs to stick up for them. Otherwise, sooner or later, it will be us."

Center for the American Founding

1311 Dolley Madison Blvd., Suite 2A
McLean, VA 22101   **Phone:** (703) 506-1790   **E-Mail:** brendahunter@earthlink.net
USA   **Fax:**   (703) 506-8085

Contact Person: Brenda Hunter.
Officers or Principals: Balint Vazsonyi, Director
Mission or Interest: "Practice and advocate discussion on national issues as they relate to America's founding principles."
Accomplishments: "Building a national constituency for a pledge, called 'Reaffirmation of the American founding'."
Products or Services: The Battle for America's Soul and other publications.
Tax Status: 501(c)(3) **Annual Report:** No. **Employees:** 3
Other Information: Affiliated with the Potomac Foundation at the same address.

Center for American Values

P.O. Box 91180
Washington, DC 20090-1180
USA

Contact Person: Deborah Stone, President.
Mission or Interest: "Dedicated to holding our elected officials accountable to the voters."
Accomplishments: Distributed thousands of abridged copies of Floyd G. Brown's book, Slick Willie: Why America Cannot Trust Bill Clinton
Tax Status: 501(c)(3)

Center for the Defense of Free Enterprise

12500 N.E. 10th Place
Bellevue, WA 98005   **Phone:**   (206) 455-5038
USA   **Fax:**   (206) 451-3959   **Internet:** http://www.CDFE.org

Contact Person: Alan Gottlieb, President.
Officers or Principals: Alan Gottlieb, President ($0); Ron Arnold, Executive Director ($0).
Mission or Interest: "The Center was established so that Americans who understood and valued the free enterprise system could contribute to the defense and promotion of the economic system that made America a prosperous nation." The Center is closely associated with the 'Wise Use' movement that advocates multiple uses of natural resources, including consumption, for the benefit of humans.
Accomplishments: The establishment of over 600 radio stations participating in a weekly public affairs project named the American Broadcasting Network. More than 400 newspapers reaching more than 8 million people participate in a network of features and columns named the American Press Syndicate. The establishment of the Free Enterprise Press. The Free Enterprise Legal Defense Fund which files "Friends of the Court Briefs" on behalf of small businesses. Greenpeace has referred to them as the "premier think tank and training center for the Wise Use movement." Earth First! leader Christopher Manes attacks the Center in his book Green Rage: Radical Environmentalism and the Unmaking of Society, as a threat to the radical environmentalist movement, and as a friend of industry.
Total Revenue: 1993 $339,289 **Total Expenses:** $321,814 **Net Assets:** $57,100
Tax Status: 501(c)(3) **Annual Report:** No. **Employees:** 3 volunteers.   **Citations:** 5:192
Board of Directors or Trustees: Samuel Slom, Merril Jacobs, Jeff Kane.
Periodicals: *The Wise Use Conservation Memo* (quarterly) and *Private Sector*.
Internships: Yes.
Other Information: Established in 1976. In 1993 the Center received $307,783, or 91% of revenue, from contributions and grants. (These grants had been growing by an average of 45% since 1989.) $30,615, or 9%, from the sale of books. The remaining revenue came from interest on savings and dividends and interest from securities. Affiliated with the Second Amendment Foundation and the Citizens' Committee for the Right to Keep and Bear Arms at the same address.

Center for Defense and Strategic Studies

Southwest Missouri State University
901 S. National Ave.
Springfield, MO 65804-0095   **Phone:**   (417) 836-4137
USA   **Fax:**   (417) 836-6667

Officers or Principals: Prof. William R. Van Cleave, Director; Associate Prof. Jack D. Crouch.
Mission or Interest: Graduate-level academic program specializing in national security policy, defense analysis, and arms control. Affiliated with Southwest Missouri State University
Products or Services: In addition to the use of SMSU's library and Government Documents Depository, the Center maintains its own library that specializes in books, journals, and documents particular to their field of study.
Tax Status: 501(c)(3)
Board of Directors or Trustees: Adjunct faculty includes: Dennis Bark, Ph.D., (Hoover Inst.), Roger Barnett, Ph.D., Captain, USN, Ret. (former Dir., Strategy and Concepts, U.S. Navy), Joseph Churba, Ph.D., (Pres., International Security Council), Angelo Codevilla, Ph.D. (Hoover Inst.), Henry Cooper, Ph.D. (former Dir., Strategic Defense Initiative organization), R. Joseph DeSutter, Ph.D., Colonel, USAF (Military Asst. to Vice Pres. Quayle), Charles Kupperman, Ph.D. (Exec. Dir., Empower America), Constantine Menges, Ph.D. (American Enterprise Inst.), Prof. Harold Hood (Claremont College).
Other Information: Established in 1987. Affiliated with, and incorporated under, Southwest Missouri State University.

Center for Economic and Policy Education

Saint Vincent College
300 Fraser Purchase Rd.
Latrobe, PA 15650   **Phone:**   (412) 537-4597   **E-Mail:** cepe@stvincent.edu
USA   **Fax:**   (412) 537-4599

Contact Person: Christine M. Bender, Program Coordinator.
Officers or Principals: Prof. Gary M. Quinlivan, Director; Asst. Prof. Lee J. Weissert, Director.
Mission or Interest: Program at St. Vincent College that hosts the Alex G. McKenna Economic Education Series Lecture and publishes a newsletter that promotes free-market economics and limited government.
Accomplishments: The Alex G. McKenna Economic Education Series Lecture has hosted Dr. Gertrude Himmelfarb (CUNY), Dr. David Henderson (Hoover Inst.), Dr. Lawrence Mead (Harvard Kennedy School of Government), Dr. Richard S. Lindzen (MIT), Robert Rector (Heritage Found.), Dr. Norman B. Ture (Institute for Research on the Economics of Taxation), and others. In 1997 the Center hosted a three-day conference, "The Political Order and Culture: Toward the Renewal of Civilization." The Conference featured Hilton Kramer (*New Criterion*), Dinesh D'Souza, Ralph McInerny (*Crisis*), Claes Ryn (National Humanities Inst.), Elizabeth Fox-Genovese (Emory Univ.), and others

Products or Services: <u>Culture in Crisis and the Renewal of Civil Life</u> (Rowman & Littlefield, 1996), <u>The Cultural Context of Economics and Politics</u> (University Press of America, 1994), other books and publications.
Tax Status: 501(c)(3)
Periodicals: *Economic Directions* (monthly newsletter).
Other Information: Established in 1991 by T. William Boxx, chairman of the Philip M. McKenna Foundation, and Prof. Gary Quinlivan. Affiliated with and incorporated under Saint Vincent College. In 1994-95 the Center received $104,000 from the Philip M. McKenna Foundation, and $1,000 from the Aequus Institute.

Center for Economic Policy Research

Stanford University
100 Encina Commons
Stanford, CA 94305
USA

Officers or Principals: Michael J. Boskin, John B. Taylor, Research Fellows.
Mission or Interest: Economic research with a free-market perspective
Tax Status: 501(c)(3)
Other Information: Affiliated with and incorporated as a part of Stanford University. Michael Boskin was the top economic advisor to President Bush. Recently, he headed the Senate commission that examined the case for revising the Consumer Price Index (CPI). John B. Taylor was an economic advisor to Republican Presidential candidate Bob Dole. In 1994-95 the Center received $135,800 from the John M. Olin Foundation, and $7,500 from the Gordon and Mary Cain Foundation.

Center for Education Reform (CER)

1001 Connecticut Ave, N.W., Suite 920
Washington, DC 20036   **Phone:**   (202) 822-9000
USA   **Fax:**   (202) 822-5077

Contact Person: Jeane Allen, President.
Officers or Principals: Jeane Allen, President/Treasurer ($15,417); Lisa Graham Keegan, Co-Chair, Education Leaders Council.
Mission or Interest: Clearinghouse for information on educational reform efforts nationwide. Hosts the Education Leaders Council, a membership project for educators.
Accomplishments: The Center claims to have the most extensive database of education reform efforts, including research, key figures, and the organizations involved. *The Washington Times* said of Jeane Allen, "She's up on who's doing what, on the national, state, county and even local level. She could tell you what bills are pending, which reforms have been effective, which groups are working toward what end. That has made her a terrific resource for the school-reform movement." In 1993 the Center spent $63,872 on its programs. This included $16,568 to hold a 'town meeting' in Detroit to assist the community in learning about the new charter school program.
Total Revenue: 1993 $120,270 **Total Expenses:** $67,867 94%/5%/1% **Net Assets:** $52,499
Products or Services: Action papers and info-packs.
Tax Status: 501(c)(3)
Board of Directors or Trustees: William Hume, G. Carl Ball, William Bennett, John Chubb, Denis Doyle, Pete DuPont, Chester Finn, Byron Lamm, Kate O'Beirne, Louise Oliver, Stephen Tracy, Polly Williams.
Periodicals: *Opportunity* (quarterly journal), newsletter.
Other Information: Established in 1993. Founder Jeane Allen was formerly with the U.S. Department of Education (1984-88) and the Heritage Foundation.   The Center received $120,270, or 99.9% of revenue, from contributions and grants awarded by foundations, businesses, and individuals. (In 1994, $10,000 from the J.M. Foundation. In 1995, $75,000 from the Scaife Family Foundation, $50,000 from the John M. Olin Foundation, $5,000 from the John William Pope Foundation, $5,000 from the Roe Foundation, and $4,000 from the Sunmark Foundation.) The remaining revenue came from interest on savings and temporary cash investments.

Center for Entrepreneurship and Free Enterprise (CEFE)

Reinhardt College
7300 Reinhardt College Parkway
Waleska, GA 30183   **Phone:**   (404) 720-5579
USA   **Fax:**   (404) 720-5602

Contact Person: Dr. Robert L. Formaini, Director.
Mission or Interest: The Center holds seminars and hosts speakers for Reinhardt College and the surrounding community. "Promotes free enterprise and, to some extent, Austrian economics."
Products or Services: All seminars are available on VHS video tape.
Tax Status: 501(c)(3) **Annual Report:** No. **Employees:** 3
Periodicals: *News and Views* (quarterly).
Other Information: Affiliated with, and incorporated under, Reinhardt College. Reinhardt College is the site of the "Renewing American Civilization" course taught by House Speaker Newt Gingrich (R-GA). (Gingrich was House Minority Whip at the time). The course is at the center of the controversy surrounding the Speaker, the heart of which is whether or not Gingrich used 501(c)(3) organizational status to promote his party and his own political ambitions.

Center for Environmental Education Research (CEER)

7049 E. Tanque Verde Rd., Suite 386
Tucson, AZ 85715   **Phone:** (520) 722-3300
USA   **Fax:**   (520) 722-3335

Contact Person: Dr. Michael Sanera, Research Fellow.
Officers or Principals: Larry Arnn, President; Chuck Heatherly, Vice President.
Mission or Interest: Focus on environmental education in the nation's schools. Critiques current education standards regarding the environment, seeks the reform of state environmental education laws, and provides "balanced and objective environmental education curriculum materials".
Accomplishments: Published Facts, not Fear: A Parents Guide to Teaching Children About the Environment. Produced studies on environmental education in Wisconsin and Alaska. "Instrumental in passage of the American Legislative Exchange Council's model environmental education legislation
Tax Status: 501(c)(3) **Annual Report:** No. **Employees:** 1
Internships: Yes, unpaid internships in Tucson, AZ, or Claremont, CA.
Other Information: Established in 1995. CEER is affiliated with, and incorporated under, the Claremont Institute. It assumes the office space and personnel (Dr. Sanera) of the Arizona Institute, now defunct. In its last year of operation, 1995, the Arizona Institute had net revenue, expenses, and assets of $9,797, $9,338, and $1,027.

Center for Equal Opportunity (CEO)

(see Equal Opportunity Foundation)

Center for Immigration Studies

1815 H St., N.W., Suite 1010
Washington, DC 20006   **Phone:** (202) 466-8185   **E-Mail:** center@cis.org
USA   **Fax:**   (202) 466-8076

Contact Person: Mark Krikorian, Executive Director.
Officers or Principals: George High, Senior Fellow ($60,323); Prof. Otis L. Graham, Jr., Chairman; Rosemary E. Jenks, Editor; Leon F. Bouvier, David E. Simcox, Senior Fellows.
Mission or Interest: "A research institute devoted to the study of immigration's economic, social, demographic and cultural impacts. . . the Center is the nation's only think tank focusing on immigration from the perspective of America's national interest."
Accomplishments: Co-published How Many Americans? Population, Immigration, and the Environment with the Sierra Club. "Featured prominently in the recent public debate over immigration. Its officers and staff have testified before Congress on numerous occasions and are quoted widely in the news media, including outlets such as *Commentary* and *The National Review*." In 1994 the Center spent $260,000 on its programs.
Total Revenue: 1994 $255,409 (-29%) **Total Expenses:** $427,367 61%/25%/15% **Net Assets:** $128,464
Products or Services: Issue Papers, studies, Backgrounders, Fifty Million Californians?, Florida in the 21st Century, Thirty Million Texans?, and other books. Internet mailing list.
Tax Status: 501(c)(3) **Annual Report:** No. **Employees:** 7   **Citations:** 168:44
Board of Directors or Trustees: Prof. Vernon Briggs, Jr. (Cornell Univ.), Thomas C.T. Brokaw, Roger Conner (American Alliance for Rights and Responsibilities), Prof. George Grayson (College of William and Mary), Eugene Katz (Planned Parenthood of NY), Malcolm Lovell, Jr. (National Planning Assoc.), Prof. Frank Morris, Sr. (Morgan State Univ.), Elizabeth Paddock, Hon. Robert Sayre, Hon. Eleanor Weinstock, Iêda Siqueira Wiarda (Library of Congress).
Periodicals: *Immigration Review* (quarterly newsletter).
Internships: Yes, paid and unpaid for graduate and undergraduate students.
Other Information: Established in 1985. The Center received $251,956, or 99% of revenue, from contributions and grants awarded by foundations, businesses, and individuals. (In 1995 these grants included $50,000 from the Carthage Foundation.) The remaining revenue came from interest on savings and temporary cash investments.

Center for Independent Thought / Laissez Faire Books

938 Howard St., Suite 202
San Francisco, CA 94103   **Phone:** (415) 541-9780   **E-Mail:** orders@lfb.org
USA   **Fax:**   (415) 541-0597   **Internet:** http://www.lfb.org/

Contact Person: Anita Anderson, Vice President.
Officers or Principals: Anita Anderson, Vice President ($40,465); Andrea Rich, President ($0); Howard Rich, Treasurer.
Mission or Interest: Distributes books, conducts forums and funds educational projects.
Accomplishments: "Laissez Faire Books is the biggest distributor of books on liberty in the world. We have also donated over 15,000 books to Eastern Europe." In 1995 the Center spent $1,323,648 on its programs. This included $16,500 in grants and awards for individual scholars. Grant recipients included $5,500 for Lysander, Inc. (an organization that supports individual scholars), and $5,000 each for Karl Hess, Jr. and Michael Mello.

Total Revenue: 1995 $1,551,685 4%(2) **Total Expenses:** $1,394,125 95%/5%/0% **Net Assets:** $927,103
Products or Services: Support independent scholars through the Roy Childs Fund. Thomas Szasz Award for outstanding achievement in civil liberties. 1995 Szasz award winners were author James Bovard and Julie Stewart. Distribution of books and journals.
Tax Status: 501(c)(3) **Annual Report:** No. **Employees:** 9   **Citations:** 1:225
Board of Directors or Trustees: Joe Stillwell, David Boaz (Cato Inst.), Eric O'Keefe.
Internships: No.
Other Information: Formerly the Libertarian Review Foundation. Name changed in 1990. The Center received $1,415,640, or 91% of revenue, from book sales. $52,086, or 3%, from royalties. $34,168, or 2%, from contributions and grants awarded by foundations, businesses, and individuals. $27,893, or 2%, from interest on savings and temporary cash investments. $20,733, or 1%, from "book fulfillment services".

Center for Individual Rights (CIR)

1300 19th St., N.W., Suite 260
Washington, DC 20036   **Phone:** (202) 833-8400   **E-Mail:** cir@mail.wdn.com
USA   **Fax:** (202) 833-8410   **Internet:** www.wdn.com/cir/index/html

Contact Person: Robert Alt, Director of Public Relations.
Officers or Principals: Michael Greve, Executive Director ($99,000); Michael McDonald, President ($99,000); Michael Rosman ($66,000).
Mission or Interest: "Defense of individual rights, with particular emphasis on civil rights, freedom of speech and the free exercise of religion, and sexual harassment law. CIR provides free legal representation to deserving clients who cannot otherwise obtain or afford legal counsel and whose individual rights are threatened."
Accomplishments: CIR joined the legal defense of the successful California Prop. 209, the "California Civil Rights Initiative." CIR has a web page devoted to Prop. 209, "http://www.wdn.com/cir/ccri.htm". CIR represented the plaintiff who challenged race-based preferential admissions at the University of Texas Law School. CIR won the case in the Fifth Circuit court's ruling on Hopwood v. State of Texas; a decision both sides agreed was an "A-bomb" dropped on affirmative action. CIR represented the plaintiffs in Rosenberger v. Rector and Visitors of the University of Virginia in which the Supreme Court held that the First Amendment barred the University from excluding a religious student publication from the University's funding system. Nat Hentoff of *The Village Voice* said "The Center is usually categorized as conservative, but I've written about a number of the cases and would describe the Center and its attorneys as Libertarian. They have taken many unpopular free-speech cases, regardless of the political views of the speaker, and their batting average is high." William Kristol of the *Weekly Standard* said, "I can't think of another group that has been equally effective in dismantling the political establishment's absurd claims to moral superiority and in fighting the ideological passions that inflame American politics." Articles by executive director Michael Greve have appeared in *The Chronicle of Higher Education*, *The Weekly Standard*, and *The Wall Street Journal*. Over 40 law firms and law professors have made pro bono contributions to CIR efforts. In the fiscal year ending March 1996, CIR spent $474,343 on its programs that included litigating 19 cases. For its litigation CIR received $41,117 in court-awarded legal fees.
Total Revenue: FY ending 3/96 $919,010 19%(2) **Total Expenses:** $650,668 73%/24%/3% **Net Assets:** $615,072
Tax Status: 501(c)(3) **Annual Report:** Yes. **Employees:** 12   **Citations:** 56:94
Board of Directors or Trustees: Gary Born, Michael Carvin, Prof. Jeremy Rabkin (Cornell Univ.). CIR has a Lawyers' Committee that includes: Christopher deMuth (AEI), Prof. Richard Epstein (Univ. of Chicago Law School), Prof. Jonathan Macey (Cornell Univ. Law School), Prof. Michael McConnell (Univ. of Chicago Law School), and others.
Periodicals: *Docket Report* (quarterly review).
Internships: Yes. Some paid full-time summer clerkships and year-round, part-time clerkships for law students with excellent academic credentials.
Other Information: Established in 1989. CIR received $872,659, or 95% of revenue, from contributions and grants awarded by foundations, businesses, and individuals. (These grants included $250,000 from the Smith Richardson Foundation, $100,000 from the Lynde and Harry Bradley Foundation, $80,000 from the John M. Olin Foundation, $25,000 from the Castle Rock Foundation, $25,000 from the Scaife Family Foundation, $25,000 from the William H. Donner Foundation, and $5,000 from the John William Pope Foundation. In 1994, $50,000 from the Gilder Foundation, $30,000 from the F.M. Kirby Foundation, $18,915 from the Alliance Defense Fund, $9,600 from the Earhart Foundation, $2,000 from the Aequus Institute.) $41,117, or 4%, from court-awarded attorney's fees. The remaining revenue came from interest on savings and temporary cash investments.

Center for Libertarian Studies (CLS)

875 Mahler Rd., Suite 150
Burlingame, CA 94010   **Phone:** (415) 692-8456
USA   **Fax:** (415) 692-8459

Contact Person: Burton S. Blumert, President.
Officers or Principals: Burton S. Blumert, President ($0); Llewellyn H. Rockwell, Jr., Secretary ($0); David Gordon, Paul Gottfried, Hans-Hermann Hoppe, Michael Levin, Justin Raimondo, Jeffrey Tucker, Contributing Editors.
Mission or Interest: Publication of classical liberal scholarship. Publication of the *Triple R*, formerly called the *Rothbard-Rockwell Report*.

Accomplishments: Pat Buchanan says of the Rothbard-Rockwell Report, it is "the one publication I read the minute I get it, front to back, every page." Joe Sobran says, "Every time I read it, I find myself thinking about it for days afterward."
Total Revenue: FY ending 6/95 $213,043 82%(2) **Total Expenses:** $185,925 97%/3%/0% **Net Assets:** $58,763
Products or Services: Publish Reclaiming the American Right. Organizers of the annual meeting of the John Randolph Club. The John Randolph Club is made up of conservatives and libertarians who come together to find common ground.
Tax Status: 501(c)(3) **Annual Report:** No. **Employees:** 3   **Citations:** 6:189
Board of Directors or Trustees: Rep. Ron Paul, M.D. (R-TX), David Keyston, Leonard Liggio (Inst. for Humane Studies), David Padden (Heartland Inst.), Joseph Peden (CUNY), George Resch, Michael Holmes, Matt Monroe.
Periodicals: *Journal of Libertarian Studies*, *Triple R* (monthly newsletter).
Internships: No.
Other Information: *Triple R* was formerly called *The Rothbard-Rockwell Report*, and was named after contributor Lew Rockwell ,and the late Murray Rothbard, Ph.D. (1926-1995). Despite his death, the *Triple R* continues to bear his name. Rothbard was considered one of the leading contemporary figures in the Austrian school of economics. Llewllyn Rockwell was formerly Chief of Staff for Rep. Ron Paul (R-TX), and is president of the Ludwig von Mises Institute. The Center received $204,646, or 96%, from newsletter subscriptions. $6,213, or 3%, from contributions and grants awarded by foundations, businesses, and individuals. The remaining revenue came from interest on savings and temporary cash investments.

Center for Market Processes

4084 University Dr., Suite 208
Fairfax, VA 22030-6815   **Phone:** (703) 934-6970   **E-Mail:** cmp@gmu.edu
USA   **Fax:**   (703) 934-1578   **Internet:** http://web.gmu.edu/departments/cmp

Contact Person: Robert N. Mottice, Executive Director.
Officers or Principals: Judy Redpath, Business Development Director ($68,588); Wayne Gable, President ($41,151); Colleen Moreeta, Secretary/Treasurer ($40,978); Robert N. Mottice, Executive Director; Charles Koch, Chairman; David Nott, Executive Vice President.
Mission or Interest: To assist George Mason students and faculty in the study of economics, particularly Austrian theory.
Accomplishments: Center President Wayne Gable and Director Jerome Ellig recently wrote the booklet, Introduction to Market-Based Management. In the fiscal year ending August 1995 the Center spent $1,090,289 on its programs. These programs included: $198,462 for educational programs to assist policy makers, including an Administrative Assistant Conference. $183,166 for the Charles G. Koch Summer Fellows for students of economics and public policy. Other programs awarded various grants and fellowships for students and faculty.
Total Revenue: FY ending 8/95 $1,069,068 8%(2) **Total Expenses:** $1,250,929 87%/9%/3% **Net Assets:** $193,982
Products or Services: Grants to aid students and faculty at George Mason University. Market-based management program which develops and applies techniques for managing decentralized organizations.
Tax Status: 501(c)(3) **Annual Report:** No. **Employees:** 12   **Citations:** 8:178
Board of Directors or Trustees: Prof. Walter Williams (syndicated columnist), Paul Brooks, Richard Fink.
Periodicals: *Market Process News* (monthly newsletter).
Other Information: Established in 1980. Previously called the Center for the Study of Market Processes until 1994. The Center received $950,653, or 89%, from contributions and grants awarded by foundations, businesses, and individuals. (These grants included $475,000 from the Charles G. Koch Charitable Foundation, $125,000 from the Claude R. Lambe Charitable Foundation, $50,000 from the David H. Koch Charitable Foundation, $25,000 from the Sarah Scaife Foundation, $7,500 from the Gilder Foundation, $2,500 from the Gordon and Mary Cain Foundation, and $1,000 from the John William Pope Foundation.) $110,876, or 10%, from the sale of publications. The remaining revenue came from interest on savings, and other miscellaneous sources.

Center for Media and Public Affairs

2101 L St., N.W., Suite 300
Washington, DC 20037   **Phone:** (202) 223-2942
USA   **Fax:**   (202) 872-4014

Contact Person: Dr. S. Robert Lichter, President .
Officers or Principals: Dr. Linda Lichter, Treasurer ($36,458); Thomas Sheehan, Executive Director ($33,594); Dr. S. Robert Lichter, President ($24,792).
Mission or Interest: To scientifically analyze how the news and entertainment media treat social and political issues.
Accomplishments: The Lichters have written widely on the role of news and entertainment media in American society. In addition to writing five books, their articles have appeared in many scientific journals, as well as the *New York Times, Washington Post*, and *Wall Street Journal*. They have discussed their work on Nightline, Today, Good Morning America, and the big three networks' evening news programs.
Total Revenue: FY ending 8/95 $725,569 23%(2) **Total Expenses:** $458,102 77%/17%/6% **Net Assets:** $471,140
Products or Services: Books, monographs. "Health Reform Pink Book," a comparison of assertions made by President Clinton and the proposals in the bill he submitted to Congress.
Tax Status: 501(c)(3) **Citations:** 29:135
Board of Directors or Trustees: David Gergen, Prof. Paul McCracken (Univ. of MI), Paul Mongerson, Hon. Robert Stuart, Jr.

Periodicals: *Media Monitor* (monthly newsletter).
Other Information: Affiliated with the 501(c)(3) Statistical Assessment Service. In the fiscal year ending July 1995, the two affiliates had combined net revenues, expenses, and assets of $1,549,559, $800,923, and $952,309. The officers Dr. S. Robert Lichter, Dr. Linda Lichter, and John Sheehan served as officers of both affiliates and received a combined $72,920, $72,916, and $61,080 respectively. The Center received $693,757, or 96% of revenue, from contributions and grants awarded by foundations, businesses, and individuals. (These grants included $50,000 from the Lynde and Harry Bradley Foundation, $40,000 from the John M. Olin Foundation, $5,000 from the Gates Foundation, $3,000 from the Vernon K. Krieble Foundation, $3,000 from the Philip M. McKenna Foundation, and $2,500 from the Roe Foundation.) $15,675, or 2%, from interest on savings and temporary cash investments. $12,359, or 2%, from the sale of publications. The remaining revenue came from capital gains on the sale of assets.

Center for Military Readiness (CMR)

P.O. Box 51600
Livonia, MI 48151   **Phone:** (313) 464-9430
USA   **Fax:**   (313) 464-6678

Contact Person: Elaine Donnelly, President.
Officers or Principals: Elaine Donnelly, President ($57,600).
Mission or Interest: Research and distribute information regarding military personnel policies and how they affect military effectiveness and preparedness. "The purpose of the military is to deter aggression or, if necessary, fight and win wars with as few casualties as possible. . . Careers and equal opportunity concerns are important, but in the making of personnel policies **military necessity** must be the primary consideration. . . the armed forces should not be used for political purposes or social experiments which put lives at risk, undermine readiness, or degrade cultural values."
Accomplishments: Influential in the debates regarding women and open homosexuality in the military. Elaine Donnelly served as a member of the 1992 Presidential Commission on the Assignment of Women in the Armed Forces. She is also a former member of the Pentagon's Defense Advisory Committee on Women in the Services. She has testified before the Senate Armed Services Manpower and Personnel Sub-Committee in opposition to the lifting of the ban on women being placed in combat positions.
Total Revenue: 1995 $126,978 6%(2) **Total Expenses:** $98,957 21%/76%/3% **Net Assets:** $32,853
Tax Status: 501(c)(3) **Annual Report:** No. **Employees:** 2
Board of Directors or Trustees: Gen. Robert Barrow, USMC, Ret. (former Commandant, U.S. Marine Corps), Allan Carlson (Pres., Rockford Institute), Vice Adm. Dudley Carlson, USN (Ret.), Linda Chavez (Manhattan Inst.), Brig. Gen. Samuel Cockerham, USA, Ret. (former Commissioner, Presidential Commission on the Assignment of Women in the Armed Forces, PCAWAF), David Horowitz (Pres., Center for the Study of Popular Culture), Beverly LaHaye (Pres., Concerned Women for America), Capt. Eugene "Red" McDaniel, USN, Ret. (Pres., American Defense Inst.), Lt Col. Oliver North, USMC (Ret.), Kate Walsh O'Beirne (former Commissioner, PCAWAF), Col. John Ripley, USMC (Ret.), Phyllis Schlafly (Pres., Eagle Forum), LTG Richard Trefry, USA (Ret.), MSGT Sarah White, USAFR (former Commissioner, PCAWAF).
Periodicals: *CMR Report, CMR Notes*.
Other Information: Established in 1992. Originally called the Coalition for Military Readiness. The Center has a Washington, DC, phone number, (202) 347-5333. The Center received $118,958, or 94% of revenue, from contributions and grants awarded by foundations, businesses, and individuals. (These grants included $1,000 from Concerned Women for America.) $8,020, or 6%, from membership dues.

Center for the New West

600 World Trade Center
1625 Broadway
Denver, CO 80202   **Phone:** (303) 572-5400   **E-Mail:** cnwinfo@newwest.org
USA   **Fax:**   (303) 572-5499

Contact Person: James A. Bane, Managing Director.
Officers or Principals: Robert K. Briggs, Senior Fellow, Regulatory Studies ($67,680); Robert Wurmsted, Director, Communications ($58,126); Colleen Murphy, Senior Fellow, Rural Policy Studies ($58,126); Philip M. Burgess, President; A. Gary Ames, Chairman; Steven T. Halverson, Secretary; Michael P. Glinsky, Treasurer.
Mission or Interest: Promotes free trade, entrepreneurship and free-market economic development, particularly in twenty western states. The Center for the New West is a bipartisan effort, and often assigns to the government a greater role in the economy than most of the other organizations listed.
Accomplishments: U.S. Senator Pete Domenici (R-NM) called the Center, "a significant player on the national scene. . . a real asset to the West." In the fiscal year ending September 1994, the Center spent $1,565,084 on its programs.
Total Revenue: FY ending 9/94 $2,062,037 21%(4) **Total Expenses:** $2,242,390 70%/30%/0% **Net Assets:** (-$118,736)
Products or Services: Papers, reports, policy studies, forums, roundtables and technical assistance.
Tax Status: 501(c)(3) **Annual Report:** Yes. **Employees:** 19   **Citations:** 138:50
Board of Directors or Trustees: Stephen Bartolin (Broadmoor Hotel), Harry Bowes, O. Mark DeMichele (Pres./CEO, Arizona Public Service Co.), Kenneth Hubbard, Thomas Levin, Barbara Nelson (Hubert H. Humphrey School), Kenneth Olson (Goldman Sachs), Sally Shelton, James Stever (U.S. West), Hon. Michael Sullivan (former Governor, D-WY), Solomon Trujillo (U.S. West Marketing), John Naisbitt (Megatrends, Inc.), Fred Palmer (Western Fuels Assoc.).

Periodicals: *Points West Chronicle* (newsletter).
Internships: Yes, for graduate and undergraduate students.
Other Information: Established in 1989. Chairman A. Gary Ames is the President & CEO of U.S. West Communications and two other members of the Board also work for U.S. West. In the period from 1989-1993, U.S. West contributed $3,820,500 to the Center. The Center received $1,151,104, or 56% of revenue, from gifts and grants awarded by foundations, businesses, and individuals. $672,730, or 33%, from contract research fees. $110,232, or 5%, from membership dues. $98,268, or 5%, from briefings fees. The remaining revenue came from the sale of publications, conferences, interest on savings and temporary cash investments, and other miscellaneous sources.

Center for Policy Studies

201 Sirrine Hall
Clemson University
Clemson, SC 29634   **Phone:** (803) 656-1346
USA   **Fax:**   (803) 656-4532

Contact Person: Prof. Bruce Yandle, Director.
Mission or Interest: Public policy institute affiliated with Clemson University that focuses on market-based solutions to public policy programs.
Accomplishments: Produced influential studies on the Safe Drinking Water Act and other issues
Tax Status: 501(c)(3)
Other Information: Affiliated with and incorporated as part of Clemson University. In 1995 the Center received $7,500 from the Claude R. Lambe Charitable Foundation, and $5,000 from the Roe Foundation.

Center for Rebuilding America's Schools

800 E. Northwest Highway, Suite 1080
Palatine, IL 60067   **Phone:** (847) 202-3060
USA   **Fax:**   (847) 202-9799

Contact Person: Joseph Walsh, Executive Director.
Mission or Interest: Dedicated to recreating the American school system based on 'school choice.' Advocates school-voucher plans that include private and religious schools
Tax Status: 501(c)(3)
Other Information: Originally a project of the Heartland Institute, it is now incorporated separately but is still located at the same address as the Heartland Institute.

Center for Security Policy (CSP)

1250 24th St., N.W., Suite 350
Washington, DC 20037   **Phone:** (202) 466-0515   **E-Mail:** info@security-policy.org
USA   **Fax:**   (202) 466-0518   **Internet:** www.security-policy.org

Contact Person: Rinelda Bliss, Associate Director of Development.
Officers or Principals: Frank Gaffney, Jr., President/Treasurer ($127,115); Rinelda Bliss, Associate Director of Development ($73,962); Amir Morgan, Paul T. Iarrobino, Research Associates.
Mission or Interest: "To stimulate and inform the national and international debate about all aspects of security policy, notably those policies bearing on the foreign, defense, economic, financial and technology interests of the United States." Rates members of Congress according to their voting records on defense matters.
Accomplishments: Testified at various congressional hearings. In 1995 Center members testified on behalf of; the dangers of Soviet-designed nuclear power plants in Cuba, the Middle East peace process, troop deployment in Bosnia, and other topics. Provided information and opposition to Clinton appointees Morton Halpern, Strobe Talbott, Derek Shearer and Sam Brown. The Center has recently been cited in *Foreign Affairs, Los Angeles Times, Washington Inquirer, Washington Times, Agence France Presse, National Journal, Insight, Defense News, Wall Street Journal, Arizona Republic, Business Week*, and others. In 1994 the Center spent $643,019 on its programs.
Total Revenue: 1994 $884,808   14%(5)   **Total Expenses:** $829,337 78%/9%/13% **Net Assets:** $19,257
Products or Services: Automated fax update system. "The World this Week" public television programming. Annual "National Security Scorecard" rating members of Congress. Annual "Keeper of the Flame" award. 1995's recipient was Pres. Ronald Reagan. Previous recipients have included former Defense Secretary Casper Weinberger, Sen. Malcolm Wallop, Margaret Thatcher, Steve Forbes, and Sen. Jon Kyl.
Tax Status: 501(c)(3) **Annual Report:** Yes. **Employees:** 5   **Citations:** 93:67
Board of Directors or Trustees: Douglas Feith, Charles Kupperman (Empower America). Advisors include: Elliott Abrams (Assistant Secretary, Inter-American Affairs, 1985-89), William Bennett (Empower America), Midge Decter (Inst. on Religion and Public Life), Edwin Feulner, Jr. (Heritage Found.), Hon. Alan Keyes (Ambassador to the U.N., 1985-87), Hon. Jeane Kirkpatrick (Ambassador to the U.N., 1981-85), Hon. John Lehman, Jr. (Secretary of the Navy, 1981-87), Hon. J. William Middendorf, II (Ambassador to the Organization of American States, 1981-85), Joshua Muravchik, Daniel Oliver, Orson Swindle, Edward Teller, Hon. Curtin Winsor, Jr. (Ambassador to Costa Rica, 1983-85).

Internships: Yes, up to eight graduate and undergraduate students during each semester and the summer.
Other Information: Established in 1988. Affiliated with the Committee on U.S. Interest in the Middle East, and the Coalition to Defend America. The Center received $694,171, or 78% of revenue, from contributions and grants awarded by foundations (56%), businesses (32%), and individuals (9%). (These grants included $125,000 from the Sarah Scaife Foundation, and $15,000 from the Aequus Institute. In 1995, $100,000 from the Carthage Foundation, $50,000 from the Lynde and Harry Bradley Foundation, $25,000 from the William H. Donner Foundation, $25,000 from the John M. Olin Foundation, $8,000 from the Sunmark Foundation, and $5,000 from the Forbes Foundation.) $150,000, or 17%, from television production. $39,860, or 4%, from fund raising events. The remaining revenue came from subscriptions.

Center for Strategic and International Studies (CSIS)

1800 K St., N.W., Suite 400
Washington, DC 20006   **Phone:** (202) 887-0200   **E-Mail:** info@csis.org
USA   **Fax:** (202) 775-3199   **Internet:** http:/www.csis.org

Contact Person: Dr. David M. Abshire, President.
Officers or Principals: Dr. David M. Abshire, President ($258,727); Richard Fairbanks, Managing Director, Domestic and International Issues ($135,913); Douglas M. Johnston, Jr., Executive Vice President/COO ($130,728); Anthony A. Smith, Executive Vice President ($128,804); Amb. Anne Armstrong, Chairman; Maurice R. Greenberg, Vice Chairman; William A. Schreyer, Chairman, Executive Committee; Judy L. Harbaugh, Secretary; David G. Hunt, Treasurer; William J. Taylor, Jr., John N. Yochelson, Vice Presidents. (Salaries reflect a nine-month fiscal year, see Other Information.)
Mission or Interest: Research institution focusing on international policy and security issues, and, to a lesser extent, domestic policy and economic issues. "Its goal is to inform and shape selected policy decisions in government and the private sector to meet the increasingly complex and difficult challenges that leaders will confront in the next century. It achieves its mission by generating strategic analysis, by convening policy makers and other influential parties, and by building leadership structures for policy action."
Accomplishments: CSIS hosts over 700 meetings, seminars, and conferences each year. The Center operates through various program areas, projects, membership groups, and endowed chairs. Endowed chairs include the Henry A. Kissinger Chair in International Politics, Diplomatic History, and National Security Policy currently held by Walter Laquer, and the William E. Simon Chair in Political Economy, Sidney Weintraub. CSIS operates the Honolulu-based Pacific Forum CSIS to research and analyze issues regarding Asia and the Pacific Rim (see separate listing). Bob Dole, the 1996 Republican Presidential candidate, made his first major campaign foreign policy speech at a CSIS forum. CSIS counselors include William E. Brock, Harold Brown, Zbigniew Brzezinski, Henry A. Kissinger, and James R. Schlesinger. In the shortened fiscal year from January through September 1995, CSIS spent $8,280,372 on its programs.
Total Revenue: FY running from 1/95 through 9/95 $15,784,340 20%(2)   **Total Expenses:** $12,134,334 68%/24%/8%
Net Assets: $20,256,942
Products or Services: Numerous books listed in a catalog and via e-mail at books@csis.org. Conferences, seminars, lectures, papers, studies, and reports.
Tax Status: 501(c)(3) **Employees:** 276   **Citations:** 690:13
Board of Directors or Trustees: Lester Aberthal, Jr., Dwayne Andreas, James Baker, III (Secretary of State, 1989-1992), William Brock, Harold Brown, Zbigniew Brzezinski (National Security Advisor to Pres. Carter), Joseph Gorman, Richard Green, Jr., Carla Hill (U.S. Trade Representative, 1989-93), Ray Hunt, James Kelly, Henry Kissinger (Secretary of State, 1973-1977), Leonard Marks, Homer Neal, John Pepper, Charles Sanders, John Sawhill, James Schlesinger, Brent Scowcroft, Robert Strauss, Murray Weidenbaum (Center for the Study of American Business), Dolores Wharton, R. James Woolsey, Stanley Zax.
Periodicals: *Washington Quarterly* (quarterly journal), *news@csis.dc* (quarterly newsletter).
Internships: Yes.
Other Information: Founded in 1962. CSIS changed its fiscal year in 1995 to begin on October 1 and end September 30. Consequently the 1995 fiscal year was only nine months, from January 1 to September 30. CSIS received $14,179,058, or 90% of revenue, from contributions and grants awarded by foundations, businesses, and individuals. (These grants included $650,000 over three years from the Pew Charitable Trusts, $200,000 from the Scaife Family Foundation, $150,000 from the Smith Richardson Foundation, $50,000 from the John M. Olin Foundation, and $25,000 from the Samuel Roberts Noble Foundation. In 1994, $470,000 from the Sarah Scaife Foundation. In 1993, $650,000 from the Starr Foundation.) $538,015, or 3%, from dividends and interest from securities. $472,376, or 3%, from contracted research paid by the federal government. $236,332, or 1%, from capital gains on the sale of securities. The remaining revenue came from the sale of publications and conferences.

Center for the Study of American Business (CSAB)

Washington University
Campus Box 1208
One Brookings Dr.
St. Louis, MO 63130-4899   **Phone:** (314) 935-5630   **E-Mail:** bat@wuecon.wustl.edu
USA   **Fax:** (314) 935-5688   **Internet:** http://csab.wustl.edu

Contact Person: Robert Batterson, Communications Director .
Officers or Principals: Murray L. Weidenbaum, Ph.D., Director; Kenneth Chilton, Ph.D., Director; Melinda Warren, Assistant Director.

Mission or Interest: Conducts scholarly research on issues affecting the American business system. Focus on environmental and safety regulations, labor relations, management issues, and taxation and fiscal issues.

Accomplishments: In 1995 the Center published "Restructuring Environmental Big Business," a study asserting that the large environmental organizations had hurt themselves financially and in terms of influence by focusing on alarmist issues and expanding their own bureaucracies. The study was featured in *The New York Times*. The Center also published "Environmental Justice in the City of St. Louis," a study contradicting the claims of the 'environmental justice' advocates who allege that racism, rather than the dynamics of the housing market, cause minorities to be more likely to live near industrial pollution. Dr. Weidenbaum testified before the House Ways and Means Committee on behalf a proposal to allow unlimited tax-free savings while eliminating the income tax and instituting a "modified consumption tax". The center has a national reputation for its work on the costs of federal regulation and the need for cost effective approaches. Center research also contributed to the 1986 Tax Reform Act

Products or Services: Occasional Papers, Contemporary Issues series, and Working Papers.

Tax Status: 501(c)(3)   **Annual Report:** Yes.   **Employees:** 12

Board of Directors or Trustees: Adjunct Scholars includes professors: James Burnham (Duquesne Univ.), Thomas DiLorenzo (Loyola College), David Henderson (Naval Postgraduate School), William Lash, III (George Mason Univ. School of Law), Dwight Lee (Univ. of Georgia), Richard McKenzie (Univ. of California, Irvine), Leo Troy (Rutgers Univ.), Richard Vedder (Ohio Univ.).

Internships: yes, in environmental policy.

Other Information: Established in 1975. Murray Weidenbaum was Chairman of Economic Advisors under President Ronald Reagan, 1981-1882. CSAB is part of, and incorporated under, Washington University. In 1995 the Center received $100,000 from the John M. Olin Foundation, $7,000 from the Sunmark Foundation, and $5,000 from the Philip M. McKenna Foundation.

Center for Study of Market Alternatives (CSMA)

P.O. Box 15749
Boise, ID 83715
USA

Phone: (208) 368-7811
Fax: (208) 368-0668

Contact Person: Barbara L. Sall, Facilitator.

Officers or Principals: Robert Rathbone, Chairman; Allen Dalton, Director.

Mission or Interest: To "transmit information on how the free-market makes for economic well-being and social harmony."

Accomplishments: Cited in news articles, published editorials. Director Dalton received media attention for an op-ed he wrote that appeared in the *Idaho Press-Tribune*. He criticized Republicans for using the rhetoric of liberty, but failing to vote or legislate that way. Idaho's then Republican state chairman responded and the debate drew wider attention.

Total Revenue: 1995 less than $25,000

Tax Status: 501(c)(3)   **Annual Report:** No.   **Employees:** 3

Board of Directors or Trustees: Harry Bettis (Foundation Press), several members associated with the Symms Fruit Ranch, Dan Symms, Dick Symms, and Jim Mertz. Academic advisors include Sen. Steve Symms (R-ID) and Prof. Steve Hanke (Johns Hopkins Univ.).

Periodicals: *Freedom Messenger* (monthly), *Classical Liberal* (bi-monthly), and other intermittent studies.

Other Information: Established in 1976.

Center for the Study of Popular Culture / *Heterodoxy*

P.O. Box 67398
Los Angeles, CA 90067
USA

Phone: (310) 843-3699
Fax: (310) 843-3692

E-Mail: 76712.3274@compuserve.com
Internet: http://www.cspc.org

Contact Person: David Horowitz, President.

Officers or Principals: John Howard, General Counsel ($95,200); Peter Collier, Director ($91,850); David Horowitz, President ($91,840); Allyson Tucker, Director, Individual Rights Foundation; Wallace Nunn, Chairman; David West, Vice Chair; Kevin Teasley, Treasurer; Judy Magilnick, Secretary.

Mission or Interest: Study American culture, particularly the popular media (television, movies, etc.) and academia. Special focus on 'political correctness' in American institutions.

Accomplishments: The style of *Heterodoxy*, reminiscent of the radical magazines of the 1960's and early 70's, has brought them much attention and many critics. In 1996 the Center co-hosted a conference with the National Review Institute at the Paramount Studios. This "Images of Ourselves" conference brought together entertainment industry professionals, their critics, and political analysts. In 1995 the Center began the "Educate America Project" on education reform issues. This Project publishes a newsletter, *Report Card*. In 1994 the Center spent $2,550,085 on its programs. The largest program, with expenditures of $415,038, was the Individual Rights Foundation, a legal project protecting First Amendment Rights. $394,287 was spent on *Heterodoxy*. $247,449 was spent on *The Defender*, the publication of the Individual Rights Foundation. $203,672 was spent on *COMINT*, a publication of the Center's Committee on Media Integrity, that monitors the media with a special focus on Public Television. Other programs included investigative journalism training, writing, and speaking engagements.

Total Revenue: 1994 $3,002,416 84%(2)   **Total Expenses:** $2,550,085 61%/10%/29%   **Net Assets:** $970,144

Products or Services: <u>Deconstructing the Left</u>, <u>The National Endowments</u>, <u>Liberal Racism</u>, and other books. Video and audio tapes. Litigation.

Tax Status: 501(c)(3)   **Citations:** 92:68

Periodicals: *Heterodoxy* (monthly tabloid), *The Defender* (bimonthly journal), *COMINT* (magazine), *Center News* (quarterly newsletter), and *Report Card* (bimonthly journal).
Other Information: Established in 1989. Peter Collier and David Horowitz are the authors of <u>Destructive Generations</u> and <u>Deconstructing the Left</u>. Both were prominent leftists in the 60's and early 70's, and published the leftist investigative journal, *Ramparts*. The two 'left the fold' after being alarmed by the Left's tolerance of violence by radical groups such as the Black Panthers, cultural nihilism, and the Left's lack of outrage at and continued support of communist governments and armies worldwide despite repeated atrocities. Their final break with the Left occurred when they wrote "Farewell To All That," an op-ed published in *The Washington Post* that publicly announced that they had voted for President Reagan, and explained why. In 1997 Horowitz's autobiography, <u>Radical Son: A Generation Odyssey</u> (The Free Press), was released. The Center received $2,522,178, or 84% of revenue, from contributions and grants awarded by foundations, businesses, and individuals. (These grants included $500,000 from the Sarah Scaife Foundation. In 1995, $545,000 from the Lynde and Harry Bradley Foundation, $275,000 from the Scaife Family Foundation, $250,000 from the Carthage Foundation, $200,000 from the John M. Olin Foundation, $50,000 from the Castle Rock Foundation, and $2,500 from the Forbes Foundation.) $373,965, or 12%, from membership dues. The remaining revenue came from conference fees, publication and paraphernalia sales, and other miscellaneous sources.

Center for the Study of Public Choice

George Mason University
Georges Hall, Mail Stop 1D3
Fairfax, VA 22030   **Phone:** (703) 993-2315
USA   **Fax:**   (703) 993-2323

Contact Person: Dr. Robert Tollison, Director.
Officers or Principals: Dr. James Buchanan, Director.
Mission or Interest: Research and education institute dedicated to using the methodology of 'Public Choice.' Public Choice is the application of economic principles and motivations to political questions - such as voting patterns, lobbying activities, and the operation of public bureaucracies. Public Choice is usually associated with Nobel Prize-winning economist James Buchanan, who, with co-author Gordon Tullock, wrote <u>The Calculus of Consent</u>, a seminal work in Public Choice. Other prominent economists in this school of thought include Dr. William Niskanen (Cato Inst.), and Dr. Robert Tollison
Tax Status: 501(c)(3)
Other Information: Affiliated with and incorporated as a part of George Mason University. In 1994-95 the Center received $100,000 from the Sarah Scaife Foundation, $25,000 from the John M. Olin Foundation, $7,000 from the John William Pope Foundation, and $6,750 from the Earhart Foundation.

Center for the Study of Taxation (CST)

695 Town Center Dr., Suite 1460
Costa Mesa, CA 92626   **Phone:** (714) 641-8067
USA   **Fax:**   (714) 641-3128

Contact Person: Patricia M. Soldano, President.
Mission or Interest: "Dedicated to preserving a healthy economic and tax climate that will be beneficial to all Americans. Concentrating on transfer taxes, CST analyzes and reports on the economic impact of legislation and administrative initiatives, provides information about potentially adverse or beneficial changes in law, and supports research on economic and tax subjects of interest and concern to individuals, families, and family businesses."
Products or Services: "Federal Estate and Gift Taxes: Are They Worth the Cost?", "Federal Estate Tax Impact Survey", Federal Transfer Taxation: A Study in Social Cost" and other studies
Other Information: Established in 1992.

Center for World Capitalism

(see the James Madison Institute)

Center of the American Experiment

12 S. 6th St., Suite 1024
Minneapolis, MN 55402   **Phone:** (612) 338-3605
USA   **Fax:**   (612) 338-3621   **Internet:** www.amexp.org

Contact Person: Mitchell B. Pearlstein, President.
Officers or Principals: Mitchell B. Pearlstein, President; Katherine A. Kersten, Chairman; Bruce A. Thomson, Vice President; K. Jeffrey Dahlberg, Treasurer.
Mission or Interest: "Brings conservative and alternative ideas to bear on the most difficult issues facing Minnesota and the nation."
Accomplishments: Former British Prime Minister Margaret Thatcher is scheduled as keynote speaker at the Center's annual dinner in May 1997. 1996's keynote speaker was William Kristol (*Weekly Standard*). Kristol said that the Center "was the best" of the state-based conservative policy organizations. Breakfast and Luncheon Forum Series has included Marvin Olasky, Mona Charen, Clint Bolick, Robert Woodson, Grover Norquist, and others.

Total Revenue: 1995 $521,268 42%(3) **Total Expenses:** $534,745 **Net Assets:** $44,907
Products or Services: Tim Penny and Vin Weber Distinguished Fellows Program, named after the two former Congressional Representatives, Penny - a moderate Democrat and Weber - a conservative Republican. (Penny had a lifetime American Conservative Union rating of approximately 30%, Weber's was 85%.) Certain Truths: Essays About Our Families, Children and Culture, book.
Tax Status: 501(c)(3)   **Annual Report:** Yes.   **Citations:** 59:92
Board of Directors or Trustees: Peter Bell, Linda Rios Brook (KLGT-TV), William Cooper (TCF Financial Corp.), Ronald Eibensteiner, Esperanza Guerrero-Anderson, Lowell Hellervik, John Hinderaker, State Sen. Gen Olson (R-Minnetrista, MN), Dean Riese, Steven Rothmeier, William Thomas, James Van Houten, Michael Wigley, Stephen Young. Advisors include: Hon. Rudy Boschwitz (former Senator, R-MN), Linda Chavez, Mayor Norm Coleman, Dave Durenberger, Chester E. Finn, Jr., Bill Frenzel, Roy Innis (Congress of Racial Equality), Prof. Glenn Loury (Boston Univ.), Michael Novak (AEI), Kate O'Beirne (*National Review*), Barbara Dafoe Whitehead, Robert Woodson (National Center for Neighborhood Enterprise).
Other Information: Established in 1990. Member of the State Policy Network. The Center received $402,216, or 77% of revenue, from contributions and grants awarded by foundations, businesses, and individuals. (These grants included $70,000 from the Lynde and Harry Bradley Foundation, and $3,000 from the Roe Foundation.) $59,536, or 11%, from conference admission fees. $55,669, or 11%, from membership fees. The remaining revenue came from the sale of publications and interest on savings and temporary cash investments.

Center on the Family in America
(see Rockford Institute)

Center on Religion & Society
(see Rockford Institute)

Central News Service
27036 Azul Dr.
Capistrano Beach, CA 92624   **Phone:**   (714) 240-8472   **Internet:** http://home.earthlink.net/~marceric/index.htm
USA

Contact Person: Marc Eric Ely.
Mission or Interest: "Raising the awareness of average Americans as to the true history of America, for the purpose of the re-establishment of a legal government in the U.S."
Accomplishments: Claims to have "spearheaded the re-organization of the Libertarian Party of Washington State, 1980; Assisted in the production of the Future of Freedom Conference, 1986; Organized the Free Territory of Ely-Chatelaine in 1975; instituted the Nation of America, 1993; incorporated and secured nonprofit tax exempt status for the Mildred Rose Memorial Foundation, Inc., and organized four homeless shelters in Orange County, CA. Published the *Territorial Herald*, 1981 to 1991."
Products or Services: Publications including "The Constitution Papers" and "Banned in America."
Tax Status: Unincorporated.
Periodicals: *The American National* (newsletter).

Centre for the New Europe (CNE)
Roularta Media Building
Research Park, De Haak
B-1731 Zellik   **Phone:**   (32-2) 467-5730   **E-Mail:** info@cne.be
BELGIUM   **Fax:**   (32-2) 467-5605   **Internet:** http://www.cne.be

Mission or Interest: Pan-European policy research institute that bases advocates "economic growth and entrepreneurial initiative in an ordered society based on personal liberty, creativity and responsibility."
Products or Services: From Welfare State to Social State, Capitalism with Capital: The Recipe for Full Employment, and other books and publications
Other Information: Established in 1994.

CEO America
208 W. Main
Bentonville, AR 72712   **Phone:** (501) 273-6957   **E-Mail:** CEOA@aol.com
USA   **Fax:**   (501) 273-9362

Contact Person: Fritz S. Steiger, President.
Officers or Principals: Fritz S. Steiger, President; James M. Mansour, Chairman; Robert Aguirre, Vice President.
Mission or Interest: CEO stands for Children's Educational Opportunity Foundation. To coordinate the expansion and replication of privately funded voucher programs across the United States of America in order to provide low-income children with greater educational opportunities."

Accomplishments: Over 22 programs established. Along with other similar programs, such as Educational CHOICE Trust, they have helped over 10,000 children attend private schools; with another 16,500 children wait-listed. These programs have attracted the attention of notable charitable organizations such as the Walton Family Foundation (the philanthropy of the Wal-Mart founders), as well as several foundations connected to National Basketball Association Teams. In 1996 CEO hosted the "First Presidential Golf Challenge" which raised $1.2 million. The golf challenge came about after Democrats filibustered $5,000,000 in scholarships as part of a bill President Clinton threatened to veto. Shortly after, President Clinton raised $76,000 for his daughter's private school by auctioning a round of golf with himself. "President Clinton challenged all of us to play golf for kids when he played golf for Chelsea's school," said the organizer

Tax Status: 501(c)(3) **Annual Report:** No. **Employees:** 2

Board of Directors or Trustees: James Leininger, M.D., George Noga (Trans America Financial Group), John Andrews, Jr., Jack Antonini, John Walton, Robert Aguirre, Thomas Lyles, J. Patrick Rooney (Chair., Golden Rule Insurance Co.), Larry Walker (Publisher/CEO, *San Antonio Express News*), John Walton.

Periodicals: *The Voucher Voice* (quarterly newsletter).

Internships: No.

Other Information: CEO America credits the idea of giving privately funded vouchers to inner-city schools to J. Patrick Rooney, Chairman of Golden Rule Insurance Company. Rooney started the Educational CHOICE Charitable Trust in Indianapolis, IN.

CHAMPION Economics & Business Association (CEBA)

P.O. Box 11471
Lynchburg, VA 24506   **Phone:**   (804) 385-0151
USA   **Fax:**   same   **Internet:** http://www.pathway.net/ceba

Contact Person: Robert N. Mateer, President.

Officers or Principals: George Champion, Chairman Emeritus; William P. Snavely, Vice President.

Mission or Interest: "To develop a value-based, free-market, limited-government message, but only as undergirded by our Judeo-Christian values, to pastors and teachers, those who influence our youth. The future of our nation can only be assured if our youth understand these principles."

Accomplishments: CEBA has sold over 9,000 copies of its video series, including 1,600 copies to churches and 300 to colleges

Products or Services: "Economics, Freedom & Values" video series featuring Prof. Ronald H. Nash with Prof. G. Dirk Mateer (Grove City College), Dr. James Gwartney (Florida State Univ.), Michael Novak (AEI), Prof. Walter E. Williams (George Mason Univ.), and Nobel Laureate Dr. James Buchanan. "Liberty: Its Preservation" video series featuring Jack Kemp, Dr. Paul Craig Roberts (Inst. for Political Economy), Dr. Robert Krieble (Krieble Inst.), Paul Weyrich (Free Congress Found.), Phyllis Schlafly (Eagle Forum), and others.

Tax Status: 501(c)(3) **Annual Report:** No. **Employees:** 1

Board of Directors or Trustees: William Ball, Robert Cannada, Jerry Falwell (Chancellor, Liberty Univ.), Dr. James Gills, M.D., Prof. James Gwartney (Florida State Univ.), Dr. D. James Kennedy (Coral Ridge Ministries), Dr, Robert H. Krieble (Krieble Inst.), Dr. Ronald Nash (Reformed Theological Seminary), Michael Novak (AEI), Dr. Paul Craig Roberts (Inst. for Political Economy), Phyllis Schlafly (Eagle Forum), Prof. Walter Williams (George Mason Univ.).

Periodicals: *Christian Perspectives: A Journal of Free Enterprise* (biannual magazine).

Internships: No.

Other Information: Established in 1988 as the Contemporary Economics and Business Association. Affiliated with the Liberty University School of Business and Government.

Charles B McFadden Co.

P.O. Box 2268
Winter Park, FL 32790   **Phone:**   (407) 629-4548
USA   **Fax:**   (407) 629-0762

Contact Person: Stephen M. Combs, Publisher.

Officers or Principals: Robert F. Dixon, Vice President/Marketing; Shelby A. Rallis, Director of Education; Ronald D. Falkner, Art Director.

Mission or Interest: Information about free-market economics and America's cultural heritage. Publishes *The Economic Monitor*, a launching pad for new economic writers

Products or Services: "The Florida Media Guides," guides to conservative media personnel in Florida.

Tax Status: For profit. **Annual Report:** No. **Employees:** 4

Board of Directors or Trustees: Not yet.

Periodicals: *The Economic Monitor* (quarterly).

Internships: Yes, for economics or finance majors in the Orlando area.

Other Information: Established in 1992.

Charles G. Koch Charitable Foundation

1450 G St., N.W., Suite 445
Washington, DC 20005   **Phone:**   (202) 393-2354
USA   **Fax:**   (202) 393-2355

Contact Person: Wanda L. Stokes, Foundations Assistant.
Officers or Principals: Richard Fink, President ($0); Elizabeth B. Koch, Vice President ($0); Victoria Hughes, Vice President ($0); Vonda Holliman, Secretary/Treasurer; Charles G. Koch, Director.
Mission or Interest: Grant-making foundation that includes conservative and free-market organizations in its awards.
Accomplishments: In 1995 the Foundation awarded $1,438,595 in grants. Recipients included: two grants totaling $475,000 for the Center for Market Processes, $50,000 each for the Pacific Research Institute and Heritage Foundation, $24,484 for the Citizens for a Sound Economy Foundation, $16,000 for the Philanthropy Roundtable, $12,000 for the Leadership Institute, and $10,000 each for the Federalist Society and Heartland Institute. The Foundation also spent $494,312 on its Youth Entrepreneurship Program that teaches business skills to students in Kansas. The Foundation also made $15,625 in venture capital grants to youths in Kansas.
Total Revenue: 1995 $10,705,434 **Total Expenses:** $2,060,885 **Net Assets:** $19,080,412 16%(3)
Tax Status: 501(c)(3)
Other Information: Established in 1981. Charles Koch is chairman and chief executive officer of Koch Industries, which is an outgrowth of Rock Island Oil and Refining Company, founded by his father, Fred C. Koch (1900-1967). Fred Koch was also a donor to the David H. Koch Charitable Foundation. Located at the same address and shares the same officers with the Claude R. Lambe Charitable Foundation. The Foundation also has a Kansas office; P.O. Box 2256, Wichita, KS 67201, (316) 828-5552. The Foundation received $10,059,154, or 94% of revenue, from contributions and grants. $361,040, or 3%, from capital gains on the sale of assets. $224,702, or 2%, from dividends and interest from securities. The remaining revenue came from interest on savings and other miscellaneous sources. The Foundation held $10,527,873, or 55% of assets, in savings and temporary cash investments. $5,143,237, or 27%, in "Tactical Asset Funds."

Chicken Little Society

9175-D, S.W., 20th St.
Boca Raton, FL 33428   **Phone:** (407) 482-0159
USA   **Fax:** (407) 479-0560

Contact Person: Tully M. Robison, Director.
Mission or Interest: "Research and education in the wise use of resources."
Total Revenue: 1993 less than $25,000
Products or Services: Annual awards for "least substantiated environmental catastrophes".
Tax Status: 501(c)(3) **Annual Report:** Yes. **Employees:** 1
Board of Directors or Trustees: Joseph Rosenbaum, Leona Brehm.
Periodicals: *Chicken Little Society Newsletter*.
Internships: No.
Other Information: Established in 1992.

Children's Educational Opportunity Foundation (CEO Michigan)

P.O. Box 230078
Grand Rapids, MI 49523   **Phone:** (616) 459-2222
USA

Officers or Principals: Dick and Betsy DeVos, Co-Chairs.
Mission or Interest: Foundation that awards scholarships to disadvantaged children, enabling them to attend the private school of their choice in Michigan
Tax Status: 501(c)(3)
Other Information: Founded in 1991 by Michigan State Senate Majority Leader Dick Posthumus (R) as the Vandenberg Foundation. Co-Chair Betsy DeVos was the Michigan Republican State Chair.

Chinese Family Alliance (CFA)

450 Taraval St., Suite 246
San Francisco, CA 94116   **Phone:** (415) 337-1007
USA   **Fax:** (415) 587-4338

Contact Person: Rev. Raymond Kwong, Executive Director.
Officers or Principals: Grace Fong, Administrative Assistant.
Mission or Interest: Traditional family values and anti-abortion organization with an emphasis on serving the Asian community in America. "Most social problems can be traced back to a weakened family structure. . . Chinese have been able to survive and thrive in economic and social hardship primarily because of a strong family structure. Unfortunately, Chinese organizations tend to be silent or passive regarding many of the issues and influences that are destroying the moral fabric of our society."
Accomplishments: Over 1,200 members. Have served as a bridge between religious and traditional values groups and the English, Cantonese, and Mandarin speaking Chinese population in the United States. CFA has appeared on CNN News, CBN News, Family News in Focus, Asian Week, and other media outlets
Tax Status: 501(c)(3)
Board of Directors or Trustees: Tom Fong, Henry Ho, John Lee, Bill Tam, Ph.D. Advisors include: Gary Gin, M.D., Pastor Joseph Wong, Melvin Wong, Ph.D., Cecilia Yau, Richard Yen, M.D., Ph.D., Frank Yuen.
Periodicals: *Chinese Family Voice* (quarterly). **Internships:** No.
Other Information: The CFA is affiliated with *Kwong's News Digest*.

Choice and Charges, All Schools

8530 Bradshaw
Lenexa, KS 66215   **Phone:**   (913) 888-4455
USA

Contact Person: John McDonough.
Mission or Interest: "Discontinuance of monopoly schooling. Free markets in school choice and charges for public schools. State aid only for those passing means tests (low income). . . Public schools and their users should be treated like private schools and their students. State and local budgets are being bashed by free public education. All who can afford to should pay user's charges for public schools."
Other Information: Called the Conservative Values Coalition until 1991.

Christ and Country Courier

6020 Old Harford Rd.
Baltimore, MD 21214   **Phone:**   (301) 426-8427
USA   **Fax:**   (301) 574-0793

Contact Person: Pastor Robert T. Woodworth, President.
Officers or Principals: Benjamin J. Woodworth, Press Owner; Claudia Barlow, Vice President.
Mission or Interest: Christ and Country Church publishes *Christ and Country Courier*; primarily biblical morality, some articles on free enterprise.
Accomplishments: Over thirty-five years of broadcasting, publishing, writing, speaking. Service on several Boards: Maryland Council on Education, Maryland Right to Life, United Christian Citizens, Inc.
Products or Services: Books, tracts, periodicals, Church services, counseling.
Tax Status: 501(c)(3) **Employees:** 10
Periodicals: *Christ and Country Courier*.
Internships: No.
Other Information: Printed by C& C Press.

Christian Action Network (CAN)

P.O. Box 606
Forest, VA 24551   **Phone:**   (800) 835-5795
USA

Contact Person: Jim Mohr, Executive Director.
Officers or Principals: Martin Mawyer, President/Founder; T. Carroll, Chairman.
Mission or Interest: Conservative Christian group that teaches its members how to engage in lobbying.
Accomplishments: Claims over 200,000 supporters nationwide. "Has successfully lobbied the U.S. Congress on issues pertaining to homosexual rights, prayer in public schools, the National Endowment for the Arts, and many other pro-family issues."
Products or Services: Numerous publications and guides on how to contact and lobby elected representatives and government officials. "Home Lobbyist Companion," a glossy manual written by the American Conservative Union's David Keene. Numerous booklets, pamphlets, and video tapes.
Tax Status: 501(c)(4)
Board of Directors or Trustees: David William, Roger Ott, Dr. Jim Dracup, Martin Mawyer.
Periodicals: *Family Alert* (monthly newsletter).
Other Information: Established in 1990.

Christian Anti-Communism Crusade

227 E. 6th St.
Long Beach, CA 90802   **Phone:**   (213) 437-0941
USA   **Fax:**   (213) 432-2074

Contact Person: Ella Doorn, Secretary.
Officers or Principals: Dr. Fred Schwarz, President/Treasurer ($84,163); Rev. James Colbert, Vice President/Chairman ($77,903); Ella Doorn, Secretary ($22,186).
Mission or Interest: "Anti-Communism educational services within the U.S.A. and abroad."
Accomplishments: One of the first and longest-lived anti-communist organizations, the Christian Anti-Communism Crusade became the model for numerous other organizations. In 1995 the Crusade spent $548,755 on its programs.
Total Revenue: 1995 $651,077 (-15%)(6) **Total Expenses:** $774,920 71%/27%/3% **Net Assets:** $1,026,119
Products or Services: Literature, audio tapes, video tapes, and seminars. You Can Trust the Communists (to be Communists) book by Dr. Fred Schwarz, first published in 1960 with over thirteen printings and over 1 million copies in print. "Why Communism Kills" and other pamphlets.
Tax Status: 501(c)(3) **Annual Report:** Yes. **Employees:** 20   **Citations:** 4:196

Board of Directors or Trustees: Floyd Burroughs, Ruth Burroughs, Ellie Riggs, Dorothy Plowman, Robert Sackett, Dr. John Schwarz, Joel Colbert, Dr. P.W. Sorenson, Dr. John Whitehall, Harry Anderson, Susan Colbert Wright, Katherine Taylor.
Periodicals: Bimonthly newsletter.
Internships: Yes.
Other Information: Established in 1955. The Crusade received $610,883, or 93% of gross revenue, from contributions and grants awarded by foundations, businesses, and individuals. (These grants included $10,000 from the Sunmark Foundation. In 1994, $14,000 from the Milliken Foundation.) $40,293, or 6%, from dividends and interest from securities. The remaining revenue came from interest on savings. The Crusade lost $3,551 on the sale of securities.

Christian Coalition

1801 Sara Dr., Suite L
Chesapeake, VA 23320   **Phone:** (757) 424-2630   **E-Mail:** letters@cc.org
USA   **Fax:** (757) 424-9068   **Internet:** http://www.cc.org/

Contact Person: Ken Hill, Chief Operating Officer.
Officers or Principals: Ralph Reed, Jr., former Executive Director ($122,556); Judy Liebert, Secretary ($62,878); Pat Robertson, President ($0). (Salaries are from 1993.)
Mission or Interest: Prominent organization of religious conservatives. Lobbies and organizes to influence public policy. "Formed. . . to speak out against anti-Christian bigotry and to make our government more responsive to the concerns of Christians and pro-family Americans."
Accomplishments: Claims more than 1.9 million members. In 1997 the Coalition announced the "Samaritan Project" that pledged to raise $1million that year to aid inner-city churches that "minister to at-risk youth." The Project aims to increase to $10 million in three years. In 1996 the Coalition sponsored 400 "Citizen Action Training Schools" nationwide to train grassroots activists; distributed 34 million voter guides; established 737 new chapters in all 50 states; distributed 17 million "Congressional Scorecards." Awarded $750,000 to 25 churches in the South to rebuild after fires. In 1994 it spent an estimated $1.4 million to defeat the Clinton health care plan; the largest lobbying effort by the Coalition. In 1995 the Coalition spent $15,646,690 on its programs. The largest program, with expenditures of $9,590,371, was legislative affairs.
Total Revenue: 1995 $19,745,323 16%(2) **Total Expenses:** $19,459,499 80%/17%/3% **Net Assets:** $1,953,719
Products or Services: Activist training, voters guides, "Congressional Scorecard", lobbying, more.
Tax Status: 501(c)(4)   **Citations:** 9,543:1
Board of Directors or Trustees: Dr. Billy McCormack, Richard Weinhold.
Periodicals: *Christian American* (monthly magazine), *Religious Rights Watch* (monthly newsletter).
Internships: Yes.
Other Information: Established in 1989. The Coalition is currently under federal investigation, having been accused of coordinating campaign efforts with specific Republican candidates. On April 23, 1997, executive director Ralph Reed, Jr., announced that he was leaving the Coalition to found his own political-consulting firm to be called Century Strategies. The firm will provide "campaign consulting services to pro-family, pro-life and pro-free-enterprise candidates." Reed had been with the Coalition since its establishment. The Coalition received $13,955,677, or 95% of revenue, from contributors. $332,524, or 2%, from program services. The remaining revenue came from interest on savings and temporary cash investments, and other miscellaneous sources.

Christian Educators Association International (CEAI)

P.O. Box 41300
Pasadena, CA 91114   **Phone:** (818) 798-1124   **E-Mail:** ceai educa@aol.com
USA   **Fax:** (818) 798-2346

Contact Person: Forrest L. Turpen, Executive Director.
Officers or Principals: Richard Nicholson, Chairman; Dr. Daniel C. Elliott, Vice Chairman; Donita Wheeler, Treasurer; Gloria Tizzano, Secretary.
Mission or Interest: "To encourage, equip and empower Christian educators serving in public and private schools."
Accomplishments: Gary Bauer of the Family Research Council has spoken at several CEAI conferences. Provided testimony before state legislators and local school boards. "Worked with teachers to help them understand options with unions." Provides teachers with alternatives to the National Education Association and American Federation of Teachers. Consulted with church leaders to help them work with public schools. In 1994 CEAI spent $286,011 on its programs.
Total Revenue: 1994 $362,547 39%(2) **Total Expenses:** $326,887 87%/10%/2% **Net Assets:** $42,733
Products or Services: CEAI provides educators in public schools "professional liability insurance and other benefits."
Tax Status: 501(c)(3) **Annual Report:** No. **Employees:** 7   **Citations:** 2:216
Board of Directors or Trustees: George Elling, Ron Kriesel, Joyce Anne Munn, Shirley Wilson.
Periodicals: *Vision* (monthly newsletter) that is included in members' copies of Focus on the Family's *Teachers in Focus* magazine.
Internships: Yes.
Other Information: Previously called the National Educators Fellowship from 1953-1981. In 1994 the CEAI received $247,487, or 68% of revenue, from membership dues. $46,991, or 13%, from contributions and grants awarded by foundations, businesses, and individuals. $42,360, or 12%, from convention and seminar income. $19,968 net, or 5%, from the sale of inventory. $5,741, or 2%, from interest on savings and temporary cash investments.

Christian Film and Television Commission

2510-G Las Posas Rd., Suite 502
Camarillo, CA 93010   **Phone:**   (805) 383-2000
USA   **Fax:**   (805) 383-4089

Contact Person: Dr. Theodore Baehr, Chairman.
Officers or Principals: Terry Harrison, Director of Advancement; Bruce Grimes, President.
Mission or Interest: The Christian Film and Television Commission seeks to redeem the values of the media according to biblical principles. They try to influence media executives and the public by not only criticizing and exposing what is wrong with the entertainment in our society and how it reflects on us, but also by praising and calling attention to the movies and shows which are a positive moral influence and respect traditional biblical values.
Accomplishments: They have won several awards, including: The Southern California Motion Picture Council Halo Award of High Esteem, The Film Advisory Board of Excellence, and the Media Angel Awards of Excellence
Products or Services: The Movieguide Radio Program, which is sent out to many independent stations and nationally syndicated programs. Also Movieguide TV Program, which is seen on several stations and small networks.
Tax Status: 501(c)(3) **Annual Report:** Yes. **Employees:** 10
Board of Directors or Trustees: The Commission's Board of Reference includes: Dr. Jimmy Allen, Dr. John Ankerberg, L. Brent Bozell, III (Media Research Center), Rev. Paul Cedar, Rev. David Collins, Rev. Paul Curtis, Joseph Farah (Western Journalism Center), Hank Hanegraaff, Rev. Harold Helms, Rev. Donald Ned Hicks, Reed Irvine (Accuracy in Media), Dr. D. James Kennedy (Coral Ridge Ministries), Beverly LaHaye (Concerned Women for America), Dr. Tim LaHaye, Rep. Steve Largent (R-OK), Dr. Marlin Maddoux (International Christian Media), Rev. Paul Marx, OSB, Ph.D. (Human Life International), Dr. Judith Reisman, Jay Sekulow (American Center for Law and Justice), Sir John Templeton, Rev. Don Wildmon (American Family Association), others.
Periodicals: *Movieguide: A Family Guide to Movies and Entertainment* (bi-weekly).
Internships: Yes.
Other Information: The Christian Film and Television Commission is an affiliate of Good News Communications, Inc.

Christian Forum Research Foundation

1111 Fairgrounds Rd.
Grand Rapids, MN 55744   **Phone:**   (218) 326-2688
USA

Contact Person: Sidney Reiners, President.
Officers or Principals: Sidney Reiners, President; Steve Reiners, Secretary; Darcy Okoenk, Board Member.
Mission or Interest: Publication of educational materials and letter-writing campaigns regarding religious persecution in the United States and world-wide.
Accomplishments: "We have participated in successful campaigns to obtain the release of prisoners of conscience. We ship Bibles and related literature to several foreign nations."
Tax Status: 501(c)(3) **Annual Report:** Yes. **Employees:** All volunteer.
Periodicals: *Christians in Crisis* (bimonthly newsletter).

Christian Legal Society

4208 Evergreen Lane, Suite 222
Annadale, VA 22003   **Phone:**   (703) 642-1070
USA   **Fax:**   (703) 642-1075

Contact Person: Samuel B. Casey, Executive Director.
Officers or Principals: Steven T. McFarland, Director ($72,975); Samuel B. Casey, Executive Director ($46,667); John R. Wylie, President ($0); Brent L. Amato, Vice President; Wallace L. Larson, Secretary; William D. Treeby, Treasurer.
Mission or Interest: "The preservation of and universal respect for religious liberty in courts, legislatures, and government agencies throughout the nation, including the U.S. Supreme Court."
Accomplishments: Claims 4,500 members, including over 800 law students and 80 law professors. In the 1980's, the Society and its members participated in nearly 80% of the religious liberty cases argued before the Supreme Court. In 1994 the Society spent $885,206 on its programs. Of this, $308,595 was spent on the Society's litigation division, the Center for Law and Religious Freedom.
Total Revenue: 1994 $1,384,098 39% **Total Expenses:** $1,695,525 52%/9%/38% **Net Assets:** (-$359,649)
Products or Services: Legal assistance, student ministries, conferences, Christian conciliation services for settling disputes outside of court. They have a directory of all members nationwide involved in the legal profession.
Tax Status: 501(c)(3) **Employees:** 20   **Citations:** 52:97
Board of Directors or Trustees: Prof. Karen Owen Bowdre (Cumberland School of Law), Prof. Lynn Buzzard (Campbell Univ., School of Law), Dean Samuel Casey (Simon Greenleaf School of Law), Rev. Ron Choong, Dr. Keith Fournier (Exec. Dir., American Center for Law and Justice), Dean Edward Gaffney (Valparaiso Univ. Law School), Prof. Mary Libby Payne (MS College, School of Law), Stephen West (U.S., Attorney's Office), many others, including many practicing attorneys.
Periodicals: *Quarterly* (quarterly).

Internships: Yes, they have a summer intern program for law school students.
Other Information: Established in 1975. The Society received $914,192, or 66% of revenue, from contributions and grants awarded by foundations, businesses, and individuals. (These grants included $50,000 from the M.J. Murdock Charitable Trust. In 1995, $59,269 from the Western Center for Law and Religious Freedom, and $41,792 from the Alliance Defense Fund.) $343,535, or 25%, from membership dues. $79,489, or 6%, from conference fees. $28,431, or 2%, from fees received by the Center for Law and Religious Freedom. The remaining revenue came from interest on savings and other temporary cash investments.

Christian Liberty Academy Satellite Schools (CLASS)

502 W. Euclid Ave.
Arlington Heights, IL 60004   **Phone:**   (708) 259-8736
USA

Contact Person: Rev. Paul D. Lindstrom, Superintendent of Schools.
Mission or Interest: A network of home schooling programs, with necessary curriculum materials and aids.
Accomplishments: "Over 22,000 students in 50 states and 56 foreign countries." *The Christian Educator* features the writing of well-known conservatives such as Phyllis Schlafly
Products or Services: Programs, books, testing materials
Periodicals: *The Christian Educator* (newspaper).
Other Information: Established in 1968 by Dr. Lindstrom, who was known at the time for his efforts to free missionaries, POW's and MIA's in Southeast Asia. In 1970 he began to organize the Satellite Schools system, and in 1972 the CLASS program officially began. The Christian Liberty Academy also operates the Christian Liberty Press at the same address. This press offer titles for home-schooling, as well as general interest.

Christian Solidarity International (CSI)

1260 Billington Rd.
Silver Spring, MD 20904   **Phone:**   (301) 989-0298
USA   **Fax:**   (301) 898-0398

Contact Person: Rev. Steven Snyder, President.
Officers or Principals: Rev. Steven Snyder, President ($47,160); Michael Farris, Chairman ($0); Dr. David Harding, Treasurer ($0); Craig Silver, Secretary.
Mission or Interest: An international, interdenominational organization which gathers information on persecuted Christians and then acts on their behalf by organizing letter and petition writing campaigns, sponsoring high-level delegations, and providing legal and material aid. Focus on the abuse of Christians in Islamic-dominated countries.
Accomplishments: CSI was the first non-governmental human rights organization to have met with government leaders in the Soviet Union, China, and Nepal. CSI campaigns has resulted in the release of many Christians from prison, and a series of legal reforms.
Total Revenue: 1994 $121,152 (-12%)(2) **Total Expenses:** $160,856 59%/41%/0% **Net Assets:** $11,431
Tax Status: 501(c)(3) **Annual Report:** Yes. **Employees:** 50 worldwide.
Board of Directors or Trustees: Fr. Stan DeBoe, OSST (Trinitarian Society), Sen. Don Nickles (R-OK), Robert Pittenger, Rev. Tom Riner, Hon. Mark Siljander (Alternate U.S. Rep. to the United Nations, 1987-88), Rev. Hans Stuckelberger, Hon. Faith Ryan Whittlesey (Ambassador to Switzerland, 1981-83 & 1985-88).
Periodicals: *Mission to the Persecuted* (newsletter).
Internships: Yes, three month or one year programs that concentrate on research, public policy, marketing, and public relations.
Other Information: They have an affiliate in Zurich, Switzerland. CSI received $95,084, or 78% of revenue, from the sale of publications. $20,370, or 17%, from gifts and grants awarded by foundations, businesses, and individuals. $4,800, or 4%, from rental income. The remaining revenue came from interest on savings and other miscellaneous sources.

Chronicles
(see the Rockford Institute)

Citizens Against Government Waste (CAGW)

1301 Connecticut Ave., N.W., Suite 400
Washington, DC 20036   **Phone:** (202) 467-5300   **E-Mail:** cagw@soho.ios.com
USA   **Fax:**   (202) 467-4253   **Internet:** http://www.GOVT-WASTE.org

Contact Person: Shannon Dubke.
Officers or Principals: Thomas A. Schatz, President ($156,250); Leslie Paige, Director of Media ($63,000); Joan Trumps, Director of Administration ($63,000); Robert J. Tedeschi, Treasurer; Jeffrey P. Altman, Secretary.
Mission or Interest: "Educate the public about government waste, fraud and abuse."
Accomplishments: Claims over 600,000 members. Since its inception, CAGW proposals for cutting government spending that have been enacted have yielded a claimed $433.5 billion in savings. CAGW has earned praise from across the political spectrum for advocating not only cuts in social spending, but military spending as well. CAGW's annual report on governmental 'pork' regularly attracts widespread media attention as CAGW lists wasteful projects and the biggest congressional offenders. These projects are spending what is "appropriated in circumvention of the normal budgetary procedures" and typically benefit a small special interest. Since 1991 CAGW has identified more than $43.5 billion of this "procedural pork." In 1994 CAGW spent $3,697,734 on its programs. Most, $3,400,881, went for public education, the rest went toward research.

Total Revenue: 1994 $5,592,510 (-7%)5 **Total Expenses:** $4,917,767 75%/7%/18% **Net Assets:** $2,480,357
Products or Services: Annual booklets, "Congressional Pig Book Summary" and "Prime Cuts Summary: Fifty Ways to Leaner Government." Numerous special reports on topics such as Medicare, children's vaccine programs, the War on Poverty's regional development organizations, and others.
Tax Status: 501(c)(3) **Annual Report:** Yes. **Employees:** 18 **Citations:** 395:27
Board of Directors or Trustees: Jack Anderson (syndicated columnist), Hon. Jack Kemp (Secretary of Housing and Urban Development, 1989-93), George Goldberger, Jeffrey Altman.
Periodicals: *Waste Watch* (quarterly newspaper).
Internships: Yes.
Other Information: Established in 1984 by columnist Jack Anderson and the late J. Peter Grace to generate public support for implementation of the Grace Commission Report. Affiliated with the 501(c)(4) Council for Citizens Against Government Waste. In 1994 the two affiliates had combined net revenues of $7,906,751, net expenses of $7,228,473, and assets of $2,641,043. CAGW received $5,338,357, or 95% of revenue, from contributions and grants awarded by foundations, businesses, and individuals. (These grants included $5,000 from the Gordon and Mary Cain Foundation, $3,000 from the Vernon K. Krieble Foundation, and $500 from the Richard & Helen DeVos Foundation.) $127,404, or 2%, from mailing list rentals. $98,992, or 2%, from interest on savings and temporary cash investments. The remaining revenue came from the sale of publications, speakers' fees, and the sale of assets. CAGW's decline in revenues occurred in 1994. Between 1993 and 1994 revenues decreased 30%. Prior to that revenues had been increasing at less than 1% per year for four years. The decline was due to a decrease in contributions and grants, which fell 31% from 1993 to 1994.

Citizens Committee for the Right to Keep and Bear Arms (CCRKBA)

Liberty Park
12500 N.E. Tenth Place
Bellevue, WA 98005   **Phone:**   (206) 454-4911
USA   **Fax:**   (206) 451-3959   **Internet:** http://www.ccrkba.org

Contact Person: Ken Jacobson, Executive Director.
Officers or Principals: John M. Snyder, Director of Public Affairs ($41,000); Alan M. Gottlieb, Chairman ($30,000); Merrill Jacobs, Secretary ($0); Jeffrey Kane, Treasurer.
Mission or Interest: Dedicated to preserving the Second Amendment. "Our founding fathers knew that freedom depends upon the ability of the individual to protect himself and his property, and upon the ability of the citizenry as a whole to protect itself from enemies internal and external."
Accomplishments: CCRKBA's promotional and educational television messages have aired on TNN, CNN, PBS, USA, and ESPN. "Since 1990, over 1,600 activists have attended Leadership Training Conferences." In 1995 CCRKBA spent $1,990,738 on its programs.
Total Revenue: 1995 $2,621,968 2%(3) **Total Expenses:** $2,656,480 75%/4%/21% **Net Assets:** $1,064,423
Products or Services: "The Failure of Gun Control" report. Lobbying, education, conferences, media services, speakers bureau, buttons, bumper stickers, films, books, other paraphernalia. Monthly "Gun Rights Defender of the Month Award." Annual "Gun Rights Policy Conference' and "Leadership Training Conference."
Tax Status: 501(c)(4) **Annual Report:** Yes. **Employees:** 25 **Citations:** 25:140
Board of Directors or Trustees: Michael Connelly, Robert Kukla, James Schneider. Their National Advisory Council and Distinguished Advisors include: Hon. Dan Quayle, Jerry Ahern, Gene Autry, Massad Ayoob (author, firearms instructor), Tom Clancy (best-selling author), M. Stanton Evans (publisher, *Consumers' Research*), Prof. Jeffery Hart (Dartmouth College), George Roche III (Pres., Hillsdale College), many more.
Periodicals: *Point Blank* (monthly newsletter).
Internships: Yes.
Other Information: Established in 1971. They are located at the same address as the Center for the Defense of Free Enterprise and the Second Amendment Foundation. CCRKBA also maintains a Capitol Hill Office, 600 Pennsylvania Ave., S.E., Suite 205, Washington, DC 20003. The Committee received $2,500,508, or 95% of revenue, from contributors. $57,831, or 2%, from mailing list rentals. $42,308, or 2%, from interest on savings and temporary cash investments. The remaining revenue came from dividends and interest from securities, and other miscellaneous sources.

Citizens for an Alternative Tax System (CATS)

10600 A Crestwood Dr.
Manassas, VA 20109   **Phone:**   (703) 368-6113
USA   **Fax:**   (703) 368-5843

Contact Person: Frank Davis, Director, Membership Services.
Officers or Principals: Vic Krohn, Executive Director ($0); Brendan Haggerty, Secretary/Treasurer ($0); Steven L. Hayes, Vice President ($0).
Mission or Interest: Replacement of the current income-tax system with a national sales tax.
Accomplishments: Claims 300-plus chapters; 3,000-plus memberships. Support of California Republican Assembly. National press attention. In 1991 CATS took out a full-page ad in *USA Today*, paid for by a grant from the International Association of Scientologists. The Church of Scientology also paid for the production of a glossy publication, "Freeing the USA from the Income Tax," distributed by CATS.

Total Revenue: 1994 $80,270 (-34%)(1) **Total Expenses:** $74,146 **Net Assets:** $11,065
Products or Services: Memberships, educational material, booklet, videos.
Tax Status: 501(c)(4) **Annual Report:** Yes. **Employees:** 7
Periodicals: Monthly newsletter.
Internships: Yes, they are pleased to have interns in their program. Interns work in the areas of economic research and administration.
Other Information: CATS received $56,586, or 70% of revenue, from membership dues. $18,304, or 23%, from contributions and grants awarded by foundations, businesses, and individuals. $4,267 net, or 5%, from the sale of inventory. The remaining revenue came from various miscellaneous sources.

Citizens for Educational Choice

P.O. Box 405
Needham, MA 02194   **Phone:** (617) 449-2643
USA   **Fax:**   (617) 444-7545

Contact Person: Chris Dobrowolski, President.
Officers or Principals: Chris Dobrowolski, President; John O'Leary, Treasurer; Kathleen Roever, Clerk.
Mission or Interest: Disseminating information regarding and promoting school choice.
Accomplishments: Radio appearances and speaking engagements
Tax Status: 501(c)(3) **Annual Report:** No. **Employees:** 0
Periodicals: *Freedom of Choice* (quarterly newsletter).

Citizens for Educational Freedom (CEF)

927 S. Walter Reed Dr.
Arlington, VA 22204   **Phone:** (703) 486-8311   **E-Mail:** CEFVoucher@aol.com
USA   **Fax:**   (703) 486-3160

Contact Person: Patrick J. Reilly, Executive Director.
Officers or Principals: James Condit, President; Rev. Peter Stravinskas, Chairman; Patrick J. Reilly, Executive Director; Mae M. Duggan, Founder/Vice President; Sr. Renee Oliver, OSU, Secretary; Dr. Daniel McGarry, Treasurer.
Mission or Interest: "Organization to lobby and build grassroots support for the right of all parents to choose the best school for their child."
Accomplishments: Successfully opposed federal aid to education that did not include students in nongovernment schools in the 1960's. Helped to obtain the support of several political leaders, including Presidents Reagan and Bush and various Governors for educational freedom of choice and instruction
Products or Services: "The ABC's of Promoting Educational Choice" manual, numerous pamphlets, videos, books and other information. Annual conference.
Tax Status: 501(c)(4) (application pending) **Annual Report:** No. **Employees:** 1
Board of Directors or Trustees: James Condit, Eugene Gremaud, Marilyn Lundy, Robert Marlowe, John McDonough, Daniel Sullivan, Robert Wittman.
Periodicals: *Parents' Choice* (semimonthly newsletter).
Internships: Yes, year-round for college students.
Other Information: Established in 1959. Affiliated with the 501(c)(3) Educational Freedom Foundation at the same address. "Citizens for Educational Freedom has founded and maintained several national organizations supportive of educational freedom, including the Educational Freedom Foundation, the Thomas J. White Educational Foundation, the Clearinghouse on Educational Choice, Parents' Rights, the Committee for Equal Rights in Education, and Americans for Choice in Education."

Citizens for Educational Freedom, Michigan

750 Berkshire Lane
East Lansing, MI 48823   **Phone:** (517) 351-9561
USA   **Fax:**   (517) 351-1944

Contact Person: Donald Hillman, Ph.D., President.
Officers or Principals: O. J. Murdick, Vice President.
Mission or Interest: Advocates "direct vouchers to parents or guardians for tuition at school of their choice without government intervention."
Accomplishments: "CEF provided the initial leadership for TEACH Michigan, and has opened the public's mind about alternatives to school's educational finance monopoly."
Tax Status: 501(c)(3) (application pending) **Employees:** All volunteer.

Citizens for Law and Order (CLO)

P.O. Box 1291
Sonoma, CA 95476   **Phone:** (707) 938-3778
USA   **Fax:**   (707) 938-8962

Contact Person: Bob Nicholas, President.
Officers or Principals: Bob Nicholas, President; Lee Chancellor, Vice President; Harold Cloer, Secretary; Doris Huntting, Treasurer; Donald Baldwin, Eastern Director; Kathy Christiansen, Governmental Affairs.
Mission or Interest: CLO believes it is a prime duty of government to "vigorously protect citizens against violent crime" and "ensure that violent criminals are swiftly and effectively prosecuted, tried and punished." They are currently focusing on reforming *habeas corpus,* the appeals process for death penalty cases. They want the procedure to be streamlined and faster.
Accomplishments: CLO played a key role in the campaign to unseat California Chief Justice Rose Bird in 1986 and two other Associate Justices from the California Supreme Court. Currently supporting the 10-20-Life initiative in California that would mandate an additional 10 years for using a gun while committing a felony, 20 years for pulling the trigger, and 25 years to life for shooting someone. Actively supported California's "Victim's Bill of Rights" in 1982 and the "Judicial Reform Act" in 1990. Their twenty-fifth anniversary luncheon featured former Attorney General Edwin P. Meese, III, as special guest speaker
Products or Services: Lobbying, recommends or opposes judicial nominations and appointments, arranges for members to attend parole hearings, public information activities.
Tax Status: Nonprofit.
Board of Directors or Trustees: Collene Campbell, Harry Davis, Albert Del Masso, Jan De Yoe, Stan Hess, Robert Kress, Cris Mack, Mike Reynolds, Harriet Salarno, Fran Schletewitz, Ronald Smith, M.D., James Tucker.
Periodicals: *CLO News* (bimonthly newsletter).
Other Information: Established in 1970. They have an Eastern regional office: 7509 Essex Ave., Springfield, VA 22150, (703) 569-8574, fax (703) 569-2367, contact Jack or Trudy Collins. CLO has established an educational organization, the Judicial Reform Foundation, to study violent crime and propose measures that will "restore respect for authority and for life within our society."

Citizens for a Sound Economy (CSE)

1250 H St., N.W., Suite 700
Washington, DC 20005   **Phone:** (202) 783-3870   **E-Mail:** cse@www.cse.org
USA   **Fax:**   (202) 783-4687   **Internet:** http://www.cse.org/cse

Contact Person: Deborah Korte, Treasurer.
Officers or Principals: Paul Beckner, President ($41,535); Deborah Korte, Treasurer ($21,478); C. Boyden Gray, Chairman ($0); Dr. Wayne Gable, Secretary.
Mission or Interest: Dedicated to "our forefathers' ideals of economic freedom and prosperity by working to inform and involve all citizens in the policy making process."
Accomplishments: 250,000 members. In 1995 CSE claims to have: authored more than 130 policy papers; distributed almost 8 million pieces of mail; almost 50 different advertising campaigns reaching nearly every state; more than 175 radio and television appearances by CSE spokesmen; 235 published op-eds; and more than 42,000 calls from CSE members to their elected representatives." CSE was especially active in telecommunications deregulation. In 1994 CSE spent $5,998,720 on its programs.
Total Revenue: 1994 $6,628,118 47%(3) **Total Expenses:** $6,802,525 88%/3%/9% **Net Assets:** $935,772
Products or Services: Lobbying, and two occasional research and legislative briefs, "Issue Analysis" and "Capitol Comment."
Tax Status: 501(c)(4) **Annual Report:** Yes. **Employees:** 50 (includes both affiliates)   **Citations:** 248:34
Board of Directors or Trustees: Carl Holst-Knudsen, Sarah Jane Atkins, F. Kenneth Iverson, David Dewhurst, David Padden, Richard Stephenson, Dirk van Dongen, Gordon Cain, Deecy Gray, James Pope, James Miller, III.
Internships: Yes. Interns work on public policy, litigation, state projects, government relations, communications, fundraising, and membership development.
Other Information: Established in 1984. Affiliated with the 501(c)(3) Citizens for a Sound Economy Educational Foundation at the same address. In 1994 the two affiliates had combined net revenues of $10,014,547, net expenses of $9,543,753, and net assets of $7,738,297. Paul Beckner serves as president of both, and received combined compensation of $89,871. Treasurer Deborah Korte received a combined $51,389. Chairman C. Boyden Gray served as a counsel to Vice President, then President Bush in various capacities from 1981-93. CSE received $6,389,115, or 96% of revenue, from contributions and grants. $185,947, or 3%, from mailing list rentals. The remaining revenue came from interest on savings and temporary cash investments, publication sales, conference fees, and other miscellaneous sources.

Citizens for a Sound Economy Educational Foundation (CSE Foundation)

1250 H St., N.W., Suite 700
Washington, DC 20005   **Phone:** (202) 783-3870   **E-Mail:** cse@www.cse.org
USA   **Fax:**   (202) 783-4687   **Internet:** http://www.cse.org/cse

Contact Person: Deborah Korte, Treasurer.
Officers or Principals: Paul Beckner, President ($48,336); Nancy Mitchell, Vice President, Policy Implementation ($50,329); Deborah Korte, Treasurer ($29,911); David H. Koch, Chairman; Dr. Wayne Gable, Secretary.

Mission or Interest: Research and education division of Citizens for a Sound Economy.
Accomplishments: The Foundation was active in advocating reform of the Food and Drug Administration "since 25 cents of every consumer dollar is touched by the FDA's regulatory apparatus." *The Washington Post* called the Foundation "one of FDA's strongest critics." The Foundation commissioned a poll of 500 executives whose businesses are regulated by the FDA and found that "the poll results more than proved that the fear of retaliation by the FDA affected decisions made by the regulated firms." In 1994 the Foundation spent $2,041,246 on its programs.
Total Revenue: 1994 $3,386,429 23%(3) **Total Expenses:** $2,741,228 74%/15%/11% **Net Assets:** $1,802,185
Products or Services: The Foundation runs training programs for congressional staff on economic and policy matters. Awards the "Jefferson Award" for Congressional lawmakers who "vote in favor of market-based economic policies 80 percent or more of the time." Lobbying: in 1995 the Foundation spent $6,274 on grassroots lobbying.
Tax Status: 501(c)(3) **Annual Report:** Yes. **Employees:** 50 (includes both affiliates).   **Citations:** 248:34
Board of Directors or Trustees: Sarah Atkins, Dr. Richard Fink (Koch Industries), Dr. Robert Tollison (George Mason Univ.), Dr. Walter Williams (George Mason Univ.).
Internships: Yes.
Other Information: Established in 1984. Affiliated with the 501(c)(4) Citizens for a Sound Economy at the same address. In 1994 the two affiliates had combined net revenues of $10,014,547, net expenses of $9,543,753, and net assets of $7,738,297. Paul Beckner serves as president of both, and received combined compensation of $89,871. Treasurer Deborah Korte received a combined $51,389. Chairman David H. Koch is the president of Koch Engineering and the David H. Koch Charitable Foundation, and was the 1980 Libertarian Vice Presidential candidate. The Foundation received $3,217,394, or 95% of revenue, from contributions and grants awarded by foundations, businesses, and individuals. (These grants included $150,000 from the Sarah Scaife Foundation, $60,000 from the Gordon and Mary Cain Foundation, $17,500 from the F.M. Kirby Foundation, and $200 from the United Educators Foundation. In 1995, $600,000 from the David H. Koch Charitable Foundation, $300,000 from the Claude R. Lambe Charitable Foundation, $100,000 from the Scaife Family Foundation, $35,000 from the John M. Olin Foundation, $35,000 from the John William Pope Foundation, $24,484 from the Charles G. Koch Charitable Foundation, $17,000 from the Philip M. McKenna Foundation, and $1,000 from the Roe Foundation.) $94,614, or 3%, from mailing list rentals. $73,150, or 2%, from interest on savings and temporary cash investments. The remaining revenue came from the sale of publications.

Citizens for Traditional Values

4407 W. St. Joseph
Lansing, MI 48917   **Phone:** (517) 321-6233
USA

Contact Person: Jeff Vissoher, Executive Director.
Officers or Principals: Jeff Vissoher, Executive Director ($15,082); James Muffett, President ($0); Randy Marcial, Chairman ($0); Guy Richardson, Vice President; Blaine Schultz, Treasurer.
Mission or Interest: Organize citizens at the grassroots level to promote political candidates who support traditional values.
Accomplishments: In 1994 the organization spent $21,820 on its programs, which included training people to be Deputy Registers in order to hold voter registration drives. Also trains people to be Precinct Delegates.
Total Revenue: 1994 $25,003 **Total Expenses:** $21,820 **Net Assets:** $287
Tax Status: 501(c)(4)
Board of Directors or Trustees: Terry Applegate, Lori Packer, Jon Thorne, Harry Veryser.
Other Information: Affiliated with the 501(c)(3) Foundation for Traditional Values at the same address. In 1994 the two affiliates had combined net revenues, expenses, and assets of $179,473, $141,809, and $51,239. Citizens for Traditional Values received $25,003, or 100% of revenue, from contributors.

Citizens Helping Achieve New Growth and Employment (CHANGE-NY)

426 Rawlinson Rd.
Rochester, NY 14617
USA

Contact Person: Melissa Mooney, Secretary.
Officers or Principals: Thomas W. Cawoll, President ($65,960); Brian D. Backstrom, Vice President ($42,565); Melissa M. Mooney, Secretary ($19,837).
Mission or Interest: "Educates the public about major public-policy issues and disseminates information on the voting records of elected officials. . . To encourage citizen support for changes needed to stimulate economic growth reform." Focus on New York state.
Accomplishments: Labeled "most influential new group in New York" after first year. Issues respected 'counter budget.' Considerable amount of media coverage. In 1994 CHANGE-NY spent $597,387 on its programs.
Total Revenue: 1994 $636,550 (-20%)(1) **Total Expenses:** $628,830 95%/4%/1% **Net Assets:** $13,833
Tax Status: 501(c)(4) **Annual Report:** No. **Employees:** 8   **Citations:** 135:51
Internships: Yes, on a project-by-project basis.
Other Information: Affiliated with the 501(c)(3) Empire Foundation. CHANGE-NY received $628,937, or 99% of revenue, from contributors. The remaining revenue came from material sales, interest on savings and other miscellaneous income.

Citizens Research Council of Michigan

625 Shelby St.
Detroit, MI 48226-4154   **Phone:**   (313) 961-5377
USA   **Fax:**   (313) 961-0648

Contact Person: Robert Queller, Executive Director.
Officers or Principals: Robert Queller, Executive Director ($105,523); Paul R. Good, Director of Research ($66,000); Robert N. McKerr, Senior Research Associate ($60,000); Louis Betanzos, President; Paul H. Martzowka, Treasurer.
Mission or Interest: The Council's special concern is with the organization, management and financing of state and local government. It investigates the problem of maximum efficiency in government when it does not have to meet such an objective test as a profit and loss statement. The Council advocate's the accountability of government to the citizens. It does not pursue less government in the conservative or libertarian sense, it pursues 'better' or 'more efficient' government.
Accomplishments: "We keep a low profile and encourage government officials to accept credit for any recommendations made by this organization. Accomplishments are too numerous to list." In 1994 the Council spent $528,895 on its programs. State and local government research was its top priority, followed by the "Michigan Constitutional Convention Project."
Total Revenue: 1994 $588,363 2%(2) **Total Expenses:** $661,363 80%/17%/3% **Net Assets:** $550,799
Products or Services: A Fellowship is offered to a student pursuing a master's degree in public administration at Wayne State University.
Tax Status: 501(c)(3) **Employees:** 10   **Citations:** 9:175
Board of Directors or Trustees: George Bashara, Jr. (Dykema Gossett), J. Edward Berry (General Motors), Michael Glusac (Chrysler Corp.), Daniel Kelly (Deloitte & Touche), Susan Kelly (Hudson's), David Kennedy (Earhart Found.), Roger Martin (Steelcase), Donald Parfet, Jerold Ring (Dow Chemical), S. Martin Taylor (Detroit Edison), Martin Zimmerman (Ford Motor Co.), and many others from the Michigan business community.
Other Information: Established in 1916. The Council received $554,734, or 94% of revenue, from contributions and grants awarded by foundations, businesses, and individuals. (These grants included $44,900 from the Earhart Foundation.) $21,086, or 4%, from dividends and interest from securities. $7,797, or 1%, from capital gains on the sale of securities. The remaining revenue came from interest on savings and temporary cash investments.

Citizens United

11094-D Lee Highway, Suite 200
Fairfax, VA 22030   **Phone:**   (703) 352-4788   **E-Mail:**   floyd@citizensunited.org
USA   **Fax:**   (703) 591-2505   **Internet:** http://www.citizensunited.org/cu

Contact Person: Floyd Brown, President.
Officers or Principals: Floyd Brown, President/Chairman ($114,675).
Mission or Interest: "Dedicated to restoring our government to citizen control. As government has continued to expand, special interests and the bureaucracy have come to dominate it at every level. This trend has isolated our government from its citizens, putting it dangerously out of touch with the people it was meant to serve. . . Our goal is to restore the founding father's vision of a free nation guided by the honesty, common sense and goodwill of its people."
Accomplishments: Citizens United has been persistent and prominent in attacking President Clinton on his Whitewater land dealings and other scandals, both publicizing them and conducting original research. Floyd Brown has been a frequent guest on radio and television shows and in the written media, having appeared in *Time, The Washington Post, New York Times*, ABC News, CBS News, NBC news, and CNN. Collected petitions opposing the United Nation's proposed "Global Tax." Sent more than 250,000 petitions to the President and Congress opposing District of Columbia statehood. Produced the television commercial "Who Will Judge the Judge" which criticized members of the Senate Judiciary Committee during the Clarence Thomas nomination to the Supreme Court. In 1994 Citizens United spent $2,424,352 on its programs.
Total Revenue: 1994 $2,850,274 (-10%)(1) **Total Expenses:** $3,159,150 77%/14%/9% **Net Assets:** (-$298,367)
Products or Services: "Talk Back to Washington" radio show, <u>Slick Willie: Why America Can Not Trust Bill Clinton</u>, and other books and publications.
Tax Status: 501(c)(4) **Employees:** 22   **Citations:** 1,307:8
Board of Directors or Trustees: Ron Robinson (Young America's Foundation), Kirby Wilbur, Brian Berry, Doug Robinson.
Periodicals: *ClintonWatch* (monthly newsletter), and *Citizens Agenda* (monthly newsletter).
Internships: Yes, for college students to work for 2½-3 months.
Other Information: Floyd Brown was the creator of the original 'Willy Horton radio ad' during the 1988 Presidential campaign. Affiliated with the 501(c)(3) Citizens United Foundation and Conservative Student Support Foundation at the same address. In 1994 Citizens United and the Citizens United Foundation had combined net revenues, expenses and assets of $2,952,813, $3,289,118, and (-$326,380). Citizens United received $2,785,045, or 98% of gross revenue, from contributions and grants. $63,189, or 2%, from mailing list rentals. The remaining revenue came from the radio show, the sale of assets, and other miscellaneous sources. The group lost $1,399 on rental properties.

Citizens United Foundation

11094-D Lee Highway, Suite 200
Fairfax, VA 22030   **Phone:**   (703) 352-4788
USA   **Fax:**   (703) 591-2505   **Internet:** http://www.citizensunited.org/cu

Contact Person: Floyd Brown, President.

Officers or Principals: Floyd Brown, President ($0); Cliff Kincaid, Director, American Sovereignty Action Project; Michael Boos, Legal Director.

Mission or Interest: Research and education affiliate of Citizens United.

Accomplishments: Created the "American Sovereignty Action Project" that advocates withdrawing from the United Nations "and preventing the world body from serving as a base for terrorist and intelligence operations against the U.S." Also launched the National Citizens Legal Network, a project dedicated to investigating the Clinton administration for criminal activity. In 1994 the Foundation spent $89,099 on its programs. The largest program, with an expenditure of $58,965, were *amicus curiae* (friend of the court) briefs on behalf of term limits before the 9th Circuit Court of Appeals and the Supreme Court. (The Supreme Court ruled against the position of the Foundation and other supporters of term limits.)

Total Revenue: 1994 $102,539 266%(1) **Total Expenses:** $129,968 69%/18%/13% **Net Assets:** (-$28,013)

Tax Status: 501(c)(3)   **Citations:** 1,307:8

Board of Directors or Trustees: Ron Robinson (Young America's Foundation), Kirby Wilbur, Brian Berry, Doug Robinson.

Periodicals: *ASAP Report* (monthly newsletter) and *Citizens Legal Advocate* (monthly newsletter).

Other Information: Established in 1993. Affiliated with the 501(c)(4) Citizens United and Conservative Student Support Foundation at the same address. In 1994 Citizens United and the Citizens United Foundation had combined net revenues, expenses and assets of $2,952,813, $3,289,118, and (-$326,380). The Foundation received $102,539, or 100% of revenue, from contributions and grants awarded by foundations, businesses, and individuals.

Citizens' Justice Programs

62 Central Ave.
Hull, MA 02045   **Phone:** (617) 925-5253   **E-Mail:** dcg3@ix.netcom.com
USA   **Fax:** (617) 925-3906   **Internet:** http://www.the.spa.com/constitution/c.s.legal.htm

Contact Person: David C. Grossack.

Mission or Interest: "Teaching the public methods of pro-se (on one's own behalf) litigation. Promoting Constitutional rights." Advocates citizens representing themselves in a court of law. Also advocates suing Judges when their rulings violate an individual's constitutional right.

Accomplishments: Grossack's legal techniques have become popular with many in the militia movement and other populist groups. According to Citizens' Justice Programs, "(Grossack's) pamphlet, 'How To Sue A Judge', caused so much chaos when it was posted on the Internet, Congress is debating legislation to eradicate the few loopholes that still allow such actions. . . In the 1980's, Congress changed the procedure for citizens contesting IRS third-party summonses after Grossack filed some discovery pleadings in a Boston case."

Products or Services: "Constitutional Warfare: A Legal Insurrection Manual for Pro Se litigants" legal manual, many other publications.

Tax Status: For profit.

Clare Boothe Luce Policy Institute

112 Elden St., Suite P
Herndon, VA 20170   **Phone:** (888) 891-4288
USA

Contact Person: Michelle Easton, President.

Officers or Principals: Michelle Easton, President ($75,000); Frank Donatelli, Secretary/Treasurer ($0); Mary Whitten Neal, Director.

Mission or Interest: "The goal of the Clare Boothe Luce Institute is to refute the widely accepted myth that feminists speak for women in America, and to focus especially on showing young professionally oriented women how to be successful in their lives. . . Clare Boothe Luce is a role model because she was a leader in the free world's opposition to communism, an outspoken advocate of the free market, and a loving wife and mother. Mrs. Luce came under the same attack from liberals and feminists of her day that modern conservative women do when they are successful."

Accomplishments: Rep. Helen Chenoweth (R-ID) said, "No nation can survive the corruption of its women. . . The Luce Institute is leading the fight to reclaim America's young women." In 1994 the Institute spent $199,676 on its programs.

Total Revenue: 1994 $173,930 445%(1) **Total Expenses:** $275,428 72%/7%/21% **Net Assets:** (-$83,578)

Products or Services: Scholarships, leadership training seminars, conferences, and speaker's bureau.

Tax Status: 501(c)(3) **Annual Report:** No. **Employees:** 2   **Citations:** 3:204

Periodicals: *Clare Boothe Luce Policy Institute Newsletter*.

Internships: No.

Other Information: Established in 1993. Named after Clare Boothe Luce (1903-1987), the editor of *Vanity Fair*, an award-winning playwright, a Congresswoman from Connecticut, the Ambassador to Italy, and "a widely admired conservative leader as well as a loving wife and mother." The Institute received $173,889, or 99.9% of revenue, from contributions and grants awarded by foundations, businesses, and individuals. (These grants included $25,000 from the Sarah Scaife Foundation, $15,000 from the J.M. Foundation, $7,500 from the F.M. Kirby Foundation.) The remaining revenue came from other miscellaneous sources.

Claremont Institute for the Study of Statesmanship and Political Philosophy

250 W. 1st St., Suite 330
Claremont, CA 91711   **Phone:** (909) 621-6825   **E-Mail:** 2026935@mcimail.com
USA   **Fax:**   (909) 626-8724   **Internet:** http://www.claremont.org

Contact Person: Larry Arnn, Executive Director.
Officers or Principals: S. Bruce Herschensohn, Distinguished Fellow ($115,875); William Rusher, Distinguished Fellow ($115,782); Thomas McClintock, Associate Director ($86,134); Charles Heatherly, Executive Vice President; Bruce Sanborn, Chairman.
Mission or Interest: "To restore the principles of the American founding to their rightful, preeminent authority in our national life." Programs include the Salvatori Center for the Study of the American Constitution, the Center for the Study of the Natural Law, the Golden State Center for Policy Studies, and the Center for Environmental Education Research.
Accomplishments: In 1996 the Center focused extensively on affirmative action, publishing at least ten papers on the subject. Through its publications and conferences the Claremont Institute has become one of the most influential conservative think tanks on the west coast. The Institute hosts a special project, Doctors for Responsible Gun Ownership, directed by Dr. Tim Wheeler. Dr. Wheeler testified before Congress against funding for the Center for Disease Control's controversial studies regarding the ownership of firearms and safety. In 1995 the Institute spent $1,641,065 on its programs. The largest program, with expenditures of $512,348, focused on public policy nationwide. $506,233 was spent on California public policy. $275,846 was spent on Pacific Rim and Asian studies "to promote a greater understanding of the economic and strategic importance of the Far East." $136,480 for academic programs to help high school teachers and journalists understand "the principles of American democracy and. . .the American founding."
Total Revenue: 1995 $1,977,032 13%(5) **Total Expenses:** $2,239,696 73%/15%/12% **Net Assets:** $1,412,385
Products or Services: Abraham Lincoln Fellows for young professionals in the field of public policy. Publius Fellows for journalism students. Annual Lincoln Day Colloquium started in 1997. Annual Winston Churchill dinner at which the Institute presents its' Statesmanship Award. Winners of this award have included President Reagan, William F. Buckley, Jr., Justice Clarence Thomas and Jack Kemp.
Tax Status: 501(c)(3) **Annual Report:** Yes. **Citations:** 111:57
Board of Directors or Trustees: Roberta Green Ahmanson, Howard Ahmanson, Richard Cammack, Nick Coussoulis, Robert Cummins, K. Jeffrey Dahlberg, Prof. Chistopher Flannery (Azusa Pacific Univ.), Tom Fuentes, Dr. Harry Jaffa, Dr. Charles Kesler (Salvatori Center, Claremont McKenna College), Don Moe, Gregory Palen, Kenneth Petersen, Pat Sajak, Dr. Peter Schramm (Ashbrook Center), Dr. Thomas Silver, Christina Snyder, Brian Sullivan.
Periodicals: *The Public View* (quarterly newsletter).
Other Information: Established in 1979. The Institute received $1,806,112, or 91% of revenue, from contributions and grants awarded by foundations, businesses, and individuals. (These grants included $75,000 from the John M. Olin Foundation, $40,000 from the Lynde and Harry Bradley Foundation, $25,000 from the William H. Donner Foundation, and $25,000 from the Philip M. McKenna Foundation. In 1994, $100,000 from the Aequus Institute, $75,000 from the Sarah Scaife Foundation, and $5,000 from the Anschutz Foundation.) $71,161, or 4%, from conference fees. $38,755, or 2%, from interest on savings and temporary cash investments. $35,583, or 2%, from capital gains on the sale of securities. $25,421, or 1%, from dividends and interest from securities.

Classics of Liberty

333 East 38th St., 10th Floor
New York, NY 10016   **Phone:** (212) 455-5000
USA   **Fax:**   (212) 682-1096

Contact Person: Richard G. Ritter, President.
Mission or Interest: "A distinguished collection of facsimile reprints of historically significant books expressing republican ideals and thought for individuals with a strong sense of the philosophic foundations of modern democracies." Authors include Locke, Mills, Burke, de Tocqueville, Montesquieu, Jefferson, Lincoln and Adam Smith
Tax Status: For profit. **Annual Report:** No.
Board of Directors or Trustees: Editorial Advisory Board includes: Prof. Thomas Barnes (Univ. of CA), William Safire (columnist), Clifton Fadiman (board member, Council for Basic Education), Milton Friedman (Nobel Laureate), Paul Johnson (historian, author), Irving Kristol (National Affairs), William E. Simon (former U.S. Treasury Secretary), Gary Wills (columnist).

Claude R. Lambe Charitable Foundation

1450 G St., N.W., Suite 445
Washington, DC 20005   **Phone:** (202) 393-2354
USA   **Fax:**   (202) 393-2355

Contact Person: Wanda L. Stokes, Foundation Assistant.
Officers or Principals: Richard Fink, President ($0); Elizabeth B. Koch, Vice President ($0); Victoria Hughes, Vice President ($0); Vonda Holliman, Secretary/Treasurer; Charles G. Koch, Director.
Mission or Interest: Grant-making philanthropy that gives almost exclusively to conservative and free-market organizations. "To advance a free and civil society through furthering the understanding and application of market-based approaches to solving critical social problems by funding academic and public policy research."

Accomplishments: In 1995 the Foundation awarded $1,785,430 in grants. Recipients included: two grants totaling $500,000 for the Cato Institute, two grants totaling $335,500 for the Institute for Humane Studies, two grants totaling $300,000 for Citizens for a Sound Economy, $120,000 for the Political Economy Research Center, $125,000 for the Center for Market Processes, two grants totaling $76,000 for the Humane Studies Foundation, $50,000 for the Reason Foundation, $40,000 for the Acton Institute, and $25,000 each for the Intercollegiate Studies Institute. The Foundation also spent $29,614 conducting its own research "in the area of education for market-based management and public policy issues."

Total Revenue: 1995 $2,797,211 **Total Expenses:** $2,198,354 **Net Assets:** $27,265,741 2%(7)
Tax Status: 501(c)(3)
Other Information: Established in 1982 by the late Claude R. Lambe. The Foundation is located at the same address and shares the same directors as the Charles G. Koch Foundation. The Foundation received $1,775,814, or 63% of revenue, from capital gains on the sale of assets. $986,632, or 35%, from dividends and interest from securities. $34,765, or 1%, from interest on savings and temporary cash investments.

Claustrophobia

400 N. High St., Suite 137
Columbus, OH 43215 **Phone:** (614) 444-2493 **E-Mail:** phobia@bronze.coil.com
USA **Fax:** (614) 879-5886

Contact Person: Dena L. Bruedigam, Publisher.
Officers or Principals: Michael D. Campbell, Editor; Donald Gallick, Assistant Editor.
Mission or Interest: Support minimal government and laissez-faire capitalism. Provide readers with articles on the principles of individualism and liberty, and a forum for alternate viewpoints. The title "relates to the people feeling somewhat claustrophobic. . . It's an offshoot of the government being so large and such a part of our lives."
Accomplishments: Begun as a newsletter distributed on the Ohio State campus in 1992, it now has an international circulation of over 100. Articles which have appeared first in *Claustrophobia* have been reprinted elsewhere
Tax Status: For profit. **Annual Report:** No. **Employees:** 6, all volunteer.
Periodicals: *Claustrophobia* (monthly).
Internships: No.
Other Information: Established in 1992.

Coalition for Vehicle Choice (CVC)

1440 New York Ave., N.W., Suite 310
Washington, DC 20005 **Phone:** (202) 628-5164
USA **Fax:** (202) 628-5168

Contact Person: Diane Steed, President.
Officers or Principals: Diane Steed, President ($183,104); Peter Pestillo, Secretary ($0); Andrew H. Card, Treasurer ($0); George A. Peapples, Chairman.
Mission or Interest: To preserve consumer choice in automobiles, rather than one that has fuel economy mandated by the government. An organization composed of members of the automotive industry, agribusiness, insurance industry and safety groups.
Accomplishments: CVC has been instrumental in fighting higher Corporate Average Fuel Economy (CAFE) standards. They produced the frequently aired television commercial which shows the effects of an auto crash on a small car versus a large car. More than 4,800 organizations have joined CVC. CVC members have participated in rule-making activities on light truck fuel economy standards.
Total Revenue: FY ending 2/95 $2,951,770 **Total Expenses:** $3,278,935 **Net Assets:** $1,393,693
Products or Services: CVC has distributed copies of the National Academy of Sciences' report on fuel economy, "Automotive Fuel Economy: How Far Should We Go?" Exhibits available for trade shows. Annual meetings and conventions. Lobbying: in the fiscal year ending February 1995 CVC spent $31,519 on lobbying, down 23% from the year before.
Tax Status: 501(c)(6) **Citations:** 44:105
Board of Directors or Trustees: James Johnson (General Motors), Derrick Crandall (American Recreation Coalition), Rob Liberatore.
Other Information: Established in 1991 by the firm of E. Bruce Harrison & Co. President Diane Steed headed the NHTSA under President Reagan. CVC received $2,898,921, or 98% of revenue, from membership dues. $52,849, or 2%, from interest on savings and temporary cash investments.

Coalition on Urban Affairs

6033 W. Century Blvd., Suite 400
Los Angeles, CA 90045 **Phone:** (310) 412-8670 **E-Mail:** cua@kybersys.com
USA **Fax:** (714) 361-6567 **Internet:** http://www.kybersys.com/cua

Contact Person: Star Parker, President.
Mission or Interest: "A social policy think tank and research center." Focuses on the black community. Supports free market community development and pro-family policies. Opposed to abortion, government controlled education, and gun control.

Accomplishments: Star Parker has appeared on CNN & Company debating Jesse Jackson, Larry King Live, Sonya Live, and Nightline. She has addressed new Republican members of the 104th Congress, the American Cause, and the Christian Coalition. Parker has been profiled on ABC's 20/20, Dr. James Dobson's *Focus on the Family*, *Readers Digest*, the *Limbaugh Letter*, and others
Products or Services: Conferences, surveys, research, publications and pilot programs.
Tax Status: 501(c)(3)
Periodicals: *Another View* (quarterly newsletter).
Other Information: Established in 1992. Star Parker was a single mother living on welfare. She returned to college and studied marketing. She started her own publishing company and produced a magazine distributed to churches in the Los Angeles area. The Los Angeles riots of 1992 destroyed many of the businesses that she relied on for advertising revenue, forcing her out of business. She says that the reaction of national black leaders who "were claiming that the gangsters, who carried out the riots, were simply victims of society," prompted her to speak out and form the Coalition on Urban Affairs. Parker is the author of <u>Pimps, Whores and Welfare Brats</u> (Simon & Schuster, 1997).

Coalitions for America

717 2nd St., N.E., Suite 209
Washington, DC 20002   **Phone:**   (202) 546-3000
USA   **Fax:**   (202) 543-8425   **Internet:** http://www.net.fcret.org

Contact Person: Eric M. Licht, President.
Officers or Principals: Eric M. Licht, President ($107,100); Paul M. Weyrich, National Chairman ($24,192); Hon. Paul Pressler, Chairman ($0); Charles A. Moser, Ph.D., Secretary/Treasurer.
Mission or Interest: Affiliate of the Free Congress Foundation that lobbies for state-level policies based on free markets and traditional values. Conducts meetings and satellite conferences.
Accomplishments: In 1994 the Coalition spent $367,395 on its programs. This included $120,600 in grants for other organizations. Recipients were; $38,500 for the League of Catholic Voters, $36,400 for Citizens for Responsible Government, $33,400 for the Catholic Network, $6,150 for the Liberation Support Alliance, $6,000 for American Land Rights, and $150 for Toward Tradition.
Total Revenue: 1994 $618,347 **Total Expenses:** $437,017 84%/9%/6% **Net Assets:** $303,718
Tax Status: 501(c)(4)   **Citations:** 80:77
Board of Directors or Trustees: Sen. James McClure, Joseph Cannon, Tony Grampsas (Coors Brewing Co.), Frank Madsen, Joseph Dioguardi.
Other Information: Affiliated with the 501(c)(3) Free Congress Foundation, 501(c)(3) Committee for Effective State Government, and the Free Congress Political Action Committee. The Coalitions received $583,866, or 94% of revenue, from contributions. $20,000, or 3%, from fees for satellite conferencing. $8,988, or 1%, from dividends and interest from securities. $5,379, or 1%, from interest on savings and temporary cash investments.

College Pro-Life Information Network

P.O. Box 10664
State College, PA 16805   **Phone:**   (814) 867-6263   **E-Mail:** sicree@geosc.psu.edu
USA

Contact Person: Andrew Sicree.
Mission or Interest: "Organizing and networking with pro-life activists on college campuses."
Tax Status: Unincorporated **Annual Report:** No. **Employees:** None.
Periodicals: *The Pro-Life Collegian* (bimonthly).
Internships: No.

College Republican National Committee

600 Pennsylvania Ave., S.E., Suite 301
Washington, DC 20003   **Phone:**   (202) 608-1411   **E-Mail:** jgalli1995@aol.com
USA   **Fax:**   (202) 608-1429   **Internet:** http://www.crnc.org

Contact Person: Fred Bartlett, Membership Director.
Officers or Principals: Joe Galli, Chairman; George Fondren, Executive Director; Caroline Boyd, Administrative Assistant.
Mission or Interest: "To recruit, organize, mobilize, empower and strengthen College Republicans across the country."
Products or Services: Lectures, seminars, distribution of pamphlets and leaflets.
Tax Status: Political party. **Employees:** 4
Board of Directors or Trustees: Vice President Dan Quayle, Honorary Co-Chairman.
Periodicals: *Broadside* (bi-monthly newspaper).
Internships: Yes. Full-time during the summer and part-time during the spring and fall.

Collegiate Network

14 S. Bryn Mawr Ave., Suite 100
Bryn Mawr, PA 19010   **Phone:**   (215) 525-7501
USA   **Fax:**   (215) 525-3315

Contact Person: Charles Horner.
Mission or Interest: Previously called the Madison Center for Educational Policy, the Collegiate Network was founded to assist conservative student newspapers and journalists. In 1995 the Collegiate Network assumed the functions of the Madison Center, and reached an agreement with the Intercollegiate Studies Institute (ISI) that places the Network under the contractual management of ISI - although ISI has no editorial control over Collegiate Network-member publications. (Contact information provided is for the Intercollegiate Studies Institute. The financial information provided is from the Madison Center's last year of independent operation.)
Accomplishments: In the fiscal year ending June 1995 the Center awarded $124,786 in grants. The majority of this went to conservative college publications.
Total Revenue: FY ending 6/95 $370,444 (-37%)(2) **Total Expenses:** $451,044 66%/34%/0% **Net Assets:** $251,875
Tax Status: 501(c)(3)
Other Information: The Center received $334,226, or 90% of revenue, from contributions and grants awarded by foundations, businesses, and individuals. (These grants included $188,000 from the Lynde and Harry Bradley Foundation, $35,000 from the Castle Rock Foundation, $25,000 from the Sarah Scaife Foundation, $17,500 from the F.M. Kirby Foundation, and $9,500 from the Earhart Foundation.) $18,224, or 5%, from dividends and interest from securities. $17,994, or 5%, from the sale of publications.

Committee for a Constructive Tomorrow (CFACT)

P.O. Box 65722
Washington, DC 20035   **Phone:**   (202) 429-2737
USA   **Fax:**   (301) 858-0944

Contact Person: Craig Rucker, Executive Director.
Officers or Principals: David M. Rothbard, President/CEO ($32,388); Craig Rucker, Executive Director ($29,999); Norval E. Carey, Vice-Chairman ($0); Mark D. Dioguardi, Second Vice-Chairman.
Mission or Interest: "To bring constructive, free-market-oriented solutions to current consumer and environmental issues."
Accomplishments: Helped stop Ralph Nader's PIRGs from collecting mandatory student fees. Helped gain federal approval of food irradiation. Helped cast public doubt on such doomsday scenarios as acid rain, ozone depletion and global warming. Reach 250,000 listeners daily with a one-minute radio commentary called "Just the Facts," heard on over fifty radio stations nationwide. In 1993 the Committee spent $115,374 on its programs.
Total Revenue: 1993 $140,875 (-less than 1%)(2) **Total Expenses:** $147,934 78%/19%/3% **Net Assets:** $16,836
Products or Services: White papers on various topics. A high-school lecture program, "The Positively Profound Power of Human Progress," that looks at man's scientific and technological progress, and how it has benefitted us. Campus outreach.
Tax Status: 501(c)(3) **Annual Report:** No. **Employees:** 6
Board of Directors or Trustees: Board of Academic / Scientific Advisors includes: Bruce Ames, Ph.D. (Chair, Dept. of Chem., Univ. of CA, Berkeley), James Bovard (Competitive Enterprise Inst.); Barbara Keating-Edh (Consumer Alert), Edward Krug, Ph.D. (Univ. of IL, Champaign), Elizabeth Whelan, Sc.D., M.P.H., (American Council on Science and Health), Robert Poole (Pres., Reason Found.), many other scientists and academics. Dixie Lee Ray served on their board until her death in 1994.
Periodicals: *Citizen Outlook* (bimonthly newsletter).
Internships: Yes. Interns work on various projects that enable them to help with research and activist coordination.
Other Information: Established in 1985. Affiliated with the 501(c)(4) Citizens for a Constructive Tomorrow at the same address, although that affiliate has been dormant since 1991. The Committee received $139,878, or 99% of revenue, from contributions and grants awarded by foundations, businesses, and individuals. (In 1995 these grants included $50,000 from the Carthage Foundation.) The remaining revenue came from interest on savings and temporary cash investments.

Committee for Monetary Research and Education

10004 Greenwood Court
Charlotte, NC 28215   **Phone:**   (704) 598-3717
USA

Contact Person: Elizabeth B. Currier, President.
Officers or Principals: Elizabeth B. Currier, President ($0); Henry Donner, Vice President ($0); Austen B. Colgate, Secretary ($0); William H. Tehan, Treasurer.
Mission or Interest: "Monetary research and education - consisting of study, evaluation, analysis and education concerning domestic and world monetary crises and their solutions."
Accomplishments: In 1995 the Committee spent $33,294 on its programs. $22,326 was spent on research and analysis, and the rest on two meetings/symposiums.
Total Revenue: 1995 $37,179 **Total Expenses:** $35,991 93%/5%/3% **Net Assets:** (-$42,206)
Tax Status: 501(c)(3)
Board of Directors or Trustees: Hon. J. William Middendorf, II (U.S. Ambassador to the Organization of American States, 1981-85), William Easman, Tracy Herrick, Frederick Toland.

Other Information: The Committee received $15,120, or 41% of revenue, from symposium fees. $9,525, or 26%, from gifts and grants awarded by foundations, businesses, and individuals. (In 1994 these grants included $300 from the United Educators Foundation. These gifts and grants have been decreasing by an average of 28% per year since 1991.) $7,150, or 19%, from membership dues. $4,510, or 12%, from dividends and interest from securities. The remaining revenue came from the sale of inventory.

Committee on Justice and the Constitution (COJAC)
P.O. Box 135
Mesa, AZ 85211   **Phone:** (602) 964-3014
USA

Contact Person: A. Rick Dalton, Executive Director.
Officers or Principals: Jack McLamb, President.
Mission or Interest: "To promote a return to the founders' principles in all areas of society." Populist/conservative organization.
Accomplishments: Crime-victims' rights legislation. Influenced policy of limiting death sentence appeals. Influence of other legislation by litigation and lobbying
Products or Services: Reports, monographs and books on constitutional issues. *The U.S. Tax Court* (monograph), The Sanctuary Movement: A Study in Deception, and the Analytical Index to the U.S. Constitution.
Tax Status: Not exempt. **Annual Report:** Yes. **Employees:** 10, all volunteer.
Internships: No.
Other Information: Jack McLamb is also the executive director of the Aid & Abet Foundation.

Committee on Media Integrity
(see Center for the Study of Popular Culture)

Committee on Population and the Economy
53 Cavendish Road
London SW12 0DQ   **Phone:** (44-81) 675 1881
UNITED KINGDOM   **Fax:**   (44-81) 675 8417

Contact Person: Robert Whelan.
Officers or Principals: Julian Simon, International Chairman; Baroness Elles, Vice President; Robert Whelan, Director.
Mission or Interest: The Committee demonstrates, through scholarship, that "population growth does not cause poverty or scarcity of resources. On the contrary, as population has increased rapidly in the West during the 19th century and in the developing countries since World War II, living standards have risen dramatically. The social, economic and environmental problems attributed to population growth are usually caused by government."
Accomplishments: Disseminated the work of scholars such as Simon Kuznets, Lord Bauer, Julian Simon, Jacqueline Kasun, Ester Boserup and Colin Clark. International Director Julian Simon is the author of The Economic Consequences of Immigration and The Ultimate Resource.
Board of Directors or Trustees: Advisory Council includes: Prof. Hubert Campbell, Allan Carlson, Prof. Jacqueline Kasun, John Kelly, FRCS, FRCOG, William Niskanen (Cato Inst.), Prof. Luis Pazos, Prof. Bryan Thwaites.
Periodicals: *People Count* (newsletter).

Committee to Restore the Constitution
P.O. Box 986
2218 W. Prospect Rd.
Fort Collins, CO 80522   **Phone:** (303) 484-2575
USA

Contact Person: Lt. Col. Archibald E. Roberts, AUS, (Ret.), Director.
Officers or Principals: Hon. John R. Rarick, Chairman; Hon. Bruce Alger, President; Arnold Kadue, Secretary; Lawrence Patterson, Treasurer; Hon. T. David Horton, Counsel.
Mission or Interest: Populist/conservative organization. "To restore interest-free money, repudiate unpayable national debt, eliminate federal deficits and reestablish freedoms of person and property guaranteed to you by the Constitution. . . Participate in the task of generating public debate on facts behind the 'New World Order'."
Accomplishments: Books, cassettes, videotapes, and work books that provide instructions for accomplishing the Committee's objectives. The Anatomy of a Revolution, The Most Secret Science ("explains how to defend your money and property against confiscatory stratagems of Federal Reserve banks") and other books and publications are published by the Committee's Betsy Ross Press
Tax Status: Colorado nonprofit.
Board of Directors or Trustees: Dr. Serban Andronescu (*New York Spectator*), Don Bell (*Don Bell Reports*), N. M. Camardese, M.D. (Pres., Americanism Found.), Hon. Frank Findlay (former Idaho State Legislator), Hon. Jack Metcalf (Washington State Sen.), Eustace Mullins (author, Secrets of the Federal Reserve), John Rakus, CFP, (Pres., National Justice Found.), Prof. Revilo Oliver, Ph.D., Dr. Frank Rogers, M.D., Major James Townsend (publisher, *National Educator*), others.

Periodicals: *CRC Bulletin* (monthly).
Other Information: Established in 1965. Lt. Col. Archibald Roberts is also the president of the 501(c)(3) Foundation for Education, Scholarship, Patriotism and Americanism, at the same address. Lt. Col. Roberts served 19 years of active duty in the Army, and fought in the Korean War. There he grew concerned over U.S. troops fighting and dying under United Nations command in a conflict that he believed they were not allowed to win. Roberts was assigned by the Army to prepare a troop information program on the responsibilities of U.S. troops overseas. The result and the content of his program was considered too political, and he was relieved of his command, and later dismissed. A military court reinstated him, but he then retired. Later in 1966, he published a book of his experience in the Korean War called <u>Victory Denied: Why Your Son Faces Death in No-Win Wars</u>.

Commonwealth Foundation for Public Policy Alternatives
3544 N. Progress Ave., Suite 101
Harrisburg, PA 17110   **Phone:**   (717) 671-1901   **E-Mail:**   COMMWEALTH@aol.com
USA   **Fax:**   (717) 671-1905

Contact Person: Clifford Frick, Communications Director.
Officers or Principals: Henry Olsen, President; Don E. Eberly, former President ($91,676); Clifford G. Frick, Communications Director ($34,232); Keith Bashore, Research Associate ($31,766); William Boxx, Chairman.
Mission or Interest: The Foundation's programs attempt to foster an economic atmosphere where entrepreneurship and private initiative can flourish. Focus on Pennsylvania.
Accomplishments: Published seven books, over 100 reports, and held conferences on such issues as privatization and education. Influential in the debate of public funding for sports stadiums. Provided testimony for state legislators. The average circulation for issues of *The Bottom Line* was 7,200 in 1993.
Total Revenue: 1993 $347,257 **Total Expenses:** $381,007 **Net Assets:** $93,126
Products or Services: Reports, conferences, monographs, testimony, speakers bureau.
Tax Status: 501(c)(3) **Annual Report:** No. **Employees:** 6   **Citations:** 4:196
Board of Directors or Trustees: Allan Meltzer, Ph.D. (Carnegie Mellon Univ.), Earl Hess, Ph.D. (Pres., Lancaster Laboratories), Sam McCullough, Frederick Anton, III (Chair, Pennsylvania Manufacturers' Assoc.), Charles Huston, III (Huston Foundation), Kevin Southeimer, Ph.D. (University of Pittsburgh), Victor Milione (Intercollegiate Studies Inst.), James Murdy (Allegheny Ludlum Corp.), James Panyard, Dr. Robert Woodson (National Center for Neighborhood Enterprise), Joanne Beyer (Pres., Allegheny Found.).
Periodicals: *The Bottom Line* (monthly).
Internships: Yes, paid internships year-round.
Other Information: Established in 1988. Affiliated with the National Fatherhood Initiative. Donald Eberly was an Executive Assistant to President Reagan. The Foundation received $332,456, or 96% of revenue, from contributions and grants awarded by foundations, businesses, and individuals. (In 1995 these grants included $108,000 from the Philip M. McKenna Foundation, $40,000 from the Lynde and Harry Bradley Foundation, $35,000 from the Scaife Family Foundation, $10,000 from the Carthage Foundation, and $3,000 from the Roe Foundation. In 1994, $51,000 from the Sarah Scaife Foundation.) $10,825, or 3%, from conference registration fees. The remaining revenue came from interest on savings, the sale of publications, and other miscellaneous sources.

Compass
P.O. Box 1769
Murphys, CA 95247
USA

Contact Person: Otto Scott, Editor/Publisher.
Mission or Interest: "Historically-rooted monthly commentary on subjects of contemporary concern, including reviews of books, movies and plays."
Accomplishments: Mr. Scott has written numerous books including biographies and companies' histories. He has worked as an editorialist, columnist and reviewer for various magazines and newspapers. In 1976 he won the "George Washington Medal" for Best Article from the Freedoms Foundation. Scott was also the keynote speaker at the 1992 U.S. Taxpayers Party's nominating convention
Tax Status: For profit.
Periodicals: *Compass* (monthly).

Competitive Enterprise Institute (CEI)
1001 Connecticut Ave., N.W., Suite 1250
Washington, DC 20036   **Phone:**   (202) 331-1010   **E-Mail:**   info@cei.org
USA   **Fax:**   (202) 331-0640   **Internet:** http://www.cei.org

Contact Person: Marlo Lewis, Jr. Executive Director.
Officers or Principals: Fred L. Smith, Jr., President ($85,778); Marlo Lewis, Jr. Executive Director ($71,744); James Heetderks, Treasurer ($37,049); Helen Hewitt, Secretary.
Mission or Interest: Devoted to free enterprise and limited government. Specializes in deregulation, science and technology issues and free-market environmentalism.

Accomplishments: *The Boston Globe* called CEI "One of Washington's feistiest think tanks." Successfully challenged the National Highway Traffic Safety Administration over the increased safety costs in higher CAFE standards (<u>CEI v. NHTSA</u>, Wash. D.C. Circuit, February 19, 1992) - the first judicial overturning of a CAFE standard in the 18-year history of the program. This was a major advance in exposing the often hidden cost of environmental regulations. In 1995 the Institute spent $1,433,625 on its programs. The largest program, with expenditures of $755,707, was the Environmental Studies program "to develop and legitimize a property-based approach to environmental protection as well as exploring methods of preserving both individual liberty and the environment." This resulted in the formation of the Center for Private Conservation. $285,123 was spent on its legal and litigation program. $236,344 was spent on economic and regulatory studies.

Total Revenue: 1995 $2,260,513 45%(3) **Total Expenses:** $1,734,297 83%/10%/7% **Net Assets:** $1,196,786

Products or Services: <u>Environmental Politics: Public Costs, Private Rewards</u> (Praeger), and <u>The True State of the Planet</u> (The Free Press, 1995), other books. Litigation. *In the Press*, an annual collection of CEI's published opinions, analyses, and media citations over the past year. "Competitive Enterprise Index", an annual analysis of congressional voting records on issues of competition and freedom. Monographs and policy studies. Jefferson Group Forum for Free Market Discussion, a bi-weekly meeting for members. Awards the annual Warren T. Brookes Fellowship in Environmental Journalism - recipients have included Ron Bailey, author of <u>Eco-Scam: The False Prophets of Ecological Apocalypse</u>, Michael Fumento, author of <u>The Myth of Heterosexual AIDS</u>, and Michelle Maglalang Malkin, a columnist at the *Los Angeles Daily News*. The <u>Free Market Environmental Bibliography</u> is published annually. It is a bibliography of books and studies on the environment and environmentalism from a free-market perspective. In 1995 the Institute lobbied for the first time, spending $2,088 on grassroots lobbying.

Tax Status: 501(c)(3) **Annual Report:** Yes. **Employees:** 15 **Citations:** 237:35

Board of Directors or Trustees: Francis Smith (Consumer Alert), Michael Greve (Center for Individual Rights), Leonard Liggio (Atlas Found.), William Dunn. Advisors include: Frank Blake (Vice Pres.,& General Counsel, General Electric), Prof. Emeritus Yale Brozen (Univ. of Chicago), Robert Brumley (former General Counsel, Commerce Dept.), Christopher DeMuth (Pres., American Enterprise Inst.), Prof. Steve Hanke (Johns Hopkins Univ.), Michael Horowitz (former General Counsel, Office of Management and Budget), Lawrence Kudlow (former Chief Economist, Bear Stearns), Thomas Gale Moore (Senior Fellow, Hoover Inst.), Robert Poole (Pres., Reason Found.), John Snow (Chair/CEO, CSX Corporation), Phil Truluck (Exec. Vice Pres., Heritage Found.).

Periodicals: *CEI Update* (monthly).

Internships: Yes, for both graduates and undergraduates.

Other Information: Established in 1984. CEI received $2,198,052, or 97% of revenue, from contributions and grants awarded by foundations, businesses, and individuals. (These grants included $150,000 from the Scaife Family Foundation, $60,000 from the Lynde and Harry Bradley Foundation, $25,000 from the David H. Koch Charitable Foundation, and $20,000 from the Claude R. Lambe Charitable Foundation. In 1994, $250,000 from the Gilder Foundation, $60,000 from the Sarah Scaife Foundation, $15,000 from the Philip M. McKenna Foundation, $10,000 from the Earhart Foundation, $10,000 from the Aequus Institute, $5,000 from the Vernon K. Krieble Foundation, $5,000 from the Roe Foundation, $5,000 from the Alex C. Walker Foundation, and $2,500 from the John William Pope Foundation.) $32,190, or 1%, from interest on savings and temporary cash investments. $12,983, or 1%, from royalties. The remaining revenue came from publication sales, dividends and interest from securities, and other miscellaneous sources.

Concerned Women for America (CWA)

370 L'Enfant Promenade, S.W., Suite 800
Washington, DC 20024   **Phone:** (202) 488-7000
USA   **Fax:**   (202) 488-0806   **Internet:** http://www.cwfa.org

Contact Person: James A. Woodall, Vice President .

Officers or Principals: Beverly LaHaye, President/Chairman ($76,915); James A. Woodall, Vice President, Management ($71,360); Lee K. LaHaye, Vice President, Finance ($70,027); Penny L. Young, Director, Legislation; Paulette Brack, Vice President; Patricia Fava, National Field Director; Laurie Tryfiates, Director of Legislative Affairs; Kathy Arrington, Chairman; Jean Crisp, Treasurer; Barrie Lyons, Secretary.

Mission or Interest: An educational and legal defense foundation that seeks to protect the family and preserve traditional Christian-American values.

Accomplishments: The largest conservative women's organization with over 600,000 members in 2,500 regional groups. Beverly LaHaye's daily radio show, "Beverly LaHaye Live," is heard by more than 500,000; and won the 1993 Best Talk Show of the Year award from the National Religious Broadcasters. CWFA's website also won an award from the National Religious Broadcasters. In the fiscal year ending June 1995 CWA spent $8,514,545 on its programs. $2,196,447 of this was spent on radio and television programming. CWA awarded $59,600 in grants. Recipients included; $20,000 for the Life Issues Institute, $9,100 for the Council for National Policy, and $1,000 for Liberty University. The remaining grants went to various colleges, universities, and for honorarium.

Total Revenue: FY ending 6/95 $10,371,563 (-4%)(2) **Total Expenses:** $10,610,865 80%/5%/14% **Net Assets:** $424,879

Products or Services: College scholarship competition for graduating high school seniors accepted at a conservative Christian college. Grassroots organizing, newsletter, annual conference, radio and television programming, grants, and lobbying. In the fiscal year ending June 1995 CWA spent $117,289 on the direct lobbying of legislators, the previous year CWA did not lobby, but this was a decrease of 7% from $126,134 two years prior and a 61% decrease from $298,183 three years prior.

Tax Status: 501(c)(3) **Employees:** 34 **Citations:** 287:31

Board of Directors or Trustees: Sandy Anderson, Kathy Arrington, Peggy Pishop, Paulette Brack, Betty Lou Martin, Shirley Peters, Jan Roberto, M.D., Maxine Sieleman.

Periodicals: *Concerned Women for America Newsletter, Family Voice* (monthly magazine).
Internships: Yes, 4-6 week internships with a stipend.
Other Information: Established in 1979 by Beverly LaHaye. President LaHaye is married to Rev. Tim LaHaye, a co-founder of the Moral Majority. Affiliated with the 501(c)(4) Concerned Women for America Legislative Action Committee at the same address. In the fiscal year ending June 1995, the two affiliates had combined net revenues, expenses, and assets of $12,908,883, $13,366,635, and $511,557. Beverly LaHaye serves as president of both and received a combined $88,915 from the two affiliates. CWA received $9,741,623, or 94% of revenue, from contributions and grants awarded by foundations, businesses, and inidivduals. (These grants included $1,226,710 from its affiliate, the CWA Legislative Action Committee, $5,000 from the Richard & Helen DeVos Foundation, and $1,400 from the Alliance Defense Fund.) $322,458, or 3%, from mailing list rentals. $136,473, or 1%, from royalties. $103,475, or 1%, from book sales. The remaining revenue came from convention fees and interest on savings.

Concerned Women for America Legislative Action Committee (CWALAC)

370 L'Enfant Promenade, Suite 800
Washington, DC 20024   **Phone:**   (202) 488-7000
USA   **Fax:**   (202) 488-0806   **Internet:** http://www.cwfa.org

Contact Person: Beverly LaHaye, President.
Officers or Principals: Beverly LaHaye, President ($12,000); Betty Lou Martin, Vice President ($0); Joanne Spence, Treasurer ($0); Linda Murphy, Secretary.
Mission or Interest: Lobbying division of Concerned Women for America. Advocates traditional values and anti-abortion-based public policy.
Accomplishments: In the fiscal year ending June 1995, the Committee spent $2,491,238 on its programs. This included a grant of $1,226,710 to its affiliate, Concerned Women for America.
Total Revenue: FY ending 6/95 $2,537,320 20%(2) **Total Expenses:** $2,755,770 90%/2%/8% **Net Assets:** $86,678
Tax Status: 501(c)(4)   **Citations:** 287:31
Board of Directors or Trustees: Debbie Beyer, Addie Anderson, Sandy Anderson, Jean Crisp, Linda Murphy, Shirley Peters, Cindy Johnson, Pam Shellenberger, Lori Scheck.
Other Information: Affiliated with the 501(c)(3) Concerned Women for America at the same address. In the fiscal year ending June 1995, the two affiliates had combined net revenues, expenses, and assets of $12,908,883, $13,366,635, and $511,557. Beverly LaHaye serves as president of both and received a combined $88,915 from the two affiliates. The Committee received $2,537,320, or 100% of revenue, from contributions.

Concord Coalition

1019 19th St., N.W., Suite 810
Washington, DC 20036   **Phone:**   (800) 231-6800
USA

Contact Person: Martha Phillips, Executive Director.
Officers or Principals: Martha Phillips, Executive Director ($126,750); Paula Price, Regional Field Director ($58,500); Peter G. Peterson, President ($0); Hon. Warren B. Rudman, Chairman; Lloyd Cutler, Secretary/Treasurer; David Sawyer, Vice Chairman, Public Relations; Dr. John White, Vice Chairman, Issues Committee; Eugene Freedman, Vice Chairman, Fundraising Committee.
Mission or Interest: Bipartisan organization "to research economic issues, and to inform the public of the problems associated with the Federal budget deficits and the national debt."
Accomplishments: Produced the "Contract With Our Grandchildren", a plan to balance the budget by the year 2002. Also developed a "Zero Deficit Plan" to eliminate the deficit in the year 2000 with a combination of spending cuts and tax increases. In 1994 the Coalition spent $1,794,378 on its programs.
Total Revenue: 1994 $3,829,806 **Total Expenses:** $2,921,687 61%/8%/31% **Net Assets:** $1,440,054
Products or Services: Publications and deficit reduction plans. "Tough Choices" Deficit Reduction Scorecard that rates House and Senate representatives on their votes. The Coalition believes that "balancing the budget takes priority over tax cuts, so cutting taxes results in a negative score. During the 104th Congress in 1995, a vote to cut taxes was double-weighted, making it an even larger negative influence on rankings.
Tax Status: 501(c)(3)   **Citations:** 999:9
Board of Directors or Trustees: Prof. John Gardner (Stanford Univ.), Prof. Hanna Gray (Univ. of Chicago), William Gray, III (United Negro College Fund), Dr. George Hatsopoulos, Paul Volker (former Chairman, Federal Reserve Board), Harvey Meyerhoff, Joseph Segel.
Periodicals: Newsletter.
Other Information: Established in 1992 by two moderate former Senators, the late Paul Tsongas of Massachusetts and Warren Rudman of New Hampshire. The Coalition received $3,475,193, or 91% of revenue, from contributions and grants awarded by foundations, businesses, and individuals. (In 1995 these grants included $51,000 from the Smith Richardson Foundation.) These contributions and grants have averaged a 141% increase per year since its founding. $342,719, or 9%, from program services. The remaining revenue came from interest on savings and temporary cash investments.

Congressional Institute

316 Pennsylvania Ave., S.E., Suite 403
Washington, DC 20003   **Phone:**   (202) 547-4600   **E-Mail:**   Change_Leader@CongInst.org
USA   **Fax:**   (202) 547-3556   **Internet:** http://www.CongInst.org

Contact Person: Carl DeMaio.
Officers or Principals: Jerome F. Climer, President; Frank Gregorsky, Editor, *We The People*.
Mission or Interest: Focus on the changing nature of representative government, with an emphasis on decentralization, increased communication, and the use of markets to allocate goods and resources. "What the nation needs now - and what we are looking to you to help provide - are transformational, visionary, and 'outside-the-box' ideas to solve the toughest domestic and international issues."
Accomplishments: Created an interactive website, through which any interested party can participate in the development of the Institute's "Strategic Plan for the 105th Congress." Morton Kondracke of *Roll Call* says "I discovered 10 years ago that (*We the People* editor) Frank Gregorsky is one of the best researchers in Washington. This magazine is the latest confirmation - it has rigor, creativity and <u>enthusiasm</u>." Has studied health care, tax reform, the environment, campaign reform, and other areas.
Tax Status: 501(c)(4)
Board of Directors or Trustees: Kenneth Duberstein, Bruce Gates, Edward Hamberger, Michael Johnson, John Maddox, Daniel Mattoon, W. Dennis Thomas.
Periodicals: *We the People* (bimonthly magazine).
Other Information: Established in 1987.

Connecticut Policy and Economic Council (CPEC)

99 Pratt St., Suite 5
Hartford, CT 06103   **Phone:**   (203) 527-8177
USA   **Fax:**   (203) 246-9790

Contact Person: Natalie G. Bancroft, Membership and Program Director.
Officers or Principals: John J. Carson, President ($106,219); Michael Levin, Vice President ($57,901); Madeline Cassavino, Secretary ($33,861); Frederick J. Boos, Treasurer; Dr. James T. Vanderslica, Chairman; Marie O'Brien, J. Yancey Brame, Vice Chairmen.
Mission or Interest: "To help elevate, clarify and influence the public debate on key issues in Connecticut and to work toward efficient state and local government at the most reasonable cost to taxpayers. . . The Council has supported a Constitutional spending limit for the state budget, a tighter state debt limit and tax reform."
Accomplishments: "Our objective, well regarded research, has been used to limit taxes and restrain state spending. The Council is a frequent source for media analysis on fiscal and economic issues and has had membership on important state commissions and task forces." Connecticut's Republican Governor John G. Rowland said of the Council, "I am pleased we had the opportunity to have a frank exchange concerning Connecticut's fiscal and economic future. I found the information you provided provocative and useful." In the fiscal year ending June 1995, the Council spent $244,278 on its programs.
Total Revenue: FY ending 6/95 $460,902 7%(2) **Total Expenses:** $479,254 51%/47%/2% **Net Assets:** $93,563
Products or Services: Biennial "Taxpayers Guide to Connecticut's Economy and Government." Numerous studies and reports. Publishes an annual analysis of 169 municipal budgets.
Tax Status: 501(c)(4)   **Citations:** 34:122
Board of Directors or Trustees: Marjorie Anderson (World Affairs Council), Janet Hansen, James Lutstein, William Malchodi (ITT Hartford), Thomas Volpe (Champion Intl. Corp.).
Periodicals: *Connecticut Watch* (bimonthly statistical report), *Budget Watch* (bimonthly state fiscal analysis), *Taxpayers News* (quarterly newsletter).
Other Information: Established in 1942. Affiliated with the 501(c)(3) CPEC Foundation at the same address. CPEC received $383,253, or 83% of revenue, from membership dues. $20,603, or 4%, from reimbursements for research performed. $19,300, or 4%, from grants from its affiliate. $16,800, or 4%, from annual meeting revenues. $11,104, or 2%, from book sales. $8,377, or 2%, from dividends and interest from securities. The remaining revenue came from interest on savings and temporary cash investments.

Connection, The

101 S. Whiting, Suite 700
Alexandria, VA 22304   **Phone:**   (703) 461-8645
USA

Contact Person: Erwin S. Strauss.
Mission or Interest: "*The Connection* is the Amateur Press Association for talk about hot potatoes like politics and religion. More a club than a magazine, members send in what they want to publish to a central mailer (E. S. Strauss), who sends a copy of each to all."
Accomplishments: Publication of *The Connection* since 1968
Tax Status: Unincorporated.
Periodicals: *The Connection*.
Internships: No.

Other Information: Members/subscribers can have one page per issue published free. . . additional pages can be bought for a nominal fee. *"The Connection* was started as *The Libertarian Connection* in 1968, and there was a stated requirement that subscribers be libertarian. In practice, this standard was rarely seriously enforced. Though most members remain libertarians, I dropped the word from the title to show that proponents of all views are welcome (it's hard to have a dialogue without foils)."

Conservative Book Club
15 Oakland Ave.
Harrison, NY 10528
USA

Mission or Interest: Serves as a clearinghouse for books of interest to conservative readers.
Accomplishments: Book club offering monthly selections of conservative books at 20-50% discounts
Products or Services: Newsletter with book reviews, club selections, and listings of conservative activities.
Tax Status: For profit.
Periodicals: *Club Bulletin.*
Other Information: Sells slightly older titles at substantial discounts. The club offers free books to new members. The Club is half-owned by Eagle Publishing, Inc. (For more information, see Eagle Publishing, Inc.)

Conservative Caucus
450 E. Maple Ave., Suite 309
Vienna, VA 22180   **Phone:** (703) 938-9626   **E-Mail:** ccrndorf@cais.com
USA   **Fax:** (703) 281-4108

Contact Person: Charles Orndorff, Vice Chairman.
Officers or Principals: Howard Phillips, Chairman ($202,333); Charles Orndorff, Vice Chairman ($65,147); Peter Thomas, Secretary ($1,500); Lawrence J. Straw, Jr., Treasurer.
Mission or Interest: "Grassroots lobbying to maximize conservative influence on the Federal government."
Accomplishments: Collected signatures for a "Congressional Impeachment Inquiry" into President Clinton and the 'Whitewater' dealings. Chairman Phillips has run for President of the United States as the candidate for the U.S. Taxpayers Party. Historically, the Conservative Caucus helped to defeat the SALT II treaty, repeal the Clark Amendment, repeal the Catastrophic Coverage Act, and restore Oliver North's Marine pension. In the fiscal year ending June 1995, the Caucus spent $1,783,972 on its programs.
Total Revenue: FY ending 6/95 $2,378,788 (-9%)(2) **Total Expenses:** $2,680,428 67%/11%/23% **Net Assets:** (-$698,608)
Products or Services: "Conservative Roundtable" weekly cable television show, publications, and lobbying.
Tax Status: 501(c)(4) **Annual Report:** No. **Employees:** 20 **Citations:** 284:32
Board of Directors or Trustees: Dr. James Lucier, Hon. J. Alan MacKay, Dr. James McClellan.
Periodicals: *Member's Message* (newsletter), *Taxpayer Scorecard.*
Internships: Yes.
Other Information: Founded in 1974. Affiliated with the 501(c)(3) Conservative Caucus Research, Analysis, and Education Foundation at the same address. Chairman Phillips' compensation was mostly in the form of funds for retirement, $111,333. The Caucus received $2,258,064, or 95% of revenue, from contributors and grants. $116,124, or 5%, from list rentals. The remaining revenue came from interest on savings and temporary cash investments.

Conservative Caucus Research, Analysis and Education Foundation
450 E. Maple Ave., Suite 309
Vienna, VA 22180   **Phone:** (703) 938-9626   **E-Mail:** ccrndorf@cais.com
USA   **Fax:** (703) 281-4108

Contact Person: Charles Orndorff, Administrative Vice President.
Officers or Principals: Helen Gombert, Executive Assistant ($50,354); Charles Orndorff, Administrative Vice President ($26,006); Howard Phillips, President ($0).
Mission or Interest: Research and education affiliate of the Conservative Caucus.
Accomplishments: In the fiscal year ending November 1994, the Foundation spent $749,831 on its programs. The largest program, with expenditures of $589,619, was public education and the dissemination of information. $107,421 was spent on research, and $52,791 was spent producing publications.
Total Revenue: FY ending 11/94 $1,065,071 **Total Expenses:** $1,015,131 74%/11%/15% **Net Assets:** (-$4,285)
Tax Status: 501(c)(3) **Citations:** 284:32
Board of Directors or Trustees: Jack Abramoff, Neuberne Brown, Dr. Martin Claussen, Mrs. Richard Conner, Mitchell Drake, Linda Bean Folkers, Jesse Grier, Hon. Louis Jenkins, Brig. Gen. Albion Knight (USA-Ret), Donald McAlvany, Edward McAteer, J.A. Parker, Carl Shipley, Lt. Col. Richard Shoff, Abe Siemens, Maj. Gen. John Singlaub (USA-Ret), Ronald Tinlin, Herbert Titus.
Internships: Yes.
Other Information: Affiliated with the 501(c)(4) Conservative Caucus. Charles Orndorff also serves as Administrative Vice Chairman for the Conservative Caucus. During the fiscal year that ended November 1994, Orndorff received total compensation of $103,068. Policy Analysis, Inc., of Vienna, VA, was contracted and paid $117,550 to conduct research. The Foundation received $763,619, or 72% of revenue, from contributions and grants awarded by foundations, businesses, and individuals. (These grants included $25,000 from the Milliken Foundation, $5,000 from the Vernon K. Krieble Foundation, $5,000 from the Richard & Helen DeVos Foundation.) $235,749, or 22%, from a series of lectures conducted as part of a tour. $24,763, or 2%, from mailing list rentals. The remaining revenue came from reimbursements from their lobbying affiliate, dividends and interest from securities, interest on savings and temporary cash investments, and other miscellaneous sources.

Conservative Chronicle

9 2nd St., N.W.
Hampton, IA 50441
USA

Phone: (515) 456-2585
Fax: (515) 456-2587

Contact Person: Joseph P. Roth, Publisher.
Mission or Interest: Weekly tabloid newspaper that publishes nationally-syndicated conservative columnists and cartoonists. Columnists include William F. Buckley, Jr., Thomas Sowell, Walter E. Williams, Don Feder, and others
Tax Status: For profit. **Annual Report:** No. **Employees:** 12
Periodicals: *Conservative Chronicle* (weekly tabloid).
Internships: No.
Other Information: Does not accept advertising.

Conservative Citizens Foundation

(see Council of Conservative Citizens)

Conservative Consensus

P.O. Box 17912
Seattle, WA 98107
USA

Phone: (206) 783-3243
Fax: same

E-Mail: ccnrs@eskimo.com
Internet: http://www.eskimo.com/~ccnrs/news.html

Contact Person: Craige A. McMillan, Publisher.
Mission or Interest: Populist/conservative newsletter featuring "honest reporting, analysis, forecasts, politics, religion, education, security, and book reviews."
Accomplishments: "Correctly forecast 1994 Congressional sweep by Republicans - down to number of seats changing hands - six weeks prior to election. Stays 3-6 months ahead on identifying major news stories."
Products or Services: Internet news release service.
Tax Status: For profit. **Annual Report:** No. **Employees:** 3
Periodicals: *Conservative Consensus* (monthly newsletter).

Conservative Political Action Conference (CPAC)

919 Prince St.
Alexandria, VA 22314
USA

Phone: (703) 739-2550
Fax: (703) 548-7657

Internet: http://www.cpac.org

Contact Person: Patricia Kempthorne, Director.
Mission or Interest: Hosts an annual conference "to provide conservative America with a place to meet its current and nurture its upcoming leaders."
Accomplishments: Since 1973, "CPAC has brought together such prominent speakers as Ronald Reagan, George Bush, Newt Gingrich, and Phil Gramm. CPAC draws many of the nation's grassroots leaders - in 1996 attendance was about 1,500."
Tax Status: 501(c)(3) **Annual Report:** No. **Employees:** 4
Board of Directors or Trustees: David Keene (American Conservative Union).
Internships: Yes.
Other Information: A program of the American Conservative Union.

Conservative Review

1307 Dolley Madison Blvd., Room 203
McLean, VA 22101
USA

Phone: (703) 893-7302
Fax: (703) 893-7273

Contact Person: Frederic N. Smith, Editor.
Officers or Principals: Frederic N. Smith, Editor; Prof. Dwight Murphey, Associate Editor; Dr. Susan Huck, Associate Editor.
Mission or Interest: A magazine dedicated to winning the culture war and arranging society on the principles of religion and tradition.
Accomplishments: Prints original articles and reprints by conservative authors including Eric Brodin, Reed Irvine, Larry Sulc, Joseph Douglas, Jr., and others. Features a poetry page and includes book reviews
Tax Status: For profit. **Annual Report:** No. **Employees:** One, several volunteers.
Periodicals: *Conservative Review* (bimonthly).
Internships: Yes, summer internship.
Other Information: Previously published by the Council for Social and Economic Studies. Currently published by Newcomb Publishers. Dr. Susan Huck is the author of Legal Terrorism: The Truth About the Christic Institute. Dr. Dwight Murphy is the author of Liberalism in Contemporary America.

Conservatives for a Constitutional Convention

P.O. Box 582
Desert Hot Springs, CA 92240   **Phone:**   (619) 251-2216
USA

Contact Person: R.D. Adams, Founder.
Mission or Interest: "To arouse public interest in government reform, by means of a call for a National Constitutional Convention, through the voice of the people, voiding illegal legislation, judicial decisions, Presidential executive orders, and bureaucratic intrusions into government operations."
Accomplishments: "A series of 15 'Concerned Patriots' Circulars' plus many other documents" have been produced and continue to be circulated, but "results have been negligible."
Tax Status: Unincorporated.
Other Information: An outgrowth of the Liberty Amendment Committee. The group is largely dormant, but "Concerned Patriots' Circulars" continue to be copied and distributed, and have "achieved recognition by a dozen National Patriotic organizations."

Constitutional Coalition

P.O. Box 37054
St. Louis, MO 63141   **Phone:**   (314) 434-7028
USA   **Fax:**   (314) 878-6294

Contact Person: Tim Weir, President.
Officers or Principals: Tim Weir, President ($0); Betty McDowell, Treasurer ($0); Harry Langengberg, Director ($0).
Mission or Interest: "Understanding, knowing and educating others about our Constitution; acknowledging absolutes as the basis of our laws and God as the giver of freedom." Research and education on constitutional issues, focusing on both the federal and Missouri's Constitutions.
Accomplishments: Has hosted nine conferences since 1985 and was a prime sponsor of The Columbus 500 conference. In 1995 the Coalition spent $81,018 on its programs.
Total Revenue: 1995 $168,437 **Total Expenses:** $167,675 48%/51%/1% **Net Assets:** $34,203
Products or Services: Publications, videos, and conferences. Voters' guides and a congressional handbook. They offer two books by former U.S. Department of Education official Donna Hearne; Paychecks and Power about federal government encroachment on employment and civil liberties, and The Dawning of the Brave New World about 'Outcome Based Education.' Study program including a book and seven videos entitled "Seven Men Who Rule the World from the Grave" about Dewey, Darwin, Freud, Keynes, Marx, and others.
Tax Status: 501(c)(3)
Periodicals: *Frontline* (occasional) covers legislators, legislation and candidates, *Policy Brief* (monthly).
Other Information: Established in 1978 and received tax-exempt status in 1981. The Coalition received $126,469, or 75% of revenue, from contributions and grants awarded by foundations, businesses, and individuals. $41,968, or 25%, from program services, including seminar fees.

Constitutionalists United Against a Constitutional Convention

P.O. Box 11117
Glendale, CA 91206   **Phone:**   (818) 247-5147
USA   **Fax:**   (818) 242-1230

Contact Person: Elliott Graham, Founder/National Chairman.
Officers or Principals: State chairmen in Montana, Michigan, Utah, Ohio, New Jersey, Pennsylvania, Oklahoma and California.
Mission or Interest: Opposed to any attempt to call for a Constitutional Convention. They fear that a Constitutional Convention would result in a 'runaway' convention which would rewrite the Constitution, granting special privileges based on race and gender rather than affirming universal rights, and taking away the right to keep and bear arms.
Accomplishments: They helped stop Constitutional Convention resolutions in Ohio, New Jersey, Michigan, Montana and California. They wrote, introduced and passed resolutions to oppose a convention at the National Rifle Association's general meeting, at the Citizen's Committee for the Right to Keep and Bear Arms, and at the Democratic Party of California. They convinced The U.S. Taxpayer's Party and the American Independent Party to make opposition to a convention part of their platform planks. Active in opposition to the proposed Conference of the States. Graham introduced a resolution at the May 1995 NRA general meeting opposing the Conference of the States; the resolution was not voted on. His opposition was based on the fact that the Conference of the States "meets the requirements for being a Constitutional Convention."
Products or Services: Video cassettes of Public Access TV shows during the Bill of Rights Bicentennial.
Tax Status: Unincorporated. **Annual Report:** No. **Employees:** All volunteers.
Internships: Yes, anyone willing to volunteer.

Constitutionists Networking Center (CNC)

442 E. 1250 Rd.
Baldwin, KS 66006   **Phone:** (913) 594-3367
USA   **Fax:**   same

Contact Person: Walter Myers, Executive Director.
Officers or Principals: Hon. Evan Mecham, Chairman.
Mission or Interest: To restore the Constitution as the supreme law of the land. CNC members are concentrated in the Western states and see special danger in the federal government's encroachment on property rights and the right to keep and bear arms. They advocate peaceful replacement of elected and federal officials with officials who honor their oath to uphold the Constitution
Products or Services: Conferences and workshops.
Tax Status: Unincorporated.
Board of Directors or Trustees: Dr. Greg Dixon (American Coalition of Unregistered Churches), Dr. Ron Carlson, Jim Thomas (Radio Amateur Freemans Association), Joseph Stumph (Committee of 50 States), John Voss.
Other Information: Chairman Evan Mecham, the former Governor of Arizona, states that CNC was formed to combat the "socialist elite one-worlders (who) have taken control over most of the news media, our educational system, and our government." He sees the actions of the "CFR/TC/Bilderberger controlled Clinton Administration" as a window of opportunity, as they have "awakened many of our fellow Americans." Participants in their workshops include Byron Dale and Brett Brough of the National Coalition to Reform Money and Taxes, Liberty Lobby radio host Tom Valentine, Kirk Lyons of the CAUSE Foundation, James Hale of the Patriot Library, Sam Turnipseed of the Council of Conservative Citizens, Fortiscue Hopkins of the Patrick Henry PAC, Vern Holland of the Freemans Association, and others.

Consumer Alert

1001 Connecticut Ave., N.W., Suite 1128
Washington, DC 20036   **Phone:** (202) 467-5809   **E-Mail:** calert@AOL.com
USA   **Fax:**   (202) 467-5814   **Internet:** http://www.his.com/~chyden/CAlert/

Contact Person: Rich Zipperer, Policy Analysis.
Officers or Principals: Frances B. Smith, Executive Director ($45,000); William C. MacLeod, Chairman ($0); Barbara Keating-Edh, President ($0); Carol Dawson, Secretary.
Mission or Interest: "To enhance understanding and appreciation of the consumer benefits of a market economy so that individuals and policy makers rely more on private rather than government approaches to consumer concerns."
Accomplishments: Published a joint study with the Media Research Center about bias in articles on public policy appearing in women's magazines (*Redbook, Good Housekeeping*, etc.). In 1996 Consumer Alert testified before congress on how "excessive use of federal authority, whether through official actions or through unofficial pronouncements, distorts market forces, drives up prices, and reduces choices for consumers." Entered comments for the record during public hearings on; the FDA's policy of restricting information pharmaceutical firms may distribute regarding their drugs, the FTC's policies regarding the internet, opposing the U.S. Department of Agriculture's plan to create a regional dairy marketing commission in New England that would "create a cartel to raise prices of dairy products and block competition from dairy farmers in other states," and opposed raising the Corporate Average Fuel Economy (CAFE) standards for passenger vans, sport utility vehicles, and light trucks which would cause "a shift to smaller vehicles (that) could dramatically decrease safety and restrict consumer choice." In 1995 Consumer Alert spent $126,856 on its programs. This included a $21,875 Science Journalism Fellowship awarded to Michael Fumento. Fumento is the author of The Myth of Heterosexual AIDS and other books.
Total Revenue: 1995 $205,315 36%(2) **Total Expenses:** $145,372 87%/13%/0% **Net Assets:** $79,353
Tax Status: 501(c)(3) **Employees:** 5
Board of Directors or Trustees: Richard Collins, Carol Dawson, Suzanne Garment, Roger Meiners (Univ. of Texas at Arlington), Terry Neese, Anthony Palladino, Hon. Denny Smith, Richard Weiss. The Advisory Council includes: Prof. Thomas DiLorenzo (Loyola College), Prof. Yale Brozen (Univ. of Chicago), Jerry Cohen, B.S., M.P.H., C.I.H. (Science Applications International Corp.), Prof. Philip Dziuk (Univ. of Illinois at Urbana-Champaign), Prof. J. Gordon Edwards (San Jose State Univ.), Hugh Ellsaesser (Lawrence Livermore Laboratory), Prof. Thomas Hazlett (Univ. of California, Davis), Ernest Hueter (National Legal Center for the Public Interest), Prof. Thomas Jukes (Space Science Laboratory, Univ. of California at Berkeley), Prof. Arthur Kantrowitz (Dartmouth College), Lawrence Kudlow (*National Review*), Prof. Margaret Maxey (Univ. of Texas, Austin), Prof. John McKetta (Univ. of Texas, Austin), Prof. Patrick Michaels (Univ. of Virginia, Charlottesville), Malcolm Ross (U.S. Geological Survey), Elizabeth Whelan (American Council on Science and Health), Prof. Walter Williams (George Mason Univ.), Prof. Bruce Yandle (Clemson Univ.), others.
Periodicals: *Consumer Comments* (newsletter).
Internships: Yes.
Other Information: Established in 1977. A member of the National Consumer Coalition. Consumer Alert received $186,289, or 91% of revenue, from contributions and grants awarded by foundations, businesses, and individuals. (In 1994-95 these grants included $13,000 from the John M. Olin Foundation, $3,000 from the Roe Foundation, and $1,000 from the Gordon and Mary Cain Foundation.) $16,709, or 8%, from membership dues. (Membership, as measured by membership fees, hit a high in 1991, then a low in 1993. Since 1993 membership dues have been growing by an average of 70% per year.) The remaining revenue came from interest on savings, conference fees, reimbursed costs, and other miscellaneous sources.

Consumers' Research

800 Maryland Ave., N.E.
Washington, DC 20002   **Phone:**   (202) 546-1713
USA   **Fax:**   (202) 546-1638

Contact Person: Peter L. Spencer, Editor.
Officers or Principals: M. Stanton Evans, President ($0); James Roberts, Vice President ($0); Ronald Pearson ($0); Allan Ryskind, Treasurer; Whitney L. Ball, Assistant Publisher.
Mission or Interest: Consumer journalism. Reports on health care, the environment, regulations, safety, and nutrition. *"Consumers' Research* is the only consumer-oriented magazine in the United States that analyzes and reports on issues with an appreciation of free-markets and an understanding of economic principles."
Accomplishments: Reports on cable TV competition, problems with generic drugs, sources of "the energy crisis," and more.
Total Revenue: 1995 $3,444 (-74%)(2)   **Total Expenses:** $71,606   **Net Assets:** (-$126,774)
Tax Status: 501(c)(3)   **Annual Report:** No.   **Employees:** 7
Board of Directors or Trustees: Daniel Oliver (Citizens for a Sound Economy), Ruth Matthews, Terrence Scanlon (Heritage Found.).
Periodicals: *Consumers' Research* (monthly magazine).
Internships: Yes, accepted periodically through the National Journalism Center.
Other Information: Published since 1928. Affiliated with the 501(c)(3) Education and Research Institute at the same address. In 1995 the two affiliates had combined revenue, expenses, and assets of $343,764, $440,728, and (-$85,379). *Consumers' Research* received $20,159, or 60% of gross revenue, from royalties. $12,077, or 36%, from rental income. $1,496, or 4%, from the sale of reprints. The organization lost $30,355 on the sale of its publication.

Contra-PC

2635 Camino del Rio South, Suite 108
San Diego, CA 92108   **Phone:**   (619) 440-1703
USA   **Fax:**   (619) 440-2532

Contact Person: Peter D. Lepiscopo, J.D., Editor.
Mission or Interest: To provide a newsletter with opinions contrary to current, `politically correct,' political, moral, social and ethical views.
Periodicals: *Contra-PC* (monthly).
Internships: Yes, unpaid internships for students of English and history who have studied the classics.
Other Information: Established in 1993.

Coral Ridge Ministries Media

5554 N. Federal Highway, Suite 200
Fort Lauderdale, FL 33308   **Phone:**   (954) 772-0404
USA   **Fax:**   (954) 491-7975   **Internet:** http://www.coralridge.org

Contact Person: John Aman, Publications Manager.
Officers or Principals: David Walters, Director of Ministry Advancement ($73,815); Mike McKee, Director of Support Services ($72,085); James Small, Director of Radio/Television Production ($61,417); Dr. D. James Kennedy, President; Jim Carlson, Vice President; Ralph Mittendorf, Treasurer; Gladys Israels, Secretary.
Mission or Interest: "Protecting religious liberty and America's Christian heritage by encouraging the application of biblical principals to all spheres of our culture and to all of life."
Accomplishments: "Reach approximately three million people weekly with radio and television broadcasts. . . Distributed more than 35,000 Christian books, tapes, and videos each month." Recently opened the Center for Christian Statesmanship in Washington, DC, that was praised by Sen. Jesse Helms (R-NC), who said "the spiritual guidance and encouragement you and your team will give to Capitol Hill will be refreshing and sorely needed." Started the Center for Reclaiming America, a grassroots network "of concerned Christians committed to the restoration of virtue in American culture." Awarded a grant of $50,000 to the Alliance Defense Fund. Sent more than 30,000 petitions to Washington, DC, urging a ban on 'partial birth abortions.' In 1995 the Ministries spent $18,051,178 on its programs.
Total Revenue: 1995 $21,447,057   **Total Expenses:** $20,523,018   88%/4%/8%   **Net Assets:** $4,608,536
Products or Services: Annual 'Reclaiming America for Christ' conference. Annual 'Christian Statesman of the Year' award. The 1996 recipient was Sen. John Ashcroft (R-MO). Radio commentaries and religious television broadcasting. Numerous books, videos, audio tapes, and publications. Lobbying: in 1995 the Ministries spent $429,448 on lobbying, $181,624 on grassroots lobbying and $247,824 on the direct lobbying of legislators. This was an increase of 28% over the previous year.
Tax Status: 501(c)(3)   **Annual Report:** Yes.   **Employees:** 125, ten employees paid over $50,000.   **Citations:** 29:135
Board of Directors or Trustees: A. Robert Coningsby, Lawrence Eldridge, Lyle Everse, Anna Mae French, Herman Hinz, Jr., Walter Koenig, Gene Sitter.
Periodicals: *IMPACT* (monthly newsletter), *The Statesmanship Statute* (monthly newsletter), *The Washington Statesman* (monthly newsletter).

Internships: Yes, for college students during the summer, fall, and spring semesters.
Other Information: Established in 1994 as a separate incorporated entity from Coral Ridge Ministries. President D. James Kennedy, Ph.D., is the Senior Pastor of the Coral Ridge Presbyterian Church, Fort Lauderdale, FL. The D. James Kennedy Center for Christian Statesmanship is located at; 214 Massachusetts Ave., N.E., Suite 220, Washington, DC 20002, (202) 547-3052, fax (202) 547-3287. The director of the Institute is Dr. Frank Wright. The Coral Ridge Ministries Media received $21,311,721, or 99% of revenue, from contributions and grants awarded by foundations, businesses, and individuals. (These grants included $1,250,000 from the Richard and Helen DeVos Foundation. Contributions and grants increased 141% over the initial year.) The remaining revenue came from interest on savings and temporary cash investments and the sale of assets.

Council for Affordable Health Insurance (CAHI)

112 S. West St., Suite 400
Alexandria, VA 22314   **Phone:** (703) 836-6200   **E-Mail:** cahi2@aol.com
USA   **Fax:**   (703) 836-6550

Contact Person: Kelly McCarthy, Manager of Public Affairs.
Officers or Principals: Greg Scandlen, former Executive Director ($112,600); David E. Lack, Executive Director; E. Rod Ross, President ($0); Mark Litow, Jeff Burman, Vice Presidents ($0); John Whelan, Treasurer; Merlinda Henry-Adams; Victoria Bunce, Director of Research and Policy.
Mission or Interest: An association of small to mid-sized insurance companies that fights for free-market solutions to health-care problems. Reforms it supports include Medical Savings Accounts and other policies that increase the patient's knowledge and decision-making power.
Accomplishments: Membership consists of over 40 "small to mid-sized" insurance companies that cover over 40 million people, as well as insurance agents, physicians, and actuaries. Published several studies on subjects such as open enrollment, community rating, children and insurance coverage, guaranteed issues (mandatory coverage regardless of risks), and benefits mandated by the states.
Total Revenue: FY ending 3/95 $1,230,097 46%(2) **Total Expenses:** $1,127,377 100%/0%/0% **Net Assets:** (-$21,478)
Products or Services: In the fiscal year ending March 1995 the Council spent $127,697 on lobbying.
Tax Status: 501(c)(6)   **Citations:** 32:125
Periodicals: *Full Coverage* (newsletter).
Other Information: Founded in March 1992. The Council received $1,056,537, or 86% of revenue, from membership dues. $132,221, or 11%, from contributions and grants awarded by foundations, businesses, and individuals. $20,049, or 2%, from the sale of publications. The remaining revenue came from annual meeting fees, royalties, interest on savings and temporary cash investments, and other miscellaneous sources.

Council for Basic Education (CBE)

1319 F St., N.W., Suite 900
Washington, DC 20004   **Phone:** (202) 347-4171
USA   **Fax:**   (202) 347-5047

Contact Person: Christopher T. Cross, President.
Officers or Principals: Christopher T. Cross, President ($133,500); Elsa M. Little, Associate Director ($76,000).
Mission or Interest: Advocates educational reform. Their three central principles are, 1) academic excellence for all schools, 2) the basic liberal arts subjects are what should be first and foremost, and 3) the premise that all children can learn.
Accomplishments: Educator Jacques Barzun, a director emeritus of the Council, said, "The Council was first in calling attention to the plight of the schools and has been first - in the other sense of outstanding - in proposing and testing remedies. That should be enough to establish its values to the country - an indispensable institution." In the fiscal year ending June 1995, the Council spent $1,934,332 on its programs.
Total Revenue: FY ending 6/95 $2,137,075 ($1,000,000, or 47%, from government grants) (-12%)(2)
Total Expenses: $2,159,860 **Net Assets:** $1,841,165
Products or Services: Several Fellowships, including: The Sci-Mat Fellowships which strengthen secondary level math and science teaching, Independent Study in the Humanities Fellowships, and the Arts Education Fellowships. They support the Writing to Learn program, which helps teachers promote writing as a thinking tool for all disciplines.
Tax Status: 501(c)(3)   **Citations:** 81:76
Board of Directors or Trustees: Mrs. J. William Fulbright, Vice Chairman, Mrs. Talcott Bates (former member, CA State Board of Education), Charles Blitzer (Woodrow Wilson Center); Donald Stewart (Pres., College Board), others.
Periodicals: *Basic Education* (monthly), *Perspective* (quarterly journal).
Other Information: Established in 1956. The Council works with organizations and foundations of all kinds. They have entered into partnerships with teachers' unions and receive funding from the National Endowment for the Humanities and the National Endowment for the Arts (NEA) for art programs. The Council received $1,000,000, or 47% of revenue, from government grants. $931,126, or 44%, from contributions and grants awarded by foundations, businesses, affiliates, and individuals. (These grants included $500,000 over three years from the Pew Charitable Trusts, $24,250 from the William H. Donner Foundation, and $15,000 from the Carthage Foundation.) $122,938, or 6%, from dividends and interest from securities. The remaining revenue came from royalties, honoraria, membership dues, interest on savings, and other miscellaneous sources.

Council for Citizens Against Government Waste

1301 Connecticut Ave., N.W., Suite 400

Washington, DC 20036	**Phone:**	(202) 467-5300	**E-Mail:** cagw@soho.ios.com
USA	**Fax:**	(202) 467-4253	**Internet:** http://www.GOVT-WASTE.org

Contact Person: Thomas Schatz, President.
Officers or Principals: Tom Schatz, President ($0); Jeffrey P. Altman, Secretary ($0); Robert J. Tedeschi, Treasurer ($0).
Mission or Interest: Lobbying affiliate of Citizens Against Government Waste.
Accomplishments: The Council's ratings of Congress, based on the Congressmen's voting record on fiscal issues, has become well known and widely cited. In 1994 the Council spent $1,770,099 on its programs.
Total Revenue: 1994 $2,314,241 34%(5) **Total Expenses:** $2,310,706 77%/6%/17% **Net Assets:** $160,686
Products or Services: Annual "Congressional Ratings Book."
Tax Status: 501(c)(4) **Annual Report:** Yes. **Citations:** 395:27
Internships: Yes.
Other Information: Affiliated with the 501(c)(3) Citizens Against Government Waste at the same address. In 1994 the two affiliates had combined net revenues of $7,906,751, net expenses of $7,228,473, and assets of $2,641,043. The Council received $2,305,031, or 99.6% of revenue, from contributions and grants. The remaining revenue came from interest on savings and temporary cash investments, and other miscellaneous sources.

Council for the Defense of Freedom

4455 Connecticut Ave., N.W., Suite 330

Washington, DC 20008	**Phone:**	(202) 364-2339
USA	**Fax:**	(202) 364-4098

Contact Person: Arthur D. Randall.
Officers or Principals: James Tyson, President ($0); William Kaufman, Vice President ($0); Joseph Goulden, Treasurer ($0); Col. Samuel T. Dickens, USAF (Ret.), Chairman/Secretary.
Mission or Interest: Studies and disseminates information on issues pertaining to national security, foreign policy, international relations, and arms control.
Accomplishments: In 1994 the Council spent $87,140 on its programs. This included $7,000 in grants; $3,000 for Accuracy in Media, and $2,000 each for Accuracy in Academia and Anger Control.
Total Revenue: 1994 $80,215 (-15%)(2) **Total Expenses:** $89,818 97%/3%/0% **Net Assets:** $38,596
Tax Status: 501(c)(3) **Annual Report:** No. **Employees:** 1
Periodicals: *Washington Inquirer* (weekly newspaper).
Internships: Yes, paid internships for journalism students.
Other Information: Established during the Korean War "to educate people about the dangers of communist expansionism." The Council received $78,742, or 98% of revenue, from contributions and grants awarded by foundations, businesses, and individuals. These grants have been steadily declining in recent years. Since 1991 they have been declining by an average of 23% per year. $1,473, or 2%, from interest on savings and temporary cash investments.

Council for National Policy (CNP)

3030 Clarendon Blvd., Suite 340

Arlington, VA 22201	**Phone:**	(703) 525-8822
USA		

Contact Person: Morton C. Blackwell, Executive Director.
Officers or Principals: Morton C. Blackwell, Executive Director ($58,500); Hon. Edwin Meese, III, President ($0); Hon. Holland H. Coors, Vice President ($0); Reed E. Larson, Secretary/Treasurer.
Mission or Interest: "To educate its members and the public on matters relating to national policy."
Accomplishments: In 1995 the Council spent $413,842 on its programs.
Total Revenue: 1995 $617,773 **Total Expenses:** $580,385 71%/29%/0% **Net Assets:** (-$25,242)
Products or Services: Three conferences per year, educational materials.
Tax Status: 501(c)(3) **Annual Report:** No. **Employees:** 3 **Citations:** 25:140
Board of Directors or Trustees: Hon. Gary Bauer (Family Research Council), Foster Friess, H. Preston Hawkins, Hon. Donald Paul Hodel (Secretary of the Interior, 1985-89), Rep. Louis Jenkins (R-LA), Marion Magruder, Jr., Sam Moore, Lt. Col. Oliver North, USMC (Ret.), Howard Phillips (Conservative Caucus), Dr. Lowell Smith (Nichols College), LaNeil Wright Spivy.
Periodicals: *Policy Counsel* (semi-annual journal that reprints speeches from Council meetings).
Internships: Yes, for periods of 3-4 months.
Other Information: Established in 1981. Affiliated with the 501(c)(4) CNP Action at the same address. The Council received $477,179, or 77% of revenue, from contributions and grants awarded by foundations, businesses, and individuals. (These grants included $5,000 from the Castle Rock Foundation, $4,000 from the Heritage Foundation, $2,500 from the John William Pope Foundation, and $1,490 from the Home School Legal Defense Foundation. In 1994, $20,000 from the Richard & Helen DeVos Foundation, $9,100 from Concerned Women for America, and $8,000 from the Aequus Institute. Contributions and grants have been erratic, and have averaged $470,296 since 1991.) $136,986, or 22%, from conference fees. The remaining revenue came from dividends and interest from securities, and other miscellaneous sources.

Council of Conservative Citizens (CCC)

P.O. Box 9683
St. Louis, MO 63122   **Phone:**   (314) 291-8474
USA

Contact Person: Gordon Lee Baum, CEO.
Officers or Principals: Gordon Lee Baum, CEO ($0); Tom Dover, President ($0); William D. Lord, Jr., Senior Field Coordinator ($0); Claire C. Bawcom, Secretary.
Mission or Interest: Represents the "No Longer Silent Majority." Building a network of conservative groups and individuals at the state and local level.
Accomplishments: Members and local chapters have been able to influence various elections. "Kept the Confederate flag flying over state house domes in South Carolina and on the Mississippi state flag." Columnist Samuel Francis says, "CCC's localism and populist activism grows out of the republican tradition - not the Stupid Party's phony republicanism that shills for Big Business and its statist and globalist agendas but the real republicanism of the Founding Fathers." Although concentrated in the South, they now have chapters and affiliates in 21 states throughout the country, members in all 50 states, 6 foreign countries, and continue to expand.
Total Revenue: 1995 $44,084 **Total Expenses:** $53,802 **Net Assets:** $14,844
Tax Status: 501(c)(4)
Periodicals: *Council Reporter* (quarterly newsletter) and *Citizen Informer* (monthly newspaper).
Internships: No.
Other Information: Established in 1990. *Citizen Informer* carries several well-known conservative columnists such as Joe Sobran, Tom Anderson, Llewellyn Rockwell, Sam Francis, Pat Buchanan, and Sen. Trent Lott (R-MS). The Council is also affiliated with the 501(c)(3) Conservative Citizens Foundation, which conducts surveys and research of both conservative opinion and the public at large. In 1995 the Foundation had gross revenues of $31,193. The Council received $43,735, or 99% of revenue, from contributors. The remaining revenue came from investment income.

Council of Volunteer Americans (CVA)

7263 Maple Place, Suite 203
Annandale, VA 22003   **Phone:**   (703) 379-9188   **Internet:** http://www.impeachclinton.org
USA

Contact Person: Ronald Wilcox, Executive Director.
Officers or Principals: Ronald Wilcox, Executive Director; Eugene A. Delgaudio, Director.
Mission or Interest: Hosts the "Clinton Investigation Commission," a project devoted to "populariz(ing) the allegations (against President Clinton) so that people can take it and understand it." Other projects include the "Committee to Impeach the President," and the "Conservative Media Commissions Project."
Accomplishments: The Council claims to have delivered 343,231 petitions to Congress calling for prosecution of President and Mrs. Clinton. Hosted a memorial service for Clinton aide Vince Foster, who the Council believes was "murdered." The service caught the attention of *The New Republic*, which called the Council more extreme than "even those on the rightmost fringe of the legitimate political spectrum." Hosted other protests and media events, including the placement of a "Drug Testing Station" outside the gates of the White House and activists dressed as "File Man" to call attention to the administration's possession of over 900 FBI files.
Total Revenue: 1995 $1,247,818 **Total Expenses:** $954,132 76%/1%/23%
Tax Status: 501(c)(4)
Board of Directors or Trustees: Scott Lauf, Mike Davis.
Periodicals: *Report to Congress* (quarterly newsletter).
Other Information: Established in 1981.

Covenant Enterprises / *Journal of Biblical Ethics in Medicine*

P.O. Box 14488
Augusta, GA 30919   **Phone:**   (706) 736-0161   **E-Mail:** famlymed.epayne@mail.mcg.edu
USA   **Fax:**   (706) 721-0758
                            Internet: http://www.usit.net/public/capo/friendly/jbem/intro_pa.htm

Contact Person: Ed Payne, M.D., Director.
Mission or Interest: "Medical ethics from Biblical foundations. . . To reach physicians with a commitment to the Bible as foundational to medical ethics."
Accomplishments: Has featured articles by Harold O.J. Brown, John Jefferson Davis, Alister McGrath, and others
Products or Services: Books, newsletters, publications and audio tapes. Back issues of the Journal are available in bound volumes. Offer copies of Patient Power, "the best current answer to the health-care dilemma," to subscribers.
Tax Status: For profit.
Periodicals: *Journal of Biblical Ethics in Medicine* (quarterly journal).
Other Information: Established in 1987.

Criminal Justice Legal Foundation (CJLF)

2131 L St.
Sacramento, CA 95816   **Phone:** (916) 446-0345   **E-Mail:** cjlf@netcom.com
USA   **Fax:**   (916) 446-1194

Contact Person: Michael Rushford, President.
Officers or Principals: Michael Rushford, President ($87,224); Kent Scheidegger, Legal Director ($82,220); Charles Hobson, Attorney ($67,463); John C. Argue, Chairman; Hon. George Deukmejin, Vice Chairman; Milan D. Smith, Jr., Secretary/Treasurer.
Mission or Interest: "To encourage precedent-setting appellate court decisions which recognize the rights of crime victims and the law-abiding public."
Accomplishments: "Since 1989 the Foundation has maintained the best win/loss ratio of any public interest group participating in cases before the United States Supreme Court." Recent victories included: Loving v. United States in which a member of the military convicted of double-homicide charged that the court-martial process violated his constitutional rights; the ACLU joined the case on his behalf. The Supreme Court ruled in favor of CJLF, saying that the military did not have to adopt what CJLF calls "the same complicated process for death penalty cases that plagues the civilian criminal justice system." United States v. Armstrong in which the Supreme Court overturned a federal court ruling that "allowed criminal defendants to make unsupported claims of racial bias to avoid trial." The Foundation has been honored by former Attorney General Edwin Meese. In the fiscal year ending July 1996 the Foundation spent $291,099 on its programs.
Total Revenue: FY ending 7/96 $428,656 **Total Expenses:** $457,822 64%/16%/20% **Net Assets:** $367,038
Products or Services: Numerous publications, law review articles, and handbooks.
Tax Status: 501(c)(3) **Annual Report:** No. **Employees:** 7   **Citations:** 35:120
Board of Directors or Trustees: Robert Carrau, Lawrence Del Santo, Osias Goren, Carl Gregory, Barron Hilton (Chair/CEO, Hilton Hotels Corp.), James Jacobson, Glen McDaniel, Lee Paul, J. Kristoffer Popovich, Charles Reed, James Rettig, Hon. Richard Riordan (mayor, Los Angeles), Mary Rudolph, Ted Westerman, Robert Wilson. Legal Advisory Committee includes: Hon. John Arguelles (former California Supreme Court Justice), Burnham Enersen (former Pres., State Bar of California), Hon. Marcus Kaufman (former California Supreme Court Justice), Prof. Phillipe Nonet (Univ. of California, Berkeley), Hon. Edward Panelli (former California Supreme Court Justice), Hon. Frank Richardson (former, California Supreme Court Justice), Prof. James Q. Wilson (UCLA).
Periodicals: *Advisory* (quarterly newsletter).
Internships: Yes, one annual fellowship for a new law school graduate.
Other Information: The Foundation received $427,425, or 99.7% of revenue, from contributions and grants awarded by foundations, businesses, and individuals. (These grants included $25,000 from the Smith Richardson Foundation, and $25,000 from the Carthage Foundation. In 1994, $12,500 from the F.M. Kirby Foundation.) The remaining revenue came from interest on savings and capital gains on the sale of assets.

Crisis: A Journal of Lay Catholic Opinion

(see Brownson Institute)

Crispus Attucks Institute

2187 Pond View Court
Reston, VA 22091   **Phone:** (703) 620-1262
USA

Contact Person: Thomas I. Ahart, President.
Officers or Principals: Thomas I. Ahart, President ($20,000); Everett Bellamy, Vice President ($0); Ezzie M. May, Secretary/Treasurer ($0).
Mission or Interest: "Promotes research and education activities that increase the understanding of economic productivity in general and capital formation in particular by African Americans. The Institute initiates activities that significantly increase the number of African Americans who actively support the principles of a free-market system."
Accomplishments: Sponsors leadership development on the formulation and management of public policy for African American corporate officers, community leaders, and government officials. Establishes Student Economic Clubs at historically African American Colleges. Sponsors Independent Researchers Awards Program for African American scholars on free-market public policy issues.
Total Revenue: 1993 less than $25,000
Tax Status: 501(c)(3) **Annual Report:** Yes. **Employees:** 5
Board of Directors or Trustees: Marion Bowden (Pres., Blacks in Government), John Castellani (Vice Pres., TRW), Albert Elder, III (Vice Pres., U.S. League of Savings Institutions), Robert Hill (Vice Pres., American Gas Assoc.), James Morrison, Earl Proctor, Walter Larke Sorg, John Wilkes.
Internships: Yes.
Other Information: Established in 1986. Crispus Attucks, a black man, was one of three killed during the Boston Massacre of 1770. He is credited with being the first to die in America's War of Independence. In 1994 the Institute received $1,000 from the Aequus Institute.

Critical Review Foundation / *Critical Review*

P.O. Box 1254
Danbury, CT 06813   **Phone:**   (203) 387-1023   **E-Mail:**   critrev@aol.com
USA   **Fax:**   (203) 794-1007   **Internet:** http:\\\www.sevenbridgespress.com

Contact Person: Jeffrey Friedman, Editor.
Officers or Principals: Richard Cornuelle, Publisher; Dawn Herron, Business Manager.
Mission or Interest: Publishes *Critical Review: An Interdisciplinary Journal of Politics and Society*, an academic journal of classic liberal thought. Specializes in review essays of books on political theory, political science, and political economy.
Accomplishments: Circulation of 3,000. Recent topics include liberalism, communitarianism, Marxism, individualism, consumerism, environmentalism, post-modernism, rational choice theory, Keynesianism, and more. The Review is indexed or abstracted in: Book Review Index, Current Contents/Social & Behavioral Sciences, Index to book Reviews in the Humanities, Political Science Abstracts, and most other social science abstracts
Products or Services: Summer seminars for college students.
Tax Status: 501(c)(3)
Board of Directors or Trustees: Advisors include: David Beito (Univ. of Nevada), Peter Boettke (New York Univ.), James Buchanan (George Mason Univ.), Richard Epstein (Univ. of Chicago), Israel Kirzner (New York Univ.), Seymour Martin Lipset (George Mason Univ.), Thomas Szasz (SUNY), many others.
Periodicals: *Critical Review* (quarterly academic journal).
Other Information: Previously located in New York city. In 1994-95 the Foundation received $15,000 from the Carthage Foundation, $15,000 from the Earhart Foundation, and $5,000 from the Claude R. Lambe Charitable Foundation.

Crystal Star Press

P.O. Box 204
Susquehanna, PA 18847-0204
USA

Contact Person: A. Alexander Stella, President.
Officers or Principals: Avram Beilitzsyn, Comptroller.
Mission or Interest: The primary mission is the revision of the current Pledge of Allegiance. The proposed new version places emphasis on the Constitution, rather than on the symbol of the flag.
Accomplishments: "So far, our organization has published several stage plays dealing with freedom. We've also gained some conventional media attention for our new Pledge of Allegiance."
Products or Services: The CSP offers copies of its play "Crystal Star" for consideration by theater groups with an interest in political analysis.
Tax Status: Unincorporated. **Employees:** Volunteers.
Internships: No.

CSW Freedom School

College of the Southwest
6610 Lovington Highway
Hobbs, NM 88240
USA

Mission or Interest: Educational program at the College of the Southwest "to impart as much knowledge about a free society - its institutions and its philosophy - to as many students as possible". . . based on "the only true world-view that gave birth to and sustained religious, political, and economic freedom in the West: Christianity."
Products or Services: Degree based on 36 academic hours in philosophy, history, politics, and economics. Curriculum materials for other colleges. Guest lecture program, booklets, books, audio and video tapes.
Tax Status: 501(c)(3)
Other Information: Incorporated as a part of the College of the Southwest, established in 1962. The College of the Southwest has approximately 540 students per academic term. The College has annual net revenues and expenses of approximately $4.4 million.

Cuban American National Foundation (CANF)

10441 S.W. 187th St.
Miami, FL 33157   **Phone:**   (305) 592-7768
USA   **Fax:**   (305) 592-7889

Contact Person: Dr. Francisco J. Hernández, President.
Officers or Principals: Mario Miranda ($52,00); Mirta Iglesias ($39,220); Rene J. Silva ($37,301); Dr. Francisco J. Hernández, President; Manuel Cutillas, Chairman; Carlos Arboleya, Vice Chairman. Feliciano Foyo, C.P.A., Treasurer; Tony Costa, Secretary.
Mission or Interest: "The Foundation supports the principles of: respect for human rights; freedom of thought and expression; freedom of religion; the right of the people to freely elect their government; the right to private property; free enterprise; and economic prosperity with social justice."

Accomplishments: Conferences and publications that have attracted such notables as Jeane Kirkpatrick, Susan Kaufman Purcell, and Mark Falcoff. In the fiscal year ending June 1994 the Foundation spent $1,202,773 on its programs. This included a grant of $114,500 for its 501(c)(4) lobbying affiliate, the Cuban American Foundation.
Total Revenue: FY ending 6/94 $1,855,657 (-17%)(1) **Total Expenses:** $2,109,525 57%/24%/14% **Net Assets:** $2,014,720
Tax Status: 501(c)(3)   **Citations:** 399:25
Board of Directors or Trustees: Donato Arguelles, M.D., Jose Bacardi, Manuel Jose Coto, M.D., Hector Hernandez (Interamerican Financial Services), Herminio Orizondo, M.D., Agustin Vazquez Leyva, M.D., and others - many from the Florida and Puerto Rican business communities.
Periodicals: *Cuban Update, Cuba Human Rights Monitor* (monthly newsletter), *Fundacion* (quarterly magazine), and *Cuba Survey* (monthly newsletter).
Other Information: Dr. Francisco Hernandez was a student leader at the University of Havana in the struggle against the Batista dictatorship, then against the Castro regime. He was a participant in the failed Bay of Pigs invasion, and served two years in Castro's jails. He returned to the United States and served in the U.S. Marine Corps. He earned his doctorate in economics from the University of Florida. The Foundation also has an office in Washington, DC: 1000 Thomas Jefferson St., N.W., Suite 505, Washington, DC 20007, (202) 265-2822. They are affiliated with the 501(c)(4) Cuban American Foundation. The National Foundation received $1,699,297, or 92%, from contributions and grants awarded by foundations, businesses, and individuals. $78,366 net, or 4%, from special fund-raising events. $45,559, or 2%, from interest on savings and temporary cash investments. The remaining revenue came from various miscellaneous sources.

Culture Wars

206 Marquette Ave.
South Bend, IN 46617   **Phone:**   (219) 289-9786
USA   **Fax:**   (219) 289-1461

Contact Person: E. Michael Jones, Ph.D., Editor.
Mission or Interest: Magazine of cultural conservatism with a Catholic emphasis.
Accomplishments: Editor E. Michael Jones is the author of numerous books, including <u>John Cardinal Krol and the Cultural Revolution</u> (Fidelity Press), and <u>Degenerate Moderns</u> (Ignatius Press), a book on the influence of Freud, Margaret Mead, Alfred Kinsey, Picasso, and others. Prof. Charles E. Rice of Notre Dame Law School said of *Culture Wars*, "This magazine can make an important contribution by dramatizing without compromise the reality that the culture wars involve the question of who is God: the real God or the autonomous individual and ultimately the state." Keith Fournier of the American Center for Law and Justice said, "I cannot recommend *Culture Wars* highly enough. It's simply the right magazine for the right time."
Tax Status: Nonprofit.
Periodicals: *Culture Wars* (monthly).
Other Information: E. Michael Jones is the long-time editor/publisher of *Fidelity* magazine, established in 1985, then *Culture Wars* in 1995. Jones has merged the two publications into *Culture Wars*, and abandoned the glossy format the magazine started with, going to the austere (and less expensive) format of *Fidelity*.

Curran Foundation

P.O. Box 1575
Wilmington, DE 19899   **Phone:**   (302) 658-4287
USA

Contact Person: Eileen Cousineau, Secretary.
Officers or Principals: Willard A. Sherman, III, President ($0); James C. Stewart, Vice President/Treasurer ($0); Eileen Cousineau, Secretary ($0).
Mission or Interest: Grant-making foundation that includes conservative and free-market organizations in its awards.
Accomplishments: In 1994 the Foundation awarded $122,000 in grants. Recipients included $35,000 for the Foundation for Economic Education, $25,000 for the Intercollegiate Studies Institute, $10,000 for the Independent Institute, $7,500 each for Hillsdale College, and the Public Policy Education Fund, $5,000 for the Institute for Humane Studies, and $2,000 each for the Delaware Council on Economic Education, and the Philadelphia Society.
Total Revenue: 1994 $112,976 **Total Expenses:** $132,840 **Net Assets:** $2,377,894 1%
Tax Status: 501(c)(3)
Board of Directors or Trustees: Edward Crane, Jr., E.W. Dykes, Charles Maddock, Prof. John Allen Sparks (Grove City College).
Other Information: The Foundation received $94,636, or 84% of revenue, from dividends and interest on savings and temporary cash investments. $14,788, or 13%, from capital gains on the sale of assets. $3,552, or 3%, from interest on savings and temporary cash investments. The Foundation held $1,882,475, or 79%, in corporate stock.

David H. Koch Charitable Foundation

4111 E. 37th St. North
Wichita, KS 67220   **Phone:**   (316) 828-5552
USA

Contact Person: Ruth E. Williams, Secretary .

Officers or Principals: David Koch, President ($0); Ruth E. Williams, Secretary ($0); Vonda Holliman, Treasurer ($0).
Mission or Interest: Grant-making foundation that includes libertarian and free-market organizations in its awards.
Accomplishments: In 1995 the Foundation awarded $9,256,760 in grants. Recipients included: $600,000 for Citizens For a Sound Economy, $500,000 each for the Cato Institute and National Foundation for Teaching Entrepreneurship, $250,000 each for the Institute for Humane Studies and Institute for Justice, $100,000 each for the Humane Studies Foundation and Reason Foundation, $50,000 each for the Center for Market Processes and Pacific Research Institute, $25,000 for the Competitive Enterprise Institute, and $10,000 for the National Center for Policy Analysis.
Total Revenue: 1995 $8,930,629 **Total Expenses:** $9,286,275 **Net Assets:** $906,799 -53%(3)
Tax Status: 501(c)(3)
Other Information: Established in 1982. The Foundation received $8,900,000, or 99.7% of revenue, from contributions and grants received from businesses and individuals. The remaining revenue came from interest on savings and temporary cash investments. The Foundation held $909,616, or 99.9% of assets, in savings and temporary cash investments.

David Hume Institute

21 George Square
Edinburgh EH8 9LD, Scotland   **Phone:**   (44-31) 650-4633   **E-Mail:**   ydhw01@srv0.law.ed.ac.uk
UNITED KINGDOM   **Fax:**   (44-31) 667-9111   **Internet:** http://www.law.ed.ac.uk/hume/home.htm

Contact Person: Kathy Mountain, Assistant.
Officers or Principals: Prof. Brian Main, Executive Director; Hector MacQueen, FRSE, Director; Gillian Lomas, Secretary; Prof. Sir Alan Peacock, FBA, FRSE, Consultant Economist; Sir John Shaw, CBE, FRSE, Chairman.
Mission or Interest: Dissemination of ideas on public policy that can be answered by combining the disciplines of law and economics, with David Hume as the inspiration.
Accomplishments: Published 18 titles in the "Hume Papers" series, 12 titles in the *Hume Papers on Public Policy* series, 50 occasional papers, 4 books and 3 Hume reprints
Products or Services: The Deregulation of Financial Markets, Governments and Small Business, as well as many papers.
Tax Status: U.K. charity.   **Annual Report:** Yes.   **Employees:** 1
Board of Directors or Trustees: Catherine Blight, Sir. Gerald Elliot, FRSE, Nick Kuenssberg, Lady Mackenzie-Stuart, Prof. John Murray, QC, Prof. John Ward, CBE. Sir Samuel Brittan, Honorary President; Prof. James Buchanan, Honorary Vice President.
Periodicals: *Hume Papers on Public Policy* (quarterly journal).
Other Information: Established in 1985 by Sir Alan Peacock, who was at the time Vice Chancellor and Professor of Economics at the University of Buckingham. The late George Stigler, Nobel Laureate in Economics, was the Institute's first honorary President. The Institute was consciously formed away from London to avoid the pitfall of placing themselves too close to the seat of political power - "this concentration sometimes develops a metropolitan perspective of economic events and a tendency to pursue 'fashionable' subjects and techniques." The site of Edinburgh, Scotland, was chosen for its long intellectual tradition in economics, including David Hume and his friend Adam Smith.

Defenders of Property Rights

6235 33rd St., N.W.
Washington, DC 20015   **Phone:**   (202) 686-4197   **E-Mail:**   DWAlmasi@aol.com
USA   **Fax:**   (202) 686-0240

Contact Person: Nancie G. Marzulla, President.
Officers or Principals: Nancie G. Marzulla, President/Chief Legal Counsel ($50,000); David W. Almasi, Director of Media Relations.
Mission or Interest: "The nation's only legal defense foundation dedicated exclusively to the protection of property rights."
Accomplishments: Numerous media and public appearances; in 1995 Defenders made 61 television and 12 radio appearances. As of 1996, Defender's had taken 15 cases as lead counsel, and won 13; an 87% winning record in court. Participated in another 61 by filing friend-of-the-court briefs and providing other assistance. Most cases, 34%, involved zoning and land-use laws, 33% environmental laws, and 16% business regulations. Filed a brief in Bennett v. Plenert, a case before the Supreme Court in which ranchers challenged the recovery plan for the Lost River sucker and shortnose sucker on the grounds that the recovery plan failed to take into account the ranchers' resulting economic damage. The 9th Circuit Court of Appeals held that only those "who allege an interest in the preservation of endangered species" may bring citizen suits under the Endangered Species Act. Assisting the plaintiffs in Terry L. And Gayle E. Beardslee v. Crawford County Road Commission, a case involving Michigan property owners whose land was bulldozed to widen a trail on their property to make a public highway. The County Road Commission sought to turn what it called an "old logging road" into a public highway without notice, public hearing, or offer of compensation. The logging trail was not indicated by a survey or title search when the Beardslees bought the property. Submitted a successful amicus curiae in the Supreme Court decision in Lucas v. South Carolina, a landmark decision that shifted the burden of proof in property-rights cases from the property owners to the government. In 1995 Defenders spent $272,961 on its programs.
Total Revenue: 1995 $355,655 **Total Expenses:** $308,427 89%/6%/6% **Net Assets:** $88,167
Products or Services: Litigation, fax network, publications.
Tax Status: 501(c)(3)   **Annual Report:** No.   **Employees:** 6   **Citations:** 64:87

Board of Directors or Trustees: Jeremy Ray Akers, Timothy Flanagan, Charles Jarvis, William Wewer. Legal Advisors include: T. Kenneth Cribb (Intercollegiate Studies Inst.), John Curry, Jr., Charles Jarvis, Hon. Mark Killian (Speaker of the House, AZ), J.B. Love, Prof. Jonathan Macey (Cornell Law School), Roger Marzulla, George Miller, Hon. Gale Norton (Attorney General, CO), Hon. Theodore Olson (Asst. Attorney General, 1981-84), Vickie O'Meara, Eric Rubin, Hon. Harold Stratton.
Periodicals: *Property Rights Reporter* (bimonthly newsletter).
Internships: Yes.
Other Information: Established in 1991. Nancie Marzulla and her husband Roger both worked in Pres. Reagan's Department of Justice, Nancie as a Trial Attorney (1986-88), and Roger as Deputy Attorney General for Land and Natural Resources (1985-88). The Marzullas recently co-authored <u>Property Rights: Understanding Government Takings and Environmental Regulation</u> (Government Institutes Press, 1997). The organization received $262,389, or 74% of revenue, from contributions and grants awarded by foundations, businesses, and individuals. (These grants included $100,000 from the Carthage Foundation, $25,000 from the Castle Rock Foundation, $10,000 from the Claude R. Lambe Charitable Foundation, and $5,000 from the John William Pope Foundation. In 1994, $10,000 from the J.M. Foundation.) $79,596, or 22%, from litigation fees. $9,481, or 3%, from membership dues. $2,609, or 1%, from interest on savings and temporary cash investments. The remaining revenue came from speakers' fees.

Defense Forum Foundation (DFF)

3014 Castle Rd.
Falls Church, VA 22044
USA

Phone: (703) 534-4313
Fax: (703) 538-6149

Contact Person: Suzanne K. Scholte, President.
Officers or Principals: Suzanne K. Scholte, President; Amb. William Middendorf, II, Chairman.
Mission or Interest: "Educating the general public and Congressional staff members about the conservative perspective on defense, foreign affairs, national security and human rights issues."
Accomplishments: Senator Jesse Helms (R-NC), Chairman of the Senate Foreign Relations Committee, said "The Defense Forum Foundation is doing outstanding work in promoting conservative principles and policies that are clearly in the best interest of the United States. Not only am I proud of you - I am grateful to you." Hosted forums that included Chinese dissident Harry Wu, South Korean Ambassador Seung-Soo Han, former Cuban Air Force Major Orestes Lorenzo (who conducted a much-publicized rescue of his wife and children from Cuba), former KGB Major Stanislav Levchenko, African scholar Dr. George B. N. Ayittey, and many others.
Total Revenue: 1996 $150,000 (est.) **Total Expenses:** $150,000 (est.) 88%/2%/10%
Tax Status: 501(c)(3) **Annual Report:** Yes. **Employees:** 1
Board of Directors or Trustees: Amb. Holly Coors, J.E.B. Carney, Chadwick Gore, Adm. James Holloway, III, USN (Ret.), Dr. Fred Ikle, Hon. Tidal McCoy, John Mucci.
Periodicals: *Defense Forum Foundation Newsletter*.
Internships: No.
Other Information: Established in 1985. In 1994-95 the Foundation received $10,000 from the Carthage Foundation, $5,000 from the Anschutz Foundation, and $1,000 from the Lynde and Harry Bradley Foundation.

Delaware Public Policy Institute (DPPI)

1201 N. Orange St., Suite 501
Wilmington, DE 19899
USA

Phone: (302) 655-7908
Fax: (302) 655-7238

Contact Person: Todd Wielar.
Officers or Principals: John H. Lopez, Executive Director; Pierre S. du Pont, IV, Chairman; Marvin N. Scoenhals, Vice Chairman.
Mission or Interest: A free-market oriented state policy institute focusing on Delaware.
Accomplishments: Held a forum on health care in November 1993 that was attended by over 400 members of the business community. Presentations were made by the Clinton Administration, Cato Institute, National Center for Policy Analysis, Delaware's governor, and local health officials. Held a "River Conference Cruise" attended by 550 business people, environmentalists, elected officials, and the media. The floating conference focused on economic development of the ports and "the need to preserve the environmental integrity of the Delaware Estuary."
Total Revenue: 1995 $310,000 37%(2) **Total Expenses:** $306,000
Products or Services: "Better Government Competition" that awards $8,500 in prize money for ideas that improve the efficiency of the public sector. "How Delaware Compares," a statistical abstract which details taxes, expenditures, and quality of life measures for Delaware, and compares them to other states. Conferences, studies, analysis of key issues.
Tax Status: 501(c)(3)
Board of Directors or Trustees: James Gilliam, Jr., Edwin Golin, Hon. Joshua Martin, III (Vice Pres., General Counsel & Corporate Secretary, Bell Atlantic), James McGinnis (former Lt. Gov., DE), David Roselle (Pres., Univ. of DE), Marvin Schoenhals (Chair, Wilmington Savings Fund Society), Patricia Schramm (former DE Secretary of the Dept. of Health and Social Services), William Vernon, A. Keith Willard.
Periodicals: *Outlook* (three times-a-year newsletter).
Other Information: Established in 1990. Recieved funding from the Bradley Foundation.

Destiny Magazine

18398 Redwood Highway
Selma, OR 97538   **Phone:**   (503) 597-4000
USA   **Fax:**   (503) 597-4800

Contact Person: Emanuel McLittle, Editor/Founder.
Officers or Principals: Stuart Pigler, Political Editor; Joseph Kearney, Associate Editor.
Mission or Interest: Political and social commentary, with a conservative bent, aimed at black America. The magazine is sub-titled, "The New Black American Mainstream."
Accomplishments: *Destiny's* readership and ability to attract advertisers makes it a flagship publication among the emerging black conservative leadership. An op-ed in *The Wall Street Journal* said it "say(s) the unpopular things that need to be said by blacks-to blacks."
Tax Status: For profit.
Board of Directors or Trustees: Advisory Board includes; John Uhlmann, Dr. Robert Woodson (Pres., National Center for Neighborhood Enterprise), Robert Unger, Dr. Joe Clark, Prof. Walter Williams (Center for Market Processes), Keith Butler (former Detroit City Councilman), Marie Kaigler (talk-show host), Lt. Drew Brown, J. A. Parker (Pres., Lincoln Inst.), Dr. Alan Keyes (Chair., Black America's PAC), Polly Williams (State Rep., D-WI), Stanley Crouch (author), Ezola Foster.
Periodicals: *Destiny Magazine* (bimonthly).

Devin - Adair Publishers / Veritas Book Club

6 N. Water St.
Greenwich, CT 06830   **Phone:**   (203) 531-7755
USA

Contact Person: R. Corbin.
Officers or Principals: Roger H. Lourie, President
Mission or Interest: Publishes books to "Promote conservative, traditional and free-market thinking in economics and national and international affairs." Many books on money, the federal reserve system, and taxes. Hosts the Veritas Book Club, a "small, personal book club" that offers Devin-Adair books as well as titles from other publishers.
Accomplishments: "Have published the largest and most significant number of conservative books in the U.S.. Extant since 1911 and always creating a forum for the distribution of free-market economic ideas."
Tax Status: For profit. **Annual Report:** No. **Employees:** 12

DeWitt Families Conduit Foundation

8300 96th Ave.
Zeeland, MI 49464   **Phone:**   (616) 875-8131
USA

Contact Person: Marvin G. DeWitt, President.
Officers or Principals: Marvin G. DeWitt, President ($0); William G. DeWitt, Vice President ($0); Gary D. DeWitt, Vice President ($0); William J. DeWitt, Secretary/Treasurer.
Mission or Interest: Grant-making foundation that primarily finances religious and civic activities, but also includes awards for conservative religious public-policy organizations.
Accomplishments: In 1994 the Foundation awarded $1,173,860 in grants. Recipients included: $140,938 for Focus on the Family, $30,200 for the Campus Crusade for Christ, $19,500 for Gospel Films, $10,500 for the Family Research Council, $9,500 for the Michigan Family Forum, $4,500 for the Prison Fellowship Ministries, $2,000 for the Billy Graham Evangelical Association, and $1,000 for the Right to Life Michigan Educational Fund.
Total Revenue: 1994 $1,177,421 **Total Expenses:** $1,182,860 **Net Assets:** $733,070 (-20%)(2)
Tax Status: 501(c)(3)
Other Information: Established in 1987. The Foundation received $1,181,773, or 99% of gross revenue, from contributions of Sarah Lee common stock, mostly from DeWitt family members. The remaining revenue came from dividends and interest from securities, and interest on savings and temporary cash investments. The Foundation lost $11,391 on the sale of assets. The Foundation held $661,416, or 90% of assets, in "institutional liquid assets" obtained with the sale of the Sarah Lee shares.

Discovery Institute

1201 3rd Ave., 39th Floor
Seattle, WA 98101   **Phone:**   (206) 287-3144
USA   **Fax:**   (206) 583-8500

Contact Person: Bruce Chapman, President.
Officers or Principals: Bruce Chapman, President ($72,983); Diane Hodgson, Vice President ($13,125); Tom A. Alberg, Chairman ($0); Charles Katz, Jr., Douglas A. Raff, Vice Presidents; Ritajean Butterworth, Secretary/Treasurer.

Mission or Interest: "Thoughtful analysis and effective action on local, regional, national, and international issues." Large emphasis on law and technological innovations.

Accomplishments: Many media appearances, including a feature article about the Institute in *Insight*. Research Fellows include president Bruce Chapman (former U.S. Ambassador; Deputy Assistant to the President; Dir., The U.S. Census Bureau; Washington State Secretary of State; co-author of The Party that Lost its Head, and the author of The Wrong Man in Uniform), George F. Gilder (author of Wealth and Poverty, The Spirit of Enterprise, Microcosm, Life After Television, and Sexual Suicide), David Hancock (Dir., Arizona-Sonora Desert Museum in Tucson; former Dir., Woodland Park Zoological Gardens in Seattle; and author of Animals and Architecture, and Master Builders of the Animal World), many others. In 1995 the Institute spent $331,203 on its programs.

Total Revenue: 1995 $911,481 37%(3) **Total Expenses:** $723,236 46%/25%/29% **Net Assets:** $209,073

Tax Status: 501(c)(3)   **Citations:** 151:46

Board of Directors or Trustees: Christopher Bayley, Deborah Bevier, Michael Darland (Pres., Digital Systems Intn'l), Robert Davidson, Richard Derham, William Glasgow, Mack Hogans, Susan Hutchison, Stanley McNaughton, John Oppenheimer, Diarmuid O'Scannlain, Paul Schell, Raymond Waldmann.

Other Information: Established in 1991. The Institute received $628,997, or 69% of revenue, from contributions and grants awarded by foundations, businesses, and individuals. (In 1994 these grants included $100,000 from the M.J. Murdock Charitable Trust, $7,500 from the Earhart Foundation.) $162,080, or 18%, from conference fees. $36,043, or 4%, from membership dues. The remaining revenue came from book sales, interest on savings, and other miscellaneous sources.

Discussion Club

319 N. 4th St., Suite 622
St. Louis, MO 63102   **Phone:** (314) 621-2033
USA   **Fax:**   (314) 421-3740

Contact Person: H.F. Langenberg, President.

Officers or Principals: H.F. Langenberg, President ($0); Boyce Meyer, Vice President ($0); Nancy B. Prentis, Secretary/Treasurer ($0); Mary Ann Jozwiak, Office Manager.

Mission or Interest: "To supply valid intellectual ammunition to the community supporting freedom and high traditional values by exploring current events, history and economic issues from a classical liberal perspective."

Accomplishments: Its yearly list of speakers is a who's who of conservative intellectuals. Previous speakers have included; F.A. Hayek, Milton Friedman, Leonard Read, William F. Buckley, Jr., Joseph Sobran, Irving Kristol, Michael Novak, Israel Kirzner, Russell Kirk, Erik von Kuehnelt-Leddihn, Henry Hazlitt, and others.

Total Revenue: 1995 $55,745 **Total Expenses:** $54,303 **Net Assets:** $3,763

Products or Services: Holds monthly dinner meetings and discussions with featured speakers.

Tax Status: 501(c)(3) **Annual Report:** No. **Employees:** 3

Board of Directors or Trustees: Advisory board includes: Prof. Gerald Dunne (Emeritus, St. Louis Univ.), Dr. Wolf Fuhrig (MacMurray College), Prof. Steve Hanke (John Hopkins Univ.), Prof. Mark Hearne (Westminster Christian Academy), Dr. James Hitchcock (St. Louis Univ.), Prof. Tom Ireland (Univ. of Missouri, St. Louis), Dr. Donald Kemmerer (Univ. of Illinois), Prof. Seung Kim (School of Business, St. Louis Univ.), Dr. William Peterson (Campbell Univ.), Prof. G. C. Wiegand (Southern Illinois Univ.).

Other Information: Established in 1955. The Discussion Club is for like-minded individuals to come together to sharpen their own knowledge. They do not exclude ideological 'adversaries,' so long as they abide by the rules of the club. They do not seek direct political involvement on the part of their members, nor do they endorse parties or candidates. Anyone interested in starting their own local discussion club should contact the St. Louis Discussion Club. They would like to help set up a network of discussion clubs and coordinate tours for the speakers from city to city. The Club received $34,977, or 63% of revenue, from contributions and grants awarded by foundations, businesses, and individuals. (These grants included $2,000 from the Sunmark Foundation. Grants have been increasing by an average of 5% per year since 1991.) $11,003, or 20%, from program service fees. $9,765, or 17%, from membership dues.

Doctors for Disaster Preparedness

2509 N. Campbell Ave., Suite 272
Tucson, AZ 85719   **Phone:** (520) 325-2680
USA

Contact Person: Dr. Jane Orient, Secretary/Treasurer.

Officers or Principals: Arthur Robinson, President ($0); Howard Long, Vice President ($0); Dr. Jane Orient, Secretary/Treasurer ($0).

Mission or Interest: Doctors, scientists, and engineers working on defense preparedness ever since the nuclear bomb was created. They are currently involved in the environmental debate.

Accomplishments: Their 13th Annual Conference in 1995, co-sponsored with *Access To Energy*, Oregon Institute of Science and Medicine, and Physicians for Civil Defense, featured; Cresson Kearny on the continuing threat of malaria and its relationship to pesticide reduction and wetlands preservation; Col. Ernest Takafuji (USAMRIID) on the threat of biological weapons; Dr. Peter Duesberg on HIV/AIDS and his dissent from the prevailing theory that HIV causes AIDS; Fred Smith (Competitive Enterprise Inst.), on risk assessment and overregulation; Dr. Arthur Robinson (*Access to Energy*) on the politicization of American Education; and many other prominent speakers. In 1995 the organization spent $30,398 on its programs; $22,644 on its conference and $7,753 on its newsletter.

Total Revenue: 1995 $34,964 **Total Expenses:** $32,959 **Net Assets:** $61,373
Tax Status: 501(c)(3)
Board of Directors or Trustees: Claud Boyd, Harvey Cain, Robert Cihak, Gerald Looney, Howard Maccabee, Paul Morris, William Nesbitt, Thomas Ruh.
Periodicals: Bimonthly newsletter.
Other Information: Doctors for Disaster Preparedness received $29,902, or 86% of revenue, from program services, including conference fees and newsletter subscriptions. $4,724, or 12%, from membership dues. The remaining revenue came from interest on savings, and contributions and grants awarded by foundations, businesses, and individuals.

Doctors for Integrity in Research & Public Policy (DIRPP)

5201 Norris Canyon Rd., Suite 140
San Ramon, CA 94583   **Phone:**   (510) 277-0333
USA   **Fax:**   (510) 277-1283

Contact Person: Edgar A. Suter, M.D., Chairman.
Mission or Interest: Examine the issue of guns and violence in America. "On the issue of guns and violence, our group has uncovered shocking incompetence, distortions and outright lies in many major medical journals. We have discovered it is quite common for *taxpayer-funded* gun control researchers to fabricate and sculpt their data to bolster their biased and foregone conclusions."
Accomplishments: Have provided testimony on proposed legislation. Filed *amicus curiae* (friend-of-the-court) briefs in certain "assault weapons" challenges.
Products or Services: Monographs: "Guns in the Medical Literature - A Failure of Peer Review," "Assault Weapons' Revisited - An Analysis of the AMA Report," and "The Right to Keep and Bear Arms - A Primer for Physicians."
Other Information: DIRPP membership includes medical school professors, researchers and practicing physicians.

Doctors for Life

39 Tealwood Dr.
St. Louis, MO 63141   **Phone:**   (314) 567-3446
USA

Contact Person: Anne E. Bannon, M.D., President.
Officers or Principals: Anne E. Bannon, M.D., President ($33,600); Manuel Comas, Secretary ($0).
Mission or Interest: "To foster, promote, coordinate, and fund. . . medical, scientific and legal research into the rights of born and unborn children."
Accomplishments: In the fiscal year ending June 1995 Doctors for Life spent $29,923 on its programs.
Total Revenue: FY ending 6/95 $37,865 **Total Expenses:** $37,387 80%/20%/0% **Net Assets:** $15,594
Tax Status: 501(c)(3)
Other Information: The organization received $37,865, or 100% of revenue, from membership dues.

Doctors for Responsible Gun Ownership

(see Claremont Institute for the Study of Statesmanship)

Dove Foundation

4521 Broadmoor, S.E.
Grand Rapids, MI 49512   **Phone:**   (616) 554-9993
USA

Contact Person: Richard K. Rolfe, Managing Director.
Officers or Principals: Richard K. Rolfe, Managing Director ($47,476); Dar Vander Ark, Secretary/Treasurer ($0).
Mission or Interest: The Dove Foundation screens movies on video cassette and issues a Dove "Family Approved" rating for films that eschew explicit sex, extreme violence, inappropriate language, and anti-social or anti-family behavior. They describe their ratings as the 'Good Housekeeping Seal of Approval' for videos.
Accomplishments: Dove's list of approved movies includes over 700 titles, and their label of approval has been accepted by approximately 150 video retailers. The Foundation, in cooperation with a local independent television station (WXON) and a 50,000 watt radio station (WJR), hosted the Dove Film Festival at theaters in the Detroit, MI area. In the fiscal year ending April 1995, the Foundation spent $188,400 on its programs.
Total Revenue: FY ending 4/95 $283,221 **Total Expenses:** $268,083 70%/30%/0% **Net Assets:** $66,673
Products or Services: The Foundation sells a complete list of Dove approved movies.
Tax Status: 501(c)(3)   **Citations:**   30:132
Board of Directors or Trustees: Lyles Carr, Bill Kanaga, Brad Curl, B. J. Weber, Ron Walton, James Buick, Jim Lane.
Other Information: Established in 1992. The Foundation received $172,926, or 61% of revenue, from retail store display fees. $106,882, or 38%, from contributions and grants awarded by foundations, businesses, and individuals. The remaining revenue came from interest on savings and temporary cash investments.

Dumont Institute for Public Policy Research

236 Johnson Ave.
Dumont, NJ 07628
USA

Phone: (201) 501-8574   **E-Mail:** Dumontinst@aol.com
Fax: (201) 387-0744   **Internet:** http://www.hili.com~dumontin

Contact Person: Robert W. McGee, President.
Mission or Interest: "Firmly grounded in the principles of individual freedom, a tradition personified by Thomas Jefferson and America's other Founding Fathers. . . Recognition of inalienable individual rights and the dignity and worth of each individual; protection of those rights through the institutions of individual private property, contract and the rule of law; voluntarism in all human relations; the self-ordering market, free trade, free migration and peace."
Accomplishments: Published many books on public policy issues, various analyses, policy briefs, working papers, as well as occasional papers on the internet
Tax Status: 501(c)(3)   **Annual Report:** No.
Board of Directors or Trustees: John Galandak (Foundation for Free Enterprise), Murray Sabrin (Alliance for Monetary Education). The Advisory Board includes: Prof. D.T. Armentano (Univ. of Hartford), Doug Bandow (Cato Inst.), Prof. Walter Block (College of the Holy Cross), Prof. Peter Boetke (New York Univ.), Prof. Emeritus Antony Flew (Univ. of Reading), Bettina Bien Greaves (Foundation for Economic Education), Hans-Herman Hoppe (UNLV), Prof. Steve Horwitz (St. Lawrence Univ.), Prof. Tibor Machan (Auburn Univ.), Prof. Yuri Maltsev (Carthage College), Prof. Steve Pejovich (Texas A&M, Univ.), Andrea Millen Rich (Laissez Faire Books), Prof. Joseph Salerno (Pace Univ.), Prof. Jeremy Shearmur (Australian National Univ.), Fred Smith, Jr. (Competitive Enterprise Inst.), Prof. Walter Williams (George Mason Univ.), Prof. Gary Wolfram (Hillsdale College).
Periodicals: *Journal of Accounting, Ethics & Public Policy* (quarterly journal).
Internships: Yes, unpaid.

Dwight D. Eisenhower Presidential Library

S.E. 4th St.
Abilene, KS 67410
USA

Phone: (913) 263-4751

Contact Person: David D. Holt, Director.
Mission or Interest: Collection of the papers of Dwight D. Eisenhower throughout his presidency and his military career.
Accomplishments: Dwight D. Eisenhower: A Selected Bibliography of Periodical and Dissertation Literature.
Other Information: Maintained by the National Archives and Records Administration.

E. L. Wiegand Foundation

165 W. Liberty St., Suite 200
Reno, NV 89501
USA

Phone: (702) 333-0310

Contact Person: Kristen A. Avansino, President.
Officers or Principals: Raymond C. Avansino, Jr., Chairman ($105,800); Kristen A. Avansino, President/Executive Director ($77,678); James T. Carrico, Treasurer ($48,063); Harvey C. Fruehauf, Jr., Vice President; Michael J. Melarkey, Secretary.
Mission or Interest: Grant-making philanthropy that includes conservative organizations in its awards. The Foundation's main focus is on medical and research institutions with a Catholic emphasis, with a geographic focus on the west coast and mountain states.
Accomplishments: In the fiscal year ending October 1995, the Foundation awarded $3,515,283 in grants. Recipients included; $100,000 for the Federalist Society, $68,000 for the Political Economy Research Center, $47,420 for the Capital Research Center, and $5,000 for the Nevada Policy Research Institute.
Total Revenue: FY ending 10/95 $5,647,748 **Total Expenses:** $4,255,182 **Net Assets:** $87,170,458 2%(2)
Tax Status: 501(c)(3)
Board of Directors or Trustees: Frank Fahrenkopf, Jr., Mario Gabelli.
Other Information: Established in 1982. The Foundation received $3,617,286, or 64% of revenue, from interest on savings and temporary cash investments. $1,237,587, or 22%, from capital gains on the sale of assets. $708,712, or 13%, from dividends and interest from securities. $84,163, or 1%, from gifts and grants. The Foundation held $28,211,088, or 32% of assets, in government bonds. $24,175,153, or 28%, in savings and temporary cash investments. $18,057,500, or 21%, from corporate stock.

Eagle Forum

P.O. Box 618
Alton, IL 62002
USA

Phone: (618) 462-5415   **E-Mail:** eagle@eagleforum.org
Fax: (618) 462-8909   **Internet:** http:/www.eagleforum.org

Contact Person: Phyllis Schlafly, President.
Officers or Principals: Phyllis Schlafly, President ($0); Cathie Adams, Secretary ($0); Margaret Gaul, Treasurer ($0); Tottie Ellis, Vice President.

Mission or Interest: Lobbying organization "to enable conservative and pro-family men and women to participate in the process of self-government and public policy-making so that America will continue to be a land of individual liberty, respect for family integrity, public and private virtue, and private enterprise."

Accomplishments: Approximately 8,000 members. Instrumental in defeating passage of the Equal Rights Amendment. Early supporter of an orbit-based missile defense system, the Strategic Defense Initiative. More recently, it was instrumental in defeating the "Conference of the States," a conference that was to be held by representatives from each state to discuss federal-state issues. The Forum believes that such a conference would have the power to become a Constitutional Convention, which it opposes on the grounds that such a convention would remove certain Constitutional rights, and create new ones. Opposition to the United Nations and "New World Order" military interventions. President Ronald Reagan said, "Eagle Forum has set a high standard of volunteer participation in the political and legislative process. . . Your work is an example to all of those who would struggle for an America that is prosperous and free." Even Eagle Forum's opponents, such as Jean Hardisty of Political Research Associates, concede that Phyllis Schlafly is the "grande dame" of the Right and "a brilliant political innovator, architect, and strategist." In 1995 Eagle Forum spent $621,624 on its programs.

Total Revenue: 1995 $989,976 **Total Expenses:** $697,605 89%/5%/6% **Net Assets:** $1,710,799

Tax Status: 501(c)(4) **Employees:** 12   **Citations:** 557:18

Board of Directors or Trustees: LaNeil Wright Spivy, Eunice Smith, Shirley Curry, Cathie Adams, Nancy Spreen.

Periodicals: *Education Reporter*, and *Phyllis Schlafly Report* (monthly newsletter).

Internships: Yes.

Other Information: Founded in 1972 as Stop ERA, then incorporated in 1975 as the Eagle Forum. Besides patriotic connotations, the eagle is a biblical reference from Isaiah 40:31, "They that wait upon the Lord shall renew their strength; they shall mount up with wings as eagles, they shall run, and not be weary; and they shall walk and not faint." Affiliated with the 501(c)(3) Eagle Forum Education and Legal Defense Fund at the same address. They also have an office in the District of Columbia; 316 Pennsylvania Ave., S.E., Suite 203, Washington, DC 20003, phone (202) 544-0353, and an office near St. Louis; 7800 Bonhomme St., Clayton, MO 63105, phone (314) 721-1213, fax (314) 721-3373. Phyllis Schlafly is also the Chairman of the Republican National Coalition for Life, located at the same address as Eagle Forum. Schlafly is best known for her opposition to the Equal Rights Amendment. She is also an expert on defense and foreign policy, having written five books on the subject. She has degrees from Washington University, Harvard, and Washington University Law School. She was married to the late Fred Schlafly, who was affiliated with the Christian Anti-Communist Crusade and led the World Anti-Communist League. Schlafly first became well-known in 1964 when she authored a book, A Choice Not An Echo, that was important in gaining the Republican presidential nomination for Barry Goldwater. Eagle Forum received $819,327, or 83% of revenue, from contributions and grants. $87,125, or 9%, from membership dues. $80,330, or 8%, from dividends and interest from securities. The remaining revenue came from other miscellaneous sources.

Eagle Forum Education and Legal Defense Fund

P.O. Box 618
Alton, IL 62002   **Phone:** (618) 462-5415   **E-Mail:** eagle@eagleforum.org
USA   **Fax:**   (618) 462-8909   **Internet:** http:/www.eagleforum.org

Contact Person: Phyllis Schlafly, President.

Officers or Principals: Phyllis Schlafly, President ($0); Helen Marie Taylor, Vice President ($0); Elizabeth Clark, Secretary ($0); Alyse O'Neill, Treasurer.

Mission or Interest: Research and education affiliate of the Eagle Forum. Conservative organization focusing on "pro-family issues, education, taxes, national defense, the Constitution, defeating ERA, the constitutional convention (Con Con), and federal babysitting."

Accomplishments: In 1994 the Fund spent $370,743 on its programs. Opposed to 'Outcome-Based Education.' Instrumental in defeating the "Conference of the States," a conference that was to be held by representatives from each state to discuss federal/state issues. The Fund believes that such a conference would have the power to become a Constitutional Convention, which it opposes on the grounds that such a convention would remove certain Constitutional rights, and create new ones.

Total Revenue: 1994 $1,003,018 27%(2) **Total Expenses:** $412,726 90%/8%/3% **Net Assets:** $3,525,144

Products or Services: Child Abuse in the Classroom, and other books by Phyllis Schlafly.

Tax Status: 501(c)(3)   **Citations:** 557:18

Board of Directors or Trustees: Najila Lataif, Linda Bean Folkers, Richard Eckburg.

Periodicals: *Phyllis Schlafly Report* (monthly newsletter).

Other Information: Affiliated with the 501(c)(4) Eagle Forum at the same address. The Fund received $838,389, or 84% of revenue, from contributions and grants awarded by foundations, businesses, and individuals. (These grants included $5,000 from the Richard & Helen DeVos Foundation. In 1995, $10,000 from the John M. Olin Foundation, and $5,000 from the John William Pope Foundation.) $72,447, or 7%, from book sales. $71,894, or 7%, from interest on savings and temporary cash investments. $23,129, or 2%, from dividends and interest from securities.

Eagle Publishing

422 First St., S.E.
Washington, DC 20003   **Phone:** (202) 546-5005
USA   **Fax:**   (202) 546-8759   **Internet:** http://www.townhall.com/eagle

Contact Person: Jeff Carneal, President.
Officers or Principals: Thomas Phillips, Chairman; Jeff Carneal, President.
Mission or Interest: Conservative publishing company. Owns *Human Events*, *Evans-Novak Political Report*, Regnery Publishing (formerly Regnery Gateway), and 50% of the Conservative Book Club
Products or Services: Books and periodicals. Also sells art prints, including works by Frederic Remington.
Tax Status: For profit. **Annual Report:** Yes. **Employees:** Over 50.
Other Information: Eagle Publishing is a division of Phillips Publishing International, Inc. Eagle Publishing used to publish the now defunct Oliver North newsletter, *Frontlines*.

Earhart Foundation

2200 Green Rd., Suite H
Ann Arbor, MI 48105   **Phone:** (313) 761-8592
USA

Contact Person: David Kennedy, President.
Officers or Principals: David Kennedy, President ($109,113); Antony T. Sullivan, Secretary ($79,024); Marilyn Bagamery, Assistant Treasurer ($53,210); Dennis L. Bark, Chairman; Edward Sichler, III, Treasurer.
Mission or Interest: Grant-making foundation that includes conservative and free-market organizations and scholars. Also provides fellowships for students.
Accomplishments: In 1994 the Foundation awarded $2,425,261 in grants. $641,229 was awarded as H.B. Earhart Fellowships for college students. $1,259,723 was awarded to organizations. Recipients included: three grants totaling $67,000 for the Intercollegiate Studies Institute, eight grants totaling $56,750 for the Atlas Foundation, two grants totaling $55,000 for the American Enterprise Institute, five grants totaling $53,300 for the Hoover Institution, seven grants totaling $44,938 for the Institute for Humane Studies at George Mason University, two grants totaling $44,900 for the Citizens Research Council of Michigan, two grants totaling $35,000 for the Social Philosophy and Policy Center, two grants totaling $33,090 for the Institute for Political Economy, two grants totaling $27,000 for the Political Economy Research Center, $25,000 for the Study of Federalism, two grants totaling $20,000 for the Federalist Society, $18,846 for the Institute for Foreign Policy Analysis, $18,000 for the Foundation Francisco Marroquin, $17,500 for the Institute for the Study of Economic Culture, and $15,000 each for *Critical Review*, the Eric Voegelin Institute, Ethics and Public Policy Center, and the Institute for World Politics. The Foundation also awarded $424,487 in Fellowship Research Grants. Recipients included: Fred McChesney of the Emory School of Law to prepare a book, Rent Extraction: The Theory and Practice of Extortion by Politicians; Bruce Yandel of Clemson University for preparation of a book, Land Rights: Escaping Feudalism by the 21st Century; Roger Meiners of the University of Texas at Arlington; Michael Sanera of the Center for Environmental Education Policy Research; Clint Bolick of the Institute for Justice; and others.
Total Revenue: 1994 $2,550,332 **Total Expenses:** $3,197,616 **Net Assets:** $55,527,727 (-5%)(1)
Tax Status: 501(c)(3)
Board of Directors or Trustees: Willa Johnson, Richard Ware, Earl Heenan, Robert Queller, Thomas Bray (*Detroit News*), Prof. Paul McCracken (Univ. of Michigan), Edward Sichler, III, Ann Irish, John Moore.
Other Information: Established in 1929. The Foundation received $2,548,612, or 99.9% of revenue, from dividends and interest from securities. The remaining revenue came from capital gains on the sale of assets. The Foundation held $37,324,901, or 67% of assets, in corporate stock. $17,969,374, or 32%, in government securities.

East Moline Christian School

900 46th Ave.
East Moline, IL 61244   **Phone:** (309) 796-1485
USA

Contact Person: Rev. James R. Patterson, Director.
Officers or Principals: Ronald J. Patrick, Principal.
Mission or Interest: Educational efforts from a conservative Christian perspective. Hosts the Douglas MacArthur Institute. "To uphold those rare and noble qualities that are imperative to the moral, spiritual, economic, and political well-being of a nation and which were so magnificently displayed in General MacArthur's life, words, and actions. . . Rebuilding the foundations of America upon the original intent of the founding fathers."
Products or Services: Produced and re-published books, speeches, and articles. Plans to institute correspondence and computer courses, create summer courses and a two-year course in the "freedom philosophy."
Tax Status: Nonprofit.
Periodicals: *MacArthur Institute Update* (newsletter), *Foundations of Liberty* (bimonthly journal that re-prints speeches, correspondence, and classical stories of American history and Americana).

Education and Research Institute

800 Maryland Ave., N.E.
Washington, DC 20002   **Phone:** (202) 546-1710
USA   **Fax:**   (202) 546-1638

Contact Person: M. Stanton Evans, Chairman.
Officers or Principals: M. Stanton Evans, Chairman ($26,000); Allan Ryskind, President ($0); Ralph Bennet, Vice President ($0); James Roberts, Secretary; Ronald Pearson, Treasurer.
Mission or Interest: Helps develop conservative writers and journalists through its National Journalism Center project.
Accomplishments: "Has educated over 1,000 young people in the principles of journalism leading to many thousands of articles and research projects." In 1995 the Institute spent $186,135 on its programs.
Total Revenue: 1995 $340,320 (-7%)(2) **Total Expenses:** $369,122 50%/46%/4% **Net Assets:** $41,395
Tax Status: 501(c)(3) **Citations:** 4:196
Board of Directors or Trustees: William Bowen, Patrick Korten, Charles Moser, Daniel Oliver (Senior Fellow, Heritage Found.), James Quayle.
Other Information: Affiliated with the 501(c)(3) *Consumers' Research* at the same address. Chairman M. Stanton Evans is a conservative journalist who got his start with *The Freeman*, then worked at *National Review* and *Human Events*. In 1995 the two affiliates had combined revenue, expenses, and assets of $343,764, $440,728, and (-$85,379). The Institute received $335,652, or 99% of revenue, from contributions and grants awarded by foundations, businesses, and individuals. (These grants included $40,000 from the Castle Rock Foundation, $40,000 from the John M. Olin Foundation, $8,000 from the Sunmark Foundation, $5,000 from the Claude R. Lambe Charitable Foundation, and $1,000 from the Forbes Foundation. In 1994, $8,000 from the Earhart Foundation, $7,000 from the Grover Hermann Foundation, $5,000 from the Gilder Foundation, $5,000 from the Milliken Foundation, $5,000 from the Vernon K. Krieble Foundation, $2,500 from the Aequus Institute, $2,500 from the John William Pope Foundation, and $1,000 from the Roe Foundation.) $4,500, or 1%, from rental income. The remaining revenue came from interest on savings.

Educational CHOICE Charitable Trust

7440 N. Woodland Dr.
Indianapolis, IN 46278   **Phone:**   (317) 293-7600
USA   **Fax:**   (317) 297-0908

Contact Person: Timothy P. Ehrgott, Executive Director.
Officers or Principals: Timothy P. Ehrgott, Executive Director ($41,600); Otto N. Frenzel, III, President ($0); Carol D'Amico, Vice President ($0); H. Patrick Callahan, Secretary; John M. Whelan, Treasurer.
Mission or Interest: "Provides tuition assistance to low-income students, serves as a model for research and legislation, and encourages all schools to improve by introducing competition in the education system."
Accomplishments: "CHOICE has assisted more than 2,200 students in Indianapolis, increasing their satisfaction with and performance in their education. Twenty-one cities across America have replicated our program, with some 10,000 students currently enrolled." In the fiscal year ending June 1995, the Trust awarded $484,578 in scholarships for low income students (as determined by federal rules for participation in free or reduced lunch programs) to attend private, mostly Christian schools.
Total Revenue: FY ending 6/95 $509,725 (-6%)(2) **Total Expenses:** $530,122 91%/9%/0% **Net Assets:** $10,433
Products or Services: Scholarships.
Tax Status: 501(c)(3) **Employees:** 2
Board of Directors or Trustees: Lorene Burkhart, William Crawford (Indiana General Assembly), Mitchell Daniels, Jr. (Vice Pres., Corporate Affairs, Eli Lilly and Co.), Carmen Hansen-Rivera, Mark Lubbers, Hon. James Payne, Larry Pitts, J. Patrick Rooney (Chair, Golden Rule Insurance), Cory SerVaas, M.D., Peter Rusthoven, William Styring, III (Vice Pres., IN Chamber of Commerce).
Other Information: The Trust received $508,721, or 99.8% of revenue, from contributions and grants awarded by foundations, businesses, and individuals. The remaining revenue came from interest on savings and temporary cash investments.

Educational Freedom Foundation (EFF)

927 S. Walter Reed Dr., Suite 1
Arlington, VA 22204   **Phone:** (703) 486-8311   **E-Mail:** CEFVoucher@aol.com
USA   **Fax:**   (703) 486-3160

Contact Person: Patrick J. Reilly, Executive Director.
Officers or Principals: Daniel D. McGarry, Ph.D., President; Dean John Vanden Berg, Vice President; Mae M. Duggan, Secretary; Paul Mecklenborg, Treasurer.
Mission or Interest: "National organization to promote educational choice by providing training, educational materials, and general assistance."
Products or Services: ABC's of Promoting Educational Choice manual.
Tax Status: 501(c)(3) **Annual Report:** No.
Board of Directors or Trustees: Burnett Bauer, Joseph Blume, James Condit, Martin Duggan, Stuart Hubbell.
Periodicals: *Parents' Choice* (bimonthly newsletter).
Internships: Yes.
Other Information: Affiliated with the 501(c)(4) Citizens for Educational Freedom at the same address. Previously located in St. Louis, MO.

Educational Research Associates

P.O. Box 8795
Portland, OR 97207   **Phone:** (503) 228-6345
USA

Contact Person: Carl W. Salser, President.
Officers or Principals: Mark R. Salser, Assistant Treasurer ($18,000); Barbara H. Salser, Executive Director ($9,600); Carl W. Salser, President ($8,400); Vernon S. White, Treasurer.
Mission or Interest: "Research in instructional and school management techniques for more effective and cost effective schools."
Accomplishments: Carl Salser is a former two-term member of the National Council on Educational Research.
Total Revenue: 1994 $313,103 (-13%)(2) **Total Expenses:** $316,177 84%/16%/0% **Net Assets:** (-$116,465)
Tax Status: 501(c)(3) **Annual Report:** Yes.   **Citations:** 34:122
Internships: No.

Edward Elgar Publishing Company

Old Post Rd.
Brookfield, VT 05036-9704   **Phone:** (802) 276-3162   **E-Mail:** elgarinfo@ashgate.com
USA   **Fax:**   (802) 276-3837

Mission or Interest: Publishes titles that focus on classical liberalism and free markets. Publishes the two-volume set, <u>Economic Thought Before Adam Smith</u> and <u>Classical Economics</u> by the late Murray Rothbard. Publishes the Locke Institute's "Shaftesbury Papers Series," including; <u>Before Resorting to Politics</u> by Anthony de Jasay, <u>Classical Liberalism in the Age of Post-Communism</u> by Prof. Norman Barry, <u>Adam Smith into the Twenty-First Century</u> by Prof. Edwin West, <u>Economic Policy in a Liberal Democracy</u> by Prof. Richard Wagner, and <u>The Political Economy of the Minimal State</u> by Prof. Charles Rowley. Publishes other books from the Locke Institute including titles that won the Sir Antony Fisher Memorial Award
Tax Status: For profit.
Other Information: United States affiliate of the U.K.'s Edward Elgar Publishing, Ltd. Distributed by Ashgate Publishing Company.

Edwards Notebook

703 Parker, Suite 5
Detroit, MI 48214   **Phone:** (313) 331-0670
USA   **Fax:**   (313) 272-5045

Contact Person: Ron Edwards, Commentator.
Officers or Principals: Debra Dawson, Producer.
Mission or Interest: Syndicated radio commentaries. Attempts to "blow away the myths and reveal the truth concerning moral, political, educational and other issues effecting our world and nation."
Accomplishments: Heard in over 40 U.S. radio markets
Tax Status: For profit. **Employees:** 2
Periodicals: *Edwards Notebook Newsletter.*
Internships: Yes, to do secretarial work, research and public relations.
Other Information: Ron Edwards is a long-time broadcast and print journalist.

Elizabethtown Center for Business and Society

Elizabethtown College
One Alpha Dr.
Elizabethtown, PA 17022   **Phone:** (717) 367-1151
USA   **Fax:**   (717) 367-7567

Contact Person: Paul Gottfried, Ph.D., Director.
Mission or Interest: Discuss common ground between business and academic communities.
Accomplishments: Held several conferences on business and society
Products or Services: Magazine and conferences.
Tax Status: 501(c)(3) **Annual Report:** No. **Employees:** 3
Periodicals: *This World: A Journal of Religion and Public Life* (annual).
Internships: No.
Other Information: Affiliated with and incorporated under Elizabethtown College. *This World* was formerly published by the Rockford Institute. Although most of the board considers themselves to be politically conservative, they do not stress their ideology in their programs or publications. They do not consider themselves to be "movement conservatives" such as "Kemp, Gingrich, or Bennett." Paul Gottfried is the author of <u>The Conservative Movement</u>, a highly regarded history of the post-World War II Right.

Empire Foundation for Policy Research

P.O. Box 825
Clifton Park, NY 12065   **Phone:** (518) 383-2877
USA   **Fax:**   (518) 383-2841

Contact Person: Brian Backstorm.
Officers or Principals: Thomas Rhodes, Chairman ($0); Thomas W. Carrol, President; Brian Backstrom, Vice President.
Mission or Interest: To develop in-depth analyses of New York State policies, and to highlight creative alternative ways of doing the "state's business" that are less expensive and more effective.
Accomplishments: Published widely-read studies on privatization, tax reduction, Medicaid reform, and an overhaul of the state's welfare programs. In 1995 the Foundation spent $48,492 on its programs.
Total Revenue: 1995 $76,046 (-18%)(3) **Total Expenses:** $48,492 **Net Assets:** $31,457
Products or Services: Studies and reports.
Tax Status: 501(c)(3) **Annual Report:** No. **Employees:** 5
Board of Directors or Trustees: Peter Flanigan, Richard Gilder, Thomas Gosnell, Irving Kristol (National Affairs), Lawrence Kudlow (*National Review*), Peggy Noonan (White House Speechwriter for Pres. Reagan and Bush), Stephen Peck, Frank Richardson (Solicitor, Dept. of the Interior, 1984-85), William Stern, Hon. Leon Weil (U.S. Ambassador to Nepal, 1984-87), Walter Wriston.
Internships: Yes, on a project-by-project, as needed basis.
Other Information: Affiliated with the 501(c)(4) CHANGE-NY. The Foundation received $89,000, or 97% of gross revenue, from gifts and grants awarded by foundations, businesses, and individuals. (These grants included $25,000 from the Lynde and Harry Bradley Foundation, $20,000 from Ronald Lauder, and $5,000 from the Grace Jones Richardson Trust. The Foundation has historically received substantial support from Ronald Lauder.) The remaining revenue came from various miscellaneous sources. The Foundation lost $15,731 on the sale of assets.

Employee Benefit Research Institute (EBRI)
2121 K St., N.W., Suite 600
Washington, DC 20037   **Phone:** (202) 659-0670
USA   **Fax:** (202) 775-6312

Contact Person: Dallas L. Salisbury, President.
Officers or Principals: Dallas L. Salisbury, President ($355,760); William Link, Chairman ($0); John H. Seiter, Vice Chairman($0); Christopher O'Flinn, Treasurer; Margaret Gagliardi, Secretary.
Mission or Interest: "To promote sound public policy on employee benefit and work-force issues." Promotes shielding income from taxation through employers providing in-kind services via benefits.
Accomplishments: Widely regarded as a leading source of information on benefit issues. In 1994 EBRI spent $2,098,197 on its programs.
Total Revenue: 1994 $2,810,866 **Total Expenses:** $2,426,797 86%/11%/3% **Net Assets:** $3,885,136
Tax Status: 501(c)(6) **Annual Report:** Yes. **Employees:** 28 **Citations:** 3:204
Board of Directors or Trustees: John Ivans (Aetna Health Plans), Margaret Gagliardi (American Express), Donald Harrington (At&T), Carl Marinacci (Amoco), Harry Cain, II (Blue Cross and Blue Shield), Dennis Crispin (Boeing), Lawrence English (CIGNA Healthcare), Martin Zuckerman (Chemical Bank), Robert Reynolds (Fidelity Investments), many others from business and industry - particularly benefit managers.
Periodicals: *Employee Benefit Notes, EBRI Issue Briefs, EBRI's Benefit Outlook.*
Internships: Yes.
Other Information: Affiliated with the 501(c)(3) Employee Benefit Research Institute Education and Research Fund at the same address. The Institute received $2,053,250, or 73% of revenue, from membership dues. $339,441, or 12%, from contributions and grants. $206,138, or 7%, from dividends and interest from securities. $185,129, or 7%, from honoraria and travel reimbursements. The remaining revenue came from interest on savings, mailing list rentals, and other miscellaneous sources.

Employment Policies Institute
607 14th St., N.W., Suite 1110
Washington, DC 20005   **Phone:** (202) 347-5178
USA   **Fax:** (202) 347-5250

Contact Person: John C. Doyle, Director of Public Affairs.
Officers or Principals: Richard B. Berman, Executive Director; John M. Baitsell, Chairman ($0); G. John Tysse, Secretary/Treasurer ($0).
Mission or Interest: Research and education organization focusing on employment policies such as minimum wage laws. "In particular, EPI research focuses on issues that affect entry-level employment. Among other issues, EPI research has quantified the impact of new labor costs on job creation, explored the connection between entry-level employment and welfare reform, and analyzed the demographic distribution of mandated benefits." Most research is conducted by contracted professors who are unaffiliated with the Institute.
Accomplishments: The Foundation received widely publicized attention for its response to a study by economists David Card and Alan B. Krueger which purported to show that an increase in the minimum wage did not result in higher unemployment in the fast-food industry in New Jersey. The Institute found that, "The Card-Krueger data set consistently reports employment losses where none actually took place and employment gains far in excess of their true values. Although the EPI analysis covered 25% of the franchised units in the Card-Krueger data set, there are very few instances in which the Card-Krueger numbers even closely resemble the actual payroll records. In fact, with one-third of the observations, the Card-Krueger data set fails to identify the correct direction of employment change. . . not only are the Card-Krueger numbers wrong, they are often catastrophically wrong." EPI turned over the data to two economists not affiliated with the Institute, David Neumark of Michigan State University and William Wascher of the Federal Reserve Board. The two economists found that the data "implies that the minimum wage increase led to a statistically significant 4.6 percent decline in fast-food employment in New Jersey relative to the Pennsylvania control group." In 1994 the Foundation spent $814,754 on its programs.

Total Revenue: 1994 $803,295 **Total Expenses:** $834,058 98%/0%/2% **Net Assets:** $101,066
Products or Services: Over twenty academic studies in the last four years.
Tax Status: 501(c)(3)   **Citations:** 59:92
Board of Directors or Trustees: William Maltarieh (TRW), Gerald Parks (General Electric), Donald Redlinger (Allied Signal), John Regnier (Shell Oil), James Robertson (Prudential Insurance), Douglas Root (ALCOA), John Rubino (Walgreen), Don Sacco (NYNEX), Frank Umanzio (Raytheon), Paul Vogel (Merck & Co.), Daniel Williams (Anheuser-Busch), Linda Workman (RJR Nabisco), others.
Other Information: Previously affiliated with the 501(c)(6) Employment Policies Institute, which was dissolved in 1995, with all assets being transferred to the 501(c)(3) Employment Policy Foundation, which then took the name Employment Policies Institute. The Institute received $593,434, or 74% of revenue, from contributions and grants awarded by foundations, businesses, and individuals. (In 1995 these grants included $75,000 from the John M. Olin Foundation, and $5,000 from the Claude R. Lambe Charitable Foundation. These grants have been growing by an average of 11% per year from 1990 till 1994.) $206,412, or 26%, from the sale of inventory. The remaining revenue came from interest on savings.

Empower America

1776 I St., N.W., Suite 890
Washington, DC 20006   **Phone:** (202) 452-8200
USA   **Fax:**   (202) 833-0388

Contact Person: Charles M. Kupperman, Executive Director.
Officers or Principals: William J. Bennett, Director ($110,875); John V. Weber, Vice Chairman ($97,868); Charles M. Kupperman, Executive Director ($94,556); William A. Dal Col, President; Linda Pell, Secretary; Sheldon M. Groner, Controller.
Mission or Interest: Dedicated to advancing freedom and democratic capitalism around the world, economic policies at home that encourage economic growth through entrepreneurship, and finding new approaches to cultural and social problems.
Accomplishments: Empwer America has received acclaim from Larry King, *The Wall Street Journal*, *The Washington Post* and others as the possible future of the Republican Party. In 1993, its first year of existence, Empower America had revenues of $8,667,054; probably the most for any lobbying organization in its first year. In 1996 two Empower America directors were involved in the Presidential election; former chairman Steve Forbes ran for the Republican Party's nomination and Jack Kemp was the party's choice for Vice President.
Total Revenue: 1994 $5,258,303 (-39%)(1) **Total Expenses:** $5,311,055 44%/23%/33% **Net Assets:** $296,509
Products or Services: Operate "Candidate Schools" which are conferences that help state and local level candidates develop a comprehensive and coherent message emphasizing conservative principles.
Tax Status: 501(c)(4)   **Citations:** 511:20
Board of Directors or Trustees: Theodore Forstmann, Founding Chairman, Jack Kemp (Secretary, Housing and Urban Development, 1989-93), Hon. Jeane Kirkpatrick (AEI).
Internships: Newsletter.
Other Information: Established in 1993. Empower America received $5,046,608, or 96% of revenue, from contributors. $133,460, or 3%, from mailing list rentals. $54,795, or 1%, from newsletter subscriptions. The remaining revenue came from the sale of merchandise and interest on savings.

Empowerment Network Foundation, The (TEN-F)

2210 Mt. Vernon Ave., Suite 301
Alexandria, VA 22301   **Phone:** (703) 548-6619
USA   **Fax:**   (703) 548-7328

Contact Person: Sharron D. Lipscomb, Executive Director.
Officers or Principals: Sharron D. Lipscomb, Executive Director ($39,000); Mary Pirault, Secretary/Treasurer ($26,000); David L. Caprara, President ($25,000); Chris Jacobs, Vice President.
Mission or Interest: Promotes legislative action on a range of 'empowerment' issues. Promotion of school choice, resident management urban homestead initiatives for the poor, enterprise zones, and other strategies.
Accomplishments: In 1994 the Foundation spent $116,247 on its programs.
Total Revenue: 1994 $209,921 503%(2) **Total Expenses:** $253,742 **Net Assets:** $7,089
Tax Status: 501(c)(3)   **Citations:** 0:233
Board of Directors or Trustees: Ed Batal, Steve Flaude (National Congress for Community Economic Development), Bill Cleveland, Alan Smith (Assoc. Vice Pres., Government Relations, Nationwide Insurance).
Other Information: Established in 1992. The Empowerment Network Foundation promotes strategies that, rather than removing welfare, try to reform it so as to create incentives which will induce the poor to earn and save, accumulate assets, and improve their immediate living conditions. Critics on the Right often agree that the current welfare system has built-in disincentives to work, save and invest, but that the 'empowerment' approach is more welfare under a new name. They argue that 'empowerment' relies on government bureaucrats, taxpayer funding and income redistribution, just as the current system does. The Foundation received $209,680, or 99.8% of revenue, from contributions and grants awarded by foundations, businesses, and individuals. (These grants included $5,000 from the Anschutz Foundation.) The remaining revenue came from interest on savings.

Enterprise Square, USA

2501 E. Memorial Rd.
Oklahoma City, OK 73136   **Phone:** (405) 425-5030
USA   **Fax:** (405) 425-5316

Contact Person: Pendleton Woods.
Officers or Principals: Dr. J. Terry Johnson, President; Dr. Guy Ross, Executive Director.
Mission or Interest: An attracton for tourist and school groups, interpreting, in an entertaining manner, the American Free-Enterprise System.
Accomplishments: Each year the center welcomes visitors from every state in the union, averaging 50,000 annually. The center has hosted visitors from more than 70 nations
Products or Services: Essay contests, forums, high school student business competitions, educational cassettes, business day camps.
Tax Status: 501(c)(3)   **Annual Report:** Yes.   **Employees:** 9 full time.
Board of Directors or Trustees: Same as the board of directors of Oklahoma Christian University of Science and Arts.
Periodicals: *Report from Enterprise Square, USA* (quarterly newsletter).
Internships: Yes, principally their own students, but others can apply for consideration.
Other Information: Affiliated with, and incorporated under, the Oklahoma Christian University of Science and Arts. Also affiliated with the National Education Program.

Entrepreneurial Leadership Center

Bellevue University
1000 Galvin Rd., S.
Bellevue, NE 68005   **Phone:** (402) 293-3743
USA   **Fax:** (402) 293-2023   **Internet:** http://bruins.bellevue.edu
Contact Person: Dr. Judd W. Patton, Director.
Officers or Principals: Dr. John Kayne, Editor; Dr. Judd W. Patton, Director.
Mission or Interest: "Dedicated to promoting a better and deeper understanding of the processes and principles of economics, the free enterprise system, and entrepreneurial skills." To carry out its mission the Center offers six 'free enterprise' classes.
Accomplishments: Distributed more than half a million copies of an article on Richard McDonald, founder of McDonald's restaurants, through reprints of the newsletter it appeared in. Only university in America to award Richard McDonald an Honorary Doctorate. The Center's telecourse, "Is Rush Right?" (a class for credit that analyzes the statements made by Rush Limbaugh, the popular radio host) has received nationwide attention
Products or Services: Classes and curriculum, annual Free Enterprise Day, and Speaker's Bureau.
Tax Status: 501(c)(3)
Periodicals: *Bottom Line* (quarterly newsletter).
Other Information: Established in 1982; part of and incorporated under Bellevue University.

Equal Opportunity Foundation

815 15th St., N.W., Suite 928
Washington, DC 20005   **Phone:** (202) 639-0803   **E-Mail:** comment@ceousa.org
USA   **Fax:** (202) 639-0827   **Internet:** http://www.ceousa.org

Contact Person: Jorge Anselle.
Officers or Principals: Linda Chavez, President; John J. Miller, Vice President.
Mission or Interest: Hosts the Center for Equal Opportunity. Promotion of a color-blind society and racial harmony. Opposes racial preferences and bilingual education. Supports making skills preferences the basis for an immigration policy and promotes immigrant assimilation.
Accomplishments: Brought the leaders of the California Civil Rights Initiative (Proposal 209) to Washington, DC for a National Press Club press conference. Hosted debates and conferences. Linda Chavez has a weekly column in *USA Today*. "Campaign for a Color-Blind America" initiative opposing racial gerrymandering
Products or Services: The Failure of Bilingual Education, Strangers at the Gates: Immigration in the 1990s, Alternatives to Afrocentrism, Index of Leading Immigration Indicators, and other books.
Tax Status: 501(c)(3)   **Annual Report:** Yes.   **Employees:** 6
Board of Directors or Trustees: Hon. Jerry Apodaca (former Gov., New Mexico), Michael Meyers (Exec. Dir., New York Civil Rights Coalition), Caesar Arredondo, Prof. Christine Rossell (Boston Univ.), Albert Shanker (Pres., American Federation of Teachers), Prof. Shelby Steele (San Jose State Univ.).
Periodicals: *The American Experiment* (quarterly).
Internships: Yes. Part-time and full-time unpaid internships.
Other Information: Linda Chavez worked for the Reagan administration as Staff Director of the U.S. Commission on Civil Rights (1983-85) and as an Assistant to the President and the Director of White House Public Liaison (1985-86). She was a senior fellow at the Manhattan Institute for six years. In 1995 the Foundation received $150,000 from the John M. Olin Foundation, $30,000 from the Lynde and Harry Bradley Foundation, $27,500 from the Scaife Family Foundation, $25,000 from the William H. Donner Foundation, and $3,200 from the Madison Center for Educational Affairs.

Eric Voegelin Institute

Louisiana State University
240 Stubbs Hall
Baton Rouge, LA 70803
USA

Phone: (504) 388-2552   **E-Mail:** evelli@unix1.sncc.lsu.edu
Fax: (504) 388-2540
Internet: http://www.lsu.edu:80/guests/poli/public-html/voegelin.html

Contact Person: Prof. Ellis Sandoz, Secretary.
Mission or Interest: Part of the College of Arts and Sciences at LSU, the Institute honors Eric Voegelin, the former LSU professor now recognized as "one of the great minds of the twentieth century." The Institute is devoted to revitalizing teaching, and understanding the great works of western civilization.
Products or Services: A Government of Laws, and Eric Voegelin's Significance for the Modern Mind, both by Ellis Sandoz. The Institute plans to publish The Collected Works of Eric Voegelin in 34 volumes through the LSU Press by 2001, several volumes have already been published. Annual Meeting since 1985.
Tax Status: 501(c)(3)
Periodicals: *Eric Voegelin Society Newsletter.*
Other Information: The Institute is incorporated under the LSU Foundation. Eric Voegelin (1901-1985) was a scholar who came to America from Germany as a refugee from the Nazis "because of his resolute scholarly opposition to Hitler." Voegelin taught at LSU from 1942-1958, and was a member of the Philadelphia Society. The Dictionary of American Conservatism says of Voegelin, "a religious historian whose overview of human social developments was inspiring to conservative intellectuals. . . denounced 'Gnosticism'." Programs of the Institute include such topics as "Voegelin contra Heidegger", "Voegelin, Kant and the Meaning of Reason", "Voegelin's Reading of the Ancients", "Nominalism, Realism, Post Modernism and Eric Voegelin", "Voegelin and Hegel in Dialogue", and "Voegelin and Saint Augustine". In 1994 the Center received $15,000 from the Earhart Foundation.

Ethan Allen Institute (EAI)

RFD 1, Box 43
Concord, VT 05824
USA

Phone: (802) 695-2555   **E-Mail:** ethallen@plainfield.bypass.com
Fax: same   **Internet:** http://plainfield.bypass.com/~ethallen/

Contact Person: John McClaughry, President.
Officers or Principals: John McClaughry, President ($30,000); Anne McClaughry, Treasurer ($0); John Mitchell, Chairman ($0).
Mission or Interest: State-level free-market public-policy think tank focusing on Vermont. The Institute strongly advocates the devolution of governing to smaller, local, bodies.
Accomplishments: The Institute and McClaughry have attracted attention outside of Vermont for their ideas on government devolution. Prior to founding the Institute, McClaughry co-published, with political science professor Frank Bryan, "The Vermont Papers: Recreating Democracy on a Human Scale." McClaughry represented the Institute at the (leftist) E.F. Schumacher Society's Decentralist Conference. McClaughry delivered the closing address at the second annual New York State Conference on Private Property Rights in 1996. His topic was "Social Property and Feudalism." In Vermont, the Institute opposed the Northeast Interstate Dairy Compact, a Commission that would control milk prices in the region, and revoke the license and fine $10,000 per day any farmer who sold milk at a lower price than set by the Commission. Supported Medical Savings Accounts in Vermont. In 1995 the Institute published 23 newspaper commentaries in 15 Vermont dailies and weeklies. Commentaries also appeared on bi-weekly four-minute pieces on Vermont Public Radio.
Total Revenue: 1995 $49,554 **Total Expenses:** $50,226 **Net Assets:** $8,777
Products or Services: Dinners, luncheons, conferences, reports, commentaries, and an annual contest for better ideas in governance.
Tax Status: 501(c)(3) **Annual Report:** Yes. **Employees:** 1
Board of Directors or Trustees: Rolan Vautour, William Sayre, Robert Hardy, Mark Waskow, Martin Adams, Marcia DeRosia, Ray Allen (Vermont Wildflower Farm).
Periodicals: *Ethan Allen Institute Newsletter* (monthly newsletter).
Internships: No.
Other Information: Established in 1993. A member of the State Policy Network. President McClaughry was a White House Senior Policy Advisor from 1981-82, a two-time State Senator, and an unsuccessful candidate for Governor of Vermont. He is also a friend and supporter of Pat Buchanan. Despite his conservative credentials, he has won *some* friends and accolades from a few on the Left, particularly environmentalists, who share his decentralist views. The Institute received $41,716, or 84% of revenue, from contributions and grants awarded by foundations, businesses, and individuals. (These grants included $2,500 from the Roe Foundation.) $6,950, or 14%, from membership dues. $874, or 2%, from special fund-raising events. The remaining revenue came from the sale of inventory.

Ethics and Public Policy Center

1015 15th St., N.W., Suite 900
Washington, DC 20005
USA

Phone: (202) 682-1200
Fax: (202) 408-0632

Contact Person: George S. Weigel, Jr., President.

Officers or Principals: George S. Weigel, Jr., President ($117,966); Robert Royal, Vice President for Research ($75,616); Michael M. Uhlmann, Senior Fellow ($66,971); Michael L. Cromartic, Senior Fellow; Carol F. Griffith, Senior Editor; Admiral E.R. Zumwalt, Jr., Chairman; Bettie Gray, Secretary.

Mission or Interest: To clarify and reinforce the Judeo-Christian moral tradition in public debate over domestic and foreign policy. Programs include research, writing, publication, and conferences. The Center studies five main areas, Religion and Society, Foreign Policy, Law and Society, Education and Society, and Business and Society.

Accomplishments: The Center has published over 60 books. Columnist George Will said of them, "Within every wise public policy there is a hard kernel of ethical understanding. The Ethics and Public Policy Center helps keep Washington conscious of and conscientious about the kernels." In 1995 the Center spent $677,448 on its programs.

Total Revenue: 1995 $1,076,829 (decrease of less than 1%)(5) **Total Expenses:** $1,042,085 77%/17%/6%
Net Assets: $2,166,522

Products or Services: Books, conferences. They present the annual "Shelby Cullom Davis Award" for integrity and courage in public life. Past recipients include; Jeane Kirkpatrick, Lech Walesa, Paul Nitze, Edward Teller, Robert Bork, and others.

Tax Status: 501(c)(3) **Annual Report:** Yes. **Citations:** 78:79

Board of Directors or Trustees: Neal Freeman (Blackwell Corp.), Prof. Mary Ann Glendon (Harvard Law School), Dr. Carl Henry, Frederick Hill, Amb. Max Kampelman , Jeane Kirkpatrick (Co-Director, Empower America), Rev. Richard John Neuhaus (Inst. on Religion and Public Life), George Tanham (Rand Corp.), Hon. W. Allen Wallis (former Chancellor, Univ. of Rochester), Hon. John Whitehead (Deputy Secretary of State, 1985-89).

Periodicals: *American Purpose,* and *Ethics and Public Policy Center Newsletter.*

Other Information: Established in 1976 by Ernest W. Lefever. The Center received $1,014,718, or 94% of gross revenue, from contributions and grants awarded by foundations, businesses, and individuals. (These grants included $258,000 from the Lynde and Harry Bradley Foundation, $125,000 from the John M. Olin Foundation, $93,000 from the Smith Richardson Foundation, and $10,000 from the Philip M. McKenna Foundation. In 1994, $200,000 from the Sarah Scaife Foundation, and $15,000 from the Earhart Foundation.) $32,198, or 3%, from dividends and interest from securities. $17,159, or 2%, from interest on savings and temporary cash investments. The remaining revenue came from royalties, capital gains on the sale of assets, and other miscellaneous sources. The Center lost $1,068 net on the sale of inventory.

Evans-Novak Political Report

1750 Pennsylvania Ave., N.W., Suite 1312
Washington, DC 20006   **Phone:** (202) 393-4340
USA   **Fax:** (202) 546-9579

Contact Person: J. Richard Pearcey, Associate Editor.

Officers or Principals: Robert D. Novak, Rowland Evans, Editors; Thomas L. Phillips, Chairman; Jeffrey J. Carneal, President.

Mission or Interest: Newsletter written by Robert Novak and Rowland Evans. Political 'insider's report' of what's happening in Washington. Covers fast-breaking political and economic developments, "What's happening. . . who's ahead. . . in politics today."

Accomplishments: Circulation of over 2,000. Novak and Evans are perhaps best known for hosting the CNN interview program, "Evans & Novak." They are also the authors of <u>Lyndon B. Johnson: The Exercise of Power</u>, <u>Nixon in the White House: The Frustration of Power</u>, and <u>The Reagan Revolution</u>.

Tax Status: For profit.

Periodicals: *Evans-Novak Political Report.*

Other Information: *Evans-Novak Political Report* is published by Eagle Publishing, Inc. (For more information see Eagle Publishing, Inc.)

Evergreen Freedom Foundation (EFF)

2111 State St., 2nd Floor
Olympia, WA 98507   **Phone:** (360) 956-3482   **E-Mail:** effwa@aol.com
USA   **Fax:** (360) 352-1874

Contact Person: Theresa Rudacille, Development Director.

Officers or Principals: G. Robert Williams, President ($45,900); Lynn Harsh, Executive Director ($40,500); Nichole Smith, Research Associate.

Mission or Interest: "Dedicated to the principles of individual liberty, free enterprise and limited, accountable government. The Foundation specializes in refocusing the role of state government around core governing principles, using free-market alternatives to government designed and managed programs." Focus on Washington state.

Accomplishments: Has been cited by Heritage's *Policy Review*, ALEC's *FYI*, and the *Wall Street Journal* for its work in government downsizing, state budgets, and education and welfare reform. "EFF published the first national study of Medical Savings Accounts which was used by state and Congressional officials to incorporate MSAs into health reform legislation." Developed an extensive grassroots network. "EFF staff members meet quarterly with Washington's Governor and hold weekly meetings with legislators during the annual legislative session." Organized "Taxpayer Action Day" in Washington. In 1995 EFF spent $134,943 on its programs.

Total Revenue: 1995 $253,323 39%(3) **Total Expenses:** $239,952 56%/25%/19% **Net Assets:** $43,821

Products or Services: Biennial State Budget Analysis, and "Reducing the Size and Cost of Government" - a guide for state lawmakers. Other handbooks and studies.

Tax Status: 501(c)(3) **Annual Report:** No. **Employees:** 4   **Citations:** 50:99
Board of Directors or Trustees: Duane Alton, Douglas Bohlke, Lyle Dickie, Harry James, Mary Jo Kahler, Andy Nisbet, Ansar Schei, Juanita Schindler, Richard Schoon, Lynne Schow, Bill Shortt, Robert Taigen, Del Vanwinkle, Brian Worden.
Periodicals: *Washington Journal* (monthly newsletter).
Internships: Yes, January through April "Legislative Session Internship" and June through August summer internships.
Other Information: A member of the State Policy Network. EFF received $252,211, or 99.5% of revenue, from contributions and grants awarded by foundations, businesses, and individuals. (These grants included $7,500 from the Roe Foundation. In 1994, $30,000 from the M.J. Murdock Charitable Trust.) The remaining revenue came from interest on savings and temporary cash investments.

Excellence in Broadcasting Network (EIB) / Rush Limbaugh Show

2 Penn Plaza, 17th Floor
New York, NY 10121   **Phone:** (212) 661-7500   **E-Mail:** rush@compuserve.com
USA   **Fax:** (212) 563-9166

Contact Person: Kit Carson, Chief of Staff.
Officers or Principals: Rush Limbaugh, Host.
Mission or Interest: Nationally syndicated talk show featuring Rush Limbaugh.
Accomplishments: The Rush Limbaugh Show is carried by over 600 stations nationwide and has over 20 million listeners during any given week. He has written two #1 bestsellers, The Way Things Ought to Be and See I Told You So
Tax Status: For profit.
Other Information: The phone number to contact the Rush Limbaugh Show on the air is (800) 282-2882.

Exodus International, North America

P.O. Box 77652
Seattle, WA 98177   **Phone:** (206) 784-7799   **E-Mail:** BobExodus@aol.com
USA   **Fax:** (206) 784-7872

Contact Person: Bob Davies, Executive Director.
Officers or Principals: Bob Davies, Executive Director ($34,725); John Smid, President ($0); Pat Allan, Vice President ($0); Bud Searcy, Secretary/Treasurer.
Mission or Interest: "Provide support and counsel for men and women seeking freedom from homosexuality. We also minister to family members and friends (of homosexuals)."
Accomplishments: A frequent reference source of religious conservatives. In 1994 Exodus spent $219,141 on its programs. The largest program, with expenditures of $114,161, was the annual conference for training ministers. Approximately 600 individuals attended the one-week conference. $47,141 was spent on assistance to local ministries in response to 200 requests. $43,825 was spent on approximately 5,000 referrals to local ministries.
Total Revenue: 1994 $304,953 **Total Expenses:** $369,557 59%/41%/1% **Net Assets:** $7,303
Products or Services: Counseling, materials, and referrals.
Tax Status: 501(c)(3) **Annual Report:** No. **Employees:** 4   **Citations:** 14:165
Board of Directors or Trustees: Mary Heathman, Bill Consiglio, Anita Worthen, John Paulk, Tony Bishop.
Periodicals: *Update* (monthly newsletter).
Internships: No.
Other Information: Established in 1976. Recently moved from San Rafael, CA. While in California, Exodus' office was invaded by the San Francisco chapter of the Lesbian Avengers, who released hundreds of crickets in the office, calling it a "plague of locusts," and shouting "we don't need to be cured!". Exodus International received $201,925, or 66% of revenue, from conference fees. $77,988, or 26%, from contributions and grants awarded by foundations, affiliates, businesses, and individuals. $11,374, or 4%, from the sale of inventory. The remaining revenue came from interest on savings, membership fees, and application fees.

Experimental Media Organization

Binghamton University
P.O. Box 6000
Binghamton, NY 13902   **E-Mail:** bc90121@bingsuns.cc.binghamton.edu
USA

Contact Person: Justin Weinberg, Editor.
Officers or Principals: Brian Taylor, Editor.
Mission or Interest: Produces *Guillotine*, a libertarian publication distributed on numerous college campuses through the Student Individualist Network.
Products or Services: Publishes papers and pamphlets, and sponsors films and speakers in the Binghamton area.
Tax Status: Unincorporated.
Periodicals: *The Guillotine* (monthly).

F. M. Kirby Foundation

17 DeHart St.
P.O. Box 151
Morristown, NJ 07963   **Phone:**   (201) 538-4800
USA

Contact Person: F. M. Kirby, President.
Officers or Principals: Paul B. Mott, Jr., Executive Director ($69,364); Thomas J. Bianchini, Secretary/Treasurer ($20,036); F. M. Kirby, President ($0); Walker D. Kirby, Vice President; Alice K. Horton, Assistant Secretary.
Mission or Interest: Grant-making foundation that includes conservative and free-market organizations in its awards. Also awards grants to left-of-center organizations.
Accomplishments: In 1994 the Foundation awarded $13,978,634 in grants. Recipients included: two grants totaling $1,560,000 for the Intercollegiate Studies Institute ($1.5 million to name the new F. M. Kirby Campus and Hall), $750,000 for the Leadership Institute (to name a wing of classrooms the F. M. Kirby National Training Center), $50,000 each for the Center on National Labor Policy, National Right to Work Legal Defense Foundation, Young America's Foundation, and National Forum Foundation, $40,000 for the Heritage Foundation, $30,000 each for the Center for Individual Rights, High Frontier, Jamestown Foundation, and the Free Congress Foundation, $20,000 each for Accuracy in Media, Federalist Society, Institute for Justice, National Association of Scholars, and the Atlantic Legal Foundation, $17,500 each for the Citizens for a Sound Economy Foundation, Media Research Center, Social Philosophy and Policy Foundation, and the Madison Center, $15,000 for the American Council on Science and Health, $10,000 each for the Federation for American Immigration Reform, Hudson Institute, U.S. Term Limits Foundation, and Hillsdale College, $7,500 each for the Clare Boothe Luce Policy Institute, and National Legal Center, $6,500 for the American Enterprise Institute, $5,000 each for the Fund for American Studies, Philanthropy Roundtable, Washington Legal Foundation, and Pacific Legal Foundation, and $3,500 for the Capital Research Center.
Total Revenue: 1994 $26,083,489 **Total Expenses:** $15,384,111 **Net Assets:** $259,143,737 (-4%)(1)
Tax Status: 501(c)(3)
Board of Directors or Trustees: Fred Kirby, III, S. Dillard Kirby, Jefferson Kirby.
Other Information: Established in 1931. The Foundation received $20,610,000, or 79% of revenue, from capital gains on the sale of assets. $5,451,646, or 21%, from dividends and interest from securities. The remaining revenue came from other miscellaneous sources. The Foundation held $241,843,534, or 93% of assets, in corporate stock.

Factsheet Five

P.O. Box 170099
San Francisco, CA 94117   **Phone:**   (415) 621-1761
USA

Contact Person: R. Seth Friedman.
Mission or Interest: Promotes free speech by reviewing independent publications of all types. *Factsheet Five* reviews and lists magazines and periodicals, mostly of the political Left, but some libertarian, populist and conservative publications are reviewed.
Accomplishments: Organizes shows of the various publications
Tax Status: For profit.
Periodicals: *Factsheet Five* (magazine).
Internships: No.
Other Information: Organizations and groups who publish newsletters and periodicals are encouraged to send a copy to *Factsheet Five* for inclusion.

Fairness to Land Owners Committee (FLOC)

1730 Garden of Eden Rd.
Cambridge, MD 21613   **Phone:**   (410) 228-3822
USA   **Fax:**   (410) 228-8357

Contact Person: Margaret Ann Reigle, Chairman/Founder.
Officers or Principals: C. Charles Jowaiszas; E. Thomas Merryweather; Melanie Merryweather.
Mission or Interest: "Restore the power and private property rights to We the People."
Accomplishments: Have assisted landowners in private property rights issues such as wetlands, endangered species, new National Wildlife Refuge designations, expansion of National parks, etc. Assisted in the enactment of a Private Property Rights bill in the 1992 session. Worked with Senator Symms (R-ID) on passage of Private Property Rights Act in the U.S. Senate. Assisted Congressman Hayes (D-LA) in provisions of a wetlands reform bill and enlisting co-sponsors. Margaret Ann Reigle has appeared on ABC's Nightline, The MacNeil/Lehrer Newshour, NBC Network News, CBS Network News, Wall Street Journal (TV) Report, Church Today (cable VISN network) and on local Washington and Baltimore stations. In the print media, they have been featured in *Forbes, Readers Digest, U.S. News & World Report,* and *Tomorrow* magazines, as well as *The New York Times, New York Newsday, U.S.A. Today, The Washington Post, The Washington Times, Philadelphia Inquirer, Chicago Tribune, The Baltimore Sun,* and other newspapers. 10,000 members in 35 states
Periodicals: *News from The FLOC* (monthly).

Family Council

1900 N. Bryant, Suite A
Little Rock, AR 72207   **Phone:** (501) 664-4566
USA   **Fax:** (501) 664-2317

Contact Person: Tom Moseley, Editor.
Officers or Principals: Jerry Cox., Director.
Mission or Interest: Promotion of "Biblical values" and family-friendly policies in Arkansas.
Products or Services: Voter guides.
Tax Status: 501(c)(3)
Periodicals: *Arkansas Citizen* (monthly newsletter included in Focus on the Family's *Citizen*), and *Arkansas Family Times* (monthly church bulletin).
Other Information: Established in 1989. Affiliated with Focus on the Family.

Family Foundation

3817-B Plaza Dr.
Fairfax, VA 22151   **Phone:** (703) 273-9555
USA   **Fax:** (703) 273-9656

Contact Person: Walt Barber, President.
Officers or Principals: Walt Barber, President ($0); John E. Towell, Vice President ($0); Charles James, Sr., Treasurer ($0); Dr. Jim Burns, Secretary; George Tryfiates, Executive Director; Marilyn Caro, Administrative Director; Margaret Bocek, Assistant Administrative Director; Robin DeJanette, Government Relations Director.
Mission or Interest: "Dedicated to strengthening Virginia's families through research, education, and public policy activities."
Accomplishments: "Largest and most influential Virginia-based organization of its kind, networking with tens of thousands of citizens." In 1995 the Foundation spent $144,996 on its programs.
Total Revenue: 1995 $201,797 **Total Expenses:** $171,076 85%/7%/8% **Net Assets:** $79,943
Products or Services: "Virginia Education Report Card." Fax Alert Network. "Report Card" rating Virginia legislators. Videos, audio tapes and books. Training seminars. Lobbying: the Foundation spent $11,295 on lobbying, $4,957 on grassroots lobbying and $6,338 on the direct lobbying of legislators. 1995 was the first year the Foundation lobbied.
Tax Status: 501(c)(3)
Periodicals: *The Virginia Citizen* (monthly newsletter inserted in Focus on the Family's *Citizen*).
Other Information: Established in 1987. Affiliated with Focus on the Family, although they receive no direct financial support. The Foundation received $200,609, or 99% of revenue, from contributions and grants awarded by foundations, businesses, and individuals. The Foundation's contributions and grants have increased by an average of 28% over the last three years. The remaining revenue came from interest on savings and temporary cash investments.

Family Research Council (FRC)

801 G St., N.W.
Washington, DC 20001   **Phone:** (202) 393-2100
USA   **Fax:** (202) 393-2134   **Internet:** http://www.frc.org

Contact Person: Gary L. Bauer, President .
Officers or Principals: Gary L. Bauer, President ($150,618); Philip V. Olsen, Vice President, Education and Development ($95,797); Douglas L. Werk, Vice President, Administration ($80,938); Charles Donovan, Editor; Robert Knight, Director, Cultural Studies; David Wagner, Director, Legal Affairs; Elizabeth Law, Director, Government Relations; William Mattox, Director, Policy; Philip V. Olsen, Vice President, Resources; Douglas L. Werk, Vice President, Administration; Kay Cole James, Vice President, Policy; Stephen Reed, Counsel.
Mission or Interest: Public policy affiliate of Focus on the Family. "Rebuilding the family must become a national priority - we would say, *the* national priority. But to rebuild the family, we must first rebuild the consensus about family. . . The FRC has endeavored to communicate the pro-family perspective to our political leaders in Washington through lobbying, research, media relations and education."
Accomplishments: The FRC has been instrumental in crafting policy and proposed legislation based on traditional values. Its newsletter, *Washington Watch*, reaches an average of 206,500 homes - *Family Policy* reaches 32,500. Distributed over 84,000 copies of "Anatomy of the Clinton Health Plan." In the fiscal year ending September 1994 the FRC spent $5,573,266 on its programs - an increase of 42% over the previous year.
Total Revenue: FY ending 9/94 $8,185,615 12%(1) **Total Expenses:** $6,933,232 80%/15%/5% **Net Assets:** $3,844,621
Products or Services: Publications, newsletters, media appearances, and lobbying. FRC spent $186,814 on lobbying, $124,133 on grassroots lobbying and $62,681 on the direct lobbying of legislators. This was an increase of 178% over the previous year.
Tax Status: 501(c)(3) **Annual Report:** No. **Employees:** 17   **Citations:** 1,361:7
Board of Directors or Trustees: Ronald Blue, James Dobson (Focus on the Family), Lee Eaton, Edgar Prince, Larry Smith.
Periodicals: *Washington Watch* (newsletter)*, Family Policy* (bimonthly).
Internships: Yes, providing interns with hands-on experience within a professional atmosphere. Internships are unpaid.

Other Information: Established in 1983, in 1988 it merged with Focus on the Family. Affiliated with the 501(c)(4) American Renewal at the same address. President Gary Bauer was Under Secretary of the Department of Education, 1985-87, and a White House Policy Advisor, 1987-88. The Council received $7,936,742, or 97% of revenue, from contributions and grants awarded by foundations, businesses, and individuals. (These grants included $10,500 from the DeWitt Families Conduit Foundation. In 1995, $55,000 from the Lynde and Harry Bradley Foundation, $10,000 from the John William Pope Foundation, and $1,000 from the Roe Foundation.) $125,732, or 2%, from interest on savings and temporary cash investments. The remaining revenue came from rental income and conference and seminar fees.

Family Research Institute (FRI)

P.O. Box 2091
Washington, DC 20013   **Phone:**   (703) 690-8536
USA   **Fax:**   same

Contact Person: Paul Cameron, Ph.D., Chairman.
Officers or Principals: Kirk Cameron, Ph.D.; Keith Abbott, J.D.; William Playfair, M.D.
Mission or Interest: "Believes that the West is making a profound mistake in trading traditional Christian sexual morality for the anarchy of the 'sexual revolution'." Their goal is to preform sound research in the fields of sociology, psychology and medicine which defends traditional values. They also critique the works of left-leaning social researchers such as the Kinsey Institute, Planned Parenthood, etc.
Accomplishments: The Institute claims it and its researchers were: The first to empirically refute the claim of the Kinsey sex survey that 10% of the population is gay. First to document the harmful effects of second-hand tobacco smoke. Demonstrated misuse of statistical analysis by the U.S. Centers for Disease Control on data regarding HIV transmission in Africa. Exposed the American Psychological Association for falsifying data. The Institute's researchers have appeared on Nightline, CBS News, Straight Talk, Crossfire, 700 Club, C-SPAN, and other television and radio shows. Chairman Paul Cameron was nominated as "the most dangerous man in America," by *The Advocate*, a magazine of homosexuals' concerns. Family Research Institute has served as a primary source of information for anti-gay rights ballot initiatives
Products or Services: Numerous pamphlets, video tapes, books, articles, audio tapes, more.
Tax Status: 501(c)(3) **Annual Report:** No. **Employees:** 11
Periodicals: Newsletter.
Other Information: Established in 1982 as the Institute for Scientific Investigation of Sexuality. The name changed in 1987.

Federal Lands Legal Foundation

P.O. Box 1633
Roswell, NM 88202   **Phone:**   (505) 622-0055
USA   **Fax:**   (505) 625-9608

Contact Person: Alice Eppers, Secretary.
Officers or Principals: Bud Eppers, President; Alice Eppers, Secretary.
Mission or Interest: Property rights legal advocacy group. Active in the County Movement. FLLF works as the legal advocacy arm of the County Movement. It has brought several lawsuits against government agencies including the Forest Service and the Fish and Wildlife Service.
Total Revenue: 1994 less than $25,000
Tax Status: 501(c)(3)
Other Information: The Foundation received $17,198 in contributions and grants.

Federalist Society for Law and Public Policy Studies

1700 K St., N.W., Suite 901
Washington, DC 20006   **Phone:**   (202) 822-8138   **E-Mail:**   fedsoc@radix.net
USA   **Fax:**   (202) 296-8061   **Internet:** http://www.fed-soc.org

Contact Person: Eugene B. Meyer, Executive Director.
Officers or Principals: Eugene B. Meyer, Executive Director ($60,000); Leonard A. Leo, Director, Lawyers Division ($51,500); Stephen G. Calabresi, President ($0); Brent O. Hatch, Treasurer; David M. McIntosh, Lee Liberman Otis, Chairmen.
Mission or Interest: Legal advocacy and watchdog group that seeks "to promote diversity in the legal profession and the legal community. . . advances traditional legal principles such as limited, constitutional government; individual freedom and responsibility; traditional values; and the rule of law."
Accomplishments: Claims 22,000 members, 145 Student Division chapters, and 60 Lawyers' Division chapters. Sen. E. Spencer Abraham (R-MI) was previously a vice president of the Society. Participants in the Society's events have included Presidents Reagan and Bush, Vice President Quayle, Supreme Court Justices William Rehnquist, Warren Burger, Anthony Kennedy, Antonin Scalia, and Clarence Thomas, as well as numerous other judges and elected officials. In 1994 the Society spent $1,056,197 on its programs.
Total Revenue: 1994 $1,236,924 21%(2) **Total Expenses:** $1,181,587 89%/4%/6% **Net Assets:** $96,548
Products or Services: "E. L. Wiegand Practice Groups" that create a network of active attorneys that support the Society's mission. Pro Bono Resource Network that refers individuals needing legal assistance. ABA Watch Project monitors the political activity of the American Bar Association and seeks to counter the ABA's becoming a "left wing advocacy group." Speakers Bureau. Annual Lawyers Convention first held in 1987, and the annual John M. Olin lectures.

Tax Status: 501(c)(3) **Employees:** 8   **Citations:** 86:71
Board of Directors or Trustees: Directors include Sen. Spencer Abraham (R-MI) and Peter Keisler. Trustees include: Co-Chairmen Robert Bork and Sen. Orrin Hatch (R-UT), Holland Coors, C. Boyden Gray (Counselor to Vice President and President Bush), Lois Haight Herrington (Assistant Attorney General, Justice Programs, 1983-86), Donald Paul Hodel (former Interior Secretary, 1985-89), Harvey Koch, Edwin Meese, III (former Attorney General, 1985-88), Hugh Overholt, William Bradford Reynolds (former Assistant Attorney General, Civil Rights, 1981-88).
Periodicals: *ABA Watch* (twice a year newsletter), and *The Federalist Paper* (monthly newsletter).
Internships: Yes.
Other Information: Established in 1982. The Society received $119,569, or 91% of revenue, from contributions and grants awarded by foundations, businesses, and individuals. (These grants included $75,000 from the Lilly Endowment, $75,000 from the Sarah Scaife Foundation, $65,000 from the William H. Donner Foundation, $20,000 from the Earhart Foundation, $20,000 from the F.M. Kirby Foundation, $20,000 from the J.M. Foundation, $10,000 from the Charles G. Koch Charitable Foundation, and $10,000 from the Milliken Foundation. In 1995, $170,000 from the John M. Olin Foundation, $126,000 from the Lynde and Harry Bradley Foundation, $100,000 from the E. L. Wiegand Foundation, $18,000 from the Philip M. McKenna Foundation, $10,000 from the John William Pope Foundation, and $1,000 from the Roe Foundation.) $108,902, or 9%, from conference registration fees. The remaining revenue came from capital gains on the sale of securities, and dividends and interest from securities.

Federation for American Immigration Reform (FAIR)

1666 Connecticut Ave., N.W., Suite 400
Washington, DC 20009   **Phone:** (202) 328-7004
USA   **Fax:** (202) 387-3447   **Internet:** http://www.fairus.comm

Contact Person: Paula Galliani.
Officers or Principals: Daniel Stein, Executive Director ($181,456); K.C. McAlpin, Deputy Director ($107,219); Marjorie Wilkinson, Director of Development ($59,867); Ira Mehlman, Director, Media Outreach; John Tanton, M.D., Chairman; Nancy Anthony, Vice Chairman; Steve Swensrud, Treasurer; Janet Harte, Secretary.
Mission or Interest: "A national pro-limits organization working to stop illegal immigration and reform legal immigration." Special focus on immigration and population-growth concerns.
Accomplishments: "FAIR played a key role in the passage of the Immigration Reform Act of 1986. FAIR helped double the manpower of the U.S. Border Patrol. In 1990, FAIR helped defeat a massive immigration increase bill in the House of Representatives. FAIR was instrumental in getting a commitment from the Bush Administration that no U.S.-Mexico Free Trade Agreement would grant Mexicans access to the U.S. labor market." Television appearances on 48 Hours, 60 Minutes, Firing Line, Eye on America, Court TV, and NBC's Today. Frequent testimony before Congressional committees. In 1995 FAIR spent $2,786,886 on its programs. This included $81,500 in grants for local immigration-restriction organizations, including; $50,000 for U.S. Inc. (MI), $30,000 for FLA187 Committee (FL), $1,000 for Citizens of Dade United (FL), and $500 for Texans for FAIR Immigration.
Total Revenue: 1995 $3,330,443 9%(5) **Total Expenses:** $3,595,705 78%/10%/12% **Net Assets:** $5,390,836
Products or Services: Monographs, articles, and a syndicated column. "Border Line" television show produced for NET-TV. Ten Steps to Ending Illegal Immigration, and other books. Lobbying: in 1995 FAIR spent $210,945 on lobbying, $44,705 on grassroots lobbying and $166,240 on the direct lobbying of legislators. This was down from 40% from 1994, but 5% over 1993 and 37% over 1992.
Tax Status: 501(c)(3) **Annual Report:** Yes. **Employees:** 16
Board of Directors or Trustees: Sharon Barnes (Zero Population Growth), Kenneth Bilby, Henry Buhl, Don Collins, Sarah Epstein (Pathfinder Fund), Otis Graham, Jr., Ph.D., (Univ. of California, Santa Barbara), Janet Harte (Planned Parenthood), Hon. Richard Lamm (Governor, D-CO, 1975-87).
Internships: Yes.
Other Information: Established in 1979. Affiliated with the 501(c)(4) FAIR Congressional Task Force. FAIR employed the Alexandria, VA, firms of Gallagher & Associates as consultants, and the MPG List Co. for mailing list management (both firms are located at the same address). The two firms were paid $118,748 and $63,770 respectively. FAIR is unusual for an organization that works with conservatives in that it is associated with abortion rights and population-growth control. Almost every member of its board is a member of Planned Parenthood, The Pathfinder Fund, Sierra Club, or Zero Population Growth. Chairman Tanton was a former President of Zero Population Growth. He states that he is "concerned about continually growing human populations, in substantial measure because of libertarian-type worries about erosions of personal liberty this will surely bring. A good way to assure an I.D. card in our future is to double our population." These connections are even more unusual since they work with the anti-abortion Free Congress Foundation and its NET-TV to produce their show, "Border Line." FAIR received $2,866,626, or 86% of revenue, from contributions and grants awarded by foundations, businesses, and individuals. (These included $20,000 from the Carthage Foundation. In 1994, $10,000 from the F.M. Kirby Foundation.) $323,874, or 10%, from dividends and interest from securities. $79,496, or 2%, from mailing list rentals. $53,785, or 2%, from interest on savings and temporary cash investments. The remaining revenue came from the sale of publications and honoraria.

FEDUP Publishing

P.O. Box 477
East Moline, IL 61244-0477
USA

Contact Person: Richard J. Jolley, Owner/Publisher.
Mission or Interest: To inform Americans about the true nature of the Constitution and the form of limited government set up by our founders. The *FEDUP News* prints original articles and reprints from other sources. It also serves as a "paper of record," printing excerpts from the Congressional Record, as well as the writings of the Founding Fathers.
Accomplishments: *FEDUP News* premiered in December of 1993
Tax Status: For profit. **Annual Report:** No. **Employees:** None.
Periodicals: *FEDUP News* (quarterly, eventually to become a weekly).
Internships: No.
Other Information: Established in 1993. FEDUP is an acronym for "Freedom is Education and Depends Upon People."

Financial Freedom Fellowship

6602 Beadnell Way, Suite 14
San Diego, CA 92117   **Phone:** (619) 277-2708
USA

Contact Person: Fred Graessle, Founder.
Mission or Interest: Populist group supporting Constitutional government, abolishment of the Federal Reserve and a return to gold-backed money
Products or Services: Lectures, newsletters, By Their Works Ye Shall Know Them booklet
Periodicals: *Financial Facts Newsletter*.

Financial Privacy Report

P.O. Box 1277
Burnsville, MN 55337
USA

Contact Person: Michael Ketcher, Editor.
Officers or Principals: Dan Rosenthal, Founder.
Mission or Interest: Newsletter on how to protect your finances, property, computer documents and personal information from government intrusion and confiscation. Also concerned with the rights of jurors
Products or Services: The Closing Door: The End of Financial Privacy in America with a forward by Rep. Ron Paul (R-TX), Your House is Under Arrest: How Police Can Seize Your Home, Car, and Business Without a Trial, and other books.
Tax Status: For profit.
Periodicals: *Financial Privacy Report* (newsletter).

Firearms Civil Rights Legal Defense Fund

11250 Waples Mill Rd.
Fairfax, VA 22030   **Phone:** (703) 267-1254
USA   **Fax:** (703) 267-3985

Contact Person: Robert Dowlut, Secretary.
Officers or Principals: George S. Knight, Chairman ($0); Robert K. Corbin, Vice Chairman ($0); Robert Dowlut, Secretary ($0); Wilson H. Phillips, Jr., Treasurer.
Mission or Interest: Legal assistance affiliate of the National Rifle Association. "Assert and defend the human, civil and constitutional rights of law-abiding Americans to keep and bear arms through precedent-setting litigation and education programs."
Accomplishments: In the fiscal year ending October 1995 the Fund spent $370,224 on its programs. Challenged the 'Brady Bill' Federal waiting period statute in several U.S. District Courts. Other cases included the defense of those who are prosecuted for defending themselves with a firearm; such as Charles Wilbur Wilson of Missouri, who shot and killed a burglar. Wilson was charged with second degree murder. The Fund spent $25,000 on his defense, and a jury acquitted him of all charges. Litigates legal challenges to shooting ranges; such as Shooting Sports, Inc., in Orlando Florida. The range was being denied permits by the city despite the location having been zoned for indoor recreation. Following $24,278 in assistance from the Fund, permits were issued and the range opened. Legal challenges to the denial of permits for concealed carry. The Fund has provided $2,000 in assistance to Bernard Goetz in his unsuccessful defense in Cabey v. Goetz. The Fund has also provided assistance in cases connected to the stand-off and conflagration at the Branch Davidian compound in Waco, TX. The Fund awarded $120,868 in grants and awards for scholarly research. Recipients included; $94,294 for the Independence Institute (this included mailings of the article "A Nation of Cowards" by Jeff Snyder. The article first appeared in *The Public Interest*.), $20,552 for Stephen P. Halbrook, Ph.D. Other recipients included Academics for the Second Amendment, and researcher David Fischer.
Total Revenue: FY ending 10/95 $578,670 (-6%)(2) **Total Expenses:** $404,421 92%/8%/0% **Net Assets:** $1,491,971
Products or Services: Writing contests and scholarships for law students. Two special award funds; the Harlon B. Carter / George S. Knight Freedom Fund for scholars and activists in support of the Second Amendment, and the Catherine Post Woodring Educational and Scholarship trust.
Tax Status: 501(c)(3) **Annual Report:** Yes. **Employees:** 2 **Citations:** 7:182
Board of Directors or Trustees: David Caplan, Prof. Robert Cottrol (George Washington Univ. School of Law), Sandra Froman, J.D., Thomas Moncure, Jr. (Clerk, Circuit Court of Stafford County, VA), Alfred Rubega (Gun Owners of New Hampshire), Paul Heath Hill (Justice of the Peace, Harris County, TX), Rep. Harold Volkmer (D-MO).

Internships: No.
Other Information: Established in 1978 by the National Rifle Association. The Fund received $504,103, or 87% of revenue, from contributions and grants awarded by affiliates, foundations, businesses, and individuals. $61,886, or 11%, from interest on savings and temporary cash investments. The remaining revenue came from other miscellaneous sources.

Focus on the Family

8605 Explorer Dr.
Colorado Springs, CO 80920 **Phone:** (719) 531-3400
USA **Fax:** (719) 531-3385

Contact Person: Tom Minnery, Vice President, Public Policy.
Officers or Principals: Paul Hetrick, Senior Vice President ($110,333); Mike Trout, Senior Vice President, Broadcasting ($100,632); Rolf Zettersten, Executive Vice President ($86,854); James C. Dobson, Jr., President/CEO; Bobb Beihl, Treasurer; Lee Eaton, Secretary; Ronald Wilson, Senior Vice President, Operations.
Mission or Interest: Through publications, radio, videos, books, and other "ministries" Focus on the Family is "Dedicated to the preservation of the home."
Accomplishments: Focus on the Family is the largest religious conservative organization. Focus works with state affiliates who, although incorporated and financially separate, work with Focus and often distribute Focus' magazine *Citizen*, with their own state-specific newsletter. These state-focused groups include; Alabama Family Alliance (AL), Capitol Resource Institute (CA), Family Council (AR), Family Foundation (VA), Free Market Foundation (TX), Illinois Family Institute (IL), Massachusetts Family Institute (MA), Michigan Family Forum (MI), North Carolina Family Policy Council (NC), North Dakota Family Alliance (ND), Oklahoma Family Policy Council (OK), Palmetto Family Council (SC), and the South Dakota Family Policy Council (SD). Focus developed the concept of "Community Impact Committees" that work through local religious leaders to coordinate and unify 'pro-family' efforts. President James Dobson is well-known for his syndicated radio show and books such as Dare to Discipline, Parenting Isn't for Cowards, and others. In the fiscal year ending September 1994, Focus spent $70,737,969 on its programs. The largest program, with expenditures of $26,511,973, was constituent services; "more than 3.2 million letters and phone calls were responded to." $17,566,330 was spent on the publication of newsletters and magazines for "over 6 million readers. Over 60 million items were distributed." $16,515,264 was spent on radio and television programming; "more than 2 million people listen to 'Focus on the Family' programs in 49 countries. Other programs included the publication of books.
Total Revenue: FY ending 9/94 $93,444,707 12%(5) **Total Expenses:** $82,975,736 85%/11%/4% **Net Assets:** $46,534,379
Products or Services: Seven Promises of a Promise Keeper, Pornography: The Human Tragedy, Children at Risk, and other books. "Adventures in Odyssey," "Life on the Edge," and other videos. Lobbying: Focus spent $410,488 on lobbying, $307,951 on grassroots lobbying, and $102,537 on the direct lobbying of legislators. This was an increase of 125% from $182,173 the year before, but down 7% from two years prior, and down 38% from $662,221 in FY 1990.
Tax Status: 501(c)(3) **Annual Report:** Yes. **Employees:** 1,300,with 196 were paid more than $30,000. **Citations:** 2,106:4
Board of Directors or Trustees: Anthony Wauterlek, Bill Hybels, Kay Coles James, Ted Enstrom, Shirley Dobson, Michael Roberts, Beth Allen Blakemore.
Periodicals: *Focus on the Family Magazine* (monthly magazine), *Citizen* (monthly public policy magazine), *Teachers in Focus* (monthly magazine for teachers), *Physician* (monthly magazine for physicians), and *Parental Guidance* (monthly review of popular culture).
Internships: No.
Other Information: Established in 1977. Affiliated with the 501(c)(3) Family Research Council in Washington, DC. The Council focuses on public policy. Dr. James Dobson is not compensated by Focus on the Family. He owns his own for-profit company, James Dobson, Inc. (JDI). JDI pays $5,000 per month to Focus for the "visibility provided to Dr. Dobson by radio programs." Books by Dr. Dobson and other officers are donated to Focus "as a resource to be offered to donors. Royalties are waived in order to avoid conflict of interest and to make possible maximum discounts." Focus on the Family is a member of The Evangelical Council for Financial Accountability; an organization that monitors financial responsibility and reporting "consistent with standards established by the American Institute of Certified Public Accountants." Focus employed the firms of Mike Joens Productions, of Glendale, CA, Set productions, of Sherman Oaks, CA, and Roger C. Ambrose Designs, of Newbury Park, CA, for film production and services. The three companies were paid $863,009, $193,194, and $191,248 respectively. Focus received $89,408,653, or 96% of revenue, from contributions and grants awarded by foundations, businesses, and individuals. (These grants included $140,938 from the DeWitt Families Conduit Foundation.) $1,568,656, or 2%, from products sold. $835,197, or 1%, from film royalties. The remaining revenue came from "events/ministries", advertising, cafeteria sales, and other miscellaneous sources.

For Limited American Government (FLAG)

601 San Juan Ct.
Irvine, TX 75062 **Phone:** (214) 717-0090
USA **Fax:** (214) 717-0296

Contact Person: Dennis McCuistion, President.
Officers or Principals: Niki Nicastro McCuistion, Editor.
Mission or Interest: Free-market organization focusing on Texas state and local issues.

Tax Status: 501(c)(3) **Annual Report:** No.
Periodicals: *The Banner* (monthly newsletter).
Other Information: Established in 1983.

Forbes Foundation

c/o Forbes, Inc.
60 5th Ave.
New York, NY 10011   **Phone:**   (212) 620-2403
USA

Contact Person: Leonard H. Yablon, Secretary/Treasurer.
Officers or Principals: Timothy C. Forbes, President ($0); Christopher Forbes, Vice President ($0).
Mission or Interest: Grant-making foundation funded by Forbes, Inc., that awards some grants to conservative organizations. Most funding is awarded to traditional charities (arts, museums, education, medical research, etc.), but a small amount is awarded to conservative and free-market organizations, with an approximately equal amount going to left-of-center organizations.
Accomplishments: In 1995 the Foundation awarded $1,171,272 in grants. Conservative recipients were: $60,000 for the Margaret Thatcher Foundation, $10,000 for the American Enterprise Institute, $5,000 each for the Atlantic Legal Foundation, Partners Advancing Values in Education, and Center for Security Policy, $2,500 for the Study of Popular Culture, $1,000 each for the American Jewish Committee, Institute for Policy Innovation, Institute for Political Economy, Education and Research Institute, National Legal Center for the Public Interest, New Jersey Citizens for a Sound Economy Foundation, and $500 for the Washington Legal Foundation. The Foundation also awarded grants to those on the other side of the political spectrum, including $18,000 for the Anti-Defamation League, $2,500 for Planned Parenthood, $1,250 for Gay Men's Health Crisis, and smaller grants (less than $1,000) for the American Foundation for AIDS Research, Amnesty International, Hetrick-Martin Institute, Nature Conservancy, and the Wilderness Society.
Total Revenue: 1995 $1,175,888 **Total Expenses:** $1,171,547 **Net Assets:** $53,635
Tax Status: 501(c)(3)
Other Information: Former Presidential candidate and Forbes Inc., CEO Steve Forbes does not sit on the board of the Forbes Foundation. According to Steve Forbes, "The Foundation is run by my three brothers and they choose to fund the organizations that they deem appropriate. My views on giving are personal and tend to follow my conservative beliefs." The Foundation received $1,175,000, or 100% of revenue, from a gift awarded by Forbes, Inc. The remaining revenue came from interest on savings.

Foreign Policy Research Institute (FPRI)

1528 Walnut St., Suite 610
Philadelphia, PA 19102   **Phone:**   (215) 732-3774
USA   **Fax:**   (215) 732-4401

Contact Person: Harvey Sicherman, President.
Officers or Principals: Harvey Sicherman, President ($96,075); Ross Munro, Researcher ($71,258); Alan Luxenberg, Vice President ($63,307); Charles B. Grace, Treasurer; Lynne Smith, Assistant Treasurer; Roger Donway, Editor; John G. Christy, Chairman; Bruce H. Hooper, Marvin Wachman, Vice Chairmen.
Mission or Interest: "Examining the political, the diplomatic, the military and the economic areas of American foreign policy. . . . we force the scholars to do more than just describe problems. They have to suggest solutions, suggest policies. We are able to bring policies a depth of perspective that is not available to the government, which is always on a short hook because of political and time pressures."
Accomplishments: FPRI scholars regularly appear in the media and provide testimony at congressional hearings. *Orbis*, the Institute's journal, is edited by Pulitzer Prize-winning historian Walter McDougall. In 1994 the Institute spent $1,035,382 on its programs.
Total Revenue: 1994 $914,458 (-22%)(2) ($125,036, or 14%, from government grants) **Total Expenses:** $1,286,063
Net Assets: (-$465,434)
Tax Status: 501(c)(3) **Annual Report:** No.   **Citations:** 62:89
Board of Directors or Trustees: W.W. Keen Butcher, Robert Fox, Susan Goldberg, Hon. Alexander Haig, Jr. (Secretary of State, 1981-82), Kenneth Hill, Bobbie Hillman, Tamall Hillman, Hon. John Lehman, Jr. (Secretary of the Navy,1981-87), David Lucterhand, Martin Meyerson (Pres. Emeritus, Univ. of Pennsylvania), Stephen Moody, Ronald Naples, Frank Piasecki, Charles Pizzi, Edward Snider, Hon. Robert Strausz-Hupè, David Wachs, William Wurster, Dov Zakheim, S. Michael Alexander, David Duncan.
Periodicals: *Orbis* (quarterly journal).
Internships: Yes. Interns work on research, administration, and editorial projects.
Other Information: Established in 1955, FPRI was originally a part of the University of Pennsylvania. In 1970 it became independent. Founded by Robert Strausz-Hupè, a professor who later served as an ambassador during the Reagan administration. FPRI received $667,252, or 73%, from contributions and grants awarded by foundations, businesses, and individuals. (These grants included $150,000 from the Sarah Scaife Foundation. In 1995, $150,000 from the John M. Olin Foundation, $48,800 from the Lynde and Harry Bradley Foundation, and $42,500 from the William H. Donner Foundation.) $125,036, or 14%, from government grants. $104,181, or 11%, from subscriptions to *Orbis*. The remaining revenue came from conference and seminar fees, interest on savings and other temporary cash investments, and other miscellaneous sources.

Foundation for the Advancement of Monetary Education (FAME)

211 E. 43rd St.
New York, NY 10017   **Phone:** (212) 818-1206
USA   **Fax:**   (212) 818-1197   **Internet:** http://www.fame.org

Contact Person: Lawrence M. Parks, Executive Director.
Officers or Principals: Lawrence M. Parks, Ph.D., Executive Director; Jonathan Parks, General Manager.
Mission or Interest: "To lay the intellectual foundation for a return to honest money - e.g., gold as money." Promotion of a currency that is redeemable for gold or silver, as it used to be. FAME states that our current, irredeemable, fiat currency is responsible for inflation, recessions, the continuation of the welfare state, greater deficits, a lower standard of living, and other social problems. "FAME's emphasis is on grassroots outreach using the Internet and conventional methods to raise public awareness."
Accomplishments: "FAME has assembled perhaps the world's largest library of information about sound money. . . Fast becoming the largest repository of intellectual ammunition in support of honest money on the internet."
Products or Services: Pamphlets, publications, research available on the internet.
Tax Status: 501(c)(3) **Employees:** 3
Board of Directors or Trustees: K. Tucker Anderson, Philip Carret, Douglas Casey, Hon. Alfred Kingon (Assistant Secretary of the U.S. Treasury, 1985-87), Herbert London, Ph.D. (New York University), Herbert Meeker, Richard Scott-Ram, Ph.D. (Economic Advisor, World Gold Council), Charles Darwin Snelling, Frederick Seitz, Ph.D. (Pres. Emeritus, Rockefeller Univ., & Past Pres., National Academy of Sciences), Robert Sturz. Advisors include: Amelia Augustus, Ph.D. (Pres., Women's Economic Round Table), Elizabeth Currier (Committee for Monetary Research & Education), Prof. Emeritus C. Lowell Harriss, Ph.D. (Columbia Univ.), Hon. Roy Innis (Congress of Racial Equality), Hon. Brewster Kopp (former Asst. Secretary of the U.S. Army), Rep. Ron Paul (R-TX), Llewellyn Rockwell (Ludwig von Mises Inst.), Hans Sennholz, Ph.D. (Foundation for Economic Education), Edwin Vieira, Jr. (National Alliance for Constitutional Money), Jude Wanniski (Polyconomics, Inc.).
Internships: No.

Foundation for Cultural Review / *New Criterion*

850 7th Avenue, Suite 400
New York, NY 10019   **Phone:** (212) 247-6980
USA   **Fax:**   (212) 247-3127

Contact Person: Roger Kimball, Managing Editor.
Officers or Principals: Hilton Kramer, Editor ($98,350); Roger Kimball, Managing Editor ($77,250); Chris Carduff, Assistant Managing Editor ($47,188); Irving Kristol, Chairman; Michael S. Joyce, Vice Chairman; James Piereson, Secretary.
Mission or Interest: Publishes *The New Criterion*, a conservative review of the arts, literature, and cultural issues edited by Hilton Kramer.
Accomplishments: *The London Times Literary Supplement* said, "As a critical periodical *The New Criterion* is probably more consistently worth reading than any other magazine in English." *The Boston Review* said, "not since H.L. Mencken and *The American Mercury* has literary America seen so much fur fly." *The New Criterion* had approximately 5,400 paid subscribers as of June 1995, up from 4,200 in 1992. The journal *New Criterion* cost $208,831 to produce and distribute, and brought in revenues of $210,857; a net gain of $2,026.
Total Revenue: FY ending 6/95 $814,806 3%(3) **Total Expenses:** $772,200 27%/73%/0% **Net Assets:** $413,775
Products or Services: Two collected works, The New Criterion Reader (The Free Press, 1988), and Against the Grain (Ivan R. Dee, 1995).
Tax Status: 501(c)(3) **Annual Report:** No. **Employees:** 6   **Citations:** 0:233
Board of Directors or Trustees: The late Samuel Lipman served as the publisher and treasurer.
Periodicals: *The New Criterion* (monthly journal).
Internships: Yes, summer internship.
Other Information: Established in 1982. The Foundation received $587,505, or 72% of revenue, from contributions and grants awarded by foundations, businesses, and individuals. (These grants included $225,000 from the John M. Olin Foundation, $215,000 from the Lynde and Harry Bradley Foundation, and $150,000 from the Sarah Scaife Foundation.) $140,175, or 17%, from journal subscriptions. $52,277, or 6%, from advertising. $13,690, or 2%, from dividends and interest from securities. $9,036, or 1%, from newsstand sales. $7,624, or 1%, from mailing list rentals. The remaining revenue came from other miscellaneous sources.

Foundation for Economic Education (FEE) / *The Freeman*

30 S. Broadway
Irvington, NY 10533   **Phone:** (914) 591-7230   **E-Mail:** freeman@westnet.com
USA   **Fax:**   (914) 591-8910   **Internet:** http://www.pg.net/fee

Contact Person: Renate T. A. Oechsner, Director.
Officers or Principals: Hans F. Sennholz, President ($60,000); W. A. Speakman, III, Chairman ($0); Sally von Behren, Vice Chairman($0); Mark Spangler, Treasurer; Felix R. Livinston, Vice President; Paige K. Moore, Secretary.
Mission or Interest: "Was founded in 1946 to combat the prevailing trend toward state intervention in human affairs. FEE's method is to study and explain the alternatives to intervention: the free market, private property, limited government concepts and the moral and spiritual principles on which this country was founded."

Accomplishments: "Since 1946 the field of free market think tanks, public policy analysis groups, and political activism has grown immensely; and we applaud our friends who have chosen other paths to sustain freedom. Many trace their beginnings to FEE." Former British Prime Minister Margaret Thatcher was the keynote speaker on the occasion of FEE's 50th anniversary celebration. FEE is supported financially by more than 10,000 individuals, foundations, and businesses. *The Freeman* has more than 30,000 subscribers. Reprints from *The Freeman* have appeared in *Reader's Digest*, *The Wall Street Journal*, and other publications. In the fiscal year ending March 1995 FEE spent $1,167,725 on its programs.

Total Revenue: FY ending 3/95 $2,103,676 47%(1) **Total Expenses:** $1,566,543 75%/16%/9% **Net Assets:** $2,260,979

Products or Services: Essay contest for high school and college students. Scholarships are awarded to the top finishers. The 'FEE School' offers classes on weekends and extended seminars on the philosophy of the free market. Book catalog. FEE maintains an extensive library, including the private collection of economist/columnist Henry Hazlitt (1894-1993). Organizes "Freeman Society Discussion Clubs" nationwide.

Tax Status: 501(c)(3) **Annual Report:** No. **Employees:** 12 **Citations:** 48:101

Board of Directors or Trustees: Manuel Ayau, Edward Barr, Prof. Gottfried Dietze (Johns Hopkins Univ.), Ridgeway Foley, Jr., E.A. Gallun, Jr., P.W. Gifford, Harry Hoiles, John Howell, Ethelmae Humphreys, David Keyston, Dr. Israel Kirzner, Robert Love, Paige Moore, Edmund Opitz, Rep. Ron Paul, M.D. (R-TX), J.S. Pritchard, M.D., Lawrence Reed (Mackinac Center for Public Policies), Ralph Smeed, Mark Spangler, W.A. Speakman, III, Philip Spicer, Steven Symms, Don Taylor, Dr. Thomas Taylor, John Van Eck, Sally Von Behren.

Periodicals: *The Freeman* (monthly journal), and *Notes from FEE* (quarterly newsletter).

Other Information: Established in 1946 by Leonard Read (1898-1983). FEE acquired *The Freeman* in 1955. The Foundation received $1,780,896, or 85% of revenue, from contributions and grants awarded by foundations, businesses, and individuals. (These grants included $35,000 from the Curran Foundation, $10,000 from the Philip M. McKenna Foundation, $10,000 from the John M. Olin Foundation, $7,000 from the Sunmark Foundation, $6,000 from the Milliken Foundation, $1,000 from the John William Pope Foundation, and $1,000 from the Charles G. Koch Charitable Foundation. These contributions and grants have grown by an average of 20% over the last five years.) $231,929, or 11%, from the sale of inventory. $83,614, or 4%, from dividends and interest from securities. The remaining revenue came from honoraria and other miscellaneous sources.

Foundation for Education, Scholarship, Patriotism and Americanism

2218 West Prospect Rd.
P.O. Box 986
Fort Collins, CO 80522   **Phone:**   (303) 484-2575
USA

Contact Person: Lt. Col. Archibald E. Roberts, AUS, Ret., President.

Officers or Principals: John W. Clements, Jr., Secretary/Treasurer; John N. Shaffer, RAdm, USN, Ret., Trustee.

Mission or Interest: "Only one course of action offers hope for the descendants of the pioneers, engineers and warriors who created this unique American civilization. Restoring and then preserving and defending the basic principles originally embodied in the Constitution of the United States is the only solution that offers grounds for hope."

Tax Status: 501(c)(3)

Other Information: Established in 1963. Affiliated with the Committee to Restore the Constitution at the same address (see the separate entry for the Committee for more information on Lt. Col. Roberts and his views).

Foundation for Florida's Future (FFF)

P.O. Box 144155
Coral Gables, FL 33114   **Phone:**   (305) 442-0414
USA   **Fax:**   (305) 442-2215

Contact Person: Sally S. Harrell, Executive Director.

Officers or Principals: Jeb Bush, Chairman; Sally S. Harrell, Executive Director; Keyla Alba, Office Administrator; Kitty Cunningham, Director of Communications; Jonathan K. Hage, Director of Research; Mark Wallace, Legal Counsel.

Mission or Interest: To further conservative principles and policy in the state of Florida.

Accomplishments: The "Citizens' Action Council," a grassroots network organized in branches in each county. Fax network. Televised "Town Hall" meetings. General lobbying.

Total Revenue: 1995 $750,000 (est.)

Tax Status: 501(c)(4)

Other Information: Established in 1995 by Jeb Bush, son of former President George Bush. Jeb Bush ran unsuccessfully for Governor of Florida in 1994. Sally Harrell and Keyla Alba both held high ranking positions in his campaign.

Foundation for Rational Economics and Education (FREE)

837 W. Plantation Dr.
Clute, TX 77531   **Phone:**   (409) 265-3034
USA   **Fax:**   (409) 265-7378

Contact Person: Deana Watts.

Officers or Principals: Lori Pyeatt, Treasurer ($18,000); Henry K. May, President ($0); Mary Jane Smith, Vice President ($0); Carol Paul, Secretary.

Mission or Interest: "To advance public understanding of the principles of limited government, free-market economics, sound money and non-interventionist foreign policy." Produces television programming on economic and social issues.

Accomplishments: In 1996 FREE founder and chairman, Ron Paul, M.D., was reelected to Congress. He had previously held a congressional seat from 1976-1984. In 1994 FREE spent $154,251 on its programs - a 70% increase over the previous year.

Total Revenue: 1994 $215,540 1%(1) **Total Expenses:** $243,387 63%/27%/10% **Net Assets:** $77,196

Products or Services: "At Issue" television series. The Case for Gold, Ten Myths About Paper Money, Abortion and Liberty, and other books and monographs.

Tax Status: 501(c)(3) **Annual Report:** Yes. **Employees:** 2 **Citations:** 0:233

Other Information: Established in 1976. Founder Ron Paul, M.D., was first elected to Congress from Texas in 1976 and he served until 1984. He was co-founder with Sen. Jesse Helms (R-NC) of the U.S. Gold Commission; "the first official examination of our monetary system and the alternative of the gold standard in over 70 years." At the end of the Commission's hearings, Dr. Paul coauthored, with Commission member Lewis E. Lehrman, The Case for Gold. In 1988 Paul ran for President on the Libertarian ticket. In 1996 he successfully ran for Congress again. The Foundation contracted David Mertz and Jay Bryant as executive director and producer of "At Issue" and paid them $64,753 and $50,873 respectively. FREE received $211,718, or 98% of revenue, from contributions and grants awarded by foundations, businesses, and individuals. $3,000, or 1%, from rent paid by the for-profit Ron Paul and Associates, Inc. The remaining revenue came from special fund-raising events and the sale of publications.

Foundation for Research on Economics and the Environment (FREE)

945 Technology Blvd., Suite 101F
Bozeman, MT 59715   **Phone:** (406) 585-1776
USA   **Fax:** (406) 585-3000

Contact Person: Dr. John Baden, Chairman.

Officers or Principals: Dr. John Baden, Chairman ($111,708).

Mission or Interest: "Our work is motivated by a commitment to foster free and responsible people in their relations with one another and their environment." Seeks to use and protect the earth and its resources through property rights and decentralized decision making. FREE differentiates itself from the "Wise-Use" movement. FREE sees the Wise-Use movement as preserving the status quo of government subsidies and privileges for timber, mining, grazing, and other special-interest users resources, to the exclusion of others. FREE sees this approach as government welfare.

Accomplishments: FREE has put together over 50 successful conferences in the past 15 years. Topics covered have included "Business and the Environment," "Conservation and the Progressive Era," and "Liberty and the Land Ethic." These programs promote and circulate new ideas and have led to articles in such publications as The Wall Street Journal and the New York Times as well as the production of numerous academic and trade books. In 1995 FREE spent $297,836 on its programs; $231,099 on conferences and seminars, and the rest on publications and newsletters.

Total Revenue: 1995 $483,581 (-6%)(4) **Total Expenses:** $466,748 64%/31%/5% **Net Assets:** (-$12,841)

Products or Services: Conferences, publications.

Tax Status: 501(c)(3) **Annual Report:** No. **Employees:** Varies. **Citations:** 25:140

Board of Directors or Trustees: Wayne Adams, Judge Danny Boggs (U.S. Court of Appeals, 6th Circuit Court), Richard Derham, Richard Duesenberg, H. Martin Gibson, Judge Douglas Ginsburg (U.S. Court of Appeals, District of Columbia Circuit), Prof. James Huffman (Environmental and Natural Resources Law program, Lewis and Clark College), James Kraft (Plum Creek Timber Co.), Dr. John Lamping (General Manager, Environmental Affairs, Amoco Corp.), John McCormack, Furman Moseley (Sasquatch Books), Thomas O'Leary (Chair, Burlington Resources), Deecy Stephens Gray, Dr. R. Neal Wilkins (Wildlife Biologist, Port Blakely Tree Farms).

Periodicals: FREE Perspectives (quarterly).

Internships: Yes, for graduated college students.

Other Information: Established in 1978. FREE has a Seattle office: 1914 North 34th St., Suite 107, Seattle, WA 98103, phone (206) 548-1776, fax (206) 548-0250. FREE received $479,989, or 99% of revenue, from contributions and grants awarded by foundations, businesses, and individuals. (These grants included $100,000 from the Carthage Foundation, and $25,000 from the John M. Olin Foundation. In 1994, $38,000 from the M.J. Murdock Charitable Trust.) The remaining revenue came from the sale of posters and interest on savings and temporary cash investments.

Foundation for Teaching Economics (FTE)

260 Russell Blvd., Suite B
Davis, CA 95616   **Phone:** (916) 757-4630
USA   **Fax:** (916) 757-4636

Contact Person: Joyce F. Gordon, Assistant to the President.

Officers or Principals: Gary M. Walton, President ($121,000); James R. Klauder, Vice President, Public Affairs ($101,578); Stephen R. Gerhart, Vice President, Administration ($73,455); W. J. Hume, Chairman; Julie A. Neithercutt, Development Coordinator; Katya L. Anderson, Administrative Assistant.

Mission or Interest: The Foundation has dedicated itself to fostering an understanding of market economics, emphasizing "the important role of individuals as productive, responsible citizens in free societies." FTE works with numerous other educational associations and they go to lengths to emphasize their nonpartisan work.

Accomplishments: Over 3,000,000 students in all 50 states have used FTE products to study economics in the classroom. In 1994 the Foundation spent $1,084,814 on its programs.

Total Revenue: 1994 $1,446,307 59%(2) **Total Expenses:** $1,431,553 76%/12%/13% **Net Assets:** $1,292,559

Products or Services: Leadership training programs, textbooks, teachers guides, films, essay contests, videos, lesson plans. They place a special emphasis on economic factors in history and work with history teachers. In 1993 they began awarding a $5,000 prize for excellence in teaching economics to high-school students.

Tax Status: 501(c)(3) **Annual Report:** Yes. **Citations:** 5:192

Board of Directors or Trustees: David Bellet, Linda Chavez (Center for Equal Opportunity), Dr. Linton Deck, Dr. Timothy Dyer (Exec. Dir., National Association of Secondary School Principals), Dr. Chester Finn (Hudson Inst.), Dr. Rose Friedman (economist, wife and collaborator of Nobel Laureate, Milton Friedman), Ted Wall, Wallace Hawley, H. Robert Heller, George Hume (Basic American Foods, Inc.), Glenn Janss, Edward Landry, Dr. Floretta McKenzie, Dr. Donald Raiff, Dr. Thomas Shannon (Exec. Dir., National School Board Assn.), Anne Stephens, C.B. Sung (Chair, Unisom Group, Inc.), Michael Towbes.

Other Information: Established in 1975. President Gary M. Walton is a Professor of Management and Economics at the University of California, Davis. He wrote his dissertation under the supervision of 1993 Nobel Laureate in Economics, Douglass C. North. He is the author of History of the American Economy (Harcourt, Brace, Jovanovich, 1994) and Understanding Economics Today (Irwin, 1994). The Foundation received $630,683, or 44% of revenue, from contributions and grants awarded by foundations, businesses, and individuals. (These grants included $15,000 from the M.J. Murdock Charitable Trust, $9,000 from the Earhart Foundation, $4,000 from the Ruth and Vernon Taylor Foundation. In 1995, $50,000 from the William H. Donner Foundation, $30,000 from the Castle Rock Foundation, $4,000 from the Sunmark Foundation, and $1,000 from the Roe Foundation. Major contributors have included Basic American Foods, McDonald's Corp., Andrew Mellon Foundation, and the Ambrose Monell Foundation.) $433,377 net, or 30%, from the sale of assets. $327,546, or 23%, from investments in partnership with Basic American Foods. $54,496, or 4%, from dividends and interest from securities. The remaining revenue came from various miscellaneous sources.

Foundation for Traditional Values

4407 W. St. Joseph
Lansing, MI 48917   **Phone:**   (517) 321-6233
USA

Contact Person: James Muffett, President.

Officers or Principals: James Muffett, President ($47,174); Kent Vanderwood, Secretary ($0); Blaine Schultz, Treasurer ($0).

Mission or Interest: Research and education promoting traditional and biblical values.

Accomplishments: In 1994 the Foundation spent $66,473 on its programs. The largest program, with expenditures of $41,473, was the "Greatest Story Never Told" seminar series. This series of seminars was held in 20 churches and parochial schools throughout Michigan, and reached approximately 4,000 people. $25,000 was spent publishing *The Liberty Lamp* newsletter that reached approximately 2,000 people.

Total Revenue: 1994 $154,470 **Total Expenses:** $119,989 55%/40%/5% **Net Assets:** $50,952

Tax Status: 501(c)(3)

Board of Directors or Trustees: Scott Gordon, Deborah Johnson, William Michell, Marianne Packer, Ronald Reed, Leesa Schram, William Swets.

Periodicals: *The Liberty Lamp* (quarterly newsletter).

Other Information: Established in 1992. Affiliated with the 501(c)(4) Citizens for Traditional Values. In 1994 the two affiliates had combined net revenues, expenses, and assets of $179,473, $141,809, and $51,239. The Foundation received $135,465, or 88% of revenue, from contributions and grants awarded by foundations, businesses, and individuals. (These contributions and grants included $5,000 from the Richard and Helen DeVos Foundation, and $500 from the Amy Foundation. These contributions and grants grew by 45% over 1993.) $6,283 net, or 4%, from special fundraising events. $5,995, or 4%, from seminar fees. $3,720, or 2%, from honoraria. The remaining revenue came from the sale of inventory.

Foundation Francisco Marroquin (FFM)

4832 S.E. Anchor Ave.
Stuart, FL 34997   **Phone:** (561) 286-6450   **E-Mail:** ffm@gate.net
USA   **Fax:**   (561) 288-0670

Contact Person: William W. Weston, President.

Officers or Principals: William W. Weston, President ($75,714); Prof. Arnold C. Harberger, Academic Director ($26,273); Elliot Abrams, Chairman ($0); Esteban A. Ferrer, Treasurer; J. Clayburn La Force, Secretary.

Mission or Interest: To encourage free-market and classical-liberal scholarship in Latin America. Provides training in free-market economics at the undergraduate and Ph.D. level throughout Latin America.

Accomplishments: Operates the Advanced Training in Economics (ATE) program, funded in part by the U.S. Agency for International Development, which trains Latin American economists in free-market economics. By the end of 1995 there were 89 graduates of the program; and FFM forecasts that by 1998 there will be 142 graduates. Most graduates have been in pre-Ph.D. programs. In the fiscal year ending March 1995, FFM spent $1,503,956 on its programs. The largest program, with expenditures of $937,172, was the ATE program funded by USAID. $275,771 was spent aiding the construction of buildings on the campus of the Univeridad Francisco Marroquin. $265,375 was spent on grants for Latin American universities. Other programs funded scholarship in Latin America.

Total Revenue: FY ending 3/95 $1,502,225 ($1,208,960, or 80%, from government grants) (-17%)(2)

Total Expenses: $1,517,497 99%/1%/1% **Net Assets:** $75,268

Products or Services: Owns the Latin American rights to the video series "Free to Choose" with Nobel Prize winning economist Milton Friedman.

Tax Status: 501(c)(3) **Annual Report:** Yes, quarterly reports.   **Citations:** 0:233

Board of Directors or Trustees: Edwin Feulner, Jr. (Heritage Found.), J. William Middendorf (Ambassador to the Organization of American States, 1981-85), Thomas Anderson Roe (Roe Found.), Curtin Winsor, Jr. (Ambassador to Costa Rica, 1983-85).

Other Information: Established in 1980. Affiliated with the Francisco Marroquin University in Guatemala. The University focuses on the work of Austrian economists Ludwig von Mises and F. A. Hayek. The Foundation's chairman, Elliot Abrams, was the Assistant Secretary of State, Inter-American Affairs, from 1985-89. Prior to that he held other State Department positions during the Reagan administration. Along with other board members Middendorf and Winsor, Abrams was a key architect of President Reagan's Latin America policies. The Foundation received $1,208,960, or 80% of revenue, in government grants from the U.S. Agency for International Development (USAID). In 1992, the last year of the Bush administration, the Foundation received $1.9 million from USAID; then this amount was reduced. $289,895, or 19%, from contributions and grants awarded by foundations, businesses, and individuals. (These grants included $35,000 from the Lynde and Harry Bradley Foundation, $18,000 from the Earhart Foundation, $500 from the Aequus Institute.) The remaining revenue came from interest on savings and other miscellaneous sources.

Fragments

P.O. Box 38
Floral Park, NY 11002
USA

Phone: (718) 776-5500

Contact Person: Dr. Jack Schwartzman.

Mission or Interest: "Philosophy of individualism, liberty, as depicted in the writings of Thoreau, Henry George, Albert Jay Nock, Leo Tolstoy, Bastiat, Herbert Spencer, Thomas Paine, Max Stirner, Ralph Waldo Emerson, etc."

Accomplishments: "Issued quarterly editions from 1963 through 1988 when fire put an end to a spectacularly brilliant magazine (3,000 readers). We shall revise it again with the first issue dedicated to Ayn Rand."

Tax Status: Unincorporated. **Annual Report:** No. **Employees:** All voluntary.

Board of Directors or Trustees: Sydney Mayers, Oscar Johannsen, Fannie De Koto.

Periodicals: *Fragments.*

Internships: No.

Other Information: "We gave birth to innumerable other individualistic, libertarian, and conservative groups. My own (Jack Schwartzman's) articles numbered over 300, reprinted numerous times. I am a professor, a lawyer, a speaker, author, and a veteran of World War II."

Fraser Institute

626 Bute St., 2nd Floor
Vancouver, BC V6E 3M1
CANADA

Phone: (604) 688-0221   **Internet:** http://www.fraserinstiute.ca

Contact Person: Michael Walker, Executive Director.

Officers or Principals: R. J. Addington, O.B.E., Chairman; T. P. Boyle, Vice Chairman; R. J. Currie, Vice Chairman; W. Korol, Vice Chairman; Michael Walker, Executive Director; Sally Pipes, Assistant Director.

Mission or Interest: "Directs public attention to the value of competitive markets and the role they can play in solving Canada's economic and social problems."

Accomplishments: Dr. Milton Friedman has said, "No organization has done more to help Canadians appreciate the importance of the marketplace - and the consequences of government interference - to their continued enjoyment of that country's standard of living." The Fraser Institute sponsored a forum called "The NAFTA Network" in conjunction with 21 other policy groups in the United States, Canada and Mexico to promote free trade through the passage of the North American Free Trade Act. Organized many conferences and roundtable lunches, and published over 100 titles. Institute editorials appear in over 50 newspapers. Focused international attention on the short-comings of the Canadian health-care system

Products or Services: Books, periodicals, Roundtable luncheon series, Adam Smith ties and scarves.

Tax Status: Nonprofit. **Annual Report:** Yes. **Employees:** 23

Periodicals: *On Balance, Fraser Forum.*

Internships: No.

Other Information: Established in 1975. In 1994-95 the Institute received $331,551 U.S. from the Lilly Endowment, $15,000 U.S. from the Lynde and Harry Bradley Foundation, and $1,000 U.S. from the John William Pope Foundation.

Free Africa Foundation (FAF)

1511 K St., N.W., Suite 1100
Washington, DC 20005
USA

Phone: (202) 783-5433

Contact Person: George B. N. Ayittey, Ph.D., President.

Officers or Principals: Isaac K. Amuah, Ph.D., Vice President ($0).

Mission or Interest: To promote intellectual, political, economic and religious freedom in Africa.

Accomplishments: Dr. Ayittey has written op-eds that have appeared in *The Wall Street Journal*. Authored a public-policy paper, "The Somali Crisis: Time for an African Solution" for the Cato Institute.

Total Revenue: 1994 $19,650   **Total Expenses:** $21,432   **Net Assets:** (-$5,451)

Products or Services: Research, books, position papers, op-eds, seminars and conferences. Collaborative efforts with non-governmental officials in Africa.

Tax Status: 501(c)(3)

Board of Directors or Trustees: Advisors include: Bruce Bartlett (Policy Dir., Cato Inst.), Larry Diamond, Ph.D. (Hoover Inst.), Audna England (Carnegie Council on Ethics and Int'l Affairs), John Fund (*Wall Street Journal*), Makaziwe Mandela, Ph.D. (African Academy of Sciences), Kojo Owusu-Nyantekyi (CEO, Crescent Oil), Jude Wanniski (CEO, Polyconomics).

Periodicals: *Freedom Bulletin* (monthly newsletter).

Internships: Yes.

Other Information: Established in 1993. Dr. Ayittey is the author of <u>Africa Betrayed</u>, which was one of five finalists for the 1993 Mencken Award. He is also a professor of economics at American University. FAF resists the temptation to impose "alien ideologies" on Africa. They state that Africa has indigenous institutions of participatory democracies, open borders, freedom of expression, free trade and free markets. FAF received $15,000, or 76% of revenue, from contributions and grants awarded by foundations, businesses, and individuals. (In 1995 these grants included $2,000 from the Heritage Foundation.) $4,000, or 24%, from program service fees. The remaining revenue came from membership dues.

Free Congress Research and Education Foundation

717 2nd St., N.E.
Washington, DC 20002   **Phone:**   (202) 546-3000
USA   **Fax:**   (202) 543-8425   **Internet:** http://www.fcref.org

Contact Person: Richard B. Dingman, Executive Vice President.

Officers or Principals: Paul M. Weyrich, President ($289,067); Burton Yale Pines, Senior Staff ($105,400); Richard B. Dingman, Executive Vice President ($104,051); John Exnicios, Senior Staff ($102,304); Jeffrey H. Coors, Chairman; Robert H. Krieble, Ph.D., Vice Chairman; John D. Beckett, Treasurer; Rep. Ralph M. Hall, Secretary; William Lind, Director, Center for Cultural Conservatism; Stephen M. Lilienthal, Director, Center for State Policy; Thomas L. Jipping, Director.

Mission or Interest: "A research and education organization institute dedicated to conservative governance, traditional values and institutional reform." Operates National Empowerment Television (see separate listing).

Accomplishments: "Has trained over 7,000 grassroots activists and organizations in the U.S. since October 1995 and continues to do so on a monthly basis through the Krieble Institute (KI/USA)." The Foundation's Center for Cultural Conservatism had a fictional short story, "Victoria," published in *The Washington Post's* "Outlook" section. In 1994 the Institute spent $8,178,278 on its programs. The largest program, with expenditures of $5,634,509, was National Empowerment Television, or NET - Political NewsTalk Network (In 1995 NET became a separate entity). $1,042,875 was spent on the Krieble Institute training grassroots activists in the U.S. and Eastern Europe. $840,346 was spent on domestic policy analysis, including monitoring judicial appointments. $292,798 was spent on CNET, monthly satellite television programming that allows "conservative groups around the country to focus on the same policy issues at the same time and act on them." Other programs included training "citizens across the country to enable them to participate more fully in their local and state governments."

Total Revenue: 1994 $9,140,413 23%(4) ($37,548, or less than 1%, from government grants)

Total Expenses: $9,246,147 88%/4%/7% **Net Assets:** $4,796,953

Products or Services: Annual "American Founders Freedom and Governance Award" since 1989. 1995 recipients were House Speaker Newt Gingrich (R-GA), Majority Leader Dick Armey (R-TX), and Majority Whip Tom Delay (R-TX). Research, publications, activist training, television programming, and lobbying. In 1994 the Foundation spent $39,034 on grassroots lobbying; this was down 62% from the previous year.

Tax Status: 501(c)(3)   **Annual Report:** Yes.   **Employees:** 43   **Citations:** 199:38

Board of Directors or Trustees: Hon. William Armstrong, Hon. Howard Callaway (Ida Cason Callaway Found.), Clifford Heinz (C.S. Heinz Found.), Ralph Hostetter, Terry Kohler (Windway Capital Corp.), Elizabeth Lurie (W.H. Brady Found.), Marion Magruder, Charles Moser, Ph.D., Thomas Roe (Roe Found.), Kathleen Teague Rothschild.

Periodicals: *Judicial Selection Monitor* (monthly newsletter), and *The New Electric Railway Journal* (tri-annual journal). *The New Electric Railway Journal* advocates the development of electric rail systems for public transportation; a long-time project of the Foundation.

Internships: Yes, unpaid.

Other Information: Established in 1977. Prior to that, a political action committee was formed called the Committee for a Free Congress in 1974. The term "Free Congress" referred to the election plans of organized labor to establish a 'veto-proof' congress that would support labor's agenda; and the Committee for a Free Congress was determined to provide a Congress 'free of union domination.' The Free Congress Foundation was founded by Paul Weyrich, who was also a founder of the Heritage Foundation. Weyrich was a leader in the late seventies and early eighties in working with religious conservatives and bringing them into the Washington, DC think tank and advocacy system. The Foundation is affiliated with the 501(c)(3) Committee for Effective State Government, 501(c)(4) Coalitions for America, and the Free Congress Political Action Committee. Paul Weyrich receives compensation from all four organizations totaling $315,679. Free Congress hired Robert Carleson of San Diego, CA, as a consultant; Crane Media Sales of New York city, for advertising sales; The Development Group of Washington, DC, for fundraising; and Conus Communications for its news service. For their services they were compensated $174,000, $97,027, $82,296, and $85,000 respectively. The Foundation received $7,336,552, or 80% of revenue, from contributions and grants awarded by foundations, businesses, and individuals. (These grants included $120,000 from the Vernon K. Krieble Foundation, $50,000 from the Milliken Foundation, $30,000 from the F.M. Kirby Foundation, $25,000 from the Samuel Roberts Noble Foundation, $10,000 from the Gilder Foundation, $7,500 from the Anschutz Foundation, and $5,000 from the Grover Hermann Foundation. In 1995, $720,000 from the Carthage Foundation, $450,000 from the Lynde and Harry Bradley Foundation, $150,000 from the Castle Rock Foundation, $55,000 from the Roe Foundation, $50,000 from the John M. Olin Foundation, $15,000 from the Philip M. McKenna Foundation, and $10,000 from the John William Pope Foundation.) $963,950, or 11%, from associate broadcasters' fees from organizations that produce programming for National Empowerment Television. $222,429, or 2%, from capital gains on the sale of securities. $205,610, or 2%, from advertising revenues. $143,659, or 1%, from publication sales. $102,195, or 1%, from dividends and interest from securities. The remaining revenue came from affiliate fees, studio fees, mailing list rentals, government grants, interest on savings and temporary cash investments, conference fees and other miscellaneous sources. The Free Congress Foundation also received a low-interest loan from the Lynde and Harry Bradley Foundation.

Free Enterprise and Government

82 Main St., P.O. Box 145
Madison, OH 44057   Phone: (216) 428-2466
USA

Contact Person: Jack Greenways.
Mission or Interest: Distributes copies of a proposed Amendment XI to the constitution. Amendment XI would repeal all previous amendments to the Constitution except for the first ten - the Bill of Rights - and every law enacted by Congress, Executive Orders, and federal regulations and mandates. Every law made after enacting this amendment would have a expiration date of not more than ten years - but could, after a one year wait, be reenacted.
Accomplishments: "Partially instrumental in defeating the proposed 'Constitution for the Newstates of America', a Rockefeller effort to overthrow our Constitutional Republic."
Tax Status: Unincorporated. **Annual Report:** No. **Employees:** 0
Other Information: Previously called Concerned American Citizens, The Last Call, Wake-Up Ohio Committee, The Judiciary Amendment, and Greenways Printing.

Free Enterprise Institute

9525 Katy Freeway, Suite 303
Houston, TX 77024-1415   Phone: (713) 984-1343   E-Mail: grehmke@aol.com
USA   Fax: (713) 984-0409

Contact Person: W. Winston Elliott, III, President.
Officers or Principals: W. Winston Elliott, III, President ($60,000); Paige K. Moore, Director of Programs ($0); Mary Palmer, Executive Assistant ($0); Greg F. Rehmke, Director of Educational Programs; Robert C. McNair, Chairman.
Mission or Interest: To serve as a clearinghouse for students and educators on free-market economics, free enterprise, and related areas. To generate programs, seminars, and conferences to disseminate this information. To promote the ideals of individual responsibility and Constitutional government as prerequisites to the sustenance of free markets.
Accomplishments: In 1994 the Center spent $302,698 on its programs
Total Revenue: 1994 $459,062 28%(3) **Total Expenses:** $430,671 70%/23%/6% **Net Assets:** $394,288
Products or Services: Speech contests for high-school students. High school debate program, "Economics in Argumentation," which provides resource materials and seminars on the national debate topic. *Economics in One Lesson* scholarship contest for high-school students. They are co-sponsoring several new episodes of the "Free to Choose" video series by Milton Friedman. The original series aired on PBS, and the new episodes will focus on restructuring in Eastern Europe. "LD Solutions," a Macintosh Hypercard and Windows 3.1 database which works as a computer filing system for information and studies from various free-market think tanks. It is updated quarterly or twice yearly with hundreds of market-oriented studies.
Tax Status: 501 (c)(3) **Annual Report:** Yes. **Citations:** 20:150
Board of Directors or Trustees: Gordon Cain, Peggy Pearce Caskey, David Dewhurst; W. A. Griffin, III, Walter Johnson, John Wilson Kelsey (Smith Barney), Charles Berdon Lawrence, S. Reed Morian (Dixie Chemical Co.), John Niemann, Jr., Roger Scott, Ed Smith, Charles Still.
Periodicals: *The Freedom Focus* (bimonthly newsletter). *Econ Update* (monthly).
Internships: Yes, Kiwanis Junior Scholars Program.
Other Information: Established in 1976 and originally called the Free Enterprise Education Center. The Institute received $326,116, or 71% of gross revenue, from contributions and grants awarded by foundations, businesses, and individuals. (These grants included $15,000 from the Gordon and Mary Cain Foundation.) $119,358, or 26%, from program registration fees. $11,788, or 3%, from dividends and interest from securities. The remaining revenue came from interest on savings and other miscellaneous sources. The Institute lost $3,531 on the sale of securities.

Free Enterprise Partnership

206 Roosevelt Building
609 Penn Ave.
Pittsburgh, PA 15222   **Phone:**   (412) 471-1504
USA   **Fax:**   (412) 471-4051

Contact Person: Sherry Bayer, President .
Officers or Principals: Sherry Bayer, President ($37,800); Nathan K. Parker, Jr., Chairman; Stuart G. Hoffman, Vice President; William B. Livingston, Secretary; Thomas J. Gillespie, Jr., Treasurer.
Mission or Interest: Helping young people understand the American free enterprise economic system before they graduate from high school.
Accomplishments: In 1995 the Partnership spent $136,471 on its programs.
Total Revenue: 1995 $284,675 2%(3) **Total Expenses:** $157,845 86%/10%/3% **Net Assets:** $179,616
Tax Status: 501(c)(3)   **Citations:** 8:178
Board of Directors or Trustees: John Bitzer, Jr., Robert Bozzone, Nancy Hammer Clay, Howard Emery, Edward Hallenberg, C. Brett Harrison, William Henderson, George Hill, Edgar Holtz, Casandra Ruane, Walter Schratz (Corporate Relations Officer, Carnegie Mellon Univ.), Bernard Stoecklein, Jr. William Lund is the Chairman Emeritus.
Internships: Yes.
Other Information: Formerly the Enterprise and Education Foundation. The Partnership received $253,327, or 89% of revenue, from contributions and grants awarded by foundations, businesses, and individuals. (These grants included $80,000 from the Scaife Family Foundation, and $18,000 from the Philip M. McKenna Foundation.) $28,031, or 11%, from the sale of inventory. The remaining revenue came from interest on savings and temporary cash investments, and other miscellaneous sources.

Free Enterprise Society

300 West Shaw Ave., Suite 205
Clovis, CA 93612   **Phone:**   (209) 294-0665
USA

Contact Person: Steven Hempfling, Director.
Officers or Principals: Shawn O'Connor, Civil Support Services Director; Robert Hawks, Legal Defense Fund Director.
Mission or Interest: Concerned with the growth of government bureaucracy, the erosion of individual rights and the expropriation of private property. They provide assistance in tax resistance and legal challenges to taxes and non-gold-backed money.
Accomplishments: They claim to have won seventeen legal cases, about a third of those tried, for their clients who refused to pay income taxes
Products or Services: Numerous books and tapes on tax and regulatory avoidance, as well as historical documents on the income tax and other subjects. The Free Enterprise Society has three additional services that members have the option to participate in for additional fees: The Civil Support Services, which gives clients information on dealing with government agencies, the IRS, how to use the Freedom of Information Act and how to prepare for a case (although it is explicitly not legal advice or assistance in the practice of law). The Traffic Support Services, which aids in ticket and licensing problems. The Legal Defense Fund, which is a trust fund set up to provide for filing fees, legal expenses and other costs relating to legal action.
Periodicals: *Free Enterprise Society.*
Other Information: Established in 1979.

Free Market Foundation

P.O. Box 740367
Dallas, TX 75374   **Phone:**   (214) 348-2801
USA   **Fax:**   (214) 348-6725

Contact Person: Steven B. Knudsen, Executive Director.
Officers or Principals: Steven Knudsen, Executive Director ($50,531); Richard Ford, President ($0); Bob Reese, Chairman ($0).
Mission or Interest: Texas foundation pursuing free markets and conservative values.
Accomplishments: The Foundation's "Living History Productions" school assembly program reached an estimated 43,000 people. Their daily radio talk show reaches approximately 50,000 people in Texas. Monthly "Satellite Forum" about public policy reaches approximately 5,000. Their "Business Network" reaches over 1,000 business leaders and employees. In 1994 the Foundation spent $142,686 on its programs.
Total Revenue: 1994 $199,633 3% **Total Expenses:** $243,063 59%/26%/16% **Net Assets:** $30,296
Products or Services: Nonpartisan voters' guides. How To / Resource Guide, a publication containing information on how to get involved in politics. It contains listings for elected officials and public policy organizations, and information on how to communicate effectively with them. They sent out over 10,000 copies of the Guide. Community Impact seminars informing local communities on how to get involved. Helped organize a prayer day in Austin, TX. Spending reports on government programs with dollar amounts, and the legislative voting records for these programs.
Tax Status: 501(c)(3) **Annual Report:** No. **Employees:** 6   **Citations:** 7:182
Board of Directors or Trustees: Robert Schoolfield, Robert Breunig, Joe Broome, Pete Gifford, James Lightner, Kyle Thompson, Fred Disney, William Robertson, Robert Reese, Jr., Tim Dunn.

Periodicals: *Lone Star Citizen* (a monthly newsletter inserted in Focus on the Family's *Citizen*).
Internships: No.
Other Information: Affiliated with the 501(c)(4) Free Market Committee. Loosely affiliated with Focus on the Family, although they receive no direct financial support. Directors of the Free Market Foundation are not paid; however, the president, Richard Ford, runs Richard Ford Associates Inc., which has been retained and paid by the Foundation since 1987 to oversee and perform all services, projects, and activities. In 1993 Richard Ford Associates Inc. was paid $76,460 by the Foundation. The Foundation received $164,426, or 82% of revenue, from contributions and grants awarded by foundations, businesses, and individuals. $33,977, or 17%, from program services, including the sale of voter guides, candidate forums, and other events. The remaining revenue came from interest on savings and temporary cash investments.

Free Market Society of Chicago

2644 N. Troy
Chicago, IL 60647   **Phone:**   (800) 556-4429   **E-Mail:**   71740.261@compuserve.com
USA   **Fax:**   (312) 276-1347

Contact Person: Patrick T. Peterson, President.
Officers or Principals: Patrick T. Peterson, President/Executive Director ($11,664); Kent Cowie, Treasurer ($5,807); Robert Davis, Vice President/Secretary ($1,792); Joseph Plauché, Chairman; Brain Wesbury, David Hershey, Seminar Leaders.
Mission or Interest: To study and promote the ideas and benefits of free-market economics. Focus on investment and business cycles issues.
Accomplishments: In 1994 the society spent $16,575 on its programs.
Total Revenue: 1994 $34,177 **Total Expenses:** $34,179 **Net Assets:** $5,132
Products or Services: Classes, private seminars, special events and an annual dinner celebrating the birthday of Ludwig von Mises.
Tax Status: 501(c)(3)
Board of Directors or Trustees: Daniel Curran, Frank Resnik, Bob Costello, Lynn Salah. Advisors include; Terrence Barnich, Robert Cooke, Robert Genetski, Robert Hessen (Hoover Inst.), Lawrence Kudlow (Chief Economist, Bear, Stearns & Co.), Arthur Laffer (Chair, A.B. Laffer, V.A. Canto & Assoc.), Yuri Maltsev (Carthage College), David Padden, Beryl Sprinkel, David Ramsay Steele, Stuart Warner.
Other Information: Established in 1993. The Society received $18,435, or 54% of revenue, from program services. $15,623, or 46%, from contributions and grants awarded by foundations, businesses, and individuals. The remaining revenue came from special fundraising events.

Free Nation Foundation (FNF)

111 West Corbin St.
Hillsborough, NC 27278   **E-Mail:**   freenation.org
USA

Contact Person: Richard O. Hammer, President.
Officers or Principals: Richard O. Hammer, President; Bobby Yates Emory, Secretary; Roderick T. Long, Editor.
Mission or Interest: "To advance the day when the coercive institutions of government can be supplanted by voluntary institutions of civil mutual consent, by developing clear and believable descriptions of those voluntary institutions, and by building a community of people who share confidence in these descriptions."
Accomplishments: *Claustrophobia*'s magazine reviewer says the Foundation "addresses these issues with a great deal of wisdom and scholarship. As governments continue to change throughout the world, the ideas expressed in *Formulations* (the Foundation's journal) are vital to the establishment of free nations everywhere."
Total Revenue: 1994 $4,060 **Total Expenses:** $4,060
Products or Services: Forums, "Toward a Free Nation" (booklet).
Tax Status: 501(c)(3) **Annual Report:** Yes. **Employees:** All volunteer.
Periodicals: *Formulations* (quarterly).
Other Information: Incorporated June, 1993. In 1995 the Foundation received $500 from the John William Pope Foundation.

Free State Constitutionalists

P.O. Box 3281
Baltimore, MD 21228
USA

Mission or Interest: Provide populist news and information to back the claim that "individuals in the United States are not required to pay income taxes" because the income tax is "voluntary." Also promotes 'jury nullification' of tax laws.

Freedom Alliance

45472 Holiday Dr., Suite 10
Sterling, VA 20166   **Phone:**   (703) 709-6620   **E-Mail:**   freedom@mail.erols.com
USA   **Fax:**   (703) 709-6615

Contact Person: Steven Davis, Director of Research and Educational Affairs.
Officers or Principals: Lt. Col. Oliver L. North, USMC (Ret.), Founder/Honorary Chairman; Hon. Steve Syms, President; Marc T. Short, Chief Executive Officer.
Mission or Interest: "The preservation of traditional American values, and institutions, the maintenance of a strong national defense, the protection of the rights and freedoms of individual citizens, and the adoption of policies that promote free enterprise."
Accomplishments: "125,000 care packages to U.S. soldiers who served in the Persian Gulf War; aided travel and educational expenses of families of Gulf War veterans; helped stop Clinton administration policy to place open homosexuals in U.S. military; participated in Presidential Commission on Women in Combat and argued against placing women in deadly combat roles; created 'Second Careers in Education' program that aids men and women who are veterans or separating from U.S. military to become outstanding role model teachers in America's troubled public school systems." Supported military personnel who refused to replace their insignia with United Nations insignia
Products or Services: "Second Careers in Education" resource manual. Issue Briefs. "Our Military Under Siege" video tape.
Tax Status: 501(c)(3) **Employees:** 6
Board of Directors or Trustees: Richard Hendershot, Carl Bohman, Thomas Cook.
Periodicals: *The Free American* (bimonthly newsletter).
Internships: No.
Other Information: Established in 1990.

Freedom Books

P.O. Box 5303, 605 Skiff St.
Hamden, CT 06517   **Phone:**   (203) 281-6791
USA   **Fax:**   (203) 287-1562

Contact Person: Irwin A. Schiff.
Mission or Interest: Publish books revealing how to "legally" avoid paying federal income tax and social security.
Accomplishments: *Life* magazine estimates 20 million Americans don't file an income tax return, Irwin A. Schiff believes that a good percentage of those people are using the methods and procedures outlined in his books. His books have received positive reviews from Dr. Walter E. Williams, Howard J. Ruff, *Publishers Weekly*, and *The Wall Street Journal*.
Products or Services: The Great Income Tax Hoax, The Social Security Swindle, How Anyone can Stop Paying Income Taxes, The Federal Mafia, and others. Books, lectures.
Tax Status: For profit. **Employees:** All work is subcontracted.
Other Information: Schiff himself has served time in prison for his failure to file and pay federal taxes.

Freedom House

120 Wall St., 26th Floor
New York, NY 10005   **Phone:**   (212) 514-8040
USA   **Fax:**   (212) 514-8050

Contact Person: Arch Puddington, Researcher.
Officers or Principals: Arch Puddington, Researcher ($108,857); Doug Payne, Survey of World Freedom ($81,450); Frank Calzon, Program Director ($78,845); Betty Bao Lord, Chairman; Ned W. Bandler, Vice Chairman; Angier Biddle Duke, Secretary; Walter J. Schloss, Treasurer.
Mission or Interest: "Established in 1941 to strengthen democratic institutions at home and abroad. It monitors human rights and political and economic freedom around the world."
Accomplishments: "Introduced the current practice of election monitoring around the world." In the fiscal year ending June 1994 Freedom House spent $1,249,091 on its programs. The largest program, with expenditures of $336,484, was the research and production of the *Comparative Survey of Freedom*. $249,613 was spent on *Freedom Review*, which monitors human rights and economic freedoms. $147,318 was spent on programs dealing with Cuba. $175,325 was spent on the monitoring conditions and elections in the Ukraine. $174,913 was spent monitoring conditions in El Salvador. Other programs included the Sakharov Archives, European Journalism Network, and Radio Free Europe.
Total Revenue: FY ending 6/94 $1,922,238 ($142,456, or 7%, from government grants)   (-30%)(1)   **Total Expenses:** $2,209,582 57%/39%/5% **Net Assets:** (-$414,311)
Tax Status: 501(c)(3) **Annual Report:** Yes. **Employees:** 30   **Citations:** 493:21
Board of Directors or Trustees: Norman Hill, Jeanne Kirkpatrick (American Enterprise Inst.), Morton Kondracke, Burns Roper.
Periodicals: *Survey of Freedom* (annual), *Freedom Review* (bimonthly magazine), and *World Survey of Economic Freedom* (annual).
Internships: Yes.
Other Information: Freedom House received $1,198,744, or 62% of revenue, from contributions and grants awarded by foundations, affiliates, businesses, and individuals. (These grants included $75,000 from the Sarah Scaife Foundation. In 1995, $304,950 from the Smith Richardson Foundation, $75,000 from the Lynde and Harry Bradley Foundation, $75,000 from the Lilly Endowment, $20,000 from the Carthage Foundation, and $20,000 from the William H. Donner Foundation.) $569,829, or 30%, from program services. $142,456, or 7%, from government grants. The remaining revenue came from interest on savings and temporary cash investments, and other miscellaneous sources.

Freedom in Medicine Foundation

c/o Affordable Health
1056 Stelton Rd.
Piscataway, NJ 08854   **Phone:** (908) 562-0033
USA   **Fax:**   (908) 463-2289

Contact Person: Dr. John Eck, M.D., Founder.
Officers or Principals: Dr. Alieta Eck, M.D., Founder, Dr. Nino Camardese, M.D., President.
Mission or Interest: Advocates the removal of government control and financing of health care. The Foundation proposes Medical Savings Accounts for most people, and pooled charitable funds administered by religious institutions for the indigent.
Accomplishments: Conference and seminar participants have included Dr. Edward Annis (past President, American Medical Association), Andrew Schlafly, Dr. Nino Camardese (Americanism Foundation), and others
Tax Status: 501(c)(3)

Freedoms Foundation at Valley Forge

Route 23
Valley Forge, PA 19481   **Phone:** (215) 933-8825
USA   **Fax:**   (215) 935-0522

Contact Person: Rear Adm. Richard C. Ustick, USN (Ret.), President .
Officers or Principals: Rear Adm. Richard C. Ustick, USN (Ret.), President; Robert Miller, former President ($88,097); Charles Hepburn, Senior Vice President, Education ($63,907); Franklin Edinger, Controller ($42,714); E. Katherine Wood-Jacobs, Vice President, Awards; Hon. Ronald H. Walker, Chairman; Hon. Arnold Burns, Vice Chairman.
Mission or Interest: "To carry out national programs of information and education that promote traditional American values and provide a better understanding of the responsibilities of citizenship." Special focus on working with educators and youths.
Accomplishments: Over 50 chapters nationwide. In the fiscal year ending June 1994 the Foundation and its affiliates spent $2,153,309 on programs. The largest program, with expenditures of $1,722,647, was educational services for teachers and students; including seminars for credit. $430,662 was spent on awards, including "certificates, medals , and cash for the best presentations in a variety of categories."
Total Revenue: FY ending 6/94 $2,800,303 **Total Expenses:** $2,682,014 80%/20%/0% **Net Assets:** $9,737,230
Products or Services: National Awards, Leavy Awards for Excellence in Private Enterprise Education, computerized mailing lists. They maintain the Medal of Honor Grove, a 52 acre national shrine dedicated to our Medal of Honor recipients. Workshops for students and teachers are held, funded in part by a grant from the M. J. Murdock Charitable Trust.
Tax Status: 501(c)(3) **Employees:** 31   **Citations:** 62:89
Board of Directors or Trustees: Hon. Rodney Brady, Hon. Arnold Burns, Hon. Red Cavaney (Pres., American Forest and Paper Assoc.), Hon. Chapman Cox, Hon. Michael McManus, Jr., Hon. Milan Panic, Blanka Rosenstiel (Pres., American Inst. of Polish Culture), Hon. Donna Tuttle, Hon. Frank Ursomarso, Hon. Ron Walker, Hon. Joseph Wright, Joseph Coors (Adolph Coors Co.), Hon. Raymond Shafer, others.
Periodicals: *Report from Valley Forge* (quarterly newsletter).
Other Information: Established in 1949. Distinguished Trustees are; Hon. Warren Burger, Hon. Ronald Reagan, and Hon. Strom Thurmond. Past Chairmen included Gen. Dwight D. Eisenhower. The Foundation received $1,191,145, or 43% of revenue, from contributions and grants awarded by foundations, businesses, and individuals. (These grants included $25,000 from the M.J. Murdock Charitable Trust, $10,000 from the Richard & Helen DeVos Foundation.) $819,788, or 29%, from educational program fees. $417,000, or 15%, from dividends and interest from securities. $154,109 net, or 6%, from the sale of assets. $96,157, or 3%, from special fund-raising events. $94,285, or 3%, from membership dues. The remaining revenue came from interest on savings.

Frontiers of Freedom

1735 N. Lynn St., Suite 1050
Arlington, VA 22209   **Phone:** (703) 527-8282
USA   **Fax:**   (703) 527-8388   **Internet:** http://www.ff.org

Contact Person: Jeffrey L. Taylor, Executive Director.
Officers or Principals: Jeffrey L. Taylor, Executive Director ($55,824); Hon. Malcolm Wallop, Chairman ($0).
Mission or Interest: "Ensure the maximum individual and economic freedom for every American." They have four main goals: 1) elimination of the current tax system and most of the IRS to be replaced by a flat tax, 2) re-affirm the right to own and control private property, 3) expose government's efforts to limit free speech, and 4) return government regulatory powers to the state and local level.
Accomplishments: Although newly formed, Frontiers has received much press attention, having been cited or featured in *The Wall Street Journal, Washington Times, Casper Star Tribune, Los Angeles Times*, and others. Frontiers is leading a coalition of property-rights, 'wise use', consumers', and industry organizations that advocate reforming the Endangered Species Act. The organization took out a full-page ad in *The Washington Times* on Earth Day 1995 stating, "The Endangered Species Act Doesn't Work. Let's Fix It!" In 1995 the organization spent $171,796 on its programs.
Total Revenue: 1995 $448,288 **Total Expenses:** $447,396 38%/36%/25% **Net Assets:** $45,902

Products or Services: Lobbying, periodic reports.
Tax Status: 501(c)(4)   **Citations:** 42:108
Board of Directors or Trustees: Lawrence Kudlow (*National Review*), J. A. Parker (Lincoln Inst.), Joseph Schuchert (Kelso & Co.), Diemer True (Chair, Wyoming Republican Party), Adjunct Prof. Warren Dean (Georgetown Univ. Law Center).
Other Information: Established in 1994. Affiliated with the 501(c)(3) Frontiers of Freedom Institute. Chairman Malcolm Wallop was a Republican Senator from Wyoming from 1976 until his retirement in 1994. Wallop retired with an American Conservative Union lifetime rating of over 91%. Frontiers received $448,288, or 100% of revenue, from contributions and grants awarded by foundations, businesses, and individuals.

Fully Informed Jury Association (FIJA)

P.O. Box 59
Helmsville, MT 59843   **Phone:** (406) 793-5550   **E-Mail:** juryinfo@aol.com
USA   **Fax:** same   **Internet:** http://fija.org/~fija/

Contact Person: Don Doig, National Coordinator.
Officers or Principals: Don Doig, National Coordinator ($18,100); Kathy Ballard, Secretary/Treasurer ($15,810); Larry Pratt, Vice President ($0); Gary Dusseljee, President.
Mission or Interest: "Dedicated to restoration of our traditional system of trial by jury, and seeks to protect it from further incursions. FIJA believes that the jury is a crucial check and balance in our system of government, and that the power of the jury to judge not only the evidence, but also the merits of the law itself is central to its historic role."
Accomplishments: "FIJA has distributed one to two million pieces of literature designed to educate the American people about the rights and responsibilities of jurors. Spokespersons have appeared on hundreds of radio and television talk shows and news programs. Active organizations have been formed in most of the 50 states. Governors of 16 states have signed FIJA's Jury Rights Day proclamations, and FIJA legislation has been introduced in 28 states. FIJA bills have been passed in the Oklahoma House of Representatives and in the Arizona Senate. FIJA is changing the perception of the legal community with respect to the role of the jury in the American political system. Articles discussing FIJA have appeared in many law review journals and other legal publications." FIJA's methods have been used by advocates across the political spectrum, although mostly by libertarians. Juries have received 'jury nullification' materials from FIJA in court cases involving physician-assisted suicide, drug possession, tax resistors, and cases involving militias. In 1995 FIJA spent $84,988 on its programs. This included responses to 10,800 requests for information, 150,000 "Jury Information Kits", 275,000 brochures, and 30,000 issues of its newspaper. FIJA applied for "continuing education for legal credits from the University of Utah."
Total Revenue: 1995 $132,272 14%(2) **Total Expenses:** $120,140 71%/26%/16% **Net Assets:** $37,487
Products or Services: Pamphlets for jury members and other publications.
Tax Status: 501(c)(3)
Board of Directors or Trustees: Larry Dodge, Honey Lanham Dodge, Doug Casey, Julie Sheppard.
Periodicals: *FIJActivist* (quarterly newspaper).
Other Information: Established in 1989. FIJA received $143,672, or 99.6% of gross revenue, from contributions and grants awarded by foundations, affiliates, businesses, and individuals. (These grants included $50,000 from the Carthage Foundation.) The remaining revenue came from interest on savings and temporary cash investments. FIJA lost $12,000 on the sale of securities.

Fund for American Studies

1526 18th St., N.W.
Washington, DC 20036   **Phone:** (202) 986-0384
USA   **Fax:** (202) 986-0390

Contact Person: Stephen E. Slattery, Director of Development.
Officers or Principals: David R, Jones, President ($196,746); Roger Rearn, Executive Vice President ($109,537); Michael W. Thompson, Vice President; William E. Tucker, Secretary; Robert S. Understein, Treasurer; Randal C. Teague, General Counsel.
Mission or Interest: A forum, held in partnership with Georgetown University, meant to instill college students with an understanding and appreciation of America's form of constitutional government and the free-enterprise system.
Accomplishments: Has hosted more than 4,000 students from all 50 states and from 39 foreign countries. Students have attended from over 700 colleges and universities. At their 25th anniversary dinner in 1995, the featured speaker was Gen. Colin L. Powell, USA (Ret.). Czech Prime Minister Václav Klaus delivered the commencement address at one of the Fund's Institutes. In the fiscal year ending September 1995 the Fund spent $1,298,268 on its programs. The majority of these expenditures went toward four annual Institutes; the Engalitcheff Institute on Comparative Economic Systems (with expenses of $399,553), the Institute on Political Journalism ($265,748), the Bryce Harlow Institute on Business and Government Affairs ($246,234), and the American Institute on Political and Economic Systems at Charles University in Prague, The Czech Republic ($252,801).
Total Revenue: FY ending 9/95 $2,382,629 **Total Expenses:** $1,887,750 69%/20%/11% **Net Assets:** $15,352,430
Products or Services: College students attend the Fund's Institutes with the help of scholarship programs such as the Goldwater Scholarships, begun in 1975 and named after Arizona Senator and Presidential candidate Barry Goldwater, and the newly established Freedom Education Trust Fund.
Tax Status: 501(c)(3) **Annual Report:** Yes. **Employees:** 9   **Citations:** 4:196
Board of Directors or Trustees: Charles Black, Daniel Branch, Don Cogman, Chapman Cox, William Hybl, James Culbertson, Patrick Daly, Mitchell Daniels, Jr., Salvador Diaz-Verson, Jr., Robert Greene, Clark Horvath, Thomas McDermott (Pres., Northwest Indiana Forum), Peter McPherson (Pres., Michigan State Univ.), David Neideffer, Jay Parker (Pres., The Lincoln Inst.), Ken Rietz, T. Timothy Ryan, Jr. (Managing Dir., J.P. Morgan), Susan Johnston Saewert (Exec. Dir., Kalamazoo Academy of Medicine), Arnold Steinberg, Gov. Donald Sundquist (R-TN), Justin Wilson, Rick Ventura, Mary Ann Zaloumis.

Periodicals: *Fastrack* (quarterly newsletter).
Internships: Yes. Students who attend one of the Institutes are placed with Congress, Executive-branch agencies, public policy organizations, business and corporate offices, lobbying groups and the media.
Other Information: Established in 1970 after being initiated by Charles Edison, former Governor of New Jersey, Secretary of the Navy, and son of inventor Thomas Alva Edison. Gov. Edison died in 1969, before the program was operational, and the project was named the Charles Edison Memorial Youth Fund by its founding members, William F. Buckley, Jr., Dr. Walter Judd, David Jones, and Marvin Liebman. The name was changed in 1987 to the Fund for American Studies, in accordance with Gov. Edison's wishes that his name be associated with the Fund for only twenty years or less. The Fund received $688,438, or 29% of revenue, from capital gains on the sale of securities. $594,273, or 25%, from dividends and interest from securities. $573,030, or 24%, from contributions and grants awarded by foundations, businesses, and individuals. (These grants included $50,000 from the Lynde and Harry Bradley Foundation, $10,000 from the Earhart Foundation, $7,000 from the Sunmark Foundation, $7,000 from the Grover Hermann Foundation, $6,000 from the Philip M. McKenna Foundation, and $5,000 from the F.M. Kirby Foundation. These grants have been growing by an average of 18% per year over the previous five years.) $486,938, or 20%, from Institute fees and tuition. The remaining revenue came from special fundraising events and interest on savings.

Fund for Stockowners Rights

P.O. Box 65563
Washington, DC 20035   **Phone:** (703) 276-3330
USA

Contact Person: Carl Olson, Chairman.
Officers or Principals: Allan Feldman, Vice Chairman.
Mission or Interest: Advocate for stock owners of corporations. Studies of total tax burdens on corporations, corporate donation patterns on tax reduction measures. Promotion of sponsoring resolutions at annual stock owner meetings to bring about more ownership control over management.
Accomplishments: The Fund's annual survey of tax burdens on corporations has been quoted twice in *The Wall Street Journal*. The Fund found that profitable U.S. corporations pay almost 300% more in taxes per share than in earnings per share
Products or Services: Model resolutions for submission at annual stockowners meetings. Information on secret ballots, anti-poison pill measures, minimum stockholdings by directors.
Tax Status: 501(c)(3) **Annual Report:** No. **Employees:** 2
Periodicals: *The Stockowners' News* (newsletter).

Future of Freedom Foundation (FFF)

11350 Random Hills Rd., Suite 800
Fairfax, VA 22030   **Phone:** (703) 934-6101   **E-Mail:** 75200.1523@compuserve.com
USA   **Fax:** (703) 352-8678   **Internet:** http://www.fff.org/freedom/daily/

Contact Person: Jacob G. Hornberger, President.
Officers or Principals: Jacob G. Hornberger, President ($43,333); Richard M. Ebeling, Vice President, Academic Affairs ($10,250); Sheldon Richman, Vice President, Policy Affairs.
Mission or Interest: "To present the uncompromising moral, philosophical, and economic case for the libertarian philosophy."
Accomplishments: Their publications have over 4,500 subscribers nationwide and in 30 foreign countries. Published four books including the award-winning Separating School & State. Prof. Walter E. Williams said, "FFF is carrying on the fine tradition of freedom in a manner that would make its predecessors proud."
Total Revenue: 1995 $348,164 19%(3) **Total Expenses:** $367,394 69%/19%/12% **Net Assets:** $40,387
Products or Services: Video and audio tapes of lectures. The Case for Free Trade and Open Immigration, The Failure of America's Foreign Wars, and The Dangers of Socialized Medicine (a collection containing articles from 12 eminent free-market scholars).
Tax Status: 501(c)(3) **Employees:** 3   **Citations:** 17:156
Board of Directors or Trustees: Sally van Behren, Paige Moore, Sarah Atkins, others.
Periodicals: *Freedom Daily* (monthly newsletter).
Internships: No.
Other Information: Established in 1989. The Foundation received $205,727, or 59% of revenue, from contributions and grants. $134,968, or 39%, from program services. The remaining revenue came from other miscellaneous sources.

G. Gordon Liddy Show

WJFK Radio
10800 Main St.
Fairfax, VA 22030   **Phone:**   (703) 934-9448
USA   **Fax:**   (703) 352-0111

Contact Person: John Popp, Producer.
Mission or Interest: Conservative radio talk show hosted by G. Gordon Liddy, former Nixon administration and Watergate figure.
Accomplishments: Heard across the country on 220 stations. Featured anonymous figure reputed to be the first to find the body of Vince Foster, an aide to President Clinton who was found dead in a park from a presumed suicide. The anonymous figure disputed the official version of the death scene as put forth in the independent counsel's report.
Other Information: The radio show is aired live weekdays from 10 am to 2 pm, Eastern Time. The phone number to be on the show is (800) 445-4339 and the fax number is (800) 937-4329.

Gates Foundation

3200 S. Cherry Creek Dr., Suite 630
Denver, CO 80209   **Phone:**   (303) 722-1881
USA   **Fax:**   (303) 698-9031

Contact Person: Thomas Stokes, Executive Director.
Officers or Principals: Thomas Stokes, Executive Director ($142,543); C. H. Turissini, Assistant Treasurer ($59,873); F. C. Froelicher, Trustee; Charles C. Gates, President; Diane G. Wallach, Vice President; Thomas J. Gibson, Treasurer.
Mission or Interest: Grant-making foundation that awards a very small percentage of its grants to conservative and free-market organizations. The Foundation's awards for these organizations have been gradually decreasing over the years.
Accomplishments: In 1994 the Foundation awarded $5,833,625 in grants. Recipients included: $5,000 each for the American Enterprise Institute, Center for Media and Public Affairs, Heritage Foundation, and the Institute for Research on the Economics of Taxation.
Total Revenue: 1994 $9,745,143 **Total Expenses:** $5,833,625 **Net Assets:** $118,266,099 1%(2)
Tax Status: 501(c)(3)
Board of Directors or Trustees: Charles Cannon, Mike Wilfley, George Beardsley, William Grant.
Other Information: The Foundation received $5,751,352, or 59% of revenue, from capital gains on the sale of assets. $3,943,048, or 40%, from dividends and interest from securities. The remaining revenue came from other miscellaneous sources. The Foundation held $74,624,463, or 63% of assets, in corporate stock.

George H. W. Bush Presidential Library

Mission or Interest: The George Bush Presidential Library Center is currently under construction on 90 acres of the Texas A&M University campus. The library will hold papers and documents from the Bush administration, and will be maintained by the National Archives. The Center will also feature the School of Government and Public Service, the Center for Presidential Studies, and the Center for Public Leadership Studies. Private funds will be raised to endow these Centers. The Centers will be accessible to scholars and students who "will write the history of one of the most exciting periods in world politics - the demise of communism and what has been termed the creation of a 'new world order.'"
Other Information: 1n 1993 the Library and Centers received $500,000 from the Starr Foundation.

George C. Marshall Institute

1730 M St., N.W., Suite 502
Washington, DC 20036   **Phone:** (202) 296-9655   **E-Mail:** 71553.3017@compuserve.com
USA   **Fax:**   (202) 296-9714

Contact Person: Dr. Jeffrey Salmon, Executive Director.
Officers or Principals: Dr. Jeffrey Salmon, Executive Director ($82,820); Dr. Robert Jastrow, President ($13,500); Frederick Seitz, Chairman.
Mission or Interest: Educational organization specializing in science and technology and how it can be applied to public policy and national security. Major focus is on global climate change, missile defense systems, and the U.S. space program.
Accomplishments: During the Bush administration, the Institute's research on global warming was widely credited with influencing the White House's decision to not sign an international treaty limiting carbon-dioxide emissions. In a June 1996 *Wall Street Journal* op-ed, Chairman Seitz asserted that the International Panel on Climate Change (IPCC), which was convened to assess scientific evidence regarding the human production of greenhouse gasses and their relation to global climate change, altered its final report after it had been approved by the supporting governmental representatives. Seitz stated that these changes made it appear as though a strong consensus among scientists existed linking greenhouse gasses and climate change - "The fact is that someone connected with the presentation of the published version. . . rewrote basic material. . . with the result that scientific doubts about man-made global warming were suppressed." His op-ed opened a contentious debate on the work of the IPCC. The Institute's reports on missile defense in the early 1980's "won over (Defense) Secretary Weinberger" to strong support for SDI , according to the *Washington Post*.
Total Revenue: 1994 $646,951 59%(2) **Total Expenses:** $456,987 78%/14%/8% **Net Assets:** $274,561
Products or Services: Numerous studies on SDI, space technology, and other scientific issues.
Tax Status: 501(c)(3) **Annual Report:** Yes. **Employees:** 5 **Citations:** 31:130
Board of Directors or Trustees: Willis Hawkins (Senior Advisor, Lockheed Corp.), John Moore (Dir., International Inst., George Mason Univ.), William Nierenburg (Scripps Inst. of Oceanography). Their Science Advisory Board includes: Sallie Baliunas (Harvard-Smithsonian Center for Astrophysics), Gregory Canavan (Los Alamos National Laboratory), Jerry Grey (American Inst. of Aeronautics & Astronautics), Richard Lindzen (Massachusetts Inst. of Technology), John McCarthy (Stanford Univ.), Kenneth McKay (AT&T / Bell Laboratories), Jerome Namias (Scripps Inst. of Oceanography), Allen Peterson (Stanford Univ.), Robert Sproull (Univ. of Rochester), Kenneth Watson (San Diego Marine Physics Laboratory), Lowell Wood (Lawrence Livermore National Laboratory).
Internships: Yes, interns assist in research and editing of technical reports and current issues, help plan seminars and identify potential new issues.
Other Information: Chairman Seitz is the former president of the National Academy of Sciences. The Institute received $633,335, or 98% of revenue, from contributions and grants awarded by foundations, businesses, and individuals. (These grants included $240,300 from the Lynde and Harry Bradley Foundation, $130,000 from the Sarah Scaife Foundation, and $15,000 from the J.M. Foundation. In 1995, $280,300 from the Lynde and Harry Bradley Foundation, $43,000 from the William H. Donner Foundation, and $40,000 from the John M. Olin Foundation.) $8,857, or 1%, from the sale of publications. The remaining revenue came from interest on savings.

George E. Coleman, Jr., Foundation
200 Madison Ave.
New York, NY 10016   **Phone:**   (212) 727-1440
USA

Mission or Interest: Grant-making Foundation that has historically included conservative public-policy organizations in its awards
Tax Status: 501(c)(3) **Net Assets:** 1992 $6,368,271
Board of Directors or Trustees: Denis Loncto, Daniel Oliver, Louise Oliver.
Other Information: Established in 1979 by George E. Coleman, Jr.

George Edward Durell Foundation
c/o Shenandoah University
1460 University Dr.
Winchester, VA 22601
USA

Contact Person: James A. Davis, Secretary/Treasurer.
Officers or Principals: Alson H. Smith, Chairman.
Mission or Interest: Grant-making philanthropy that has historically included some funding for conservative organizations.
Accomplishments: In 1994 the Foundation awarded $680,088 in grants. Most of this, $400,000, went to Shenandoah University. Other recipients included $50,000 each for America's Future, and the Christian Observer.
Net Assets: 1994 $16,800,088
Tax Status: 501(c)(3)
Board of Directors or Trustees: G. Britton Durell, James Landaker, R.D. Patrick Mahoney, Elizabeth Racer.
Other Information: Established in 1985.

Georgia Public Policy Foundation
4340 Georgetown Sq., Suite 608
Atlanta, GA 30338   **Phone:**   (770) 455-7600   **E-Mail:**   gppf@america.net
USA   **Fax:**   (770) 455-4355

Contact Person: Joseph G. Doyle, President.
Officers or Principals: Joseph G. Doyle, President ($92,055); Kelly McCutcheon, Executive Director ($40,579); Henry McCamish, Jr., Chairman ($0); H. Stephen Merlin, Secretary.
Mission or Interest: Public policy organization focusing on Georgia offering solutions based on free markets, deregulation, and private enterprise. Works on health care, crime, tax and fiscal issues, school reform and vouchers, and welfare reform.
Accomplishments: Filed Amicus brief in the case of Lucas v. S.C. Coastal Council. Stopped Atlanta housing ordinance against private property. Lots of media appearances. Public seminars and forums held featuring Justice Clarence Thomas, Pat Buchanan, Bill Kristol, Hon. Jack Kemp, and Gov. Carrol Campbell. Leadership Breakfasts have featured guest speakers Lt. Gov. Pierre Howard (GA), Attorney General Michael Bowers (GA), John Fund (editorial writer, *The Wall Street Journal*), Rep. Newt Gingrich (R-GA), State Sen. Terrell Starr, Robert Woodson, and others. In 1995 the Foundation spent $355,764 on its programs.
Total Revenue: 1995 $636,625 2%(2) **Total Expenses:** $740,288 48%/23%/29% **Net Assets:** $22,371
Tax Status: 501(c)(3)   **Citations:** 40:113
Board of Directors or Trustees: Thomas Perdue, J. Gordon Beckham, Jr.
Periodicals: *Georgia Policy* (quarterly journal).
Internships: Yes.
Other Information: Established in 1991. Member of the State Policy Network. The Foundation received $635,718, or 99.8% of revenue, from contributions and grants awarded by foundations, businesses, and individuals. (These grants included $33,000 from the Samuel Roberts Noble Foundation.) The remaining revenue came from dividends and interest from securities, the sale of publications, and other miscellaneous sources.

Georgians for Freedom in Education
209 Cobb St.
Palmetto, GA 30268   **Phone:**   (404) 463-3719
USA

Contact Person: Billie Jean Bryant, State Coordinator.
Officers or Principals: Mary Ann Cauther, Secretary; Teresa Ditto, CEO; Linda Ramey, Editor.
Mission or Interest: Support, education, and networking of, for and by home educators and others.
Accomplishments: "Instrumental in passing (Georgia) homeschool law."
Products or Services: Materials and resources for home schooling, state contact list, book and tape library.
Tax Status: Nonprofit. **Employees:** All volunteer.
Board of Directors or Trustees: Sharon Kurtzberg, Billie Jean Bryant, others.
Periodicals: *Georgians for Freedom in Education Newsletter* (quarterly newsletter).
Other Information: Established in 1983.

Gerald R. Ford Presidential Library

1000 Beal Ave.
Ann Arbor, MI 48109   **Phone:** (313) 668-2218
USA   **Fax:**   (313) 668-2341

Officers or Principals: Frank Mackaman, Director; Dennis Daellenbach, Assistant Director; David Horrocks, Supervising Archivist; Richard Holzhausen, Archivist.
Mission or Interest: Federal repository for the papers and records of the Ford Administration. Collections of various other papers.
Other Information: Maintained by the National Archives and Records Administration.

Gilder Foundation

912 5th Ave.
New York, NY 10021   **Phone:** (212) 765-2500
USA

Contact Person: Richard Gilder, Jr., President.
Officers or Principals: Richard Gilder, Jr., President ($0); Richard Schneidman, Secretary ($0); Thomas L. Rhodes, Vice President ($0); David Howe, Treasurer.
Mission or Interest: Grant-making foundation that includes conservative and free-market organizations in its awards.
Accomplishments: In 1994 the Foundation awarded $4,750,180 in grants. Recipients included: $250,000 for the Competitive Enterprise Institute, two grants totaling $100,000 for the Manhattan Institute, four grants totaling $67,000 for the National Center for Neighborhood Enterprise, $50,000 for the Center for Individual Rights, $25,000 each for U.S. Term Limits and *Commentary*, two grants totaling $12,500 for the Reason Foundation, $10,000 for the Free Congress Foundation, $7,500 for the Center for the Study of Market Processes, $5,000 each for the Young Americas Foundation, Education and Research Institute, National Fatherhood Initiative, and Philanthropy Roundtable, and $1,500 for the National Tax Limitation Committee. Many large grants went to environmental conservation organizations; including four grants totaling $1,105,542 for the Central Park Conservatory and $125,000 for the Environmental Defense Fund.
Total Revenue: 1994 $4,815,949 **Total Expenses:** $5,372,298 **Net Assets:** $24,628,077
Tax Status: 501(c)(3)
Other Information: The Foundation received $5,020,581, or 84% of gross revenue, from a gift of stock from Richard Gilder. $851,339, or 14%, from dividends and interest from securities. The remaining income came from other miscellaneous sources. The Foundation lost $1,150,170 on the sale of assets. The Foundation held $16,348,788, or 66% of assets, in government bonds. $5,002,036, or 20%, in savings and temporary cash investments.

Goldwater Institute for Public Policy

201 N. Central Ave., Concourse
Phoenix, AZ 85003   **Phone:** (602) 256-7018
USA   **Fax:**   (602) 256-7045

Contact Person: Jeff Flake, Executive Director.
Officers or Principals: Jeff Flake, Executive Director ($67,117); Michael Block, President ($0); Dale Garman, Treasurer ($0); Norma McClella, Chairman; John Norton, Vice Chairman; Roy Miller, Secretary; Jock Patton, Counsel.
Mission or Interest: "Serves as the leading voice of free market and limited government policy initiatives in Arizona."
Accomplishments: The Majority Leader of the Arizona State Senate, Sen. Tom Patterson, said, "The Goldwater Institute has a well-deserved reputation for thoughtful, hardhitting analysis of public issues. The Institute's reports and seminars make a significant difference for policy makers in state government." In the fiscal year ending June 1995, the Institute spent $275,152 on its programs. These included the publication of over 20 studies on issues of state governance, and almost a dozen speeches and policy briefings. Print media coverage included *National Review*, *Washington Times*, *Arizona Republic*, *Phoenix Gazette*, *Arizona Daily Star*, and many other papers state-wide.
Total Revenue: FY ending 6/95 $400,148 75%(2) **Total Expenses:** $369,523 74%/18%/8% **Net Assets:** $131,792
Products or Services: Annual Goldwater Institute Award; the 1995 recipient was Pres. Ronald Reagan.
Tax Status: 501(c)(3)   **Citations:** 2:216
Board of Directors or Trustees: Barry Aarons, Jonathan Rose (Arizona State Univ.), Hon. Lewis Tambs (former Ambassador to Costa Rica, 1985-87), Prof. Gordon Tullock (Univ. of Arizona), Vernon Smith (Univ. of Arizona), many others.
Other Information: Established in 1988. Formerly called the Barry Goldwater Institute for Public Policy. The Institute received $396,494, or 99% of revenue, from contributions and grants awarded by foundations, businesses, and individuals. (These grants included $25,000 from the J.M. Foundation, $25,000 from the John M. Olin Foundation, $10,000 from the Roe Foundation, and $10,000 from the Earhart Foundation.) The remaining revenue came from interest on savings and temporary cash investments.

Gordon and Mary Cain Foundation

8 Greenway Plaza, Suite 702
Houston, TX 77046   **Phone:** (713) 877-8257
USA

Contact Person: James D. Weaver, President.
Officers or Principals: James D. Weaver, President ($60,000); Gordon A. Cain, Chief Executive Officer ($0); William C. Oehmig, Secretary/Treasurer ($0).
Mission or Interest: Grant-making foundation that includes free-market organizations in its awards. Also awards grants to left-of-center organizations.
Accomplishments: In 1994 the Foundation awarded $1,619,170 in grants. Recipients included: three grants totaling $140,000 for the Cato Institute, two grants totaling $100,000 for the Bionomics Institute, four grants totaling $66,000 for Citizens for a Sound Economy, two grants totaling $37,500 for the Landmark Legal Foundation, $15,000 for the Free Enterprise Education Center, $10,000 each for the National Center for Policy Analysis, Texas Public Policy Foundation, and the Reason Foundation, $7,500 for the Center for Economic Policy Research, Stanford University, $5,000 each for Citizen's Against Government Waste and the Institute for Policy Innovation, $2,500 each for the Center for Market Processes and the Institute for Energy Research, and $1,000 for Consumer Alert.
Total Revenue: 1994 $20,087,289 **Total Expenses:** $1,861,907 **Net Assets:** $59,105,956 49%(2)
Tax Status: 501(c)(3)
Board of Directors or Trustees: Mary Cain, Margaret Oehmig, Sharyn Weaver, John Sullivan.
Other Information: Established in 1988. The Foundation received $18,843,750, or 92% of gross revenue, from a single gift. $1,697,275, or 8%, from dividends and interest from securities. The remaining revenue came interest on savings and temporary cash investments. The remaining revenue came from various miscellaneous sources. The Foundation lost $492,610 on the sale of assets.

Grover Hermann Foundation

c/o Schiff, Hardin & White
7200 Sears Tower
Chicago, IL 60606   **Phone:**   (312) 258-5625
USA

Contact Person: Paul K. Rhoads, President.
Officers or Principals: Paul K. Rhoads, President ($0); John T. Hayes, Secretary ($0); Katheryn V. Rhoads, Treasurer ($0).
Mission or Interest: Grant-making foundation that includes conservative and free-market organizations in its awards.
Accomplishments: In 1994 the Foundation awarded $2,129,050 in grants. Recipients included: $165,000 for the Heritage Foundation, $100,000 for the Media Research Center, $40,000 for the Pacific Legal Foundation, $35,000 for the Intercollegiate Studies Institute, $15,000 for the Reason Foundation, $12,000 for the National Tax Limitation Foundation, $10,000 each for the Young America's Foundation, Cato Institute, and American Spectator Education Fund, $7,000 each for the Washington Legal Foundation, Fund for American Studies, $5,000 each for the Free Congress Foundation, Philanthropy Roundtable, and the American Legislative Exchange Council, $3,000 for the American Cause, $2,500 each for the Capital Research Center, Legislative Studies Institute, and the Institute for Research on the Economics of Taxation, and $2,000 for the Pacific Legal Foundation. The Foundation's award for the Heritage Foundation includes funding for the Grover Hermann Fellow in Federal Budgetary Affairs, currently held by Scott A. Hodge.
Total Revenue: 1994 $448,911 **Total Expenses:** $2,216,900 **Net Assets:** $3,904,497 (-35%)(2)
Tax Status: 501(c)(3)
Other Information: Established in 1955. The Foundation received $235,631, or 52% of revenue, from dividends and interest from securities. $203,076, or 45%, from capital gains on the sale of assets. $10,204, or 3%, from interest on savings and temporary cash investments. The Foundation held $2,049,000, or 52% of assets, in corporate stock. $1,132,300, or 29%, in corporate bonds.

Gun Owners of America

8001 Forbes Place, Suite 102
Springfield, VA 22151   **Phone:**   (703) 321-8585
USA   **Fax:**   (703) 321-8408

Contact Person: Larry Pratt, Executive Director.
Officers or Principals: Sen. H. L. Richardson, Chairman ($18,000); Larry Pratt, Executive Director ($0).
Mission or Interest: "Advocacy on behalf of individual firearms rights." Gun Owners of America views gun ownership as a freedom issue, and disagree with the compromising approach frequently used by the NRA. They feel the NRA's approach - to reshape legislation which the NRA cannot stop - is ultimately wrong-headed as it chips away at freedoms and allows legislators off the hook by letting them vote for anti-gun legislation which has been altered by the NRA. Pratt is an advocate of citizen militias.
Accomplishments: Initiation of active pro-gun legislation. Supported a background check that would instantly check for a criminal record, but would not keep records of who owns guns. Drafted model legislation for the federal and state levels that deals with crime problems. In 1994 the organization spent $1,116,818 on its programs, an increase of 67% over the previous year. Programs included legal defense and litigation.
Total Revenue: 1994 $1,664,439 111% **Total Expenses:** $1,567,262 71%/17%/12% **Net Assets:** $181,924
Products or Services: Lobbying. Various videos, books and backgrounders.
Tax Status: 501(c)(4) **Annual Report:** Yes. **Employees:** 10   **Citations:** 176:41
Board of Directors or Trustees: Tim Macy, Harry Sanford, Dave Bauer, Gary Marbut.
Periodicals: *The Gun Owners* (newsletter).

Internships: Yes. A limited number of positions are available to do office work and research.
Other Information: Affiliated with the 501(c)(3) Gun Owners Foundation. Larry Pratt had been a co-chair of Pat Buchanan's Presidential campaign until the Center for Public Integrity released a report saying that Pratt has spoken at conferences organized by white supremacists, a charge that Pratt denies. Gun Owners of America received $1,656,545, or 99.5% of revenue, from contributors. The remaining revenue came from mailing list rentals and interest on savings.

Gun Owners of Macomb County (GOMAC)
P.O. Box 46364
Mt. Clemens, MI 48045   **Phone:** (810) 463-4032
USA   **Fax:**   (810) 463-4032

Contact Person: Michael P. Sessa, Chairman.
Officers or Principals: C. Bradley Shoenburg, Vice Chairman/Treasurer.
Mission or Interest: Encouraging grassroots participation in the political process on behalf of gun-owners' rights.
Accomplishments: Leading gun owners' rights group in Michigan. Were able to put together a rally on short notice which attracted 6-9,000 participants. Encouraged gun owners to become precinct delegates. Fax network
Tax Status: Nonprofit recreational association. **Annual Report:** No. **Employees:** All volunteer.
Board of Directors or Trustees: Advisors include MI State Rep. David Jaye.
Periodicals: *On Target.*
Internships: No.
Other Information: Chairman Michael Sessa is the Macomb County Commissioner. Although COMAC is centered in one county, they have members throughout Michigan. Affiliated with Gun Owners of America.

Headway
13555 Bammel N. Houston Rd., Suite 227
Houston, TX 77066   **Phone:** (713) 444-4265   **E-Mail:** grichardson@ghgcorp.com
USA   **Fax:**   (713) 583-9534   **Internet:** http://www.townhall.com/headwaymag

Contact Person: Gwen Daye Richardson, Editor.
Officers or Principals: Willie A. Richardson, Publisher; John F. Guest, Profiles Editor; Deroy Murdock, Sharon Brooks Hodge, Social/Cultural Correspondent.
Mission or Interest: National monthly magazine of news and opinions featuring black conservative columnists. Formerly called *National Minority Politics*. Promotes "strong families, individual responsibility, free enterprise, limited government, strong defense, community-based problem solving, good taste and common sense in popular culture, and compassionate conservatism."
Accomplishments: Rep. J.C. Watts, Jr. (R-OK), said, "It's rare that a magazine comes along that so accurately reflects what's current with the nation's most critical issues. *Headway* fills the bill." Featured columnists include Dr. Thomas Sowell, Dr. Walter E. Williams, Joseph H. Brown, Ezola Foster, and Errol Smith. Their 1994 National Leadership Conference featured keynote speakers, Dr. Mildred Jefferson (Pres., Right to Life Crusade), Prof. Walter Williams (George Mason Univ.), Sen. Kay Bailey Hutchison (R-TX), Rep. Gary Franks (R-CT), and Sen. Phil Gramm (R-TX)
Tax Status: For profit.
Periodicals: *Headway* (monthly magazine).
Internships: Not now, but perhaps in the future.
Other Information: Established in 1989 as *National Minority Politics*.

Heartbeat International
7870 Olentangy River Rd., Suite 304
Columbus, OH 43235   **Phone:** (614) 885-7577   **E-Mail:** heartbeat@qn.net
USA   **Fax:**   (614) 885-8746   **Internet:** www.qn.net/~heartbeat/

Contact Person: Margaret H. Hartshorn, President.
Officers or Principals: Margaret H. Hartshorn, president ($25,000); Anne Pierson, Vice President ($0); Tom Glessner, J.D., Secretary/Treasurer ($0).
Mission or Interest: Anti-abortion group that seeks "To create an environment where every human heart is cherished and protected - within the womb and within strong families. . . We start and strengthen existing pregnancy help centers (crisis pregnancy centers, maternity homes, nonprofit adoption agencies, medical clinics) all over the world."
Accomplishments: "350 affiliated centers in 45 states and 12 foreign countries, major training conference held annually for 25 years." In 1995 the conference had 300 participants. In 1995 Heartbeat spent $83,629 on its programs.
Total Revenue: 1995 $115,059 **Total Expenses:** $113,500 74%/18%/9% **Net Assets:** $2,634
Products or Services: Worldwide Directory of Life-Affirming Pregnancy Services listing 4,000 crisis pregnancy centers, and Model Program manuals for centers.
Tax Status: 501(c)(3) **Annual Report:** No. **Employees:** 4
Board of Directors or Trustees: Michael Hartshorn, J.D., Gregory Loesch, Janet Trenda.
Periodicals: *Heartbeat International* (quarterly newsletter).

Internships: No.
Other Information: Established in 1971, previously called Alternatives to Abortion. Heartbeat received $58,265, or 51% of revenue, from contributions and grants awarded by foundations, businesses, and individuals. Although its major source of funding in 1995, contributions and grants have been sporadic in the past, $50,092 in 1994, $114,566 in 1993, $5,070 in 1992, and $0 in 1991. $25,719, or 22%, from conference fees. $18,174, or 16%, from membership dues. $7,871, or 7%, from the sale of manuals and books. The remaining revenue came from the sale of tapes, jewelry, and other paraphernalia, consultations, and computer applications.

Heartland Institute

800 E. Northwest Highway, Suite 1080
Palatine, IL 60067   **Phone:** (847) 202-3060   **E-Mail:** think@heartland.org
USA   **Fax:** (847) 202-9799   **Internet:** http://www.heartland.org

Contact Person: Diane Carol Bast.
Officers or Principals: Joseph L. Bast, President ($40,135); Herbert J. Walberg, Chairman ($0).
Mission or Interest: Free-market policy organization that focuses on the Midwest. Heartland aims to be "the world's fastest, most convenient, most comprehensive, and most reliable source of public policy information." Emphasizes the electronic transfer of public policy information.
Accomplishments: Operates the "PolicyFax" system which faxes nearly 3,000 documents from 90 different think tanks, publications, and trade associations. During 1995 PolicyFax sent nearly 5,000 documents. In May 1996 PolicyFax sent out a record 967 documents. Eco-Sanity: A Common-Sense Guide to Environmentalism by Peter Hill and Richard Rue (published by Heartland), won the 1996 Sir Antony Fisher International Memorial Award for books "that made the greatest contributions to the understanding of the free market." Produced and distributed over 140,000 copies of a tabloid newspaper, *Earth Day '96*, to students, legislators, and others on Earth Day. The paper "focused on sound science and giving facts you need to make up your own mind," and focused on "government policies that are cost effective and don't needlessly infringe on people's rights." A follow-up survey of state legislators found that (among those responding) 100% said they learned "quite a lot" or "a lot" from *Earth Day '96*, and 69% would like to receive and distribute copies in 1997. Recommended economists to Rep. Phil Crane's (R-IL) office for a public hearing on free trade. In March of 1996, Heartland's web page attracted 23,852 'hits.' In 1995 the Institute spent $490,094 on its programs.
Total Revenue: 1995 $716,196 (-5%)(2) **Total Expenses:** $655,664 75%/12%/14% **Net Assets:** (-$13,603)
Products or Services: PolicyFax service offering faxed studies from Heartland, free-market policy organizations and others, including Planned Parenthood. Research and publications. Annual "Liberty Prizes."
Tax Status: 501(c)(3) **Annual Report:** No. **Employees:** 9   **Citations:** 48:101
Board of Directors or Trustees: Robert Buford, Ronald Docksai, Ph.D. (Vice Pres., Federal Government Relations, Bayer Corp.), Theodore Eck, Ph.D. (Chief Economist, Amoco Corp.), Dan Hales, John Hosemann (Chief Economist, American Farm Bureau Federation), James Johnston, Roy Marden (Corporate Relations, Philip Morris Co.), David Padden, Frank Resnik, Leslie Rose, Al St. Clair (Proctor & Gamble), Herbert Walberg, Lee Walker.
Periodicals: *Intellectual Ammunition* (bimonthly magazine), *Heartlander* (monthly newsletter), and *The Eco-Sanity Report* (monthly newsletter featuring reviews of over 50 publications on environmental issues).
Internships: Yes, unpaid.
Other Information: The methods of the Heartland Institute have shifted in focus somewhat. When it was founded in 1984, Heartland worked through regional offices throughout the Midwest in Michigan, Missouri, Ohio, and Wisconsin. These regional offices were to take advantage of economies of scale and distribute research more efficiently than separate organizations could on their own. These offices have since closed and the Institute now operates solely out of its Palatine office. The focus has also shifted away from original research to disseminating the research and studies of others. Following a "Total Quality Management" review, Heartland decided to focus on "the best available information on public policy issues," and to deliver it in "the world's fastest, most convenient, most comprehensive manner possible." Heartland still produces original research, but the amount has dropped, from 36% of the program budget in 1993 to 21% in 1995. Heartland is affiliated with the Center for Rebuilding America's Schools; a 501(c)(3) organization that began as a project of the Heartland Institute. Heartland received $583,909, or 82% of revenue, from contributions and grants awarded by foundations, businesses, and individuals. (These grants included $25,000 from the Lynde and Harry Bradley Foundation, $10,000 from the Charles G. Koch Charitable Foundation, and $5,000 from the Roe Foundation. In 1994, $10,000 from the J.M. Foundation, and $2,000 from the United Educators Foundation.) $131,352, or 18%, from program services including the sale of publications and PolicyFaxes. The remaining revenue came from interest on savings and temporary cash investments.

Heather Foundation

2430 Juan Tabo, N.E., Suite 153
Albuquerque, NM 87112   **Phone:** (505) 275-4960
USA

Contact Person: Spencer H. MacCallum.
Officers or Principals: Emalie E. MacCallum.
Mission or Interest: "Furthering understanding of society as an evolving natural phenomenon of spontaneously patterned cooperation among freely-acting individuals. Taxation and other institutionalized coercions are viewed as evidence of insufficient development of social organization, a condition to be outgrown. The Foundation sponsors research, lectures and publications."

Accomplishments: Edited and published two books from the papers of E.C. Riegel; three titles in preparation from the papers of Spencer Heath. Harry Browne, 1996 Libertarian candidate for president, said of one of Riegel's books, "The best explanation of the free market I've seen." "Drafting a Constitution for Orbis" project of "designing a social structure of a hypothetical free-standing proprietary (nonpolitical) community, anticipating such communities in the future."
Products or Services: Flight from Inflation and The New Approach to Freedom by E.C. Riegel, Citadel, Market and Altar by Spencer Heath, and The Art of Community by Spencer Heath. Other articles and papers
Internships: Yes, for scholars interested in the philosophies of Spencer Heath, Arthur C. Holden, or E.C. Riegel.

Herbert Hoover Presidential Library

West Branch, IA 52358   **Phone:**   (319) 643-5301
USA   **Fax:**   (319) 643-5825

Officers or Principals: Richard Norton Smith, Director; Mildred Mather, Librarian/Archivist.
Mission or Interest: Manuscripts of Herbert Hoover and his administration.
Other Information: Maintained by the National Archives and Records Administration.

Heritage Foundation

214 Massachusetts Ave., N.E.
Washington, DC 20002   **Phone:** (202) 546-4400   **E-Mail:** Insider@heritage.org
USA   **Fax:**   (202) 546-8328   **Internet:** http://www.heritage.org or www.townhall.com

Contact Person: Dr. Edwin Feulner, Jr., President.
Officers or Principals: Dr. Edwin Feulner, Jr., President/CEO ($458,344); Phillip N. Truluck, Executive Vice President ($261,574); Edwin Meese, Distinguished Scholar ($232,953); William Bennett, Distinguished Scholar ($215,680); John Von Kannon, Vice President/Treasurer ($167,373); Herb B. Berkowitz, Vice President ($157,298); Stuart M. Butler, Vice President ($154,594); Marshall Breger, Distinguished Scholar ($151,590); Peter E. S. Pover, Vice President ($136,997); Adam Meyerson, Vice President ($132,094); Kim R. Holmes, Vice President ($123,094); Lewis F. Gayner, Vice President ($120,928); David Winston, Distinguished Scholar ($103,806); Dr. David R. Brown, Chairman; Richard M. Scaife, Vice Chairman.
Mission or Interest: "A research and educational institute - a think tank - whose mission is to formulate and promote conservative public policies based on the principles of free enterprise, limited government, individual freedom, traditional American values, and a strong national defense."
Accomplishments: Heritage is the largest conservative think tank, and the most frequently quoted in the media. According to *The Wall Street Journal*, "With the Republicans' rise to control of Congress, think tank power in the nation's capital has shifted to the right. And no policy shop has more clout than the conservative Heritage Foundation." Heritage claims that its 240,000 contributors make it the most broadly supported think tank in America. Heritage's research is widely credited has having been influential in the passage of NAFTA, welfare reform, telecommunications reform, agricultural subsidies reform, and other laws that have been enacted. It is also influential in the debate on Medicare reform, regulatory reform, tax reduction, immigration and other issues. Heritage was instrumental in the creation of SDI, the Strategic Defense Initiative (for more information see High Frontier). With a grant from the Roe Foundation, Heritage has created an econometric forecasting model "similar in detail and sophistication to those used by the Congressional Budget Office, Federal Reserve Board, and Office of Budget and Management." In 1995 Heritage spent $20,850,116 on its programs. The largest expenditure, $10,515,478, went to research. $5,909,452 was spent on educational programs. $4,425,186 was spent on media and government relations, through which Heritage has gained a reputation as an excellent promoter of its research. Heritage awarded $57,480 in grants. Recipients included: $20,000 for the National Commission on Economic Growth and Tax Reform, $15,000 for the Philadelphia Society, $5,000 for the Atlas Economic Research Institute, $4,000 for the Council for National Policy, and $2,000 for the Free Africa Foundation.
Total Revenue: 1995 $28,812,513 10%(5) **Total Expenses:** $25,055,050 83%/3%/14% **Net Assets:** $38,358,736
Products or Services: Research, publications, conferences and forums. Town Hall computer network. Resource Bank of over 2,000 conservative public policy experts. Fellowships and scholarships.
Tax Status: 501(c)(3) **Annual Report:** Yes. **Employees:** Over 160; 37 employees paid over $50,000.   **Citations:** 3,108:3
Board of Directors or Trustees: Jeb Bush (Foundation for Florida's Future), Grover Coors, Midge Decter (Inst. on Religion and Public Life), William Hume, Dr. Robert Krieble (Krieble Associates), Hon. J. William Middendorf, II (U.S. Ambassador to the Organization of American States), J. Frederic Rench, Thomas Rhodes (Pres., National Review), Thomas Roe (Roe Found.), Hon. Frank Shakespeare (U.S. Ambassador to the Vatican, 1986-93), Jay Van Andel (founder, Amway Corp.), Preston Wells.
Periodicals: *Policy Review* (bimonthly magazine). In 1996 *Policy Review* received a new format, changed from quarterly to bimonthly, added the subtitle "The Journal of American Citizenship," and saw circulation pass 30,000. *The Insider* (monthly update of events and publications of interest to conservatives).
Internships: Yes.
Other Information: Established in 1973. Preisdent Ed Feulner was a counsellor to 1996 Republican Vice Presidential candidate Jack Kemp. Heritage co-owns the for-profit computer network, Town Hall, with *National Review*. In 1995 Town Hall brought in $311,328 in income, and was valued at $48,296. Town Hall was started and expanded with a loan of $500,000 from the Lynde and Harry Bradley Foundation. President Ed Feulner, Jr., also sits on the boards of the Roe Foundation, Sarah Scaife Foundation and the Aequus Institute, for which he was paid $500, $3,344 and $8,000 respectively. In 1995 the Aequus Institute contributed $100,000 to the Heritage Foundation. The Foundation contracted various consulting firms: Factor Direct of Los Angeles and Winchell and

Associates of Arlington, VA, performed membership services, and were paid $488,791 and $422,504 respectively. Newton and Associates of Washington, DC, were paid $128,000 for public relations. Jack Kemp was hired for public policy research, and paid $136,364. Heritage received $24,628,126, or 85% of revenue, from contributions and grants awarded by foundations, businesses, and individuals. (These grants included $875,000 from the Lynde and Harry Bradley Foundation, $635,000 from the Carthage Foundation, $581,400 from the John M. Olin Foundation, $450,000 from the Samuel Roberts Noble Foundation, $100,000 from the Castle Rock Foundation, $75,000 from the Philip M. McKenna Foundation, $55,000 from the Roe Foundation, $50,000 from the Charles G. Koch Charitable Foundation, $45,000 from the John William Pope Foundation, $35,000 from the Sunmark Foundation, $12,500 from the Ruth and Vernon Taylor Foundation, and $5,000 from the Gates Foundation. In 1994, $600,000 from the Sarah Scaife Foundation, $165,000 from the Grover Hermann Foundation, $125,000 from the M.J. Murdock Charitable Trust, $100,000 from the Aequus Institute, $85,000 from the Alex C. Walker Foundation, and $40,000 from the F.M. Kirby Foundation. Heritage states that individuals make up the largest portion of these grants, followed by foundations, and then businesses.) $2,077,826, or 7%, comes capital gains on the sale of assets. $707,445, or 2%, from mailing list rentals. $491,934, or 2%, from the sale of publications and subscriptions. $460,036, or 2%, from dividends and interest from securities. The remaining revenue came from interest on savings and temporary cash investments, a real estate tax write-off, advertising, and other miscellaneous sources.

Heritage Preservation Association (HPA)

P.O. Box 98209
Atlanta, GA 30359   **Phone:** (770) 928-2714   **E-Mail:** HPA@america.net
USA   **Fax:**   (770) 928-2719   **Internet:** www.hpa.org

Contact Person: R. Lee Collins, President.
Officers or Principals: R. Lee Collins, President ($0); P. Charles Lunsford, Vice President ($0); David L. Watson, Treasurer/General Counsel ($0).
Mission or Interest: "To protect Southern symbols and Southern heritage. . . Southern heritage is a part of American heritage but the political correctness movement wants to change that. Their version of a multi-cultural society allows everyone to honor their heritage and culture, *except* Southerners!"
Accomplishments: Chapters in ten states, with members in 48 states and six countries. Prominent in its support of the Southern 'Stars and Bars' flag and its display. "In Georgia we have helped elect pro-Southern legislators. To educate voters, we distributed over 60,000 flag facts brochures. We collected over 50,000 petitions, defeated an anti-flag boycott and lobbied the General Assembly to help save the Georgia state flag." Similar efforts in Virginia, South Carolina, and other states.
Total Revenue: 1994 $38,185 **Total Expenses:** $26,439 **Net Assets:** $14,949
Tax Status: 501(c)(4)
Board of Directors or Trustees: Olga Lucia Barrera, R. Wayne Byrd Sr., Tony Carr, Sr., Darren Wheeler.
Periodicals: *The Front Line* (quarterly newsletter).
Other Information: Established in 1993. The Association received $30,689, or 80% of revenue, from membership dues. $7,184, or 19%, from contributors. The remaining revenue came from other miscellaneous sources.

High Frontier

2800 Shirlington Rd., Suite 405A
Arlington, VA 22206   **Phone:** (703) 671-4111   **E-Mail:** highfrontier@bix.com
USA   **Fax:**   (703) 931-6432

Contact Person: Bernice Coakley.
Officers or Principals: Robert C. Richardson, III, Secretary/Treasurer ($24,965); J. Milnor Robert, Director ($11,400); Amb. Henry Cooper, Chairman.
Mission or Interest: To educate the public, and promote strategic defense issues, space, and commercialization of space issues. In particular they focus on the Strategic Defense Initiative (SDI), a space-based anti-missile system, commonly called "Star Wars".
Accomplishments: In 1981 founder Gen. Graham organized a team of scientists, engineers, and strategists in an effort to find a method "to defend the nation against attack by ballistic missiles." The study was done under the aegis of the Heritage Foundation. The result, "High Frontier: A National Strategy," was issued to government officials in 1982 - and in the following year the concept was adopted by President Reagan as the "Strategic Defense Initiative." "High Frontier is the nation's leading non-government pro-SDI group, and is often called upon to comment on SDI and related issues. . . Gen. Graham is the nation's leading advocate for SDI, and is known as the father of SDI. Origin of Brilliant Pebbles concept, as well as SSTO--Single-Stage-To-Orbit Vehicle." The group's newsletter has a per copy circulation of about 25,000. The quarterly journal has a circulation of about 2,000. In 1995 High Frontier spent $268,009 on its programs.
Total Revenue: FY ending 11/95 $541,357 (-6%)(2) **Total Expenses:** $532,037 50%/24%/26% **Net Assets:** $111,074
Tax Status: 501(c)(3) **Employees:** 8, plus consultants and volunteers.   **Citations:** 40:113
Board of Directors or Trustees: Dr. Werner Glatt.
Periodicals: *The Shield* (bimonthly newsletter), and a quarterly journal.
Internships: Yes, Summer internship program for high school, college and graduate students. Paid internships are involved with administrative work and special projects.

Other Information: Established in 1981. Affiliated with the 501(c)(6) Space Transportation Association. Previously affiliated with the now-defunct 501(c)(4) Americans for the High Frontier. Founder Lt. Gen. Daniel O. Graham (1925-96) was a West Point graduate whose military career included receiving the Distinguished Service Medal, Distinguished Intelligence Medal, and Legion of Merit with two oak-leaf clusters; as a civilian he received NASA's highest award, the Distinguished Public Service Medal. He served as military advisor to Ronald Reagan during the 1976 and 1980 Presidential campaigns. The organization received $517,971, or 96% of revenue, from contributions and grants awarded by foundations, businesses, and individuals. (These grants included $35,000 from the Carthage Foundation. In 1994, $30,000 from the F.M. Kirby Foundation, $5,000 from the Richard & Helen DeVos Foundation.) $10,959, or 2%, from conference fees. $6,069, or 1%, from mailing list rentals. The remaining revenue came from periodical subscriptions, interest on savings, and other miscellaneous sources.

Hillsdale College

33 E. College St.
Hillsdale, MI 49242   **Phone:**   (517) 439-1524, ext. 2318
USA   **Fax:**   (517) 437-0654   **Internet:** http://www.hillsdale.edu

Contact Person: Lissa Roche, Director of Seminars.
Officers or Principals: George C. Roche, III, President ($348,395); John Cervini, Vice President, Development ($142,335); F. LaMar Fowler, Secretary ($111,142); H. Kenneth Cole, Treasurer ($104,218).
Mission or Interest: "Coeducational liberal arts residential college with an enrollment of approximately 1,100 students." Hillsdale's curriculum focuses on the free market and traditional liberal arts disciplines and course materials. Hillsdale accepts no government tuition assistance, and has withdrawn from the Pell Grant and other student loan programs. Free of direct government support, Hillsdale does not need to conform to affirmative action requirements or Department of Education regulations.
Accomplishments: "Published *Imprimis*, the world's largest speech digest and sponsors the largest lecture series in higher education." *Imprimis* has a circulation of approximately 500,000 readers. The lecture series, the Center for Constructive Alternatives, has hosted over 1,500 presentations on campus. Past speakers have included Fred Barnes, William Bennett, Pat Buchanan, William F. Buckley, Jr., George Bush, Eleanor Clift, William Sloane Coffin, Midge Decter, Steve Forbes, Newt Gingrich, Jesse Jackson, Jack Kemp, Michael Kinsley, Jeane Kirkpatrick, George McGovern, Malcolm Muggeridge, Ralph Nader, Leonard Nimoy, P.J. O'Rourke, Colin Powell, Dan Quayle, Ronald Reagan, Thomas Sowell, Margaret Thatcher, Tom Wolfe, and others. "Hillsdale was the first college in the nation to have a policy of nondiscrimination written into its state charter. . . Hillsdale admitted women, blacks and minorities on par with white males almost two decades before the Civil War. . . Hillsdale successfully fought against segregated ROTC units during World War I."
Total Revenue: FY ending 6/95 $44,934,236 (-4%)(2) **Total Expenses:** $35,584,249 74%/13%/13% **Net Assets:** $133,452,018
Products or Services: Center for Constructive Alternatives lecture series. Shavano Institute for National Leadership, an 'off-campus' lecture series. Catalog of books, tapes and publications.
Tax Status: 501(c)(3) **Annual Report:** Yes. **Employees:** 300.
Board of Directors or Trustees: William Atherton, Walter Auch, David Belew, Jeffrey Coors, Rep. Philip Crane (R-IL), Arthur Decio, Jack Eckerd, Martin Edwards, Harvey Fruehauf, Hazel Hare, Trefle Harnois, Stephen Higley, Thomas Jordan, Jr., William Killgallon, Charles Kirsch, Paul Leutheuser, Rodney Linton, C. Fabian McGraw, Charles McIntyre, III, C. Donald Miller, Jr., Lovett Peters (Pioneer Inst.), J. Eric Plym, James Quayle, Robert Richardson, John Riecker, Melissa Sage, Lawrence Selhorst, Hon. Frank Shakespeare (former Ambassador to the Vatican), D. Curtis Shaneour, Jr., Duane Stranahan, Jr., John Tormey, Jay Van Andel (Chair, Amway Corp.).
Periodicals: *Imprimis* (monthly reprint of lectures).
Other Information: The College received $18,515,505, or 41% of revenue, from contributions and grants awarded by foundations, businesses, and individuals. (These grants included $152,000 from the Castle Rock Foundation, $20,000 from the J.M. Foundation, $10,000 from the F.M. Kirby Foundation, $8,000 from the Sunmark Foundation, $7,500 from the Curran Foundation, $5,000 from the Vernon K. Krieble Foundation, $5,000 from the Aequus Institute, $2,500 from the Winchester Foundation, $2,000 from the United Educators Foundation, and $1,000 from the John William Pope Foundation.) $12,553,823, or 28%, from tuition and fees. $2,842,086, or 6%, from dividends and interest from securities. $2,781,167, or 6%, from capital gains on the sale of assets. The remaining revenue came from various other activities associated with a college; cafeteria, sports complex membership, etc. The College held $89,865,718, or 67% of assets, in securities. $37,106,969, or 28%, in land, buildings and equipment.

Hoffman Education Center for the Family

2323 Bell Rd.
Montgomery, AL 36123   **Phone:**   (334) 271-1530
USA   **Fax:**   same

Contact Person: Mrs. Bobbie H. Ames, Administrator.
Officers or Principals: David P. Ames, Business Manager; Jeanne Riley, Register; Helen Carroll, Administrative Assistant.
Mission or Interest: Operates a "demonstration school" that advocates a "Biblical Principle Approach and Classical Education similar to that of the Founding Fathers of America." Also focuses on free-market economics.
Accomplishments: Operating for over 30 continuous years. In the fiscal year ending June 1994 the Center spent $592,549 on its programs.
Total Revenue: FY ending 6/94 $517,489 41%(2) **Total Expenses:** $598,700 99%/0%/1% **Net Assets:** $255,811

Products or Services: The Education of James Madison by Mary-Elaine Swanson and other publications.
Tax Status: 501(c)(3)
Board of Directors or Trustees: John Ames, John Chism, Donald Coffee.
Internships: Yes.
Other Information: Previously known as the Dallas Christian School. The Center received $411,640, or 80% of revenue, from tuition and fees. $100,488, or 19%, from contributions and grants awarded by foundations, businesses, and individuals. The remaining revenue came from interest on savings and other miscellaneous sources.

Holy Spirit Association for Unification of World Christianity / Unification Church of America

4 W. 43rd St.
New York, NY 10036 **Phone:** (212) 997-0050 **E-Mail:** admin@hsanahq.org
USA **Fax:** (212) 768-0791

Contact Person: Peter D. Ross.
Officers or Principals: Dr. Tyler O. Hendricks, President; Dr. Edwin Ang, Vice President; Michael Inglis, Treasurer; Kaye Allen, Secretary.
Mission or Interest: "The future of Christianity, family values and ethics." Religious organization associated with Rev. Sun Myung Moon.
Accomplishments: The Unification Church is adamantly anti-communist, and has worked with conservative organizations to oppose the spread of communism as well as on issues of traditional values and morality. Supported the publication of *The Washington Times* and its sister publications. An organization within the Unification Church, the Professors World Peace Academy, bought the University of Bridgeport, in Connecticut, a private academy. The Unification Church claims a worldwide membership of over three million
Products or Services: "Practical personal and social ministry, teaching Rev. Moon's 'Divine Principle,' which explains the meaning of The Bible and Second Coming."
Tax Status: 501(c)(3) **Annual Report:** Yes.
Board of Directors or Trustees: Dr. Mose Dunst (Global Economic Action Institute); Dr. Edwin Ang (Unification Theological Seminary); Dr. William Bergman (World Health Institute).
Periodicals: *Unification News.*
Internships: Yes, three-day, one-week, and three-week workshops. Many affiliated activities.
Other Information: Founder is the Rev. Sun Myung Moon of Korea. Perhaps best known for their well-publicized mass marriages of thousands of arranged partners. Although members are commonly called "Moonies", they view this name as a slur, and most of the major news organizations have concurred. Rev. Moon was a Presbyterian Sunday school teacher in Korea when he claims that Jesus came to him and asked him to "complete the task of establishing God's kingdom on earth and bringing His peace to humankind." In 1981 Rev. Moon, who had come to America in 1972, was indicted for evading income taxes and sentenced to 18 months in prison. The Church says that the U.S. Justice Department offered to waive the prison sentence if he would leave America and not come back. On his behalf, 40 friend of the court briefs were filed by Christian organizations and civil liberties groups. Most maintained that the financial practices that Rev. Moon was convicted of were fairly common place among religious organizations, and necessary for their operations - a view largely reached by a Senate subcommittee that examined the issue. Although many in the conservative movement find Rev. Moon's views heretical, he has been influential in the conservative movement through funding and a large following.

Home School Legal Defense Association

P.O. Box 159
Paeonian Springs, VA 22129 **Phone:** (703) 882-3838
USA **Fax:** (703) 338-1952

Contact Person: Michael Farris, President.
Officers or Principals: Michael Farris, President ($0); J. Michael Smith, Vice President ($0); Jeff Ethel, Secretary/Treasurer ($0).
Mission or Interest: To "protect and advance the freedom to home educate, and protect the fundamental rights of families."
Accomplishments: In the fiscal year ending March 1995, the Association spent $309,298 on its programs. The largest program, with expenditures of $132,998, was the provision of legal information, publications, and representation. Other programs included publications, a radio broadcast, and seminars.
Total Revenue: FY ending 3/95 $1,708,317 **Total Expenses:** $353,300 88%/22%/0% **Net Assets:** $1,355,017
Tax Status: 501(c)(4) **Citations:** 63:88
Board of Directors or Trustees: George Stroh, Ken Johnson, Richard Honaker.
Other Information: Established in 1994. Affiliated with the Home School Legal Defense Foundation at the same address. In the fiscal year ending March 1995, the two affiliates had combined net revenues, expenses, and assets of $4,192,969, $3,131,543, and $3,443,899. The Association received $1,533,011, or 90% of revenue, from membership dues. $110,908, or 6%, from dividends and interest from securities. $59,560, or 3%, from program services including the sale of publications and seminar fees. The remaining revenue came from interest on savings.

Home School Legal Defense Foundation

P.O. Box 159
Paeonian Springs, VA 22129   **Phone:** (703) 882-3838
USA   **Fax:**   (703) 338-1952

Contact Person: Michael Farris, President.
Officers or Principals: Michael Farris, President ($173,940); J. Michael Smith, Vice President ($159,386); Dewitt Black, III, Senior Counsel ($91,574); Chris Klicka, Senior Counsel; Charles Hurst, Membership Director; Scott Somerville, Legal Counsel; Inge Cannon, Associate Director; Jeff Ethell, Secretary/Treasurer.
Mission or Interest: Provide legal assistance for members who home school their children.
Accomplishments: In the fiscal year ending March 1995, the Foundation spent $1,816,232 on its programs. This included $19,490 in grants; $12,000 for Family Protection Ministries, $6,000 for the National Challenged Home Schoolers Association Network, and $1,490 for the Council on National Policy.
Total Revenue: FY ending 3/95 $2,484,652 (-7%)(2) **Total Expenses:** $2,778,243 65%/35%/0% **Net Assets:** $2,088,882
Products or Services: Legal advice and counsel. Standardized testing services for home schooled children. Advise home schoolers on legislation and organizing. Lobbying: the Association spent $109,683 on lobbying, $38,631 on grassroots lobbying, and $71,052 on the direct lobbying of legislators. This was an increase of 27% over the previous year, and 129% over two years prior.
Tax Status: 501(c)(3)   **Citations:** 63:88
Board of Directors or Trustees: George Stroh, Ken Johnson, Richard Honaker.
Periodicals: Newsletter.
Other Information: Affiliated with the 501(c)(4) Home School Legal Defense Association. In the fiscal year ending March 1995, the two affiliates had combined net revenues, expenses, and assets of $4,192,969, $3,131,543, and $3443,899. President Michael Farris campaigned unsuccessfully for Lieutenant Governor of Virginia. Although he lost, he is widely credited for energizing the conservative religious vote and helping the Republicans win the Governor's race. The Foundation received $2,452,627, or 88% of gross revenue, from membership dues. $93,150, or 3%, from dividends and interest from securities. $82,867, or 3%, from seminar and publication fees. $73,333, or 3%, from rental income. $21,777, or 1%, from interest on savings and temporary cash investments. The remaining revenue came from other miscellaneous sources. The Foundation lost $293,273 on the sale of securities.

Hong Kong Centre for Economic Research (HKCER)

The University of Hong Kong
Pokfulam Road   **Phone:** (852-5) 547-8313   **E-Mail:** hcker@econ.hku.hk
HONG KONG   **Fax:**   (852-5) 548-6319

Contact Person: Prof. Richard Y. C. Wong, Director.
Officers or Principals: Dr. Alan Siu, Executive Director; Francis T.F. Yuen, Chairman; Dr. Yim-Fai Luk, Chief Editor; Prof. Kwok-Chiu Fung, Associate Director; Prof. Pak-Wai Liu, Research Director.
Mission or Interest: To provide policy research relying on the market mechanism to solve social and economic problems.
Accomplishments: Currently undertaking a large economic study project that encompasses over 30 economic studies of different aspects of Hong Kong.
Products or Services: The Scheme of Control on Electricity Companies by Pun-Iee Lam, The China Miracle, and other books. Research monographs, monthly lunch talk.
Tax Status: Charitable trust. **Annual Report:** No.
Board of Directors or Trustees: Vincent Cheng, Po Chung, John Greenwood, Raymond Kwok, Antony Leung, Dr. Lo Ka-Shui, Moses Tsang, Patrick Wang, Henry Woo. Academic Advisors include: Prof. Yale Brozen (Univ. of Chicago), Prof. Steven N. S. Cheung (Univ. of Hong Kong), Lord Harris of High Cross (Inst. of Economic Affairs, London), Prof. Sir Alan Peacock (David Hume Inst., Edinburgh), Dr. Alvin Rabushka (Hoover Inst.), Prof. Julian Simon (Univ. of MD), Prof. Gordon Tullock (Univ. of AZ), Prof. Sir Alan Walters (American International Group), others.
Periodicals: HKCER Letters (bimonthly newsletter).
Internships: No.
Other Information: Established in 1987. Many publications in English, Chinese, and Japanese.

Hoover Institution on War, Revolution and Peace

Stanford University
Stanford, CA 94305   **Phone:** (415) 723-1754   **E-Mail:** horaney@Hoover.Stanford.edu
USA   **Fax:**   (415) 723-1687   **Internet:** http://www-hoover.stanford.edu

Contact Person: Michele M. Horaney, Press Relations Officer.
Officers or Principals: John Raisian, Director; Herbert Hoover, III, Chairman; W. Kurt Hauser, Vice Chairman; Bowen H. McCoy, Development Chairman; Thaddeus N. Taube, Communications Chairman.
Mission or Interest: "The Institution supports the Constitution of the United States, its Bill of Rights, and its method of representative government. Both our social and economic systems are based on private enterprise from which springs initiative and integrity. . . More than one hundred scholars examine major issues in economics, political science, legal studies, education, history, and sociology."

Accomplishments: Established in 1919, Hoover is the oldest conservative research institute. Perhaps currently best known for its Research Fellows and their efforts, Hoover was founded as an archive, and remains one of the most important holding sites for documents. William L. Shirer used the Institution's primary source materials extensively for The Rise and Fall of the Third Reich. Aleksandr Solzhenitsyn made extensive use of the archives, as did Barbara Tuchman. Hoover's archives have been prominent in collecting documents from the former Soviet-bloc, and has opened an office in Warsaw, Poland. The Institution is affiliated with three Nobel Laureates. Senior Fellows include: Richard V. Allen, Martin Anderson, Robert J. Barro, Gary S. Becker, Michael J. Boskin, Robert Conquest, Milton Friedman, Robert Hall, Seymour Martin Lipset, Edwin Meese, III, James Miller, III, Alvin Rabushka, Paul Craig Roberts, George Shultz, Thomas Sowell, Shelby Steele, James Bond Stockdale, Edward Teller, Harry Wu, and many others. Recent activities undertaken by these Fellows included: Michael Boskin chaired the U.S. Senate Finance Committee's investigation into revamping the Consumer Price Index. Robert Hall and Alvin Rabushka, the authors of The Flat Tax, were central in defending and promoting a flat tax. Harry Wu returned from imprisonment in China and wrote his autobiography, Troublemaker: One Man's Crusade against China's Cruelty.

Total Revenue: FY ending 8/96 $19,500,000 (est.) ($496,000, or 2%, from government grants) (no change)(2)

Total Expenses: $19,500,000 **Net Assets:** $171,900,000

Products or Services: "Uncommon Knowledge" weekly television program produced with PBS affiliate KTEH in San Jose, CA. Hoover Institution Press publishes numerous books, including The Essence of Becker, Frontiers of Tax Reform, Imposters in the Temple, Private Vouchers, and The Effect of Japanese Investment on the World Economy. Many studies and forums. Extensive archive and library.

Tax Status: 501(c)(3) **Annual Report:** Yes.

Board of Directors or Trustees: William Barclay Allen, Dwayne Andreas, Hon. George Deukmejian (former Governor, R-CA), Andrew Hoover, Jeremiah Milbank, Jeremiah Milbank, III, Richard Scaife, Charles Schwab, William Simon (Secretary of the Treasury, 1974-77), Prof. Walter E. Williams (George Mason Univ.), many others.

Periodicals: *Hoover Institution Newsletter* (quarterly newsletter), and *Hoover Digest* (quarterly academic journal).

Internships: Yes.

Other Information: Established in 1919 by Hebert Hoover before he was elected the thirty-first President of the United States. The Institution was created as a specialized collection of documents on the causes and consequences of the first World War. Affiliated with and incorporated as a part of Stanford University. Hoover received $9,384,000, or 42% of revenue, from contributions and grants awarded by foundations, businesses, and individuals. (These grants included $410,000 from the Sarah Scaife Foundation, $260,000 from the Sarah Scaife Foundation, $135,000 from the Lynde and Harry Bradley Foundation, $132,500 from the John M. Olin Foundation, $66,800 from the Earhart Foundation, $20,000 from the J.M. Foundation, and $10,000 from the Carthage Foundation.) $7,538,000, or 34%, from its Endowment Fund. $4,061,000, or 18%, from Stanford University for operating the Hoover Library and Archives. $708,000, or 3%, from royalties and the sale of publications. $496,000, or 2%, from government grants. The remaining revenue came from other miscellaneous sources.

Horatio R. Storer Foundation

419 7th St., N.W.
Washington, DC 20004   **Phone:** (202) 626-8800
USA

Contact Person: Wanda Franz, President.

Officers or Principals: Wanda Franz, President ($0); Robert Powell, Executive Vice President ($0); Emma N. O'Steen, Secretary ($0); Geline Williams, Chairman; Anthony J. Lauinger, Treasurer.

Mission or Interest: Foundation promoting anti-abortion and anti-euthanasia issues.

Accomplishments: Co-sponsored a seminar with the National Legal Center for the Medically Dependent and Disabled on the theme "Current Controversies in the Right to Life and Right to Die." Also co-sponsored publication of *Issues in Law and Medicine* with the National Legal Center. In the fiscal year ending April 1995 the Foundation spent $40,099 on its programs. This included a grant of $30,000 for the National Legal Center for the Medically Dependent and Disabled.

Total Revenue: FY ending 4/95 $44,009 1%(2) **Total Expenses:** $41,591 96%/4%/0% **Net Assets:** $2,474

Tax Status: 501(c)(3)

Periodicals: *Issues in Law and Medicine* (bimonthly).

Other Information: Affiliated with National Right to Life PAC, 501(c)(4) National Right to Life Committee, 501(c)(3) National Right to Life Committee Educational Trust Fund, and the 501(c)(4) National Right to Life Conventions at the same address. In the fiscal year ending April 1995, the four nonprofit affiliates had estimated combined net revenues, expenses, and assets of $11,508,000, $11,483,000, and $2,264,794. This represented an average 1% per year increase in revenue over the last three years. The Foundation received $42,500, or 97% of revenue, from the National Right to Life Committee Educational Trust Fund. $1,493, or 3%, from contributions and grants awarded by foundations, businesses, and individuals. The remaining revenue came from the sale of educational materials.

Howard Jarvis Taxpayers Association

621 S. Westmoreland Ave., Suite 3202
Los Angeles, CA 90005   **Phone:** (213) 384-9656
USA

Contact Person: Joel Fox, President.
Officers or Principals: Joel Fox, President ($107,000); Joseph Ransom, CPA, Treasurer ($60,000); Trevor Grimm, Secretary ($54,000); John Suttie, Vice President, Finance; Lucille Marquez, Assistant Treasurer; Mark Dolon, Chairman; Estelle Jarvis, Honorary Chairman.
Mission or Interest: Attempts to lower taxes in California by lobbying public officials, and grassroots efforts.
Accomplishments: In the fiscal year ending June 1995, the Association spent $2,814,389 on its programs. The largest program, with expenditures of $1,241,703, was lobbying. $828,712 was spent on educational material. $283,334 on litigation. $460,640 was awarded in grants to other organizations.
Total Revenue: FY ending 6/95 $5,056,968 (-2%)(2) **Total Expenses:** $6,267,874 45%/36%/14% **Net Assets:** $493,731
Products or Services: Lobbying, public education, litigation.
Tax Status: 501(c)(4)   **Citations:** 303:30
Board of Directors or Trustees: Ralph Horowitz, Delores Tuttle.
Periodicals: *Taxing Times* (quarterly newsletter).
Other Information: Affiliated with the Howard Jarvis Taxpayers Foundation, the American Tax Reduction Movement, and the Howard Jarvis Taxpayers PAC at the same address. The late Howard Jarvis was the leader of California's Proposition 13 in 1978. Proposition 13 limited property taxes to 1% of assessed value at that time. Taxes have since risen above that level. The Association received $5,094,872, or 99.5% of gross revenue, from contributors. The remaining revenue came from interest on savings. The Association lost $64,350 on the sale of inventory.

Hudson Institute

5395 Emerson Way
Herman Kahn Center
P.O. Box 26-919
Indianapolis, IN 46226   **Phone:**   (317) 545-1000
USA   **Fax:**   (317) 545-9639   **Internet:** http://www.hudson.org/hudson

Contact Person: Leslie Lenkowsky, President.
Officers or Principals: Leslie Lenkowsky, President ($139,156); Chester E. Finn, Jr., Senior Fellow ($135,000); Michael Horowitz, Senior Fellow ($133,956); Alan A. Reynolds, Director of Economics ($109,928); Walter P. Stern, Chairman; Daniel F. Evans, Jr., Vice Chairman; Pat Hasselblad, Secretary.
Mission or Interest: Research institute specializing in economics, political institutions, education, welfare, health care, science and technology, urban affairs, national security and other related areas. Has a continuing interest in domestic and international technological change and its impact on society.
Accomplishments: Hosts the Educational Excellence Network founded by Chester E. Finn, Jr., and Diane S. Ravitch. In the fiscal year ending September 1995 the institute spent $7,412,644 on its programs.
Total Revenue: FY ending 9/95 $9,328,664 ($305,752, or 3%, from government contracts) 15%(3)
Total Expenses: $9,312,850 80%/19%/2% **Net Assets:** $3,281,473
Products or Services: Monographs, seminars, conferences, books, articles, papers. Awards grants to individuals for educational fellowships.
Tax Status: 501(c)(3) **Annual Report:** Yes. **Employees:** 72   **Citations:** 581:17
Board of Directors or Trustees: Thomas Bell, Jr. (Burson-Marsteller), Linden Blue (General Atomics), Mitchell Daniels, Jr. (Eli Lilly & Co.), Thomas Donohue (American Trucking Assoc.), Joseph Epstein (*The American Scholar*), Mrs. Herman Kahn, Prof. Herbert London (New York Univ.), Vice President Dan Quayle, Hon. Roger Semerad (Asst. Secretary, Employment & Training, Dept. of Labor, 1985-87), Max Singer (Potomac Organization), Dr. Barbara Taylor, Hon. Jay Van Andel (Amway Corp.), others.
Periodicals: *Visions*, *Foresight*, and *Outlook.*
Internships: Yes, contact Linda McDonald.
Other Information: Established in 1961 by the late Herman Kahn. The Institute has offices in Washington, DC, Madison, WI, Brussels, and Montreal. Affiliated with the for-profit Hudson Analytical Service. Operates the Educational Excellence Network. The Institute received $5,962,988, or 64% of revenue from research contracts. $2,541,543, or 27%, from contributions and grants awarded by foundations, businesses, and individuals. (These grants included $828,000 from the Lilly Endowment, $400,000 over two years from the Pew Charitable Trusts, $395,000 from the Lynde and Harry Bradley Foundation, $215,000 from the Carthage Foundation, $150,000 from the John M. Olin Foundation, $144,881 from the Smith Richardson Foundation, $35,000 from the J.M. Foundation, $25,000 from the William H. Donner Foundation, $20,000 from the Sarah Scaife Foundation, $10,000 from the F.M. Kirby Foundation, $6,000 from the Sunmark Foundation, and $1,000 from the John William Pope Foundation.) $305,752, or 3%, from government contracts. $238,739, or 3%, from interest on savings and temporary cash investments. The remaining revenue came from book sales, royalties, and other miscellaneous sources.

Human Events

422 1st St., S.E.
Washington, DC 20003   **Phone:**   (202) 546-5006
USA   **Fax:**   (202) 549-9579

Contact Person: Thomas Winter, Editor.

Officers or Principals: Jeffrey Carneal, President; Mark Ziebarth, Vice President.
Mission or Interest: Weekly newspaper of news and conservative opinion. The name refers to the beginning of the Declaration of Independence, which states "When in the course of Human Events..." "In reporting the news, *Human Events* is objective; it aims for accurate presentation of the facts. But it is not impartial. It looks at events through eyes that are biased in favor of limited constitutional government, local self-government, private enterprise and individual freedom."
Accomplishments: Former President Ronald Reagan said, "As you know, I became a *Human Events* reader years ago, and I continue to regard it as essential reading. *Human Events* contains aggressive reporting, superb analysis, and one of the finest collections of conservative columnists to be found." Circulation of approximately 50,000
Tax Status: For profit. **Employees:** 30
Periodicals: *Human Events* (weekly newspaper).
Internships: Yes, accepts interns from the National Journalism Center.
Other Information: Established in 1944. Owned by Eagle Publishing.

Human Life
2725 152nd Ave., N.E.
Redmond, WA 98052   **Phone:**   (206) 882-4397
USA

Contact Person: Ken VanDerhoef, President.
Officers or Principals: Ken VanDerhoef, President ($0); Eileen Geller, Vice President ($0); Jef Geller, Treasurer ($0); Mary Jo Kahler, Vice President.
Mission or Interest: "Prolife education" and "promoting awareness of the life issues."
Accomplishments: The organization's newsletter has a circulation of 54,000. In 1995 Human Life spent $115,027 on its programs.
Total Revenue: 1995 $256,493 **Total Expenses:** $237,832 48%/34%/18% **Net Assets:** $31,621
Tax Status: 501(c)(4)
Board of Directors or Trustees: Dr. Robin Bernhoft, Hope Braun, Rosetta Brumbaugh, Willard Crow, Dorothy Gill, Dr. James McClellan, Lance Sorensen, Fr. Robert Spitzer, Carrie Stemen, Joan Sullivan, Bob Witter.
Other Information: Human Life received $186,812, or 73% of revenue, from contributors and affiliates. $54,763, or 21%, from program services. $14,511, or 6%, from membership dues. The remaining revenue came from interest on savings.

Human Life Foundation / *Human Life Review*
150 E. 35th St.
New York, NY 10016   **Phone:**   (212) 679-7330
USA

Contact Person: Faith A. McFadden, Secretary .
Officers or Principals: Faith A. McFadden, Secretary ($23,200); James P. McFadden, President ($0); Edward A. Capano, Vice President/Treasurer ($0); Robert A. McFadden, CEO.
Mission or Interest: Publishes *Human Life Review*. The *Review* includes original articles as well as excerpts and reprints from other sources. Awards grants to local organizations.
Accomplishments: Contributors include; Kay Ebeling, Ellen Wilson Fielding, Elena Muller Garcia, James Hitchcock, Erik von Kuehnelt-Leddihn, Jo McGowan, Mary Meehan, John Muggeridge, John Wauck, and Chilton Williamson, Jr. They distribute approximately 10,000 copies per issue of *Human Life Review*. In 1994 the Foundation spent $338,916 on its programs. This included $62,300 in grants for local anti-abortion organizations and crisis pregnancy centers.
Total Revenue: 1994 $521,567 6%(1) **Total Expenses:** $535,964 63%/17%/20% **Net Assets:** $214,722
Tax Status: 501(c)(3)
Board of Directors or Trustees: Faith Abbott, Pricilla Buckley, Msgr. Eugene Clark, Mrs. Charles Teetor.
Periodicals: *Human Life Review* (quarterly scholarly journal).
Other Information: Established in 1974. The Foundation received $498,799, or 96% of revenue, from contributions and grants awarded by foundations, businesses, and individuals. $12,531, or 2%, from mailing list rentals. $4,672, or 1%, from dividends and interest from securities. The remaining revenue came from the sale of inventory, interest on savings, and other miscellaneous sources.

Human Life International (HLI)
7845 Airpark Rd., Suite E
Gaithersburg, MD 20879   **Phone:**   (301) 670-7884
USA   **Fax:**   (301) 869-7363

Contact Person: Rev. Paul Marx, OSB, Ph.D., Chairman.
Officers or Principals: Robert Lalonde, Vice President ($82,042); Michele Lapalm, Assistant Vice President ($43,561); Rev. Paul Marx, Ph.D., Chairman; Fr. Matthew Habiger, President; Magaly Llaguno, Treasurer; Barnabas Laubach, Secretary.
Mission or Interest: "The world's largest pro-life / pro-family organization."
Accomplishments: Oversees 84 branches in 56 countries. Has 12 chapters in the United States. Pope John Paul II has said of Fr. Marx, "You are the Apostle of Life." Mother Teresa of Calcutta said of Fr. Marx and HLI, "In protecting the pre-born so beautifully by using the gift that God has given you...you have indeed made your own lives precious to God. May you continue to protect, promote and build up life and uphold its sanctity." In 1993 they held a World Conference in Houston which was attended by 2,000 people representing 46 countries. In the fiscal year ending September 1994, HLI spent $4,083,850 on its programs. Of this, $156,301 was spent on the Population Research Institute program (see separate listing).

Total Revenue: FY ending 9/95 $6,347,885 22%(2) **Total Expenses:** $5,017,920 81%/7%/12% **Net Assets:** $2,276,523
Products or Services: Information and materials about abortion, euthanasia, infanticide and sterilization. Operates "Magdalene Mission" for the helping and rehabilitation of prostitutes, primarily in third-world countries. "Mary Corps," a ministry to the former Soviet Union. "The Next Generation" program for pro-life youth. World Conference.
Tax Status: 501(c)(3) **Employees:** 80   **Citations:** 41:110
Board of Directors or Trustees: Advisors include: Brian Clowes, Ph.D., Edgar Debany, Michael Doherty, Michael Engler, John Finn, Hymie Gordon, M.D., Richard and Elaine Healy, Carl Karcher, John Little, Peg Luksik, Daniel McGivern, Barbara McGuigan, Charles Rice, J.S.D., Ted and Vivian Rowell, Rev. Albert Salmon, Joseph Scheidler, Bishop Austin Vaughan, Joseph Woltering.
Periodicals: *HLI Reports* (monthly newsletter), *Seminarians for Life International Newsletter*, *Escoge LA Vida* (in Spanish).
Other Information: Established in 1981. Affiliated with the HLI Endowment at the same address. Human Life International received $4,029,659, or 63% of revenue, from contributions and grants awarded by foundations, businesses, and individuals. $948,279, or 15%, from the sale of special reports. $369,225, or 6%, from *HLI Reports* subscriptions. $191,968, or 3%, from the sale of literature. $95,054, or 3%, from HLI's World Conference fees. The remaining revenue came from the Pro-Life Seminarians project, Latin American outreach, interest on savings, and other miscellaneous sources.

Ignatius Press
2515 McAllister St.
San Francisco, CA 94118   **Phone:** (415) 387-2324
USA   **Fax:**   (914) 835-8406

Officers or Principals: Rev. Joseph Fessio, S.J., Editor; Carolyn Lemon, Production Editor; Anthony Ryan, Marketing Manager; Mary Jennett, Business Manager.
Mission or Interest: Publishes books, magazines, and audio tapes on religion, philosophy and social issues from a conservative Catholic viewpoint. Publishes the magazine, *Catholic World Report*.
Accomplishments: Over $2.5 million in sales annually. Former Rep. Robert K. Dornan (R-CA) said of *Catholic World Report*, "Taking its cue from outspoken leaders like Pope John Paul II, Mother Teresa, Cardinal O'Connor, *Catholic World Report* gives accurate, original and lively reporting on critical issues. With a no-fear journalistic approach and a nose for controversy, *Catholic World Report* doesn't just report the news - it makes it."
Products or Services: The Ratzinger Report by Joseph Cardinal Ratzinger, The Quotable Chesterton by George Marlin, The Collected Works of G.K. Chesterton, Joan of Arc by Mark Twain, Degenerate Moderns and Dionysos Rising by E. Michael Jones, The Truth About Homosexuality by Fr. John Harvey, OSFS, and other books.
Tax Status: For profit.
Periodicals: *Catholic World Report*.
Other Information: They accept unsolicited manuscripts. They also distribute for Veritas Publishers.

Illinois Family Institute (IFI)
799 W. Roosevelt Rd., Bldg. 3, Suite 218
Glen Ellyn, IL 60137   **Phone:** (708) 790-8370
USA   **Fax:**   (708) 790-8390

Contact Person: Joe E. Clark, Executive Director.
Officers or Principals: Joe E. Clark, Executive Director ($0).
Mission or Interest: "To create an environment in which families can flourish by equipping churches and influencing public policy makers through leadership, information, and training, Our work includes: social policy research and informative publications, educating and mobilizing citizens for social action, advocacy for citizens acting on behalf of family issues."
Accomplishments: "Organized grassroots and lobbying efforts to pass a bill banning same-sex marriage, and American Heritage Act; organized 'Family Institute Action Teams' in all 118 state representative districts." In 1995 the Institute spent $205,851 on its programs.
Total Revenue: 1995 $286,020 **Total Expenses:** $282,921 73%/26%/1% **Net Assets:** $65,206
Products or Services: Publications, community organizing, fax updates, and lobbying. In 1995 the Institute spent $4,280 on lobbying; $3,186 on grassroots lobbying, and $1,094 on the direct lobbying of legislators.
Tax Status: 501(c)(3) **Annual Report:** No. **Employees:** 3   **Citations:** 15:163
Board of Directors or Trustees: Warren Anderson, Jim Blinn, Steve Baer, Stephanie Hayes, Jim Matson, Leslie Frazier, Byron Tabbut, M.D., John Koehler.
Periodicals: *Illinois Family Citizen* (monthly newsletter inserted in Focus on the Family's *Citizen*), *Community Impact Leader Notes* (monthly newsletter for religious leaders).
Internships: No.
Other Information: Affiliated with Focus on the Family. IFI received $270,842, or 95% of revenue, from contributions and grants awarded by foundations, businesses, and individuals. These contributions and grants have increased by an average of 88% over the last three years. $13,533, or 5%, from the sale of books, tapes, and materials. The remaining revenue came from interest on savings and temporary cash investments, and other miscellaneous sources.

Illinois Public Policy Caucuses (IPPC)
151 North Michigan Ave., Suite 2815
Chicago, IL 60601   **Phone:**   (312) 565-7522
USA   **Fax:**   (312) 565-4460

Contact Person: Larry Horist, Executive Director.
Officers or Principals: Alex Seith, President; Jameson Campaigne, Secretary; Dan Hales, General Counsel.
Mission or Interest: Public policy advocacy with a conservative emphasis on free markets, limited government and traditional values. The organization operates on a unique caucus system. Caucuses will form and dissolve around specific issues as the need arises. The caucuses will serve as catalysts for activists and develop lobbying strategies and plans of action. Caucuses may develop their own divisional budgets, plan special events, and raise funds for their activities. IPPC officers and staff will function "largely as an administrative vehicle and professional support system for the caucuses."
Accomplishments: IPPC's inaugural event featured David Keene, Chairman of the American Conservative Union. Keene was impressed with the caucus concept and wrote a letter to conservative leaders and organizations countrywide calling IPPC "a new and exciting state-based conservative advocacy organization. . . (and) . . . a unique concept with tremendous potential." IPPC has been successful in attracting conservative Democrats to work with a number of the Caucuses. In fact, president Smith is a registered Democrat, and a Democratic state representative and senator have joined as liaison to conservative Democrats
Products or Services: Lobbying, media relations, speakers bureau, conferences and seminars. "Freedom Impact Statements" that evaluates how specific pieces of legislation will affect individual freedoms. "Freedom Score" that rates Illinois legislators based on their votes.
Tax Status: 501(c)(4)   **Annual Report:** No.   **Employees:** 2
Board of Directors or Trustees: Diane Atwood (Alpha Square Television), Frank Avila (Illinois Citizens for School Choice), Jameson Campaigne, Jr. (American Conservative Union), Ralph Conner, Maryalice Erickson (Chief of Staff to Rep. Ray LaHood, [R-18th District]), Daniel Hales, Case Hoogendoorn, Jill Horist, James Perlstein (Heartland Inst.).
Periodicals: *Quick Read* (newsletter).
Internships: Yes. IPPC will design projects for college and high school students for credit.
Other Information: Established in 1995.

Independence Institute
14142 Denver West Parkway, Suite 185
Golden, CO 80401   **Phone:**   (303) 279-6536
USA   **Fax:**   (303) 279-4176   **Internet:** http://www.i2i.com

Contact Person: Tom Tancredo, President.
Officers or Principals: David Kopel, Research Director ($68,000); Thomas Tancredo, President ($57,200); Steve Schuck, Chairman; Patty Price, Vice President; Carolyn DeRaad, Parent Information Center Director.
Mission or Interest: Promoting limited government and free markets in Colorado and the Rocky Mountain region. Promotion of school-choice programs.
Accomplishments: *The Denver Post* said, "In the great debate over the proper role of government in America, the Independence Institute is convincing many Coloradans that government should be limited in scope." Symposiums and conferences have featured speakers such as David Blankenhorn of the Institute for American Values, Gov. Tommy Thompson (R-WI), and Dr. Marvin Olasky. The Institute has a special program, the "Parent Information Center," to inform parents on the conditions and performance of "almost every public school in Colorado," and to promote school choice. In the fiscal year ending June 1995 the Institute spent $357,688 on its programs.
Total Revenue: FY ending 6/95 $472,753 31%(2)   **Total Expenses:** $449,214 80%/9%/12%   **Net Assets:** $89,605
Products or Services: "Independence Issue Papers," public school report cards, video tapes, and other publications.
Tax Status: 501(c)(3)   **Annual Report:** No.   **Employees:** 5   **Citations:** 88:69
Board of Directors or Trustees: John Andrews, Vern Bickel (Colorado Union of Taxpayers), Jeff Coors, Cordlandt Dietler, Lloyd King, Herb Koether, Gary Loo, James MacDougald, Paul Miller, Chris Paulson, Burton Yale Pines (National Empowerment Television), Greg Stevinson, Paul Swalm.
Periodicals: *Declarations of Independence* (monthly essays).
Internships: Yes, unpaid research positions.
Other Information: Founded in 1985. Research Director David Kopel is the author of The Samurai, the Mountie, and the Cowboy, a book about cultural differences and its impact on gun control efforts. The Institute received $206,500, or 44% of revenue, from contributions and grants awarded by foundations, businesses, and individuals. (These grants included $37,500 from the William H. Donner Foundation, $30,000 from the Castle Rock Foundation, and $3,500 from the Roe Foundation.) $93,704, or 20%, from membership dues. $75,000, or 16%, from a contracted project. $28,314, or 6%, from the sale of publications. $21,573, or 5%, from seminar fees. The remaining revenue came from expense reimbursements, interest on savings and temporary cash investments, and other miscellaneous sources.

Independent Institute / *The Independent Review*
134 98th Ave.
Oakland, CA 94603   **Phone:**   (510) 632-1366   **E-Mail:**   independ@dnai.com
USA   **Fax:**   (510) 568-6040   **Internet:** http://www.independent.org

Contact Person: David J. Theroux, President.

Officers or Principals: David J. Theroux, President ($69,110); Robert Higgs, Ph.D., Research Director; Mary L.G. Theroux, Vice President; Harrison Shaffer, Publications Director; Carl Close, Public Affairs Director.

Mission or Interest: "To conduct and disseminate non-politicized studies of the origins and solutions to critical social and economic problems." Covers a wide range of issues.

Accomplishments: In the fiscal year ending June 1995, the Institute spent $796,913 on its publications. The largest expenditure, $441,187, was for the publication of books and papers. Many Institute books have won the Sir Antony Fisher International Memorial Award from the Atlas Economic Research Foundation. These included The Academy in Crisis edited by John Sommer, Out of Work: Unemployment and Government in Twentieth-Century America by Richard Vedder and Lowell Gallaway, and Beyond Politics: Markets, Welfare and the Failure of Bureaucracy by William Mitchell and Randy Simmons. $268,455 was spent on public policy research. $57,890 was spent producing and distributing a newsletter. $29,381 was spent on conferences and forums. These forums included a luncheon honoring Richard Epstein, professor of law at the University of Chicago and author of Takings and Simple Rules for a Complex World. Other luncheons honored human-rights activist Harry Wu, and David Packard of Hewlett-Packard. David and Mary Theroux attended a private conference at the Vatican on the problems facing the institution of families. Participants included Pope John Paul II, and Nobel Laureate economist Gary Becker.

Total Revenue: FY ending 6/95 $1,179,401 15%(2) **Total Expenses:** $1,010,360 79%/14%/7% **Net Assets:** $780,704

Products or Services: Numerous books, studies, and conferences. The Institute hosts a "Summer Seminar in Political Economy" for high school students. Olive W. Garvey Fellowships for college students

Tax Status: 501(c)(3) **Employees:** 12   **Citations:** 125:53

Board of Directors or Trustees: Robert Erwin, James Fair, III, Ellen Hill, Bruce Jacobs, William Koch, Ph.D., Willard Speakman, III. The Institute also has a Board of Advisors that includes: Martin Anderson (Hoover Inst.), James Buchanan (Nobel Laureate in Economics, George Mason Univ.), Richard Epstein (Univ. of Chicago), George Gilder (Discovery Inst.), Nathan Glazer (Harvard Univ.), Forrest McDonald (Univ. of Alabama), Merton Miller (Nobel Laureate in Economics, Univ. of Chicago), Charles Murray (American Enterprise Inst.), William Niskanen (Cato Inst.), Paul Craig Roberts (Institute of Political Economy), Robert Tollison (Center for Study of Public Choice, George Mason Univ.), Gordon Tullock (Univ. of Arizona), Sir Alan Walters, Walter Williams (George Mason Univ.), and many other academics.

Periodicals: *The Independent* (newsletter), *Independent Policy Report* (monthly essays and studies), *The Independent Review* (quarterly scholarly journal), and *LibertyTree* (semi-annual catalog and review of books). *The Independent Review* is a new academic journal produced by the Institute. Introduced in June 1996, the *Review* is carried by bookstore chains such as Barnes & Noble, and Borders.

Internships: Yes.

Other Information: Affiliated with the David and Mary Theroux Foundation. The Institute received $818,873, or 68% of gross revenue, from contributions and grants awarded by foundations, businesses, and individuals. (These grants included $10,000 from the Curran Foundation, $10,000 from the J.M. Foundation, $10,000 from the David H. Koch Charitable Foundation, and $5,000 from the John William Pope Foundation.) $247,362, or 21%, from the sale of books. $59,829, or 5%, from conferences and luncheons. $27,391, or 2%, from advertising. $17,421, or 1%, from interest on savings and temporary cash investments. $11,623, or 1%, from dividends and interest from securities. The Institute lost $16,733 on the sale of securities.

Independent Women's Forum (IWF)

2111 Wilson Blvd., Suite 550
Arlington, VA 22201   **Phone:** (703) 243-8989
USA   **Fax:**   (703) 243-9230   **Internet:** www.iwf.org

Contact Person: Anita K. Blair, Secretary/Treasurer.

Officers or Principals: Anita K. Blair, Secretary/Treasurer ($12,000); Elizabeth B. Lurie, President ($0); Louise Oliver, Vice President ($0); Barbara Ledeen, Executive Director of Policy; Grace Paine Terzian, Publisher.

Mission or Interest: "Fostering interaction between, and professional development of, women and men who support the basic tenets of limited government, individual responsibility and economic rights."

Accomplishments: Produced, in cooperation with the American Enterprise Institute, a study entitled "Women's Figures: the Economic Progress of Women in America" that contradicts the "major thesis of popular media culture that women are victims of their social condition. According to that theory, women suffer from substantial discrimination that leaves them less well-off than men. The apostles of that women-as-victims perspective use selected statistics and anecdotes to illustrate their theory. . . the monograph (Women's Figures) shows how women's wages and education levels are closing the gap with those of men; how occupational choices have influenced wages; and how women are playing an important role in creating small business."

Although recently formed and comparatively small, IWF has received extensive media attention, including appearances or citations on PBS's "Charlie Rose," Comedy Central's "Politically Incorrect," CNN's "Crossfire," NPR's "All Things Considered," "CNN & Co.," and print media including *The Washington Times, Washington Post, New York Times, Boston Globe*, and others. IWF representatives have appeared before Congress testifying against affirmative action, for de-funding the Violence Against Women Act, and urging Congress to reject the U.N.'s Fourth World Conference on Women. The attention received by the IWF has caused critics on the Left, such as Fairness and Accuracy In Reporting, to allege that "After years of ignoring the expertise of women's organizations. . . popular pressure continued to demand a space for women in media discourse. When a group of conservative females came along, they were a convenient way to fill the gender gap." In the fiscal year ending August 1995 IWF spent $166,496 on its programs.

Total Revenue: FY ending 8/95 $145,316 **Total Expenses:** $261,807 64%/22%/14% **Net Assets:** $16,384

Products or Services: <u>Media Directory of Women Experts</u>.
Tax Status: 501(c)(3)
Board of Directors or Trustees: Lynne Cheney (Chair, National Endowment for the Humanities, 1986-93), Midge Decter (Inst. on Religion and Public Life), Wendy Lee Graham (Director of Economics, Federal Trade Commission, 1983-85), Heather Higgins, R. Gaull Silberman.
Periodicals: *Ex Femina* (monthly newsletter), *The Women's Quarterly* (quarterly journal).
Other Information: Established in 1992. IWF received $133,885, or 92% of revenue, from contributions and grants awarded by foundations, businesses, and individuals. (These grants included $100,000 from the Carthage Foundation, $50,000 from the John M. Olin Foundation, $40,000 from the Lynde and Harry Bradley Foundation, and $4,000 from the Sunmark Foundation.) $8,204, or 6%, from membership dues. $3,199, or 2%, from program services such as the sale of publications.

Indiana Family Institute

9100 Meridian Square
70 E. 91st, Suite 210
Indianapolis, IN 46240   **Phone:**   (317) 582-0300
USA

Contact Person: William Smith, Jr., Executive Director.
Officers or Principals: William Smith, Jr., Executive Director ($50,000); Larry and Judy Summers, Presidents ($0); Dr. Ed and Nancy Fitzgerald, Secretaries ($0); Ardie and Leann Bucher, Treasurers.
Mission or Interest: "Provide educational material to thousands of individuals, churches and organizations on issues that concern the family."
Accomplishments: In 1994 the Institute spent $220,273 on its programs, a 25% increase over the previous year.
Total Revenue: 1994 $275,633 32%(1) **Total Expenses:** $271,152 81%/10%/9% **Net Assets:** $35,007
Tax Status: 501(c)(3)   **Citations:** 37:118
Board of Directors or Trustees: James and Marvel Butcher, Maggie Arnold, Dr. Peter and Suzy Scott, Tom and Margie Moore, Donna Hennessee, Richard and Susan Linson, Dan and Diana Hallman.
Other Information: The Institute received $275,633, or 100% of revenue, from contributions and grants awarded by foundations, businesses, and individuals.

Indiana Policy Review Foundation

320 N. Meridian, Suite 904
Indianapolis, IN 46204   **Phone:**   (317) 236-7360
USA   **Fax:**   (317) 236-7370

Contact Person: Thomas Hession, President.
Officers or Principals: William Styring, III, Research Director ($89,250); T. Craig Ladwig, Editor ($65,000); Thomas Hession, President ($32,500); Charles S. Quilhot, Chairman; Stephen E. Williams, Treasurer.
Mission or Interest: Publishes the *Indiana Policy Review*, "a journal concerning human liberty, free competitive enterprise and freedom."
Accomplishments: In 1994 the Foundation spent $408,127 on its programs.
Total Revenue: 1994 $415,033 (-3%)(2) **Total Expenses:** $408,127 100%/0%/0% **Net Assets:** $2,622
Tax Status: 501(c)(3)   **Citations:** 10:173
Periodicals: *Indiana Policy Review* (bimonthly journal).
Other Information: Established in 1989. The Foundation received $415,033, or 100% of revenue, from contributions and grants awarded by foundations, businesses, and individuals. (In 1995 these grants included $10,000 from the Roe Foundation.)

Individual Rights Foundation

(see Center for the Study of Popular Culture)

Ingersoll Foundation

(see the Rockford Institute)

Initiators

806 Devon Rd.
S. Venice, FL 34293   **Phone:**   (813) 497-3887
USA

Contact Person: Marie G. McAfee, Chairman.
Mission or Interest: Helps individuals work for Constitutional rights. Repeal the Federal Reserve Act. Distributes articles from other sources.
Accomplishments: "Information Bureau on all issues."
Tax Status: Unincorporated.
Other Information: Adheres to the line by Emerson, "Every institution that has contributed to American progress has been built upon the initiative and enthusiasm of an individual."

Insight on the News

3600 New York Ave., N.E.
Washington, DC 20002   **Phone:** (202) 636-8800   **E-Mail:** 76353.2113@compuserve.com
USA   **Fax:**   (202) 529-2484

Officers or Principals: Paul M. Rodriguez, Managing Editor; Jamie Dettmer, Senior Editor.
Mission or Interest: Weekly glossy newsmagazine published by *The Washington Times* Corporation. "*Insight* delivers hard-hitting news for those who want a conservative viewpoint with the unvarnished truth! It is a magazine written by the 'old school' of journalists who are, first and foremost, 'dig it out with a pickax and let the chips fall where they may' investigative reporters."
Accomplishments: Managing editor Paul Rodriguez, while an investigative reporter at *The Washington Times*, broke the stories about "the House Post Office, the House Bank" and the Clinton's computer database for tracking supporters and opponents
Tax Status: For profit.
Periodicals: *Insight on the News* (weekly magazine).

Institute for American Values

1841 Broadway, Suite 211
New York, NY 10023   **Phone:**   (212) 246-3942
USA

Contact Person: David Blankenhorn, III, President.
Officers or Principals: David Blankenhorn, III, President ($109,548); Barbara Dafoe Whitehead, Vice President ($68,881); Vesna Neskow, Secretary ($50,806); Jean Bethke Elshtain, Ph.D., Chairman; JoAnn Luehring, Treasurer.
Mission or Interest: "Devoted to research, publication, and public education on issues of family well-being, family policy, and civic values. The Institute's primary mission is to examine the status and future of the family as a social institution. Its more general mission is to examine the social sources of competence, character, and citizenship in American society."
Accomplishments: Vice President Barbara Dafoe Whitehead authored "Dan Quayle was Right," an article that appeared in *The Atlantic*. Blankenhorn authored the book, Fatherless America. Institute Associate William Galston became a domestic-policy aide to President Clinton. Blankenhorn has testified in favor of reforming no-fault divorce laws before state legislators in Michigan. In the fiscal year ending February 1995, the Institute spent $336,476 on its programs.
Total Revenue: FY ending 2/95 $460,029 (-2%)(2) **Total Expenses:** $400,925 84%/12%/4% **Net Assets:** $173,013
Products or Services: Affiliate Scholars program that funds academic research. Rebuilding the Nest: A New Commitment to the American Family.
Tax Status: 501(c)(3)   **Citations:** 174:42
Board of Directors or Trustees: Charles Ballard (National Inst. for Responsible Fatherhood & Family Development), Prof. Don Browning (Divinity School of the Univ. of Chicago), Thomas Garth (Pres., Boys & Girls Club of America), Sylvia Ann Hewlett, Ph.D. (National Parenting Assoc.), Alphonso Jackson (Pres., Housing Authority of the City of Dallas), Louise Oliver (Independent Women's Forum), Samuel Peabody (Chair, Citizens' Committee for Children of New York), J. Douglas Phillips, Prof. David Popenoe (Rutgers Univ.), Bernard Rapoport (Chair, American Income Life Insurance), Ivan Stacks.
Other Information: Established in 1987 by "former liberal activist" David Blankenhorn. The Institute received $449,266, or 98% of revenue, from contributions and grants awarded by foundations, businesses, and individuals. (These grants included $75,000 from the William H. Donner Foundation, $37,500 from the Lynde and Harry Bradley Foundation, and $5,000 from the Philip M. McKenna Foundation.) $6,438, or 1%, from book royalties. The remaining revenue came from interest on savings and temporary cash investments, and the sale of scholarly papers.

Institute for Children

18 Brattle St., Suite 253
Cambridge, MA 02138   **Phone:**   (617) 491-4614
USA   **Fax:**   (617) 491-4673

Contact Person: Angelica Marin, Director of Programs.
Officers or Principals: Conna Craig, President ($24,056); Edward D. Barlow, Clerk ($0); John Blundell, Director ($0).
Mission or Interest: "To stop and reverse the huge growth of state-run, state-funded foster care and to rehabilitate private adoption." Works, mostly at the state level, to make adoption easier and get children out of 'temporary' state care.
Accomplishments: Worked as the only outside consultant to Massachusetts Governor Weld's Adoption reform project in 1994. Many other states have adopted or considered recommendations made by the Institute. The Institute has been featured in editorials in *The Wall Street Journal*, *The Dallas Morning News*, *The Boston Globe*, and in a nationally syndicated column by Mona Charen. Conna Craig has written a feature article that appears in the Heritage Foundation's *Policy Review*.
Total Revenue: 1995 $100,035 **Total Expenses:** $91,339 59%/35%/6% **Net Assets:** $39,105
Tax Status: 501(c)(3)
Other Information: Established in 1994. The Institute promotes cross-racial adoption, and president Craig was herself adopted into a multi-ethnic family. The Institute received $92,520, or 93% of revenue, from contributions and grants awarded by foundations, businesses, and individuals. (These grants included $18,750 from the William H. Donner Foundation. Contributions and grants increased 46% over the previous year, its first year of existence.) The remaining revenue came from expense reimbursements and other miscellaneous sources.

Institute for Christian Economics (ICE)

P.O. Box 8000
Tyler, TX 75711   **Phone:** (903) 593-9124
USA   **Fax:** (903) 593-1577

Contact Person: Lynn Dwelle.
Officers or Principals: Gary North, President ($0); Sharon North, Director ($0).
Mission or Interest: "Publishing Christian, free-market economics, educational materials, newsletters, and books."
Accomplishments: Published approximately 40 books over the last 18 years. In 1994 the Institute spent $165,893 on its programs.
Total Revenue: 1994 $180,312 (-7%)(2) **Total Expenses:** $212,940 78%/22%/0% **Net Assets:** $1,567,810
Products or Services: Catalog of publications.
Tax Status: 501(c)(3) **Employees:** 2   **Citations:** 0:233
Board of Directors or Trustees: Larry Pratt (Gun Owners of America), Robert Thoburn (Thoburn Christian School).
Periodicals: *Biblical Economics Today* (bimonthly newsletter), *Christian Reconstruction* (bimonthly newsletter), *Biblical Chronology* (monthly newsletter).
Other Information: The Institute received $97,573, or 53% of gross revenue, from contributions and grants awarded by foundations, businesses, and individuals. $75,419, or 41%, from book sales. $8,782, or 5%, from dividends and interest from securities. $2,447, or 1%, from capital gains on the sale of assets. The remaining revenue came from interest on savings and oil royalties. The Institute lost $5,087 on rental properties and other investments.

Institute for Contemporary Studies (ICS)

720 Market St.
San Francisco, CA 94102   **Phone:** (415) 981-5353 **E-Mail:** icspress@hooked.net
USA   **Fax:** (415) 986-4878

Contact Person: Perenna Flemming, Chief Operating Officer.
Officers or Principals: Robert Hawkins, President ($120,181); L. Chickering, Executive Director ($102,417); Barry Sklar, Director ($75,345); William Kendall, Chairman; Dr. Henry Lucas, Vice Chairman.
Mission or Interest: "To promote a self-governing and entrepreneurial way of life." Focus on developing third-world countries.
Accomplishments: "Develop and assist resident management corporations in public-housing developments. Have published eight Nobel laureates. Offer books, videos, and training materials on managing common property resources through self-governance. Played a key role at the U.N.'s Summit for Social Development." In the fiscal year ending June 1995, the ICS spent $4,306,446 on its programs. The largest program, with expenditures of $3,175,149, went to sponsoring "research projects and conferences that examine economic growth in underdeveloped communities and countries" through the International Center for Economic Growth (ICEG). Findings are published in books and reports by the ICS Press. These projects receive government funding and $788,079 was awarded in grants to organizations outside the U.S. $503,545 was spent on the ICS Press. $464,123 was spent on the International Center for Self-Governance that produces materials for an international audience, and $163,629 on the Center for Self-Governance that focuses on domestic entrepreneurship.
Total Revenue: FY ending 6/95 $4,894,777 (-1%)(2) ($3,141,451, or 64%, from government grants)
Total Expenses: $4,890,223 88%/11%/1% **Net Assets:** $247,198
Products or Services: ICS Press that publishes approximately eight titles each year; catalog available. Recent titles include: Restoring Hope in America: The Social Security Solution by Sam Beard, Break These Chains: The Battle for School Choice by Daniel McGroaty, Crime edited by James Q. Wilson, and others.
Tax Status: 501(c)(3) **Annual Report:** No. **Employees:** 15 **Citations:** 18:154
Board of Directors or Trustees: Sen. David Nething, James Stack.
Internships: No.
Other Information: Established in 1972. ICS received $3,141,451, or 64% of revenue, from government grants. $1,530,897, or 31%, from contributions and grants awarded by foundations, businesses, and individuals. (These grants included $354,965 from the Lynde and Harry Bradley Foundation, $175,000 from the Lilly Endowment, $100,000 from the Sarah Scaife Foundation, $85,350 from the Smith Richardson Foundation, $40,500 from the John M. Olin Foundation, $24,000 from the Carthage Foundation, and $10,000 from the Earhart Foundation.) $203,616, or 4%, from book royalties. The remaining revenue came from dividends and interest from securities, rental income, and other miscellaneous sources. Compared to two years prior, ICS had increased revenues from every source except for government grants. An average decrease of 5% per year over the last two years in government grants accounts for the average 1% decrease in overall revenues.

Institute for Energy Research (IER)

6219 Olympia
Houston, TX 77057   **Phone:** (713) 974-1918
USA   **Fax:** same

Contact Person: Robert L. Bradley, Jr., President.
Officers or Principals: Robert L. Bradley, Jr., President ($16,000); Nancy C. Bradley, Secretary/Treasurer ($4,000).
Mission or Interest: "Promote free-market approaches to energy and environmental policy." Awards honorarium and grants to scholars and organizations for research and writing on specific energy topics.

Accomplishments: The head of the California Energy Commission has said, "IER's free-market positions on state-level electric regulation have provided much-needed balance to the interventionist coalitions of our day." President Bradley has written articles for Citizens Against Government Waste, Citizens for a Sound Economy, Free Enterprise Education Center, Hillsdale College, and the Texas Public Policy Foundation. His research and publications are widely circulated in the fossil fuels and energy industry, and he has provided testimony before Congressional committees. In 1994 the Institute spent $22,812 on its programs. The largest expenditure, $10,333, went toward the publication of books and articles including <u>Done in Oil</u> and <u>Oil, Gas, and Government, the U.S. Experience</u> (University Press of America, 1993). The Institute awarded $2,283 in grants. Recipients included; $1,500 for the Competitive Enterprise Institute to "prepare and present electricity industry testimony to the CPUC," $500 for the Cato Institute to support the "New Horizons in Electricity Deregulation Conference," and $283 for the California Independent Petroleum Association to write an article on "elimination of the oil export ban."
Total Revenue: 1994 $29,288 21%(2) **Total Expenses:** $32,868 **Net Assets:** $14,431
Tax Status: 501(c)(3)
Board of Directors or Trustees: Jim Clarkson, Prof. Wayne Gable (Center for the Study of Market Processes), Howard Gano, Jr., Dr. James Johnston, Dr. William Leffler (Shell Oil Co.).
Internships: Yes, for researchers.
Other Information: Established in 1989. The Institute received $28,339, or 97% of revenue, from contributions and grants awarded by foundations, businesses, and individuals. (These grants included $2,500 from the Gordon and Mary Cain Foundation. In 1995, $3,000 from the Claude R. Lambe Charitable Foundation.) Historically the Foundation has received support from the American Gas Association, California Independent Petroleum Association, Koch Industries, Southwire Co., Williams Natural Gas and others in the industry.) $855, or 3%, from program services. The remaining revenue came from investments.

Institute for Foreign Policy Analysis

675 Massachusetts Ave.
Cambridge, MA 02139   **Phone:** (617) 492-2116
USA

Contact Person: Robert Pfaltzgraff, Jr., President.
Officers or Principals: Robert Pfaltzgraff, Jr., President ($170,000); David Tanks, Senior Staff ($87,566); Mark Edington, Senior Staff ($56,650); Edmund A. Gullion, Chairman; Marjorie Duggan, Executive Secretary; Andrew Dagle, Treasurer.
Mission or Interest: Examination of the United State's foreign policy and formulation of policy options.
Accomplishments: In the fiscal year ending June 1995 the Institute spent $1,175,343 on its programs.
Total Revenue: FY ending 6/95 $1,837,092 **Total Expenses:** $1,800,317 65%/33%/2% **Net Assets:** $71,751
Products or Services: Presentation of analysis before government agencies and the general public. Training students for careers in foreign policy analysis. Fellowships for pre-doctoral candidates and recent Ph.D. recipients.
Tax Status: 501(c)(3)   **Citations:** 7:182
Board of Directors or Trustees: Charles Francis Adams, William Edgerly, Jon Kutler, Richard Ware (Pres., Earhart Found.), William Smith, Hon. Casper Weinberger (Secretary of Defense, 1981-87), Hon. Frank Carlucci (Secretary of Defense, 1987-88), Stephen Ritterbush, Neil Russell.
Other Information: Owns the for-profit consulting firm, National Security Planning Associates. In the fiscal year ending June 1995 the firm lost $37,932, and had assets of $273,644. The Institute received $941,952, or 51% of revenue, from contributions and grants awarded by foundations, businesses, and individuals. (These grants included $420,000 from the Sarah Scaife Foundation, $101,875 from the William H. Donner Foundation, $100,000 from the Carthage Foundation, $96,000 from the Smith Richardson Foundation, $25,000 from the John M. Olin Foundation, and $18,846 from the Earhart Foundation.) $877,313, or 48%, from contributions and grants awarded by foundations, businesses, and individuals. The remaining revenue came from interest on savings, investments, and other miscellaneous sources.

Institute for Human Rights

800 N.W. Loop 410, Suite 350 South
San Antonio, TX 78216   **Phone:** (210) 525-1500
USA   **Fax:**   (210) 525-9323

Contact Person: Ben A. Wallis, President.
Officers or Principals: John McClaughry, Chairman; Dr. Nathan Wright, Jr., Vice President; Joan Mery, Secretary.
Mission or Interest: Advancement and protection of private property rights. Information resource for property rights groups
Products or Services: Cataloging of property rights abuses. Produced model legislation. Research papers.
Tax Status: 501(c)(3) **Annual Report:** No. **Employees:** All volunteer.
Internships: Yes, during summer.
Other Information: Established in 1978. Previously called the Institute for Human Rights Research.

Institute for Humane Studies (IHS)

4084 University Dr., Suite 101
Fairfax, VA 22030   **Phone:** (703) 934-6920   **E-Mail:**   ihs@osf1.gmu.edu
USA   **Fax:**   (703) 352-7535   **Internet:** http://osf1.gmu.edu/~ihs/

Contact Person: Collette Ridgeway, Director of Student Applications.
Officers or Principals: David Nott, President/CEO ($75,901); Marty Zupan, Vice President ($39,147); Odell Huff, Assistant Secretary ($33,514); Charles Koch, Chairman; William Beach, President; Walter Grinder, Vice President; Andrea Arbore. Secretary/Treasurer; Odell Huff, Assistant Secretary; Leonard Liggio, Distinguished Senior Scholar.
Mission or Interest: Hosts academic seminars "exploring the meanings and implications of liberty, justice, order, tolerance and other values that are the basis of a free society." Recent seminars included "The First Amendment and Beyond," "Scholarship and the Free Society," and "Liberty in Film & Fiction."
Accomplishments: In the fiscal year ending August 1995, the Institute spent $1,457,024 on its programs. The largest program, with expenditures of $1,125,820, was the awarding of 147 fellowships and 4 grants. $183,433 was spent on "student mentoring, career guidance, and academic reference support" for over 200 students in the humanities; also provided these students with books and other materials. $115,053 was spent on their conferences and seminars. The Institute spent $32,718 to sponsor one issue of the *Harvard Journal of Law and Public Policy*, and publish a career guide.
Total Revenue: FY ending 8/95 $1,694,299 2%(5) **Total Expenses:** $1,806,625 81%/11%/8% **Net Assets:** $2,446,282
Products or Services: Awards academic fellowships to attend Institute seminars. Grants to assist the development of young professionals. Annual Felix Morley Memorial Journalism Competition. Residential Fellowships to develop the skills of students planning to work in the nonprofit public-policy sector. Claude R. Lambe Fellowships. Smith Fellowships. John M. Olin Fellowships. Hayek Fund for Scholars. Leonard P. Cassidy Fellowships. Earhart Fellowships.
Tax Status: 501(c)(3) **Annual Report:** Yes. **Citations:** 0:233
Board of Directors or Trustees: Roger Silk, C. W. Anderson, John Blundell, Timothy Browne, Robert Case, Richard Fink, J. M. Fullinwider, David Humphreys, Henry Langenberg, R. A. Liebig, Robert Love, Julio Morales, Arthur Neis, Francis O'Connell, Jr., Eric O'Keefe, Gerald O'Shaughnessy, James Pope, Andrea Rich, William Sumner.
Periodicals: *Humane Studies Review* (quarterly scholarly journal), *Account* (quarterly newsletter).
Other Information: Established in 1961 by Dr. F. A. Harper, a former professor of economics at Cornell University. Located at George Mason University, but separately incorporated. Affiliated with the 501(c)(3) Institute for Humane Studies, Europe, at the same address. The Institute received $1,578,590, or 93% of revenue, from contributions and grants awarded by foundations, businesses, and individuals. (These grants included $335,500 from the Claude R. Lambe Charitable Foundation, $250,000 from the David H. Koch Charitable Foundation, $61,438 from the Earhart Foundation, $30,000 from the John William Pope Foundation, $18,000 from the Sunmark Foundation, $15,000 from the Philip M. McKenna Foundation, $10,000 from the John M. Olin Foundation, $5,000 from the Curran Foundation, $5,000 from the Aequus Institute, $1,000 from the Roe Foundation, and $500 from the United Educators Foundation.) $91,677, or 5%, from interest on savings and temporary cash investments. $23,632, or 2%, from program services, including publication sales and conference fees. The remaining revenue came from the sale of assets.

Institute for Humane Studies, Europe

4084 University Dr.
Fairfax, VA 22030   **Phone:** (703) 934-6920   **E-Mail:** IHS@gmu.edu
USA   **Fax:** (703) 352-7535

Contact Person: Leonard Liggio, Director.
Officers or Principals: Henri LePage, Vice Chairman ($20,353); Dr. Jean-Pierre Centi, Director ($15,000); Dr. Jacques Garello, President/Chairman ($14,226); Dr. Bertrand Lemennicier, Secretary.
Mission or Interest: Awards scholarships and hosts seminars promoting "the principles of the classical liberal tradition" in Europe.
Accomplishments: In 1995 the Institute spent $481,372 on its programs, including $222,237 in grants.
Total Revenue: 1995 $485,389 **Total Expenses:** $596,644 81%/12%/7% **Net Assets:** (-$3,594)
Tax Status: 501(c)(3)
Board of Directors or Trustees: John Blundell, David Nott.
Other Information: The Institute received $485,000, or 99.9% of revenue, from contributions and grants awarded by foundations, businesses, and individuals. (These grants included $120,000 from the Carthage Foundation.) Affiliated with the 501(c)(3) Institute for Humane Studies at the same address. The remaining revenue came from program services and interest on savings and temporary cash investments.

Institute for Independent Education (IIE)

1313 N. Capitol St., N.E.
Washington, DC 20002   **Phone:** (202) 745-0500   **E-Mail:** iie@prodigy.com
USA

Contact Person: Joan Ratteray, President.
Officers or Principals: Joan Davis Ratteray, Ph.D., President ($58,362); Pluria Marshall, Vice President ($0); Alice Bullock, Secretary/Treasurer ($0).
Mission or Interest: African-American organization promoting independent community-based schools and school choice. They emphasize self-help and the need for entrepreneurial skills.
Accomplishments: In 1994 IIE spent $125,360 on its programs, including conferences, workshops, scholarships, teacher in-service programs, and institutional development.
Total Revenue: 1994 $184,926 (-18%)(1) **Total Expenses:** $147,506 85%/13%/2% **Net Assets:** $4,296

Products or Services: Presents several "Excellence in Education Awards" 1996 recipients included State Rep. Polly Williams (D-WI) and Skylar Byrd, a former student of the Roots Activity Learning Center (an independent community-based school in Washington, DC) who earned a perfect score on the Scholastic Aptitude Test.
Tax Status: 501(c)(3)
Board of Directors or Trustees: Oswald M. T. Ratteray.
Periodicals: *American Choices* (monthly newsletter).
Other Information: Established in 1984. Many of the independent schools represented have Christian or Muslim affiliations. The IIE helps develop African-centered curriculums. Although they pursue the goal of more independence from government control, they frequently work with those on the Left. The 1994 Annual Awards dinner featured poet Maya Angelou. IIE received $139,934, or 92% of revenue, from contributions and grants awarded by foundations, businesses, affiliates and individuals. $7,087, or 5%, from the sale of publications. $4,907, or 3%, from interest on savings and temporary cash investments.

Institute for Justice

1717 Pennsylvania Ave., N.W., Suite 200
Washington, DC 20006   **Phone:** (202) 955-1300
USA   **Fax:** (202) 955-1329   **Internet:** http://www.instituteforjustice.org

Contact Person: John Kramer, Director of Communication.
Officers or Principals: William H. (Chip) Mellor III, President/General Counsel ($138,398); Clint Bolick, Vice President/Director of Litigation ($116,146); John Kramer, Director of Communications ($57,853).
Mission or Interest: A public interest group dedicated to the advancement of 'natural rights.' Specializes in litigation directed toward free-market economics, private property rights, and the free exchange of ideas. Also devotes time to educating other lawyers and students about the necessary skills to pursue this kind of public-interest litigation.
Accomplishments: Bolick represented two African-style hair-braiders who were being denied the right to practice their craft in Washington, DC, without an expensive "cosmetology license." Bolick's advocacy won out when the city council allowed them to stay in business. Another case won involved the right of a man to hire homeless people to sell shoe-shines. Bolick was the author of "Quota Queen," an op-ed piece that appeared in *The Wall Street Journal* and was crucial in defeating President Clinton's appointment of Lani Guinier to the top Civil Rights post. In the fiscal year ending June 1995 the Institute spent $1,508,745 on its programs.
Total Revenue: FY ending 6/95 $1,508,745 21%(2) **Total Expenses:** $1,291,642 81%/9%/10% **Net Assets:** $945,739
Products or Services: Legal activism. Since 1992 they have held annual expenses-paid conferences for law students. Clint Bolick is the author of Grassroots Tyranny: The Limits of Federalism (Cato Institute Books, 1993).
Tax Status: 501(c)(3) **Annual Report:** No. **Employees:** 9   **Citations:** 782:11
Board of Directors or Trustees: Manuel Klausner, Gerrit Wormhoudt, David Kennedy (Pres., Earhart Found.), James Lintott, Abigail Thernstrom.
Internships: Yes, year-round, paid and unpaid or school credit.
Other Information: Clint Bolick was formerly with the Landmark Legal Foundation and had worked at the Equal Employment Opportunity Commission and Department of Justice from 1985-87. William Mellor worked in the Department of Energy from 1984-86. The Institute received $1,471,280, or 98% of revenue, from contributions and grants awarded by foundations, businesses, and individuals. (These grants included $250,000 from the David H. Koch Charitable Foundation, $77,500 from the Lynde and Harry Bradley Foundation, $60,000 from the Sarah Scaife Foundation, $50,000 from the John M. Olin Foundation, $35,000 from the John William Pope Foundation, $25,000 from the J.M. Foundation, $20,000 from the F.M. Kirby Foundation, $10,000 from the John Brown Cook Foundation, $3,430 from the Claude R. Lambe Charitable Foundation, $3,000 from the Roe Foundation, and $2,000 from the Ruth and Vernon Taylor Foundation.) $35,190, or 2%, from interest on savings and temporary cash investments. The remaining revenue came from honoraria and royalties.

Institute for Objectivist Studies (IOS)

82 Washington St., Suite 207
Poughkeepsie, NY 12601   **Phone:** (914) 471-6100   **E-Mail:** ios@ios.org
USA   **Fax:** (914) 471-6195   **Internet:**http://www.artsci.wustl.edu/~diana/objectivism/ios/

Contact Person: David Kelley, Executive Director.
Officers or Principals: David Kelley, Executive Director ($56,000); Donald Heath, Secretary/Treasurer ($50,000).
Mission or Interest: "Research and education on Objectivism, the philosophy originated by Ayn Rand. . . Objectivism is a secular worldview that stresses reason, individualism, respect for achievement, and liberty. Institute research, conferences, seminars, and publications deal with Objectivism at every level, from advanced theoretical questions to its applications to political and personal issues."
Accomplishments: In 1994 the Institute spent $205,825 on its programs, including lectures, seminars, publications, and scholarships.
Total Revenue: 1994 $280,424 40%(2) **Total Expenses:** $299,761 69%/21%/10% **Net Assets:** $21,204
Products or Services: Annual "Objectivism Today" conference. Week-long academic "Summer Seminar." Unrugged Individualism: The Selfish Basis of Benevolence by David Kelly and other books. "Principal Source" mail-order service for books and audio tapes.

Tax Status: 501(c)(3) **Annual Report:** Yes. **Employees:** 4   **Citations:** 0:233
Board of Directors or Trustees: Frank Bond (Chair, Foundation Group), Walter Donway, Ed Snider (Founder, Spectator/Philadelphia Flyers), Prof. Emeritus George Walsh (Salisbury State Univ.). The Advisory Board includes; Michael Berger, Frank Bubb (Vice Pres./General Counsel, The Sports Authority), Howard Dickman, Ph.D. (Senior Staff Editor, *Reader's Digest*), Roger Donway (Foreign Policy Research Inst.), Robert Hessen, Ph.D. (Hoover Institution), Prof. James Lennox (Univ. of Pittsburg), Prof. Kenneth Livingston (Vassar College), Prof. Fred Miller (Bowling Green State Univ.), Victor Niederhoffer, Ph.D., Lawrence Parks, Ph.D. (Foundation for the Advancement of Monetary Education), Robert Poole, Jr. (Reason Foundation), Prof. Mario Rizzo (New York Univ.), David Ross, Ph.D. (Senior Research Scientist, Eastman Kodak Research Labs), Ray Stata.
Periodicals: *IOS Journal* (monthly newsletter).
Internships: No.
Other Information: Established in 1990. IOS received $219,041, or 78% of revenue, from contributions and grants awarded by foundations, businesses, and individuals. $60,796, or 22% of revenue, from program services. The remaining revenue came from interest on savings and investments and other miscellaneous sources.

Institute for Policy Innovation (IPI)

250 South Stemmons, Suite 306
Lewisville, TX 75067   **Phone:**   (214) 219-0811   **E-Mail:** ipi@i-link.net
USA   **Fax:**   (214) 219-0372   **Internet:** http://www.ipi.org

Contact Person: Tom Giovanetti, President.
Officers or Principals: Tom Giovanetti, President; David Hobbs, former President ($84,000); Rep. Dick Armey, Chairman; Lisa Hyde, Secretary ($0).
Mission or Interest: "Conduct research, aid development, and widely promote innovative and nonpartisan solutions to today's public policy problems." Focus on 'dynamic' and 'supply-side' analysis, as opposed to 'static' models.
Accomplishments: IPI operates a tax-policy analysis division called TaxAction Analysis. TaxAction Analysis studies the effects of taxes and government spending on the U.S. economy. TaxAction bases its forecasts on a general equilibrium econometric model of the U.S. economy, the Fiscal Associates model, created by research associates Gary and Aldona Robbins, both of whom are former U.S. Treasury Department economists.
Total Revenue: 1993 $373,267 **Total Expenses:** $323,613 45%/21%/34% **Net Assets:** $357,818
Tax Status: 501(c)(3) **Annual Report:** No.
Periodicals: *Issue Brief* (monthly), *IPI Insights* (bimonthly), and *Economic Scorecard* (quarterly publication of the TaxAction Analysis division).
Other Information: Established in 1987. IPI received $364,744, or 98% of revenue, from contributions and grants awarded by foundations, businesses, and individuals. (In 1995 these grants included $75,000 from the Lynde and Harry Bradley Foundation, $60,000 from the John M. Olin Foundation, $50,000 from the Carthage Foundation, and $1,000 from the Forbes Foundation. In 1994, $5,000 from the Vernon K. Krieble Foundation, and $5,000 from the Gordon and Mary Cain Foundation.) $8,523, or 2%, from interest on savings and temporary cash investments.

Institute for Political Economy

1000 Massachusetts Ave., N.W.
Washington, DC 20001   **Phone:**   (202) 789-5260
USA

Contact Person: Paul Craig Roberts, Chairman.
Officers or Principals: Paul Craig Roberts, Chairman ($75,000).
Mission or Interest: Economic research and education organization headed by Dr. Paul Craig Roberts, noted supply-side economist and columnist.
Accomplishments: Published entries on supply-side economics in two economic and financial encyclopedias. Provided 236 media interviews in 1992. Published an article and prepared a book manuscript on Latin American economic transformation. Hosted a lecture by Lord Peter T. Bauer on population growth and economic development. In the fiscal year ending March 1995 the Institute spent $158,221 on its programs.
Total Revenue: FY ending 3/95 $611,610 **Total Expenses:** $239,633 66%/27%/7% **Net Assets:** $2,739,151
Products or Services: Articles, research, columns and op-eds.
Tax Status: 501(c)(3)   **Citations:** 41:110
Board of Directors or Trustees: Gordon Dean Booth, George Champion, Robert Krieble.
Other Information: Chairman Roberts was the U.S. Treasury Department Assistant Secretary for Economic Policy 1981-82. The Institute received $521,991, or 82% of revenue, from contributions and grants awarded by foundations, businesses, and individuals. (These grants included $100,000 from the John M. Olin Foundation, $33,090 from the Earhart Foundation, $25,000 from the Vernon K. Krieble Foundation, $10,000 from the Samuel Roberts Noble Foundation, $5,000 from the Sunmark Foundation, $2,000 from the Fanwood Foundation, $2,000 from the Charles G. Koch Charitable Foundation, and $1,000 from the Forbes Foundation.) $105,760, or 17%, from interest on savings and temporary cash investments. $10,277, or 1%, from dividends and interest from securities. The Institute lost $25,468 on the sale of securities.

Institute for Republican Women

P.O. Box 65301
Washington, DC 20035   **Phone:** (202) 862-2604
USA   **Fax:**   (202) 466-8554

Contact Person: Carolyn S. Parlato, President.
Officers or Principals: Theresa L. Conroy, Ph.D., Vice President.
Mission or Interest: To foster the involvement of Republican women in informed public policy debate. The Institute seeks to "provide critical thinking regarding the challenges of the 21st century." The Institute "will not address narrow 'women's issues'"
Products or Services: One-day conferences, and seminar-type programs around the country.
Tax Status: 501(c)(4)   **Annual Report:** No.
Board of Directors or Trustees: Hon. Elise duPont, Sallie James, Lisa Britton Nelson, Gleaves Rhodes, Judith Taggart.
Periodicals: *Forum* (quarterly).
Internships: No.
Other Information: Established in 1993.

Institute for Research on the Economics of Taxation (IRET)

1300 19th St., N.W., Suite 240
Washington, DC 20036   **Phone:** (202) 463-1400
USA   **Fax:**   (202) 463-6199

Contact Person: Dr. Norman B. Ture, President .
Officers or Principals: Dr. Norman B. Ture, President ($161,549); Stephen J. Entin, Resident Scholar ($94,000); Michael A. Schuyler, Senior Economist ($53,000); Bud Murphy, Chairman; Red Cavanery, Vice Chairman; Robert T. Scott, Treasurer; Rady Johnson, Secretary; Karen McClurg, Controller.
Mission or Interest: Promotes tax and fiscal policies that do a minimum to distort the free-market system.
Accomplishments: "Established reputation for informing public-policy makers of the economic consequences of their actions." IRET has employed many economists who have gone on to other institutions, including Dr. Roy Cordato (Lundy Chair, Campbell University), and Aldona and Gary Robbins (Institute for Policy Innovations). In 1996 IRET published analysis of the two parties' Presidential candidates' economic and budget plans. In 1994 the Institute spent $326,321 on its programs.
Total Revenue: 1994 $639,982   (an increase of less than 1%)(1)   **Total Expenses:** $616,628   53%/36%/12%
Net Assets: (-$83,203)
Products or Services: Numerous reports and periodicals.
Tax Status: 501(c)(3)   **Employees:** 8   **Citations:** 19:151
Board of Directors or Trustees: Randolf Aires (Vice Pres., Sears, Roebuck and Co.), Prof. C. Lowell Harriss (Columbia Univ.), E. Noel Harwerth (Vice Pres. & Chief Tax Officer, Citicorp/Citibank), John Hogan (Dean, College of Business and Industry, GA State Univ.), Paul Huard (Vice Pres., Taxation and Fiscal Policy, National Organization of Manufacturers), John Kent (Vice Pres., Taxes, GTE Corp.), Lawrence Kudlow (former Chief Economist, Bear, Stearns & Co.), Gerald Mossinghoff (Pres., Pharmaceutical Manufacturers Assoc.), Hon. Martha Seger (former Gov., Federal Reserve Board), Dr. Walter Williams (George Mason Univ.), many other members of the business community.
Periodicals: *Byline, Economic Policy Bulletin, Congressional Advisory,* and *Fiscal Issues.*
Internships: Yes. Full-time summer, or part-time fall and spring, for upper-classmen and graduate-level students.
Other Information: Established in 1977. Dr. Ture served as Under Secretary of the Treasury for Tax and Economic Affairs from 1981-82. Resident scholar Stephen Entin served as Deputy Assistant Secretary for Economic Policy at the Treasury Department from 1981-88. IRET received $637,020, or 99.5% of revenue, from contributions and grants awarded by foundations, businesses, and individuals. (These grants included $70,000 from the Sarah Scaife Foundation, $60,000 from the Lilly Endowment, $15,000 from the Vernon K. Krieble Foundation, $5,000 from the Gates Foundation, and $2,500 from the Grover Hermann Foundation. In 1995, $8,000 from the Philip M. McKenna Foundation.) The remaining revenue came from the sale of publications, and interest on savings.

Institute for the Study of Economic Culture

Boston University
10 Lenox St.
Brookline, MA 02146   **Phone:** (617) 353-9050
USA   **Fax:**   (617) 353-6408

Contact Person: Peter L. Berger, Director.
Officers or Principals: Marilyn Halter, Laura Nash, Robert Weller, Research Associates; Robert Hefner, Associate Director.
Mission or Interest: "A research center at Boston University committed to systematic study of the relationships between economic development and sociocultural change."
Accomplishments: Director Peter Berger is the author of numerous books, including; <u>A Far Glory: The Quest for Faith in an Age of Incredulity</u>, <u>Invitation to Sociology</u>, <u>The War over the Family</u>, and <u>The Capitalist Revolution</u>, a book released in 1986 making an empirical case for the superiority of free markets over socialism. Berger defends capitalism as empirically proven to be the superior form of economic organization from the point of view of enhancing the welfare of individuals. But he argues that countries can tolerate a large amount of social spending and welfare, as long as the means of production remain in private hands.

Products or Services: Research. Black Entrepreneurship in America (1990, Transaction Books), The Spirit of Chinese Capitalism (1990, de Gruyter), The Capitalist Spirit: Toward a Religious Ethic of Wealth Creation (1991, ICS Press), The Culture of Entrepreneurship (1991, ICS Press), and other books.
Tax Status: 501(c)(3)   **Employees:** 5
Board of Directors or Trustees: Joan Estruch (Universidad Autonama de Barcelona), Arturo Fontaine Talavera (Centro de Estudios Publicos), Gillian Godsell (University of the Witwatersrand), Ashis Gupta (University of Calgary), Michael Hsiao (Academia Sinica). Paolo Jedlowski (University of Calabria), Hansfried Kellner (Goethe Universitaet), Bernice Martin (University of London), David Martin (London School of Economics), Gordon Redding (University of Hong Kong Business School), Anton Zijderveld (Erasmus Universiteit).
Other Information: Established in 1985. Affiliated with and incorporated under Boston University. In 1995 the Institute received $120,000 from the Lynde and Harry Bradley Foundation. In 1994, $100,000 from the Sarah Scaife Foundation, $17,500 from the Earhart Foundation.

Institute of Economic Affairs (IEA)

2 Lord North St.
London, SW1P 3LB, England   **Phone:** (44-71) 799-3745 **E-Mail:** iea@iea.org.uk
UNITED KINGDOM   **Fax:** (44-71) 799-2137 **Internet:** http://www.iea.org.uk

Contact Person: John Blundell, Director General.
Officers or Principals: Lord Vinson of Roddam Dene, LVO, Chairman; C. Robinson, Editorial Director; David Green, Health Program Director; Roger Bate, Environment; J. Tooley. Education; G. Frost, Trade & Development.
Mission or Interest: "To bring market analysis to bear on society's pressing problems and then to bring the results of that work to the attention of today's and tomorrow's opinion leaders around the world."
Accomplishments: IEA has redirected attention to the importance of microeconomics and the limits of Keynesian macroeconomics. Influential not only in the U.K., but worldwide. IEA and its founder, Sir Antony Fisher, have been instrumental in creating market-based think tanks around the world. In the U.S., Sir Fisher founded the Atlas Economic Research Foundation, which in turn helped to create most of the current state-based think tanks. The Economist called IEA, "The grandaddy of the think tanks." Currently concentrating on deepening understanding in Britain of the relationship between law and economics.
Products or Services: Books, conferences, seminars, and video tapes.
Tax Status: U.K. charity. **Annual Report:** Yes. **Employees:** 20
Board of Directors or Trustees: Managing Trustees: Prof. Michael Beesley, Michael Fisher, Sir Ronald Halstead, Malcolm McAlpine, Sir Edward Nixon CBE, DL, Prof. Sir Alan Peacock, Sir Michael Richardson, Prof. Harold Rose, Sir Peter Walters, Mrs. Linda Whetstone, Prof. Geoffrey Wood.
Periodicals: Economic Affairs (bimonthly magazine).
Other Information: Established in 1955 by Sir Antony Fisher (1915-1988). The Institute is well known for publishing books and series of booklets written by some of the world's top economists. IEA operates two additional units: the Health and Welfare Unit, directed by Dr. David Green, and the Environment Unit, directed by Roger Bate. These two units are located at the same address as IEA. In 1994-95 IEA received $35,000 U.S. from the William H. Donner Foundation, $30,000 U.S. from the Earhart Foundation, and $1,000 U.S. from the Roe Foundation.

Institute of World Politics

1521 16th St., N.W.
Washington, DC 20036   **Phone:** (202) 462-2101
USA

Contact Person: Tom Copeland, Director of Student Services.
Officers or Principals: Dr. John Lenczowski, Director ($65,000); Kenneth E. DeGraffenreid, Professor ($30,000).
Mission or Interest: Academic institution offering classes in foreign affairs and world politics.
Accomplishments: Passed a high-level evaluation of their curriculum undertaken by the Provost of Boston University. The Director, Dr. Lenczowski, testified before Congress and made a number of public appearances. Past faculty and guest faculty have included; Elliz Sandoz (LSU), Valentin Aksilenko (former KGB officer), Joshua Muravchik (AEI), Walter Berns (Georgetown Univ.), Edwin Feulner, Jr. (Heritage Found.), Francis Fukuyama (RAND Corp.), Michael Novak (AEI), Daniel Pipes (Middle East Quarterly), Ben Wattenberg (AEI), Kenneth DeGraffenreid (Dir., Intelligence Programs, National Security Council, 1981-87), John Walcott (US News & World Report), Michael Ledeen (AEI), and many others. In 1994 the Institute offered 17 classes that attracted 80 students, and had 11 principal guest faculty and 50 guest lecturers of national stature. In 1994 the Institute spent $198,262 on its programs.
Total Revenue: 1994 $417,316 31%(1) **Total Expenses:** $379,171 52%23%/25% **Net Assets:** $88,965
Products or Services: Academic courses.
Tax Status: 501(c)(3)   **Citations:** 1:255
Board of Directors or Trustees: Terry Balderson, Donald Bently, Kenneth Crosby (Diplomatic Liaison, Merrill Lynch), James George Jatras (U.S. Senate Staff), Hon. Faith Whittlesey (U.S. Ambassador to Switzerland, 1981-83 & 1985-88), Thomas Phillips (Phillips Publishing).
Other Information: Dr. John Lenczowski worked in the State Department and on the National Security Council from 1981-87 and specialized in European and Soviet affairs. The Institute received $319,230, or 76% of revenue, from contributions and grants awarded by foundations, businesses, and individuals. (These grants included $15,000 from the Earhart Foundation, $10,000 from the Vernon K. Krieble Foundation.) $95,496, or 23%, from application and tuition fees. The remaining revenue came from interest on savings, dividends and interest from securities, and other miscellaneous sources.

Institute on Religion and Public Life / *First Things*

156 5th Ave., Suite 400
New York, NY 10010   **Phone:**   (212) 627-1985
USA   **Fax:**   (212) 627-2184   **Internet:** http://www.firstthings.com

Contact Person: Davida Goldman, Assistant Director.
Officers or Principals: Rev. Richard John Neuhaus, President ($98,778); James Nuechterlain, Editor ($79,770); Midge Podhoretz, Distinguished Fellow ($69,459); Matthew Berke, Managing Editor; David Novak, Vice President; George Weigel, Secretary/Treasurer.
Mission or Interest: "Religion and Public Life is an interreligious, nonpartisan research and education institute whose purpose is to advance a religiously informed public philosophy for the ordering of public life." Publication of *First Things*.
Accomplishments: *First Things* has over 27,000 subscribers. In 1996 the Institute held a symposium entitled "The End of Democracy? The Judicial Usurpation of Politics." The symposium asked the question, 'if the judicial branch makes our moral decisions for us (on such questions as abortion and euthanasia), is our democracy legitimate? And if our democracy allows abortion to occur, is our form of government legitimate?' The symposium concluded that it may be time for "noncompliance to resistance to civil disobedience to morally justified revolution." The controversial symposium received wider attention than most; and some participants, such as historian Gertrude Himmelfarb, considered some of the conclusions dangerous because, "Americans, including most conservative Americans, are too sensible and prudent to entertain such extreme ideas." Judge Robert Bork says of *First Things*, "In a welter of magazines specializing in the ephemeral, *First Things* stands apart by living up to its name. Unfailingly intelligent, graceful, and lucid, it is precisely what one expects from Richard John Neuhaus." Richard John Neuhaus was awarded first place in the 1993 Amy Writing Awards competition for his op-ed, "The Truth About Freedom," which appeared in *The Wall Street Journal*. In 1994 the Institute spent $1,171,633 on its programs. The publication of *First Things* cost $968,704.
Total Revenue: 1994 $1,331,306 **Total Expenses:** $1,483,860 79%/18%/3% **Net Assets:** $379,988
Products or Services: Conferences, consultations, research projects, public education events, and a fellows program. Dulles and Ramsey Seminars, continuing discussions regarding theological issues and natural law.
Tax Status: 501(c)(3) **Annual Report:** Yes. **Employees:** 6   **Citations:** 19:151
Board of Directors or Trustees: James Burtchaell (Congregation of Holy Cross), Thomas Derr (Smith College), Jean Bethke Elshtain (Univ. of Chicago Divinity School), Ernest Fortin (Boston College), Mary Ann Glendon (Harvard Law), Bruce Hafen (Brigham Young Univ.), Stanley Hauerwas (Duke Divinity School), Russell Hittinger (Univ. of Tulsa), Glenn Loury (Boston Univ.), David Novak (Univ. of Toronto), George Weigel (Ethics and Public Policy Center), Robert Wilken (Univ. of Virginia).
Periodicals: *First Things: A Monthly Journal of Religion and Public Life* (monthly magazine).
Internships: Not at the present time.
Other Information: Established in 1989, *First Things* began publishing in 1990. Rev. Richard John Neuhaus was a prominent liberal Protestant religious leader during the 1960's civil rights movement and was a friend of Dr. Martin Luther King, Jr. Rev. Neuhaus later converted to Catholicism and shifted toward conservatism. The Institute received $780,390, or 59% of revenue, from contributions and grants awarded by foundations, businesses, and individuals. (These grants included $100,000 from the Sarah Scaife Foundation, $61,930 from the Lilly Endowment. In 1995, $400,000 from the Lynde and Harry Bradley Foundation, $100,000 from the John M. Olin Foundation, $35,000 from the Carthage Foundation, and $10,000 from the Castle Rock Foundation.) $484,739, or 36%, from subscriptions and magazine sales. $49,859, or 4%, from advertising. The remaining revenue came from interest on savings. Production and distribution of *First Things* cost $968,704, and revenues associated with its publication (subscriptions, sales, advertising, etc.) were $534,598; so it required net subsidization of $434,106.

Intercollegiate Studies Institute (ISI)

14 S. Bryn Mawr Ave., Suite 100
Bryn Mawr, PA 19010   **Phone:**   (215) 525-7501   **E-Mail:** isi@tefl.attmail.com
USA   **Fax:**   (215) 525-3315

Contact Person: Christopher Long, Vice President of Programs.
Officers or Principals: T. Kenneth Cribb, Jr., President ($190,400); John F. Lulves, Jr., Executive Vice President ($95,700); H. Spencer Masloff, Vice President ($92,700); Louise Oliver, Chairman; Charles H. Hoeflich, Secretary; Richard M. Larry, Vice Chair.
Mission or Interest: "To further in successive generations of American college youth a better understanding of the economic, political, and spiritual values that sustain a free society."
Accomplishments: Supreme Court Justice Antonin Scalia said, "It's my pleasure to support ISI, which is an organization that I was affiliated with long before I was who I am in Washington. I was a professor at Columbia University when I first began to take part in ISI's program of trying to stimulate the intellectual debate in the nation's capital." ISI has volunteer representatives at more than 1,090 colleges and more than 53,000 student and faculty members. Over 300 events a year are held at college campuses nationwide each year. Recently opened the F.M. Kirby Campus and Hall. In the fiscal year ending March 1995 ISI spent $2,738,960 on its programs. This included $81,455 awarded in fellowships. Since its establishment, ISI has awarded over 400 fellowships.
Total Revenue: FY ending 3/95 $4,746,850 34%(2) **Total Expenses:** $3,176,465 86%/8%/6% **Net Assets:** $3,372,280
Products or Services: Lectures, conferences, week-long summer programs for college students, Richard M. Weaver Fellowships for graduate students in liberal arts and social sciences, Salvatori Fellowships for graduate students studying the American Founding, training programs for high-school teachers, and the annual Henry Salvatori Lecture. Numerous books and publications - many offered free of charge to college students.

Tax Status: 501(c)(3) **Annual Report:** Yes. **Employees:** 21   **Citations:** 7:182
Board of Directors or Trustees: Edwin Feulner, Jr. (Heritage Found.), E. Victor Milione, Richard Allen, T. William Boxx (Treasurer, Philip McKenna Found.), James Burnley, IV, Prof. William Campbell (LSU), George Carey, Holland Coors, Rep. Philip Crane (R-IL), Richard DeVos (Amway Corp.), James Evans, M. Stanton Evans (National Journalism Center), Ralph Husted, Robert Krieble (Krieble Inst.), Thomas Pauken, William Regnery, Paul Craig Roberts (former Assistant Secretary for Economic Policy, Treasury Dept., 1981-82), Thomas Roe (Roe Found.), John Ryan, Wayne Valis, Robert Miller.
Periodicals: *Campus: America's Student Newspaper* (tri-annual paper distributed free on campuses), *Intercollegiate Review* (biannual scholarly journal), *Modern Age* (quarterly scholarly journal), *Political Science Reviewer* (annual scholarly journal).
Internships: Yes, fellowships.
Other Information: Established in 1953. ISI's first president was William F. Buckley, Jr. ISI is under contract to manage the Collegiate Network (see separate listing). The Institute paid author Dinesh D'Souza $94,000 for a series of lectures. ISI received $4,207,050, or 89% of revenue, from contributions and grants awarded by foundations, businesses, and individuals. (These grants included $1,560,000 from the F.M. Kirby Foundation, $400,000 from the Allegheny Foundation, $400,000 from the Sarah Scaife Foundation, $200,000 from the John M. Olin Foundation, $122,500 from the Philip M. McKenna Foundation, $90,000 from the Lilly Endowment, $75,000 from the Richard & Helen DeVos Foundation, $70,000 from the Lynde and Harry Bradley Foundation, $67,000 from the Earhart Foundation, $65,500 from the Aequus Institute, $50,000 from the Castle Rock Foundation, $50,000 from the M.J. Murdock Charitable Trust, $40,000 from the Roe Foundation, $36,300 from the Carthage Foundation, $35,000 from the J.M. Foundation, $35,000 from the Grover Hermann Foundation, $25,000 from the Curran Foundation, $25,000 from the Claude R. Lambe Charitable Foundation, $10,000 from the Samuel Roberts Noble Foundation, $10,000 from the Vernon K. Krieble Foundation, $8,000 from the Sunmark Foundation, $5,000 from the Milliken Foundation, $3,000 from the John William Pope Foundation, and $1,000 from the Winchester Foundation.) $383,608, or 8%, from program fees. $90,308, or 2%, from publication sales and journal subscriptions. The remaining revenue came from dividends and interest from securities, and advertising.

International Center for Economic Growth
(see the Institute for Contemporary Studies)

International Christian Concern (ICC)
2020 Pennsylvania Ave., N.W., Suite 941
Washington, DC 20006   **Phone:** (301) 989-1708   **E-Mail:** icc@wingnet.net
USA   **Fax:**   (301) 989-1709   **Internet:** http://www.wingnet.net/~icc

Contact Person: Rev. Steven Snyder, President.
Officers or Principals: Rev. Steven Snyder, President/CEO; Craig Silver, Chairman; Prof. Frank T. Robb, Vice Chairman; Dr. David Harding, Secretary; James J. Schnabel, P.E., Development Director; Le Roy A. Witt, Treasurer.
Mission or Interest: "An advocacy and educational organization for human rights and the defense of Christian faith and values. . . Militant Islam, Communism and other forces continue to represent a serious and hostile threat to Christians."
Accomplishments: "Launched a major grassroots campaign to draw public and political attention to the rise of worldwide persecution of Christians."
Tax Status: 501(c)(3) **Annual Report:** Yes. **Employees:** 3
Board of Directors or Trustees: The Baroness Caroline Cox (House of Lords, UK), Rep. Chris Smith (R-NJ).
Periodicals: *Concern* (monthly newsletter that chronicles human rights abuses committed against Christians).
Internships: Yes.
Other Information: Established in 1995.

International Christian Media
P.O. Box 30
Dallas, TX 75221   **Phone:** (214) 484-3900
USA

Contact Person: Marlin Maddoux.
Officers or Principals: Pris Waldie, Director of Marketing.
Mission or Interest: Produces the daily radio show, "Point of View." Focus on conservative and populist topics from a Christian point of view. Opposed to U.S. involvement in the United Nations and to 'globalism'. Focus on 'New Age' education in public schools.
Accomplishments: Point of View is a daily radio talk show hosted by Marlin Maddoux. *Christianity Today* calls Point of View "The most popular Christian call-in show." Majority Leader Dick Armey (R-TX), says, "I don't know what this country would do without Point of View's insights and interpretations. . . Point of View has done wonders to help the American people." Guests in 1996 included; Lady Margaret Thatcher, Gary Bauer (Family Research Council), Morton Blackwell (Leadership Inst.), Hon. William Casey (former Governor, D-PA), Howard Phillips (Conservative Caucus), and James Stewart (author, *Blood Sport*).
Tax Status: Nonprofit.
Periodicals: *Freedom Club Report* (monthly newsletter).

International Christian Studies Association (ICSA)

2828 3rd St., Suite 11
Santa Monica, CA 90405   **Phone:** (213) 396-0519
USA

Mission or Interest: ICSA is an international, multi-disciplinary, non-denominational, non-profit educational society dedicated to the exploration of knowledge and its integration with Judeo-Christian ethical and spiritual values. Co-publishes the *Journal of Interdisciplinary Studies* (JIS) with the Institute for Interdisciplinary Research.
Accomplishments: An issue of JIS on "Christian Political Economy" included conservatives Fr. Robert Sirico (Acton Inst.), and Ronald Nash (Reformed Theological Seminary)
Products or Services: Publications, activities.
Tax Status: 501(c)(3)
Periodicals: *ICSA Newsletter*, and *Journal of Interdisciplinary Studies*.
Other Information: Established in 1983. Affiliated with the Institute for Interdisciplinary Research at the same address.

International Churchill Society

181 Burrage Rd.
Hopkinton, NH 03229   **Phone:**   (603) 746-4433
USA   **Fax:**   (603) 746-4260

Contact Person: Merry L. Alberigi, Director of Development.
Officers or Principals: Richard M. Langworth, President; Ambassador Paul Robinson, Jr., Chairman; Lady Soames, D.B.E., Patron.
Mission or Interest: The Society consists of four non-profit, charitable-educational organizations in Australia, Canada, the United Kingdom, and the United States, plus individual members in other countries around the world, all of whom work together to promote interest in and the study on the life, times, philosophy, speeches and writings of The Rt. Hon. Sir Winston Spencer Churchill, K.G. (1874-1965), and to preserve his memory for future generations.
Accomplishments: Speakers at Society conferences have included Alistair Cooke, biographer William Manchester, Hon. John Sununu, Hon. Casper Weinberger, and others
Products or Services: Conferences, benefits, books, audio tapes, news quarterly.
Tax Status: 501(c)(3) **Annual Report:** Yes. **Employees:** 2
Board of Directors or Trustees: Marianne Almquist, Derek Brownleader, R. Alan Fitch, William Ives, Richard Knight, Jr., Cdr. Larry Kryske, George Lewis, Alfred Lurie, Dr. Cyril Mazansky, James Muller, Jean Smalling.
Periodicals: *Finest Hour* (quarterly), *Proceedings of the Churchill Societies*, (bi-annual), various special publications.
Other Information: Established in 1968. In 1994 the Society received $5,000 from the Aequus Institute.

International Life Services

2606½ W. 8th St.
Los Angeles, CA 90057   **Phone:**   (213) 382-2156
USA   **Fax:**   (213) 382-4359

Contact Person: Sister Paula Vandegaer, President.
Officers or Principals: Sister Paula Vandegaer, President ($10,635); Gary Shuberg, Treasurer ($0); Ann Biondi, Secretary ($0).
Mission or Interest: "Promoting the sanctity of human life from the moment of conception to its natural end and promulgating the high moral ethics expressed in the Judeo-Christian tradition."
Accomplishments: In 1995 International Life Service spent $313,552 on its programs.
Total Revenue: 1995 $539,413 **Total Expenses:** $511,431 **Net Assets:** $246,236
Products or Services: Material support and medical services for pregnant women. Conferences, seminars, video and audio tapes. Pro-Life Resource Directory.
Tax Status: 501(c)(3)   **Citations:** 2:216
Board of Directors or Trustees: Jacki Stuart, Becky Grothues, Felix McGinnis, Licia Nicassio, Louise Walsh, Louise Zeko.
Periodicals: *Living World* (quarterly magazine).
Other Information: Affiliated with the 501(c)(3) International Human Life Services Foundation, and the Scholl Institute of Bioethics. International Life Service received $468,079, or 87% of revenue, from contributions and grants awarded by foundations, businesses, and individuals. (These contributions and grants have been growing by an average of 9% a year since 1990.) $39,210, or 7%, from the sale of publications and videos. $22,167, or 4%, from conference fees. $7,364, or 1%, from dividends and interest from securities. The remaining revenue came from interest on savings and temporary cash investments.

International Life Services Foundation

2606½ W. 8th St.
Los Angeles, CA 90057   **Phone:**   (213) 382-2156
USA   **Fax:**   (213) 382-4359

Contact Person: Mary Barkow, Secretary.
Officers or Principals: Roger Sullivan, President ($0); Walter Conn, Vice President ($0); Robert Barbera, Treasurer ($0).
Mission or Interest: Foundation established to assist International Life Services.
Total Revenue: 1993 $10,086 **Total Expenses:** $3,201 **Net Assets:** $6,885
Tax Status: 501(c)(3)   **Citations:** 2:216
Other Information: Established in 1993. Affiliated with the 501(c)(3) International Life Services and the Scholl Institute of Bioethics. The Foundation received $10,058, or 99.7% of revenue, from contributions and grants awarded by foundations, businesses, and individuals. The remaining revenue came from investments.

International Republican Institute (IRI)

1212 New York Ave., N.W., Suite 900
Washington, DC 20005   **Phone:**   (202) 408-9450   **E-Mail:** iri@iri.org
USA   **Fax:**   (202) 408-9462

Contact Person: R. Bruce McColm, President.
Officers or Principals: R. Bruce McColm, President ($123,746); Lorne W. Craner, Vice President ($98,659); Grace Moe, Vice President ($92,331); Hon. John McCain, Chairman; Michael Kostiw, Vice Chairman; Hon. J. William Middendorf, II, Chairman.
Mission or Interest: Dedicated to advancing democracy worldwide. Although not officially part of the Republican Party structure, they draw on the "talents and resources" of many Republicans.
Accomplishments: Sali Berisha, President of Albania, said "My 1992 election would not have occurred without IRI's help. Albania's first election in 1991 resulted in a communist victory because we democrats lacked the means to compete effectively. IRI responded by training democratic leaders in campaign techniques and by supplying equipment for campaigning in Albania's mountainous terrain. You have proved to be our most reliable friends." In the fiscal year ending September 1995, IRI spent $8,431,273 on its programs. This included $1,118,956 in grants to other organizations.
Total Revenue: FY ending 9/95 $10,731,751 ($10,381,656, or 97%, from government grants) 4%(1)
Total Expenses: $10,573,329 80%/20%/0% **Net Assets:** $400,242
Products or Services: Equipment and training for democratic elections abroad. Computers and printing equipment for democracy activists. Voting monitors. "Freedom Awards" given to persons who have worked to bring democracy to their countries. The recipients of the first award in 1995 were former President of El Salvador, Alfredo F. Christiani, and Nicaraguan Cardinal Obando y Bravo.
Tax Status: 501(c)(3) **Annual Report:** Yes. **Employees:** About 50 in Washington, DC. Many more abroad. **Citations:** 128:52
Board of Directors or Trustees: Rep. David Drier (R-CA); Hon. Lawrence Eagleburger (former Secretary of State, 1992), Mayor Susan Golding, Wendy Lee Graham; Hon. Jeane Kirkpatrick (former ambassador to the U.N., 1981-85), Rep. Bob Livingston (R-LA), Sen. Connie Mack (R-FL), Brent Scowcroft, many others.
Periodicals: *IRI* (quarterly newsletter).
Other Information: Established in 1983 along with sister organizations representing the Democratic Party, Chamber of Commerce, and AFL-CIO. Together they make up the core programs of the National Endowment for Democracy. In addition to private support, IRI receives funding from the U.S. government through the National Endowment for Democracy and the U.S. Agency for International Development. In 1993 IRI received about $3,535,697 from the National Endowment for Democracy. IRI maintains offices in Albania, Bulgaria, Cambodia, Lithuania, Peru, Romania, Russia, Slovakia, South Africa, and the Ukraine. The IRI received $10,381,656, or 97%, from indirect public support via the taxpayer-funded National Endowment for Democracy and U.S. Agency for International Development. $346,969, or 3%, from contributions and grants awarded by foundations, businesses, and individuals. The remaining revenue came from interest on savings and temporary cash investments.

International Society for Individual Liberty (ISIL)

1800 Market St.
San Francisco, CA 94102   **Phone:**   (415) 864-0952   **E-Mail:** 71034,2711@compuserve.com
USA   **Fax:**   (415) 864-7506   **Internet:** http://www.isil.org

Contact Person: Vince Miller, President.
Officers or Principals: Vince Miller, President ($0); James Ellwood, Vice President ($0).
Mission or Interest: International libertarian organization. "Association of individuals and organizations dedicated to building a peaceful world, respect for individual rights and liberties, and an open and competitive economic system based on voluntary exchange and free trade."
Accomplishments: ISIL sponsors free memberships for over 300 members in Central and Eastern Europe and the third world. ISIL's news magazine is distributed to members in over 80 countries. Holds an annual conference - in 1996 it was held in Whistler, British Columbia, Canada. In 1994 it was held in Merida, Yucatan, Mexico. Translates books on free-market economics for Lithuania, Russia, and Romania. In 1994 the Society spent $84,275 on its programs - a 24% increase over the previous year.
Total Revenue: 1994 $140,607 18%(1) **Total Expenses:** $153,679 55%/27%/18% **Net Assets:** (-$3,878)
Products or Services: Books, videos, pamphlets and computer network services.
Tax Status: 501(c)(3)
Periodicals: *Freedom Network News* (bimonthly newsletter).

Other Information: ISIL received $88,896, or 63% of revenue, from contributions and grants awarded by foundations, businesses, and individuals. (In 1995 these grants included $1,000 from the John William Pope Foundation. These contributions and grants have been steadily increasing over the last five years, averaging 14% growth per year since 1990.) $21,192, or 15%, from conference registration fees. $15,125, or 11%, from the sale of inventory. $10,400, or 7%, from the sale of pamphlets. $2,388, or 2%, from advertising. The remaining revenue came from interest on savings, mailing list rentals, and other miscellaneous sources.

Iowans for Tax Relief

2610 Park Ave.
Muscatine, IA 52761   **Phone:**   (319) 264-8080
USA   **Fax:**   (319) 264-2413

Contact Person: Debbie A. Martin.
Officers or Principals: David M. Stanley, President; Hilarius L. Heying, Vice President; Cloyd E. Robinson, Vice President; Jane A. Miller, Secretary; Don Carver, C.P.A., Treasurer; Herbert A. Wilson, Finance Chairman; Edward D. Failor, Sr., Chief of Staff; Jeffrey R. Boeyink, Executive Director; Robert G. Morrison, Education Director; Kim A. Neal-Smith, Information Services Director; Robert H. Solt, Research Director; Roger J. Fletcher, Administrative Assistant; Linda J. Hafner, Development Director.
Mission or Interest: Limit and reduce taxes and spending at all levels of government. Revamp the entire tax system to encourage work, savings and capital formation.
Accomplishments: The group claims more than 51,000 members. Supported and won various limits on property and other local taxes. Claims 34 major victories in 16 years. Supported Iowa's Legislative Resolution calling for a U.S. Balanced Budget Constitutional Amendment. Helped to defeat numerous tax increases and repealed others. The National Taxpayers Union, with whom they are affiliated, called them, "the most effective state taxpayers' group in the country." The *Des Moines Register* says they "turned up some white-hot heat against higher taxes. Legislative leaders say the group is gaining in influence around the state." In 1994 the group spent $613,882 on its programs. This included a grant of $70,000 for the National Taxpayers Union.
Total Revenue: 1994 $798,573   **Total Expenses:** $669,970 92%/1%/7%   **Net Assets:** $1,377,006
Products or Services: "Within Our Means: A Taxpayers' Rights Amendment" program manual.
Tax Status: 501(c)(4)   **Citations:** 21:46
Board of Directors or Trustees: Anthony Berardi, John Giblin, Riley Gillette, Hugh Greig, Edwin Hicklin, Marjorie Kreager, Donald Racheter, Donald Shaw, Jean Leu Stanley, Tom Vance, Keith Vetter, Peter Voorhees, C.H. Woodward.
Periodicals: *Tax Action Alerts.*
Other Information: Affiliated with the National Taxpayers Union and the 501(c)(3) Tax Education Foundation at the same address. Iowans for Tax Relief received $451,152, or 55% of gross revenue, from membership dues. $273,010, or 33%, from other organizations for services. $49,258, or 6%, from a "capital gain reinvestment." $44,232, or 5%, from dividends and interest from securities.

Issues & Views Open Forum Foundation / *Issues & Views*

P.O. Box 467
New York, NY 10025   **Phone:**   (212) 655-7847
USA

Contact Person: Elizabeth Wright, Executive Director.
Officers or Principals: Elizabeth Wright, Executive Director ($21,600); J.A. Parker, Vice President ($0); Dr. Walter E. Williams, Secretary ($0).
Mission or Interest: Publication of *Issues & Views*, a newsletter focusing on "self-help and economic development within the black community."
Accomplishments: Over 4,000 subscribers. One of the first outlets for the opinions of conservative black intellectuals.
Total Revenue: FY ending 2/96 $76,867 (-7%)(3)   **Total Expenses:** $87,320 51%/49%/0%   **Net Assets:** $37,498
Products or Services: Sells books with the theme of entrepreneurship and free-market economic development.
Tax Status: 501(c)(3)   **Employees:** 1
Periodicals: *Issues & Views* (quarterly newsletter).
Internships: No.
Other Information: The Issues & Views Open Forum Foundation received $69,039, or 90% of revenue, from contributions and grants awarded by foundations, businesses, and individuals. (These grants included $15,000 from the Lynde and Harry Bradley Foundation, and $15,000 from the Carthage Foundation. Issues & Views has a record of erratic gift and grant support. In the fiscal year ending February 1995 the Foundation received $37,550, in 1994, $135,850, in 1993 $85,000, and $42,350 in 1991.) $5,763, or 7%, from membership dues. (Membership had been steadily increasing, from $4,931 in 1992 to $13,117 in 1995; then falling in the current year.) $1,323, or 2%, from the sale of books. The remaining revenue came from interest on savings and temporary cash investments.

J. M. Foundation

60 E. 42nd St., Suite 1651
New York, NY 10165   **Phone:** (212) 687-7735
USA

Contact Person: Chris Olander, Executive Director.
Officers or Principals: Chris K. Olander, Executive Director ($133,400); Astrid Kukk, Administrative Assistant ($58,075); Lynn Bruhn, Assistant Secretary ($57,308); Margaret M. Bogert, Vice President; William Lee Hanley, Jr., Treasurer; Daniel G. Tenney, Jr., Secretary.
Mission or Interest: Grant-making foundation that includes conservative and free-market organizations in its awards. Most nonpublic policy awards go to medical research and services for the handicapped.
Accomplishments: In 1994 the Foundation awarded $1,344,870 in grants. Recipients included: $35,000 each for the Hudson Institute, National Fatherhood Initiative, and Intercollegiate Studies Institute, $25,000 each for the Washington Legal Foundation, Institute for Justice, Goldwater Institute, National Center for Neighborhood Enterprise, and NFIB Education Foundation, $20,000 each for the Federalist Society, Hoover Institution, Manhattan Institute, National Taxpayers Union Foundation, U.S. Term Limits Foundation, and Hillsdale College, $15,000 each for Americans for Tax Reform, George C. Marshall Institute, Young America's Foundation, and the Clare Boothe Luce Policy Institute, $10,000 each for the Andrew Jackson Institute, Josiah Bartlett Center, Children's Educational Opportunity Foundation, Independent Institute, Defenders of Property Rights, National Center for Public Policy Research, Buckeye Center, Heartland Institute, John Locke Foundation, and the Center for Education Reform, and $5,000 for the American Studies Center.
Total Revenue: 1994 $1,260,156 **Total Expenses:** $2,127,613 **Net Assets:** $19,663,537 (-7%)(2)
Tax Status: 501(c)(3)
Board of Directors or Trustees: Jeremiah Bogert, Mary Caslin Ross, Jeremiah Milbank, III, Peter Morse, Michael Sanger.
Other Information: Established in 1924 by investment-firm owner Jeremiah Milbank (1887-1972). Milbank was the founder of the Red Cross Institution for Crippled Soldiers and Sailors, later to become the Institute for the Crippled and Disabled now known as the ICD. He was also a driving force behind the Boys and Girls Clubs of America. Milbank financed the Cecil B. DeMille film, "King of Kings." The Foundation received $600,936, or 48% of revenue, from capital gains on the sale of assets. $548,589, or 44%, from dividends and interest from securities. $110,631, or 8%, from interest on savings and temporary cash investments. The Foundation held $8,681,616, or 44% of assets, in various investment partnerships that included real estate, foreign stocks, and others. $5,981,500, or 30%, in corporate stock.

J. S. Sanders & Company / Caliban Books

P.O. Box 50331
Nashville, TN 37205   **Phone:** (615) 790-8951
USA   **Fax:**   (615) 790-2594   **Internet:** http://www.pointsouth.com/sanders.htm

Contact Person: John Stoll Sanders, President/Publisher.
Mission or Interest: J.S. Sanders and Company is a publisher of books by important 19th and 20th century authors in its "Southern Classics Series." The Company publishes fiction, autobiography, biography, history, and poetry. Although not conservative in the sense of the modern conservative movement, titles show an appreciation for social orders defined by traditions, religion, and common heritage.
Accomplishments: Publishes works by Robert Penn Waren, Jefferson Davis and Stonewall Jackson by Allen Tate, Destruction and Reconstruction by Richard Taylor (son of President Zachary Taylor), and others.
Tax Status: For profit.
Internships: No.
Other Information: Caliban Books is an imprint of J.S. Sanders & Co. for conservative political books. Unsolicited manuscripts welcome.

James Madison Institute

2017 Delta Blvd., Suite 102
Tallahassee, FL 32303   **Phone:** (904) 386-3131   **E-Mail:** MadisonJMI@aol.com
USA   **Fax:**   (904) 386-1807   **Internet:** http://JamesMadison.org

Contact Person: John Clendinen, Director of Communications.
Officers or Principals: J. Stanley Marshall, Chairman/CEO ($86,000); John R. Smith, Vice President ($42,713); Susan Christian, Director of Administration.
Mission or Interest: "To influence the public policy process in Florida and the nation with such timeless principles as economic liberty, limited government, federalism, the rule of law, traditional values, and individual liberty coupled with individual responsibility. . . To educate American and world leaders about the economic and moral superiority of democratic capitalism."
Accomplishments: Released a study in 1996 that found "corporate welfare" violated Florida's constitution. The study received statewide attention, and was mentioned in the *Wall Street Journal*. Pres. Ronald Reagan said of the Institute, "The work of your institute, and others like it, will help to ensure that future generations may enjoy the blessings of liberty and prosperity." In 1994 the Institute merged with the Center for World Capitalism. In 1995 the Institute spent $830,737 on its programs.

Total Revenue: 1995 $1,436,773 **Total Expenses:** $1,063,691 78%/15%/7% **Net Assets:** $706,482
Products or Services: Annual International Prize awarded by the Center for World Capitalism. The 1996 recipient was Dave Thomas, the founder of Wendy's restaurants. Previous winners included Nobel Prize winning economist Milton Friedman, Michael Novak, and Czech Republic prime minister Vaclav Klaus. Annual essay competition for college students, the J.E. Davis Writing Award. Eastern European Student Scholarship Program.
Tax Status: 501(c)(3) **Annual Report:** Yes. **Employees:** 10   **Citations:** 35:120
Board of Directors or Trustees: Hoyt Barnett, Jacob Belin, Louise Courtelis, A. Dano Davis (Winn-Dixie Stores), Tom Feeney, Hon. Mallory Horne (former President of the Florida Senate), Victor Kiam (Remington Products), Jean McCully, Wayne Mixson (former Florida Governor), Ann Murphey, Carlos Palomares, Frank Shaw, Jr., Jay Skelton, Paul Tipton (Jacksonville Univ.), Billy Walker, Rebecca Walter. The Advisory Council includes: Randall Holcombe (FL State Univ.), James Buchanan (George Mason Univ.), Peter Aranson (Emory Univ.), Don Bellante (Univ. of South FL), Bruce Benson (FL State Univ.), Kenneth Clarkson (Univ. of Miami), David Denslow (Univ. of FL), Thomas Dye (FL State Univ.), James Gwartney (FL State Univ.), Dwight Lee (Univ. of GA), Susan MacManus (Univ. of South FL.), Richard Wagner (George Mason Univ.), Laurin Wollan, Jr. (FL State Univ.), Bruce Yandle (Clemson Univ.).
Periodicals: *The Madison Journal* (quarterly journal), *Madison Review* (quarterly journal) and *James Madison Messenger* (monthly newsletter).
Internships: Yes, for high-school students.
Other Information: Member of the State Policy Network. In December 1994 the James Madison Institute absorbed the Institution for World Capitalism located on the campus of Jacksonville University, and renamed it James Madison's Center for World Capitalism. The address for the Center is: 2800 University Blvd., North, Jacksonville, FL 32211, (904) 744-9986, fax (904) 744-9987. The Institute founded a new professional association for Florida educators, the Professional Educators Network (PEN), with a grant of $15,000 in 1995. The Institute received $1,326,535, or 91% of gross revenue, from contributions and grants awarded by foundations, businesses, and individuals. (These grants included $7,500 from the Roe Foundation.) $117,572, or 8%, from program services including publications, conferences, and seminars. $19,382, or 1%, from dividends and interest from securities. The Institute lost $26,716 on rents.

Jeffersonian Health Policy Foundation

136 John Tyler Highway
Williamsburg, VA 23185   **Phone:**   (757) 253-2729
USA   **Fax:**   (757) 253-1481

Contact Person: John A. Lanzalotti, M.D., Policy Director.
Officers or Principals: Robert Nirschl, M.D., Chairman.
Mission or Interest: Jeffersonian principles of limited government and local and individual control applied to health care. "Americans should have the liberty, the freedom and the means to choose not only the doctor they prefer, but the treatment they determine is in their best interest. Health care rationing, price controls and limitations on treatment by a third party through third party reimbursement are alien concepts and are abhorrent to many Americans." Supports Medical Savings Accounts.
Accomplishments: Developed "The American Health Care Plan" designed to "provide financing mechanisms and political/economic strategies for government to use in reshaping the medical market place."
Tax Status: For profit. **Annual Report:** No.
Board of Directors or Trustees: Louis Williams, M.D., John O'Banyon, III, M.D., Harold Williams, M.D.
Other Information: Established in 1993. Chairman Robert Nirschl, M.D., is the director of the Arlington Hospital Virginia Sports Medicine Institute Orthopedic Fellowship Program. Program director and vice chairman John Lanzalotti, M.D., is an Associate Professor at the College of William and Mary.

Jesse Helms Center Foundation

3918 U.S. Highway 74 East
Wingate, NC 28174   **Phone:**   (704) 233-1776
USA   **Fax:**   (704) 233-1787

Contact Person: John Dodd, President.
Officers or Principals: C. C. Dickson, Chairman.
Mission or Interest: "To preserve and promote the principals of traditional values, democratic government and free enterprise upon which U.S. Senator Jesse Helms (R-NC) has built his life and his career."
Accomplishments: Hosted U.S. Secretary of State Madeleine Albright at Wingate College, where she delivered a major foreign policy speech at a "Jesse Helms Lecture."
Tax Status: 501(c)(3)   **Annual Report:** No.   **Employees:** 3
Products or Services: Lecture series, Free Enterprise Leadership Conference for high-school students, and archives of Senator Helms's Senate papers.
Periodicals: *The Standard* (newsletter).
Other Information: Established in 1990, began program operations in 1994. Senator Helms gained prominence in the 1960s as a conservative radio commentator. In 1972 he was elected to the U.S. Senate from North Carolina, where he has served since. He currently chairs the Senate Foreign Relations Committee. Senator Helms's papers were donated to the archives at Wingate College, but they are on "permanent loan" to the Foundation. The Foundation also makes frequent use of Wingate College's facilities, but the two are separately incorporated. In 1995 the Foundation received $35,000 from the John William Pope Foundation, and $25,000 from the John M. Olin Foundation.

Jewish Policy Center (JPC)

415 2nd St., N.E., Suite 100
Washington, DC 20002   **Phone:** (202) 547-7706   **E-Mail:** 73512.2351@compuserve.com
USA   **Fax:** (202) 544-2434

Contact Person: Joseph Rubin, Coordinator.
Officers or Principals: Matthew Brooks, Executive Director ($39,704); Sheldon Kamins, Chairman ($0); Michael Epstein, Vice Chairman ($0); Marshall Breger, Vice Chairman; .
Mission or Interest: To "identify politically conservative Jews, and to convince the historically liberal Jewish community that conservative answers to today's problems are more effective than the failed liberalism of the last 30 years."
Accomplishments: JPC Fellow Midge Decter testified before the House Ways and Means Committee on behalf of the proposed per-child tax credit. JPC has sponsored seminars and conferences featuring its Board of Fellows, including film critic Michael Medved, Irving Kristol (National Affairs), Norman Podhoretz (*Commentary*), and Dennis Prager (Center for Ethical Monotheism).
Total Revenue: 1995 $136,367 **Total Expenses:** $145,480 62%/28%/10% **Net Assets:** (-$72,450)
Tax Status: 501(c)(3) **Annual Report:** No. **Employees:** 7
Board of Directors or Trustees: Herbert Ascherman, J. Morton Davis, Richard Fox, Norman Freidkin, Dr. Paul Friedman, Gary Polland, Betty Sembler, Steven Some, Arnold Thaler. Fellows include: Midge Decter (Inst. on Religion and Public Life), Prof. Rabbi Samuel Dresner (Jewish Theological Seminary in NY), Murray Friedman (Center for American Jewish History, Temple Univ.), Irving Kristol (National Affairs), Rabbi Daniel Lapin (Toward Tradition), Michael Medved (film critic), Prof. David Novak (Union for Traditional Judaism), Daniel Pipes (Foreign Policy Research Inst.), Norman Podhoretz (former editor-in-chief, *Commentary*), Dennis Prager (Center for Ethical Monotheism), Prof. Ruth Wisse (Harvard Univ.).
Periodicals: *Details* (quarterly newsletter), and *For the Record* (periodic commentaries).
Internships: Yes, paid.
Other Information: Affiliated with the 501(c)(4) National Jewish Coalition at the same address. The Center received $134,571, or 99% of revenue, from contributions and grants awarded by foundations, businesses, and individuals. (These contributions have been growing by an average of 8% a year since 1991.) The remaining revenue came from interest on savings, and interest and dividends from securities.

Jews for the Preservation of Firearms Ownership (JPFO)

2872 S. Wentworth Ave.
Milwaukee, WI 53207   **Phone:** (414) 769-0760
USA   **Fax:** (414) 483-8435

Contact Person: Aaron S. Zelman, Executive Director.
Officers or Principals: Aaron S. Zelman, Executive Director ($26,795); Jay Edward Simkin, Research Director; Alan M. Rice, Board Member.
Mission or Interest: Firearms owners' rights organization. JPFO concentrates on the Jewish people and their need for self-defense (although JPFO is open to anyone).
Accomplishments: Approximately 5,300 members. JPFO has a reputation in the firearms owners' rights community as being single minded and unwilling to compromise. "Until JPFO was established. . . gun-grabbers were almost immune from criticism: they could silence a critic with an accusation of 'anti-semitism.' JPFO members believe they have a duty to their misguided brothers and sisters. . . In the last 2,000 years, Jews have suffered horribly because they were almost always disarmed." Have produced numerous studies appearing in *The Wall Street Journal, Guns & Ammo, The Orlando Sentinel, The Washington Times, Shotgun News,* and others. JPFO published the controversial book, Gun Control: Gateway to Tyranny, showing, through translations and analysis, the parallels between the United States' Gun Control Act of 1968 and gun control laws passed in Nazi Germany. Produced posters and bumper stickers depicting Adolph Hitler giving the Nazi straight-arm salute, accompanied with the statement "All in Favor of Gun Control Raise Your Right Hand." In 1995 JPFO spent $99,504 on its programs.
Total Revenue: 1994 $114,186 **Total Expenses:** $110,264 90%/10%/0% **Net Assets:** $132,078
Products or Services: Reports, op-eds, analysis, more.
Tax Status: 501(c)(3) **Annual Report:** Yes. **Employees:** One full-time, several volunteers.
Periodicals: *The Firearms Sentinel* (monthly academic magazine).
Internships: No.
Other Information: Established in 1989. JPFO received $106,011, or 93% of revenue, from membership dues. (Membership dues were down from $175,061 in 1994, but up considerably from $2,600 in 1993.) $4,545 net, or 4%, from the sale of inventory. $3,630, or 3%, from interest on savings and temporary cash investments.

John Birch Society

770 Westhill Blvd.
Appleton, WI 54914   **Phone:** (414) 749-3780   **E-Mail:** birch@execpc.com
USA   **Fax:** (414) 749-5062   **Internet:** http://www.jbs.org

Contact Person: John F. McManus, President.

Officers or Principals: John F. McManus, President; G. Vance Smith, CEO; Thomas G. Gow, Vice President.

Mission or Interest: "To create an informed electorate through programs of education and action by a grassroots organization of citizens dedicated to proclaiming the constitutional values of Americanism in order to bring about less government, more responsibility, and with God's help, a better world." Primarily concerned with protecting American sovereignty from perceived elite global conspirators, and protecting individual rights from government encroachment. Strongly opposed to United States involvement with the United Nations.

Accomplishments: The John Birch Society has experienced renewed popularity in the last decade. National membership has been estimated to be at least 40,000 members. The Society's populism and belief that a socialist "New World Order" is being imposed on Americans by elites in government, business and the media have made them influential in the militia movement and other anti-big-government movements, especially in the West and Midwest. A 1995 speech by president McManus in Michigan drew more than 400 people. Membership growth has occurred largely among people under 40 years of age. The Society helped defeat the proposed "Conference of the States" in 1995. The Conference was going to be a meeting of representatives from all 50 states to discuss the roles of governing at various levels of government. The John Birch Society took a leading role among populists and conservatives in opposing the Conference based on the belief that it could become a Constitutional Convention, and threaten the Bill of Rights. Furthermore, the Society maintained that the proper roles of state and federal government was already set forth in the 10th Amendment. Also opposed other calls for a Constitutional Convention. "Distributed more than 8 million" congressional report cards. Created the TRIM (Tax Reform IMmediately) project to advocate lower taxes and reduced government. In 1996 the Society's flagship magazine, *The New American*, became accessible through newsstands nationwide.

Products or Services: Voters' guides. The Insiders: Architects of the New World Order and other books. Speakers bureau. Licenses a "small chain of bookstore franchises" called American Opinion.

Tax Status: Nonprofit, but without the Federal nonprofit designation of 501(c)(3), which it has never sought.

Annual Report: No. **Employees:** 90

Periodicals: *The New American* (bi-weekly magazine), and *JBS Bulletin* (monthly newsletter).

Internships: No.

Other Information: Established in 1958 by candy manufacturer Robert Welch (1899-1985). The Society is named after Capt. John Birch who was a Christian missionary in China at the start of World War II. During the war he was an intelligence officer behind enemy lines in Japan where he directed U.S. raids by radio and rescued Col. Jimmy Doolittle after his bombing mission. After World War II he served in China, were he was killed by Chinese Communists, making him "the first casualty of the Cold War." Affiliated with the for-profit American Opinion Publishing that produces *The New American* and other products, and the nonprofit Robert Welch University. The Society believes that powerful elites seek to govern the world through a single, socialist, world government. Central to this conspiracy are the United Nations, Council on Foreign Relations (CFR), Trilateral Commission, Bilderbergers, and the Rockefeller family. The Society believes that because institutions such as the Council on Foreign Relations were founded largely by socialists, and American involvement in the United Nations was heavily influenced by Soviet agents such as Alger Hiss, Harry Dexter White, and Victor Perlo, they are irrevocably opposed to the American democratic system and represent a significant threat. Furthermore, the fact that the CFR and the Trilateral Commission have memberships composed of so many prominent elites from government, the media, and business, the conspiracy must be very powerful and far-reaching. According to the Society, because organizations advocating socialism and multi-national or world governance exist, any movement toward socialism or world government in the United States can only be explained as the result of these organizations' efforts; no other correlation or coincidence can explain it.

John Brown Cook Foundation

205 Church St., 9th Floor
New Haven, CT 06509
USA

Contact Person: William R. Murphy, Secretary.

Officers or Principals: Marian M. Cook, Chairman ($0); Harold C. Ripley, Vice Chairman ($0); Gregory M. Cook, President ($0); Leo C. McKenna, Treasurer; Wallis Cook, Vice President; Bruce Lewellyn, Assistant Secretary.

Mission or Interest: Grant-making foundation that includes conservative groups in its awards.

Accomplishments: In the fiscal year ending October 1995 the Foundation awarded $165,000 in grants. Recipients included: $10,000 each for the Washington Legal Foundation, Institute of Justice, and the National Center for Neighborhood Enterprise.

Total Revenue: FY ending 10/95 $227,196 **Total Expenses:** $182,031 **Net Assets:** $2,076,457

Tax Status: 501(c)(3)

Other Information: The Foundation received $120,000, or 53% of revenue, from a grant from the Marian Miner Cook 1987 Charitable Annuity Trust. $87,669, or 39%, from dividends and interest from securities. $16,942, or 7%, from capital gains on the sale of assets. The remaining revenue came from interest on savings and temporary cash investments. The Foundation held $1,198,259, or 58% of assets, in corporate stock. $346,433, or 17%, in corporate bonds.

John Locke Foundation

1304 Hillsborough St.
Raleigh, NC 27605   **Phone:** (919) 828-3876   **E-Mail:** locke@interpath.com
USA   **Fax:**   (919) 821-5117

Contact Person: John Hood, Vice President.
Officers or Principals: Marc E. Rotterman, President ($53,012); John Hood, Vice President ($32,786); Art Zeidman, Secretary/Treasurer ($0); Arthur Pope, Chairman.
Mission or Interest: "State policy think tank with a free-market orientation and interest in issues such as health care, taxes, state budget, and education."
Accomplishments: "Succeeded in pushing budget reforms in the state legislature and tenure and teaching reforms at state universities." Numerous media appearances. In the fiscal year ending June 1994 the Foundation spent $359,116 on its programs.
Total Revenue: FY ending 6/94 $425,712 81%(1) **Total Expenses:** $403,751 **Net Assets:** $22,042
Products or Services: Luncheons, studies, publications.
Tax Status: 501(c)(3) **Annual Report:** Yes. **Employees:** 4 **Citations:** 1:225
Board of Directors or Trustees: Bruce Babcock, John Carrington, N.W. Chalmers, Thomas Fetzer, William Graham, Kevin Kennelly, Robert Luddy, Ralph McMillan, Burley Mitchell, Robert Pittenger, Tula Carter Robbins, David Stover, Arthur Zeidman.
Periodicals: *Carolina Journal* (bimonthly magazine).
Internships: Yes, for students at local colleges.
Other Information: Established in 1990. Member of the State Policy Network. The Foundation received $373,174, or 88% of revenue, from contributions and grants awarded by foundations, businesses, and individuals. (These grants included $131,000 from the John William Pope Foundation, $15,000 from the Smith Richardson Foundation, $10,000 from the J.M. Foundation, $8,500 from the Atlas Economic Research Foundation, and $7,000 from the Roe Foundation. In 1995, $82,000 from the John William Pope Foundation, and $12,000 from the Charles G. Koch Charitable Foundation.) $52,179, or 12%, from conference fees and the sale of publications. The remaining revenue came from interest on savings and temporary cash investments.

John M. Ashbrook Center for Public Affairs

Ashland University
Ashland, OH 44805   **Phone:** (419) 289-5411
USA   **Fax:**   (419) 289-5425

Contact Person: Tom Roepke, Assistant to the Director.
Officers or Principals: Dr. Bradford P. Wilson, Deputy Director; Dr. Peter Schramm, Coordinator of Special Programs; Fred Lennon, Chairman Emeritus; William Rusher, Chairman; Thomas Van Meter, Vice Chairman.
Mission or Interest: The Ashbrook Center is an" academic forum for the study, research and discussion of the principles and practices of American constitutional government and politics." Named after conservative Congressman John Ashbrook who died in 1982 while campaigning for the U.S. Senate.
Accomplishments: Sponsoring a scholarship program, campus lecture series, and aiding students with career preparations.
Products or Services: Publications.
Tax Status: 501(c)(3) **Employees:** 5
Board of Directors or Trustees: Rep. Philip Crane (R-IL), Phyllis Schlafly (Pres., Eagle Forum), Victor Lasky, many others.
Periodicals: *Ashbrook Essays, Res Publica* (student publication).
Internships: Yes, internship program available for all scholars.
Other Information: Established in 1983. In 1994-95 the Center received $1,780 from the Earhart Foundation, and $1,000 from the John William Pope Foundation.

John M. Olin Foundation

330 Madison Ave., 22nd Floor
New York, NY 10017   **Phone:** (212) 661-2670
USA   **Fax:**   (212) 661-5917

Contact Person: James Piereson, Executive Director.
Officers or Principals: James Piereson, Executive Director ($293,750); Caroline McMullen Hemphill, Director of Special Programs ($125,000); William Voegeli, Program Officer ($118,750); William E. Simon, President; George J. Gillespie, III, Secretary/Treasurer.
Mission or Interest: "To provide support for projects that reflect or are intended to strengthen the economic, political and cultural institutions upon which the American heritage of constitutional government and private enterprise is based."
Accomplishments: In 1995 the Foundation awarded $16,190,207 in grants. Recipients included: six grants totaling $649,185 for the American Enterprise Institute, five grants totaling $581,400 for the Heritage Foundation, six grants totaling $322,500 for the Manhattan Institute, $250,000 for the production of "Firing Line" with William F. Buckley, Jr., two grants totaling $225,000 for the Foundation for Cultural Review, $200,000 each for the Center for the Study of Popular Culture, and Intercollegiate Studies Institute, $170,000 for the Federalist Society, $150,000 each for the Equal Opportunity Foundation, Hudson Institute, and Foreign Policy Research Institute, $132,500 for the Hoover Institution, $125,000 each for the Ethics and Public Policy Center, and National Association of Scholars, $115,000 for Radio America, $100,000 each for the Brookings Institution, Center for the Study of American Business, Institute for Political Economy, Institute on Religion and Public Life, National Alumni Forum, National Center for Policy Analysis, National Right to Work Legal Defense Foundation, New Citizenship Project, Social Philosophy and Policy Center, Washington Legal Foundation, and Council on Foreign Relations, $80,000 each for the Center for Individual Rights, and Progress & Freedom Foundation, $75,000 each for the American Spectator Educational Foundation, Employment Policy Foundation, National

Affairs, Statistical Assessment Service, and Claremont Institute, $60,000 each for the American Jewish Committee, National Taxpayers Union Foundation, Pacific Legal Foundation, and Institute for Policy Innovation, $50,000 each for the American Council on Science and Health, Becket Fund for Religious Liberty, Cato Institute, Center for Education Reform, Center for New Black Leadership, Center for Strategic and International Studies, Free Congress Foundation, Independent Women's Forum, Institute for Justice, Media Research Center, Pacific Research Institute, Philanthropy Roundtable, and Political Economy Research Center. The Foundation also funded a number of fellowships, chairs, and research grants for various professors, including: Christina Hoff Sommers (Clark Univ.), Walter E. Williams (George Mason Univ.), Eliot Cohen (Johns Hopkins Univ.), Herbert London (New York Univ.), Diane Ravitch (New York Univ.), Michael Boskin (Stanford Univ.), Gary Becker (Univ. of Chicago), Richard Epstein (Univ. of Chicago), and George Priest (Yale Law School).

Total Revenue: 1995 $12,338,632 **Total Expenses:** $18,626,716 **Net Assets:** $121,670,261 9%(6)
Tax Status: 501(c)(3) **Annual Report:** Yes. **Employees:** 7
Board of Directors or Trustees: Peter Flanigan, Richard Furlaud, Charles Knight, Eugene Williams, Jr.
Internships: Yes, one per year.
Other Information: Established in 1953 by John Merrill Olin (1892-1982). The Foundation received $6,181,926, or 74% of revenue, from capital gains on the sale of assets. $3,173,311, or 26%, from dividends and interest from securities. $1,819,033, or 15%, from contributions and grants. $1,164,362, or 9%, from interest on savings and temporary cash investments. The Foundation held $54,171,005, or 44% of assets, in mutual funds. $25,504,666, or 21%, in corporate stock.

John Templeton Foundation

P.O. Box 8322
Radnor, PA 19087   **Phone:** (610) 687-8942   **E-Mail:** info@templeton.org
USA   **Internet:** http://www.templeton.org

Contact Person: Frances Schapperle, Director.
Officers or Principals: Frances Schapperle, Director ($55,000); Harvey M. Templeton, III, Secretary ($3,053); Ann Cameron, Treasurer ($2,575); Dr. John Marks Templeton, Jr., President; Sir John Marks Templeton, Chairman.
Mission or Interest: Grant-making philanthropy that focuses on religion, scientific research, and free enterprise.
Accomplishments: In the fiscal year ending March 1993 the Foundation awarded $765,237 in grants. Recipients included; $20,000 for the American Family Association, $13,497 for the Foundation for Economic Education, and $2,000 for the Institute for Humane Studies.
Total Revenue: FY ending 3/93 $2,593,185 **Total Expenses:** $993,060 **Net Assets:** $6,715,816
Products or Services: Awards the "John Templeton Foundation Honor Roll for Free Enterprise Teaching" to higher education programs that "teach the principles and benefits of free market economic systems." The Foundation for Economic Education is commissioned to review the college and university programs. Also awards the "Templeton Prize for Progress in Religion" to "recognize frontier thinking in religion that contributes to humanity's understanding of God, spirituality and the universe."
Tax Status: 501(c)(3)
Board of Directors or Trustees: Dr. Anne Zimmerman, Dr. Paul Davies, Dr. Robert Herrmann, Rev. Bryant Kirkland, Rev. Glenn Mosley, Dr. David Myers, S.B. Rymer, Hon. William Simon (John M. Olin Found.), Dr. Russell Stannard.
Other Information: Established in 1988 by John Marks Templeton, successful mutual fund investment manager and creator of the Templeton Growth Fund. In 1987 Templeton was knighted by Queen Elizabeth. The Foundation received $2,002,000, or 77% of revenue, from gifts awarded by Sir John M. Templeton, Sr., and Dr. John M. Templeton, Jr. $326,796, or 13%, from interest on savings and temporary cash investments. $262,511, or 10%, from dividends and interest from securities. The remaining revenue came from capital gains on the sale of assets.

John William Pope Foundation

3401 Greshams Lake Rd.
Raleigh, NC 27615   **Phone:** (919) 876-6000
USA   **Fax:**   (919) 790-9526

Contact Person: James Arthur Pope, President.
Officers or Principals: James Arthur Pope, President ($43,050); Joyce W. Pope, Chairman ($0); John W. Pope, Vice President ($0); Amanda Joyce Pope, Director.
Mission or Interest: Grant-making institution that awards money to public policy organizations and higher education programs, often with a conservative or free-market emphasis.
Accomplishments: During the fiscal year ending June 1996 the Foundation awarded $822,500 in grants. Recipients included; $100,000 for the Campbell University Business School, eight grants totaling $82,000 for the John Locke Foundation, $45,000 each for the Heritage Foundation, and the National Alumni Forum, $35,000 each for the Jesse Helms Center Foundation, Cato Institute, Institute for Justice, and Center for a Sound Economy, $30,000 for the Institute for Humane Studies, $25,000 for the Washington Legal Foundation, $20,000 for the Atlas Economic Research Foundation, $15,000 for the Reason Foundation, $10,000 each for the Free Congress Foundation, Family Research Council, Federalist Society, North Carolina Taxpayers United Educational Foundation, Alexis de Tocqueville Institution, South Carolina Policy Council, Tax Foundation, U.S. Term Limits, National Center for Policy Analysis, and Capitol Research Center, $5,000 each for the American Academy for Liberal Education, Americans for Tax Reform Foundation, Center for Individual Rights, Pacific Research Institute, Defenders of Property Rights, Political Economy Research Center, Independent Institute, Campbell University Lundy Chair, Eagle Forum Education Center, and the Center for Education Reform.

Total Revenue: FY ending 6/96 $252,696 **Total Expenses:** $868,545 **Net Assets:** $8,464,611 89%(3)
Tax Status: 501(c)(3)
Other Information: Established in 1986. The Foundation received $246,236, or 97% of revenue, from capital gains on the sale of assets. $6,460, or 3%, from interest on savings and temporary cash investments. The Foundation held $8,343,000, or 99% of assets, in corporate stock.

Josiah Bartlett Center for Public Policy

7 S. State St.
Concord, NH 03301   **Phone:** (603) 224-4450   **E-Mail:** jbcpp@tiac.net
USA   **Fax:** (603) 224-4329

Contact Person: Emily Mead, President.
Officers or Principals: Edgar Mead, Vice President/Treasurer; Jennifer A. Shipe, Executive Director.
Mission or Interest: Public policy in New Hampshire with a free-market emphasis.
Accomplishments: Published influential studies including an analysis of New Hampshire's Business Enterprise Tax, a version of a Value Added Tax (VAT).
Products or Services: "Ideas for New Hampshire" contest for ideas on reforming state government in the areas of education, welfare, health care, and taxation. Winning ideas are published in a book and distributed to legislators and others.
Tax Status: 501(c)(3) **Employees:** 4 part-time.
Board of Directors or Trustees: Joan Fowler, Hans. Kuttner, John Stabile.
Periodicals: *Ideas* (quarterly newsletter).
Internships: Yes.
Other Information: Established in 1993. A member of the State Policy Network. Named after Josiah Bartlett, the first governor of New Hampshire and a signer of the Declaration of Independence. Bartlett was also a founder of the state medical society, a militia colonel, and a Chief Justice of the state courts. In 1994-95 the Center received $10,000 from the J.M. Foundation, and $1,500 from the Roe Foundation.

Justice Journal

P.O. Box 8636
Independence, MO 64054   **Phone:** (816) 833-1907
USA

Contact Person: Jack Rifen.
Mission or Interest: Populist newsletter describing how to avoid paying federal income tax.
Accomplishments: "Revealed how income tax can be reduced 100% - legally!"
Products or Services: Free at Last - From the IRS book.
Tax Status: Unincorporated. **Annual Report:** No. **Employees:** 1
Periodicals: *Justice Journal*.   **Internships:** No.

Kansas Intelligencer

211 W. Elizabeth Ave.
Morganville, KS 66502   **Phone:** (913) 926-3131
USA

Contact Person: R. W. Clack, Editor/Publisher.
Mission or Interest: "Celebrating constitutional, representative self-government, the competitive free market and the conviction that human intellect is more than a Darwinian fluke."
Tax Status: Unincorporated. **Annual Report:** No.
Periodicals: *The Kansas Intelligencer* (monthly).
Internships: Yes, unpaid.
Other Information: After more than ten years of publishing, retired nuclear engineer Clack says,"I have to conclude it has had negligible impact. Haven't even been able to make anybody mad even though I periodically attack the Greens, the ACLU, Barney Frank, the homosexual lobby and other targets of opportunity."

Kansas Public Policy Institute

P.O. Box 780712
Wichita, KS 67278   **Phone:** (316) 683-0261   **E-Mail:** KPPI@aol.com
USA   **Fax:** (316) 683-0734

Contact Person: Bryan Riley, Executive Director.
Officers or Principals: Martin K. Eby, Jr., Chairman ($0); Vonda Holliman, Secretary/Treasurer ($0).
Mission or Interest: "Promote principals of open markets, limited government, and individual freedom and responsibility in Kansas."

Accomplishments: "Sixty press citations, events with Michael Tanner, James Guartney, and Marvin Olasky, five research papers."
Total Revenue: 1995 $7,993 **Total Expenses:** $12,415 **Net Assets:** (-$4,422)
Tax Status: 501(c)(3) **Employees:** 1
Board of Directors or Trustees: Gerrit Wormhoudt, George Pearson.
Internships: Yes, unpaid.
Other Information: Established in 1995, formerly called the Veritas Fund. The Institute received $7,275, or 91% of revenue, from contributions and grants awarded by foundations and individuals. (These grants included $7,000 from the Atlas Economic Research Foundation.) $585, or 6%, from event fees. The remaining revenue came from interest on savings and temporary cash investments.

Keene Report

12500 Fairlakes Circle, Suite 155
Fairfax, VA 22033   **Phone:**   (703) 684-0550
USA

Contact Person: David A. Keene, Editor.
Mission or Interest: David Keene's analysis of news and events.
Accomplishments: Bob Dole has said of him, "David Keene is one of the best political minds in the country." Michael Barone of The Almanac of American Politics says, "David Keene is a shrewd and clear-sighted analyst of political trends and politicians. . . his words are worth heeding."
Tax Status: For profit.
Periodicals: *The Keene Report* (monthly newsletter).
Other Information: David Keene is the chairman of the American Conservative Union.

Knowledge Equals Freedom (K=F)

2790 Wrondel Way, Suite 41
Reno, NV 89502
USA

Mission or Interest: Populist directory and clearinghouse that serves the "Freedom Movement."
Tax Status: For profit.

Kwong's News Digest

450 Taraval, Suite 246
San Francisco, CA 94116   **Phone:**   (415) 587-8825
USA

Officers or Principals: Rev. Raymond Kwong, Editor.
Mission or Interest: A newsletter focusing on issues of religion and public life, education, politics and other subjects - often with a special emphasis on the Chinese-American community.
Periodicals: *Kwong's News Digest* (monthly newsletter).
Other Information: Rev. Raymond Kwong is the Executive Director of the Chinese Family Alliance.

Labor Policy Association

1015 15th St., N.W., Suite 1200
Washington, DC 20005   **Phone:**   (202) 789-8670
USA

Contact Person: Jeffrey C. McGuiness, President.
Officers or Principals: Jeffrey C. McGuiness, President ($0); Bruce Carswell, Chairman ($0); Clifford J. Ehrlich, J. Roger King, Vice Chairman ($0).
Mission or Interest: Professional organization representing large employers, "encouraging and conducting research and study of governmental policies and legislation affecting employee-employer relations." Concerned with labor laws and legislation.
Total Revenue: 1994 $1,655,053 8%(1) **Total Expenses:** $1,443,617 **Net Assets:** $1,121,219
Products or Services: Research, litigation, lobbying. In 1994 the Association spent $1,227,074 on lobbying and political expenditures. The previous year it spent less than $2,000.
Tax Status: 501(c)(6)   **Citations:** 42:108
Board of Directors or Trustees: The Board of Directors consists of 29 members, most of whom are key human resources or administration personnel at Mobil, U.S. West, Pfizer, Motorola, Goodyear, General Electric, Lockheed, Union Pacific, Chrysler, Gannett, AT&T, Boeing, Eastman Kodak, 3M, Ford, UPS, and other major U.S. corporations.
Other Information: The Association received $1,511,164, or 91% of revenue, from membership dues. $125,955, or 8%, from meeting registration fees. $17,934, or 1%, from interest on savings and temporary cash investments.

Laissez Faire Books
(see Center for Independent Thought)

Laissez Faire Institute

828 N. Poplar Ct.
Chandler, AZ 85226   **Phone:** (602) 940-9824
USA

Contact Person: John Semmens.
Officers or Principals: John Semmens, Economist; Dianne Kresich, Director.
Mission or Interest: Promotion of free-market public policies. Focus on transportation policies. Have advocated "innovative ideas" for privatizing roads, drivers' licensing, and vehicle registration.
Accomplishments: Played a "critical role" in several public referenda, such as the defeat of an $8 billion transit system in Phoenix. Articles by Semmens and Kresich have been published in *Policy Review, Liberty, The Freeman, Transportation Quarterly*, and numerous daily papers in Arizona.
Tax Status: For profit.

Lambda Report on Homosexuality

P.O. Box 45252
Washington, DC 20026   **Phone:** (703) 491-7975   **E-Mail:** peter@aimgate.aim.org
USA

Contact Person: Peter LaBarbera, Publisher.
Officers or Principals: Brian Fitzpatrick, Assistant Editor; Peter LaBarbera, Publisher.
Mission or Interest: "Monitoring the homosexual activist movement in American politics and culture."
Accomplishments: First to publish news stories on subjects such as: federal agencies demanding Christian employee groups recognize different "sexual orientations;" major corporate media funding and recruiting at homosexual journalists' convention; "biased coverage" of reporting on homosexual gene research; the National Endowment for the Arts funding a book claiming St. Paul, St. Augustine, King David and others were homosexuals.
Periodicals: *Lambda Report on Homosexuality* (bimonthly newspaper).
Other Information: Publisher LaBarbera can be reached during the day at Accuracy in Academia at (202) 364-3085, ext. 106.

Land Rights Foundation

P.O. Box 1111
Gloverville, NY 12078   **Phone:** (518) 725-1090   **E-Mail:** landrights@aol.com
USA   **Fax:** (518) 725-8239

Contact Person: David B. Howard, President/Editor.
Mission or Interest: "Education and distribution of information concerning private property rights."
Accomplishments: "Maintains an extensive archive of property rights information covering all 50 states."
Tax Status: 501(c)(3) **Employees:** 1
Board of Directors or Trustees: Joanna Wuagh (Alliance for America).
Periodicals: *Land Rights Letter* (monthly newsletter).
Internships: No.

Landmark Legal Foundation

2345 Grand Ave., Suite 2310
Kansas City, MO 64108   **Phone:** (816) 474-6600   **E-Mail:** hutchp@aol.com
USA   **Fax:** (816) 474-6609

Contact Person: Jerald L. Hill, President.
Officers or Principals: Jerald L. Hill, President ($113,046); Mark J. Bredemeier, General Counsel ($101,717); Mark R. Levin, Director, DC Office ($85,000); Menlo F. Smith, Chairman; William J. Hume, Vice Chairman; William Bradford Reynolds, Treasurer; R.T. Amis, Secretary.
Mission or Interest: Litigation and legal aid on behalf of conservatives and conservative causes.
Accomplishments: One of the first conservative litigation organizations. Represented former Attorney General Edwin Meese III in litigation surrounding the final report issued by Iran-Contra Independent Counsel Lawrence Walsh. Challenged the exclusion of religious schools from Milwaukee's Parental Choice Program. In 1994 Landmark spent $550,761 on its programs. Involved in litigation including: Burke, et al. v. Roberts, "to require State Governor to carry out welfare reform measures approved through voter referendum." Miller, et al. v. John T. Benson, "to vindicate equal protection and free exercise of religious rights of low income families wishing to choose sectarian schools in school voucher program." In re Central Nebraska Public Power and Irrigation District concerning "federal relicensing of power and irrigation project with focus on property rights implications of license requirements' environmental restrictions." For its litigation Landmark received $5,000 in court-awarded attorneys fees.

Total Revenue: 1994 $909,320 **Total Expenses:** $937,985 59%/19%/23% **Net Assets:** $801,631
Products or Services: Review of Attorney General Janet Reno's performance. Litigation, research.
Tax Status: 501(c)(3)   **Citations:** 142:49
Board of Directors or Trustees: John Dodd, Charles Matthews, Louise Oliver (Intercollegiate Studies Inst.), Edwin Meese, III (U.S. Attorney General, 1985-88).
Other Information: Also operates the Landmark Legal Foundation, Center for Civil Rights, One Farragut Square S., 9th Floor, Washington, DC 20006, (202) 393-3360. Landmark received $872,115, or 96% of revenue, from contributions and grants awarded by foundations, businesses, and individuals. (These contributions and grants have increased by an average of 5% a year over the last five years. These grants included $75,000 from the Lilly Endowment, $50,000 from the Sarah Scaife Foundation, and $37,500 from the Gordon and Mary Cain Foundation. In 1995, $225,000 from the Scaife Family Foundation, $125,000 from the Carthage Foundation, $40,000 from the Allegheny Foundation, $25,000 from the Sunmark Foundation, and $25,000 from the John M. Olin Foundation.) $18,805, or 2%, from interest on savings and temporary cash investments. $13,400, or 1%, from rental income. The remaining revenue came from court-awarded attorneys fees.

Law Enforcement Alliance of America (LEAA)

7700 Leesburg Pike, Suite 421
Falls Church, VA 22043   **Phone:**   (703) 847-2677
USA   **Fax:**   (703) 766-8578

Contact Person: Ted Deeds, Operations Director.
Officers or Principals: James J. Fotis, Executive Director ($58,850); Ted Gogol, Chief of Staff ($58,850); Richard Beckman, President; John Chapman, First Vice President; Christine Long-Wagner, Second Vice President; Bryant G. Jennings, Third Vice President; Carl T. Rowan, Treasurer; John Washco, Secretary; William F. Seaman, Jr., Sargeant-at-Arms.
Mission or Interest: A coalition of over 50,000 law enforcement professionals, crime victims and private citizens fighting for measures that will reduce violent crime and assist crime victims and peace officers. Strong support for the Second Amendment right of law-abiding citizens to own and use firearms.
Accomplishments: LEAA played a major role in the effort to persuade Time Warner to drop rap singer Ice-T from their label after they released his "Cop Killer" song. They support and have drafted legislative efforts such as: a bill which will allow off-duty and retired police officers to carry a concealed weapon; the "Three Strikes and You're Out" bills that mandate a life sentence for a third violent criminal offense; and the bill that created a national registry of criminals convicted of crimes against minors to be used by child-care centers, schools, scouts, etc. Drafted legislation banning weight-lifting equipment from federal prisons that passed in the U.S. House, and was adopted by the American Legislative Exchange Council and passed in several states. Testified on behalf of civilian "Right to Carry" laws allowing citizens to carry concealed weapons. In 1995 the Alliance spent $682,891 on its programs.
Total Revenue: 1995 $1,058,508 **Total Expenses:** $1,096,283 62%/5%/33% **Net Assets:** (-$52,312)
Products or Services: Video of police officers testifying before Congress in 1995 calling for the repeal of the "1994 Clinton Gun Ban". Books and videos on criminal justice and crime prevention. Discounts on pepper spray.
Tax Status: 501(c)(4)   **Citations:** 66:86
Board of Directors or Trustees: Ronald Allen (Westfield, NJ, Police Dept., 2nd Vice Pres., National P.A.L.), David Lindman (Minneapolis, MN, Police Dept.), Ray Maples (Memphis, TN, Police Dept., Pres., Memphis Police Assc.), Jimmy Trahin (Los Angeles, CA, Police Dept., Ret.).
Periodicals: *LEAA Advocate* (quarterly newsletter).
Other Information: LEAA was originally formed in 1989 when New Jersey Police Officer, Tom Aveni, formed Law Enforcement for the Preservation of the Second Amendment (LEPSA). In a few months it grew to over 1,000 police officers. In November 1990 LEPSA was dissolved and merged into LEAA. LEAA received substantial support from the National Rifle Association. Affiliated with the 501(c)(3) Law Enforcement Alliance of America Foundation, at the same address. In 1993 the Foundation had revenues and expenses of less than $10,000. LEAA received $643,722, or 61% of revenue, from contributors. $320,472, or 30%, from membership dues. $91,587, or 9%, from program services. The remaining revenue came from interest on savings.

Lawyers' Second Amendment Society (LSAS)

18034 Ventura Blvd., Suite 329
Encino, CA 91316   **Phone:** (818) 734-3066   **E-Mail:** DJShultz1@aol.com or GUNnut Esq@aol.com
USA

Contact Person: Daniel J. Schultz, President.
Officers or Principals: Steven A. Silver, Vice President; David L. DePasquale.
Mission or Interest: An organization of lawyers (non-lawyers may be members as well) dedicated to preserving the Second Amendment right to keep and bear arms. "The legal community must be educated... Attorneys, judges and justices frequently hold the patently false belief that the Second Amendment only guarantees the states the right to maintain militias. This, even when the most superficial research immediately reveals the right to keep and bear arms is, and always was, an inalienable *individual* right."
Tax Status: 501(c)(4) (status application pending)
Periodicals: *The Liberty Pole* (bimonthly).
Other Information: Established in 1994.

Leadership Councils of America (LCA)

P.O. Box 373
Valparaiso, IN 46384   **Phone:**   (219) 462-3728
USA

Contact Person: Martin Henrichs, President.
Officers or Principals: Martin Henrichs, President; Dan Schreiber, Vice President, Public Policy; Jim Stanton, Vice President, Finance; George Bloyer, Vice President, Administration; Joan Chirby, Secretary; John Murvihill, Treasurer.
Mission or Interest: "To educate, unite, and empower citizens to achieve conservative solutions to America's problems." Members vote on resolutions, and act on these resolutions. Focus on Indiana.
Tax Status: 501(c)(3)
Board of Directors or Trustees: Betty Gabriel, John Kerr, John Jagiella, Gordon Bloyer, Bill Matthews, Carol Gumulauskis, Irene Johnson.
Periodicals: *The American Sentry* (monthly newsletter).
Other Information: Established in 1984.

Leadership Institute

1101 N. Highland St.
Arlington, VA 22201   **Phone:**   (703) 247-2000   **E-Mail:**   lead@townhall.com
USA   **Fax:**   (703) 247-2001   **Internet:**   http://www.lead-inst.org

Contact Person: Kevin Gentry, Executive Vice President.
Officers or Principals: Kevin Gentry, Executive Vice President ($84,348); William Forrest, Vice President, Programs ($63,842); Richard E. Hendrix, Director, Finance ($58,912); Morton C. Blackwell, President; Mark Z. Montini, Vice President, Operations.
Mission or Interest: Trains conservative students and activists "to increase the number and effectiveness of conservative public policy leaders." Conducts various "schools," including Youth Leadership School, Student Publications School, Broadcast Journalism School, Capitol Hill Staff Training School, Campaign Leadership School, Candidate Development School, Public Relations School, Legislative Project Management School, Direct Mail School, Rhetoric and Campaign Communication School, and the Foreign Service Opportunity School. Helps establish conservative campus newspapers.
Accomplishments: "Since its founding in 1979, the Leadership Institute has trained more than 13,000 conservatives for effective leadership. In 1995 the total number of students trained by the Institute was 2,429 -- a 51% increase over 1994's record total of 1,609. Since the 1994 elections, the Institute has placed hundreds of conservatives in positions of influence with the new Congress on Capitol Hill." Revenue has been increasing dramatically, averaging 41% growth annually for the last six years and more than doubling from 1993 to 1994. In 1994 the Institute spent $691,602 on these Schools. $106,423 was spent on journalism internships. $82,182 was spent producing publications and $62,632 was spent on the annual leadership conference.
Total Revenue: 1994 $4,717,172 35%(7) **Total Expenses:** $2,239,659 58%/5%/37% **Net Assets:** $3,167,304
Products or Services: Leadership Training Schools. Salvatori Leadership Speakers Bureau. "The Conservative Organizational Entrepreneur," a guide to establishing, financing, and promoting a nonprofit advocacy organization. A study of business and association political action committees and their contribution patterns in 1993-94. Adam Smith neckties.
Tax Status: 501(c)(3) **Annual Report:** Yes. **Employees:** 21   **Citations:** 555:19
Board of Directors or Trustees: M. Dennis Daugherty (former Vice Pres., Legal Services Corp., 1982-85), Baker Armstrong Smith, Craig Murphy (Press Secretary to Rep. Joe Barton, R-TX), Kevin Richardson (Vice Pres., Government Relations, Electronic Industries Assoc.), William Blackwell, Beverly Danielson, Rev. Fred Fowler III, John Maxwell, Fred Sacher, Louis Weiss.
Periodicals: *Building Leadership* (bimonthly newsletter).
Internships: Yes, typically accepts three groups of twelve throughout the year.
Other Information: Established in 1979. Graduates of the Institute's training include: Gov. Terry Branstad (R-IA), Sen. Mitch McConnell (R-KY), Virginia Attorney General Jim Gilmore, Rep. Jack Fields (R-TX), Rep. Dave McIntosh (R-IN), Rep. Mark Souder (R-IN), Rep. Steve Stockman (R-TX), Kerry Knott (Chief of Staff to House Majority Leader Dick Armey), and many others. The Institute received $4,655,990, or 99% of revenue, from contributions and grants awarded by foundations, businesses, and individuals. (These grants included $750,000 from the F.M. Kirby Foundation, $245,000 from the M.J. Murdock Charitable Trust, $50,000 from the Milliken Foundation, $10,000 from the Vernon K. Krieble Foundation, $10,000 from the Richard & Helen DeVos Foundation. In 1995, $107,000 from the Sunmark Foundation, $25,000 from the Lynde and Harry Bradley Foundation, $25,000 from the Castle Rock Foundation, $12,000 from the Charles G. Koch Charitable Foundation, and $1,000 from the John William Pope Foundation.) $33,703, or 1%, came from training tuition. The remaining revenue came from dividends and interest from securities, and other miscellaneous sources.

League of Private Property Voters (LPPV)

30218 N.E., 82nd Ave.
Battle Ground, WA 98604   **Phone:**   (360) 687-2471   **E-Mail:**   alra@pacifier.com
USA   **Fax:**   (360) 687-2973

Contact Person: Chuck Cushman, Chairman.

Mission or Interest: Rates Congressional Representatives and Senators on their votes affecting private property issues.
Accomplishments: Published the *Private Property Congressional Vote Index* every election year since 1990. Published and delivered 250,000 copies in 1994, 500,000 copies in 1996.
Products or Services: *Private Property Congressional Vote Index.* Provides bulk copies to other organizations.
Tax Status: Nonprofit incorporated in the state of Washington. **Employees:** 8
Periodicals: *Private Property Congressional Vote Index* (semi-annual).
Internships: Yes.
Other Information: Affiliated with the American Land Rights Association.

Legal Affairs Council (LAC)

3554 Chain Bridge Rd., Suite 301
Fairfax, VA 22033   **Phone:** (703) 591-7767
USA   **Fax:**   (703) 273-4514

Contact Person: Richard A. Delgaudio, President.
Officers or Principals: Richard A. Delgaudio, President ($49,106); Donald A. Derham, Jr., Chairman ($0).
Mission or Interest: "To educate the public regarding national legal and constitutional issues and to serve as a legal aid fund to ensure equal access to the courts for those individuals whose first amendment rights have been, or are threatened with being abridged or denied."
Accomplishments: In 1997 the Council created the "Stop Ebonics / Save our Children" program. Assisted Oliver North in his legal defense. Helped defeat the push for Washington, DC statehood. Assisted former Defense Secretary Casper Weinberger following his indictment by Special Prosecutor Lawrence Walsh. Working to uphold congressional term limits. In 1994 the Council spent $868,552 on its programs. This included $7,750 in grants. Recipients included; $4,000 for the Paula Corbin Jones Legal Trust Fund, $1,000 each for the U.S. Justice Foundation, the Arkansas State Troopers who were assigned to transport and protect then-Governor Clinton, and the Sidewalk Defense Fund, $500 for Stone & Feeley, and $250 for the Officer L. Powell Defense Fund.
Total Revenue: 1994 $972,436 **Total Expenses:** $1,185,918 73%/17%/10% **Net Assets:** (-$452,727)
Products or Services: Legal assistance, conservative attorney referral, publications.
Tax Status: 501(c)(4) **Annual Report:** Yes. **Citations:** 7:182
Board of Directors or Trustees: Ben Fegan.
Internships: *Legal Briefs Bulletin* (monthly).
Other Information: Established in 1986. Affiliated with the 501(c)(4) National Security Center, and the for-profit Right Lists, Inc., and the Richard A. Delgaudio Corp. In 1994 the two nonprofit affiliates had combined net revenues, expenses, and assets of $1,834,581, $1,951,810, and (-$565,175). Richard Delgaudio served as president of both and received combined compensation of $67,906. The Council received $889,165, of 91% of revenue, from contributors. $67,562, or 7%, from mailing list rentals. The remaining revenue came from other miscellaneous sources.

Lehrman Institute

42 North Ave., Suite L
New Rochelle, NY 10805   **Phone:** (914) 632-7000
USA

Contact Person: Angel Burgos.
Officers or Principals: Lewis Lehrman, Chairman ($0); Frank P. Trotta, President ($0); Peter Schattenfield, Treasurer ($0); Patricia Blake, Secretary; Susan Yu, Assistant Secretary.
Mission or Interest: Private foundation that conducts direct charitable activities and research. Has, in the past, awarded grants to organizations including the Manhattan Institute.
Accomplishments: Funded the research of Dr. Alvin Rabushka, of the Hoover Institution, who is best known for his work on a flat tax. In the fiscal year ending July, 1994, the Institute awarded no grants, but spent $146,920 on its own educational activities. $103,832 was spent on a survey of 1,200 New York city and state residents in cooperation with the Empire State Foundation. The 1993 survey topic was immigration and in 1994 it was welfare. $8,572 was spent on seminars relating to the survey topics. $19,970 was spent on the Cali Project, a joint effort with Columbia University and the Universidad de Valle in Cali, Columbia. The Cali Project studied the effects of non-governmental organizations on development in Columbia, and sponsored a two-day conference on "Cali: The Entrepreneurial Spirit" at Columbia University. $10,673 was spent on studies of Latin American foreign policy with the Heritage Foundation.
Total Revenue: FY ending 7/94 $76,444 **Total Expenses:** $174,825 **Net Assets:** $3,687,981 (-29%)(2)
Tax Status: 501(c)(3)
Other Information: The Institute received $58,000, or 76% of revenue, from contributions awarded by two foundations; $30,000 from the Empire Foundation and $28,000 from the Lynde and Harry Bradley Foundation. $18,093, or 24%, from capital gains on the sale of assets. The remaining revenue came from dividends and interest from securities, and rents. The Foundation held $3,637,903, or 99% of assets, in occupied land, buildings, and equipment. $39,600, or 1%, was held in fine art.

Liberals Always Waffle Newsletter (LAWN)

2490 Black Rock Turnpike, Suite 422
Fairfield, CT 06430　　　　**Phone:** (203) 368-1862　　**E-Mail:** Prodigy: PMDK87A
USA

Contact Person: Robert K. Morgan, Publisher..
Mission or Interest: A satirical look at the Clinton administration and 'political correctness'.
Tax Status: For profit.　**Annual Report:** No.　**Employees:** 1 full time, 2 part time.
Periodicals: *Liberals Always Waffle Newsletter* (bimonthly).
Internships: Contact the publisher.
Other Information: Established in 1993. Printed on un-recycled paper.

Libertarian Party - USA

2600 Virginia Ave., N.W., Suite 100
Washington, DC 20037　　　　**Phone:** (202) 333-0008　　**E-Mail:** lphq@access1.digex.net
USA　　　　　　　　　　　　　　　　　　　　　　　　　**Internet:** http://www.lp.org/

Contact Person: Perry Willis, National Director.
Officers or Principals: Stephen Dasbach, Chairman.
Mission or Interest: "Libertarians believe the answer to America's political problems is the same commitment to freedom that earned America its greatness: a free-market economy and the abundance and prosperity it brings; a dedication to civil liberties and personal freedom that marks this country above all others; and a foreign policy of non-intervention, peace, and free trade as prescribed by America's founders."
Accomplishments: Third largest political party in the United States. Libertarian candidates have campaigned in every presidential election since 1972. Several thousand others have run for state, local, and federal level executive office. In the 1996 elections, over 2 million people voted for Libertarian candidates. There were, as of April 1994, 116 elected Libertarian officials in the United States. In 1996, former Libertarian Party Presidential candidate Dr. Ron Paul wasre-elected to Congress as a Republican. In 1972 Vice Presidential candidate Tonie Nathan became the first women to receive an electoral vote. In 1980 Presidential candidate Ed Clark received almost 1 million votes.
Products or Services: Literature for outreach purposes, tools for campaigns and research/logistical services for Libertarian Party candidates and lobbyists around the country.
Tax Status: Tax-exempt political party.　**Annual Report:** No.
Periodicals: *Libertarian Party News*.
Internships: Yes, positions are available year-round to do entry-level political work.
Other Information: Established in 1971 at the home of David Nolan.

Libertarians for Gay and Lesbian Concerns (LGLC)

P.O. Box 447
Chelsea, MI 48118
USA

Contact Person: James Hudler, International Coordinator.
Officers or Principals: Raymond Warner, Secretary.
Mission or Interest: Organization dedicated to promoting individual liberty, with an emphasis on homosexuals' concerns.
Accomplishments: Organized a contingent for the April, 1993 "March on Washington for Lesbian, Gay and Bisexual Equal Rights and Liberation," and held their own events there.
Periodicals: *LGLC Newsletter* (quarterly).

Libertarians for Life (LFL)

13424 Hathaway Dr.
Wheaton, MD 20906　　　　**Phone:** (301) 460-4141　　**E-Mail:** DORIS.GORDON@IAD.blkcat.com
USA　　　　　　　　　　　　　　　　　　　　　　　　　**Internet:** http://www.members.aol.com/brentjass/LFL

Contact Person: Doris Gordon, National Coordinator.
Mission or Interest: "Founded to show why abortion is wrong, not a right. Being libertarian, we insist that everyone's unalienable rights be respected. The proper function of government is to defend rights. It should not side with aggressors against their victims. Legalized abortion is legalized aggression. . . LFL's reasoning is expressly philosophical rather than religious."
Accomplishments: Doris Gordon has had an op-ed published in *The Washington Post*. Facilitated and instigated debates within the Libertarian Party on its abortion-rights stance.
Products or Services: Numerous articles and literature.
Tax Status: Unincorporated.
Periodicals: *LFL Reports* (quarterly newsletter).
Other Information: Established in 1976 by Doris Gordon at the Libertarian Party Convention.

Liberty Alliance

P.O. Box 190
Forest, VA 24551   **Phone:**   (804) 534-8588
USA

Contact Person: Randy Scott, President.
Officers or Principals: Randy Scott, President ($0); George McGann, Secretary ($0).
Mission or Interest: "Educating the American public and elected officials about various events affecting traditional values, morals and education of American children."
Accomplishments: In 1993 the Alliance spent $2,536,138, a 274% increase over the previous year.
Total Revenue: 1993 $3,225,655 310%(1) **Total Expenses:** $3,200,162 79%/7%/13% **Net Assets:** $39,457
Products or Services: Lobbying, publications.
Tax Status: 501(c)(4)   **Citations:** 21:146
Board of Directors or Trustees: Eugene Ferris, Charlie Harbin, Jerry Falwell.
Other Information: Director Rev. Jerry Falwell is the former leader of the Moral Majority. The Alliance received $3,230,907, or 100% of gross revenue, from contributors. The Alliance lost $5,252 on bad checks and refunds.

Liberty Foundation / *Liberty*

P.O. Box 1181
Port Townsend, WA 98368   **Phone:**   (360) 385-5097
USA   **Fax:**   (360) 385-3704   **Internet:** http://www.LibertySoft.com.liberty

Contact Person: Timothy Virkkala.
Officers or Principals: R. W. Bradford, Publisher/Editor; Stephen Cox, Senior Editor.
Mission or Interest: Publishes *Liberty*, a classical liberal/libertarian review, and monographs.
Accomplishments: According to *The Whole Earth Review*, *Liberty* is "the leading theoretical journal of the libertarian movement, and a literate commentary on our times." Milton Friedman said, "I find *Liberty* a lively, idiosyncratic publication, often presenting fresh and original comments from a liberal (in the true sense) point of view."
Products or Services: Conferences, videotapes, audiotapes, monographs.
Tax Status: 501(c)(3)
Periodicals: *Liberty* (bimonthly magazine).
Internships: Yes, designed for aspiring journalist with interests in economics, social philosophy, etc.
Other Information: *Liberty* was briefly published by the Invisible Hand Foundation. The late Karl Hess was a senior editor. He is probably best known for his speech-writing for Barry Goldwater. Hess wrote the famous phrase, "Extremism in the defense of liberty is no vice. . . Moderation in the pursuit of justice is no virtue."

Liberty Fund

8335 Allison Pointe Trail, Suite 300
Indianapolis, IN 46250   **Phone:**   (817) 842-0880
USA   **Fax:**   (817) 577-9067

Contact Person: William C. Dennis, Senior Program Officer.
Officers or Principals: Charles King, President ($202,389); Emilio J. Pacheco, Director of Education ($85,000); James McClellan, Director of Publications ($84,500); Alan Russell, Chairman; Enid Goodrich, Vice Chairman; Ruth E. Connolly, Secretary; Chris L. Talley, Treasurer.
Mission or Interest: "A private educational foundation established to encourage study of the ideal of a society of free and responsible individuals." Conducts private conferences, awards grants, and publishes reprints of classic books.
Accomplishments: In the fiscal year ending April 1995 the Fund awarded $200,000 in grants to pre-selected organizations. Recipients included; $50,000 for the Intercollegiate Studies Institute, $25,000 for the Foundation Francisco Marroquin, $15,000 each for the Foundation for Economic Education and Institute for Humane Studies, $10,000 each for the Acton Institute, Cato Institute, Center for the Study of Federalism, Fraser Institute, Political Economy Research Center, Rockford Institute, Social Affairs Unit, and Social Philosophy and Policy Foundation, $7,500 each for the Institute for Political Economy, and the Pacific Research Institute. $233,695 was spent on private seminars and colloquiums on topics such as "Liberty, the Bill of Rights, and the Fourteenth Amendment," "The State, Law, and Society in Humboldt, Mill and Stephen," and "Liberty, Law, and Economics." Some of these colloquia were held in cooperation with the Locke Institute. $832,209 was spent on printing and publications.
Total Revenue: FY ending 4/95 $12,470,757 **Total Expenses:** $6,465,742 **Net Assets:** $170,241,620
Products or Services: Catalog of books. Recently added titles include <u>Cato's Letters: Essays on Liberty</u>, <u>The American Commonwealth</u> by James Bryce, and numerous other works by authors such as Albert Jay Nock, Wilhelm von Humboldt, Edmund Burke, John C. Calhoun, Michael Oakeshott, Irving Babbitt, Richard Weaver, Jacques Barzun, F. A. Hayek, David Hume, Lord Acton, Adam Smith, and Ludwig von Mises. Video tapes on Adam Smith, the Industrial Revolution, Hong Kong, and the American Constitution.
Tax Status: 501(c)(3) **Annual Report:** No. **Employees:** 22

Board of Directors or Trustees: Manuel Ayau, Roseda Decker, Ralph Husted, George Martin, Edward McLean, Irwin Reiss, Richard Ware, Don Welch.
Internships: No.
Other Information: Established in 1960 by Pierre F. Goodrich, an Indianapolis businessman and lawyer. The Fund received $6,522,462, or 52% of revenue, from capital gains on the sale of assets. $3,698,009, or 30% of revenue, from interest on savings and temporary cash investments. $2,012,955, or 16%, from dividends and interest from securities. The remaining revenue came from contributions and grants, and other miscellaneous sources. The Fund held $82,873,172, or 49% of assets, in corporate stock. $25,815,506, or 15%, in government bonds.

Liberty Lobby

300 Independence Ave., S.E.
Washington, DC 20003   **Phone:**   (202) 546-5611
USA

Contact Person: Paul Croke, Vice Chairman, Executive Committee.
Officers or Principals: Vince Ryan, Chairman; Willis A. Carto, Treasurer; Anne Cronin, Secretary.
Mission or Interest: Populist institution that advocates reduced government intervention and resistance to "The New World Order." Advocates several conspiracy and historical revisionist theories.
Accomplishments: Claims a membership of 100,000. Claims to have gross revenues of approximately $4 million per year. Founded the Populist Party in 1984. Hosts the show "Radio Free America," with Tom Valentine, that is heard on over 50 stations nationwide and on shortwave radio. Prominent in the opposition to NAFTA.
Products or Services: Liberty Library catalog of books on various topics. Radio shows, video and audio tapes.
Tax Status: "Nonprofit. No exemption and no taxes paid." **Employees:** 35
Board of Directors or Trustees: "We have a Board of Policy with 19,000 members who direct policy of the institution. They are polled by mail."
Periodicals: *The Spotlight* (weekly newspaper).
Other Information: Established in 1955 by Willis Carto. The Lobby is considered anti-Semitic by groups such as the Simon Weisenthal Center and the Anti-Defamation League of B'nai B'rith. The Lobby responds that it is not anti-Semitic, but critical of the state of Israel and of Zionism. In 1985 the Lobby was sued by William F. Buckley, Jr., after *Spotlight* accused him of supporting pedophilia and the American Nazi movement.

Life Cycle Books

P.O. Box 420
Lewiston, NY 14092   **Phone:**   (416) 690-5860
USA   **Fax:**   (416) 690-8532

Contact Person: Paul Broughton, Proprietor.
Mission or Interest: Books and educational products concerning abortion.
Products or Services: "Life Catalogue" of products, including models of fetal development.
Tax Status: For profit.
Other Information: Established in 1973.

Life Education and Resource Network (LEARN)

704 Chenevert St.
Houston, TX 77003-3012
USA

Contact Person: Akua Furlow, Assistant Director.
Officers or Principals: Pastor Johnny Hunter, National Director; Dr. Haywood Robinson, Finance Chairman.
Mission or Interest: A network of African-American anti-abortion activists.
Accomplishments: The Network has called attention to the role African-Americans play in the anti-abortion movement. They have also focused attention on the racial views and involvement in eugenics of Planned Parenthood founder Margaret Sanger. The Network's 1994 conference was called "Halting the Genocide of Targeted Minorities: Networking for Survival."
Products or Services: Brochures, conferences, protest organization and activist training. Support library of books, articles and documents.
Board of Directors or Trustees: Mignonne Anderson (Single Mothers United for Christ), Barbara Bell (Massachusetts Blacks for Life), Delores Grier (Black Catholics for Life), Janet Hudspeth (California Blacks for Life), Rev. Eugene Pack, Juliette Bartlett Pack (Texas Blacks for Life), Sylvia Parker (Frontline Outreach), Paulette Roseberry (Black Americans for Life), Deacon John Tyler (African-American Association for the Preservation of Life and Family).
Other Information: Established in 1993 at the African American Pro-life Planning Conference.

Life Issues Institute

1721 W. Galbraith Rd.
Cincinnati, OH 45239
USA

Phone: (513) 729-3600
Fax: (513) 729-3636

E-Mail: lifeissues@aol.com
Internet: http://www.lifeissues.org

Contact Person: Brad Mattes, Executive Director.
Officers or Principals: Bradley J. Mattes, Executive Director ($43,037); John C. Willke, M.D., President ($0); Sandra Keefer, Vice President ($0); Roger Mall, Treasurer.
Mission or Interest: "Pro-life leaders came to the inescapable conclusion that the pro-life movement had to change with the times. We had to update and alter the way we disseminate our message. Abortion was becoming too familiar. America was showing signs of enduring it. . . Life Issues Institute was founded to reverse this alarming trend, and rejuvenate and reinvigorate a nation-wide educational awakening." Produces "first-of-its kind market research, international development and networking, writings and publications."
Accomplishments: Radio broadcasts heard on over 250 radio stations. In 1994 the Institute spent $183,089 on its programs.
Total Revenue: 1994 $258,431 **Total Expenses:** $253,664 72%/6%/22% **Net Assets:** $46,612
Products or Services: "Life Jewels" compact disk containing 58 sixty-second "fact-filled" messages on abortion and related issues. The disk has been distributed to over 1,000 Christian radio stations. "Abortion Questions and Answers" and other pamphlets.
Tax Status: 501(c)(3) **Annual Report:** No. **Employees:** 4 **Citations:** 23:144
Board of Directors or Trustees: Barbara Willke, William Butterfield.
Periodicals: *Life Issues Connector* (monthly newsletter), and *The RU486 Report*.
Internships: No.
Other Information: Established in 1991. The Institute received $256,891, or 99% of revenue, from contributions and grants awarded by foundations, businesses, and individuals. (These grants included $20,000 from Concerned Women for America. This was a slight decrease; since its establishment, the Institute has averaged $272,681 in contributions.) The remaining revenue came from interest on savings and temporary cash investments.

Life Legal Defense Foundation (LLDF)

P.O. Box 2105
Napa, CA 94558
USA

Phone: (707) 224-6675
Fax: (707) 224-6676

Contact Person: Mary Riley.
Officers or Principals: Mary Smedley, Administrator ($28,963); John A. Streett, President/Chairman ($0); Stephen D. Lopez, Vice President ($0); Andrew W. Zepeda, Vice President.
Mission or Interest: Legal defense of anti-abortion activists. "LLDF attorneys promote and defend the human and civil rights of individuals through litigation addressing civil, constitutional, criminal and appellate issues."
Accomplishments: LLDF represented the case of Planned Parenthood v. Williams before the California Supreme Court. The case, which deals with the rights of anti-abortion protesters to hold signs in close proximity to abortion clinics, will be ruled on by the United States Supreme Court, when it rules on Schenk v. Prochoice Network, a similar case. LLDF took the case of Robert Wedland "who had been slated by his wife and the hospital medical ethics committee for death by starvation and dehydration while he was in a coma." LLDF took the case on behalf of his sister and prevented the removal of his feeding tube. "Wedland unexpectedly awoke shortly thereafter, and is now off life support and mobile in a wheelchair." In 1994 LLDF spent $27,824 on its programs; $23,538 on litigation, and the remainder to produce its newsletter.
Total Revenue: 1994 $121,114 6%(2) **Total Expenses:** $109,548 25%/43%/32% **Net Assets:** $14,115
Tax Status: 501(c)(3)
Board of Directors or Trustees: Ann Kindt, Gregg Cunningham.
Periodicals: *Lifeline* (quarterly newsletter).
Other Information: Established in 1989 "as an ad hoc effort to provide legal counsel for hundreds of Operation Rescue protesters" in Sunnyvale, CA. Although the LLDF files its tax returns and accepts contributions, it has not yet received confirmation of its nonprofit status from the IRS. The LLDF received $118,958, or 98% of revenue, from contributions and grants awarded by foundations, businesses, and individuals. $1,241, or 1%, from the sale of securities. The remaining revenue came from a fund-raising banquet, mailing list rentals, interest on savings and temporary cash investments, and other miscellaneous sources.

Lilly Endowment

P.O. Box 88068
Indianapolis, IN 46208
USA

Phone: (317) 924-5471
Fax: (317) 926-4431

Contact Person: William M. Goodwin, Treasurer .
Officers or Principals: Thomas H. Lake, Honorary Chairman ($671,024); Thomas M. Lofton, Chairman ($390,055); N. Clay Robbins, President ($212,736); William M. Goodwin, Secretary/Treasurer ($212,372); Craig R. Dykstra, Vice President, Religion ($203,576); Charles A. Johnson, Vice President, Development ($189,726); William C. Bonifield, Vice President, Education ($142,589); Ralph E. Lundgren, Vice President, Education ($155,457).

Mission or Interest: Grant-making foundation that awards funds for religious, educational, and community development. The Foundation includes awards for conservative and free-market organizations.

Accomplishments: In 1994 the Endowment awarded $101,854,052 in grants. Recipients included: three grants totaling $828,000 for the Hudson Institute, $375,000 for the Atlas Economic Research Foundation, two grants totaling $331,551 for the Fraser Institute, $250,000 for the Manhattan Institute, $175,000 for the Institute for Contemporary Studies, $131,400 for the Reason Foundation, $112,500 for the American Enterprise Institute, two grants totaling $90,000 for the Intercollegiate Studies Institute, two grants totaling $85,000 for the National Center for Policy Analysis, $75,000 each for Freedom House, Landmark Legal Foundation, Pacific Legal Foundation, and the Federalist Society, two grants totaling $70,000 for the Social Philosophy and Policy Foundation, $61,930 for the Institute on Religion and Public Life, two grants totaling $60,000 for the Institute for Research on the Economics of Taxation, $50,000 each for the Capitol Research Center, and Washington Legal Foundation, $40,000 each for the Atlantic Legal Foundation, Pacific Research Institute, Political Economy Research Center, and New England Legal Foundation, and two grants totaling $39,678 for the Center for Policy Research.

Total Revenue: 1994 $119,503,183 **Total Expenses:** $113,212,504 **Net Assets:** $2,788,660,989 11% (1)
Tax Status: 501(c)(3)

Board of Directors or Trustees: Otis Bowen, William Enright, Earl Herr, Byron Hollett, Eli Lilly, II, Eugene Ratliff, Herman Wells.

Other Information: The Endowment was established in 1937 by Josiah Kirby Lilly. Josiah Lilly was the son of Eli Lilly, founder of the pharmaceutical giant, Eli Lilly and Co. The Endowment was initially funded with stock from the company. Today the Endowment holds approximately 47 million shares of common stock in Eli Lilly and Co., which was valued at $2.7 billion in 1994. The Endowment received $117,368,355, or 98% of revenue, from dividends and interest from securities. $1,074,071, or 1%, from the return of unused grant money. The remaining revenue came from interest on savings and temporary cash investments, contributions and grants, and other miscellaneous sources. The Endowment held $2,772,827,387, or 99.4% of assets, in Eli Lilly and Co. common stock.

Limbaugh Letter

366 Madison Ave.
New York, NY 10017
USA

Mission or Interest: Newsletter written by radio host Rush Limbaugh.
Tax Status: For profit.

Lincoln Institute for Research and Education

1001 Connecticut Ave., N.W., Suite 1135
Washignton, DC 20036   **Phone:**   (703) 759-4599
USA

Contact Person: Jay A. Parker, President .

Officers or Principals: James B. Taylor, Secretary/Treasurer ($10,500); Jay A. Parker, President ($0); Thomas P. Walsh, Jr., Vice President ($0); Darin J. Waters, Director.

Mission or Interest: Conservative organization that publishes *The Lincoln Review*. Also produces radio commentary and educational materials.

Accomplishments: In the fiscal year ending September 1994 the Institute spent $419,651 on its programs. This included $8,100 in grants. Recipients included; $7,000 for the Fund for American Studies, $500 for the James Madison University, and $100 for *The Dartmouth Review*.

Total Revenue: FY ending 9/94 $664,113 **Total Expenses:** $692,000 61%/10%/29% **Net Assets:** (-$73,131)
Tax Status: 501(c)(3)   **Citations:** 3:204
Periodicals: *The Lincoln Review* (journal).

Other Information: Jay Parker is an employee of Jay Parker and Associates, a for-profit organization that performs management services for the Institute. Jay Parker is also the president of the 501(c)(4) Abraham Lincoln Foundation. The Institute received $641,083, or 97% of revenue, from contributions and grants awarded by foundations, businesses, and individuals. (These contributions and grants have been declining by an average of 7% per year since 1991.) $22,946, or 3%, from mailing list rentals. The remaining revenue came from interest on savings.

Lincoln Institute of Public Opinion Research

453 Springlake Rd.
Harrisburg, PA 17112   **Phone:** (717) 671-0776   **E-Mail:** 74157.243@Compuserve.com
USA   **Fax:**   (717) 671-1176

Contact Person: Lowman S. Henry, Chairman/CEO.

Officers or Principals: Lowman S. Henry, Chairman/CEO ($12,800); John Hanks, Jr., Executive Director ($6,886); Jane R. Gordon, Secretary/Treasurer ($6,820); Robert W. Keibler, Vice Chairman.

Mission or Interest: "To promote the ideals of free-market economics, individual liberty and limited government through the conduct of public opinion research and related educational projects." Focus on Pennsylvania. Conducts polls on the nation and Pennsylvania's economy; the popularity of the President, Federal Reserve Chairman Alan Greenspan, and other public figures; Pennsylvania households' economic well-being; and the business climate in Pennsylvania. Uses the results of these polls to advance public policy.
Accomplishments: In 1995 the Institute spent $79,101 on its programs.
Total Revenue: 1995 $126,489 **Total Expenses:** $89,485 88%/9%/2% **Net Assets:** $41,884
Products or Services: Produces a bimonthly radio program aired on 56 stations. Occasional special reports.
Tax Status: 501(c)(3) **Annual Report:** Yes. **Employees:** 4
Board of Directors or Trustees: James Canova, Hilary Holste (Strongland, PA, Chamber of Commerce), Doris O'Donnell (Allegheney Found.), Joseph Geiger, Charles Huston, III (Commonwealth Found.), Albert Paschall (Pres., King of Prussia, PA, Chamber of Commerce), James Trammell.
Periodicals: *Sindlinger Economic Report* (quarterly survey data).
Internships: No.
Other Information: Established in 1993. The Institute received $123,175, or 97% of revenue, from contributions and grants awarded by foundations, businesses, and individuals. (This was a 147% increase over the previous year. These grants included $85,000 from the Allegheny Foundation.) $2,260, or 2%, from a fund-raising golf outing. The remaining revenue came from interest on savings and temporary cash investments, and other miscellaneous sources.

Lincoln Legal Foundation

100 West Monroe St., Suite 1600
Chicago, IL 60603   **Phone:** (312) 606-0951
USA   **Fax:**   (312) 606-0879

Contact Person: Joseph A. Morris, President/General Counsel.
Officers or Principals: Joseph A. Morris, President ($0); Robert T. Palmer, Secretary ($0); Theophil C. Kammholz, Vice President ($0); Peter G. Gallanis, Treasurer; Henry Pitts, Chairman.
Mission or Interest: To represent the public interest through legal action in defense of individual liberty, free enterprise, and limited constitutional government.
Total Revenue: 1995 $70,917 **Total Expenses:** $44,522 **Net Assets:** (-$9,392)
Products or Services: *Pro bono publico* casework. They take on cases that have broad implications for law and public policy.
Tax Status: 501(c)(3)
Board of Directors or Trustees: Leon Bronfin, Fred Eichhorn, Michael Freeborn, Morris Leibman, K. Thor Lundgren, Terence MacCarthy, Jeremiah Marsh, Robert Palmer, J. D. Thorne, Joseph Wright, Jr.
Other Information: The Foundation received $64,643, or 91% of revenue, from contributions and grants awarded by foundations, businesses, and individuals. (These contributions and grants have been erratic, but 1995's were the highest in the last five years.) $6,269, or 9%, from program services. The remaining revenue came from interest on savings.

Live and Let Live

P.O. Box 613
Redwood Valley, CA 95470
USA

Contact Person: James N. Dawson, Publisher.
Mission or Interest: "A Journal which seeks to explore and develop a theory and strategy of fetal and animal rights from a libertarian-individualist (as opposed to a left-collectivist) framework and also provide a forum for libertarian and other animal-rights advocates outside the political, philosophical and religious mainstream outside of the animal-rights movement."
Accomplishments: Received fairly good reviews in *Factsheet 5*, *Incite Information*, and others.
Tax Status: Unincorporated. **Annual Report:** No.
Periodicals: *Live and Let Live*, (irregularly published journal, 2-4 a issues a year).
Internships: No.
Other Information: Mr. Dawson is a long-time advocate of animal rights. He became involved with libertarianism and became a Libertarian after seeing commercials for 1980 Libertarian presidential candidate Ed Clark.

Live Free International

P.O. Box 1743
Harvey, IL 60426   **Phone:** (312) 821-5483
USA

Contact Person: James C. Jones, Executive Director.
Mission or Interest: "To promote and support self-sufficiency, self-reliance, self-protection and freedom for responsible people of all races, religions and nationalities. . . Live Free started as a small Chicago area sports and wilderness survival club in the 1960s and slowly expanded its interests to include disaster preparedness and self-reliance advocacy. When 'survivalist' and 'survivalism' suddenly became the subjects of media madness and distortions in the 1980s, Live Free fought to preserve the reputation of the responsible survivalist and did much to define the true philosophy of survivalism as a positive and constructive concept."

Accomplishments: "Live Free has consistently received favorable press in such publications as *American Survival Guide, The Journal of Civil Defense*, the *Chicago Tribune* and dozens of other publications, radio programs and TV programs."
Products or Services: "Survivalist Papers," a series of guides to emergency preparedness, wilderness survival, and self-reliant skills. Cash prizes for new ideas for the series. "Certified Survival Instructor" program.
Tax Status: 501(c)(3) **Annual Report:** No. **Employees:** All volunteer.
Periodicals: *Directions* (monthly newsletter). **Internships:** No.

Living Free

P.O. Box 29, Hiler Branch
Buffalo, NY 14223
USA

Contact Person: Jim Stumm.
Mission or Interest: "Newsletter that discusses practical methods for increasing personal freedom. Forum for freedom-seekers, libertarians, survivalists, anarchists, and outlaws since 1979."
Products or Services: "Published 97 issues of *Living Free* since 1979, and have dozens of reports available for sale."
Tax Status: For profit.
Board of Directors or Trustees: *Living Free* newsletter.

Living Truth Ministries

1708 Patterson Rd.
Austin, TX 78733   **Phone:** (512) 263-9780
USA   **Fax:** (512) 263-9793

Contact Person: Wanda J. Marrs, Vice President.
Officers or Principals: Texe W. Marrs, President; Wanda J. Marrs, Vice President (the Marrs did not receive a salary; they did, however, share $260,000 in book royalties); Sharon Norris, Trustee ($0).
Mission or Interest: "Christian education and promotion of patriotism within a Biblical framework." Opposition to 'The New World Order' and other "long-standing, serpentine networks of international revolutionaries and facist ideologues whose goal is to end American sovereignty and bring about a global, Marxist paradise."
Accomplishments: "International newsletter distributed in 70 countries. Publisher of books, a number of which are Christian bestsellers." In 1994 the Ministries spent $1,096,813 on its programs. The largest expenditure, $1,027,213, was the production and distribution of "195,000 books, 480,000 newsletters, 7,220 videos, 19,520 audiotapes, 56,000 tracts and booklets." Other programs included speaking engagements and counseling.
Total Revenue: 1994 $1,439,359 36%(1) **Total Expenses:** $1,157,701 95%/5%/0% **Net Assets:** $312,897
Products or Services: Books by the Marrs, including Dark Majesty: The Secret Brotherhood and the Magic of A Thousand Points of Light, Project L.U.C.I.D.: The Beast 666 Universal Human Control System, and Big Sister is Watching You about Hillary Rodham Clinton. Audio and video tapes. Shortwave radio program heard on 7435 kHz.
Tax Status: 501(c)(3) **Employees:** 12 **Citations:** 3:204
Periodicals: *Flashpoint* (monthly newsletter).
Internships: No.
Other Information: The Ministry received $1,288,703, or 90% of revenue, from the sale of books and recordings. $143,200, or 10%, from contributions and grants awarded by foundations, businesses, and inidividuals. The remaining revenue came from interest on savings and temporary cash investments.

Local Government Center

(see Reason Foundation)

Locke Institute

4084 University Dr., Suite 103
Fairfax, VA 22030   **Phone:** (703) 934-6960
USA   **Fax:** (703) 352-9747 **Internet:** http://www.his.com/~chyden/locke

Contact Person: Prof. Charles K. Rowley, General Director.
Officers or Principals: Amanda J. Owens, Director, Legal Services; Marjorie I. Rowley, Program Director; Arthur Seldon, Editorial Director; Robert S. Elgin, Financial Director.
Mission or Interest: "Dedicated to pursuit of individual liberty, private property rights, limited government and the rule of law."
Accomplishments: Awarded first place for the Sir Antony Fisher Memorial Award in 1994, 1995, and 1996. Published 8 books and 8 monographs, all receiving positive reviews. Organized colloquia in cooperation with the Liberty Fund for economics students and the general public.
Products or Services: Locke Institute books published by Edward Elgar Publishing Ltd., include: The Right to Justice, Property Rights and the Limits of Democracy, Public Goods and Private Communities, and Bureaucracy and Public Economics.
Tax Status: 501(c)(3)

Other Information: Established in 1989. In 1995 the Institute received $4,000 from the Sunmark Foundation.

Lofton Letter

P.O. Box 1142
Laurel, MD 20725   **Phone:**   (301) 490-0104
USA   **Fax:**   (301) 953-3423

Contact Person: John Lofton.
Mission or Interest: A monthly newsletter (10-15,000 words) of "the real, red-meat of the orthodox, Biblical faith," written by John Lofton.
Accomplishments: Mr. Lofton has spoken on numerous campuses, to home-school groups, has been a guest on "Good Morning America," "Nightline," "The Today Show," "CBS Morning News," "Crossfire," and the major television talk shows. His writings have appeared in *The Washington Post, Harper's, Christianity Today, USA Today, Human Events, National Review* and *The American Spectator.* He is the first place prize winner of the 1987 Amy Writing Awards.
Tax Status: For profit.
Periodicals: *The Lofton Letter* (monthly newsletter).

Louisiana Citizens for a Sound Economy

P.O. Box 80362
Baton Rouge, LA 70898   **Phone:**   (504) 387-2242
USA   **Fax:**   (504) 387-2244

Contact Person: Beverly Smiley, Director.
Mission or Interest: Louisiana affiliate of Citizens for a Sound Economy. Advocates lower taxes, less spending, and less regulation of the economy.
Accomplishments: Over 2,500 members statewide.
Products or Services: Lobbying, research and educational activities.
Tax Status: 501(c)(4)
Other Information: Like Citizens for a Sound Economy in Washington, DC, they also have a 501(c)(3) foundation, Louisiana Citizens for a Sound Economy Foundation at the same address.

Ludwig von Mises Institute

Auburn University
Auburn, AL 36849   **Phone:**   (334) 844-2500   **E-Mail:**   lvmises@mail.auburn.edu
USA   **Fax:**   (334) 844-2583   **Internet:** http://www.mises.org

Contact Person: Llewellyn H. Rockwell, Jr., President.
Officers or Principals: Llewellyn H. Rockwell, Jr., President ($59,000); Patricia Heckman, Vice President ($50,000); Burton S. Blumert, Director; John V. Denson, Director.
Mission or Interest: ". . .fills a gap in American academic and public life through economics education in the tradition of the Austrian School of economics. Our goal is to renew interest in logical methods in economics and the social sciences generally, and provide a radical but nonpartisan critique of all government intervention, a defense of unfettered capitalism, a case for the restoration of sound money, and a call for international conflicts to be settled through free trade, not protectionism, embargoes, or warfare." The Austrian School of economics emphasizes the deductive method for discovering immutable and universal laws of economics. Theory is favored over quantitative statistical and mathematic methods. The Austrian School was founded on the theories of 19th century economists Carl Menger and Eugen von Böhm-Bawerk. The Institute is named for economist Ludwig von Mises (1881-1973), "the century's exemplar of the tradition." Among Mises's prominent works are Human Action and Socialism. He was the mentor of Nobel Laureate economist F. A. Hayek, as well as Murray Rothbard, Henry Hazlitt, Israel Kirzner and others.
Accomplishments: Austrian Scholars Conference brought together scholars from ten countries to hear and critique 60 academic papers. Published many new academic works and translations; has also brought back many out-of-print works by Austrian scholars. The Cuban Ministry of Economy and Planning has requested to be placed on the Institute's mailing list. In 1994 the Institute spent $752,623 on its programs. The largest expenditure, $304,115 was spent on conferences and seminars. $251,661 was spent on publications. $128,741 was spent on student fellowships and research grants.
Total Revenue: 1994 $1,483,303 43%(2) **Total Expenses:** $953,909 79%/8%/13% **Net Assets:** $1,233,797
Products or Services: Annual summer program for students. Annual catalog of publications. Academic workshops, seminars, conferences, scholarships, more.
Tax Status: 501(c)(3) **Annual Report:** Yes. **Employees:** 7   **Citations:** 30:132

Board of Directors or Trustees: Prof. Roger Garrison (Auburn Univ.), Prof. Hans-Hermann Hoppe (UNLV), Prof. Yuri Maltsev (Carthage College), Prof. Walter Block (Holy Cross College), Prof. Jeffrey Herbener (Washington & Jefferson College), Prof. David Gordon (UCLA).

Periodicals: *The Free Market* (monthly newsletter), *The Mises Review* (quarterly book review journal), *The Austrian Economics Newsletter* (quarterly newsletter), *Mises Memo* (quarterly newsletter of Institute activities), and *The Review of Austrian Economics* (biannual academic journal).

Internships: Yes.

Other Information: Established in 1982 by Llewellyn Rockwell, former Chief of Staff for Rep. Ron Paul (R-TX). Murray Rothbard (1926-1995) was Director of Academic Affairs at the Institute from its founding until his death. The Institute received $1,408,586, or 95% of revenue, from contributions and grants awarded by foundations, businesses, and individuals. (In 1995 these grants included $1,000 from the Roe Foundation.) $34,109, or 2%, from interest on savings and temporary cash investments. $23,443, or 2%, from conference fees. The remaining revenue came from mailing list rentals and the sale of inventory. Despite strong opposition to the Federal Reserve system, the Institute's single largest investment holding in 1994 was $149,741 held in a U.S. Treasury Reserve Note.

Lundy Chair of Philosophy of Business

Campbell University
P.O. Box 1145
Buies Creek, NC 27501   **Phone:** (910) 893-1410   **E-Mail:**   cordato@camel.campbell.edu
USA   **Fax:**   (910) 893-1424

Contact Person: Roy E. Cordato, Lundy Professor.

Mission or Interest: "To educate students and the community in the principles of individual liberty and responsibility, free enterprise, and limited government." Program and endowed chair that stresses free-markets and classical liberal thought. With Campbell University's Adam Smith Club, the program provides a curriculum, hosts speakers through its "Foundations of Rational Economic Education" (FREE) program, and conducts other educational events.

Accomplishments: Recent FREE speakers included columnist Joseph Sobran, author James Bovard, and Doug Bandow of the Cato Institute.

Products or Services: Occasional papers, curricula, and speakers.

Tax Status: 501(c)(3) **Annual Report:** No. **Employees:** 2

Board of Directors or Trustees: Patrons and supporters of the Adam Smith Club include; Arthur Pope (Pope Found.), Prof. Walter E. Williams (George Mason Univ.), Howard and Andrea Rich, and others.

Periodicals: *Campbell Entrepreneur* (quarterly newsletter).

Internships: No.

Other Information: Affiliated with and incorporated under Campbell University. The Lundy Chair is named after the late Burrows T. Lundy, the founder of the Lundy Packing Company. Previous holders of the Lundy Chair included Dr. Eric Brodin and Dr. William H. Peterson. The current holder, Dr. Roy E. Cordato, has written for *The Christian Science Monitor, Washington Times, Journal of Commerce, Human Events,* and *The Free Market* - a publication of the Ludwig von Mises Institute. Cordato is considered a key contemporary economist in the Austrian school of economics. He is the author of Welfare Economics and Externalities in an Open Ended Universe (Kluwer Academic Publishers, 1992). In 1995-96 the Campbell University Business School received $100,000 from the John William Pope Foundation, and the Lundy Chair specifically received another $5,000 from the Pope Foundation.

Lutherans for Life

1229 South G Ave., Building B, Suite 100
Nevada, IA 50201   **Phone:** (515) 382-2077
USA   **Fax:**   (515) 382-3020

Contact Person: Dr. James I. Lamb, Executive Director.

Officers or Principals: Linda Bartlett, President ($0); Rev. David Wende, Vice President ($0); Joyce Gierke, Secretary ($0); Diane Schroeder, Treasurer.

Mission or Interest: "Lutherans for Life believes that the Church is compelled by God's Word to speak and act on behalf of those who are vulnerable and defenseless. The crisis of our time is the repudiation of Biblical truth manifested in the wanton destruction of innocent human life through legalized abortion-on-demand and the growing threat to the lives of others through legalized assisted suicide and euthanasia."

Accomplishments: Has assisted in the formation of Lutherans for Life organizations in Canada, Germany, Austria, and other countries. Helped to establish a K-junior high "Celebrate the Life" curriculum. LFL has filed two friend-of-the-court briefs to the U.S. Supreme Court. Past president Dr. Jean Garton is the author of Who Broke the Baby?, a key book in the anti-abortion movement.

Total Revenue: 1995 $232,115 **Total Expenses:** $233,600 100%/0%/0% **Net Assets:** $71,856

Products or Services: Radio programming, curricula and educational materials, books and videos.

Tax Status: 501(c)(3) **Annual Report:** No. **Employees:** 3   **Citations:** 22:145

Board of Directors or Trustees: Jerry Hiller, Joan Engel, Rev. Don Richman, Rev. David Renfro, Rev. Frank Maurer, Jerry Heise, Margaret Mesmer, Marilyn Goad.

Periodicals: *Living* (magazine), and *Life Date* (newsletter).
Internships: No.
Other Information: Previously located in Benton, Arkansas. LFL received $175,510, or 76% of revenue, from contributions and grants awarded by foundations, businesses, and individuals. (These contributions and grants have been growing by an average of 12% per year since 1991.) $55,509, or 24%, from membership dues. The remaining revenue came from interest on savings.

Lynde and Harry Bradley Foundation

P.O. Box 92848
Milwaukee, WI 53202   **Phone:** (414) 291-9915
USA   **Fax:**   (414) 291-9991

Contact Person: Michael S. Joyce, President.
Officers or Principals: Michael S. Joyce, President ($454,805); Hillel G. Fradkin, Vice President, Academic Programs ($230,591); Robert N. Berkopec, Treasurer/CFO ($156,467); I. Andrew Rader, Chairman ($155,859); Daniel P. Schmidt, Vice President, Operations ($134,595); William Schambra, ($122,590); Allen M. Taylor, Vice Chairman; Wayne J. Roper, Secretary.
Mission or Interest: Grant-making foundation that includes conservative and free-market-oriented organizations in its awards. "Devoted to strengthening American democratic capitalism and the institutions, principles, and values which sustain and nurture it."
Accomplishments: In 1995 the Foundation awarded $24,040,012 in grants. Recipients included: nine grants totaling $1,824,100 for Partners Advancing Values in Education, seven grants totaling $875,000 for the Heritage Foundation, four grants totaling $740,000 for the American Enterprise Institute, ten grants totaling $545,000 for the Center for Popular Culture, four grants totaling $460,000 for the Wisconsin Policy Research Institute, four grants totaling $450,000 for the Free Congress Foundation, four grants totaling $400,000 for the Institute on Religion and Public Life, four grants totaling $400,000 for National Affairs, seven grants totaling $395,000 for the Hudson Institute, five grants totaling $394,900 for the Institute for Contemporary Studies, five grants totaling $375,000 for the National Bureau of Economic Research, three grants totaling $300,000 for the Ronald Reagan Presidential Foundation, seven grants totaling $258,000 for the Ethics and Public Policy Center, five grants totaling $280,300 for the George C. Marshall Institute, $225,000 for the National Center for Neighborhood Enterprise, $215,000 for the Foundation for Cultural Review, $193,750 for the Institute for International Studies, $188,000 for the Madison Center, $185,000 for the New Citizenship Project, $165,000 for the American Spectator, five grants totaling $153,500 for the Black Research Organization, $150,000 each for the National Association of Scholars, National Fatherhood Initiative, and Of the People Foundation, $126,000 for the Federalist Society, $120,000 for the Institute for the Study of Economic Culture, $100,000 each for the Center for Individual Rights, and National Forum Foundation, $90,000 for the Brownson Institute, $85,000 for the Reason Foundation, $77,500 for the Institute for Justice, $75,000 each for the American Jewish Committee/*Commentary*, Institute for Policy Innovation, Hoover Institution, and Philanthropy Roundtable, $70,000 each for the Center of the American Experiment, and Intercollegiate Studies Institute, $60,000 each for the Competitive Enterprise Institute, and Progress & Freedom Foundation, $55,500 for the Environmental Defense Fund, $55,000 for the Family Research Council, $50,000 each for the American Academy of Liberal Education, Center for Media and Public Affairs, Center for Security Policy, Fund for American Studies, National Alumni Forum, National Center for Policy Analysis, and Political Economy Research Center.
Total Revenue: 1995 $34,506,420 **Total Expenses:** $29,295,659 **Net Assets:** $461,043,169 4%(3)
Tax Status: 501(c)(3)
Board of Directors or Trustees: Sarah Barder, Hon. Frank Shakespeare (former Ambassador to the Vatican), David Uihlein, J. Clayburn La Force, Reed Coleman, Wayne Roper, Allen Taylor.
Other Information: Established in 1985 when the Allen-Bradley Company, founded in 1903 by two brothers -- Lynde and Harry Bradley, was sold to Rockwell International. The Foundation received $19,503,841, or 57% of revenue, from capital gains on the sale of securities. $13,696,658, or 40%, from dividends and interest from securities. $1,305,921, or 3%, from interest on savings and temporary cash investments. The Foundation held $316,796,981, or 69% of assets, in corporate stock. $66,227,060, or 14%, in government bonds.

M. J. Murdock Charitable Trust

703 Broadway, Suite 710
Vancouver, WA 98660   **Phone:** (206) 694-8415
USA

Contact Person: Ford A. Anderson, II, Executive Director.
Officers or Principals: James R. Martin, Chief Financial Officer ($160,080); Ford A. Anderson, II, Executive Director ($121,800); Neal O. Thorpe, Senior Program Officer ($94,944); Joanna S. Wilson, John M. Woodyard, Program Officers; Bonnie J. O'Donnell, Administrative Officer.
Mission or Interest: "The Trust's primary function is to provide 'up-front' or venture capital, along with that of other donors and the applicant's own resources, in the testing and validation of promising concepts and in the launching of well thought-out programs which have the potential to thrive beyond the stage of initial funding." The Trust focuses on various social problems, and includes conservative and free-market organizations in its grants. An example of this is the Trust's funding of pilot programs to establish the efficacy of "medical savings accounts" through grants to the National Center for Policy Analysis and the Evergreen Freedom Foundation. Focus on the Rocky Mountain states.

Accomplishments: In 1994 the Trust awarded $17,492,509 in grants. Recipients included: two grants totaling $245,000 for the Leadership Institute, $150,000 for the National Strategy Information Center, $125,000 for the Heritage Foundation, $100,000 each for the Discovery Institute, and the National Center for Policy Analysis, $50,000 each for the Intercollegiate Studies Institute, Pacific Legal Foundation, and Christian Legal Society, $38,000 for the Foundation for Research on Economics and the Environment, $30,000 each for the Cascade Policy Institute and Evergreen Freedom Foundation, $25,000 each for Freedoms Foundation at Valley Forge, Washington Research Council, and Montana Land Reliance, $20,000 for the Acton Institute, and $15,000 for the Foundation for Teaching Economics.

Total Revenue: 1994 $27,357,680 **Total Expenses:** $21,872,571 **Net Assets:** $262,451,053 (Decrease of less than 1%)(1)
Tax Status: 501(c)(3)
Board of Directors or Trustees: James Castles, Walter Dyke, Lynwood Swanson.
Other Information: Established in 1975 as a provision in the will of M.J. (Jack) Murdock (1917-1971). Jack Murdock was a founder and chairman of Tektronix. Murdock, a pilot, died in a small-plane crash. Subsequently, small-plane safety has been a concern of the Trust. The Trust received $18,466,863, or 68% of revenue, from capital gains on the sale of assets. $8,882,799, or 32%, from dividends and interest from securities. The remaining revenue came from interest on savings and temporary cash investments. The Trust held $189,410,123, or 72% of assets, in corporate stock. $41,458,879, or 16%, in government securities.

Mackinac Center for Public Policy

119 Ashman St., P.O. Box 568
Midland, MI 48640   **Phone:** (517) 631-0900   **E-Mail:** mcpp@mackinac.org
USA   **Fax:**   (517) 631-0964   **Internet:** http://www.mackinac.org

Contact Person: Joseph G. Lehman, Director of Communications.
Officers or Principals: Lawrence W. Reed, President ($90,000); David Cotten, Development Director ($70,069); Richard D. McLellan, Secretary ($0); Joseph Overton, Vice President; D. Joseph Olson, Chairman; Robert P. Hunter, Director of Labor Policy.
Mission or Interest: "Provide research and education to advance sound economic policy proposals which show Michigan citizens and leaders the benefits of free markets and civil society."
Accomplishments: "Dozens of policy proposals have been adopted by Michigan state government in areas including education reform, privatization, government waste, welfare reform, taxation, state infrastructure, collective bargaining, and others." In 1996 the Center received an award of $250,000 for its endowment fund from the Herbert H. And Grace A. Dow Foundation. The Center, in cooperation with the Institute for Justice, trained attorneys to defend the rights of entrepreneurs and individuals. In 1994 the Center spent $463,260 on its policies.
Total Revenue: 1994 $598,773 34%(2) **Total Expenses:** $634,603 73%/10%/17% **Net Assets:** $38,634
Products or Services: "Free Market Moments" radio commentaries heard throughout Michigan. "Viewpoint" print commentary series. Training programs for high-school teachers in economics and history. Debate workshops for high-school students. Private Cure for Public Ills: The Promise of Privatization, edited by Larry Reed. Catalog of numerous studies and publications.
Tax Status: 501(c)(3) **Annual Report:** No. **Employees:** 14   **Citations:** 77:80
Board of Directors or Trustees: Peter Cook, Hon. Paul Gadola, Lynne Galligan, Harry Hutchison, IV, Mara Letica, Bruce Maguire, Jr., Richard McLellan, James Rodney, Linda Shinkle. The Center's Board of Advisors includes: Dick DeVos (Pres., Amway Corp.), Mark Bissell, John Canepa, Kevin Cusack, Betsy DeVos, Dan DeVos, Dan Gordon, Doyle Hayes, David Hooker, J. C. Huizenga, Michael Jandernoa, Hank Meijer (Vice Chairman, Meijer, Inc.), Bob Powers, Owen Pyle, Amb. Peter Secchia (former ambassador to Italy, 1989-93), Ginny Seyferth, Dick Simmons, Charles Stoddard.
Periodicals: *IMPACT!* (quarterly newsletter), *Privatization Report* (quarterly report).
Internships: Yes, both paid and unpaid.
Other Information: Member of the State Policy Network. The Center received $598,322, or 99.9% of revenue, from contributions and grants awarded by foundations, businesses, and individuals. (These grants included $10,000 from the Earhart Foundation, and $5,000 from the Richard & Helen DeVos Foundation. In 1995, $30,000 from the Lynde and Harry Bradley Foundation, and $10,000 from the Roe Foundation.) The remaining revenue came from interest on savings and temporary cash investments.

Madison Center for Educational Affairs

(see the Collegiate Network)

Manhattan Institute for Public Policy Research

52 Vanderbilt Ave.
New York, NY 10017   **Phone:** (212) 599-7000   **E-Mail:** mi@manhattan-institute.org
USA   **Fax:**   (212) 599-3494   **Internet:** http://www.manhattan-institute.org

Contact Person: David DesRosiers.
Officers or Principals: Peter Huber, Senior Fellow ($180,000); Lawrence J. Mone, President ($173,538); Myron Magnet, Editor, *City Journal.* ($133,269); John Elwell, Senior Fellow ($112,538); Walter Olson, Senior Fellow ($108,000); Agnes Richardson, Director, Center for Educational Innovation ($100,000); Midge Richardson, Executive Director, Center for Educational Innovation; Andrew Cowlin, Executive Director, Center for Civic Innovation; Andrew Hazlett, Acting Director, Center for Judicial Studies.
Mission or Interest: "Produces original scholarship on a variety of public policy topics, disseminates information and ideas, and operates units which take a direct role in initiating reforms." Focus on New York.

Accomplishments: Publication of more than 100 books, including; <u>Losing Ground</u> by Charles Murray, <u>The Litigation Explosion: What Happened When America Unleashed the Lawsuit</u> by Walter K. Olson, <u>Miracle in East Harlem</u> by Seymour Fliegel, <u>Fixing Broken Windows</u> by George Kelling and Catherine Coles, <u>The Growth Experiment</u> by Lawrence B. Lindsey, and others. Opened "Young Women's Leadership School," an all-girls' public school in East Harlem specializing in science education for children from poor, minority communities. Hosted major conferences on "Junk Science in the Classroom," "Reinventing Government: The Indianapolis Experience" and "Charter Schools: What Are They." In 1996 the Institute spent $5,517,298 on its programs.
Total Revenue: 1996 $6,241,342 10%(4) **Total Expenses:** $5,517,298 92%/4%/4% **Net Assets:** $1,528,786
Products or Services: Operates the Center for Educational Innovation. The Center is active in restructuring low-performing schools in Brooklyn, Maryland, Philadelphia, and elsewhere.
Tax Status: 501(c)(3) **Annual Report:** No. **Employees:** 30   **Citations:** 233:36
Periodicals: *The City Journal* (quarterly), *CEI Notes* (publication of the Center for Educational Innovation), *Civil Justice Memo*, and *Civic Bulletin*.
Internships: Yes.
Other Information: Established in 1978 as the International Center for Economic Policy Studies. Name changed to Manhattan Institute in 1980. The Institute received $6,102,800, or 98% of revenue, from contributions and grants awarded by foundations, businesses, and individuals. (In 1994-95 these grants included $322,500 from the John M. Olin Foundation, $250,000 from the Lilly Endowment, $175,000 from the Sarah Scaife Foundation, $100,000 from the Gilder Foundation, $100,000 from the Smith Richardson Foundation, $37,500 from the William H. Donner Foundation, $25,000 from the Carthage Foundation, $7,500 from the Earhart Foundation, $5,000 from the Milliken Foundation, $2,500 from the John William Pope Foundation, and $2,500 from the Fanwood Foundation.) $101,260, or 2%, from programs service revenues. The remaining revenue came from dividends and interest from securities, interest on savings, rental income, and other miscellaneous sources.

Margaret Thatcher Foundation

1901 L St., N.W., Suite 707
Washington, DC 20036   **Phone:**   (202) 775-1455
USA   **Fax:**   (202) 775-1415

Contact Person: Katherine Strobel Carraway, Program Manager.
Officers or Principals: Katherine Strobel Carraway, Program Manager ($36,000).
Mission or Interest: Committed to democracy and market economies in developing nations and the emerging nations of Eastern Europe.
Total Revenue: 1993 $1,321,706 **Total Expenses:** $473,531 27%/20%/54% **Net Assets:** $1,270,168
Products or Services: In 1993 the Foundation awarded $127,500 in grants to organizations aiding the development of skills and technology in developing countries.
Tax Status: 501(c)(3)   **Citations:** 3:204
Other Information: Established in 1992. In 1995 the Foundation received $60,000 from the Forbes Foundation.

Massachusetts Family Institute

381 Elliot St.
Newton Upper Falls, MA 02164   **Phone:**   (617) 928-0800   **E-Mail:**   mafamily@aol.com
USA   **Fax:**   (617) 928-1515

Contact Person: Debby Keogh, Office Manager.
Officers or Principals: Daniel White, President ($37,516); Robert H. Bradley, Chairman ($0); Joseph C. Cunningham, Vice Chairman ($0); Anita W. Fritze, Secretary; Walter H. Weld, Treasurer.
Mission or Interest: "To equip and encourage the citizens of Massachusetts to create communities where families are valued and nurtured. . . Committed to strengthening the family and restoring Judeo-Christian values to our culture. . . We provide credible information on a variety of crucial issues such as welfare reform, sex education, educational choice, gambling, pornography, abortion, adoption, taxation, euthanasia, homosexuality, drug abuse, and criminal justice."
Accomplishments: In the fiscal year ending September 1995, the Institute spent $43,164 on its programs.
Total Revenue: FY ending 9/95 $122,848 **Total Expenses:** $122,520 35%/51%/13% **Net Assets:** $6,930
Products or Services: Research, analysis, networking with churches and professional organizations, and lobbying. In 1995 the Institute spent $760 on lobbying; this was the first time it had engaged in lobbying.
Tax Status: 501(c)(3)
Board of Directors or Trustees: Ronald Brandt, Gregory Dunn, Charles Gogolak, Gail Mills, Mary Shahian, Hope Vassos, Warren Wise, William Payne, John Daniel, Thomas Owens.
Periodicals: *Massachusetts Family Report* (bimonthly newsletter), and *Massachusetts Citizen* (monthly newsletter included in Focus on the Family's *Citizen*).
Other Information: Established in 1991. Affiliated with Focus on the Family. The Institute combines its newsletter with Focus' *Citizen*, but does not receive any direct financial assistance from Focus. The Institute received $121,797, or 99% of revenue, from contributions and grants awarded by foundations, businesses, and individuals. (These contributions have grown at an average rate of 22% over the last five years.) The remaining revenue came from newsletter subscriptions, an annual banquet, and interest on savings and temporary cash investments.

Massachusetts Taxpayers Foundation

24 Province St.
Boston, MA 02108   **Phone:**   (617) 720-1000
USA

Contact Person: Michael J. Widmer, President.
Officers or Principals: Michael J. Widmer, President ($177,667); Susanne E. Tompkins, Vice President ($94,752); Gina Beauchemin, Assistant Treasurer ($16,952).
Mission or Interest: Analysis of taxation and fiscal issues in the state of Massachusetts "to ensure state fiscal stability and promote healthy economic growth."
Accomplishments: In 1994 the Foundation spent $488,884 on its programs. The largest expenditure, $146,665, was on state budget analysis, monitoring the appropriations process, and a fiscal year report and assessment. $122,221 was spent on local government analysis. $97,777 for economic and tax forecasting using their own model. Other programs included an annual report on municipal data, a report on welfare reform, and a voter's guide to state ballot questions.
Total Revenue: 1994 $841,622 (-1%)(1) **Total Expenses:** $795,191 61%/24%/15% **Net Assets:** $493,301
Products or Services: Research, analysis, forecasting, and lobbying. Annual tax conference. The Foundation spent $33,320 on lobbying, $19,950 on grassroots lobbying and $13,370 on the direct lobbying of legislators. This was a 194% increase over the previous year.
Tax Status: 501(c)(3)   **Citations:** 108:61
Board of Directors or Trustees: F. Gregory Ahern, Dennis Austin, James Conway, III, Albert Cornelio, Robert Dubiel, William Hogan, Jr., Daniel Holland, Mitchell Kertzman, John Killian, Joanna Lau, Pamela McDermott, Thomas Moloney, Thomas Olsen, Alison Taunton-Rigby, Clifford Tuttle, Robert Weinberg, Elizabeth Whitehead.
Internships: Yes.
Other Information: The Foundation received $817,803, or 97% of revenue, from contributions and grants awarded by foundations, businesses, and individuals. $9,952, or 1%, from tax conference fees. $7,237, or 1%, from interest on savings and temporary cash investments. The remaining revenue came from the sale of publications and other miscellaneous sources.

Media Associates Resource Coalition (MARC)

P.O. Box 5100
Zionsville, IN 46077-5100   **Phone:**   (317) 873-6649
USA   **Fax:**   same

Contact Person: Jean A. Elmore, Executive Director.
Officers or Principals: Mike Wilson, President ($0); Vincent Cannon, Vice President ($0); Greg Wallace, Vice President ($0); Jean Elmore, Secretary/Treasurer.
Mission or Interest: Providing free media referral service to anti-abortion and traditional-values organizations. Matches skilled professionals such as graphic artists, videographers, photographers, musicians, speakers, journalists, writers, broadcasters and others with organizations that need their services.
Accomplishments: In the first 18 months of existence the Coalition has identified over 65 associates throughout the United States. At least two-thirds of these professionals have been referred once or more to organizations needing their skills. In the fiscal year ending April 1995 the Coalition spent $7,142 on its programs.
Total Revenue: FY ending 4/95 $9,538 **Total Expenses:** $7,142 **Net Assets:** $7,025
Products or Services: In addition to their referral service they have distributed two radio spots, and a crisis pregnancy video. Professionals who wish to make themselves available as associates for referral pay no fee
Tax Status: 501(c)(3) **Annual Report:** No. **Employees:** All volunteer.
Periodicals: *MARConnections* (quarterly newsletter).
Internships: Possibly. Contact for more details.
Other Information: Established in 1991. The Coalition received $9,438, or 99% of revenue, from contributions and grants awarded by foundations, businesses, and individuals. The remaining revenue came from the sale of inventory and other miscellaneous sources.

Media Bypass

P.O. Box 5326
Evansville, IN 47716   **Phone:**   (812) 477-8670
USA

Contact Person: Eric J. Neese, Editor-in-Chief.
Officers or Principals: Troy L. Underhill, Assistant Editor.
Mission or Interest: Populist/conservative magazine of news and opinion.
Tax Status: For profit.
Periodicals: *Media Bypass: The Uncensored National News* (monthly magazine).
Other Information: Established in 1993.

Media Research Center (MRC)

113 S. West St., Suite 200
Alexandria, VA 22314   **Phone:** (703) 683-9733
USA   **Fax:**   (703) 683-9736   **Internet:** http://www.mediaresearch.org

Contact Person: Brent Baker, Executive Director.
Officers or Principals: L. Brent Bozell, Chairman ($154,887); Richard Kimble, Director of Finance ($69,141); Brent H. Baker, Secretary/Treasurer ($52,524); Sandra Crawford, Entertainment Division Director.
Mission or Interest: "Educating the public on bias in the media." Focus on leftist bias in news reporting and the entertainment industry.
Accomplishments: In 1996 MRC launched its "Tell the Truth Campaign," a campaign "to expose the lies and distortions of the national news media. MRC pledged to spend $2.8 million on the campaign. Developed a database of major print and broadcast news sources and prime time entertainment programming. The database contains over 80,000 hours of programing dating back to 1987, and is the largest database of its kind. MRC has over 10,000 members who receive publications. Operates through four divisions: the News Division, Entertainment Division, Parents' Television Council, and the Free Enterprise and Media Institute. In 1994 MRC spent $2,190,362 on its programs.
Total Revenue: 1994 $2,736,511 23%(1) **Total Expenses:** $2,505,976 87%/5%/7% **Net Assets:** $881,106
Products or Services: "Daily CyberAlert" e-mail updates sent to a network of over 1,700 recipients. Books include; And That's the Way It Isn't: A Reference Guide to Media Bias, How to Identify, Expose and Correct Liberal Media Bias, and Out of Focus: Network Television and the American Economy. Occasional special reports. MRC's Press Picks, a directory of conservative spokespersons and press figures (including liberals) who have "earned an overall reputation for fairness to conservatives."
Tax Status: 501(c)(3) **Annual Report:** Yes. **Employees:** 25   **Citations:** 398:26
Board of Directors or Trustees: Burton Yale Pines, William Rusher, Harold Clark Simmons, Curtis Winsor, Jr., Leon J. Weil.
Periodicals: *MediaWatch* (monthly newsletter), *Notable Quotables* (bimonthly newsletter "compilation of the most outrageous examples of bias from the media), *Hollywood Watch* (monthly newsletter covering the entertainment industry), *MediaNomics* (monthly newsletter covering business and economics issues and reporting).
Internships: Yes, "to train young conservatives in their pursuit to bring balance to journalism."
Other Information: Established in 1987. In 1994 MRC sublet office space to the Conservative Victory Committee PAC. MRC contracted the Alexandria, VA, public relations firm of Creative Response Concepts, paying the firm $72,000. MRC received $2,188,997, or 80% of revenue, from contributions and grants awarded by foundations, businesses, and individuals. (These grants included $100,000 from the Grover Hermann Foundation, $17,500 from the F.M. Kirby Foundation. In 1995, $50,000 from the John M. Olin Foundation, and $37,500 from the William H. Donner Foundation.) $472,699, or 17%, from publication subscriptions. $58,958, or 2%, from mailing list rental income. The remaining revenue came from interest on savings and temporary cash investments, and rental income (from the Conservative Victory Committee).

Men's Defense Association

17854 Lyons St.
Forest Lake, MN 55025   **Phone:** (612) 464-7887   **E-Mail:** mensdefens@aol.com
USA   **Fax:**   (612) 464-7135   **Internet:** http://mensdefense.org

Contact Person: Richard F. Doyle, President.
Officers or Principals: Richard F. Doyle, President/Treasurer ($0); Frank Zepezauer, Secretary ($0); Reuben Kidd, Vice President ($0).
Mission or Interest: "To salvage the family through equal rights and equal dignity for the male sex." Views government programs and "left wing politics" as having removed males from their place in society. "Government administered divorce, entitlement programs, and Affirmative Action programs subordinate individuals sovereignty to political fashions and arbitrarily redistribute property, sabotaging free enterprise and violating basic human rights."
Accomplishments: "Have stemmed the denigration of the male to some extent." The Association's newsletter, *The Liberator*, is "the original and flagship news forum of the international men's movement, (and) predates modern 'feminism'." In 1994 the Association spent $30,593 on its programs. In that time the Association referred an estimated 404 members to attorneys and to like-minded organizations in their home states.
Total Revenue: 1994 $31,932 **Total Expenses:** $32,474 **Net Assets:** $753
Products or Services: Books including The Rape of the Male (Poor Richard's Press, 1976) and The Men's Manifesto (Poor Richard's Press, 1992).
Tax Status: 501(c)(3) **Annual Report:** No. **Employees:** 2
Periodicals: *The Liberator* (monthly tabloid newsletter).
Internships: No.
Other Information: *The Liberator* has been published since 1968. The Men's Defense Association (then known as the Men's Rights Association) was founded in 1972. The Association received $11,263, or 35% of revenue, from subscriptions and sales of *The Liberator*. $8,073, or 25%, from membership dues. $5,505, or 17%, from the sale of advertisements. $3,663, or 11%, from contributions and grants. The remaining revenue came from the sale of literature and other miscellaneous sources.

Micah Center for Ethical Monotheism

10573 W. Pico Blvd., Suite 167
Los Angeles, CA 90064   **Phone:**   (310) 558-3958
USA   **Fax:**   (310) 558-4241

Contact Person: Dennis Prager, President.
Officers or Principals: Mark Wilcox, Vice President ($30,000); Dennis Prager, Founder/President.
Mission or Interest: "To promote Judeo-Christian based ethics and values as well as combat secular extremism."
Accomplishments: Produced two ethics-based comedy films directed by David Zucker of "Airplane" and "The Naked Gun" fame. Conducted several programs to bring together blacks and whites after the 1992 Los Angeles riots. Dennis Prager is the host of the highest-rated radio talk show in its time slot in Southern California. He was invited to speak on Vatican radio, and has been a guest on the Christian Broadcasting Network's "700 Club," speaking about anti-Semitism. In 1994 the Center spent $32,900 on its programs.
Total Revenue: 1994 $94,038 (-37%)(2) **Total Expenses:** $85,980 38%/39%/23% **Net Assets:** $24,282
Products or Services: Films, books, lectures, radio show.
Tax Status: 501(c)(3) **Annual Report:** No. **Employees:** 2
Periodicals: *Ultimate Issues* (quarterly).
Internships: Yes, for production assistants and writers.
Other Information: Established in 1991. Dennis Prager does not necessarily consider himself a conservative in the political sense. He was appointed by President Reagan to be a member of the United States delegation to the Vienna Review Conference on the Helsinki Accords to negotiate human rights with the former Soviet Union. He was national spokesman of the Student Struggle for Soviet Jewry and a delegate to the first Brussels World Conference on Soviet Jewry. The Center received $60,524, or 64% of revenue, from contributions and grants awarded by foundations, businesses, and individuals. $32,500, or 35%, from "fundraising residuals." The remaining revenue came from interest on savings and temporary cash investments, and other miscellaneous sources.

Michael Reagan Show, The

American Entertainment Network
P.O. Box 1548
La Jolla, CA 92038   **Phone:**   (619) 754-3333
USA   **Fax:**   (619) 754-3344

Contact Person: Peggie Ballard, Director of Network Operations.
Mission or Interest: Conservative radio show hosted by Michael Reagan, the son of former President Reagan, heard nationwide.
Accomplishments: Currently carried on over 75 stations nationwide. His show receives, on average, 3,000 - 6,000 calls a night, although only about 26 make it on the air.
Other Information: The phone number to reach the show while on the air is (800) 345-3113. The show is broadcast weeknights from 9-12:00 EST.

Michigan Family Forum (MFF)

611 S. Walnut
Lansing, MI 48933   **Phone:**   (517) 374-1171
USA   **Fax:**   (517) 374-6112

Contact Person: Patricia Payne.
Officers or Principals: Randall Hekman, Executive Director ($125,141); Kevin Cusak, Chairman ($0); Mile Wierda, Treasurer ($0).
Mission or Interest: Religious organization promoting "steady improvement in our state's schools, strengthening of marriage laws, a reduction of crime, a curbing of teen sexual activity and drug and alcohol use."
Accomplishments: In 1996 MFF's advocacy on behalf of no-fault divorce reform attracted national attention, appearing in the *New York Times, Los Angeles Times, Wall Street Journal*, and ABC's "World News Tonight." Distribution of over 500,000 voter guides for the 1996 general election. Recruited and trained 200 citizens to be activists. In 1995 MFF spent $616,136 on its programs.
Total Revenue: 1995 $1,026,211 **Total Expenses:** $839,513 73%/16%/11% **Net Assets:** $323,191
Products or Services: Prayer network, activist training, pamphlets, and other books and publications. Lobbying: in 1995 MFF spent $6,479 on lobbying; $5,050 on grassroots lobbying, and $1,429 on the direct lobbying of legislators. This was an increase of 117% over the previous year.
Tax Status: 501(c)(3)   **Citations:** 26:138
Board of Directors or Trustees: Gunnar Klarr, Louise Klarr, Michael Miller, Wayne VanDamm, Len Crowley, Don DeWitt, Jack DeWitt, Mary DeWitt, Victor Eagan, Emerson Eggerichs, Christine Gettel, Paul Hontz, Jerry Horne, J. C. Huizenga, Robert Igrisan, Paul Johnson, Herman Kanis, Richard Merillat, John Miller, Kelly Miller, Mark Saur, Tom Schram, Brian Sikma, William Sterk, Todd van Dyk, Jerry VanderLugt, James Wright.
Other Information: Affiliated with the 501(c)(4) Public Interest Forum at the same address. In 1995 the Public Interest Forum had revenues of only $100 and expenses of $129. Distributes copies of Focus on the Family's *Citizen* magazine. MFF received $997,862, or 97% of revenue, from contributions and grants awarded by foundations, businesses, and individuals. (In 1994 these grants included $100,000 from the Richard & Helen DeVos Foundation, $9,500 from the DeWitt Families Conduit Foundation.) $28,236, or 3%, from program services, including the sale of publications and conference fees. The remaining revenue came from interest on savings and temporary cash investments.

Mid America Legal Foundation (MALF)

120 W. Forest
Wheaton, IL 60187   **Phone:**   (630) 668-5488
USA

Contact Person: William Price, General Counsel.
Officers or Principals: William Price, General Counsel; Martha A. Churchill, former President ($32,609); James T. Harrington, Vice President ($0).
Mission or Interest: Free-market education and judicial action. MALF participates in legal matters which are likely to affect the economies of the Midwestern region.
Accomplishments: Filed a brief urging multiple punitive damages be eliminated in <u>Dunn v. Hovic</u>.
Total Revenue: 1994 $34,175 (-33%)(1) **Total Expenses:** $35,431 91%/2%/7% **Net Assets:** $1,037
Tax Status: 501(c)(3) **Employees:** 2
Board of Directors or Trustees: M. P. Venema, Edward Weber, Jr. (Acme Metals), Paul Meyer (Ashland Petroleum), Stephan Beyer, James Backham, Jr. (Potomac Communications Group), Ronald Ganim (Amoco).
Internships: No.
Other Information: Established in 1975 by various business organizations to promote "free enterprise principles in the courts." The Foundation received $33,775, or 99% of revenue, from contributions and grants awarded by foundations, businesses, and individuals. The remaining revenue came from a payment from the American Council on Science and Health for an article written by former president Martha Churchill.

Middle East Forum

1920 Chestnut St.
Philadelphia, PA 19103   **Phone:**   (215) 569-9225   **E-Mail:**   meforum@aol.com
USA   **Fax:**   (215) 569-9229

Contact Person: Amy Shargel, Associate Director.
Officers or Principals: Daniel Pipes, Director ($52,000); Amy Shargel, Associate Director ($40,000); Albert J. Wood, Founding Chairman; Leonard A. Sylk, Chairman; Thomas Tropp, Vice Chairman.
Mission or Interest: "Seeks to define and promote U.S. interests in the Middle East through its publications, research, education, media outreach, and activism. . . (Through its *Middle East Quarterly*) supports strong ties with Israel, Turkey, and other democracies as they emerge; urges strong measures to eradicate terrorism and control both conventional and unconventional arms proliferation; works for human rights throughout the region; seeks a stable supply and low price of oil; and promotes peaceful settlement of regional and international disputes."
Accomplishments: "Exposes anti-American attitudes among Middle East specialists in American universities." Articles from the *Middle East Quarterly* have been reprinted by publications such as the *Los Angeles Times, Miami Herald Tribune, National Review, Wall Street Journal, Washington Post*, and various international journals. In 1995 the Forum spent $305,249 on its programs. The largest program, with expenditures of $196,225, was the "administration of book publications regarding Muslim extremists, Kuwait, and various conspiracy theories".
Total Revenue: 1995 $544,478 **Total Expenses:** $458,333 67%/33%/0% **Net Assets:** $108,377
Products or Services: Annual dinner honoring an "individual who has made important contributions to the attainment of peace in the Middle East or has enhanced American understanding of that region". Past recipients have included A.M. Rosenthall (*New York Times*), Martin Peretz (*New Republic*), Oliver Revell (FBI), and Hon. Jeane Kirkpatrick. Morris Sidewater Lecture Series.
Tax Status: 501(c)(3) **Annual Report:** No. **Employees:** 6   **Citations:** 8:178
Board of Directors or Trustees: Andrew Allen, Howard Casper, D. David Eisenhower, II, Seymour Kaplan, Maurice Rosen, Jerry Sorkin, and 34 others.
Periodicals: *Middle East Quarterly* (quarterly journal) and *Wire* (newsletter).
Internships: Yes, unpaid semester-long.
Other Information: Established in 1994. The Forum received $293,600, or 54% of revenue, from the sale of publications and research. $164,449, or 30%, from contributions and grants awarded by foundations, businesses, and individuals. (These grants included $46,400 from the Smith Richardson Foundation, $25,000 from the Carthage Foundation. These contributions and grants declined 48%, from $318,760 in 1994.) $36,552, or 7%, from journal subscriptions. $35,591, or 7%, from dinners and conferences. $10,439, or 2%, from lectures. The remaining revenue came from dividends and interest from securities.

Milken Institute for Job & Capital Formation (MIJCF)

1250 4th St., 2nd Floor
Santa Monica, CA 90401   **Phone:**   (310) 998-2600   **E-Mail:**   bzw@mijcf.org
USA   **Fax:**   (310) 998-2626   **Internet:** http://www.mijcf.org

Contact Person: Lewis C. Solomon, President/Editor.
Officers or Principals: Lewis C. Solomon, President/Editor; Michael Milken, Chairman; Benjamin Zycher, Vice President; Lisa Hoffstein, Executive Director, University-Community Outreach Program; Beverly Z. Werber, Managing Editor.

Mission or Interest: "To encourage discussion of current issues of economic policy relating to economic growth, job creation, and capital formation."

Periodicals: *Jobs & Capital* (quarterly magazine).

Other Information: Founded by Michael Milken, the financier convicted of securities and exchange violations. Milken was associated with the use of high-risk, high-yield 'junk bonds' to finance corporate mergers and raise start-up capital. The Institute is not as conservative or libertarian as most other organizations, but it is generally free-market oriented. Contributors to *Jobs & Capital* have included ABC News's John Stossel and the Hudson Institute's Chester E. Finn, as well as self-described "dangerous leftist," Prof. Paul Krugman of MIT.

Milliken Foundation

c/o Citibank, N.A.
153 E. 53rd St.
New York, NY 10043   **Phone:**   (212) 559-2604
USA

Contact Person: L. Heagney, Foundation Manager.

Mission or Interest: Grant-making foundation that includes conservative and free-market organizations in its awards.

Accomplishments: In 1994 the Foundation awarded $1,288,166 in grants. Recipients included: $50,000 each for the Leadership Institute, and Free Congress Foundation, $25,000 for the Conservative Caucus Foundation, $14,000 for the Christian Anti-Communism Crusade, $10,000 each for Accuracy in Media, South Carolina Policy Council Education Foundation, and the Federalist Society, $6,000 for the Foundation for Economic Education, $5,000 each for the American Spectator Education Foundation, Manhattan Institute, and Intercollegiate Studies Institute, and $2,500 each for America's Future, and the Capital Research Center.

Total Revenue: 1994 $1,166,936 **Total Expenses:** $1,306,195 **Net Assets:** $5,502,428 1%

Tax Status: 501(c)(3)

Board of Directors or Trustees: Roger Milliken, Minot Milliken, Gerrish Milliken, Dr. Thomas Malone.

Other Information: The Foundation received $1,019,844, or 87% of revenue, from contributions and grants awarded by individuals, primarily Roger Milliken. $95,155, or 8%, from interest on savings and temporary cash investments. $51,937, or 5%, from dividends and interest from securities. The Foundation held $3,086,596, or 56%, in government securities. $2,271,478, or 41%, in corporate bonds.

Minnesota Family Council

2855 Anthony Lane, S., Suite 150
Minneapolis, MN 55418   **Phone:** (612) 789-8811   **E-Mail:** mfc@primenet.com
USA   **Fax:**   (612) 789-8858   **Internet:** http://www.mfc.org

Contact Person: Thomas Prichard, Executive Director.

Officers or Principals: Thomas Prichard, Executive Director ($40,000); Tom Aslesen, Chairman ($0); Justin Bratnober, Vice Chairman ($0); Marty Gavic, Secretary; Chuck Betz, Treasurer.

Mission or Interest: "Dedicated to the promotion and preservation of traditional Judeo-Christian values" in Minnesota.

Accomplishments: Worked for the passage of key legislation. In the fiscal year ending September 1995, the Council spent $317,487 on its programs

Total Revenue: FY ending 9/95 $495,613 25%(2) **Total Expenses:** $495,613 64%/26%/10% **Net Assets:** $60,064

Products or Services: Backgrounders on key issues and lobbying. Distributes 100,000 copies of its newspaper every month. In the fiscal year ending September 1995 the Council spent $18,562 on lobbying, $14,164 on grassroots lobbying and $4,393 on the direct lobbying of legislators. The lobbying expenditures have been steadily growing, increasing by an average of 56% per year over the last four years.

Tax Status: 501(c)(3) **Annual Report:** No. **Employees:** 16 **Citations:** 30:132

Board of Directors or Trustees: Wendell Brown, David Henningson, Charlie Betz, Dorothy Fleming, Cary Humphries.

Periodicals: *Pro-Family News* (monthly newspaper).

Internships: Yes, for college students.

Other Information: Established in 1982. Previously called the Berean League. The Council received $463,351, or 93% of revenue, from contributions awarded by foundations, businesses, and individuals. (These grants included $69,739 from the Alliance Defense Fund.) $23,476, or 5%, from conference fees. The remaining revenue came from the sale of literature, dividends and interest from securities, interest on savings, and other miscellaneous sources.

Mississippi Family Council

P.O. Box 13514
Jackson, MS 39236   **Phone:** (601) 969-1200
USA   **Fax:**   (601) 969-1600

Contact Person: Forest M. Thigpen, Executive Director.

Officers or Principals: Forest M. Thigpen, Executive Director ($51,250); Steve Barnes, Research Director.

Mission or Interest: Public policy institution dedicated to strengthening the family and lessening government intrusion in the lives of families.

Accomplishments: Created draft legislation outlawing the possession of child pornography in Mississippi that was passed and signed into law. They have been contacted by the governor's office soliciting a recommendation for an appointment to the Southern Regional Infant Mortality Project (a project of the Southern Governor's Association). Their recommendation, Dr. Steve Mills, was appointed. Thigpen testified before the Mississippi House Ways and Means Committee stressing the importance of eliminating the "marriage penalty" in the Mississippi tax code. In the fiscal year ending September 1995, the Council spent $102,737 on its programs. $10,985 of this was spent on the conference, "Leading People out of Poverty: What Churches and Individuals Can Do," that featured Marvin Olasky, author of <u>The Tragedy of American Compassion</u>, Virgil Gulker, the founder of a network of church volunteers called "Love Inc.," and John Perkins, the publisher of *Urban Family Magazine*.

Total Revenue: FY ending 9/95 $135,367 **Total Expenses:** $139,428 74%/21%/6% **Net Assets:** $30,398

Products or Services: "Mississippi Index of Leading Cultural Indicators." Briefings and luncheons for state legislators. Conferences and seminars. Lobbying: the Council spent $761 on lobbying, $48 on grassroots lobbying and $713 on the direct lobbying of legislators. This was an increase of 6% over the previous year.

Tax Status: 501(c)(3)

Periodicals: *Business & Family* (monthly).

Other Information: Established in 1990. The Council received $132,749, or 98% of revenue, from contributions and grants awarded by foundations, businesses, and individuals. (These contributions and grants have been steadily growing at an average increase of 90% per year over the last four years.) $1,864, or 1%, from conference fees. The remaining revenue came from interest on savings.

Monetary Realist Society

P.O. Box 31044
St. Louis, MO 63131   **Phone:**   (314) 997-9898
USA

Contact Person: Ken Bush.

Officers or Principals: Paul Hein, M.D., President; Charles Harrison, Secretary.

Mission or Interest: "Explores the nature of modern money and its role in shaping our lives. . . Monetary Realists believe that money should be a material thing produced by people, owned by people, and traded for other things, or services." Monetary Realists advocate a return to tangible money and currency redeemable for precious metals.

Accomplishments: Participant on the Phil Donahue show. Articles about the Society in *Time, People*, and elsewhere. Many local television and radio talk shows.

Tax Status: For profit.   **Annual Report:** No.   **Employees:** Volunteers.

Periodicals: *The Bulletin of the Monetary Realist Society* (newsletter).

Internships: No.

Monetary Science Publishing

P.O. Box 86
Wickliffe, OH 44092
USA

Contact Person: Peter Cook, President.

Mission or Interest: "Educating the general public on the mechanics of money, banking, the Federal Reserve system, and interest-free government credit."

Products or Services: <u>Do Banks Create & Destroy Money?</u>, numerous other books and pamphlets on the Federal Reserve system and money.

Tax Status: For profit.

Moneychanger, The

P.O. Box 341753
Memphis, TN 38184   **Phone:**   (901) 853-6136
USA   **Fax:**   (901) 854-5138

Contact Person: Franklin Sanders.

Mission or Interest: Monthly newsletter on politics and economics from a populist/Christian viewpoint. Focus on the Federal Reserve and the fractional-reserve banking system. "Our goal is to help Christians prosper with their morals intact in an age of monetary and spiritual chaos."

Tax Status: Unincorporated.   **Annual Report:** No.   **Employees:** 1

Periodicals: *The Moneychanger.*

Internships: No.

Other Information: Franklin Sanders was arrested in 1987 for "conspiring to evade federal taxes" by operating a precious metals exchange. Sanders maintained that he "used the exchange to buy gold as a hedge against a collapse of the credit banking system." In 1991 Sanders and 17 co-defendants were acquitted. According to the Memphis *Commercial Appeal*, "The trial was the longest federal trial in recent memory in west Tennessee."

Mont Pèlerin Society

P.O. Box 7031
Alexandria, VA 22307
USA

Contact Person: Dr. Edwin J. Feulner, Jr., Treasurer.
Officers or Principals: Prof. Pascal Salin, President ($0); Dr. Carl-Johan Westholm, Secretary ($0); Dr. Edwin J. Feulner, Jr., Treasurer; Dr. R.M. Hartwell, Senior Vice President; Dr. Gary Becker, Dr. John H. Moore, Ricardo A. Ball, Vice Presidents.
Mission or Interest: The Mont Pèlerin Society was founded in 1947 by Friedrich A. Hayek. Its mission was to bring together individuals from the fields of economics, history, philosophy and other social sciences to share ideas. At that time the world seemed to be headed inevitably toward a socialist society and Hayek was frustrated that the relatively few individuals who were still willing to defend classical liberalism and a market economy where scattered and lacked the opportunity to gather and compare ideas. He felt that if freedom was to survive they would not have to propagandize to the masses, but rather convince intellectuals and the elites who deal second hand in ideas. Attendees at the first meeting, in Mont Pèlerin, Switzerland, included several who would go on to win Nobel Prizes in Economics -- Hayek himself, George Stigler, and Milton Friedman. Other members included Ludwig von Mises, British philosopher Karl Popper, Max Eastman, Jacques Rueff, Henry Hazlitt, and Walter Lippman. Membership is by election only.
Accomplishments: Although it has a small budget, and few people are aware of its existence, the Society is highly influential. Its membership has included the most prominent conservative and free-market thinkers of this century. Over 500 members from 35 nations. Past presidents were: F.A. Hayek, Wilhelm Röpke, John Jewkes, Friedrich Lutz, Bruno Leoni, Günter Schmölders, Milton Friedman, Arthur Shenfield, Gaston Leduc, George Stigler, and Manuel Ayau. In the fiscal year ending March 1995, the Society spent $119,689 on its programs.
Total Revenue: FY ending 3/95 $98,185 1%(2) **Total Expenses:** $126,078 95%/5%/0% **Net Assets:** $298,243
Products or Services: Conferences, Olive W. Garvey Fellowships essay contest.
Tax Status: 501(c)(3)
Board of Directors or Trustees: Prof. Peter Bernholz, Carolina de Bolivar (Instituto Cultural Ludwig von Mises), Dr. Motoo Kaji (University of the Air), M. Henri Lepage (Institut Euro 92), Prof. Harold Demsetz, Greg Lindsay (Centre for Independent Studies), Dr. Roland Vaubel (University of Mannheim), Dr. Michael Walker (Fraser Inst.).
Other Information: Established in 1947. The Society is very exclusive and not publicly oriented. Communicating with the Society is difficult, and they are not responsive to requests for information. The Society received $55,300, or 56% of revenue, from contributions and grants awarded by foundations, businesses, and individuals. (These grants included $14,800 from the Earhart Foundation, $11,500 from the Aequus Institute, $5,000 from the Lynde and Harry Bradley Foundation, $5,000 from the Vernon K. Krieble Foundation, $5,000 from the Carthage Foundation, and $5,000 from the Roe Foundation.) $32,458, or 33%, from membership dues. $6,815, or 7%, from dividends and interest from savings. $3,612, or 4%, from interest on savings and temporary cash investments.

Morality In Media (MIM)

475 Riverside Dr.
New York, NY 10115   **Phone:** (212) 870-3222
USA   **Fax:**   (212) 870-2765

Contact Person: Patrick McGrath, Director of Public Affairs.
Officers or Principals: Paul J. McGeady, General Counsel ($59,700); Robert W. Peters, President ($45,000); Ed Hynes, Executive Vice President ($35,000); Robert L. Cahill, Jr., Chairman; Evelyn Dukovic, Vice President; Edward Hynes, Treasurer.
Mission or Interest: "The criminal traffic in hardcore pornography degrades men and women, violates children, destroys marriages, serves as a training manual for sexual psychopaths in our midst, threatens public health and causes deterioration of entire neighborhoods. The well-being and safety of individuals, families and communities are thereby threatened on many levels." Disseminates information on pornography and its effects. Operates as a clearinghouse on obscenity law through its National Obscenity Law Center.
Accomplishments: MIM has filed 'friend of the court' briefs in numerous legal cases and appeals. In 1995 MIM filed an amicus curiae brief in a case that was upheld on appeal that "empowers cable operators to eliminate indecent programming on leased/public access channels on cable." Proposes and aids in the drafting of legislation. In 1996 MIM proposals were included in a bill approved by Congress that would regulate indecency on computer networks. Works with state legislatures, attorneys general, and local organizations. Also opposes sex and violence on television and informs the public and sponsors on program content. In 1994 MIM spent $411,950 on its programs. The largest program, with expenditures of $171,769 was spent on research and publications. $102,984 was spent on the National Obscenity Law Center and its publication, *The Obscenity Law Bulletin*, that publishes information on relevant legislation and court cases.
Total Revenue: 1994 $641,432 (-3%)(1) **Total Expenses:** $587,735 70%/25%/5% **Net Assets:** $183,764
Products or Services: Legislation, litigation, research, publications, and lobbying. In 1994 MIM spent $1,201 on lobbying. Lobbying expenditures have been steadily decreasing, down 57% from 1993, down 74% from 1992, and down 89% from $10,462 in 1991.
Tax Status: 501(c)(3) **Employees:** 10   **Citations:** 40:113
Board of Directors or Trustees: Robert Peters, Kevin Beattie, Robert Cahill, Sophia Casey, Thomas Donnelly, Evelyn Dukovic, Rev. John Fisk, Msgr. Paul Hayes, David Hopkins, Richard Hughes, Msgr. James Lisante, Paul McGlinchey, Rabbi Dr. Morton Pomerantz, John Reilly, Frank Russo, Jr., Victor Sayegh, John Walsh, Kathleen Reilly Zawacki, Grace Rinaldi.

Periodicals: *Obscenity Law Bulletin* (monthly law bulletin), and *The Morality in Media Newsletter* (bimonthly newsletter).
Other Information: Founded as a local concern in 1962 as Operation Yorkville. In 1968 the name was changed to Morality in Media. The National Obscenity Law Center was established in 1976. MIM received $617,254, or 96% of revenue, from contributions and grants awarded by foundations, businesses, and individuals. $12,878, or 2%, from subscriptions and publications sales. The remaining revenue came from disability insurance proceeds, interest on savings and temporary cash investments, and other miscellaneous sources.

Mountain States Legal Foundation (MSLF)

707 17th St., Suite 3030
Denver, CO 80202   **Phone:**   (303) 292-2021
USA   **Fax:**   (303) 292-1980

Contact Person: William Perry Pendley, President.
Officers or Principals: William Perry Pendley, President ($147,000); Beverly Kinard, Vice President ($82,951); Todd S. Welch, Lawyer ($80,445); George Yates, Chairman; John Dendahl, Treasurer.
Mission or Interest: Public-interest law firm focusing on property rights.
Accomplishments: In 1995 the Foundation spent $694,142 on its programs. Litigation included: Adarand Constructors, Inc. v. Pena, et al., where the Foundation assisted the plaintiff, a construction contractor who was denied a federal contract, despite offering the lowest bid, in favor of a minority applicant. The 10th Circuit Court ruled in favor of the defendants, but the case made its way to the U.S. Supreme Court, which told the circuit court to retry the case using a standard of scrutiny more favorable to the Foundation and Adarand. The Foundation assisted and helped to win Bear Lodge Multiple Use Association, et al. v. Liggett, et al., on behalf of a 'multiple use' group seeking to preserve the practice of climbing guides working on Devil's Tower, a national monument. The National Parks Service sought to prohibit the practice during the month of June "in respect for the reverence many American Indians hold for Devils Tower as a sacred site." The Foundation filed an amicus brief on behalf of the plaintiffs in Catron County Board of Supervisors v. Babbitt, et al. The County held that federal law entitles them to participate in wildlife recovery plans issued by the U.S. Fish and Wildlife Service, but that no such notice had been given in the recovery plans of the spikedace and loach minnows. The Foundation and Catron County won this case, and it was upheld on appeal.
Total Revenue: 1995 $1,063,017 10%(2) **Total Expenses:** $946,361 73%/13%/13% **Net Assets:** $528,759
Tax Status: 501(c)(3)   **Citations:** 51:98
Board of Directors or Trustees: Bill Armstrong, George Alcorn, Hon. Tim Babcock, Steven Banzhaf, Denise Bode (Pres., Independent Petroleum Assoc. of America), Peter Botting, John Burke, Glenn Chancellor, Scott Crozier, John Dendahl, Byron Farrell, Gus Fleischli, David Flitner, Gerald Freeman, Ronald Graves, Hon. Clifford Hansen, Raymond Hanson, Mark Hooper, Dallas Horton, DVM, MS, James Lucas, David McClure (Pres., Montana Farm Bureau), Hon. James McClure, Charles Mcrea, Cecil Miller, Roger Bill Mitchell (Pres., Colorado Farm Bureau), J. Larry Nichols, Jack Parson, Jr., William Reeds, W. Thomas Richards (Pres./CEO, Idaho Forest Industries), David Rovig, Jack Scwabacher, Jerry Sheffels, Harold Short, Diemer True (True Companies), many others.
Other Information: Established in 1976 with James Watt (Secretary of the Interior, 1981-83) as its first president. Current president William Perry Pendley was the Department of the Interior's Assistant Secretary, Energy and Minerals, from 1983-84. The Foundation received $1,031,857, or 97% of revenue, from contributions and grants awarded by foundations, businesses, and individuals. (These grants included $35,000 from the Castle Rock Foundation, and $10,500 from the Ruth and Vernon Taylor Foundation. In 1994 these grants included $5,000 from the Anschutz Foundation.) $14,076, or 1%, from dividends and interest from securities. $13,656, or 1%, from the sale of inventory. The remaining revenue came from investments and other miscellaneous sources.

Movie Morality Ministries

1309 Seminole Dr.
Richardson, TX 75080   **Phone:**   (972) 231-9910
USA   **Fax:**   (972) 669-9040   **Internet:** http://www.cyserv.com/preview

Contact Person: John H. Evans, President.
Officers or Principals: Don Spear, Vice President.
Mission or Interest: "Persuading the public to avoid morally degenerate movies and those with liberal and anti-Christian messages. . . Publishes a twice-monthly movie guide based on traditional values. Also provides recorded and live radio shows to Christian and secular communities."
Tax Status: 501(c)(3) **Annual Report:** No. **Employees:** 3 full-time, 4 part-time.
Board of Directors or Trustees: Bill Garrett, Rev. Don Wildmon (American Family Association).
Periodicals: *Preview: Family Movie & TV Review* (biweekly entertainment reviewer).
Internships: No.
Other Information: Established in 1986.

Nathan Hale Institute

104 North Carolina Ave., S.E.
Washington, DC 20003   **Phone:**   (202) 546-2293
USA   **Fax:**   (202) 546-3091

Contact Person: Lawrence B. Sulc, President.

Officers or Principals: Frederic N. Smith, Vice President; Lawrence B. Sulc, President.

Mission or Interest: To support the U.S. intelligence community. "Research in the area of domestic and foreign intelligence with particular emphasis on the role of intelligence operations in a free society."

Accomplishments: President Reagan said, "As we strive to keep ourselves strong and prosperous, organizations like The Hale Foundation are helping to remind Americans that vigilance against the enemies of our nation is an essential part of safeguarding the freedoms we enjoy."

Products or Services: Occasional pamphlets.

Tax Status: 501(c)(3)

Periodicals: *Nathan Hale Newsletter* (quarterly).

Internships: Yes.

Other Information: Established in 1976. They also operate a 501(c)(4) lobbying organization, the Hale Foundation, at the same address. The Hale Foundation was formed by Lawrence Sulc in response to the unmasking of U.S. agents abroad by members of the U.S. radical Left. Some of these unmaskings were linked to the subsequent death of the agent. The Hale Foundation supports the efforts of the U.S. government to acquire information, and in particular supports the human operations officers. Vice President Smith is the publisher of *Conservative Review*. Named after Capt. Nathan Hale (1755-1776), the War of Independence figure perhaps best known for his statement, "I only regret that I have but one life to lose for my country".

National Affairs

1112 16th St., N.W., Suite 530
Washington, DC 20036   **Phone:**   (202) 467-4884
USA   **Fax:**   (202) 467-0006

Contact Person: Owen Harries, Editor in Chief.

Officers or Principals: Owen Harries, Secretary/Treasurer ($84,500); Irving Kristol, President ($0); Nathan Glazer, Vice President ($0); Adam Garfinkle, Executive Editor.

Mission or Interest: Publishes two journals. *The National Interest* - a quarterly of foreign policy issues, and *The Public Interest* - a quarterly of domestic issues. The publisher of both is one of the most prominent 'neo-conservatives,' Irving Kristol.

Accomplishments: Published such influential articles as "The End of History" by Francis Fukuyama, "America First, Second, and Third," by Patrick Buchanan, and "A Nation of Cowards" by Jeffrey Snyder. In the fiscal year ending April 1996, National Affairs spent $705,823 to publish and distribute its two journals.

Total Revenue: FY ending 4/96 $864,962 3%(3) **Total Expenses:** $746,410 95%/5%/0% **Net Assets:** $935,917

Tax Status: 501(c)(3) **Annual Report:** No.

Board of Directors or Trustees: The advisory board for *The National Interest* includes: Midge Dector, Samuel Huntington, Francis Fukuyama, Jeane Kirkpatrick (Empower America), Chalmers Johnson, Henry Kissinger, Charles Krauthammer, Edward Luttwak, Daniel Pipes, and several others. The publications committee for *The Public Interest* includes: Martin Feldstein, Prof. Glenn Loury (Boston Univ.), Sen. Daniel Moynihan (D-NY), Charles Murray, Martin Segal, Irwin Stelzer, James Q. Wilson, and others.

Periodicals: *The National Interest* (quarterly journal), *The Public Interest* (quarterly journal).

Other Information: *The National Interest* was established in 1985. The subscription address is P.O. Box 622, Shrub Oak, NY 10588-0622, (914) 962-6297. National Affairs attracted unwanted attention recently from the defection of executive editor Michael Lind. Lind denounced conservatives, particularly neo-conservatives, for associating with religious conservatives, gun-rights activists, and populists; then went on to write several books, including Up from Conservatism (a play on William F. Buckley, Jr.'s 1959 book, Up from Liberalism) chastising the conservative movement. National Affairs received $585,000, or 68% of revenue, from contributions and grants awarded by foundations, businesses, and individuals. (These grants included $400,000 from the Lynde and Harry Bradley Foundation, $75,000 from the Smith Richardson Foundation, and $75,000 from the John M. Olin Foundation.) $223,655, or 26%, from subscriptions. $28,153, or 3%, from royalties. $27,779, or 3%, from interest on savings and temporary cash investments. The remaining revenue came from advertising income. The journals cost $705,823 to publish, and provided $252,183 in revenues (subscriptions, advertising, etc.), requiring subsidization of $453,640.

National Alliance of Senior Citizens (NASC)

1700 18th St., N.W., Suite 401
Washington, DC 20009   **Phone:**   (202) 986-0117
USA

Contact Person: Peter J. Luciano, CEO .

Officers or Principals: Peter J. Luciano, CEO ($5,500); John E. Wilbur, President; Robert S. Carter, Vice President; Ruth B. Clinkscales, Vice President.

Mission or Interest: Promoting seniors' interests in state and federal legislation.

Accomplishments: Worked for the repeal of mandatory retirement age, raising Social Security earning limit, and the repeal of Catastrophic Act of 1988. In 1994 the Alliance spent $44,203 on its programs.

Total Revenue: 1994 $48,991 (-40%)(2) **Total Expenses:** $64,356 69%/31%/0% **Net Assets:** (-$25,778)

Tax Status: 501(c)(4) **Annual Report:** No. **Employees:** 3

Periodicals: *The Senior Guardian*.

Internships: No.

Other Information: NASC owns 75% of a for-profit insurance company, Seniorcare Insurance Services. In 1994 this subsidiary provided the Alliance with $2,413 in revenue. In 1994 the Alliance received loans totaling $25,255 with 10% annual interest from CEO Luciano "to provide NASC with working capital until new members and programs yield sufficient revenues." The Alliance received $38,579, or 79% of revenue, from membership dues. $9,923, or 20%, from royalties. The remaining revenue came from list rentals and interest on savings.

National Alliance of Stocking Gun Dealers

P.O. Box 187
Havelock, NC 28532   **Phone:**   (919) 447-3544
USA

Contact Person: Bill Bridgewater, Executive Director.
Officers or Principals: Carole Bridgewater, Secretary ($0).
Mission or Interest: Organization representing professional licensed firearms dealers (as opposed to licensed dealers who work from their residence) that lobbies on behalf of gun owners' rights.
Total Revenue: 1994 $27,309 **Total Expenses:** $38,866 **Net Assets:** $22,076
Products or Services: Lobbying: in 1994 the Alliance spent less than $2,000 on lobbying.
Tax Status: 501(c)(6)
Other Information: The Alliance received $33,125, or 99% of revenue, from membership dues. The remaining revenue came from interest on savings and temporary cash investments. The Alliance lost $6,130 hosting special events.

National Alumni Forum (NAF)

1625 K St., N.W., Suite 310
Washington, DC 20006   **Phone:**   (202) 467-6787   **E-Mail:**   naf@naf.org
USA   **Fax:**   (202) 467-6784   **Internet:** http://www.naf.org

Contact Person: Colleen Aylward.
Officers or Principals: Jerry L. Martin, President ($107,813); Anne D. Neal Petri, Vice President ($19,638); Lynne Munson, Secretary ($0); Jeffrey Wallin, Treasurer; Lynne V. Cheney, Chairman; Gov. Richard D. Lamm, Vice Chairman.
Mission or Interest: "Organization of alumni and college trustees dedicated to academic freedom and excellence. . . In recent years, scholars from across the political spectrum have warned about growing political intolerance on our nation's campuses. . . Now that the threat is from within, members of the larger academic community, including alumni and trustees, must step forward in defense of the life and liberty of the mind." By influencing the $2.9 billion awarded to colleges and universities annually by alumni, the Forum works to counter 'political correctness.'
Accomplishments: Though newly established in 1994, by 1995 the Forum received $641,800 in contributions and grants. In 1995 the Forum spent $256,145 on its programs. These programs included organizing alumni by specific schools and regions. Also helped alumni "target programs and activities worthy of support."
Total Revenue: 1995 $663,412 **Total Expenses:** $320,839 80%/20%/0% **Net Assets:** $340,665
Tax Status: 501(c)(3) **Employees:** 5   **Citations:** 99:64
Board of Directors or Trustees: Sen. Hank Brown (R-CO), Chester Finn, Jr. (former Assistant Secretary of Education, 1985-88), James Higgins (former CEO, Mellon Bank Corp.), Irving Kristol (editor, *Public Interest*), Sen. Joseph Lieberman (D-CT), Philip Merrill (publisher, *The Washingtonian*), Martin Peretz (*The New Republic*), Hon. Laurence Silberman (U.S. Circuit Judge, U.S. Court of Appeals), William Tell, Jr. (Senior Vice Pres., Texaco), Herman Wells (Chancellor, Indiana Univ.).
Internships: Yes.
Other Information: Established in 1994. Chairman Lynne Cheney was formerly the chair of the National Endowment for the Humanities from 1986-1993. Vice Chairman Richard D. Lamm was formerly the Democratic Governor of Colorado. The Forum received $641,800, or 97% of revenue, from contributions and grants awarded by foundations, businesses, and individuals. (These grants included $100,000 from the John M. Olin Foundation, $50,000 from the Lynde and Harry Bradley Foundation, $45,000 from the John William Pope Foundation, $40,000 from the National Association of Scholars, and $35,000 from the William H. Donner Foundation.) $16,271, or 2%, from membership dues. $5,341, or 1%, from interest on savings and temporary cash investments.

National Association for Neighborhood Schools (NANS)

1800 W. 8th St.
Wilmington, DE 19805   **Phone:**   (302) 658-1856
USA

Contact Person: William D. D'Onofrio, President.
Officers or Principals: Dan Seale, Vice President; Joyce Haws, Secretary.
Mission or Interest: "To discredit and end the policy of racial-balance school busing."
Accomplishments: "There have been no major busing orders issued over the past decade. . . NANS has been an integral part of the political process, to bring this about. Our direction is now toward relieving the communities under existing busing orders."
Tax Status: 501(c)(4) **Annual Report:** No. **Employees:** All volunteer.

Board of Directors or Trustees: Kaye Cook, Lillian Dannis, Mary Eisel, others.
Periodicals: Bimonthly newsletter.
Internships: No.
Other Information: Established in 1976. The Association also operates NANS-PAC, a political action committee.

National Association of Scholars (NAS)

575 Ewing St.
Princeton, NJ 08540   **Phone:**   (609) 683-7878
USA   **Fax:**   (609) 683-0316

Contact Person: Dr. Stephen H. Balch, President.
Officers or Principals: Dr. Stephen H. Balch, President/Executive Director ($100,500); Rita Zurcher, Research Director ($38,695); Dr. Glenn Ricketts, Public Affairs Director ($37,000); Stanley Rothman, Chairman; Dr. B. Nelson Ong, Secretary/Treasurer; Joseph Horn, Bradford Wilson, Prof. Carol Iannone, Vice Presidents.
Mission or Interest: Promotion of 1) high academic standards, 2) intellectual tolerance and openness, 3) opposition to gender and race-based quotas for academic placement. Founded because, "Concepts like 'political correctness' and 'multiculturalism' (along with the latter's handmaiden, 'diversity') had laid an iron grip on college and university campuses across America, threatening freedom of thought and expression, and destroying traditional measurements of academic achievement. Even worse, the rigorous curriculum I had known as an undergraduate was being increasingly diluted and trivialized."
Accomplishments: Nearly 4,000 members and affiliates in 36 states and the District of Columbia. In 1996 NAS published "The Dissolution of General Education: 1914-1993" which attracted media attention, and was cited in *The New York Times, U.S. News and World Reports, Chronicle of Higher Education, Wall Street Journal, Washington Times, Forbes,* and *USA Today.* Assisted in the formation of the National Alumni Forum. Helped create the American Academy for Liberal Education, a recognized accreditation agency. NAS members formed the Association of Literary Scholars and Critics. NAS members helped design an undergraduate course of study at the University of Wisconsin, Milwaukee. In 1995 NAS spent $531,450 on its programs. The largest program with expenditures of $250,802, was the publication of the journal *Academic Questions.* This included a payment of $80,068 to the publisher, Transactions Publishers. The NAS awarded $98,600 in grants to various affiliates at the state, college and university level, as well as $40,000 for the National Alumni Forum, and $2,000 for the First Amendment Coalition.
Total Revenue: 1995 $889,929 **Total Expenses:** $853,215 62%/36%/2% **Net Assets:** $912,572
Products or Services: Fellows program, publications, conferences, and lobbying. NAS spent $5,230 on the direct lobbying of legislators. This was down 35% from 1993, NAS did not lobby in 1994.
Tax Status: 501(c)(3)   **Citations:** 77:80
Board of Directors or Trustees: Board of Advisors includes: Jacques Barzun, Peter Diamandopoulos, Chester E. Finn, Eugene Genovese, Gertrude Himmelfarb, Irving Horowitz, Harry V. Jaffa, Robert Jastrow, Donald Kagan, Jeane Kirkpatrick, Irving Kristol, Richard Lamm, Seymour Martin Lipset, Glenn Loury, Nelson Polsby, John Silber, Ernest van den Haag, Edward Wilson, James Q. Wilson.
Periodicals: *Academic Questions* (quarterly academic journal), *NAS Update* (quarterly newsletter).
Other Information: Established in 1987. NAS received $742,925, or 83% of revenue, from contributions and grants awarded by foundations, businesses, and individuals. (These grants included $150,000 from the Lynde and Harry Bradley Foundation, $125,000 from the John M. Olin Foundation, $105,000 from the Smith Richardson Foundation, and $25,000 from the Castle Rock Foundation. In 1994, $300,000 from the Sarah Scaife Foundation, and $20,000 from the F.M. Kirby Foundation. These contributions and grants have been declining by an average of 6% for the last four years.) $111,159, or 12%, from membership dues. Membership dues have been increasing an average of 16% for the last four years. $17,213, or 2%, from interest on savings and temporary cash investments. $15,323, or 2%, from dividends and interest from securities. The remaining revenue came from royalties.

National Association to Protect Individual Rights (NAPIR)

P.O. Box 90030
Washington, DC 20077-7387   **Phone:**   (800) 825-8688
USA

Mission or Interest: To protect the freedoms of individuals from encroachment by governments. In particular, they see use of the tax codes to alter behavior as especially dangerous. They also strongly object to governments gathering and storing information about individuals' personal lives. "In the time since ratification of the Constitution, the power of federal, state and local governments, large bureaucracies, and private institutions and organizations has increased largely at the expense of individual rights and liberties. This continued centralization of power is at odds with the concept of limited government and expansive individual rights and liberties established in the Constitution."
Products or Services: Surveys, alerts on fast-breaking issues.
Tax Status: 501(c)(4)
Periodicals: Quarterly newsletter.
Other Information: Established in 1991.

National Black Republican Council (NBRC)

375 South End Ave., Plaza 400-8U
New York, NY 10280   **Phone:**   (212) 662-1335
USA

Contact Person: Fred Brown, Chairman
Mission or Interest: Black Republicans working to get more blacks elected to state, federal, and local positions as Republicans..
Accomplishments: 25,000 members, and 44 state groups.
Products or Services: Speakers bureau, annual meeting.
Other Information: Established in 1972. Auxiliary of the Republican National Committee.

National Center for Neighborhood Enterprise

1367 Connecticut Ave., N.W.
Washington, DC 20036   **Phone:**   (202) 331-1103
USA

Contact Person: Robert L. Woodson, President.
Officers or Principals: Robert L. Woodson, President ($143,171); Lee Earl, Project Director ($52,823); Sydney Stakely, Project Director ($50,916); Robert B. Hill, Ph.D., Chairman; Frank K. Ross, Secretary/Treasurer.
Mission or Interest: Promotes economic development, crime prevention, family preservation, and alternative education through neighborhood-based groups.
Accomplishments: In 1994 the Center spent $1,374,858 on its programs. The largest program, with expenditures of $708,119, was technical assistance and educational materials for inner-city students and residents in the basics of business and entrepreneurship. $359,449 was spent to "provide training and capital to inner-city businesses, including public-housing residents assuming management of their projects." Other programs included anti-drug and crime reduction efforts.
Total Revenue: 1994 $1,572,433 ($202,005, or 13%, from government grants) (-33%)(2)
Total Expenses: $1,550,739 89%/2%/9% **Net Assets:** (-$676,245)
Products or Services: Studies, books, leaflets, monographs, including Race and Economic Opportunity, by Robert L. Woodson, and Entrepreneurial Enclaves in the African-American Experience, by John Sibley Butler and Kenneth Wilson. Technical business assistance for inner-city organizations. Projects for crime and drug prevention. Family preservation programs.
Tax Status: 501(c)(3) **Employees:** 14   **Citations:** 115:54
Board of Directors or Trustees: Maurice Barksdale, Michael Castine, Pamela Haber, Carl Hardick, John McKnight, Don Speaks, Richard Treibick, Rita Wilson, Robert Hill, Ph.D., Jack Kemp (Secretary, Housing and Urban Development 1989-93), Dave Roberson.
Periodicals: *Agenda* (newsletter).
Other Information: Affiliated with the for-profit Neighborhood Capital Corporation at the same address. The Corporation makes low-interest loans to qualified businesses. The Center employed the District of Columbia firm of Betah Associates as consultants, and paid the firm $67,275. The Center received $1,344,868, or 86%, from contributions and grants awarded by foundations, businesses, and individuals. (These grants included $67,000 from the Gilder Foundation, $27,000 from the J.M. Foundation, and $10,000 from the John Brown Cook Foundation. In 1995, $245,000 from the Scaife Family Foundation, $225,000 from the Lynde and Harry Bradley Foundation, $25,000 from the John M. Olin Foundation, and $15,000 from the Sunmark Foundation.) $202,005, or 13%, from government grants. The remaining revenue came from program fees, membership dues, interest on savings, and other miscellaneous sources.

National Center for Policy Analysis (NCPA)

12655 N. Central Expressway, Suite 720
Dallas, TX 75243   **Phone:**   (214) 386-6272   **E-Mail:**   ncpa@onramp.net
USA   **Fax:**   (214) 386-0924

Contact Person: Jeanette W. Nordstrom, Executive Vice President.
Officers or Principals: Dr. John C. Goodman, President ($203,877); Jeanette W. Nordstrom, Executive Vice President ($94,672); Dorman Cordell, Vice President, Publications ($68,756); Jere W. Thompson, Chairman; H. Martin Gibson, Secretary; Jan Faiks, Vice President, External Affairs; Thom Golab, Vice President, Development; Merrill Matthews, Vice President, Domestic Policy.
Mission or Interest: "The primary goal of the NCPA is to develop and promote private alternatives to government regulation and control, solving problems by relying on the strengths of the competitive, entrepreneurial private sector."
Accomplishments: Widely credited with the repeal of the Medicare Catastrophic Coverage Act in 1989, "the first repeal of a major federal welfare program in 100 years." NCPA research demonstrated that the Act would impose a very high marginal tax rate on the elderly. NCPA has been the driving force behind Medical Savings Accounts, producing the research and econometric analysis demonstrating cost savings and cost containment that would result from widespread implementation of these accounts. NCPA produced a study on the average time of incarceration for convicted felons, showing that as expected punishment decreased, crime rose. This study was widely cited. Op-eds by NCPA authors have appeared in *The Wall Street Journal, Investor's Business Daily, Barron's,* and *USA Today.* "In 1994, the NCPA's media coverage was the equivalent of $4.3 million in advertising and reached the equivalent of more than 220 million households. . . Per Burrelles clip service, NCPA 1995 media coverage was the equivalent of $13.8 million in advertising equivalence with a reach of 920 million households. Also per Burrelles during that same period we received 46,000 column inches of coverage." In 1995 NCPA spent $2,430,455 on its programs.

Total Revenue: 1995 $2,991,754 21%(5) **Total Expenses:** $3,029,444 80%/11%/9% **Net Assets:** $1,032,815
Products or Services: Lecture series, international conferences, policy briefings. Numerous studies and publications.
Tax Status: 501(c)(3) **Annual Report:** Yes. **Employees:** 25 in Dallas, 4 in Washington, DC. **Citations:** 411:23
Board of Directors or Trustees: Dan Cook, III (Goldman Sachs Group), Robert Dedman, Hon. Pete du Pont (former Governor of Delaware-R), James Middleton (Atlantic Richfield), G.N. Parrott, Henry Smith.
Periodicals: *Executive Alert* (monthly research brief).
Internships: Yes, for graduates and graduate students.
Other Information: Established in 1983. Member of the State Policy Network. NCPA recently opened an office in the District of Columbia: 727 15th St., N.W., 5th Floor, Washington, DC 20005, (202) 628-6671, fax (202) 628-6474. NCPA received $2,817,988, or 94% of revenue, from contributions and grants awarded by individuals (56%) businesses (29%) and foundations (15%). (These grants included $105,000 from the Sarah Scaife Foundation, $100,000 from the John M. Olin Foundation, $50,000 from the Lynde and Harry Bradley Foundation, $25,000 from the Claude R. Lambe Charitable Foundation, $10,000 from the John William Pope Foundation, and $10,000 from the David H. Koch Charitable Foundation. In 1994, $100,000 from the M.J. Murdock Charitable Trust, $85,000 from the Lilly Endowment, $10,000 from the Richard & Helen DeVos Foundation, $10,000 from the Gordon and Mary Cain Foundation, $10,000 from the Alex C. Walker Foundation, $5,000 from the Philip M. McKenna Foundation, $1,000 from the Roe Foundation, and $500 from the United Educators Foundation.) $148,148, or 5%, from conference fees. The remaining revenue came from interest on savings, publication sales, royalties, and dividends and interest from securities. NCPA lost $998 on the sale of securities.

National Center for Public Policy Research

300 I St., Suite 3
Washington, DC 20002   **Phone:** (202) 543-1286   **E-Mail:** ncppr@aol.com
USA   **Fax:** (202) 543-4779   **Internet:** http://www.nationalcenter.inter.net

Contact Person: Amy Moritz, President .
Officers or Principals: Amy Moritz, President ($63,953); David Ridenour, Vice President/Secretary ($48,263); Burton Yale Pines, Chairman; Edmund Peterson, Chairman, Project 21.
Mission or Interest: To promote grassroots conservatism and work on fast-breaking issues. Operates a program, Project 21, that focuses on the problems of blacks in America and works with black conservatives. Project 21 was created in the wake of the Los Angeles riots.
Accomplishments: In 1994 the Center had 78 op-eds published -- a record for them, and six "conservative movement coalition meetings" were chaired or co-chaired by Center personnel. Helped Rep. Tom DeLay (R-TX) to launch Project Relief that focuses on regulatory reform. The Project Relief coalition now includes over 200 business and nonprofit groups. Project Relief can be reached via e-mail at "ReliefRprt@aol.com". In 1994 the Center spent $240,657 on its programs. The largest program, with expenditures of $100,884 was Project 21. Project 21 improved the visibility of black conservatives through public forums such as radio programing, television programming, and newspaper op-ed pages. $40,909 was spent producing 44 weekly editions of "Scoop TV" for NET - Political NewsTalk Network (see separate listing). $29,699 was spent on looking "for ways to develop and protect the nation's environment in such a manner that does not harm communities and the economy" through the Environmental Policy Task Force. $29,482 was spent on issues related to health-care reform.
Total Revenue: 1994 $1,539,915 70%(2) **Total Expenses:** $1,505,636 16%/3%/81% **Net Assets:** $56,542
Products or Services: Directory of Environmental Scientists and Economists. "Black America: A New Beginning," a 130-page report. "Scoop" fax update network that covers Capital Hill activities for radio talk-show hosts. "Relief Report" fax updates. "Budget Watch" fax updates.
Tax Status: 501(c)(3) **Annual Report:** Yes. **Employees:** 7   **Citations:** 38:117
Board of Directors or Trustees: William Bradford Reynolds.
Internships: Yes, unpaid.
Other Information: Established in 1982. When first created, the Center focused largely on U.S. policy in Nicaragua and Latin America and in assisting conservative Catholics "who were challenging some of the political assertions of far-Left Catholic leaders on issues such as nuclear deterrence and the economy." Vice President David Ridenour was previously the executive director of the U.S. Youth Council from 1985-86. The Center received $1,535,064, or 99.7% of revenue, from contributions and grants awarded by foundations, businesses, and individuals. (These grants included $10,000 from the J.M. Foundation. In 1995, $100,000 from the Carthage Foundation, and $25,000 from the Castle Rock Foundation.) The remaining revenue came from the sale of publications, interest on savings and temporary cash investments, and rental income.

National Chamber Foundation

1615 H St., N.W.
Washington, DC 20062   **Phone:** (202) 463-5552
USA   **Fax:** (202) 463-3174

Contact Person: Margaret A. Elgin, Director.
Officers or Principals: Nancy Turnbull, Manager ($57,739); Margaret A. Elgin, Director ($54,305); Roger C. Jask, Vice President ($24,535); Dr. Thomas C. Schreck, Chairman; Richard L. Lesher, President; Martin Regalia, Executive Vice President; Lawrence B. Kraus, Secretary; Roy C. Fletcher, Treasurer.

Mission or Interest: Research and education in areas of tax, regulation and social cost, health care and employee benefits.
Total Revenue: 1994 $1,618,114 (-14%)(2) **Total Expenses:** $1,580,954 94%/6%/0% **Net Assets:** $713,523
Products or Services: Center for Leadership Development which creates and implements programs for the general public. Library used by businesses and the general public. Scholarships.
Tax Status: 501(c)(3) **Employees:** 15   **Citations:** 0:233
Board of Directors or Trustees: Kenneth Crosby (Merrill Lynch & Co.), Gene Gambale, William Good, CAE (National Roofing Contractors Association), Dr. Carl Grant (Senior Vice Pres., Communications, U.S. Chamber of Commerce), E. Noel Harwerth (Vice Pres., & Chief Tax Officer, CitiCorp/CitiBank), Bruce Josten (U.S. Chamber of Commerce), Joseph Lema (National Coal Association), Dr. Richard Lesher (Pres., U.S. Chamber of Commerce), Hon. Edwin Meese (Heritage Found.), William Modahl (Digital Equipment Corp.), Barbara Schaye, Burton Siegel, Joan Verplanck, Thomas Wall, Harry Zachem (Senior Vice Pres., External Affairs, Ashland Oil).
Periodicals: Produced several publications on domestic and international tax issues. Also produces a monthly journal of regulation and social cost.
Internships: Yes, their internships are unpaid.
Other Information: Affiliated with the 501(c)(6) United States Chamber of Commerce. The Foundation received $1,543,676, or 95% of revenue, from membership dues. $73,837, or 5%, from contributions and grants awarded by foundations, businesses, and individuals. The remaining revenue came from interest on savings and temporary cash investments.

National Coalition for Public Lands and Natural Resources (NCPLNR)

301 N. Main St., Suite 306
Pueblo, CO 81003   **Phone:** (719) 543-8421   **E-Mail:** pfw@usa.net
USA   **Fax:** (719) 543-9473   **Internet:** www.usa.net~pfw

Contact Person: Jeffrey Harris, Executive Director.
Officers or Principals: Robert E. Quick, Jr., Chairman/President; Jeffrey Harris, Executive Director.
Mission or Interest: Advocating the 'wise use' of natural resources and private property rights. "Balancing environmental protection and economic growth." Operates the People for the West! campaign.
Accomplishments: In 1994 three People for the West! members were elected to congress: Reps. J.D. Hayworth (R-AZ), Scott McInnis (R-CO), and Helen Chenoweth (R-ID). Held many rallies and demonstrations. "Organized a five-mile-long convoy to the Arizona State Capitol building to call attention to a logging injunction in Arizona and New Mexico national forests. . . Members turn out in force at 45 of the 48 hearings scheduled throughout the country by Interior Secretary Bruce Babbitt as part of his plan to radically alter federal rangeland law. . . Seventeen PFW families traveled to Washington, DC to deliver 400,000 petition signatures of public land users who support multiple use and resource production."
Tax Status: 501(c)(6) **Annual Report:** No. **Employees:** 14
Board of Directors or Trustees: Bruce Vincent (Alliance for America).
Periodicals: *People for the West!* (monthly tabloid).
Internships: No.
Other Information: Formerly called the Western States Public Lands Coalition. Affiliated with several other coalitions and groups, including Western States Coalition, Alliance for America, Wind River Multiple Use, Coalition of Arizona/New Mexico Counties for Stable Economic Growth.

National Commodity and Barter Association (NCBA)

P.O. Box 2255
Longmont, CO 80502   **Phone:** (303) 337-9617
USA

Contact Person: John Voss, President.
Officers or Principals: Brett Brough, Political Action Coordinator; John Voss, President.
Mission or Interest: Abolition of the Internal Revenue Service, return to gold and/or silver-backed currency.
Accomplishments: Rep. Ron Paul (R-TX) said, "I congratulate the NCBA on its fine work exposing the evil tactics of the IRS. Keep up the good work."
Products or Services: Post Office vigils, gold rallies, growing coalition activities in the national arena, letters to Congressmen, lobbies in Washington, economic research, Congressional directory, NCBA Freedom Books, "legal assistance challenging government abuse."
Tax Status: Unincorporated. **Employees:** Volunteers.
Periodicals: *The Petitioner, NCBA Reports.*
Other Information: Established in 1978. The Association operates the National Commodity Exchange, a warehouse exchange system that allows members to exchange goods and services without paperwork or the exchange of money issued by the federal government to avoid scrutiny by the IRS. According to the NCBA, these exchanges have come under heavy IRS scrutiny. Publicly released memorandum show the IRS warning regional offices about these exchanges and requesting that the offices "initiate covert action." Members who have participated in such exchanges have faced criminal prosecution. NCBA offices have been searched and, in the case of Voss, Grandbouche, et al. v. Agents Bergsgaard, et al., a court ruled that the IRS agents' warrant was illegal.

National Defense Council Foundation

1220 King St., Suite 1
Alexandria, VA 22314   **Phone:**   (703) 836-3443
USA   **Fax:**   (703) 836-5402

Contact Person: Major F. Andy Messing, Jr., Executive Director.
Officers or Principals: Milton R. Copulas, President ($59,106); Major F. Andy Messing, Jr., Executive Director ($52,550); Catherine C. Dickey, Vice President ($0); Rep. Dan Burton, (R-IN), Chairman; Hon. Robert K. Dornan, Vice Chairman.
Mission or Interest: "Provide primary-source research regarding low-intensity conflict, drug trade, and environmental/energy policy as they pertain to U.S. National Security."
Accomplishments: "Distributed 137 tons ($17 million) of food and medicine to the hottest combat zones in the world; taken over 100 members of Congress, key opinion makers, and media on fact-finding missions to wars worldwide; published and distributed nearly 90 studies and reports that were widely published in the nation's top newspapers." Instrumental in preserving the Navy SEAL program. Former President Ronald Reagan said, "The efforts of the NDCF have been invaluable in offering hope and promise where there was only despair. The inspirational programs undertaken by the NDCF. . . will help the cause of freedom. (The NDCF's) work is in the highest tradition of this great nation." In 1995 the Council spent $126,626 on its programs. These included the delivery of medical supplies to Haiti.
Total Revenue: 1995 $148,331 6%(3) **Total Expenses:** $169,922 75%/14%/12% **Net Assets:** (-$11,285)
Products or Services: Annual "Conflict List" detailing all current conflicts worldwide. Lobbying: in 1995 the Council spent $2,910 on the direct lobbying of legislators. This represents a steady increase over the last four years, averaging a 23% increase per year.
Tax Status: 501(c)(3)
Board of Directors or Trustees: Sen. Trent Lott (R-MS), Rep. Newt Gingrich (R-GA).
Internships: Yes, for a small stipend.
Other Information: Received $147,514, or 99% of revenue, from contributions and grants awarded by foundations, businesses, and individuals. (These grants included $1,000 from the Roe Foundation. In 1994, $5,000 from the Aequus Institute.) The remaining revenue, came from the sale of a video tape to CBS News, and interest on savings and temporary cash investments.

National Education Program (NEP)

P.O. Box 11000
Oklahoma City, OK 73136   **Phone:**   (405) 425-5040
USA

Contact Person: Dr. Guy Ross, Editor-in-Chief.
Officers or Principals: Pendleton Woods.
Mission or Interest: "Dedicated to promoting an understanding among the American people of the importance of our faith in God, strictly limited constitutional government, and the private ownership and control of property."
Tax Status: 501(c)(3)
Periodicals: *National Program Letter* (monthly newsletter).
Other Information: Established in 1936.

National Fatherhood Initiative (NFI)

600 Eden Rd., Bldg. E
Lancaster, PA 17601   **Phone:** (717) 581-8860   **E-Mail:**   trimbath@aol.com
USA   **Fax:**   (717) 581-8862

Contact Person: Jeffrey S. Trimbath, Secretary/Treasurer.
Officers or Principals: Wade F. Horn, Ph.D., Program Director ($76,539); Don. E. Eberly, President ($25,000); Jeffrey S. Trimbath, Secretary/Treasurer ($19,231); David Blankenhorn, Chairman.
Mission or Interest: "To restore responsible fatherhood in America." To challenge "the myth of the superfluous father."
Accomplishments: "Convened a national summit sponsored by ten leading civic groups, unveiled an Ad Council campaign; mentioned in over 1,000 media outlets." Promoted statistics and research showing the negative consequences of fatherless children. In 1996 NFI received a grant from the Virginia Department of Health to initiate a statewide fatherhood promotion campaign. In 1994 the Initiative spent $263,643 on its programs.
Total Revenue: 1994 $402,031 **Total Expenses:** $361,669 73%/17%/11% **Net Assets:** $38,268
Products or Services: Pamphlets, videos, books, and other products.
Tax Status: 501(c)(3) **Annual Report:** No. **Employees:** 3 full-time, 3 part-time.   **Citations:** 114:55
Board of Directors or Trustees: Eloise Anderson (Director, Social Services, State of California), Marilyn Benoit, M.D., William Bennett, Ph.D. (Empower America), Everett Christmas (YMCA), James Cox (Boys and Girls Clubs), Guarione Diaz (Cuban American National Council), James Egan, M.D., Amitai Etzioni, Ph.D. (Communitarian Network), Ofra Fisher (B'nai B'rith Intl.), George Gallup (Chair, Gallup Intl.), Richard Harwood, James Earl Jones (actor), Jeff Kemp (Washington Family Council), Michael Lamb, Ph.D., Rep. Steve Largent (R-OK), Stephen Lawson (Exec. Vice Pres., U.S. Junior Chamber of Commerce), Robert Lerman, Ph.D. (American Univ.), Lynn Mapes (Deputy Director, Partnership for a Drug-Free America), Willard Scott (Today Show), Michael Singletary, Bill Stepheny, Hon. Louis Sullivan (former Secretary, Health and Human Services, 1989-93), Josephine Velasquez, Judith Wallerstein, Ph.D. (Center for Families in Transition), Jerry Wiener, M.D. (George Washington Univ.).

Periodicals: *Fatherhood Today* (quarterly newsletter).
Internships: No.
Other Information: Established in 1993. Affiliated with the Commonwealth Foundation for Public Policy Alternatives. NFI received $400,276, or 99.5% of revenue, from contributions and grants awarded by foundations, businesses, and individuals. (These grants included $35,000 from the J.M. Foundation, $5,000 from the Gilder Foundation. In 1995, $200,000 from the Scaife Family Foundation, $150,000 from the Lynde and Harry Bradley Foundation.) The remaining revenue came from interest on savings and temporary cash investments.

National Federal Lands Conference (NFLC)

P.O. Box 847
Bountiful, UT 84011   **Phone:**   (801) 298-0858
USA   **Fax:**   (801) 295-0173

Contact Person: Jim Faulkner.
Officers or Principals: Kent Howard, President; Burt Smith, Vice President; Dick Manning, Vice President; Ruth Kaiser, Executive Director.
Mission or Interest: NFLC works to inform "Americans of their private rights in Federal Lands." Protection of private property rights and the right to use federally owned land. Active in the 'Wise Use Movement' and 'County Movement'. The County Movement is headquartered in the Western and Mountain states, and advocates local county control over land use, not the Federal government.
Accomplishments: The leftist Southwest Environmental Center says "To a large extent the National Federal Lands Conference *is* the county movement." Hosted organizing seminars throughout the West.
Products or Services: Numerous books, pamphlets, video and audio tapes, and other materials. Sells the seminal works of the County Movement, such as Mark Pollot's Grand Theft & Petit Larceny.
Tax Status: 501(c)(3)   **Annual Report:** No.   **Employees:** 0
Board of Directors or Trustees: DeMar Dahl, Joe Fallini, Ronald Mann, Loyd Sorensen, Von Sorensen. Advisors include: Ron Arnold (Center for the Defense of Free Enterprise), Bud Eppers (Federal Lands Legal Foundation), Richard Johnson (Farm and Ranch Investments-Exchanges), Ronald Mayer (Farm & Ranch Sales/Appraisals), Mark Pollot, Esq. (Dir., Stewards of the Range Constitutional Law Center), others, including many ranchers, and mining and timber executives.
Periodicals: *Update* (monthly).
Other Information: NFLC has called for and supported the formation of citizen militias.

National Federation of the Grand Order of Pachyderm Clubs

7306 Wise Ave., Suite 100
St. Louis, MO 63117   **Phone:**   (314) 874-3688   **Internet:** http://www.pachyderms.org
USA

Contact Person: William A. Kay, Jr., Executive Director.
Officers or Principals: William C. Phelps, President.
Mission or Interest: "Social organizations, separate from the politics of county committees, working to educate Republicans on national issues at weekly luncheons."
Tax Status: Not exempt.
Other Information: Auxiliary of the Republican Party.

National Federation of Republican Women (NFRW)

124 N. Alfred St.
Alexandria, VA 22314   **Phone:**   (703) 548-9688   **E-Mail:** nfrw@worldweb.net
USA   **Fax:**   (703) 548-9836   **Internet:** http://nfrw.org

Contact Person: Frederika ver Hulst, Executive Director.
Officers or Principals: Marilyn Thayer, President; Carole Jean Jordon, Secretary; Heidi Smith, Treasurer.
Mission or Interest: To elect Republican women to office.
Accomplishments: Over 115,000 members in 2,300 clubs nation-wide.
Products or Services: Various programs and publications. Candidate training and seminars. Llovelyn Evans Memorial Scholarships awarded annually to minority women. Pathfinder Scholarships for women studying substance-abuse prevention. Betty Rendel scholarships for undergraduate women majoring in government, political science, or economics. Mamie Eisenhower Library Project that contributes NFRW-approved books to libraries, hospitals, and schools.
Tax Status: Not exempt.   **Annual Report:** No.   **Employees:** 10
Periodicals: *The Republican Woman* (quarterly magazine).
Internships: Yes, the Dorothy Kabis Memorial Internship program.
Other Information: Established in 1938.

National Flag Foundation (NFF)

Flag Plaza
Pittsburgh, PA 15219   **Phone:**   (412) 261-1776
USA

Contact Person: Daniel R. Fleck, President.
Officers or Principals: Daniel R. Fleck, President ($53,722); George F. Cahill, Director ($31,552); William J. Copeland, Vice President ($0); C.J. Queenan, Jr., Chairman.
Mission or Interest: "To inspire love and pride of country in our children, to invigorate America's attachment to freedom, and to promote frequent and proper display of our national emblem."
Accomplishments: "It is believed that NFF has produced and distributed more pieces of flag-related patriotic literature than any other private sector effort." In 1994 the Foundation spent $259,078 on its programs.
Total Revenue: 1994 $86,261 (-76%)(1) **Total Expenses:** $275,215 94%/5%/1% **Net Assets:** $482,406
Products or Services: Books, flags, pins, banners, prints, other flag-related products.
Tax Status: 501(c)(3) **Annual Report:** Yes. **Employees:** 2
Board of Directors or Trustees: E.F. Andrews, James Crawford, Thomas Marshall, James Rohr, Wesley von Schack, James Will.
Periodicals: *The New Constellation.*
Internships: No.
Other Information: Established in 1968. The Foundation received $45,815, or 49%, from contributions and grants awarded by foundations, businesses, and individuals. $27,781 net, or 30%, from the sale of inventory. $19,016, or 20%, from interest on savings and temporary cash investments. The remaining revenue came from royalties and other miscellaneous sources. The Foundation lost $7,525 on the sale of securities.

National Forum Foundation (NFF)

511 C St., N.E.
Washington, DC 20002   **Phone:**   (202) 543-3515
USA   **Fax:**   (202) 547-4101

Contact Person: James S. Denton, Secretary/Treasurer .
Officers or Principals: James S. Denton, Secretary/Treasurer ($101,985); Alan Dye, President.
Mission or Interest: Promotion of political and economic freedom through a variety of international projects, including the sponsorship of conferences, election observer teams and extensive training programs. The Foundation provides direct support to the newly emerging democratic states of Europe. Through a variety of public education activities, including conferences, media outreach and publications, they encourage American policy makers to adopt policies that promote democracy and free-market economics here and abroad.
Accomplishments: Before the collapse of the Soviet Union, the Forum had provided support to the underground press and human-rights activists in Central Europe. The NFF's "Second Thoughts Project" brings together former members of the political Left to discuss their shift toward conservatism. The Project has produced several books about the effects of the 1960's legacy on American politics and culture. These were reviewed by every leading magazine and newspaper in the country. One of the books, Destructive Generation, was a *Washington Post* best seller. In the spring of 1990, the project sponsored a major conference that brought together liberals and conservatives to discuss the troubling issue of race in America. In 1994 the Forum spent $1,138,419 on its programs, most of which went to programs dealing with Eastern Europe. This included $64,689 in grants for organizations working in Estonia and Poland.
Total Revenue: 1994 $1,441,643 ($988,307, or 69%, from government grants) 14%(5)
Total Expenses: $1,477,661 77%/22%/1% **Net Assets:** $267,510
Tax Status: 501(c)(3) **Annual Report:** Yes. **Employees:** 8   **Citations:** 6:189
Board of Directors or Trustees: J.P. Bolduc (WR Grace & Co.), Pete Collier (Institute for the Study of Popular Culture), Mara Liasson (White House Correspondent for NPR), P.J. O'Rourke (best-selling author), Dean Paul Wolfowitz..
Periodicals: *NFF Update* (newsletter).
Internships: Yes, available in the summer for American students. They also operate the largest internship training program in the U.S. for emerging leaders of Central and Eastern Europe.
Other Information: The Forum received $988,307, or 69% of revenue, from government grants. $443,008, or 31%, from contributions and grants awarded by foundations, businesses, and individuals. (These grants included $50,000 from the F.M. Kirby Foundation. In 1995, $100,000 from the Lynde and Harry Bradley Foundation, $86,164 from the Smith Richardson Foundation.) The remaining revenue came from interest on savings, and other miscellaneous sources.

National Home Education Research Institute (NHERI)

P.O. Box 13939
Salem, OR 97301   **Phone:** (503) 364-1490   **E-Mail:** mail@nheri.org
USA   **Fax:**   (503) 364-2827   **Internet:** http://www.nheri.org

Contact Person: Brian D. Ray, Ph.D., President.

Officers or Principals: Brian D. Ray, Ph.D., President ($13,395); Thomas E. Glogau, Secretary ($0); Gregg Harris, Director ($0); Thomas Tinker, M.D.

Mission or Interest: Research and distribution of academic studies on home schooling. Works with scholars, attorneys, home educators, legislators, and the media.

Accomplishments: Co-researcher in federally-funded study conducted in three Western states. The Institute has provided expert testimony in court cases, and has completed basic research on home schooling in the U.S. and Canada. In 1995 the Institute spent $46,202 on its programs.

Total Revenue: 1995 $46,202 **Total Expenses:** $43,576 96%/4%/0% **Net Assets:** $3,437

Products or Services: Research, lectures, expert testimony.

Tax Status: 501(c)(3) **Annual Report:** No. **Employees:** 2

Periodicals: *Home School Researcher* (quarterly, academic journal).

Internships: Yes, but no stipend.

Other Information: Established in 1985. The Institute received $16,317, or 35% of revenue, from subscriptions. $11,731, or 25%, from contributions and grants awarded by foundations, businesses, and individuals. $11,695, or 25%, from research grants. $5,712, or 12%, from speaking fees. The remaining revenue came from investments.

National Humanities Institute

214 Massachusetts Ave., N.E., Suite 470
Washington, DC 20002   **Phone:** (202) 544-3158   **E-Mail:** nhi@access.digex.net
USA   **Fax:**   same   **Internet:** http://www.access.digex.net/~nhi

Contact Person: Joseph Baldacchino, President.

Officers or Principals: Joseph F. Baldacchino, President ($16,800); Dr. Claes G. Ryn, Chairman ($7,440); Mark L. Melcher, Treasurer ($0).

Mission or Interest: The Institute was founded to "deal with social decline at its ultimate sources in the moral, intellectual, and aesthetical life of society." They see political activism and public policy advocacy as, at best, of limited use. They see the root of problems in our culture, that "over time shapes the will, the mind, and the imagination of a people -- for good or ill. It forms society's sense of reality, its basic likes and dislikes."

Total Revenue: 1995 $56,252 7%(2) **Total Expenses:** $55,991 **Net Assets:** $53,502

Products or Services: Research and writing in areas pertaining to culture. Publication of books and articles. Conferences, symposia, and lectures. Programs to help visiting foreign students and journalists understand American and Western culture. The Institute also has launched a Center for Constitutional Studies. In 1995 the Institute spent $37,865 on its programs, mostly on books and publications.

Tax Status: 501(c)(3)

Board of Directors or Trustees: Edward Babbitt, Jr., William Benton, Mrs. Herbert Dow Doan, Hon. Robert Ellsworth, Sture Eskilsson (Chair, Enterprise Foundation), Anthony Harrigan, Mark Melcher, Mrs. David Scott, Clyde Sluhan. President Richard Nixon was Honorary Chairman until his death. The Academic Board includes: John Aldridge (Univ. of Michigan), Jude Dougherty (Dean, Catholic Univ. of America), Paul Gottfried (Elizabethtown College), Forrest McDonald (Univ. of Alabama), George Panichas (Univ. of Maryland), Peter Stanlis (Rockford College). The late historian Robert Nisbet was on the Board, and Russell Kirk was Chairman of the Academic Board until his death.

Periodicals: *Humanitas* (quarterly journal), *National Humanities Bulletin* (newsletter).

Other Information: Established in 1984. The Institute received $42,259, or 75% of revenue, from contributions and grants awarded by foundations, businesses, and individuals. (These grants included $11,000 from the John M. Olin Foundation. In 1994, $12,000 from the Earhart Foundation.) $13,213, or 23%, from program services. The remaining revenue came from the sale of inventory, and investments.

National Institute for Labor Relations Research

8001 Braddock Rd., Suite 510
Springfield, VA 22151   **Phone:** (703) 321-8510   **E-Mail:** info@nrtw.org
USA   **Fax:**   (703) 321-9613   **Internet:** http://www.nrtw.org

Contact Person: Reed E. Larson, Executive Director.

Officers or Principals: Reed E. Larson, Executive Director ($33,350); John Wilson, Chairman ($0); Virginia A. Smith, Secretary/Treasurer ($0).

Mission or Interest: Educational research affiliate of the National Right to Work Committee. "The Institute maintains a research library; responds to requests for research and information; sponsors educational research, writings, and symposia; and publishes and distributes educational materials."

Accomplishments: In 1994 the Institute spent $252,878 on its programs.

Total Revenue: 1994 $239,573 **Total Expenses:** $289,125 87%/5%/7% **Net Assets:** $289,549

Tax Status: 501(c)(3)   **Citations:** 4:196

Board of Directors or Trustees: Morton Blackwell (Leadership Inst.), Camille Bradford, Roy Cook, N. Carl Monroe, Thomas Quinlan, R. Bruce Simpson, John Wilson.

Other Information: Affiliated with the 501(c)(4) National Right to Work Committee, and its Concerned Educators Against Forced Unionism division, and the 501(c)(3) National Right to Work Legal Defense and Education Foundation. In 1994 the three affiliates had combined revenues of $11,983,356. Reed Larson serves as executive director for all three and in 1994 he received a combined $255,225. The Institute received $236,834, or 99% of revenue, from contributions and grants. (In 1995, $25,000 from the Sunmark Foundation.) The remaining revenue came from dividends and interest from securities.

National Institute for Public Policy

3031 Javier Rd., Suite 300
Fairfax, VA 22031   **Phone:** (703) 698-0563   **E-Mail:** nippnsr@delphi.com
USA   **Fax:**   (703) 698-0566

Contact Person: Keith Payne, President.
Officers or Principals: Keith Payne, President ($82,873); Amy Moltaji, Secretary ($32,410); John Kohout, III ($25,437).
Mission or Interest: Foreign policy and national defense research institute.
Accomplishments: Provided testimony before Congress, and articles for scholarly journals.
Total Revenue: FY ending 11/95 $1,058,362 ($392,748, or 37%, from government grants) 51%(2)
Total Expenses: $995,656 94%/4%/2% **Net Assets:** $598,476
Tax Status: 501(c)(3)   **Citations:** 11:170
Board of Directors or Trustees: Colin Gray, Meta Jane Mortensen, Felix Hampton, Frank Molton.
Other Information: Owns 100% of the for-profit National Security Research, Inc., that had a yearly income of $11,767,782, and assets valued at $447,400. The Institute received $655,591, or 61% of gross revenue, from contributions and grants awarded by foundations, businesses, and individuals. (These grants included $273,762 from the Smith-Richardson Foundation.) $392,748, or 37%, from government grants. $10,882, or 1%, from interest on savings and temporary cash investments. The remaining revenue came from dividends and interest from securities, royalties, and publication sales. The Institute lost $8,103 net on the sale of securities.

National Interest

(see National Affairs)

National Jewish Coalition (NJC)

415 2nd St., N.E., Suite 100
Washington, DC 20002   **Phone:** (202) 547-7701
USA   **Fax:**   (202) 544-2434

Contact Person: Shari Hillman.
Officers or Principals: Matthew Brooks, Executive Director ($54,574); Cheryl Halpern, National Chairman ($0); S. Daniel Abraham, Vice Chairman ($0); Herbert Linsenberg, Treasurer; Jeffery P. Altman, Secretary/Counsel.
Mission or Interest: "To act as a bridge between the American Jewish community and Republican decision makers."
Accomplishments: "The NJC has built the only national grassroots network of Jewish Republicans and has a growing roster of local chapters in key cities and states." Strongly backed the Supreme Court nomination of Justice Clarence Thomas. Supported aid and loan guarantees for Israel. In 1994 the Coalition spent $159,871 on its programs.
Total Revenue: 1994 $297,562 (-13%)(2) **Total Expenses:** $257,830 62%/24%/14% **Net Assets:** $244,965
Tax Status: 501(c)(4)   **Citations:** 19:151
Board of Directors or Trustees: Max Fisher, Richard Fox, Sam Fox, Hon. Joseph Gildenhorn, George Klein, Michael David Epstein, Sheldon Kamins, Hon. Mel Sembler, Robert Snyder. The Advisory Committee includes: Sen. Rudy Boschwitz, Hon. Marshall Breger, Hon. Harriet Derman, Rep. Jon Fox, Rep. Ben Gilman, Mayor Stephen Goldsmith, Rep. Steven Schiff, Sen. Arlen Specter, Hon. Susan Weiner.
Periodicals: *NJC Bulletin* (bimonthly newsletter).
Internships: Yes, during the fall, spring, and summer semesters.
Other Information: Established in 1985. Affiliated with the 501(c)(3) Jewish Policy Center at the same address. The Coalition received $286,562, or 96% of revenue, from contributions and grants. $10,390, or 4%, from membership dues. The remaining revenue came from interest on savings and temporary cash investments.

National Journalism Center

(see Education and Research Institute)

National Justice Foundation of America

1617 16th St.
Sacramento, CA 95814   **Phone:** (916) 442-0537
USA

Contact Person: John Rakus, President.
Mission or Interest: Support "the national sovereignty of the United States of America and our form of government as a constitutional republic. . . Secures to Americans the right of private property." Advocates a return to the gold standard and an end to race-based quotas.
Products or Services: Pamphlets and booklets.
Tax Status: 501(c)(3)
Board of Directors or Trustees: James Townsend (*The National Educator*), Robert Von Esch, Jr. (Judge pro tem, Fullerton, CA), Ormond Howard, Arnold Giesbret, M.D., Russell Granata, John Grady, M.D. (American Rifle and Pistol Assn.), John Rarick, G. G. Baumen, others.

National Legal Center for the Public Interest

1000 16th St., N.W., Suite 301
Washington, DC 20036   **Phone:** (202) 296-1683
USA   **Fax:**   (202) 293-2118

Contact Person: Ernest B. Hueter, President.
Officers or Principals: Ernest B. Hueter, President ($141,624); Roger Clegg, Vice President/General Counsel ($103,476); Irene A. Jacoby, Vice President ($85,531); Gov. Raymond P. Shafer, Treasurer; Patsy R. Williams, Secretary.
Mission or Interest: Educational and public-service foundation concerned with the role of the judiciary, the effectiveness and fairness of the judicial process in dispute resolution, and broad issues of public policy that relate to law or justice administration. They do not litigate. "The Center's philosophical base rests on regard for the constitutional system of the United States and for the traditional values that have sustained the nation, including the rights of individuals, freedom of enterprise, private ownership of property, balanced use and protection of private and public resources and limited government."
Accomplishments: "The Center fulfills an ever-expanding agenda of diverse programs, each of the quality and professionalism which has earned the respect of the judiciary, the Congress, and the executive branch alike." In 1994 the Center spent $598,130 on its programs; $374,964 was spent on publications, and the rest on a conference series attended by approximately 500.
Total Revenue: 1994 $858,174 14%(1) **Total Expenses:** $887,390 67%/18%/15% **Net Assets:** $838,907
Products or Services: Newsletters, monographs, conferences and special projects.
Tax Status: 501(c)(3) **Annual Report:** Yes. **Employees:** 4   **Citations:** 2:216
Board of Directors or Trustees: Hon. Joan Aikens (Commissioner, Federal Election Commission), Curtis Barnette (Chair/CEO, Bethlehem Steel), Hon. Griffin Bell (Attorney General, 1977-79), Joseph Coors (Adolph Coors Co.), Dr. David Davenport (Pres., Pepperdine Univ.), Arnaud de Borchgrave (Center for Strategic and International Studies), Livio DeSimone (Chair/CEO, 3M), Hon. Glen Holden (Ambassador to Jamaica, 1989-93), Dean Kleckner (Pres., American Farm Bureau Federation), Shirley Peterson (Pres., Hood College), Enrique Sosa (Pres., Dow North America), Hon. Robert Strauss, Hon William Webster (Director, CIA, 1987-1993), Hon. Casper Weinberger (Chair., *Forbes;* Secretary of Defense, 1981-87), Prof. Walter Williams (George Mason Univ.), others.
Periodicals: *National Legal Center for the Public Interest News*, and *Judicial Legislative Watch Report.*
Internships: Yes, interns assist in monitoring decisions of the Supreme Court and other courts, act as research assistants to scholars and senior staff members, and are assigned research projects.
Other Information: Established in 1976. The Center received $809,925, or 94% of revenue, from contributions and grants awarded by foundations, businesses, and individuals. (These grants included $7,500 from the F.M. Kirby Foundation, $1,000 from the Earhart Foundation, $1,000 from the United Educators Foundation. In 1995, $1,000 from the Forbes Foundation.) $39,576, or 5%, from dividends and interest from securities. The remaining revenue came from the sale of monographs, and interest on savings.

National Legal Foundation

6477 College Park Square, Suite 306
Virginia Beach, VA 23464   **Phone:** (804) 424-4242   **E-Mail:** Netlegal@Norfolk.INSI.net
USA   **Fax:**   (804) 420-0855

Contact Person: Steven W. Fitschen, Executive Director.
Officers or Principals: Robert K. Skelrood, President ($87,500); Steven W. Fitschen, Executive Director ($36,755); Barry C. Hodge, Staff Attorney ($32,873); Leonard J. Nelson, III, John Wheeler, Vice Presidents; William Patrick Crowder, Secretary/Treasurer.
Mission or Interest: "A Christian legal advocacy firm dedicated to the preservation of America's freedom and constitutional rights...We do not merely wish to carve out a 'safe haven' for religion. Nor do we want to go back to some better day. Rather, we want to go on to something greater than we have ever known before."
Accomplishments: Launched an effort to challenge the implementation of "Outcome Based Education," or OBE in Oregon. The Institute's efforts are led by Dr. Herbert W. Titus, Dean of the Law School at Regent University. Successfully involved in Parker v. Stern that allowed a religious assembly in New York's Central park; Westside Community Schools v. Mergens that allowed high school students to organize a Bible Club in school; Equality Foundation v. City of Cincinnati that allowed the city charter to repeal homosexuals' rights legislation, and prohibit the future passage of such laws. Unsuccessful in support of Colorado's Amendment 2, which the Foundation helped draft, before the Supreme Court. Amendment 2, which was passed by popular vote in Colorado, disallowed "granting special rights to homosexuals" and was ruled unconstitutional by the Supreme Court by a vote of 6 to 3 in Romer v. Evans. In the fiscal year ending April 30, 1995, the Foundation spent $442,978 on its programs. $231,607 was spent on legal action. $211,371 was spent on public information and education; for example, handling approximately 200 telephone requests for information regarding legal issues such as Bible clubs in schools.
Total Revenue: FY ending 4/95 $659,112 **Total Expenses:** $828,208 53%/15%/32% **Net Assets:** (-$164,746)
Products or Services: Litigation. Numerous pamphlets, booklets, and other paraphernalia. Daily radio program.
Tax Status: 501(c)(3) **Annual Report:** Yes. **Employees:** 7   **Citations:** 17:156
Board of Directors or Trustees: David Barton, Michael Johnston, Jim Woodall.
Periodicals: *The Minuteman* (quarterly newsletter).
Other Information: Founded in 1985. Previously called the Freedom Council. The Foundation has an office in Tennessee; P.O. Box 341283, Memphis, TN 38184-1283. The Foundation received $628,802, or 95% of revenue, from contributions and grants awarded by foundations, businesses, and individuals. $25,871, or 4%, from clients' fees. The remaining revenue came from the sale of publications and mailing lists.

National Legal and Policy Center (NLPC)

8321 Old Courthouse Rd., Suite 270
Vienna, VA 22182   **Phone:**   (703) 847-3088
USA   **Fax:**   (703) 448-8341

Contact Person: Peter Flaherty, President.
Officers or Principals: Ken Boehm, Chairman ($60,000); Peter T. Flaherty, President/Secretary ($35,000); Sarah F. Krouch, Director ($0).
Mission or Interest: "Promotes ethics in government through the distribution of the code of ethics for government and through research, education and legal action."
Accomplishments: NLPC was a plaintiff in the suit that forced the Clintons to turn over documents relating to the Health Care Task Force. NLPC has been an ardent opponent of the federally funded Legal Services Corporation, and due in part to its efforts through the Legal Services Accountability Project, the LSC's funding was reduced from $400 million to $278 million. In February 1997 the Center led a coalition of 36 business and policy groups in calling for an end to all funding for the Corporation. NLPC was one of the first organizations to pursue the firing of the White House travel office staff, filing a complaint with the Federal Election Commission alleging illegal contributions to the Clinton candidacy by Harry Thomason and that the travel office business was given to Thomason as repayment. In 1995 the Center spent $246,254 on its programs, $135,187 to research the Legal Services Corporations and its grantees, and $111,067 to "make the Food and Drug Administration accountable by monitoring compliance with the Federal Advisory Committee Act, the Freedom of Information Act and the Sunshine in Government Act.
Total Revenue: 1995 $511,183 **Total Expenses:** $384,241 64%/18%/18% **Net Assets:** $112,670
Products or Services: The Case Against the Legal Services Program book, fax network, FDA Watch program, more. Lobbying: in 1995 the Center spent $2,850 on lobbying, mostly through media advertisements.
Tax Status: 501(c)(3) **Annual Report:** No. **Employees:** 6   **Citations:** 32:125
Periodicals: *Ethics Watch* (quarterly newsletter).
Internships: Yes.
Other Information: Established in 1992. The Center received $487,524, or 95% of revenue, from contributions and grants awarded by foundations, businesses, and individuals. (These grants included $62,000 from the Carthage Foundation, $50,000 from the Scaife Family Foundation. These contributions and grants have grown by an average of 48% per year since 1993. Grants have historically included money from R.J. Reynolds.) $20,735, or 4%, from program service fees. $2,924, or 1%, from interest on savings and temporary cash investments.

National Monitor of Education

P.O. Box 402
Alamo, CA 94596   **Phone:**   (510) 945-6745
USA

Contact Person: Betty Arras, Editor/Publisher.
Mission or Interest: Inform citizens concerning current educational developments in school reform, school choice, bussing programs, parental rights, legislation, and curriculum content in nonacademic, "psycho-social" school programs.
Tax Status: Unincorporated. **Annual Report:** No. **Employees:** 2
Periodicals: *National Monitor of Education* (10 times a year).
Internships: No.

National Motorists Association (NMA)

6678 Pertzborn Rd.
Dane, WI 53529   **Phone:** (608) 849-6000   **E-Mail:** nma@genie.geis.com
USA   **Fax:**   (608) 849-8697   **Internet:** http://www.motorists.com

Contact Person: James J. Baxter, President.
Mission or Interest: Supports the rights of citizens to own and drive automobiles without undue burden. They oppose excessive taxation on cars and fuel, heavy-handed regulation such as mandatory fuel economy standards and other such environmental laws, and support the raising of the federally mandated speed limit. "Over twelve years ago, we realized that the American motorist was on the road to being taxed, regulated, and fined into oblivion."
Accomplishments: They have received positive publicity in *Car and Driver* and *Automobile* magazines. *Car and Driver* called president Jim Baxter, "the only genuine crusader for drivers' rights." They have over 15,000 members. In 1987 (under a previous name, Citizens for Rational Traffic Laws) they were instrumental in getting the 55 mph speed limit raised to 65 mph. Influential in passing the 1995 legislation that repealed the national maximum speed limit. Direct involvement in raising the speed limit in approximately 20 states. Successfully opposed universal vehicle emissions inspections. Promoted remote sensing as an alternative to emission inspection.
Products or Services: They offer a "Legal Resources Kit," to help motorists fight and win in traffic court, as well as an "Attorney Referral Service" for those who choose not to represent themselves. They have a unique Traffic Justice Program intended to fight "unjust" speeding tickets. If after one year of continuing membership, you receive a speeding ticket, plead "not guilty," and lose, they will pay your fine. NMA publishes Special Alerts when legislation or regulations affecting drivers or automobiles are being considered. Also publish Motorists Guide to State Traffic Laws. Other services are offered.

Tax Status: For profit. **Annual Report:** No. **Employees:** 5
Periodicals: *NMA News* (bimonthly).
Other Information: Name changed from Citizens for Rational Traffic Laws in 1989.

National Obscenity Law Center
(see Morality in Media)

National Organization of Episcopalians for Life (NOEL)
10523 Main St.
Fairfax, VA 22030   **Phone:** (703) 591-6635
USA   **Fax:**   (703) 385-0415

Contact Person: L. Roberts, Administrative Assistant.
Officers or Principals: Marilyn Heigl, Executive Director ($20,292); Rev. Rebecca C. Spanos, President ($0); Mary Haines, Vice President ($0); Thelma Barto, Secretary; Daniel F. Derrick, Jr., Treasurer.
Mission or Interest: National Episcopalian anti-abortion organization. "NOEL supports women who choose life, teens who choose chastity, families who choose healing after abortion."
Accomplishments: In 1994 NOEL spent $74,262 on its programs. The largest program, with expenditures of $38,745, was the production and distribution of *NOEL News* -- 32,000 copies were mailed. $31,265 was spent on their general convention at the tri-annual meeting of the National Episcopal Church attended by 5,000. Other programs produced literature and audio tapes, and held the convocation.
Total Revenue: 1994 $66,183 (-4%)(1) **Total Expenses:** $74,262 **Net Assets:** $7,611
Tax Status: 501(c)(3)
Board of Directors or Trustees: Rev. Kenneth Cook, Rev. Sudduth Cummings, David Mills (Trinity Episcopal School for Ministry), Rev. Dr. Robert Munday (Trinity Episcopal School for Ministry), Rev. Wesley Nelson, Richard Schwaab, Kathleen Sweet. The Board of Advisors includes: The Very Rev. David Collins, The Rt. Rev. Alex Dickson, Carolyn Gerster, M.D., Rt. Rev. John Howe, Rt. Rev. Terence Kelshaw, Robert Lewis, M.D., Rt. Rev. Edward MacBurney, Rev. Dr. John Rodgers (Trinity Episcopal School for Ministry), Rt. Rev. Harry Shipps, Dr. Stephen Smith (Trinity Episcopal School for Ministry), Rt. Rev. William Stevens, Rev. Carey Womble, M.D., and others.
Periodicals: *NOEL News* (newsletter).
Other Information: NOEL Vice President Mary Haines is married to the Right Reverend Ronald Haines, Episcopal Bishop of Washington. Bishop Haines is a prominent abortion-rights advocate and is "one of the Episcopal Church's most liberal spokesmen." NOEL received $60,960, or 92% of revenue, from contributions and grants awarded by foundations, businesses, and individuals. $2,525, or 4%, from program services including the sale of materials. $2,310, or 3%, from membership dues. The remaining revenue came from investment income.

National Policy Forum
229 ½ Pennsylvania Ave., S.E.
Washington, D.C. 20003   **Phone:** (202) 544-2900
USA   **Fax:**   (202) 544-0296   **Internet:** http://www.npf.org

Contact Person: Michael Baroody, President.
Mission or Interest: Created to hold a series of meetings across the country to find what Americans feel are the most pressing current problems, and possible solutions. The results of these forums will be evaluated, and reported back to the Republican party.
Tax Status: 501(c)(4)
Board of Directors or Trustees: Sen. Don Nickles (R-OK), Hon. Bob Michel (former Rep., R-IL), Gov. George Voinovich (R-OH), Sen. Teresa Lubbers (State Sen., R-IN), Mayor James Garner (Hempstead, NY), Gaddi Vasquez, Oren Benton, William Brock, Gwendolyn King.
Periodicals: *Common Sense: A Republican Journal of Thought and Opinion* (quarterly), and *Ideas Matter* (monthly newsletter).
Other Information: Established in 1993.

National Republican Club of Capitol Hill
300 First St., S.E.
Washington, DC 20003   **Phone:** (202) 484-4590
USA   **Fax:**   (202) 479-9110

Contact Person: Michael Dineen, President.
Officers or Principals: Michael Dineen, President ($0); Barbara Bush, First Vice President ($0); Haley Barbour, Second Vice President ($0); Phyllis M. McGovern, Third Vice President; Tom Lankford, Chairman; Gerald F. Hurley, Treasurer; M. Elizabeth Powell, Secretary.
Mission or Interest: Social and political club for those involved with, or seeking to join, the Republican Party.
Total Revenue: 1994 $2,969,511 **Total Expenses:** $2,993,177 **Net Assets:** $2,447,074

Products or Services: Newsletter, social activities.
Tax Status: 501(c)(7) (Social and Recreational Club)
Board of Directors or Trustees: Kurt Branham, Jim Bunning, Conrad Burns, Dorothy Cavanaugh, Elford Cederberg, Theodore Doremus, George Esherick, William Hildenbrand, Clifton Hilderley, Mary Lou O'Brien Jackson, John Magill, Tom Martin, Robert McClory, Doe McCullough, Constance Morella, John Myers, Molly Singerling, Arlan Stangeland, Don Sundquist, George Thompson, Ralph Vinovich, David Williams, Jr.
Periodicals: *Capitol Hill Club Newsletter* (quarterly).
Other Information: The Club received $1,342,243 net, or 45% of revenue, from the sale of inventory. $1,242,835, or 42%, from membership dues. The remaining revenue came from service fees, room rentals, and interest on savings.

National Republican Congressional Committee (NRCC)

320 1st St., S.E.
Washington, DC 20003   **Phone:** (202) 479-7000   **Internet:** http://www.nrcc.org
USA

Contact Person: Maria Cino, Executive Director.
Officers or Principals: Rep. Bill Paxton (R-NY), Chairman.
Mission or Interest: "Provides public relations and direct-mail assistance to Republicans running for the House of Representatives."
Tax Status: Not exempt.

National Republican Heritage Council

310 1st St., S.E.
Washington, DC 20003   **Phone:** (202) 608-1404
USA

Contact Person: Theodore Perros, Chairman.
Mission or Interest: "Assists the Republican Party to strengthen its ties with Americans of ethnic heritage."
Tax Status: Not tax-exempt.
Periodicals: *GOP Nationalities News* (quarterly newsletter).
Internships: Yes.
Other Information: Established in 1971.

National Republican Senatorial Committee (NRSC)

425 2nd St., N.E.
Washington, DC 20002   **Phone:** (202) 675-6000   **Internet:** http://www.nrsc.org
USA

Contact Person: John Heubusch, Executive Director.
Officers or Principals: Sen. Al D'Amato (R-NY), Chairman.
Mission or Interest: Coordinates Republican policy in the Senate and assists candidates in fund-raising.
Tax Status: Not exempt.

National Review

215 Lexington Ave.
New York, NY 10016   **Phone:** (212) 679-7330   **Internet:** http://www.nationalreview.com
USA   **Fax:**   (212) 849-2835

Officers or Principals: John O'Sullivan, Editor; Edward A. Capano, Publisher; Thomas L. Rhodes, President; William F. Buckley Jr., Editor-at-Large; William J. Bennett, Senior Editor.
Mission or Interest: National biweekly conservative magazine of politics and culture.
Accomplishments: *National Review* has played a major role in defining modern American conservatism. The Dictionary of American Conservatism calls the *National Review* "the central journal of American conservatism." *National Review* currently has a circulation of over 225,000. The typical *National Review* subscriber is male, college educated, with a median household income of $88,500.
Products or Services: "Town Hall" internet web site, various books.
Periodicals: *National Review* (biweekly magazine).
Other Information: Established in 1955. *National Review* owns half of the "Town Hall" internet site, along with the Heritage Foundation (see Town Hall's separate listing). National Review's editors and contributing editors include Peter Brimlow (author, Alien Nation), Richard Brookhiser, Priscilla Buckley, Jeffrey Hart, Kate O'Beirne, David Klinghoffer, Elliott Abrams (Asst. Secretary of State, Inter-American Affairs 1985-89), Wick Allison, Tom Bethell (*American Spectator*), Andrew Ferguson, Florence King, Lawrence Kudlow (White House Associate Director, Economic Policy, 1981-83) , Erik von Kuehnelt-Leddihn, Stephen Moore (Cato Inst.), Richard John Neuhaus (Inst. on Religion and Public Life), Paul Craig Roberts (Inst. for Political Economy), Peter Samuel (*Toll Roads*), John Simon, Ernest van den Haag, and others.

National Review Institute

215 Lexington Ave., 4th Floor
New York, NY 10016   **Phone:** (212) 679-7330   **Internet:** http://www.nationalreview.com
USA   **Fax:**   (212) 849-2835

Contact Person: Kelly Luce Forsberg, Executive Director.
Officers or Principals: Hon. Pete du Pont, Chairman.
Mission or Interest: "Explores and advances conservative ideas on education, environment, culture and economics through its conferences, lectures, debates and publications." Founded by William F. Buckley, Jr., the Institute parallels the goals of the magazine, *National Review*, but is organizationally and financially separate.
Accomplishments: Has sponsored three Conservative Summits in Washington, DC, and regional conferences in Chicago, San Diego, Charleston, Los Angeles and Dallas. It has held four international seminars under the chairmanship of Margaret Thatcher.
Tax Status: 501(c)(3)
Other Information: Established in 1991. In 1994 the Institute received $20,000 from the Richard & Helen DeVos Foundation.

National Rifle Association of America (NRA)

11250 Waples Mill Rd.
Fairfax, VA 22030   **Phone:** (703) 267-1000   **E-Mail:** listproc@nra.org
USA   **Internet:** http://www.nra.org

Contact Person: Wayne R. LaPierre, Jr., Executive Vice President.
Officers or Principals: Wayne R. LaPierre, Jr., Executive Vice President ($189,412); Wilson H. Phillips, Jr., Treasurer ($164,412); Don W. Rakestraw, Executive Director, General Operations ($164,412); Tanya Metaksa, Executive Director ($155,147); Warren Creek, Secretary ($101,187); Marion P. Hammer, President; Neal Knox, Vice President; James Jay Baker, Executive Director. (Salaries are from 1994.)
Mission or Interest: "To protect and defend the Constitution of the United States, especially with reference to the inalienable right of the individual American citizen guaranteed by such constitution to acquire, possess, transport, carry, transfer ownership of, and enjoy the right to use arms, in order that the people may always be in a position to exercise their legitimate individual rights of self preservation and defense of family, person, and property, as well as to serve effectively in the appropriate militia for the common defense of the Republic and the individual liberty of its citizens."
Accomplishments: Largest and most powerful gun-rights lobby, over 3 million members. Over the last five years the NRA has averaged 12% growth in revenue per year. In 1995 the NRA celebrated its 125th year. Executive Vice President Wayne LaPierre's book, Guns, Crime, and Freedom (Regnery Press, 1994), was #11 on the *New York Times* bestseller list in 1994. Numerous commentators and President Clinton himself credited the NRA's efforts on behalf of candidates in 1994 for electing the Republican majority. In 1994 the NRA spent $109,124,977 on its programs. The largest program, with expenditures of $52,458,638, was membership services. $16,315,827 was spent on publications, including membership magazines and various books and pamphlets. $15,976,945 was spent on the Institute for Legislative Action, or ILA, the primary lobbying body of the NRA. In 1994 the NRA-ILA focused on state efforts to allow citizens to legally carry concealed handguns. $7,476,566 was spent on public affairs, including hunter safety and training, wildlife and game conservation, and firearms-safety classes. $3,284,465 was spent on shooting-sports competitions. $1,999,276 was spent on hunter services. $1,256,258 was spent on activities with law enforcement. $694,641 was spent on "Women's Issues," including the "Refuse to Be a Victim Program." The NRA awarded $60,756 in grants. $17,000 in college scholarships were awarded through the Jeanne E. Bray Fund. $36,501 was awarded to researchers to study topics related to hunting and wildlife management. $7,500 was awarded to other firearms rights organizations; $2,500 each to the Arizona State Rifle & Pistol Association, Rhode Island State Rifle & Pistol Association, and the South Carolina Shooting Association.
Total Revenue: 1995 $155,719,137 12%(5) **Total Expenses:** $148,962,702 82%/12%/6% **Net Assets:** (-48,007,307)
Products or Services: Lobbying, publications, scholarships. Sybil Ludington Women's Freedom Award (named after a Revolutionary War heroine) presented to "recognize women's contributions toward the cause of Second Amendment freedom." "Eddie Eagle" gun safety program for children. National Firearms Museum. CrimeStrike program that advocates harsher sentencing and ending parole for violent criminals.
Tax Status: 501(c)(4) **Annual Report:** Yes.   **Citations:** 5,892:2
Board of Directors or Trustees: Rex Applegate, Lt. Col. Robert Brown, USAR, Ret. (*Soldier of Fortune*), David Caplan, Ph.D., Jeff Cooper (author/instructor), Robert Corbin, Sen. Larry Craig (R-ID), Hon. Joe Foss (former SD Governor, former NRA Pres.), Roy Innis (Congress on Racial Equality), John Milius (screenwriter or director of "Dirty Harry," "Conan the Barbarian," "The Wind and the Lion," "Red Dawn," and others), Ted Nugent (rock musician, Pres., World Bowhunters), Prof. Joseph Olson (Academics for the Second Amendment), Lt. Harry Thomas, Judge Paul Heath Till, Glen Voorhees, Jr., Hon. Donald Young.
Periodicals: *American Rifleman* (monthly magazine), *American Hunter* (monthly magazine).
Other Information: Established in 1871 by two Union officers, Col. William C. Church and Gen. George Wingate, who deplored the state of marksmanship among Union troops during the Civil War. Gen. Ambrose E. Burnside was the NRA's first president. For its first century the NRA focused on marksmanship for military duty, law enforcement, hunting and self defense. In 1957 NAACP affiliates in Monroe, NC, received firearms instruction from the NRA to defend against the Ku Klux Klan. Presidents Theodore Roosevelt and John F. Kennedy were among the many presidents who were life members. In the late sixties and early seventies the NRA began to focus more on opposing gun control, culminating in the 1977 annual meeting in Cincinnati where "legislative and political action became the Association's priority." Affiliated with the 501(c)(3) NRA Special Contribution Fund,

Firearms Civil Rights Legal Defense Fund, NRA Foundation, National Firearms Museum, and the NRA Political Victory Fund PAC. The NRA is currently being audited by the IRS. The IRS has demanded that the NRA turn over confidential membership lists, a move the NRA says it will not comply with and will challenge in court. The NRA, despite increased revenues, had run large deficits from 1991-1994, so that at the end of 1994 the Association was a net debtor of $57,425,392. Much of this debt was taken on with the purchase of a new headquarters in Fairfax, VA. In 1995 the NRA was again in the black for the year, and reduced its net debt by $5,914,438 to $48,007,307. In 1995 the NRA elected it first female president, Marion Hammer (a "life-long Democrat"), to replace the late Tom Washington, who died while holding that office. NRA received $78,190,602, or 50% of revenue, from membership dues. $36,850,588, or 24%, from contributors. $22,725,092 or 15%, from program fees, including advertising and subscription income. $9,719,446, or 6%, from investment income. $2,651,319, or 2%, from royalties. The remaining revenue came from various miscellaneous sources.

National Right to Life
(see "Right to Life, National")

National Right to Read Foundation (NRRF)
P.O. Box 490
The Plains, VA 20198   **Phone:** (800) 468-8911   **E-Mail:** NRRF@pop.erob.com
USA   **Fax:** (540) 349-3065   **Internet:** http://www.jwor.com/nrrf.htm

Contact Person: Robert W. Sweet, Jr., President.
Mission or Interest: To return phonics-based reading education to public schools and promote decentralized education reform. "Return direct, systematic phonics to every first grade classroom in America."
Accomplishments: Legislation to require phonics in Wisconsin, Ohio, California, North Carolina, Texas, and several other states. Sweet testified before the House Committee on Economic and Educational Opportunities Subcommittee on Early Childhood, Youth and Families in July 1995. NRRF has supplied materials to the authors of articles on the "whole language" vs. phonetics debate that have appeared in *Atlantic Monthly, Forbes, Destiny, News & Views,* and *CQ Researcher* (published by *Congressional Quarterly*). NRRF helped raise public awareness when the Federal Trade Commission charged "Hooked on Phonics," a commercially available learning aid, with misleading advertising.
Products or Services: Publications and learning aids to help teach the phonetic method of reading. They publish a list of educators and researchers who support and can provide evidence for the superiority of learning to read using phonics. NRRF is establishing the Restore America Literacy Project. They hope to have Project chapters in every state and community.
Tax Status: 501(c)(3)   **Annual Report:** No.   **Employees:** 4
Board of Directors or Trustees: Marjorie Alfonso, Joseph Brown (former Pres., Adult Education Assoc.), Virginia Carey (founder, Nellie Thomas Literacy Inst.), Marva Collins (Dir., Westside Preparatory School), John Corcoran (National Literacy Council), Prof. Emeritus Patrick Groff (San Diego State Univ.), Judge David Grossman (Pres., Nat. Assoc. of Family and Juvenile Court Judges), Hon. William Hansen (former CFO, U.S. Dept. of Education), Dominic Herbst (Dir., Bethesda Day Treatment Center), James Jacobson (former White House advisor), Prof. Constantine Menges (George Washington Univ.), Robert Unger.
Periodicals: *Right to Read Report* (bimonthly).
Internships: Not at this time.
Other Information: Robert Sweet, Jr., was Deputy Director of the National Institute of Education from 1982-3. He was also White House Deputy Executive Secretary for Domestic Policy from 1985-89. Under President Bush he headed the Office of Juvenile Justice and Delinquency Prevention at the Department of Justice.

National Right to Work Committee
8001 Braddock Rd., Suite 600
Springfield, VA 22160   **Phone:** (703) 321-8510   **E-Mail:** info@nrtw.org
USA   **Fax:** (703) 321-9613   **Internet:** http://www.nrtw.org

Contact Person: Stephen O. Goodrick, Vice President.
Officers or Principals: Stephen O. Goodrick, Vice President ($79,553); Mark A. Mix, Vice President ($71,910); Reed E. Larson, President ($44,168); John Wilson, Chairman; Virginia Smith, Secretary.
Mission or Interest: "Conducts an educational-lobbying program on a state and national level to oppose compulsory unionism. Among other objectives, the Committee strives to protect the existing 21 states' Right to Work laws and the Federal employees' Right to Work law, as well as to encourage other states and the federal government to adopt Right to Work laws protecting all workers affected by compulsory unionism." Also operates Concerned Educators Against Forced Unionism.
Accomplishments: Founded in 1955 by Rep. Fred Hartley. Hartley was the co-author of the 1947 Taft-Hartley Act, a law that protects the right of workers *not* to join a union. The Committee has historically lobbied to retain that right and has been critical in gaining the right for workers to not have their compulsory union dues pay for political activities. In 1994 the Committee spent $6,192,486 on its programs.
Total Revenue: 1994 $7,846,645 9%(3) **Total Expenses:** $7,834,641 79%/3%/18% **Net Assets:** $968,901
Products or Services: Concerned Educators Against Forced Unionism provides two annual $1,000 scholarships.
Tax Status: 501(c)(4)   **Citations:** 47:104

Board of Directors or Trustees: Walter Allen, Carol Applegate, Buell Baclesse, Langdon Barber, Morton Blackwell (Leadership Inst.), Camille Bradford, Howard Brown, James Cecil, Roy Cook, R. R. Ebbing, Barbara Fernsten, Annabelle Fetterman, Cornell Gethmann, Dr. Roland Goode, Greg Hagenston, E. M. Hammond, Sidney Hammond, Thomas Harris, Susan Havas, Giles Heroy, Harriette Hughes, Bruce Jacobs, Dr. Abner McCall, N. Carl Monroe, Elizabeth Mudge Mann, Thomas Quinlan, Rev. Norman Ream, Franklin Severance, R. Bruce Simpson, Mary Smith, Jon Sween, W.L. Thornton, John Waldum, Louis Weiss, George Whyte, John Wilson.

Periodicals: *National Right to Work Newsletter* (monthly newsletter), and *Insider's Report* (quarterly newsletter of Concerned Educators Against Forced Unionism).

Other Information: Established in 1955. Affiliated with the 501(c)(3) National Institute for Labor Relations Research and the 501(c)(3) National Right to Work Legal Defense and Education Foundation. In 1994 the three affiliates had combined revenues of $11,983,356. Reed Larson serves as executive director for all three and in 1994 he received a combined $255,225. The Committee is also affiliated with the Right to Work PAC. The Committee owns 100% of a for-profit telecommunications company, the Liberty Phone Center. In 1994 the Liberty Phone Center had gross revenues of $197,000 and assets of $44,138. The Committee received $7,688,346, or 98% of gross revenue, from contributions and grants. The remaining revenue came from dividends and interest from securities, interest on savings and other temporary cash investments, and other miscellaneous sources. The Committee lost $4,217 on the sale of assets.

National Right to Work Legal Defense and Education Foundation

8001 Braddock Rd., Suite 600
Springfield, VA 22160   **Phone:** (703) 321-8510   **E-Mail:** info@nrtw.org
USA   **Fax:**   (703) 321-9613   **Internet:** http://www.nrtw.org

Contact Person: Timothy M. McConville, Vice President.
Officers or Principals: Rex H. Reed, Executive Vice President/Secretary ($177,707); Edith D. Hakola, Vice President/Treasurer ($166,024); Hugh Reilly, Staff Attorney ($115,874); Raymond Lajeunesse, Staff Attorney ($114,354); Milton Chappell, Staff Attorney ($102,840); Bruce Cameron, Staff Attorney ($102,342); Reed E. Larson, President; Dr. Frederick Fowler, III, Chairman; Howard R. Brown, Vice Chairman.
Mission or Interest: Legal action affilliate of the National Right to Work Committee. "Free legal aid to employees whose human or civil rights have been violated by abuses of compulsory unionism."
Accomplishments: "Since 1968 the Foundation has fought for the rights of more than 30,000 employees in over 1,500 cases, from arbitration hearings to the U.S. Supreme Court, where our attorneys have never lost a case. Foundation attorneys have shaped the law to protect the basic constitutional rights of American workers. The Foundation's communications staff has educated millions of employees - as well as opinion leaders and members of the media." Won the Beck v. Communication Workers of America case, which was upheld in 1988 by the U.S. Supreme Court. Beck allowed employees who worked in a union shop, but declined to join the union, to only pay union fees for contract negotiations and similar services, but not be required to pay dues for political and lobbying activities. In 1994 the Foundation spent $3,410,468 on its programs. For its litigation, the Foundation received $11,930 in court-awarded attorney's fees. (This was down substantially from its previous four-year average of $221,907.)
Total Revenue: 1994 $3,897,138 **Total Expenses:** $4,066,493 84%/6%/10% **Net Assets:** $1,504,272
Products or Services: Litigation, brochures, and guides detailing workers' rights.
Tax Status: 501(c)(3)   **Citations:** 47:104
Board of Directors or Trustees: Langdon Barber, Thomas Faria, Robert Gaylord, Jr., Harriette Hughes, Henry Jansen, Dr. Abner McCall, Menlo Smith, Ben Tate, Jr., Louis Weiss.
Periodicals: *Foundation Action* (bimonthly newsletter).
Internships: Yes, legal internships available.
Other Information: Established in 1968. Affiliated with the 501(c)(4) National Right to Work Committee, and its Concerned Educators Against Forced Unionism division, as well as the 501(c)(3) National Institute for Labor Relations Research. In 1994 the three affiliates had combined revenues of $11,983,356. Reed Larson serves as executive director for all three and in 1994 he received a combined $255,225. The Foundation received $3,710,913, or 95% of revenue, from contributions and grants awarded by foundations, businesses, affiliates and individuals. (These grants included $50,000 from the F.M. Kirby Foundation, $8,000 from the Ruth and Vernon Taylor Foundation, $5,000 from the Vernon K. Krieble Foundation, and $2,000 from the United Educators Foundation. In 1995, $100,000 from the John M. Olin Foundation, $60,000 from the Sunmark Foundation, and $1,000 from the Roe Foundation.) $57,898, or 1%, from rental income. $50,759, or 1%. From interest on savings and temporary cash investments. $39,084, or 1%, from capital gains on the sale of assets. The remaining revenue came from dividends and interest from securities, and court-awarded attorney's fees.

National Security Center

3554 Chainbridge Rd., Suite 301
Fairfax, VA 22030   **Phone:** (703) 273-0788
USA

Contact Person: Richard A. Delgaudio, President.
Officers or Principals: Richard A. Delgaudio, President ($18,800); Donald A. Derham, Jr., Chairman ($0); Captain G. Russell Evans, USCG, (Ret.), Project Advisor; Hon. David B. Funderburk, Project Advisor.

Mission or Interest: Dedicated to preserving the national security. Current projects include calling attention to potential terrorist attacks on the Panama Canal, and fighting the Clinton Administration's 'social engineering' of the military.
Accomplishments: In 1994 the Center spent $555,348 on its programs.
Total Revenue: 1994 $862,145 (-6%)(3) **Total Expenses:** $1,002,083 **Net Assets:** $28,118
Tax Status: 501(c)(4)   **Citations:** 1:255
Periodicals: *National Security Report* (newsletter).
Other Information: Affiliated with the 501(c)(4) Legal Affairs Council, the for-profit Right Lists, Inc., and the for-profit Richard A. Delgaudio Corp. In 1994 the two nonprofit affiliates had combined net revenues, expenses, and assets of $1,834,581, $1,951,810, and (-$565,175). Richard Delgaudio served as president of both and received combined compensation of $67,906. The Center received $683,815, or 79% of revenue, from contributors. $156,061, or 18%, from mailing list rentals. The remaining revenue came from other miscellaneous sources.

National Tax Limitation Committee

151 N. Sunrise Ave., Suite 901
Roseville, CA 95661   **Phone:** (916) 786-9400
USA   **Fax:** (916) 786-8163

Contact Person: Lewis K. Uhler, President.
Officers or Principals: Lewis K. Uhler, President ($96,000); Diane K. Sekafetz, Secretary/Treasurer ($54,000).
Mission or Interest: Pursues fundamental structural change at the federal, state, and local levels to control fiscal excesses, restore balance between branches and levels of government, reduce the size and scope of government at all levels and promote the free-enterprise system.
Accomplishments: Hosts a coalition of organizations promoting privatization called "Americans for Responsible Privatization." In the fiscal year ending September 1994 the Committee spent $275,488 on its programs.
Total Revenue: FY ending 9/94 $368,847 (-13%)(2) **Total Expenses:** $501,701 55%/29%/16% **Net Assets:** (-$248,257)
Products or Services: Conferences, publications, book <u>Setting Limits: Constitutional Control of Government</u>.
Tax Status: 501(c)(4)   **Citations:** 37:118
Board of Directors or Trustees: Robert Carlson, Prof. Craig Stubblebine (Claremont McKenna College).
Other Information: Established in 1975. Affiliated with the 501(c)(3) National Tax Limitation Foundation (which received $12,000 from the Grover Hermann Foundation, $1,500 from the Gilder Foundation in 1994), and the National Tax Limitation Political Action Committee. The Committee received $208,279, or 56% of revenue, from fees for services provided to affiliates. $160,532, or 44%, from contributors. The remaining revenue came from dividends and interest from securities.

National Taxpayers Union (NTU)

108 N. Alfred St.
Alexandria, VA 22314   **Phone:** (703) 683-5700
USA   **Fax:** (703) 683-5722   **Internet:** http://www.ntu.org.

Contact Person: Peter J. Sepp, Vice President for Communications.
Officers or Principals: David Keating, Executive Vice President ($68,075); James Dale Davidson, Chairman ($34,200); David M. Stanley, President ($0); Edward D. Failor, Vice President; Mark Frazier, Treasurer.
Mission or Interest: "The nation's largest and oldest citizen taxpayer organization. NTU mobilizes taxpayers at the grassroots, educates and informs the public and the press, and lobbies all levels of government on behalf of lower taxes, less wasteful spending, and accountability from public officials."
Accomplishments: "Helped to win income tax indexing, a line-item veto, a Taxpayer Bill of Rights, and dozens of state and local tax limitations. Helped to defeat national health care plans in the 103rd Congress, several congressional pay hikes, and 90% of the major tax hikes that have appeared on state ballots in the past five years." *Dollars and Sense* has an average circulation of over 75,000 per issue. In June 1996 David Keating was named to the National Commission to Restructure the IRS, a bipartisan, 17-member panel of tax experts who will recommend IRS reforms. In 1994 the NTU spent $3,756,352 on its programs. The largest expenditure, $1,373,816, went toward lobbying. $1,237,185 went toward research and education; this included NTU's annual Congressional vote ratings. $835,852 was spent on membership development, and the rest was spent on the Union's publications.
Total Revenue: 1994 $4,754,774 11%(2) **Total Expenses:** $4,665,648 81%/5%/15% **Net Assets:** (-$171,679)
Products or Services: Annual "Congressional Spending Study" rating members of Congress on their votes. (In 1995 Republicans received an average score of 86% in the House and 83% in the Senate, while Democrats received 23% and 28%.) Numerous brochures and books.
Tax Status: 501(c)(4) **Annual Report:** Yes. **Employees:** 20   **Citations:** 621:16
Board of Directors or Trustees: Scott Burns (*Dallas Morning News*), James Clark, Sol Erdman, E. A. Morris, Cloyd Robinson, Gail Schoettler, George Snyder, Herbert Wilson.
Periodicals: *Dollars and Sense* (ten times-a-year newsletter), *Tax Saving Report* (ten times-a-year newsletter featuring tax saving tips).
Internships: Yes, paid.
Other Information: Established in 1969 by James Dale Davidson, then a graduate student in political science at the University of Maryland. Affiliated with the 501(c)(3) National Taxpayers Union Foundation at the same address. In 1994 the two affiliates had combined revenues of $5,692,243, expenses of $5,770,001, and a net debt $96,923. NTU received $4,744,466, or 99.7% of revenue, from contributions and grants. (These grants included $70,000 from Iowans for Tax Relief). The remaining revenue came from interest on savings and temporary cash investments, and dividends and interest from securities.

National Taxpayers Union Foundation (NTUF)

108 N. Alfred St.
Alexandria, VA 22314   **Phone:** (703) 683-5700
USA   **Fax:**   (703) 683-5722   **Internet:** http://www.ntu.org.

Contact Person: Peter J. Sepp, Vice President for Communications.
Officers or Principals: David Keating, President; Paul Hewitt, Executive Director; James Davidson, Chairman.
Mission or Interest: Research and education affiliate of the National Taxpayers Union.
Accomplishments: In 1994 the Foundation spent $791,711 on its programs.
Total Revenue: 1994 $937,469 10%(2) **Total Expenses:** $1,104,353 72%/25%/3% **Net Assets:** $74,756
Tax Status: 501(c)(3)   **Citations:** 621:16
Board of Directors or Trustees: Gregory Barnhill, William Bonner, Mark Cannon, Mark Frazier, Curtin Winsor.
Periodicals: *Capital Ideas* (bimonthly newsletter).
Internships: Yes.
Other Information: Established in 1978. The Foundation received $860,325, or 92% of revenue, from contributions and grants awarded by foundations, businesses, and individuals. (These grants included $100,000 from the Sarah Scaife Foundation, and $20,000 from the J.M. Foundation. In 1995, $60,000 from the John M. Olin Foundation, $31,250 from the William H. Donner Foundation, and $5,000 from the Claude R. Lambe Charitable Foundation.) The remaining revenue came from interest and dividends from securities, and other miscellaneous sources.

National Taxpayers Union of Ohio

51 Jefferson Ave.
Columbus, OH 43215   **Phone:** (614) 220-4000   **E-Mail:** NTUOhio@aol.com
USA   **Fax:**   (614) 220-4004

Contact Person: Scott A. Pullins, Executive Director.
Officers or Principals: Dr. Richard Vedder, Chairman.
Mission or Interest: "Eliminating government waste. Limiting taxes and government spending at all levels."
Accomplishments: "Won increases in personal exemption for Ohio taxpayers. Exemptions will increase to $950 in 1998 and to $1,050 in 1999 and thereafter. Won $400 million in cuts in state income taxes for all Ohio taxpayers. Won passage of the Ohio Taxpayer Protection Amendment in the Ohio House. This measure requires a supermajority of the legislature or a statewide vote of the people to increase taxes or impose new ones."
Tax Status: 501(c)(4) **Annual Report:** No. **Employees:** 2
Board of Directors or Trustees: Advisory Council includes: Prof. Richard Vedder (Ohio Univ.), Phillip Connolly, Paul Kalmbach, Lee Koenig.
Other Information: Organized under the incorporation of the National Taxpayers Union.

National Teen Age Republicans (TARS)

10620-C Crestwood Dr.
P.O. Box 1896
Manassas, VA 22110   **Phone:** (703) 368-4214
USA   **Fax:**   (703) 368-0830

Contact Person: Barby Wells, National Director.
Mission or Interest: "The TAR organization is dedicated to educating teenagers in the traditional principles of free enterprise, constitutional government, and patriotism. TARS is also involved in training young people in the techniques of precinct organization to help elect Republican candidates to local, state, and national office."
Accomplishments: More than 300,000 teenagers have attended TAR workshops. TAR directors operate in all 50 states. Thousands of TAR clubs work on voter registration and get-out-the-vote efforts.
Products or Services: Drug and alcohol abuse prevention programs. Literature, books, pamphlets, video tape library featuring films on patriotism, national defense, free enterprise, and campaign techniques. Speakers bureau.
Tax Status: 501(c)(4)
Periodicals: *TARGET* (quarterly newsletter).
Other Information: Established in 1966. Affiliated with the national Republican Party and the 501(c)(3) Teen Age Research Services Foundation at the same address.

National Wetlands Coalition (NWC)

1050 Thomas Jefferson St., N.W., Suite 600
Washington, DC 20007   **Phone:** (202) 298-1905
USA   **Fax:**   (202) 338-2146

Contact Person: Kimberly Putens, Executive Director.
Officers or Principals: Kimberly Putens, Executive Director ($0); H. Leighton Steward, Chairman ($0).

Mission or Interest: Coalition of businesses and other organizations interested in reforming the nation's wetlands policies; making it less restrictive and favoring individuals' property rights. Specifically, NWC seeks the reformation of Section 404 of the Clean Water Act.

Accomplishments: NWC helped lobby former Vice President Quayle's Council on Competitiveness, who proposed a restricted definition of wetlands. (This restricted definition was enacted by the Bush administration, then overturned by the EPA during the transition to the Clinton administration.) NWC helped draft H.R. 1330, the Comprehensive Wetlands Conservation and Management Act, which would compensate property owners for legal fees and financial loss when their property is designated as protected wetlands. In 1994 NWC spent $14,332 on lobbying.

Total Revenue: 1994 $369,502 (-40%)(2)   **Total Expenses:** $414,613   **Net Assets:** (-$70,033)

Tax Status: 501(c)(6)   **Citations:** 1:255

Board of Directors or Trustees: William Berry (Louisiana Land and Exploration Co.), L. Ronald Forman (Audubon Inst.), James Keys (Exec. Dir., Tenneco Gas), Oliver Leavitt (Vice Pres., Arctic Slope Regional Corp.), Frank Walk (Chair, Walk, Haydel & Assoc.), Damian Zamias, Donovan Ross (National Stone Assoc.), Hon. Tom Fink (Mayor, Municipality of Anchorage), Mark Maslyn (American Farm Bureau Fed.), Stuart Wells (Legislative Director, National Association of Home Builders), Robert Jones, Clayton Doherty (Oglethorpe Power Co.).

Other Information: The Coalition received $367,085, or 99% of revenue, from membership dues. This was an average increase of 5% over the last two years. The remaining revenue came from interest on savings and temporary cash investments.

National Wilderness Institute (NWI)

P.O. Box 25766
Washington, DC 20007
USA

Phone: (703) 836-7404
Fax: (703) 548-8024   **Internet:** http://www.nwi.org

Contact Person: Robert E. Gordon, Executive Director.

Officers or Principals: Robert E. Gordon, Executive Director ($25,224).

Mission or Interest: Promotion of the "wise management of renewable resources" and "the need for the private sector to be more proactive in managing renewable resources." Emphasis on free markets and property rights.

Accomplishments: Attracted nationwide press attention. Developed the NWI Network, a database of environmental experts. In 1997 NWI submitted petitions to Interior Secretary Bruce Babbitt requesting that he remove 16 "imaginary" animals and plants from the List of Endangered and Threatened Wildlife and Plants. In 1994 NWI spent $206,946 on its programs.

Total Revenue: 1994 $324,335 63%(2)   **Total Expenses:** $268,257 77%/12%/11%   **Net Assets:** $58,825

Products or Services: Videos, t-shirts, conferences and seminars.

Tax Status: 501(c)(3)   **Citations:** 3:204

Board of Directors or Trustees: Hon. George Dunlop (former Asst. Secretary of the Interior, 1986-1989), Hon. Becky Norton Dunlop (former Asst. Secretary of the Interior, 1987-1989), Earl Gjelde, Stephen Conger, Sr.

Periodicals: *NWI Resource* (newsletter).

Internships: Yes.

Other Information: Established in 1990. NWI received $265,035, or 82% of revenue, from contributions and grants awarded by foundations, businesses, and individuals. (In 1995, these grants included $25,000 from the John M. Olin Foundation.) $56,5305 or 17%, from the sale of publications. The remaining revenue came from interest on savings and temporary cash investments, the sale of t-shirts, and other miscellaneous sources.

NET - Political NewsTalk Network

717 2nd St., N.E.
Washington, DC 20002
USA

Phone: (800) 638-0660   **Internet:** http://www.net.fcret.org

Contact Person: Robert W. Swanner, Vice President/General Manager.

Mission or Interest: A 24-hour television broadcasting network. NET was originally a project of the Free Congress Foundation, and is now "a separate corporation." NET broadcasts a variety of public affairs shows, many of them produced by, or in cooperation with, other nonprofit organizations. Programming includes: "Borderline" produced by the Federation for American Immigration Reform, "Business Voice" by the U.S. Business and Industrial Council, "Cato Forum" by the Cato Institute, "On Target" by the National Rifle Association, "The Other Side of the Story" by Accuracy in Media, "Christian Coalition Live" by the Christian Coalition, and "Straight Talk" by the Family Research Council. (See the Free Congress Foundation for more information.)

Tax Status: 501(c)(3)

Other Information: Established in 1993, it currently reaches "more than 11 million homes." Originally named National Empowerment Television. In 1994 NET's budget, as part of the Free Congress Foundation, was $5,634,509. It brought in revenues for the Free Congress Foundation of $963,950 from fees paid by the contracting organization that produce programming, $205,610 in advertising revenues, and $50,530 in studio fees paid by contracting organizations for the use of the Foundation's studio and equipment; a total of $1,220,090. In 1994-95 NET-TV received $50,000 from the Richard & Helen DeVos Foundation, and $1,000 from the Ruth and Vernon Taylor Foundation.

Nevada Families Eagle Forum

P.O. Box 656
Sparks, NV 89432   **Phone:**   (702) 356-9055
USA   **Fax:**   (702) 356-0727

Contact Person: Janine Hansen.
Mission or Interest: Nevada affiliate of the Eagle Forum. Especially active opposing a Constitutional Convention. Also active in the Western land disputes with the Federal government.

Nevada Freedom Coalition

675 Fairview Drive, Suite 246
Carson City, NV 89701   **Phone:**   (702) 883-2894
USA

Contact Person: Dave Horton.
Officers or Principals: Tom Thompson, Managing Editor.
Mission or Interest: To promote liberty through the reduction of government and adherence to the Constitution. Also opposed to any transfer of sovereignty from the citizens of the United States to the United Nations and the "New World Order." Supports states' rights and the creation of a State Bank of Nevada.
Accomplishments: Active in the "County Movement." Sponsored a "Meet the Candidates" rally in October 1994, attended by several hundred people. Won an award for their parade entry in the 1995 Nevada Day Parade. Dave Horton can be heard on KPTL Talk Radio, AM 1300, in Carson City.
Products or Services: "Nevada's Public Lands: An Analysis of the Position of Nevada in Asserting Ownership over the Public Lands within the State" booklet.
Board of Directors or Trustees: Members of the Coalition include; American Pistol and Rifle Association, Central Nevada Farm Bureau, Central Nevada People for the West, Committee to Restore the Constitution, County Alliance to Restore the Economy and Environment, Gun Owners of America, Independent American Party, Knowledge Equals Freedom, Libertarian Party, Nevada Business Services, Nevada Eagle Forum, Nevada State Rifle and Pistol Association, Nevada TRIM Committee, People for the Best, Republicans for Home Rule, Sons of Liberty, United We Stand America-NV, others.
Periodicals: *Nevada Sentinel* (monthly).
Other Information: The County Movement is centered in the western United States where county governments are asserting authority over Federal lands, claiming that the only Constitutional authority for the Federal government to hold land is set forth in Article I, Section 8, Clause 17, "for the erection of forts, magazines (military storage, ed.), dock-yards and other needful buildings."

Nevada Policy Research Institute (NPRI)

800 W. 2nd St.
Reno, NV 89503   **Phone:** (702) 786-9600   **E-Mail:**   npri@policy.reno.nv.us
USA   **Fax:**   (702) 786-9604   **Internet:** http://www.npri.org

Contact Person: Marilyn Medina, Business Manager.
Officers or Principals: Judy M. Cresanta, President; Dick Young, Vice President; Jason Barrett, Manager of Administration; Erica Olsen, Research Analyst; Jamie Clark, Chairman; Robert Achurra, Treasurer.
Mission or Interest: Free-market based public policy organization focusing on Nevada.
Accomplishments: Hosted guest speakers including Prime Minister Lady Margaret Thatcher and Hon. Jack Kemp. "By the end of 1997 our radio commentaries will be able to be heard nationwide. Our national spokesperson will be J. C. Watts."
Total Revenue: FY ending 8/93 $73,593 **Total Expenses:** $53,685 **Net Assets:** $27,691
Products or Services: "You Think About It," weekly television show on KTVN, Channel 2, in Reno. Speaker's bureau.
Tax Status: 501(c)(3)   **Employees:** 6
Board of Directors or Trustees: David and Lexi Allen, Dorine Dominguez, Stephen Dow, M.D., Paul Fisher, Hal Furman, Sally Furman, Gary Foote, James Gallaway, Bernie Horn-Bostel, Howard Hoffman, M.D., Lewis Laughlin, Sally McKinney, Lewis Shuman, David Papandrea, Lexey Parker, M.D., Randall Rumph. Advisors include: Hon. Morton Blackwell (Leadership Inst.), Hon. Holland Coors (Women of Our Hemisphere), Jeffrey Coors (Coors Found.), Don Devine (former Director, White House Office of Personnel, 1981-85), Hon. Edwin Meese, III (U.S. Attorney General, 1985-88), Grover Norquist (Americans for Tax Reform), Burton Pines (National Center for Public Policy Research), Hon. Paul Pressler (former Justice, Texas Court of Appeals).
Periodicals: *Online Nevada* (bimonthly journal).
Other Information: Established in 1991. Member of the State Policy Council. The Institute received $73,123, or 99% of revenue, from contributions and grants awarded by foundations, businesses, and individuals. (In 1995 these grants included $50,000 from the Castle Rock Foundation, $7,500 from the Roe Foundation, and $5,000 from the E. L. Wiegand Foundation.) The remaining revenue came from other miscellaneous sources.

New Century Foundation (NCF)

P.O. Box 1674
Louisville, KY 40201   **Phone:** (502) 637-9324   **E-Mail:**   amren@clever.net
USA   **Fax:**   (502) 637-9324   **Internet:** http://www.amren.com

Contact Person: Samuel Jared Taylor, Editor.

Officers or Principals: Samuel Jared Taylor, Editor ($0); George Resch, Trustee ($0); Louis March, Trustee ($0); Thomas Jackson, Assistant Editor; George McDaniel, Web Page Editor.

Mission or Interest: Publishes the newsletter *American Renaissance*. "We treat in a thoughtful way subjects that other publications prefer to avoid: immigration, race, and the preservation of our heritage. We believe that these questions lie close to the heart of many of the problems facing our nation." Promotion of white-racial consciousness, but not animus toward other races. They promote segregation and racial identity. Editor Taylor says, "Unless whites, as a race, can disengage from non-whites, they are doomed as a people and as a culture. . . I have a first loyalty to my people, to my race and culture. It is not because they are the best - however much I may like them - but because they are mine."

Accomplishments: Jared Taylor is the author of Paved With Good Intentions, a book on "the failure of race relations" that *National Review* called, "The most important book to be published on the subject in many years." Taylor's articles have been published in *The Wall Street Journal, Los Angeles Times, Chicago Tribune, Baltimore Sun*, and others. The Foundation has hosted two conferences in the last three years. Participants have included: columnists Joseph Sobran and Samuel Francis, and professors Philippe Rushton, Father Ronald Tacelli, S.J., and Michael Levin. One of the conferences was cited in Dinesh D'Souza's book The End of Racism as a "white supremacist" gathering. According to Jared Taylor, "D'Souza had invented passages from speeches (which had been recorded) and deliberately falsified 'quotations' from *American Renaissance*. . . D'Souza's falsehoods were so egregious that the Free Press (his publisher) took the extraordinary step of junking the entire first print run." Former *Washington Times* editor and columnist Samuel Francis stated that his participation in the conference and the subsequent "publication of the book (The End of Racism) and of a factually flawed excerpt from it by. . .*The Washington Post*" caused him to lose his position at *The Washington Times*. In 1995 the Foundation spent $19,746 on its programs. This included $800 in grants; $500 for Prof. Michael Levin to copy and distribute his research, and $300 for Allan Silliphant for assistance in producing a video on the effects of immigration.

Net Revenue: 1995 $35,527 **Total Expenses:** $23,555 **Net Assets:** $90,441

Tax Status: 501(c)(3) **Annual Report:** No.

Board of Directors or Trustees: Samuel Francis (syndicated columnist), Wayne Lutton.

Periodicals: *American Renaissance* (monthly newsletter).

Other Information: Established in 1994 and previously called the Jefferson Institute. The Foundation received $25,841, or 73% of revenue, from program services including newsletter subscriptions. $6,406, or 18%, from contributions and grants awarded by foundations, businesses, and individuals. $3,280, or 9%, from investment income.

New Citizenship Project

1150 17th Street, N.W., Suite 510
Washington, DC 20036   **Phone:** (202) 822-8333
USA   **Fax:** (202) 822-8325

Contact Person: John Walters, President.

Mission or Interest: "To restore American self-government and civil society." Public-policy organization focusing on: the AmeriCorps program, drugs and crime, affirmative action, and other issues.

Tax Status: 501(c)(3)

Other Information: The Project is undergoing reorganization and its office and staff have merged with the Philanthropy Roundtable. In 1994-95, the Project received $185,000 from the Lynde and Harry Bradley Foundation, $100,000 from the John M. Olin Foundation, $75,000 from the Sarah Scaife Foundation, $50,000 from the Scaife Family Foundation, $20,000 from the William H. Donner Foundation, $2,500 from the Roe Foundation, and $1,000 from the John William Pope Foundation.

New Criterion
(see Foundation for Cultural Review)

New England Institute for Public Policy

P.O. Box 146, State House
Boston, MA 02133   **Phone:** (617) 821-5939
USA   **Fax:** same

Contact Person: Larry Overlan, President.

Mission or Interest: Encourages privatization of state-run programs. Advocates education vouchers.

Accomplishments: Cited in both the *Boston Globe* and *Boston Herald*. Wrote columns that were published in the *Boston Globe* and *The American Enterprise*.

Tax Status: 501(c)(3) **Annual Report:** No. **Employees:** 3

Internships: No.

Other Information: Founded in 1993. Larry Overlan has been the president of the Conservative Society of Massachusetts since 1994.

New England Legal Foundation (NELF)

150 Lincoln St.
Boston, MA 02111   **Phone:** (617) 695-3660
USA

Contact Person: Stephen Ostrach, Legal Director.

Officers or Principals: Stephen Ostrach, Legal Director ($104,262); Edward A. Schwartz, President ($85,992); Patrick W. Hanifin, Staff Attorney ($58,756); Richard Scipione, Chairman; Robert L. Paglia, Treasurer; Gary A. Spiess, Secretary.

Mission or Interest: Legal advocacy group. Pursues property rights and cases which advance free-market principles.

Accomplishments: Won <u>Paul and Patricia Preseault v. United States</u>, in the Federal Circuit Court, that decided "whether the United States can, without paying compensation, transfer to a third party a permanent easement over landowners' property." <u>Preseault v. U.S.</u>, unless it is reviewed and overturned by the U.S. Supreme Court, is an important decision in the property rights battle in that it focused on a "rails-to-trails" case. "Rails-to-trails" is a common strategy of environmentalists/conservationists that transfers the property easement given for use by the railways to be used for nature trails on private property. Helped change a Rhode Island law which held landowners responsible for injuries to trespassers. The change makes owners liableonly for "willful and wanton" injuries to trespassers on their property. Challenged the EPA's withholding of internal documents that show there is no scientific basis for requiring the use of oxygenated auto fuel. Representing the Vermont Farm Bureau in a case challenging state and local land use regulation as "taking" private property without just compensation. Other cases included: <u>Leger v. Commissioner of Revenue</u> which would decide if "Massachusetts (can) place a lien on a person's home, without prior notice or judicial hearing to collect an allegedly due sales tax." <u>Conservation Law Foundation v. U.S. Dept. of the Air Force</u> to decide "can a state redevelop a closed military base without violating federal environmental laws?" In 1994 the Foundation spent $365,473 on its programs.

Total Revenue: 1994 $578,614 (-5%)2 **Total Expenses:** $651,025 56%/15%/29% **Net Assets:** $684,205

Tax Status: 501(c)(3)   **Citations:** 5:192

Board of Directors or Trustees: John Cabot, John Besser, William Buccella, George Calver, Karen Crider, Kenneth Decko, John Delaney, Richard deLima, Madelyn DeMatteo, John Douglas III, Edward Finn, Harrison Fitch, Charles Gooley, Frederick Greenman, Edwin Hebb, Christopher Hoffman, Edward Lane-Reticker, Steve Lauwers, Thomas Lemberg, Lisa Lopez, Sandra Lynch, Margaret Marshall, Edward Masterman, Peter Meade, M. Brian Moroze, Joseph Norberg, Alice Richmond, Donald Robbins, John Sartore, Deming Sherman, John Michael Shepherd, Marshall Simonds, David Warren, Robert Wax, Morrison Webb, Fletcher Wiley.

Other Information: The Foundation received $558,082, or 96% of revenue, from contributions and grants awarded by foundations, businesses, and individuals. (These grants included $50,000 from the Sarah Scaife Foundation, $40,000 from the Lilly Endowment.) $7,621, or 1%, from interest on savings and temporary cash investments. The remaining revenue came from other miscellaneous sources.

New Intellectual Forum

9400 S. Damen Ave.
Chicago, IL 60620   **Phone:**   (312) 233-8684   **E-Mail:**   jenright@home.interaccess.com
USA   **Internet:** http://www.mcs.net/~tshell/aif.com

Contact Person: Marsha Enright.

Mission or Interest: Objectivist discussion group to, "foster open discussion on the ideas of Ayn Rand and related topics, including those related to the requirements of a free society."

Accomplishments: Co-hosted a conference with the Free Market Society of Chicago and the Heartland Institute. The conference was titled "Ayn Rand, Friedrich Hayek, and the New Radicalism," featuring Chris Matthew Sciabarra, Ph.D., the author of <u>Ayn Rand: The Russian Radical</u> and <u>Marx, Hayek, and Utopia</u>.

Tax Status: Unincorporated discussion club.

New Jersey Conservative Party (NJCP)

P.O. Box 1088
Point Pleasant Beach, NJ 08742   **Phone:**   (908) 458-5887
USA   **Fax:**   (908) 458-5754

Contact Person: Tom Blomquist, Trustee.

Officers or Principals: Agnes James, Stu Emanuel.

Mission or Interest: Participates in the electoral and political process in New Jersey to exert influence on behalf of NJCP platform proposals.

Accomplishments: In 1993 (for the first time in New Jersey history), the Party fielded a third-party legislative ticket. In the 1996 New Jersey Senate race the NJCP candidate, Richard J. Pezzullo, received 50,971 votes, the highest total ever for a third-party candidate for statewide (other than presidential) office in New Jersey.

Products or Services: State and federal New Jersey Conservative Party Platforms.

Tax Status: Incorporated in the state of New Jersey. **Annual Report:** No. **Employees:** All volunteer.

Board of Directors or Trustees: 25-member State Organizing Committee.

Internships: Yes, high school and college students have been accepted.

New Nation USA (NNUSA)

P.O. Box 441
Morongo Valley, CA 92256   **Phone:**   (619) 364-2588
USA

Contact Person: S. A. Freeman, and Phil Marsh..

Mission or Interest: Populist organization that seeks to create an alternative government based on the Constitution, the Bill of Rights, and common law. "NNUSA does not seek to overthrow the existing government. We simply intend to co-exist to provide the option of a lawful government as distinguished from an unlawful government." They hope that after enough members join the New Nation, it will be accepted as the de facto government. This new government will abolish the Federal Reserve and fractional reserve banking system, institute a common-law justice system with "strict penalties and no chance of appeal," and "the church will once again become the center of the community activity. Everyone will tithe to the church and these funds will go where they are supposed to, helping those who have come upon some misfortune. . . You think this won't work? This concept worked in England for 723 years and it would still be their way of life had not usury banking been introduced."

Accomplishments: The New Nation's methods have been used by various organizations and individuals, including the Montana Freemen, who have claimed that their membership in the New Nation removes their obligation to the federal government. Members have claimed that New Nation citizenship ends their military service contract and removes liens on their property imposed by the IRS.

Tax Status: Unincorporated.

Periodicals: *The Connector* (newsletter) and *The Citizen's Claw* (bimonthly newsletter).

Other Information: Established in 1984. Affiliated with another unincorporated organization, Citizens for Constitutional Law at the same address. NNUSA opposed the "First New World Order War" in the Middle East against Iraq. NNUSA advocates flying the flag upside down until "Americans have the courage to defend their constitution."

New Puritan Library

91 Lytle Rd.
Fletcher, NC 28732   **Phone:** (704) 628-2185
USA   **Fax:** same

Contact Person: Patricia O. Brooks, Editor.

Officers or Principals: Richard F. Brooks, President; Patricia O. Brooks, Vice President.

Mission or Interest: Christian and patriotic publishing. "Our books are written for those who are able to understand that America is a country now under divine judgement. . . Destruction is certain without repentance. God is calling intercessors to meet this challenge. It is now either 'repent or perish.' Repentance will involve a return to the most wholesome kind of free enterprise in the economic realm, and a wholesale rejection of socialism, such as is now being seen in New Zealand."

Accomplishments: Three Christian bestsellers: Should a Christian be a Mason? by E. M. Storms, Return of the Puritans and Healing of the Mind by Pat Brooks.

Products or Services: Honest Money, Honest Government, Freedom or Slavery. Books for children include; The Pilgrim Primer, Puritan Primer, Patriot Primer and Pioneer Primer. Catalog available on request.

Tax Status: For profit. **Annual Report:** No.

Other Information: Spring Arbor Distributors distributes some of their titles.

New York State Conservative Party

486 78th St.
Brooklyn, NY 11209   **Phone:** (718) 921-2158
USA   **Fax:**   (718) 921-5268

Contact Person: Laura Schreiner.

Officers or Principals: Michael R. Long, State Chairman; James P. Molinaro, State Vice Chairman; Anthony M. Rudmann, Executive Director.

Mission or Interest: Promotion and development of conservative ideals and the election of conservative candidates throughout the state of New York.

Accomplishments: Third largest political party in the state of New York. Election of U.S. Senator James L. Buckley in 1970 on the Conservative Party line.

Products or Services: Annual Legislative Platform and brochure.

Tax Status: Not exempt. **Annual Report:** No. **Employees:** 4

Periodicals: *The NY Conservative* (monthly newsletter).

Internships: No.

Nixon Center for Peace and Freedom

1620 I St., N.W., Suite 900
Washington, DC 20006   **Phone:** (202) 887-1000
USA   **Fax:**   (202) 887-5222

Contact Person: Dimitri K. Simes, President.

Officers or Principals: Peter W. Rodman, Director of National Security Programs.

Mission or Interest: A bipartisan policy institute committed to analysis of foreign policy.

Accomplishments: In March 1995 the Center held a conference entitled "After Victory: Defining an American role in an uncertain world." Chaired by Henry Kissinger, the conference featured addresses by President Bill Clinton, Senate Majority Leader Bob Dole, House Speaker Newt Gingrich, and Secretary Kissinger.

Products or Services: "Study Group on National Security" chaired by former Defense Secretary James Schlesinger. The "Washington Task Force on Russia"in conjunction with the Council on Foreign Relations. "Congressional Leadership Luncheon Series" co-chaired by Rep. Lee Hamilton (D-IN) and Sen. John McCain (R-AZ).

Board of Directors or Trustees: Dwayne Andreas (Chair. Archer Daniels Midland); George Argyros (former Seattle Mariners owner); Tricia Nixon Cox; Julie Nixon Eisenhower; Hon. Robert Ellsworth (former Ambassador to NATO); Maurice Greenberg (Chair, American International Group); Hon. Henry Kissinger (Secretary of State 1973-77); Eugene Lawson (Pres., U.S.-Business Council); Sen. Joseph Lieberman (D-CT); C. William Maynes (editor, *Foreign Policy*); Sen. John McCain (R-AZ); Hon. Ann McLaughlin (Secretary of Labor 1987-89); Lionel Olmer (former Undersecretary of Commerce for International Trade); James Perrella (Chair, Ingersoll-Rand); Hon. James Schlesinger (Secretary of Defense 1973-74); Hon. Robert Strauss (former Chair, Democratic National Committee and Ambassador to the Soviet Union); and John Taylor (Dir., Richard Nixon Library and Birthplace).

Other Information: The Center is a subsidiary of the Nixon Foundation that also operates the Richard M. Nixon Library and Birthplace (for more on the Foundation, see the separate listing for the Richard M. Nixon Presidential Library and Birthplace.).

Nixon Foundation
(see Richard M. Nixon Presidential Library and Birthplace)

Nockian Society, The
42 Leathers Rd.
Fort Mitchell, KY 41017
USA

Mission or Interest: "Help keep green the memory of Albert Jay Nock (1870-1945)." Nock was a writer best known for his libertarian views as an editor of *The Freeman* (1920-24), and as the author of books such as <u>Our Enemy, The State</u>, <u>Memoirs of a Superfluous Man</u>, and <u>The State of the Union</u> (Liberty Press, 1991). He believed that government should be limited to "negative" interventions - that is when the power of the government is used to protect one individual's rights from another - not 'positive' interventions, such as the provision of social services and compulsory education. Nock was a proponent of Henry George's proposed single tax on land.

Products or Services: Books and photocopies of out-of-print books by Nock.

Tax Status: Unincorporated.

Periodicals: Periodic newsletter.

Other Information: <u>The Dictionary of American Conservatism</u> lists Nock as an "eccentric conservative whose work broke ground for modern conservatism in some respects."

North Carolina Family Policy Council
P.O. Box 2567
Raleigh, NC 27602   **Phone:**   (919) 834-4090
USA   **Fax:**   (919) 834-0045

Contact Person: Bill Brooks, President.

Officers or Principals: Dick Douglas, Chairman; Anna Smith, Administrator; John McConnell, Community Impact Director.

Mission or Interest: "To serve as a voice for families and traditional family values in the public policy arena." Focus on North Carolina.

Accomplishments: The 1995 session of the North Carolina General Assembly "(from a pro-family standpoint) has to be regarded as one of the most successful sessions in years. . . the difference this year, can be explained by several factors. . . (including) groups like the NC Family Policy Council (who) are working to research and educate the citizens on the impact of laws on the basic family unit."

Tax Status: 501(c)(3)

Periodicals: *North Carolina Citizen* (monthly newsletter included in Focus on the Family's *Citizen*), and *North Carolina Family Policy News* (monthly newsletter).

Other Information: Established in 1992. Affiliated with Focus on the Family.

North Dakota Family Alliance (NDFA)
4007 N. State St.
Bismarck, ND 58501   **Phone:**   (701) 223-3575   **E-Mail:**   NDFA@aol.com
USA   **Fax:**   (701) 223-3675

Contact Person: Rev. Clinton Birst, Executive Director.

Officers or Principals: Gail Biby, Assistant Editor; Rev. Clinton Birst, Executive Director.

Mission or Interest: "Focus on the effects of public policies and cultural issues on the Family." Advocates policies based on, "the unique, divine inspiration, entire trustworthiness and authority of the Bible."

Products or Services: Radio show on 3 stations. Voters' guides.

Tax Status: 501(c)(3) **Employees:** 2
Periodicals: *Family Alliance Report* (monthly newsletter), and *North Dakota Citizen* (monthly newsletter included in Focus on the Family's *Citizen*).
Internships: No.
Other Information: Affiliated with Focus on the Family, although it receives no direct financial support. Formerly called the North Dakota Alliance.

Northwest Legal Foundation

P.O. Box 5327
Tacoma, WA 98415   **Phone:**   (206) 274-0708
USA

Contact Person: Jeanette Burrage, Executive Director.
Officers or Principals: Jeanette Burrage, Executive Director ($40,800); Robert L. Hale, President ($0); Richard Sanders, Vice President ($0); Suzanne Burke, Treasurer.
Mission or Interest: Public interest law firm dedicated to protecting the constitutional rights of individuals, with a focus on privacy and property.
Accomplishments: Litigated Seattle v. McCready, a case involving privacy in one's own home, and Robinson v. Seattle, a case involving damages and due process; others. In 1993 the Foundation spent $94,803 on its programs.
Total Revenue: 1993 $82,244 **Total Expenses:** $123,505 77%/14%/10% **Net Assets:** $3,241
Products or Services: Seminars, "Property as a Civil Right" and "Property Law Symposium." Speaking engagements. Lobbying: in 1993 the Foundation spent $5,000 on the direct lobbying of legislators; and increase of 25% over the year before.
Tax Status: 501(c)(3) **Annual Report:** No. **Employees:** 2
Internships: Yes, law students work for school credit.
Other Information: The Foundation received $72,960, or 89% of revenue, from contributions and grants awarded by foundations, businesses, affiliates, and individuals. (These grants have been declining by an average of 25% per year for the last three years.) $4,425, or 5%, from seminar and registration fees. $2,117, or 3%, from a tax refund. The remaining revenue came from legal services, the sale of products, and interest on savings.

NOT-SAFE (National Organization Taunting Safety and Fairness Everywhere)

Box 5743-APL
Montecito, CA 93150
USA

Contact Person: Dale Lowdermilk.
Mission or Interest: Waging a sarcastic war against society's preoccupation with safety, and against law makers "who have nothing to do except pass laws which save us from ourselves."
Accomplishments: Membership of over 650. Lowdermilk has been removed from the Food and Drug Administration's mailing list. Featured in *Insight*, and *The Economist* magazines. Lowdermilk was named Man-of-the-Year by *Satire* magazine. Lowdermilk's proposals include requiring that all aircraft taxi to their destinations (airborne is much to dangerous), and that if they must leave the ground they should only go one at a time (to prevent mid-air crashes). Airline passengers should travel naked making it (nearly) impossible to smuggle a gun or bomb on board.
Tax Status: Unincorporated.
Other Information: Lowdermilk, a former air-traffic controller, is a member of the Libertarian Party.

NRA Foundation

11250 Waples Mill Rd.
Fairfax, VA 22030   **Phone:**   (703) 267-1000   **E-Mail:** listproc@nra.org
USA   **Internet:** http://www.nra.org

Officers or Principals: John Woods, President ($0); Wayne Sheets, Executive Director ($0); Wilson H. Phillips, Jr., Treasurer ($0); Sandra Froman, Vice President; Michael Patrick Murray, Secretary.
Mission or Interest: Grant-making affiliate of the National Rifle Association.
Accomplishments: In 1993 the Foundation awarded $335,009 in grants, 100% of its operating budget. Of this, $310,000 went to the NRA to support programs in firearms safety, hunting, and competition. Other recipients included $18,000 for Academics for the Second Amendment, and $7,009 for the Southern Arizona Firearms Educators for safety classes.
Total Revenue: 1993 $915,006 **Total Expenses:** $488,453 69%/6%/25% **Net Assets:** $385,839
Tax Status: 501(c)(3)
Board of Directors or Trustees: Tanya Metaksa, Richard Carone, Wayne LaPierre, Jr., Neal Knox, Joe Olson.
Other Information: Established in 1991. The Foundation received $892,976, or 98% of revenue, from contributions and grants awarded by foundations, businesses, and individuals. ($595,875, or 67% of contributions, came from "Friends of the NRA" fundraising events - mostly from individuals. Contributions and grants grew by 70% over the previous year.) $22,030, or 2%, from interest on savings and temporary cash investments.

NRA Special Contribution Fund

P.O. Box 700
Raton, NM 87740   **Phone:** (505) 445-3615
USA

Contact Person: Michael Ballew, Executive Director.
Officers or Principals: Michael Ballew, Executive Director ($60,000); Kayne Robinson, Chairman ($0); Clifford Burgess, Jr., Secretary ($0); Wilson H. Philips, Jr., Treasurer.
Mission or Interest: Affiliate of the National Rifle Association that provides educational materials and firearms training.
Accomplishments: In 1994 the Fund spent $813,151 on its activities.
Total Revenue: 1994 $2,015,124 18% **Total Expenses:** $2,148,615 38%/28%/34% **Net Assets:** $2,884,484
Tax Status: 501(c)(3)
Other Information: Affiliated with the 501(c)(3) National Rifle Association. The Fund received $1,470,548, or 73% of revenue, from program services. $309,548, or 15%, from contributions and grants awarded by foundations, businesses, and individuals. $135,102, or 7%, from membership dues. $54,331, or 3%, from interest on savings and temporary cash investments. $41,695, or 2%, from the sale of inventory. The remaining revenue came from the rents and other miscellaneous sources.

Objectivist Club of Michigan

1175-D Kirts Blvd.
Troy, MI 48084   **Phone:** (810) 543-0155   **Internet:** http://www.rustnet/~lc/
USA

Contact Person: Karen Reedstrom, Editor.
Officers or Principals: Rick Minto, David Oyerly.
Mission or Interest: Study and promote Objectivism. Enjoy the company of objectivists.
Accomplishments: Although primarily a local group, their newsletter *Full Context* has gained subscribers throughout the U.S. and Canada, as well as in England and Norway. As subscribers are technically members, they believe they might be the largest objectivist club in the world. Back issues are available, as well as a package of articles on the controversy surrounding the origins and causes of AIDS, which includes an interview with Dr. Peter Duesberg from the February 1992 *Full Context*.
Products or Services: Produce a local access cable television talk show, hold monthly meetings (except during July and August), and host an occasional lecture. Back issues of *Full Context* available.
Tax Status: 501(c)(3) **Annual Report:** No. **Employees:** All volunteer.
Periodicals: *Full Context* (monthly, except for July and August, newsletter).
Internships: No.
Other Information: Publishing *Full Context* since 1988.

Of the People Foundation

2111 Wilson Blvd., Suite 700
Arlington, VA 22201   **Phone:** (703) 351-5051
USA   **Fax:** (703) 351-0937

Contact Person: Courtney Atherton.
Officers or Principals: Jeffery Bell, President/Chairman ($43,125); Greg D. Erken, Executive Director ($35,500); Ralph J. Benko, President ($16,000); Robert C. Heckman, Senior Vice President; Francis P. Cannon, Treasurer.
Mission or Interest: Stressing the importance of values and parents' rights. Advocates the passage of a "Parental Rights Amendment" to state and the federal constitutions. The wording of the amendment is as follows: "1. The rights of parents to direct the upbringing and education of their children shall not be infringed. 2. The legislature shall have the power to enforce, by appropriate legislation, the provisions of this article."
Accomplishments: "National clearinghouse for Parental Rights." In 1994 the Foundation spent $60,650 on its programs.
Total Revenue: 1994 $143,148 112% **Total Expenses:** $169,786 36%/26%/38% **Net Assets:** $25,048
Tax Status: 501(c)(3) **Annual Report:** Yes. **Employees:** 10
Board of Directors or Trustees: John Mueller, Lewis Lehrman.
Periodicals: Newsletter.
Internships: Yes, for general administration and staff assistance.
Other Information: Established in 1993. Affiliated with the 501(c)(4) Of the People. The Foundation maintains that the U.S. Supreme Court has already upheld parental rights in <u>Meyer</u> and <u>Pierce</u>, but that lower-court judges nationwide do not abide by these decisions - hence the need for a Constitutional amendment. The Foundation received $142,530, or 99.5% of revenue, from contributions and grants awarded by foundations, businesses, and individuals. (In 1995 these grants included $150,000 from the Lynde and Harry Bradley Foundation, $50,000 from the Scaife Family Foundation.) The remaining revenue came from interest on a note receivable from Of the People.

Ohio Rifle and Pistol Association (ORPA)

P.O. Box 43083
Cincinnati, OH 45243
USA

Contact Person: Frank Fecke, President.
Officers or Principals: Frank Fecke, President ($0); Craig Swihart, Vice President ($0); Diana Stankiewicz, Secretary ($0); Susan Antolik, Treasurer.
Mission or Interest: Organization promoting the safe ownership of firearms.
Accomplishments: Won the "Outstanding State Association Award" from the NRA. In the fiscal year ending September 1994 the Association spent $108,012 on its programs.
Total Revenue: FY from 1/94 to 9/94 $129,648 32%(2) **Total Expenses:** $125,275 86%/14%/0% **Net Assets:** $98,563
Products or Services: Lobbying, firearm competitions, safety classes, annual meeting, hunting classes, more.
Tax Status: 501(c)(4)
Periodicals: *Gunsmoke* (newsletter).
Other Information: Established in 1934. The Association received $83,587, or 64% of revenue, from shooting tournament fees. $32,302, or 25%, from membership dues. $12,417, or 10%, from contributors. The remaining revenue came from other miscellaneous sources.

Oklahoma Council of Public Affairs (OCPA)

100 W. Wilshire, Suite C-3
Oklahoma City, OK 73116   **Phone:** (405) 843-9212   **E-Mail:** ocpathink@aol.com
USA   **Fax:** (405) 843-9436   **Internet:** http://www.ocpathink.org

Contact Person: Brett A. Magbee, Executive Director.
Officers or Principals: Brett A. Magbee, Executive Director; David R. Brown, M.D., Chairman; Brandon T. Dutcher, Research Director; Paulette Jones, Development Coordinator.
Mission or Interest: "Formulating and promoting public-policy analysis consistent with the principles of free enterprise, limited government, and individual initiative."
Accomplishments: "Research quoted in print, broadcast news stories in Oklahoma; op-ed columns have appeared in newspapers throughout the state."
Products or Services: Annual Citizenship Award; the first recipient, in 1997, is Jeane Kirkpatrick. Briefings, luncheons, and publications.
Tax Status: 501(c)(3) **Annual Report:** No. **Employees:** 3
Board of Directors or Trustees: Ralph Abercrombie, William Avery, Steve Beebe, G.T. Blankenship, John Brock, Aaron Burleson, Jim Cantrell, Fred Fox, Jr., Josephine Freede, Kent Frizzell, Paul Hitch, Henry Kane, Thurman Magbee, Tom McCasland, III, Lew Meibergen, Lloyd Noble, II, Robert Reece, Patrick Rooney, Earl Shipp, Richard Sias, Dean Sims, John Snodgrass, William Thurman, M.D., Betty Lou Lee Upsher, Lew Ward, Harold Wilson.
Periodicals: *OCPA Perspective* (bimonthly newsletter).
Internships: Yes.
Other Information: Established in 1993. Chairman Dr. David Brown is also chairman of the Heritage Foundation.

Oklahoma Family Policy Council

5101 N. Classen Blvd.
Oklahoma City, OK 73118   **Phone:** (405) 840-3005
USA   **Fax:** (405) 840-4288

Contact Person: David Dunn, Director .
Officers or Principals: David Dunn, Director of Research and Policy Analysis ($34,000); Lloyd McAlister, Chairman ($0); Beth Hammons, Secretary ($0); Scott Duncan, Treasurer; Bill Held, Director.
Mission or Interest: Educating Oklahomans on public policy as it affects the family and promotes responsible citizenship.
Accomplishments: Influential during the 1992 legislative consideration of HB 1893, a living-will reform bill.
Total Revenue: FY ending 9/95 $114,497 (-14%)(2) **Total Expenses:** $125,850 0%/100%/0% **Net Assets:** $6,893
Products or Services: Several publications and a radio program.
Tax Status: 501(c)(3) **Annual Report:** Yes. **Employees:** 3
Periodicals: *Oklahoma Citizen* (monthly newsletter included in Focus on the Family's *Citizen*).
Internships: Yes, for undergraduates and post-graduates.
Other Information: Established in 1989 as the Resource Institute of Oklahoma. In the fiscal year ending September 1995, the Council underwent an organizational change, changing its name and physical location. All expenditures that year went to overhead costs. Affiliated with Focus on the Family, although they receive no direct support from them. The Council received $114,374, or 99.9% of revenue, from contributions and grants awarded by foundations, businesses, and individuals. (These grants included $10,000 from the Roe Foundation. The Council has historically received financial support from the J. M. Foundation and Samuel Roberts Noble Foundation.) The remaining revenue came from interest on savings.

Operation Rescue

P.O. Box 1180
Binghamton, NY 13902   **Phone:** (607) 723-4012
USA

Officers or Principals: Randall A. Terry
Mission or Interest: "To save children from being killed by abortion, mothers from exploitation, and help to restore to America a respect for life." Anti-abortion group that gained prominence in the late 1980s and early 1990s by using tactics of civil disobedience and passive resistance to block access to abortion clinics.
Accomplishments: "From 5/88 to 6/91 over 634 children have been saved from abortion, Operation Rescue has helped to make abortion the number-one issue in America, and has drawn countless numbers of people into the fight for life."
Products or Services: Pro-life materials.
Tax Status: Not exempt. **Annual Report:** No.
Periodicals: *The National Rescuer* (bimonthly newsletter).
Internships: No.

Oregon Institute of Science and Medicine

2251 Dick George Rd.
Cave Junction, OR 97523   **Phone:** (503) 592-4142
USA   **Fax:**   same

Contact Person: Arthur B. Robinson, Ph.D., President.
Officers or Principals: Arthur B. Robinson, Ph.D., President ($14,133); Arnold Hunsberger, Vice President ($0); Richard McIntyre, Secretary ($0).
Mission or Interest: Health research, civil defense, and home-schooling curriculum development. Health research focuses primarily on the molecular biology of cancer and aging.
Accomplishments: In 1995 the Institute spent $62,851 on its programs.
Total Revenue: 1995 $145,275 32%(3) **Total Expenses:** $75,030 84%/8%/8% **Net Assets:** $376,625
Products or Services: Various books, scientific publications, and video tapes. Plans for chemical, biological and nuclear shelters.
Tax Status: 501(c)(3) **Employees:** All volunteer.
Periodicals: *Fighting Chance* (monthly newsletter).
Other Information: Dr. Robinson taught chemistry at the University of California, San Diego. He was a professor at the age of 25 and had published over 50 research papers by the age of 32. He home schooled his six children with his wife, Laurelee, until her death in 1988. He continues their schooling himself. In addition to the Oregon Institute of Science and Medicine, Dr. Robinson has taken over the publication of *Access to Energy*, following the death of its founder, Petr Beckmann. The Institute received $119,722, or 82% of revenue, from contributions and grants awarded by foundations, businesses, and individuals. $23,901 net, or 16%, from the sale of inventory. $1,652, or 2%, from interest on savings and temporary cash investments.

Oregon Lands Coalition

247 N.E. Commercial St.
Salem, OR 97301   **Phone:** (503) 363-8582
USA   **Fax:**   (503) 363-6067

Contact Person: Chris Chandler, State Coordinator.
Officers or Principals: Chris Chandler, State Coordinator ($32,000); Jean Nelson, Office Manager ($15,600); Valerie Johnson Eves, External Vice Chair ($0); Pat Anderes, Internal Vice Chair; Tom Hirons, Chair; Mel Schmidt, Treasurer; Deb Crisp, Secretary.
Mission or Interest: 'Wise use' group working "to heighten public understanding of benefits derived from the use of natural resources without compromising the ability of future generations to do the same."
Accomplishments: Brought together 67 member groups - including grassroots organizations and organizations representing industries affected by environmental legislation - representing 82,000 people. In 1989 they led a boycott of the broadcasting of "Ancient Forests: Rage Over Trees," by the Turner Broadcasting System. The documentary was produced by the National Audubon Society and was felt to portray logging in a very unfavorable manner. The boycott caused various sponsors to drop their support, costing TBS $250,000 in lost revenue. In 1994 the Coalition spent $74,116 on its programs.
Total Revenue: 1994 $100,738 23%(2) **Total Expenses:** $105,880 70%/25%/5% **Net Assets:** $6,675
Products or Services: Rallies, parades, seminars, letter/phone/fax campaigns. Monthly strategy sessions.
Tax Status: 501(c)(4) **Employees:** 2
Board of Directors or Trustees: Terri Moffett, Judy Wortman, Rita Kaley, Evelyn Badger, Mark Simmons, Loydee Grainger, Rod Harder, Audrey Barnes, Larry George, Stan Barg, Bob Haitmanek.
Periodicals: *Network News* (newsletter).   **Internships:** Yes.

Oregonians for Food and Shelter (OFS)

567 Union St., N.E.
Salem, OR 97301   **Phone:** (503) 370-8092
USA   **Fax:**   (503) 370-8565

Contact Person: Terry Witt, Executive Director.

Officers or Principals: Terry Witt, Executive Director ($86,396); Dee Bridges, President ($0); Charles Henry, Secretary ($0).
Mission or Interest: 'Wise use' organization, representing agricultural interests in Oregon, that fights excessive environmental regulations, particularly certain restrictions on pesticide use. Seeks reformation of the Endangered Species Act.
Total Revenue: 1993 $277,375 **Total Expenses:** $263,599 **Net Assets:** $47,573
Tax Status: 501(c)(6)   **Citations:** 3:204
Board of Directors or Trustees: Fred Cholick (Willamette Valley Potato Growers), Bill Egan (Oregon Assn. of Nurserymen), Dean Freeborn (Oregon Farm Bureau Federation), Charles Henry (Oregon Horticulture Society), Mike Kerr (Oregon Hop Growers Assn.), Denise McPhail (Portland General Electric), Norm Parker (Western Helicopter Services), Jim Rombach (Weyerhaeuser), Bob Wix (DuPont Agricultural Products), and many other members representing agribusiness in Oregon.
Periodicals: Newsletter.
Other Information: The organization received $273,180, or 98% of revenue, from membership dues. $3,520, or 1%, from the sale of educational materials. The remaining revenue came from interest on savings and temporary cash investments.

Oregonians in Action (OIA)

P.O. Box 230637
Tigard, OR 97281   **Phone:** (503) 620-0258   **E-Mail:** oiaec@teleport.com
USA   **Fax:** (503) 639-6891

Contact Person: Lawrence George, Executive Director.
Officers or Principals: Lawrence George, Executive Director ($31,404); Frank Nims, President ($0); Bill Moshofsky, Vice President; Dave Hunnicutt, Director of Legal Affairs; Jasper Coombes, Secretary; Matt Cyrus, Treasurer.
Mission or Interest: "Protection of private property rights" through lobbying and litigation. Focus on the 5th Amendment and on regulatory 'takings,' particularly in Oregon.
Accomplishments: "Staff attorneys won the landmark U.S. Supreme Court case Dolan v. City of Tigard." The Court ruled that the City of Tigard acted improperly when it required that a portion of the Dolan's property be given for public use in order for the Dolan's requested permit to expand their plumbing supply store to be approved. The Court said in the case, "We see no reason why the Takings Clause of the Fifth Amendment, as much a part of the Bill of Rights as the First Amendment or Fourth Amendment, should be relegated to the status of poor relation." In 1994 the organization spent $176,862 on its programs. The largest program, with expenditures of $79,334, was litigation. $48,764 was spent seeking regulatory reform at the state's agencies. $36,573 was spent on public education, and $12,191 was spent "educating landowners about regulatory and legislative actions that impact them and the state's economy."
Total Revenue: 1994 $328,874 8%(2) **Total Expenses:** $279,070 63%/21%/15% **Net Assets:** $50,666
Tax Status: 501(c)(4) **Annual Report:** No. **Employees:** 8   **Citations:** 18:154
Board of Directors or Trustees: David Clem, Don Duhrkopf, Kristi Halvorsen, Leslie Lewis, Susan Mast, Susie Cahill, Rita Swyers.
Periodicals: *Looking Forward* (bimonthly newsletter), and *Horizons* (annual journal).
Internships: No.
Other Information: Affiliated with the Oregonians in Action Education Center and Oregonians in Action Legal Center, both 501(c)(3). The OIA received $214,313, or 65% of revenue, from contributions and grants. $111,295, or 34%, from administration services provided for its two affiliates. The remaining revenue came from other miscellaneous sources.

Oregonians in Action Education Center

P.O. Box 230637
Tigard, OR 97281   **Phone:** (503) 620-0258   **E-Mail:** oiaec@teleport.com
USA   **Fax:** (503) 639-6891

Contact Person: Larry George, Executive Director.
Officers or Principals: Frank Nims, President ($0); Rita Swyers, Vice President ($0); Wallace Cegavske, Secretary/Treasurer ($0).
Mission or Interest: Research and education affiliate of Oregonians in Action.
Accomplishments: The newsletter the Center co-publishes with Oregonians in Action "reaches more than 15,000 homes." In 1995 the Center spent $99,278 on its programs, including public meetings, forums, radio and television ads.
Total Revenue: 1995 $175,061 **Total Expenses:** $150,953 66%/18%/16% **Net Assets:** $121,669
Tax Status: 501(c)(3)   **Citations:** 18:154
Board of Directors or Trustees: David Clem, Jasper Coombes, Matt Cyrus, Don Duhrkopf, Kristi Halvorson, Leslie Lewis, Carl Neuburger.
Other Information: Established in 1992. Affiliated with the 501(c)(4) Oregonians in Action and the 501(c)(3) Oregonians in Action Legal Center at the same address. The Center received $168,671, or 96% of revenue, from contributions and grants awarded by foundations, businesses, and individuals. $4,934, or 3%, from interest on savings and temporary cash investments. $1,456, or 1%, from dividends and interest from securities.

Oregonians in Action Legal Center

P.O. Box 230637
Tigard, OR 97281   **Phone:** (503) 620-0258   **E-Mail:** oiaec@teleport.com
USA   **Fax:** (503) 639-6891

Contact Person: Larry George, Executive Director.

Officers or Principals: William J. Moshofsky, President ($0); Frank L. Nims, Vice President ($0).
Mission or Interest: Litigating affiliate of Oregonians in Action. "To protect Constitutional rights of landowners by gathering excessive land-use regulations through litigation."
Accomplishments: In 1995 the Center spent $45,158 on its programs.
Total Revenue: 1995 $51,991 **Total Expenses:** $53,036 85%/11%/4% **Net Assets:** $111,904
Tax Status: 501(c)(3)   **Citations:** 18:154
Board of Directors or Trustees: Kristi Halvorson, John Shonkwiler, J. Kenneth Brody, Lon Bryant, James Huffman.
Other Information: Affiliated with the 501(c)(4) Oregonians in Action and the 501(c)(3) Oregonians in Action Education Center at the same address. The Legal Center received $48,924, or 94% of revenue, from contributions and grants awarded by foundations, businesses, and individuals. $2,043, or 4%, from interest on savings and temporary cash investments. The remaining revenue came from dividends and interest from securities, and other miscellaneous sources.

Pacific Academy for Advanced Studies

1333 19th St., Suite 6
Santa Monica, CA 90404   **Phone:**   (310) 208-7735
USA

Contact Person: Dr. J. Clayburn La Force, President.
Mission or Interest: Develops economic programs for Latin America.
Tax Status: 501(c)(3)
Other Information: President La Force is Dean Emeritus of the UCLA Graduate School of Management, and is secretary of the Foundation Francisco Marroquin. In 1994-5 the Institute received $600,000 from the Lilly Endowment, and $60,000 from the Carthage Foundation.

Pacific Forum CSIS

1001 Bishop St.
Pauahi Tower, Suite 1150
Honolulu, HI 96813   **Phone:**   (808) 521-6745
USA   **Fax:**   (808) 599-8690

Contact Person: Ralph A. Cossa, Executive Director.
Officers or Principals: Amos A. Jordan, President; L. R. Vasey, Founder and Senior Advisor; Lt. Gen. Brent Scrowcroft, USAF (Ret.), Chairman; Thomas Hayward, Adm., USN (Ret.), Hahn Been Lee, Lloyd R. Vasey, Rear Adm., USN (Ret.), Vice Chairmen; Jane Khanna, Development and Program Associate; Stanley Katz, Linda Paul, Senior Associates.
Mission or Interest: Analyzes political, economic, and security interests and trends in the Asia-Pacific region.
Products or Services: "International Business and Economics Program." Several "Political and Security Programs," that include the "United States-Korean Wisemen Council." This council brings together six experienced and senior officials from both countries to meet and discuss various issues. The Pacific Forum maintains the autonomous Ocean Policy Institute (OPI), that provides a forum for analysis of marine issues. OPI's Director is Dr. Melvin Peterson. The Forum also assumes management responsibility for the Pacific Basin Economic Council (PBEC). This Council is an association of business executives representing approximately 1,000 corporations in 17 member countries. PBEC's International Director General is Robert G. Lees.
Tax Status: 501(c)(3)
Board of Directors or Trustees: Adm. Ronald Hays, USN, Ret. (former U.S. Commander in Chief, Pacific Command), James Kelly (former Special Asst. For National Security Affairs to Pres. Reagan), Ann McLaughlin (former Secretary of Labor, 1987-89), many other prominent members of the business, diplomatic, and military communities.
Periodicals: *PacNet Newsletter* (weekly fax).
Other Information: Established in 1975. In 1989 the Forum merged operations with the Center for Strategic and International Studies in Washington, DC, although it remains autonomous as a nonprofit organization. (For more information, see the Center for Strategic and International Studies.) In 1995 the Forum received $60,000 from the Carthage Foundation.

Pacific Legal Foundation (PLF)

2151 River Plaza Dr., Suite 305
Sacramento, CA 95833   **Phone:**   (916) 641-8888
USA   **Fax:**   (916) 920-3444

Contact Person: Ronald A. Zumbrun, President.
Officers or Principals: Anthony T. Caso, Director of Litigation ($138,529); Robin L. Rivett, Chief, Environmental Law ($118,316); Richard R. Bradley, Director, Strategy & Development ($92,222); James S. Burline, Chief, Property Rights; Ronald A. Zumbrun, President; Thomas R. Pascoe, Vice President; Douglas C. Jacobs, Secretary/Treasurer.
Mission or Interest: Public interest law in defense of individual and economic freedoms. Private property and government 'takings' are of particular interest.

Accomplishments: Successful U. S. Supreme Court Cases, including <u>Nollan v. California Coastal Commission</u> and <u>Keller v. State Bar</u>. Filed an amicus curiae (friend of the court) brief in <u>Dolan v. City of Tigard</u>, a case that held that local permit costs must be proportionate to damage that land use could cause. Using the precedent set in *Dolan* to argue other cases. Defending a New York landlord whose apartment building burned down. Because rebuilding the apartments was not cost effective, the landlord decided against using the land for new apartments. For this reason he is being sued by the former tenants because they want to resume living in apartments at their old rent-controlled rates. The Foundation holds that requiring him to rebuild apartments is an uncompensated 'taking'. PLF asked the California Supreme Court to hear the case of <u>Clark v. City of Hermosa Beach,</u> in which an Appeals Court ruled that a government agency's failure to approve a permit for building does not deny due process unless the agency meets the strict criteria of conduct so outrageous that it "shocks the conscience." In 1994 PLF spent $2,587,820 on its programs.

Total Revenue: 1994 $3,490,127 (-2%)(4) **Total Expenses:** $4,024,083 64%/17%/18% **Net Assets:** $2,914,778

Products or Services: *Pro bono* legal representation. Limited Government Project to ease government regulations. College of Public Interest Law (CPIL) which trains recent law school graduates. An extensive library of case information and analysis.

Tax Status: 501(c)(3) **Annual Report:** Yes. **Employees:** 50   **Citations:** 172:43

Board of Directors or Trustees: Robin Arkley, James Busby, Ward Connerly (American Civil Rights Inst.), Ben Gantt, Jr., Catherine Goodrich, Douglas Jacob (Arthur Anderson & Co.), Thomas May, Robert McCarthy, April Morris (Standard Pacific), Fess Parker (actor), Thomas Paton (Chair, Blue Shield of Calif.), Jerry Schauffler, John Schwabe, Michael Thomas, Ronald Van Buskirk, Brooks Walker, Jr.

Internships: Yes, public interest law fellowships, law clerkships.

Other Information: Established in 1973. Has offices in Alaska and Seattle. The PLF paid $524,199 to the San Francisco firm of Arthur Andersen for financial services; a member of PLF's Board is a managing partner in that firm. PLF also contracted the Sacramento firm of Zumbrun, Best & Findley for management and legal services. The firm was paid $212,661. The firm is affiliated with PLF president, Ronald Zumbrun, who is paid as an independent contractor through this firm. PLF received $3,418,973, or 95% of gross revenue, from contributions and grants awarded by foundations, businesses, and individuals. (These grants included $75,000 from the Sarah Scaife Foundation, $75,000 from the Lilly Endowment, $50,000 from the M.J. Murdock Charitable Trust, $42,000 from the Grover Hermann Foundation, $5,000 from the F.M. Kirby Foundation, and $5,000 from the Anschutz Foundation. In 1995, $60,000 from the John M. Olin Foundation, $25,000 from the Castle Rock Foundation, and $10,000 from the Philip M. McKenna Foundation.) $69,999, or 2%, from court-awarded attorney fees. $68,724, or 2%, from interest on savings and temporary cash investments. The remaining revenue came from dividends and interest from securities, and, other miscellaneous sources. PLF lost $61,099 on special events, and $29,994 on the sale of securities.

Pacific Research Institute for Public Policy (PRI)

755 Sansome St., Suite 450
San Francisco, CA 94111   **Phone:** (415) 989-0833   **E-Mail:** pripp@aol.com
USA   **Fax:**   (415) 989-2411   **Internet:** http://www.ideas.org

Contact Person: Sally Pipes, President.

Officers or Principals: Sally Pipes, President ($109,500); Dr. Steven Hayward, Research Director; Pamela Riley, Director, Public Affairs; James W. Fuller, Chairman; Samuel Husbands, Jr., Vice Chairman; Thomas C. Magowan, Secretary/Treasurer.

Mission or Interest: Research into all areas of public policy and how it can be improved using market-based solutions. Emphasis on California.

Accomplishments: Provided testimony before California's Board of Regents' Meeting on behalf of California's Civil Rights Initiative (Prop. 209). Have received media coverage in *Newsweek*, *The Economist*, *New York Times*, *Chief Executive*, *Los Angeles Times*, and on ABC's "20/20". In 1995 the Institute spent $1,001,521 on its programs.

Total Revenue: 1995 $1,657,304 11%(2) **Total Expenses:** $1,311,357 71%/14%/15% **Net Assets:** $843,224

Products or Services: Research, conferences and seminars.

Tax Status: 501(c)(3) **Annual Report:** No. **Employees:** 17   **Citations:** 99:64

Board of Directors or Trustees: Howard Leach, C. Derek Anderson, Robert Ernst, III, Daniel Gressel, Kenneth Grubbs, Jr. (*Orange County Register*), David Keystone, Roy Marden (Philip Morris Co.), Francis O'Connell (John M. Olin Found.), Daniel Oliver (Heritage Found.), Jeffery Stein, Jean Wente; F. Christian Wignall.

Periodicals: *Ideas in Action* (quarterly newsletter), *Pacific Outlook* (quarterly newsletter), *President's Quarterly* (quarterly newsletter).

Internships: Yes. Available year-round in areas of research, public affairs, and events coordination.

Other Information: Established in 1979 and known as the Pacific Institute for Public Policy Research until 1984. The Institute received $1,525,489, or 92% of revenue, from contributions and grants awarded by foundations, businesses, and individuals. (These grants included $50,000 from the David H. Koch Charitable Foundation, $50,000 from the Charles G. Koch Charitable Foundation, $50,000 from the John M. Olin Foundation, $20,000 from the Lilly Endowment, $8,000 from the Philip M. McKenna Foundation, and $2,500 from the Magowan Family Fund. In 1994, $150,000 from the Sarah Scaife Foundation, $50,000 from the William H. Donner Foundation, $40,000 from the Lilly Endowment, $7,500 from the Earhart Foundation, $5,000 from the Aequus Institute, $2,000 from the Ruth and Vernon Taylor Foundation, and $1,500 from the Charles G. Koch Charitable Foundation.) $70,996, or 4%, from the sale of publications. $48,356, or 3%, from conference registration fees. $11,047, or 1%, from interest on savings and temporary cash investments. The remaining revenue came from mailing list rentals.

Palmer R. Chitester Fund

9008 Main Place, Suite 3
McKean, PA 16426-0266   **Phone:** (814) 476-7721   **E-Mail:** cca@erie.net
USA   **Fax:**   (814) 476-1283   **Internet:** http://www.ideachannel.com

Contact Person: Robert J. Chitester, President.
Officers or Principals: Robert J. Chitester, President ($0); James Currie, Jr., Secretary ($0); Bertram Hopeman, Chairman ($0).
Mission or Interest: To develop television programs "examining the prerequisites of a free society."
Accomplishments: Robert Chitester was the president of the Erie, PA Public Broadcasting Station and was the producer of the "Free to Choose" series featuring Nobel Laureate in Economics, Milton Friedman.
Total Revenue: 1994 $39,660 11%(2) **Total Expenses:** $30,326 57%/43%/0% **Net Assets:** (-$520)
Products or Services: Produces "The Idea Channel" available on cable in Philadelphia. Sells video cassettes of interviews and discussions with prominent conservatives and libertarians. Series includes: Nobel Prize-winning economists Gary Becker, James Buchanan, and Milton Friedman, Charles Murray (AEI), Dr. Walter E. Williams (George Mason Univ.), scientist Bruce Ames (UC, Berkeley), Midge Decter (Inst. on Religion and Public Life), Ed Feulner (Heritage Foundation), Reed Larson (National Right to Work Committee), Julian Simon (Univ. of MD), and others.
Tax Status: 501(c)(3) **Annual Report:** No.
Board of Directors or Trustees: Annelise Anderson (Hoover Institution), Maurice Baker, Prof. J.R. Clark (Univ. of Tenn.), Phil Cooper, Johnnie Crean, James Currie, Jr., Dr. George D'Angelo, Dave Jorgensen, Don Saurer, Arnold Schwarzenegger (actor).
Internships: No.
Other Information: The Fund received $39,355, or 99% of revenue, from contributions and grants awarded by foundations, businesses, and individuals. The remaining revenue came from the sale of assets, and other miscellaneous sources.

Palmetto Family Council

P.O. Box 211634
Columbia, SC 29221   **Phone:** (803) 731-4313   **E-Mail:** 75607.1134@compuserve.com
USA   **Fax:**   (803) 731-4314

Contact Person: Dr. G. Steven Suits, President/Executive Director.
Officers or Principals: G. Steven Suits, M.D., Executive Director ($16,002); Kevin M. Caiello, Office Director ($9,796); Ken and Margaret Charles, Chairmen ($0); Brad and Debbie Jordan, Vice Chairmen; Charles and Peggy McCreight, Treasurers; Don and Teresa Jenkins, Secretaries.
Mission or Interest: Preservation of the family and biblical morals in South Carolina.
Accomplishments: In 1995 the Council sent the health education directors in the state's 91 school districts a "Save Sex" poster. Held two conferences and made several media appearances, including citations in *The State* and *The Greenville News*. Worked with the South Carolina Coalition of Black Church Leaders to improve race relations. Worked with churches throughout the state as part of the Community Impact Project. In 1994 the Council spent $4,992 on its programs, primarily the distribution of a voter guide.
Total Revenue: 1994 $126,253 **Total Expenses:** $56,356 9%/85%/6% **Net Assets:** $107,791
Products or Services: Prayer network, voters' guides, family issues surveys, books, brochures and other publications.
Tax Status: 501(c)(3) **Annual Report:** No. **Employees:** 3
Board of Directors or Trustees: Gary and Heath Brown, Barry and Susan Huey, Alva and Debbie Humphries, Gregg and Becky McKenzie, J.D. and Nancy Martin, Ben and Brenda Dawkins, Joey and Pat Haney, Jim and Claudia Sanders, Brandt and Pam Shelbourne, Jack and Deborah Tingle, David and Lynn Vandewater.
Periodicals: *South Carolina Citizen* (monthly newsletter included in Focus on the Family's *Citizen*).
Internships: Yes.
Other Information: Established in 1993. Affiliated with Focus on the Family, but receives no direct financial assistance. The Council received $124,638, or 99% of revenue, from contributions and grants awarded by foundations, businesses, and individuals. (In 1995 these grants included $1,000 from the Roe Foundation.) The remaining revenue came from interest on savings and temporary cash investments.

Parents' Music Resource Center (PMRC)

1500 Arlington Blvd., Suite 130
Arlington, VA 22209   **Phone:** (703) 524-9466
USA   **Fax:**   (703) 525-4462

Contact Person: Barbara P. Wyatt, Director.
Officers or Principals: Barbara P. Wyatt, Director ($7,000); Sally Nevius, President ($0); Susan Baker, Vice President ($0); Pam Howar, Treasurer/Secretary; Tipper Gore, Founder.
Mission or Interest: Education of the public, and particularly parents, of messages and themes contained in popular music. They favor a voluntary warning label system to alert the public to music which contains sex, violence, profanity, Satanism, misogyny, substance abuse and other themes that are harmful.
Accomplishments: "The American Medical Association, American Academy of Pediatrics, and the PTA support our position relative to the harmful effects explicit and violent lyrics have on children." Numerous media appearances and congressional hearings. "Involved Dr. William Bennett, Dr. C. DeLores Tucker, and Sen. Bob Dole in this issue." In 1985 the Recording Association of America adopted a warning label system after discussions with the PMRC.

Total Revenue: 1993 $28,648 (-45%)(2) **Total Expenses:** $34,401 44%/31%/25% **Net Assets:** $2,521
Products or Services: "Rising to the Challenge" video.
Tax Status: 501(c)(3) **Annual Report:** No.
Board of Directors or Trustees: Sharon Archer, Elayne Bennett, B. A. Bentsen, Vicki Campbell, Sharon Danforth, Debbie Dingell, William Gorong, Sheila Griffin, Ann Hand, Peatsy Hollings, Frank Jones, Olivia Jones, William McSweeny, Jane Sloat, Kim Swindall, Rosemary Trible, Carol Vander Jagt, Barbara Wyatt.
Internships: No.
Other Information: Established in 1985. The Center's revenues from contributions and grants have been steadily falling since 1989 by an average of 62% per year. The Center received $23,568, or 82% of revenue, from the sale of publications and videos. $5,005, or 18%, from contributions and grants awarded by foundations, businesses, and individuals. The remaining revenue came from interest on savings.

Parents' Rights Organization

12571 Northwinds Dr.
St. Louis, MO 63146   **Phone:** (314) 434-4171
USA

Contact Person: Mrs. Mae Duggan, President.
Officers or Principals: Dr. Daniel D. McGarry, Director; John R. McCormack, Treasurer.
Mission or Interest: "To establish and defend, by appropriate legal action, the right of parents to choose the kind of education their children receive." Supports educational vouchers that include religious schooling.
Accomplishments: Initiated and joined in amicus briefs and other litigation.
Products or Services: They provide numerous publications, brochures, legal briefs, more. Materials for home-schooling.
Board of Directors or Trustees: Dr. Roger Freeman (Hoover Inst.), Harvey Johnson, Sr. M. Raymond McLaughlin, O.S.B., Ph.D., Dr. Daniel McGarry (St. Louis Univ.), Anthony Nollet, Dr. Charles Rice (Notre Dame, School of Law), Dr. William Super, M.D., Albert Walsh.
Other Information: Established in 1967 by Mrs. Mae Duggan following a radio debate with atheist Madalyn Murray O'Hair.

Partners Advancing Values in Education (PAVE)

1434 W. State St.
Milwaukee, WI 53233   **Phone:** (414) 342-1505
USA

Contact Person: Daniel M. McKinley, Executive Director.
Officers or Principals: Daniel M. McKinley, Executive Director ($75,900).
Mission or Interest: Awards grants to low-income students to subsidize their attendance at religious and other private schools.
Accomplishments: "PAVE is the nation's largest privately-funded school choice program that most closely resembles (Wisconsin) Governor Thompson's recently expanded Milwaukee Parental Choice Program. . . (a) first-year evaluation of the program (conducted by Family Service America) reported high levels of parent satisfaction (96%) and involvement (97%) from the 960 (63%) families who completed a survey. The second-year evaluation investigated seventh grader's academic achievement, and reported that PAVE students scored higher in reading and math than did representative samples from Milwaukee Public Schools." In the fiscal year ending June 1995 PAVE awarded $1,961,760 in grants.
Total Revenue: FY ending 6/95 $2,030,771 **Total Expenses:** $2,130,112 92%/8%/0% **Net Assets:** $1,319,525
Tax Status: 501(c)(3)   **Citations:** 43:106
Board of Directors or Trustees: Richard Abdoo (Wisconsin Electric Power), Patricia Apple (Apple Family Found.), T. Michael Bolger (Pres., Medical College of Wisconsin), Dr. Peter Danner (Prof. Emeritus, Marquette Univ.), Ricardo Diaz (Dir., Housing Mgt., City of Milwaukee), Leonard Goldstein (Ret. Chair, Miller Brewing Co.), James Keyes (Chair/CEO, Johnson Controls), The Most Rev., Rembert Weakland, O.S.B., and many others, mostly from the Wisconsin business community.
Other Information: Established in 1991. PAVE received $1,964,983, or 97% of revenue, from contributions and grants awarded by foundations, businesses, and individuals. (These grants included $1,824,100 from the Lynde and Harry Bradley Foundation, $5,000 from the Forbes Foundation. These contributions and grants have grown by an average of 35% per year since its founding.) $65,788, or 3%, from dividends and interest from securities.

Patriot Network

515 Concord Ave.
Anderson, SC 29621   **Phone:** (803) 225-3061
USA

Contact Person: Robert Clarkson.
Officers or Principals: Ron Brown.
Mission or Interest: Populist/libertarian organization that seeks to abolition the IRS and the Federal Reserve, and advocates a return to gold money.

Accomplishments: "Formed over 100 Tax Patriot Clubs, helped 8,000 people stop filing income tax returns."
Products or Services: Books, videos, tapes.
Tax Status: Unincorporated. **Annual Report:** No.
Periodicals: *The Patriot Cannon.*
Internships: Yes.
Other Information: "We are Tax Patriots, anti-statists and we reach out to the public. Thousands of Americans want to stop paying income tax. We show them how."

Paul Gann's Spirit of 13

9745-D Business Park Dr.
Sacramento, CA 95827   **Phone:**   (916) 366-3500
USA   **Fax:**   (916) 336-8267

Officers or Principals: Richard Gann, President ($0); Nell Gann, Vice President ($0); Linda Gann Stone, Secretary/Treasurer ($0).
Mission or Interest: Education and lobbying for lower taxes in California.
Total Revenue: 1995 less than $25,000
Tax Status: 501(c)(4)
Other Information: Spirit of 13 refers to Proposition 13, which passed in California in 1978. This Proposition limited property taxes to 1% of assessed value. It was widely seen as the beginning of the modern grassroots anti-tax movement.

Paul Harvey

333 N. Michigan Ave.
Chicago, IL 60601   **Phone:**   (312) 899-4000
USA   **Fax:**   (312) 899-4088

Contact Person: Paul Harvey.
Mission or Interest: One of America's leading news commentators.
Accomplishments: Mr. Harvey is also a very successful author and columnist, with over 100 of his broadcasts and columns reprinted in the Congressional Record. As a radio personality for over 50 years, he is the dean of conservative broadcasters appealing to a broad range of the American public opinion. His wife of 52 years, Lynn Cooper, whom he calls "Angel," is the producer of his nationally syndicated radio programs heard in every major U.S. market.

Pennsylvania Family Institute

3544 N. Progress Ave., Suite 104
Harrisburg, PA 17110   **Phone:**   (717) 545-0600
USA

Contact Person: Michael Geer, President.
Officers or Principals: Michael Geer, President ($46,229); Max Bingaman, Vice President ($0); Clyde W. Horst, Secretary ($0); James M. Herr, Chairman; Robert B. Hayward, Jr., Treasurer.
Mission or Interest: Promotion of pro-family public policy.
Accomplishments: In 1994 the Institute spent $196,892 on its programs.
Total Revenue: 1994 $281,097 30%(2) **Total Expenses:** $293,277 67%/18%/14% **Net Assets:** $18,719
Products or Services: Voter guides, research, conferences.
Tax Status: 501(c)(3)   **Citations:** 16:160
Board of Directors or Trustees: Raymond Speicher, Debra Cruel, James Krieder, Dr. Lisa Jenkins Cahill, Tony deCaro, Dr. and Mrs. Kevin Moore.
Periodicals: Newsletter.
Other Information: Established in 1989. The Institute received $274,434, or 98% of revenue, from contributions and grants awarded by foundations, businesses, and individuals. $6,394, or 2%, from conference registration fees. The remaining revenue came from interest on savings.

Pennsylvania Leadership Council (PLC)

225 State St., Suite 330
Harrisburg, PA 17101   **Phone:**   (717) 232-5919
USA   **Fax:**   (717) 232-1186

Contact Person: Gorden Blain, President.
Officers or Principals: Sean Duffy, former President ($47,168); Susan Staub, Secretary/Treasurer ($0); Frederick W. Anton, Chairman ($0); Gorden Blain, President.
Mission or Interest: Push for state-level reform of taxing, spending, and education in Pennsylvania. Helps other grassroots organizations.

Accomplishments: Helped derail legislative pay raise. Well-known opposition to teachers' unions. Expanded state "Sunshine Law," and sued entire State House Leadership for Sunshine Law violation. Their "Pennsylvania Leadership Conference" has attracted top names such as William Bennett, Newt Gingrich, columnist Robert Novak, Lynne Cheney, former U.N. Ambassador Alan Keyes and others. In 1994 the Council spent $177,793 on its programs.
Total Revenue: 1994 $192,631 15%(1) **Total Expenses:** $203,701 87%/10%/3% **Net Assets:** (-$7,391)
Products or Services: Lobbying. Report Card on Pennsylvania public education. "FastFax Network" that faxes news and updates to participants across the state. Presents the "Golden Paperclip Award" for outrageous abuses of taxpayers' money in Pennsylvania.
Tax Status: 501(c)(4) **Annual Report:** No. **Employees:** 4   **Citations:** 14:165
Board of Directors or Trustees: Guy Ciarrocchi, Tom Humbert, Ann Monteith, John Knoell, Charles Beckley, Eugene Hickok, Irma Zimmer, David Transue.
Periodicals: *The Right Word* (monthly), *Taxpayer Advocate* (quarterly), *Pennsylvania Education Review* (quarterly), *Business / Consumer Quarterly* (quarterly).
Internships: Yes. Wide variety of duties including lobbying, public relations, and publication editing.
Other Information: The Council received $170,133, or 88% of revenue, from contributors. $21,667, or 11%, from conference fees. The remaining revenue came from periodical subscriptions and interest on savings.

People for the West!
(see National Coalition for Public Lands and Natural Resources)

Pew Charitable Trusts
2005 Market St., Suite 1700
Philadelphia, PA 19103   **Phone:** (215) 575-9050
USA   **Fax:** (215) 575-4939   **Internet:** http://www.pewtrusts.com/

Officers or Principals: Rebecca W. Rimel, President; Nadya K. Shmavonian, Executive Vice President.
Mission or Interest: The Pew Charitable Trusts are one of the nation's largest philanthropies, with approximately $3.8 billion in assets shared by the seven member Trusts. The seven Trusts awarded approximately $180 million in 1995. The Trusts were founded by the Pew family, heirs to the Sun Oil Company founded by Joseph N. Pew. Joseph Pew's four children, Joseph Howard, Mary Ethel, Joseph Newton, and Mabel all endowed Trusts upon their deaths. Joseph Pew and his two sons were staunch capitalists, and the Trusts that bear their names, the J. Howard Freedom Trust and the J. N. Pew, Jr., Charitable Trust, were initially created to fund organizations promoting Christian values, hard work, and the free-enterprise system. Initially, these Trusts funded conservative and free-market organizations, but currently almost all such funding has ceased. In 1995 the Trusts awarded only $1.55 million in grants (0.08% of total awards) to three moderate/conservative organizations; $650,000 over three years for the Center for Strategic and International Studies, two grants totaling $500,000 over three years for the Council for Basic Education, and $400,000 over two years for the Hudson Institute's Educational Excellence Network. Numerous left-of-center organizations received grants.
Board of Directors or Trustees: Susan Catherwood, Thomas Langfitt, M.D., Robert McDonald, J. Howard Pew, II, J. N. Pew, III, Joseph Pew, IV, M.D., R. Anderson Pew, Richard Pew, William Richardson.

Philadelphia Society
105 W. Main St.
North Adams, MI 49262   **Phone:** (517) 287-4266   **E-Mail:** SPBL37A@Prodigy.com
USA   **Fax:** (517) 287-5814

Contact Person: Don Campbell, Secretary.
Officers or Principals: M. Stanton Evans, President; Barbara von der Heydt, First Vice President; James McClellan, Second Vice President; William F. Campbell, Secretary; David P. Stuhr, Treasurer; Daniel B. Hales, Assistant Secretary.
Mission or Interest: "To sponsor the interchange of ideas through discussion and writing, in the interest of deepening the intellectual foundations of a free and ordered society, and broadening the understanding of its basic principles and traditions. In pursuit of this end we shall examine a wide range of issues: economic, political, social, cultural and philosophic. We shall seek understanding, not conformity."
Accomplishments: Distinguished Members include: Dr. Glenn Campbell (Hoover Inst.), Prof. Milton Friedman, Dr. John A. Howard (Rockford Inst.), Prof. Gerhart Niemeyer, Francis A. O'Connell, Jr. Distinguished members who have died included Albert Campbell, F.A. Hayek, W.H. Hutt, Henry Regnery, Eliseo Vivas, and Eric Voegelin.
Tax Status: 501(c)(3)
Board of Directors or Trustees: Larry Arnn (Claremont Inst.), William Campbell, John Cooper, T. Kenneth Cribb, Jr. (Intercollegiate Studies Inst.), James Evans, Jeffrey Gayner, Annette Kirk, Forrest McDonald, Fernando Monterroso, Daniel Peters, Ronald Robinson, Bridgett Wagner.
Other Information: Established in 1964 by Don Lipsett (1930-95). Lipsett was active in the early post-World War II conservative movement and worked at *National Review* and *The Freeman*. He returned to his native Indiana, were he became the Intercollegiate Studies Institute's midwestern director. While active in Indiana, he was instrumental in organizing and connecting conservatives there and was key in introducing a small college publication at the University of Indiana, *The American Spectator*, to established writers and funding sources. Lipsett is also remembered for popularizing the Adam Smith necktie, which he sold through the Decatur Shop he ran with his wife Norma, that was worn by numerous members of the Reagan administration. In 1994-95 the Society received $15,000 from the Lynde and Harry Bradley Foundation, $15,000 from the Heritage Foundation, $10,000 from the John M. Olin Foundation, $10,000 from the Earhart Foundation, $5,000 from the Aequus Institute, $2,500 from the Roe Foundation, $2,000 from the Curran Foundation, and $1,500 from the Winchester Foundation.

Philanthropy Roundtable

1150 17th St., Suite 503
Washington, DC 20036   **Phone:** (202) 822-8333   **E-Mail:** philtable@aol.com
USA   **Fax:**   (202) 822-8325   **Internet:** http://philanthropyroundtable.org

Contact Person: Lara Y. Stead, Director, Associate Series.
Officers or Principals: John P. Walters, President; Whitney L. Ball, Executive Director; James F. X. O'Gara, Director of Research; Jessica L. Gavora, Director of Publications.
Mission or Interest: "To support America's pluralist system of private initiative, free institutions, and entrepreneurship through an enhancement of private philanthropy." Assists grantmakers in finding appropriate institutions to fund, and in insuring that the funds are used as intended. Conservative emphasis.
Accomplishments: In 1995 the Roundtable spent $151,946 on its programs. The largest program, with expenditures of $110,224, was the hosting of conventions and meetings "to promote innovative ideas for philanthropic giving." $41,482 was spent on the publication of *Philanthropy*. The rest was spent producing monographs.
Total Revenue: 1995 $587,176 10%(2) **Total Expenses:** $455,329 33%/67%/0% **Net Assets:** $649,071
Products or Services: Hold meetings for grant-makers, provide consulting services, publish monographs.
Tax Status: 501(c)(3) **Annual Report:** No. **Employees:** 5   **Citations:** 9:175
Board of Directors or Trustees: James Piereson (John M. Olin Found.), Joanne Beyer (Scaife Family Found.), Paul Rhoads (Grover Hermann Found.), David Kennedy (Earhart Found.), Chris Olander (J. M. Found.), Louise Oliver (George Coleman, Jr., Found.), Daniel Peters (Proctor & Gamble).
Periodicals: *Philanthropy* (quarterly).
Internships: Yes, to assist with research.
Other Information: Incorporated in 1991, after having operated since the late 1970's as part of the Institute for Educational Affairs. The Roundtable recently moved to the District of Columbia from Indianapolis, IN. The Roundtable received $513,750, or 85% of revenue, from contributions and grants awarded by foundations, businesses, and individuals. (These grants included $70,000 from the Lynde and Harry Bradley Foundation, $50,000 from the John M. Olin Foundation, $25,000 from the Smith Richardson Foundation, $25,000 from the leftist Tides Foundation, $16,000 from the Charles G. Koch Charitable Foundation, $10,000 from the William H. Donner Foundation, $10,000 from the Allegheny Foundation, $5,000 from the Castle Rock Foundation, $4,000 from the Roe Foundation, and $1,000 from the John William Pope Foundation. In 1994, $25,000 from the Sarah Scaife Foundation, $10,000 from the Earhart Foundation, $5,000 from the Grover Hermann Foundation, $5,000 from the Gilder Foundation, $5,000 from the F.M. Kirby Foundation, $3,474 from the Sunmark Foundation, and $1,000 from the Philip M. McKenna Foundation.) $56,545, or 10%, from conference fees. $14,940, or 3%, from interest on savings and temporary cash investments. $14,367, or 2%, from dividends and interest from securities. The remaining revenue came from the sale of publications, and other miscellaneous sources.

Philip M. McKenna Foundation

P.O. Box 186
Latrobe, PA 15650   **Phone:** (412) 537-6900
USA   **Fax:**   (412) 537-6906

Contact Person: T. William Boxx, Chairman.
Officers or Principals: T. William Boxx, Chairman ($31,748); Norbert J. Pail, Secretary/Treasurer ($0).
Mission or Interest: Grant-making foundation that focuses on conservative and free-market public policy organizations.
Accomplishments: In 1995 the Foundation awarded $914,670. Recipients included: $122,500 for the Intercollegiate Studies Institute, $108,000 for the Commonwealth Foundation, $104,000 for St. Vincent College's Center for Economic and Policy Education, $75,000 for the Heritage Foundation,$38,000 for the Pennsylvanians for Effective Government Education Committee, $35,000 for the Capital Research Center, and $25,000 for the Claremont Institute.
Total Revenue: 1995 $1,515,204 **Total Expenses:** $1,087,088 **Net Assets:** $14,150,503 2%(2)
Tax Status: 501(c)(3)
Board of Directors or Trustees: Richard Larry, Zan McKenna Rich, Alex McKenna, Donald McKenna.
Other Information: The Foundation received $762,362, or 50% of revenue, from capital gains on the sale of securities. $450,935, or 30%, from dividends and interest from securities. $275,000, or 18%, from a grant awarded by the Katherine Mabis McKenna Foundation. The remaining revenue came from investments and other miscellaneous sources.

Phillips Foundation

7811 Montrose Rd.
Potomac, MD 20854   **Phone:** (301) 340-2100   **E-Mail:** jfarley@phillips.com
USA   **Fax:**   (301) 424-9245

Contact Person: John Farley.
Officers or Principals: Thomas L. Phillips, Chairman; Robert D. Novak, Director; Alfred S. Regnery, Director.
Mission or Interest: Foundation that offers fellowships to print journalists with less than five years' experience for a project of their choosing "focusing on journalism supportive of American culture and a free society." The Foundation's mission is, "to advance constitutional principles, a democratic society, and a vibrant free enterprise system."

Products or Services: Fellowships for young journalists - full-time $50,000 fellowships, and part-time $25,000 fellowships.
Tax Status: 501(c)(3)
Internships: No.
Other Information: Established in 1990. Thomas Phillips is the owner of Phillips publishing, which owns Eagle Publishing, which in turn owns Regnery Publishing, whose CEO is Phillips Foundation director Alfred S. Regnery. (See separate listing Regnery Publishing.)

Phoenix Enterprises

P.O. Box 1900
Arvada, CO 80001   **Phone:**   (303) 421-7619
USA

Contact Person: Fred Holden, President.
Mission or Interest: Educate the public on the adverse effects of the growing size and power of government.
Accomplishments: Mr. Holden has been recognized for his many books and articles, as well as his "Two Percent Solution," which would hold federal spending to an annual increase of 2%, balancing the budget in six years. He is also known for his work as Director of Economic Affairs and Director of Public Affairs Research at the Adolph Coors Company before he left to found Phoenix Enterprises. He also sits on the *Rocky Mountain News* Board of Economists.
Products or Services: Numerous articles, speaking engagements, talk radio appearances and two books, The Phoenix Phenomenon and Total Power of One in America.
Tax Status: For profit.

Phoenix Letter

4400 Loma Vista Dr.
Billings, MT 59106   **Phone:**   (406) 652-2355
USA   **Fax:**   (406) 656-3075

Contact Person: Anthony C. Sutton, D.Sc..
Mission or Interest: Publishes the *Phoenix Letter: A Report on the Abuse of Power*, a populist/conservative monthly newsletter.
Accomplishments: In print for over 16 years.
Tax Status: For profit.
Periodicals: *Phoenix Letter* (monthly newsletter).
Other Information: Published by the Liberty House Press, which also publishes the newsletter *Future Technology Intelligence Report*.

Pioneer Institute

85 Devonshire St., 8th Floor
Boston, MA 02109   **Phone:**   (617) 723-2277   **E-Mail:**   75374.6430@Compuserve.com
USA   **Fax:**   (617) 723-1880   **Internet:** http://www.his.com/~chyden/pithink

Contact Person: Robert Chatfield, Operations Manager.
Officers or Principals: James Peyser, Executive Director ($65,000); Lovett Peters, Chairman ($0); Morris Gray, Treasurer ($0).
Mission or Interest: "To change the intellectual climate in Massachusetts by promoting free-market solutions to public policy problems."
Accomplishments: In 1994 the Institute spent $349,804 on its programs. The largest program, with expenditures of $182,653, was the "Better Government Competition" - a contest for new ideas on reducing the state's government and saving taxpayers' money. The Institute awards research stipends to contest finalists with a demonstrated financial need. "Our annual Better Government Competition has saved Massachusetts over $200 million." Winners in 1995 included Massachusetts Attorney General Scott Harshbarger who proposed that the tort judgements for negligence decided against state agencies be paid out of the agency's budget, rather than a general fund, so as to make the agencies more responsible for their actions. Indianapolis Mayor Stephen Goldsmith proposed a method of pricing government services based on the private sector. William Mellor and John Kramer of the Institute for Justice proposed a deregulation plan for Boston taxicabs. Other winning proposals included community policing, wastewater reform, trucking deregulation, and more. $79,720 was spent publishing Agenda for Leadership, a book on public policy topics in Massachusetts. Other programs included the Charter School Resource Center that helps to set up charter schools, coordinates with businesses and foundations to sponsor the schools, assists in management, performs legal research, and researches policy. Also hosts programs focusing on special education in Massachusetts.
Total Revenue: 1994 $685,953 23%(5) **Total Expenses:** $601,217 58%/24%/18% **Net Assets:** $363,640
Products or Services: Numerous studies and publications, "Pioneer Papers" series.
Tax Status: 501(c)(3) **Annual Report:** Yes. **Employees:** 8   **Citations:** 86:72
Board of Directors or Trustees: Prof. Charles Baker, Sr. (Northeastern Univ.), James Carlin, Gerard Doherty (former Chair, Massachusetts Democratic Party), William Edgerly (Chair, Foundation for Partnerships), David Evans, Colby Hewitt (Chair, Health Action Forum of Greater Boston), Cindy Johnson, Thomas McDermott, Joseph McNay, Peter Nessen, John Rowe (Chair, Massachusetts Business Roundtable), Raymond Shamie (former Chair, Massachusetts Republican Party), Diana Spencer (Shelby Cullom Davis Found.), Thornton Stearns, Virginia Strauss (former Exec. Dir., Pioneer Inst.).

Internships: Yes.
Other Information: Established in 1988 by Lovett Peters, a businessman with a background in oil and gas. The Institute received $657,050, or 96% of revenue, from contributions and grants awarded by foundations, businesses, and individuals. (In 1995 these grants included $50,000 from the David H. Koch Charitable Foundation, and $1,000 from the Roe Foundation.) $11,730, or 2%, from the sale of publications. $8,655, or 1%, from luncheon fees. The remaining revenue came from other miscellaneous sources.

Plymouth Rock Foundation

Sandwich Rd.
Plymouth, MA 02360   **Phone:**   (508) 746-1120
USA

Contact Person: John G. Talcott, President.
Officers or Principals: Russell S. Walton, Program Director ($34,625); John G. Talcott, President ($0); Allen C. Emery, Treasurer ($0).
Mission or Interest: To promote biblical principles of government, education, and economics. "To preserve the facts concerning America's Christian heritage."
Accomplishments: "*FAC-Sheet* widely recognized as prime source of data regarding Biblical principles as they relate to contemporary issues. Books selected as among top 10 in Christian publishing. Developed Foundation's Christian Committees of Correspondence program in cities and towns throughout the U.S."
Total Revenue: 1994 $162,964 23%(2) **Total Expenses:** $160,209 **Net Assets:** (-$9,247)
Products or Services: "The Christian and Civil Government" video tape series. Books, periodicals, audio and video tapes. Seminars and workshops. Annual art and essay contests for high-school level Christian schools.
Tax Status: 501(c)(3) **Annual Report:** Yes. **Employees:** 4
Periodicals: *Letter From Plymouth Rock* (monthly), *The Correspondent* (monthly), and *FAC-Sheet* (occasional).
Other Information: The Foundation received $94,967, or 58% of revenue, from contributions and grants awarded by foundations, businesses, and individuals. $67,997, or 42%, from the sale of publications and videos.

Political Dynamite

P.O. Box 467939
Atlanta, GA 31146   **Phone:**   (800) 728-2288
USA   **Fax:**   (770) 399-0815

Contact Person: John Elvin, Editor-in-Chief.
Mission or Interest: Newsletter by the former "Inside the Beltway" columnist for the *Washington Times*, John Elvin.
Tax Status: For profit.
Periodicals: *Political Dynamite* (monthly newsletter).

Political Economy Research Center (PERC)

502 S. 19th Ave., Suite 211
Bozeman, MT 59715   **Phone:**   (406) 587-9591   **E-Mail:**   perc@perc.org
USA   **Fax:**   (406) 586-7555

Contact Person: Terry L. Anderson, Executive Director .
Officers or Principals: Monica Lane Guenther, Treasurer ($31,364); Terry L. Anderson, Executive Director ($6,000); Donald R. Leal, Senior Research Associate; P. J. Hill, Jane S. Shaw, and Richard L. Stroup, Senior Associates.
Mission or Interest: Research in applying free-market economics to environmental and natural resource issues.
Accomplishments: Greenpeace describes PERC's approach as; "Under PERC's 'free-market environmentalism alternative', market forces would fully regulate the rate of environmental preservation and destruction. Assure landowners of their constitutionally guaranteed 'property rights', and PERC promises that they'll voluntarily protect their own land to preserve its value." PERC hosted a conference bringing together environmental organizations and free-market think tanks. Participants included the Wilderness Society, National Wildlife Federation, World Resources Institute, Environmental Law Institute, Cato Institute, and the Competitive Enterprise Institute. Numerous appearances in the print and television media. In 1995 PERC spent $371,829 on its programs. $253,741 was spent on various educational projects, and $118,088 was spent on conferences and seminars.
Total Revenue: 1995 $988,512 33%(2) **Total Expenses:** $816,269 46%/50%/4% **Net Assets:** $780,739
Products or Services: Free Market Environmentalism, Bureaucracy vs. Environment, Economics: Private and Public Choice, Natural Resources: Bureaucratic Myths and Environmental Management, and other books, conferences, fellowships and lectures.
Tax Status: 501(c)(3)   **Citations:** 28:137
Board of Directors or Trustees: Thomas Bray (Editorial Page Editor, *Detroit News*), Prof. Ryan Amacher (Univ. of Texas, Arlington), Jean Briggs (Asst. Managing Editor, *Forbes*), Dave Cameron (rancher), Kimberly Dennis (Philanthropy Roundtable), William Dunn, Lorents Grosfield, Thomas Magowan, Adam Meyerson (Vice Pres., Heritage Found.), E. Wayne Nordberg, Jerry Perkins, Leigh Perkins (CEO, Orvis Co.), Scott Rasmussen (North Carolina Term Limits), Hardy Redd (Charles Redd Found.), John Tomlin.

Periodicals: *PERC Reports, PERC Viewpoints.*
Other Information: Established in 1981. PERC received $965,446, or 98% of revenue, from contributions and grants awarded by foundations, businesses, and individuals. (These grants included $120,000 from the Claude R. Lambe Charitable Foundation, $68,000 from the E. L. Wiegand Foundation, $50,000 from the Lynde and Harry Bradley Foundation, $50,000 from the John M. Olin Foundation, $7,500 from the Ruth and Vernon Taylor Foundation, $5,000 from the John William Pope Foundation, $4,000 from the Roe Foundation, and $1,000 from the Magowan Family Fund. In 1994, $150,000 from the Sarah Scaife Foundation, $40,000 from the Lilly Endowment, and $15,000 from the Earhart Foundation.) $23,066, or 2%, from interest on savings and temporary cash investments.

Polyconomics Inc.

86 Maple Ave.
Morristown, NJ 07960   **Phone:**   (201) 267-4640
USA

Contact Person: Ronald De La Rosa, Administrative Manager.
Officers or Principals: Jude Wanniski, President.
Mission or Interest: Political and economic consulting for clients.
Products or Services: Consulting.
Tax Status: For profit.
Other Information: Established in 1978. Jude Wanniski is the author of The Way the World Works, and is an enthusiastic supply-sider who has worked for the editorial page of *The Wall Street Journal* and for Ronald Reagan's 1980 presidential campaign.

Population Renewal Office

36 W. 58th St.
Kansas City, MO 64113   **Phone:**   (816) 363-6980
USA

Contact Person: Frances Frech, Director.
Mission or Interest: "To reveal the fallacies of population control. . . but we've branched out into other causes. We supply, at no charge, information on population, abortion, AIDS, and teen pregnancy to students, teachers, journalists, and anyone else who wants it."
Accomplishments: "Piggy-backed" on other groups to attend three United Nations conferences and present papers. Given testimony at legislative hearings. Served as 'expert witnesses' for anti-abortion organizations.
Tax Status: Unincorporated.

Population Research Institute (PRI)

5119 A Leesburg Pike, Suite 295
Falls Church, VA 22041   **Phone:**   (540) 622-5240   **E-Mail:**   popri@ik.netcom.com
USA   **Fax:**   (540) 622-2728   **Internet:** http://www.pop.org

Contact Person: David Morrison, Associate Editor.
Officers or Principals: Steven W. Mosher, Executive Director.
Mission or Interest: "To articulate and promote authentic economic development through models which recognize the material and social benefits of moderate (population) growth. To make a case against the widely held, but fundamentally wrong-headed, development paradigm which places economic and population growth in opposition to each other. To document and publicize abuses of human rights in the name of population control."
Accomplishments: Op-eds have appeared in *The Wall Street Journal* and other publications.
Total Revenue: FY ending 9/95 $156,301
Products or Services: Articles, workshops, research, talks, debates.
Tax Status: 501(c)(3) **Employees:** 7
Board of Directors or Trustees: Advisors include: Lawrence Adekoya, KSS (Nigeria), Rene Bel, SSS (Benin), Siegried Ernst, M.D. (Germany), Hymie Gordon, M.D. (USA), Nestor Gregorini, M.D. (Argentina), Jaqueline Kasun, Ph.D. (USA), Jerome Lejeune, M.D., Ph.D. (France), Claude Newbury, M.D. (South Africa), Marie Mignon Mascarenhas, MBBS, DPH, MFCMRCP (India), Peggy Norris, MB, BCh (United Kingdom), Charles Rice, Esq. (USA), Michael Schooyans, Ph.D., PhLD, STD (Belgium), Anthony Zimmerman, SVD, STD (Japan).
Periodicals: *PRI Review* (bimonthly academic newsletter).
Other Information: Incorporated under Human Life International. Executive director Mosher is the author of A Mother's Ordeal: One Woman's Fight Against One-Child China (HarperCollins, 1994).

Pragmatist

P.O. Box 392
Forest Grove, PA 18922   **Phone:**   (215) 794-8368
USA

Contact Person: Jorge Amador, Editor.

Officers or Principals: Hans Schroeder, Publisher.
Mission or Interest: *The Pragmatist* promotes libertarianism and the benefits of free markets and social tolerance. They explore alternatives to all government services and combine an "unashamed free-market approach with concern for the poor."
Products or Services: Occasional issue papers and article reprints.
Tax Status: Not exempt.
Periodicals: *The Pragmatist* (bimonthly magazine).
Other Information: Established in 1983.

Prison Fellowship International

P.O. Box 17500
Washington, DC 20041   **Phone:**   (703) 478-0100
USA   **Fax:**   (703) 478-0452

Contact Person: Charles W. Colson, Chairman.
Officers or Principals: Ronald Nikkel, President ($75,233); Frank J. Lofaro, Executive Director ($55,000); Ivan Sotirov, Director, Eastern Europe ($50,088); Charles Colson, Chairman; Mernardo Jimenez, Vice Chairman; Jaime Crosby, Treasurer; Paul Kuck, Secretary; Sir Mari Kapi, Chairman, International Council.
Mission or Interest: A ministry founded by Chuck Colson, the former aide to President Nixon, dedicated to the task, "that all those involved in and directly impacted by crime will experience the grace and peace of Jesus Christ." Actively involved with conservative religious organizations.
Accomplishments: In 1994 the Fellowship spent $1,428,918 on its programs.
Total Revenue: 1994 $1,898,791 28%(1) **Total Expenses:** $1,792,793 80%/17%/3% **Net Assets:** $347,377
Products or Services: Numerous ministries for prisoners, such as bible studies, periodic in-prison seminars, pen-pal programs, more. Hosts the "BreakPoint" radio show.
Tax Status: 501(c)(3)   **Citations:** 334:28
Board of Directors or Trustees: David Hajjar (Director, Middle East), Timothy Khoo (Director, Asia), Gregory Strong, M. Balakrishnan (Sri Lanka), Angus Creighton (Scotland), Allan Curtis (New Zealand), Richard Hudson (Canada), Carl Lam (Hong Kong), Simon Nandjui (Cote d'Ivoire), Silvio Marques Neto (Brazil), Herve Odermatt (France), Oscar Oqueli (Honduras), S. K. Parmar (India), Tom Pratt, Eva Sanderson (Zambia), Reg Worthy (Australia).
Other Information: Prison Fellowship is a member of the Evangelical Council for Financial Accountability. The Fellowship received $1,150,653, or 61%, from membership dues. $733,502, or 39%, from contributions and grants awarded by foundations, businesses, and individuals. (These grants included $60,000 from the Richard & Helen DeVos Foundation, $4,500 from the DeWitt Families Conduit Foundation, $1,200 from the Amy Foundation.) The remaining revenue came from interest on savings, and other miscellaneous sources.

Privacy Journal

P.O. Box 28577
Providence, RI 02908   **Phone:**   (401) 274-7861
USA

Contact Person: Andrea Blair.
Officers or Principals: Robert E. Smith, Publisher.
Mission or Interest: Independent monthly publication on privacy in a computer age. Focus on how to keep personal information private and out of the hands of various government agencies, credit companies, etc.
Products or Services: Privacy: How to Protect What's Left of It, Workrights, and other books and publications.
Tax Status: For profit. **Annual Report:** No.
Internships: *Privacy Journal* (monthly journal).

Private Enterprise Research Center

Texas A&M University
459 Blocker Building
College Station, TX 77843   **Phone:** (409) 845-7559   **E-Mail:** PERC@tamu.edu
USA   **Fax:**   (409) 845-6636   **Internet:** http://www.tamu.edu/perc/

Contact Person: Thomas R. Saving, Director.
Officers or Principals: Leslie Appelt, Chairman; Thomas R. Saving, Director.
Mission or Interest: "Established to study the elements of the great American experiment in individual freedom which produced the economic miracle that is the United States of America." Conducts research and assists educators at all levels in teaching about private enterprise and a market economy.
Accomplishments: Fifteen years of research on important public-policy issues. They have sponsored programs on public policy at the state, national and worldwide level.
Products or Services: Research working papers.

Tax Status: 501(c)(3) **Annual Report:** No.
Board of Directors or Trustees: Dr. Edwin Feulner, Jr. (Heritage Found.). Sen. Phil Gramm (R-TX).
Periodicals: *PERCspectives* (quarterly newsletter).
Internships: No.
Other Information: Established in 1977. The Center operates independently of any college on the Texas A&M campus, but reports to the Office of the Provost of Texas A&M and is incorporated under the Universities 501(c)(3) status. It was previously known as the Center for Education, Research and Free Enterprise.

Privatization Research Organization
Center for Management, Baruch College / CUNY
17 Lexington Ave.
New York, NY 10010   **Phone:** (212) 447-3550
USA   **Fax:**   (212) 447-3574

Contact Person: Dr. E. S. Savas, Director.
Mission or Interest: Research and dissemination of information on privatization.
Accomplishments: Professor Savas' book, <u>Privatization: The Key to Better Government</u>, has been published in: English, Spanish, French, Portuguese, Greek, Arabic, Indian, Urdu, Polish, Hungarian, Russian, Bulgarian, Turkish, and Serbo-Croation. Further Eastern European and a Chinese translation are expected.
Products or Services: Numerous research products have been published, including: <u>Privatization for New York: Competing for a Better Future</u>, which was edited by Dr. Savas and prepared for the New York State Senate, <u>The Private Sector in Public Transportation in New York City: A Policy Perspective</u> and <u>A Comparative Study of Public and Private Bus Operations in New York City</u>, as well as others.
Tax Status: 501(c)(3) **Annual Report:** Yes.
Other Information: Incorporated as a part of the City University of New York.

Pro-Family Forum
P.O. Box 8907
Fort Worth, TX 76124   **Phone:** (817) 531-3605
USA

Contact Person: Lottie Beth Hobbs, President.
Officers or Principals: Kate Houlihan, Treasurer; Lottie Beth Hobbs, President.
Mission or Interest: Pursues traditional values from a Christian perspective. Special focus on alerting families to 'New Age' teachings in schools.
Accomplishments: Members in all 50 states. Primary organizer of the Pro-Family Rally held in the Astro-Arena in Houston attended by approximately 20,000.
Products or Services: Numerous books, cassette tapes, video tapes, newsletter.
Tax Status: Nonprofit.
Periodicals: *The Family Educator* (bimonthly newsletter).
Other Information: Established in 1975. Lottie Beth Hobbs is an acclaimed author and speaker. Among her accolades are: Honorary citations in Personalities of America and Outstanding Personalities of the Southwest. Awarded The Outstanding Christian Literature Award. Voted Woman of the Year by Women for Constitutional Government. Cited by the Fort Worth Press Club as an Outstanding Female Newsmaker of the year in 1977. Appointed to President Reagan's Commission on Family Matters.

Pro-Life Action League
6160 N. Cicero Ave., Suite 210
Chicago, IL 60646   **Phone:** (312) 777-2900
USA   **Fax:**   (312) 777-3061

Contact Person: Joseph Scheidler, Chairman.
Officers or Principals: Joseph M. Scheidler, Chairman ($52,800); Ann Scheidler, Secretary ($20,193); Elizabeth Lewis, Treasurer ($0).
Mission or Interest: Development of active strategies and techniques for stopping abortion.
Accomplishments: Joe Scheidler is recognized by most as one of the top anti-abortion figures. Operation Rescue's Randall Terry says, "The Pro-Life Action League and Joe Scheidler are a tremendous inspiration to pro-life activists everywhere." In the fiscal year ending May 1995 the League spent $193,875 on its programs. The League specializes in "sidewalk counseling" at abortion clinics.
Total Revenue: FY ending 5/95 $341,021 (-4%)(2) **Total Expenses:** $344,014 56%/35%/8% **Net Assets:** $12,318
Products or Services: "Meet the Abortion Providers," a video featuring former abortionists who now oppose the procedure. <u>Closed: 99 Ways to Stop Abortion</u>, a book of strategies and tactics. Annual "Protector" award. Many Brochures.
Tax Status: 501(c)(3) **Annual Report:** No. **Employees:** 6   **Citations:** 60:91
Board of Directors or Trustees: Elizabeth Lewis, Tonnasine Romano.

Periodicals: *Action News* (quarterly newspaper).
Internships: No.
Other Information: Established in 1980. The League received $304,555, or 88% of gross revenue, from contributions and grants awarded by foundations, businesses, and individuals. $41,747 net, or 12%, from special fund-raising events. The remaining revenue came from dividends and interest from securities. The League lost $5,460 net on the sale of inventory.

Pro-Life Action Ministries

1163 Payne Ave.
St. Paul, MN 55101   **Phone:**   (612) 771-1500
USA

Contact Person: William Rush, President.
Officers or Principals: Gil Mathews, Vice President ($0); Greg Troy, Treasurer ($0); Paul Bernabei, Secretary ($0).
Mission or Interest: Minnesota anti-abortion organization.
Accomplishments: In the fiscal year ending June 1995, the Ministries spent $141,218 on its programs. The largest program, with expenditures of $63,548, was the production of educational materials. $42,365 was spent on "sidewalk counseling and exercise of constitutional liberties educating the public." Other programs included public speaking engagements and attendance at conventions and fairs.
Total Revenue: FY ending 6/95 $131,651 **Total Expenses:** $155,008 91%/7%/2% **Net Assets:** $13,870
Tax Status: 501(c)(3)
Periodicals: Newsletter.
Other Information: The Ministries received $128,487, or 98% of revenue, from contributions and grants awarded by foundations, businesses, and individuals. (These contributions and grants have been decreasing by an average of 21% over the last five years.) $3,095, or 2%, from the sale of educational materials. The remaining revenue came from interest on savings.

Pro-Life Alliance of Gays and Lesbians (PLAGAL)

P.O. Box 33292
Washington, DC 20033   **Phone:** (202) 223-6697   **E-Mail:** plagalone@aol.com
USA   **Fax:**   (202) 265-9737

Contact Person: Philip Arcidi, President.
Mission or Interest: "To advance the pro-life cause in the lesbian, gay, and bisexual community." They compare the treatment of the fetus by abortion to the frequent treatment of homosexuals; that is because they are seen as less than human "they are denied the basic human rights of life, liberty and the pursuit of happiness." A particular concern of theirs; "If, as recent scientific discoveries suggest, homosexuality has a genetic basis, the day is not far off when doctors will be able to determine if a child is predisposed to be gay. Once medical science achieves this ability, it will be possible. . .by legal, surgical procedure. . .to eliminate lesbians and gays once and for all."
Accomplishments: They have been able to bring an anti-abortion message to people and organizations that would normally not listen to a pro-life organization. Hosted information booths at parades and conventions. "We have taken a lead in exposing the link between abortion and breast cancer. We have uncovered and challenged the diversion of funds from various 'AIDS Walks' to abortion providers." Mailing list of over 550 members.
Products or Services: Annual meeting.
Tax Status: 501(c)(3) **Annual Report:** No. **Employees:** All volunteer.
Periodicals: *PLAGAL Memorandum* (monthly newsletter).
Internships: No.
Other Information: Established in 1990 as Gays Against Abortion. Name changed in 1991. Their motto, "Human rights start when human life begins."

Pro-Life Council of Connecticut (PLCC)

411 Townsend Ave.
New Haven, CT 06512   **Phone:**   (203) 469-9185
USA

Contact Person: Regina Smith, Executive Director.
Officers or Principals: Regina Smith, Executive Director ($25,608); Sandra Bobowski, President ($0); Ken Kusmerski, Vice President ($0); Rosemarie Young, Secretary; Frances Calzetta, Treasurer.
Mission or Interest: Connecticut affiliate of National Right to Life Committee. "Supports human rights of everyone especially the unborn, the ill, the aged, and the mentally and physically handicapped."
Total Revenue: 1993 $59,138 **Total Expenses:** $52,164 **Net Assets:** $18,497
Products or Services: Books, films, video and audio cassettes.
Tax Status: 501(c)(3)
Board of Directors or Trustees: Pasquale Pepe, Catherine Foley, Margaret Curtin, David McElroy, Salvatore Aresco, Carol Zukowski, Barbara Pierolo, Linda Hardgrove, Most Rev. Walter Curtis, Eileen Lussier, Mary Ellen Pascale, Marilyn Kosche, Cathy Campbell.
Other Information: The Council received $58,999, or 99.6% of revenue, from contributions and grants awarded by foundations, businesses, and individuals. The remaining revenue came from interest on savings.

Pro-Life Minnesota

P.O. Box 18874
Minneapolis, MN 55418
USA

Contact Person: Mary Ann Kuharski, President.
Officers or Principals: John H. Kuharski, Treasurer ($0); Dorothy Fleming, Vice President ($0); Michael Fleming, Secretary ($0).
Mission or Interest: Minnesota anti-abortion organization, "promot(ing) dignity and respect for all human life."
Accomplishments: In the fiscal year ending November 1995, Pro-Life Minnesota spent $350,261 on its programs. These included 130 presentations before a total audience of approximately 32,000; eight types of brochures produced and a total of 23,000 were distributed; funded crisis pregnancy clinics; placed educational messages on 516 billboards state-wide; placed ads on 16 television stations and numerous newspapers state-wide.
Total Revenue: FY ending 11/95 $308,495 **Total Expenses:** $350,261 87%/2%/10% **Net Assets:** $12,723
Tax Status: 501(c)(3)   **Citations:** 2:216
Other Information: Pro-Life Minnesota received $307,195, or 99.6% of revenue, from contributions and grants awarded by foundations, businesses, and individuals. (These contributions and grants have been growing by an average of 14% per year over the last five years.) The remaining revenue came from interest on savings.

Progress & Freedom Foundation

1250 H St., N.W., Suite 550
Washington, DC 20005   **Phone:**   (202) 484-2312   **E-Mail:** mail@pff.org
USA   **Fax:**   (202) 484-9326   **Internet:** http://www.pff.org

Contact Person: Eric Michael.
Officers or Principals: Jeffrey A. Eisenach, President; Bethany A. Noble, Vice President; George Keyworth, II, Ph.D., Chairman.
Mission or Interest: "Dedicated to creating a positive vision of the future founded in the historic principles of the American idea." The Foundation recently created the Center for Effective Compassion. The Center seeks to help the needy through a "people-focused approach that is personal, challenging and spiritual." Their approach is heavily based on the work of Senior Fellow and co-founder Dr. Marvin Olasky as typified in his book The Tragedy of American Compassion (Regnery 1994). The Center is Chaired by Senior Fellow Arianna Huffington. They intend to publish the philanthropic habits of public officials, entertainers, and others in the public eye. If the practice of the person in question is different from their public pronouncements, (i.e., they criticize the government and taxpayers for not doing enough while they personally donate little) they will be placed on a "Hypocrisy Index." The expected budget for the Center is $750,000 for the first 12 months beginning in September 1995.
Accomplishments: The Foundation's president, Jeffrey Eisenach is a close advisor to House Speaker Newt Gingrich. In the first six months of 1995 the Foundation has received revenues of $1.3 million. This compares to $1.7 million in its first two years of existence. Their goal is $6 million in a year. The Foundation has received much attention for its plan to eliminate the Federal Communications Commission (FCC) and let businesses own parts of the radio spectrum; buying, selling or leasing them like real estate.
Total Revenue: 1995 $3,000,000 (est.)
Products or Services: The Foundation distributes tapes of Newt Gingrich's televised academic course series "Renewing American Civilization." Tapes of the 1993 and 1994 course offerings are available. These courses are the broadcasts of ten-week, academic-credit classes taught by Congressman Newt Gingrich at Reinhardt College in Waleska, Georgia. The Foundation also hosts conferences for volunteer teachers who will use the video course to teach different audiences. The course can also be seen on National Empowerment Television. The Progress & Freedom Foundation also produces a show called "The Progress Report" for National Empowerment Television.
Tax Status: 501(c)(3) **Annual Report:** No. **Employees:** 10
Board of Directors or Trustees: Frank Hanna, III (CEO, HBR Capital), Arianna Huffington (author, The Fourth Instinct), R. Mark Lubbers (Senior Vice Pres., Corporate Affairs, Associated Group), James Miller, III (Counsel, Citizens for a Sound Economy), William Roesing (Vice Pres., Public Policy, Joseph E. Seagram & Sons). Senior Fellows include: Prof. Michael Block (Univ. of Arizona), heads the "Competition in Electric Power" project, Jane Fortson, Finance and Urban Development, Heather Higgins, Director of the Council on Culture & Community, Thomas Lenard, Director of Regulatory Studies, William Myers, Director of Programs and Activities, Marvin Olasky, Michael Vlahos, Foreign Policy, Hon. Vin Weber, Domestic Politics.
Periodicals: Future Insight.
Internships: Yes. Unpaid research interns accepted.
Other Information: The Foundation has been caught in the center of the controversy surrounding House Speaker Gingrich's ethics. Critics maintain that Gingrich's course, Renewing American Civilization, was funded as a 501(c)(3) project with tax-deductible money, then used to build support for the Republican Party, an activity prohibited by tax laws governing organizations with 501(c)(3) status. Critics also point out that the course received funding from GOPAC, a political action committee, (about whose involvement the Speaker and his lawyer had given conflicting evidence to Congress) and cite this as evidence of party building. Defenders of the program maintain that the course promoted ideals, not a partisan strategy, many 501(c)(3) organizations promote a political philosophy, and that the Speaker avoided any overt promotion of his party. In 1994-95 the Foundation received $80,000 from the John M. Olin Foundation, $60,000 from the Lynde and Harry Bradley Foundation, $10,000 from the Charles G. Koch Charitable Foundation, and $5,000 from the Samuel Roberts Noble Foundation.

Project 21
(see the National Center for Public Policy Research)

Project for the Republican Future (PRF)
1150 17th St., N.W., 5th Floor
Washington, DC 20036   **Phone:**   (202) 293-4900
USA

Contact Person: James Pitts, Vice President.
Officers or Principals: William Kristol, Chairman ($130,000); James Pitts, Vice President ($80,000); Jennifer Komosa, Treasurer ($32,500); Jay P. Lefkowitz, Secretary.
Mission or Interest: Think tank devoted to influencing Republican strategies.
Accomplishments: PRF and Kristol played a part in the health-care debate by encouraging Republicans to take the position that there is no health-care crisis, at least not one serious enough to destroy the current system. They have also published influential works on how the party should handle the abortion issue. In 1994 the Project spent $940,016 on its programs.
Total Revenue: 1994 $1,053,814 **Total Expenses:** $1,130,072 83%/16%/1% **Net Assets:** $240,890
Products or Services: "Town Meetings." Research.
Tax Status: 501(c)(4)   **Citations:** 2:216
Board of Directors or Trustees: Virginia Gilder, Michael Joyce (Lynde and Harry Bradley Found.), Thomas Rhodes (*National Review*).
Other Information: Established in 1993. William Kristol is the son of key neo-conservative Irving Kristol and historian Gertrude Himmelfarb. He served as chief-of-staff for Vice President Quayle, where he created and over-saw the Competitiveness Council. The PRF grew out of the now defunct Bradley Project on the 90's, also chaired by Kristol. The Project received $1,046,997, or 99% of revenue, from contributors. The remaining revenue came from interest on savings, and other miscellaneous sources.

Property Rights Foundation of America
P.O. Box 75
Stony Creek, NY 12878   **Phone:**   (518) 696-5748
USA

Contact Person: Carol W. LaGrasse, President.
Officers or Principals: Carol W. LaGrasse, President ($0); Bruce Dederick, Vice President ($0); Robert Prentiss, Director ($0).
Mission or Interest: "To defend and enhance the Constitutional right to own and use private property." Special focus on New York state.
Accomplishments: Called attention to the methods used by 'land trusts', such as the Nature Conservancy and the Trust for Public Land, whereby governments purchase land through these organizations without going through the process of public hearings and meetings subject to the Freedom of Information Act. Rep. Richard Pombo (R-CA) said to the Foundation, "It is important that we can call on an unbiased source such as you and count on the reliability of your information. The staff values your articles on private property rights issues." New York State Senate Vice President Pro Tempore Owen Johnson said, "since you formed The Property Rights Foundation of America the public debate in New York on property rights issues has been elevated to a higher level." In 1995 the Foundation spent $51,971 on its programs.
Total Revenue: 1995 $53,372 **Total Expenses:** $55,464 **Net Assets:** $3,799
Products or Services: Annual conference since 1995. Annual award for "Defenders of Property Rights." Rep. Gerald Solomon (R-NY) was the first recipient. Lobbying: in 1995 the Foundation spent $529 on lobbying.
Tax Status: 501(c)(3) **Employees:** All volunteer.
Board of Directors or Trustees: Advisory Board includes: Nate Dickinson, Arleen Hanson (No Wolf Option Committee), Marilyn Haymen (Citizens for Responsible Zoning and Landowner Rights), Kenneth McCasland, John McClaughry (Ethan Allen Inst.), Kay Nordyke (Colusa County, CA, Supervisor), Larry Peterson (Protect America's Rights and Resources), Margery Pinkerton, Scott Robbins (Vice Chair, Michigan Forest Resources), Guy Shefstead, Leon Somerville, Jr., John and Sandra Wall.
Periodicals: *New York Property Rights Clearinghouse* (quarterly newsletter), and *Positions on Property* (quarterly journal).
Other Information: Established in 1994. The Foundation received $43,465, or 81% of revenue, from contributions and grants awarded by foundations, businesses, and individuals. (These contributions and grants increased 150% over the Foundation's initial year.) $9,753, or 18%, from programs services including conference fees and the sale of publications. The remaining revenue came from investment income and other miscellaneous sources.

Protecting Marriage
22 Mountainview Trail
Chadds Ford, PA 19317   **Phone:**   (610) 459-8474
USA   **Fax:**   (610) 348-3432

Contact Person: Phyllis H. Witcher, President.
Officers or Principals: Marty Stevensin, Program Director; Dr. Douglas Herrmann, Secretary/Treasurer.

Mission or Interest: "Pledged to end the divorce plague." Challenging the current 'no-fault' divorce laws in the United States. Witcher contends that current 'no-fault' laws allow the dissolution of the marriage contract when only one party wants the dissolution. Under no other contract law is that allowed without penalty. Since the party not wanting dissolution may not challenge the breaking of the contract, Witcher contends that they are denied due process. She maintains that the ease of these one sided 'no-fault' laws have created an atmosphere that encourages divorce and that the legal system has set up "wife disposal laws." Witcher was divorced under no-fault laws and has challenged her "erasure of constitutional due process" in the Pennsylvania courts.
Accomplishments: In the last four years Phyllis Witcher has given more than eighty interviews nationwide. Her correspondence has been published in legal journals. Her lawsuit challenging her own no-fault divorce was aided by the Free Congress Foundation who set up a fund to help pay for her appellate litigation. The Men's Defense Association followed her case closely. Chuck Colson of *Break Point* has written about her crusade. In addition to finding a niche in the family values movement, Witcher's efforts have received support from states' rights advocates, to help reverse the existing federal laws that "were intended to fertilize the divorce rate juggernaut."
Tax Status: 501(c)(3)
Board of Directors or Trustees: Mr. & Mrs. Thomas McMullin, Capt. Peter Fullinsider, USNR, Dr. Douglas Herrmann (Indiana State Univ.), Carole Hessler, Peter Weyrich (Free Congress Found.), Michael Schwartz (Progress & Freedom Found.), William Reil, Gary Robinson.
Other Information: Established in 1992.

Public Advocate of the United States

5613 Leesburg Pike, Suite 9
Falls Church, VA 22041   **Phone:**   (703) 845-1808
USA

Contact Person: Eugene Delguadio, Executive Director.
Officers or Principals: Ronald W. Pearson, President ($0); Charles Floto, Secretary ($0); William McCarthy, Director ($0).
Mission or Interest: "To expose and fight federal government waste, fraud, and abuse. To drive corrupt officials from office."
Accomplishments: Media coverage of highly visible protests against Sen. Ted Kennedy (D-MA) (dressing in scuba gear and calling themselves the "Ted Kennedy Swim Team"), Rep. Barney Frank (D-MA) (forming a "house-sitting" squad after it was revealed that Frank's lover had used the congressman's house for prostitution), former House Speaker Jim Wright, Gov. Michael Dukakis, and others. In 1995 the organization spent $667,796 on its programs.
Total Revenue: 1995 $962,938 16%(5) **Total Expenses:** $931,220 72%/5%/23% **Net Assets:** $73,164
Products or Services: "Take No Prisoners" video tape, demonstrating how to gain media attention.
Tax Status: 501(c)(4) **Employees:** 1   **Citations:** 0:233
Other Information: Although not compensated directly by the organization, Eugene Delguadio owns the for profit Eugene Delgaudio & Associates, Inc. The Associates were paid $80,000 for service provided during the year, including rent and utilities. Public Advocate received $928,823, or 96% of revenue, from contributors. $34,115, or 4%, from royalties.

Public Interest
(see National Affairs)

Public Interest Institute

600 N. Jackson
Mt. Pleasant, IA 52641   **Phone:**   (319) 385-3462   **E-Mail:** piiatiwc@seiowa.net
USA   **Fax:**   (319) 385-3799

Contact Person: Dr. Don Racheter, Executive Director.
Officers or Principals: David M. Stanley, President; I. Maurene Failor, Vice President/Secretary; Jeffrey R. Boeyink, Stanley M. Howe, Dr. Robert J. Prins, Vice Presidents; Jane A. Miller, Treasurer.
Mission or Interest: "Provide a forum for identifying practical solutions to critical national, state, and local issues." Focus on Iowa.
Accomplishments: Hosted a "Leadership Iowa Seminar" sponsored by the Iowa Association of Business and Industry. Publishes an annual "Statistical Profile of Iowa". Published a report showing that Iowa's government employees receive higher wages and salaries than private sector employees. In 1994 the Institute spent $309,190 on its programs.
Total Revenue: 1994 $521,337 **Total Expenses:** $340,276 91%/8%/1% **Net Assets:** $3,210,257
Tax Status: 501(c)(3) **Annual Report:** No. **Employees:** 5   **Citations:** 9:175
Periodicals: *Institute Brief* (monthly single-issue briefs), *Facts and Opinions* (quarterly newsletter), *Limits* (quarterly newsletter), *Imprint* (monthly newsletter), and *Iowa Economic Scorecard* (quarterly data sheet).
Internships: Yes.
Other Information: Located on the campus of Iowa Wesleyan College. In 1994 the Institute received $253,546, or 49% of revenue, from capital gains on the sale of securities. $127,050, or 24%, from contributions and grants awarded by foundations, businesses, and individuals. (In 1995 these grants included $5,000 from the Roe Foundation.) $95,620, or 18%, from dividends and interest from securities. $29,983, or 6%, from program services, including conference fees and a research grant. The remaining revenue came from membership dues, and interest on savings and temporary cash investments.

Public Policy Institute of New York State

152 Washington Ave.
Albany, NY 12210   **Phone:**   (518) 465-7511
USA

Mission or Interest: Public policy in New York state with a focus on deregulation and reduced taxation.
Accomplishments: A study titled "A Revolution in Regulation: New York Must Treat Employers as Customers to Compete for the Growth and Jobs We Need" was widely circulated and received media attention.
Tax Status: Nonprofit.

Public Service Research Council

527 E. Maple Ave., 3rd Floor
Vienna, VA 22180   **Phone:**   (703) 242-3575   **E-Mail:**   publicsr@erols.com
USA   **Fax:**   (703) 242-3579

Contact Person: David Denholm, President.
Officers or Principals: David Y. Denholm, President ($62,748); Carol Applegate, Chairman ($0); Rev. Frederick C. Fowler, Secretary/Treasurer ($0).
Mission or Interest: Focuses on the influence of organized labor on public policy with a special emphasis on public-sector unions.
Accomplishments: "Led the campaign for public support of President Reagan's firm handling of the PATCO strike. Filed the lawsuit in 1978 which prevented a nationwide Postal strike. Supported legislation which was enacted to prevent unionization of the armed forces. Delivered more than 1.5 million petitions to Congress demanding repeal of the Davis-Bacon Act." In the fiscal year ending September 1994, the Council spent $836,513 on its programs. The largest program, with expenditures of $321,282, was public information and legislative activities through its "Americans Against Union Control of Government" division. $299,897 was spent on membership services, and $215,334 on education and research.
Total Revenue: FY ending 9/94 $1,044,598 (-21%)(1) **Total Expenses:** $1,045,661 80%/8%/12% **Net Assets:** (-$107,624)
Tax Status: 501(c)(4) **Employees:** 6   **Citations:** 7:182
Board of Directors or Trustees: Louis Weiss, Jesse Smith, Jr., Eugene Frazier, George Whyte, George Boys.
Other Information: Established in 1973. Affiliated with the 501(c)(3) Public Research Foundation at the same address. The Council received $996,703, or 95% of revenue, from contributions and grants. $44,819, or 4%, from royalties on mailing lists and other materials. $3,076, or 1%, from dividends and interest from securities.

Public Service Research Foundation

527 E. Maple Ave., 3rd Floor
Vienna, VA 22180   **Phone:**   (703) 242-3575   **E-Mail:**   publicsr@erols.com
USA   **Fax:**   (703) 242-3579

Contact Person: David Denholm, President.
Officers or Principals: David Denholm, President.
Mission or Interest: Research and education affiliate of the Public Service Research Council.
Products or Services: Beyond Public Sector Unionism: A Better Way, book.
Tax Status: 501(c)(3) **Employees:** 6   **Citations:** 7:182
Periodicals: Government Union Review (quarterly journal).
Other Information: Affiliated with the 501(c)(4) Public Service Research Council at the same address.

Putting Liberty First (PLF)

13873 Park Center Rd., Suite 316
Herndon, VA 20171   **Phone:**   (703) 925-0881   **E-Mail:**   APC@Nicom.com
USA   **Fax:**   (703) 925-0991   **Internet:** http://www.americanPolicy.com

Contact Person: Tom DeWeese, President.
Officers or Principals: Kathleen Marquardt, Executive Director; Tom DeWeese, President; Carolyn Craig, Secretary.
Mission or Interest: "Libertarian educational foundation defending property rights, individual liberty, and opposing animal rights."
Accomplishments: "Exposed the Earth First-Unabomber connection. Forced President Clinton to back down on the threat to boycott Norway over Minke whaling. Got extremist Chris DeRose off TV's 'Hard Copy'." Convinced Northwest Airlines to resume shipment of lab animals. Defended hunters' rights and started "Hunters for the Hungry," a program which distributes venison, and other game meat, to the needy in 28 states. Greenpeace calls Kathleen Marquardt "the rising star of the Wise Use movement." Kathleen Marquardt was the "inspiration to William Perry Pendley (Mountain States Legal Foundation) for his book, It Takes A Hero."
Products or Services: Animal Scam by Kathleen Marquardt, "the first book to reveal the truth behind the activist's often deceptive claims. It exposes the threat they pose to the fundamental political, ethical, and religious values Americans cherish. Describes the consequences their terrorist actions have on science, medicine, health, our economy, food, and other aspects of life we take for granted."

Tax Status: 501(c)(3) **Annual Report:** No. **Employees:** 2
Periodicals: *Self Evident* (monthly newsletter).
Internships: No.
Other Information: Established in 1992 and formed by merging with Putting People First. Maintains a Montana office; P.O. Box 1707, Helena, MT 59601, phone (406) 442-5700, fax (406) 449-0942. Affiliated with the 501(c)(3) American Policy Foundation, 501(c)(4) American Policy Center, and the for-profit DeWeese Company.

Quality Education
Route 10, P.O. Box 52-A
Florence, SC 29501
USA

Contact Person: John T. Harllee, Editor.
Officers or Principals: Robert Brakeman, Associate Editor.
Mission or Interest: Publishes a newsletter that collects articles and cartoons from various sources to buttress a libertarian point of view. Freedom from "Damn Yankees and other oppressive governments."
Accomplishments: "Ridicule of public officials."
Products or Services: Harleian Miscellany Club, books, posters, postcards, bumper stickers.
Tax Status: Unincorporated.
Periodicals: *The Southern Libertarian Messenger.*   **Internships:** No.

Radio Free Europe / Radio Liberty Fund
1201 Connecticut Ave., N.W., Suite 1100
Washington, DC 20036   **Phone:** (202) 457-6900
USA   **Fax:** (202) 457-6997

Officers or Principals: E. Nicholas P. Gardiner, President ($0); Richard M. Schmidt, Jr., Secretary ($0); Michael R. Marchetti, Treasurer ($0); Leonard H. Marks, Chairman.
Mission or Interest: Provide funding for regular radio broadcasts to communist and formerly-communist countries.
Total Revenue: FY ending 6/94 $14,282 (-93%)(1) **Total Expenses:** $30,784 **Net Assets:** $116,427
Products or Services: Research projects. Visiting scholars.
Tax Status: 501(c)(3)
Board of Directors or Trustees: H. Ross Johnson, Kevin Klose, Robert Gillette, R.T. Curran.
Internships: Yes.
Other Information: The Fund received $7,536, or 53% of revenue, from investment income. $6,746, or 47%, from contributions and grants awarded by foundations, businesses, and individuals.

Rampart Institute
P.O. Box 22231
Carmel, CA 93922-0231
USA   **Phone:** (408) 624-2604

Contact Person: Lawrence Samuels, President.
Officers or Principals: Lawrence Samuels, President; Jane Heider, Secretary.
Mission or Interest: Radical libertarian thought. "An effort to privatize the world and make government obsolete."
Accomplishments: Organized the "Future of Freedom" series, published Robert LeFevre's book, The Fundamentals of Liberty.
Products or Services: Catalog of books and audio and video tapes.
Tax Status: 501(c)(3) **Employees:** All volunteers.
Board of Directors or Trustees: Lorne Strider, Harry Hoiles, Samuel Oglesby, Robert Ormsbee.
Periodicals: *Rampart Individualist.*
Other Information: Established in 1980.

Rational Conservative, The
R.R. 2, Box 6880
Fair Haven, VT 05743
USA   **Fax:** (802) 537-4362   **Internet:** 73641.175@compuserve.com

Officers or Principals: Valery Chalidze, Editor
Accomplishments: Monthly magazine of conservative news and opinion focusing on the role of private property and contract in a free society.
Tax Status: For profit. **Annual Report:** No.
Periodicals: *The Rational Conservative* (monthly magazine).
Other Information: Established in 1994. Mr. Chalidze has written several books and articles defending the rule of law and freedom. He was awarded a MacArthur Fellowship, and a Sakharov Fellowship from the Blaustein Institute. Self-published books include Hierarchical Instinct and Human Evolution, and Ethan and Ira Allen: Collected Works. These books and The Rational Conservative are published by Chalidze Publications.

Reagan Alumni Association

7212 Valon Ct.
Alexandria, VA 22307-2045
USA

Contact Person: Louis J. Cordia, Executive Director.
Mission or Interest: Appointees and campaign staff of President Ronald Reagan working to further the objectives and ideals that characterized the Reagan administration.
Products or Services: Publishes a directory of Reagan and Bush administration appointees that lists their current whereabouts and employment. Offers placement services for members.
Tax Status: For profit.
Periodicals: *Reagan Alumni Directory* (annual), *Reagan Alumni Newsletter* (periodic).
Other Information: Formerly Reagan Appointees Alumni Association. Louis Cordia is also the executive director of the Washington Executive Bank, at the same address. Cordia served in several different positions with the Reagan Administration, mostly with the EPA.

Reason Foundation / *Reason*

3415 Sepulveda Blvd., Suite 400
Los Angeles, CA 90034   **Phone:** (310) 391-2245   **E-Mail:** rich@reason.org
USA   **Fax:**   (310) 391-4395   **Internet:** http://www.reason.org/

Contact Person: Robert W. Poole, Jr., President.
Officers or Principals: Robert W. Poole, Jr., President ($104,487); Bryan E. Snyder, Executive Vice President ($91,904); P. Lynn Scarlett, Vice President, Research ($86,520); Virginia I. Postrel, Editor; Janet Levine, Development Director; William Eggers, Privatization Director; Janet Beales, Policy Analyst.
Mission or Interest: Libertarian research institute promoting a free society, including privatization and deregulation. Conducts privatization research on a consulting basis for local governments through a subsidiary, named the Local Government Center. Publishes *Reason* magazine.
Accomplishments: *Reason* has the highest circulation of any libertarian magazine with an average monthly circulation of over 45,000. Many of the Reason Foundation's plans for privatization and deregulation have been implemented at the state and local level. The Foundation is often considered the most effective libertarian group at producing 'nuts-and-bolts' strategies for reducing government. In the fiscal year ending September 1995, the Foundation spent $2,777,130 on its programs.
Total Revenue: FY ending 9/95 $3,353,184 12%(2) **Total Expenses:** $3,416,412 81%/6%/13% **Net Assets:** (-$471,816)
Tax Status: 501(c)(3)   **Citations:** 159:45
Board of Directors or Trustees: Bernard Baltic, Frank Bond, William Dunn, Manuel Klausner, David Koch (Chair., Citizens for a Sound Economy), Harry Teasly, Jr., Prof. Walter Williams (George Mason Univ.), Stina Hans.
Periodicals: *Reason* (monthly magazine), *Privatization Watch* (monthly newsletter), *Reason Report* (quarterly newsletter), and *Issue Paper*.
Other Information: Established in 1978. Contributing Editors to *Reason* include: Ronald Bailey (author, Eco-Scam: The False Prophets of Ecological Apocalypse), Prof. Thomas Hazlett (Univ. of CA, Davis), Prof. David Henderson (Naval Postgraduate School), John Hood (Vice Pres., John Locke Found.), Brink Lindsey (Cato Inst.), John McClaughry (Pres., Ethan Allen Inst.), Charles Oliver, Paul Craig Roberts (Center for Strategic and International Studies), Prof. Thomas Szasz (SUNY), William Tucker (writer, *Forbes*), Martin Morse Wooster, Cathy Young, others. The Foundation received $2,146,001, or 64% of revenue, from contributions and grants awarded by foundations, businesses, and individuals. (These grants included $131,400 from the Lilly Endowment, $100,000 from the David H. Koch Charitable Foundation, $85,000 from the Lynde and Harry Bradley Foundation, $75,000 from the Sarah Scaife Foundation, $64,680 from the Smith Richardson Foundation, $55,000 from the John M. Olin Foundation, $50,000 from the Claude R. Lambe Charitable Foundation, $42,201 from the William H. Donner Foundation, $15,000 from the Grover Hermann Foundation, $12,500 from the Gilder Foundation, $10,000 from the Gordon and Mary Cain Foundation, $5,000 from the Aequus Institute, $5,000 from the Alex C. Walker Foundation, $3,000 from the Roe Foundation, $3,000 from the Sunmark Foundation, and $1,000 from the Winchester Foundation.) $706,556, or 21%, from *Reason* subscriptions. $222,736, or 7%, from research income. $141,950, or 4%, from advertising income. $107,372, or 3%, from mailing list rentals. The remaining revenue came from interest on savings and other miscellaneous sources.

Reason Papers: A Journal of Interdisciplinary Normative Studies

MCB University Press Ltd.
60/62 Toller Lane
Bradford, BD8 9BY   **Phone:** (44-1274) 777-700
UNITED KINGDOM   **Fax:**   (44-1274) 785-200

Contact Person: Prof. Tibor R. Machan, Book Review Editor..
Officers or Principals: A journal of libertarian philosophy. Subject matter covers issues in moral, social, and political philosophy. Interdisciplinary in approach, the journal publishes the work of historians, sociologists, economists, psychologists and others.
Tax Status: For profit.
Periodicals: *Reason Papers* (annual academic journal).
Other Information: Books editor Dr. Tibor Machan is a professor of philosophy at Auburn University.

Regal Foundation

2300 Jetport Dr.
Orlando, FL 32809   **Phone:**   (407) 851-4360
USA

Contact Person: Carol Kuck, Secretary.
Officers or Principals: Paul Kuck, Chairman ($0); A. William Forness, Jr., Treasurer ($0); Carol Kuck, Secretary ($0).
Mission or Interest: Grant-making philanthropy focusing on religious, traditional-values, and anti-abortion organizations.
Accomplishments: In the fiscal year ending July 1993 the Foundation awarded $26,836 in grants Recipients included; $3,000 each for Focus on the Family and Prison Fellowship International, and $1,000 each for the American Family Association, Coral Ridge Ministries, Family Research Council, Florida Family Council, and Florida Right to Life Education Foundation.
Total Revenue: FY ending 7/93 $37,615 **Total Expenses:** $64,862 **Net Assets:** $20,497 (-27%)(4)
Products or Services: Mayor's Prayer Breakfast and Seminole County Prayer Breakfast featuring nationally renowned speakers.
Tax Status: 501(c)(3)
Board of Directors or Trustees: Jared Billings, W. Charles Stark.
Other Information: Established in 1984. Affiliated with Regal Marine Industries. The Foundation received $34,202, or 91% of revenue, from Prayer Breakfast receipts. $2,535, or 7%, from contributions from local organizations and businesses. The remaining revenue came from interest on savings. All assets were held in cash.

Regnery Publishing

422 First St., S.E.
Washington, DC 20003   **Phone:**   (202) 546-5005   **Internet:** http://www.townhall.com/eagle
USA

Officers or Principals: Alfred S. Regnery, CEO
Mission or Interest: Book publishing.
Accomplishments: Publishes books of particular interest to conservatives. Published the classic The Conservative Mind, by the late Russell Kirk. Regnery has recently had a string of strong successes. Starting with Guns, Crime, and Freedom by NRA executive Wayne LaPierre, Regnery has had several books make the bestseller lists. Unlimited Access by retired FBI agent Gary Aldridge reached number 1 on the *New York Times* bestseller list and stayed there several weeks. Boy Clinton by *American Spectator* editor R. Emmett Tyrell, Jr., reached the bestseller list. Most recently, Murder in Brentwood by Mark Fuhrman, a detective on the Nicole Brown Simpson murder case, reached number 1 on the *New York Times* bestseller list. Other recent titles include The Next War by former Secretary of Defense (1981-87) Casper Weinberger.
Tax Status: For profit. **Annual Report:** No. **Employees:** 15
Board of Directors or Trustees: Thomas Phillips (Eagle Publishing), William Lee Hanley, Jr.
Other Information: Previously called Regnery Gateway. Now owned by Eagle Publishing, Inc. (For more information, see Eagle Publishing, Inc.)

Religion and Society / *St. Croix Review*

P.O. Box 244
Stillwater, MN 55082   **Phone:**   (612) 439-7190
USA   **Fax:**   (612) 439-7017

Contact Person: Argus MacDonald, Ph.D., Editor/Publisher.
Officers or Principals: Dr. O. Guy Johnson, Chairman.
Mission or Interest: Publishes *The St. Croix Review*, a journal that serves as a clearing house for a number of think tanks in an attempt to publish the best and most influential studies and articles.
Accomplishments: Nobel Laureate Milton Friedman says, "*The St. Croix Review* is an extension of the basic values and high standards of its editor. They make it a unique, and uniquely valuable, journal."
Tax Status: 501(c)(3) **Annual Report:** Yes. **Employees:** 3
Board of Directors or Trustees: William & Kay Hempel, Richard Herreid, Jack & Joyce Hooley, Marilyn Johnson, James & Sharon Lammers, Rema MacDonald, Gregor MacDonald, Mitzi Olson.
Periodicals: *St. Croix Review*.
Internships: No.
Other Information: Established in 1968.

Religious Heritage of America

1750 S. Brentwood Blvd., Suite 502
St. Louis, MO 63144   **Phone:**   (314) 962-0001
USA   **Fax:**   (314) 961-8716

Contact Person: Barbara J. Eichhorst, Executive Director.

Officers or Principals: Barbara J. Eichhorst, Executive Director ($13,869); Catherine Martini, Administrative Assistant ($2,070); Tommy P. Thompson, President ($0); Dr. William J. Simmons, Secretary; C.E. Harris, Treasurer; Ruth Dudley, Founder/Trustee.
Mission or Interest: "To help America reclaim the religious values upon which it was founded by demonstrating how these values add to the quality of life."
Accomplishments: Instrumental in the inclusion of the words "under God" in the Pledge of Allegiance and in establishing a National Day of Prayer.
Total Revenue: 1995 $25,228 (-41%)(2) **Total Expenses:** $33,675 **Net Assets:** (-$11,484)
Products or Services: Oratory contest for high school students. Annual awards for religious leaders, teachers, clergy, and active citizens. Since its establishment, over 700 people have been honored.
Tax Status: 501(c)(3) **Employees:** 2
Board of Directors or Trustees: Dr, Theodore Baehr (Christian Film and Television Commission); George Fernau (The Futures of America), Art Fleming, Sarah Belk Gambrell, C.E. Harris, J. Paul Klinger, John Latshaw, Carl Mays, Judy Moore (JM Productions), E. Raymond Parker, Gary Rieman, Dr. Arthur Sharron (Psycheconomics), Dr. William Simmons, W. Robert Stover.
Periodicals: *Religious Heritage of America Newsletter* (quarterly).
Internships: No.
Other Information: Established in 1951 as the Washington Pilgrimage, then changed to Religious Heritage of America in 1957. The organization received $25,795, or 97% of gross revenue, from contributions and grants awarded by foundations, businesses, and individuals. (These grants included $500 from the Richard & Helen DeVos Foundation.) The remaining revenue came from investment income. The organization lost $612 net on special fundraising events.

Religious Roundtable

P.O. Box 11467
Memphis, TN 38111   **Phone:**   (901) 458-3795
USA   **Fax:**   (901) 324-0265

Contact Person: Edward E. McAteer, President.
Officers or Principals: Edward E. McAteer, President ($11,160); John Beckett, Secretary/Treasurer ($0); Jack Stewart, Vice President ($0).
Mission or Interest: Coalition building between organized groups of religious conservatives.
Accomplishments: In 1994 the Roundtable spent $34,009 on its programs.
Total Revenue: 1994 $75,207 (-20%)(2) **Total Expenses:** $86,466 **Net Assets:** $11,809
Products or Services: Literature distribution, seminars, and rallies. Conservative issues information.
Tax Status: 501(c)(3) **Annual Report:** Yes. **Employees:** 5
Board of Directors or Trustees: T. O. Barnett, J. W. Bell, K. Q. Chedester, Nancy Leigh DeMoss, Robert Hackman, Ron Hale, E. V. Hill, Clifton Hollis, Ben Marshall, Mark Merrill, Lowry Shrader, Mark Siljander, Tom Snyder, Michael Valerio.
Periodicals: *The Roundtable Report*, and *The Roundtable Update*.
Internships: Have hired interns in the past. Write for information.
Other Information: Also serves as organizer for the "National Affairs Briefing," a convention first held in 1980, and repeated in 1992, in Dallas. The first was a water-shed event for what became known as the 'Religious Right'. They are affiliated with the 501(c)(4) Roundtable Issues & Answers, which is located at the same address with the same officers and directors. The Roundtable received $75,105, or 99.8% of revenue, from contributions and grants awarded by foundations, businesses, and individuals. The remaining revenue came from interest on savings.

Renaissance Foundation

205 3rd St., S.E.
Washington, DC 20003   **Phone:**   (205) 546-4142
USA   **Fax:**   (703) 790-0070

Officers or Principals: Nina May, Founder.
Mission or Interest: "Supports and promotes traditional family values and believes the right of a woman to stay home and raise children is just as important, as the right of a woman to compete openly and equally in the market place."
Accomplishments: Operates through its Renaissance Women project. Spokesmen for the group have testified before the Senate Foreign Relations Committee, the Platform Committee of the Republican National Conventions, and before the United Nations General Assembly.
Products or Services: Provides scholarships toward a two-year degree or trade school, with the support and assistance of the Virginia Department of Social Services, for women currently on welfare.
Tax Status: 501(c)(3)
Periodicals: *Paradigm 2000* (quarterly magazine).
Other Information: Established in 1983 as Renaissance Women. In 1989 the name was changed to Renaissance Foundation, and the original name was given to its primary program. The Foundation has an office in Seoul, South Korea.

Republican Coalition for Choice (RCFC)

P.O. Box 40070
Washington, DC 20016   **Phone:**   (202) 364-3446   **E-Mail:** rcfc@aol.com
USA   **Fax:**   (202) 362-4127

Contact Person: Susan R. Cullman, Director.
Mission or Interest: Organization of Republicans supporting abortion rights. Works to make abortion rights a part of the Republican platform.
Other Information: Established in 1989 by Mary Dent.

Republican Governors' Association (RGA)

310 1st St., S.E.
Washington, DC 20003   **Phone:**   (202) 863-8587
USA   **Fax:**   (202) 863-8820   **Internet:** http://www.rga.org

Contact Person: Brian Kennedy, Executive Director.
Mission or Interest: Coordinates the Republican Party and Republican Governors. Works directly with candidates.
Products or Services: Annual conference.
Other Information: Established in 1963.

Republican Liberty Caucus (RLC)

611 Pennsylvania Ave., S.E., Suite 370
Washington, DC 20003   **Phone:**   (202) 546-8749   **E-Mail:** rlc@rlc.org
USA   **Fax:**   same   **Internet:** http://www.rlc.org

Contact Person: T. Mike Griffin, Executive Director.
Officers or Principals: Clifford Thies, Ph.D., Chairman; Mike Holmes, Treasurer; Laura Kotelman, Secretary; Alan Turin, General Counsel; Tom Walls, State Liaison; Gregory Koontz, Congressional Liaison.
Mission or Interest: "The RLC represents the libertarian wing of the GOP. It assists libertarian Republican candidates (via its PAC) and in passing legislation which respects individual rights and restores limits on government power."
Accomplishments: Has affiliates in 26 states. Assisted in numerous political campaigns, mostly on the state legislative level. Recruited 12 Republican congressmen to its Advisory Board. Its PAC contributed over $17,000 to 23 candidates in 1996.
Board of Directors or Trustees: Roger MacBride, Rep. Helen Chenowith (R-ID), Rep. Brian Bilbray (R-CA), Rep. Mark Foley (R-FL), Rep. J.D. Hayworth (R-AZ), Rep. Sam Johnston (R-TX), Rep. Jack Metcalf (R-WA), Rep. Ron Paul (R-TX), Rep. Frank Riggs (R-CA), Rep. Matt Salmon (R-AZ), Rep. John Shadegg (R-AZ), Rep. Nick Smith (R-MI), Rep. Todd Tiahrt (R-KS), others.
Periodicals: *Republican Liberty* (quarterly + annual outreach issue).
Internships: Yes.
Other Information: Established in 1988. They see themselves as libertarians working within the GOP. They are not conservatives and disagree with conservatives on social issues such as drug legalization and abortion. Caucus Trustee Roger MacBride cast his 1972 vote as a Republican presidential elector for the Libertarian Party's candidate, John Hospers. This was the only electoral college vote ever received by a Libertarian candidate.

Republican National Coalition for Life (RNC/Life)

P.O. Box 618
Alton, IL 62002   **Phone:**   (214) 387-4160
USA   **Fax:**   (214) 387-3830

Contact Person: Colleen Parro.
Officers or Principals: Phyllis Schlafly, Founder.
Mission or Interest: Dedicated to preserving the Republican Party platform's "pro-life plank".
Accomplishments: In 1992 the Coalition delivered over 100,000 pledges of support for the plank, including 3,500 signatures from elected Republican officials. Successfully defended the plank in 1996.
Tax Status: 501(c)(4)
Board of Directors or Trustees: Gary Bauer (Family Research Council), Beverly LaHaye (Concerned Women for America), Morton Blackwell (Leadership Inst.), J. Patrick Rooney (Golden Rule Insurance), Marylin Shannon (Vice Chairman, GOP of Oregon), Jerome Urbik.
Other Information: Established in 1990 by Phyllis Schlafly. Mrs. Schlafly is the president of the Eagle Forum, which is located at the same address.

Republican National Committee (RNC)

310 1st St., S.E.
Washington, DC 20003   **Phone:**   (202) 863-8500   **E-Mail:**   72662.1234@compuserve.com
USA   **Fax:**   (202) 863-8820   **Internet:** http://www.rnc.org

Officers or Principals: Jim Nicholson, Chairman; Patricia Harrison, Co-Chairman; Howard Leach, National Finance Chairman.

Mission or Interest: The main objective of the RNC is to aid in the election of Republican candidates on federal, state and local levels.

Accomplishments: In 1994 the Republican Party won control of both houses of the national Congress. In 1996 the RNC broke its previous record for fundraising in a year, raising approximately $112.2 million. This came from approximately 1.2 million donors, 300,000 of whom were first-time donors.

Tax Status: Nonprofit political party. **Annual Report:** Yes. **Employees:** 375

Board of Directors or Trustees: The members of the Republican National Committee with three representatives from each state or territory.

Internships: Yes, Eisenhower Internship Program during summer months.

Other Information: Auxiliaries affiliated with the RNC are; College Republican National Committee, National Black Republican Council, National Federation of the Grand Order of Pachyderm Clubs, National Federation of Republican Women, National Republican Heritage Groups Council, Republican National Hispanic Assembly, Republicans Abroad International, and Young Republican National Federation.

Republican National Hispanic Assembly (RNHA)

600 Pennsylvania Ave., S.E., Suite 300
Washington, DC 20003   **Phone:**   (202) 662-1355
USA   **Fax:**   (202) 662-1408

Contact Person: Jaime Guzman-Fournier, Executive Director.

Officers or Principals: Cesar Gonzalez, Assistant Executive Director; Antonio Monroig, National Chairman; Grace Ramos, First Co-Chair; Manual Villalon, Second Co-Chair; Jose R. Santaballa, Treasurer; Jesus Lapera, Assistant Treasurer; Diana Dominguez-Weir, Secretary; Jose Charley Gomez, Assistant National Secretary.

Mission or Interest: Better government, fair voter registration, political education and communication, candidate recruitment, issue development, liaison to Hispanic organizations.

Accomplishments: Held its first annual convention in 1995. Recruited candidates for office, actively involved in the fast-track free trade approval for NAFTA, active fund raisers.

Tax Status: Not exempt. **Employees:** 1

Internships: No, but they are working on a scholarship database.

Other Information: Established in 1974 as a official auxiliary of the Republican National Committee. It was founded as an outgrowth of the Hispanic Finance Committee formed in 1972.

Republican Network to Elect Women (RENEW)

1555 King St.
Alexandria, VA 22313-0507   **Phone:**   (703) 836-2255   **Internet:** http://users.aol.com/gorenew/
USA

Contact Person: Karen Roberts, Co-Director.

Officers or Principals: Margaret Barton, Co-Director.

Mission or Interest: "RENEW backs women who acknowledge that protecting the sound, fundamental Republican tenets of individual responsibility and free markets keeps the nation strong and the economy growing."

Other Information: Auxiliary of the Republican Party.

Republican Youth Majority

P.O. Box 75885
Washington, DC 20013   **Phone:**   (202) 4-CHOICE
USA   **Fax:**   (202) 546-7212

Contact Person: Nicole Schlinger, National Chairman.

Officers or Principals: Josh Vichness, National Coordinator; Lori Shook, Field Recruiter; Richard Wheeler, Managing Director.

Mission or Interest: "To promote a broad based Republican party on college campuses nationwide." Emphasis on the right to have an abortion.

Accomplishments: Featured in *Human Events*. Active on over 40 college campuses.

Republicans Abroad International

440 1st St., N.W.
Washington, DC 20001   **Phone:**   (202) 662-1390   **Internet:** http://www.cyberserv.com/rqi/
USA

Contact Person: Michael Jones, Executive Director.

Officers or Principals: Barbara Hayward, Chairman.

Mission or Interest: "Provides up-to-date briefings on issues of national importance to Republicans living overseas in diplomatic, personal, and professional capacities."

Other Information: Auxiliary of the Republican Party.

Rescue Task Force

P.O. Box 2926
San Bernardino, CA 92406   **Phone:**   (714) 864-5863
USA

Contact Person: Gary D. Becks, President.
Officers or Principals: Gary D. Becks, President; Joseph Douglas, Vice President.
Mission or Interest: International relief and support for anti-communist "freedom fighters".
Accomplishments: Direct aid to the Nicaraguan Contras and their families. Initiated General Accounting Office audit of United Nations operations in Central America. "Instrumental in causing U.S. Congressional interest, and (in shaping) legislation regarding Central America."
Tax Status: 501(c)(3) **Annual Report:** Yes. **Employees:** 2
Board of Directors or Trustees: Bob Schroeder, Art Bowen, Robin Shidler, James Baxter.
Periodicals: Newsletter.
Internships: Yes, unpaid.

Research Center for Religion and Human Rights in Closed Societies

475 Riverside Dr., Suite 828
New York, NY 10115   **Phone:**   (212) 870-2481
USA

Contact Person: Olga S. Hruby, Executive Director.
Officers or Principals: The Very Rev. F. Leonid Kishkovsky, President ($0); Col. Carl Henry, Vice President ($0); Bryan B. Sterling, Vice President/Treasurer ($0); Rev. James R. Corgee, Chairman; Frances N. Sterling, Secretary.
Mission or Interest: Research, analysis, and publication of information concerning violations of human rights, religious freedom, attitudes and practices of totalitarian governments, and development in post-Communist societies.
Accomplishments: Recognition for service expressed by President Reagan, Mr. and Mrs. Alexander Solzhenitsyn, President Vaclev Havel of the Czech Republic, members of Congress and others. Successful campaigns for the persecuted in the USSR and East-Central Europe. Contributed to the documentation of violations of religious and other human rights. Analyses of discriminatory laws. Testimony before Congressional committees, etc. In 1994 the Center spent $5,087 on its programs; all of which was spent producing the periodical, *Religion in Communist Dominated Areas*.
Total Revenue: 1994 $7,656 (-36%)(2) **Total Expenses:** $15,198 **Net Assets:** (-$6,591)
Products or Services: Extensive archives. Annual conferences in NYC and DC.
Tax Status: 501(c)(3) **Annual Report:** Yes. **Employees:** 5
Board of Directors or Trustees: Prof. Charles Ford, Dr. Carol Rae Hansen, Suzanne Hruby, James Mulholland, Jr., Nicolas Pentcheff, Jeffrey Ross, Ph.D., J. Ruthvan Ryan, Jacob van Rossum.
Periodicals: *RCDA* (quarterly, acronym for Religion in Communist Dominated Areas).
Internships: Yes, unpaid. Students may receive credit.
Other Information: Established in 1962. The Center received $4,825, or 63% of revenue, from contributions and grants awarded by foundations, businesses, and individuals. (These contributions and grants have been steadily declining by an average of 43% per year since 1989.) $2,768, or 36%, from program services including journal subscriptions. The remaining revenue came from interest on savings.

Resistance International

P.O. Box 70265, S.W.
Washington, DC 20024   **Phone:**   (202) 488-7453
USA

Contact Person: Michael Makarenko, President.
Officers or Principals: Dr. Paul Lindstrom, National Director; Gregory Burnside, Secretary.
Mission or Interest: Organization of former Soviet dissidents in the United States who sought to expose the crimes of the Soviet Union and aid those in the Soviet Union who were persecuted.
Accomplishments: Helped found the first legal Christian school in the USSR. Helped found the first Christian radio station. Distributed tons of clothing, Christian books and Bibles, medical supplies, and other materials.
Tax Status: 501(c)(3)
Other Information: Established in 1983.

Richard and Helen DeVos Foundation

126 Ottawa Ave., N.W., Suite 500
Grand Rapids, MI 49503   **Phone:**   (616) 454-4114
USA

Contact Person: Jerry L. Tubergen, Secretary/Treasurer.

Officers or Principals: Richard M. DeVos, President ($0); Helen J. DeVos, Vice President ($0); Jerry L. Tubergen, Secretary/Treasurer ($0); Robert H. Schierbeek, Assistant Secretary/Treasurer.

Mission or Interest: Grant-making philanthropy that focuses on conservative and religious organizations.

Accomplishments: In 1994 the Foundation awarded $8,264,945 in grants. Recipients included: $1,025,200 for the Butterworth Foundation, $570,000 for the Compassionate Capitalism Project, $400,000 for Gospel Films, $315,000 for the Northwood University/Institute, $100,000 for the Michigan Family Forum, $75,000 each for Friends of the Americas, and the Intercollegiate Studies Institute, $60,000 for the Prison Fellowship Ministries, $50,000 each for Coral Ridge Ministries, Right to Life of Michigan, Teach Michigan Education Fund, and the National Empowerment Television, $25,000 each for the Alliance Defense Fund and National Family Legal Foundation, $20,000 each for the Council for National Policy and National Review Institute, $10,000 each for Freedoms Foundation at Valley Forge, Students for America Foundation, Leadership Institute, U.S. Term Limits Foundation, and the National Center for Policy Analysis, $8,000 for Life Advocacy Resource Project, $7,500 for the Campus Crusade for Christ, $6,000 for U.S. English, $5,000 each for the Acton Institute, Conservative Caucus Foundation, Eagle Forum, Foundation for Traditional Values, High Frontier, Mackinac Center for Public Policy, National Right to Life, and Concerned Women for America, and $500 each for Citizens Against Government Waste and Religious Heritage of America.

Total Revenue: 1994 $12,604,166   **Total Expenses:** $9,660,475   **Net Assets:** $148,071,451   11%(3)

Tax Status: 501(c)(3)

Other Information: Established in 1969 by the DeVos family, owners of the Amway Corporation. The Foundation received $5,560,538, or 44% of revenue, from dividends and interest from securities. $5,008,291, or 40%, from contributions and grants, primarily from members of the DeVos family and the Amway Corp. $1,267,947, or 10%, from capital gains on the sale of assets. The remaining revenue came from various miscellaneous sources. The Foundation held $136,410,907, or 92% of assets, in corporate stock.

Richard M. Nixon Presidential Library and Birthplace / Nixon Foundation

18001 Yorba Linda Blvd.
Yorba Linda, CA 92686   **Phone:**   (714) 993-3393
USA

Officers or Principals: John Taylor, Director.

Mission or Interest: Library and museum of articles, papers, and presentations of the Nixon Presidency and its era.

Other Information: Unlike other Presidential Libraries, the Nixon Library does not serve as a federal repository for the Administrations' papers. These materials were taken from the late President by Congress, and are held by the National Archives. For information on the Presidential Papers at the National Archives, contact: The Nixon Project, 8601 Adelphi Rd., College Park, MD 20740, phone (301) 713-6950, fax (301) 713-6916. The Library is not affiliated with the federal government. It was built with private donations to the Nixon Foundation. The Nixon Foundation funds and operates the Library and the Nixon Center for Peace and Freedom (see separate listing for the Center). Recently, the Foundation came under criticism for its plan to accept $5 million from the estate of pharmaceutical tycoon Elmer Bobst, a friend of President Nixon, to establish the Bobst Institute as a part of the Nixon Library complex. It was revealed, in personal letters to the President that are now held in the National Archives, that Bobst had written anti-Semitic comments such as, "The Jews have troubled the world from the very beginning." The Foundation and the Nixon family are reportedly divided as to whether or not to accept the donation.

Right NOW!

333 E. Maple Ave., Suite 225
Vienna, VA 22180
USA

Officers or Principals: Derek Turner, Editor

Mission or Interest: British conservative magazine now for sale in the United States that frequently includes American writers such as syndicated columnist Samuel Francis, Thomas Fleming (*Chronicles*), David Horowitz (Center for the Study of Popular Culture), and others.

Tax Status: For profit.

Board of Directors or Trustees: Patrons include: The Rt. Hon. Viscount Massereene and Ferrard, Rt. Hon. Lord Sudeley, FSA, Brian Crozier, Prof. H.J. Eysenck, Prof. Anthony Flew, Prof. David Marsland, Prof. Dwight Murphey (*Conservative Review*), Peter Robinson, MP, Fr. James Thornton, Bill Walker, MP.

Periodicals: *Right NOW!* (bimonthly magazine).

Other Information: Established in 1993. The U.K. address is: BCM Right, London, WC1N 3XX.

Right to Life, National Committee

419 7th St., N.W., Suite 500
Washington, DC 20004   **Phone:**   (202) 626-8800
USA   **Fax:**   (202) 737-9189

Contact Person: Wanda Franz, Ph.D., President.

Officers or Principals: Wanda Franz, Ph.D., President ($0); Robert Powell, Executive Vice President ($0); Geline B. Williams, Chairperson ($0); Anthony Lauinger, Treasurer ($0); Emma O'Steen, Secretary; James Bopp, Jr., General Counsel.

Mission or Interest: Opposes abortion, euthanasia, and infanticide.

Accomplishments: Largest anti-abortion lobbying organization. Sub-groups in all 50 states, and over 3,000 local groups. In the fiscal year ending April 1995 the Committee spent $5,299,897 on its programs.

Total Revenue: FY ending 4/95 $9,102,230 (-2%)(2) **Total Expenses:** $9,212,313 58%/8%/34% **Net Assets:** $1,786,745

Products or Services: Books, pamphlets, brochures, audio-visual and other educational materials. Lobbying, voters' guides, aid to prolife candidates.

Tax Status: 501(c)(4)   **Citations:** 699:12

Board of Directors or Trustees: William Keyes, Marice Rosenberg, Kim Himble, 50 others, each state affiliate contributes one director.

Periodicals: *National Right to Life News* (biweekly newsletter).

Other Information: Established in 1973. Affiliated with National Right to Life PAC, 501(c)(3) National Right to Life Committee Educational Trust Fund, Horatio R. Storer Foundation, and the 501(c)(4) National Right to Life Conventions at the same address. In the fiscal year ending April 1995, the four nonprofit affiliates had estimated combined net revenues, expenses, and assets of $11,508,000, $11,483,000, and $2,264,794. This represented an average 1% per year increase in revenue over the last three years. The Committee received $8,703,453, or 96% of revenue, from contributors. $128,672, or 1%, from newsletter subscriptions. $73,100, or 1%, from interest on savings and temporary cash investments. The remaining revenue came from a long distance service program, fees from affiliates, services, advertising, seminars, and other miscellaneous sources.

Right to Life, National Committee Educational Trust Fund

419 7th St., N.W., Suite 500
Washington, DC 20004   **Phone:** (202) 626-8800
USA   **Fax:**   (202) 737-9189

Contact Person: Wanda Franz, Ph.D., President.

Officers or Principals: Richard W. Kimble, Development Associate ($68,860); Randall O'Bannon, Director of Research ($28,670); Wanda Franz, President ($0); Anthony Lauinger, Executive Vice President; Geline B. Williams, Chairman; Rev. Dennis C. Day, Treasurer; Emma O'Steen, Secretary.

Mission or Interest: Anti-abortion and euthanasia organization. "Develops pro-life strategy to overturn Roe v. Wade and protect unborn life. . . provide information to right-to-life leaders and grassroots members about the activities and strategy of abortion supporters and providers."

Accomplishments: In the fiscal year ending April 1995 the Fund spent $1,692,934 on its programs. The largest program, with expenditures of $565,528, was the production and distribution of educational information. $263,925 for a "Media Impact Campaign" to research and plan television advertisements. Other programs include working with foreign anti-abortion groups, litigation, newsletter, and state-level research. The Fund awarded $229,159 in grants. Recipients included $42,300 for the International Right to Life Federation, $40,800 for the affiliated Horatio Storer Foundation, and $137,560 for various state affiliates.

Total Revenue: FY ending 4/96 $2,223,163 16%(2) **Total Expenses:** $2,090,020 81%/6%/13% **Net Assets:** $607,679

Tax Status: 501(c)(3)   **Citations:** 699:12

Board of Directors or Trustees: William Keyes, Marice Rosenberg, Kim Humble, 50 other members, one from each state affiliate.

Other Information: Affiliated with National Right to Life PAC, 501(c)(4) National Right to Life Committee , 501(c)(3) Horatio R. Storer Foundation, and the 501(c)(4) National Right to Life Conventions at the same address. In the fiscal year ending April 1995, the four nonprofit affiliates had estimated combined net revenues, expenses, and assets of $11,508,000, $11,483,000, and $2,264,794. This represented an average 1% per year increase in revenue over the last three years. The Fund received $2,102,954, or 95% of gross revenue, from contributions and grants awarded by foundations, businesses, and individuals. (In 1994 these grants included $5,000 from the Richard & Helen DeVos Foundation.) $49,030, or 2%, from interest on savings and temporary cash investments. $37,595, or 2%, from the sale of educational materials. The remaining revenue came from reimbursements from affiliates for services, and other miscellaneous sources. The Fund lost $1,666 on the sale of securities.

Right to Life, National Conventions

419 7th St., N.W., Suite 500
Washington, DC 20004   **Phone:** (202) 626-8800
USA   **Fax:**   (202) 737-9189

Contact Person: Wanda Franz, Ph.D., President.

Officers or Principals: Wanda Franz, Ph.D., President ($0); Robert Powell, Executive Vice President ($0); Anthony Layinger, Treasurer ($0); Emma O'Steen, Secretary.

Mission or Interest: Funds and coordinates National Right to Life conventions.

Accomplishments: In the fiscal year ending April 1995 the organization spent $99,629 on its programs.

Total Revenue: FY ending 4/95 $138,779 6%(2) **Total Expenses:** $99,629 71%/29%/0% **Net Assets:** $1,039

Products or Services: Banquets, workshops, programs, more.

Tax Status: 501(c)(4)

Board of Directors or Trustees: Jeanne Head, Geline Williams, Rev. Dennis Day, Larry Hell, Carol Long.

Other Information: Affiliated with National Right to Life PAC, the 501(c)(3) National Right to Life Committee Educational Trust Fund, Horatio R. Storer Foundation, and the 501(c)(4) National Right to Life Committee at the same address. In the fiscal year ending April 1995, the four nonprofit affiliates had estimated combined net revenues, expenses, and assets of $11,508,000, $11,483,000, and $2,264,794. This represented an average 1% per year increase in revenue over the last three years.   NRL Conventions received $74,859, or 54% of revenue, from affiliates. $32,635, or 24%, from registration fees. $17,320, or 12%, from special fund-raising events. The remaining revenue came from exhibits, advertising revenue, and other miscellaneous sources.

Right to Life, California (League of Southern California)

1028 N. Lake Ave., Suite 102
Pasadena, CA 91104   **Phone:** (818) 398-6100
USA   **Fax:**   (818) 398-6101

Contact Person: Teresa Reisser, Executive Director.
Officers or Principals: Teresa Reisser, Executive Director ($22,800); Mary Vanis, President ($0); Kathy Wachter, First Vice President; Peggy Mew, Second Vice President; Mike Webber, Treasurer; Ruby de Vera, Secretary.
Mission or Interest: Anti-abortion services and education.
Accomplishments: "The oldest pro-life organization." Since its inception, more than 1 million people have heard League speakers. In 1995 the league spent $591,375 on their programs. The League's 15 crisis pregnancy centers serve over 24,750 women. Sponsored the "West Coast Maternity Home Association", a network of seven homes that assisted 181 women. The League's abstinence program was presented 35 times to more than 9,640 students. The Annual Education Conference was attended by over 400 people. The League's newsletter was mailed to more than 20,000 households.
Total Revenue: 1995 $944,403 1%(3) **Total Expenses:** $841,497 70%/16%/14% **Net Assets:** $455,342
Products or Services: Crisis pregnancy counseling. "Sex, Love and Choices" abstinence program. Pays room and board for pregnant women at three special homes. Public speakers. Presents the annual "Protector Award."
Tax Status: 501(c)(3) **Annual Report:** Yes. **Employees:** 6   **Citations:** 0:233
Board of Directors or Trustees: Bob Berry, Dan Cathcart, Otilla Collins, Kathleen Crow, Kim Davison, Jacque Fehner, Gloria Griffin, Tim Jones, Msgr. John Moretta, Bill and Barbara Schnieder, Don Sherrin, Jack Wilson, M.D., Holly Wood, Bishop Gabino Zavala. The Advisory Board includes the Hon. Richard P. Byrne; Rev. Donald Merrifield, S.J.; entertainers Pat Boone, Gordon Jump and Ricardo Montalban; others.
Periodicals: *Right to Life League of Southern California* (quarterly newsletter).
Internships: No.
Other Information: Established in 1967 at the behest of Cardinal McIntyre. The League received $929,140, or 98% of revenue, from contributions and grants awarded by foundations, businesses, and individuals. (These grants included $10,000 from the Doheney Foundation, $3,800 from the Knights of Malta Foundation, $2,000 from the Hayden Foundation, and $500 from the Shea Foundation.) $8,373, or 1%, from interest on savings and temporary cash investments. $6,890 net, or 1%, from the sale of inventory.

Right to Life, Connecticut

(see Pro-Life Council of Connecticut)

Right to Life, Florida (Lee County)

4720 S.E. 15th Ave., Suite 103
Cape Coral, FL 33904   **Phone:** (941) 542-5433
USA   **Fax:**   (941) 542-5087

Contact Person: Bernadette Reilly, Executive Director.
Officers or Principals: Kathy Miller, former Executive Director ($16,380); Bob Morley, Vice President; Paul Shoot, Treasurer; Mary Dufner, Secretary.
Mission or Interest: "Committed to preserving the right to life through the legislative process, education, and prayer."
Accomplishments: Hosted Celebrity Dinners with columnist Cal Thomas, Judge Robert Bork, Fred Barnes (*Weekly Standard*), Gary Bauer (Family Research Council), and Jay Sekulow (American Center for Law and Justice). Opened the "Lifeline Family Center," a home for women with trouble pregnancies - in its first year the Center helped 31 women and housed 10. Blocked a Planned Parenthood program from being implemented in Lee County Schools. In 1995 the organization spent $55,642 on its programs.
Total Revenue: 1995 $53,268 **Total Expenses:** $55,642 **Net Assets:** $18,477
Tax Status: 501(c)(4) **Annual Report:** Yes. **Employees:** 2
Board of Directors or Trustees: Guy Strayhorn, Dr. Konnie Yankopolus, Mary Massaro, Suzanne Specht, Wendell Garrett, Rosemary Ryan, Toni Holmund.
Periodicals: *Lifeline* (monthly newsletter).
Internships: No.
Other Information: Established in 1981. The organization received $48,400, or 91% of revenue, from contributors. $4,604 net, or 8%, from special fund-raising events. The remaining revenue came from investment income.

Right to Life, Idaho

P.O. Box 1705
Boise, ID 83701
USA

Contact Person: Ramolia Burbidge, Office Director.

Officers or Principals: Julie Katzenberger, Vice President ($0); Debbie Roper, Secretary ($0); Debbie Vance, Treasurer ($0).
Mission or Interest: Idaho Right to Life organization that encompasses three affiliates across the state. "Pro-life news and information."
Accomplishments: In 1995 the affiliates spent $8,887 on their programs. This included an annual conference, a booth at the state fair, and an event commemorating Roe v. Wade.
Total Revenue: 1995 $32,560 **Total Expenses:** $24,688 **Net Assets:** $14,220
Products or Services: Videos, publications, audio tapes, public events.
Tax Status: 501(c)(4)
Board of Directors or Trustees: Charlotte Homolka, Kerry Uhlenkott, Karen Hefner, Don Wind, Gerti Creighton.
Other Information: The affiliates received $21,368, or 66% of revenue, from contributors. $9,250, or 28%, from membership dues. $1,942, or 6%, from program service revenue including fees for conferences.

Right to Life, Illinois Committee
343 S. Dearborn St., Suite 1217
Chicago, IL 60604   **Phone:** (312) 922-1918
USA

Contact Person: Richard J. O'Connor, Executive Director.
Officers or Principals: Richard J. O'Connor, Executive Director ($33,182); Robert Ciesla, Chairman/Treasurer ($0); Laurence A. Theriault, Vice Chairman; Mary Anne Hackett, President; Mary-Lynn Davison, R.N., Vice President; Joyce E. Keen, Secretary.
Mission or Interest: Illinois affiliate dealing with "abortion, euthanasia and pro-life issues."
Accomplishments: In the fiscal year ending March 1995 the Committee spent $136,758 on its programs. The largest expenditure, $56,071, went toward exhibits and displays at parades, fairs, churches, hospitals, and other public gatherings. $43,763 was spent on billboard campaigns. $17,778 was spent on sexual abstinence promotion. The rest was spent producing and distributing a newsletter.
Total Revenue: FY ending 3/95 $189,678 **Total Expenses:** $197,193 69%/28%/2% **Net Assets:** $24,203
Products or Services: Advertising, billboards, publications, teaching abstinence kit, more.
Tax Status: 501(c)(3)   **Citations:** 20:150
Board of Directors or Trustees: Maureen Bland, Rev. Jaime Canty, Rafael Carreira, M.D., Fran Fortier.
Periodicals: Newsletter.
Other Information: The Committee received $84,572, or 45% of revenue, from contributions and grants awarded by foundations, businesses, and individuals. (These grants have been steadily growing by an average of 17% per year over the last five years.) $61,725 net, or 33%, from special fund-raising events, including a raffle, benefit auction, flower sale, and golf outing. The remaining revenue came from the sale of materials and literature, and other miscellaneous sources.

Right to Life, Kansas
214 S.W. 6th St., Suite 208
Topeka, KS 66603
USA

Contact Person: Elmer L. Feldkamp, President.
Officers or Principals: Mary Ann Lickteig, Vice President ($0); Grace M. Lallement, Secretary ($0); Audrey Feldkamp, Treasurer ($0).
Mission or Interest: Kansas anti-abortion affiliate.
Accomplishments: In the fiscal year ending July 1995 the organization spent $30,820 on its programs. The largest program, with expenditures of $16,720, was the publication and distribution of a newsletter to approximately 13,000 subscribers. $8,430 was spent on a convention attended by 125 people and a rally attended by approximately 950. The rest was spent producing and distributing other educational materials.
Total Revenue: FY ending 7/95 $52,352 **Total Expenses:** $51,171 **Net Assets:** $6,384
Tax Status: 501(c)(4)
Other Information: Right to Life of Kansas received $42,928, or 82% of revenue, from contributors. $6,595, or 12%, from advertising in their convention program. $2,829, or 5%, from membership dues.

Right to Life, Michigan (Lifespan)
28200 7 Mile Rd., Suite 127
Livonia, MI 48152   **Phone:** (313) 533-9090
USA

Contact Person: Ann Sands, President.
Officers or Principals: Ann Sands, President/Treasurer ($14,494); Patricia Holscher, Director ($10,100); Margaret Bradley, Secretary ($8,426).
Mission or Interest: "To promote respect for human life."

Accomplishments: In 1995 Lifespan spent $94,601 on its programs. This included $2,662 in grants awarded to local groups and to organizations providing material goods for unwed mothers and their children.
Total Revenue: 1995 $166,069 **Total Expenses:** $144,339 66%/22%/12% **Net Assets:** $78,028
Tax Status: 501(c)(4)
Board of Directors or Trustees: Paula Ervin, Diane Fagelman, Margaret Joyce, Karen Patrosso, Carol Smith, Phyllis Sullivan, Diane Trombley.
Periodicals: Newsletter.
Other Information: Lifespan received $57,463 net, or 35% of revenue, from the sale of inventory. $53,825, or 32%, from contributors. $31,185 net, or 19%, from special fund-raising events, including a "Mother of the Year" dinner, Bowling for Life event, a garage sale and a bake sale. The remaining revenue came from a "Legislative Breakfast", and interest on savings.

Right to Life, Michigan Educational Foundation Legal Defense Fund

2340 Porter, S.W.
Grand Rapids, MI 49509   **Phone:**   (616) 532-2300
USA

Contact Person: Barbara Listing, President.
Officers or Principals: Joseph Kincaid, M.D., Vice President ($0); Dee DeKryger, Legislative Director ($0); Margaret Baker, Secretary; Bill Schafer, Treasurer; Barbara Listing, President; Fred Patin, Trustee.
Mission or Interest: A trust formed by the affiliated Right to Life of Michigan Educational Fund to pay legal fees "to defend pro-life legislation."
Accomplishments: In 1995 the Legal Defense Fund spent $3,771 on its programs.
Total Revenue: 1995 $1,648 **Total Expenses:** $3,788 **Net Assets:** $11,334
Tax Status: 501(c)(3)   **Citations:** 83:74
Other Information: Affiliated with the 501(c)(4) Right to Life of Michigan and the 501(c)(3) Right to Life of Michigan Educational Fund. The Legal Defense Fund received $1,281, or 78% of revenue, from contributions and grants awarded by foundations, businesses, and individuals. (The contributions and grants have been sharply declining by an average of 76% per year since 1992.) $367, or 22%, from investment income.

Right to Life, Michigan Educational Foundation

2340 Porter, S.W.
Grand Rapids, MI 49509   **Phone:**   (616) 532-2300
USA

Contact Person: Barbara Listing, President.
Officers or Principals: Barbara Listing, President ($29,059); Paul Miller, Chairman ($0); Dr. Joseph Kincaid, M.D., Vice President ($0); Margaret Baker, Secretary; Bill Schafer, Treasurer; Dee DeKryger, Vice President of Legislation.
Mission or Interest: Michigan Right to Life affiliate promoting the "education of the public on pro-life issues."
Accomplishments: *The Detroit Free Press*, in a special report, said, "Right to Life of Michigan, which started 25 years ago as a loosely banded group of 'little old Catholic ladies in tennis shoes,' now rivals organized labor as a power on the state's political scene. If you're a Democrat, it's nearly impossible to win your party's nomination without labor's blessing. And if you're a Republican, Right to Life's endorsement carries comparable weight." Has 125 affiliates state-wide, 180,000 dues paying members, and a mailing list of 500,000 households. In 1995 the Fund spent $1,021,655 on its programs.
Total Revenue: 1995 $1,542,110 **Total Expenses:** $1,340,185 76%/15%/9% **Net Assets:** $562,645
Products or Services: Weekly radio program, billboard and ad campaigns, speakers bureau, video tapes, and other educational materials.
Tax Status: 501(c)(3)   **Citations:** 83:74
Board of Directors or Trustees: Ellie Baas, Peg Brennan, Dr. Laurence Burns, Carolyn DeKryger, Rusty Dutkiewicz, Evelyn Fennema, Joanna Haddix, Rita Herman, Rae Ann Houbeck, Marybeth Kaak, Elaine Kavanaugh, Judy Lachniet, Earl McAlary, Diane Mulder, Jane Muldoon, Linda Palazzolo, Fred Patin, Anthony Ross, Rosemary Ryan, Michelle Salgat, Michael Schulz, Rita Skidmore, Dee Sporleder, Paul Sutphen, Mary Zick.
Other Information: Affiliated with the 501(c)(4) Right to Life of Michigan and the 501(c)(3) Right to Life of Michigan Educational Legal Defense Fund. The Foundation received $1,404,309, or 91% of revenue, from contributions and grants awarded by foundations, businesses, affiliates, and individuals. (In 1994 these grants included $50,000 from the Richard & Helen DeVos Foundation, $1,000 from the DeWitt Families Conduit Foundation. These contributions and grants have been steadily growing by an average of 57% per year since 1991.) $59,878 net, or 4%, from special fund-raising events, including a radio-a-thon, auctions, oratory contest, and fund-raising dinner. $45,550, or 3%, from fees for educational activities. $22,823, or 1%, from the sale of inventory. The remaining revenue came from rental income, interest on savings, and other miscellaneous sources.

Right to Life, Missouri (Western Missouri)

9411 E. 63rd St.
Raytown, MO 64133   **Phone:**   (816) 353-4113
USA

Contact Person: Alexandra Colbert, Office Manager.

Officers or Principals: Alexandra Colbert, Office Manager ($11,580); Mary Kay Culp, Public Relations ($5,040); George Jeffries, Chairman ($0); Ernest W. Reed, Treasurer.
Mission or Interest: Western Missouri affiliate promoting "the sanctity of life."
Accomplishments: In 1995 the organization spent $37,523 on its programs.
Total Revenue: 1995 $36,239 **Total Expenses:** $37,523 100%/0%/0% **Net Assets:** $135
Tax Status: 501(c)(4)
Other Information: The organization received $23,371, or 64% of revenue, from contributors. $7,458 net, or 20%, from the sale of carnations. $4,030 net, or 11%, from hosting two banquets. $1,379, or 4%, from the sale of educational items.

Right to Life, New Mexico Committee

2800 San Mateo, N.E.
Albuquerque, NM 87110   **Phone:**   (505) 881-4563
USA

Contact Person: Dauneen Dolce, Director.
Officers or Principals: Dauneen Dolce, Director ($21,562); Tom McBride, President ($0); Verna Pochop, Treasurer ($0); Catherine Podvin, Secretary.
Mission or Interest: New Mexico anti-abortion affiliate.
Accomplishments: In 1994 the Committee spent $69,912 on its programs.
Total Revenue: 1994 $78,323 **Total Expenses:** $69,912 **Net Assets:** $14,390
Tax Status: 501(c)(3)
Other Information: The Committee received $47,679, or 61% of revenue, from contributions and grants awarded by foundations, businesses, and individuals. $15,380, or 20%, from membership dues. $7,736 net, or 10%, from special fund-raising events. $7,438 net, or 9%, from the sale of inventory. The remaining revenue came from investment income.

Right to Life, Ohio

8 E. Broad St., 13th Floor
Columbus, OH 43215
USA

Officers or Principals: Edward P. Markovich, Executive Director, Greater Akron ($15,384); Sue McGue, President, Lima & Allen County ($0); Peggy Lehner, President, Greater Dayton($0); Donald Kelly, President, Greater Cleveland.
Mission or Interest: Ohio affiliate of the National Right to Life. (This entry is an effort to construct the Ohio activities of the Right to Life affiliate by combining the activities of five affiliates in the state; Lima & Allen County, Greater Dayton, Greater Akron, Greater Cincinnati, and Greater Cleveland. All financial figures except salaries are estimates, and probably err on the short side.)
Accomplishments: In 1995 the affiliates spent approximately $206,801 on their programs.
Total Revenue: 1995 $313,246 **Total Expenses:** $342,724 **Net Assets:** $235,969
Tax Status: 501(c)(4)
Other Information: Affiliated with several local 501(c)(3) educational and research organizations. The five affiliates received $246,247, or 79% of revenue, from contributors.

Right to Life, Oklahoma Crusade

P.O. Box 2703
Tulsa, OK 74101
USA

Contact Person: Jim Bothell, Treasurer.
Officers or Principals: Dr. Mildred F. Jefferson, President ($0); David O'Steen, Secretary ($0).
Mission or Interest: Anti-abortion lobbying organization.
Total Revenue: FY ending 5/94 $248,723 **Total Expenses:** $253,409 0%/68%/32% **Net Assets:** $23,729
Tax Status: 501(c)(4)   **Citations:** 0:233
Other Information: The Crusade received $248,723, or 100% of revenue, from contributors.

Right to Life, Oregon

4335 N. River Rd.
Salem, OR 97303
USA

Contact Person: Gayle Atteberry, Executive Director.
Officers or Principals: Gayle Atteberry, Executive Director ($0); Becky Moore, President ($0); Cindy Rahm, Vice President ($0); Thomas Glogau, Treasurer; Beverly Bresnahan, Secretary.
Mission or Interest: Oregon anti-abortion affiliate lobbying "regarding the sanctity of human life."

Accomplishments: In 1995 RTL spent $187,239 on its programs. The largest program, with expenditures of $169,114, was the provision of educational materials. This included $4,000 in grants for various nonprofit organizations to provide care for unwed mothers. Other programs included $15,009 to host an annual convention, $2,358 to send delegates to national meetings, and $758 for an annual rally at the state capital.
Total Revenue: 1995 $460,929 **Total Expenses:** $427,196 43%/13%/43% **Net Assets:** $67,460
Tax Status: 501(c)(4)   **Citations:** 48:101
Board of Directors or Trustees: Rita Wheeler, Cathy Harper, Nedora Counts, Ray Martin, Tom Fee, Ruth Fee, Lloyd Lowry, Joseph Wetzel, Doug VandeGriend, Jane Groff, Carl Rosseti, Barbara Craig, Brenda Cosby, Jim Coskey, Pat Epperly, Jake Walsh, Kyle Miller, Roxanna Dial.
Other Information: Affiliated with the 501(c)(3) Oregon Right to Life Education Foundation. The organization received $362,688, or 79% of revenue, from contributors. $95,190, or 20%, from affiliates. $3,051, or 1%, from interest on savings and temporary cash investments.

Right to Life, Tennessee

P.O. Box 158024
Nashville, TN 37215   **Phone:**   (615) 256-7991
USA

Contact Person: Suzanne Sevier, Executive Director.
Officers or Principals: Stan Schulz, President ($0); Doris Henderson, Secretary ($0); John Hubbard, Treasurer ($0); Laurie Moore, Lobbyist; Brian Harris, Vice President.
Mission or Interest: "Pro-life education to achieve pro-life laws."
Accomplishments: In 1995 the organization spent $74,614 on its programs. This included $4,190 in grants to various local affiliates and crisis pregnancy centers. The organization's newsletter is sent to approximately 3,000 people.
Total Revenue: 1995 $141,844 **Total Expenses:** $137,973 54%/17%/29% **Net Assets:** $19,702
Tax Status: 501(c)(4)
Board of Directors or Trustees: Murvin Perry, Robert McMillan, Steve Brumit, Lynnae Franks, Maureen O'Brien, Bernie Barton, Tom Boles.
Periodicals: Newsletter.
Other Information: Right to Life, Tennessee received $84,289, or 59% of revenue, from contributors. $39,895 net, or 28%, from special fund-raising events, including a golf tournament, and a yard and craft sale. $5,955, or 4%, from revenues raised by placing ads. $4,835, or 3%, from membership dues. The remaining revenue came from banquets, rose sales, dividends and interest from securities, interest on savings, and other miscellaneous sources.

Right to Life, Texas Committee

6776 Southwest Freeway, Suite 430
Houston, TX 77074
USA

Contact Person: Jim Graham.
Mission or Interest: Texas affiliate of the National Right to Life Committee. "State-wide builders of a pro-life Texas."
Tax Status: 501(c)(4)

Right to Life, Vermont Committee

P.O. Box 1079
Montpelier, VT 05601   **Phone:**   (802) 229-4885
USA   **Fax:**   same

Mission or Interest: "To engage in educational, charitable, and scientific projects or purposes including. . . detailed and factual information upon which the public may make an informed decision about the various topics of fetal development, abortion, alternatives to abortion, euthanasia and infanticide."
Total Revenue: 1995 $72,687 **Total Expenses:** $73,246 **Net Assets:** $6,456
Tax Status: 501(c)(4)
Other Information: The Committee received $59,542, or 82% of revenue, from contributors. $11,524, or 16%, from program services. The remaining revenue came from special fund-raising events, investments, and other miscellaneous sources.

Right to Life, Wyoming

P.O. Box 1208
Casper, WY 82602
USA

Contact Person: Larry Hell, President.

Officers or Principals: Mary Schroeder, Vice President ($0); Cheryl Rodgers, Secretary ($0); Margaret Webb, Treasurer ($0).
Mission or Interest: Wyoming anti-abortion affiliate. "Public education on life issues."
Accomplishments: In the fiscal year ending April 1995 the affiliate spent $14,359 on its programs. This included publication of a newsletter with a circulation of 13,000, newspaper advertisements that had a potential audience of 18,000 readers, and educational presentations at state and county fairs. The organization also awarded $445 in grants to various organizations to help women with crisis pregnancies.
Total Revenue: FY ending 4/95 $28,131 **Total Expenses:** $29,747 **Net Assets:** $15,479
Tax Status: 501(c)(4)
Periodicals: Newsletter.
Other Information: The organization received $25,966, or 92% of revenue, from contributors. $1,145, or 4%, from mailing list rentals. The remaining revenue came from special events, the sale of inventory, and prize money from award-winning parade floats.

Ripon Society

501 Capitol Court, N.E., Suite 300
Washington, DC 20002   **Phone:** (202) 546-1292   **E-Mail:** riponsoc@aol.com
USA   **Fax:** (202) 547-6560

Contact Person: Michael Dubke, Executive Director.
Officers or Principals: Hon. Nancy Landon Kassebaum, Chairman ($0); Hon. Bill Frenzel, President ($0); Masu Kusume Dyer, Vice President ($0); John M. Vorperian, Secretary; Stephen R. Rolandi, Treasurer.
Mission or Interest: "To help make the Republican party the permanent majority party in the United States. . . to promote moderate Republican principles in our party, government and society. . . Ripon is a voluntary organization financed almost entirely by contributors who believe in its programs and principles. Through their support, moderate Republicans have a growing voice among all the shouting from the well-financed Far Right and New Left."
Accomplishments: Received praise from *Time Magazine*, *The Boston Globe*, and columnist David Broder. In 1996 the Society ran a two-part "Moderate Manifesto" in its magazine, *Ripon Forum*. Although the Ripon executive director stated that it is not necessarily the Ripon creed, it was created by Ripon members and contributors. The Manifesto called for, among other things; increased federal involvement in education, public school vouchers, and increased student loans; expanded federal and international oversight - not local - on environmental protection and maintained funding for the EPA; place a time limit on welfare, then provide government jobs - through private contractors - for the unemployable; federal laws on health care that require insurance companies to cover those with pre-existing conditions, and experiment with Medical Savings Accounts; support abortion rights and the Roe v. Wade decision, which, although the Court "may have overreached its authority in this decision. . . it was a good Solomonic solution"; increased restrictions on handgun ownership and no liberalization of concealed carry laws; and other positions. In 1995 the Society spent $122,366 on its programs.
Total Revenue: 1995 $167,427 2%(2) **Total Expenses:** $215,617 57%/14%/29% **Net Assets:** $7,483
Products or Services: "A Salute to Republican Women Leadership" video. Conferences, issue papers, more.
Tax Status: 501(c)(4)
Board of Directors or Trustees: Members include: Gov. William Weld, Gov. Christine Todd Whitman, Sen. John Chafee, Sen. William Cohen, Sen. Olympia Snowe, Sen. Arlen Specter, Sen. Ted Stevens, Rep. William Clinger, Rep. Steve Gunderson, Rep. Jim Leach, Rep. Susan Molinari, and others.
Periodicals: *Ripon Forum* (bimonthly magazine).
Other Information: The Society received $84,255 net, or 50% of revenue, from special fund-raising events. $60,220, or 36%, from contributors. $8,572, or 5%, from rental income. $8,080, or 5%, from conferences. $5,162, or 3%, from membership dues. The remaining revenue came from interest on savings and other miscellaneous sources.

Robert A. Taft Institute of Government

420 Lexington Ave.
New York, NY 10170   **Phone:** (212) 682-1530
USA   **Fax:** (212) 953-1927

Contact Person: Maryann M. Feeney, President .
Officers or Principals: Maryann M. Feeney, President ($79,552); Prescott S. Bush, Jr., Chairman ($0); Clark MacGregor, Birch E. Bayh, Jr., William F. May, Vice Chairmen ($0); Marion J. Epley, III, Esq., Secretary/Counsel; Beatrice Mitchell, Treasurer.
Mission or Interest: Founded in memory of Senator Robert A. Taft of Ohio, the Institute's mission is to continue his life-long ideals of political education, awareness and participation. Co-sponsors seminars in American constitutional government and politics with various universities.
Accomplishments: "For three decades, Taft has been highly regarded for the excellence of its teacher training programs - the Taft Seminars for Teachers. These courses, initiated in 1963, have graduated over 20,000 educators and have brought improved civic education instruction to millions of school children in all 50 states." In 1994 the Institute spent $273,983 on its programs.
Total Revenue: 1994 $411,098 (-18%)(4) (see **Other Information**) **Total Expenses:** $437,446 63%/16%/21%
Net Assets: $106,579
Products or Services: Taft Seminars for Teachers, Taft Seminar Presidential Library Series, videos.
Tax Status: 501(c)(3) **Annual Report:** Yes.   **Citations:** 0:233

Board of Directors or Trustees: Hon. Hugh Carey (former Mayor of NYC), Gil Carmichael, Robert Trent Jones, Jr., William Wood Prince, Charles Coyle, Robert Alter, Justin Wilson, Louis Bantle, Robert McCauley, Peggy Woodford Forbes, Louis Cordia (Reagan Alumni Assn.), Harry Peter, III, Fernando Mateo, William Radison, Suzanne Schutte, John van Gorder.
Other Information: Established in 1963. Robert A. Taft (1889-1953) was a Republican Senator representing Ohio. Taft is remembered for his staunch opposition to the New Deal and his opposition to U.S. involvement in World War II and the Korean War - although he supported the United Nations. Taft's most famous legislative accomplishment was the Taft-Hartley Act of 1947, a law that curtailed the power of unions. Taft sought the Republican Presidential nomination in 1952, but lost to Eisenhower. The Institute experienced a sharp drop in revenue in 1992 when it no longer received the government grants it had been receiving. In 1992, the last year it received these grants, it received $419,424. In 1994 the Institute received $380,889, or 93% of revenue, from contributions and grants awarded by foundations, businesses, and individuals. (In 1995 these grants included $1,000 from the Lynde and Harry Bradley Foundation.) $17,200, or 4%, from trust-fund revenue. $9,100 or 2%, from seminar registration fees. The remaining revenue came from publication and video sales, and interest on savings.

Rockford Institute / *Chronicles*

934 N. Main St.
Rockford, IL 61103   **Phone:** (815) 964-5053   **E-Mail:** rkfdinst@bossnt.com
USA   **Fax:**   (815) 965-1826

Contact Person: Christopher Check, Executive Vice President.
Officers or Principals: Dr. Allan Carlson, President ($82,946); Michael Warder, Vice President/Treasurer ($74,124); Thomas Fleming, Editor, *Chronicles* ($67,362); George O'Neill, Jr., Chairman; William Andrews, Vice Chairman; Harold O.J. Brown, Editor, *Religion & Society Report*; Theodore Pappas, Managing Editor, *Chronicles*.
Mission or Interest: Center of 'paleo-conservative' thought and writing. Frequently challenges 'neo-conservatives' on issues. "The Institute, informed by the distinctive accents of the Midwest, the South, and the West, defines and shapes national and international debates. We believe that a society in turmoil cannot be saved through mere legislation. Therefore, we devote our labors not to ephemeral political fashions but to the defense of these institutions without which there can be no civilization. In the broadest sense, we strive to contribute to the renewal of Christendom in this time and place through: the defense of the family; the promotion of liberty; the decentralization of political and economic life; the celebration of literary and artistic inheritance of our civilization; the adherence to Truth, revealed through Scripture and tradition."
Accomplishments: The Institute serves as the focal point of 'paleo-conservative' thought. It has been credited with setting the national debate by *The Wall Street Journal, New York Times, New Republic, National Review, Weekly Standard, National Journal*, and individuals such as Patrick Buchanan, the late sociologist Robert Nisbet, *Forbes'* Peter Brimlow, Milton Friedman and others. The Idea Brokers lists it as one of the 30 leading think tanks in the United States. *Chronicles* is listed in the 1992 Media Guide as one of the 40 most influential periodicals. In 1997 the Institute held a conference on American intervention in the Balkans. "Yugoslavia has become a potent symbol, not only of the persistence of ethnic hostilities, but also of what the New World Order holds in store for us. Today Bosnia, tomorrow Chicago." In the fiscal year ending July 1995, the Institute spent $1,196,866 on its programs. The largest expenditure, $635,500, went toward production and distribution of *Chronicles*. $197,700 was spent on the "Center on the Family in America" program. $169,500 on communications and public affairs. $155,400 on the "Center on Religion and Society" program, and $84,742 on the Ingersoll Foundation.
Total Revenue: FY ending 7/95 $1,388,970 4%(4) **Total Expenses:** $1,412,369 85%/15%/0% **Net Assets:** $352,660
Products or Services: The Ingersoll Foundation awards two prizes, the T.S. Eliot Award for Creative Writing and the Richard M. Weaver Award for Scholarly Letters. Winners of the Eliot Award include Zbigniew Herbert, Wendell Berry, Mario Vargas Llosa, Walker Percy, V.S. Naipaul, and Jorge Luis Borges. Weaver Award winners included François Furet, Eugene Genovese, John Lukacs, Forrest McDonald, and the late Murray Rothbard, Robert Nisbet, and Russell Kirk.
Tax Status: 501(c)(3) **Annual Report:** Yes. **Employees:** 21   **Citations:** 24:143
Board of Directors or Trustees: William Andrews, William Diehl, David Hartman, Mary Kohler (Windway Found.), William Nelson, Clyde Sluhan, Clayton Gaylord, Ellen Hill, Prof. Forrest McDonald (Univ. of Alabama), Dallin Oaks (The Council of the Twelve, Church of Jesus Christ of Latter-Day Saints), Robert Sandblom, Kathleen Sullivan (Illinois Eagle Forum).
Periodicals: *Chronicles: A Magazine of American Culture* (monthly magazine), *The Family in America* (monthly newsletter of sociology and research), *Religion and Society Report* (monthly newsletter) and *Main Street Memoranda* (monthly newsletter).
Internships: No.
Other Information: Established in 1976. The Institute received $917,835, or 66% of revenue, from contributions and grants awarded by foundations, businesses, and individuals. (These grants included $10,000 from the Alex C. Walker Foundation, $2,500 from the United Educators Foundation.) $301,615, or 22%, from subscriptions. $42,640, or 3%, from a management fee from the Ingersoll Foundation. $24,309, or 2%, from investment income. $13,746, or 1%, from conference fees. The remaining revenue came from the sale of literature, interest on savings, royalties, mailing list rentals, advertising, and other miscellaneous sources.

Rocky Mountain Family Council

P.O. Box 13619
Denver, CO 80201   **Phone:** (303) 292-1800
USA

Contact Person: Mark Anderson, Director of Communication.

Officers or Principals: Thomas H. McMillen, Executive Director ($28,458); Barry Arrington, President ($0); Jackie Watkins, Treasurer ($0); Stan Myers, Secretary.
Mission or Interest: Religious organization "dedicated to strengthening families in Colorado."
Accomplishments: Executive director Tom McMillen writes a weekly column that has been published in the *Holyoke Enterprise, Flagler News, Rangely Times* and the *Ranchland News*.
Total Revenue: FY ending 6/95 $114,852 **Total Expenses:** $124,863 **Net Assets:** (-$10,231)
Tax Status: 501(c)(3)
Board of Directors or Trustees: Gib and Ethel Bowman, Dick Brusco, Shawn Caldwell, Diane Goldie, Michael Hegarty, Dick MacWherter, Michael Norton, Jerry Popham, Jeff Reddy, Linda Stine, Phil Sura, Peter Trost, Ernest Witucki.
Periodicals: *Advisor* (monthly newsletter).
Other Information: Established in 1992. The Council received $118,378, or 99.9% of gross revenue, from contributions and grants awarded by foundations, businesses, and individuals. (This was down 1% from the previous year.) The remaining revenue came from other miscellaneous sources. The Council lost $3,578 on a Fourth of July festival.

Roe Foundation

712 Crescent Ave.
Greenville, SC 29601   **Phone:** (864) 242-5007
USA   **Fax:**   (864) 242-5014

Contact Person: Thomas A. Roe, Director.
Officers or Principals: Dr. Edwin Feulner, Jr., Co-President ($500); Paul W. Weyrich, Co-President ($500); Thomas A. Roe, Director ($500).
Mission or Interest: Grant-making foundation that believes, "The maximum potential of a free people is achieved when they are free to control their own destiny. . . The greatest threat to these freedoms is intrusive government. . . The Judeo Christian tradition represents the underpinnings of a just society."
Accomplishments: In 1995 the Foundation awarded $500,000 in grants. Recipients included; $55,000 each for the Free Congress Foundation, Heritage Foundation, and South Carolina Policy Council, $40,000 for the Intercollegiate Studies Institute, $25,000 for the State Policy Network, $10,000 each for the Cascade Policy Institute, Indiana Policy Review Foundation, Mackinac Center, Arkansas Policy Foundation, Resource Institute of Oklahoma, and Goldwater Institute, $9,000 for the Capital Research Center, $7,500 each for U.S. Term Limits Foundation, Evergreen Freedom Foundation, Madison Institute, Nevada Policy Research Institute, and the Buckeye Center, $5,000 each for the Acton Institute, Americans for Tax Reform Foundation, Atlas Economic Research Foundation, Cato Institute, Center for Educational Reform, Center for Policy Studies, Competitive Enterprise Institute, Mont Pelerin Society, Public Interest Institute, Golden State Center for Policy Studies, Heartland Institute, John Locke Foundation, and Texas Public Policy Foundation.
Total Revenue: 1995 $727,942 **Total Expenses:** $697,278 **Net Assets:** $14,604,615 8%(3)
Tax Status: 501(c)(3)
Board of Directors or Trustees: Shirley Roe, Roger Meiners (Center for Policy Studies), Bryan Lamm (State Policy Network).
Other Information: Established in 1968 by Thomas Anderson Roe. Co-Presidents Edwin Feulner and Paul Weyrich are the respective leaders of the Heritage Foundation and Free Congress Foundation. The Foundation received $389,818, or 54% of revenue, from interest on savings and temporary cash investments. $174,317, or 24%, from capital gains on the sale of securities. $163,446, or 22%, from dividends and interest from securities. The Foundation held $10,935,772, or 75% of assets, in corporate stock.

Ronald Reagan Presidential Foundation

40 Presidential Drive, Suite 200
Simi Valley, CA 93065   **Phone:** (805) 522-2977
USA

Contact Person: John J. Midgley, Executive Director.
Officers or Principals: Larry Bumgardner, Deputy Director ($103,405); Lynda Schuler, Deputy Director ($79,004); John L. O'Leary, Financial Administrator ($65,000); Richard Norton Smith, Executive Director; Lodwrick Cook, Chairman; Frederick Ryan, Jr., Secretary.
Mission or Interest: Funds and operates a Presidential library, museum, and Center for Public Affairs. In 1991 the National Archives and Records Administration assumed operating responsibility for the library. Although the National Archives and Records Administration assumed operating and maintenance responsibility for the Presidential Library, the Foundation remains responsible for certain portions of the facility, including the Foundation's offices and the gift shop.
Accomplishments: In 1994 the Foundation spent $2,867,568 on its programs. The Center for Public Affairs was dormant until 1994, when it held three conferences; 'What is Wrong with Conservative Politics?', 'Perils of Democracy in the former Soviet Union,' and 'Do Conservatives have a sense of Humor?'
Total Revenue: 1994 $7,052,128 (-4%)(2) **Total Expenses:** $4,996,294 57%/16%/27% **Net Assets:** $73,209,329
Products or Services: The Center for Public Affairs hosts conferences and "Reagan Forums."
Tax Status: 501(c)(3) **Annual Report:** No. **Citations:** 14:165
Board of Directors or Trustees: Joe Allbritton, Amb. Walter Annenberg, Walter Beran, Gordon Binder, Steve Forbes, Jr. (*Forbes* magazine), Rupert Murdoch, James Pattison, Nancy Reagan, President Ronald Reagan, Frederick Ryan, Jr., George Shultz (Secretary of State, 1982-89), Lew Wasserman, Mary Jane Wick.

Periodicals: *Tomorrow* (newsletter).
Other Information: Established in 1985. On November 5, 1994 former President Reagan released a handwritten letter telling America that he had been diagnosed with Alzheimer's disease. President Reagan can be reached through his Presidential Office, 1100 Wilshire Blvd., Los Angeles, CA 90024. The Foundation paid the Franklin, MA, firm of L.W. Robbins Associates $253,764 for fundraising. The Foundation received $6,539,877, or 93% of revenue, from contributions and grants awarded by foundations, businesses, and individuals. (These grants included $300,000 from the Bradley Foundation, $250,000 from the Oriental Daily News, $225,000 from L. Bob Hope, and $125,000 from the J.W. Kluge Foundation. In 1995, $300,000 from the Lynde and Harry Bradley Foundation. The Foundation has historically received large grants from director Walter Annenberg, the Government of Japan, the Republic of China, and the Sultan of Brunei.) $361,036 net, or 5%, from the sale of inventory. $151,215, or 2%, from interest on savings and temporary cash investments.

Ruth and Vernon Taylor Foundation

1670 Denver Club Building
Denver, CO 80202   **Phone:**   (303) 893-5284
USA

Contact Person: Vernon F. Taylor, Jr., Trustee.
Mission or Interest: Grant-making foundation that includes conservative and free-market organizations in its awards.
Accomplishments: In the fiscal year ending June 1995, the Foundation awarded $1,499,751 in grants. Recipients included: $12,500 for the Heritage Foundation, $10,500 for the Mountain States Legal Foundation, $8,000 for the National Right to Work Legal Defense Fund, $7,500 for the Political Economy Research Center, $4,000 for the Foundation for Teaching Economics, $3,000 each for the Cato Institute and George C. Marshall International Center, $2,000 each for Accuracy in Media, American Council for Capital Formation Center for Policy Research, Institute for Justice, and Pacific Institute for Public Policy research, and $1,000 for National Empowerment Television.
Total Revenue: FY ending 6/95 $1,928,561   **Total Expenses:** $1,589,048   **Net Assets:** $30,824,088 2%(2)
Tax Status: 501(c)(3)   **Employees:** 0
Board of Directors or Trustees: Sara Taylor Swift, Ruth Taylor Campbell, Friday Green.
Other Information: The Foundation received $974,036, or 51% of revenue, from dividend and interest from securities. $807,761, or 42%, from capital gains on the sale of assets. $120,040, or 6%, from interest on the savings and temporary cash investments. The remaining revenue came from various miscellaneous sources. The Foundation held $25,310,341, or 82% of assets, in corporate stock.

Rutherford Institute

1445 E. Rio Road
Charlottesville, VA 22906   **Phone:**   (804) 978-3888   **E-Mail:**   rutherford@fini.com
USA   **Fax:**   (804) 978-1789   **Internet:** http://rutherford.org

Contact Person: Nisha N. Mohammed, Media Coordinator.
Officers or Principals: John W. Whitehead, President/Chairman ($205,800); Alexis I. Crow, Legal Coordinator ($81,039); John C. Thomas, Vice President ($0); Louis A. Larson, Secretary/Treasurer.
Mission or Interest: Legal and educational organization that defends First Amendment rights with particular emphasis on freedom of religion.
Accomplishments: "Have helped thousands of people with our educational materials to stand up for their religious rights and have fought in court for religious liberty, family rights, and the sanctity of human life." A staff reporter for *The Wall Street Journal* wrote that Rutherford "is the most active Christian legal group these days." In the fiscal year ending June 1995 the Institute spent $4,025,177 on its programs. The largest program, with expenditures of $2,071,366, was the production and distribution of educational materials - over 89,422 pamphlets, monographs, books, and tapes were distributed, and its periodicals were sent to over 75,000 readers. $1,701,915 was spent on legal research and litigation - approximately 750 people were aided by litigation or dispute resolution, and 8,750 people attended the Institute's legal seminars. Other programs included research on religious freedom internationally.
Total Revenue: FY ending 6/95 $5,464,716 (-7%)(2) **Total Expenses:** $5,142,927 78%/13%/9% **Net Assets:** $2,971,194
Products or Services: Radio program heard on 1083 stations, publications, seminars. Student chapters at law schools nationwide.
Tax Status: 501(c)(3)   **Annual Report:** No. **Employees:** 51   **Citations:** 189:39
Board of Directors or Trustees: James Buchfuehrer, Donovan Campbell, Jr.
Periodicals: *Rutherford* (monthly magazine), *Freedom Under Fire* (monthly, for radio stations), *Religious Liberty Bulletin* (monthly).
Internships: Yes, summer internships for law students.
Other Information: Established in 1982. The Institute has seven regional offices in the United States: Sacramento, CA; Atlanta, GA; Honolulu, HI; Grand Rapids, MI; Nashville, TN; Dallas, TX; and Fredericksburg, VA. It also has international offices in Bolivia, Hungary, and England. The Institute is named after Samuel Rutherford, a 17th century theologian who challenged the "divine right of kings" in his book Lex Rex (The Law and the Prince). The Institute received $5,310,440, or 97% of gross revenue, from contributions and grants awarded by foundations, businesses, and individuals. (These grants included $1,300 from the Amy Foundation.) $96,242, or 2%, from interest on savings and temporary cash investments. The remaining revenue came from legal settlements, royalties, dividends and interest from securities. The Institute lost $7,762 on the sale of securities and other assets.

Safe Streets Alliance

919 18th St., N.W.
Washington, DC 20006   **Phone:** (202) 822-8100
USA   **Fax:**   (202) 822-8149

Contact Person: James Wootton, President.
Officers or Principals: James Wootton, President ($75,779); Lt. Gen. Bill Etnyre, Chairman ($0); Alan Dye, Secretary/Treasurer ($0).
Mission or Interest: "To educate the American public about the inadequacies of the criminal justice system."
Accomplishments: Many media appearances. In 1994 the Alliance spent $157,258 on its programs.
Total Revenue: 1994 $233,433 100%(2) **Total Expenses:** $205,518 77%/17%/7% **Net Assets:** (-$11,786)
Products or Services: Slide presentation and other educational materials.
Tax Status: 501(c)(3)   **Citations:** 17:156
Board of Directors or Trustees: G. Ray Arnett, Grace Bender, Gloria Borland, Alfred Regnery (CEO, Regnery Publishing), Robbie Calloway (Boys Club of America), Ron Crawford, Susan Davis, Thomas Doughty, Thomas Donnelly, Jr., Chief Rueben Greenberg (Charleston, SC), Dr. Douglas Johnston, Jr. (Center for Strategic and International Studies), Emmanuel Kampouris (American Standard), Hon. Virginia Knauer (Director, U.S. Consumer Affairs, Department of Health and Human Services, 1983-89), John Phillips (National Executive Service Corps.), Gov. Ray Shafer, Robert Smith (Olin Corp.), Pat Stern, Claire Tweedie (American Cynamid), Ilene Nagel (U.S. Sentencing Commission), James Grego (Citizens Against Violent Crime).
Other Information: Established in 1992. Affiliated with the 501(c)(4) Safe Streets Coalition. The Alliance received $233,193, or 99.8% of revenue, from contributions and grants awarded by foundations, businesses, and individuals. (These grants included $75,000 from the Sarah Scaife Foundation. In 1995, $50,000 from the Scaife Family Foundation, and $1,000 from the Roe Foundation.) The remaining revenue came from interest on savings and other miscellaneous sources.

Sahara Club USA

4492 Camino De La Plaza, Suite 1251
San Ysidro, CA 92173-3097
USA

Contact Person: Rick Sieman, President.
Officers or Principals: Louis McKey, Vice President; Arlene Valdez, Art Director; Corrinne Jensen, Office Manager/Secretary; Pat Martin, Systems Operation; Rocky Nunzio, Security.
Mission or Interest: The Sahara Club was founded to counter-attack the loss of lands used for recreation caused by environmental regulations. Their methods are direct and controversial. The Club refers to Greenpeace as "a bunch of lying, evil, cretinous, scum-sucking, larcenous, vile, money-grubbing bastards." The Club publishes the names, addresses, and even vehicle licence plate numbers of environmentalists.
Accomplishments: President Rick Sieman has appeared on CBS's "60 Minutes," as well as in other interviews and articles.

Salisbury Review

33 Canonbury Park S.
London NI 2JW, England   **Phone:** (44-71) 226-7791
UNITED KINGDOM   **Fax:**   (44-71) 354-0383

Contact Person: Merrie Cave, Managing Editor.
Officers or Principals: Roger Scruton, Editor; Ian Crowther, Literary Editor.
Mission or Interest: A quarterly magazine of conservative thought, politics, philosophy, literature, and culture.
Tax Status: For profit. **Annual Report:** No. **Employees:** 1
Periodicals: *Salisbury Review* (quarterly journal).
Internships: No.
Other Information: Established in 1982. Named for The Third Marquess of Salisbury (1830-1903). For subscription information in the United States or Canada, contact: ISI, 3901 Centerville Rd., P.O. Box 4431, Wilmington, DE 19807-0431, (800) 526-7022.

Salvatori Center for Academic Leadership

The Heritage Foundation
214 Massachusetts Ave., N.E.
Washington, DC 20002   **Phone:** (202) 546-4400
USA   **Fax:**   (202) 546-8328

Officers or Principals: Leonard P. Liggio, Chairman.
Mission or Interest: A project of the Heritage Foundation, the Salvatori Center assists young faculty and doctoral candidates in the social sciences and humanities by awarding fellowships. Recipients participate in an annual faculty colloquium.
Accomplishments: Each year the Center selects 25 to 40 recipients to serve as fellows for a two-year term.

Tax Status: 501(c)(3)

Board of Directors or Trustees: Herman Belz (Univ. of Maryland), William Bennett (Empower America), George Carey (Georgetown Univ.), Robert Conquest (Hoover Inst.), T. Kenneth Cribb, Jr. (Intercollegiate Studies Inst.), Midge Dector (Inst. on Religion and Public Life), Edwin Delattre (Boston Univ.), Robert Jastrow (Pres., George C. Marshall Inst.), Charles Kesler (Claremont McKenna College), Harvey Mansfield, Jr. (Harvard Univ.), Forest McDonald (Univ. of Alabama), Hon. Edwin Meese, III (Attorney General, 1985-88), Roger Meiners (Univ. of Texas, Arlington), Jacob Neusner (Univ. of S. Florida), Jennifer Roback (George Mason Univ.), Bernard Sheehan (Indiana Univ.), Wilcomb Washburn (Dir., American Studies Program, Smithsonian Inst.).

Other Information: Incorporated as a part of the Heritage Foundation and initially funded by the now-defunct Henry Salvatori Foundation. Henry Salvatori was born in Italy. He earned his degrees at the University of Pennsylvania and Colombia University, then started his own oil-exploration and contracting businesses. He is an original member of Ronald Reagan's 'Kitchen Cabinet,' a group of California civic and business leaders who helped Reagan run for governor, than served as advisors for over two decades. Salvatori has been a long-time patron of education.

Samuel Francis Letter

P.O. Box 19627
Alexandria, VA 22320
USA

Mission or Interest: Newsletter written by syndicated conservative columnist Samuel Francis.

Tax Status: For profit.

Periodicals: *The Samuel Francis Letter* (monthly newsletter).

Other Information: Established in 1996. Samuel Francis was previously an editor at *The Washington Times*. According to Francis he lost his position there due to his affiliation and work with the New Century Foundation, publisher of *American Renaissance*. Francis' column is still carried by the *Times*. *The Samuel Francis Letter* is published by Tribune Media Services.

Samuel Roberts Noble Foundation

2510 Sam Noble Parkway
Ardmore, OK 73401   **Phone:**   (405) 223-5810
USA

Contact Person: Michael A. Cawley, President.

Officers or Principals: Michael A. Cawley, President ($279,358); Richard A. Dixon, Plant Director ($119,544); George H. Hedger, Horticulturist ($108,321); Larry A. Pulliam, Treasurer/CFO ($106,458); Elizabeth A. Aldridge, Secretary.

Mission or Interest: Foundation that concentrates on agriculture and horticulture, but also awards grants to conservative organizations.

Accomplishments: In the fiscal year ending October 1995, the Foundation spent $14,555,063 on its own projects researching plant biology and agriculture. The Foundation awarded $11,392,705 in grants. Recipients included: $450,000 for the Heritage Foundation, $33,000 for the Georgia Public Policy Foundation, $25,000 each for the Center for Strategic and International Studies, Southeastern Legal Foundation, and Free Congress Foundation, $20,000 for Students for America, $10,000 each for the Capital Research Center, Institute for Political Economy, Intercollegiate Studies Institute, Leadership Institute, and Citizens for Budget Reform, and $5,000 for the Progress and Freedom Foundation.

Total Revenue: FY ending 10/95 $29,090,835 **Total Expenses:** $29,179,976 **Net Assets:** $578,644,517 1%(2)

Tax Status: 501(c)(3)

Board of Directors or Trustees: Robert Geurin, Ann Noble Brown, D. Randolph Brown, Jr., David Brown, Vivian Noble DuBose, Bill Goddard, W.R. Goddard, E.E. Noble, Mary Jane Noble, Nick Noble, Russell Noble, Marianne Rooney, John Snodgrass.

Other Information: Established in 1945 by oilman Lloyd Noble, founder of the Noble Drilling and Samedan Oil companies. The Foundation was named for Lloyd Noble's father. The Foundation received $14,644,078, or 50% of revenue, from dividends and interest from securities. $12,735,613, or 44%, from capital gains on the sale of securities. $729,683 or 3%, from interest on savings and temporary cash investments. The remaining revenue came from contributions and grants, the sale of inventory, and miscellaneous investments. The Foundation held $456,998,915, or 79% of assets, in corporate stock. This included approximately 14% of the outstanding shares of Noble Affiliates and 7% of the outstanding shares of Noble Drilling Co.

Sarah Scaife Foundation

Three Mellon Bank Center
525 William Penn Place, Suite 3900
Pittsburgh, PA 15219   **Phone:**   (412) 392-2900
USA

Contact Person: Richard M. Larry, President.

Officers or Principals: Richard M. Larry, President ($326,744); Barbara L. Slaney, Vice President ($201,594); Donald C. Sipp, Treasurer ($148,244); Richard M. Scaife, Chairman.

Mission or Interest: Grant-making foundation that includes conservative and free-market organizations in its awards.

Accomplishments: In 1994 the Foundation awarded $11,335,000 in grants. Recipients included: $600,000 for the Heritage Foundation, $500,000 for the Center for the Study of Popular Culture, $470,000 for the Center for Strategic and International Studies, $420,000 for the Institute for Foreign Policy Analysis, two grants totaling $415,000 for the American Enterprise Institute, $400,000 for the Intercollegiate Studies Institute, $350,000 for the Social Philosophy and Policy Foundation, $300,000 for the National Association of Scholars, $275,000 for the Capital Research Center, $260,000 for the Hoover Institution, $200,000 for the Ethics and Public Policy Center, two grants totaling $185,000 for the American Spectator Educational Foundation, $150,000 each for Citizens for a Sound Economy, Pacific Research Institute, Political Economy Research Center, and Foundation for Cultural Review, $135,000 for the Cato Institute, $130,000 for the George C. Marshall Institute, $125,000 for the Center for Security Policy, $100,000 each for the National Taxpayers Union Foundation, Institute for Contemporary Studies, Institute on Religion and Public Life, Institute for the Study of Economic Culture at Boston University, Center for Study of Public Choice and the Law and Economics Center at George Mason University, and the Catalyst Institute, $75,000 each for the American Academy for Liberal Education, Federalist Society, Foreign Policy Research Institute, Freedom House, Reason Foundation, and Claremont Institute, $70,000 for the Institute for Research on the Economics of Taxation, and $60,000 each for the Competitive Enterprise Institute, and Institute for Justice.
Total Revenue: 1994 $9,886,199 **Total Expenses:** $13,545,258 **Net Assets:** $202,780,262 (-2%)(2)
Tax Status: 501(c)(3)
Board of Directors or Trustees: T. Kenneth Cribb, Jr. (Intercollegiate Studies Inst.), Anthony Bryan, William Bennett (Empower America), James Walton, Dr. Allan Meltzer (Carnegie Mellon Univ.).
Other Information: The Foundation received $9,048,420, or 92% of revenue, from dividends and interest from securities. $444,037, or 4%, from interest on savings and temporary cash investments. $389,560, or 4%, from capital gains on the sale of assets. The remaining revenue came from various miscellaneous investments. The Foundation held $101,782,692, or 50% of assets, in corporate stock. $30,280,822, or 15%, in corporate bonds.

Scaife Family Foundation

Three Mellon Bank Center, Suite 3900
Pittsburgh, PA 15219
USA

Contact Person: Joanne B. Beyer, Vice President.
Officers or Principals: Jennie K. Scaife, David N. Scaife, Co-Chairmen; Sanford B. Ferguson, President.
Mission or Interest: Grant-making foundation that includes conservative organizations in its awards.
Accomplishments: In 1995 the Foundation awarded $5,314,800 in grants. Recipients included: $275,000 for the Center for the Study of Popular Culture, $245,000 for the National Center for Neighborhood Enterprise, $225,000 for the Landmark Legal Foundation, $200,000 each for the Center for Strategic and International Studies and National Fatherhood Initiative, $150,000 for the Competitive Enterprise Institute, $125,000 for the American Enterprise Institute, $100,000 each for the Acton Institute, Citizens for a Sound Economy Education Foundation, and Allegheny Institute for Public Policy, $80,000 for the Free Enterprise Partnership, $75,000 each for the Center for Education Reform, and the Social Philosophy and Policy Foundation, $50,000 each for the Collegiate Network, National Legal and Policy Center, Of the People Foundation, Safe Streets Alliance, and Capital Research Center, $35,000 for the Commonwealth Foundation for Public Policy Alternatives, $27,500 for the Education Policy Institute, $25,000 each for the Center for Individual Rights, and Equal Opportunity Foundation, and $15,000 for Accuracy in Media.
Total Revenue: 1995 $6,912,509 **Total Expenses:** $5,878,981 **Net Assets:** $131,210,610
Tax Status: 501(c)(3)
Other Information: The Foundation received $4,135,928, or 60% of revenue, from dividends and interest from securities. $2,764,778, or 40%, from capital gains on the sale of assets. The Foundation held $57,832,000, or 44%, in corporate stocks, $33,503,312, or 26%, in government securities. /

Scholl Institute of Bioethics

2606½ W. 8th St.
Los Angeles, CA 90057   **Phone:** (213) 382-2156
USA   **Fax:** (213) 382-4359

Mission or Interest: "An organization that addresses bioethical issues including euthanasia, the withholding or withdrawing of food and water from non-dying patients, brain death, organ transplantation, genetic engineering, surrogacy, and the disabled or mentally ill."
Accomplishments: Former Governor George Deukmejian (R-CA), regarding proposed assisted-suicide legislation, credited the Institute with being "helpful (to me) in reaching my decision to veto this legislation." Professor Emeritus Walter R. Trinkaus of Loyola Law School of Los Angeles, said "The high quality of your research and information is vital in this time of crisis."
Tax Status: 501(c)(3)
Other Information: The Institute is named after Hans and Sophie Scholl, brother and sister who "were members of the White Rose, a group of university students who resisted the policies of the Third Reich including the 'mercy' killings of disabled and mentally ill persons in Nazi Germany. Hans and Sophie were executed as traitors by the Nazis on February 22, 1943."

Science and Environmental Policy Project (SEPP)

4084 University Dr., Suite 101
Fairfax, VA 22030   **Phone:**   (703) 934-6940
USA   **Fax:**   (703) 352-7535

Contact Person: Fred Singer, Ph.D., President.
Officers or Principals: Frederick Seitz, Ph.D., Chairman.
Mission or Interest: "SEPP supplies sound scientific information to decision-makers, the media, and the public. SEPP is particularly active in networking with active scientists in order to involve them more directly in shaping environmental policies based on scientific fact rather than hype and emotion."
Accomplishments: Over 50 publications have been authored by Fred Singer, Gehard Stohrer, and other SEPP-affiliated scientists. Prominent in the greenhouse/global-warming and ozone-depletion debates. In both cases Singer and the Project maintain that no serious environmental threat exists. In a 1996 debate regarding the Intergovernmental Panel on Climate Change's report on global warming, Singer criticized the Panel for changing the wording of scientific material after it had been approved by government representatives. These changes made it appear as if there was a strong consensus among scientists as to the link between human production of greenhouse gasses and global temperature; and that, "in this crusade to provide a scientific cover for political action, they are misusing the work of respected scientists who never made extravagant claims about future warming."
Tax Status: 501(c)(3)   **Annual Report:** Yes.
Board of Directors or Trustees: Charles Gelman, M.S., David Hill, Ph.D. The Board of Scientific Advisors includes: Bruce Ames, Ph.D. (Univ. of California, Berkeley), Martin Apple, Ph.D. (Council of Scientific Society Presidents), C. J. F. Böttcher, Ph.D. (Global Inst. for the Study of Natural Resources, The Hague), Tor Ragnar Gerholm, Ph.D. (Univ. of Stockholm), Michael Higatsberger, Ph.D. (Univ. of Vienna), Henry Linden, Ph.D. (Illinois Inst. of Technology), Sir William Mitchell, Ph.D. Univ. of Oxford), William Nierenberg, Ph.D. (Scripps Inst. of Oceanography), Michel Salomon, M.D. (Intl. Centre for Scientific Ecology, Paris), Chauncey Starr, Ph.D. (Electric Power Research Inst.).
Other Information: Established as an independent nonprofit organization in 1994. Prior to that it was affiliated with the Institute for Contemporary Studies.

Second Amendment Foundation (SAF)

12500 N.E. 10th Place
Bellevue, WA 98005   **Phone:**   (206) 454-7012
USA

Contact Person: Alan Gottlieb, Director.
Officers or Principals: Alan Gottlieb, Director ($39,000); Joe Tartaro, President ($32,500); John M. Snyder, Treasurer ($10,200); Jeffrey D. Kane, Vice President; Sam Slom, Secretary; Talcott J. Franklin, Research Director.
Mission or Interest: Protection of gun owner's rights.
Accomplishments: Numerous publications and paraphernalia produced by the Foundation are used by other organizations. Its publication, *Women & Guns* has been published since 1991 and has a circulation of approximately 18,000. In 1994 the Foundation spent $2,357,095 on its programs. Some of this, $40,366 was spent on litigation on behalf of specific gun-owners and Second Amendment rights in general. Also awarded a grant of $5,000 to Academics for the Second Amendment, and $7,478 for tuition for seven students.
Total Revenue: 1994 $3,448,404 14%(1) **Total Expenses:** $3,358,701 70%/13%/27% **Net Assets:** $921,043
Products or Services: Research reports, newsletter. That Every Man Be Armed, book. Presents annual James Madison Award for excellence in journalism promoting the right to keep and bear arms. Hosts annual Gun Rights Policy Conference.
Tax Status: 501(c)(3) **Annual Report:** No. **Employees:** 16   **Citations:** 11:170
Periodicals: *Gun News Digest* (quarterly magazine), *Women & Guns* (monthly magazine), *Gun Week* (weekly tabloid), and *The Gottlieb - Tartaro Report* (monthly newsletter).
Internships: Yes.
Other Information: The Foundation received $2,721,439, or 79% of revenue, from contributions and grants awarded by foundations, businesses, and individuals. $492,067, or 14%, from subscriptions. $166,288, or 5%, from advertising. $31,043, or 1%, from interest on savings and temporary cash investments. The remaining revenue came from mailing list rentals, dividends and interest from securities, and other miscellaneous sources.

Second Renaissance Book Service

143 West St.
New Milford, CT 06776   **Phone:** (800) 729-6149   **E-Mail:** 74222.2330@compuserve.com
USA   **Fax:**   (860) 355-7161

Contact Person: Edward A. Podritske, Vice President.
Officers or Principals: Peter Schwartz, President; Edward A. Podritske, Vice President.
Mission or Interest: Sells a selection of books and audio tapes on the subjects of, reason, free markets, individualism, and intellectual history with a special focus on the works of Ayn Rand and other objectivists.

Accomplishments: "Pre-eminent audio publisher of works by Ayn Rand and Leonard Peikoff with customers in over 40 countries."
Products or Services: 32-page catalog of books and audio cassettes. "A Philosopher Looks at the O.J. Verdict" cassettes by Leonard Peikoff. Peikoff looks at notions of truth and reason that came into play in the O.J. Simpson criminal trial, and traces the cause for Simpson's acquittal to emotionalism over reason and its philosophical origins in Immanuel Kant's work. Other cassettes with Peikoff feature discussions of literature, drama, reason, and objectivism.
Tax Status: For profit. **Employees:** No.

Seniors Coalition, The

11166 Main St., Suite 302
Fairfax, VA 22030   **Phone:**   (703) 591-0663
USA   **Fax:**   (703) 591-0679

Contact Person: Hugh C. Newton, Public Relations Counsel.
Officers or Principals: Paul A. Bramell, President/CEO ($114,260); Jake Hansen, Executive Director ($96,980); George McDonnell, Chairman ($61,000); Karl Lady, Treasurer.
Mission or Interest: Represents the nation's senior citizens on a wide variety of issues. Advocates primarily on behalf of: sound and self-funding Social Security and Medicare systems, a fiscally responsible government which balances its budgets, responsible health care reform which insures availability and quality, and policies which strengthen the family. Their motto is,"Protecting the Future You Have Earned."
Accomplishments: With more than two million members, it is now the third largest senior citizens' organization.
Total Revenue: 1995 $10,582,490 **Total Expenses:** $11,679,654 73%/12%/16% **Net Assets:** $481,355
Products or Services: Original research, book - <u>What Everyone Should Know About Social Security</u>. Lobbying on behalf of senior citizens. In 1995 the Coalition spent $8,472,248 on its programs.
Tax Status: 501(c)(4)   **Citations:** 102:62
Board of Directors or Trustees: Warren Stewart, James Carlen, Kim Pearson. National Advisors include, Robert Myers (Exec. Dir., National Commission on Social Security Reform 1982-83), Chairman, Lt. Gen. Quinn Becker, USA, Ret. (former Surgeon General of the Army), Dr. Timothy Covington (Chairman, Dept. of Pharmacy, Samford Univ.), Prof. Charles Schewe (Univ. of Massachusetts, Amherst), Hon. Paul Shaw (Honorary Dir., New York Teachers Pension Assn.).
Periodicals: *The Senior Class* (bimonthly newspaper), *Senior Alert* (bimonthly newsletter).
Other Information: Affiliated with the 501(c)(3) Seniors Foundation. Jake Hansen is a former executive director of the American Conservative Union. The Coalition's publications regularly feature conservative authors and researchers. The Coalition received $9,844,560, or 93% of revenue, from contributors. $559,337, or 5%, from advertising income. $119,995, or 1%, from mailing list rentals. The remaining revenue came from capital gains on the sale of securities, dividends and interest from securities, and other miscellaneous sources.

Sentinel Communications

15113 Steele Creek Rd.
Charlotte, NC 28273   **Phone:**   (704) 587-0898
USA   **Fax:**   (704) 587-0195

Contact Person: Jerry McManus.
Mission or Interest: "Publication and distribution of conservative activist newsletter, *The American Sentinel*."
Tax Status: For profit. **Employees:** 2
Periodicals: *The American Sentinel*.
Internships: No.

Sequoia Institute

3479 Beaver Ford Rd.
Woodbridge, VA 22192   **Phone:**   (703) 590-0496
USA   **Fax:**   (703) 730-1156

Contact Person: Jerry B. Jenkins, President.
Officers or Principals: Jerry B. Jenkins, President ($3,249).
Mission or Interest: Increasing consumer choice in the formulation, implementation, and effects of public policies, with particular application to developing countries. Examining the viability of overhauling the Social Security system, here and in similar programs abroad, to create a system where the ownership of savings is not monopolized by the government.
Accomplishments: The Sequoia Seminar Publications (Institute for Contemporary Studies Press) are now on the tenth book in the series, <u>Development By Consent: The Voluntary Supply of Public Goods and Services</u>. The Sequoia Institute published some of the first assessments of school choice and educational vouchers.
Total Revenue: FY ending 6/95 $7,271 (-81%)(2)(see **Other Information**) **Total Expenses:** $30,409 **Net Assets:** $5,442
Tax Status: 501(c)(3) **Employees:** No.
Board of Directors or Trustees: 1 full-time, 2 part-time.

Internships: No.
Other Information: The Institute experienced a rapid drop in revenue, from $200,393 in 1993 to $7,271 in 1995. This rapid drop was due to the loss of government grants. Sequoia had been the recipient of $1.6 million from the U.S. Agency for International Development to study economic development. This government funding had accounted for 97% of its funding in the fiscal year ending June 1993. In the fiscal year ending June 1995 the Institute received $6,993, or 96% of revenue, from contributions and grants awarded by foundations, businesses, and individuals. $278, or 4%, from the sale of inventory.

Sex and Family Education (SAFE)

1608 S. 13th Ave., Suite 112
Birmingham, AL 35205   **Phone:**   (205) 939-0302
USA   **Fax:**   (205) 939-0394

Contact Person: Mrs. Ruth E. Wooten, Director.
Mission or Interest: "Motivate and equip teens with strategies to be sexually abstinent until marriage. Live classroom presentations in public schools and churches, and through the four-part `You Are Unique' video series."
Accomplishments: Live presentations have been made to more than 15,000 public school students in Birmingham. Twenty-eight SAFE affiliates in eight states. Curriculum in use in Africa, Latin America, Romania, and Canada. Nationwide distribution of the video series.
Products or Services: Teaching manuals: "You Are Unique," "God Made You Unique," "Unique Parenting," "Chastity Counseling."
Tax Status: 501(c)(3)   **Employees:** 1 full time, 2 part time, 60 volunteers.
Periodicals: *SAFE Update* (quarterly).
Internships: No.
Other Information: Sex and Family Education is a project of Sav-A-Life, Inc.

Sherwood Sugden & Company, Publishers

315 5th St.
Peru, IL 61354   **Phone:**   (815) 223-2520
USA   **Fax:**   (815) 223-4486

Contact Person: Sherwood Sugden, Publisher.
Mission or Interest: Publishes new titles and reprints in philosophy, history, religion, literary criticism and Christian apologetics. "A certain sympathy for Roman Catholicism, the West, Canada, and the American South may mark our publications."
Accomplishments: 32 books currently in print. Favorable reviews in *First Things*, *National Review*, *New Oxford Review*, *Chronicles*, *University Bookman*, and the *New York Times Review of Books*.
Products or Services: Titles include works by Russell Kirk, M.E. Bradford, G.K. Chesterton, E. Michael Jones (*Culture Wars*), Hilaire Belloc, and others.
Tax Status: For profit.

Small Business Legislative Council

1156 15th St., N.W., Suite 510
Washington, DC 20005   **Phone:**   (202) 639-8888
USA

Contact Person: John S. Satagaj, President.
Officers or Principals: John S. Satagaj, President ($10,000); Benjamin Y. Cooper, Chairman ($0); Matthew B. Coffey, Treasurer ($0); David Gorin, Secretary.
Mission or Interest: Organization that represents associations of small businesses, explaining the impact of legislation to them and lobbying on their behalf.
Total Revenue: 1995 $177,333 **Total Expenses:** $176,690 3%/97%/0% **Net Assets:** $63,296
Products or Services: Guides to the Americans With Disabilities Act and Occupational Safety and Health Administration regulations. In 1995 the Council spent $112,560 on lobbying, 63% of its total budget.
Tax Status: 501(c)(6)   **Citations:** 2:216
Board of Directors or Trustees: (Directors represent member organizations) Elaine Acevedo (Florists' Transworld Delivery Assn.), Paula Calimafde (Small Business Council of America), W. Dewey Clower (NATSO), Philip Chisholm (Petroleum Marketers Assn.), Robert Dolibois (American Assn. of Nurserymen), Gary Donnelly (Natl. Lumber & Building Material Dealers Assn.), Stephen Driesler (Natl. Assn. of Realtors), Philip Friedlander (Natl. Tire Dealers & Retreaders Assn.), Raymond Hall (Electronics Representatives Assn.), Charles Hawkins (Associated Builders & Contractors), Michael Jenkins (American Warehouse Assn.), Frank Jensen (Helicopter Assn. Intl.), Robert Morgan (Council of Growing Companies), Allen Neece (Assn. of Small Business Development Centers), Colette Nelson (American Subcontractors Assn.), Joseph O'Neil (American Council of Independent Laboratories), Neil Offen (Direct Selling Assn.), Ted Olson (Promotional Products Assn. Intl.), Susan Perry (American Business Assn.), John Rector (Natl. Assn. of Retail Druggists), Peter Ruane (American Road & Transportation Builders Assn.), Bennie Thayer (Natl. Assn. for the Self-Employed).
Other Information: Affiliated with the 501(c)(3) Small Business Research and Education Council.

Small Business Survival Committee

1320 18th St., N.W., Suite 200
Washington, DC 20036
USA

Phone: (202) 785-0238
Fax: (202) 822-8118

E-Mail: rstikes@sbsc.org
Internet: http://www.sbsc.org

Contact Person: Karen Kerrigan, President.
Officers or Principals: Karen Kerrigan, President ($82,414); Grover Norquist, Treasurer ($0); Svdnet Hoff-Hay, Secretary ($0); Raymond Keating, Chief Economist.
Mission or Interest: An advocate for small business. Opposed to taxes, regulation, and pending legislation at all levels of government that imposes "unfair burdens on American businesses and impedes economic growth."
Accomplishments: Nearly 36,000 activist members nationwide. Testified before Congress on a variety of issues including the EPA's Superfund Program, broadcasting spectrum allocations and auctions, the Commerce Department, and reforming OSHA. Op-eds have appeared in the *Wall Street Journal, New York Times, Washington Times, Investor's Business Daily*, and others. Television appearances include CNN, C-SPAN, CNBC, America's Talking, NET-TV, ABC, PBS affiliates, and others. In the fiscal year ending June 1996, the Committee spent $173,483 on its programs.
Total Revenue: FY ending 6/96 $368,646 **Total Expenses:** $419,888 41%/58%/1% **Net Assets:** $20,045
Products or Services: "Small Business Hill Alert" weekly fax alert. Twice-monthly conferences. Annual "National Small Business Summit".
Tax Status: 501(c)(4)   **Citations:** 76:82
Periodicals: *Small Business and the Economy* (bimonthly newsletter).
Other Information: Affiliated with the 501(c)(3) Small Business Survival Foundation. (In 1995 the Foundation received $38,000 from the John M. Olin Foundation.) The Committee received $273,815, or 74% of revenue, from contributors. $93,982, or 25%, from reimbursements from the Foundation. The remaining revenue came from interest on savings.

Smith Center for Private Enterprise Studies

California State University
Hayward, CA 94542
USA

Phone: (510) 885-2640
Fax: (510) 885-4222

E-Mail: dmittels@csuhayward.edu

Contact Person: Donna Mittelstedt.
Officers or Principals: Charles W. Baird, Ph.D., Sam Basu, Ph.D., Co-Directors.
Mission or Interest: Educational activities for college students promoting entrepreneurship and free-market economics. Located in the School of Business and Economics, at the University of California, Hayward.
Accomplishments: Past speakers have included Nobel Laureate, Milton Friedman, former Secretary of Education, William Bennett, and former Secretary of Labor, Lynn Martin, Robert Bork, Dr. Erik Von Kuehnelt-Leddihn, Thomas DiLorenzo, Robert Hessen, the late Dr. Murray Rothbard, Dr. Bruce Ames, Edwin Fuelner, and others.
Products or Services: Government in Healthcare: Lessons from the U.K., by W. Duncan Reekie. Two-week summer economics program for high-school teachers, and essay contests and speakers for high-school students. Research grants and student grants. Conferences and seminars. Videos of lectures and speeches.
Tax Status: 501(c)(3) **Annual Report:** No. **Employees:** 3
Board of Directors or Trustees: Advisors include: Annelise Anderson (Hoover Inst.), John Baden (Foundation for Research on Economics and the Environment), Roger Garrison (Auburn Univ.), M. Bruce Johnson, Shyam Kamath (California State Univ., Hayward), Dwight Lee (Univ. of Georgia), William Mellor, III (Inst. for Justice), W. Duncan Reekie (Univ. of Witwatersrand), Stephen Shmanske (California State Univ., Hayward), Karen Vaughn (George Mason Univ.).
Periodicals: *Smith Center Journal.*
Internships: No.
Other Information: Founded in 1991 by entrepreneurs Owen R. and Emma F. Smith of California. Director Charles Baird is a member of the Mont Pelerin Society, and has been affiliated with the Cato Institute, Foundation for Economic Education, and the Ludwig von Mises Institute. He has written extensively on Austrian economics.

Smith Richardson Foundation

230 N. Elm St., Suite 1600
Greensboro, NC 27401
USA

Contact Person: P. L. Richardson, President.
Officers or Principals: P. L. Richardson, President ($219,041); Marin J. Strmecki, Program Director ($190,547); Arvid R. Nelson, Secretary ($179,225); R. L. Coble, Treasurer ($163,593); Cheryl A. Keller, Senior Program Officer ($114,008); H. S. Richardson, Jr., Chairman.
Mission or Interest: "Supports scholarly research on issues of public policy. All Smith Richardson grants share an emphasis on pragmatic policy-relevant research. Proposals are evaluated based on the project's relevance to public policy, the soundness of its methodology, the significance of its contribution to the existing literature, and the principal investigator's expertise and qualifications to carry out the project." Includes grants for free-market organizations.

Accomplishments: In 1995 the Foundation awarded $10,369,480 in grants. Recipients included: $273,762 for the National Institute for Public Policy, $250,000 for the Center for Individual Rights, $210,050 for the American Enterprise Institute, $150,000 each for the Center for Strategic and International Studies, and National Affairs, $144,881 for the Hudson Institute, $125,000 for the Ethics and Public Policy Center, $86,164 for the National Forum Foundation, $85,350 for the Institute for Contemporary Studies, $51,000 for the Concord Coalition, $50,000 for the American Jewish Committee, $46,400 for the Middle East Forum, $25,000 for the Philanthropy Roundtable, and $24,750 for the Social Philosophy and Policy Foundation. The Foundation also gave to some left-of-center policy groups, including $310,500 for the Brookings Institution, and $85,000 for the Wisconsin Project on Nuclear Arms Control.
Total Revenue: 1995 $36,521,527 **Total Expenses:** $16,092,499 **Net Assets:** $390,383,075 3%(2)
Tax Status: 501(c)(3)
Board of Directors or Trustees: R.R. Richardson, Robert DeMichele, Diana Washburn, Robert Mulreany, Heather Higgins, Stuart Richardson, Adele Richardson Ray, Gary Brewer, L. Richardson Preyer, Lundsford Richardson, Jr., Henry Rowen, E. William Stetson, III, Zbigniew Brzezinski, Edward Meyer, Edward Zigler, William Odom, Doug Besharov, Isabel Sawhill, Marc Trachtenberg, Michel Oksenberg, Rebecca Maynard, Larry Mead, Sara McLanahan, John Aber.
Other Information: Established in 1935. (The following financial data includes three affiliated 501(c)(2) title-holding companies.) The Foundation received $22,064,197, or 60% of revenue, from capital gains on the sale of assets. $10,538,195, or 29%, from dividends and interest from securities. $3,315,560, or 9%, from an investments partnership. The remaining revenue came from interest on savings and temporary cash investments, dividends and interest from securities, and other miscellaneous sources. The Foundation held $261,201,749, or 67% of assets, in corporate securities.

Sobran's

P.O. Box 565
Herndon, VA 22070   **Phone:**   (800) 513-5053
USA

Mission or Interest: Newsletter written by conservative columnist Joe Sobran.
Tax Status: For profit.
Periodicals: *Sobran's* (newsletter).
Other Information: Joe Sobran was formerly a senior editor at *National Review*, until he had a falling out with William F. Buckley, Jr. The rift was caused by (according to Sobran) Sobran's public criticism of and feuding with 'neo-conservatives'. Previously, Buckley publicly examined some of Sobran's writings in the *National Review* after Norman Podhoretz (*Commentary*) and other neo-conservatives raised the possibility that Sobran's views were anti-Semitic. Buckley examined the charges, and in a lengthy article "In Search of Anti-Semitism," decided that although Sobran had been sharply critical of Israel's policies (in regard to Christians and Palestinians living in Israel), he was not anti-Semitic. The newsletter is published by The Vere Company.

Social Philosophy and Policy Foundation

P.O. Box 938
Bowling Green, OH 43402   **Phone:**   (419) 372-2536
USA   **Fax:**   (419) 372-8738

Contact Person: Fred D. Miller, Jr., President.
Officers or Principals: Fred D. Miller, Jr., President ($0); Ellen F. Paul, Vice President ($0); Jeffrey E. Paul, Secretary ($0); Duane Stranahan, Trustee.
Mission or Interest: Supports publications, conferences, and fellowships in philosophy and public policy.
Accomplishments: In 1995 the Foundation spent $484,173 on its programs. This included $429,158 in grants, which resulted in the publication of 11 books and numerous articles on public policy. The recipient of the largest grant was $323,100 for the Social Philosophy and Policy Center (see **Other Information**). Other recipients included Edward Jay Epstein, Myron Lieberman, Charlene Harr, and William McGowan - all of whom are writing books.
Total Revenue: 1995 $1,746,725 18%(2) **Total Expenses:** $661,771 73%/21%/5% **Net Assets:** $12,178,181
Tax Status: 501(c)(3)   **Citations:** 2:216
Other Information: Supports the Social Philosophy and Policy Center, an academic institution affiliated with and incorporated under, Bowling Green State University that can be reached through the Foundation. The Foundation received $760,980, or 44% of revenue, from contributions and grants awarded by foundations, businesses, and individuals. (These included $125,000 from the Carthage Foundation, $100,000 from the John M. Olin Foundation, $75,000 from the Scaife Family Foundation, $39,930 from the Lynde and Harry Bradley Foundation, $24,750 from the Smith Richardson Foundation, $15,000 from the Philip M. McKenna Foundation, and $1,000 from the John William Pope Foundation. In 1994, $350,000 from the Sarah Scaife Foundation, $70,000 from the Lilly Endowment, $35,000 from the Earhart Foundation, and $17,500 from the F.M. Kirby Foundation.) $515,082, or 29%, from dividends and interest from securities. $425,640 net, or 24%, from capital gains on the sale of securities. $43,552, or 2%, from interest on savings and temporary cash investments. The remaining revenue came from other investments.

Society for Environmental Truth (SET)

5535 E. Rosewood St.
Tucson, AZ 85711   **Phone:**   (520) 518-0430
USA   **Fax:**   (520) 519-0433

Contact Person: R. S. Bennett, Executive Director.

Officers or Principals: Randy Jones, President.
Mission or Interest: To promote private ownership and private management of land and resources. "Environmental law based on sound science." Operates through six sections; general, forests and wilderness, wildlife management and endangered species, range resources, mineral resources, and energy.
Accomplishments: Delayed or stopped the transfer of some lands from private ownership to government ownership.
Total Revenue: 1993 less than $25,000
Products or Services: Position papers, newsletter.
Tax Status: 501(c)(3) **Annual Report:** No. **Employees:** 1
Board of Directors or Trustees: Dr. Jane Orient (Exec. Dir., American Association of Physicians and Surgeons), Director, General Section; Walter Armer, Sr. (past Pres., Arizona Cattlemen's Association), Range Resources Section; Dennis Parker (Univ. of AZ, Elderhostel), Wildlife Management and Endangered Species Section; Richard Leisure, Mineral Resources Section; Dr. Charles Osterberg (former Asst. Dir. of Environment at the Atomic Energy Commission and Dir., International Laboratory of Marine Radioactivity at Monaco).
Periodicals: *The Torch* (nine times a year).
Internships: No.
Other Information: Established in 1992. R.S. Bennet is a former forestry instructor.

Soldier of Fortune

5735 Arapahoe Road
Boulder, CO 80303   **Phone:** (303) 449-3750
USA

Contact Person: Articles editor.
Officers or Principals: Robert K. Brown, Editor; Janice L. Brown, Associate Publisher; Tom Slizewski, Executive Editor; Don McLean, Senior Editor.
Mission or Interest: Magazine of weaponry and weapon owners' rights, history, military and para-military information.
Accomplishments: *Soldier of Fortune* currently has a circulation of about 23,000 subscribers and 80,000 in newsstand sales. *Soldier of Fortune* provides military analysis of various conflicts throughout the globe, information from the field which is seldom published in the mainstream news media. The magazine is recovering financially from a court decision that held the magazine liable for running a classified ad which turned out to be a request for a hit-man - although the ad was not worded as such. In addition to their usual material, the magazine has given considerable attention to analyzing the stand-off between Federal agents and the Branch Davidians in Waco, Texas - the events that led up to it, and the federal government's investigation following the fatal fire. Publisher Robert K. Brown sits on the Board of Directors of the National Rifle Foundation. *Soldier of Fortune* has recently challenged the claims of various conspiracy theorists, including the American Justice Federation and the Liberty Lobby.
Tax Status: For profit.
Periodicals: *Soldier of Fortune* (monthly).

Sound Dollar Committee

P.O. Box 226
Fort Lee, NJ 07024   **Phone:** (201) 224-6037
USA

Contact Person: Richard L. Solyom.
Mission or Interest: Reform of U.S. monetary system to restore "Constitutional money, i.e. specie money."
Accomplishments: Carried out two money-issue test cases through the lower courts to the U.S. Supreme Court. Funded and published the book by Dr. Erwin Vieira, Pieces of Eight, which "has become the standard reference book for those engaged in monetary reform."
Products or Services: Pieces of Eight, pamphlets. "Dr. Vieira and I expect to continue the campaign for sound, constitutional money. The next lawsuit will probably be: The Gold Bond Case. . . I have acquired a total of 15 World War I Liberty Loan Bonds with a total face value of about $1,000 which we plan to use as the basis for our claim to be paid in the amount of present-day paper currency that represents their present-day value in gold. This claim will be based on the Supreme Court's decision in Perry v. U.S. 294 U.S. 330 (1935)."
Tax Status: Unincorporated. **Annual Report:** No. **Employees:** 1

South Carolina Association of Taxpayers (SCAT)

P.O. Box 50799
Columbia, SC 29250   **Phone:** (803) 782-6913
USA

Contact Person: Rufine Anderson, Secretary.
Officers or Principals: Aurelia Hood, President; Joe Mitchum, Bob Moore, Dick Winchell, Vice Presidents; Rufine Anderson, Secretary; Mary Williams, Treasurer.

Mission or Interest: Responsible government and lower taxes at federal, state, and local levels.
Tax Status: Nonprofit.
Board of Directors or Trustees: Rex Bailey, Elizabeth Davis, Rose Pennington, Robert Josey, William O'Reilly, John Harllee (Quality Education).
Periodicals: *Tax Watch*, which includes reprints of articles, editorials, cartoons, and other interesting news items.

South Carolina Policy Council Education Foundation

1419 Pendleton St.
Columbia, SC 29201   **Phone:** (803) 779-5022   **E-Mail:** SCPC9@mail.idt.net
USA   **Fax:** (803) 779-4953

Contact Person: Ed McMullen, President.
Officers or Principals: Ed McMullen, President ($51,000); Nancy Hawk, Chairman ($0); Claudette Holliday, Director of Public Relations ($0); Michael S. Hubbard, Senior Policy Analyst; Thomas Roe, Founding Chairman.
Mission or Interest: "To educate our members and all South Carolinians about state and local public policy based on traditional South Carolina values of individual liberty and responsibility, free enterprise, and limited government."
Accomplishments: In 1994 the Foundation spent $177,916 on its programs. This included research and the publication of papers which gained media attention and resulted in print, television, and radio interviews.
Total Revenue: 1994 $258,726 4%(1) **Total Expenses:** $237,220 75%/20%/5% **Net Assets:** $8,423
Products or Services: Reclaiming the Legacy: A New Public Policy Agenda for South Carolina edited by Thomas Moore, other books, Capital Comments (brief issue analysis), Issue Papers (in-depth analysis), Factsheets, and Capital Comments which often appear as op-eds in the state's papers.
Tax Status: 501(c)(3) **Annual Report:** No. **Employees:** 3
Board of Directors or Trustees: Donald Boudreaux, James Clarkson, III, Robert Coleman, E. Ervin Dargan, David Lucas, Larry Merchant, J.J. Mahoney, James Martin, Henry McMaster, Harold Eberle, W. Wesley Giles, W. Sylvia Greer, Dr. Henry Jordan, Alex Kiriakides, III, Lawrence Rowland, David Smith, Robert Thompson, Joe Willis.
Periodicals: *The Insider* (monthly newsletter).
Internships: Yes, for graduate and undergraduate students of public policy.
Other Information: Affiliated with the 501(c)(4) South Carolina Policy Council. Member of the State Policy Network. The Foundation received $255,991, or 99% of revenue, from contributions and grants awarded by foundations, businesses, and individuals. (These grants included $10,000 from the Milliken Foundation. In 1995, $55,000 from the Roe Foundation, amd $10,000 from the John William Pope Foundation.) The remaining revenue came from interest on savings and temporary cash investments, and other miscellaneous sources.

South Dakota Family Policy Council

P.O. Box 88007
Sioux Falls, SD 57109   **Phone:** (605) 335-8100   **E-Mail:** sdfamily@aol.com
USA   **Fax:** (605) 338-0240

Contact Person: John H. Paulton, Executive Director.
Officers or Principals: Robert Fischer, President ($0); Gene Christensen, Vice President ($0); Marsha Hubner, Secretary ($0); Craig Uthe, Treasurer.
Mission or Interest: "Strengthening South Dakota families through research and education on issues impacting South Dakota."
Accomplishments: "Led successful 1996 legislative effort to define marriage as the union of one man and one woman. Distributed nearly 200,000 non-partisan voter's guides during the fall of 1996. Among leaders of efforts to roll back gambling in South Dakota." In 1994 the Council spent $73,140 on its programs.
Total Revenue: 1994 $57,983 **Total Expenses:** $73,140 **Net Assets:** $6,083
Products or Services: Research, education, and lobbying. In 1994 the Council spent $6,309 on lobbying. Most of this, $5,824, was spent on an ad that appeared in nine newspapers opposing video gambling on the statewide ballot. Other efforts included health care and an obscenity bill.
Tax Status: 501(c)(3) **Annual Report:** No. **Employees:** 2
Board of Directors or Trustees: Donna Niemann, Aaron Shives, Arie Van Vuren, Dwight Beukelman.
Periodicals: *South Dakota Citizen* (monthly newsletter included in a copy of Focus on the Family's *Citizen*), and *Family News* (newsletter).
Internships: No.
Other Information: Affiliated with Focus on the Family, but receives no direct financial support. The Council received $57,786, or 99.7% of revenue, from contributions and grants awarded by foundations, businesses, and individuals. These contributions and grants have grown an average of 18% since 1990. The remaining revenue came from investment income.

Southeastern Legal Foundation (SLF)

3340 Peachtree Rd., N.E., Suite 2515
Atlanta, GA 30326   **Phone:** (404) 365-8500
USA

Contact Person: Matthew J. Glavin, President.

Officers or Principals: G. Stephen Parker, Legal Director ($70,000); Henry D. Granberry, Vice President/General Counsel ($70,000); Matthew J. Glavin, President ($70,000); Elaine Thurston, Vice President.
Mission or Interest: Public interest law firm challenging government regulations and tax policies in Georgia and the South.
Accomplishments: Representing former FBI agent Gary Aldrich, author of the best-selling book Unlimited Access, against "government agencies that want to sue him for the book proceeds and possibly imprison him for writing it." In 1995 SLF brought suit challenging the Georgia "Intangibles Tax" (a tax on stocks and bonds of out-of-state corporations) in Lombard v. State of Georgia. The state conceded SLF's case, and in 1996 the legislature repealed the tax. In 1996 SLF disclosed the possible illegality of a $1 billion surplus in Georgia's unemployment insurance tax fund; this resulted in the legislature calling for a $65 million tax cut. Brought suit against the Stephens County School district in Earls v. Stephens County School District for alleged violations of parents' rights by transporting minor children to a county health clinic "where they received HIV/AIDS tests, PAP smears, condom and birth control medications - all without the parents' consent. The parents were also denied access to the results of the test." Challenged minority set-aside contracts in Prior Tire v. Fulton Board of Education. Other lawsuits supported school-voucher programs, and challenged government grants to nonprofit institutions. In the fiscal year ending June 1995, the Foundation spent $259,542 on its programs.
Total Revenue: FY ending 6/95 $416,024 36%(2) **Total Expenses:** $374,918 69%/14%/17% **Net Assets:** $91,944
Tax Status: 501(c)(3) **Annual Report:** Yes. **Employees:** 4 **Citations:** 82:75
Periodicals: *Action Update* (monthly newsletter).
Other Information: Established in 1977 by former U.S. Rep. Ben Blackburn (R-GA). President Matthew Glavin was formerly president of the Georgia Public Policy Foundation. SLF received $327,198, or 79% of revenue, from contributions and grants awarded by foundations, businesses, and individuals. (These grants included $50,000 from the Sarah Scaife Foundation, $25,000 from the Samuel Roberts Noble Foundation, $25,000 from the Castle Rock Foundation, $3,000 from the Roe Foundation, and $2,500 from the John William Pope Foundation.) $87,987, or 21%, from a "Celebrate America" special fund-raising event. The remaining revenue came from interest on savings and temporary cash investments, and other miscellaneous sources.

Speak Out America

P.O. Box 831
Highland, MI 48357   **Phone:** (810) 887-4919
USA   **Fax:** same

Contact Person: Karen Mazzarella, Director.
Officers or Principals: Gary Stewart, Director.
Mission or Interest: To hold elected officials accountable. Their slogan is, "The least served special interest is the American Taxpayer." Opposed to bigger government, more taxes, more spending and waste.
Accomplishments: Co-sponsored and helped organize the "National March on Washington," October 16, 1993.
Tax Status: 501(c)(3) **Employees:** All volunteer.
Periodicals: Newsletter. **Internships:** No.

St. Antoninus Institute for Catholic Education in Business

4110 Fessenden St., N.W.
Washington, DC 20016   **Phone:** (202) 686-0849   **E-Mail:** antoninus@crnet.org
USA   **Fax:** same

Contact Person: Jean-Francois Orsini, TOP, Ph.D., President/Executive Director.
Mission or Interest: "To develop, explain and promote the social teachings of the Catholic Church. We are inspired by the realistic thinking of St. Thomas Aquinas. Economic followers of St. Thomas were all for free-markets."
Accomplishments: An extensive grassroots membership.
Products or Services: Publish the "Pro-Life Shopping Guide" that lets consumers know which companies support abortion. A management textbook (in electronic form) that incorporates Catholic social teachings, thomistic philosophy and supports a strong entrepreneurial position. Hosts a business and economics computer network forum, CRNET (Catholic Resources Network).
Tax Status: 501(c)(3)
Board of Directors or Trustees: Rev. Bartholomew de la Torre, OP, Mrs. Frances Griffin, TOP (Griffin Communications), Robert Royal, TOP (Ethics and Public Policy Center). Advisors include; Rev. Pierre Conway, OP, Rev. Ernest Fortin (Boston College), Rev. Matthew Habiger, OSB (Human Life Int'n.), Rev. John Madigan, OP (Molloy College), Capt. Tad Stanwick, USN (Ret.). Russell Kirk was an advisor until his death.
Periodicals: *St. Antoninus Institute Newsletter* (quarterly).
Internships: Not at this time.
Other Information: Established in 1989. Dr. Orsini is also the president of the Washington chapter of the Society of Catholic Social Scientists. St. Antoninus was the Archbishop of Florence, "a realistic although demanding confessor who commented on the writing of St. Thomas in the fields of business and economics."

State Department Watch

P.O. Box 65398
Washington, DC 20035   **Phone:** (703) 241-3700
USA   **Fax:** (818) 223-8080

Contact Person: Carl Olson, Chairman.

Officers or Principals: Mark Seidenberg, Vice Chairman ($0); David Nolan, Secretary ($0).
Mission or Interest: "To be a voice for the American public's interest in foreign policy." Concerns include; preventing the importation of "slave-made goods" from China, preventing the giveaway of eight "strategic and resource-rich" islands in the Arctic and Bering Sea to the Russians, and the collection of "billions of dollars owed to the U.S. Treasury by the Russians."
Accomplishments: Supported bills in the California, Massachusetts and Alaska state legislatures that prohibited the states from purchasing "foreign slave-made goods." Introduced a similar resolution at the annual AT&T shareholders meeting was endorsed by millions of share holders despite opposition from the board of directors. Supported resolutions in the Alaska and California state legislatures that opposed the U.S.'s giveaway of the eight islands in the Arctic and Bering seas. Numerous letters to the editor published in national and international journals and newspapers including *The Economist, Business Week, Wall Street Journal, Forbes,* and others. In 1994 State Department Watch spent $90,565 on its programs, an increase of 13% over the previous year.
Total Revenue: 1994 $113,499 10%(1) **Total Expenses:** $119,782 76%/7%/18% **Net Assets:** (-$29,615)
Tax Status: 501(c)(4) **Annual Report:** No. **Employees:** 3
Periodicals: *State Department Watch* (periodic newsletter), *The Bad News Bulletin* (periodic newsletter).
Internships: No.
Other Information: Affiliated with the 501(c)(3) American Sovereignty Task Force. In 1994 the two organizations had combined revenues of $364,672. State Department Watch received $93,269, or 82% of revenue, from contributions and grants. $20,229, or 18%, from mailing list rentals.

State Policy Network

816 Mill Lake Rd.
Ft. Wayne, IN 46845   **Phone:** (219) 637-7778
USA   **Fax:** (219) 637-7779

Contact Person: Byron Lamm, Executive Director.
Officers or Principals: Byron Lamm, Executive Director ($42,500); Lawrence Reed, President ($0); Charles L. Heatherly, Chairman ($0); Joseph Bast, Secretary; Edward T. McMullen, Jr., Treasurer.
Mission or Interest: To provide a support network for state-based policy organizations in order to facilitate the transference of information, provide speakers, establish a library, scholarship programs, etc. Member organizations include; Alabama Family Alliance (AL), Arkansas Family Policy Council (AR), Buckeye Institute (OH), Cascade Policy Institute (OR), Center for the American Experiment (MN), Ethan Allen Institute (VT), Evergreen Freedom Foundation (WA), Georgia Public Policy Institute (GA), James Madison Institute (FL), John Locke Foundation (NC), Josiah Bartlett Center (NH), Mackinac Center (MI), National Center for Policy Analysis (TX), Nevada Policy Research Institute (NV), South Carolina Policy Council (SC), Sutherland Institute (UT), and the Yankee Institute for Public Policy (CT).
Accomplishments: In 1994 the Network spent $77,672 on its programs.
Total Revenue: 1994 $93,246 (-36%)(2) **Total Expenses:** $122,460 63%/38%/0% **Net Assets:** $85,659
Products or Services: Book on issues related to term limits, Gridlock in Government. Media guide for use by members.
Tax Status: 501(c)(3)
Board of Directors or Trustees: Thomas Roe (Roe Foundation), Judy Cresanta (Nevada Policy Research Inst.), Tracie Sharp (Cascade Policy Inst.), Mitch Pearlstein (Center of the American Experiment), Gary Palmer (Alabama Family Alliance), John Goodman (National Center for Policy Analysis), Michael Sanera (Arizona Inst.), William Myers (ALEC Foundation), John Andrews, Chris Olander (JM Foundation).
Other Information: Established in 1992. The Network received $86,830, or 93% of revenue, from contributions and grants awarded by foundations, businesses, and individuals. (In 1995, these grants included $40,000 from the John M. Olin Foundation, and $25,000 from the Roe Foundation.) $4,381, or 5%, from dividends and interest from securities. The remaining revenue came from interest on savings, and other miscellaneous sources.

Statistical Assessment Service (STATS)

2100 L St., N.W., Suite 300
Washington, DC 20037   **Phone:** (202) 223-3193   **E-Mail:** STATS2100@aol.com
USA   **Fax:** (202) 872-4014

Contact Person: John Thomas Sheehan, Executive Director.
Officers or Principals: Dr. S. Robert Lichter, President ($48,125); Dr. Linda Lichter, Director ($36,458); John Sheehan, Executive Director ($27,486); David Murray, Director of Research; Thomas Riley, Senior Analyst.
Mission or Interest: "Countering questionable statistics before the media transform them into political 'facts'. . . The biggest problem for sound policy is not the absence of information but the abundance of misinformation. Everybody complains about the false 'facts' and distorted data that plague the policy arena, but nobody knows how to get rid of them. Advocacy groups regularly use the media to pollute the policy debate with misleading or unverified statistics about purported social and economic problems. These claims are often refuted but rarely dislodged from the public consciousness, where they continue to distort rational debate."
Accomplishments: Has published critiques of studies on medical inflation, sperm count reduction, child abductions, population concerns, domestic violence, women and guns, and others. In the fiscal year ending July 1995, STATS spent $203,013 on its programs.
Total Revenue: FY ending 7/95 $823,990 **Total Expenses:** $342,821 59%/41%/0% **Net Assets:** $481,169

Products or Services: "Fishiest Facts of 1996" annual compilation of "the year's silliest moments in science and statistical reporting," and the "1996 Dubious Data Awards" for "most misleading stories of things as they aren't."

Tax Status: 501(c)(3)   **Citations:** 41:110

Board of Directors or Trustees: Sallie Baliunas (George Marshall Inst. and Harvard Smithsonian Center for Astrophysics), Prof. Thomas Childers (Univ. of Pennsylvania), Prof. John Diolulio (Princeton Univ.), Wolfgang Donsbach (Pres., World Association of Opinion Research), Nicholas Eberstadt (Harvard Univ. Center for Population Studies), Everett Ladd (Roper Public Opinion Center, Univ. of Connecticut), Prof. Elisabeth Noelle-Neumann (Univ. of Chicago), Nelson Polsby (Institute of Government Studies, UC Berkeley), Prof. Harrison Pope (Harvard Medical School), Humphrey Taylor (Pres./CEO, Louis Harris & Associates), Prof. Stanley Rothman (Smith College), Prof. James Q. Wilson (UCLA).

Periodicals: *STATS 2100* (monthly newsletter).

Internships: Yes.

Other Information: Established in 1994. Affiliated with the 501(c)(3) Center for Media and Public Affairs, a media 'watchdog' that has consistently found a left-leaning bias in the media. In the fiscal year ending July 1995, the two affiliates had combined net revenues, expenses, and assets of $1,549,559, $800,923, and $952,309. The officers Dr. S. Robert Lichter, Dr. Linda Lichter, and John Sheehan served as officers of both affiliates and received a combined $72,920, $72,916, and $61,080 respectively. STATS received $801,806, or 97% of revenue, from contributions and grants awarded by foundations, businesses, and individuals. (These grants included $75,000 from the John M. Olin Foundation, and $66,667 from the William H. Donner Foundation.) $22,084, or 3%, from interest on savings and temporary cash investments. The remaining revenue came from royalties.

Stewards of the Range

802 W. Bannock, Suite 601
Boise, ID 83702   **Phone:** (208) 336-5922
USA   **Fax:** (208) 336-7054

Contact Person: Margaret H. Gabbard, Executive Director.

Officers or Principals: Mark L. Pollot, Director, Stewards Constitutional Law Center ($91,500); Margaret H. Gabbard, Executive Director ($28,600); Frank Duran, President ($0); Martin Andrews, Vice President; Elisa Pendergrass, Business Manager; Pam Swatzel, Office Manager; Dean McLaughlin, Production Manager.

Mission or Interest: Public-interest law firm protecting the rights of private property owners and users of federal lands and the adjacent areas.

Accomplishments: Testified before the U.S. House of Representatives' Task Force on Second Amendment Rights and Excessive Use of Government Force held in Boise, Idaho, as well as other oversight hearings. Appeared on numerous radio and television shows, including ABC's "Nightline" and the "American Agenda" with Peter Jennings. Contributed to the legal team of rancher Wayne Hage. Hage is the author of Storm Over Rangelands, a key book in the western land dispute. Hage claims, in his lawsuit Hage v. United States, of physical harassment from the Forest Service and being singled out for regulatory persecution. Hage v. United States is pending before the United States Federal Court of Claims. Other cases included: Participation in United States v. Nye County regarding the Federal government's jurisdiction over land within County borders. Diamond Bar v. U.S. Forest Service challenging "whether the U.S. Forest Service can arbitrarily reduce the use of grazing rights without paying just compensation." In the fiscal year ending June 1995 Stewards of the Range spent $232,026 on its programs. Most went toward educational programs, $99,702 was spent on public interest litigation.

Total Revenue: FY ending 6/95 $377,317 **Total Expenses:** $398,460 58%/34%/7% **Net Assets:** (-$21,143)

Products or Services: Stewards Constitutional Law Center that files cases, teaches litigation, and consults on cases involving property rights and regulatory 'takings.' Conferences and seminars. Catalog of books and publications. Lobbying: in the fiscal year ending June 1995 Stewards spent $3,279 on the direct lobbying of legislators.

Tax Status: 501(c)(3)   **Citations:** 3:204

Board of Directors or Trustees: David Theroux (Pres., Independent Inst.), Tom Kelly. The Litigation Committee screens cases for public interest relevance. The committee includes: Sam Elliot (Actor), Prof. Bernard Seigan (Univ. of San Diego, School of Law), Leighton Hills, Sandra Mitchell.

Periodicals: *Cornerstone* (monthly). Formerly called *Stewards of the Range NEWS*.

Internships: Yes.

Other Information: Established in 1994. Previously Stewards operated as a project of the Center for the Defense of Free Enterprise's Free Enterprise Legal Defense Fund. Director Mark Pollot was formerly an official in the Justice Department under President Reagan. He authored the "Takings Executive Order" signed by President Reagan in 1988. Pollot is the author of Grand Theft and Petit Larceny, available through Stewards. In its first year, Stewards received $328,144, or 87% of revenue, from contributions and grants awarded by foundations, businesses, and individuals. (These grants included $2,470 from the American Policy Foundation.) $46,611, or 12%, from programs and the sale of publications. The remaining revenue came from special events and interest on savings.

Stop Promoting Homosexuality Hawaii (SPHH)

P.O. Box 27843
Honolulu, HI 96827   **Phone:** (808) 523-7739
USA

Contact Person: Mike Gabbard, President.

Mission or Interest: To challenge the acceptance and promotion of homosexuality as a normal and healthy alternative lifestyle. "We are all God's children. Those who engage in homosexual activity warrant the respect and compassion that all people deserve. But real compassion is not shown by pretending that homosexual behavior is normal and healthy. We aren't expected to relate to alcoholics by glorifying their alcoholism or to drug addicts by celebrating their addiction. It's not compassionate to encourage people to take pride in behavior that is destroying themselves."
Products or Services: Weekly talk-radio show, weekly community-access cable show, newsletter.
Tax Status: Applying for 501(c)(3). **Annual Report:** No.
Board of Directors or Trustees: Leon Siu, Carol Gabbard.
Periodicals: *Stop Promoting Homosexuality Hawaii* (monthly newsletter).
Internships: No.
Other Information: Established in 1991.

Straight Talk
P.O. Box 60
Pigeon Forge, TN 37868   **Phone:**   (615) 453-8237
USA

Contact Person: Linda Parton.
Officers or Principals: Tom Anderson, Publisher.
Mission or Interest: Conservative newsletter. "Truth beyond the media coverage - facts, without fear or favor."
Accomplishments: Senator Jesse Helms (R-NC) says, "Tom Anderson's *Straight Talk* is precisely that - straight talk, honest, forthright, courageous. For years it has been an oasis in a journalistic desert - a voice of sanity daring to level with the American people, telling them the truth about the direction in which our nation is headed."
Tax Status: For profit.
Board of Directors or Trustees: *Straight Talk* (weekly).
Other Information: Tom Anderson has run for President in 1976 on the American Party's ticket. He has received several Freedom Awards from Freedom's Foundation at Valley Forge.

Students for America Foundation
P.O. Box 10469
Charlotte, NC 28212   **Phone:**   (704) 535-7321
USA   **Fax:**   (704) 535-8507

Contact Person: Jeffrey M. McCraw, Programs Director.
Officers or Principals: Jonathan C. Roberts, Executive Director ($14,233).
Mission or Interest: National conservative student group founded on Judeo-Christian values. Works with local chapters on college campuses through their Campus Steering Committees.
Accomplishments: Sen. Jesse Helms (R-NC) said, "I'm proud of all you young people associated with Students for America." In 1995 the Foundation spent $49,064 on its programs. This included $425 in academic awards.
Total Revenue: FY ending 5/95 $98,040 **Total Expenses:** $82,499 **Net Assets:** $13,818
Products or Services: Leadership training seminars, foreign policy summit, Roger Milliken Scholarship Program, national convention, fall recruitment effort, speakers bureau.
Tax Status: 501(c)(3) **Annual Report:** 5
Board of Directors or Trustees: Darin Waters, Ed Noble, Mike Crisp, Kyle Stallings, Stephen Maye, Kevin Parsons, E. Bigham, Prof. Charles Rice (Notre Dame Univ.), Jonathan Roberts.
Internships: Yes, they help with the placement of summer interns in public policy positions.
Other Information: Established in 1984. Anyone can join, but students pay a lower membership fee. The Foundation received $97,460, or 99% of revenue, from contributions and grants awarded by foundations (51%), individuals (44%), and businesses (1%). (These grants included $20,000 from the Samuel Roberts Noble Foundation, $10,000 from the Richard & Helen DeVos Foundation, $5,000 from the Carthage Foundation, and $1,000 from the Roe Foundation.) The remaining revenue came from membership dues, and investment income.

Students in Free Enterprise (SIFE)
1959 E. Kerr
Springfield, MO 65803   **Phone:** (417) 831-9505   **E-Mail:**   SIFEHQ@aol.com
USA   **Fax:**   (417) 831-6165   **Internet:** http://www.SIFE.org

Contact Person: Alvin W. Rohrs, President.
Officers or Principals: Alvin W. Rohrs, President/CEO ($133,031); Richard J. Laird, Vice President, University Relations ($68,224); Thomas J. Payne, Vice President ($11,750); Jack Kahl, Chairman; Robert H. Cowan, Secretary; Thomas J. Hoeppner, Treasurer.
Mission or Interest: To establish and direct student-generated free-market education programs at colleges and universities bringing America's collegians and other citizens a better understanding and greater appreciation for the free-enterprise system.

Accomplishments: "Over 30,000 students on 354 college campuses across the country and beyond U.S. borders." Recently SIFE held its first regional entrepreneurship competition in Central Asia, "including 11 SIFE teams from three different countries." In the fiscal year ending August 1995, SIFE spent $1,413,916 on its programs. $380,000 of this went toward awards and scholarships.
Total Revenue: FY ending 8/95 $2,172,312 **Total Expenses:** $1,902,447 74%/7%/19% **Net Assets:** $1,844,440
Tax Status: 501(c)(3) **Annual Report:** Yes. **Employees:** 6   **Citations:** 109:60
Board of Directors or Trustees: Over 55 top executives from major corporations make up the Board of Directors.
Periodicals: *SIFE Lines* (quarterly newsletter).
Internships: No.
Other Information: Established in 1985. SIFE received $2,127,904, or 98% of revenue, from contributions and grants awarded by foundations, businesses, and individuals. (These grants included $7,500 from the Castle Rock Foundation, and $4,000 from the Sunmark Foundation.) $29,267, or 1%, from dividends and interest from securities. The remaining revenue came from interest on savings and temporary cash investments, capital gains on the sale of securities, and other miscellaneous sources.

Sunmark Foundation

510 Maryville College Dr., Suite 210
St. Louis, MO 63141   **Phone:** (314) 453-9700
USA

Contact Person: Menlo F. Smith, Trustee.
Officers or Principals: John Reed, Trustee ($0); John Prentiss, Trustee ($0).
Mission or Interest: Grant-making foundation that focuses on conservative and free-market organizations.
Accomplishments: In the fiscal year ending January 1996, the Foundation awarded $708,248 in grants. Recipients included: $107,000 for the Leadership Institute, $60,000 for the National Right to Work Legal Foundation, $35,000 for the Heritage Foundation, $25,000 each for the Center on National Labor Policy and the National Institute for Labor Relations, $20,000 for the Atlas Economic Foundation, $15,000 each for the Cato Institute, Young America's Foundation, and National Center for Neighborhood Enterprise, $12,000 for the Capital Research Center, $10,000 each for the Acton Institute and the Christian Anti-Communism Crusade, $8,000 for the George Mason University's Law and Economics Center, $7,000 each for the Foundation for Economic Education, and the Center for the Study of American Business, $6,000 for the Hudson Institute, $5,000 each for the American Legislative Exchange Council, Institute for Political Economy, and National Coalition Against Pornography, $4,000 each for Students in Free Enterprise and the Independent Women's Forum, $3,475 for the Philanthropy Roundtable, $2,000 each for the American Spectator Educational Foundation, American Enterprise Institute, and the St. Louis Discussion Club, and $500 for the Cardinal Mindszenty Foundation.
Total Revenue: FY ending 1/96 $1,189,240 **Total Expenses:** $711,153 **Net Assets:** $2,351,853 26% (1)
Tax Status: 501(c)(3)
Other Information: The Foundation received $700,000, or 59% of revenue, from contributions and grants awarded by foundations, businesses, and individuals. $417,221, or 35%, from capital gains on the sale of assets. $44,925, or 4%, from dividends and interest from securities. $27,094, or 2%, from interest on savings and temporary cash investments.

Sutherland Institute

Independence Square
111 E. 5600 South, Suite 208
Murray, UT 84107   **Phone:** (801) 281-2081   **E-Mail:** Sutherland@utah-inter.net
USA   **Fax:**   (801) 281-2414

Contact Person: David F. Salisbury, Ph.D., President.
Officers or Principals: David F. Salisbury, Ph.D., President ($51,400); Louis James, Vice President, Project Development; Gaylord Swim, Chairman.
Mission or Interest: "To positively affect the state's economic, social and political climate by disseminating workable ideas to the important decision makers in our state: government officials, business and education leaders." Focus on Utah.
Accomplishments: "Recently held a successful legislative workshop on streamlining government privatization and a local government workshop on privatization and contracting out." In the fiscal year ending June 1996 the Institute spent $91,109 on its programs.
Total Revenue: FY ending 6/96 $156,821 **Total Expenses:** $157,371 58%/19%/24% **Net Assets:** $28,342
Products or Services: Seminars, "Issues & Ideas" luncheons, conferences, "Focus on Utah" report series, "To the Point" perspective series, audio tapes of speeches, more.
Tax Status: 501(c)(3) **Annual Report:** No. **Employees:** 3
Board of Directors or Trustees: Richard Headlee, Maxwell Miller, Mark Rinehart, James Parker. The Board of Scholars includes: Prof. Emeritus B. Delworth Gardner (BYU), Prof. Emeritus Jay Bagley (Utah State Univ.), Prof. Paul Cassell (Univ. of Utah), Prof. Chris Fawson (Utah State Univ.), Prof. Bruce Godfrey (Utah State Univ.), Prof. Brad Hainsworth (BYU), Prof. John Keith (Utah State Univ.), Assoc. Prof. Val Lambson (BYU), Prof. Cris Lewis (Utah State Univ.), Assoc. Prof. Peter McNamara (Utah State Univ.), Prof. Noel Reynolds (BYU), Prof. Richard Sherlock (Utah State Univ.), Prof. Randy Simmons (Dir., Inst. for Political Economy, Utah State Univ.), Prof. Richard Vetterli (BYU), Prof. Larry Wimmer (BYU).
Internships: Yes, unpaid for academic credit.
Other Information: Established in 1994. Member of the State Policy Network. The Institute received $150,000, or 96% of revenue, from contributions and grants awarded by foundations, businesses, and individuals. (These contributions and grants increased by 362% over the previous, initial, year.) $6,319, or 4%, from program services, including the sale of books and publications, and workshop fees. The remaining revenue came from interest on savings.

Tamarack Foundation

P.O. Box 23894
Tigard, OR 97223
USA

Phone: (503) 639-7320

Contact Person: Dal Ferry, President.
Officers or Principals: Dal Ferry, President; B. J. Rogers, Secretary/Treasurer.
Mission or Interest: National and statewide education on the subjects of land use, property rights, education, economics, and taxes. Primary focus on property rights. Publishes *Counterpoint* newspaper.
Tax Status: Oregon nonprofit. **Annual Report:** No. **Employees:** All volunteers.
Board of Directors or Trustees: Mildred Sundeleaf, Tom Dennehey, Shirley Bryant, Ann Buehner, others.
Periodicals: *Counterpoint* (published about 8 times per year).
Internships: No, but may in future.
Other Information: Established in 1984.

Tax Foundation

1250 H Street, N.W., Suite 700
Washington, DC 20005
USA

Phone: (202) 783-2760

Contact Person: Stephen Gold, Director of Communications.
Officers or Principals: J.D. Foster, Executive Director ($82,000); Stephen Gold, Director of Communications ($60,504); Gaye Bennett, Director ($59,920); Wayne Gable, President.
Mission or Interest: Fiscal and management aspects of federal, state, and local government, including studies on expenditures, the federal budget, taxation, and public administration. Serves as a national information agency for individuals and organizations concerned with problems of government expenditures, taxation, and debt.
Accomplishments: In 1994 the Foundation spent $784,180 on its programs.
Total Revenue: 1994 $1,315,662 (-5%)(2) **Total Expenses:** $1,283,983 61%/21%/18% **Net Assets:** (-$13,869)
Products or Services: Research published in various forms, sponsors Annual National Tax Conference and Tax Seminars. Their library has 16,000 volumes on state, federal, and local finance and taxation.
Tax Status: 501(c)(3) **Annual Report:** Yes. **Employees:** 13   **Citations:** 666:15
Board of Directors or Trustees: Richard Fink, David Koch, Larry Landon, Dominic Tarantino, James Riordan.
Periodicals: *Tax Features, Library Bulletin, Federal Tax Policy Memo,* and *Facts and Figures on Government Finance* (annual).
Other Information: Established in 1991. Affiliated with Citizens for a Sound Economy and Citizens for the Environment. The Foundation received $1,025,760, or 76% of gross revenue, from contributions and grants awarded by foundations, businesses, and individuals. (In 1995 these grants included $25,000 from the Carthage Foundation, $10,000 from the John William Pope Foundation, and $10,000 from the Philip M. McKenna Foundation.) $277,469, or 21%, from conference fees. $32,939, or 2%, from the sale of publications. The remaining revenue came from interest on savings. The Foundation lost $31,927 on special events.

Tax Free America

11015 Cumpston St.
North Hollywood, CA 91601
USA

Phone: (818) 763-1000
Fax: (818) 769-4996

Contact Person: Boris Isaacson, President.
Mission or Interest: To replace all city, county, state, and federal taxes, fees, excises, and assessments with a 1% trade charge on all trade, retail, wholesale and otherwise. "Our only goal is fair government funding, to take the power to tax away from all legislators and give it to the voters directly."
Accomplishments: Circulated petitions in several states to place the 1% trade charge on the ballot. Was on Montana ballot and received 40% of the vote.
Tax Status: 501(c)(4) **Annual Report:** No. **Employees:** All volunteer.

TEACH Michigan Education Fund

913 W. Holmes, Suite 265
Lansing, MI 48910
USA

Phone: (517) 394-4870
Fax: (517) 394-0093

Contact Person: Robert J. Wittmann, President.
Officers or Principals: William Broadwick, former Executive Director ($16,108); Paul N. DeWeese, M.D., Chairman ($0); Carolyn Andrews, Treasurer ($0).
Mission or Interest: To sponsor research and conduct educational forums on behalf of educational choice.
Accomplishments: Coauthored book on educational choice, submitted major research proposal to New American Schools Development Corp. Provided financial assistance for the Michigan Center for Charter Schools, an organization that assists charter schools in their development. In 1995 the Fund spent $136,838 on its programs.

Total Revenue: 1995 $168,666 **Total Expenses:** $207,642 66%/29%/5% **Net Assets:** (-$113,818)
Products or Services: Op-Eds, occasional research. Lobbying: the Fund spent $10,000 on the direct lobbying of legislators. This was down 76% from $41,871 the previous year, and down 87% from $75,023 in 1993.
Tax Status: 501(c)(3) **Annual Report:** Yes. **Employees:** 4
Board of Directors or Trustees: Dr. Margaret Betts, Larry Meyer (Michigan Retailers Assn.).
Periodicals: *Teach Michigan Newsletter* (bimonthly).
Internships: Yes, both volunteer and paid.
Other Information: Affiliated with the 501(c)(3) Michigan Center for Charter Schools, and the 501(c)(4) TEACH Michigan. The Fund received $166,193, or 99% of revenue, from contributions and grants awarded by foundations, businesses, and individuals. (In 1994 these grants included $50,000 from the Richard & Helen DeVos Foundation. These grants and contributions have been erratic, and have averaged $308,247 in the previous four years.) $2,324, or 1%, from rental income. The remaining revenue came from interest on savings.

Teaching Home, The
P.O. Box 20219
Portland, OR 97294   **Phone:** (503) 253-9633
USA   **Fax:** (503) 253-7345

Contact Person: Sue Welch, Publisher.
Officers or Principals: Pat Welch, Publisher.
Mission or Interest: Magazine to provide information, inspiration, and support to Christian home-school families and organizations.
Accomplishments: Publishing since 1981. Contains a column on the legal aspects of home-schooling by Michael Farris of the Home School Legal Defense Association.
Tax Status: For profit.
Periodicals: *The Teaching Home* (bimonthly magazine).
Other Information: Established in 1981. Member of the Evangelical Press Association.

Teen Age Research Services Foundation (TARS Foundation)
10620-C Crestwood Dr.
Manassas, VA 22110   **Phone:** (703) 368-0830
USA   **Fax:** same

Contact Person: Megan Beth Lott, Executive Director.
Officers or Principals: Barbara W. Gilbert, President/Treasurer ($0); Joyce H. Armendaris, Secretary ($0); Janet Kraft, Assistant Treasurer ($0).
Mission or Interest: Education for teens in the principles of free enterprise, constitutional government and patriotism.
Accomplishments: TARS has instructed high school students for over 27 years.
Total Revenue: FY ending 4/94 $45,136 **Total Expenses:** $35,520 **Net Assets:** $9,616
Products or Services: Leadership Training Schools which are held across the country and help teach the fundamental principles of a free society and the skills needed for debate and public speaking. "Stop Drugs" campaign. Program teaching America's heritage and achievements.
Tax Status: 501(c)(3) **Annual Report:** Yes. **Employees:** 5
Board of Directors or Trustees: Carol Browning, Cassandra Scholte. Advisors include: William Bennett (Empower America), William Brock, Paula Hawkins, Jack Kemp (Empower America), Col. and Mrs. R. H. Kreuter, Edwin Meese, III (former Attorney General), J. William Middendorf, Fred Sacher, William Simon (former U.S. Treasury Secretary), Prof. Walter Williams (George Mason Univ.).
Periodicals: *TARGET Newsletter*.
Internships: No.
Other Information: Affiliated with the National Teen Age Republicans at the same address. The Foundation received $45,136, or 99.7% of revenue, from contributions and grants awarded by foundations, businesses, and individuals. The remaining revenue came from other miscellaneous sources.

Texans United for Life
4424 Spring Valley Rd.
Dallas, TX 75244   **Phone:** (214) 490-3430
USA   **Fax:** (214) 490-3434

Contact Person: William E. Price, President.
Officers or Principals: William E. Price, President ($35,723); Gillian L. Jeffrey, Treasurer ($12,503).
Mission or Interest: Lobbying organization that "distributes pro-life literature and supports pro-life activities throughout Texas."
Accomplishments: In 1995 the organization spent $189,717 on its programs. This included $68,034 in grants for crisis pregnancy centers and homes for unwed mothers.

Total Revenue: 1995 $306,070 **Total Expenses:** $323,173 59%/12%/29% **Net Assets:** $16,529
Tax Status: 501(c)(4)   **Citations:** 182:40
Board of Directors or Trustees: Tom Brown, Robert Farrell, Jim Fregia, D.D.S. (West Texans for Life), Susie Hoeller, Patrick McCarty, M.D., J. D. McCaslin, Susan Heller Stanzel (Cardinal Mindszenty Found.), Janet Storey, Kyleen Wright (Pres., Greater Tarrant Right to Life).
Other Information: Affiliated with the 501(c)(3) Texans United for Life Educational Foundation at the same address. The organization received $305,877, or 99.9% of revenue, from contributions and grants awarded by foundations, businesses, and individuals. The remaining revenue came from the sale of program materials.

Texans United for Life Educational Foundation

4424 Spring Valley Rd.
Dallas, TX 75244   **Phone:**   (214) 490-3430
USA   **Fax:**   (214) 490-3434

Contact Person: William E. Price, President.
Officers or Principals: William E. Price, President ($24,363); Gillian L. Jeffrey, Treasurer ($12,396).
Mission or Interest: "Education and research on pro-life issues."
Accomplishments: "Oldest and largest pro-life group in Texas." In 1994 the Foundation spent $97,319 on its programs. These included $3,911 in grants to local organizations and crisis pregnancy centers.
Total Revenue: 1994 $157,203 12%(2) **Total Expenses:** $167,441 58%/25%/17% **Net Assets:** $57,939
Products or Services: Banquets and seminars. Pamphlets, bumper-stickers and other materials.
Tax Status: 501(c)(3) **Annual Report:** Yes. **Employees:** 5   **Citations:** 182:40
Board of Directors or Trustees: Tom Brown, Robert Farrell, Jim Fregia, D.D.S. (West Texans for Life), Susie Hoeller, Patrick McCarty, M.D., J. D. McCaslin, Susan Heller Stanzel (Cardinal Mindszenty Found.), Janet Storey, Esq., Kyleen Wright (Pres., Greater Tarrant Right to Life).
Internships: No.
Other Information: Affiliated with the 501(c)(4) Texans United for Life at the same address. The Foundation received $165,316, or 99.7% of gross revenue, from Contributions and grants awarded by foundations, businesses, and individuals. The remaining revenue came from the sale of assets. The Foundation lost $5,727 on special events, and $2,797 on the sale of inventory.

Texas Justice Foundation (TJF)

8122 Datapoint Dr., Suite 812
San Antonio, TX 78229   **Phone:**   (210) 614-7157
USA   **Fax:**   (210) 614-6656

Contact Person: Yvette Smith, Media Director.
Officers or Principals: Allan Parker, J.D., President.
Mission or Interest: Legal advocacy organization focusing on Texas. Focuses on, "limited government, free markets, private property and parental rights."
Accomplishments: TJF is representing State Rep. John Shields in his motion to intervene in a lawsuit by the Sierra Club against those who draw water from the Edwards Aquifer, Sierra Club v. San Antonio, et al. The Sierra Club held that the federal government can and should place limits on the removal of water from the Aquifer by the citizenry (over a million people rely on this water), because the water level affects endangered species. TJF and others claim that this federal government control violates the Tenth Amendment and is not covered by the Commerce Clause, using the reasoning of U.S. v. Lopez, a 1995 Supreme Court decision limiting government authority. The case is before the Fifth Circuit Court of Appeals. TJF has been selected by the State Board of Education as one of five official evaluators of the "Open-Enrollment Charter Schools." Numerous media appearances.
Tax Status: Texas nonprofit. **Employees:** 4
Board of Directors or Trustees: Dr. James Leininger, Tim Lyles, Fritz Steiger, Cass Stevens.
Other Information: Established by the Texas Public Policy Foundation, and is a separate incorporated entity.

Texas Public Policy Foundation (TPPF)

8122 Datapoint Dr., Suite 816
San Antonio, TX 78229   **Phone:**   (210) 614-0080   **E-Mail:** pppf@txdirect.net
USA   **Fax:**   (210) 614-2649   **Internet:** http://www.praxistechnology/tppf/com

Contact Person: Jeff M. Judson, President.
Officers or Principals: James B. Cardle, Vice President, Development.
Mission or Interest: "Advances those timeless principles which have made Texas one of the most prosperous and powerful states in the nation: Free Enterprise, Limited Government, and Individual Responsibility."
Accomplishments: In 1996 TPPF received more than twice its operating budget in media coverage. TPPF "would have had to spend $1.5 million to receive the same amount of radio, television, and newspaper coverage that was earned." Influential in tort reform and education reform. Hosts the Texas Justice Foundation (see separate listing). In 1995 TPPF spent $232,612 on its programs.

Total Revenue: 1995 $1,000,621 (-7%)(2) **Total Expenses:** $624,428 37%/52%/11% **Net Assets:** $369,082
Products or Services: <u>Sundown on Big Government</u>, book. Conferences, studies, publications, and video tapes.
Tax Status: 501(c)(3) **Annual Report:** Yes. **Employees:** 6   **Citations:** 76:82
Board of Directors or Trustees: Phil Adams, R.C. Allen, Buddy Barfield, Scott Bennett, Michael Burke, James Cicconni, David Dewhurst, Bruce Gibson, David Hartman, James Huffines, John Kerr, James Leininger, M.D., Tim Lyles, James Mansour, Cindy Maser, Brig. Gen. Robert McDermott, USAF (Ret.), William McMinn, Robert Mosbacher (Secretary of Commerce, 1989-1992), Gerry Pate, P.E., Fritz Steiger (CEO America), Michael Williams, Judy Petty Wolf (Department of Transportation, Director of Public and Consumer Affairs, 1985-86).
Internships: Yes, inquire for further details.
Other Information: The Foundation received $927,581, or 93% of revenue, from contributions and grants awarded by foundations, businesses, and individuals. (These grants included $5,000 from the Roe Foundation. In 1994, $10,000 from the Gordon and Mary Cain Foundation.) $16,657, or 2%, from special events. $16,234, or 2%, from the sale of inventory. The remaining revenue came from the "recovery of administrative costs," the sale of assets, and interest on savings.

Thoreau Institute
14417 S.E. Laurie
Oak Grove, OR 97267   **Phone:** (503) 652-7049   **E-Mail:** rot@ti.org
USA   **Fax:** same   **Internet:** http://www.teleport.com/~rot

Contact Person: Randal O'Toole, Executive Director.
Officers or Principals: Randal O'Toole, Executive Director ($0); Karl Hess, Jr., Contributing Editor ($0).
Mission or Interest: "Research and education aimed at environmental protection without big government. . . *there are no enemies of the environment - only people with different incentives.* . . labeling people 'environmental enemies' becomes a self-fulfilling prophesy as it turns these people into enemies, not of the environment but of environmentalists." Opposed to government subsidies of logging, mining, etc.
Accomplishments: "Research studies of Forest Service, Park Service, and other federal agencies that have greatly influenced both agency and congressional policies." Op-eds have appeared in *Forbes* and other publications. "Has roots in both the environmental movement and conservative organizations, so it is providing a bridge between the two views." In 1995 the Institute spent $62,019 on its programs.
Total Revenue: 1995 $43,684 **Total Expenses:** $65,137 **Net Assets:** $37,510
Tax Status: 501(c)(3) **Annual Report:** No. **Employees:** 4
Board of Directors or Trustees: John Baden (Foundation for Research on Economics and the Environment), Doug Crandall (Vice Pres., American Forest and Paper Assoc.), Prof. William Ferrell (Oregon State Univ.), Dean James Huffman (Northwest School of Law), Andy Stahl (Association of Forest Service Employees for Environmental Ethics).
Periodicals: *Different Drummer* (quarterly journal).
Internships: Yes.
Other Information: Established in 1975 as the Cascade Holistic Economic Consultants. The name was changed in 1995. The Institute received $30,220, or 69% of revenue, from contributions and grants awarded by foundations, businesses, and individuals. (These included the Lazar Foundation. Contributions and grants have been sporadic, $16,155 in 1994, $118,970 in 1993, and $68,838 in 1992.) $11,065, or 25%, from program services, including consulting and publication sales.

Toll Roads
301 E. Third St.
Frederick, MD 21701   **Phone:** (301) 631-1148   **E-Mail:** tollroads@aol.com
USA   **Fax:** (301) 631-1248

Contact Person: Peter Samuel, Editor/Publisher.
Mission or Interest: Publication of a newsletter. "The general thrust of change is to make more use of user-fees (tolls) and market forces, so as to tap the capital markets and get management that is focused on consumer responsive highway service. The $48 billion/year cost lines of stop-&-go traffic on our 'free' roads are an analog of the lines of people at the empty stores that the Russians used to suffer before the collapse of communism. . . Our present 'highway communism' is equally unsustainable."
Tax Status: For profit.
Periodicals: *Toll Roads* (monthly newsletter).
Other Information: Established in March 1996.

Toward Tradition
P.O. Box 58
Mercer Island, WA 98040   **Phone:** (206) 236-3046   **E-Mail:** Yardenw@aol.com
USA   **Fax:** (206) 236-3288

Contact Person: Yardin Weidenfeld, Executive Director.
Officers or Principals: Rabbi Daniel Lapin, President; Jack Abramoff, Chairman.

Mission or Interest: "Creating a national movement of Jewish conservatives and a new political alliance between Jewish and Christian conservatives, supplying intellectual ammunition linking conservatism to its religious origins, and offering a pro-business defense of capitalism based on the intrinsic morality of the free market."

Accomplishments: Took out two advertisements in *The New York Times* in 1994. One, entitled "Should Jews Fear the 'Christian Right'?", defended Christian conservatives against unjust charges of anti-Semitism. The other, entitled "Mazel Tov, Speaker Gingrich - We Know All About 10 Point Contracts," affirmed that Jewish principles are rooted in the Jewish tradition. Articles have appeared in *The Wall Street Journal, Orange County Register,* and *Crisis Magazine.* They co-hosted an October 1994 conference with the Claremont Institute and the Jewish Policy Center attended by over 400. The theme of the conference was "Toward a New Alliance: American Jews and Political Conservatism." Participants included Elliott Abrams (Hudson Inst.), Midge Decter (Inst. on Religion and Public Life), Don Feder (columnist), David Horowitz (Center for the Study of Popular Culture), Roy Innis (Congress of Racial Equality), Irving Kristol (National Affairs), William Kristol (Project for the Republican Future), Michael Medved (movie critic, author), Adam Meyerson (*Policy Review*), Grover Norquist (Americans for Tax Reform), Norman Podhoretz, Ralph Reed (Christian Coalition), Father Robert Sirico (Acton Inst.), and others.

Products or Services: Conferences, articles, cassette tape series.

Tax Status: 501(c)(3) **Annual Report:** Yes. **Employees:** 5

Board of Directors or Trustees: David Altschuler, Hart Hasten, David Holder, Lewis Kaufman, Howard Klein, Michael Lapin, Graig Lewis (Exec. Vice Pres., MBNA America), Judd Magilnick, Michael Medved (film critic), Joseph Morris, Adam Pruzan, Dr, Martin Rabin (Univ. of Washington Dental School). Sr. Minton Ritter, Dr. Roberta Ritter, Dr. Jeffrey Satinover, Larry Smith, Leo Strauss, Benjamin Waldman, Barrie Wexler.

Periodicals: *Perspectives* (quarterly newsletter).

Internships: Yes, to work on publications and policy analysis.

Other Information: In 1995 Toward Tradition received $15,000 from the Carthage Foundation, and $10,000 from the Lynde and Harry Bradley Foundation. In 1994, $150 from Coalitions for America.

Town Hall

214 Massachusetts Ave., N.E.
Washington, DC 20002   **Phone:** (800) 441-4142
USA   **Fax:**   (202) 544-7330   **Internet:** http://www.townhall.com

Mission or Interest: Computer network linking web pages of various conservative organizations. Member organizations are: Heritage Foundation, *National Review,* Frontiers of Freedom Institute, Family Research Council, Progress and Freedom Foundation, Small Business Survival Committee, Americans for a Balanced Budget, Media Research Center, American Association of Christian Schools, American Conservative Union, Bradley Foundation, Landmark Legal Foundation, Empower America, American Legislative Exchange Council, State Policy Network, Claremont Institute, Discovery Institute, Federalist Society, Americans Back in Charge, Americans for Tax Reform, Capital Research Center, Leadership Institute, *Washington Times National Weekly,* Savers & Investors League, Young America's Foundation, Eagle Publishing, Foundation for Research on Economics and the Environment, Center for Individual Rights, Intercollegiate Studies Institute, Citizens Against Government Waste, and *Headway Magazine.*

Accomplishments: *U.S. News & World Report* called Town Hall, "The premier Web site on the right. . . links to and information about almost every conservative group." Records as many as 4 million hits per month. Town Hall's average user is male, 42 years old; 93% have a college degree, and 24% have a graduate degree.

Tax Status: For profit.

Other Information: Established in 1995 with a loan of $500,000 from the Lynde and Harry Bradley Foundation. Co-owned 50/50 by the Heritage Foundation and *National Review.*

True Foundation

P.O. Drawer 2360
Casper, WY 82602   **Phone:** (307) 237-9301
USA

Contact Person: Cherie Miller.

Officers or Principals: H. A. True, Jr., Trustee ($0).

Mission or Interest: Grant-making philanthropy that includes conservative groups in its awards.

Accomplishments: In the fiscal year ending November 1993 the Foundation awarded $214,111 in grants. Recipients included; $33,000 for the Mountain States Legal Foundation, $5,000 for the Political Economy Research Center, $3,000 for the Capital Research Center, $2,000 each for the Leadership Institute, and National Center for Policy Analysis, $1,050 for the Heritage Foundation, $1,000 each for Hillsdale College, and the Institute for Justice, and grants of less than $1,000 for the American Council for Capital Formation, U.S. English Foundation, America's Future, Fund for American Studies, Accuracy in Media, Media Research Center, Defenders of Property Rights, Free Congress Foundation, Citizens Against Government Waste, Citizens for a Sound Economy Foundation, Competitive Enterprise Institute, Hudson Institute, U.S. Term Limits, National Legal Center for the Public Interest, Southwestern Legal Foundation, Washington Legal Foundation, National Right to Work Legal Defense Foundation, High Frontier, and Prison Fellowship. Also awards scholarships to True Oil Company employees.

Total Revenue: FY ending 11/93 $77,632 **Total Expenses:** $215,816 **Net Assets:** $2,769,240

Tax Status: 501(c)(3)

Other Information: Established in 1958. The True Foundation is sponsored by the True Oil Company. The Foundation received $77,632, or 100% of revenue, from interest on savings and temporary cash investments. The Foundation held $2,246,062, or 81% of assets, in U.S. Treasury bonds.

Unification Church of America
(see Holy Spirit Association for Unification of World Christianity)

United Citizens for Legal Reform (UCLR)
2801V Eubank, N.E., Suite 167
Albuquerque, NM 87112   **Phone:** (800) 505-6555
USA

Contact Person: Sammy S. Jenkins, Jr., Executive Director.
Mission or Interest: To reform our legal system by acting as a clearinghouse for information on abuses and legal reform efforts across the country.
Accomplishments: Published <u>Dracula in Charge of the Bloodbank: An Expose of the American Judicial System</u>, through American Trend Publishing, Inc., at the same address.
Tax Status: Nevada nonprofit.
Periodicals: *Legal Watch* (monthly newsletter).
Other Information: Jenkins is also the author of <u>Mecham, Arizona's Fighting Governor</u>, which describes the 1988 impeachment of Governor Mecham of Arizona as, "a showcase example of political persecution under the guise of judicial prosecution."

United Educators Foundation
900 Armour Dr.
Lake Bluff, IL 60044   **Phone:** (708) 234-3700
USA

Contact Person: Robert C. Davis, President.
Officers or Principals: Robert C. Davis, President/Treasurer ($0); Warren T. Davis, Jr., Vice President/Secretary ($0); Robert C. Davis, III, Director ($0).
Mission or Interest: Grant-making foundation that includes conservative organizations in its awards.
Accomplishments: In 1994 the Foundation awarded $26,950 in grants. The recipients included: $2,500 for the Rockford Institute, $2,000 each for the Heartland Institute, Hillsdale College, and National Right to Work Foundation, $1,000 for the National Legal Center for Public Interest, $500 each for the Institute for Humane Studies, American Institute for Economic Research, Accuracy in Media, and National Center for Policy Analysis, $300 for the Committee for Monetary Research and Education, and $200 for the Citizens for a Sound Economy Foundation.
Total Revenue: 1994 $12,592 **Total Expenses:** $27,230 **Net Assets:** $333,259 (-4%)(1)
Tax Status: 501(c)(3)
Other Information: The Foundation received $12,592, or 100% of revenue, from interest on savings and temporary cash investments. The Foundation held all of its assets in cash or savings and temporary cash investments.

United Republican Fund (URF)
151 North Michigan Ave, Suite 2815
Chicago, IL 60601   **Phone:** (312) 565-4497
USA   **Fax:** (312) 565-4496

Contact Person: Larry P. Horist, Vice President.
Officers or Principals: Denis Healy, President; William C. Croft, Chairman; Jill B. Horist, Vice President/Operations Director.
Mission or Interest: To promote conservative candidates and causes. "The United Republican Fund melds conservative principles with 'street smarts'. They seek out support and cooperation in urban and minority communities."
Accomplishments: Founded the Illinois Educational Choice Coalition. Helped defeat tax increases. Active in getting a GOP majority elected in the Illinois State Senate.
Tax Status: 501(c)(4) **Employees:** 15
Other Information: Established in 1934.

United Seniors Association (USA)
12500 Fair Lakes Circle, Suite 125
Fairfax, VA 22033   **Phone:** (703) 803-6747
USA   **Fax:** (703) 803-6853

Contact Person: Sandra L. Butler, President.
Officers or Principals: Sandra L. Butler, President ($70,688); Kathleen A. Patten, Secretary ($67,856); Jon B. Utley, Director ($1,500); Richard A. Viguerie, Co-Founder; Mrs. George (Bette) Murphy, Honorary Chairman; Hon. Beau Boulter, Legislative Director.
Mission or Interest: "The *right* voice for senior Americans. . . Founded to provide an independent organization for senior citizens who support lower taxes, less federal spending, and the American free enterprise system."

Accomplishments: Claims over 400,000 members. In 1996 USA co-sponsored hospitality suites at the Republican National Convention in San Diego. In 1994 USA distributed more than 1.5 million copies of its newsletter. Over 11 million letters were sent out, "educating and informing" seniors on issues. Delivered a petition to Congress signed by 23,974 USA members and other seniors opposing "Clinton-style health care reform plans that cut Medicare." Lobbied on behalf of Social Security, Medicare, and pension reforms. Supports Medical Savings Accounts-based health care reforms. Co-founded Citizens Against Rationing Health with the American Conservative Union. In 1994 USA spent $2,499,981 on its programs.

Total Revenue: 1994 $6,676,908 8%(2) **Total Expenses:** $6,524,469 38%/17%/45% **Net Assets:** (-$844,484)

Products or Services: "Reflections" radio show. "Resolving the Medicare Crisis: A Proposal for Rescuing Seniors and Taxpayers" by Peter Ferrara (Senior Fellow, National Center for Policy Analysis), and other publications. "The Senior Line" fax updates. Discounts on insurance and pharmaceuticals for seniors. "Murphy Awards" for elected officials who "significantly contribute to the betterment of senior citizens. In 1994 the award was given to 24 elected officials, including Rep. Newt Gingrich (R-GA), Rep. Dick Armey (R-TX), Sen. Daniel Patrick Moynihan (D-NY), and Sen. Paul Simon (D-IL).

Tax Status: 501(c)(4)   **Citations:** 39:116

Board of Directors or Trustees: Anne Edwards, Anthony Fabrizio, Anne Keast, Jim Minarik, Jon Utley, Michael Valerio. Advisory Board includes: Walt Bragg (General Dynamics), G, Thatcher Darwin (founder, American Conservative Party), Peter Ferrara (NCPA), H. Lynn Hopewell, Rev. Edmund Opitz (contributing editor, *The Freeman*), Dr. Jane Orient (Association of American Physicians and Surgeons), W. H. Regnery, John Ryan (former chairman, U.S. Postal Rate Commission), Otto Scott, Terree Wasley.

Periodicals: *The Senior American* (bimonthly newsletter).

Other Information: Established in 1991 by former U.S. Senator George Murphy (1902-1992) and direct mail fundraiser Richard A. Viguerie. USA received $6,514,163, or 98% of revenue, from contributions and grants. $162,745, or 2%, from royalties.

United States Business and Industrial Council

122 C St., N.W., Suite 815
Washington, DC 20001   **Phone:** (202) 628-2211
USA

Contact Person: Steven V. Hill.

Officers or Principals: Kevin Kearns, President ($47,950); C. Bryan Little, Assistant Treasurer ($31,722); Steven Hill, Secretary ($5,230); Frank Buhler, Treasurer; Frank Buhler, Chairman; H. Norman Saurage, III, Vice Chairman.

Mission or Interest: Conservative business advocacy organization committed to preserving American economic preeminence.

Accomplishments: "Leading coalitions on budget and tax; helped defeat strike breaker bill; leading spokesman on issues, including trade, and economic security."

Total Revenue: 1994 $926,596 52%(2) **Total Expenses:** $790,305 **Net Assets:** $189,758

Products or Services: Fax board for "Action Alerts" to members, position papers, special *Issues Briefings*, newsclip booklets, radio programs, lectures, and articles. Produces the "Business Voice" program on National Empowerment Television. Lobbying: in 1994 the Council spent $86,852 on lobbying.

Tax Status: 501(c)(6) **Employees:** 7   **Citations:** 2:216

Board of Directors or Trustees: Abraham Goldfarb (National Banner Co.), Cornelius Hubner (American Felt and Filter Co.), John Nash (Milliken & Co.), Jack Whelan (Golden Rule Insurance), Anthony Grampsas (Adolph Coors Co.), Diemer True (True Drilling Co.), Hank True (Eighty-Eight Oil Co.), many others from business and industry.

Periodicals: *Business Bulletin* (newsletter).

Internships: Yes.

Other Information: Affiliated with the 501(c)(3) U.S. Industrial Council Educational Foundation. The Council received $463,765, or 50% of revenue, from contributions and grants awarded by foundations, businesses, and individuals. $415,475, or 45%, from membership dues. The remaining revenue came from meeting registration fees, interest on savings, and other miscellaneous sources.

United States Chamber of Commerce

1615 H St., N.W.
Washington, DC 20062   **Phone:** (202) 659-6000
USA   **Fax:** (202) 463-5836   **Internet:** http://www.USChamber.ORG/Chamber

Contact Person: Milton E. Mitler, Vice President.

Officers or Principals: Roger C. Jask, Vice President ($98,138); Dr. Richard L. Lesher, President.

Mission or Interest: "To achieve human progress through an economic, political and social system based on individual freedom, incentive, initiative, opportunity and responsibility."

Accomplishments: Maintaining vigilance on legislative issues impacting upon the economy and the American business community, developing policy on those issues and articulating that policy to members, the general public, the press, members of Congress and the Administration.

Products or Services: Intelligence on legislative issues affecting the American business community.

Tax Status: 501(c)(6) **Annual Report:** Yes. **Employees:** 1,200

Periodicals: *The Business Advocate* (bimonthly), *Nation's Business* (monthly).

Internships: Yes, U.S. Chamber accommodates interns, college juniors and seniors, who are authorized by their schools to participate for point credit. Chamber does not pay salary, just a stipend.

United States English

1747 Pennsylvania Ave., N.W., Suite 1100
Washington, DC 20006   **Phone:**   (202) 833-0100
USA   **Fax:**   (202) 833-0108

Contact Person: Mauro E. Mujica, Chairman/CEO.
Officers or Principals: Mauro E. Mujica, Chairman/CEO; Norman D. Shumway, Secretary; Rodney A. Smith, Treasurer.
Mission or Interest: Lobbying organization promoting English as the official language of the United States.
Accomplishments: In 1996 U.S. English assisted Rep. Duke Cunningham in passing H.R. 123, "The Bill Emerson English Language Empowerment Act of 1996" that passed in the House, 259-169. This bill was introduced by the late Rep. Bill Emerson (R-MO) and makes English the official language of the federal government. U.S. English worked with Sen. Richard Shelby (R-AL) in the Senate, but the Senate adjourned for the session and the bill died. With the help of U.S. English, 23 states have enacted measures making English the official language.
Total Revenue: 1995 $7,236,358 **Total Expenses:** $6,616,924 69%/11%/35% **Net Assets:** $1,291,295
Tax Status: 501(c)(4)   **Citations:** 112:56
Other Information: Established in 1984. Affiliated with the 501(c)(3) U.S. English Foundation at the same address. In 1995 the two affiliates had combined revenues of $6,303,536, expenses of $4,829,514, and net assets of $1,064,494.

United States English Foundation

1747 Pennsylvania Ave., N.W., Suite 1100
Washington, DC 20006   **Phone:**   (202) 833-0100
USA   **Fax:**   (202) 833-0108

Contact Person: Mauro E. Mujica, Chairman/CEO.
Officers or Principals: Mauro E. Mujica, Chairman/CEO ($0); Jerry M. Mosier, Secretary ($0); Rodney A. Smith, Treasurer ($0); Richard Shelby, Director.
Mission or Interest: Promotion of the English language as the official language of the United States. "Represents the interests of Official English advocates before the courts, promotes opportunities for people living in the United States to learn English, disseminates information on Offical English and English teaching methods, sponsors educational programs, and develops English instructional materials."
Accomplishments: Claims 750,000 members nationwide. In 1995 the Foundation spent $300,644 on its programs.
Total Revenue: 1995 $786,884 (-8%)(3) **Total Expenses:** $300,644 65%/23%/12% **Net Assets:** $807,392
Products or Services: "Bilingual Education in the United States" a joint study with the American Legislative Exchange Council. National Volunteer Organization Directory. Basic English language audio-tapes and language teaching program assistance.
Tax Status: 501(c)(3)   **Annual Report:** Yes.   **Citations:** 112:56
Board of Directors or Trustees: Advisors include: Jacques Barzun, Ph.D., Saul Bellow, Alistair Cooke, Sen. Joseph Corcoran, Midge Decter, George Gilder, Nathan Glazer, Ph.D., Sen. Barry Goldwater, Charlton Heston, Sen. Eugene McCarthy, Norman Podhoretz, Henry Salvatori, Arnold Schwarzenegger, Alex Trebek.
Other Information: Founded in 1983 by the late Sen. S. I. Hayakawa (D-CA). In 1994 the Foundation paid the American Legislative Exchange Council $156,675 for its part in their joint study. Affiliated with the 501(c)(4) U.S. English at the same address. In 1995 the two affiliates had combined revenues of $6,303,536, expenses of $4,829,514, and net assets of $1,064,494. The Foundation received $529,218, or 67% of revenue, from contributions and grants awarded by foundations, businesses, and individuals. $195,904, or 25%, from mailing list rentals. $39,470, or 5%, from capital gains on the sale of securities. $22,292, or 3%, from interest on savings and temporary cash investments.

United States Strategic Institute (USSI)

P.O. Box 15618, Kenmore Station
Boston, MA 02215   **Phone:**   (617) 353-8700
USA   **Fax:**   (617) 353-7330

Contact Person: Mackubin T. Owens, Editor.
Officers or Principals: Abigail DuBois, Managing Editor ($54,776); Mackubin T. Owens, Editor-in-Chief ($23,292); Dr. Arthur G. B. Metcalf, Chairman ($0); Gen. Bruce K. Holloway, President; Richard R. Glendon, Treasurer/Secretary; Lt. Gen. Victor H. Krulak, Vice Chairman.
Mission or Interest: Publishes *Strategic Review*, a quarterly journal devoted to foreign policy and national defense.
Accomplishments: "*Strategic Review* is known and respected for its steadfast role in support of the vital interests and security of the United States." In the fiscal year ending February 1995 *Strategic Review* was sent to approximately 1,600 subscribers, mostly university and military libraries. USSI spent $105,846 on the publication and distribution of *Strategic Review*.
Total Revenue: FY ending 2/95 $43,319 (-58%)(2) **Total Expenses:** $128,964 82%/18%/0% **Net Assets:** $73,005
Tax Status: 501(c)(3)
Board of Directors or Trustees: Richard Allen, Gen. T. R. Milton, USAF (Ret.), Adm. Thomas Moorer, USN (Ret.), Gen. F. Michael Rogers, USAF (Ret.), Dr. John Silber (Boston Univ.), Gen. Fred C. Weyand, USA (Ret.), Gen. Fred F. Woerner, Jr., USA (Ret.).
Periodicals: *Strategic Review* (quarterly journal).

Other Information: USSI publishes *Strategic Review* in association with the Center for International Relations at Boston University. USSI is given "modest" office space and pays no rent. The Institute received $24,154, or 46% of gross revenue, from subscription fees. $13,890, or 26%, from contributions and grants awarded by foundations, businesses, and individuals. $7,475, or 14%, from membership dues. $7,209, or 14%, from dividends and interest from securities. The remaining revenue came from interest on savings and temporary cash investments. Revenues were offset by $5,024 in unrealized losses on securities, and $4,437 from the sale of securities for a loss. From February 1993 to 1995, subscription revenues dropped 23%; but the large loss in net revenue was due primarily to an overall drop of 82% in contributions and grants.

United States Taxpayers Alliance (USTA)

450 E. Maple Ave.
Vienna, VA 22180   **Phone:**   (703) 281-9426
USA   **Fax:**   (703) 281-4108

Contact Person: Alison Potter.
Officers or Principals: Mark Weaver, President ($48,080); Howard Phillips, Chairman ($0); Charles Orndorff, Treasurer ($0); David Crowell, Secretary; Rus Walton, Vice President.
Mission or Interest: Lobbying on public-policy matters to limit the scope of government and promote traditional values.
Accomplishments: In the fiscal year ending March 1995, USTA spent $140,018 on numerous conferences and training seminars. Conference participants included Larry Pratt of Gun Owners of America, Franklin Sanders of *The Moneychanger*, Randall Terry of Operation Rescue, George Grant of Legacy Communications, Dr. Herb Titus, Dean of Regent University Law School, and various elected officials.
Total Revenue: FY ending 3/95 $191,376 21%(2) **Total Expenses:** $248,519 56%/23%/21% **Net Assets:** (-$173,450)
Products or Services: Books and video tapes of conferences.
Tax Status: 501(c)(4) **Annual Report:** No. **Employees:** 4   **Citations:** 1:225
Board of Directors or Trustees: Margie Godsey, David Drye, Jesse Grier, Robert Meucci, Roger Milliken (Milliken Foundation), Gerrish Milliken (Milliken Foundation), Dorothy Robinson, Abe Siemens, Gertrude Sumph.
Periodicals: *Weaver Report* (monthly newsletter).
Internships: No.
Other Information: Chairman Howard Phillips is the perennial presidential nominee of the U.S. Taxpayers Party. According to Phillips, "The real struggle today is not between liberals and conservatives or Republicans and Democrats. It is, in fact, a conflict between those who recognize that God, the Creator and Sovereign, is the true source of law and authority, and, those who, on the other hand, falsely assume that either man's flawed reason or the civil government's imperfect authority can somehow alter or ignore, without consequence, the laws of the universe." The Alliance received $191,361, or 99.9% of revenue, from contributions and grants awarded by foundations, businesses, and individuals. The remaining revenue revenue came from interest on savings and temporary cash investments.

Unied States Term Limits

1511 K St., N.W., Suite 540
Washington, DC 20008   **Phone:**   (202) 393-6440
USA   **Fax:**   (202) 393-6434   **Internet:** http://www.termlimits.org

Contact Person: Jonathan Ferry, Communications Director.
Officers or Principals: Sally Reed-Impastato, Vice President ($59,583); Paul Jacob, Executive Director ($55,833); Shannon A. McCloskey, Secretary ($7,917); Howard S. Rich, President; Christina N. Liptak, Treasurer.
Mission or Interest: Attempt to restore citizen control of government by supporting term limits for Congress, as well as state and local officials.
Accomplishments: 23 states have passed congressional term limits. 21 state legislative term limits laws. Approximately 3,000 cities and towns under local limits.
Total Revenue: 1992 $1,700,733 **Total Expenses:** $3,105,065 **Net Assets:** (-$1,406,112)
Products or Services: Lobbying for term limits. Provides funding for state initiatives. "Outlook" research series.
Tax Status: 501(c)(4) **Annual Report:** No. **Employees:** 10   **Citations:** 408:24
Board of Directors or Trustees: Peter Ackerman, Steven Baer, Terrence Considine, Edward Crane (Pres., Cato Inst.), Cora Fields, Mike Ford, F. Philip Handy, Cecil Heftel, Mike Hepple (Dir. of Marketing, Time Life, Inc.), M. Blair Hull, Michael Keiser, Kenneth Langone, Ronald Lauder, William Long, Rob Mosbacher, Eric O'Keefe, Paul Raynault, Pete Schabarum, Joseph Stilwell (Center for Independent Thought).
Periodicals: *No Uncertain Terms* (ten times-a-year newsletter).
Internships: Yes. Full and part-time paid positions are available.
Other Information: Affiliated with the 501(c)(3) U.S. Term Limits Foundation at the same address. The organization received $1,671,684, or 98% of revenue, from contributions. The remaining revenue came from interest on savings and other miscellaneous sources.

United States Term Limits Foundation

1511 K St., N.W., Suite 540
Washington, DC 20005   **Phone:**   (202) 393-6440
USA   **Fax:**   (202) 393-6434   **Internet:** http://www.termlimits.org

Contact Person: Jonathan Ferry, Communications Director.

Officers or Principals: Paul Jacob, Executive Director ($72,083); Sally Reed-Impastato, Vice President ($56,667); John T. Buckley, Secretary ($24,000); Howard S. Rich, President.
Mission or Interest: Research and education affiliate of U.S. Term Limits.
Accomplishments: In 1994 the Foundation spent $1,201,773 on it programs.
Total Revenue: 1994 $929,824 304%(2) **Total Expenses:** $1,768,751 68%/27%/5% **Net Assets:** (-$832,235)
Products or Services: Conferences, research projects, policy papers.
Tax Status: 501(c)(3)   **Citations:** 408:24
Board of Directors or Trustees: Steven Baer, Terrence Considine, Edward Crane (Pres., Cato Inst.), Cora Fields, Mike Ford, F. Philip Handy, Cecil Heftel, Mike Hepple (Dir. of Marketing, Time Life, Inc.), M. Blair Hull, Michael Keiser, Kenneth Langone, Ronald Lauder, William Long, Rob Mosbacher, Eric O'Keefe, Paul Raynault, Pete Schabarum, Joseph Stilwell (Center for Independent Thought).
Periodicals: *The Legal Limit* (monthly newsletter)
Other Information: Established in 1990. Affiliated with the 501(c)(4) U.S. Term Limits at the same address. The Foundation received $924,692, or 99% of revenue, from contributions and grants awarded by foundations, businesses, and individuals. (These grants included $25,000 from the Gilder Foundation, $20,000 from the J.M. Foundation, $10,000 from the Richard & Helen DeVos Foundation, $10,000 from the F.M. Kirby Foundation. In 1995, $25,000 from the Lynde and Harry Bradley Foundation, $10,000 from the Philip M. McKenna Foundation, $10,000 from the John William Pope Foundation, and $7,500 from the Roe Foundation.) The remaining revenue came from interest on savings, and the sale of books and paraphernalia.

United Taxpayers of New Jersey

P.O. Box 103
Cedar Grove, NJ 07009   **Phone:** (201) 890-0271   **E-Mail:** utnj@aol.com
USA   **Fax:**   same   **Internet:** http://www.3wnet/utnj/

Contact Person: Sam Perelli, State Chairman.
Mission or Interest: "To operate as a government watchdog by proposing and supporting legislation which benefits the state's taxpayers."
Accomplishments: "Participated in passage of binding arbitration for paid police and firefighters, state mandate-state pay, and uniform recall act (any elected official can be recalled). Supported and participated in institution of reduction of state income and sales taxes."
Tax Status: Nonprofit.

University Centers for Rational Alternatives

570 7th Ave., Suite 1007
New York, NY 10018   **Phone:**   (212) 391-2396
USA

Contact Person: Dr. Miro M. Todorovich, Executive Secretary.
Officers or Principals: Lewis Feuer, President ($0); Gray L. Dorsey, Vice President ($0); Miro M. Todorovich, Executive Secretary ($0).
Mission or Interest: An organization of academics who promote scholarship as the criteria of academia.
Accomplishments: Newsletter *Measure* sent to about 3,000. In 1995 the organization spent $66,482 on its programs.
Total Revenue: 1995 $86,939 8%(3) **Total Expenses:** $81,076 **Net Assets:** $22,827
Tax Status: 501(c)(3)
Board of Directors or Trustees: Gertrude Himmelfarb (historian), Morton Kaplan, Eugene Rostow, others.
Periodicals: *Measure* (newsletter founded by Sidney Hook).
Other Information: Many of those associated with University Centers for Rational Alternatives are neo-conservatives - former leftists who have moved to the Right. The organization received $60,180, or 69% of revenue, from contributions and grants awarded by foundations, businesses, and individuals. The remaining revenue came from rental income, newsletter subscriptions, investment income, and other miscellaneous sources.

Utah Taxpayers Association

1578 W. 1700 S., Suite 201
Salt Lake City, UT 84401   **Phone:** (801) 972-8814   **E-Mail:** 72640,1711@compuserve.com
USA   **Fax:**   (801) 973-2324

Contact Person: Howard Stephenson, President.
Officers or Principals: Howard Headlee, Legislative Director; Greg A. Fredde, Research Analyst; Dr. Kelly Matthews, Chairman; Reed Crockett, Vice Chairman; Philip Despain, Secretary/Treasurer.
Mission or Interest: Utah-based organization working for less taxes and "efficient use of our tax dollars".
Accomplishments: "$160 million in state tax cuts over the past two years; passage of several pro-business sales tax exemptions; review of the budgets of Utah's 29 counties, 40 school districts, and 13 major cities."
Products or Services: Educational materials, annual budget analysis, and studies that compare Utah to other states in terms of tax burdens.

Tax Status: 501(c)(4) **Employees:** 4 full time, 5 part time.
Periodicals: *The Utah Taxpayer* (monthly newsletter).
Internships: Yes, paid legislative intern position available from January through March.
Other Information: "Since 1922."

Vernon K. Krieble Foundation

P.O. Box 389
Marlborough, CT 06447
USA

Contact Person: Helen K. Fusscas, President.
Officers or Principals: Helen K. Fusscas, President ($0); Frederick K. Krieble, Treasurer ($0); Collette C. Krieble, Vice President ($0); Nancy B. Krieble, Secretary.
Mission or Interest: Grant-making foundation that includes conservative and free-market organizations in its awards.
Accomplishments: In 1994 the Foundation awarded $510,000 in grants. Recipients of these grants included: $35,000 for the Free Congress Foundation, $25,000 for the Institute for Political Economy, $15,000 each for the George Mason University's Department of Economics and the Law and Economics Center, and the Institute for Research on the Economics of Taxation, $10,000 each for the Institute of World Politics, Leadership Institute, and Intercollegiate Studies Institute, $5,000 each for the Cato Institute, Competitive Enterprise Institute, Conservative Caucus Foundation, Mont Pelerin Society, National Endowment for Democracy, National Right to Work Foundation, Tax Policy Analysis, Institute for Policy Innovation, and Hillsdale College, $4,000 for the American Foundation for Resistance International, and $3,000 each for Accuracy in Media, American Enterprise Institute, Center for Media and Public Affairs, and Citizens Against Government Waste.
Total Revenue: 1994 $933,006 **Total Expenses:** $655,897 **Net Assets:** $10,082,147 2%(2)
Tax Status: 501(c)(3)
Board of Directors or Trustees: Robert Krieble, Amanda Fusscas, Christopher Fusscas, Frederick Fusscas.
Other Information: Established in 1985. The Foundation received $745,293, or 81% of revenue, from capital gains on the sale of assets. $162,226, or 17%, from dividends and interest from securities. $5,995, or 1%, from interest on savings and temporary cash investments. The remaining revenue came from miscellaneous sources. The Foundation held $7,940,363, or 79% of assets, in mutual funds and common stocks.

Virginians for Property Rights

9205-D Vassau Court, Conner Center
Manassas Park, VA 20111   **Phone:** (703) 368-1878
USA   **Fax:**   (703) 330-1924

Contact Person: Patricia A. Bradhorn, President.
Officers or Principals: William Frazier, Vice President; Jim Menks, Treasurer; Sue Hansohn, Secretary.
Mission or Interest: "Maintain, restore, and protect private property rights. Eliminate abuses and perversions of enabling legislation which was originally designed to protect, conserve and enhance quality of life such as: The Outdoor Recreation Act of 1963, Land and Water Conservation Act of 1914, National Historic Preservation Act of 1966, National Trails System 1968, National Wild and Scenic Rivers Act 1968."
Accomplishments: Helped pass legislation "which makes it impossible to nominate or designate private property for historical purposes without property owners permission."
Products or Services: Legal referrals for landowners. Pamphlets and publications, grassroots organizing.
Tax Status: 501(c)(3) **Employees:** All volunteer.
Board of Directors or Trustees: Alice Menks, Robert Sansom, Elizabeth Parker, Peter Gyory, Claire Rollins, Suzanne Wright, Gladys Frazier, Leri Thomas, Steve McIntyre.

Voice of Liberty

692 Sunnybrook Dr.
Decatur, GA 30033   **Phone:** (404) 633-3634
USA

Contact Person: Martha O. Andrews, Executive Director.
Mission or Interest: Populist/conservative newsletter "exposing the enemies of God and Country".
Tax Status: Unincorporated. **Annual Report:** All volunteer.
Periodicals: *Voice of Liberty* (quarterly).

Voluntaryists

P.O. Box 1275
Gramling, SC 29348   **Phone:** (864) 472-2750
USA

Contact Person: Carl Watner, Editor/Publisher.
Mission or Interest: Non-political strategies to achieve a free society and de-legitimization of the state through education. They advocate the withdrawal of the cooperation and tacit consent on which government power relies.
Products or Services: Books, Neither Bullets nor Ballots and Truth is Not a Half-Way Place, by Robert Lefevre.
Periodicals: *The Voluntaryist* (monthly newsletter).
Other Information: Established in 1982. They do not try to change things through the electoral process. They believe elections give the government an "aura of moral legitimacy. . . Governments must cloak their actions in an aura of moral legitimacy in order to sustain their power, and political methods invariably strengthen that legitimacy."

W. H. Brady Foundation
P.O. Box 610
Maggie Valley, NC 28751   **Phone:** (704) 926-1413
USA   **Fax:**   (704) 926-0167

Contact Person: Elizabeth B. Lurie, President.
Officers or Principals: Joy M. Barnes, Secretary; Peter Lettenberger, Vice President.
Mission or Interest: Grant-making philanthropy that includes conservative organizations in its awards. The Foundation's motto is the conservative maxim, "Ideas have consequences."
Accomplishments: In the fiscal year ending June 1995 the Foundation awarded $367,333 in grants.
Net Assets: FY ending 6/95 $7,000,000 (est.)
Tax Status: 501(c)(3)
Board of Directors or Trustees: Heather Higgins, Kim Dennis, Sherry Hoel, Phillip McGoohan.
Other Information: Established in 1956.

Wake-Up Call America
P.O. Box 280488
Lakewood, CO 80228   **Phone:** (303) 526-5023
USA   **Fax:**   (303) 526-2043

Contact Person: Greg R. Carroll.
Officers or Principals: Rick Barton.
Mission or Interest: Bimonthly newspaper with a populist/conservative viewpoint. "To inform people of critical information not available from the mainstream media from a pro-Constitutional, limited government point of view. . . We cover much material about the New World Order/United Nations plans to create a one-world socialist dictatorship to eliminate America's Constitutional freedoms. Our goal is to literally 'wake up' a sleeping America to the reality of the day and the plans of the enemy's of freedom."
Tax Status: Colorado nonprofit.
Periodicals: *Wake-Up Call America* (bimonthly tabloid).
Other Information: Established in 1994.

Wanderer, The
201 Ohio St.
St. Paul, MN 55107   **Phone:** (612) 224-5733
USA

Contact Person: A. J. Matt, Jr., Editor.
Officers or Principals: Peggy Moen, Associate Editor; Paul Likoudis, News Editor; Frank Morriss, John J. Mulloy, Edith Myers, Charles R. Pulver, Contributing Editors.
Mission or Interest: A national weekly of news and conservative Catholic opinion. Carries syndicated columnists Pat Buchanan, Joe Sobran, Samuel Francis, and other conservatives.
Tax Status: For profit.
Periodicals: *The Wanderer* (weekly newspaper).
Other Information: Established in 1867.

Washington Institute for Policy Studies
P.O. Box 24645
Seattle, WA 98124   **Phone:** (206) 938-6300   **E-Mail:** wips@wips.org
USA   **Fax:**   (206) 938-6313   **Internet:** http://www.wips.org

Contact Person: Daniel Mead Smith, Project Manager.
Officers or Principals: R. William Baldwin, President ($62,425); John Carlson, Chairman ($36,000); John Hamer, Vice President Communications ($32,518); William Polk, Vice Chairman; Ed McMillan, Treasurer; Dave LaCourse, Research Analyst.
Mission or Interest: Policy research center founded on the principles of individual freedom, free enterprise, more accountability for the spending of tax dollars, and the development of private-sector solutions for social problems. Focus on Washington State. Works through "Washington Institute Network Groups," or WINGs, local activists in various regions of the state who work with their local Chamber of Commerce, Rotary, and other people and groups.

Accomplishments: Instrumental in passing the "Three Strikes and You're Out" law in Washington State. Featured on the "MacNeil-Lehrer News Hour," Paul Harvey's radio commentary, CNN's "Both Sides with Jesse Jackson," also in the *Congressional Quarterly*, the *National Journal*, *Forbes*, and the *Wall Street Journal*. In addition they have won praise from Barry Goldwater, William F. Buckley, Jr., Charlton Heston, Peter Grace, and Judge Robert Bork who have appeared at the Institute's Annual Dinner. In 1995 the Institute spent $364,009 on its programs.

Total Revenue: 1995 $523,627 33%(2) **Total Expenses:** $482,621 75%/12%/13% **Net Assets:** $66,587

Products or Services: Various studies, briefs, public addresses, more.

Tax Status: 501(c)(3) **Annual Report:** No. **Employees:** 5 **Citations:** 100:63

Board of Directors or Trustees: James Allison, R. William Baldwin, M. Lamont Bean, Ron Cohn, Conrad Denke, Hon. Kemper Freeman, Jr., Hon. Jeannette Hayner, Patricia Herbold, Tom Isenberg, Jeff Kuney, Gregg MacDonald, David Maryatt, John McEachern, Ed McMillan, Stanley McNaughton, Carl Meitzen, Amb. Della Newman, Brent Orrico, Steven Phelps, William Rademaker, Jr., Michale Schlitt, M.D., James Shaenfield, Thomas Stewart, Janet True, James Udelhoven, Larry Wells, Howard Wright.

Periodicals: *CounterPoint* (nine times a-year media critique), and *Institute Quarterly* (quarterly newsletter).

Internships: Yes. Two students per quarter conduct research, perform administrative tasks and help with mailings.

Other Information: Established in 1986. The Institute received $473,050, or 90% of revenue, from contributions and grants awarded by foundations, businesses, and individuals. (These grants included $38,000 from the Lynde and Harry Bradley Foundation, and $1,000 from the Roe Foundation.) $46,559, or 9%, from seminar fees. The remaining revenue came from special events, dividends and interest from securities, and interest on savings.

Washington Legal Foundation (WLF)

2009 Massachusetts Ave., N.W.
Washington, DC 20036   **Phone:** (202) 588-0302
USA   **Fax:** (202) 588-0386   **Internet:** http://www.wlf.org

Contact Person: Constance Claffey Larcher, Vice President.

Officers or Principals: Daniel J. Popeo, Chairman/President ($212,636); Constance Claffey Larcher, Vice President/Treasurer ($184,602); Paul D. Kamenar, Director of Litigation ($141,361); Richard A. Samp, Attorney ($109,065); John A. Popeo, Secretary.

Mission or Interest: Public interest law firm with a conservative and free-market emphasis.

Accomplishments: Successfully litigated Washington Legal Foundation v. Texas Equal Access to Justice Foundation, which held that interest on pooled clients' funds belongs to the clients. This interest had "generated approximately $150 million annually nationwide, which is used to supplement Legal Services Corporation funding for activist organizations." WLF participated on behalf of the plaintiff in BMW v. Gore, a lawsuit won by BMW by a vote of 5 to 4 in the U.S. Supreme Court. The ruling held that the amount of punitive damages awarded by a jury was excessive. Participating in Bennett v. Plenert, a case before the U.S. Supreme Court that will determine whether persons affected economically by the Endangered Species Act have a standing before the court to challenge government decisions. The 9th Circuit Court of Appeals had ruled that only environmentalists had standing to challenge government agency decisions in court to protect the species. WLF is representing 22 U.S. Senators and Representatives in Skaggs V. Carle. The suit defends the constitutionality of adopting a 3/5 majority needed in Congress to raise taxes. In 1994 WLF spent $1,475,319 on its programs. The largest program, with expenditures of $940,021, included legal analysis, legal intern programs, briefs and litigation. $535,298 was spent on the production and distribution of surveys and educational materials. This included a research grant of $90,000 for the Fund for Living American Government.

Total Revenue: 1994 $3,094,451 10%(4) **Total Expenses:** $2,420,709 61%/34%/5% **Net Assets:** $8,754,439

Tax Status: 501(c)(3) **Citations:** 68:85

Other Information: Established in 1977 by Daniel Popeo, a former staffer for the Nixon and Ford administrations. Affiliated with the 501(c)(3) American Legal Foundation, a financial "support group." WLF received $2,856,899, or 92% of gross revenue, from contributions and grants awarded by foundations, businesses, and individuals. (These grants included $50,000 from the Lilly Endowment, $25,000 from the J.M. Foundation, $10,000 from the John Brown Cook Foundation, $7,000 from the Grover Hermann Foundation, $5,000 from the F.M. Kirby Foundation, and $5,000 from the Anschutz Foundation. In 1995, $450,000 from the Carthage Foundation, $100,000 from the John M. Olin Foundation, $5,000 from the Philip M. McKenna Foundation, and $500 from the Forbes Foundation.) $130,778, or 4%, from dividends and interest from securities. $113,424, or 4%, from interest on savings and temporary cash investments. The remaining revenue came from the sale of publications. The Foundation lost $23,116 on the sale of securities.

Washington Research Council (WRC)

1301 Fifth Ave., Suite 2810
Seattle, WA 98101   **Phone:** (206) 357-6643
USA   **Fax:** (206) 754-2193

Contact Person: Richard S. Davis, President.

Officers or Principals: Richard S. Davis, President ($74,861); John S. Archer, Research Director ($45,455).

Mission or Interest: "Promoting effective public policy and efficient government through independent and objective fiscal analysis of policy." Focus on Washington state.

Accomplishments: In 1994 the Council spent $223,775 on its programs.

Total Revenue: 1994 $319,149 (-4%)(1) **Total Expenses:** $334,420 67%/25%/8% **Net Assets:** $71,546

Tax Status: 501(c)(3) **Citations:** 34:122

Periodicals: *In Context* (monthly graphic representation of fiscal issues).
Internships: Yes.
Other Information: Established in 1932. The Council received $270,090, or 85% of revenue, from contributions and grants awarded by foundations, businesses, and individuals. (These grants included $25,000 from the M.J. Murdock Charitable Trust.) $35,852, or 11%, from special contracted research. $3,014, or 1%, from the sale of publications. The remaining revenue came from interest on savings and temporary cash investments, and other miscellaneous sources.

Washington Times National Weekly Edition
3600 New York Ave., N.E.
Washington, DC 20002   **Phone:** (800) 636-4918   **E-Mail:** nated@infi.net
USA   **Fax:**   (202) 832-8285   **Internet:** http://www.WashTimes-Weekly.com

Contact Person: Wesley Pruden, Editor-in-Chief.
Officers or Principals: Wesley Pruden, Editor-in-Chief; Josette Shiner, Managing Editor; Tod Lindberg, Editorial Page Editor; Robert Morton, Assistant Managing Editor.
Mission or Interest: Weekly edition of the daily *Washington Times*, a newspaper with a distinctly conservative editorial policy. The weekly edition is generally more conservative than the daily, and is marketed as such.
Accomplishments: *The Washington Times* has a daily circulation in the DC area of over 101,000, and is the fastest growing daily in a major metropolitan area. The *National Weekly Edition* has a circulation of over 50,000 nationwide. *The Wall Street Journal* said of the *Times*, "A controversial Washington newspaper scoops its loftier rivals on Whitewater." *The Village Voice* said, "It's become impossible to have an informed discussion of Whitewater with anyone who's not reading *The Washington Times*." The Ombudsman of *The Washington Post* said, "*The Times* also beat *The Post* on several developments that *The Post*, I think, underestimated."
Tax Status: For profit.
Periodicals: *The Washington Times National Weekly Edition* (weekly newspaper).
Other Information: The *Times* began publishing in 1982. The former managing editor was Arnaud de Borchgrave. The *Times* is published by News World Communications, whose board is made up of members of Rev. Sun Myung Moon's Unification Church. Early on there were charges of editorial interference by the Church, and some editors and journalists resigned. Today, few of the paper's editors or managers are members of the Unification Church. The paper has been said (in *The New York Times*) to have consistently lost money and required subsidization. A commonly held reason for why the Unification Church continues to fund a money-losing enterprise is that the prestige of owning a widely-read newspaper, which was read by Presidents Reagan and Bush, confers a legitimacy on Rev. Moon and his organization that they might not otherwise have. (For more information see the Holy Spirit Association for Unification of World Christianity.) News World Communications also publishes the glossy weekly *Insight*, and the journal *World & I* (see separate listings).

We the People Institute (WTP) / Middle American News
6600 Six Forks Rd., Suite 103
Raleigh, NC 27615   **E-Mail:** manews@manews.org
USA   **Internet:** http://www.manews.org

Contact Person: Palmer Stacy.
Officers or Principals: Jerry Woodruff, Editor.
Mission or Interest: Populist/conservative lobbying organization. Publishes *Middle American News*, a monthly newspaper of news and opinion.
Accomplishments: Lobbied on behalf of term limits.
Products or Services: The Great Betrayal, book.
Tax Status: 501(c)(4)
Periodicals: *Middle American News* (monthly newspaper).

Weekly Standard, The
1150 17th St., N.W., 5th Floor
Washington, DC 20036   **Phone:** (202) 293-4900
USA   **Fax:**   (202) 293-4901

Contact Person: William Kristol, Editor/Publisher.
Officers or Principals: Fred Barnes, Executive Editor; John Podhoretz, Deputy Editor; David Tell, Opinion Editor; David Brooks, Senior Editor; Andrew Ferguson, Senior Editor; P.J. O'Rourke, David Frum, Charles Krauthammer, Contributing Editors.
Mission or Interest: A new weekly magazine of news and opinion with a conservative viewpoint.

Accomplishments: Claimed readership of over 60,000. The three editors are well-known in political circles. William Kristol was Chief of Staff for Vice President Quayle, he is now chairman of the Project for the Republican Future and is regarded as one of the most prominent Republican strategists. Fred Barnes was the chief political correspondent for *The New Republic*, and a regular on Public Television's "The McLaughlin Group." John Podhoretz has worked at numerous publications, including *Time*, *U.S. News and World Report*, *The New York Post*, *The Washington Times* and *The American Spectator*. Other featured writers include best selling author and humorist P.J. O'Rourke, Pulitzer-Prize winning columnist Charles Krauthammer, <u>Dead Right</u> author David Frum, *Wall Street Journal* editorial-features editor David Brooks, and former President Bush's speech writer Andrew Ferguson. *The Standard* has been praised in *Time*, *Newsweek* and *The New Yorker* for collecting strong talent.
Tax Status: For profit.
Periodicals: *The Weekly Standard* (weekly magazine).
Other Information: First issue published September 1995. Initial financing was provided by media giant Rubert Murdoch.

Wendell Cox Consultancy

P.O. Box 8083
Belleville, IL 62222   **Phone:** (618) 632-8507   **E-Mail:** policy@publicpurpose.com
USA   **Fax:** (618) 632-8538   **Internet:** http://www.publicpurpose.com/

Contact Person: Wendell Cox, Consultant.
Mission or Interest: Research and consulting on public policy issues including privatization, labor policy, competitive contracting, economic policy, and overall domestic policy. "To facilitate the ideal of government as the servant of the people by identifying and implementing strategies to achieve public purposes at a cost that is no higher than necessary."
Accomplishments: Cox frequently consults for the American Legislative Exchange Council. In 1994 he was paid $153,259 for his work for the Council. He has also done research for the Reason Foundation and Fraser Institute.
Tax Status: For profit. **Annual Report:** No.

Western Center for Law and Religious Freedom (WCLRF)

317 Court St., N.E., Suite 203
Salem, OR 97301   **Phone:** (503) 364-7612
USA

Contact Person: Douglas Vande Griend, Secretary.
Officers or Principals: Douglas Vande Griend, Secretary ($21,433); Beverly Ellis, President ($0); William Rehwald, Vice President ($0); Victor L. Smith, Treasurer.
Mission or Interest: Legal services and litigation with an emphasis on "religious freedom issues, pro-life questions, and student and parent rights in the public school system."
Accomplishments: The Center's litigation included: Successfully representing the Oregon Right to Life Education Foundation before the Oregon Department of Revenue, after the Foundation's application for real estate tax exemption was denied because the Foundation "wanted to persuade people of a certain point of view." Opposed the inclusion of a seminar, "Homosexuality, Christianity and Coming Out," in a government-sponsored conference. The Center stated that the seminar "purported to correct incorrect beliefs about the Bible's view of homosexuality," and successfully argued that the government could not espouse a particular position on religious issues. The seminar was removed from the conference. The Center spent $134,080 on its programs. This included $59,269 in grants made to the Christian Legal Society.
Total Revenue: 1995 $106,696 **Total Expenses:** $156,453 86%/14%/1% **Net Assets:** $17,271
Products or Services: Litigation, legal counsel. "CLSNet," an internet service for Christian attorneys, law students, law professors, and other legal professionals.
Tax Status: 501(c)(3)
Board of Directors or Trustees: J. Gregory Casey, David Llewellyn, Steve McFarland (Center for Law and Religious Freedom), Jim Eriksen (Jews for Jesus), Darren Walker, Samuel Casey (Christian Legal Society), William Ball, Susan Rankin, Julius Poppinga.
Other Information: The Center received $95,242, or 89% of revenue, from contributions and grants awarded by foundations, businesses, and individuals. (These grants included $29,617 from the Alliance Defense Fund. Contributions and grants have been steadily falling by an average of 32% since 1991.) $1,653, or 2%, from CLSNet income. The remaining revenue came from other miscellaneous sources, including the refund of unused portions of advances paid to other law firms.

Western Journalism Center (WJC)

P.O. Box 2450
Fair Oaks, CA 95628   **Phone:** (916) 852-6300
USA   **Fax:** (916) 852-6302   **Internet:** http://www.e-truth.com

Contact Person: Joseph Farah, Executive Director.
Officers or Principals: Cindy L. Gibson, Secretary/Treasurer ($15,254); Joseph Farah, Executive Director ($0); James Smith, Director ($0); Mike Antonnicci, Managing Editor.
Mission or Interest: "To promote investigative reporting, especially into government fraud, waste, and corruption; to sponsor training of a new generation of journalists, who are philosophically diverse."

Accomplishments: Focused attention on the "questions and inconsistencies behind the death of White House Deputy Counsel Vincent Foster Jr." For its investigation into the death of Vincent Foster, the Center believes it has become the target of politically-based scrutiny from the IRS. In a 1996 *Wall Street Journal* op-ed, Joseph Farah states that the IRS began auditing the Center just months after final approval of the Center's tax-exempt status. Furthermore, Farah says that the investigators were not interested in bookkeeping or financial records, but with the Center's choice of investigations. According to Farah one of the IRS field agents told him, "Look, this a political case, and it's going to be decided at the national level." Also according to Farah, a supporter of the Center whose corporation relies on federal contracts was contacted by Energy Secretary Hazel O'Leary, who told him that his continued support of the Center would jeopardize his government business. Other programs of the Center have forced the California Legislature to open public records. In 1995 the Center spent $346,309 on its programs.
Total Revenue: 1995 $501,318 **Total Expenses:** $486,546 71%/14%/15% **Net Assets:** $29,183
Products or Services: Vincent Foster: The Ruddy Investigation by Christopher Ruddy. Annual "Courage in Journalism" award.
Tax Status: 501(c)(3) **Annual Report:** No. **Employees:** 3 **Citations:** 80:77
Board of Directors or Trustees: James Smith (former publisher, Sacramento Union and Washington Star), Darryl Schmidt, Jack Stevens, Chuck Bell, John Roux. Advisors include: William Rusher (former publisher, *National Review*), John Kurzweil (*California Political Review*), Arianna Huffington, Marvin Olasky, Ph.D., Don Clark (anchorman, ABC affiliate in Bakersfield, CA), Bill Lee (publisher, *Sacramento Observer*), Dennis Prager (Micah Center), Linda Bowles (columnist), Sally Pipes (Pacific Research Inst.).
Periodicals: *Dispatches* (semi-weekly news and media review) and *Inside California* (monthly newsletter).
Internships: Yes.
Other Information: Established in 1993. Joseph Farah is a former editor of the *Sacramento Union* and also runs a for-profit consulting business, Farah & Associates. The Center received $500,887, or 99.9% of revenue, from contributions and grants awarded by foundations, businesses, and individuals. (These grants included $230,000 from the Carthage Foundation, and $1,000 from the Roe Foundation. The grants increased by 68% from $297,711 the previous year.) The remaining revenue came from interest on savings.

William H. Donner Foundation

500 5th Ave., Suite 1230
New York, NY 10010   **Phone:** (212) 719-9290
USA   **Fax:**   (212) 302-8734

Contact Person: James J. Capua, President.
Officers or Principals: James J. Capua, President ($135,751); William T. Alpert, Senior Program Officer ($80,372); Jacalyn Schwartz, Financial Manager ($40,150); Curtin Winsor, Jr., Secretary; William D. Roosevelt, Treasurer. (Compensation is from FY ending 10/92.)
Mission or Interest: Grant-making philanthropy that awards grants for education, and "Human Capitol Development." Includes grants for conservative organizations.
Accomplishments: In the fiscal year ending October 1995 the Foundation awarded $2,366,765 in grants. Recipients included; two grants totaling $101,875 for the Institute for Foreign Policy Analysis, $75,000 for the Institute for American Values, $66,667 for the Statistical Assessment Service, $65,000 for the Federalist Society, $50,000 each for the Pacific Research Institute for Public Policy, and Foundation for Teaching Economics, $43,000 for the George C. Marshall Institute, $42,500 from the Foreign Policy Research Institute, $42,201 for the Reason Foundation, $37,500 each for the American Council on Science and Health, Manhattan Institute, Media Research Center, and Independence Institute, $35,000 each for the National Alumni Forum, and Institute of Economic Affairs (U.K.), $31,250 for the National Taxpayers Union Foundation, and $25,000 each for the Center for Individual Rights, Center for Security Policy, Claremont Institute, Equal Opportunity Foundation, and Hudson Institute.
Net Assets: FY ending 10/95 $77,635,836 6%(3)
Tax Status: 501(c)(3)
Board of Directors or Trustees: James Balog, Peter Cannell, Timothy Donner, John Hagenbuch, Louise Oliver, Deborah Donner Roy, Monica Winsor Washburn, Wilcomb Washburn.
Other Information: Established in 1961 by the estate of William H. Donner. William Donner (1864-1953) was a businessman who was successful in grain milling, real estate, tin plate manufacturing, and then steel production in partnership with the Mellon brothers. Donner married Nora Mellon.

Winchester Foundation

100 S. Meridian St.
Winchester, IN 47394   **Phone:** (317) 584-3501
USA

Contact Person: Chris Talley, Chairman.
Officers or Principals: Chris Talley, Chairman ($0); Enid Goodrich, Vice Chair ($0); Terri E. Matchett, Secretary ($0); Linda Pugh, Assistant Secretary.
Mission or Interest: Grant-making foundation that includes conservative and free-market organizations in its awards. Also awards college scholarships to graduates of Winchester Community High School.
Accomplishments: In 1994 the Foundation awarded $90,409 in grants. Most of this, $66,309, went to scholarships. Conservative recipients were; $2,500 for Hillsdale College, $1,500 for the Philadelphia Society, and $1,000 each for the Reason Foundation and the Intercollegiate Studies Institute.
Total Revenue: 1994 $139,854 **Total Expenses:** $110,764 **Net Assets:** $3,207,375 3%(2)

Tax Status: 501(c)(3)
Board of Directors or Trustees: Don Welch, Ruth Connally, Helen Garlotte.
Other Information: The Foundation received $85,402, or 61% of revenue, from dividends and interest from securities. $50,053, or 36%, from interest on savings and temporary cash investments. $4,399, or 3%, from contributions and grants from individuals and businesses. The Foundation held $1,304,252, or 41% of assets, in corporate stock. $938,549, or 29%, in cash and temporary savings. $928,700, or 29%, in government securities.

Wisconsin Policy Research Institute (WPRI)

11516 N. Port Washington Rd., Suite 103
Mequon, WI 53092   **Phone:** (414) 241-0514
USA   **Fax:**   (414) 241-0774

Contact Person: James Miller, President.
Officers or Principals: James Miller, President ($127,950); Robert Buchanan, Chairman ($0); Richard Gallagher, Secretary/Treasurer ($0).
Mission or Interest: To conduct research on public policy in the state of Wisconsin with an emphasis on free markets and private enterprise. "The focus of the Institute's activities will direct attention and resources to study the following issues: education, welfare and social services, criminal justice, taxes and spending, and economic development."
Accomplishments: Have received press coverage in *USA Today, New York Times, Wall Street Journal, Washington Post, Chicago Tribune* and numerous local papers throughout Wisconsin. In the fiscal year ending March 1995 the Institute spent $539,345 on its programs.
Total Revenue: FY ending 3/95 $663,290 20%(2) **Total Expenses:** $567,733 95%/5%/0% **Net Assets:** $1,495,800
Tax Status: 501(c)(3)   **Citations:** 87:70
Board of Directors or Trustees: Roger Fitzsimonds, Michael Grebe, Roger Hauck, Sheldon Lubar, Brenton Rupple, Paul Schierl, Edward Zore.
Periodicals: *Wisconsin Interest* (biannual journal).
Internships: Yes.
Other Information: Established in 1987 with a grant from the Lynde and Harry Bradley Foundation. The Institute received $572,159, or 86% of revenue, from contributions and grants awarded by foundations, businesses, and individuals. (These grants included $460,000 from the Lynde and Harry Bradley Foundation, $17,500 from the John M. Olin Foundation, and $1,000 from the Roe Foundation.) $91,131, or 14%, from interest on savings and temporary cash investments.

Women's Freedom Network (WFN)

4410 Massachusetts Ave., N.W., Suite 179
Washington, DC 20016
USA   **Fax:**   (202) 885-2907

Contact Person: Rita J. Simon, Editor.
Mission or Interest: Conservative women's organization.
Products or Services: From Data to Public Policy: Affirmative Action, Sexual Harassment, Domestic Violence and Social Welfare, book.
Tax Status: 501(c)(3)
Other Information: In 1995 the Network received $20,000 from the John M. Olin Foundation.

World

P.O. Box 2330
Asheville, NC 28802   **Phone:** (704) 253-8063
USA   **Fax:**   (704) 253-1556

Contact Person: Harriet McKenna, Office Manager.
Officers or Principals: Joel Belz, Editor/Publisher; Nickolas S. Eicher, Managing Editor; Marvin Olasky, Editor-At-Large; Courtney Miller, Director of Operations; Fred Barnes, Larry Burkett, Doug LeBlanc, Charles Colson, Contributing Editors; John Prentis, Chairman; John White, Vice Chairman; Nelson Somerville, Secretary; Lanny Moore, Treasurer.
Mission or Interest: "To help Christians apply the Bible to their understanding of and response to everyday current events. To achieve this by reporting the news on a weekly basis in an interesting, accurate, and arresting fashion."
Accomplishments: Syndicated columnist Cal Thomas says, "*World* has material that is of interest to Christians and non-Christians alike and does the best job I've seen of stimulating thought, encouraging action, and reporting news from a perspective that is available virtually nowhere else."
Tax Status: For profit.
Board of Directors or Trustees: Mariam Bell, Henry Boss, Robert Case, Duane Jacobs, William Joseph, Bronwyn Leonard, Bentley Rayburn, David Strassner, Joseph Tolbert, W. Jack Williamson.
Periodicals: *World* (weekly news magazine).
Other Information: They have a toll free number for subscriptions, (800) 951-6397.

World & I

34000 New York Ave., N.E.
Washington, DC 20002
USA

Phone: (202) 635-4000
Fax: (202) 526-5724   **Internet:** http://www.worldandi.com

Contact Person: Morton A. Kaplan, Editor/Publisher.
Officers or Principals: Morton A. Kaplan, Editor/Publisher; Michael Marshall, Executive Editor; Eric P. Olsen, Associate Executive Editor; Lee Edwards, Senior Editor; Cynthia Grenier, Senior Contributing Editor.
Mission or Interest: Journal of news, politics, history, and culture.
Accomplishments: The Dictionary of Literary Biography calls it, "One of the most extraordinary magazines in America."
Tax Status: For profit.
Periodicals: *World & I* (monthly magazine).
Other Information: Published by the News World Communications, which also publishes *The Washington Times*.

World Climate Review

Department of Environmental Sciences
Clark Hall, University of Virginia
Charlottesville, VA 22903
USA

Contact Person: Patrick J. Michaels, Ph.D., Chief Editor.
Officers or Principals: Patrick J. Michaels, Ph.D., Chief Editor; Philip J. Stenger, Research Coordinator; Paul C. Knappenberger, Technical Supervisor; Robert J. Wood, Research Assistant.
Mission or Interest: *World Climate Review* is a quarterly devoted to global climate change and the issues that surround it.
Accomplishments: Patrick J. Michaels is the author of Sound and Fury: The Science and Politics of Global Warming (Cato Publishing, 1992). *World Climate Review* publishes various articles, understandable to the layman, on the latest research regarding global warming. Included in each issue is the latest satellite data on world temperatures. The data consistently shows that global temperatures fall below what is predicted by the computer models that are the basis for dangerous greenhouse-effect scenarios.
Tax Status: 501(c)(3)
Periodicals: *World Climate Review* (quarterly).
Other Information: *World Climate Review* is affiliated with and incorporated under the University of Virginia. Dr. Michaels is an Associate Professor of Environmental Sciences at the University of Virginia. He also serves as Virginia State Climatologist and is a senior fellow at the Cato Institute. He is a former President of the American Association of State Climatologists and was Program Chair for the Committee on Applied Meteorology of the American Meteorological Society.

Wyoming Heritage Society

139 W. 2nd St., Suite 3E
Casper, WY 82601
USA

Phone: (307) 577-8000
Fax: (307) 577-8003

Contact Person: William C. Schilling, Executive Director.
Officers or Principals: William C. Schilling, Executive Director ($18,537); Tom Thorson, President ($0); Stan Bader, Vice President ($0); Thomas J. Lien, Secretary/Treasurer.
Mission or Interest: Coalition representing a broad spectrum of business interests, promoting Wyoming's quality of life and the free enterprise system. Pays particular attention to the areas of Wyoming's economy driven by natural resources and their extraction. The Society advocates the 'wise-use' of natural resources.
Accomplishments: Coordinates twelve public-interest groups in Wyoming who support the 'multiple use' of resources. In the fiscal year ending September 1995 the Society spent $42,164 on its programs.
Total Revenue: FY ending 9/95 $92,653 1%(2) **Total Expenses:** $55,245 76%/24%/0% **Net Assets:** $143,773
Products or Services: Public forums, partnership with local Chambers of Commerce, public opinion surveys, policy briefs and reports, speakers bureau, twice-weekly radio show, more. Lobbying: the Society spent $6,209 on lobbying.
Tax Status: 501(c)(6) **Annual Report:** No. **Employees:** 4
Board of Directors or Trustees: Eli Bebout (Nucor Drilling), Cynthia Lummis, Dave Raynolds (Table Mountain Ranch), H.A. True (Eighty-Eight Oil Co.), Roger Harris (Tg Soda Ash), Tom Lockhart (Pacific Power & Light).
Periodicals: *Heritage Report, Heritage Action Alert*
Internships: No.
Other Information: Affiliated with the 501(c)(3) Wyoming Heritage Foundation at the same address. The Society received $87,987, or 95% of revenue, from contributions and grants from businesses and individuals. $4,666, or 5%, from interest on savings and temporary cash investments.

Yankee Institute for Public Policy

117 New London Turnpike
Glastonbury, CT 06033
USA

Phone: (860) 633-8188
Fax: (860) 657-9444

Contact Person: Laurence D. Cohen, Executive Director.

Officers or Principals: Laurence D. Cohen, Executive Director ($3,788); William Lee Hanley, Jr., President/Chairman ($0); William H. Campbell, Treasurer ($0); John M. Horak, Secretary.
Mission or Interest: "Education reform, individual liberty, taxation and regulation reform in Connecticut."
Accomplishments: Despite its relatively small size, the Yankee Institute has been called "Connecticut's premier conservative think tank," by the *Hartford Advocate*, and Republican Governor John Rowland said "the ideas that the Yankee Institute promotes have helped to shift public opinion and drive the public debate in Hartford and across the state." The Institute has been cited in the *Boston Globe, Chicago Tribune, Connecticut Post, Dallas Morning News, Hartford Courant, New York Times, Hartford Advocate, Associated Press, U.S. News and World Report, Criminal Justice Digest*, and many other local papers. Numerous radio and television appearances. In 1995 the Institute spent $14,798 on its programs.
Total Revenue: 1995 $13,523 **Total Expenses:** $14,798 **Net Assets:** $1,474
Products or Services: Public affairs television programming broadcast on cable systems statewide. Seminars and conferences. Research papers.
Tax Status: 501(c)(3) **Annual Report:** Yes. **Employees:** 1
Board of Directors or Trustees: Gordon Allen, Harvey Backmender, Joseph Bentivegna, Joseph Broder, Gwendolyn Bronson, Benton Brown, Larry Brown, Jean Castagno, Stephen Courtney, John Cunnane, Dr. Gerald Gunderson, Cheryl Hillen, Patrick Kennedy, Charles Klein, Michael Lattman. Academic Advisory Board includes: Prof. William Alpert (Univ. of Connecticut), Prof. Dominick Armentano (Univ. of Hartford), Prof. Peter Berman (Univ. of New Haven), Prof. Ward Curran (Trinity College), Gerald Gunderson (Trinity College), Prof. Charles Logan (Univ. of Connecticut), Prof. Arthur Wright (Univ. of Connecticut).
Periodicals: *Policy Perspectives* (quarterly journal).
Internships: Yes, unpaid for graduate or undergraduate students.
Other Information: Member of the State Policy Network. The Institute received $7,005, or 52% of revenue, from contributions and grants awarded by foundations, businesses, and individuals. (These grants included $2,500 from the Roe Foundation.) Contributions and grants have been declining for the Institute, down an average of 36% per year for the last five years. $6,518, or 48%, from special fund-raising events.

Yellow Ribbon Coalition

P.O. Box 240
Springfield, OR 97477   **Phone:** (503) 747-5874
USA   **Fax:**   (503) 747-0612

Contact Person: Merrilee Peay, Executive Director.
Officers or Principals: Jim Larson, President; Bonnie Morgan, Wilbur Heath, Steve Ward, Vice Presidents; Suzanne Penegor, Secretary; Debbie Howell, Treasurer.
Mission or Interest: "To heighten community awareness and knowledge about the importance of wise multiple use of nature's renewable resources and responsible environmentalism by balancing resource production with resource protection."
Accomplishments: Provided a hands-on forestry-education program for over 10,000 students. Forty-foot forest-products display trailer has made two national tours, and over a hundred local visits.
Products or Services: Rallies, lectures, speakers, letter-writing campaigns and other media events.
Tax Status: 501(c)(6) **Annual Report:** No. **Employees:** 1 full-time, 2 part-time.
Board of Directors or Trustees: 31 board members, many from the timber industry.
Periodicals: *Yellow Ribbon Coalition Newsletter* (monthly).
Internships: No.
Other Information: The Yellow Ribbon Coalition is a member of the Oregon Lands Coalition and the Alliance for America.

Young Americans for Freedom (YAF)

1208 N. DuPont St.
Wilmington, DE 19806   **Phone:** (302) 427-3827
USA

Contact Person: Jon C. Pastore, National Chairman.
Mission or Interest: Organization of college-age conservative activists.
Accomplishments: "The nation's oldest, largest and most active conservative youth organization." Claims over 50,000 active members. Operates on numerous college campuses, often known for their confrontational and combative style.
Tax Status: Nonprofit.
Periodicals: *New Guard* (quarterly).
Other Information: Established in 1960 by members of the Young Republicans who had campaigned for Richard Nixon. Co-founders included William F. Buckley, Jr. Throughout the 1990's, YAF's national organization has been in constant flux, and at times non-existent. Throughout this, however, college chapters have remained active.

Young Americans for Social Security Reform (YASSR)

1801 Crystal Dr., Suite 1117
Arlington, VA 22202   **Phone:** (703) 685-7547
USA

Contact Person: Marc Ross, Founder.

Mission or Interest: "Promotes a complete overhaul of the current program to ensure the viability of a retirement system that allows for a better rate of return for American workers without an increase in taxation."
Tax Status: Nonprofit.
Periodicals: *3rd Rail* (biweekly newsletter).
Other Information: Established in 1997, YASSR made its public debut at the March 1997 Conservative Political Action Conference (CPAC).

Young America's Foundation

110 Elden St.
Herndon, VA 22070   **Phone:** (703) 318-9608   **E-Mail:** YngAmerica@aol.com.
USA   **Fax:** (703) 318-9122   **Internet:** http://www.yaf.org

Contact Person: Ron Robinson, President.
Officers or Principals: Ron Robinson, President ($183,625); James Taylor, Executive Director ($94,833); Darla Anzalone ($70,432); Ronald Pearson, Vice President; Frank Donnatelli, Secretary/Treasurer; Kristen Kingsley, Conference Director; Matthew Schenk, Publications.
Mission or Interest: "National outreach campaign to bring conservative ideas to America's schools."
Accomplishments: "Nation's largest campus outreach program." Over the last five years the Foundation has averaged 12% annual revenue growth. Foundation Program Officer Ron Rosenberg was the successful plaintiff in the Supreme Court's ruling on Rosenberg v. Rector and the Visitors of the University of Virginia. The ruling held that the school had discriminated against a Christian student newspaper founded by Rosenberg by denying it equal access to funds for student activities. In 1995 the Foundation spent $2,345,149 on its programs. This included the distribution of over 100,000 free posters, books, monographs, and videos to students. The largest expenditure, $1,815,238, went to general research and education programs. $266,291 was spent on four campus lecture series; the Henry Salvatori Distinguished Lecture Series, Grover Hermann Freedom Lecture Series, William Flowers Lecture Series, and the William J. Casey Lecture Series. Recent lectures featured; Justice Clarence Thomas, Speaker Newt Gingrich, Walter E. Williams, William F. Buckley, Jr., Vice President Dan Quayle, Michael Medved, Sen. Trent Lott, Jack Kemp, M. Stanton Evans, Armstrong Williams, Oliver North, P.J. O'Rourke, and MTV's Kennedy. $85,993 was spent on their publications. $18,500 was spent on scholarships "for needy students involved in campus issues."
Total Revenue: 1995 $3,657,661 42%(1) **Total Expenses:** $3,339,597 70%/7%/23% **Net Assets:** $9,896,924
Products or Services: Annual "National Conservative Student Conference," and regional conferences. The Myth of the Robber Barons by Burton W. Folsom, Jr., Columbus on Trial by Robert Royal, and other books. "Comedy and Tragedy," a bound collection of college course descriptions from Ivy League schools that are "bizarre" in their advocacy of diversity and multi-culturalism. Conservative Guide to Campus Activism handbook.
Tax Status: 501(c)(3) **Annual Report:** Yes. **Employees:** 14 **Citations:** 25:140
Board of Directors or Trustees: Frank Donatelli (White House Director of Political Affairs, 1987-89), James Lacy, T. Kenneth Cribb (Intercollegiate Studies Inst.), Wayne Thorburn (former Exec. Dir., Young Americans for Freedom).
Periodicals: *Campus Leader* (monthly newspaper mailed to campus activists for distribution), *Libertas* (bimonthly newsletter), *Continuity* (biannual scholarly history journal).
Internships: Yes. Paid positions and academic tuition available. Sarah T. Hermann Scholarships for qualified interns.
Other Information: Established in 1969. The Foundation received $1,852,496, or 51% of revenue, from contributions and grants awarded by foundations, businesses, and individuals. (These grants included $15,000 from the Sunmark Foundation. In 1994, $50,000 from the F.M. Kirby Foundation, $15,000 from the J.M. Foundation, $10,000 from the Grover Hermann Foundation, $5,000 from the Gilder Foundation.) $799,069, or 22%, from capital gains on the sale of securities. $766,064, or 21%, from dividends and interest from securities. $93,737, or 3%, from lecture series admission fees. $86,951, or 2%, from summer-school tuition. $32,051, or 1%, from mailing list rentals. The remaining revenue came from the sale of publications, interest on savings and temporary cash revenues, and other miscellaneous sources.

Young Republican National Federation (YRNF)

440 1st St., N.W.
Washington, DC 20001   **Phone:** (202) 662-1340
USA

Contact Person: Kelly Heinrich, Executive Director.
Officers or Principals: Larry Kidwell, Chairman.
Mission or Interest: "Works to promote Republican Party principles and the Republican Party platform in young Americans, ages 18 to 40."
Accomplishments: "Provide a strong volunteer base to assist Republican candidates."
Tax Status: Not exempt.

Zenger News Service (ZNS)

P.O. Box 98950
Seattle, WA 98198   **Phone:** (206) 874-2704   **E-Mail:** zns@interserv.com
USA   **Fax:** (206) 815-0265   **Internet:** http://www.zns.com

Contact Person: James E. Ewart, President.

Mission or Interest: "ZNS syndicates articles, feature stories, and opinion pieces to newspapers and other print media. Syndicated items reflect traditional American values and focus on important topics not covered adequately by the dominant media. ZNS also produces in-depth reports on special topics for private researchers, attorneys, broadcasters and the public."

Accomplishments: "ZNS syndication packets regularly reach editors of newspapers whose aggregate circulation is about 12 million."

Tax Status: For profit.

Periodicals: *Principia* (newsletter).

Internships: No.

Other Information: Established in 1982. James Ewart previously operated the now-defunct National Victory Alliance. Named in honor of John Peter Zenger (1697-1746), a colonial-American publisher, arrested by the British for his out-spoken opinions against the Crown. His trial was a key point in establishing American freedom of the press.

Zychik Chronicles

E-Mail: jzychik@via.net

Internet: http://www.via.net/~jzychik

Contact Person: Joe Zychik.

Mission or Interest: Libertarian commentaries on daily news stories.

STATUS UNKNOWN

The organizations listed in this section were identified as being active in the conservative or free-market movement. However, they did not respond to our questionnaires nor did we receive any notification from the Postal Service that their address had changed. The organizations may be defunct or simply not responsive to the public's interest. Readers may pursue them, but <u>The Right Guide</u> can not verify any of these groups' aims, responses, or operations. If users of <u>The Right Guide</u> can provide any information about these groups, we would be happy to include it in future editions. We have listed their address and, when available, their phone number and a contact person.

1789 Committee
P.O. Box 12421
El Cajon, CA 92020
Bill Reichenbach

A.L.P.H.A.
439 Marsh St.
San Luis Obispo, CA 93401
(805) 541-3367

Activist
P.O. Box 501
Phoenix, AZ 85001

Adroit Press
P.O. Box 680365
Franklin, TN 37068

Advance to Liberty
933 Colorado Ave.
Palo Alto, CA 94303

Afghanistan Forum
19 Fanning Ave.
East Hampton, NY 11937

African Research Center for Public Policy and Market Process
21 Charles Lane
Storrs, CT 06268
(203) 486-3027, fax (203) 429-1048

Alabama Conservative Union
P.O. Box 7123
Montgomery, AL 36107

Alabama Family Advocates
P.O. Box 1230
Birmingham, AL 36102
Tom Parker

Alabama Pro-Life Coalition
3501 Pine Ridge Rd.
Birmingham, AL 35213
Mrs. Claire Downey

Alaska Support Industry Alliance (ASIA)
4220 B St., Suite 200
Anchorage, AK 99503
Lowell Humphrey, President

Alaskans for Legislative Reform
P.O. Box 672289
Chugiak, AK 99567-2289

Albanian Catholic Information Center
1032 Irving St., Suite 518
San Francisco, CA 94122

Alexander Solzhenitsyn Society
P.O. Box 4654
Boulder, CO 80306

Alliance for a Responsible CFC Policy
2111 Wilson Blvd., Suite 850
Arlington, VA 22201
James Wolf, Chairman

Alliance for Affordable Health Care
1725 K St., N.W., Suite 310
Washington, DC 20006
Jere W. Glover, Director

Alliance for Border Enforcement
3510 Addison St.
San Diego, CA 92106
Pete Nunez, Director
(619) 224-8837

Alliance of California Taxpayers
P.O. Box 330
Aptos, CA 95001-0330
Jane Armstrong, Director
(408) 688-8986

Alliance to Save America's Future
5 Thomas Circle, N.W.
Washington, DC 20005
Thad Heath, President
(202) 667-6728

Alpha 66
P.O. Box 420067
Miami, FL 33142

Alpha Publications
P.O. Box 92
Sharon Center, OH 44274

Alternative, The
P.O. Box 720
Santa Ynez, CA 93460
Helen Pappas, Director
(805) 688-8688

America 21
100 12th Ave., S.
Nashville, TN 37203

America Catholic Monthly
106 W. 56th St.
New York, NY 10019
(212) 581-4640

America First
P.O. Box 1887
Washington, DC 20013

America First Committee
R.R. 4, Box 369
Spokane, WA 99204

America Today
9400 Fairview Ave.
Manassas, VA 22110

America's Hope Monthly
PO Box 72
Hopkins, MN 55343

American - African Affairs Association
1001 Connecticut Ave., N.W., Suite 1135
Washington, DC 20036
Max Gallimore, Chairman
(202) 223-5110

American Answer
P.O. Box 631747
Nacogdoces, TX 75963

American Anti-Persecution League (AAPL)
504 South Beach Blvd., Suite 426
Anaheim, CA 92804
Jeff White, Director
(800) 501-2275

American Association of Crimean Tartars
4509 New Utrecht Ave.
Brooklyn, NY 11219

American Association of Pro Life Obstetricians and
Gynecologists
850 Elm Grove Rd.
Elmgrove, WI 53122
Robert Herzog, Director

American Business Conference
1730 K St., Suite 1200
Washington, DC 20006
Barry K. Rogstad

American Citizens & Lawman Association
P.O. Box 8712
Phoenix, AZ 85066

American Citizens Alliance
5238 W. Dakin St.
Chicago, IL 60641

American Citizens Together
P.O. Box 3788
Alhambra, CA 91803
Rod Irvine, President
(818) 666-6321

American Civil Responsibilities Union (ACRU)
P.O. Box 17099
Anaheim, CA 92817
Howard Garber, Director
(714) 998-6007

American Commerce for Traditional Values
139 C St., S.E.
Washington, DC 20003
(202) 547-8570

American Constitution Committee
7777 Leesburg Pike, Suite 304
Falls Church, VA 22043
Michael Smith, President
(703) 790-5580

American Council of Christian Churches
P.O. Box 816
Valley Forge, PA 19482

American Cultural Traditions
P.O. Box 540204
Grand Prairie, TX 75054

American Defenders
1013 West Greenfield Ave.
Milwaukee, WI 53204
David Bethke

American Education Forum
1820 E. Colfax Ave.
South Bend, IN 46617

American Fair Trade Council
1001 Bridgeway, Suite 301
Sausalito, CA 94965
Duncan Dwelle

American Family Association of Alabama
2180 Woodley Rd.
Montgomery, AL 36111

American Family Defense Coalition
P.O. Box 2611
Santa Maria, CA 93456
(805) 937-2097

American Forum
P.O. Box 1854
Andalusia, AL 36420
(800) 240-4446

American Foundation for Resistance International
101 East 52nd St., 12th Floor
New York, NY 10022
Albert Jolis, Director
(212) 759-3434, fax (212) 207-8173

American Freedom Movement
P.O. Box 309
Irwin, PA 15642

American Friends of the Anti-Bolshevik Bloc of Nations
136 Second Ave.
New York, NY 10003

American Independent Party
8158 Palm St.
Lemon Grove, CA 92045
Eileen M. Shearer

American Independent Party
274 Magnolia St.
Orange, CA 92666
Kirk Robinson, Chairman

American Information Newsletter
3500 Mountain View Dr.
Boise, ID 83704
(208) 343-3790

American Institute of Economics
P.O. Box 136
New Wilmington, PA 16142

American Institute of Fellows in Free Enterprise
P.O. Box 217
Houston, DE 19954
Cal Hollis, Director

American Latvian Association
P.O. Box 432
Rockville, MD 20805

American Media
P.O. Box 4646
Westlake Village, CA 91359

American Militia Organization
P.O. Box 194
St. John, WA 99171

American News Analyst
215 E 3rd St.
Des Moines, IA 50309

American Party
Route 2, Box 1072
Roseburg, OR 97470
Frank Varnum, Director

American Patriot
P.O. Box A
Scottsdale, AZ 85252

American Pistol and Rifle Association
Rt. 2, Box 164
Benton, TN 37307
John Grady, M.D., President
(615) 338-2328

American Policy Institute
P.O. Box 11839
Alexandria, VA 22312
Jerry Woodruff, President

American Redneck
c/o AR Publications
312 W. 6th St.
Corona, CA 91720

American Rights Coalition
3104 Paradise Acres
Hoover, AL 35244
Becky Bower, Director

American Sentry Report
P.O. Box 653
Ashland, OH 44805

American Society of Educated Citizens
15322 Spring St.
Union Grove, WI 53182

American Sovereignty Task Force
P.O. Box 65631
Washington, DC 20035

American Students for Populism
2415 Beekay Ct.
Vienna, VA 22180

American Tax Reduction Movement
621 S. Westmoreland Ave., Suite 202
Los Angeles, CA 90005
Joel Fox, Director

American Tax Reduction Movement
6302 30th St., N.W.
Washington, DC 20015

American Tract Society
P.O. Box 402008
Garland, TX 75040

American Yorktown Eagle
P.O. Box 20446
Salt Lake City, UT 84120

Americanism Educational League
P.O. Box 5986
Buena Park, CA 90622
Edward S. Rankin, Director

Americans Against Socialized Medicine
P.O. Box 1485
Shawnee, OK 74801

Americans Back in Charge!
1873 South Bellaire St., 17th floor
Denver, CO 80222
(303) 758-7343

Americans for a Better America
RR #3, Box 66
Grantham, NH 03753

Americans for a Second Bill of Rights
P.O. Box 550
Sour Lake, TX 77659

Americans for Action
9205 S.E. Clackamas, Suite 1776
Clackamas, OR 97015

Americans for America
P.O. Box 59833
Potomac, MD 20854

Americans for an Informed Public
P.O. Box 1529
Sugar Land, TX 77487
Mike Richards, Director

Americans for Constitutional Government
P.O. Box 7012
Watchung, NJ 07060

Americans for Constitutional Government
P.O. Box 1544
Billings, MT 59103

Americans for Constitutional Rights
P.O. Box 331
Howland, ME 04448

Americans for Freedom Always
P.O. Box 9561
Arlington, VA 22219-9561
John Holland, President
(703) 351-9326

Americans for Human Rights in Ukraine
43 Midland Pl.
Newark, NJ 07106
Bozhena Olshaniwsky, Director

Americans for Immigration Control
717 2nd St., N.E., Suite 307
Washington, DC 20002
Palmer Stacy, Director

Americans for Legal Reform
1319 F St., N.W., Suite 300
Washington, DC 20004

Americans for Legal Reform
10 E St., S.E.
Washington, DC 20003

Americans for Medical Freedom
P.O. Box 4228-B
Westlake Village, CA 91359

Americans for Responsible Television
P.O. Box 627
Bloomfield Hills, MI 48303
Terry Rakolta, President
(313) 646-4248

Americans to Limit Congressional Terms
900 2nd St., N.E.
Washington DC 20002

Americans Under God
P.O. Box 75275
Los Angeles, CA 90075

Americans United
915 Stone Rd.
Laurel Springs, NJ 08021

Americans United
P.O. Box 1122
Malibu, CA 90265

Americans United for God & Country
P.O. Box 183
Merion Station, PA 19066
Thomas A. Bierling, Director

Americas Society
608 Park Ave.
New York, NY 10021

Analysis and Outlook
P.O. Box 1167
Pt. Townmail, WA 98368

Anger Control
P.O. Box 1000
Selma, OR 97538

Anglo-European Fellowship
P.O. Box 3380
Kailua Kona, HI 96740

Angry Environmentalist
P.O. Box 146
Silver Bay, MN 55614

Anti-Bolshevik League of Nations
136 2nd Ave.
New York, NY 10003

Anti-Communist Conference of Polish Freedom Fighters
18 Boardman St.
Salem, MA 01970

Anti-Communist International
P.O. Box 1095, Grand Central Station
New York, NY 10163
Dr. John Speller

Anti-Lawyer Party
6308 24th Ave.
Kenosha, WI 53140

Anumeralist
P.O. Box 2084
Norristown, PA 19404

Arizonans for Immigration Control
P.O. Box 32552
Tucson, AZ 85751

Armed Citizens News
P.O. Box 78336
Seattle, WA 98178

Armenian National Committee
419A W. Colorado, Suite 3
Glendale, CA 91204
Garen Yeghparian, Director

Armenian Revolutionary Federation
80 Bigelow Ave.
Watertown, MA 02172
John Megerdichian, Director

Asian-Americans for Border Control
P.O. Box 921634
Sylmar, CA 91312
Gil Wong, Director
(619) 899-7409

Asset Guardian
P.O. Box 513
Franklin, NJ 07416

Association for California Tort Reform
1121 L St., Suite 100
Sacramento, CA 95814
Fred Heistand, Director
(916) 448-5100

Association for the Liberation of the Ukraine
P.O. Box 106
New York, NY 10003

Association of America to Save Africa
P.O. Box 525
Marshall, VA 22115

Association of Conservative Hispanic Americans
756 E. 40th St.
Hialeah, FL 33013

Association of Former Intelligence Officers
6723 Whittier Ave., Suite 303A
McLean, VA 22101
David Atlee Phillips, Director

Association of Independent Methodists
P.O. Box 4274
Jackson, MS 39216

Association of New Jersey Rifle and Pistol Clubs
P.O. Box 66
Highland Lakes, NJ 07422
James M. Furno, Editor
(201) 661-0634

Association of Pragmatic Individuals
P.O. Box 392
Forest Grove, PA 18922

Association of Private Enterprise Education
P.O. Box 8012
Waco, TX 76798
Calvin A. Kent, Director

Atlas Shrugged Network
P.O. Box 8606
Portland, OR 97207
Samantha Johnston
(503) 241-8467, e-mail: sxj@aol.com

Austrian Economics Program
269 Mercer St., 7th Fl.
New York, NY 10003

B.R.A.V.O.
23917 Craftsmen Rd.
Calabasas, CA 90029

Backwoods Home Magazine
1257 Siskiyou Blvd., Suite 312-I
Ashland, OR 97520
(503) 488-2053

Baltic American Freedom League
P.O. Box 29657
Los Angeles, CA 90029

Baltic Womens Council
162 Highcrest Dr.
West Milford, NJ 07480

Baltic World Conference
243 E. 34th St.
New York, NY 10016

Baltic World Council
19102 Stedwick Dr.
Gaithersburg, MD 20879
Maido Kari, Director

Bankers Research Institute
P.O. Box 1105
Staunton, VA 24401

Baptist Joint Committee
200 Maryland Ave., N.E.
Washington DC 20002

Barristers Inn
P.O. Box 9411
Boise, ID 83707

Battle Axe News
Route 2, Box 404
Dandridge, TN 37725

Best Friends
5505 Connecticut Ave., N.W., Suite 264
Washington, DC 20015
Elayne Bennett, Executive Director

Better America
P.O. Box 424
Coolidge, AZ 85228

Between the Lines
65 Conduit St.
Annapolis, MD 21401

Bible-Science Association
P.O. Box 32457
Minneapolis, MN 55432-0457
(612) 755-8606

Biblical Evangelist
P.O. Box 940
Ingleside, TX 78362

Billy Falling Publishing
27217 Oakmont Rd.
Valley Center, CA 92082

Birthright California
277 N. Rancho Santa Fe Rd., Suite S
San Marcos, CA 92069
Grace Denny, Director
(619) 744-1313

Black Americans for Family Values
2554 Lincoln Blvd., Suite 264
Venice, CA 90291
Ezola Foster, Founder

Black Americans for Life
P.O. Box 3722
Capitol Heights, MD 20743
Paulette Roseboro, Director
(301) 249-7230

Blue Ribbon Coalition (BRC)
P.O. Box 5449
Pocatello, ID 83202
Joani DuFourd, President

Blue-Book Publishers
64 Prospect St.
White Plains, NY 10606

Blumenfeld Education Letter
P.O. Box 45161
Boise, ID 83711
Samuel L. Blumenfeld, Publisher

Bohica Concepts
P.O. Box 546
Randle, WA 98371

Books For All Times
P.O. Box 2
Alexandria, VA 22313

Boston Tea Party
1051 N Grand
Mesa, AZ 85201

Breaking Free Ministries
P.O. Box 225 DTS
Boone, NC 28607

Brian Bex Report
100 Country Club Rd.
Hagerstown, IN 47346

Bubba's Journal
9214 Ridgefield Circle
Frederick, MD 21701

Bulgarian National Committee
109 Amherst St.
Highland Park, NY 08904

Bureaucracy Unlimited
P.O. Box 1705
Santa Rosa, CA 95402

By The People
3707 E. La Palma Ave.
Anaheim, CA 92806

Byelorussian Congress Committee
85-26 125th St.
Queens, NY 11415

Byelorussian Liberation Front
6526 Anita Dr.
Cleveland, OH 44130

Byelorussian-American Association
P.O. Box 178
Jamaica, NY 11431

Byelorussian-American Youth Association
P.O Box 1123
New Brunwick, NJ 08903

C and S Research
P.O. Box 43191
Louisville, KY 40243

C.R.E.D.O.
243 Ferndale Way
Redwood City, CA 94062

C.U.S.A.
P.O. Box 1120
Yucca Valley, CA 92284

California Coalition for Immigration Reform
5942 Edinger, Suite 113-117
Huntington Beach, CA 92649
Barbara Coe, Chairman
(714) 921-7142

California Committee for the Preservation of Individual Rights
445 Mariner Point Way
Sacramento, CA 95831
(916) 424-8120

California Family Woman
18640 Perego Way
Saratoga, CA 95070

California Home Education Clearinghouse
8241 E. Hidden Lakes Dr.
Roseville, CA 95678
(916) 791-4467

California Organization for Public Safety
1451 S. Rimpau Ave., Suite 214
Corona, CA 91719
Mike McNolty, Director
(909) 279-9953

California Republican Assembly
26781 Winter Court
Tehachapi, CA 93581
Greg Hardcastle, Chairman
(916) 349-7834

California Review
4846 Rancho Grande
Del Mar, CA 92014

California Shooting Camps
14330 Woodland Dr.
Victorville, CA 92392
Marsha Moody, Director
(619) 243-4620

California Voters Alliance
22647 Ventura Blvd., Suite 402
Woodland Hills, CA 91367
Jerry Allen, Director
(818) 884-1857

Californians for America
1105 E. Commonwealth Ave., Suite A
Fullerton, CA 92631
William Dannemeyer, President
(714) 284-5990

Californians for Fair Rent Laws
621 S. Westmoreland Ave.
Los Angeles, CA 90005

Californians for Freedom to Work
P.O. Box 996
Sacramento, CA 95812
(916) 448-7872

Californians for Immigration Control
P.O. Box 1574
Anderson, CA 96007
Dewey Carter, Director
(916) 365-6822

Californians for Population Stabilization
926 J St., Suite 915
Sacramento, CA 95814
Julee Malinowski, Director
(916) 446-1033

Californians for Responsible Immigration
P.O. Box 3133
Orange, CA 92665
Doug Thompson, Director
(714) 637-3019

Campaign for America
113 N. Foushee St.
Richmond, VA 23220

Canal Watchers Association
P.O. Box 246
Milton, NC 27305

Cape of Good Hope Foundation
Foundation Center 228-77
Pasadena, CA 91125
Dr. Edwin S. Munger, Director
(818) 356-3634

Capitol Hill Publishing
325 Pennsylvania Ave., S.E.
Washington, DC 20003

Capitol Report
P.O. Box 2700
Washington, DC 20013

Censor
P.O. Box 295
San Fernando, CA 91341

Center for Bio-Ethical Reform
P.O. Box 2483
Corona, CA 91719
Gregg Cunningham, Executive Director
(909) 736-9950

Center for Christian Studies
237 N. Michigan
South Bend, IN 46601

Center for Financial Freedom and Accuracy in Financial Reporting
P.O.Box 37812
Cincinnati, OH 45222

Center for International Private Enterprise
1615 H St., N.W.
Washington, DC 20062

Center for Media and Values
1962 S. Shenandoah St.
Los Angeles, CA 90034
Elizabeth Thoman, Executive Director
(310) 559-2944

Center for Public Policy and Contemporary Issues
University Park
Denver, CO 80208

Center for Social Thought
37 W. 20th St., Suite 902
New York, NY 10011

Center for Strategic Studies
8 Galleria Dr.
San Antonio, TX 78257
Dr. Francis X. Kane, Director

Center for the California Taxpayer
151 N. Sunrise Ave., Suite 901
Roseville, CA 95661
Tom McClintock, Director
(916) 786-9400

Center for the New East
175 Fairway Dr.
Princeton, NJ 08542
Steve Schlosstein, President
(609) 924-4290

Center for the Survival of Western Democracies
3419 Irwin Ave.
Riverdale, NY 10463
Lev Navrozov, Director

Central In Constitutionality
3210 Leonard Rd.
Martinsville, IN 46151

Central News Service
P.O. Box 7075
Laguna Niguel, CA 92677

Chalcedon Foundation
P.O. Box 158
Vallecito, CA 95251

Chesapeake Research Institute
601-J Hammonds Ferry Rd.
Linthicum, MD 21090
(410) 636-0280

Choices
P.O. Box 2124
Yorba Linda, CA 92686
(714) 777-3345

Christian Action League
P.O. Box 6216
Santa Barbara, CA 93111

Christian Advocate
P.O. Box 6321
Lakeland, FL 33807

Christian Advocate Serving Evangelism
P.O. Box 450349
Atlanta, GA 30345

Christian Challenge, The
1215 Independence Ave., S.E.
Washington, DC 20003

Christian Citizens' Crusade
12 Treasure Dr.
Riverdale, GA 30296

Christian Civic League of Maine
70 Sewall St.
Augusta, ME 04330
Michael Heath, Executive Director
(207) 622-7634, fax (207) 622-7635

Christian Civil Liberties Association
Afton Rd.
Afton, TN 37616

Christian Crusade
P.O. Box 977
Tulsa, OK 74102

Christian Crusade for Truth
Star Route 2, Box 39
Deming, NM 88030

Christian Defense Coalition
P.O. Box 75168
Washington, DC 20013
(202) 547-1735

Christian Economist
2255 Short Cut Rd.
Urbana, OH 43078

Christian Educator
1828 Mayfair Dr., N.E.
Grand Rapids, MI 49503

Christian Family Renewal
P.O. Box 73
Clovis, CA 93612

Christian Focus on Government
3028 Highgate Lane
Bedford, TX 76021
Glen Dickerson, Director

Christian Forum
P.O. Box 881
Oracle, AZ 85623

Christian Freedom Letter
P.O. Box 368
Fall Hills, NJ 07931

Christian Heritage Center
1941 Bishop Ln., Suite 205
Louisville, KY 40218
Dr. N. Burnett Magruder, Director

Christian Legal Defense and Education Foundation
P.O. Box 1088
Fairfax, VA 22030
(703) 818-7150

Christian Media
P.O. Box 448
Jacksonville, OR 97530
James Lloyd, Director

Christian Mission to the Communist World, International
P.O. Box 2947
Torrance, CA 90509

Christian News
P.O. Box 168
New Haven, MO 63068

Christian Parents Educational Fellowship
310 Blue Bonnet Dr.
Findlay, OH 45840

Christian Patriot
P.O. Box 4690
Sevierville, TN 37864

Christian Patriot Women
P.O. Box 504
Evanston, WY 82930

Christian Patriots Committee
412 Paddock Lane
Montgomery, AL 36109

Christian Patriots Defense League
P.O. Box 565
Flora, IL 62839

Christians for Better Government
P.O. Box 754
Lancaster, PA 17603

Christians for Justice
P.O. Box 711
Jacksonville, FL 32201

Christians for Life
4901 Lloyd Nolan Parkway
Fairfield, AL 35064
Rev. Jim Pinto, Director

Citizen Action
P.O. Box 90
Hull, MA 02045

Citizen Congress for Private Enterprise
220 10th Ave.
Grand Falls, MN 56241

Citizen Government Direction Council
509 Daisy Ave.
Lodi, CA 95240

Citizen Legal Defense Alliance
1935 Alpha Rd., Suite 366
Glendale, CA 91208

Citizen Legal Protective League
5456 Lake Ave.
Sanford, FL 32771

Citizen Rights in Education
P.O. Box 705
St. Cloud, MN 56301

Citizen Taxpayer
P.O. Box 1911
Bothell, WA 98041

Citizen's Claw
P.O. Box 441
Morongo Valley, CA 92256

Citizens Advocating Responsible Education
6157 Stevens Forest Rd.
Columbia, MD 21045

Citizens Against Research Bans
1140 23rd St., N.W., Suite 806
Washington, DC 20037

Citizens Committee for Second Amendment Rights
P.O. Box 2757
Camarillo, CA 93011

Citizens for a Balanced Budget
103 Martin Dr.
Harrison, AR 72601
Jerry Cash, Director

Citizens for Action Now
P.O. Box 2744-117
Huntington Beach, CA 92649
Barbara Coe, Director
(714) 647-2369

Citizens for Affordable Health Care
2 Suydam Lane
Bayport, NY 11705
Robert C. Forman, Director

Citizens for America
P.O. Box 3366
Shawnee Mission, KS 66217

Citizens for America Committee
25250 W. Main St.
Barstow, CA 92311

Citizens for Energy and Freedom
P.O. Box 283
Broomfield Hights, CO 44109

Citizens for God and Country
P.O. Box 137
McLean, VA 22101

Citizens for Governmental Restraint
212 W. Franklin Ave.
Minneapolis, MN 55404
M. Jacquelin Stevenson, Director

Citizens for Honest Government
504 Mary St.
Carson City, NV 89703
Mike Oliver
(702) 883-0903, (702) 883-6408 fax

Citizens for Judicial Reform
P.O. Box 2764
Sacramento, CA 95812

Citizens for Just Taxation
P.O. Box 368
Dolton, IL 60419

Citizens for Sensible Taxation
11109 Richland Valley Dr.
Great Falls, VA 22066
(703)430-6792

Citizens for Tax Reduction
6132 Flat Rock Rd.
Hoagland, IN 46745

Citizens for Term Limits
20675 S. Western Ave., Suite 204
Torrance, CA 90501-1809
Peter Schabarum, Chairman

Citizens for Total Energy
P.O. Box 563
Sunol, CA 94586
Helen Hubbard, President

Citizens Informer
P.O. Box 2494
Saint Louis, MO 63114

Citizens Law Enforcement and Research Committee
P.O. Box 169
North Powder, OR 97867

Citizens Right of Referendum Movement
P.O. Box 11351
Memphis TN 38111

Civilian Military Assistance
P.O. Box 3012
Decatur, AL 35602
Thomas V. Posey, Director

Claustrophobia
1402 Upland Dr.
Portland, OR 97221

Clean Up TV Campaign
5807 Charlotte Ave.
Nashville, TN 37209
John Hurt, Director

Clearlight Publications
13026 N. 18th St.
Phoenix, AZ 85022

Closing Abortuaries Now (CAN)
2046 Maple Ave., Suite C
Costa Mesa, CA 92627

Coalition for Academic Excellence
3524 Bermuda Dr.
Irondale, AL 35210
Mrs. Joan Kendall, Director

Coalition for Children
7485 Vance Dr., Suite 301
Arvada, CO 80003

Coalition for Constitutional Rights
6365 Canby Ave.
Reseda, CA 91335
Tom Richie, Director
(818) 881-3449

Coalition for New Republicans
P.O. Box 11457
Fresno, CA 93773-1457
John Estrada, Director

Coalition for Wisconsin
13259 Lakewood Dr.
Mequon, WI 53092

Coalition of Women Aware
P.O. Box 233
Alamagordo, NM 88310

Coalition Organized for Parental Equality
68 Deering St.
Portland, ME 04101

Cogitations
1004 Broad Branch
McLean, VA 22101

Colorado Council on Economic Education
225 East 16th Ave., Suite 740
Denver, CO 80203
(303) 832-8480, fax (303) 832-8474

Comics Commando
9530 Elvis Lane
Lanham, MD 20706

Committee for Constitutional Integrity
P.O. Box 17752
Raleigh, NC 27619

Committee for Constitutional Taxation
3327 Morning Glory Rd.
Philadelphia, PA 19154

Committee for Defense Preparedness
3337 Reservoir Rd.
Washington, DC 20007

Committee for Freedom of Choice in Medicine
1180 Walnut Ave.
Chula Vista, CA 92011

Committee for Human Rights in Romania
P.O. Box J, Gracie Station
New York, NY 10028

Committee for Monetary Reform
P.O. Box 2200
Newport Beach, CA 92663

Committee for Panama-US Relations
1860 Venice Park Dr., Suite 220
North Miami, FL 33181

Committee for Positive Education
301 Old Oak Dr.
Cortland, OH 44410

Committee for Responsible Youth Politics
3128 North 17th St.
Arlington, VA 22201

Committee to Cap the National Debt
9848 Business Park Dr., Suite B
Sacramento, CA 95827
Richard Gann, Director

Committee to Protect the Family
8001 Forbes Place, Suite 102
Springfield, VA 22151

Committee to Remember
P.O. Box 4690
Sevierville, TN 37864

Committee to Save the Panama Canal
1235 E. Portner
West Covina, CA 91790

Common Sense Press
Route 1, Box 6
Cleveland, OK 74020

Commonwealth Foundation of Virginia
220 University Boulevard, Suite 302
Harrisonburg, VA
Walter Curt, President
(800) 296-9751, fax (703) 432-9430

Community Anti-Drug Coalitions of America
701 N. Fairfax St.
Alexandria, VA 22314

Compete
1 Farragut Square South, N.W.
Washington, DC 20006

Concerned American Citizen
76 W. Main St.
Madison, OH 44057

Concerned Citizens for the Constitution
P.O. Box 44590
Indianapolis, IN 46244

Concerned Citizens League
870 Sunup Dr.
Bartown, FL 33830

Confederate Society of America
HCR 3, Box 73-A
Peyton, TX 79070

Congress of Racial Equality (CORE)
30 Cooper Square
New York, NY 10003
Roy Innis, Chairman
(212) 598-3568

Connecticut Legal Fund
110 Sleepy Hallow Rd.
New Canaan, CT 06840

Consent Clause
626 Flowerdale
Ferndale, ME 48220

Conservative Action Foundation
316 Pennslyvania Ave., S.E., Suite 401
Washington, DC 20003
R. David Finzer, Director

Conservative Alliance
1315 Duke St., Suite 200
Alexandria, VA 22314
J. Barry Bitzer, Director

Conservative Forum for Unitarian Universalists
12101 Parkin Lane
Fenton, MI 48430
Dean Drake, Editor

Conservative Libertarian Party
1828 Vinewood Blvd.
Ann Arbor, MI 48104

Conservative Majority for Citizen's Rights
302 Briarwood Circle, N.W.
Ft. Walton Beach, FL 32548-3904
James Stanley Harkins, Director

Conservative Network Foundation
1000 Water St., S.W., Suite 62
Washington, DC 20024
Rob Brooks, Director
(703) 971-0692

Conservative Order of Good Guys
235 East Fourth Ave.
Escondido, CA 92025

Conservative Party of Kansas
R.R. 1, Box 52
Florence, KS 66851

Conservative Research Center
P.O. Box 97009
Washington, DC 20090
Charles Via, Chairman

Conservative Think Tank
4601 Pinecrest Office Park Dr., Suite F
Alexandria, VA 22312
Howard Grove, Chairman
(703) 914-9279

Conservatives for Freedom
P.O. Box 190
Buies Creek, NC 27506
Dr. David B. Funderburk, Director

Conservatives for Good Government
P.O. Box 1311
Southern Pines, NC 28287

Conservatives Organized Against the Usurpation of Political Power
P.O. Box 1864
Tustin, CA 92681
David S. Whitley, Publisher

Constitution of the Confederate States of America
1269 Huffman Rd.
Birmingham, AL 35215
Dr. C. E. Booklet, Director

Constitution Party
7752 Las Palmas Way
Jacksonville, FL 33216

Constitutional Caucus Clearinghouse
1405 S. Glendale
Sioux Falls, SD 57105

Constitutional Civil Liberties Union
100-A East Clairborne
Greenwood, MS 38930

Constitutional Freedom Committee
P.O. Box 157
Linwood, NJ 08221

Constitutional Liberties Foundation
P.O. Box 1637
Ranch Santa Fe, CA 92067

Constitutional Militia of 1791
P.O. Box 601
Cornville, AZ 86325

Constitutional Research Association
P.O. Box 550
South Holland, IL 60473

Constitutional Taxpayers
1617 Engleman Rd.
Grand Island, NE 68801

Coordinating Committee of Hungarian Organizations
4101 Blackpool Rd.
Rockville, MD 20853

Coping With Turbulent Times
Box 4630 SFA Station
Nacagdoches, TX 75961
Reynold Griffith, Director

Copperweld Foundation
Four Gateway Ctr., 22nd Floor
Pittsburgh, PA 15222-1211
(412) 263-3200
Douglas E. Young, Trustee

Cornerstone Curriculum
2006 Flat Creek Place
Richardson, TX 75080

Correspondent Committee
P.O. Box 9283
Missoula, MT 59807

Council for Educational Freedom
14517 Colonels Choice
Upper Marlboro, MA 20747
Dr. Rudolph Wilhelm, President
(301) 350-0979

Council for Government Reform
6867 Elm St., Suite 101
McLean, VA 22101
Geoff Peters, Director
(703) 356-8702

Council of Minnesota Taxpayers Associations
628 Stryker Ave.
St. Paul, MN 55107

Council on Crime in America
1150 17th St., N.W., Suite 510
Washington, DC 20036
(202) 822-8333, fax (202) 822-8325

Council on Culture and Community
255 E. 49th St., Suite 23C
New York, NY 10017
Candace De Russy, Director
(212) 752-7315

Council on Imprisoned and Missing Americans
P.O. Box 339
Muncy, PA 17756

Council on Property Rights
P.O. Box 706
Mount Pleasant, SC 29465
David Lucas, Chairman
(803) 886-4654, fax (803) 886-4654

Counsel of Chalcedon
3032 Hacienda Court
Marietta, GA 30066

Covert Intelligence Letter
P.O. Box 67
St. Charles, MO 63301

Criminal Politics
P.O. Box 37812
Cincinnati, OH 45222

Croatian National Congress
10 Ackerman Rd.
Saddle River, NJ 07458
Dr. Matthew Mestrovic, Director

Crusade for Life
18030 Brookhurst, Box 372
Fountain Valley, CA 92708
Beverly Cielnicky, President
(714) 963-4753

Curriculum and Textbook Development
560 J St., Suite 290
Sacramento, CA 95814
Glen Thomas, Director

Czechoslovak National Council
2137 S. Lombard Ave.
Chicago, IL 60650

Dallas Institute
2719 Routh St.
Dallas, TX 75201
Dr. Gail Thomas, Director

Dandelion
1985 Selby Ave.
St. Paul, MN 55104

Dawn Enterprises
P.O. Box 90913
Los Angeles, CA 90009

Dayspring Publications
P.O. Box 7677
Texarkana, TX 75505

Defenders Publications
P.O. Box 11134
Las Vegas, NV 89111

Defense of Freedom Council
7 Buttonwood Lane
Darien, CT 06280

Delaware Family Foundation
P.O. Box 3747
Wilmington, DE 19807
Duane Higgins, Director

Deleware Council on Economic Education
110 Purnell Hall
University of Delaware
Newark, DE 19716

Delta Press
P.O. Box 1625
El Dorado, AR 71730

Deregulator
P.O. Box 17343
Raleigh, NC 27619

Deseret Political Journal
17 S. Cleveland Ave.
Blackfoot, ID 83221

Desert Stream
12488 Venice Blvd.
Los Angeles, CA 90066
(310) 572-0140

Destiny of America Foundation
Route 2, Box 452
Berryville, AK 72616

Destiny Research Foundation
P.O. Box 333
Salem, OH 44460
Frank A. Fiebiger, Director

Diane Books
P.O. Box 2948
Torrance, CA 90509

Diogenes
426 E. North St., Suite 101
Waukesha, WI 53188

Dodge Jones Foundation
400 Pine, Suite 900
Abilene, TX 79601
Joseph Edwin Canon, Executive Director

Doughty Report
6321 S. 72nd E. Place
Tulsa, OK 74133

Durell Publishing Company
P.O. Box 586
Berryville, VA 22611

Eagle Forum of Alabama
4200 Stone River Circle
Birmingham, AL 35213

Eagle Forum of Wisconsin
5238 N. 48th St.
Milwaukee, WI 53218

Eclectic Reader
Star Route Box 286
Topton, NC 28781

Economic Awareness Foundation
P.O. Box 399
Casper, WY 82602

Economic Education Enterprises
7618 Gazette Ave.
Canoga Park, CA 91306
Nancy Spillman, Director

Economic Institute for Research and Education
3870 Cloverleaf Dr.
Boulder, CO 80304
Dr. Fred Glahe, Director

Economics Press
12 Daniel Rd.
Fairfield, NJ 07006

Education Service Council
P.O. Box 271
Elm Grove, WI 53122

Educational Research and Analysis
P.O. Box 7518
Longview, TX 75601

Educational Research and Analysis
3625 Urband Lane
Lakeland, FL 33813

Educational Research Bureau
P.O. Box 2194
Roanoke, VA 24009

Educational Services International
1183 S.E. Godsey Rd.
Dallas, OR 97338

Educator Publishing
1110 S. Pomona Ave.
Fullerton, CA 92632

Efficacy
P.O. Box 92260
Santa Barbara, CA 93190-3260

End Poverty in America Society
P.O. Box 6163
San Bernardino, CA 92412
Carl Fredericks, Director

English First
8001 Forbes Place, Suite 102
Springfield, VA 22151
George Tryfiates, Director
(703) 321-8818

Enough!
P.O. Box 402036
Miami, FL 33140

Enterprise
P.O. Box 1145
Buies Creek, NC 27506

Enterprise Publications
155 Maplewood Dr.
Laflin, PA 18702

Entrepreneur
Grove City College
Grove City, PA 16127

Environment Betrayed - A Newsletter of Science, Philosophy, and Uncommon Sense
P.O. Box 1161
Winona, MN 55978

Environmental Conservation Organization
P.O. Box 191
Hollow Rock, TN 38342
Henry Lamb, Director
(901) 986-0099

Environmental Conservation Organization
1300 Maybrook Dr.
Maywood, IL 60153
Robert Vicks, Chairman

Esping Center of Free Enterprise
Bellevue College
Bellevue, NE 68005

Estonian American National Council
243 E. 34th St.
New York, NY 10016

Ethnic Review
P.O. Box 441
New York, NY 10028

Evangelical Child & Family Agency
1530 N. Main St.
Wheaton, IL 60187
(708) 653-6400

Extrophy
1129 W. 30th St., Apt. 8
Los Angeles, CA 90007

Fact Finder
P.O. Box 10555
Phoenix, AZ 85064
Harry T. Everingham, Publisher

Facts About Cuba
65 Green St.
Jamaica Plain, MA 02130

Fair Government Foundation
1317 F St., N.W., Suite 950
Washington, DC 20004
(202) 637-9779

Faith and Freedom Sentinel
P.O. Box 1020
Alton, IL 62002-1020
Ron Cowan, Editor
(618) 463-0844

Families for Life
P.O. Box 206
Ronkonkoma, NY 11779

Families for Moral Government
7615 Decatur Dr.
Fayetteville, NC 28303

Family Action Network
44648 W. 15th St.
Lancaster, CA 93534
(714) 947-6627

Family Concern
P.O. Box 900
Morrison, CO 80465
J. Allen Petersen, Director
(303) 697-1202

Family Defense Council
P.O. Box 310478
Jamaica, NY 11431
Dr. Howard Hurwitz, Chairman
(718) 591-6392

Family Foundation
263 Cochran Rd.
Lexington, KY 40522
Kent Ostrander, Executive Director
(606) 255-5400, fax (606) 233-3330

Family Institute
200 S. 12th Ave.
Nashville, TN 37203
Jeff Whitesides, Executive Director
(615) 254-3917, fax (615) 782-6695

Family Institute of Connecticut
P.O. Box 58
Southport, CT 06490
Charles P. Stetson, Chairman
(203) 254-1039

Family Life League
P.O. Box 293
River Forest, IL 60305

Family Life Ministries
370 L'Enfant Promenade, S.W., Suite 801
Washington, DC 20024
Dr. Tim LaHaye, President
(202) 488-0700

Family Protection Ministries
910 Sunrise Ave., Suite A1
Roseville, CA 95661

Family Report
P.O. Box 9
Washougal, WA 98671

Family Research Institute of Wisconsin
111 King St., Suite 25
Madison, WI 53703-3339
Marvin Munyon, Executive Director
(608) 256-3228, fax (608) 256-3370

Farmers Alliance for Improved Regulation
2300 N St., N.W., Suite 600
Washington, DC 20037
James Moody, Coordinator
(202) 663-9011

Federal Research Institute
P.O. Box 66129
Seattle, WA 98166

Federation for American-Afghan Action
P.O. Box 1876
Washington, DC 20013

Federation of New Jersey Taxpayers
P.O. Box 86
Summit, NJ 07901

Fellowship of Christian Home Educators
4734 Kirkwell Dr.
Mobile, AL 36619

Fellowship of Concerned Churches
P.O. Box 505
Amherst, VA 24521

Firearms Coalition
P.O. Box 6537
Silver Spring, MD 20906
Neal Knox, President
(301) 871-3006

Firearms Education Institute
P.O. Box 2193
El Segundo, CA 90245
Randall N. Herrst, Director
(310) 322-7244

Firing Line
P.O. Box 5966
Columbia, SC 29250

First Amendment Rights
1733 Burgundy Boulevard
Tallahassee, FL 32303
Richard Bjornseth, Chairman
(904) 574-3177

Fiscal Policy Council
100 E. 17th St.
River Beach, FL 33404

Florida Action Committee for Education
8434 S. Lamento Ave.
Jacksonville, FL 32239

Florida Christian Task Force Against Anti-Semitism
4781 N. Congress Ave., Suite 247
Lantana, FL 33462

Florida Family Council
101 E. Kennedy Blvd., Suite 1320
Tampa, FL 33602
Randall Knox, Director
(813) 222-8300, fax (813) 222-8301

Florida Independent
P.O. Box 6771
Lake Worth, FL 33466

Florida Right to Life Education Foundation
3348 Edgewater Dr.
Orlando, FL 32804

Floridians for Immigration Control
P.O. Box 187
Boca Raton, FL 33429

FOCUS Magazine
P.O. Box 1197
Thousand Oaks, CA 91358
Mimi Jaffe, Editor
(805) 494-1115

Footprints Newsletter
P.O. Box 45057
Boise, ID 83711

For America
614 Walnut St.
Arcadia, CA 91006

For Producers Only
P.O. Box 156
Springtown, PA 18081

Forerunner
P.O. Box 1799
Gainesville, FL 32602

Foresight Institute
P.O. Box 61058
Palo Alto, CA 94306

Forfeiture Endangers American Rights (FEAR)
1735 N. Broadway
Walnut Creek, CA 94596
Brenda Grantland, Editor
(510) 930-3298

Forsberg Focus
24331 Muirlands Blvd., Suite 4-311
Lake Forest, CA 92630
Robert W. Forsberg
(714) 581-2900

Forum
101 N. 5th St.
Fargo, ND 58102

Foundation Endowment
611 Cameron St.
Alexandria, VA 22314

Foundation for a New Freeman
1909 Beacon St.
Brookline, MA 02146

Foundation for Africa's Future
5316 Inverchapel Rd.
Springfield, VA 22151

Foundation for American Christian Education
P.O. Box 27035
San Francisco, CA 94127

Foundation for Christian Theology
1215 Independence Ave., S.E.
Washington, DC 20003

Foundation for Economic Liberty
130 3rd St., S.E.
Washington, DC 20003
Tom Valentine, Director

Foundation for International Studies
P.O. Box 219
Buies Creek, NC 27506
Eric Brodin, Director
(919) 893-8786

Foundation for Reconciliation
P.O. Box 40125
Pasadena, CA 91104
John M. Perkins, Founder
(818) 791-7439

Foundation for Religous Action in the Social and Civil Order
160 Longleaf Rd.
Southern Pines, NC 28387
Charles W. Lowry, Director

Foundation for Student Communication
Aaron Burr Hall
Princeton, NJ 08540

Foundation for Thought and Ethics
P.O. Box 830721
Richardson, TX 75083
Jon Buell, Director

Foundation to Defend the First Amendment
300 Independence Ave., S.E.
Washington, DC 20003

Foundation to End Totalitarianism
1332 2nd St.
Gulfport, MS 39501

Fourth World Review
708 Montgomery
San Francisco, CA 94111

Frank Hawkins Kenan Institute of Private Enterprise
CB#3440 The Kenan Center
Chapel Hill, NC 27514
Rollie Tillman, Director

Free American New Service
P.O. Box 3125
Denver, CO 80201

Free Citizen
100 Dartmouth Rd.
Raleigh, NC 27609

Free Enterprise Institute
7575 E. Fulton Rd.
Ada, ME 48355

Free Lithuania
2618 W. 71st St.
Chicago, IL 60629

Free Man's Press
P.O. Box 861
Bowling Green, KY 42101
Donovan Freeman, Editor

Free Marin Forum
P.O. Box 367
Kentfield, CA 94914

Free Market Committee
P.O. Box 740367
Dallas, TX 75374
(214) 348-2801

Free Speech Coalition
904 Massachusetts Ave., N.E.
Washington, DC 20002

Free the Masons Ministries
P.O. Box 1077
Issaquah, WA 98027

Free2B
P.O. Box 612
Baton Rouge, LA 70821

Freeaction Newsletter
4895 Macarthur Blvd., N.W.
Washington, DC 20007

Freedom
P.O. Box 375
Bellevue, WA 98009

Freedom Calendar
704 Edgerton
St. Paul, MN 55101

Freedom Council
1210 Timber Ridge Dr.
Euless, TX 76039

Freedom Enterprise
15765 Main Market Rd.
Burton, OH 44021

Freedom Federation
415 2nd St., N.E., Suite 100
Washington, DC 20002

Freedom First in California
2141 Stradella Rd.
Los Angeles, CA 90077

Freedom Forum
740 N. Washington Ave.
Minneapolis, MN 55401

Freedom Information Center
1332 N. Lake Ave.
Pasadena, CA 91104

Freedom League
4207 Patricia St.
Fremont, CA 94536

Freedom League
721 2nd St., N.E.
Washington, DC 20002

Freedom Network
3242 N. Pulaski Rd.
Chicago, IL 60641

Freedom Now
1317 Lakewood Dr.
Ft. Collins, CO 80521

Freedom School Library
P.O. Box 6100-161
Costa Mesa, CA 92628

Freedom Task Force
1404 N. Catalina St.
Los Angeles, CA 90029

Freedom Through Truth Foundation
801 S. Home Ave.
Oak Park, IL 60304

Freedom to Express
422 S.W. 5th., Suite B
Grants Pass, OR 97526

Freedom Unlimited
P.O. Box 38
Aztec, NM 87401

Freedom Writer
P.O. Box 773
Ft. Smith, AR 72902

Freeman Institute
4084 N.E. 5th Dr.
Gresham, OR 97030

Freeperson Magazine
50 Maplewood Dr.
Monroe, CT 06468

Friends of Freedom
704 Edgerton
St. Paul, MN 55101

Friends of Lithuania Front
1634 49th Ave.
Chicago, IL 60650

Friends of the Americas
1024 N. Foster Dr.
Baton Rouge, LA 70806
Woody Jenkins, Director
(504) 926-5707

Friends of the Farm
Route 1, Box 32
Dalton City, IL 61925

Front Range Objectivist Group
8700 Dover Ct.
Westminster, CO 80005
Lin Zinser, Director
(303) 431-2525

Frontiers of Freedom
10235 S.E. 13th Place
Bellevue, WA 98004

Fund for America's Future
P.O. Box 2634
La Plata, MD 20646

Fund for Sane Environmental Laws
Board of Trade Center, Suite 501
Wichita, KS 67202
Toby Elster, Director

Fund to Punish Criminals
P.O. Box 863525
Flushing, NY 11386

Geneva Ministries
708 Hamvasy Lane
Tyler, TX 75701

Georgia Conservative Union
160 Peachtree Way, N.E.
Atlanta, GA 30305

Georgia Family Education and Research Council
3937 Holcomb Bridge Rd., Suite 301
Norcross, GA 30092
Richard Hamme, Executive Director
(404) 242-0001, fax (404) 242-0501

Georgia Objectivists
4565 Duron Place
Mableton, GA 30059
Karyn Volk, Director
(770) 739-1900

Gila Constitutional Defenders
1903 Bighorn
Stafford, AZ 85546

Global Glance
P.O. Box 28240
Tempe, AZ 85285

God's Last Call
P.O. Box 426
Scappoose, OR 97056

God's World Publications
P.O. Box 2330
Asheville, NC 28802

Gold Standard Review
P.O. Box 1311
Germantown, MD 20875
Harold E. Thomas, President

Golden Mean Society
P.O. Box 2904
Pasco, WA 99302

Golden State Center
2012 H St., Suite 101
Sacramento, CA 95814

Good Society
P.O. Box 655
Tujunga, CA 91042

Gospel Outreach
P.O. Box 801188
Houston, TX 77280

Gospel Tract Society
P.O. Box 1118
Independence, MO 64051

Government Waste Report
P.O. Box 14151
Shawnee, KS 66215

Grass Rooters
457 S. Arden
Los Angeles, CA 90005

Grass Roots
P.O. Box 27932
Houston, TX 77227

Groom Books
1800 Diagonal Rd., Suite 600
Alexandria, VA 22314

Groundswell, USA
1421 23rd St.
Manhattan Beach, CA 90266

Guardians of Education
Rt. 68, Box 124
Cushing, ME 04563

Guardians of Traditional Education
P.O. Box 606
Bowie, MD 20715

Gun Owners of California
3440 Viking Dr., Suite 106
Sacramento, CA 95827
John E. Stoos, Executive Director
(916) 361-2827

Gun Rights Committee
P.O. Box 414
East Sullivan, NH 03445
Al Rubega, Chairman

Gun World Magazine
34249 Camino Capistrano
Capistrano Beach, CA 92624
Jack Lewis, Editor

Gunsite Press
P.O. Box 401
Paulden, AZ 86334

Halycon House
P.O. Box 8795
Portland, OR 97207

Heart of America Conservative Club
9631 Catalina
Overland Park, KS 66207

Heritage Education and Review Organization
P.O. Box 202
Jarettsville, MD 21084

Heritage Enterprises
P.O. Box 1483
Everett, WA 98206

Heritage House '76
919 S. Main St.
Snowflake, AZ 85937
(602) 536-7592

Hillaire du Berrier Report
P.O. Box 786
St. George, UT 84770

His Heart Ministries
12162 E. Mississippi Ave.
P.O. Box 12321
Aurora, CO 80011
(303) 369-2961

Hispanic Coalition for a Free America
415 2nd St., N.E., Suite 100
Washington, DC 20002

Hispanics for Life
P.O. Box 9086
Torrance, CA 90501
Louis Madrid, Director
(213) 549-4182

Holy Land State Committee
2005 N. Nelson St.
Washington, DC 22207

Honest Money for America
202 Institutions Building
Olympia, WA 98504

Hudson Valley Objectivists
28 Jackson Rd.
Poughkeepsie, NY 12603
Nancy Tellin, Director
(914) 462-2716

Humanist Century
P.O. Box 84116
San Diego, CA 92138

Hungarian Freedom Fighters
P.O. Box 441
New York, NY 10028

I.E.C. Newsletter
805 S. Randolph
Arlington, VA 22204

I'm a Patriot
301 Soule Ave.
Pleasant Hill, CA 94523

Idaho Citizens for Educational Reform
P.O. Box 166
Riggins, ID 83549

Idaho Family Forum
5301 Emerald St.
Boise, ID 83706
Dennis Mansfield, Executive Director
(208) 344-9009, fax (208) 344-1808

Immigration Legislative Network
915 L St., Suite C-292
Sacramento, CA 95814
Kathy Nelson Turner, Director
(916) 442-3700

Independent Americans
P.O. Box 2501
Salt Lake City, UT 84110
Dr. Joye Wyatt, Director

Independent Bar Association
88838 Hale Rd.
Noti, OR 97461

Independent Entrepeneur
P.O. Box 546
El Cajon, CA 92020

Independent Populist Party
205 Hanley
Plainfield, IN 46168

Indiana Citizens for Life
70 East 91st St., Suite 210
Indianapolis, IN 46340
Mike Fichter, Executive Director
(317) 574-1896, fax (317) 582-1438

Indispensable Rights School
4305 172nd, N.W.
Lynwood, WA 98036

Individual Rights Committee
P.O. Box 32024
Long Beach, CA 98832
Robert Barney, Director
(310) 634-3339

Individualist Journal
P.O. Box 33486
Seattle, WA 98133

Individualist Research Foundation
P.O. Box 7486
Beverly Hills, CA 90212

Information Council of the Americas
P.O. Box 53371
New Orleans, LA 70153

Information Digest
2805 St. Paul St.
Baltimore, MD 21218

Inland Empire Citizens Against Crime
1910-3 W. Palmyra Ave.
Orange, CA 92668
Michael Reeder, Director
(714) 634-3635

Inland Empire Conservative Coalition
24103 Ironbark Rd.
Moreno Valley, CA 92557
Rosemary Peters, Director
(909) 243-7729

Institute for Business Ethics
DePaul University
243 South Wabash Ave.
Chicago IL 60604

Institute for Creation Research
10946 N. Woodside Ave.
El Cajon, CA 92021
Dr. Henry Morris, Director
(619) 448-0900

Institute for Cultural Conservatism
717 Second St., N.E.
Washington, DC 20002
William Lind, Director
(202) 546-3004

Institute for East-West Security Studies
360 Lexington Ave.
New York, NY 10017

Institute for Law and Policy Analysis
551 Bermuda Run
Advance, NC 27006
Dr. Sylvester Petro, Director
(910) 940-5922

Institute for Regional and International Studies
P.O.Box 693
Boulder, CO 80306
Alexander McColl, Director

Institute for the Study of Christianity and Marxism
Wheaton College
Wheaton, IL 60187
Mark Elliott, Director
(708) 260-5917

Institute of Religion
865 Stanford Ave.
Palo Alto, CA 94306
Dr. Gerald E. Jones, Director

Institute on Public Policy and Private Enterprise
Grove City College
Grove City, PA 16127

Institute on Religion and Democracy
1331 H St., N.W., Suite 900
Washington, DC 20005
Rev. Ed Robb, Chairman
(202) 393-3200

Institute on Strategic Trade
3420 Annandale Rd.
Falls Church, VA 22042

Intelligence Digest
P.O. Box 2100
Rolling Hills Estates, CA 90274

Intercessors for America
P.O. Box 2639
Reston, VA 22090
Gary Bergel, President
(703) 471-0913

International Cultural Foundation
1015 18th St., N.W., Suite 300
Washington, DC 20036
(202) 293-7440

International Intercessors
P.O. Box 0
Pasadena, CA 91109

Iowa Basic Freedoms Association
Route 5
Iowa City, IA 52240

Iowans for Moral Education
P.O. Box 304
Kalona, IA 52247

Islamic Home School Association of North America
610 S.W. 21 Rd.
Warrensburg, MO 64093
Janet Akremi, Editor, *The Muslim Family*

Issues Research and Educational Foundation
2920 Kirby Dr.
Houston, TX 7798

Jamestown Foundation
1528 18th St., N.W.
Washington, DC 20036
Lawrence Uzzell, Vice President
(202) 438-8888

Jefferson Educational Foundation
7414 Benjamin Franklin Station
Washington, DC 20044
David H. Barron, Director

Jeremiah Films
P.O. Box 1710
Hemet, CA 92546
(800) 828-2290

Jewish Institute for National Security Affairs
1717 K St., N.W.
Washington, DC 20036
Tom Neumann, Executive Director
(202) 833-0020, fax (202) 296-6452

Jews for Morality
P.O. Box 262
Brooklyn, NY 11223
Isaac Levy, Director
(718) 336-0063

Joint Baltic American National Committee
400 Hurley Ave.
Rockville, MD 20850
Sandra Aistars, Director

Josh McDowell Ministry
P.O. Box 1000
Dallas, TX 75221
(214) 907-1000

Journal of Social and Political Science
1133 13th St., N.W., Suite 2
Washington, DC 20005

Judicial Reform Foundation
P.O. Box 1455
Pebble Beach, CA 93953

Judicial Watch
501 School St., S.W., Suite 725
Washington, DC 20024
(202) 646-5172

Junta Patriotica Cubana
P.O. Box 350-492
Miami, Fl 33135

Justice Fellowship
1856 Old Reston Ave.
Reston, VA 22090
Roberto Rivera, Director
(703) 478-0100, fax (703) 478-9679

Kansas Family Research Institute
2250 N. Rock Rd., Suite 118-224
Wichita, KS 67226
David Payne, Executive Director
(316) 634-2428, fax (316) 634-2622

Keep America Independent
6609 Edenvale Rd.
Baltimore, MD 21209
Alfred I. Aaronson, Director

Keep the Faith
810 Belmont Ave.
North Haledon, NJ 07508

Kentucky Journal
1548 Alexandria Dr., Suite 2B
Lexington, KY 40504

Knights of Lithuania
164 Burns St.
Forest Hills, NY 11375

Kona Torch
RR 1, Box 157
Captain Cook, HI 96704

L.I.F.E.
2501 E. Central Ave.
Wichita, KS 67214

L'Abri Cassettes
P.O. Box 2035
Michigan City, IN 46360

La Hojada de Combate
P.O. Box 420952
Miami, FL 33142

Larsen File
P.O. Box 4080
Torrance, CA 90510

Last Stand Publishing
1129 East Cliff Rd.
Burnsville, MN 55337
Nick Guarino, Director

Latvian Information Services
4325 17th St., N.W.
Washington, DC 20011

Law and Economics Center
P.O. Box 248000
Coral Gables, FL 33124
Kenneth W. Clarkson, Director
(305) 284-6174, fax (305) 662-9159

Lawyers for Life
P.O. Box 217
Lakeville, CT 06039

Laymens Educational Guild at Law
9600 Cedar Lake Rd.
Pinckney, MI 48169

Leadership Foundation
7945 MacArthur Blvd.
Cabin John, MD 20818

Legal Action for Women
1145 Candlewood Circle
Pensacola, FL 32514
(904) 474-1091

Legislative Action
10764 Southview Loop, S.E.
Jefferson, OR 97352

Legislative Alert
P.O. Box 404
Merrifield, VA 22116

Legislative Research
7515 Goldenrod
Sacramento, CA 95828

Libertarian Action
3818 Lakeview Terrace
Falls Church, VA 22041

Libertarian Agenda
1200 Hamilton Ave.
Palo Alto, CA 94301

Libertarian Banner
P.O. Box 6651
Providence, RI 02940

Libertarian Digest--Gutenburg Press
1920 Cedar St.
Berkeley, CA 94709

Libertarian E-Mail Directory
447 Merrick St.
Shreveport, LA 71104

Libertarian Familist Movement
P.O. Box 4826
El Paso, TX 79914-4826
(915) 755-6940

Libertarian Forum
P.O. Box 341
New York, NY 10010

Libertarian Gun Owners Caucus
3861 Mentone Ave., Suite 44
Culver City, CA 90232
Bob Weber, Chairman
(310) 204-0612

Libertarian Letters
4250 Yukon Ave.
Simi Valley, CA 93063

Libertarian Library
2009 S. Fisher Court
Pasadena, TX 77502

Libertarian Publishers
P.O. Box 6022
San Rafael, CA 94903

Libertarian S.I.G.
P.O. Box 142
Port Hueneme, CA 93041

Libertarian Transition Caucus
1910 N. Morianna, Suite 311
Los Angeles, CA 90032

Libertarian-Republican Alliance
1149 E. 32nd St.
Brooklyn, NY 11210

Liberty
1149 Villa Ave.
Indianapolis, IN 46203

Liberty Action Council
P.O. Box 730
Clinton, AR 72031

Liberty Counsel
P.O. Box 540774
Orlando, FL 32854
(407) 875-2100, fax (407) 875-8008

Liberty Federation
P.O. Box 190
Forest, VA 24551
Jerry C. Nims, Director

Liberty Forum
1420 Locust St., Suite 360
Philadelphia, PA 19102

Life Advocate Magazine
P.O. Box 13656
Portland, OR 97207
Andrew Burnett, Editor

Life After Abortion
210 S. Illinois Ave., Apt. 1
Anaheim, CA 92805
Ron Stoltenberg, Director
(714) 774-7510

Life Decisions International
P.O. Box 419
Amherst, NY 14226
Douglas Scott, Director
(716) 839-4420

Lincoln Caucus
2907 North 2nd St.
Phoenix, AZ 85012
Sydney Hoff Hay, President
(602) 230-2981

Lincoln Center for Legal Studies
P.O. Box 15
Great Falls, VA 22066
William Stanmeyer, President
(703) 759-5227

Lincoln Club of Orange County
2344 S. Pullman Ave.
Santa Ana, CA 92705
Don Henley, President
(714) 852-2147

Lininger Information Services
501 Faculty
Concordia, MO 64020

Lithuanian American Community
6940 Hartwell
Dearborn, MI 48126

Lithuanian National League
P.O. Box 241
Addison, IL 60101

Lithuanian Regeneration Association
6821 S. Maplewood
Chicago, IL 60629

Lithuanian-American Council
788 E. Broadway
South Boston, MA 02127

Live and Let Live
300 Frandor Ave.
Lansing, MI 48912

Louisiana Caucus Club
2101 New School Rd.
Lake Charles, LA 70605

Lutherans Alert National
P.O. Box 7186
Tacoma, WA 98407

M.S. Fair
P.O. Box 612816
San Jose, CA 95161

Mackay Society
P.O. Box 131
New York, NY 10023

Mantooth Report
R.R. 1, Box 387
Salem, IN 47167

March for Life Education and Defense Fund
P.O. Box 90300
Washington, DC 20090
Nellie J. Gray, President
(202) 626-8810

Margaret Thatcher Institute
3714 Dale Ave.
Tampa, FL 33609
(818) 876-1204

Marple Mountain Constitutional Patriots
P.O. Box 926
Happy Camp, CA 96039

Massachusetts Blacks for Life
140 Sharon
West Bedford, MA 02155

Massachusetts Taxpayers Foundation
24 Province St.
Boston, MA 02109
Richard Manley, Director

Mastermedia International
330 N. Sixth St., Suite 110
Redlands, CA 92734-3312
(909) 335-7353

McAlvany Intelligence Advisor
P.O. Box 84904
Phoenix, AZ 85071

Media & Values Magazine
1962 S. Shenandoah St.
Los Angeles, CA 90034
Elizabeth Thoman, Executive Director
(310) 559-2944

Media Action Coalition
P.O. Box 134
Whippany, NJ 07981

Medical Action Committee for Education (MACE)
P.O. Box 1667
Elkins, WV 26241
Jerry Arnett, Director
(304) 636-8416

Medical Institute of Sexual Health
P.O. Box 4919
Austin, TX 78765
(800) 892-9484, fax (512) 451-7599
Dr. Joe McIlhaney, M.D., Founder

Methodists for Life
12105 Livingston St.
Wheaton, MD 20902-2131
Olga Fairfax, Ph.D., Director
(301) 942-1627

Michigan Alliance of Families
P.O. Box 241
Flushing, MI 48433

Michigan Christian Heritage
2101 Cook Rd.
Owosso, MI 48867

Michigan Committee for Freedom
4407 West Saint Josephs Highway
Lansing, MI 48917

Mid-America Commodities and Bartering
P.O. Box 374
Wheeling, IL 60090

Mid-Atlantic Research Association
P.O. Box 1523
Washington, DC 20013

Mid-East Publishing House
5519 N. 77th Place
Scottsdale, AZ 85253

Midway Review
600 N. Aubrey Cir.
Greenwood, MS 38930

Military Veteran's Forum
15106A Frederick Rd., Plaza 136
Rockville, MD 20850

Minimum Wage Coalition to Save Jobs
P.O. Box 27414
Washington, DC 20038
Richard Berman, Director

Minuteman Alert
P.O. Box 30
Conneaut, OH 44030

Missionary Crusader
2451 34th St.
Lubbock, TX 79411

Mississippi Conservative
P.O. Box 519
Ocean Springs, MS 39564
(601) 875-5373

Missouri Emergency Committee
7232 Ward Parkway
Kansas City, MO 64114

Missouri Family Council
P.O. Box 480018
Kansas City, MO 64148-0018
Paul Scianna, Executive Director
(816) 943-1776, fax (816) 943-0550

Money Matters
P.O. Box 25
Iola, WI 54945

Monist
P.O. Box 600
LaSalle, IL 61301

Montana Sunflower
2459 Hi Hi Tah
St. Ignatius, MT 59865

Montgomery Street Foundation
235 Montgomery St., Suite 1107
San Francisco, CA 94104

Moore Foundation
P.O. Box 1
Camas, WA 98607

Morality in Medicine
475 Riverside Dr.
New York, NY 10115
Bob Peters, President
(212) 870-3222

Morningside Review
206 Lewisohn Hall, CU
New York, NY 10027

Movement for Independence and Democracy in Cuba
10020 S.W. 37th Terrace
Miami, FL 33153

Moviemento Nacionalista Cuba
614 Franklin St.
Elizabeth, NJ 07206

Music Box, The
3606 Edwin Ave.
Cincinnati, OH 45204

N.C.B.A. Reports
P.O. Box 2255
Longmont, CO 80501

N.E.T. Program
P.O. Box 91
Pinesdale, MT 59841

National Animal Interest Alliance
P.O. Box 66579
Portland, OR 97290
Patti Strand, Executive Director

National Association for Crime Victims Rights
P.O. Box 16161
Portland, OR 97416

National Association for the Self-Employed
P.O. Box 612067
Dallas-Fort Worth Airport, TX 75261

National Association of Evangelicals
1023 15th St., N.W., Suite 500
Washington, DC 20005
(202) 789-1011

National Association of Legal Support for Alternative Schools
P.O. Box 2823
Santa Fe, NM 87501

National Association of Pro America
Rt. 1 Box 156
Craig, NE 68019
Tyrone E. Grothe, Director

National Association of Pro America
2101 Connecticut Ave., N.W.
Washington, DC 20008
Joan L. Hueter, Director

National Association to Keep and Bear Arms
P.O. Box 78336
Seattle, WA 98178

National Captive Nations Committee
P.O. Box 1171
Washington, DC 20013
Lev Dobriansky, Director

National Center for Fathering
10200 W 75th St., Suite 267
Shawnee Mission, KS 66204-2223

National Center for the Study of History
RR 1, Box 679
Cornish, ME 04020
Robert Pomeroy, III, Director
(207) 637-2873

National Center on Education and the Economy
39 State St., Suite 500
Rochester, NY 14614
Marc Tucker, President
(716) 546-7620, fax (716) 546-3145

National Christian Association
P.O. Box 40945
Washington, DC 20016

National Coalition Against Pornography
800 Compton Rd., Suite 9224
Cincinnati, OH 45231
Dr. Jerry Kirk, President
(513) 521-6227

National Coalition of IRS Whistleblowers
P.O. Box 4283
Pocatello, ID 83201
Paul J. DesFosses, Director

National Coalition of Patriotic Americans
426 N. Ellsworth
Salem, OH 44460
Frank A. Fiebiger, Director

National Coalition to Legalize Freedom
P.O. Box 92260
Santa Barb, CA 93190

National Committee for a Human Life Amendment
1511 K St., N.W., Suite 335
Washington, DC 20005
Michael Taylor, Executive Director
(202) 393-0703

National Committee to Restore Internal Security
P.O. Box 234
Mantoloking, NJ 08738

National Confederation of Ethnic Groups
728 Ridge St.
Newark, NJ 07104

National Conservative Foundation
618 Alfred St.
Alexandria, VA 22314

National Coordinating Council for Constructive Action
P.O. Box 12340
Reno, NV 89510

National Council for Adoption
1930 17th St., N.W.
Washington, DC 20009
Mary Beth Style, Vice President
(202) 328-1200, fax (202) 332-0935

National Council of Sons and Daughters of Liberty
420 Stokes Mill Rd.
Stroudsburg, PA 18360

National Council to Support the Democracy Movements
101 E. 52nd St., 12th Floor
New York, NY 10022

National Criminal Justice Association
444 N. Capital Hill St., N.W., Suite 618
Washington, DC 20001
Barbara McDonald, President
(202) 347-4900

National Determination Party
P.O. Box 5100
Charleston, WV 25361

National Educator, The
1110 S. Pomona Ave.
P.O. Box 333
Fullerton, CA 92632
James H. Townmail, Publisher

National Federation of Cuban-American Republican Women
2119 S. Webster St.
Ft. Wayne, IN 46802
Dr. Graciela Beecher, Director

National Federation of Independent Business
600 Maryland Ave., S.W., Suite 695-700
Washington, DC 20024
Jack Faris, President
(202) 554-9000

National Foundation for Educational Choice
P.O. Box 781025
San Antonio, TX 78278
Patsy O'Neill, Executive Director
(210) 408-7890

National Gun Owners Association
2309 Cipriani Blvd
Belmont, CA 94002

National Health Federation
P.O. Box 688
Monrovia, CA 91016

National Institute for Traditional Black Leadership
7612 Sheffield Green Way
Lorton, VA 22079
Phyllis Berry Myers, Director
(703) 339-9809

National Institute of Family and Life Advocates
P.O. Box 42060
Fredericksburg, VA 22404

National Law Center for Children and Families
3975 University Dr., Suite 320
Fairfax, VA 22030

National Life Center
686 North Broad St.
Woodbury, NJ 08096
Denise F. Cocciolone, President
(609) 848-1819

National Methodist Restoration
P.O. Box 3
Waynesboro, GA 30830

National Pro-Family Coalition
717 2nd St., N.E.
Washington, DC 20002
Eric Lich, Director

National Tax Research Committee
1000 Louisiana, Suite 3600
Houston, TX 77002

National Teens for Life
419 7th St., N.W., Suite 402
Washington, DC 20004
(202) 626-8800

National Traditionalist Caucus
P.O. Box 971
New York, NY 10116
Don Rosenberg, Director

National Victim Center
307 W. 7th St., Suite 1001
Fort Worth, TX 76102
Anne Seymour, Director

National Writers Network
P.O. Box 1197
Thousand Oaks, CA 91358
Mimi Jaffe, Founder

Naturist Society
P.O. Box 132
Oshkosh, WI 54902

Network for Citizen Enlightment
P.O. Box 1475
Clackamas, OR 97015

Nevada Posse Association
P.O. Box 2760
Reno, NV 89505
Sam Margolies, Director
(702) 826-6277

New Banner Institute
P.O. Box 711
Columbia, SC 29202

New Beginnings
P.O. Box 228
Waynesville, NC 28786

New Coalition for Economics and Social Change
300 South Wacker Dr., Suite 601
Chicago, IL 60606
Lee Walker, President
(312) 427-1290, fax (312) 427-1291

New Exodus
911 S.W. 1st Ave.
Miami, FL 33130

New Forces
8816 Manchester Rd., Suite 167
St. Louis, MO 63144

New Jersey Constitutionality
70 Island Rd.
Mahwah, NJ 07430

New Life Treatment
570 Glenneyre Ave., Suite 10
Laguna Beach, CA 92651
(800) 227-LIFE

New Mexico Foundation for Economic Research
P.O. Box 1216
Albuquerque, NM 87103
(505) 243-5400

New York Citizens for a Sound Economy
110 Beachview Ave., Suite 226
Bridgeport, CT 06605

Nicaraguan Information Center
P.O. Box 607
St. Charles, MO 63302

NOMOS
9857 S. Damen Ave.
Chicago, IL 60643

None of the Above Committee
P.O. Box 61212
Pasadena, CA 91106

North Carolina Citizens for Business and Industry
P.O. Box 2508
Raleigh, NC 27602

North Carolina Congress
P.O. Box 18848
Raleigh, NC 27619

North Carolina Council on Economic Education
P.O. Box 5086
Greensboro, NC 27403

North Star Mission
1414 S. Independence Blvd.
Chicago, IL 60623

North-South Institute
1015 S. Gaylord St., Suite 174
Denver, CO 80209

Northeastern Ohio Roundtable
31005 Solon Rd.
Solon, OH 44139
David Zanotti, President
(216) 349-3393, fax (216) 349-0154

Northern Virginia Victory Committee
P.O. Box 404
Merrifield, VA 22116

Northpoint Team
Rt. 1, Box 246
Andrews, NC 28901

Northwest Regional Report
533 E. Curling Dr.
Boise, ID 83702

Notes from the Underground
4291 Van Dyke Place
San Diego, CA 92116

Novis M. Shmitz Foundation
3700 N. 24st St.
Phoenix, AZ 85016

Novus Ordo Research Foundation
P.O. Box 382
Carson City, NV 89702
Mark Williams, D.M.A., Research Director
(702) 884-3566

Objectivism
P.O. Box 177
New York, NY 10016

Objectivists 'R' Us
12301 Hardy St.
Overland Park, KS 66213
Tom McKiernan, Director
(913) 338-5131

Ohana Policy Center
P.O. Box 1544
Kaneohe, HI 96744
Rebbecca Walker, Executive Director
(808) 247-8476, fax (808) 247-8836

Oklahoma Citizens for a Sound Economy
P.O. Box 2181
Edmon, OK 73034
Larry Stein, Director
(405) 330-4002

Oklahoma Conservative
P.O. Box 950
Norman, OK 73070
E. Z. Million

Oklahoma Free Enterprise Institute
2709 N.W. 39th St.
Oklahoma City, OK 73112
Judy Swafford, Director

One Nation Under God
640 Kempsville Rd.
Virginia Beach, VA 23464

Operation Enterprise
P.O. Box 88
Hamilton, NY 13346

Order of the Cross Society
P.O. Box 7638
Ft. Lauderdale, FL 33338
Rev. K. Chandler, Director

Oregonians to Limit Congressional Terms
2971 East Devil's Lake Dr., N.E.
Otis, OR 97368

Organization for Free Poland
3 E. 15th St.
New York, NY 10036

Organization for the Defense of Ukraine
P.O. Box 304
New York, NY 10003

Organization to Defend Human Rights in the Ukraine
P.O. Box 561
Ellicot City, MD 21043

Other Side
P.O. Box 632
Big Bar, CA 96010

Outrider Newsletter
P.O. Box 810
Hildale, UT 84784

Overcomers
5445 N. Clark
Chicago, IL 60640
(312) 334-5159

P.A.R.E.N.T.S.
6706 3rd Ave.
Kenosha, WI 53140

P.E.N.C.I.L.
314 Bryn Mawr Ave.
Bryn Mawr, PA 19010

Pacific Insitute
P.O. Box 33111
San Diego, CA 92103

Pacific Islands Washington Office
1615 New Hampshire Ave., N.W., Suite 400
Washington, DC 20009

Paralegal Patriots
P.O. Box 60184
Sacramento, CA 95860

Parenting for Christ Centered Families
1902 Coleman Lane
Fredericksburg, VA 22407

Parents Advocating Choice In Education
P.O. Box 154
Chandler, AZ 85244

Parents and Students United
P.O. Box 331178
Pacoima, CA 91331
Eadie Gieb, President
(818) 362-3273

Parents Involved in Education (PIE)
1912 Indian Hills Rd.
Hartsell, AL 35640

Parents' Alliance to Protect Our Children
44 E. Tacoma Ave.
Latrobe, PA 15650
Dr. Naomi King, Director

Patriot Review
P.O. Box 314
Clackamas, OR 97015

Patriotic Order of Sons of America
P.O. Box 1847
Valley Forge, PA 19481

Patriotic Pubs Review
222 Cedar
Perryville, MO 63775

Penn Kemble Foundation for Democratic Education
3425 O St., N.W.
Washington, DC 20007
Dr. Gay Johnson, Director

Pennsylvania Constitutional Rights Protection Association
P.O. Box 85
Georgetown, PA 15043

Pennsylvania Parents Commission
182 Gilbert St.
Johnstown, PA 15906

People's Advocate
3385 Arden Way
Sacramento, CA 98525
Paul Gann, Founder
(916) 482-6175

Pernicious Trash
12743 Ross Rd.
St. Louis, MO 63127

Philosophers Guild
P.O. Box 3092
Orange, CA 92665

Physicians for Life
P.O. Box 19173
Birmingham, AL 35219
Sue Turner, Director

Pilgrim Institute
52549 Gumwood Rd
Granger, IN 46530

Pink Sheet
P.O. Box 467939
Atlanta, GA 30346-7939
W. W. Wood, Publisher

Pittsburgh Leadership Foundation
100 Ross St.
Pittsburgh, PA 15219

Pittsburgh Nightmare Legal Defense Fund
2875 Cherry St., Dept. CA-43
Pittsburgh, PA 15102
(412) 833-9101

Placer Gold
P.O. Box 165
Loomis, CA 95650

Point Man Ministries
P.O. Box 440
Mountlake Terrace, WA 98043

Politically Incorrect Apparel
P.O. Box 20441
Riverside, CA 92516
(800) 707-4448

Populist Party
P.O. Box 550
Whippany, NJ 07981
Don Wassall, Chairman

Post Eagle
P.O. Box 2127
Clifton, NJ 07015

Post-Modernity Project
University of Virginia
B5 Garret Hall
Charlottesville, VA 22903
Dr. James Davison Hunter

Potomac
502 Garwood Ave.
Mt. Prospect, IL 60056

Presbyterian Lay Committee
1489 Baltimore Pk., Suite 301
Springfield, PA 19064

Preserving the Nation
4875 Hartnett Ave.
Richmond, CA 94804

Prisoner Bulletin
P.O. Box 1188
Elkhart, IN 46515

Private Enterprise Market System Program
Allegheny Intermediate Unit
200 Commerce Court Building
Pittsburgh, PA 15219

Pro Life / Pro Family Media Coalition
P.O. Box 1028
Pasadena, CA 91102
Gina Becker, Director
(818) 449-4834

Pro Se B.B.S.
P.O. Box 2192
Kearney, NE 68848

Pro-America Newsletter
1305 Bennet Dr.
Pasadena, CA 91103

Pro-Family Christian Coalition
P.O. Box 656
Sparks, NV 89431

Pro-Family Coalition
P.O. Box 1633
Hunt Beach, CA 92647

Pro-Family Press Association
9400 Fairview Ave.
Manassas, VA 22110

Pro-Life Office
P.O. Box 19173
Birmingham, AL 35219

Pro-Life Taxpayers Association
P.O. Box 1057
Morton Grove, IL 60053
Lyn Mangan, Director

Probe Ministries
1900 Firman Dr., Suite 100
Richardson, TX 75081
(214) 480-0240

Prohibition National Committee
P.O. Box 2635
Denver, CO 80201

Project Research
P.O. Box 187
College Place, WA 99324

Project Respect
1850 E. Ridgewood
Glenview, IL 60025
Kathleen Sullivan, Director

Promise Keepers
P.O. Box 18376
Boulder, CO 80308
(303) 421-2800

Property Owners Protection League
P.O. Box 902
Valley Cent., CA 92082

Protect America's Children
5266 Citizens Parkway
Selma, AL 36701

Protect Oregon Property Society
23500 S.E. Stark St.
Gresham, OR 97030

Public Affairs Council
1019 19th St., N.W.
Washington, DC 20036
(202) 835-8343

Public Affairs Research Institute of New Jersey
212 Carnegie Center, Suite 100
Princeton, NJ 08540
Donald Linky, President
(609) 452-0220, fax (609) 452-1788

Public Information Systems
P.O. Box 1014
Columbia Station, OH 44028

Public Lands Council (PLC)
1301 Pennsylvania Ave., N.W., Suite 300
Washington, DC 20004
Pamela Neal, President

Public Policy Education Fund
P.O. Box 123
Grove City, PA 16127

Puebla Institute
1319 18th St., N.W., 2nd Floor
Washington, DC 20036
Nina Shea, President
(202) 296-8050, fax (202) 296-5078

Puff - It!
Route 1, Box 43
Stanton, TX 79782

Radio Association Defending Airwave Rights
4949 S 25A
Tripp City, OH 45371

RAMA
P.O. Box 793
Carthage, MO 64836

Rational Focus
P.O. Box 9191
Akron, OH 44305

REACH
P.O. Box 1283
Harrisburg, PA 17108-1283

Reality Magazine
6822 N. 22nd Ave., Suite 414
St. Petersburg, FL 33710

Reasons to Believe
P.O. Box 5978
Pasadena, CA 91117
Hugh Ross, President
(818) 335-1480

Reconstruction Press
P.O. Box 7999
Tyler, TX 75711

Redeem Our Country
1110 S. Pomona Ave.
Fullerton, CA 92632

Refugee Relief International
1105 Balmora Dr.
Lafayette, CO 80026

Remnant
2539 Morrison Ave.
St. Paul, MN 55117

Report
42640 N. 10th St., W.
Landcaster, CA 93534
(805) 940-700

Republic Research
701 Sturm Ave.
New Haven, IN 46774

Republic Research
P.O. Box 156
Johnson, KS 67855

Restoration News Service
19 Churchill Dr.
New Hyde Park, NY 11040

Rethinking AIDS
2040 Polk St., Suite 321
San Francisco, CA 94109

Return Americas Prosperity
P.O. Box 1124
Bedford, TX 76021

Revolutionary Rationalists
P.O. Box 6492
Glendale, CA 91205

Right Mind
P.O. Box 2047
Carmichael, CA 95609
Mike Antonucci, Editor

Right Perspective
28 Grove St.
Salinas, CA 93901

Roger Sherman Society
P.O. Box 3116
Grass Valley, CA 95945

Roger Williams Review
4344 Bryant St.
Denver, CO 80211

Rosalind Kress Haley Library
5424 16th St.
Lubbock, TX 79416

Roscoe Report
100 Union St.
Ervin, TN 37560

Rothenberg Political Report
717 2nd St., N.E.
Washington, DC 20002

Roundtable Issues and Answers
11916 Lilita Lane
Clifton, VA 22024

Rutherford Institute of Alabama
2100 Southbridge Pkwy., Suite 376
Birmingham, AL 35209

S.R.C.E.
P.O. Box 1772
Santa Rosa, CA 95402

Saint Gerard Foundation
3041 Braeloch Circle East
Clearwater, FL 34621

Salon: Journal of Aesthetics
305 W. Magnolia, Suite 386
Fort Collins, CO 80521

Samizdat
700 New Hampshire, N.W., Suite 701
Washington, DC 20037

San Gabriel Valley Gun Owners Coalition
P.O. Box 1848
Monterey Park, CA 91754
Joel Friedman, Director
(818) 795-3701

Sangre de Cristo Newsnote
P.O. Box 89
Westcliffe, CO 81252

Sarmation Review
P.O. Box 79119
Houston, TX 77279

Save Our State
P.O. Box 3121
Tustin, CA 92681

Save Our Supplements
P.O. Box 26288
Santa Ana, CA 92799

Savers and Investors League
14200 S. Centerville Square, Suite 175
Centerville, VA 22020

Savers and Investors League
72 N. Valley Rd., RD3
Malvern, PA 19355

Saxon Foundation
P.O. Box 950
Oswego, IL 60543

School of Common Law
P.O. Box 297
Isabella, MO 65767

Schumacher Society
Box 76, RFD 3
Great Barrington, MA 01230

Scientists and Engineers for Secure Energy
570 7th Ave., Suite 1007
New York, NY 10018
Miro Todorovich, Executive Director
(212) 840-6595, fax (212) 840-6597

Second Amendment Action
1524 Goettens Way
St. Cloud, MN 56301
Neal Knox, Chairman

Second Chance
P.O. Box 578
Central Lake, MI 49622

Self Reliant Living
P.O. Box 467939
Atlanta, GA 30346-7939
Carl Krupp, Publisher
(800) 728-2288

Selous Foundation
325 Pennsylvania Ave., S.E.
Washington, DC 20003
Marx Lewis, Director

Separation of School and State Alliance
4578 N. 1st St., Suite 310
Fresno, CA 93726
Marshall Fritz, Founder
(888) 338-1776

Sessions Book Sales
P.O. Box 9593
Birmingham, AL 35220

Sex, Love and Choices
1028 N. Lake Ave., Suite 102
Pasadena, CA 91104
Wendi Lehman, Director
(818) 398-6106

Shield of Roses
P.O. Box 9053
Glendale, CA 91226-0053
(818) 242-3912

Signal Books
P.O. Box 940
Carrboro, NC 27510

Silver Fox
P.O. Box 2192
Pasco, WA 99302

Silver Standard Committee
Route 1, Box 29-B
Johnson City, TX 78636

Slick Times
P.O. Box 1710
Valley Center, CA 92082

Slick Willie Wire
12437 Seal Beach Blvd., Suite 121
Seal Beach, CA 90740

Slovak League of America
870 Rifle Camp Rd.
West Patterson, NJ 07424

Society Against Government Abuse
P.O. Box 81034
Wellesley, MA 02181

Society of Vietnamese
P.O. Box 29965
Atlanta, GA 30359

Soldiers of Christ
P.O. Box 100
Kenosha, WI 53141

Sons and Daughters of the South
P.O. Box 94
Eclectic, AL 36024

Sons of Confederate Veterans
9441 River Rd.
Petersburg, VA 23803
(800) 359-9000

Sons of Liberty
P.O. Box 503
Brisbane, CA 94005
Joseph W. Kerska, Director

Sound of Fife
1200 Hamilton Ave.
Palo Alto, CA 94301

South Carolinians to Limit Congressional Terms
616 Harbor Circle Place
Charleston, SC 29412

South Florida Objectivists
12995 S.W. 75th Ave.
Miami, FL 33156
Calixto Lopez, Director

South Foundation
P.O. Box 7121
Knoxville, TN 37931

South Louisiana Citizens Council
P.O. Box 9448
Metairie, LA 70055
Jackson G. Ricau, Director

Southern Partisan, The
P.O. Box 11708
Columbia, SC 29211
Richard M. Quinn, Editor

Southern Political Report
P.O. Box 15507
Washington, DC 20003

Southie News
410 W. 4th St.
South Boston, MA 02127

Sovereignty
P.O. Box 782
Freeport, IL 61032

Sparticans
P.O. Box 696
Lead, SD 57754

Spatula Ministries
P.O. Box 444
La Habra, CA 90631

Stand Up For Your Rights
P.O. Box 41138
Providence, RI 02940-1138
Dan Edmonds, Director

Statewide Committee Opposing Regulation
3306 Mannington
Cincinnati, OH 45226

Stop Forced Busing
P.O. Box 133
South Boston, MA 02127
Charlie Ross, Director

Stop Planned Parenthood (STOPP)
P.O. Box 8
La Grangeville, NY 12540
Jim Sedlak, Director

Stop the Tax!
P.O. Drawer L
Winston-Salem, NC 27108

Stormont Center for Original American Values
P.O. Box 13
Urbanna, VA 23175
(804) 758-4663

STRAPPED!
P.O. Box 2371
Grand Island, NE 68802

Strategy Letter
P.O. Box 4130
Medford, OR 97501

Strider Commentary
P.O. Box 554
Laytonville, CA 95454

Student Attorney Firearm Enthusiasts
1121 Prospect St.
Westfield, NJ 07090

SunStar Press
P.O. Box 342
Kalamazoo, MI 49005
Dr. Mary Ruwart

Support Centers of America
2001 O St., N.W.
Washington, DC 20036
Randy Bryant, Director
(202) 296-3900

Support Our POW-MIAs
6811 Santa Rita Ave.
Garden Grove, CA 92645

Survival in 20th Century
2020 Pennsylvania Ave., S.W., Suite 210
Washington, DC 20006

Survive Magazine
5735 Arapaho Ave.
Boulder, CO 80303

Sword & Spirit Ministries
P.O. Box 1466
Chino, CA 91710
Mark Ritter, Director
(909) 947-3136

Sword Enterprises
5010 Gosnold Ave.
Norfolk, VA 23508

T.A.T.
400 W. 15th, Suite 400
Austin, TX 78701

Tax Action
P.O. Box 13
Placerville, CA 95667

Tax Rebellion Committee of Ohio
1921 W. Washington
Springfield, OH 45506

Tax Reform Action Coalition
1725 K St., N.W., Suite 710
Washington, DC 20006
Dirk Van Dongen, Director

Tax Reformers United Endeavor
P.O. Box 424
Altadena, CA 91001

Tax Revolt Association
276 Trenton Ave.
Patterson, NJ 07503

Tax Strike
2211 Afton Way
Colorado Springs, CO 80909

Taxpayers Action Fund
325 Pennsylvania Ave.
Washington, DC 20003

Taxpayers Action Network
10461 Margarita
Fountain Valley, CA 92728
Richard Avard, Director
(714) 775-6090

Taxpayers Advocate
P.O. Box 4283
Pocatello, ID 83201

Taxpayers Education Lobby
11166 Main St., Suite 302
Fairfax, VA 22030

Taxpayers Network
262 N248 Washington Ave., Suite 201
Cedarburg, WI 53012

Taxpayers United for Michigan
29610 Southfield
Southfield, MI 48076

Taxpayers' Committee
133 North Carolina Ave., S.E.
Washington, DC 20003
Floyd K. Haskell, Director

TEACH America
550 Sheridan Square, Apt. 3B
Evanston, IL 60202

Tennessee Council on Economic Education
Cordell Hall Building, Room C3-301
Nashville, TN 37219

Term Limits Legal Institute
900 Second St., N.E., Suite 200A
Washington, DC 20002
Cleta Deatheridge Mitchell, President
(202) 371-0450, fax (202) 371-0210

Texas Bureau for Economic Understanding
1139 Parkway Central Building
611 Ryan Plaza Dr.
Arlington, TX 76011

Texas Citizens for a Sound Economy
P.O. Box 2165
Austin, TX 78768-2165
Peggy Venable, Director
(512) 476-5905, fax (512) 476-5906

Texas Review Society
P.O. Box 8440
Austin, TX 78713

Third Continental Congress
201 Columbia Bldg.
Tulsa, OK 74114
George Washington, Director

Thoburn Press
P.O. Box 6941
Tyler, TX 75711

Thomas J. White Foundation
One Gateway Ctr.
Newton, MA 02158

Thomas Jefferson Equal Tax Society
1469 Spring Vale Ave.
McLean, VA 22101

Thomas Jefferson Institute
P.O. Box 2934
Laguna Hills, CA 92654

Three Strikes and You're Out Committee
P.O. Box 277940
Sacramento, CA 95827-7940
Mike Reynolds, Founder
(209) 221-0288

Tidbits
P.O. Box 268
Cuyahoga Falls, OH 44222

Tocqueville Foundation
515 Madison Ave., 40th Floor
New York, NY 10022

Today and Tomorrow
P.O. Box 1281
Orangevale, CA 90405

Today's Family Magazine
Route 2, Box 656
Grottoes, VA 24441
(703) 249-4368

Tolerant Majority
P.O. Box 92260
Santa Barbara, CA 93190

Toward Utility Rate Normalization
625 Polk St., Suite 403
San Francisco, CA 94102
Sylvia M. Siegel, President

Traditional Values Coalition
139 C St., S.E.
Washington, DC 20003
Andrea Sheldon, Director
(202) 547-8570, fax (202) 546-6403

Triangle Conservative Alliance
1004 West Markham Ave.
Durham, NC 27701

Truth in Taxation
11012 Ventura Blvd., Suite 239
Studio City, CA 91604

Turkestanian American Association
2302 W. 13th St.
Brooklyn, NY 11223

Turn the Hearts America
P.O. Box 487
Cedar Glen, CA 92321
Pastor Tom Cizmar, Director
(909) 336-1952

Twentieth Century Reform
801 Haddon Ave.
Collingswood, NJ 08108

Twin Circle Publishing Co.
86 Riverside Dr.
New York, NY 10024

U.S. - Baltic Foundation
1211 Connecticut Ave., N.W., Suite 506
Washington, DC 20036
Linas J. Kojelis, President
(202) 986-0380, fax (202) 234-8130

U.S. Constitutional Rights Legal Defense Fund
3360 E. Terrell Branch Court
Marietta, GA 30067
Baker Smith, Secretary/Treasurer
(404) 980-0921, fax (404) 955-0841

Ukrainian American Association
P.O. Box 20462
St. Petersburg, FL 33742

Ukrainian Congress Committee of America
203 Second Ave.
New York, NY 10003
Ignatius M. Billinsky, Director

Ukrainian Liberation Front
136 Second Ave.
New York, NY 10003

Ukrainian National Association
30 Montgomery St.
Jersey City, NJ 07302

Ukrainian National Information Service
214 Massachusetts Ave., N.E., Suite 225
Washington, DC 20002
Irena Chelupa, Director

Ukrainian Political Science Association in the United States
P.O. Box 12963
Philadelphia, PA 19108
Petro Diachenko, Director

Underground Conservative
P.O. Box 104
Sandy Spring, MD 20860

United Conservatives of Indiana
4530 Wycombe Lane
Indianapolis, IN 46204

United Libertarian Fellows
1220 Larnel Place
Los Altos, CA 94022

United Mining Councils
202 E. Airport Dr., Suite 120
San Bernardino, CA 92408

United Neighbors of America
3612 S. Stevens Ave.
Minneapolis, MN 55409

United Sovereigns of America
8827 Ogden Ave., Suite 132
Brookfield, IL 60513

United States Coalition for Life
P.O. Box 315
Export, PA 15632

United States Council for Energy Awareness
1776 I St. N.W.
Washington, DC 20006
Phillip Bayne, President

United States Council for International Business
1212 Avenue of the Americas
New York, NY 10036

United States Day Committee
P.O. Box 35
Necedah, WI 54646

United States Defense Committee
3238 Wynford Dr.
Fairfax, VA 22031
Henry Walther, President

United States Institute of Peace
1550 M St., N.W., Suite 700
Washington, DC 20005

University Bookman
Piety Hill
Mecosta, MI 49332

Urban Family
P.O. Box 32
Jackson, MS 39205
(601) 354-1563

Utah Association of Women
5141 Clover Meadow
Murray, UT 84123

Veritas
P.O. Box 10041
Silver Spring, MD 20914
Adam H. Kalish, Publisher

Veritas Institute for Public Policy Research
3317 N. Charles
Wichitaw, KS 67204
Timothy J. Hurley, President
(316) 838-5637

Veterans Coalition for Life
P.O. Box 7232
San Buenaventure, CA 93006

Veterans for an Honorable Commander-in-Chief
757 N. Fort Ebey
Coupeville, WA 98239

Virginia Citizens for a Sound Economy
P.O. Box 7551
Charlottesville, VA 22906
Lethia Fisher, Director
(703) 863-8612, fax (703) 863-8614

Virginians for Conservative Government
P.O. Box 662
Richmond, VA 23219

Virginians for Family Values
10644 Gunston Rd.
Lorton, VA 22079

Vision
La Revista Latinoamericana
310 Madison Ave., Suite 1412
New York, NY 10017

Voice of Americanism
P.O. Box 90
Glendale, CA 91200

Voice of Citizens Together
13601 Ventura Blvd., Suite 163
Sherman Oaks, CA 91423
Glenn Spencer, Chairman
(818) 501-2061

Voice of Conservative Feminism
P.O. Box 371
Palo Alto, CA 94301

Voice of Cuban Christians
P.O. Box 2181
Montclair, CA 91763

Voice of Freedom
625 N. Grand
Santa Ana, CA 92701

Walter Williams Boosters
P.O. Box 361
Cool, CA 95614

Wanderer Forum Foundation
3505 Owens St.
Wheat Ridge, CO 80033
Dr. Frank Morriss, Director
(303) 421-1246

Washington Dateline
P.O. Box 5687
Baltimore, MD 21210

Washington Development Capital Corporation
888 17th St., N.W., 12th Floor
Washington, DC 20006

Washington Institute
1015 18th St., N.W. Suite 300
Washington, DC 20036
(202) 293-7440

Washington International Studies Center
901 6th St., S.W., Suite 713A
Washington, DC 20024
Dr. Robert Schuettinger, Director

Washington Observer
9433 Forest Haven Dr.
Alexandria, VA 22309

Washington Report
P.O. Box 10309
St. Petersburg, FL 33733

Washington's Vision
Route 2, Box 179-G
Eclectic, AL 36024

Watch
P.O. Box 5
Harmans, MD 21077

Way International
P.O. Box 328
New Knoxville, OH 45871

Wayfarer Press
P.O. Box 2187
Rolling Hills Estates, CA 90274

Wayfield Report
P.O. Box 699
Vineyard Haven, MA 02568

We Are AWARE
P.O. Box 242
Bedford, MA 01730

We, The People
P.O. Box 609
Huntsville, AL 35804

We, The People, A.C.T.
32930 Franklin St.
Wayne, MI 48184

We The People, United
P.O. Box A
Scottsdale, AZ 85252
Harry Everingham, Director

West Virginia Family Council
P.O. Box 443
Scott Depot, WV 25560
Alice Hunt, Director
(304) 562-9472, fax (304) 562-0899

West Virginians for Religious Freedom
P.O. Box 7504
Charleston, WV 25356

Western Regulatory Digest
P.O. Box 20694
Billings, MT 59104
Chris Cull, Director

Westside Libertarian
2739 Westgate Ave.
Los Angeles, CA 90034

White Hat Underground
Box 4191
Utica, NY 13504

Wilderness Impact Research Foundation
491 4th St.
Elko, NV 89801
A. Grant Gerber, Chairman
(702) 738-2009

Wilhelm Roepke Institute
P.O. Box 93
Clarksville, MD 21029

Wilmington Institute
10th and Market Sts.
Wilmington, DE 19801

Wind River Multiple Use Advocates
P.O. Box 1126
Riverton, WY 82501

Wisconsin Forum
235 N. Executive Dr., Suite 100
Brookfield, WI 53005

Wisconsin Legislative and Research Committee
P.O. Box 45
Brookfield, WI 53005

Women for Independent Thought
P.O. Box 585
Alexandria, VA 22313

Women's Association for the Defense of Four Freedoms for
Ukraine
136 Second Ave.
New York, NY 10003
Dasha Procyk, Director

Women's Lobby
P.O. Box 961
Fair Oaks, CA 95628
Barbara Alby, Director

Womens Committee for Responsible Government
3615 E. Laurel Creek Dr.
San Mateo, CA 94403

World Association of Estonians
243 E. 34th St.
New York, NY 10016

World Economic Review
P.O. Box 507
Chalmette, LA 70044

World Federation of Free Latvians
400 Hurley Ave.
P.O. Box 4016
Rockville, MD 20850
Linard Lukss, Director

World Federation of Hungarian Freedom Fighters
201 Raymond Ave.
South Orange, NJ 07079

World Federation of the Cossack Liberation Movement of
Cossackia
21 S. Western Hwy.
Blauvelt, NY 10913
Maj. Gen. Nicholas G. Nazarenko, Director

World Freedom Information Network
1421 Grand Ave., Suite 137
Grover Beach, CA 93433

World Organization for the Family
2020 Pennsylvania Ave., N.W., Suite 274
Washington, DC 20006
Anne Higgins, Director
(202) 298-6899

World Research Library
P.O. Box 582
Scottsdale, AZ 85251

World Technology Foundation
1501 Trombone Ct.
Vienna, VA 22180
Dr. James Arnold Miller, Director

Yankee Ruminator
P.O. Box 2065
Port Washington, NY 11050

Yellow Dog Political Fund
12837 N.E. Portland Rd.
Gervais, OR 97026

Yorktown Eagle
P.O. Box 70446
Salt Lake City, UT 84170

You've a Right to Know
P.O. Drawer E
St. Francisville, LA 70775

NO FORWARDING ADDRESS

The organizations listed in this section were identified as active in the conservative movement. However, mail sent to their last known address was returned, marked as "No Forwarding Address." We suspect that some of these organizations are no longer in existence, some reorganized under different names, and others moved but their forwarding order expired or their new address is not available. We have listed their last known address and, when available, a contact person. One use of this section is to update correspondence and referral files. If users of The Right Guide can provide valid addresses or the status of these organizations, we would be pleased to contact them for the next edition.

About My Father's Business
173 Woodland Ave.
Lexington, NY 40502

Academic Freedom Coalition
48 Elm St., Suite 6
Stoneham, MA 01880

Accuracy in Textbooks
3411 W. Gadsten St.
Pensacola, FL 32505

ACTS
1025 E. Clayton Rd.
Ballwin, MO 63011

Adam Smith Foundation
P.O. Box 470210
Tulsa, OK 74145

Advanced International Studies Institute
P.O. Box 15705
Fort Wayne, IN 46885

Agricultural Watchdog
P.O. Box 967
Hereford, TX 79045

Agriculture Education Foundation
111 G St., Suite 31
Davis, CA 95616

Alabama Liberty
P.O. Box 11514
Birmingham, AL 35202

Alabama Nurses for Life
P.O. Box 20984
Birmingham, AL 35216
Sarah Barbor, Director

Albanian Kosovar Youth in the Free World
439 W. 46th St.
New York, NY 10036
Maliq Arigaj, Director

Alliance for Environment and Resources (AER)
1311 I St., Suite 100
Sacramento, CA 95814
Kathy L. Kvarda, Director

Alternative Voice
P.O. Box 22
Beaver, PA 15009

Amagin
P.O. Box 10
Erie, PA 16514

America First Club
910 Henry St.
Anderson, IN 46001

America, Wake Up!
840 Bear Creek Trail
Victor, MN 59875

America's Manifest Destiny
2922 164th St.
Flushing, NY 11358

American Advisor
P.O. Box 1086
Salpulpa, OK 74066

American Agriculture News
P.O. Box 100
Iredell, TX 76649

American Anti-Terrorism Institute
910 17th St., N.W., Suite 320
Washington, DC 20006
Marion H. Smoak, Director

American Bureau of Economic Research
PO Box 8595
Tyler, TX 75711

American Catholic Committee
127 East 35th St.
New York, NY 10016
James J. McFadden, Director

American Citizens Militia
P.O. Box 200115
Denver, CO 80220

American Citizens To Inform Our Nation
P.O. Box 1656
Hemet, CA 92546
Alana Bell, Secretary

American Citizenship Center
Route 1, Box 141
Oklahoma City, OK 73111

American Citizenship Education Program
P.O. Box 954
Searcy, AR 72143

American Coalition for Traditional Values
5801 16th St., N.W.
Washington, DC 20011
Rev. Tim LaHaye, Director

American Constitutional and Civil Rights University
18055 S.W. Jay St.
Aloha, OR 97006

American Constitutional Law Foundation
601 S. Broadway, Suite U
Denver, CO 80209

American Council for Coordinated Action
1010 Vermont Ave., N.W., Suite 1017
Washington, DC 20005

American Council on Free Asia
214 Massachusetts Ave., N.E., Suite 120
Washington, DC 20003

American Defense Committee
325 Pennsylvania Ave., S.E.
Washington, DC 20003

American Defense Prepared Association
1700 N. Moore St.
Arlington, VA 22209

American Education Coalition
721 2nd St., N.E.
Washington, DC 20002

American Enterprise Teaching Notes
708 3rd Ave.
New York, NY 10017

American Entrepenuers Association
2311 Pontius Ave.
Los Angeles, CA 90064

American Family Corporation
1300 19th St., N.W., Suite 402
Washington, DC 20036

American Federation of Small Business
18200 Sherman St.
Lansing, IL 60438

American Foreign Policy Council
1023 Springvale Rd.
Great Falls, VA 22066

American Free Enterprise Productions
1 E. 42nd St.
New York, NY 10017

American Informants Network
2521 N. Grand Ave., Suite 780
Santa Ana, CA 92701

American Information Network
2521-F N. Grand Ave., Suite 780
Santa Ana, CA 92701
R. E. Forest, Director

American Institute for the Republic
5480 Katella Ave., Suite 203
Los Alamitos, CA 90720

American Institute of Cooperation
1800 Massachusetts Ave., N.W.
Washington, DC 20036

American Jewish League Against Communism
39 E. 68th St.
New York, NY 10021

American Libertarian
21715 Park Brook Dr.
Katy, TX 77450

American Liberty Association
13773 N. Central Expressway, Suite 1653
Dallas, TX 75243

American Media Network
499 S. Capitol St.
Washington, DC 20070

American Mercury
P.O. Box 1306
Torrance, CA 90505
Robert Kuttner, Director

American Patriot
2422 E. Indian School Rd.
Phoenix, AZ 85016

American Patriot News
P.O. Box 3868
Prescott, AZ 86302

American Productivity Center
1700 West Loop, South
Houston, TX 77027

American Renaissance School
468 Rosedale Ave.
White Plains, NY 10605

American Renewal Foundation
P.O. Box 835110
Richardson, TX 75083

American Space Frontier Council
4300 Evergreen Ln., Suite 205
Annandale VA 22003

American Way Ministries
3990 Stonewall Tell Rd.
College Park, GA 30349

Americans for a Conservative Congress
11 S. Meridian, Suite 815
Indianapolis, IN 46204

Americans for Competitive Enterprise System
1801 N. Front St.
Harrison, PA 17102

Americans for Constitutional Action
955 L'Enfant Plaza North, S.W.
Washington, DC 20024

Americans for Decency
P.O. Box 218
Staten Island, NY 10302
Paul J. Gangemi, Director

Americans for Freedom
P.O. Box 10524
McLean, VA 22102
Karen McKay, President

Americans for Generational Equity
605 Massachusetts Ave, N.E.
Washington, DC 20002
J.J. Wuerthner, Director

Americans for God
P.O. Box 124
Gaithersburg, MD 20760

Americans for Health and Human Rights
P.O. Box 1555
Dallas, TX 75221

Americans for Historical Accuracy
P.O. Box 372
Lawndale, CA 90260
Lillian Baker, Director

Americans for Judicial Reform
5809-C S. Broadway
Littleton, CO 80121

Americans for Nuclear Energy
2525 Wilson Blvd.
Arlington, VA 22201
Douglas O. Lee, Director

Americans for Patriotic Action
111 N. Windsor
Los Angeles, CA 90004

Americans to Free Captive Nations
P.O. Box A-380
New York, NY 10017

Andrew Jackson Institute
P.O. Box 190472
Nashville, TN 37219
Nelson Griswold, President

Ann Watson Report
P.O. Box 22296
San Diego, CA 92122

Anti-Communist Committee
P.O. Box 1832
Kansas City, MO 64141
Jack N. Stone, Director

Anti-Communist League of America
3100 Park Newport, Suite 101
Newport Beach, CA 92660
John K. Crippen, Director

Anti-Communist World Freedom Council
8001 MacArthur
Cabin John, MD 20818

Anti-Soviet Research Center of Together International
P.O. Box 3465
McLean, VA 22103

Apologia
111 E. Drake, Suite 7032
Ft. Collins, CO 80525

Apple Valley Gun Club Action Committee
15180 Prado Court
Victorville, CA 92392
Kevin Shaughnessy, Director

Area Council for Economic Education
1617 JFK Boulevard, Suite 1169
Philadelphia, PA 19103

Arizona Citizens for Limited Terms
1430 E. Missouri, Suite 105
Phoenix, AZ 85014

Arizona Family Research Center
3550 N. Central, Suite 1025
Phoenix, AZ 85012

Arizona State Rifle and Pistol Association
3455 E. Mulberry St.
Scottsdale, AZ 85257

Arizonans for National Security
P.O. Box 28286
Tempe, AZ 85285

Arms, Law & Society
ALS Publications
P.O. Box 2881
Fairfax, VA 22031
Jeff Snyder, Publisher

Assembly of Captive European Nations
150 5th Ave., Suite 832
New York, NY 10011
Feliks Gadomski, Director

Association for Family Finances in America (AFFA)
2300 N St., N.W., Suite 600
Washington, DC 20037
Pat Fagan, President

Association for Public Justice
321 8th St., N.E.
Washington, DC 20002
James Skillen, Executive Director

Association for Rational Economic Alternatives
256 Alpine Rd.
West Palm Beach, FL 33401
Richard Bjornseth, Director

Association for Rational Environmental Alternative
P.O. Box 27043
Houston, TX 77027

Association of Business Education
P.O. Box 2152
Sepulveda, CA 91343

Association of Concerned Taxpayers
1301 Connecticut Ave., N.W., Suite 450
Washington, DC 20036
Drew Clark, Director

Association of Objectivist Students
312 Wildwood Ave.
Piedmont, CA 94611

Association of Productive Working People
P.O. Box 28594
Sacramento, CA 95828

Association to Unite the Democracies
1506 Pennsylvania Ave., S.E.
Washington, DC 20003-3116

Atlantis News
P.O. Box 7973
Jacksonville, FL 32238

Bamboo Connection
P.O. Box 1713
Kinston, NC 28501

Barbara Morris Report
P.O. Box 2166
Carlsbad, CA 92008

Basic Education Association
P.O. Box 5387
Pasadena, CA 91107

Battle Cry Sounding
P.O. Box 572
Biggs, CA 95977

Beat the Bankers
84145 E. Camelback, Suite 161
Scottsdale, AZ 85251

Behavioral Research Center
7515 Greenville Ave., Suite 912
Dallas, TX 75231
Dr. David Graham Hubbard, Director

Bell Ringer
P.O. Box 3654
Memphis, TN 38103

Betsey Ross Press
483 S. Kirkwood Rd., Suite 137
Kirkwood, MO 63122

Between the Lines
2701 S. Colfax Ave.
Minneapolis, MN 55408

Bill of Rights Legal Foundation
P.O. Box 1219
Olympia, WA 98057

Bob Synder Newsletter
P.O. Box 15
Safety Harbor, FL 33572

Body Politik, The
333 E. Jefferson Ave., Suite 230-102
Detroit, MI 48226

Border Solution Task Force
330 G St., Suite 402
San Diego, CA 92101

Business Economic Education Foundation
5258 Griggs, Midway Building
1821 University Ave.
Saint Paul, MN 55104

Business for Conservative Government
1234 Market St., 17th Floor
Philadelphia, PA 19107

Caliber
9550 Warner Ave., Suite 250
Fountain Valley, CA 92708

California Business League
3040 Explorer Way, Suite G-6
Sacramento, CA 95821

California Care Coalition
221 E. Walnut, Suite 242
Pasadena, CA 91101

California Heritage Protective
1245 Cunningham Dr.
Dixon, CA 95620

California Pro-Life Council
926 J St., Suite 1100
Sacramento, CA 95814
Brian Johnston, Director

California War Veterans for Justice
P.O. Box 13949
Sacramento, CA 95853

Campus Coalition for Democracy
Box 20132, Columbus Circle Station
New York, NY 10023

Campus Review
1688 5th St.
Coralville, IA 52241

Capital Legal Foundation
700 E St., S.E.
Washington, DC 20003

Capitol Connection International News Service
801 Pennsylvania Ave., N.W., Suite 1024
Washington, DC 20004
Kenneth Shellan, President

Captive Nations Committee
P.O. Box 540
New York, NY 10028
Dr. Lev Dobriansky, Director

Care Net
101 W. Borad St., Suite 500
Falls Church, VA 22046

Carribean-Central American Action
1333 New Hampshire Ave., N.W., Suite 1010
Washington, DC 20036

Carry Concealed Weapons Sheriff
P.O. Box 11,117
Glendale, CA 91206
Elliott Graham, Chairman

Catholic Home Study Institute
9 Loudoun St., S.E.
Leesburg, VA 22075

Catholic League
111 Cabot St.
Needham, MA 02194
Philip F. Lawler, Director

Catholic League for Religious and Civil Rights
1010 Vermont Ave., N.W., Suite 712
Washington, DC 20005
Patrick Riley, Director

Catholic Study Council
214 Massachusetts Ave., N.E., Suite 580
Washington, DC 20002

Catholic World Report
P.O. Box 6718
Syracuse, NY 13217-7912

Causa USA
4301 Harewood Rd., N.E.
Washington, DC 20017
Joe Tully, Director

Center for Action
P.O. Box 9
Boulder City, NV 89005
Jerry Gillispy, Director

Center for Business Information
90 Madison St.
Worcester, MA 01608

Center for Cuban Analysis
1712 New Hampshire Ave., N.W.
Washington, DC 20009

Center for Economic Education
9939 Sunset Ave.
La Mesa, CA 92041

Center for Educational Freedom
854 Washington Building
Washington, DC 20005

Center for Entrepreneurial Management
311 Main St.
Worcester, MA 01608

Center for Family Business
5862 Mayfield Rd.
Cleveland, OH 44124

Center for International Relations
27 15th St., N.W., 8th Floor
Washington, DC 20005
Lee Edwards, President

Center for International Security
905 16th St., N.W.
Washington, DC 20006

Center for International Studies
5702 Newington
Bethesda, MD 20816
Dr. Lee Edwards, President

Center for Judicial Studies
Route 2, Box 93
Cumberland, VA 23040
Dr. James McClellan, Director

Center for Peace and Freedom
214 Massachusetts Ave., N.E., Suite 360
Washington, DC 20002

Center for Privatization
2000 Pennslyvania Ave., N.W., Suite 2500
Washington, DC 20006
Gordon Johnson, Director

Center for Values Research
13771 North Central Expressway
Keystone Park, Suite 1010
Dallas, TX 75243

Central Jersey Objectivists
P.O. Box 5165
Hazlet, NJ 07730
Daniel Ust, Director

Centre for a Free Society
1701 Pennsylvania Ave.
Washington, DC 20069

Children's Educational Opportunity Foundation
P.O. Box 17447
San Antonio, TX 78217

Children's Legal Foundation
P.O. Box 10050
Phoenix, AZ 85064

Choice in Currency Commission
325 Pennsylvania Ave., S.E.
Washington, DC 20003

Christian Action Council
101 W. Broad St., Suite 500
Falls Church, VA 22046
Thomas A. Glessner, J.D., Director

Christian American Advocate
P.O. Box 944
Mooreland, OK 73852

Christian and Protestant Order Guild
P.O. Box 715
St. George, UT 84770

Christian Family Builders
P.O. Box 93
Coopersburg, PA 18036

Christian Mandate for America
P.O. Box 2500
Culpepper, VA 22701

Christian Posse
RR 2, Box 287-A
Tigerton, WI 54486

Christian Voters League
456 E. Grand Ave., Suite 305
Escondido, CA 92025

Christian Yellow Pages
P.O. Box 840555
Houston, TX 77284

Christians on Point
P.O. Box 4624
Tyler, TX 75712

Church of Christian Liberty
3675 N. Calhoun Rd.
Brookfield, WI 53005

Church of Eternal Life and Liberty
10251 Oak Park Blvd.
Oak Park, MI 48237

Citizen Bar Association
P.O. Box 935
Medford, OR 97501

Citizen Councils of America
666 North St., Suite 102-A
Jackson, MS 39202

Citizens Against Pornography
P.O. Box 180067
Austin, TX 78718

Citizens Against Pornography of Alabama
P.O. Box 1245
Gadsden, AL 35902
Jean Faucett, Executive Director

Citizens Council
666 North St., Suite 102A
Jackson, MS 39202

Citizens for America
214 Massachusetts Ave., N.E., Suite 480
Washington, DC 20002
Donald Devine, Director

Citizens for Biblical Government
1220 Monroe, N.E.
Washington, DC 20017

Citizens for Common Sense
770 L St., Suite 810
Sacramento, CA 95814
Brian F. Lungren, Director

Citizens for Common Sense
44-489 Town Center Dr.
Palm Desert, CA 92660
Dr. Lorraine Day, President

Citizens for Congressional Reform
470 L'Enfant Plaza, S.W.
East Building Suite 7112
Washington, DC 20024

Citizens for Conservative Causes
P.O. Box 1177
Purcellville, VA 22132

Citizens for Decency
821 S. Bronson
Los Angeles, CA 90005

Citizens for Excellence in Education
2800 S. Main St., Suite F
Santa Ana, CA 92707
Shirley Kelly, Director

Citizens for Parental Rights
1945 Pawtucket Ave.
Schenectady, NY 12309

Citizens for Responsible Government
12191 Ralston Rd., Suite 103
Arvada, CO 80004

Citizens' Choice
1615 H St., N.W.
Washington, DC 20062

Citizens' Economic Forum
P.O. Box 47712
Dallas, TX 75247

Citizens' Economic Foundation
7322 S.W. Freeway, Suite 605
Houston, TX 77074

Clearinghouse on Educational Choice
1611 North Kent St., Suite 805
Arlington, VA 22209

Clinton Quarterly
P.O. Box 3073
Chapel Hill, NC 27514

Coalition for Constitutional Justice
25108 Margaret Parkway, Suite B245
Mission Viejo, CA 92692

Coalition for Democracy in Central America
P.O. Box 76461
Washington, DC 20013

Coalition for Freedom
P.O. Box 19458
Raleigh, NC 27619

Coalition for Monetary Education
708 Pendleton St.
Alexandria, VA 22314

Coalition for Religous Freedom
515 Wythe St., Suite 201
Alexandria, VA 22314

Coalition for Revival
89 Pioneer Way
Mountain View, CA 94941

Coalition for the Preservation of Family
905 W. Lansing
Broken Arrow, OK 74012

Coalition of Concerned North Carolinians
P.O. Box 247
Raleigh, NC 27602

Cognitive Dissidents
291 Laburnam Crescent
Rochester, NY 14620

Coloradans Back In Charge
P.O. Box 13366
Denver, CO 80201

Colorado Alliance for a Sound Economy
P.O. Box 11056
Denver, CO 80211

Colorado Liberty
2186 S. Holly, Suite 207B
Denver, CO 80222

Comfort
P.O. Box 12891
Wichita, KS 67213

Comments and Corrections
P.O. Box 15902
Salt Lake City, UT 84115

COMMIT
251 N. Illinios, Suite 1800
Indianapolis, IN 46204

Committee for a Conservative Virginia
P.O. Box 4244
Lynchburg, VA 24502

Committee for a Free Afghanistan
721 2nd St., N.E.
Washington, DC 20003

Committee for Economic Development
1700 K St., N.W.
Washington, DC 20006

Committee for Improved Education
2304 S.E. Belmont
Portland, OR 97214

Committee for the Restoration of the Republic
127-01 101st Ave.
Richmond, NY 11419

Committee on the Present Danger
905 16th St., N.W., Suite 207
Washington, DC 20006
Charles Tyroler, Director

Committee to Abolish the Fed
325 Pennsylvania Ave.
Washington, DC 20335
Llewellyn H. Rockwell, Director

Common Sense
188-A Onville Rd.
Stafford, VA 22554
Craig Sadick, Executive Director

Common Sense
P.O. Box 20258
Raleigh, NC 27619

Common Sense For America
1101 30th St., N.W., Suite 500
Washington, DC 20007
Peter O'B. Moore, Executive Director

Common Sense Viewpoint
P.O. Box 471
Corona Del Mar, CA 92625

Competitive Economy Foundation
410 1st St., S.E.
Washington, DC 20003

Concerned Christians
P.O. Box 88523
Atlanta, GA 30338

Concerned Christians
P.O. Box 5181
Golden, CO 80401

Concerned Citizens
P.O. Box 94
Cortland, NY 13045

Concerned Citizens Committee
P.O. Box 4144
Spartanburg, SC 29303

Concerned Citizens for Constitutional Government
P.O. Box 1985
Springfield, OH 45501

Concerned Citizens for the Nuclear Breeder
P.O. Box 3
Ross, OH 45061
Harry Horner, Director

Concerned Voters Association
6230 N.W. 173rd St.
Hialeah, FL 33015

Concord Books
755719 Ali Dr., Suite 320
Kailua-Kona, KY 40291

Conference of American Small Business Organizations
407 South Dearborn St.
Chicago, IL 60605

Conference on Economic Progress
2610 Upton St., N.W.
Washington, DC 20008

Conservative Action
P.O. Box 1233
Concord, NH 03301

Conservative Alliance
1001 Prince St., Suite 100
Alexandria, VA 22314

Conservative Books
P.O. Box 1653
Arlington Heights, IL 60006

Conservative Calendar
P.O. Box 44084
Washington, DC 20026

Conservative Campaign Fund
1156 15th St., N.W., Suite 500
Washington, DC 20005
Peter Flaherty, Chairman

Conservative Discussion Group
P.O. Box 296
Dunellen, NJ 08812
Herb Levenson, Director

Conservative Legal Defense and Education Fund
1815 H St., N.W., Suite 600
Washington, DC 20006

Conservative National Committee
2101 Wilson Blvd., Suite 523
Arlington, VA 22201

Conservative Network
400 1st St., N.W., Suite 809
Washington, DC 20001
Jack Rohrer, Director

Conservative Speakers Bureau
501 Church St.
Vienna, VA 22180

Conservative Television Network
P.O. Box 3711
Fairfax, VA 22038
Floyd G. Brown, Chairman

Conservative Viewpoint
P.O. Box 17091, Dulles Airport
Washington, DC 20041

Conservatives Do Care
7322 Southwest Freeway, Suite 605
Houston, TX 77074

Constitution Parties of the United States
P.O. Box 608
White Fish, MT 59937
Dr. Clarence Martin, Director

Constitutional Commission
P.O. Box 195
Natalia, TX 78059
Parker Abell, Director

Constitutional Money
P.O. Box 5611
San Bernardino, CA 92412

Constitutional Outreach
223 Shoal Creek Dr.
Deatsville, AL 36022

Constitutional Rights Foundation
P.O. Box 2362
Texas City, TX 77592
Dean Allen, Director

Constructive Action
P.O. Box 4006
Whittier, CA 90607

Consumers for World Trade
1346 Connecticut Ave., N.W.
Washington, DC 20036

Correspondent
P.O. Box 9283
Missoula, MT 59807

Council for a Competitive Economy
410 1st St., S.E.
Washington, DC 20003

Council for Educational Freedom in America
2105 Wintergreen Ave.
Forestville, MD 20747

Council for National Defense
7015 Old Keen Mill Rd.
Springfield, VA 22150

Council for National Defense
2100 Gallows Rd.
Vienna, VA 22180

Council for Social and Economic Studies
1133 13th St., Suite C-2, N.W.
Washington, DC 20005

Council for Social and Economic Studies
1629 K St., N.W., Suite 509
Washington, DC 20006
Roger Pearson, Director

Council for the National Interest
1900 18th St., N.W.
Washington, DC 20009

Council of Free Czechoslovakia
P.O. Box 5153
New York, NY 10163

Council on American Affairs
1785 Massachusettts Ave, N.W., Suite 210
Washington, DC 20036
Dr. Roger Pearson, Director

Council on Domestic Relations
P.O. Box 138
Carlinville, IL 62626
Jackie Patru, Director

Council on Southern Africa
P.O.Box 22484
Denver, CO 80222
Barbara Dygert, Director

Criminal Court Classroom
P.O. Box 12846
Fort Worth, TX 76116

Crusade for Forgotten Veterans
P.O. Box 690
Mount Shasta, CA 96067

Cuban Representation
1784 W. Flagler St., Suite 21
Miami, FL 33135

Dawson Newsletter
P.O. Box 332
Fayetteville, AR 72702

Decentralize
P.O. Box 3521
Washington, DC 20007

Democracy International
214 Massachusetts Ave., N.E., Suite 32
Washington, DC 20002
Lewis Lehrman, Director

Dialogue on Liberty
601 Canyon Blvd.
Boulder, CO 80302

Diebold Institute for Public Policy Studies
475 S. Park Ave.
New York, NY 10016

Directory of Rightist Publications Throughout the World
P.O. Box 4016
Lutherville, MD 21093

Distant Drums
4016 Degardner Circle
St. Francis, MN 55070

Dittoheads of America Fan Club
P.O. Box 362
Penfield, NY 14526

Dominion News and Digest
P.O. Box 1855
Manassas, VA 22110

Drake Intelligence Service
P.O. Box 1207
Stone Park, IL 60165

Economic Education for Clergy
6410 Rockledge Dr., Suite 302
Bethesda, MD 20817

Economic Literacy Council of California
400 Golden Shore, Suite 218
Long Beach, CA 90802

Edgar Bundy Ministries
P.O. Box 530525
Miami, FL 33153

Educational Books
871 Post Ave.
Glendale, MO 63122

Educational Freedoms
4337 15th N.E., Dept. 819
Seattle, WA 98105

Educational Research Council of America
Rockefeller Building
614 W. Superior Ave.
Cleveland, OH 44113

Educational Reviewer
P.O. Box 3070, Grand Central Station
New York, NY 10017

End Times
P.O. Box 1063
Chapel Hill, NC 27514

End Times Prophecy Newsletter
P.O. Box 19020-277
Las Vegas, NV 89132

Enlightened Redneck
West Branch Enterprises
P.O. Box 19649U
Denver, CO 80219

Enough is Enough
10523 Main St., Suite D
Fairfax, VA 22030

Enterprise Mentors
1600 S. Brentwood Blvd., Suite 770
St. Louis, MO 63144
Charles Cozzens, Director

Entrepreneurship Institute
90 E. Wilson Rd., Suite 247
Worthington, OH 43085

Ergo
3 Ames St.
Cambridge, MA 02139

Ethnic American Heritage News
P.O. Box 1765
Albany, NY 12201

Evergreen Foundation
3979 Crater Lake Highway
Medford, OR 97504
James D. Peterson, Executive Director

Excellence Through Choice in Education League
2250 E. Imperial Highway, Suite 220
El Segundo, CA 90245
Kevin Teasley, Executive Director

Exile Press
241 South Temelec Circle
Sonoma, CA 95476

F.A.C.T.S.
4209 164th St., N.W.
Lynnwood, WA 98037

F.A.C.T.S.
422 S.W. 5th St.
Grants Pass, OR 97526

Fairness in Media
P.O. Box 25099
Raleigh, NC 27611

Family Concerns Coalition
N96 W18221 County Line Rd.
Menomonee Falls, WI 53051

Family First
P.O. Box 885
Needham, MA 02192

Federalists
P.O. Box 6292
Vacaville, CA 95696

Federation for Restoration of the Republic
127-01 101st Ave.
Rich Hill, NY 11419

Federation of Constitutional Government
P.O. Box 50086
New Orleans, LA 70150

Fideles Et Veres
P.O. Box 10150
Kansas City, MO 64141

Financial Freedom Fellowship
6602 Beadnell Way, Suite 14
San Diego, CA 92117

Firing Line
12062 Valley View St., Suite 107
Garden Grove, CA 92645
John W. Sherburn, Editor

First Amendment Press
P.O. Box 67
Lowell, MI 49331

Florida Conservative Union
20 S.E. 8th St.
Miami, FL 33131

For Liberty
1120 NASA Blvd., Suite 104
Houston, TX 77058

ForthRight Communications
P.O. Box 3771
Merrifield, VA 22116
Patrick Moore, Director

Foundation for Constitutional Education
P.O. Box 954
Herndon, VA 22070-0954

Foundation for Free Enterprise
411 Hackensack St., Suite 500
Hackensack, NJ 07601

Foundation for Oregon Research and Education
1708 S.W. Columbia St.
Portland, OR 97201

Foundation to Defend the First Amendment
P.O. Box 70392
Washington, DC 20024
James P. Tucker, Jr., Director

Free Cuba Patriotic Movement
1635 S.W. 98th Ct.
Miami, FL 33165

Free Enterprise Fund
P.O. Box 23500, L'Enfant Plaza
Washington, DC 20024

Free Friends of Captive Nations
P.O. Box 7
Hazelwood, MO 63042

Free Market Advertiser
1515 W. MacArthur Ave., Suite 19
Costa Mesa, CA 92626

Free Market Environmentalist
1572 D Sycamore, Box 32
Hercules, CA 94547

Free Market Foundation:USSR
P.O. Box 27251
Tucson, AZ 85726-7251

Free Market Institute
9707 S. Gessner
Houston, TX 77071

Free Market Perspectives
P.O. Box 471
Barrington, IL 60010

Free Market Policy News
6114 La Salle Ave., Suite 102
Oakland, CA 94611
Jim Christie, Publisher

Free Market Yellow Pages
P.O. Box 224
Long Beach, CA 90801

Free Press Association
P.O. Box 8099
Columbus, OH 43201

Free Press International
401 5th Ave.
New York, NY 10016

Free the Eagle
25 E St., N.W., 8th Floor
Washington, DC 20002

Freedom
1301 N. Catalina St.
Los Angeles, CA 90027

Freedom at Issue
48 E 21st St.
New York, NY 10010

Freedom Church of Maryland
RR 2, Box 119
Oakland, MD 21550

Freedom Country
550 Old Mill Rd.
Campobello, SC 29322

Freedom Fighter
P.O. Box 8469
La Jolla, CA 92038

Freedom Forum
P.O. Box 185
Shelby, NC 28150

Freedom Group
P.O. Box 650
Vancouver, WA 98660

Freedom in History
1236 S. Taylor St., Suite A
Arlington, VA 22204

Freedom Leadership Foundation
1635 Connecticut Ave., N.W.
Washington, DC 20009

Freedom Products
P.O. Box 224
Long Beach, CA 90801

Freedom Research Foundation
505 2nd St., N.E.
Washington, DC 20002
Dr. Jack Wheeler, Director

Freedom Unlimited
P.O. Box 11
Haddon Heights, NJ 08035

Freedom's Friends
P.O. Box 515
Addison, TX 75001

Freeman Institute
5288 S. 320 West, Suite B158
Salt Lake City, UT 84107
Jim Barleson, President

Freeman Institute
3201 Kensington Rd.
Avondale Estates, GA 30002

Friends of Free China
1629 K St., N.W.
Washington, DC 20006

Friends of Right to Work
P.O. Box 1092
Waco, TX 76703

Friends of the U.S.A.
P.O. Box 13051
Washington, DC 20009

Frontier Journal
P.O. Box 10665
Fairbanks, AK 99710

Full Disclosure
P.O. Box 8775
Ann Arbor, MI 48107
Glen Roberts, Publisher

Fund for Education in Economics
1120 Connecticut Ave., N.W.
Washington, DC 20036

G.O.P. Women's Political Action League
P.O. Box 66011
Washington, DC 20035
Maureen E. Reagan, Director

Geo-Libertarian Society
P.O. Box 9875
Berkeley, CA 94709

German American Information and Education Association
P.O. Box 23169
Washington, DC 20026

Ginter Tapes
P.O. Box 471
Black Eagle, MT 59414

Global Economic Action Institute
1718 Connecticut Ave., N.W., Suite 410
Washington, DC 20009

Goodhope Press
P.O. Box 29115
Indianapolis, IN 46227

Gordon Kahl Memorial Committee
RR 1, Box 93-A
Smithville, AR 72466

Gun Owner's Foundation
5881 Leesburg Pike
Falls Church, VA 22041

Gun Owners Action Committee
862 Granite Circle
Anaheim, CA 92806
T. J. Johnston, Director

Gun Owners Action League
11 Main St., Box 272
Southboro, MA 01772

Gun Rights Committee
10742 Los Almitos Blvd.
Los Angeles, CA 90721

Hannibal Hamlin Institute
119 Water St.
Hallowell, ME 04347

Haugh Foundation
4280 North Campbell Ave., Suite 200
Tucson, AZ 85718
Robert G. Schwartz, Director

Health in America
P.O. Box 841
Lincolnshire, IL 60069
Eric Meyer, Director

Helms Institute for American Studies and Foreign Policy
P.O. Box 19458
Raleigh, NC 27619

Help Wake Up America
P.O. Box 2286
Vista, CA 92083

Historical Research Foundation
700 S. 4th St.
Harristown, NJ 07029

Home School Headquarters
P.O. Box 366
Fremont, NE 68025

Horizon
Institute for Policy Research
1111 N. Westshore Blvd., Suite 210
Tampa, FL 33607

Idea
P.O. Box 4010
Madison, WI 53711

In Form
P.O. Box 636
Littleton, CO 80160

Independent American
P.O.Box 636
Littleton, CO 80160

Independent Conservative Party
P.O. Box 1103
Prescott, AZ 86301

Independent News Service
2245 Swaim Circle, N.W.
Huntsville, AL 35810

Industrial Information
6219 Market St.
Youngstown, OH 44512

Information Council for the Environment (ICE)
1000 Connecticut Ave., N.W.
Washington, DC 20036

Ink Stains
P.O. Box 210093
Bedford, TX 76095
Matt Miller, Editor

Institute for Business and Economic Education
P.O. Box 16207
Lubbock, TX 79407

Institute for Democracy in Eastern Europe
48 E 21st St., 3rd Floor
New York, NY 10010

Institute for Education Affairs
10 E 40th St.
New York, NY 10017

Institute for Free Enterprise Education
Royal Central Tower
11300 N. Central, Suite 302
Dallas, TX 75243

Institute for Western Values
P.O. Box 11463
Alexandria, VA 22312

Institute of American Relations
325 Constitutional Ave., N.E.
Washington, DC 20002

Institute on Money and Inflation
314 E. Capitol St., Suite B-1
Washington, DC 20003

Intellectual Activist
131 5th Ave., Suite 101
New York, NY 10003

International Center for Economic Policy Studies
20 W. 40th St.
New York, NY 10018

International Conservative Policy Alliance
1255 23rd St., N.W., Suite 500
Washington, DC 20037

International Freedom Foundation
200 G St., N.E., Suite 300
Washington, DC 20002

International Institute for Economic Research
1100 Glendon Ave., Suite 1625
Los Angeles, CA 90024

International League of Human Rights
236 46th St.
New York, NY 10017

International Management and Development Institute
2600 Virginia Ave., N.W., Suite 905
Washington, DC 20037

International Security Council
1155 15th St., N.W., Ste. 502
Washington, DC 20005

Intrepid Books
P.O. Box 179
Rough and Ready, CA 95975

Intrepid Productions
1415 Blue Spruce Dr., Suite 2
Fort Collins, CO 80524
Arthur Maranjian, Director

Invest-in-America
2400 Chestnut St., Suite 3308
Philadelphia, PA 19103
James Panyard, Director

Invest-in-America National Council
Architects Building, Suite 906
17th and Sansom
Philadelphia, PA 19103

Iowa Caucus Club
P.O. Box 433
Le Claire, IA 52753

Justice for All
P.O. Box 665
Taft, CA 93268

Justice for All
P.O. Box 3487
Kent, WA 98032

Justice Times
P.O. Box 562
Clinton, AR 72031

Kahn's Commentary
7023 Constance Ave.
Chicago, IL 60649

Knowledge Products
P.O. Box 100340
Nashville, TN 37224

Latvian Press Society
P.O. Box 48
Dorchester, MA 02122

Law Enforcement Lobby
666 N 2nd St.
San Jose, CA 95112
Leroy Pyle, Executive Director

League of Men Voters
P.O. Box 128
Glenview, IL 60025

League of Rights
940 R St.
Gering, NE 69341

Legislative Research Association
P.O. Box 2973
Springfield, IL 62708

Libertarian Congregational Church
23 River Rd.
North Arlington, NJ 07032

Libertarian Defense Caucus
P.O. Box 7761
Thousand Oaks, CA 91359

Libertarian Forum
P.O. Box 341, Madison Square Station
New York, NY 10010

Libertarian Frontier
P.O. Box 1066
Waukesha, WI 53187

Libertarian Futurist Society
89 Gephart Rd.
Penfield, NY 14526
Victoria L. Varga, Director

Libertarian Health Association
8316 Arlington Blvd., Suite 232
Fairfax, VA 22031

Libertarian Information Service
P.O. Box 817802
Hollywood, FL 33081
Claude Pinsonneault, Director

Libertarian International
9308 Farmington Dr.
Richmond, VA 23229

Libertarian Library
P.O. Box 24269
Denver, CO 80224

Libertarian Lifeline
3960 E 14th St.
Oakland, CA 94601

Libertarian Press
Spring Mills, PA 16875

Libertarian Republican Organizing Committee
444 Castro St., Suite 301
Mountain View, CA 94041
Colin Hunter, Director

Libertarian Student Network
3910 Nara Dr.
Florrisant, MO 63033

Libertarian Student Network
P.O. Box 64
Trenton, MI 48183

Libertarians for Animal Rights
7829 Cayuga Ave.
Bethesda, MD 20817
Joseph Armour, Director

Libertas
11800 Sunrise Valley Dr., Suite 812
Reston, VA 22091

Libertas Update
2727 S. Croddy Way, Suite J
Santa Ana, CA 92704

LiberTech Project
8726 S. Sepulveda, Suite B253
Los Angeles, CA 90045

Liberty Activists Unlimited
P.O. Box 28186
Dallas, TX 75228
Wayne L. Burnham, President

Liberty Amendment Committee, U.S.A.
P.O. Box 20888
El Cajon, CA 92021
Armin R. Moths, Director

Liberty and Democracy International
1732 Wisconsin Ave., N.W.
Washington, DC 20007

Liberty and Property
P.O. Box 546
Shingle Springs, CA 95682

Liberty Audio and Film Service
824 W. Broad St.
Richmond, VA 23220

Liberty Institute
1377 K St., N.W., Suite 708
Washington, DC 20005

Liberty Newsletter
8 Marsh St.
Lowell, MA 01854

Liberty's Torch
P.O. Box 42
Anaheim, CA 92805

Library of Truth
Box 19523
Denver, CO 80219

Life Line Foundation
10511 Wyatt St.
Dallas, TX 75218

Lift-Off
8 North Liberty Ave.
Endicott, NY 13760

Limit Government
1235 Coral Way
Coral Gables, FL 33134

Lincoln Educational Foundation
299 Madison Ave.
New York, NY 10017

Lithuanian American Council
2606 W 63rd St.
Chicago, IL 60629

Lithuanian Human Rights Committee
5808 King Arthur Way
Glen Dale, MD 20109

Lithuanian-American Community in the United States
9660 Pine Rd.
Philadelphia, PA 19115

Livable Parables
P.O. Box 187
Loomis, CA 95650

Log Cabin
P.O. Box 90201
Washington, DC 20090

Lone Star 2000 Education Foundation
5151 Flynn Parkway
Corpus Christi, TX 78411-4318
Gwen Pharo, President

Long House
P.O. Box 3
New Canaan, CT 06840

Love in Action
P.O. Box 265
San Rafael, CA 94912

Lysander Spooner Society
P.O. Box 433
Willimantic, CT 06226

Maine Paper
P.O. Box 71
Hallowell, ME 04347

Manion Forum
P.O. Box 1258
South Bend, IN 46624

Massachusetts Foundation
111 Cabot St.
Needham, MA 02194

Media Institute
3017 M St., N.W.
Washington, DC 20007

Media Spotlight
P.O. Box 1288
Costa Mesa, CA 92628

Media Studies
P.O. Box 16541
Raytown, MO 64133

Men's Defense Network
P.O. Box 24305
Williamsport, PA 17703

Menconi Ministries
P.O. Box 969
Cardiff, CA 92007

Mercy Fund
1000 Potomac St., N.W.
Washington, DC 20007

Michael Fund
400 Penn Center Blvd., Room 721
Pittsburgh, PA

Michigan Conservative Union
411 Fort St.
Port Huron, MI 48060

Minuteman Media
3419 Via Lido, Suite 314
Newport Beach, CA 92663
Erick Kyle, President

Mississippi Center for Public Policy Studies
P.O. Box 5064
University, MS 38677
Scott J. Relan, Director

Modern Media Publishers
P.O. Box 1326
Provo, UT 84601

Monetary Reform Task Force
370 Altair Way, Suite 176
Sunyvale, CA 94086

Money Information Network
6602 Beadness Way, Suite 14
San Diego, CA 92117

Mott Media
1000 E. Huron
Milford, MI 48042

Movement for Human Rights in Vietnam
13482 El Prado
Garden Grove, CA 92640

Mozambique Information Office
25 E St., N.W., 8th Floor
Washington, DC 20001

Municipal Officials for Redevelopment Reform (MORR)
1501 E. Chapman, Suite 184
Fullerton, CA 92631
Chris Norby, Director

N.C.E.
P.O. Box 06631
Portland, OR 97206

National Alliance for Constitutional Money
7500 Diplomat Dr.
Manassas, VA 22110

National Alliance for Family Life
225 Jericho Turnpike, Suite 4
Floral Park, NY 11001

National Association for Abstinence Education
6201 Leesburg Pike, Suite 404
Falls Church, VA 22044

National Association for Free Enterprise
1101 New Hampshire Ave., N.W., Suite 107
Washington, DC 20037

National Association for Men
381 S. Park Ave.
New York, NY 10016

National Center for Constitutional Studies
5288 S. 320 West, No. B-158
Salt Lake City, UT 84107
Zeldon Nelson, Director

National Chastity Association
P.O. Box 402
Oak Forest, IL 60452

National Citizens Action Network
1055 E. 5800 South
Ogden, UT 84405

National Civil Liberties League
104 Hillcrest
Washington, IL 61571

National Coalition for a Free Cuba
3735 Coral Way
Miami, FL 33145

National Coalition for Children
6542 Hitt Ave.
McLean, VA 22101

National Coalition on TV Violence
P.O. Box 2157
Champaign, IL 61820

National Committee for Monetary Reform
4425 W. Napoleon Ave.
Metairie, LA 70001

National Congress for Men
68 Deering St.
Portland, ME 04101

National Congressional Club
P.O. Box 18848
Raleigh, NC 27619

National Council for Better Education
1800 Diagonal Rd.
Alexandria, VA 22314
Sally Reed, Chairman

National Council for Environmental Balance
P.O. Box 7732
Louisville, KY 40207
Irwin W. Tucker, Ph.D., President

National Council for Labor Reform
4065 Plymouth Ct.
Chicago, IL 60605

National Endowment for Liberty
18333 Egret Bay Blvd., Suite 265
Houston, TX 77058
Hon. Ron Paul, M.D., Director

National Endowment for Preservation of Liberty
305 4th St., N.E.
Washington, DC 20002

National Environmental Trust
146 Clarkson Executive Park
Ellisville, MO 63011
Harold Burson-Marstellar, Director

National Family Legal Foundation
5353 N. 16th St., Suite 400
Phoenix, AZ 85016

National Foundation for Economic Research
111 Cabot St.
Needham, MA 02194

National Hamiltonian Party
3314 Dillian Rd.
Flushing, MI 48433

National Intelligence Book Center
1700 K St., N.W., Suite 607
Washington DC 20006

National Leadership Institute
500 W. 13th St.
Austin, TX 78701

National Parents League
P.O. Box 3987
Portland, OR 97208

National Republican Youth Retreat
P.O. Box 830737
Richardson, TX 75083

National Schools Committee for Economic Education
P.O. Box 326
Old Greenwich, CT 06870

National Support Movement for Resistance in Viet Nam
P.O. Box 468
Annandale, VA 22003

National Venture Capital Association
1667 K St., N.W., Suite 900
Washington, DC 20006

New American Foundation
1253 7th St.
Santa Monica, CA 90401

New American Review
15 Burchfield Ave.
Cranford, NJ 07016

New American View
132 3rd St.
Washington, DC 20003

New Covenant
840 Airport Blvd.
Ann Arbor, MI 48107
Rhonda DeLong, Director

New Dimensions
P.O. Box 811
Grants Pass, OR 97526

New Hampshire Citizens for Choice in Education
56 Sherwood Circle
Salem, NH 03079

New Jersey Citizens for a Sound Economy
204 West State St.
Trenton, NJ 08608

New Jersey Coalition of Concerned Parents
P.O. Box 35
Little Silver, NJ 07739

New Leadership Fund
P.O. Box 3543
Washington, DC 20007
Anne Neal Petri, Director

New Libertarian
P.O. Box 1748
Long Beach, CA 90801
Samuel Edward Konkin, Director

News-Watch Alert
P.O. Box 99253
Seattle, WA 98199

Newsletter Digest
P.O. Box 2335
Huntsville, AL 358001

Newswatch Magazine
11824 Beaverton
Bridgeton, MO 63044

Nicaraguan Resistance Educational Foundation
44880 Falcon Place, Suite 109
Sterling, VA 22170
Lucia Salazar, President

Norfolk Intelligence
1324 Maplewood Dr.
Norfolk, VA 23503

North Carolina Center for Independent Higher Education
1300 St. Mary's St., Suite 204
Raleigh, NC 27605

North Carolina Foundation for Research and Economic Education
530 Blount St.
Raleigh, NC 27604

North Carolina Policy Council
1201 E. Boulevard
Charlotte, NC 28203

Oasis
P.O. Box H
Hopewell, NJ 08525

Objectivist Forum
P.O. Box 5311
New York, NY 10150

Oklahomans for Property Tax Reform
4100 Perimeter Center, Suite 145
Oklahoma City, OK 73112
Daniel Brown, Director

On Guard
P.O. Box 25
Aztec, NM 87410

On Principle
601 Ewing St., Suite B-7
Princeton, NJ 08542

Or Give Me Death
P.O. Box 940605
Rockaway Park, NY 11694

Ordo Christi Regis
Route 1, Box 295
Calhoun, TN 37309

Oregon Citizens Alliance
9150 S.W. Pioneer Court, Suite W
Wilsonville, OR 97070

Oregon Commentator
P.O. Box 30178
Eugene, OR 97403

Pacific Basin Economic Council
534 Kearny St., Suite 200
San Francisco, CA 94133
Dr. R. Sean Randolph, Director

PAL Books
P.O. Box 661
Oregon City, TX 75683

Panamanian Committee for Human Rights
607 G St., S.W.
Washington, DC 20024

Panarchy Dialectic
P.O. Box 353f
Reseda, CA 91333

Parents for Educational Choice
277 South Rancho Santa Fe, Suite C
Santa Marcos, CA 92024

Patriot Prayer
P.O. Box 5155
Sacramento, CA 95817

Patriotic Education
P.O. Box 2121
Daytona Beach, FL 32015

Patriotic Populist Party
P.O. Box 384
Okoboji, IA 51355

Patriotic Publishers
496 Tullulah Rd.
Lantana, FL 33462

Paul Revere Network
666 N. Second St.
San Jose, CA 95112
Leroy Pyle, Executive Director

Peace Through Knowledge
68 Spring St., Suite 2
Watertown, MA 2172
Dr. Yuri Tuvim, Director

Pennsylvania Committee to Save Local Government
P.O. Box 16042
Philadelphia, PA 19114

Pennsylvanians for Term Limits
RD 5, Box 156
Blairsville, PA 15717

Personal Protection Digest
P.O. Box 22586
Minneapolis, MN 55442

Philadelphia Christian Action Council
P.O. Box 24362
Philadelphia, PA 19120

Physicians for Moral Responsibility
P.O. Box 98257
Tacoma, WA 98498

Pine Tree Press
3646 Aspen Village Way
Santa Ana, CA 92704

PIX Report
P.O. Box 160
Oroville, CA 98844

Plain and Simple Truth
4314 W. Main
Decatur, IL 62522

Political Economist
P.O. Box 2478
Mission Viejo, CA 92690

Political Economy Research Institute
1410 Promenade Bank
Richardson, TX 75080

Political Gun News
7777 Leesburg Pike
Falls Church, VA 22043

Populist Conservative Tax Coalition
7777 Leesburg Pike
Falls Church, VA 22043

Populist Forum
P.O. Box 16007
Alexandria, VA 22302

Populist Party
P.O. Box 1988
Ford City, PA 16226

Populist Renaissace Party
P.O. Box 194
Chaska, MN 55318

Post-Abortion Counseling and Education
P.O. Box 35032
Tucson, AZ 35032

Posterity Press
5147 S. Harvard, Suite 139
Tulsa, OK 74135

Private Practice
P.O. Box 12489
Oklahoma City, OK 73157

Privatization Council
1101 Connecticut Ave., N.W., Suite 700
Washington, DC 20036
Jenny L. Hefferon, Director

Pro-American Press
P.O. Box 41
Gering, NE 69341

Pro-Life Political Report
7777 Leesburg Pike, Suite 305
Falls Church, VA 22046

Probe Foundation
320 Strawberry Hill Ave.
Norwalk, CT 06851

Producing Citizens
P.O. Box 1566
Aurora, IL 60507

Psychologists for the Advancement of Conservative Thought
14 Wesley Place
Tuscaloosa, AL 35400

Public Forum
Rt. 1, Box 14-B
Eastsound, WA 98245

Public Information Systems
6528 W. North Ave.
Wauwatosa, WI 53213

Public Policy Education Fund
161 E. Pine St.
Grove City, PA 16127
John A. Sparks, Director

Public Research Syndicated
4650 Arrow Highway, Suite D-6
Montclair, CA 91763

Radical Capitalist
701 7th Ave., Suite 9W
New York, NY 10036

Reality Theory Newsletter
7439 La Palma, Suite 263
Buena Park, CA 90620

Reason and Liberty
P.O. Box 8071
Tacoma, WA 98408

Rebirth of a Nation
P.O. Box 968
Austin, TX 78767

Regressive
P.O. Box 12942
Scottsdale, AZ 85267

Religion in Communist Dominated Lands
6226 29th St., N.W.
Washington, DC 20015

Remnant Review
P.O. Box 8204
Fort Worth, TX 76112

Republican Exchange Satellite Network
511 Union St., Suite 947
Nashville, TN 37219

Republican Mainstream Committee
6 Library Ct., S.E.
Washington, DC 20003
Ken Ruberg, Director

Research Reports
P.O. Box 70224
Seattle, WA 98107

Retail Industry Action Coalition
1616 H St., N.W.
Washington, DC 20006
Joseph P. O'Neill, Director

Revelations
P.O. Box 655
Eagle, ID 83616

Right Press
5 Magnolia Dr.
Groton, CT 06340

Right Woman
400 1st St., S.E.
Washington, DC 20003

Romanian National Council
P.O. Box 111
New York, NY 10101

Roundtable
4031 University Dr.
Fairfax, VA 22030

Samaritan News
1512 S.W. Fairview
Dallas, OR 97338

Samizdat Bulletin
P.O. Box 6128
San Mateo, CA 94403

Save Our Schools
655 15th St., Suite 310
Washington, DC 20005

Save the Free Enterprise System
P.O. Box B
Temple, NH 03084

Scholl Foundation
111 W. Washington St., Suite 2137
Chicago, IL 60602

Security and Intelligence Foundation
2800 Shirlington Rd., Suite 405
Arlington, VA 22206

Senator Joseph R. McCarthy Foundation
212 W. Wisconsin Ave.
Milwaukee, WI 53203
Thomas Bergen, Director

Shenandoah Letters Monthly
18 Green Rd.
Newport, NH 03773

Slepak Foundation
230 S. 15th St., Suite 300
Philadelphia, PA 19102
Steven L. Carter, Director

Society for Christian Wage Earners
P.O. Box 55533
Houston, TX 77255

Society for Libertarian Life
P.O. Box 4
Fullerton, CA 92632
Howard H. Hinman, Director

Soldiers of Freedom
P.O. Box 105
Rochester, NH 03867

Sons and Daughters of Liberty
200 N. Roselle Rd.
Schaumberg, IL 60172

South Boston Marshall
P.O. Box 1431
Boston, MA 02205

Southern California Ayn Rand Society
289 S. Robertson Blvd., Suite 300
Beverly Hills, CA 90211
Joshua Zader, Director

Southern Republican Exchange
4833 Caldwell Mill Lane
Birmingham, AL 35243

Southern Review of Law and Public Policy
P.O. Box 1959
Buies Creek, NC 27506
Michael Byrne, Director

Southwest Policy Institute
2403 N.W. 39th St., Suite 200
Oklahoma City, OK 73112

Sovereign Citizens Association National
P.O. Box 671054
Dallas, TX 75367
Michael K. Benn, Director

Special Forces Elite Society
P.O. Box 174
Bryson, TX 76027

Split Over the Issues
P.O. Box 4731
Anaheim, CA 92803

Spooner Press
P.O. Box 1165
Grand Island, NY 14072
Richard D. Fuerle, Director

St. Thomas League
14838 S.E. 10th Place
Bellevue, WA 98007

Stacey Koon Defense Fund
107 E. Broadway
Glendale, CA 91205

Students Advocating Valid Education - SAVE
P.O. Box 49051
Minneapolis, MN 55449
Peter J. Jungmann, Director

Students for a Better America
214 Massachusetts Ave., N.E., Suite 500
Washington, DC 20002

Students for Excellence in Education
214 Massachusetts Ave., N.E., Suite 580
Washington, DC 20002

Tacoma Study Club
1105 N. L St.
Tacoma, WA 98043

Tax Facts Council
525 E. Baseline Rd.
Mesa, AZ 85204

Taxpayers Against Gephardt
P.O. Box 515305
St. Louis, MO 63151

Tech-Group
P.O. Box 1132
Fremont, CA 94538

Teen-Aid
22 W. Mission
Spokane, WA 99201

Texans for an Informed Public
1716 Mangum St., Suite 308
Houston, TX 77092

Texas Tax Equity Party
3725 Acorn Circuit
Beaumont, TX 77703

Thomas Jefferson Research Center
202 S. Lake Ave., Suite 240
Pasadena, CA 91101
Dr. B. David Brooks, Director

Thomas Paine Review
84 Washington St., Suite 138
Penacook, NH 03303
Gary McGath, Director

Time for Liberty
P.O. Box 5039
Fresno, CA 93755

Together International Bulletin
P.O. Box 3465
McLean, VA 22103

Tommorrow's America Foundation
529 East Blvd.
Charlotte, NC 28203

Tortoise Report
2001 S. Barrington Ave., Suite 216
Los Angeles, CA 90025

Trinity Foundation
P.O. Box 700
Jefferson, MD 21755
John Robbins, President

Troopergate Whistle-Blowers Fund
P.O. Box 5344
Little Rock, AR 72215
Cliff Jackson, Director

Truth in Government
45-12 74th St.
Elmhurst, NY 11373

Ultraphase
P.O. Box 31632
Richmond, VA 23294

Underground Evangelism
5189 Verdugo Way
Camarillo, CA 93010

Understanding Defense
1633 Best Lane
Eugene, OR 97401
E. G. Ross, Editor

United American and Captive Nations Patriotic Movement
P.O. Box 8161
Akron, OH 44320
Dr. Balint, Director

United Families of America
P.O. Box 6096
Arlington, VA 22206

United Sovereigns of California
P.O. Box 168
Long Beach, CA 90801

United States Anti-Communist Congress
8001 MacArthur Blvd.
Washington, DC 20034

United States Border Control
P.O. Box 1188
Springfield, VA 22151

United States Business and Industry Council
220 National Press Bldg.
Washington, DC 20045

United States Constitution Rights Legal Defense Fund
5 Hickory Hill Lane
Fisherville, VA 22939

United States Council for World Freedom
2621 E. Camelback Rd., Suite 145
Phoenix, AZ 85016
John Singlaub, Director

United States Day Committee
P.O. Box 6525
Tulsa, OK 74156

United States Global Strategy Council
1800 K St., N.W., Suite 1102
Washington, DC 20006

United States Justice Foundation
2091 E. Valley Parkway, Suite 1-C
Escondido, CA 92027

United States of America Foundation
214 Massachusetts Ave., N.E., Suite 540
Washington, DC 20002

United Taxpayers Association
P.O. Box 04552
Milwaukee, WI 53204

Universal Society of Individualists
P.O. Box 664
Berkeley, CA 94701

Upright Ostrich
P.O. Box 11691
Milwaukee, WI 53211

Utah Caucus Club
P.O. Box 702
St. George, UT 84770

Vermont Heritage Institute
P.O. Box 98
South Barre, VT 05670

Voice of Freedom
18542 Rembrandt Terrace
Dallas, TX 75252

Volunteers for America
P.O. Box 75285
Washington, DC 20013

Washington International Institute
1900 M St., N.W., Suite 350
Washington, DC 20036

We Fight On
P.O. Box 7269
Phoenix, AZ 85011

We, The People
601 S.W. 8th Ave.
Conrad, MT 59425

Western Goals
111 S. Columbus St.
Alexandria, VA 22314
Linda C. Guell, Director

Western Information Network
Star Route, Box 71
Payson, AZ 85541

Western New York Freeman
P.O. Box 295
Amherst, NY 14226

Western World Press
P.O. Box 366
Sun City, CA 92381

Why Newsletter
902 Riverside
Medford, OR 97501

Wisconsin Society of Educated Citizens
3343 Royal Rd.
Janesville, WI 53546

Wisdom Publications
P.O. Box 575
Winona Lake, IN 46590
Skeet Savage, Publisher

Witherspoon Foundation
23126 L'Enfant Plaza Station
Washington DC 20026

Women Exploited by Abortion
24823 Nogal St.
Moreno Valley, CA 92388

World Freedom Foundation
111 S. Columbus St.
Alexandria, VA 22314
L. Brent Bozell, Chairman

World News Digest
1350 Center Dr., Suite 100
Dunwoody, GA 30338
Robert K. Kroening, Editor

World War III Battle Cry
7314 Mohawk Dr.
Dallas, TX 75235

World Youth Crusade for Freedom
1735 De Sales St., N.W., Suite 802
Washington, DC 20036

Worldwide Information Resources
1717 K St., N.W., Suite 706
Washington, DC 20006
Richard J. Whalen, Director

Young American Independent
P.O. Box 46
Fairdale, KY 40118

Young Conservative Council of America
P.O. Box 500014
San Diego, CA 92150

Young Conservative Foundation
1326 G St., S.E.
Washington, DC 20003

DEFUNCT

The organizations listed here have been confirmed to no longer exist. Their last known address and contact person are listed, as is any pertinent information regarding their dissolution.

Al Janny Newsletter
P.O. Box 1088
Fairfax, VA 22030

Allied Organizations for Freedom
P.O. Box 1252
New London, NH 03257

American Cause, The
P.O. Box 3170
Merrifield, VA 22116
Pat Buchanan, Chairman

American Enterprise Forum
228 Willow Bend
Huntsville, TX 77340
        The American Enterprise Forum dissolved in July 1994.
For its last seven months of operation the Forum compensated its
executive vice president, Sheridan Nichols, Ph.D., with $281,823.
This effectively depleted the Forum's accumulated assets. In the
two previous years, he was paid $57,000 and $58,708. The
Forum's Board of Trustees included Rep. Dick Armey (R-TX),
John Goodman, Ph.D. (National Center for Policy Analysis), and
other prominent conservatives.

Americanist
Route 1, Box 50
Ravenna, NE 68869

Arab American Republican Federation
918 16th St., N.W., Suite 501
Washington, DC 20006
Nader Sayegh, Director

Basic Education for America
P.O. Box 2369
Zanesville, OH 43701

Berkeley Citizens United
P.O. Box 44
Berkeley, CA 94701

Boston Conservative Society
P.O. Box 1870
Boston, MA 02205-1870
Dr. John Strang, Director

Bradley Project on the 90s
1150 17th St., N.W., 10th Floor
Washington, DC 20036
Bill Kristol, Director

Citizen Law Enforcement and Rescue
12115 N.E. 144th St.
Brush Prairie, WA 98606

Committee for a Free Lithuania
71-67 58th Rd.
Maspeth, NY 11378
Dr. Bronius Nemickas, Director

Committee for a Free China
P.O. Box 65012
Washington, DC 20035

Committee for the Free World
211 E. 51st St.
New York, NY 10022
Midge Decter, Director

Compassionate Capitalism Project
P.O. Box 455
Muskegon, MI 49443

Conservative Digest
529 14th St., Suite 1210
Washington, DC 20045

Constitutional Council
1888 S. 2500 East
Salt Lake City, UT 84108

Constitutional Revival
P.O. Box 3182
Enfield, CT 06083
Andrew Melechinsky

Council for Inter-American Security
1700 K St., N.W., Suite 650
Washington, DC 20006
        The Council for Inter-American Security, as well as its
affiliated organizations, the Council for Inter-American Security
Foundation and the National Security Advisory Board disbanded.
Legal proceedings are taking place against some of the former
officers for mismanagement of funds.

ESTATE
315 Panorama Dr.
Bakersfield, CA 93305

Facts are Facts Intelligence Service
405 Matthew St.
Haines City, FL 33844

Foundation of the American Economic Council
9595 Wilshire Blvd., Suite 200
Beverly Hills, CA 90212
Kenneth J. Gerbino, Director

Free Albania Organization
397-B W. Broadway
South Boston, MA 02127

Free Pacific Association
86 Riverside Dr.
New York, NY 10024
Rev. Paul Chan, Director

Free Spirit Press
P.O. Box 677
Bolivar, MO 65613

Freedom Inc.
P.O. Box 609
Wauna, WA 98395

Gloria Dei Press
919 Vogan Toll Rd.
Jackson, CA 95642
Margaret Scott, Director

Gould Cartoons
2010 Second St.
Long Beach, MS 39560

Greater Nebraskan
1330 Turner Blvd.
Omaha, NE 68105

Greentrack
P.O. Box 99
Libertytown, MD 2176
Peter Samuel, Director

Henry Salvatori Foundation
1901 Avenue of the Stars, Suite 230
Los Angeles, CA 90067

Independent Doctors of America
13412 E. Russell St.
Whittier, CA 90602
Frank A. Rogers, M.D., Director
        Merged with the Association of American Physicians and
Surgeons. Dr. Frank A. Rogers now operates the National
Coordinating Council.

International Freedom Council
200 G St., N.E., Suite 300
Washington, DC 20002

Jack Kemp Letter
422 1st St., S.E., Suite 300
Washington, DC 20003
Tom Phillips, Publisher

JAG
10 E. Charles St.
Oelwein, IA 50662

Joseph Story Society
107 2nd St., N.E.
Washington, DC 20002

June Ramsey Library
Route 3, Box 1192
Spicewood, TX 78669

Memory Hole
P.O. Box 94
Long Beach, CA 90801

Movement of Czechoslovak Christian Democrats
247 South St.
Hartford, CT 06114

National Center of Economic Education for Children
Lesley College
35 Mellen St.
Cambridge, MA 02138

National Commission on Economic Growth and Tax Reform
1133 Connecticut Ave., N.W., Suite 103
Washington, DC 20036
        A Commission composed of businessmen, public-policy
experts, and elected officials that reexamined the U.S. tax code and
proposed changes. The Commission recommended a flat tax at a
lower rate with large personal exemptions. Other recommendations
included a two-thirds super-majority in Congress to increase tax
rates, and reducing taxation on savings and investments. The
Commission was, in large part, organized by the Heritage
Foundation, and the Commission's recommendations can be
accessed on Heritage's website. Funding was provided by the
Heritage Foundation ($20,000), Carthage Foundation ($20,000),
and the Lynde and Harry Bradley Foundation ($20,000).

National Council for a Responsible Firearms Policy
7216 Stafford Rd.
Alexandria, VA 22307
David J. Steinberg, Director

National Security Advisory Board
1700 K St., N.W., Suite 650
Washington, DC 20006
        See the entry for the Council for Inter-American Security
in this Defunct section.

News Behind the News
5909 E. 26th St.
Tulsa, OK 74114

Oklahomans for Constitutional Taxation
Route 1, Box 15-A
Erick, OK 73645

Ollie North's Front Lines
7811 Montrose Rd.
Potomac, MD 20854

One Term Times
4641 N. 38th St.
Milwaukee, WI 53209

People Concerned About Today's Education
RR1, Box 235A
Monee, IL 60449

Private Doctors of America
3422 Bienville St.
New Orleans, LA 70119

Problems of Communism
U.S. Information Agency
United States of America
301 4th St., S.W.
Washington, DC 20402

Prolife Direct Action League
P.O. Box 11881
St. Louis, MO 63105

Religious Coalition for a Moral Drug Policy
3421 M St., N.W., Suite 351
Washington, DC 20007

Science and Engineering Committee for a Secure World
P.O. Box 76220
Washington, DC 20013
Dr. Fred Seitz, Director

Truth in Money
P.O. Box 30
Chagrin Falls, OH 44022

United States Council for an Open World Economy
7216 Stafford Rd.
Alexandria, VA 22307
David J. Steinberg, Director

University Professors for Academic Order
2412 Hathway Circle
Wichita, KS 67226

PERIODICALS

This section contains the names and addresses of the periodicals offered by organizations listed in the **Profiles** section of this guide. For more information, the researcher should refer to the corresponding profile.

3rd Rail
Young Americans for Social Security Reform (YASSR)
1801 Crystal Dr., Suite 1117
Arlington, VA 22202

AAPS News
Association of American Physicians and Surgeons (AAPS)
1601 N. Tucson Blvd., Suite 9
Tucson, AZ 85716

ABA Watch
Federalist Society for Law and Public Policy Studies
1700 K St., N.W., Suite 901
Washington, DC 20006

Academic Questions
National Association of Scholars (NAS)
575 Ewing St.
Princeton, NJ 08540

Access to Energy
P.O. Box 1250
Cave Junction, OR 97523

Account
Institute for Humane Studies (IHS)
4084 University Dr., Suite 101
Fairfax, VA 22030

Action News
Pro-Life Action League
6160 N. Cicero Ave., Suite 210
Chicago, IL 60646

Action Update
Southeastern Legal Foundation (SLF)
3340 Peachtree Rd., N.E., Suite 2515
Atlanta, GA 30326

ACTIV News
Alliance of California Taxpayers & Involved Voters (ACTIV)
P.O. Box 330
Aptos, CA 95001-0330

Acton Notes
Acton Institute for the Study of Religion and Liberty
161 Ottawa Ave., N.W., Suite 301
Grand Rapids, MI 49503

ADI News
American Defense Institute (ADI)
1055 N. Fairfax St., 2nd Floor
Alexandria, VA 22314

Advisor
Rocky Mountain Family Council
P.O. Box 13619
Denver, CO 80201

Advisory
Criminal Justice Legal Foundation (CJLF)
2131 L Street
Sacramento, CA 95816

AEI Newsletter
American Enterprise Institute for Public Policy Research (AEI)
1150 17th St., N.W.
Washington, DC 20036

AFCM Pulse
Americans for Free Choice in Medicine (AFCM)
1525 Superior Ave., Suite 100
Newport Beach, CA 92665

Agenda
National Center for Neighborhood Enterprise
1367 Connecticut Ave., N.W.
Washington, DC 20036

Aid and Abet Police Newsletter
Aid & Abet Foundation
P.O. Box 8787
Phoenix, AZ 85066

AIM Report
Accuracy in Media (AIM)
4455 Connecticut Ave., N.W., Suite 330
Washington, DC 20008

Alabama Citizen
Alabama Family Alliance
P.O. Box 59468
Birmingham, AL 35259

ALF News
Association of Libertarian Feminists (ALF)
P.O. Box 20252, London Terrace
New York, NY 10011

ALL About Issues
American Life League (ALL)
1179 Courthouse Rd.
Stafford, VA 22554

Alliance for America Newsletter
Alliance for America Foundation
P.O. Box 449
Caroga Lake, NY 12078

Alternatives in Philanthropy
Capital Research Center (CRC)
727 15th St., N.W., Suite 800
Washington, DC 20005

American Choices
Institute for Independent Education (IIE)
1313 N. Capitol St., N.E.
Washington, DC 20002

American Education Association Newsletter
American Education Association
P.O. Box 463
Center Moriches, NY 11934

American Enterprise
American Enterprise Institute for Public Policy Research (AEI)
1150 17th St., N.W.
Washington, DC 20036

American Experiment
Equal Opportunity Foundation
815 15th St., N.W., Suite 928
Washington, DC 20005

American Family Association Journal
American Family Association (AFA)
P.O. Drawer 2440
Tupelo, MS 38803

American Focus
P.O. Box 711599
Santee, CA 92072

American Hunter
National Rifle Association of America (NRA)
11250 Waples Mill Rd.
Fairfax, VA 22030

American Justice News
American Justice Federation
3850 South Emerson Avenue, Suite E
Indianapolis, IN 46203

American National
Central News Service
27036 Azul Dr.
Capistrano Beach, CA 92624

American Purpose
Ethics and Public Policy Center
1015 15th St., N.W., Suite 900
Washington, DC 20005

American Renaissance
New Century Foundation (NCF)
P.O. Box 1674
Louisville, KY 40201

American Rifleman
National Rifle Association of America (NRA)
11250 Waples Mill Rd.
Fairfax, VA 22030

American Sentinel
Sentinel Communications
15113 Steele Creek Rd.
Charlotte, NC 28273

American Sentinel
Radio Center, Suite 2E
3229 South Boulevard
Charlotte, NC 28209

American Sentry
Leadership Councils of America (LCA)
P.O. Box 373
Valparaiso, IN 46384

American Spectator
American Spectator Educational Foundation
2020 N. 14th St., Suite 750
Arlington, VA 22216

American Survival Guide
774 S. Placentia Ave.
Placentia, CA 92870

American Tax Reformer
Americans for Tax Reform Foundation
1320 18th St., N.W., Suite 200
Washington, DC 20036

American Tax Reformer
Americans for Tax Reform Foundation
1320 18th St., N.W., Suite 200
Washington, DC 20036

America's Future
7800 Bonhomme Ave.
St. Louis, MO 63105

Another View
Coalition on Urban Affairs
6033 W. Century Blvd., Suite 400
Los Angeles, CA 90045

Anti-VAT Report
Americans for Tax Reform Foundation
1320 18th St., N.W., Suite 200
Washington, DC 20036

AntiShyster: A Critical Examination of the American Legal System
P.O. Box 540786
Dallas, TX 75354

AOB News
Association of Objectivist Businessmen (AOB)
P.O. Box 370
Beverly, MA 01915

Aristos: The Journal of Esthetics
Aristos Foundation
P.O. Box 1105
New York, NY 10101

Arkansas Citizen
Family Council
1900 N. Bryant, Suite A
Little Rock, AR 72207

Arkansas Family Times
Family Council
1900 N. Bryant, Suite A
Little Rock, AR 72207

ASAP Report
Citizens United Foundation
11094-D Lee Highway, Suite 200
Fairfax, VA 22030

Ashbrook Essays
John M. Ashbrook Center for Public Affairs
Ashland University
Ashland, OH 44805

Austrian Economics Newsletter
Ludwig von Mises Institute
Auburn University
Auburn, AL 36849

AV Report
American Vision
10 Perimeter Way, Suite B-175
Atlanta, GA 30339

Bad News Bulletin
State Department Watch
P.O. Box 65398
Washington, DC 20035

Banner, The
For Limited American Government (FLAG)
601 San Juan Ct.
Irvine, TX 75062

Basic Education
Council for Basic Education (CBE)
1319 F St., N.W., Suite 900
Washington, DC 20004-1152

Battleline
American Conservative Union (ACU)
1007 Cameron St.
Alexandria, VA 22314

Beeson Report
42640 W. 10th St.
Lancaster, CA 93534

Berean Call, The
P.O. Box 7019
Bend, OR 97708

Biblical Chronology
Institute for Christian Economics (ICE)
P.O. Box 8000
Tyler, TX 75711

Biblical Economics Today
Institute for Christian Economics (ICE)
P.O. Box 8000
Tyler, TX 75711

Bionomic Perspectives
Bionomics Institute
2173 E. Francisco Blvd., Suite C
San Rafael, CA 94901

Black Economic Times
2303 W. Ledbetter, Suite 432
Dallas, TX 75224

Border Watch
American Immigration Control Foundation (AICF)
P.O. Box 525
Monterey, VA 24465

Boston Review
E53-407, MIT
Cambridge, MA 02139

Bottom Line
Commonwealth Foundation for Public Policy Alternatives
3544 N. Progress Ave., Suite 101
Harrisburg, PA 17110

Bottom Line
Entrepreneurial Leadership Center
Bellevue University
1000 Galvin Rd., S.
Bellevue, NE 68005

Brainwash
America's Future Foundation
1508 21st St., N.W.
Washington, DC 20036

Broadside
College Republican National Committee
600 Pennsylvania Ave., S.E., Suite 301
Washington, DC 20003

Budget Watch
Connecticut Policy and Economic Council (CPEC)
99 Pratt St., Suite 5
Hartford, CT 06103

Building Leadership
Leadership Institute
1101 N. Highland St.
Arlington, VA 22201

Bulletin of the Monetary Realist Society
Monetary Realist Society
P.O. Box 31044
St. Louis, MO 63131

Business & Family
Mississippi Family Council
P.O. Box 13514
Jackson, MS 39236

Business Advocate
United States Chamber of Commerce
1615 H St., N.W.
Washington, DC 20062

Business Bulletin
United States Business and Industrial Council
122 C St., N.W., Suite 815
Washington, DC 20001

Business / Consumer Quarterly
Pennsylvania Leadership Council (PLC)
225 State St., Suite 330
Harrisburg, PA 17101

Byline
Institute for Research on the Economics of Taxation (IRET)
1300 19th St., N.W., Suite 240
Washington, DC 20036

C.S. Lewis Institute Report
C. S. Lewis Institute
4208 Evergreen Lane, Suite 222
Annandale, VA 22003

Cal-Tax Letter
California Taxpayers Association
921 11th St., Suite 800
Sacramento, CA 95814

Cal-Tax News
California Taxpayers Association
921 11th St., Suite 800
Sacramento, CA 95814

California Citizen
Capitol Resource Institute
1314 H St., Suite 203
Sacramento, CA 95814

California Political Review
California Public Policy Foundation
P.O. Box 931
Camarillo, CA 93011

Calvert Comment
Calvert Institute for Policy Research
2806 N. Calvert St.
Baltimore, MD 21218

Calvert News
Calvert Institute for Policy Research
2806 N. Calvert St.
Baltimore, MD 21218

Campaign Update
Catholic Campaign for America (CCA)
1620 I St., N.W., Suite 916
Washington, DC 20006

Campbell Entrepreneur
Lundy Chair of Philosophy of Business
Campbell University
P.O. Box 1145
Buies Creek, NC 27501

Campus: America's Student Newspaper
Intercollegiate Studies Institute (ISI)
14 S. Bryn Mawr Ave., Suite 100
Bryn Mawr, PA 19010

Campus Leader
Young America's Foundation
110 Elden St.
Herndon, VA 22070

Campus Report
Accuracy in Academia (AIA)
4455 Connecticut Avenue, N.W., Suite 330
Washington, DC 20008

Capital & Liberty
P.O. Box 694
Wayne, MI 48184

Capital Formation
American Council for Capital Formation (ACCF)
1750 K St., N.W., Suite 400
Washington, DC 20006

Capital Ideas
National Taxpayers Union Foundation (NTUF)
108 N. Alfred St.
Alexandria, VA 22314

Capitol Comments
American Association of Christian Schools (AACS)
P.O. Box 2189
Independence, MO 64055

Capitol Hill Club Newsletter
National Republican Club of Capitol Hill
300 1st St., S.E.
Washington, DC 20003

CapitolWatch
601 Pennsylvania Ave., N.W., South Bldg., Suite 900
Washington, DC 20004

Carolina Journal
John Locke Foundation
1304 Hillsborough St.
Raleigh, NC 27605

Cascade Update
Cascade Policy Institute
813 S.W. Adler, Suite 707
Portland, OR 97205

Catholic Family News (CFN)
P.O. Box 743
Niagara Falls, NY 14302

Catholic World Report.
Ignatius Press / Guadalupe Associates
2515 McAllister St.
San Francisco, CA 94118

Cato Journal
Cato Institute
1000 Massachusetts Ave., N.W.
Washington, DC 20001

CEI Notes
Manhattan Institute for Public Policy Research
52 Vanderbilt Ave.
New York, NY 10017

CEI Update
Competitive Enterprise Institute (CEI)
1001 Connecticut Avenue, N.W., Suite 1250
Washington, DC 20036

Center News
Center for the Study of Popular Culture
P.O. Box 67398
Los Angeles, CA 90067

Chain Breaker
The Atlantis Project
4132 S. Rainbow Blvd., Suite 387
Las Vegas, NV 89103

Chicken Little Society Newsletter
Chicken Little Society
9175-D, S.W., 20th St.
Boca Raton, FL 33428

Chinese Family Voice
Chinese Family Alliance (CFA)
450 Taraval St., Suite 246
San Francisco, CA 94116

Christ and Country Courier
6020 Old Harford Rd.
Baltimore, MD 21214

Christian American
Christian Coalition
1801 Sara Drive, Suite L
Chesapeake, VA 23320

Christian Educator
Christian Liberty Academy Satellite Schools (CLASS)
502 W. Euclid Ave.
Arlington Heights, IL 60004

Christian Perspectives: A Journal of Free Enterprise
CHAMPION Economics & Business Association (CEBA)
P.O. Box 11471
Lynchburg, VA 24506

Christian Reconstruction
Institute for Christian Economics (ICE)
P.O. Box 8000
Tyler, TX 75711

Christians in Crisis
Christian Forum Research Foundation
1111 Fairgrounds Rd.
Grand Rapids, MN 55744

Chronicles: A Magazine of American Culture
Rockford Institute
934 N. Main St.
Rockford, IL 61103

Church Writing Group Newsletter
Amy Foundation
P.O. Box 16091
Lansing, MI 48901-6091

Citizen
Focus on the Family
8605 Explorer Dr.
Colorado Springs, CO 80920

Citizen Informer
Council of Conservative Citizens (CCC)
P.O. Box 9683
St. Louis, MO 63122

Citizen Outlook
Committee for a Constructive Tomorrow (CFACT)
P.O. Box 65722
Washington, DC 20035

Citizens Agenda
Citizens United
11094-D Lee Highway, Suite 200
Fairfax, VA 22030

Citizens Legal Advocate
Citizens United Foundation
11094-D Lee Highway, Suite 200
Fairfax, VA 22030

Citizen's Claw
New Nation USA (NNUSA)
P.O. Box 441
Morongo Valley, CA 92256

City Journal
Manhattan Institute for Public Policy Research
52 Vanderbilt Ave.
New York, NY 10017

Civic Bulletin
Manhattan Institute for Public Policy Research
52 Vanderbilt Ave.
New York, NY 10017

Civil Justice Memo
Manhattan Institute for Public Policy Research
52 Vanderbilt Ave.
New York, NY 10017

Clare Boothe Luce Policy Institute Newsletter
Clare Boothe Luce Policy Institute
112 Elden St., Suite P
Herndon, VA 20170

Classical Liberal
Center for Study of Market Alternatives (CSMA)
Suite 828, P.O. Box 15749
Boise, ID 83715

Claustrophobia
400 N. High St., #137
Columbus, OH 43215

ClintonWatch
Citizens United
11094-D Lee Highway, Suite 200
Fairfax, VA 22030

CLO News
Citizens for Law and Order (CLO)
P.O. Box 13308
Oakland, CA 94661

Club Bulletin
Conservative Book Club
15 Oakland Ave.
Harrison, NY 10528

CMR Notes
Center for Military Readiness (CMR)
P.O. Box 51600
Livonia, MI 48151

CMR Report
Center for Military Readiness (CMR)
P.O. Box 51600
Livonia, MI 48151

COMINT
Center for the Study of Popular Culture
P.O. Box 67398
Los Angeles, CA 90067

Commentary
American Jewish Committee
165 E. 56th St.
New York, NY 10022

Common Sense: A Republican Journal of Thought and Opinion
National Policy Forum
229 ½ Pennsylvania Avenue, S.E.
Washington, D.C. 20003

Community Impact Leader Notes
Illinois Family Institute (IFI)
799 W. Roosevelt Rd., Bldg. 3, Suite 218
Glen Ellyn, IL 60137

Compass
P.O. Box 1769
Murphys, CA 95247

Concern
International Christian Concern (ICC)
2020 Pennsylvania Ave., N.W., Suite 941
Washington, DC 20006

Concerned Women for America Newsletter
Concerned Women for America (CWA)
370 L'Enfant Promenade, S.W., Suite 800
Washington, DC 20024

Congressional Advisory
Institute for Research on the Economics of Taxation (IRET)
1300 19th St., N.W., Suite 240
Washington, DC 20036

Connecticut Watch
Connecticut Policy and Economic Council (CPEC)
99 Pratt St., Suite 5
Hartford, CT 06103

Connection, The
101 S. Whiting, Suite 700
Alexandria, VA 22304

Connector
New Nation USA (NNUSA)
P.O. Box 441
Morongo Valley, CA 92256

Conservative Chronicle
9 2nd St., N.W.
Hampton, IA 50441

Conservative Consensus
P.O. Box 17912
Seattle, WA 98107

Conservative Review
1307 Dolley Madison Blvd., Room 203
McLean, VA 22101

Consumer Comments
Consumer Alert
1001 Connecticut Ave., N.W., Suite 1128
Washington, DC 20036

Consumers' Research
800 Maryland Ave., N.E.
Washington, DC 20002

Continuity
Young America's Foundation
110 Elden St.
Herndon, VA 22070

Contra-PC
2635 Camino del Rio South, Suite 108
San Diego, CA 92108

Cornerstone
Stewards of the Range
802 W. Bannock, Suite 601
Boise, ID 83702

Correspondent
Plymouth Rock Foundation
Sandwich Rd.
Plymouth, MA 02360

Council Reporter
Council of Conservative Citizens (CCC)
P.O. Box 9683
St. Louis, MO 63122

Counterpoint
Tamarack Foundation
P.O. Box 23894
Tigard, OR 97223

CounterPoint
Washington Institute for Policy Studies
P.O. Box 24645
Seattle, WA 98124

CRC Bulletin
Committee to Restore the Constitution
P.O. Box 986
2218 W. Prospect Rd.
Fort Collins, CO 80522

Crisis
Brownson Institute
1511 K St., N.W., Suite 525
Washington, DC 20005

Critical Review
P.O. Box 1254
Danbury, CT 06813

Cuba Human Rights Monitor
Cuban American National Foundation (CANF)
10441 S.W. 187th St.
Miami, FL 33157

Cuba Survey
Cuban American National Foundation (CANF)
10441 S.W. 187th St.
Miami, FL 33157

Cuban Update
Cuban American National Foundation (CANF)
10441 S.W. 187th St.
Miami, FL 33157

Culture Wars
206 Marquette Ave.
South Bend, IN 46617

Culture Watch
Capital Research Center (CRC)
727 15th St., N.W., Suite 800
Washington, DC 20005

Declarations of Independence
Independence Institute
14142 Denver West Parkway, Suite 185
Golden, CO 80401

Defender
Center for the Study of Popular Culture
P.O. Box 67398
Los Angeles, CA 90067

Defense Forum Foundation Newsletter
Defense Forum Foundation (DFF)
3014 Castle Rd.
Falls Church, VA 22044

Desert News Letter
California Desert Coalition (CDC)
6192 Magnolia Ave., Suite D
Riverside, CA 92506

Destiny Magazine
18398 Redwood Highway
Selma, OR 97538

Details
Jewish Policy Center (JPC)
415 2nd St., N.E., Suite 100
Washington, DC 20002

DeWeese Report
American Policy Center
13873 Park Center Rd., Suite 316
Herndon, VA 20171

Different Drummer
Thoreau Institute
14417 S.E. Laurie
Oak Grove, OR 97267

Directions
Live Free International
P.O. Box 1743
Harvey, IL 60426

Dispatches
Western Journalism Center (WJC)
P.O. Box 2450
Fair Oaks, CA 95628

Docket Report
Center for Individual Rights (CIR)
1300 19th St., N.W., Suite 260
Washington, DC 20036

Dollars and Sense
National Taxpayers Union (NTU)
108 N. Alfred St.
Alexandria, VA 22314

Doublethink
America's Future Foundation
1508 21st St., N.W.
Washington, DC 20036

EBRI Issue Briefs
Employee Benefit Research Institute (EBRI)
2121 K St., N.W., Suite 600
Washington, DC 20037

EBRI's Benefit Outlook.
Employee Benefit Research Institute (EBRI)
2121 K St., N.W., Suite 600
Washington, DC 20037

Eco-Sanity Report
Heartland Institute
800 E. Northwest Highway, Suite 1080
Palatine, IL 60067

Econ Update
Free Enterprise Institute
9525 Katy Freeway, Suite 303
Houston, TX 77024-1415

Economic Affairs
Institute of Economic Affairs (IEA)
2 Lord North St.
London, SW1P 3LB, England
UNITED KINGDOM

Economic Directions
Center for Economic and Policy Education
Saint Vincent College
300 Fraser Purchase Rd.
Latrobe, PA 15650

Economic Education Bulletin
American Institute for Economic Research
P.O. Box 1000, Division St.
Great Barrington, MA 01230

Economic Monitor
Charles B McFadden Co.
P.O. Box 2268
Winter Park, FL 32790

Economic Policy Bulletin
Institute for Research on the Economics of Taxation (IRET)
1300 19th St., N.W., Suite 240
Washington, DC 20036

Economic Scorecard
Institute for Policy Innovation (IPI)
250 South Stemmons, Suite 306
Lewisville, TX 75067

Education in Focus
Books for All Times
P.O. Box 2
Alexandria, VA 22313

Education Insight
Cascade Policy Institute
813 S.W. Adler, Suite 707
Portland, OR 97205

Education Reporter
Eagle Forum
P.O. Box 618
Alton, IL 62002

Edwards Notebook Newsletter
Edwards Notebook
703 Parker, Suite 5
Detroit, MI 48214

Employee Benefit Notes
Employee Benefit Research Institute (EBRI)
2121 K St., N.W., Suite 600
Washington, DC 20037

EPA Watch
American Policy Center
13873 Park Center Rd., Suite 316
Herndon, VA 20171

Eric Voegelin Society Newsletter
Eric Voegelin Institute
Louisiana State University
240 Stubbs Hall
Baton Rouge, LA 70803-5466

Escoge La Vida (in Spanish).
Human Life International (HLI)
7845 Airpark Road, Suite E
Gaithersburg, MD 20879

Ethan Allen Institute Newsletter
Ethan Allen Institute (EAI)
RFD 1, Box 43
Concord, VT 05824

Ethics & Public Policy
Dumont Institute for Public Policy Research
236 Johnson Ave.
Dumont, NJ 07628

Ethics and Public Policy Center Newsletter
Ethics and Public Policy Center
1015 15th St., N.W., Suite 900
Washington, DC 20005

Ethics Watch
National Legal and Policy Center (NLPC)
8321 Old Courthouse Rd., Suite 270
Vienna, VA 22182

Evans-Novak Political Report
1750 Pennsylvania Ave., N.W., Room 1312
Washington, DC 20006

Ex Femina
Independent Women's Forum (IWF)
2111 Wilson Blvd., Suite 550
Arlington, VA 22201

Executive Alert
National Center for Policy Analysis (NCPA)
12655 N. Central Expressway, Suite 720
Dallas, TX 75243

FAC-Sheet
Plymouth Rock Foundation
Sandwich Rd.
Plymouth, MA 02360

Facts and Figures on Government Finance
Tax Foundation
1250 H Street, N.W., Suite 700
Washington, DC 20005-3908

Facts and Opinions
Public Interest Institute
600 N. Jackson
Mt. Pleasant, IA 52641

Factsheet Five
P.O. Box 170099
San Francisco, CA 94117

Family Alert
Christian Action Network (CAN)
P.O. Box 606
Forest, VA 24551

Family Alliance Report
North Dakota Family Alliance (NDFA)
4007 N. State St.
Bismarck, ND 58501

Family Educator
Pro-Family Forum
P.O. Box 8907
Fort Worth, TX 76124

Family in America
Rockford Institute
934 N. Main St.
Rockford, IL 61103

Family News
South Dakota Family Policy Council
P.O. Box 88007
Sioux Falls, SD 57109

Family Policy
Family Research Council (FRC)
801 G St., N.W.
Washington, DC 20001

Family Voice
Concerned Women for America (CWA)
370 L'Enfant Promenade, S.W., Suite 800
Washington, DC 20024

Fastrack
Fund for American Studies
1526 18th St., N.W.
Washington, DC 20036

Fatherhood Today
National Fatherhood Initiative (NFI)
600 Eden Rd., Bldg. E
Lancaster, PA 17601

Federal Tax Policy Memo
Tax Foundation
1250 H Street, N.W., Suite 700
Washington, DC 20005-3908

Federalist Paper
Federalist Society for Law and Public Policy Studies
1700 K St., N.W., Suite 901
Washington, DC 20006

FEDUP News
FEDUP Publishing
P.O. Box 477
East Moline, IL 61244-0477

Fighting Chance
Oregon Institute of Science and Medicine
2251 Dick George Road
Cave Junction, OR 97523

FIJActivist
Fully Informed Jury Association (FIJA)
P.O. Box 59
Helmsville, MT 59843

Financial Facts Newsletter
Financial Freedom Fellowship
6602 Beadnell Way, Suite 14
San Diego, CA 92117

Financial Privacy Report
P.O. Box 1277
Burnsville, MN 55337

Finest Hour
International Churchill Society
181 Burrage Rd.
Hopkinton, NH 03229

Firearms Sentinel
Jews for the Preservation of Firearms Ownership (JPFO)
2872 S. Wentworth Ave.
Milwaukee, WI 53207

Firing Line
California Rifle and Pistol Association
271 E. Imperial Highway, Suite 620
Fullerton, CA 92635

First Things: A Monthly Journal of Religion and Public Life
Institute on Religion and Public Life
156 5th Ave., Suite 400
New York, NY 10010

Fiscal Issues
Institute for Research on the Economics of Taxation
1300 19th St., N.W., Suite 240
Washington, DC 20036

Flashpoint
Living Truth Ministries
1708 Patterson Rd.
Austin, TX 78733

FMF Report
Free Market Foundation of Southern Africa (FMF)
105 Central St.
Houghton 2198
SOUTH AFRICA

Focus on the Family Magazine
Focus on the Family
8605 Explorer Dr.
Colorado Springs, CO 80920

For the Record
Jewish Policy Center (JPC)
415 2nd St., N.E., Suite 100
Washington, DC 20002

Foresight
Hudson Institute
5395 Emerson Way
Herman Kahn Center
P.O. Box 26-919
Indianapolis, IN 46226

Formulations
Free Nation Foundation (FNF)
111 West Corbin Street
Hillsborough, NC 27278

Forum
Institute for Republican Women
P.O. Box 65301
Washington, DC 20035

Foundation Action
National Right to Work Legal Defense and Education Foundation
8001 Braddock Rd., Suite 600
Springfield, VA 22160

Foundation Watch
Capital Research Center (CRC)
727 15th St., N.W., Suite 800
Washington, DC 20005

Foundations of Liberty
East Moline Christian School
900 46th Ave.
East Moline, IL 61244

Fragments
P.O. Box 38
Floral Park, NY 11002

Fraser Forum
Fraser Institute
626 Bute St., 2nd Floor
Vancouver, BC V6E 3M1
CANADA

Free American
Freedom Alliance
45472 Holiday Dr., Suite 10
Sterling, VA 20166

Free Enterprise Society
Free Enterprise Society
300 West Shaw Avenue, Suite 205
Clovis, CA 93612

Free Market
Ludwig von Mises Institute
Auburn University
Auburn, AL 36849

FREE Perspectives
Foundation for Research on Economics and the Environment (FREE)
945 Technology Blvd., Suite 101F
Bozeman, MT 59715

Freedom Bulletin
Free Africa Foundation (FAF)
1511 K St., N.W., Suite 1100
Washington, DC 20005

Freedom Club Report
International Christian Media
P.O. Box 30
Dallas, TX 75221

Freedom Daily
Future of Freedom Foundation (FFF)
11350 Random Hills Rd., Suite 800
Fairfax, VA 22030

Freedom Focus
Free Enterprise Institute
9525 Katy Freeway, Suite 303
Houston, TX 77024-1415

Freedom Messenger
Center for Study of Market Alternatives (CSMA)
Suite 828, P.O. Box 15749
Boise, ID 83715

Freedom Network News
International Society for Individual Liberty (ISIL)
1800 Market St.
San Francisco, CA 94102

Freedom of Choice
Citizens for Educational Choice
P.O. Box 405
Needham, MA 02194

Freedom Review
Freedom House
120 Wall St., 26th Floor
New York, NY 10005

Freedom Under Fire
Rutherford Institute
1445 E. Rio Road
Charlottesville, VA 22906

Freeman
Foundation for Economic Education (FEE)
30 S. Broadway
Irvington, NY 10533

Front Line
Heritage Preservation Association (HPA)
P.O. Box 98209
Atlanta, GA 30359

Frontline
Constitutional Coalition
P.O. Box 37054
St. Louis, MO 63141

Full Context
Objectivist Club of Michigan
1175-D Kirts Blvd.
Troy, MI 48084

Full Coverage
Council for Affordable Health Insurance (CAHI)
112 S. West St., Suite 400
Alexandria, VA 22314

Fundacion
Cuban American National Foundation (CANF)
10441 S.W. 187th St.
Miami, FL 33157

Future Insight
Progress & Freedom Foundation
1250 H St., N.W., Suite 550
Washington, DC 20005

FYI
American Legislative Exchange Council (ALEC)
910 17th St., N.W., 5th Floor
Washington, DC 20006

Georgia Policy
Georgia Public Policy Foundation
4340 Georgetown Sq., Suite 608
Atlanta, GA 30338

Georgians for Freedom in Education Newsletter
Georgians for Freedom in Education
209 Cobb St.
Palmetto, GA 30268

GOP Nationalities News
National Republican Heritage Council
310 1st St., S.E.
Washington, DC 20003-1801

Gottlieb - Tartaro Report
Second Amendment Foundation (SAF)
12500 N.E. 10th Place
Bellevue, WA 98005

Government Union Review
Public Service Research Foundation
527 E. Maple Ave., 3rd Floor
Vienna, VA 22180

Guillotine, The
Experimental Media Organization
Binghamton University
P.O. Box 6000
Binghamton, NY 13902

Gun News Digest
Second Amendment Foundation (SAF)
12500 N.E. 10th Place
Bellevue, WA 98005

Gun Owners
Gun Owners of America
8001 Forbes Place, Suite 102
Springfield, VA 22151

Gun Week
Second Amendment Foundation (SAF)
12500 N.E. 10th Place
Bellevue, WA 98005

Gunsmoke
Ohio Rifle and Pistol Association (ORPA)
P.O. Box 43083
Cincinnati, OH 45243

Headway
13555 Bammel N. Houston Rd., Suite 227
Houston, TX 77066

Heartbeat International
Heartbeat International
7870 Olentangy River Rd., Suite 304
Columbus, OH 43235

Heartlander
Heartland Institute
800 E. Northwest Highway, Suite 1080
Palatine, IL 60067

Heritage Action Alert
Wyoming Heritage Society
139 W. 2nd St., Suite 3E
Casper, WY 82601

Heritage Report
Wyoming Heritage Society
139 W. 2nd St., Suite 3E
Casper, WY 82601

Heterodoxy
Center for the Study of Popular Culture
P.O. Box 67398
Los Angeles, CA 90067

Highlights
Atlas Economic Research Foundation
4084 University Dr., Suite 103
Fairfax, VA 22030

HKCER Letters
Hong Kong Centre for Economic Research (HKCER)
The University of Hong Kong
Pokfulam Road
HONG KONG

HLI Reports
Human Life International (HLI)
7845 Airpark Road, Suite E
Gaithersburg, MD 20879

Hollywood Watch
Media Research Center (MRC)
113 S. West St., Suite 200
Alexandria, VA 22314

Home School Researcher
National Home Education Research Institute (NHERI)
P.O. Box 13939
Salem, OR 97301

Hoover Digest
Hoover Institution on War, Revolution and Peace
Stanford University
Stanford, CA 94305

Hoover Institution Newsletter
Hoover Institution on War, Revolution and Peace
Stanford University
Stanford, CA 94305

Horizons
Oregonians in Action (OIA)
P.O. Box 230637
Tigard, OR 97281

Human Events
422 1st St., S.E.
Washington, DC 20003

Human Life Review
Human Life Foundation
150 E. 35th St.
New York, NY 10016

Humane Studies Review
Institute for Humane Studies (IHS)
4084 University Dr., Suite 101
Fairfax, VA 22030

Humanitas
National Humanities Institute
214 Massachusetts Avenue, N.E., Suite 470
Washington, DC 20002

Hume Papers on Public Policy
David Hume Institute
21 George Square
Edinburgh EH8 9LD, Scotland
UNITED KINGDOM

ICSA Newsletter
International Christian Studies Association (ICSA)
2828 3rd St., Suite 11
Santa Monica, CA 90405

Ideas
Josiah Bartlett Center for Public Policy
7 S. State St.
Concord, NH 03301

Ideas in Action
Pacific Research Institute for Public Policy (PRI)
755 Sansome St., Suite 450
San Francisco, CA 94111

Ideas Matter
National Policy Forum
229½ Pennsylvania Avenue, S.E.
Washington, D.C. 20003

Illinois Family Citizen
Illinois Family Institute (IFI)
799 W. Roosevelt Rd., Bldg. 3, Suite 218
Glen Ellyn, IL 60137

Immigration Review
Center for Immigration Studies
1815 H St., N.W., Suite 1010
Washington, DC 20006

IMPACT
Ayn Rand Institute: The Center for the Advancement of Objectivism
4640 Admiralty Way, Suite 715
Marina Del Rey, CA 90292

IMPACT
Coral Ridge Ministries Media
5554 N. Federal Highway, Suite 200
Fort Lauderdale, FL 33308

IMPACT!
Mackinac Center for Public Policy
119 Ashman St., P.O. Box 568
Midland, MI 48640

Imprimis
Hillsdale College
33 E. College St.
Hillsdale, MI 49242

Imprint
Public Interest Institute
600 N. Jackson
Mt. Pleasant, IA 52641

In Context
Washington Research Council (WRC)
1301 Fifth Ave., Suite 2810
Seattle, WA 98101

Independent Policy Report
Independent Institute
134 98th Ave.
Oakland, CA 94603

Independent Review
Independent Institute
134 98th Ave.
Oakland, CA 94603

Independent, The
Independent Institute
134 98th Ave.
Oakland, CA 94603

Indiana Policy Review
Indiana Policy Review Foundation
320 N. Meridian, Suite 904
Indianapolis, IN 46204

Inside California
Western Journalism Center (WJC)
P.O. Box 2450
Fair Oaks, CA 95628

Insider
Heritage Foundation
214 Massachusetts Ave., N.E.
Washington, DC 20002

Insider, The
South Carolina Policy Council Education Foundation
1419 Pendleton St.
Columbia, SC 29201

Insider's Report
National Right to Work Committee
8001 Braddock Rd., Suite 600
Springfield, VA 22160

Insider's Report
American Policy Center
13873 Park Center Rd., Suite 316
Herndon, VA 20171

Insight on the News
3600 New York Ave., N.E.
Washington, DC 20002

Institute Brief
Public Interest Institute
600 N. Jackson
Mt. Pleasant, IA 52641

Institute Quarterly
Washington Institute for Policy Studies
P.O. Box 24645
Seattle, WA 98124

Intellectual Ammunition
Heartland Institute
800 E. Northwest Highway, Suite 1080
Palatine, IL 60067

Intercollegiate Review
Intercollegiate Studies Institute (ISI)
14 S. Bryn Mawr Ave., Suite 100
Bryn Mawr, PA 19010

IOS Journal
Institute for Objectivist Studies (IOS)
82 Washington St., Suite 207
Poughkeepsie, NY 12601

Iowa Economic Scorecard
Public Interest Institute
600 N. Jackson
Mt. Pleasant, IA 52641

IPI Insights
Institute for Policy Innovation (IPI)
250 South Stemmons, Suite 306
Lewisville, TX 75067

IRI
International Republican Institute (IRI)
1212 New York Ave., N.W., Suite 900
Washington, DC 20005

Issue Brief
Institute for Policy Innovation (IPI)
250 South Stemmons, Suite 306
Lewisville, TX 75067

Issue Paper
Reason Foundation
3415 Sepulveda Blvd., Suite 400
Los Angeles, CA 90034

Issues & Views
Issues & Views Open Forum Foundation
P.O. Box 467
New York, NY 10025

Issues in Law and Medicine
Horatio R. Storer Foundation
419 7th St., N.W.
Washington, DC 20004

James Madison Messenger
James Madison Institute
2017 Delta Blvd., Suite 102
Tallahassee, FL 32303

JBS Bulletin
John Birch Society
770 Westhill Blvd.
Appleton, WI 54914

Jobs & Capital
Milken Institute for Job & Capital Formation (MIJCF)
1250 4th St., 2nd Floor
Santa Monica, CA 90401

Journal of Accounting
Dumont Institute for Public Policy Research
236 Johnson Ave.
Dumont, NJ 07628

Journal of Biblical Ethics in Medicine
Covenant Enterprises
P.O. Box 14488
Augusta, GA 30919

Journal of Civil Defense
The American Civil Defense Association (TACDA)
118 Court St.
Starke, FL 32091

Journal of Interdisciplinary Studies
International Christian Studies Association (ICSA)
2828 3rd St., Suite 11
Santa Monica, CA 90405

Journal of Libertarian Studies
Center for Libertarian Studies (CLS)
875 Mahler Rd., Suite 150
Burlingame, CA 94010

Judicial Legislative Watch Report.
National Legal Center for the Public Interest
1000 16th St., N.W., Suite 301
Washington, DC 20036

Judicial Selection Monitor
Free Congress Research and Education Foundation
717 2nd St., N.E.
Washington, DC 20002

Judicial Watch
Abraham Lincoln Foundation for Public Policy Research
10315 Georgetown Pike
Great Falls, VA 22066

Justice Journal.
P.O. Box 8636
Independence, MO 64054

Kansas Intelligencer
211 W. Elizabeth Ave.
Morganville, KS 66502

Keene Report
12500 Fairlakes Circle, Suit 155
Fairfax, VA 22033

Kwong's News Digest
450 Taraval, Suite 246
San Francisco, CA 94116

Lambda Report on Homosexuality
P.O. Box 45252
Washington, DC 20026-5252

Land Rights Advocate
American Land Rights Association (ALRA)
30218 N.E. 82nd Ave.
Battle Ground, WA 98604

Land Rights Letter
Land Rights Foundation
P.O. Box 1111
Gloverville, NY 12078

LEAA Advocate
Law Enforcement Alliance of America (LEAA)
7700 Leesburg Pike, Suite 421
Falls Church, VA 22043-2618

Legal Briefs Bulletin
Legal Affairs Council
3554 Chain Bridge Rd., Suite 301
Fairfax, VA 22033

Legal Limit
U.S. Term Limits Foundation
1511 K St., N.W., Suite 540
Washington, DC 20005

Legal Watch
United Citizens for Legal Reform (UCLR)
2801V Eubank, N.E., Suite 167
Albuquerque, NM 87112

Letter From Plymouth Rock
Plymouth Rock Foundation
Sandwich Rd.
Plymouth, MA 02360

LFL Reports
Libertarians for Life (LFL)
13424 Hathaway Dr.
Wheaton, MD 20906

LGLC Newsletter
Libertarians for Gay and Lesbian Concerns (LGLC)
P.O. Box 447
Chelsea, MI 48118

Liberals Always Waffle Newsletter (LAWN)
2490 Black Rock Turnpike, Suite 422
Fairfield, CT 06430

Liberator, The
Men's Defense Association
17854 Lyons St.
Forest Lake, MN 55025

Liberator
Advocates for Self-Government
1202 N. Tennessee St., Suite 202
Cartersville, GA 30120

Libertarian Party News
Libertarian Party
2600 Virginia Ave., N.W., Suite 100
Washington, DC 20037

Libertarian Student
Alliance of Libertarian Student Organizations
25 Red Lion Square
London WC1R 4RL, England
UNITED KINGDOM

Libertas
Young America's Foundation
110 Elden St.
Herndon, VA 22070

Liberty
Liberty Foundation
P.O. Box 1181
Port Townsend, WA 98368

Liberty Lamp
Foundation for Traditional Values
4407 W. St. Joseph
Lansing, MI 48917

Liberty Pole
Lawyer's Second Amendment Society (LSAS)
18034 Ventura Blvd., Suite 329
Encino, CA 91316

LibertyTree
Independent Institute
134 98th Ave.
Oakland, CA 94603

Library Bulletin
Tax Foundation
1250 H Street, N.W., Suite 700
Washington, DC 20005-3908

Life Date
Lutherans for Life
1229 S. G Ave., Building B, Suite 100
Nevada, IA 50201

Life Issues Connector
Life Issues Institute
1721 W. Galbraith Rd.
Cincinnati, OH 45239

Lifeletter
Ad Hoc Committee in Defense of Life
150 E. 35th St.
New York, NY 10016

Lifeline
Life Legal Defense Foundation (LLDF)
P.O. Box 2105
Napa, CA 94558

Lifeline
Right to Life, Florida (Lee County)
4720 S.E. 15th Ave., Suite 103
Cape Coral, FL 33904

Limbaugh Letter
366 Madison Ave.
New York, NY 10017

Limits
Public Interest Institute
600 N. Jackson
Mt. Pleasant, IA 52641

Lincoln Review
Lincoln Institute for Research and Education
1001 Connecticut Ave., N.W., Suite 1135
Washignton, DC 20036

Live and Let Live
P.O. Box 613
Redwood Valley, CA 95470

Living
Lutherans for Life
1229 S. G Ave., Building B, Suite 100
Nevada, IA 50201

Living Free
P.O. Box 29, Hiler Branch
Buffalo, NY 14223

Living World
International Life Services
2606½ W. 8th St.
Los Angeles, CA 90057

Lofton Letter
P.O. Box 1142
Laurel, MD 20725

Lone Star Citizen
Free Market Foundation
P.O. Box 740367
Dallas, TX 75374

Looking Forward
Oregonians in Action (OIA)
P.O. Box 230637
Tigard, OR 97281

MacArthur Institute Update
East Moline Christian School
900 46th Ave.
East Moline, IL 61244

Madison Journal
James Madison Institute
2017 Delta Blvd., Suite 102
Tallahassee, FL 32303

Madison Review
James Madison Institute
2017 Delta Blvd., Suite 102
Tallahassee, FL 32303

Main Street Memoranda
Rockford Institute
934 N. Main St.
Rockford, IL 61103

MARConnections
Media Associates Resource Coalition (MARC)
P.O. Box 5100
Zionsville, IN 46077-5100

Market Process News
Center for Market Processes
4084 University Drive, Suite 208
Fairfax, VA 22030-6815

Massachusetts Citizen
Massachusetts Family Institute
381 Elliot St.
Newton Upper Falls, MA 02164

Massachusetts Family Report
Massachusetts Family Institute
381 Elliot St.
Newton Upper Falls, MA 02164

Measure
University Centers for Rational Alternatives
570 7th Ave., Suite 1007
New York, NY 10018

Media Bypass: The Uncensored National News
P.O. Box 5326
Evansville, IN 47716

Media Monitor
Center for Media and Public Affairs
2101 L St., N.W., Suite 300
Washington, DC 20037

MediaNomics
Media Research Center (MRC)
113 S. West St., Suite 200
Alexandria, VA 22314

MediaWatch
Media Research Center (MRC)
113 S. West St., Suite 200
Alexandria, VA 22314

Medical Sentinel
Association of American Physicians and Surgeons (AAPS)
1601 N. Tucson Blvd., Suite 9
Tucson, AZ 85716

Member's Message
Conservative Caucus
450 E. Maple Ave., Suite 309
Vienna, VA 22180

Middle American News
We the People Institute (WTP)
6600 Six Forks Rd., Suite 103
Raleigh, NC 27615

Middle East Quarterly
Middle East Forum
1920 Chestnut St.
Philadelphia, PA 19103

Mindszenty Report
Cardinal Mindszenty Foundation (CMF)
P.O. Box 11321
St. Louis, MO 63105

Minuteman, The
National Legal Foundation
6477 College Park Square, Suite 306
Virginia Beach, VA 23464

Mises Memo
Ludwig von Mises Institute
Auburn University
Auburn, AL 36849

Mises Review
Ludwig von Mises Institute
Auburn University
Auburn, AL 36849

Mission to the Persecuted
Christian Solidarity International (CSI)
1260 Billington Rd.
Silver Spring, MD 20904

Modern Age
Intercollegiate Studies Institute (ISI)
14 S. Bryn Mawr Ave., Suite 100
Bryn Mawr, PA 19010

Moneychanger, The
P.O. Box 341753
Memphis, TN 38184

Morality in Media Newsletter
Morality In Media (MIM)
475 Riverside Dr.
New York, NY 10115

Movieguide: A Family Guide to Movies and Entertainment
Christian Film and Television Commission
2510-G Las Posas Rd., Suite 502
Camarillo, CA 93010

NAS Update
National Association of Scholars (NAS)
575 Ewing St.
Princeton, NJ 08540

Nathan Hale Newsletter
Nathan Hale Institute
104 North Carolina Ave., S.E.
Washington, DC 20003

Nation's Business
United States Chamber of Commerce
1615 H St., N.W.
Washington, DC 20062

National Humanities Bulletin
National Humanities Institute
214 Massachusetts Avenue, N.E., Suite 470
Washington, DC 20002

National Interest
National Affairs
1112 16th St., N.W., Suite 530
Washington, DC 20036

National Legal Center for the Public Interest News
National Legal Center for the Public Interest
1000 16th St., N.W., Suite 301
Washington, DC 20036

National Monitor of Education
P.O. Box 402
Alamo, CA 94596

National Program Letter
National Education Program (NEP)
P.O. Box 11000
Oklahoma City, OK 73136

National Rescuer
Operation Rescue
P.O. Box 1180
Binghamton, NY 13902

National Review
215 Lexington Ave.
New York, NY 10016

National Right to Life News
Right to Life, National Committee
419 7th St., N.W., Suite 500
Washington, DC 20004

National Right to Work Newsletter
National Right to Work Committee
8001 Braddock Rd., Suite 600
Springfield, VA 22160

National Security Report
National Security Center
3554 Chainbridge Road, Suite 301
Fairfax, VA 22030

NCBA Reports
National Commodity and Barter Association (NCBA)
P.O. Box 2255
Longmont, CO 80502

Network News
Oregon Lands Coalition
247 N.E. Commercial St.
Salem, OR 97301

New American, The
John Birch Society
770 Westhill Blvd.
Appleton, WI 54914

New Constellation
National Flag Foundation (NFF)
Flag Plaza
Pittsburgh, PA 15219

New Criterion, The
Foundation for Cultural Review
850 7th Avenue, Suite 400
New York, NY 10019

New Electric Railway Journal
Free Congress Research and Education Foundation
717 2nd St., N.E.
Washington, DC 20002

New Guard (quarterly).
Young Americans for Freedom (YAF)
1208 N. DuPont St.
Wilmington, DE 19806

New York Property Rights Clearinghouse
Property Rights Foundation of America
P.O. Box 75
Stony Creek, NY 12878

News and Views
Center for Entrepreneurship and Free Enterprise (CEFE)
Reinhardt College
7300 Reinhardt College Parkway
Waleska, GA 30183

News from The FLOC
Fairness to Land Owners Committee (FLOC)
1730 Garden of Eden Road
Cambridge, MD 21613

news@csis.dc
Center for Strategic and International Studies (CSIS)
1800 K St., N.W., Suite 400
Washington, DC 20006

NewsLink
Beacon Hill Institute for Public Policy Research
Suffolk University, 8 Ashburton Place
Boston, MA 02108

NFF Update
National Forum Foundation (NFF)
511 C St., N.E.
Washington, DC 20002

NJC Bulletin
National Jewish Coalition (NJC)
415 2nd St., N.E., Suite 100
Washington, DC 20002

NMA News
National Motorists Association (NMA)
6678 Pertzborn Road
Dane, WI 53529

No Statesman Magazine
Alliance of Libertarian Student Organizations
25 Red Lion Square
London WC1R 4RL, England
UNITED KINGDOM

No Uncertain Terms
U.S. Term Limits
1511 K St., N.W., Suite 540
Washington, DC 20008

NOEL News
National Organization of Episcopalians for Life (NOEL)
10523 Main St.
Fairfax, VA 22030

North Carolina Citizen
North Carolina Family Policy Council
P.O. Box 2567
Raleigh, NC 27602

North Carolina Family Policy News
North Carolina Family Policy Council
P.O. Box 2567
Raleigh, NC 27602

North Dakota Citizen
North Dakota Family Alliance (NDFA)
4007 N. State St.
Bismarck, ND 58501

Notable Quotables
Media Research Center (MRC)
113 S. West St., Suite 200
Alexandria, VA 22314

Notes from FEE
Foundation for Economic Education (FEE)
30 S. Broadway
Irvington, NY 10533

NWI Resource
National Wilderness Institute (NWI)
P.O. Box 25766
Washington, DC 20007

NY Conservative
New York State Conservative Party
486 78th St.
Brooklyn, NY 11209

Obscenity Law Bulletin
Morality In Media (MIM)
475 Riverside Dr.
New York, NY 10115

OCPA Perspective
Oklahoma Council of Public Affairs (OCPA)
100 W. Wilshire, Suite C-3
Oklahoma City, OK 73116

Ohio Education Report
Buckeye Institute for Public Policy Solutions
131 N. Ludlow St., Suite 317
Dayton, OH 45402

Oklahoma Citizen
Oklahoma Family Policy Council
5101 N. Classen Blvd.
Oklahoma City, OK 73118

On Balance
Fraser Institute
626 Bute St., 2nd Floor
Vancouver, BC V6E 3M1
CANADA

On Target
Gun Owners of Macomb County (GOMAC)
P.O. Box 46364
Mt. Clemens, MI 48045

Online Nevada
Nevada Policy Research Institute (NPRI)
800 W. 2nd St.
Reno, NV 89503

Opportunity
Center for Education Reform (CER)
1001 Connecticut Ave, N.W., Suite 920
Washington, DC 20036

Orbis
Foreign Policy Research Institute (FPRI)
1528 Walnut St., Suite 610
Philadelphia, PA 19102

Organization Trends
Capital Research Center (CRC)
727 15th St., N.W., Suite 800
Washington, DC 20005

Origins & Design
Access Research Network (ARN)
P.O. Box 38069
Colorado Springs, CO 80937

Outlook
Delaware Public Policy Institute (DPPI)
1201 N. Orange St., Suite 501
Wilmington, DE 19899

Outlook
Hudson Institute
5395 Emerson Way
Herman Kahn Center
P.O. Box 26-919
Indianapolis, IN 46226

Pacific Outlook
Pacific Research Institute for Public Policy (PRI)
755 Sansome St., Suite 450
San Francisco, CA 94111

PacNet Newsletter
Pacific Forum CSIS
1001 Bishop St.
Pauahi Tower, Suite 1150
Honolulu, HI 96813

Paradigm 2000
Renaissance Foundation
205 3rd St., S.E.
Washington, DC 20003

Parent Update
American Association of Christian Schools (AACS)
P.O. Box 2189
Independence, MO 64055

Parental Guidance
Focus on the Family
8605 Explorer Dr.
Colorado Springs, CO 80920

Parents' Choice
Educational Freedom Foundation (EFF)
927 S. Walter Reed Dr., Suite 1
Arlington, VA 22204

Patriot Cannon
Patriot Network
515 Concord Ave.
Anderson, SC 29621

Pennsylvania Education Review
Pennsylvania Leadership Council (PLC)
225 State St., Suite 330
Harrisburg, PA 17101

People Count
Committee on Population and the Economy
53 Cavendish Road
London SW12 0DQ, England
UNITED KINGDOM

People for the West!
National Coalition for Public Lands and Natural Resources
(NCPLNR)
301 N. Main St., Suite 306
Pueblo, CO 81003

PERC Reports
Political Economy Research Center (PERC)
502 S. 19th Ave., Suite 211
Bozeman, MT 59715

PERC Viewpoints
Political Economy Research Center (PERC)
502 S. 19th Ave., Suite 211
Bozeman, MT 59715

PERCspectives
Private Enterprise Research Center
Texas A&M University
459 Blocker Building
College Station, TX 77843

Perspective
Council for Basic Education (CBE)
1319 F St., N.W., Suite 900
Washington, DC 20004-1152

Perspective on Current Issues
Buckeye Institute for Public Policy Solutions
131 N. Ludlow St., Suite 317
Dayton, OH 45402

Perspectives
Toward Tradition
P.O. Box 58
Mercer Island, WA 98040

Petitioner, The
National Commodity and Barter Association (NCBA)
P.O. Box 2255
Longmont, CO 80502

Philanthropy
Philanthropy Roundtable
1150 17th St., Suite 503
Washington, DC 20036

Philanthropy, Culture, and Society
Capital Research Center (CRC)
727 15th St., N.W., Suite 800
Washington, DC 20005

Phoenix Letter
4400 Loma Vista Dr.
Billings, MT 59106

Phyllis Schlafly Report
Eagle Forum
P.O. Box 618
Alton, IL 62002

Physician
Focus on the Family
8605 Explorer Dr.
Colorado Springs, CO 80920

PLAGAL Memorandum
Pro-Life Alliance of Gays and Lesbians (PLAGAL)
P.O. Box 33292
Washington, DC 20033

Point Blank
Citizens Committee for the Right to Keep and Bear Arms
(CCRKBA)
Liberty Park
12500 N.E. Tenth Place
Bellevue, WA 98005

Points West Chronicle
Center for the New West
600 World Trade Center
1625 Broadway
Denver, CO 80202

Policy Brief
Constitutional Coalition
P.O. Box 37054
St. Louis, MO 63141

Policy Counsel
Council for National Policy (CNP)
3030 Clarendon Blvd., Suite 340
Arlington, VA 22201

Policy Note
Buckeye Institute for Public Policy Solutions
131 N. Ludlow St., Suite 317
Dayton, OH 45402

Policy Perspectives
Yankee Institute for Public Policy
117 New London Turnpike
Glastonbury, CT 06033

Policy Review
Heritage Foundation
214 Massachusetts Ave., N.E.
Washington, DC 20002

Political Dynamite
P.O. Box 467939
Atlanta, GA 31146

Political Science Reviewer
Intercollegiate Studies Institute (ISI)
14 S. Bryn Mawr Ave., Suite 100
Bryn Mawr, PA 19010

Positions on Property
Property Rights Foundation of America
P.O. Box 75
Stony Creek, NY 12878

Pragmatist
P.O. Box 392
Forest Grove, PA 18922

President's Quarterly
Pacific Research Institute for Public Policy (PRI)
755 Sansome St., Suite 450
San Francisco, CA 94111

Preview: Family Movie & TV Review
Movie Morality Ministries
1309 Seminole Dr.
Richardson, TX 75080

PRI Review
Population Research Institute (PRI)
5119-A Leesburg Pike, Suite 295
Falls Church, VA 22041

Principia
Zenger News Service (ZNS)
P.O. Box 98950
Seattle, WA 98198

Priorities
American Council on Science and Health (ACSH)
1995 Broadway, 16th Floor
New York, NY 10023-5860

Privacy Journal
P.O. Box 28577
Providence, RI 02908

Private Property Congressional Vote Index
League of Private Property Voters (LPPV)
30218 N.E. 82nd Ave.
Battle Ground, WA 98604

Private Sector
Center for the Defense of Free Enterprise
12500 N.E. 10th Place
Bellevue, WA 98005

Privatization Report
Mackinac Center for Public Policy
119 Ashman St., P.O. Box 568
Midland, MI 48640

Privatization Watch
Reason Foundation
3415 Sepulveda Blvd., Suite 400
Los Angeles, CA 90034

Pro-Family News
Minnesota Family Council
2855 Anthony Lane, S., Suite 150
Minneapolis, MN 55418-3265

Pro-Life Collegian
College Pro-Life Information Network
P.O. Box 10664
State College, PA 16805

Proceedings of the Churchill Societies
International Churchill Society
181 Burrage Rd.
Hopkinton, NH 03229

Property Rights Reporter
Defenders of Property Rights
6235 33rd St., N.W.
Washington, DC 20015

Public Interest
National Affairs
1112 16th St., N.W., Suite 530
Washington, DC 20036

Public View
Claremont Institute for the Study of Statesmanship and Political Philosophy
250 W. 1st St., Suite 330
Claremont, CA 91711

Quarterly
Christian Legal Society
4208 Evergreen Lane, Suite 222
Annandale, VA 22003

Quick Read
Illinois Public Policy Caucuses (IPPC)
151 North Michigan Ave., Suite 2815
Chicago, IL 60601

Rampart Individualist
Rampart Institute
P.O. Box 22231
Carmel, CA 93922-0231

Rational Conservative, The
R.R. 2, Box 6880
Fair Haven, VT 05743

RCDA (acronym for Religion in Communist Dominated Areas)
Research Center for Religion and Human Rights in Closed Societies
475 Riverside Dr., Suite 828
New York, NY 10115

Reagan Alumni Directory
Reagan Alumni Association
7212 Valon Ct.
Alexandria, VA 22307-2045

Reagan Alumni Newsletter
Reagan Alumni Association
7212 Valon Ct.
Alexandria, VA 22307-2045

Reason
Reason Foundation
3415 Sepulveda Blvd., Suite 400
Los Angeles, CA 90034

Reason Papers: A Journal of Interdisciplinary Normative Studies
MCB University Press Ltd.
60/62 Toller Lane
Bradford, BD8 9BY, England
UNITED KINGDOM

Reason Report
Reason Foundation
3415 Sepulveda Blvd., Suite 400
Los Angeles, CA 90034

Regulation
Cato Institute
1000 Massachusetts Ave., N.W.
Washington, DC 20001

Religion & Liberty
Acton Institute for the Study of Religion and Liberty
161 Ottawa Ave., N.W., Suite 301
Grand Rapids, MI 49503

Religion and Society Report
Rockford Institute
934 N. Main St.
Rockford, IL 61103

Religious Heritage of America Newsletter
Religious Heritage of America
1750 S. Brentwood Blvd., Suite 502
St. Louis, MO 63144

Religious Liberty Bulletin
Rutherford Institute
1445 E. Rio Road
Charlottesville, VA 22906

Religious Rights Watch
Christian Coalition
1801 Sara Drive, Suite L
Chesapeake, VA 23320

Report Card
Center for the Study of Popular Culture
P.O. Box 67398
Los Angeles, CA 90067

Report from Enterprise Square, USA
Enterprise Square, 2501 E. Memorial Rd., Box 11000
Oklahoma City, OK 73136-1100

Report from Valley Forge
Freedoms Foundation at Valley Forge
Route 23
Valley Forge, PA 19481

Report to Congress
Council of Volunteer Americans (CVA)
7263 Maple Place, Suite 203
Annandale, VA 22003

Republican Liberty
Republican Liberty Caucus (RLC)
611 Pennsylvania Ave., S.E., Suite 370
Washington, DC 20003

Republican Woman
National Federation of Republican Women (NFRW)
124 N. Alfred St.
Alexandria, VA 22314

Res Publica
John M. Ashbrook Center for Public Affairs
Ashland University
Ashland, OH 44805

Research Reports
American Institute for Economic Research
P.O. Box 1000, Division St.
Great Barrington, MA 01230

Review of Austrian Economics
Ludwig von Mises Institute
Auburn University
Auburn, AL 36849

Right NOW!
333 E. Maple Ave., Suite 225
Vienna, VA 22180

Right to Life League of Southern California Newsletter
Right to Life League of Southern California
1028 N. Lake Ave., Suite 102
Pasadena, CA 91104

Right to Read Report
National Right to Read Foundation (NRRF)
P.O. Box 490
The Plains, VA 20198

Right Word
Pennsylvania Leadership Council (PLC)
225 State St., Suite 330
Harrisburg, PA 17101

Ripon Forum
Ripon Society
501 Capitol Court, N.E., Suite 300
Washington, DC 20002

Roundtable Report
Religious Roundtable
P.O. Box 11467
Memphis, TN 38111

Roundtable Update
Religious Roundtable
P.O. Box 11467
Memphis, TN 38111

RU486 Report
Life Issues Institute
1721 W. Galbraith Rd.
Cincinnati, OH 45239

Rutherford
Rutherford Institute
1445 E. Rio Road
Charlottesville, VA 22906

SAFE Update
Sex and Family Education (SAFE)
1608 13th Ave., South, Suite 112
Birmingham, AL 35205

Salisbury Review
33 Canonbury Park S.
London NI 2JW, England
UNITED KINGDOM

Samuel Francis Letter
P.O. Box 19627
Alexandria, VA 22320

Self Evident
Putting Liberty First (PLF)
13873 Park Center Rd., Suite 316
Herndon, VA 20171

Seminarians for Life International Newsletter
Human Life International (HLI)
7845 Airpark Road, Suite E
Gaithersburg, MD 20879

Senior Alert
The Seniors Coalition
11166 Main Street, Suite 302
Fairfax, VA 22030

Senior American
United Seniors Association (USA)
12500 Fair Lakes Circle, Suite 125
Fairfax, VA 22033

Senior Class
The Seniors Coalition
11166 Main Street, Suite 302
Fairfax, VA 22030

Senior Guardian
National Alliance of Senior Citizens (NASC)
1700 18th St., N.W., Suite 401
Washington, DC 20009

Senior Voice
60 Plus Association
1655 N. Fort Meyers Dr., Suite 355
Arlington, VA 22209

Sentinel of Freedom
Nevada Freedom Coalition
675 Fairview Dr., Suite 246
Carson City, NV 89701

Shield
High Frontier
2800 Shirlington Rd., Suite 405A
Arlington, VA 22206

SIFE Lines
Students in Free Enterprise (SIFE)
1959 E. Kerr
Springfield, MO 65803

Sindlinger Economic Report
Lincoln Institute of Public Opinion Research
453 Springlake Rd.
Harrisburg, PA 17112

Small Business and the Economy
Small Business Survival Committee
1320 18th St., N.W., Suite 200
Washington, DC 20036

Small Property Owner
American Association for Small Property Ownership (AASPO)
4200 Cathedral Ave., N.W., Box 515
Washington, DC 20016

Smith Center Journal
Smith Center for Private Enterprise Studies
California State University
Hayward, CA 94542

Sobran's
P.O. Box 565
Herndon, VA 22070

Soldier of Fortune
5735 Arapahoe Road
Boulder, CO   80303

South Carolina Citizen
Palmetto Family Council
P.O. Box 211634
Columbia, SC 29221

South Dakota Citizen
South Dakota Family Policy Council
P.O. Box 88007
Sioux Falls, SD 57109

Southern Libertarian Messenger
Quality Education
Route 10, P.O. Box 52-A
Florence, SC 29501

Spotlight
Liberty Lobby
300 Independence Ave., S.E.
Washington, DC 20003

St. Antoninus Institute Newsletter
St. Antoninus Institute for Catholic Education in Business
4110 Fessenden St., N.W.
Washington, DC 20016

St. Croix Review
Religion and Society
P.O. Box 244
Stillwater, MN 55082

Standard, The
Jesse Helms Center Foundation
3918 U.S. Highway 74 East
Wingate, NC 28174

State Department Watch
State Department Watch
P.O. Box 65398
Washington, DC 20035

State Factor
American Legislative Exchange Council (ALEC)
910 17th St., N.W., 5th Floor
Washington, DC 20006

Statesmanship Statute
Coral Ridge Ministries Media
5554 N. Federal Highway, Suite 200
Fort Lauderdale, FL 33308

STATS 2100
Statistical Assessment Service (STATS)
2100 L St., N.W., Suite 300
Washington, DC 20037

Stockowners' News
Fund for Stockowners Rights
P.O. Box 65563
Washington, DC 20035

Stop Promoting Homosexuality Hawaii Newsletter
Stop Promoting Homosexuality Hawaii (SPHH)
P.O. Box 27843
Honolulu, HI 96827

Straight Talk
P.O. Box 60
Pigeon Forge, TN 37868

Strategic Review
United States Strategic Institute (USSI)
P.O. Box 15618, Kenmore Station
Boston, MA 02215

Survey of Freedom
Freedom House
120 Wall St., 26th Floor
New York, NY 10005

TACDA Alert
The American Civil Defense Association
118 Court St.
Starke, FL 32091

TARGET
National Teen Age Republicans (TARS)
10620-C Crestwood Dr.
P.O. Box 1896
Manassas, VA 22110

TARGET Newsletter
Teen Age Research Services Foundation (TARS Foundation)
10620-C Crestwood Drive
Manassas, VA 22110

Tax Action Alerts
Iowans for Tax Relief
2610 Park Ave.
Muscatine, IA 52761

Tax Features
Tax Foundation
1250 H Street, N.W., Suite 700
Washington, DC 20005-3908

Tax Saving Report
National Taxpayers Union (NTU)
108 N. Alfred St.
Alexandria, VA 22314

Tax Watch
South Carolina Association of Taxpayers (SCAT)
P.O. Box 50799
Columbia, SC 29250

Taxing Times
Howard Jarvis Taxpayers Association
621 S. Westmoreland Ave., Suite 3202
Los Angeles, CA 90005

Taxpayer Advocate
Pennsylvania Leadership Council (PLC)
225 State St., Suite 330
Harrisburg, PA 17101

Taxpayer Scorecard
Conservative Caucus
450 E. Maple Ave., Suite 309
Vienna, VA 22180

Taxpayers News
Connecticut Policy and Economic Council (CPEC)
99 Pratt St., Suite 5
Hartford, CT 06103

Teach Michigan Newsletter
TEACH Michigan Education Fund
913 W. Holmes, Suite 265
Lansing, MI 48910

Teachers in Focus
Focus on the Family
8605 Explorer Dr.
Colorado Springs, CO 80920

Teaching Home, The
P.O. Box 20219
Portland, OR 97294

TFP Campus Update
American Society for the Defense of Tradition, Family and Property
P.O. Box 1868
York, PA 17405

TFP Newsletter
American Society for the Defense of Tradition, Family and Property
P.O. Box 1868
York, PA 17405

TFP Prolife Update
American Society for the Defense of Tradition, Family and Property
P.O. Box 1868
York, PA 17405

These Orwellian Times
Awake America
P.O. Box 22431
St. Louis, MO 63126

This World: A Journal of Religion and Public Life
Elizabethtown Center for Business and Society
Elizabethtown College
One Alpha Drive
Elizabethtown, PA 17022

Toll Roads
301 E. Third St.
Frederick, MD 21701

Tomorrow
Ronald Reagan Presidential Foundation
40 Presidential Drive, Suite 200
Simi Valley, CA 93065

Torch, The
Society for Environmental Truth (SET)
5535 E. Rosewood St.
Tucson, AZ 85711

Triple R
Center for Libertarian Studies (CLS)
875 Mahler Rd., Suite 150
Burlingame, CA 94010

Ultimate Issues
Micah Center for Ethical Monotheism
10573 W. Pico Blvd., Suite 167
Los Angeles, CA 90064

Unification News
Holy Spirit Association for Unification of World Christianity
4 W. 43rd St.
New York, NY 10036

Update
National Federal Lands Conference (NFLC)
P.O. Box 847
Bountiful, UT 84011

Update
Exodus International, North America
P.O. Box 77652
Seattle, WA 98177

Update on the Institute
Allegheny Institute for Public Policy
7 Parkway Center, Suite 612
Pittsburgh, PA 15220

Utah Taxpayer
Utah Taxpayers Association
1578 W. 1700 S., Suite 201
Salt Lake City, UT 84401

Virginia Citizen
Family Foundation
3817-B Plaza Dr.
Fairfax, VA 22151

Vision
Christian Educators Association International (CEAI)
P.O. Box 41300
Pasadena, CA 91114

Visions
Hudson Institute
5395 Emerson Way
Herman Kahn Center
P.O. Box 26-919
Indianapolis, IN 46226

Voice of Liberty
692 Sunnybrook Dr.
Decatur, GA 30033

Voluntaryist, The
Voluntaryists
P.O. Box 1275
Gramling, SC 29348

Voucher Voice
CEO America
208 W. Main
Bentonville, AR 72712

Wake-Up Call America
P.O. Box 280488
Lakewood, CO 80228

Wanderer, The
201 Ohio Street
St. Paul, MN 55107

Washington Inquirer
Council for the Defense of Freedom
4455 Connecticut Ave., N.W., Suite 330
Washington, DC 20008

Washington Journal
Evergreen Freedom Foundation (EFF)
2111 State St., 2nd Floor
Olympia, WA 98507

Washington Quarterly
Center for Strategic and International Studies (CSIS)
1800 K St., N.W., Suite 400
Washington, DC 20006

Washington Statesman
Coral Ridge Ministries Media
5554 N. Federal Highway, Suite 200
Fort Lauderdale, FL 33308

Washington Times National Weekly Edition
3600 New York Ave., N.E.
Washington, DC 20002

Washington Watch
Family Research Council (FRC)
801 G St., N.W.
Washington, DC 20001

Waste Watch
Citizens Against Government Waste (CAGW)
1301 Connecticut Ave., N.W., Suite 400
Washington, DC 20036

We the People
Congressional Institute
316 Pennsylvania Ave., S.E., Suite 403
Washington, DC 20003

Weaver Report
United States Taxpayers Alliance (USTA)
450 E. Maple Ave.
Vienna, VA 22180

Weekly Standard, The
1150 17th St., N.W., 5th Floor
Washington, DC 20036

Wire
Middle East Forum
1920 Chestnut St.
Philadelphia, PA 19103

Wisconsin Interest
Wisconsin Policy Research Institute (WPRI)
11516 N. Port Washington Rd., Suite 103
Mequon, WI 53092

Wise Use Conservation Memo
Center for the Defense of Free Enterprise
12500 N.E. 10th Place
Bellevue, WA 98005

Women & Guns
Second Amendment Foundation (SAF)
12500 N.E. 10th Place
Bellevue, WA 98005

Women's Quarterly
Independent Women's Forum (IWF)
2111 Wilson Blvd., Suite 550
Arlington, VA 22201

World
P.O. Box 2330
Asheville, NC 28802

World & I
Washington Times News Corp.
34000 New York Ave., N.E.
Washington, DC 20002

World Climate Review
Department of Environmental Sciences
Clark Hall, University of Virginia
Charlottesville, VA 22903

World Survey of Economic Freedom
Freedom House
120 Wall St., 26th Floor
New York, NY 10005

Yellow Ribbon Coalition Newsletter
Yellow Ribbon Coalition
P.O. Box 240
Springfield, OR 97477

GEOGRAPHIC LISTING

This section contains a listing of the organizations from the **Profiles** section, listed by the states and the District of Columbia. There are no listings for three states; Alaska, Maine, and West Virginia.

ALABAMA

Alabama Family Alliance
American Textbook Committee
Hoffman Education Center for the Family
Ludwig von Mises Institute
Sex and Family Education (SAFE)

ARIZONA

Aid & Abet Foundation
Alliance Defense Fund
American Health Legal Foundation
Arizona School Choice Trust
Association of American Physicians and Surgeons (AAPS)
Center for Environmental Education Research (CEER)
Committee on Justice and the Constitution (COJAC)
Doctors for Disaster Preparedness
Goldwater Institute for Public Policy
Laissez Faire Institute
Society for Environmental Truth (SET)

ARKANSAS

Accrediting Association of Bible Colleges
Arkansas Policy Foundation (APF)
CEO America
Family Council

CALIFORNIA

A. B. Laffer, V. A. Canto & Associates
Aequus Institute
Alliance of California Taxpayers & Involved Voters
American Christian History Institute
American Civil Rights Institute
American Focus
American Survival Guide
Americans for Free Choice in Medicine (AFCM)
Americans for Voluntary School Prayer
Ayn Rand Institute: The Center for the Advancement of Objectivism
Beeson Report
Bionomics Institute
Bluestocking Press
Brotherhood Organization of a New Destiny (BOND)
California Desert Coalition (CDC)
California Public Policy Foundation
California Rifle and Pistol Association
California Taxpayers Association
Capitol Resource Institute
Center for Economic Policy Research
Center for Independent Thought / Laissez Faire Books
Center for Libertarian Studies (CLS)
Center for the Study of Popular Culture / *Heterodoxy*
Center for the Study of Taxation (CST)

Central News Service
Chinese Family Alliance (CFA)
Christian Anti-Communism Crusade
Christian Educators Association International (CEAI)
Christian Film and Television Commission
Citizens for Law and Order (CLO)
Claremont Institute for the Study of Statesmanship and Political Philosophy
Coalition on Urban Affairs
Compass
Conservatives for a Constitutional Convention
Constitutionalists United Against a Constitutional Convention
Contra-PC
Criminal Justice Legal Foundation (CJLF)
Doctors for Integrity in Research & Public Policy
Factsheet Five
Foundation for Teaching Economics (FTE)
Free Enterprise Society
Hoover Institution on War, Revolution and Peace
Howard Jarvis Taxpayers Association
Ignatius Press / Guadalupe Associates
Independent Institute / *The Independent Review*
Institute for Contemporary Studies (ICS)
International Christian Studies Association (ICSA)
International Life Services
International Life Services Foundation
International Society for Individual Liberty (ISIL)
Kwong's News Digest
Lawyer's Second Amendment Society (LSAS)
Life Legal Defense Foundation (LLDF)
Live and Let Live
Micah Center for Ethical Monotheism
Milken Institute for Job & Capital Formation (MIJCF)
National Justice Foundation of America
National Monitor of Education
National Tax Limitation Committee
New Nation USA (NNUSA)
NOT-SAFE (National Organization Taunting Safety and Fairness Everywhere)
Pacific Academy for Advanced Studies
Pacific Legal Foundation (PLF)
Pacific Research Institute for Public Policy (PRI)
Paul Gann's Spirit of 13
Rampart Institute
Reason Foundation / *Reason*
Rescue Task Force
Right to Life, California (League of Southern California)
Ronald Reagan Presidential Foundation
Sahara Club USA
Scholl Institute of Bioethics
Smith Center for Private Enterprise Studies
Tax Free America
Western Journalism Center (WJC)

COLORADO

Access Research Network (ARN)
Anschutz Foundation
Castle Rock Foundation
Center for the New West
Committee to Restore the Constitution
Focus on the Family
Foundation for Education, Scholarship, Patriotism and
    Americanism
Gates Foundation
Independence Institute
Mountain States Legal Foundation (MSLF)
National Coalition for Public Lands and Natural
Resources (NCPLNR)
National Commodity and Barter Association (NCBA)
Phoenix Enterprises
Rocky Mountain Family Council
Ruth and Vernon Taylor Foundation
Soldier of Fortune
Wake-Up Call America

CONNECTICUT

Connecticut Policy and Economic Council (CPEC)
Devin - Adair Publishers / Veritas Book Club
Freedom Books
John Brown Cook Foundation
Liberals Always Waffle Newsletter (LAWN)
Pro-Life Council of Connecticut (PLCC)
Second Renaissance Book Service
Vernon K. Krieble Foundation
Yankee Institute for Public Policy

DELAWARE

Curran Foundation
Delaware Public Policy Institute (DPPI)
National Association for Neighborhood Schools
Young Americans for Freedom (YAF)

DISTRICT OF COLUMBIA

Accuracy in Academia (AIA)
Accuracy in Media (AIM)
Advocates for a Competitive Economy
American Academy for Liberal Education (AALE)
American Association for Small Property Ownership
American Council for Capital Formation (ACCF)
American Council for Capital Formation Center for
Policy Research
American Enterprise Institute for Public Policy Research
    (AEI)
American Legal Foundation
American Legislative Exchange Council (ALEC)
American Renewal
American Sovereignty Task Force

American Studies Center / Radio America
Americans for a Balanced Budget (ABB)
Americans for a Sound AIDS / HIV Policy
Americans for Tax Reform (ATR)
Americans for Tax Reform Foundation
Americans for Tax Reform Foundation
America's Future Foundation
Becket Fund for Religious Liberty
Brownson Institute / *Crisis*
Business Coalition for Affordable Health Care
Capital Research Center (CRC)
CapitolWatch
Catholic Campaign for America (CCA)
Cato Institute
Center for American Values
Center for Education Reform (CER)
Center for Immigration Studies
Center for Individual Rights (CIR)
Center for Media and Public Affairs
Center for Security Policy (CSP)
Center for Strategic and International Studies (CSIS)
Charles G. Koch Charitable Foundation
Citizens Against Government Waste (CAGW)
Citizens for a Sound Economy (CSE)
Citizens for a Sound Economy Educational Foundation
Claude R. Lambe Charitable Foundation
Coalition for Vehicle Choice (CVC)
Coalitions for America
College Republican National Committee
Committee for a Constructive Tomorrow (CFACT)
Competitive Enterprise Institute (CEI)
Concerned Women for America (CWA)
Concerned Women for America Legislative Action
Committee (CWALAC)
Concord Coalition
Congressional Institute
Consumer Alert
Consumers' Research
Council for Basic Education (CBE)
Council for Citizens Against Government Waste
Council for the Defense of Freedom
Defenders of Property Rights
Eagle Publishing
Education and Research Institute
Employee Benefit Research Institute (EBRI)
Employment Policies Institute
Empower America
Equal Opportunity Foundation
Ethics and Public Policy Center
Evans-Novak Political Report
Family Research Council (FRC)
Family Research Institute (FRI)
Federalist Society for Law and Public Policy Studies
Federation for American Immigration Reform (FAIR)
Free Africa Foundation (FAF)
Free Congress Research and Education Foundation
Fund for American Studies

Fund for Stockowners Rights
George C. Marshall Institute
Heritage Foundation
Horatio R. Storer Foundation
Human Events
Insight on the News
Institute for Independent Education (IIE)
Institute for Justice
Institute for Political Economy
Institute for Republican Women
Institute for Research on the Economics of Taxation
Institute of World Politics
International Christian Concern (ICC)
International Republican Institute (IRI)
Jewish Policy Center (JPC)
Labor Policy Association
Lambda Report on Homosexuality
Libertarian Party - USA
Liberty Lobby
Lincoln Institute for Research and Education
Margaret Thatcher Foundation
Nathan Hale Institute
National Affairs
National Alliance of Senior Citizens (NASC)
National Alumni Forum (NAF)
National Association to Protect Individual Rights
National Center for Neighborhood Enterprise
National Center for Public Policy Research
National Chamber Foundation
National Forum Foundation (NFF)
National Humanities Institute
National Jewish Coalition (NJC)
National Legal Center for the Public Interest
National Policy Forum
National Republican Club of Capitol Hill
National Republican Congressional Committee (NRCC)
National Republican Heritage Council
National Republican Senatorial Committee (NRSC)
National Right to Life Committee
National Right to Life Committee Educational
    Trust Fund
National Right to Life Conventions
National Wetlands Coalition (NWC)
National Wilderness Institute (NWI)
NET - Political NewsTalk Network
New Citizenship Project
Nixon Center for Peace and Freedom
Philanthropy Roundtable
Prison Fellowship International
Pro-Life Alliance of Gays and Lesbians (PLAGAL)
Progress & Freedom Foundation
Project for the Republican Future (PRF)
Radio Free Europe / Radio Liberty Fund
Regnery Publishing
Renaissance Foundation
Republican Coalition for Choice (RCFC)
Republican Governors' Association (RGA)

Republican Liberty Caucus (RLC)
Republican National Committee (RNC)
Republican National Hispanic Assembly (RNHA)
Republican Youth Majority
Republicans Abroad International
Resistance International
Ripon Society
Safe Streets Alliance
Salvatori Center for Academic Leadership
Small Business Legislative Council
Small Business Survival Committee
St. Antoninus Institute for Catholic Education in
    Business
State Department Watch
Statistical Assessment Service (STATS)
Tax Foundation
Town Hall
U.S. English
U.S. English Foundation
U.S. Term Limits
U.S. Term Limits Foundation
United States Business and Industrial Council
United States Chamber of Commerce
Washington Legal Foundation (WLF)
Washington Times National Weekly Edition
Weekly Standard, The
Women's Freedom Network (WFN)
World & I
Young Republican National Committee (YRNF)

FLORIDA

American Civil Defense Association, The (TACDA)
Charles B McFadden Co.
Chicken Little Society
Coral Ridge Ministries Media
Cuban American National Foundation (CANF)
Foundation for Florida's Future (FFF)
Foundation Francisco Marroquin (FFM)
Initiators
James Madison Institute
Regal Foundation
Right to Life, Florida (Lee County)

GEORGIA

Advocates for Self-Government
American Vision
Center for Entrepreneurship and Free Enterprise
Covenant Enterprises / *Journal of Biblical Ethics in
    Medicine*
Georgia Public Policy Foundation
Georgians for Freedom in Education
Heritage Preservation Association (HPA)
Political Dynamite
Southeastern Legal Foundation (SLF)
Voice of Liberty

HAWAII

Pacific Forum CSIS
Stop Promoting Homosexuality Hawaii (SPHH)

IDAHO

Center for Study of Market Alternatives (CSMA)
Right to Life, Idaho
Stewards of the Range

ILLINOIS

Americans United for Life (AUL)
Banfield Analytical Services
Catalyst Institute
Christian Liberty Academy Satellite Schools (CLASS)
Eagle Forum
Eagle Forum Education and Legal Defense Fund
East Moline Christian School
FEDUP Publishing
Free Market Society of Chicago
Grover Hermann Foundation
Heartland Institute
Illinois Family Institute (IFI)
Illinois Public Policy Caucuses (IPPC)
Lincoln Legal Foundation
Live Free International
Mid America Legal Foundation (MALF)
New Intellectual Forum
Pro-Life Action League
Republican National Coalition for Life (RNC/Life)
Right to Life, Illinois Committee
Rockford Institute / *Chronicles*
Sherwood Sugden & Company, Publishers
United Educators Foundation
United Republican Fund (URF)
Wendell Cox Consultancy

INDIANA

American Justice Federation
Culture Wars
Educational CHOICE Charitable Trust
Hudson Institute
Indiana Family Institute
Indiana Policy Review Foundation
Leadership Councils of America (LCA)
Liberty Fund
Lilly Endowment
Media Associates Resource Coalition (MARC)
Media Bypass
State Policy Network
Winchester Foundation

IOWA

Basic Freedoms
Conservative Chronicle
Herbert Hoover Presidential Library
Iowans for Tax Relief
Lutherans for Life
Public Interest Institute

KANSAS

Choice and Charges, All Schools
Constitutionists Networking Center (CNC)
David H. Koch Charitable Foundation
Dwight D. Eisenhower Presidential Library
Kansas Intelligencer
Kansas Public Policy Institute
Right to Life, Kansas

KENTUCKY

Catholics United for Life (CUL)
New Century Foundation (NCF)
Nockian Society, The

LOUISIANA

Eric Voegelin Institute
Louisiana Citizens for a Sound Economy

MARYLAND

Calvert Institute for Policy Research
Christ and Country Courier
Christian Solidarity International (CSI)
Fairness to Land Owners Committee (FLOC)
Free State Constitutionalists
Human Life International (HLI)
Libertarians for Life (LFL)
Lofton Letter
Pillips Foundation
Toll Roads

MASSACHUSETTS

American Institute for Economic Research
Association of Objectivist Businessmen (AOB)
Beacon Hill Institute for Public Policy Research
Boston Review
Citizens for Educational Choice
Citizens' Justice Programs
Institute for Children
Institute for Foreign Policy Analysis
Institute for the Study of Economic Culture
Massachusetts Family Institute
Massachusetts Taxpayers Foundation
New England Institute for Public Policy
New England Legal Foundation (NELF)
Pioneer Institute
Plymouth Rock Foundation
United States Strategic Institute (USSI)

MICHIGAN

Acton Institute for the Study of Religion and Liberty
Alliance for Medical Savings Accounts
American Council on Economics and Society
Amy Foundation
Capital & Liberty
Center for Military Readiness (CMR)
Children's Educational Opportunity Foundation
        (CEO Michigan)
Citizens for Educational Freedom, Michigan
Citizens for Traditional Values
Citizens Research Council of Michigan
DeWitt Families Conduit Foundation
Dove Foundation
Earhart Foundation
Edwards Notebook
Foundation for Traditional Values
Gerald R. Ford Presidential Library
Gun Owners of Macomb County (GOMAC)
Hillsdale College
Libertarians for Gay and Lesbian Concerns (LGLC)
Mackinac Center for Public Policy
Michigan Family Forum (MFF)
Objectivist Club of Michigan
Philadelphia Society
Richard and Helen DeVos Foundation
Right to Life, Michigan (Lifespan)
Right to Life, Michigan Educational Foundation
        Legal Defense Fund
Right to Life, Michigan Educational Foundation
Speak Out America
TEACH Michigan Education Fund

MINNESOTA

Academics for the Second Amendment
Applied Foresight, Inc.
Center of the American Experiment
Christian Forum Research Foundation
Financial Privacy Report
Men's Defense Association
Minnesota Family Council
Pro-Life Action Ministries
Pro-Life Minnesota
Religion and Society
Wanderer, The

MISSISSIPPI

American Family Association (AFA)
Mississippi Family Council

MISSOURI

American Association of Christian Schools (AACS)
America's Future

Awake America
Cardinal Mindszenty Foundation (CMF)
Center for Defense and Strategic Studies
Center for the Study of American Business (CSAB)
Constitutional Coalition
Council of Conservative Citizens (CCC)
Discussion Club
Doctors for Life
Justice Journal
Landmark Legal Foundation
Monetary Realist Society
National Federation of the Grand Order of
        Pachyderm Clubs
Parents' Rights Organization
Population Renewal Office
Religious Heritage of America
Right to Life, Missouri (Western Missouri)
Students in Free Enterprise (SIFE)
Sunmark Foundation

MONTANA

Foundation for Research on Economics and the
Environment (FREE)
Fully Informed Jury Association (FIJA)
Phoenix Letter
Political Economy Research Center (PERC)

NEBRASKA

Entrepreneurial Leadership Center

NEVADA

Nevada Families Eagle Forum
Nevada Freedom Coalition
Nevada Policy Research Institute (NPRI)

NEW HAMPSHIRE

International Churchill Society
Josiah Bartlett Center for Public Policy

NEW JERSEY

Americans for Hope, Growth and Opportunity (AHGO)
Dumont Institute for Public Policy Research
F. M. Kirby Foundation
National Association of Scholars (NAS)
New Jersey Conservative Party (NJCP)
Polyconomics Inc.
Sound Dollar Committee
United Taxpayers of New Jersey

NEW MEXICO

Atlantis Project, The
CSW Freedom School
E. L. Wiegand Foundation
Federal Lands Legal Foundation
Heather Foundation
Knowledge Equals Freedom (K=F)
NRA Special Contribution Fund
Right to Life, New Mexico Committee
United Citizens for Legal Reform (UCLR)

NEW YORK

Ad Hoc Committee in Defense of Life
Alliance for America Foundation
American Council on Science and Health (ACSH)
American Education Association
American Jewish Committee / *Commentary*
Aristos Foundation
Association of Libertarian Feminists (ALF)
Atlantic Legal Foundation (ALF)
Catholic Family News (CFN)
Citizens Helping Achieve New Growth and Employment
Classics of Liberty
Conservative Book Club
Empire Foundation for Policy Research
Excellence in Broadcasting Network (EIB) /
      Rush Limbaugh Show
Experimental Media Organization
Forbes Foundation
Foundation for Cultural Review / *New Criterion*
Foundation for Economic Education (FEE) /
      The Freeman
Foundation for the Advancement of Monetary Education
Fragments
Freedom House
George E. Coleman, Jr., Foundation
Gilder Foundation
Holy Spirit Association for Unification of World
      Christianity / Unification Church of America
Human Life Foundation / *Human Life Review*
Institute for American Values
Institute for Objectivist Studies (IOS)
Institute on Religion and Public Life / *First Things*
Issues & Views Open Forum Foundation / *Issues &
Views*
J. M. Foundation
John M. Olin Foundation
Land Rights Foundation
Lehrman Institute
Life Cycle Books
Limbaugh Letter
Living Free
Manhattan Institute for Public Policy Research
Milliken Foundation
Morality In Media (MIM)

National Black Republican Council (NBRC)
National Review
National Review Institute
New York State Conservative Party
Operation Rescue
Privatization Research Organization
Property Rights Foundation of America
Public Policy Institute of New York State
Research Center for Religion and Human Rights in
Closed Societies
Robert A. Taft Institute of Government
University Centers for Rational Alternatives
William H. Donner Foundation

NORTH CAROLINA

American Sentinel
CAUSE Foundation
Committee for Monetary Research and Education
Free Nation Foundation (FNF)
Jesse Helms Center Foundation
John Locke Foundation
John William Pope Foundation
Lundy Chair of Philosophy of Business
National Alliance of Stocking Gun Dealers
New Puritan Library
North Carolina Family Policy Council
Sentinel Communications
Smith Richardson Foundation
Students for America Foundation
W. H. Brady Foundation
We the People Institute (WTP) / *Middle American News
      World*

NORTH DAKOTA

North Dakota Family Alliance (NDFA)

OHIO

American Portrait Films
Americanism Foundation
Buckeye Institute for Public Policy Solutions
Claustrophobia
Free Enterprise and Government
Heartbeat International
John M. Ashbrook Center for Public Affairs
Life Issues Institute
Monetary Science Publishing
National Taxpayers Union of Ohio
Ohio Rifle and Pistol Association (ORPA)
Right to Life, Ohio
Social Philosophy and Policy Foundation

OKLAHOMA

Enterprise Square
National Education Program (NEP)
Oklahoma Council of Public Affairs (OCPA)
Oklahoma Family Policy Council
Right to Life, Oklahoma Crusade
Samuel Roberts Noble Foundation

OREGON

Access to Energy
Americans for Constitutional Democracy
Berean Call, The
Blackstone Audio Books
Cascade Policy Institute
Destiny Magazine
Educational Research Associates
National Home Education Research Institute (NHERI)
Oregon Institute of Science and Medicine
Oregon Lands Coalition
Oregonians for Food and Shelter (OFS)
Oregonians in Action (OIA)
Oregonians in Action Education Center
Oregonians in Action Legal Center
Right to Life, Oregon
Tamarack Foundation
Teaching Home, The
Thoreau Institute
Western Center for Law and Religious Freedom
Yellow Ribbon Coalition

PENNSYLVANIA

Alex C. Walker Educational and Charitable Foundation
Allegheny Foundation
Allegheny Institute for Public Policy
American Enterprise Publications
American Society for the Defense of Tradition, Family
        and Property (TFP)
Carthage Foundation
Center for Economic and Policy Education
College Pro-Life Information Network
Collegiate Network
Commonwealth Foundation for Public Policy
Alternatives
Crystal Star Press
Elizabethtown Center for Business and Society
Foreign Policy Research Institute (FPRI)
Free Enterprise Partnership
Freedoms Foundation at Valley Forge
Intercollegiate Studies Institute (ISI)
John Templeton Foundation
Lincoln Institute of Public Opinion Research
Middle East Forum
National Fatherhood Initiative (NFI)
National Flag Foundation (NFF)

Palmer R. Chitester Fund
Pennsylvania Family Institute
Pennsylvania Leadership Council (PLC)
Philip M. McKenna Foundation
Pragmatist
Protecting Marriage
Sarah Scaife Foundation
Scaife Family Foundation

RHODE ISLAND

Privacy Journal

SOUTH CAROLINA

Center for Policy Studies
Palmetto Family Council
Patriot Network
Quality Education
Roe Foundation
South Carolina Association of Taxpayers (SCAT)
South Carolina Policy Council Education Foundation
Voluntaryists

SOUTH DAKOTA

South Dakota Family Policy Council

TENNESSEE

J. S. Sanders & Company / Caliban Books
Moneychanger, The
Religious Roundtable
Right to Life, Tennessee
Straight Talk

TEXAS

AntiShyster
Associated Conservatives of Texas (ACT)
Black Economic Times
Buffalo Creek Press
For Limited American Government (FLAG)
Foundation for Rational Economics and Education
Free Enterprise Institute
Free Market Foundation
Gordon and Mary Cain Foundation
Headway
Institute for Christian Economics (ICE)
Institute for Energy Research (IER)
Institute for Human Rights
Institute for Policy Innovation (IPI)
International Christian Media
Life Education and Resource Network (LEARN)
Living Truth Ministries
Movie Morality Ministries

National Center for Policy Analysis (NCPA)
Private Enterprise Research Center
Pro-Family Forum
Right to Life, Texas Committee
Texans United for Life
Texans United for Life Educational Foundation
Texas Justice Foundation (TJF)
Texas Public Policy Foundation (TPPF)

UTAH

National Federal Lands Conference (NFLC)
Sutherland Institute
Utah Taxpayers Association

VERMONT

Edward Elgar Publishing Company
Ethan Allen Institute (EAI)
Rational Conservative, The
Right to Life, Vermont Committee

VIRGINIA

60 Plus Association
Abraham Lincoln Foundation for Public Policy Research
Alexis de Tocqueville Institution (AdTI)
American Center for Law and Justice (ACLJ)
American Christian Cause
American Conservative Union (ACU)
American Council for Health Care Reform
American Defense Institute (ADI)
American Freedom Coalition
American Immigration Control Foundation (AICF)
American Life League (ALL)
American Policy Center
American Policy Foundation
American Security Council (ASC)
American Security Council Foundation
American Spectator Educational Foundation / *American Spectator* (TAS)
Americans for Moral Government
Athens Institute
Atlas Economic Research Foundation
Books for All Times
C. S. Lewis Institute
Center for Market Processes
Center for the American Founding
Center for the Study of Public Choice
CHAMPION Economics & Business Association
Christian Action Network (CAN)
Christian Coalition
Christian Legal Society
Citizens for an Alternative Tax System (CATS)
Citizens for Educational Freedom (CEF)
Citizens United
Citizens United Foundation

Clare Boothe Luce Policy Institute
Connection, The
Conservative Caucus
Conservative Caucus Research, Analysis and Education Foundation
Conservative Political Action Conference (CPAC)
Conservative Review
Council for Affordable Health Insurance (CAHI)
Council for National Policy (CNP)
Council of Volunteer Americans (CVA)
Crispus Attucks Institute
Defense Forum Foundation (DFF)
Educational Freedom Foundation (EFF)
Empowerment Network Foundation, The (TEN-F)
Family Foundation
Firearms Civil Rights Legal Defense Fund
Freedom Alliance
Frontiers of Freedom
Future of Freedom Foundation (FFF)
George Edward Durell Foundation
Gun Owners of America
High Frontier
Home School Legal Defense Foundation
Independent Women's Forum (IWF)
Institute for Humane Studies (IHS)
Institute for Humane Studies, Europe
Jeffersonian Health Policy Foundation
Keene Report
Law Enforcement Alliance of America (LEAA)
Leadership Institute
Legal Affairs Council (LAC)
Liberty Alliance
Locke Institute
Media Research Center (MRC)
Mont Pèlerin Society
National Defense Council Foundation
National Federation of Republican Women (NFRW)
National Institute for Labor Relations Research
National Institute for Public Policy
National Legal and Policy Center (NLPC)
National Legal Foundation
National Organization of Episcopalians for Life (NOEL)
National Rifle Association of America (NRA)
National Right to Read Foundation (NRRF)
National Right to Work Committee
National Right to Work Legal Defense and Education Foundation
National Security Center
National Taxpayers Union (NTU)
National Taxpayers Union Foundation (NTUF)
National Teen Age Republicans (TARS)
NRA Foundation
Of the People Foundation
Parents' Music Resource Center (PMRC)
Population Research Institute (PRI)
Public Advocate of the United States
Public Service Research Council

Public Service Research Foundation
Putting Liberty First (PLF)
Reagan Alumni Association
Republican Network to Elect Women (RENEW)
Right NOW!
Rutherford Institute
Samuel Francis Letter
Science and Environmental Policy Project (SEPP)
Seniors Coalition, The
Sequoia Institute
Sobran's
Teen Age Research Services Foundation (TARS
Foundation)
United Seniors Association (USA)
United States Taxpayers Alliance (USTA)
Virginians for Property Rights
World Climate Review
Young Americans for Social Security Reform (YASSR)
Young America's Foundation

WASHINGTON

American Land Rights Association (ALRA)
Center for the Defense of Free Enterprise
Citizens Committee for the Right to Keep and Bear Arms
Conservative Consensus
Discovery Institute
Evergreen Freedom Foundation (EFF)
Exodus International, North America
Human Life
League of Private Property Voters (LPPV)
Liberty Publishing / *Liberty*
M. J. Murdock Charitable Trust
Northwest Legal Foundation
Second Amendment Foundation (SAF)
Toward Tradition
Washington Family Council
Washington Institute for Policy Studies
Washington Research Council (WRC)
Zenger News Service (ZNS)

WISCONSIN

Blum Center for Parental Freedom in Education
Jews for the Preservation of Firearms Ownership (JPFO)
John Birch Society
Lynde and Harry Bradley Foundation
National Motorists Association (NMA)
Partners Advancing Values in Education (PAVE)
Wisconsin Policy Research Institute (WPRI)

WYOMING

Abundant Wildlife Society of North America
Right to Life, Wyoming
True Foundation
Wyoming Heritage Society

OTHER INFORMATION SOURCES

This section contains additional sources of information on conservative and free-market organizations. Some of these publications cover organizations such as trade associations and Chambers of Commerce. Other publications include listings of radicals such as Nazis and hate-groups.

The Activist's Almanac, 1993, A Fireside Book Published by Simon & Schuster, 1230 Avenue of the Americas, New York, NY 10020, (212) 245-6400. Softbound, 431 pp.

Written by David Walls. This directory lists 105 organizations, of which only eleven could be considered conservative or free-market. The listings include contact information, annual budget, tax status, and an in-depth history and description of the organization.

Dictionary of American Conservatism, 1987, Philosophical Library, 200 W. 57th Street, New York, NY 10019. Distributed by Alpha Book Distributors. Hardbound, 380 pp.

Authored by Louis Filler, this dictionary includes personalities, movements, titles, terms, and organizations of interest to conservatives. It does not carry many current organizations or any addresses or contacts. It does, however, have brief histories of some of the larger and long-established organizations.

Encyclopedia of Associations, 32nd Edition, Gale Research Co., 835 Penobscot Building, Detroit, MI 48226-4094, (313) 961-2242. Three volumes.

Contains more than 23,000 organizations encompassing a wide range of the political spectrum. Listings of conservative groups are less extensive. Approximately 66% of the organizations profiled in The Right Guide are not included in the Encyclopedia.

The Greenpeace Guide to Anti-Environmental Organizations, 1993, Odonian Press, Box 7776, Berkeley, CA 94707, (510) 524-4000. Softbound, 110 pp.

Edited by Carl Deal, includes 54 organizations that Greenpeace considers anti-environment. Includes free-market oriented environmental groups, and members of the 'wise-use' movement. Listings include contact information, key personnel, corporate sponsors, and a half-page description of each group.

A Guide to the American Right, Editorial Research Services, P.O. Box 2047, Olathe, KS 66061. Plastic-comb softbound.

Written and published by Laird Wilcox. Lists names and addresses of over 2,500 American and British Commonwealth organizations. The list contains conservative, pro-family, racial nationalist, Nazi, anti-abortion, pro-gun, libertarian, and free-market organizations. It includes a one-letter code to identify each organization's interest. Also includes a bibliography of books and other information sources about the American Right, in addition to newspaper articles about the author. No page numbers or index.

Guide to Public Policy Experts, 1995-96, Heritage Foundation, 214 Massachusetts Ave., N.E., Washington, DC 20002, (202) 546-4400. Softbound, 412 pp.

Edited by Thomas C. Atwood. This source contains a list of conservative experts categorized by area of expertise. Listings include contact information and the expert's organizational affiliations. Affiliations primarily consist of universities and research institutions. Includes thorough descriptions of the Heritage Foundation's own experts. There is a complete index by name, and a geographic index by region. There is also a six-page index of approximately 150 policy organizations, listed alphabetically by the name of the organization with the name of a contact person.

The National Archives and Records Administration. National Archives Building, 8th St. and Pennsylvania Ave., N.W., Washington, DC.

The National Archives maintains the Federal repository system which includes the Presidential Libraries. With the exception of the Richard M. Nixon Presidential Library, all are operated under this federal system (see Richard M. Nixon Presidential Library in the **Profiles** section). They are subject to the oversight of the House Sub-committee for Government Information, Justice, and Agriculture. Researchers should contact the specific Presidential Library first, but if they are unable to obtain a timely response directly from the library or have other problems, they should contact the Presidential Libraries Department at the National Archives, voice (202) 501-5705, fax (202) 208-6938.

The Public Eye, Political Research Associates, 678 Massachusetts Ave., Suite 205, Cambridge, MA 02139, (617) 661-9313.

A newsletter from the left-wing Public Research Associates, a 501(c)(3) organization that researches right-wing organizations. Political Research Associates is profiled in The Left Guide, published by Economics America, Inc. They maintain a library of information on right-of-center organizations and leaders. The PRA publishes monographs and provides speakers.

KEYWORD INDEX

This index includes the organizations and publications mentioned in <u>The Right Guide</u>. Each reference has been indexed by its full name with the number of the page or pages on which it appears. In addition, each name has been cross-referenced by the keywords in its name. For example, Foundation for Research on Economics and the Environment will be listed under:

⬧Foundation for Research on Economics and the Environment . . . .
Research on Economics and the Environment ⬧Foundation for . . . .
Economics and the Environment ⬧Foundation for Research on . . . .
Environment ⬧Foundation for Research on Economics and the . . . .

and under their commonly used acronym:

FREE ⬧Foundation for Research on Economics and the Environment . . . .

In each case the "⬧" denotes the beginning of the group's name, while the first word on the line indicates where it is located alphabetically within the **Keyword Index**. The organization is listed in several places so researchers can find it even if they don't know its full name.